McDougal Littell

CLASSZONE

Visit classzone.com and get connected.

ClassZone resources provide instruction, practice and learning support for students and parents.

Help with the Math

- @Home Tutor enables students to focus on the math and be more prepared for class, using animated examples and instruction.

Games and Activities

- Crossword puzzles, memory games, and other activities help students connect to essential math concepts.
- Math Vocabulary Flipcards are a fun way to learn math terminology.

Math

- Engaging activities with animated problem-solving graphics support each lesson.
- Online resources include direct correlations to hands-on games and activities at the SHODOR website.

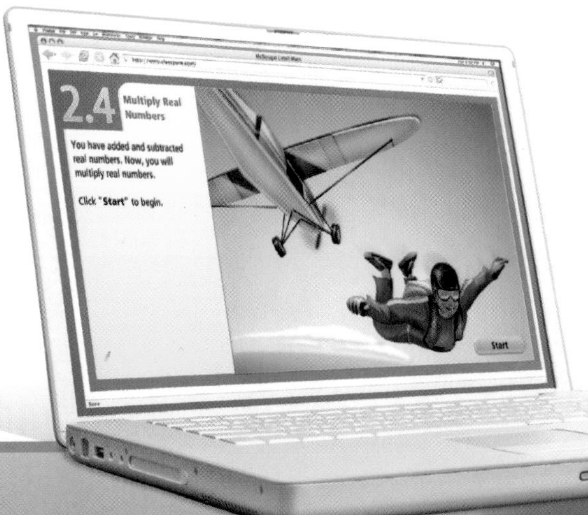

Access the online version of your textbook at classzone.com

Your complete text is available for immediate use!

McDougal Littell

Where Great Lessons Begin

NEW EDITION

Senior Authors

Rick Billstein
Jim Williamson

BOOK 3

Photography Acknowledgments

Cover: *Anasazi Ruin in Alcove Zion National Park* © Tom Till/Alamy; *Cross Section of Chambered Nautilus Shell* © Josh Westrich/zefa/Corbis; *Canal Bridge in Magdeburg, Germany* © Eckehard Schulz/AP Images.

Table of Contents: **iv** © Don Mason/Corbis; **v** © Richard Chung/Reuters/Corbis; **vi** © Craig Lovell/Corbis; **vii** © John D. Russell/AP Images; **viii** © Eckehard Schulz/AP Images; **ix** © Firefly Productions/Corbis; **x** © BSIP/Photo Researchers, Inc.; **xi** © Josh Westrich/zefa/Corbis.

Scavenger Hunt: **xxi** Jorge Alban/McDougal Littell/Houghton Mifflin Co.

Further acknowledgments for copyrighted material can be found at the end of the book and constitute an extension of this page.

THE STEM PROJECT *McDougal Littell Math Thematics®* is based on the field-test versions of The STEM Project curriculum. The STEM Project was supported in part by the

under Grant No. ESI-0137682. Opinions expressed in *McDougal Littell Math Thematics®* are those of the authors and not necessarily those of the National Science Foundation.

ISBN-13: 978-0-618-65608-0
ISBN-10: 0-618-65608-1

123456789-VJM-11 10 09 08 07

Internet Web Site: http://www.mcdougallittell.com

McDOUGAL LITTELL

MATH*Thematics*

Book 3

SENIOR AUTHORS

Rick Billstein Department of Mathematical Sciences, The University of Montana, Missoula, Montana

Jim Williamson Department of Mathematical Sciences, The University of Montana, Missoula, Montana

REVISION WRITERS

Lyle Andersen, Jean Howard, Deb Johnson, Bonnie Spence

MATHEMATICS CONSULTANTS

Dr. Ira Papick The University of Missouri, Columbia, Missouri

Dr. David Barker Illinois State University, Normal, Illinois

PROJECT EVALUATOR

Dr. Ted Hodgson Montana State University, Bozeman, Montana

CONSULTING AUTHORS

Perry Montoya, Jacqueline Lowery, Dianne Williams

STEM WRITERS

Mary Buck, Clay Burkett, Lynn Churchill, Chris Clouse, Roslyn Denny, William Derrick, Sue Dolezal, Doug Galarus, Paul Kennedy, Pat Lamphere, Nancy Merrill, Perry Montoya, Sallie Morse, Marjorie Petit, Patrick Runkel, Thomas Sanders-Garrett, Richard T. Seitz, Bonnie Spence, Becky Sowders, Chris Tuckerman, Ken Wenger, Joanne Wilkie, Cheryl Wilson, Bente Winston

STEM TEACHER CONSULTANTS

Melanie Charlson, Polly Fite, Jean Howard, Tony Navarro, Paul Sowden, Linda Tetley, Marsha Vick, Patricia Zepp

AMAZING FEATS and FACTS

Pre-Course Features

Module Features

Assessment Options

1

Connecting the Theme *Towering talents and amazing facts will capture your imagination, as you see how mathematics can be used to describe incredible accomplishments and surprising relationships.*

AT THE MALL

Connecting the Theme *Malls combine shopping with entertainment. Mathematics helps store owners plan inventory, and helps shoppers compare prices. You'll learn the mathematics that operates behind the scenes.*

Module Features

Assessment Options

The MYSTERY of BLACKTAIL CANYON

Connecting the Theme *Be on the lookout as a mystery unfolds. As you read, you'll rely on mathematics to help you piece together clues to catch a thief. Then, you'll use rules of logic to try solving the mystery.*

Module Features

Assessment Options

INVENTIONS

Connecting the Theme *How do inventors get new ideas? They brainstorm, experiment, and carefully calculate. You'll see how mathematics has helped in perfecting inventions from the tin can to the Braille alphabet to the combination lock.*

Module Features

Assessment Options

ARCHITECTS and ENGINEERS

Connecting the Theme *From blueprint to model to construction site, a structure takes shape. As you give form to your own constructions, you'll see how measurement and mathematics are tools of the construction trade around the world.*

Module Features

Assessment Options

VISUALIZING CHANGE

Connecting the Theme *It may be impossible to see the future. Still, many professionals need to predict coming trends. From economics to environmental science, you'll learn how mathematical models can help people see patterns of change.*

Module Features

Assessment Options

The ALGEBRA CONNECTION

Connecting the Theme *Algebra plays and important role in the world both inside and outside of the classroom. You will see algebra at work in the careers of scientists, mathematicians, engineers, and artists from ancient times to the present.*

Module Features

Assessment Options

MATH-THEMATICAL MIX

Connecting the Theme *In this module, you will connnect and expand mathematical topics you studied in earlier modules. You will use mathematics to find, describe, and compare patterns, relationships and measurements.*

Module Features

Assessment Options

STUDENT RESOURCES

COURSE OVERVIEW

ORGANIZATION OF THE BOOK

This book contains eight modules. To get an overview of the modules and their themes, look at the Table of Contents starting on p. iv.

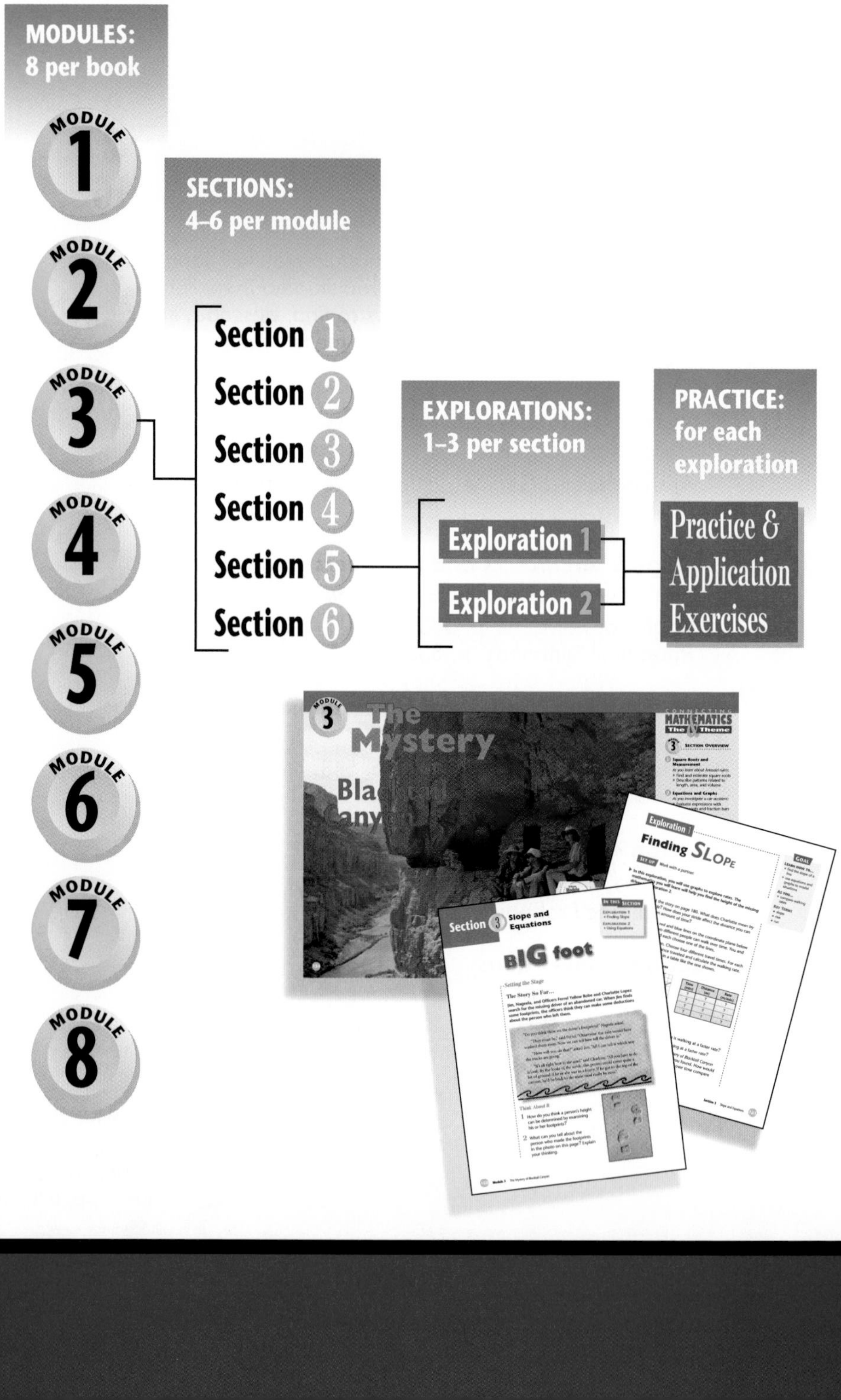

MODULES: 8 per book

Module 1, Module 2, Module 3, Module 4, Module 5, Module 6, Module 7, Module 8

SECTIONS: 4–6 per module

Section 1, Section 2, Section 3, Section 4, Section 5, Section 6

EXPLORATIONS: 1–3 per section

Exploration 1, Exploration 2

PRACTICE: for each exploration

Practice & Application Exercises

MODULE THEME & PROJECT

Each module's theme connects the mathematics you are learning to the real world. *The Mystery of Blacktail Canyon* is the theme of Module 3. At the end of each module is a Module Project that relates to the module theme.

Connecting Mathematics and the Theme
The math topics you'll be learning and the settings in which you'll be learning them.

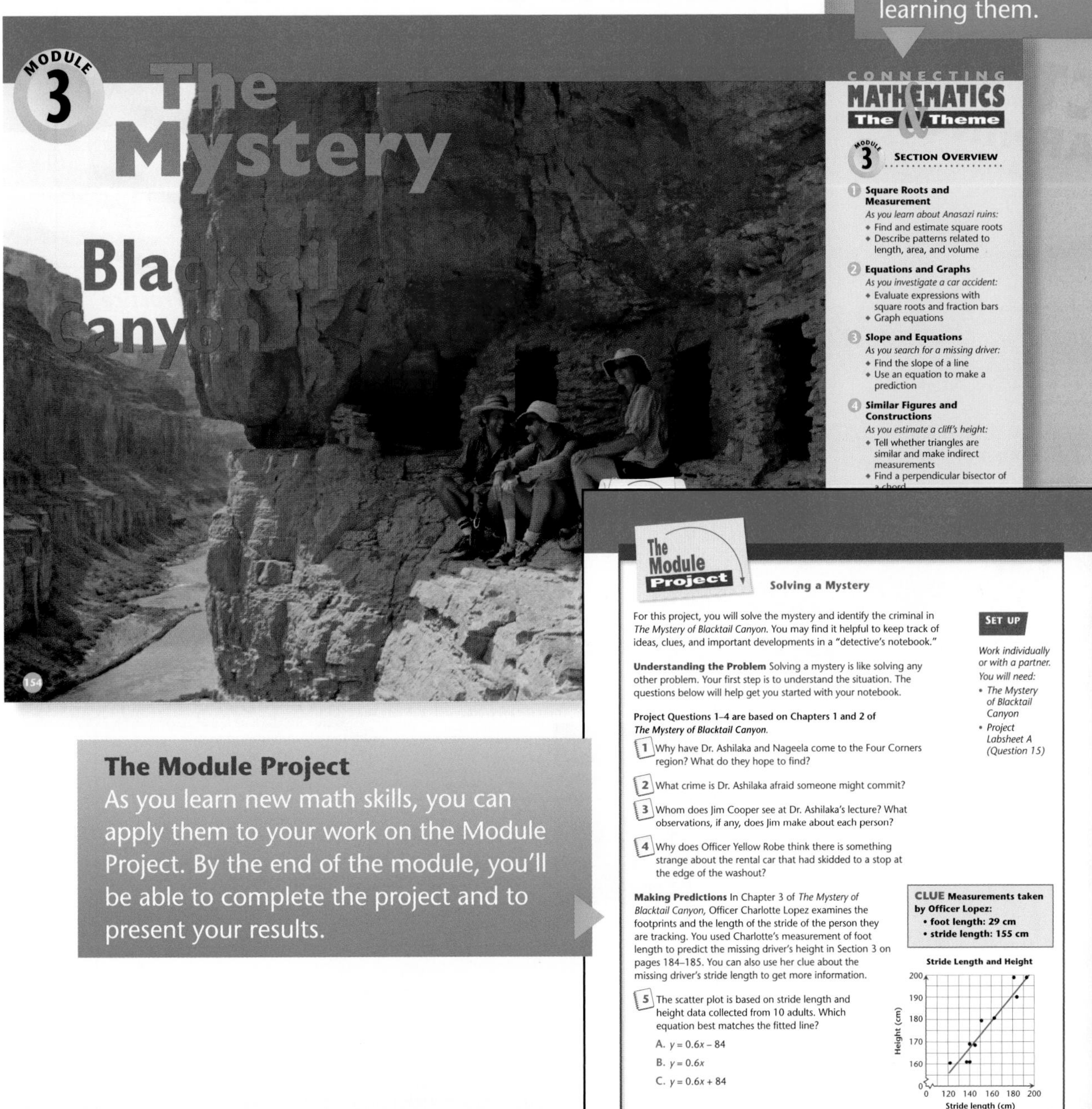

The Module Project
As you learn new math skills, you can apply them to your work on the Module Project. By the end of the module, you'll be able to complete the project and to present your results.

SECTION OVERVIEW

SECTION ORGANIZATION

The diagram below illustrates the organization of a section:

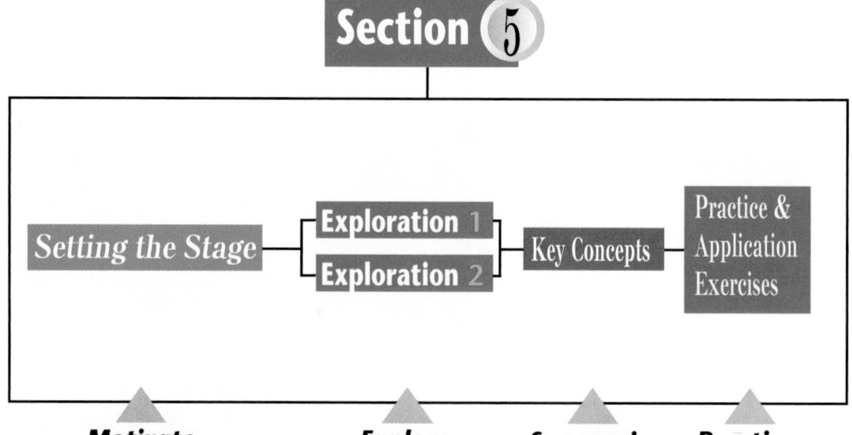

Motivate **Explore** **Summarize** **Practice**

Scientific Notation and Decimal Equations

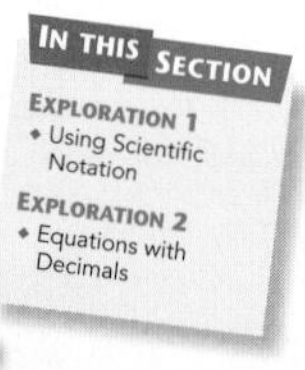

Forgotten BONES

Section Title and Mathematics Focus
The title of Section 5 is *Forgotten Bones.* Its math focus is *Scientific Notation and Decimal Equations.*

Setting the Stage

SET UP *You will need Labsheet 5A.*

The Story So Far...

Setting the Stage begins with a reading, graph, activity, or game to introduce the section.

▶ **Nageela visits Dr. Beatrice Leschensky, a s... analyzing the bones found at the site. Dr. ... how she uses *carbon dating* to estimate th...**

"Every living creature contains a certain amount of a radioactive substance known as *carbon-14*. After a plant or an animal dies, the carbon-14 decays, so that there is less and less carbon-14 over time. After about 5730 years, only half the carbon-14 remains. After another 5730 years or so, only one fourth the carbon-14 remains. After each additional 5730 years, only half the previous amount of carbon-14 remains. By measuring the amount of carbon-14 in these bones, I was able to estimate their age. That's all there is to it."

Think About It

1 Scientists say that carbon-14 has a half-life of 5730 years. Why is *half-life* a good term to use?

2 What fraction of carbon-14 is left in an 11,460-year-old bone? in a 17,190-year-old bone? How do you know?

3 **Use Labsheet 5A.** Use a table and a graph to model the *Half-Life of Carbon-14.*

▶ **In this section, you will use mathematics to find out more about the bones found in the cliff dwelling in *The Mystery of Blacktail Canyon.***

204 **Module 3** The Mystery of Blacktail Canyon

EXPLORATIONS & KEY CONCEPTS

In the explorations you'll be actively involved in investigating mathematics concepts, learning mathematics skills, and solving problems.

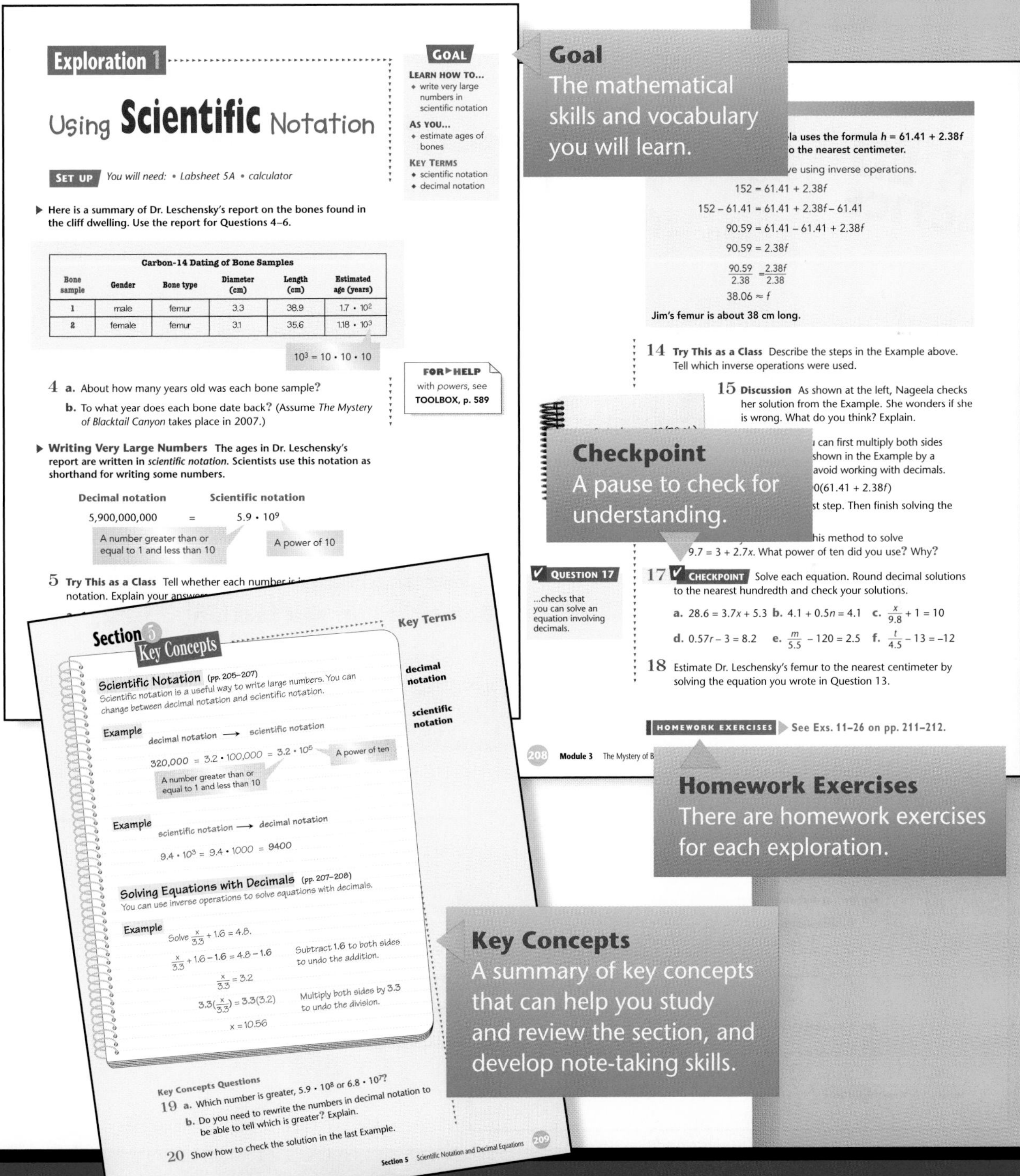

SECTION OVERVIEW

PRACTICE & APPLICATION

Practice and Application Exercises will give you a chance to practice the skills and concepts in the explorations and apply them in solving many types of problems.

Balanced Practice
These exercises develop algebra, geometry, numerical, and problem solving skills and help you communicate mathematical ideas.

Section 5 Practice & Application Exercises

YOU WILL NEED
For Ex. 7:
- calculator

For Exercises 1–4, write each number in decimal notation.

1. Approximate age of Earth: at least $4.5 \cdot 10^9$ years
2. The distance from Earth to the sun: about $9.3 \cdot 10^7$ mi
3. Speed of light: about $1.86 \cdot 10^5$ mi/sec
4. Distance light travels in a year: about $5.88 \cdot 10^{12}$ mi
5. Which numbers below are written in scientific notation? Explain.
   A. $7.987 \cdot 10^2$ B. $3.57 \cdot 10^{99}$ C. $82.1 \cdot 10^3$ D. $5.13 \cdot 2^{10}$

Astronomy **A *light-year* is the distance that light travels in a vacuum in one year. One light-year ≈ $5.88 \cdot 10^{12}$ miles. Use this fact and the bar graph below for Exercises 6–8.**

the
ite
art
les

The Mystery of Blacktail Canyon

Reflecting on the Section
exercises help you communicate ideas through oral reports, journal writing, visual thinking, research, and discussion.

25. **Open-ended** If you buy shoes from another country, you may need to know your European shoe size. The formulas below relate European size *e* to United States size *u*. Write a word problem that can be solved by using one or both of the formulas.

Men's shoes	Women's shoes
$e = 1.29u + 30.8$	$e = 1.24u + 28.7$

RESEARCH
Exercise 26 checks that you know how scientific notation is applied.

Reflecting on the Section

26. Find three large numbers in a newspaper or encyclopedia. Write them in scientific notation and add labels that explain what the numbers mean.

Spiral Review

27. $\triangle ABC \sim \triangle ADE$. Find the length of $\overline{DE}$. (Module 3, p. 198)

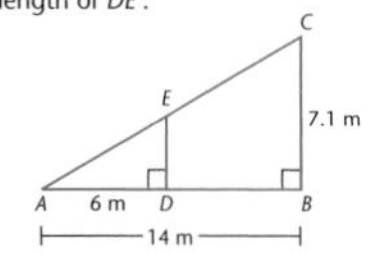

Find each sum or difference. (Module 2, p. 86)

28. $-8 + 7$ 29. $6 - (-11)$ 30. $92 + (-2)$ 31. $-15 - (-21)$
32. $-50 + 50$ 33. $0 - (-12)$ 34. $-18 - (-5)$ 35. $3 - 5 + 8$

Use the box-and-whisker plots. (Module 1, p. 23)

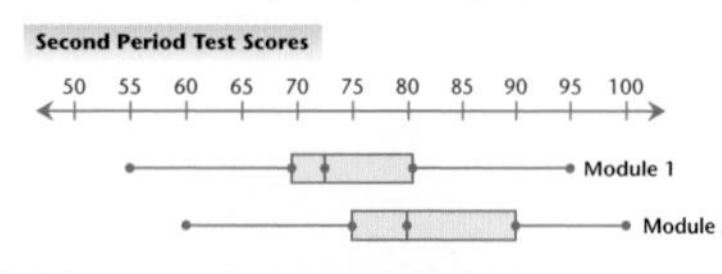

36. Estimate the median score on the Module 2 test.
37. Estimate the high score on the Module 1 test.

212 **Module 3** The Mystery of Blacktail Canyon

Spiral Review
exercises help you maintain skills by revisiting material from previous sections in the book.

ADDITIONAL PRACTICE

At the end of every section, you will find Extra Skill Practice. If needed, you can use these exercises for extra practice on important skills before you begin the next section.

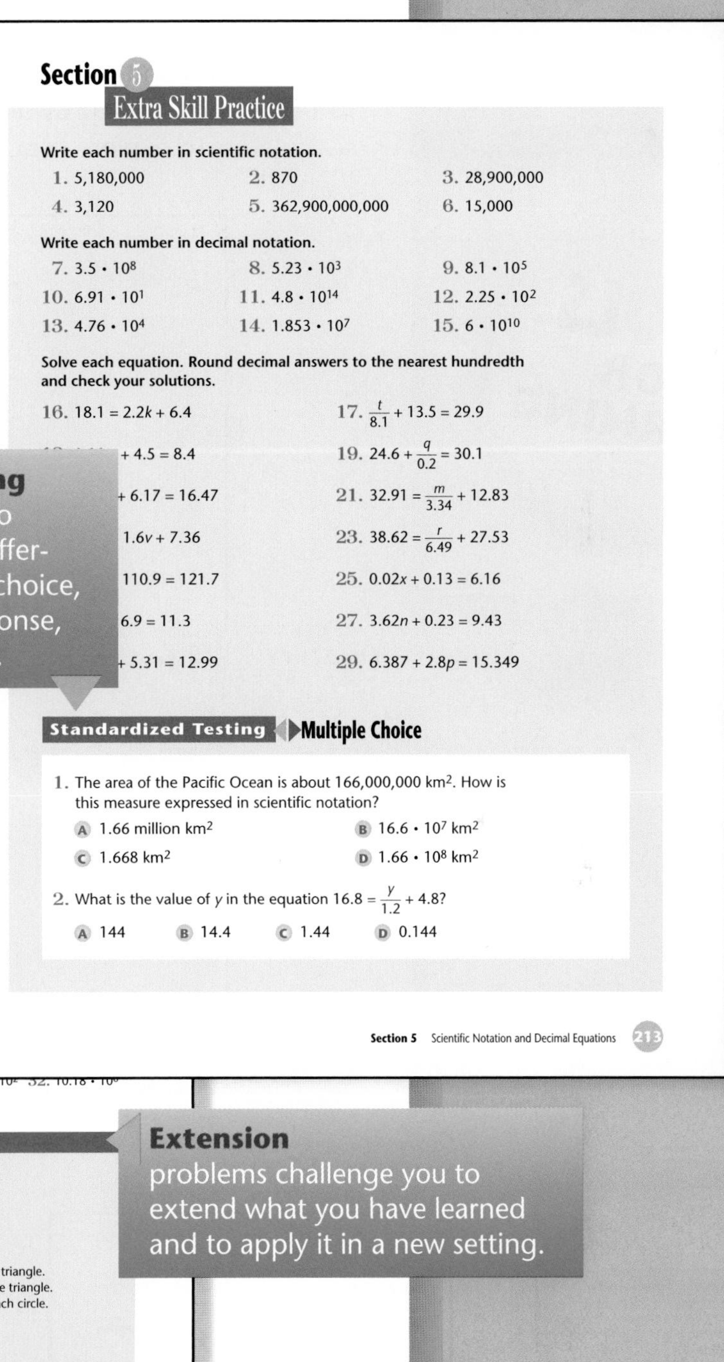

Section 5

Extra Skill Practice

Write each number in scientific notation.

1. 5,180,000
2. 870
3. 28,900,000
4. 3,120
5. 362,900,000,000
6. 15,000

Write each number in decimal notation.

7. $3.5 \cdot 10^8$
8. $5.23 \cdot 10^3$
9. $8.1 \cdot 10^5$
10. $6.91 \cdot 10^1$
11. $4.8 \cdot 10^{14}$
12. $2.25 \cdot 10^2$
13. $4.76 \cdot 10^4$
14. $1.853 \cdot 10^7$
15. $6 \cdot 10^{10}$

Solve each equation. Round decimal answers to the nearest hundredth and check your solutions.

16. $18.1 = 2.2k + 6.4$
17. $\frac{t}{8.1} + 13.5 = 29.9$

$+ 4.5 = 8.4$

19. $24.6 + \frac{q}{0.2} = 30.1$

$+ 6.17 = 16.47$

21. $32.91 = \frac{m}{3.34} + 12.83$

$1.6v + 7.36$

23. $38.62 = \frac{r}{6.49} + 27.53$

$110.9 = 121.7$

25. $0.02x + 0.13 = 6.16$

$6.9 = 11.3$

27. $3.62n + 0.23 = 9.43$

$+ 5.31 = 12.99$

29. $6.387 + 2.8p = 15.349$

Standardized Testing ▶Multiple Choice

1. The area of the Pacific Ocean is about 166,000,000 km². How is this measure expressed in scientific notation?

   A 1.66 million km²
   B $16.6 \cdot 10^7$ km²
   C 1.668 km²
   D $1.66 \cdot 10^8$ km²

2. What is the value of y in the equation $16.8 = \frac{y}{1.2} + 4.8$?

   A 144　B 14.4　C 1.44　D 0.144

Section 5　Scientific Notation and Decimal Equations　213

Standardized Testing develops your ability to answer questions in different formats: multiple-choice, open-ended, free response, and performance task.

Spiral ▶Review

Plot each pair of points on a coordin… through them. Find the slope of the…

20. (1, 1) and (–3, 3)

Find each percent of change. (Modul…

22. A $45.00 book sells for $30.00.

23. A tree grows from 4 ft to 5 ft 6 i…

24. In 1850, New Mexico's populati… it was about 61,547.

Find each product. (Toolbox, p. 589)

25. $3.6 \cdot 10^2$　26. $0.4 \cdot 10^1$

29. $75.3 \cdot 10^4$　30. $9.87 \cdot 10^5$

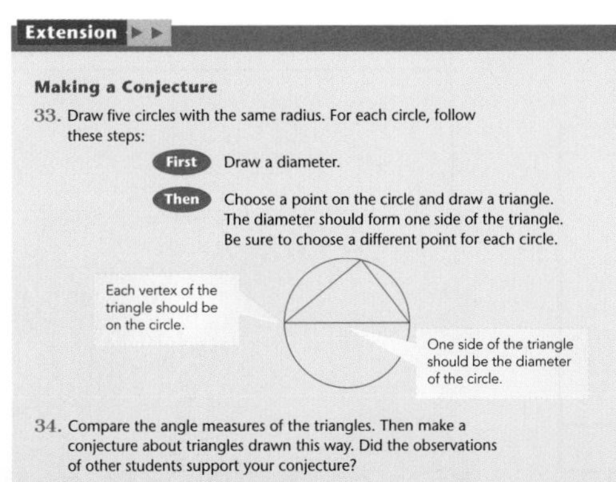

Extension ▶▶

Making a Conjecture

33. Draw five circles with the same radius. For each circle, follow these steps:

    First　Draw a diameter.

    Then　Choose a point on the circle and draw a triangle. The diameter should form one side of the triangle. Be sure to choose a different point for each circle.

34. Compare the angle measures of the triangles. Then make a conjecture about triangles drawn this way. Did the observations of other students support your conjecture?

Extension problems challenge you to extend what you have learned and to apply it in a new setting.

TECHNOLOGY OVERVIEW

CALCULATORS & COMPUTERS

There are many opportunities to use calculators, as well as mental-math and paper-and-pencil methods. Online resources and a Technology Book provide opportunities to use computers and calculators to explore concepts and solve problems.

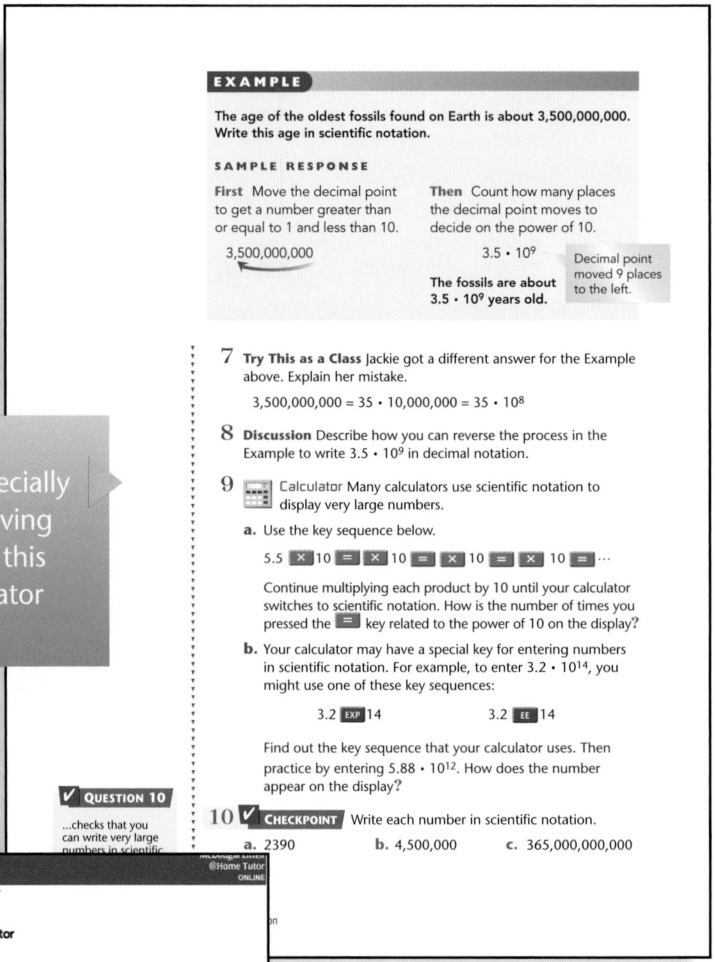

EXAMPLE

The age of the oldest fossils found on Earth is about 3,500,000,000. Write this age in scientific notation.

SAMPLE RESPONSE

First Move the decimal point to get a number greater than or equal to 1 and less than 10.

3,500,000,000

Then Count how many places the decimal point moves to decide on the power of 10.

$3.5 \cdot 10^9$

Decimal point moved 9 places to the left.

The fossils are about $3.5 \cdot 10^9$ years old.

7 **Try This as a Class** Jackie got a different answer for the Example above. Explain her mistake.

$3{,}500{,}000{,}000 = 35 \cdot 10{,}000{,}000 = 35 \cdot 10^8$

8 **Discussion** Describe how you can reverse the process in the Example to write $3.5 \cdot 10^9$ in decimal notation.

9 Calculator Many calculators use scientific notation to display very large numbers.

a. Use the key sequence below.

5.5 [×] 10 [=] [×] 10 [=] [×] 10 [=] [×] 10 [=] ...

Continue multiplying each product by 10 until your calculator switches to scientific notation. How is the number of times you pressed the [=] key related to the power of 10 on the display?

b. Your calculator may have a special key for entering numbers in scientific notation. For example, to enter $3.2 \cdot 10^{14}$, you might use one of these key sequences:

3.2 [EXP] 14   3.2 [EE] 14

Find out the key sequence that your calculator uses. Then practice by entering $5.88 \cdot 10^{12}$. How does the number appear on the display?

QUESTION 10

...checks that you can write very large numbers in scientific

10 **CHECKPOINT** Write each number in scientific notation.

a. 2390   **b.** 4,500,000   **c.** 365,000,000,000

Using Calculators

Calculators can be especially useful as a problem solving tool. The questions on this page help make calculator use meaningful.

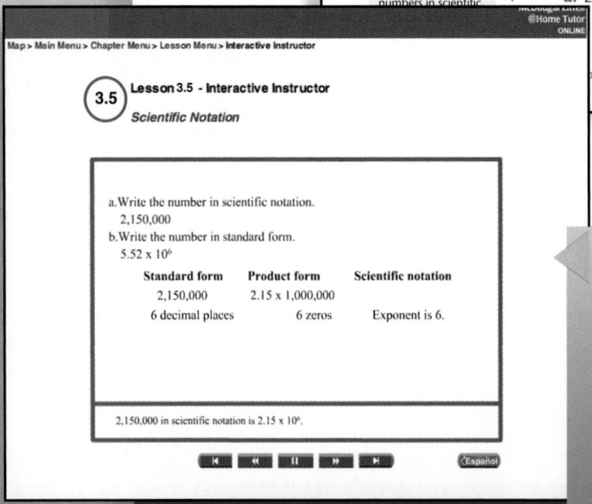

@Home Tutor ONLINE

Map > Main Menu > Chapter Menu > Lesson Menu > Interactive Instructor

3.5 **Lesson 3.5 - Interactive Instructor**

Scientific Notation

a. Write the number in scientific notation.
2,150,000
b. Write the number in standard form.
5.52×10^6

Standard form	Product form	Scientific notation
2,150,000	$2.15 \times 1{,}000{,}000$	
6 decimal places	6 zeros	Exponent is 6.

2,150,000 in scientific notation is 2.15×10^6.

Español

Using Computers

The @Home Tutor is an interactive program that provides additional instruction and practice. The tutorial, and other resources, can be accessed at classzone.com.

ASSESSMENT OVERVIEW

ASSESSMENT & PORTFOLIOS

In each module there are a number of questions and projects that help you check your progress and reflect on what you have learned. These pages are listed under *Assessment Options* in the Table of Contents.

E^2 stands for Extended Exploration—a problem solving project that you'll want to add to your portfolio.

The Situation

Try the following puzzle. Is mystery or mathematics at work?

- Pick an integer between 1 and 10.
- Multiply your number by 6.
- Add 12.
- Divide by 3.
- Subtract 4.
- Divide by your original number.
- Add 4.
- Match the number with the corresponding letter of the alphabet (1 = A, 2 = B, *and so on*).
- Think of a state in the United States that begins with that letter.
- Look at the third letter of the name of the state. Think of a fruit that begins with that letter and grows in that state.
- Turn your book upside-down and look at the bottom of the page to complete the mystery.

The Problem

Explain why the mystery puzzle works. Then create a puzzle of your own and explain why it works.

Something to Think About

- How might examining a mystery puzzle with fewer steps help you?
- Does this puzzle work for any positive integer? Would it work for negative integers? decimals? fractions?

Present Your Results

Write your puzzle on a sheet of paper. Include the solution on the back. Explain why the puzzle above works, and why your mystery puzzle works.

Student Self-Assessment Scales

Student Resource

If your score is in the shaded area, explain why on the back of this sheet and stop.

The star indicates that you excelled in some way.

Problem Solving

0 I did not understand the problem well enough to get started or I did not show any work.
2 4 I understood the problem well enough to make a plan and to work toward a solution.
6 I made a plan, I used it to solve the problem, and I verified my solution.

Mathematical Language

0 I did not use any mathematical vocabulary or symbols, or I did not use them correctly, or my use was not appropriate.
2 4 I used appropriate mathematical language, but the way it was used was not always correct or other terms and symbols were needed.
6 I used mathematical language that was correct and appropriate to make my meaning clear.

Representations

0 I did not use any representations such as equations...
2 4 ...ropriate representa- ...o solve the problem or ...lain my solution, but ...t always correct or ...ntations were needed.
6 I used appropriate and correct representations to solve the problem or explain my solution.

... and used them to ...on to other cases, ...hat this problem ...roblems, mathe- ...pplications.
6 I extended the ideas in the solution to the general case, or I showed how this problem relates to other problems, mathematical ideas, or applications.

...my solution ...r in most ...s may have trouble understanding parts of it.
6 The presentation of my solution and reasoning is clear and can be understood by others.

Toolbox 599

Assessing Problem Solving

For each E^2, you can use the Student Self-Assessment Scales on page 599. They will help you become a better problem solver.

MODULE 3 Review and Assessment

You will need • *graph paper* (Exs. 9–12) • *compass, ruler, and Review and Assessment Labsheet* (Ex. 18)

Find each value. Describe your method. Tell whether your answer is exact or an estimate. (Sec. 1, Explor. 1)

1. $\sqrt{0.09}$
2. $\sqrt{16,000}$
3. $-\sqrt{96}$
4. $\sqrt{\frac{4}{81}}$

5. Keith claims that the large can will hold twice as much as the small can. Is he correct? Explain. (Sec. 1, Explor. 2)

Find each value. (Sec. 2, Explor. 1)

6. $\frac{3(4) + 21}{\sqrt{102 + 19}}$
7. $\sqrt{\frac{8(3) + 2(-4)}{36}}$
8. $\frac{5^2}{4(-3) + 87}$

Graph each equation. Tell whether the graph is *linear* or *nonlinear*. (Sec. 2, Explor. 2)

Module Review and Assessment

Each module ends with exercises to help you review and assess what you've learned.

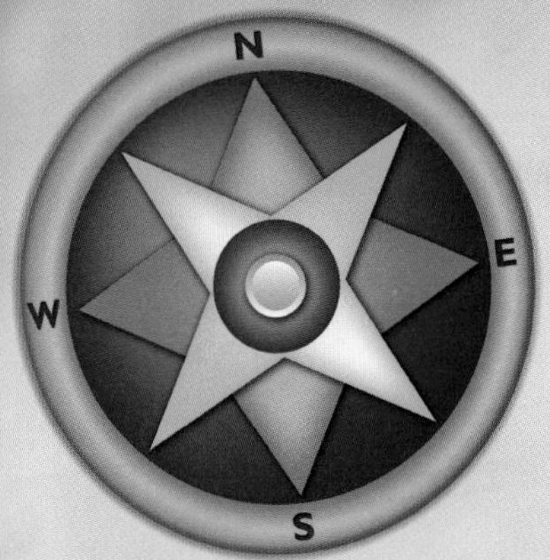

Scavenger Hunt

Your textbook will be an important tool in your study of mathematics this year. Complete the scavenger hunt below to learn more about your textbook and its various resources.

The following resources will help you on your Scavenger Hunt:

- **Table of Contents**
- **Test-Taking Skills**
- **Toolbox**
- **Tables**
- **Glossary**
- **Index**
- **Selected Answers**

1. Why do you think the title of the book is *Math Thematics*?

2. According to the book, what does STEM stand for?

3. What are the titles of the eight modules you will be studying?

4. In which module and section will you learn about "Slope-Intercept Form"?

5. In Module 7 Section 3, what math will you be learning?

6. a. On what page does the Student Resources section begin?

   b. What is the eighth math topic that is reviewed in the Toolbox?

   c. Use the Table of Symbols to find the meaning of the symbol $\approx$.

   d. In which of the Student Resources can you find the definition of independent events?

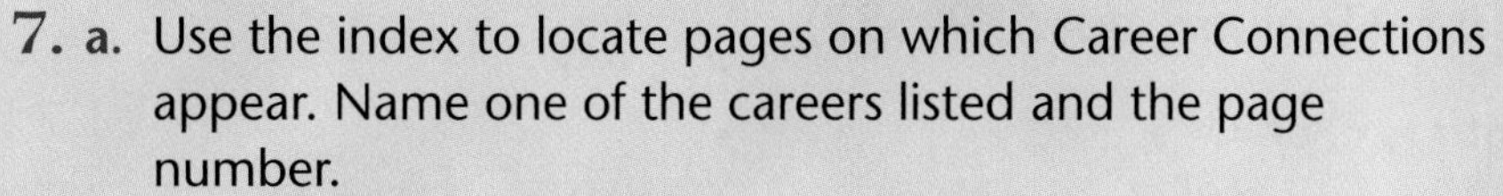

7. a. Use the index to locate pages on which Career Connections appear. Name one of the careers listed and the page number.

   b. Turn to that page and list the person's name and the module theme.

8. What is the title of the Extended Exploration (E^2) in Module 1?

9. On what page are inequalities first discussed?

10. Give a brief summary of the Module 2 Module Project.

11. What does every Key Concepts page have in common?

12. What is the suggested homework assignment for Exploration 2 of Module 4 Section 2?

13. What is the goal of Module 8 Section 3 Exploration 1?

14. How many exercises are in the Review and Assessment for Module 6?

15. What is the internet address that you can use to find online resources about a module?

16. Use the Table of Measures to find the normal body temperature in degrees Celsius.

17. What is the definition of algorithm?

18. For more help with Exercise 22 of the Spiral Review on page 346, what page would you review?

PRE-COURSE TEST

NUMBERS AND OPERATIONS

Decimal Concepts (Toolbox, pp. 579–582)

Replace each __?__ with >, <, or =.

1. 0.650 __?__ 0.65
2. 0.9 __?__ 0.99
3. 0.2 __?__ 0.02

Find each product.

4. 251×0.9
5. 7.65×1.2
6. 0.088×0.06

Find each quotient. If necessary, round each answer to the nearest hundredth.

7. $10\overline{)560.5}$
8. $16\overline{)780}$
9. $2.7\overline{)26.46}$

Divisibility, Factors, and Multiples (Toolbox, pp. 583–584)

Test each number for divisibility.

10. Is 636 divisible by 4?
11. Is 3852 divisible by 6?
12. Is 52,418 divisible by 8?

Find the GCF and the LCM of each pair of numbers.

13. 18, 45
14. 17, 50
15. 225, 240

Fraction Concepts (Toolbox, pp. 585–588)

Replace each __?__ with the number that will make the fractions equivalent.

16. $\frac{5}{9} = \frac{?}{18}$
17. $\frac{7}{8} = \frac{?}{40}$
18. $\frac{12}{56} = \frac{?}{14}$

Find each sum, difference, product, or quotient. Write each answer in lowest terms.

19. $\frac{1}{8} + \frac{2}{5}$
20. $\frac{4}{7} - \frac{3}{8}$
21. $\frac{7}{15} + \frac{1}{3}$
22. $\frac{1}{7} \cdot \frac{7}{8}$
23. $\frac{3}{5} \div \frac{6}{25}$
24. $1\frac{1}{8} \cdot \frac{5}{9}$

Write each fraction as a decimal and as a percent.

25. $\frac{3}{25}$
26. $\frac{9}{10}$
27. $\frac{17}{20}$

Order of Operations and Integers (Toolbox, pp. 589–590)

Find each answer.

28. $70 - 20 \cdot 3 + 5$
29. $50 - 4^2 \cdot 2$
30. $2(3 + 2)^2$

Use a number line to write each group of integers in order from least to greatest.

31. 2, 1, –2
32. 0, 6, –5, 3
33. 4, –5, 3, –3

GEOMETRY AND MEASUREMENT

Locating Points in a Coordinate Plane (Toolbox, p. 591)

Use the diagram at the right. Give the coordinates of each point.

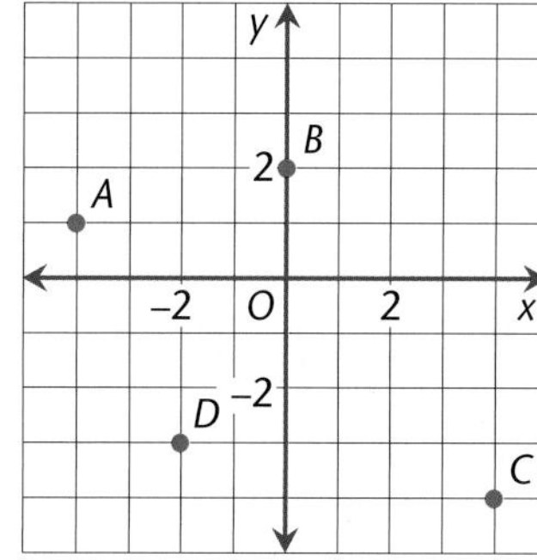

34. *A*
35. *B*
36. *C*
37. *D*

Angles and Triangles (Toolbox, pp. 592–594)

Tell whether each triangle is (a) *acute, right,* or *obtuse* and (b) *scalene, isosceles,* or *equilateral.*

38. 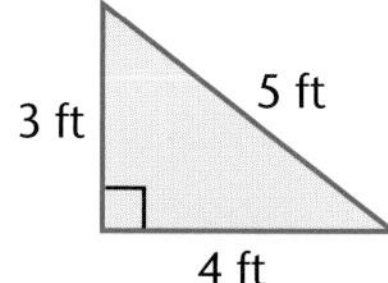

39. 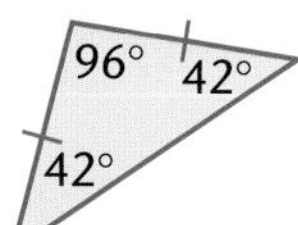

40. 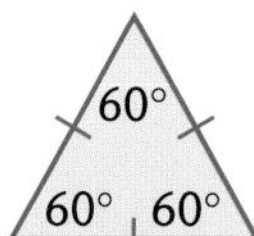

41. Explain why the figure in Exercise 40 is a regular polygon.

Using Formulas from Geometry (Toolbox, p. 595)

Find the volume of each right rectangular prism.

42. base length: 7 m, base width: 3 m, height: 4 m
43. base length: 5 cm, base width: 4 cm, height: 8 cm

DATA ANALYSIS

Finding the Mean, Median, Mode, and Range (Toolbox, p. 596)

Find the mean, the median, the mode(s), and the range of each set of data.

44. 20, 18, 7, 18, 20, 13, 16
45. 56, 51, 47, 61, 58, 59, 48, 60

TEST-TAKING SKILLS

READING AND SOLVING WORD PROBLEMS

Reading a Word Problem

Before you can solve a word problem, you have to understand the information being given and the question being asked.

- Read quickly through the problem once to get a general sense of what the problem is about.
- Read carefully through the problem a second time, focusing on those things that relate to solving the problem.

Problem

Anna is planning a vegetable garden. She wants the garden to be 6 ft wide and in the shape of a rectangle that is not a square. She paid $144 for fencing that cost $4 per linear foot, and she plans to use all of it to fence her garden. If Anna decides to make a square garden wider than 6 ft, how much more or how much less area will the garden cover?

Solving a Word Problem

- Underline, jot down, and/or make a quick sketch of any information that can be used to solve the problem.

Fencing: Total cost = $144
Cost = $4 per foot

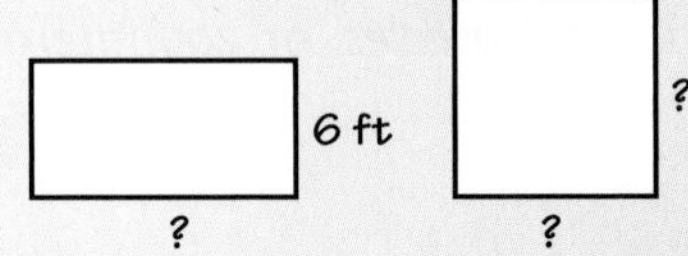

- Decide which math topic(s) relate to the problem. Think of procedures, formulas, and definitions related to that topic that can be used to solve the problem.

Total feet = total cost ÷ cost per foot
Perimeter = sum of the side lengths
Area = length x width

- Solve the problem, making sure that the question answered is the question asked. If the problem asks more than one question, make sure you answer every question

Total feet = 144 ÷ 4 = 36 feet

The two lengths of the garden use 36 ft – 12 ft = 24 ft of fencing. So, the garden's length is 24 ft ÷ 2, or 12 ft.

Area of rectangle = 12 ft x 6 ft = 72 ft^2

Area of square = 9 ft x 9 ft = 81 ft^2, because one side is 36 ft ÷ 4, or 9 ft.

The area of the square garden is greater by 9 square feet, because 81 – 72 = 9.

- Check your work.

4 x (6 + 6 + 12 + 12) = 4 x 36 = 144 ✓
4 x (9 + 9 + 9 + 9) = 4 x 36 = 144 ✓

Keep up with the course.

Ask questions about things you don't understand. Take advantage of extra-help sessions. If you get a problem wrong on a test or on your homework, try to figure out why you got it wrong. If you are absent, find out what material you missed and make up the work.

Become familiar with the test.

Make sure you know the answers to the following questions before you take the test:

- How much time do I have to complete the test?
- How many points are assigned to each type of question?
- About how much time should I spend answering a multiple choice question? a short response question? an extended reponse question?
- If I can't answer a multiple choice question, is it better to guess, or to leave a blank?
- Am I better off answering the easy, or the more difficult questions first, or should I just answer the questions as they come?
- Is paper provided for scrap work, or should it be done in the white space of the test booklet?
- On which, if any, parts of the test may I use a calculator?

During the Test

- As soon as the test begins, jot down on scrap paper or in the white space of the test booklet any formulas or procedures you're afraid you'll forget.
- Quickly scan the entire test to get an idea of which problems will probably take you the most time to do. Some people prefer to do those problems first. Others do them last.
- Skip over any question you are stuck on. Make a mark next to the question in your test booklet so that you can go back to it later if you have time. Be sure to leave a blank on your answer sheet for the answer to the question.
- Read an entire problem carefully before you start to answer it. Don't assume you know the question that will be asked.
- When answering a multiple choice question, don't assume your answer is correct because it is one of the choices. Always double check your work.
- If you think you can't do a multiple choice question, try substituting each choice back into the problem to see if it is the correct choice.
- If you must guess on a multiple choice question, first try to eliminate any choices that are obviously wrong because they have the wrong units or sign, for example.
- As you write the answer to an extended or short response question, imagine that you are writing an explanation for a fellow student who doesn't know how to solve the problem.
- If you can do part, but not all, of an extended or short response question, write down what you can do. Something written may receive partial credit. Nothing written definitely receives no credit.

BUILDING TEST-TAKING SKILLS (For use after Module 2.)

Strategies for Answering

Multiple Choice Questions

You can use the 4-step approach to solving problems on page 64 to solve any problem. If you have difficulty solving a problem involving multiple choice, you may be able to use one of the strategies below to choose the correct answer. You may also be able to use these strategies and others to check whether your answer to a multiple choice question is reasonable.

Strategy: Estimate the Answer

Problem 1

The table shows how many nickels you save each day. If the pattern continues, what is the first day you will save more than fifty dollars' worth of nickels?

You need 1000 nickels to equal fifty dollars.

Day	1	2	3
Nickels	$3^1 = 3$	$3^2 = 9$	$3^3 = 27$

A. day 5
B. day 6
C. day 7
D. day 8

Estimate: $3^5 = 27 \times 3 \times 3 \approx 27 \times 9$. A low estimate is $25 \times 8 = 200$. A high estimate is $30 \times 10 = 300$. So 3^5 is between 200 and 300. Since $3^6 = 3^5 \times 3$; 3^6 is between 600 and 900. Since $3^7 = 3^6 \times 3$, 3^7 is between 1800 and 2700. The correct answer is C.

Strategy: Use Visual Clues

Problem 2

How many feet of fencing do you need to enclose the square dog pen shown?

625 ft²

The dog pen's area is 625 square feet. Use the guess and check strategy to find the length of one side of the pen. Each side of the pen is 25 feet long.

F. 25 ft
G. 50 ft
H. 75 ft
I. 100 ft

Multiply the side length by 4 to find the total amount of fencing needed. To enclose the dog pen, you need 100 ft of fencing. The correct answer is I.

Strategy: Use Number Sense

Problem 3

When multiplying a positive fraction less than one by a positive mixed number, the product is __?__.

Think of some examples of a fraction less than 1 times a mixed number, such as $\frac{1}{3} \cdot 1\frac{1}{2}$.

A. greater than the mixed number

B. less than the mixed number

A positive fraction less than 1 times any positive number is less than the number, so the correct answer is B.

C. less than the fraction

D. equal to the fraction

Eliminating Unreasonable Choices

The strategies used to find the correct answers for Problems 1–3 can also be used to eliminate answer choices that are unreasonable or obviously incorrect.

Strategy: Eliminate Choices

Problem 4

A bicycle helmet is on sale at 25% off the original price. The sale price of the bicycle helmet is $48. What was the original price?

Read the problem carefully. The *discount* is 25%, so the sale price is 75% of the original price, not 25%.

F. $12

Not the correct answer: the original price must be greater than the sale price.

G. $56.25

H. $64

48 = 0.75(64). The correct answer is H.

I. $192

Watch Out!
An answer that appears to be correct may be an incorrect answer that you get if you make a common error.

TRY THIS

Explain why the highlighted answer choice is unreasonable.

1. The length of the rectangular top of a picnic table is twice the width. If the perimeter of the table is 18 feet, what is the length?

   A. 3 ft B. 6 ft C. 7 ft D. 9 ft

2. A bathrobe originally priced at $60 is now on sale for $24. What is the percent of decrease in the price?

   F. 40% G. 52% H. 55% I. 60%

3. What is the product –3(–7)(–18)?

   A. –378 B. –278 C. 378 D. 421

Multiple Choice

1. Mary runs 3.5 miles in 28 minutes 42 seconds. What is her average time per mile?

   A. 14 min 21 sec B. 8 min

   C. 9 min 14 sec D. 8 min 12 sec

2. The stem-and-leaf plot shows the number of minutes Sasha spent talking on her cell phone on each of 15 days. What is the mode of the data?

Stem	Leaves
0	0 5 7 7
1	2 7 7
2	1 2 2 2
3	5 6 9
4	0

Key: 3 | 5 represents 35 minutes.

   F. 7 G. 12 H. 17 I. 22

3. You are drawing a circle graph to display the results of a survey. Which angle measure would you use for a sector that represents 55% of the data?

   A. 55° B. 99° C. 180° D. 198°

4. The amount that Pria made life-guarding this week is $5 less than twice the amount she made baby-sitting. If Pria made $185 life-guarding this week, which equation can be used to find the amount she made baby-sitting?

   F. $185 = 2b - 5$ G. $185 = 2b + 5$

   H. $185 = 5b - 2$ I. $185 = 5b + 2$

5. In a survey of 96 randomly selected students at a high school, 12 said that they took art. If there are a total of 642 students enrolled at the high school, how many would you expect take art?

   A. 7 B. 12 C. 80 D. 90

6. The translation $(x + 2, y + 3)$ is applied to a figure with vertices $A(4, 5)$, $B(2, 6)$, $C(0, 3)$, and $D(6, 0)$. Which point is *not* a vertex of the image?

   F. (4, 9) G. (−2, 6)

   H. (6, 8) I. (8, 3)

7. Which expression has the greatest value?

   A. 24% of 752

   B. 49% of 398

   C. 67% of 315

   D. 79% of 240

8. The class treasurer records the amount of money spent and made at the school dance. His notes are shown below. What is the sum of the amounts?

Ticket Sales	**+$423**
Disc Jockey	**−$349**
Decorations	**−$65**

   F. −$9 G. $7

   H. $9 I. $74

9. Six red marbles and 4 blue marbles are in a bag. A marble is randomly drawn from the bag. What is the probability that it is a blue marble?

   A. $\frac{1}{4}$ B. $\frac{2}{5}$

   C. $\frac{3}{5}$ D. $\frac{2}{3}$

BUILDING TEST-TAKING SKILLS (For use after Module 4.)

Strategies for Answering

Short Response Questions

Scoring Rubric

FULL CREDIT
- answer is correct, *and*
- work or reasoning is included

PARTIAL CREDIT
- answer is correct, but reasoning is incorrect, *or*
- answer is incorrect, but reasoning is correct

NO CREDIT
- no answer is given, *or*
- answer makes no sense

A *short response* question should take about five minutes to answer. A solution should always include the work or reasoning that leads to a correct answer. The three ways a solution can be scored are listed above.

Problem

Your father hires you to work in his store after school. He pays you $35 the first week. You can then choose from 2 payment plans. With Plan A, you earn a 10% raise each week. With Plan B, you earn a $4 raise each week. Which plan is a better deal?

FULL CREDIT SOLUTION

Week	1	2	3	4	5	6
Plan A pay	$35.00	$38.50	$42.35	$46.59	$51.25	$56.38
Plan A total	$35.00	$73.50	$115.85	$162.44	$213.69	$270.07
Plan B pay	$35.00	$39.00	$43.00	$47.00	$51.00	$55.00
Plan B total	$35.00	$74.00	$117.00	$164.00	$215.00	$270.00

Data are used to justify the solution.

If you work 5 weeks or less, Plan B is better. If you work more than 5 weeks, Plan A is better, because the total pay is greater and the 10% weekly raise will continue to be more than $4.

The question is answered clearly and in complete sentences.

PARTIAL CREDIT SOLUTION

Week	1	2	3	4	5	6
Plan A	$35.00	$38.50	$42.35	$46.59	$51.25	$56.38
Plan B	$35.00	$39.00	$43.00	$47.00	$51.00	$55.00

The calculations are correct.

Plan B is better if you work 4 weeks or less, but Plan A is better if you work more than 4 weeks.

The reasoning is faulty, because the total amount earned was not considered.

PARTIAL CREDIT SOLUTION

Plan B is the better plan. The table shows that more money is earned with Plan B in each of the first 4 weeks.

The table does not include data past week 4. So, the answer is incorrect.

Week	1	2	3	4
Plan B	\$35.00	\$39.00	\$43.00	\$47.00
Plan A	\$35.00	\$38.50	\$42.35	\$46.59
Difference	\$0	\$1.50	\$0.65	\$0.41

The calculations are correct.

NO CREDIT SOLUTION

Plan B is the better plan.

The answer is incorrect.

Week	1	2	3	4	5
Plan A	\$35.00	\$38.50	\$42.00	\$45.50	\$49.00
Plan B	\$35.00	\$39.00	\$43.00	\$47.00	\$51.00

The calculations are not done correctly.

TRY THIS

Score each solution to the short response question below as *full credit, partial credit,* or *no credit.* Explain your reasoning.

Watch Out!
Be sure to explain your reasoning clearly.

Problem

You have a set of glasses. Each glass has the shape of a cylinder with a diameter of 6 cm and a height of 6 cm. You have a 1750 cm^3 bottle of juice. About how many glasses can you fill to the brim? Explain.

1. $V = 2\pi rh \approx 2(3.14)(6)(6) \approx 108$, so the volume of the glass is about 100 cm^3 and $2000 \div 100 \approx 20$; 20 times.

2. $V = \pi r^2 h \approx (3.14)(9)(6) = 169.56 \approx 170$, so the volume of the glass is about 170 cm^3. Because $1750 \div 170 \approx 10$, I can fill about 10 glasses. I rounded the actual volume up and the quotient $1750 \div 170$ down, so I'm sure I have enough juice to fill 10 glasses.

Short Response

1. If the side length of a square is doubled, by what factor does the perimeter increase? By what factor does the area increase? Explain your reasoning.

2. Jen works as a waitress. During one shift, Jen kept track of the total bill (rounded to the nearest dollar) for each customer and the corresponding tip she received. The data are shown below. Make a scatter plot of the data. Estimate Jen's tip for a total bill of $40.00. Explain your method.

Bill	Tip
$13.00	$2.00
$72.00	$13.00
$51.00	$10.00
$44.00	$7.00

Bill	Tip
$24.00	$4.50
$30.00	$4.00
$31.00	$6.00
$63.00	$9.50

3. Sheri is buying a square tarp for a camping trip. The package says that the tarp has an area of 182 square feet. What is the approximate side length of the tarp? Show your work.

4. Glen used fencing to enclose a rectangular garden that is 40 feet long and 25 feet wide. He wants to take down the fencing and enclose a square garden. What are the dimensions of the largest square garden he can build using the existing fence? Explain your method.

5. There are a total of 39 girls on the soccer and lacrosse teams. Seven of the girls play both sports. There are 2 more girls on the soccer team than on the lacrosse team. Make a Venn diagram that shows the relationship between the members of the soccer and lacrosse teams. Then tell how many girls play lacrosse, but not soccer.

6. The radius of Cylinder A is half that of Cylinder B. The height of Cylinder A is twice that of Cylinder B. Which cylinder has greater volume? Explain your reasoning.

7. Clarice asked a group of 112 students which of two televised sports they had watched in the last week. The number of students who watched neither was twice the number who watched both. The rest of the results are shown in the Venn diagram. To the nearest whole percent, what percent of the students surveyed watched both sports? Show your work.

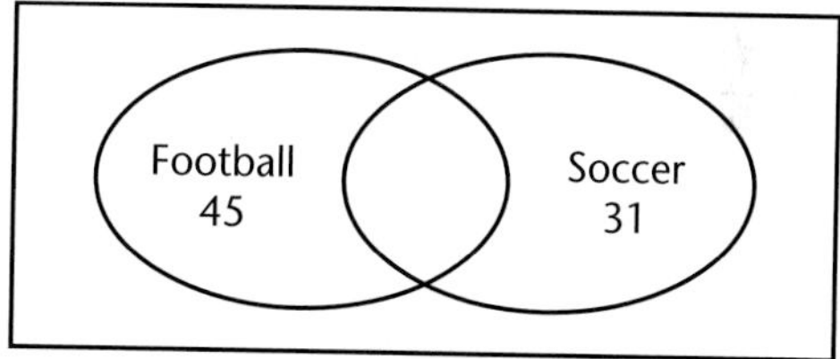

8. The figure shows the floor of one room in a house under construction. The builder is having a hardwood floor installed in the unshaded region at a cost of $16 per square foot, and ceramic tile installed in the shaded region at a cost of $10 per square foot. Find the total cost of installing the floors. Show your work.

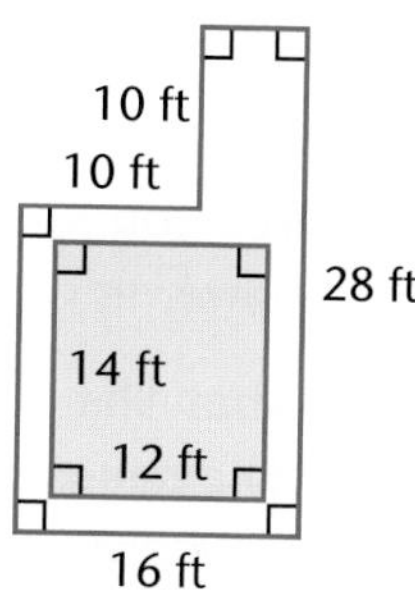

BUILDING TEST-TAKING SKILLS (For use after Module 6.)

Strategies for Answering

Context-Based Multiple Choice Questions

Some of the information you need to solve a context-based multiple choice question may appear in a table, a diagram, or a graph.

Problem 1

You made an angel food cake. The cake is approximately cylindrical, with a cylindrical hole through the center. If you want to frost the top and side of the cake, what is the surface area you need to frost?

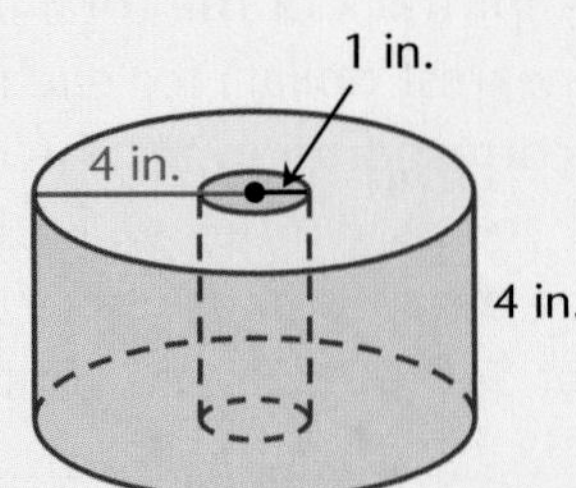

A. 47 in.^{2} B. 101 in.^{2}

C. 148 in.^{2} D. 179 in.^{2}

Solution

1) To find the area of the top of the cake, you first need to find the area of the outer circle and the area of the inner circle.

Read the problem carefully. Decide what calculations you need to make to solve the problem.

Area of outer circle:

$$A = \pi r^2 = \pi \cdot 4^2 = 16\pi$$

Area of inner circle:

$$A = \pi r^2 = \pi \cdot 1^2 = \pi$$

2) Area of top of cake = Area of outer circle − Area of inner circle

$A = 16\pi - \pi = 15\pi$

Use the areas of the outer and inner circles to find the area of the top of the cake.

3) Area of cake side = 2π • Radius of outer circle • Height of cake

$A = 2\pi \cdot 4 \cdot 4 = 32\pi$

4) Add the area of the top of the cake and the area of the side:

$A = 15\pi + 32\pi = 47\pi \approx 148$

The surface area you need to frost is about 148 square inches. The correct answer is C.

5) Check to see that the answer is reasonable. Estimate the area of the top of the cake: $\pi \cdot 4^2 - \pi \cdot 1^2 \approx 3 \cdot 16 - 3 \cdot 1 = 48 - 3 = 45$. Estimate the area of the cake side: $2\pi \cdot 4 \cdot 4 \approx 96$. Since $96 + 45 \approx 140$ square inches, C is the most reasonable choice.

Problem 2

Vanessa has paced off her distance from a clock tower she knows to be 48 feet high. Her eye is 5 feet above the ground, and she is standing about 30 feet from the base of the tower. About how long is the line of sight from her eye to the top of the tower?

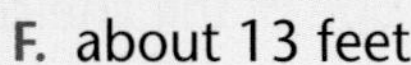

F. about 13 feet G. about 52 feet

H. about 57 feet I. about 73 feet

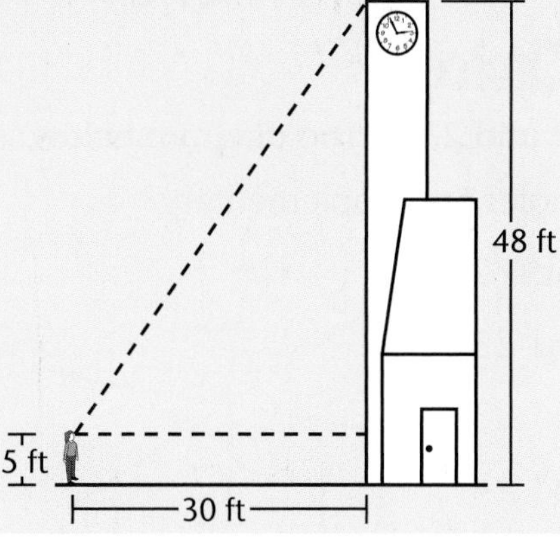

Solution

1) Find the height of the tower above Vanessa's eye level:

$48 - 5 = 43$ ft

Subtract the height of Vanessa's eye level from the height of the clock tower.

2) Let x = the length of Vanessa's line of sight.

Use the Pythagorean theorem to write and solve an equation.

$x^2 = 30^2 + 43^2$

$x^2 = 900 + 1849$

$x^2 = 2749$

$x \approx 52.4$

Vanessa is about 52 feet from the base of the clock tower.

The correct answer is G.

TRY THIS

1. In Problem 2, if Vanessa were 35 feet from the tower, how long would her line of sight be?

A. about 8 ft B. about 55 ft

C. about 59 ft D. about 78 ft

Watch Out!
Be sure that you know what question you are asked to answer. Some choices given may be intended to distract you.

In Exercises 2–3, use the spinner shown.

2. What is the probability of spinning an even number?

F. 0.125 G. 0.25

H. 0.375 I. 0.625

3. What is the probability of landing on a shaded section?

A. 0.375 B. 0.4

C. 0.5 D. 0.75

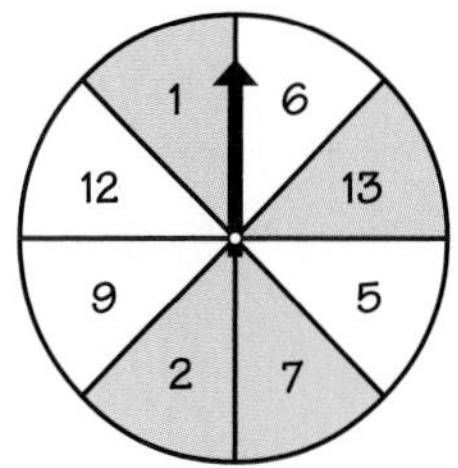

Multiple Choice

In Exercises 1 and 2, use the diagram below.

1. Which angles are supplementary?

   A. ∠1 and ∠2

   B. ∠2 and ∠3

   C. ∠1 and ∠3

   D. ∠2 and ∠4

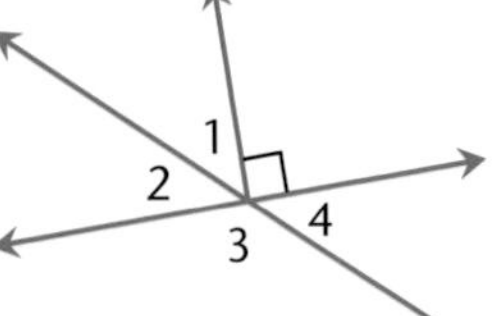

2. Which angles are vertical angles?

   F. ∠1 and ∠2 G. ∠2 and ∠3

   H. ∠1 and ∠3 I. ∠2 and ∠4

3. A can of soup is shown. Which are reasonable dimensions for the label?

   A. 27 cm by 11 cm B. 27 cm by 14 cm

   C. 54 cm by 11 cm D. 54 cm by 14 cm

4. A bagel shop offers the bagel and cream cheese choices shown below. How many different bagel and cream cheese combinations are possible?

Bagels	**Cream Cheese**
plain	plain
poppy seed	chive
onion	smoked salmon
sesame seed	

   F. 7 G. 9

   H. 12 I. 16

5. Carmen and Joey each buy notebooks at an office supply store. Information about their purchases is shown in the table. If the data were graphed and connected with a line, what would the slope of the line be?

Number of notebooks, x	3	7
Total cost, y	\$8.25	\$19.25

   A. 2.25 B. 2.75 C. 4.75 D. 11

In Exercises 6 and 7, use the diagram below. In the diagram, lines m and n are parallel.

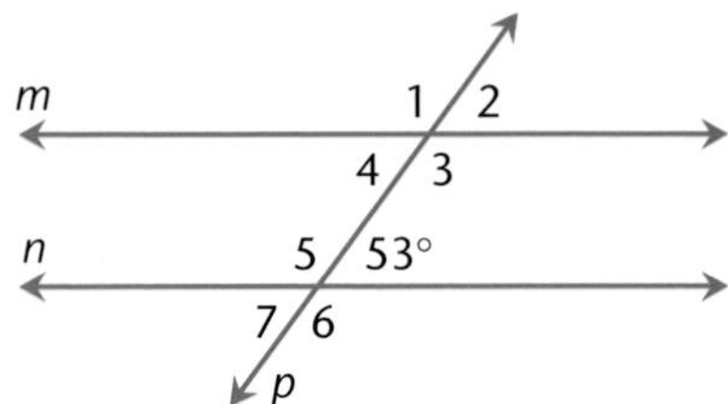

6. What is the measure of ∠7?

   F. 37° G. 53°

   H. 127° I. 143°

7. What is the measure of ∠3?

   A. 37° B. 53°

   C. 127° D. 143°

8. A block of cheese as shown below is being cut into 4 equal pieces to be wrapped and sold at a grocery store. What is the surface area of one piece of cheese?

   F. 408 cm^2

   G. 472.5 cm^2

   H. 472.5 cm^3

   I. 1002 cm^2

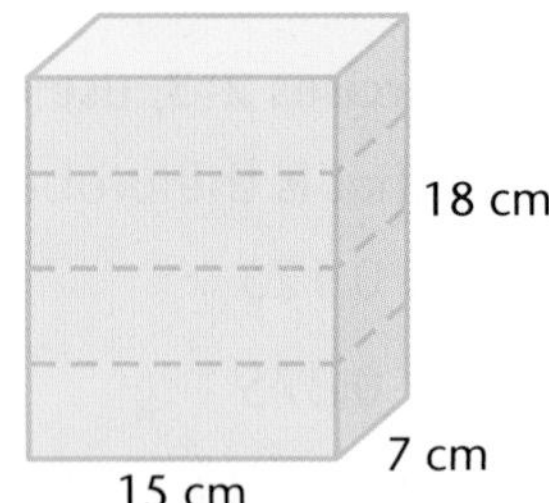

Building Test-Taking Skills (For use after Module 8.)

Strategies for Answering

Extended Response Questions

Scoring Rubric

Full Credit
- answer is correct, *and*
- work or reasoning is included

Partial Credit
- answer is correct, but reasoning is incorrect, *or*
- answer is incorrect, but reasoning is correct

No Credit
- no answer is given, *or*
- answer makes no sense

Problem

In a certain city, a taxicab ride costs $2.25 for entry into the taxicab plus $1.50 per mile traveled. Make a table and draw a graph that shows the cost of a taxicab ride as the distance traveled increases. If you have exactly $9.00 to spend on the taxicab fare, how far can you travel? Explain how you found your answer.

Full Credit Solution

In the graph, the horizontal axis shows the miles traveled and the vertical axis shows the cost of the taxicab ride.

Miles	Cost
0	$2.25
1	$3.75
2	$5.25
3	$6.75
4	$8.25
5	$9.75
6	$11.25
7	$12.75

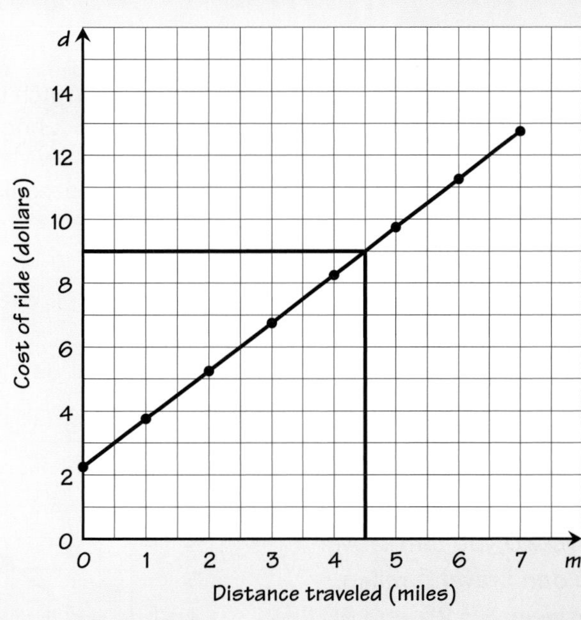

The table and graph are correct and reflect an understanding of the problem.

For $9.00, you can travel 4.5 miles in a taxicab.

The answer is correct.

To find my answer, I found $9.00 on the vertical axis of the graph. I then looked across and saw that where the line has a y-value of $9.00, the corresponding x-value is 4.5.

The reasoning behind the answer is explained clearly.

Partial credit solution

Miles	Cost
0	$2.25
1	$3.75
2	$5.25
3	$6.75
4	$8.25

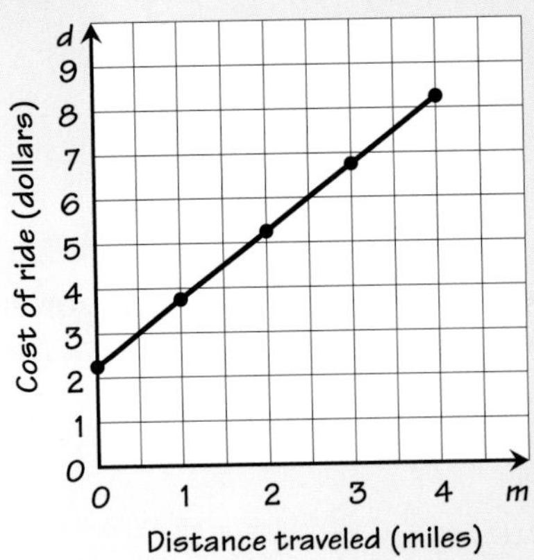

The table and graph are correct.

The taxicab costs $1.50 per mile. Since $9.00 ÷ $1.50 = 6, you can travel 6 miles for $9.00.

The answer is incorrect.

No credit solution

Miles	0	1	2	3	4
Cost	$2.25	$3.75	$5.25	$6.75	$8.25

The table is correct, but there is no graph.

You can travel 5 miles for $9.00.

The answer is incorrect, and there is no explanation.

Try This

1. A student's answer to the problem on the previous page is given below. Score the solution as *full credit*, *partial credit*, or *no credit*. Explain your choice. If you choose *partial credit* or *no credit*, explain how you would change the answer to earn a score of *full credit*.

Watch Out!
Scoring is often based on how clearly you explain your reasoning.

Miles	0	1	2	3	4	5
Cost	$2.25	$3.75	$5.25	$6.75	$8.25	$9.75

You can travel 4.5 miles in a taxicab for $9.00.

The table shows that for $8.25 you can travel 4 miles, and for $9.75 you can travel 5 miles. Since $9.00 is halfway between $8.25 and $9.75, the distance you can travel for $9.00 must be halfway between 4 miles and 5 miles. Since 4.5 miles is halfway between 4 miles and 5 miles, you can travel 4.5 miles.

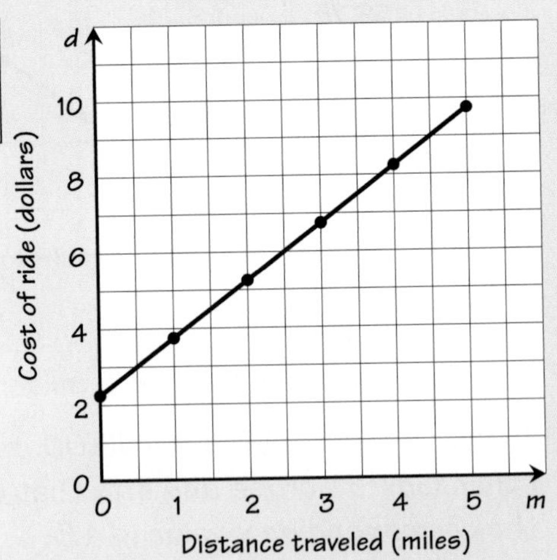

Extended Response

1. You are deciding which of two gyms to join. Gym A has a membership fee of \$75 and a monthly fee of \$45. Gym B has no membership fee and has a monthly fee of \$60. Write an equation for each gym that models the cost of the gym in terms of the number of months you go to the gym. Graph each equation in the same coordinate plane. What is the point of intersection and what does it represent? Describe under what conditions you would choose to join each gym.

2. Describe how to move triangle ABC to triangle $A'B'C'$ using a series of transformations that includes a reflection, a rotation, and a translation. Tell what the new coordinates of triangle ABC are after each transformation.

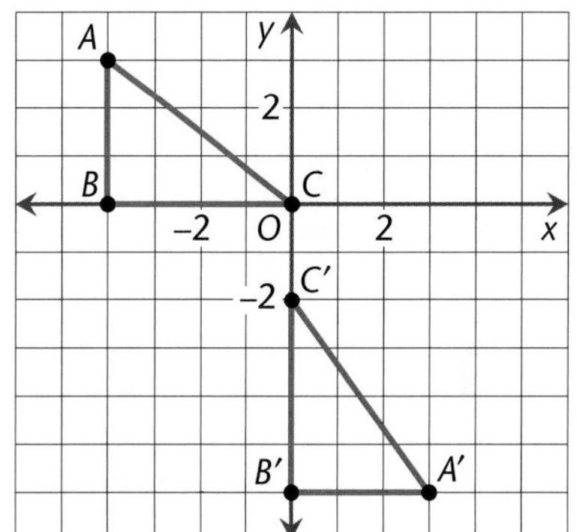

3. Adrianne has \$50 to put in a savings account or to buy a savings bond. With \$50, she can buy a savings bond that will be worth \$100 in 20 years. With the savings account, Adrianne's money will earn 3% interest compounded annually. With which option will Adrianne have more money in 20 years? About how long will it take for the money in the savings account to equal \$100? Explain your reasoning.

4. The table below gives the population of a town from 1995 to 2004. Make a scatter plot of the data. Does the data have a *negative correlation*, a *positive correlation*, or *no correlation*? What do you predict the population of the town will be in 2007? Explain how you made your prediction.

Year	1995	1996	1997	1998	1999
Population	11,750	11,850	11,800	11,320	11,290
Year	2000	2001	2002	2003	2004
Population	11,500	11,290	11,150	10,900	10,780

5. The stem-and-leaf plot shows the ages of fans in the front row of a concert. Use the data to make a histogram, a box-and-whisker plot, and a circle graph. Which of the four displays would you use to find the median of the data? Which of the displays would you use to find the mode? Which of the displays would you use to find the numerical interval containing the greatest number of data? Explain your choices.

Ages of Fans in the Front Row of a Concert

1	6 6 8 9 9 9
2	0 2 3 3 5 7 8
3	4 6 6
4	0 5 8
5	1

Key: 3 | 4 represents 34.

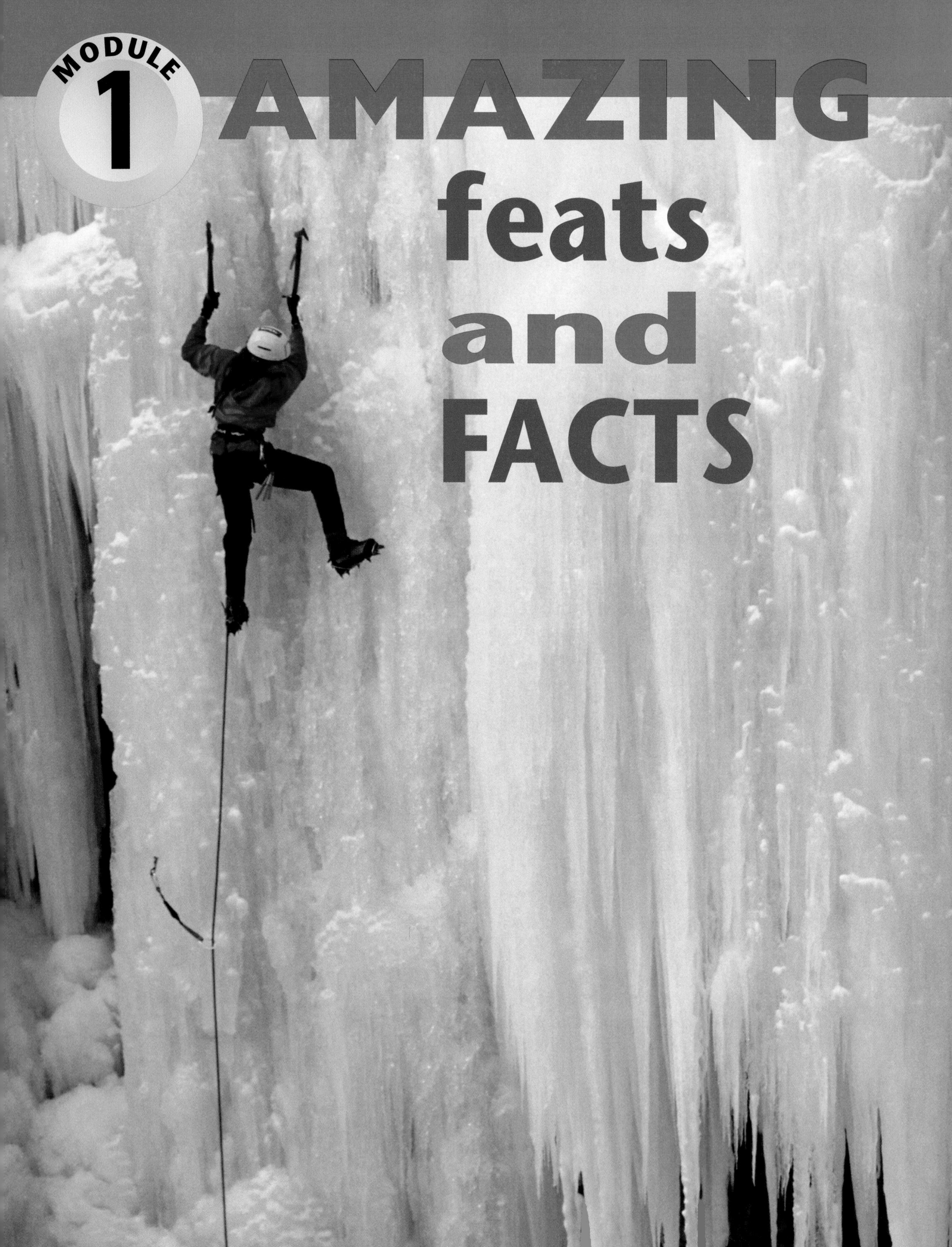
MODULE
1
AMAZING
feats
and
FACTS

CONNECTING
MATHEMATICS & The Theme

Section Overview

1 **Rates and Data Displays**
As you determine if facts are realistic:
- Find rates and unit rates
- Draw and interpret circle graphs and histograms

2 **Displaying Data**
As you compare musical performers:
- Construct stem-and-leaf plots
- Use and create box-and-whisker plots
- Choose appropriate data displays

3 **Equations and Expressions**
As you investigate various rules of thumb:
- Write and solve equations
- Simplify expressions

4 **Scatter Plots**
As you study athletic record-makers:
- Organize data in a scatter plot
- Use a fitted line to make predictions

5 **Problem Solving and Mathematical Models**
As you learn about the Lake of the Ozarks:
- Use a 4-step problem-solving approach
- Model relationships using tables, graphs, and equations

The Module Project

Fact or Fiction

Every day you are bombarded with claims that seem amazing or incredible. In this project, you will use mathematics to uncover the truth in some of these claims. Then you will display your own amazing claims on a poster to share with your class.

More on the Module Project
See pp. 72–73.

INTERNET
Resources and practice at
classzone.com

Rates and Data Displays

IN THIS SECTION

EXPLORATION 1
- Using Rates

EXPLORATION 2
- Circle Graphs and Histograms

It's AMAZING!?

Setting the Stage

SET UP *Work in a group of 2 or 3.*

Every day news reports on radio and TV, in newspapers and magazines, and online use numbers to describe the world. The facts are often phrased to make a powerful impact. Are the claims accurate? Are they really amazing? In this section, you will use rates and statistics to decide.

◀ Gentoo penguins, the fastest swimming underwater birds, can swim about 132 meters in one minute!

One rapper was able to rap 723 syllables in 51.27 seconds!

On average, Americans eat 36,500 acres of pizza each year!

In the two weeks before it leaves the nest, a baby robin may eat 14 ft of earthworms!

◀ In 2006, the record speed for typing a text message was 160 characters in 41.52 seconds!

Think About It

1 Choose one of the facts above and tell why it seems amazing.

2 How many kilometers could a Gentoo pengin swim in an hour? Does that seem more amazing?

▶ **In this module you will read about some amazing people and use mathematics to investigate some amazing claims.**

Exploration 1

Using RATES

GOAL

LEARN HOW TO...
- use rates
- find equivalent rates

AS YOU...
- determine if facts are realistic

KEY TERMS
- rate
- equivalent rates
- unit rate

▶ **A *rate* was used to describe each fact in the *Setting the Stage.* A rate is a ratio that compares two quantities measured in different units. Rates can be expressed in many different yet equivalent ways.**

EXAMPLE

"On average, Americans eat 36,500 acres of pizza each year!"

The rate compares the number of acres of pizza to the number of years.

Other rates:

73,000 acres in 2 years

100 acres per day

$4{,}356{,}000 \text{ ft}^2$ per day

1 acre = $43{,}560 \text{ ft}^2$
100 acres = $4{,}356{,}000 \text{ ft}^2$

1 year = 365 days

$$\frac{36{,}500 \text{ acres}}{365 \text{ days}} = \frac{100 \text{ acres}}{1 \text{ day}}$$

3 Try This as a Class

a. On average, about how many square inches of pizza do Americans eat each day? ($1 \text{ ft}^2 = 144 \text{ in.}^2$)

b. The population of the United States is about 300,000,000. On average, about how many square inches of pizza does each American eat per day?

c. Based on your answer to part (b) do you find the amount of pizza Americans eat to be amazing? Why or why not?

For Questions 4 and 5, use the fact that a baby robin may eat 14 ft of earthworms in two weeks.

4 What two quantities are being compared in the rate?

5 Write an equivalent rate using the given units.

a. feet per week **b.** feet per day **c.** inches per hour

6 Discussion Which of the rates from Question 5 gives you a better idea of how many earthworms a baby robin may eat? Explain.

FOR ▶ HELP with *ratios*, see **TOOLBOX, p. 585**

▶ **The rates you wrote in Question 5 are *equivalent*. Equivalent rates are equal rates that may be expressed using different units. For example, 1 gal/sec and 60 gal/min are equivalent rates.**

FOR ▶ HELP with *measures*, see **TABLE OF MEASURES, p. 601**

7 Tell whether the given rates are equivalent.

a. 50 mi/hr; 1 mi/min **b.** 48 oz/box; 3 lb/box

▶ **Unit Rates To make a rate easier to understand, it may be helpful to change it to a unit rate. A unit rate is a ratio that compares a quantity to one unit of another quantity.**

EXAMPLE

Change the rate to a unit rate:

A rapper rapped 723 syllables in 51.27 seconds!

SAMPLE RESPONSE

$$\frac{723 \text{ syllables}}{51.27 \text{ sec}} = \frac{723 \text{ syllables} \div 51.27}{51.27 \text{ sec} \div 51.27}$$

$$\approx \frac{14.1 \text{ syllables}}{1 \text{ sec}}$$ or **14.1 syllables per second**

For Questions 8–10, use the fact that a Gentoo penguin can swim 132 m in 1 min.

8 Explain why it might be difficult to picture this rate.

9 **Try This as a Class** Write the rate using the given units.

a. mm/sec **b.** cm/min **c.** km/hr

10 **Discussion**

a. Which of the rates from Question 9 gives you a better idea of how fast a Gentoo penguin can swim? Explain.

b. Which rate would you use to amaze someone? Why?

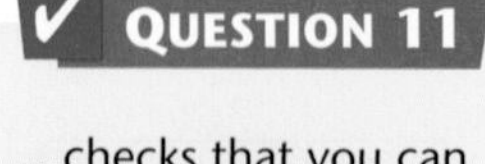

...checks that you can use equivalent rates.

11 **✓ CHECKPOINT** At top speed, a cheetah, the fastest animal on 4 legs, can run about 2060 yd in 1 min.

a. Write an equivalent rate that makes it easier to understand how fast a cheetah can run.

b. Explain why the rate in part (a) makes it easier to understand how fast a cheetah can run.

HOMEWORK EXERCISES ▶ **See Exs. 1–13 on pp. 10–11.**

Exploration 2

Circle Graphs and HISTOGRAMS

GOAL

LEARN HOW TO...
- draw and interpret circle graphs
- draw and interpret histograms

AS YOU...
- examine facts about computer usage and access to the Internet

KEY TERMS
- frequency table
- frequency
- circle graph
- sector
- histogram

SET UP *Work with a partner. You will need:* • *Labsheets 1A and 1B* • *calculator* • *compass* • *protractor*

▶ **The rapid increase in Internet use is one of the most amazing phenomena of our time. In the year 2003, more than 3 in 5 U.S. households had Internet access—over three times the number that had access in 1997, the first year the Census Bureau kept records on Internet access. The number of adults who used the Internet at home in 2003 is displayed below using a *frequency table* and a *circle graph*.**

Frequency Table

Adults Who Used the Internet at Home in 2003	
Age Group	**Number**
18 to 24	16,438,000
25 to 34	23,951,000
35 to 44	29,391,000
45 to 54	27,563,000
55 and over	28,413,000
Total	125,756,000

A **frequency table** shows the **frequency**, or number of items in each category or numerical interval.

Circle Graph

Adults Who Used the Internet at Home in 2003

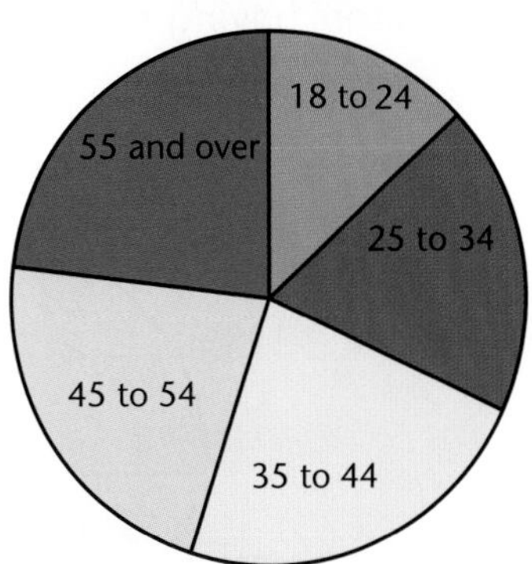

A **circle graph** shows the division of a whole into parts, each represented by a slice called a **sector**.

12 **Use Labsheet 1A.** The Labsheet shows a larger version of the *Circle Graph* above.

a. Follow the directions to complete the table on the labsheet.

b. **Discussion** Describe how you can make a circle graph from a frequency table.

FOR ▶ HELP
with *writing percents*, see **TOOLBOX, p. 588**
with *measuring angles*, see **TOOLBOX, p. 592**

EXAMPLE

A software company asked 60 computer owners what they use their computers for most. Of these owners, 21 said Internet access, 18 said word processing, 6 said spreadsheets, and 15 had other responses. Use a circle graph to display these results.

SAMPLE RESPONSE

Step 1 Organize the data in a table. Find the percent of computer owners giving each response. Use these percents to find the angle measures of the sectors of the circle graph.

FOR ▶ HELP with *multiplying decimals*, see **TOOLBOX, p. 580** with *writing fractions, decimals, and percents*, see **TOOLBOX, p. 588**

Response	Number	Percent	Angle measure
Internet access	21	$\frac{21}{60} = 35\%$	$0.35 \times 360° = 126°$
word processing	18	$\frac{18}{60} = 30\%$	$0.30 \times 360° = 108°$
spreadsheets	6	$\frac{6}{60} = 10\%$	$0.10 \times 360° = 36°$
other	15	$\frac{15}{60} = 25\%$	$0.25 \times 360° = 90°$

Step 2 Use a compass to draw a circle. Then use a protractor to draw sectors having the angle measures found in Step 1.

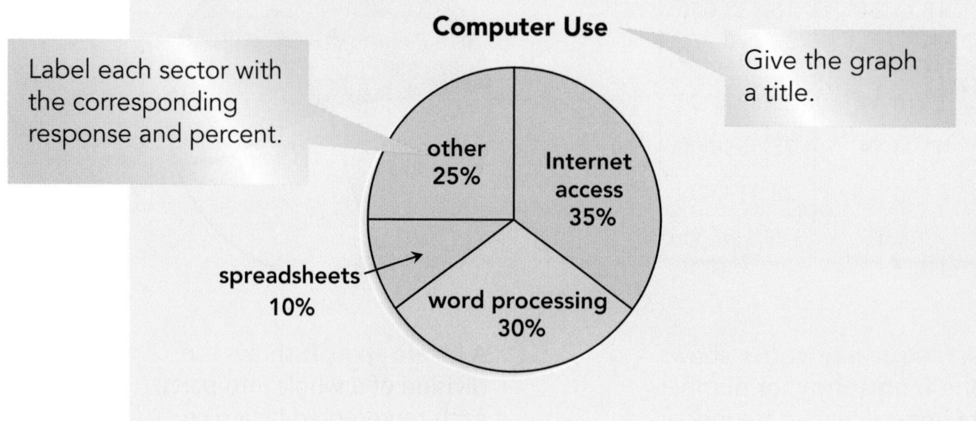

13 Find the sum of the percents and the sum of the angle measures in Step 1 of the Example. How does this help you check your work when making a circle graph?

14 ✓ CHECKPOINT Children are also using the Internet at home. Draw a circle graph of the data in the frequency table to compare the number of Internet users in each age group.

Children Who Used the Internet at Home in 2003	
Age Group	**Number**
3–9	17,493,000
10–14	14,407,000
15–17	9,023,000
Total	40,923,000

✓ QUESTION 14

...checks that you can draw a circle graph.

▶ **To measure demand for Internet access at school, the computer club at Garfield Middle School asked 50 students to estimate the number of times per month they access the Internet at home. The results are displayed below in a frequency table and a *histogram*.**

Frequency Table

Internet Access at Home	
Times per Month	**Frequency**
0–4	3
5–9	5
10–14	9
15–19	7
20–24	14
25–29	12

Histogram

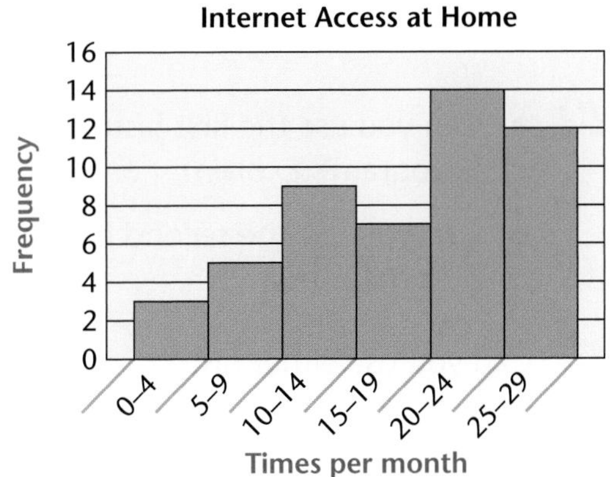

A **histogram** shows the frequencies of numerical values that fall within intervals of equal width.

15 **Discussion** How are bars in the histogram related to the frequencies in the table?

16 How is a histogram like a bar graph? How is it different?

17 Can you tell from the histogram exactly how many students said they access the Internet 10 times per month? Explain.

18 **a.** Draw a circle graph that displays the data in the frequency table. What does each sector of the circle graph tell you?

b. How does the information given by the histogram differ from the information given by the circle graph?

FOR▶HELP with *bar graphs*, see **STUDENT RESOURCE, p. 597**

▶ **The Garfield computer club raises money to pay a provider for Internet access. Then the club monitors the number of times students access the Internet at school. The numbers of students who access the Internet at school each day for 30 days are shown.**

16, 27, 26, 5, 11, 33, 23, 17, 15, 20, 3, 14, 29, 21, 23,
31, 16, 8, 14, 28, 19, 20, 24, 35, 7, 12, 22, 27, 18, 20

Use Labsheet 1B for Questions 19–23.

19 Follow the directions on the Labsheet to complete the *Frequency Tables* and draw the *Histograms*.

20 Compare the shapes of the two histograms you drew.

a. How are they alike?

b. How are they different?

21 Which histogram gives more information? Explain.

22 **a.** Can you use the first histogram to make the second histogram? Explain.

b. Can you use the second histogram to make the first histogram? Why?

23 Can you use either histogram to recover the original data values? Why or why not?

✓ QUESTION 24

...checks that you know how to use a histogram to display data.

24 **✓ CHECKPOINT** Tell whether each data set can be displayed using a histogram. If it can, draw a histogram of the data. If it cannot, explain why not.

a. weekly high temperatures (in °F) for 20 consecutive weeks:

15, 18, 30, 22, 25, 37, 33, 35, 40, 47,
38, 49, 52, 59, 51, 62, 68, 65, 70, 74

b. days on which weekly high temperatures occurred for 20 consecutive weeks:

Wed, Sat, Mon, Fri, Wed, Sun, Mon, Thurs, Thurs, Fri, Tues, Fri, Wed, Sat, Sun, Fri, Mon, Tues, Sat, Sun

HOMEWORK EXERCISES ▶ **See Exs. 14–23 on pp. 12–13.**

Section 1 Key Concepts

Key Terms

Rates (pp. 3–4)

A rate is a ratio that compares two quantities measured in different units. A unit rate gives an amount per one unit.

rates

unit rate

Example Suppose you pay $24 for 4 movie tickets. You can convert this rate to a unit rate of $6 per ticket. Both rates describe how the amount of money you pay depends on the number of tickets you buy.

Equivalent Rates (pp. 3–4)

equivalent rates

Equivalent rates are equal rates that may be expressed using different units. You can use equivalent rates to make a rate easier to understand or to make a more powerful impact.

Example Each person in the United States eats an average of 3 oz of sugar per day. To impress upon someone how much sugar this is, you might convert to pounds per year.

$$\frac{3\text{ oz}}{\text{day}} = \frac{3\text{ oz}}{1\text{ day}} \cdot \frac{1\text{ lb}}{16\text{ oz}} \cdot \frac{365\text{ days}}{1\text{ year}} \approx 68.4\text{ lb/year}$$

Circle Graphs (pp. 5–6)

circle graph

sector

A circle graph shows the division of a whole into parts. Each part is represented by a slice, or sector, of the circle graph.

Example

This circle graph compares the number of adults with access to the Internet by different household incomes.

Household Income of Adults with Internet Access

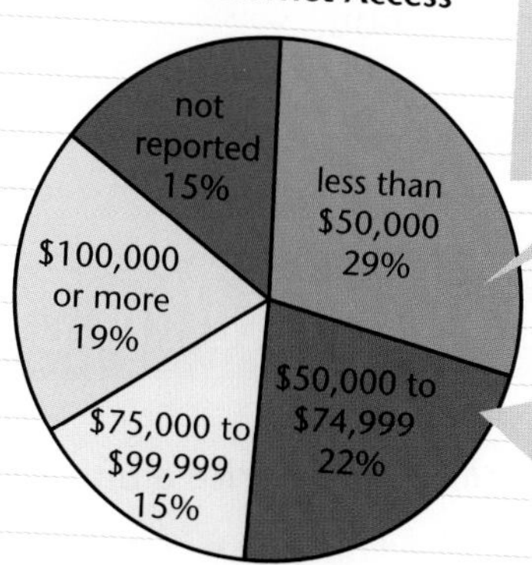

The angle measure of this sector is 29% of 360°, or 104.4°.

If the percents have not been rounded, their sum should be 100%.

25 **Key Concepts Question** Use a rate other than ounces per day or pounds per year to specify the average amount of sugar eaten by each person in the United States. Describe a situation where it would make sense to use the rate you chose.

Section 1 Key Concepts

Key Terms

histogram

frequency

frequency table

Histograms (pp. 7–8)

A histogram shows the frequencies of numerical values that fall within intervals of equal width.

Example The histogram below displays the test score data given in the frequency table.

Test Scores	
Score	Frequency
51-60	3
61-70	6
71-80	10
81-90	8
91-100	4

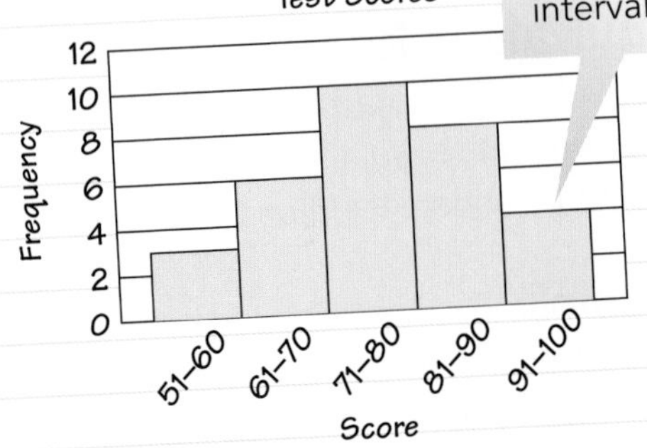

The height of each bar is the frequency of test scores in the corresponding interval.

26 Key Concepts Question Refer to the circle graph in the Example on page 9. Tell whether the data displayed in the graph can be displayed in a histogram. If it can, explain how to do so. If it cannot, explain why not.

Section 1 Practice & Application Exercises

YOU WILL NEED

For Exs. 1–8:
- Table of Measures on p. 601

For Ex. 17:
- compass and protractor

Name the units in each rate. Then write a unit rate.

1. 360 mi in 6 hr
2. 1.5 lb for $3.00

Copy and complete each equation.

3. 8000 lb/min = ? lb/hr
4. 60 in./year = ? in./month

Tell whether the given rates are equivalent.

5. 5 cars/min; 300 cars/sec
6. 20 lb/day; 3.65 tons/year

7. **Open-ended** Use an equivalent rate to rewrite this statement so that it makes a more amazing fact: "A person must consume about 2.5 quarts of water per day in order to survive."

8. **Open-ended** Use an equivalent rate to rewrite this statement so that it is easier to understand: "The three-toed sloth moves along the ground at an average speed of about 0.07 mi/hr." Explain why you chose the rate.

9. **World Records** California middle school teacher Constance Constable set a footbag record for women's singles in 1998 in Monterey, California, with 24,713 kicks in about 4 hr 9 min.

   a. Find Constance's "kick rate" in kicks per minute. Round to the nearest whole number.

   b. The overall open singles record set in 1997 is 63,326 kicks in about 8 hr 51 min. Compare this kick rate with Constance Constable's kick rate.

The modern game of *footbag* is based on an old Native American game. The game involves keeping a small stuffed cloth bag in the air by kicking it with your foot.

Write a word problem for each calculation. Solve the problem.

10. 55 mi/hr • 8 hr

11. $0.99 per oz • 6 oz

12. **Challenge** A light-year is the distance light travels in one year. Light travels at a speed of 186,282 mi/sec.

    a. Change the rate 186,282 mi/sec to mi/hr.

    b. How fast does light travel in mi/day?

    c. How far does light travel in one year?

    d. The sun is about 93 million miles from Earth. Estimate the amount of time it takes light from the sun to reach Earth.

13. It took about 21 months for the space probe Pioneer 10 to travel from Mars to Jupiter. This distance was about 620,000,000 mi. Write Pioneer 10's average speed using the given units.

    a. miles per month

    b. miles per day (Assume an average of 30.4 days per month.)

    c. miles per hour

    d. Which rate gives you the best sense of how fast Pioneer 10 was traveling? Explain.

For Exercises 14–16, use the circle graph below.

14. What percent of computer joysticks cost more than $100? How do you know?

15. Ten joysticks were reviewed. How many cost $100 or less?

16. Without measuring, give the angle measure of the sector for joysticks that cost less than $50.

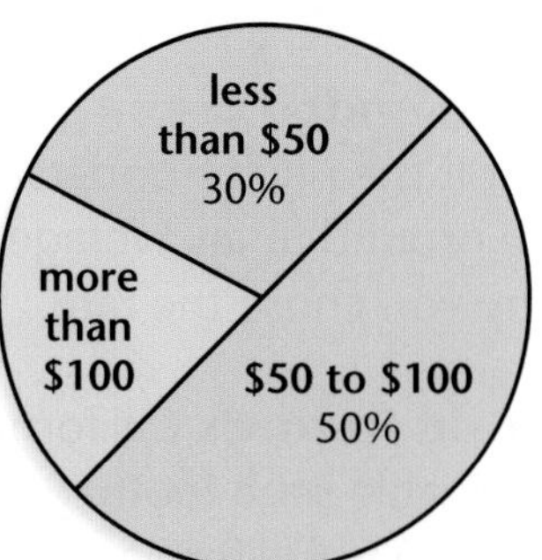

17. **Social Studies** The gross domestic product (GDP) of a country is the total market value of all the goods and services produced by the country in a given year. For each country in the table, draw a circle graph that shows the sources of the country's GDP in 2004.

	Source of GDP in 2004 (in billions of U.S. dollars)			
	Country	Agriculture	Industry	Services
a.	China	1,000	3,842	2,418
b.	India	783	883	1,682
c.	Pakistan	78	84	185

Tell what is wrong with each circle graph.

18.

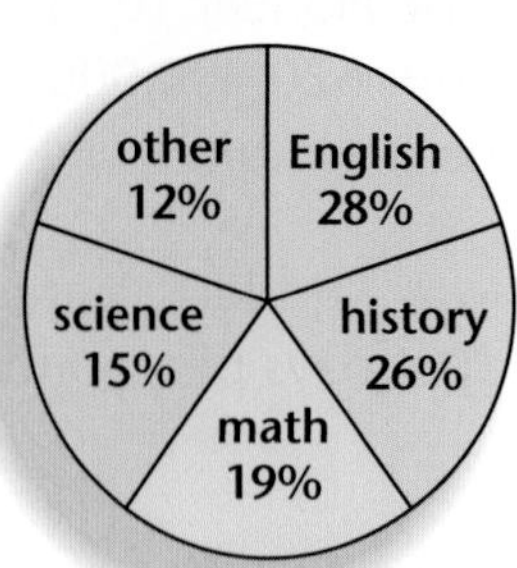

19.

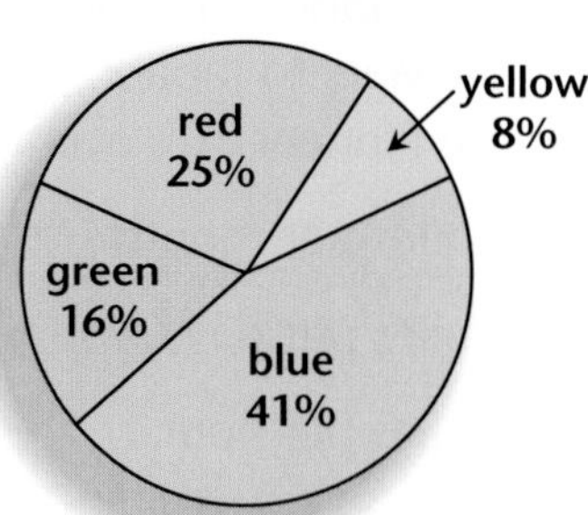

Psychology In 1978, D. H. Foster performed an experiment to see how people process visual patterns. Participants were shown 96 pairs of patterns like those at the left. They were asked if the two patterns contained the same number of dots. The numbers of correct responses from the 24 participants are given below.

55, 60, 58, 50, 57, 59, 61, 59, 65, 58, 49, 63,
54, 55, 56, 48, 50, 62, 66, 55, 51, 54, 62, 61

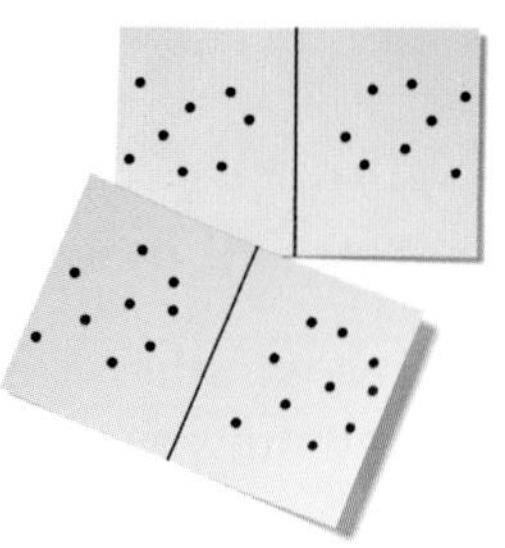

▲ Without counting, can you tell which card shows two patterns with the same number of dots?

20. a. Using intervals of 2, make a frequency table of the data. The first interval should be 48–49, then 50–51, and so on.

    b. Draw a histogram of the data using the intervals of 2 from your table in part (a).

21. Draw a histogram of the data using intervals of 5.

22. a. Explain how you can draw a histogram with intervals of 10 using only the histogram from Exercise 20.

    b. Explain how you can draw a histogram with intervals of 10 using only the histogram from Exercise 21.

    c. **Open-ended** Use one of the methods you described in parts (a) and (b) to draw a histogram with intervals of 10.

23. **Writing** Explain why you cannot use the histogram from Exercise 20 to draw the histogram from Exercise 21.

Reflecting on the Section

Be prepared to discuss your response to Exercise 24 in class.

24. Suppose you are writing an article for a science magazine and need to describe the distance from Earth to Mars. Look up the distance from Earth to Mars. To make this fact as interesting as possible, you may want to compare the distance to Mars to distances that are familiar to most people.

RESEARCH

Exercise 24 checks that you can use rates.

Spiral Review

25. Find the mean, median, mode(s), and range of the ice skater's competition scores shown below. **(Toolbox, p. 596)**

    10, 10, 9.8, 9.8, 10, 9.9, 9.7, 9.8, 9.6

Write each percent as a fraction in lowest terms. **(Toolbox, p. 588)**

26. 40% 27. 80% 28. 20% 29. 35%

Section 1 Extra Skill Practice

You will need: • *compass* (Ex. 7) • *protractor* (Ex. 7)

Tell whether the given rates are equivalent.
You may need to use the Table of Measures on page 601.

1. \$365,000/year; \$100/day
2. 15 gal/min; 2 pt/sec

For Exercises 3–5, use the circle graph at the right.

Calorie Sources

carbohydrates 60%
protein
fat 30%

3. What percent of calories should come from protein? How do you know?
4. Without measuring, give the angle measure of the sector that represents fat. How did you get your answer?
5. John takes in about 2000 calories each day. How many of these calories should come from carbohydrates?
6. The record low temperatures (in °F) for each month in Phoenix, Arizona, are 17, 22, 25, 32, 70, 50, 61, 60, 47, 34, 25, and 22. Draw a histogram of the data using intervals of 10.
7. Draw a circle graph that compares the areas of the five boroughs of New York City.

Borough	Area
Manhattan	23 mi^2
The Bronx	41 mi^2
Staten Island	56 mi^2
Brooklyn	73 mi^2
Queens	110 mi^2

Standardized Testing ▶ Multiple Choice

The histogram shows a person's monthly telephone bills for one year.

1. Which interval contains the greatest frequency of the data?

   A. \$30–\$39 B. \$40–\$49
   C. \$50–\$59 D. \$60–\$69

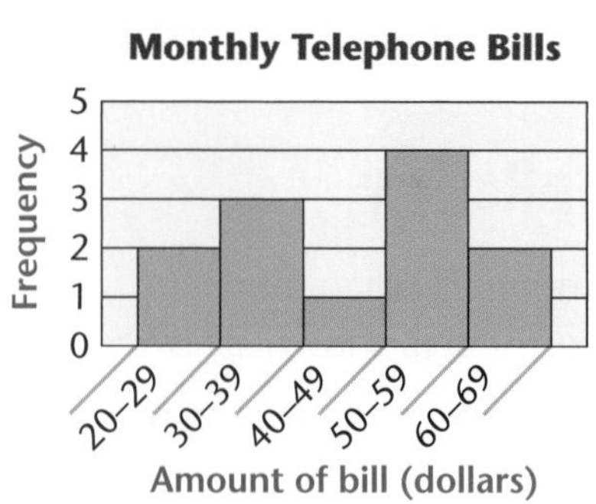

2. How many bills are for at least \$40?

   A. 6 B. 7
   C. 10 D. 12

Section 2 Displaying Data

IN THIS SECTION

EXPLORATION 1
- Stem-and-Leaf Plots

EXPLORATION 2
- Box-and-Whisker Plots

EXPLORATION 3
- Choosing a Data Display

Amazing Musicians

Setting the Stage

How would you like to have a hit song at the age of 13? Stevie Wonder had a #1 hit single at only 13. He ranks in the top four of solo pop artists for 1955-1999.

How unusual is it for a musician to have a #1 single at age 13? One way to answer this question is to look at the ages of musicians when they had their first #1 single.

Stevie Wonder was 13 when his song *Fingertips Pt 2* made it to the #1 position on *Billboard's* Top 40 chart in July, 1963.

Age of Top 20 Solo Pop Artists When They Had Their First #1 Singles

21, 25, 26, 13, 14, 29, 20, 25, 21, 20,
29, 22, 26, 18, 26, 29, 21, 31, 25, 21

Think About It

1 For the data above, find each average.

a. mean **b.** median **c.** mode

FOR ▶ HELP with *mean, median, and mode*, see **TOOLBOX, p. 596**

2 Which average do you think best represents the data? Explain.

3 How do you think the data above would compare to data about musicians of this millennium? Why?

In this section you will learn how to represent data in both *stem-and-leaf* and *box-and-whisker plots*. Then you will create different displays for musical accomplishments in the current decade.

GOAL

LEARN HOW TO...
- make and use stem-and-leaf plots

AS YOU...
- analyze the ages of famous pop and country musicians

KEY TERMS
- stem-and-leaf plot
- stem
- leaf

Exploration 1

STEM and LEAF Plots

One way to organize data is in a stem-and-leaf plot. The stem-and-leaf plot below shows the ages of the top 20 solo pop musicians when they had their first #1 singles. These musicians were rated as the top artists from 1955 to 1999.

Ages of Top 20 Solo Pop Artists When They Had Their First #1 Singles

```
1 | 3 4 8
2 | 0 0 1 1 1 1 2 5 5 5 6 6 6 9 9 9
3 | 1
```

1 | 3 represents the data item 13.

Each stem represents a tens digit.

The leaves are written in order from least to greatest.

4 **a.** The table at the right lists the names and ages of three musicians from the stem-and-leaf plot. Find their ages in the plot.

Pop Artist	Age
Elton John	25
Prince	26
Ricky Nelson	18

b. Mariah Carey's age is listed right after Ricky Nelson's. Find Mariah's age at her first #1 single.

c. Of the artists in the plot, Billy Joel was the oldest when he had his first #1 single. How old was he when he had his first #1 hit?

5 **Try This as a Class** Use the stem-and-leaf plot above.

a. How were the numbers for the stems chosen?

b. How were the numbers for the leaves chosen?

c. Find the range of the data in the stem-and-leaf plot.

d. Which averages (mean, median, and mode) can be found easily using the stem-and-leaf plot? Explain.

FOR▶HELP with *range*, see **TOOLBOX, p. 596**

▶ **Comparing Data** **You can use back-to-back stem-and-leaf plots to compare two sets of data.**

EXAMPLE

The back-to-back stem-and-leaf plot below compares the ages when the top 10 solo pop musicians of the 1950s and the top 10 of the 1980s had their first #1 record.

Age at First #1 Hit Single for Top 10 Musicians

of the 1950s		of the 1980s
	0	
8 5	**1**	4
6 4 1 1 1 1	**2**	1 5 6 6
9	**3**	0 1 2 3 5
5	**4**	

5 | **4** | represents an age of 45.

| **3** | 2 represents an age of 32.

6 **Discussion** Use the example above.

a. How old was the youngest musician in the 1950s? in the 1980s?

b. How do the oldest musicians' ages in each decade compare?

c. Based on the plot, what statements could you make to compare the ages of the musicians in the 1950s to those in the 1980s?

7 The ages of the top 20 solo country artists of the 1900s when they had their first #1 records are 28, 27, 24, 34, 29, 30, 24, 30, 30, 42, 33, 36, 27, 28, 21, 28, 30, 31, 32, 27.

Make a back-to-back stem-and-leaf plot of the ages of the top 20 country artists and the ages of the top 20 pop artists on page 15. (Be sure to put the same amount of space between the leaves.)

8 ✓ **CHECKPOINT** Use the back-to-back stem-and-leaf plot you created in Question 7.

a. What does the plot tell you about the two groups of musicians?

b. Compare the ranges of the two sets of data. What do the ranges tell you about the ages of the two groups of musicians?

c. One artist, Linda Ronstadt, had her first #1 pop hit and her first #1 country hit when she was 28. Is this age unusual for pop musicians? for country musicians? Explain.

...checks that you can interpret stem-and-leaf plots.

HOMEWORK EXERCISES ▶ See Exs. 1–2 on p. 24.

GOAL

LEARN HOW TO...
- use box-and-whisker plots to analyze and compare data

AS YOU...
- investigate the achievements of famous musicians

KEY TERMS
- box-and-whisker plot
- lower extreme
- upper extreme
- lower quartile
- upper quartile

Exploration 2

BOX and WHISKER Plots

SET UP *You will need Labsheets 2A and 2B.*

▶ **Age is only one way that artists may be deemed amazing. Another way is to examine how many of their songs were popular. The stem-and-leaf plot and the box-and-whisker plot below both show the number of Top 40 singles each of the top 25 artists of the 1960s had during that decade.**

Number of Top 40 Singles Each Artist Had from 1960–1969

Stem	Leaves
1	7 7 7 7 8 8 8 9
2	0 1 2 2 3 4 5 5 5 6 7 7 7 7 9
3	
4	4
5	1

2 | 1 means 21 Top 40 singles.

During the 60s, two artists stood out among the top 25 of the decade, Elvis Presley who produced 51 Top 40 hits and the Beatles who produced 44.

Number of Top 40 Singles Each Artist Had from 1960–1969

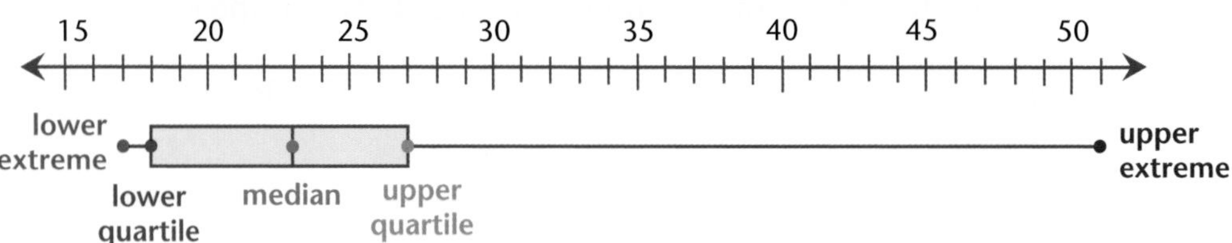

9 **a.** Find the least and greatest data items in the stem-and-leaf plot. How are these shown in the box-and-whisker plot and what are they called?

b. Use the stem-and-leaf plot to find the median of the data. How does the box-and-whisker plot show the median?

10 Use the box-and-whisker plot on page 18.

a. The upper whisker extends from 27 to 51. What are possible values in the lower whisker?

b. About what fraction of the data lies in the box between the lower and upper quartiles? What percent is this?

▶ **The steps for constructing a box-and-whisker plot are given below. You will use them to construct a box-and-whisker plot of the number of Top 40 hits each of the top 25 artists of the 90s had during that decade.**

The **upper quartile** is the median of the data values that occur after the median in an ordered list.

Creating a Box-and-Whisker Plot

Step 1 Put the data in order from least to greatest.

Step 2 Find the upper and lower extremes of the data.

Step 3 Find the median.

Step 4 Find the lower quartile and the upper quartile.

Step 5 Plot the lower extreme, lower quartile, median, upper quartile, and upper extreme below a number line. Use these values to draw the box and the whiskers.

Use Labsheet 2A for Questions 11–14.

11 **Discussion** Use the *Top 40 Hits Stem-and-Leaf Plot* on the Labsheet to answer the following questions.

a. How do you calculate the lower quartile?

b. What differences do you notice between the data for the 1960s and the data for the 1990s?

c. How do you think the differences you noticed in part (b) will be represented in the box-and-whisker plots?

12 **Try This as a Class** Use the steps for creating a box-and-whisker plot and the instructions on the Labsheet to complete the *Top 40 Hits Box-and-Whisker Plots.*

13 Discussion The box-and-whisker plot is divided into four regions. Each of these regions represents about the same number of data items.

a. About what percent of the data fall into each region of the box-and-whisker plot?

b. Why is the upper whisker longer than the upper portion of the box?

c. Consider the two box-and-whisker plots. For the 1960s the median lies close to the center of the box, but for the 1990s it does not. Explain what this means about the two sets of data.

✓ QUESTION 14

...checks that you can use box-and-whisker plots to compare data sets.

14 ✓ CHECKPOINT Which group of musicians do you think is more amazing? Use the box-and-whisker plots from the Labsheet to support your choice.

▶ **Comparing Data As you have seen, a box-and-whisker plot can stand alone to report data or be used with other box-and-whisker plots on the same number line to compare data.**

15 Use Labsheet 2B. Box-and-whisker plots can be used to compare other musicians of the 1960s to those of the 1990s.

a. Follow the directions on Labsheet 2B.

b. Use the plots from part (a) to write a short article about how the winners of the 1960s and 1990s compare.

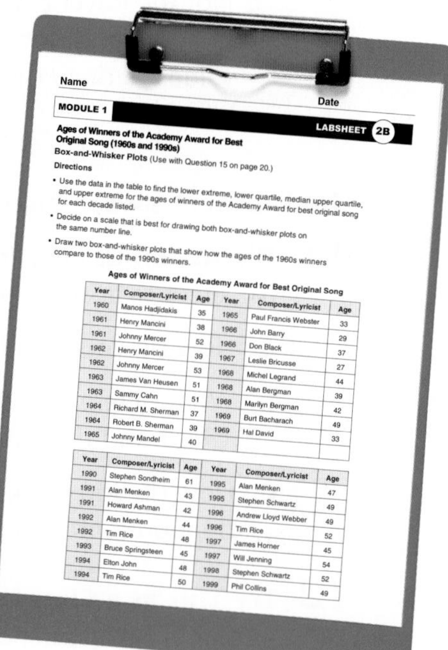
Name

Date

MODULE 1 LABSHEET 2B

Ages of Winners of the Academy Award for Best Original Song (1960s and 1990s)

Box-and-Whisker Plots (Use with Question 15 on page 20.)

Directions

- Use the data in the table to find the lower extreme, lower quartile, median upper quartile, and upper extreme for the ages of winners of the Academy Award for best original song for each decade listed.
- Decide on a scale that is best for drawing both box-and-whisker plots on the same number line.
- Draw two box-and-whisker plots that show how the ages of the 1960s winners compare to those of the 1990s winners.

Ages of Winners of the Academy Award for Best Original Song

Year	Composer/Lyricist	Age	Year	Composer/Lyricist	Age
1960	Manos Hadjidakis	35	1965	Paul Francis Webster	33
1961	Henry Mancini	38	1966	John Barry	29
1961	Johnny Mercer	52	1966	Don Black	37
1962	Henry Mancini	39	1967	Leslie Bricusse	27
1962	Johnny Mercer	53	1968	Michel Legrand	44
1963	James Van Heusen	51	1968	Alan Bergman	39
1963	Sammy Cahn	51	1968	Marilyn Bergman	42
1964	Richard M. Sherman	37	1969	Burt Bacharach	49
1964	Robert B. Sherman	39	1969	Hal David	33
1965	Johnny Mandel	40			

Year	Composer/Lyricist	Age	Year	Composer/Lyricist	Age
1990	Stephen Sondheim	61	1995	Alan Menken	47
1991	Alan Menken	43	1995	Stephen Schwartz	49
1991	Howard Ashman	42	1996	Andrew Lloyd Webber	49
1992	Alan Menken	44	1996	Tim Rice	52
1992	Tim Rice	48	1997	James Horner	45
1993	Bruce Springsteen	45	1997	Will Jenning	54
1994	Elton John	48	1998	Stephen Schwartz	52
1994	Tim Rice	50	1999	Phil Collins	49

HOMEWORK EXERCISES ▶ See Exs. 3–12 on pp. 25–28.

Exploration 3

Choosing a Data Display

GOAL

LEARN HOW TO...
- choose the best display for a given situation

AS YOU...
- look at accomplishments of famous musicians

At age 14, Rachel Barton was the first American, and the youngest artist ever, to win the gold medal at the Quadrennial J.S. Bach International Violin Competition in Leipzig, Germany. Rachel is from Chicago, where at age 10, she performed with the Chicago Symphony. Because she was home schooled, Rachel had many hours to practice the violin.

Research has shown that practice can make the difference between good violinists and the best violinists. The displays below represent the number of hours per week different students might say they practice.

Weekly Hours of Practice

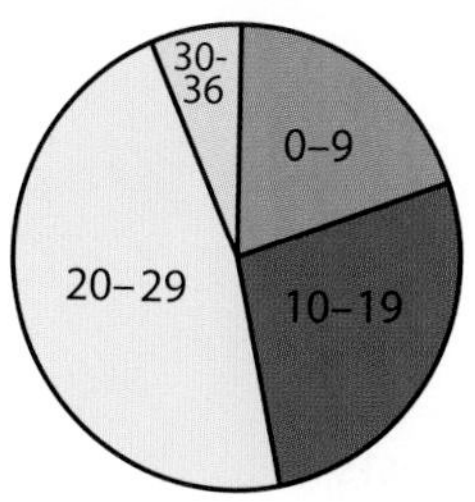

Weekly Hours of Practice

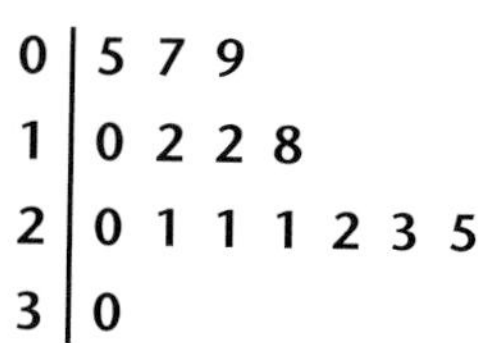

1 | 2 means 12 hours.

Weekly Hours of Practice

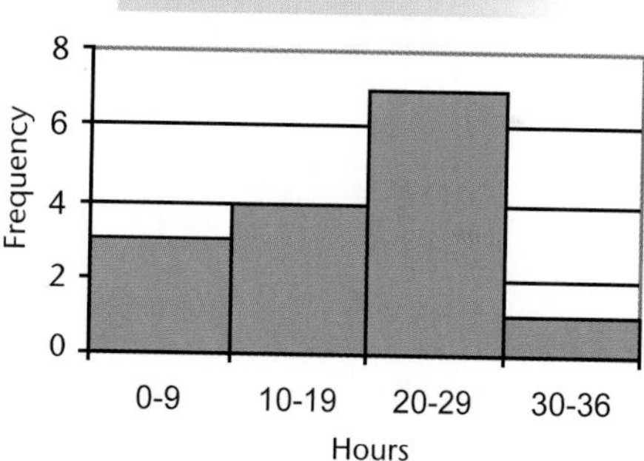

16 Which display best shows that almost half the students practice an average of 20–29 hours a week?

17 **a.** How are the histogram and the stem-and-leaf plot alike?

b. How are they different?

18 Which display gives you the actual hours?

19 Given the actual hours of practice, can you make a histogram different from the one above? a stem-and-leaf plot different from the one above? Explain.

20 What information might you want that the displays do not give?

21 Use the box-and-whisker plot below to find the median, the quartiles, the extremes, and the range of the data.

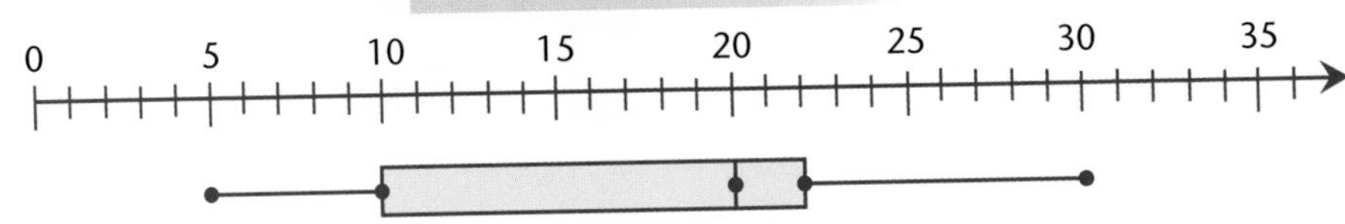

22 Can you find the information in Question 21 using each data display? Explain.

a. circle graph **b.** stem-and-leaf plot **c.** histogram

23 **Discussion** What information can you estimate quickly from the circle graph, stem-and-leaf plot, or histogram that the box-and-whisker plot does not show?

▶ **The data displays you have seen so far display singular numerical data. *Scatter plots* like the one shown below display *paired* numerical data. You will learn more about scatter plots in Section 4 of this module.**

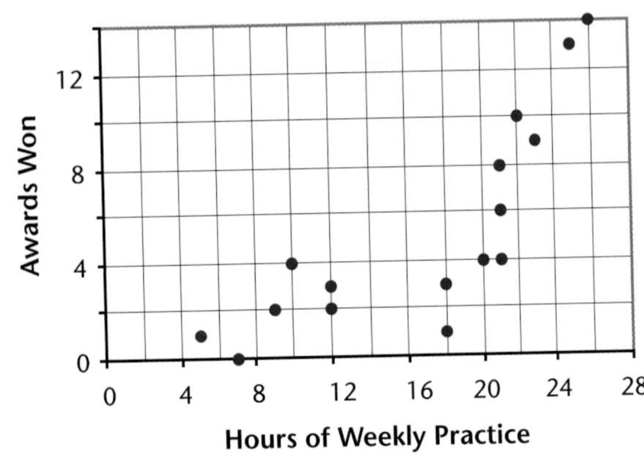

24 What does the data point (20, 4) on the scatter plot represent?

25 ✓ **CHECKPOINT** Use the Student Resource on page 597. Tell which type of display would best do each of the following.

a. Compare the ages at which artists began playing a musical instrument.

b. Give the median age at first performance in Carnegie Hall.

c. Show the number of Grammys earned and the yearly income for various musicians.

d. Show the percentage of artists who had only one hit this year.

e. Show that four musicians made the cover of *Rolling Stone Magazine* at age 18.

✓ **QUESTION 25**

...checks that you understand when to use different types of displays.

HOMEWORK EXERCISES ▶ **See Exs. 13–18 on pp. 28–29.**

Section 2 Key Concepts

Stem-and-Leaf Plots (pp. 16–17)

A stem-and-leaf plot displays data in an organized format. The data items are usually ordered from least to greatest.

John Lennon's Top 40 Singles: Highest Position Reached on the Top 40 Charts

stem	leaf
0	1 1 2 3 3 5 9
1	0 1 4 8
2	0
3	0

1 | 8 represents #18 on the Top 40 chart.

Box-and-Whisker Plots (pp. 18–20)

A box-and-whisker plot shows how data are distributed by dividing the data into 4 groups. Each group contains about 25% of the data items. The lower quartile is the median of the data values that occur before the median in an ordered list. The upper quartile is the median of the data values that occur after the median.

Highest Positions Reached By John Lennon's Top 40 Singles

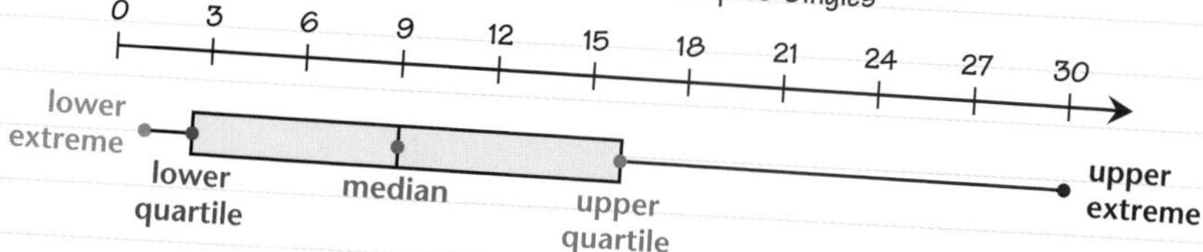

Choosing a Display (pp. 21–22)

You can use bar graphs, histograms, box-and-whisker plots, stem-and-leaf plots, scatter plots, line graphs, and circle graphs to display data. When deciding what type of display to use, consider the type and number of data sets you have as well as what aspect of the data you want to emphasize.

Key Terms

stem-and-leaf plot

stem

leaf

box-and-whisker plot

lower extreme

upper extreme

lower quartile

upper quartile

26 **Key Concepts Question** Use the displays above.

a. How many #1 singles did John Lennon have? Which display doesn't give you this information?

b. Which display(s) can you use to find the mean of the data? the median? the modes? Find each of these averages.

c. About what percent of John Lennon's Top 40 singles made it to the 16th through 30th positions of the charts?

d. What other displays would be appropriate for reporting the given data about John Lennon's music?

Section 2
Practice & Application Exercises

1. The table lists the Grammy Award winners for best female vocal performance for both country music and pop music from 1995–2006. The table also shows the artists' ages when they received the award.

Age when Awarded Grammy for Best Female Vocal Performance				
Year Awarded	Country		Pop	
	Name	Age	Name	Age
1995	Mary Chapin Carpenter	37	Sheryl Crow	33
1996	Alison Krauss	24	Annie Lennox	41
1997	LeAnn Rimes	14	Toni Braxton	30
1998	Trisha Yearwood	33	Sarah McLachlan	30
1999	Shania Twain	33	Celine Dion	30
2000	Shania Twain	34	Sarah McLachlan	32
2001	Faith Hill	33	Macy Gray	30
2002	Dolly Parton	56	Nelly Furtado	23
2003	Faith Hill	35	Norah Jones	23
2004	June Carter Cash	74	Christina Aguilera	23
2005	Gretchen Wilson	31	Norah Jones	25
2006	Emmylou Harris	48	Kelly Clarkson	23

a. Use the data to make a back-to-back stem-and-leaf plot that compares the ages by type of music.

b. Compare the shapes of the two stem-and-leaf plots. What do the shapes tell you about the ages of the best female vocal performance Grammy winners for country music and pop music?

2. a. Find the mean, the median, and the mode for each data set.

b. How does LeAnn's age compare with the ages of the other country winners?

c. How does LeAnn's age affect the mean for the country winners?

d. Which average from part (a) do you think best represents each data set? Explain your thinking.

The table shows history test scores for two classes. The data were used to make the box-and-whisker plots. Use the table and the box-and-whisker plots for Exercises 3–6.

History Test Scores			
Class A		Class B	
66	100	78	64
54	90	76	77
68	72	87	93
86	64	45	47
100	59	78	80
59	100	76	76
68	84	90	100
85	100	45	83

History Test Scores

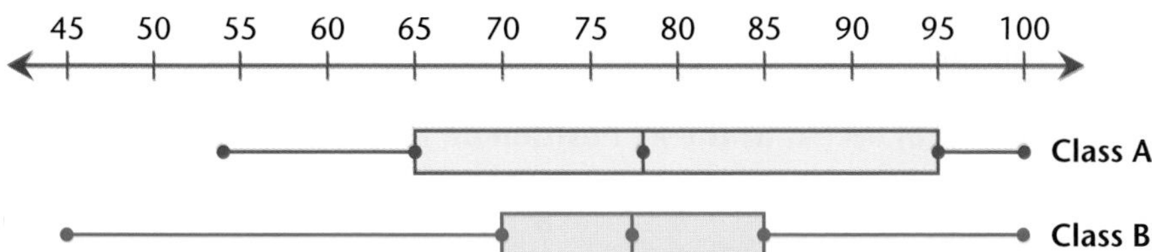

3. For each box-and-whisker plot, find the values below.
   a. the lower extreme
   b. the upper extreme
   c. the lower quartile
   d. the upper quartile

4. a. **Writing** Explain how to use the box-and-whisker plots to compare the median test scores for the two classes.
   b. Find the mean test score for each class. Which class had at least 50% of its test scores greater than its mean?

5. **Challenge** Diana says that you can tell from looking at the box-and-whisker plots that the mean test score for class A is higher than the mean test score for class B. Do you agree? Explain.

6. a. About what percent of each class's test scores are included in the box portion of each box-and-whisker plot?
   b. What do the sizes of the box portions tell you about the test scores for each class?

7. Elvis Presley had 104 singles make the Top 40 charts. The box-and-whisker plot below shows data about the highest position reached on the Top 40 charts by those singles.

Highest Positions Reached By Elvis Presley's 104 Top 40 Singles

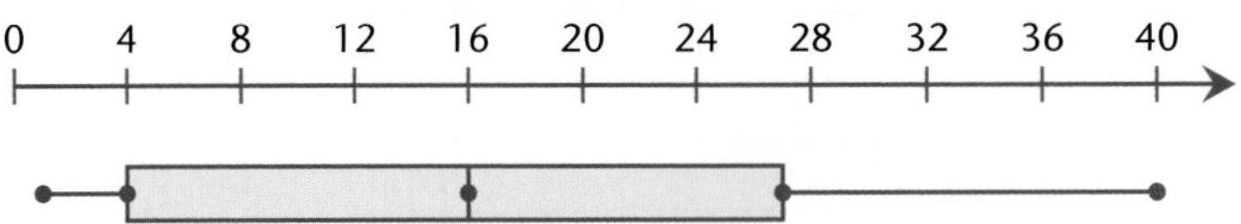

a. Identify the lower extreme and the upper extreme. What information do these values give you about the data?

b. Find the median of the data.

c. About what percent of Elvis Presley's Top 40 singles reached positions 1 though 16?

8. Use the box-and-whisker plots below.

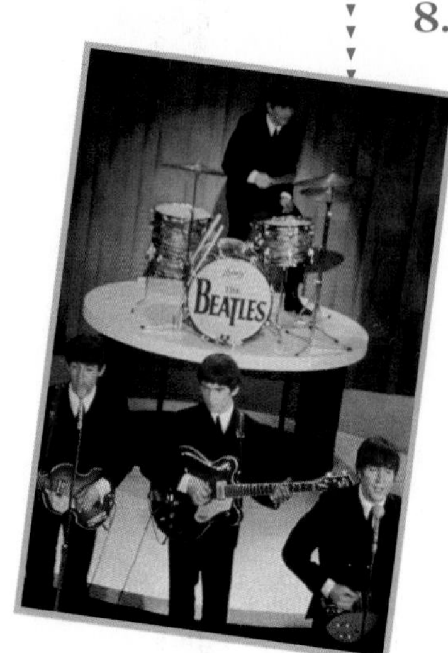

Number of Weeks at the #1 Position on the Chart

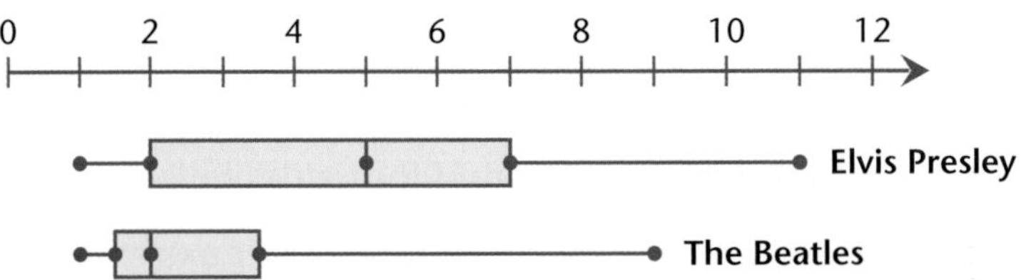

The Beatles hit "Hey Jude" stayed #1 for 9 weeks.

a. What is the range for each data set?

b. About what percent of the Beatles' #1 hit singles stayed at the #1 position for two weeks or less?

c. About what percent of Elvis Presley's #1 hit singles stayed at the #1 position for two weeks or less?

d. For each set of data, about what percent of the data items are represented by the box portion of the box-and-whisker plot?

e. Why are the sizes of the boxes different?

9. a. About 50% of Elvis Presley's #1 hit singles stayed at the #1 position for 5 to 11 weeks. About 50% of the Beatles' #1 hits stayed at the #1 position for 2 or more weeks. How do the box-and-whisker plots above show this information?

b. Who do you think is more amazing, Elvis Presley or the Beatles? Use the box-and-whisker plots above to support your choice.

10. By the end of the 1900s Mariah Carey ranked #3 to the Beatles and Elvis Presley in most #1 singles.

a. Using the clues below, sketch a box-and-whisker plot to represent the number of weeks Mariah Carey's hits held on to the #1 position.

- All but one of her songs remained in the #1 position for more than a week.
- 50% of the songs were hits for 3 weeks or longer.
- Her longest running hit, "One Sweet Day," sung with Boyz II Men topped the charts for 16 weeks.
- 5 of her 14 #1 hits stayed at #1 for 2 weeks.
- 25% of the hits remained at #1 for 4 weeks or longer.

b. Compare your sketch to the box-and-whisker plots in Exercise 8. What part of the plot could you use to convince someone that Mariah Carey is more amazing than the Beatles or Elvis Presley?

11. a. Use the data in the table below to construct a box-and-whisker plot of the number of times a composer's work was performed by American orchestras during the 2005–2006 season.

Number of Times a Composer's Work Was Performed by American Orchestras			
Name (year of birth)	**Performances**	**Name (year of birth)**	**Performances**
Handel (1685)	163	Mahler (1860)	226
Bach (1685)	201	Strauss (1864)	325
Haydn (1737)	249	Sibelius (1865)	251
Mozart (1756)	1453	Rachmaninoff (1873)	270
Beethoven (1770)	948	Ravel (1875)	277
Mendelssohn (1809)	220	Bartok (1881)	161
Schumann (1819)	196	Stravinsky (1881)	227
Brahms (1883)	495	Prokofiev (1891)	248
Tchaikovsky (1840)	581	Copland (1900)	201
Dvorak (1841)	302	Shostakovich (1906)	314

b. Use the same number line to create two more box-and-whisker plots for the data in the table: one for the composers born before 1850 and one for composers born after 1850.

c. **Writing** Use the box-and-whisker plots along with related vocabulary such as extreme, quartile, percent, and median to write a summary comparing the data for the two groups.

12. **Challenge** The Beatles had 50 singles that made the Top 40 charts. Of these hit singles, 20 made it to the #1 position. How does this fact explain why there is no lower whisker on the box-and-whisker plot below?

Highest Position Reached by the Beatles' Top 40 Singles

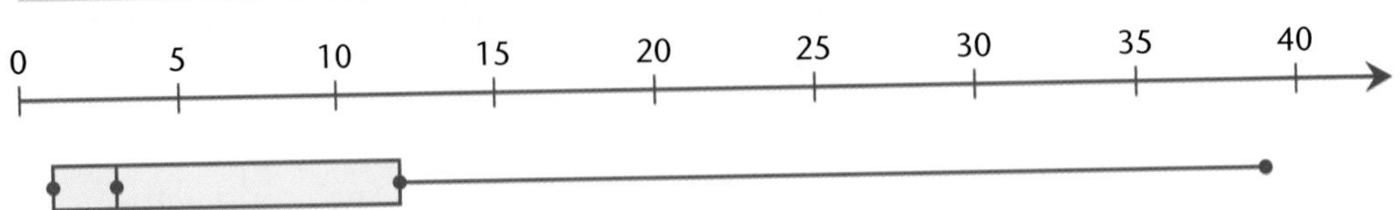

13. **Open-ended** Describe a data set that can be shown using the given type of display.

    a. histogram
    b. stem-and-leaf plot
    c. circle graph
    d. scatter plot

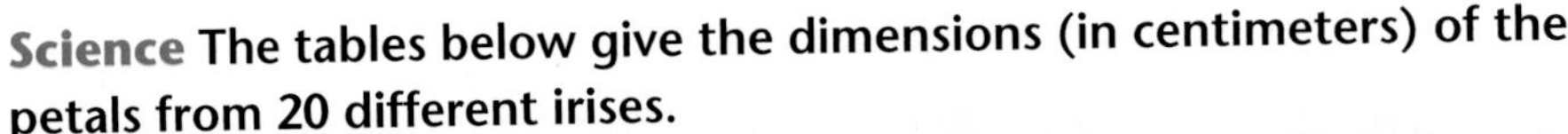

Science The tables below give the dimensions (in centimeters) of the petals from 20 different irises.

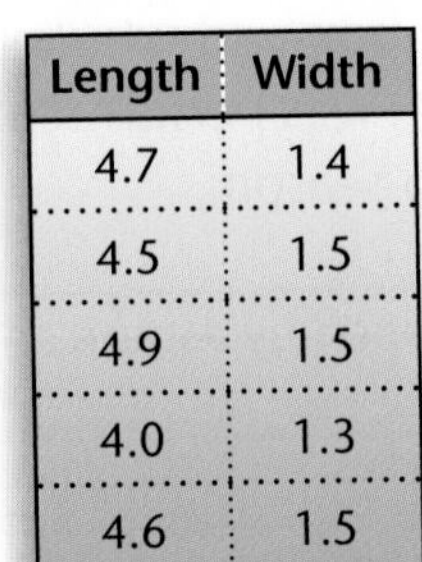

Length	Width
4.7	1.4
4.5	1.5
4.9	1.5
4.0	1.3
4.6	1.5

Length	Width
4.5	1.3
4.7	1.6
3.3	1.0
4.6	1.3
3.9	1.4

Length	Width
3.5	1.0
4.2	1.5
4.0	1.0
4.7	1.4
3.6	1.3

Length	Width
4.4	1.4
4.5	1.5
4.1	1.0
4.5	1.5
3.9	1.1

14. For each statement below, make a display that shows the information specified. Tell why you chose that type of display.

    a. the number of irises whose petals are 4.0–4.1 cm long
    b. the percent of irises whose petals are 1.3 cm wide
    c. the median petal length compared to the median petal width

15. **Open-ended** Suppose you conduct a survey to find out how often people ride bicycles during the month of July. You decide to give sample responses for people to choose from.

    a. What are four sample responses you could give if you want to display your survey results in a histogram?
    b. What are four sample responses you could give if you want to display your survey results in a bar graph?
    c. Why must your sample responses for part (b) be different from your sample responses for part (a)?

16. **Challenge**

a. Given a stem-and-leaf plot of a data set, can you always make a box-and-whisker plot? Explain.

b. Given a box-and-whisker plot of a data set, can you always make a stem-and-leaf plot? Explain.

17. **Research**

a. Research data about musicians in the current decade.

b. Decide upon two different appropriate displays and use them to present the findings of your research.

c. Discuss an advantage that each display has over the other.

Reflecting on the Section

Be prepared to discuss Exercise 18 in class.

Discussion

Exercise 18 checks that you can interpret stem-and-leaf plots and box-and-whisker plots.

18. Aretha Franklin is another amazing musician. During a career that spans five decades, she has won nearly twenty Grammy Awards and she is known as the "Queen of Soul." The stem-and-leaf plot below shows data about her singles that reached the top 40 on the U.S. Hot 100 chart as of 2007.

Highest Positions Reached by Aretha Franklin's Hits on the U.S. Hot 100 Chart

Stem	Leaves
0	1 1 2 2 2 2 3 3 3 4 5 5 5 6 6 7 7 8 9 9
1	0 1 3 3 4 6 6 7 8 9 9 9
2	0 1 2 3 4 6 6 6 8 8 8
3	1 3 7 7

3|1 represents position number 31.

a. Suppose a box-and-whisker plot was constructed from the data above. What value would be the lower extreme? the upper extreme? the median?

b. Where would the data value 11 be on the box-and-whisker plot? For example, would it be on the lower whisker?

c. Which whisker would be longer, the upper whisker or the lower whisker? Explain.

d. Use the data to create another type of display. Describe the advantages this display has over the stem-and-leaf and box-and-whisker plots.

Spiral Review

Copy and complete each equation.
(Module 1, p. 12; Table of Measures, p. 601)

19. 4.8 m/min = ? m/hr

20. 55 mi/hr = ? mi/min

21. 8 lb/ft^2 = ? lb/in.^{2}

22. \$0.75 per day = \$? per week

Test each number for divisibility by 2, 3, and 5. (Toolbox, p. 583)

23. 615

24. 2189

25. 41,852

26. 111

Replace each ? with > or <. (Toolbox, p. 590)

27. –6 ? –10

28. 3 ? – 4

29. –12 ? –22

Career Connection

Career Counselor: Charles Cunningham

School counselors like Charles Cunningham may use a box-and-whisker plot to help you understand your score on a standardized test such as the SAT. A counselor can help you find where your score falls in comparison to the scores of the other students.

2006 SAT Mathematics Test Scores

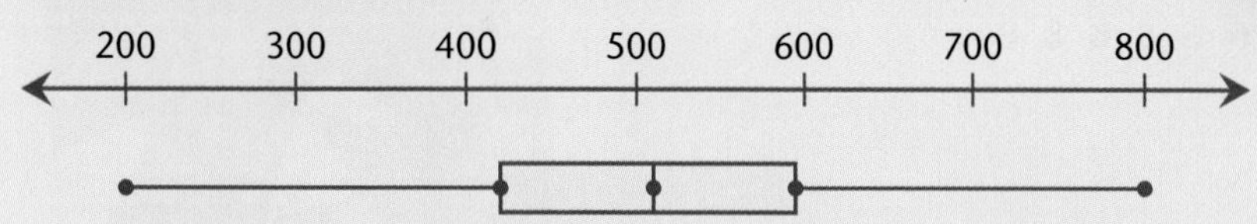

Charles Cunningham helps students research college options.

30. Would a score of 550 qualify you for an honors program that requires you to score in the top 25% of those who took the exam? Explain.

31. Give three sample scores that would lie in the lower 50%.

32. About what fraction of the data values are in the interval from 510 to 595?

Section 2 Extra Skill Practice

Use the data in the table for Exercises 1 and 2.

Ages of Academy Award Winners, 1980–2003	
Best Actor ages	Best Actress ages
43, 26, 47, 36, 40, 46, 60, 45, 31, 38, 37, 52, 57, 42, 32, 54, 43, 61, 35, 45, 52, 39, 76, 37	28, 35, 33, 33, 25, 25, 34, 39, 49, 45, 35, 33, 29, 42, 80, 26, 41, 21, 61, 38, 49, 33, 74, 31

1. a. Make a back-to-back stem-and-leaf plot for Best Actor and Best Actress ages.
   b. What do the shapes of the stem-and-leaf plots tell you about the ages of female award winners and male award winners?
   c. Find the mean, the median, and the mode(s) for each data set. Which average best represents each data set? Why?
2. Using one number line, create two box-and-whisker plots to represent the data in the table.
3. Jessica Tandy was 80 years old when she received the Best Actress Award. How unusual is it for an 80-year-old actress to receive this award? Explain.

Tell which type of display best does each of the following. Explain your thinking.

4. Shows the relationship between height and shoe size.
5. Compares the populations of New York, Los Angeles, and Chicago.
6. Shows that a company's profit has increased each year since 1992.
7. Tells what percent of the United States population is self-employed.

Standardized Testing ▶ Multiple Choice

1. Tell which values *cannot* be found using a box-and-whisker plot.

   (A) range (B) extremes (C) median (D) mean

2. Tell which display does *not* indicate the range of a data set.

   (A) histogram (B) table
   (C) stem-and-leaf plot (D) box-and-whisker plot

Section 3 Equations and Expressions

IN THIS SECTION

EXPLORATION 1
- Writing Equations

EXPLORATION 2
- Solving Equations

EXPLORATION 3
- Simplifying Expressions

Extraordinary Rules of Thumb

Setting the Stage

Rules of thumb have been passed from one generation to the next for hundreds of years. These rules help people estimate things like the temperature outdoors. Many rules are about ordinary events, but they seem extraordinary because someone noticed patterns and made connections.

Rule 1

Your adult height will be twice your height at age 2.

Rule 2

You can tell how many miles you are from a thunderstorm by counting the seconds between the lightning and the thunder and dividing by five.

Rule 3

To estimate the temperature outdoors in degrees Fahrenheit, count the number of times one snowy tree cricket chirps in fifteen seconds and add thirty-nine.

Think About It

1 Suppose your height at age 2 years was 2 ft 10 in. How tall should you be as an adult?

2 How many miles are you from a thunderstorm if you count 25 sec between the lightning and the thunder?

Exploration 1

Writing E=quations

SET UP *You will need Labsheet 3A.*

GOAL

LEARN HOW TO...
- write equations from words

AS YOU...
- investigate rules of thumb

KEY TERMS
- variable
- constant

▶ **Many rules of thumb can be written as mathematical formulas or equations using *variables*. A variable is a symbol used to represent a quantity that is unknown or that can change. For example, the rule of thumb for finding your adult height from your height at age 2 can be represented as an equation.**

EXAMPLE

Write an equation for predicting a person's height from his or her height at age 2.

First Choose a variable to represent each of the quantities that are unknown or may change.

Let c = height at age 2. Let a = adult height.

Then Represent the word relationships with symbols and variables.

$$a = 2c$$

3 **Discussion** Refer to the example above.

a. Why is each height represented by a variable?

b. How is *twice* represented?

c. For any height, toddler or adult, what will always remain the same in the equation?

▶ **Any quantity that does not change is a constant.**

4 When buying the right size refrigerator for your family, one rule of thumb states that you need about 10 cubic feet of fresh food space for two people, plus 1 cubic foot for each additional family member.

a. Which quantities in this rule are unknown or might change?

b. Which quantities in this rule are constants?

5 Which of the equations below can you use to represent the rule of thumb in Question 4? Explain your choice and what the variables r and f represent.

a. $r = 10 + 1 \cdot f$ **b.** $r = 10f$ **c.** $f + r = 10$ **d.** $r = 1 + 10f$

Use Labsheet 3A for Question 6.

6 **Try This as A Class** Follow the directions on the labsheet to practice translating various rules of thumb into equations.

✓ QUESTION 7

...checks that you can translate a word sentence into an equation.

7 **✓ CHECKPOINT** Write an equation for each rule of thumb. Be sure to tell what each variable represents.

a. The highest price you should pay for a car you are buying with a car loan is one-half your annual salary.

b. To estimate the surface area of your body, multiply the surface area of the palm of your hand by 50.

c. A set of steps will be comfortable to use if two times the height of one riser plus the width of one tread is equal to 25 in.

d. Separate a calf from its mother when the calf has gained 15 lb over its birth weight.

▲ The Council of American Building Officials recommends that risers be not more than $8\frac{1}{4}$ in. and treads not less than 9 in.

▶ **For an equation like $a = 2c$, you can find the value of a if you know the value of c.**

EXAMPLE

Trinja was 2 ft 9 in. tall at age 2. Estimate her adult height using the rule of thumb on page 32.

SAMPLE RESPONSE

Write the rule of thumb as an equation.

$$a = 2c$$
$$= 2(2.75)$$
$$= 5.5$$

2 ft 9 in. = 2.75 ft
Substitute 2.75 for the variable c.

Trinja's adult height would be 5.5 ft, or 5 ft 6 in.

FOR ▶ HELP with *order of operations*, see **TOOLBOX, p. 589**

8 **a.** To find h, the equivalent human age for a 6-year-old dog, substitute 6 for d in the equation $h = 15 + 4d$.

b. To evaluate $15 + 4d$ when $d = 6$, which operation is performed first, addition or multiplication? Why?

c. What is the equivalent human age for a 6-year-old dog?

d. What is the equivalent human age for an 11-year-old dog?

9 ✓ **CHECKPOINT** **Use Labsheet 3A.** Use an equation from the Labsheet to estimate each quantity.

a. A pilot is at an altitude of 24,000 feet. How far from the landing point should the pilot begin to descend?

b. The temperature is 15°C. What is it in degrees Fahrenheit?

c. How many pounds of gravel should be in a 55 gallon aquarium?

✓ **QUESTION 9**

...checks that you can evaluate an expression.

HOMEWORK EXERCISES ▶ **See Exs. 1–8 on pp. 44–45.**

Exploration 2

Solving Equations

GOAL

LEARN HOW TO...
- solve equations

AS YOU...
- work with rules of thumb

KEY TERMS
- solution
- solve an equation
- inverse operations

10 **a.** Face one wall of your classroom directly and hold your thumb at arm's length. Focus on the wall. Now close one eye and open the other. Switch eyes and estimate how far left or right your thumb jumped along the wall.

b. Multiply the estimated distance by 10. This is the approximate distance from you to the wall.

▶ **This rule of thumb for estimating distances can be represented by the following equation.**

Let d = the distance from you to the object.

$$d = 10e$$

Let e = the estimated distance that your thumb moved.

11 **Discussion** Suppose the distance from you to an object is 25 ft. How far should you expect your thumb to appear to move when you view it through one eye and then the other?

▶ **When you answered Question 11, you *solved the equation* $25 = 10e$. The value of a variable that makes an equation true is a solution of the equation. The process of finding solutions is called solving an equation.**

12 **Try This as a Class** Each folder contains a pair of equations.

1	2	3	4
$6 + n = 15$	$2w = 7$	$y - 7 = 21$	$\frac{a}{3} = 6$
$n = 15 - 6$	$w = \frac{7}{2}$	$y = 28$	$a = 18$

a. Do the equations in each pair have the same solution? How do you know?

b. Which operation (addition, subtraction, multiplication, or division) is used in the first equation in each box?

c. Which operation can you use to get from the first equation to the second equation in each box?

13 Addition is the *inverse operation* of subtraction. **Inverse operations** are operations that undo each other.

a. What is the inverse operation of multiplication?

b. How were inverse operations used in Question 12?

▶ **The Example below shows how to use math symbols and inverse operations to solve the equation $23 = t + 18$.**

EXAMPLE

Solve $23 = t + 18$ using math symbols and inverse operations.

SAMPLE RESPONSE

$$23 = t + 18$$
$$23 - 18 = t + 18 - 18$$
$$5 = t + 0$$
$$5 = t$$

$t + 0 = t$

14 **Discussion** When you solve an equation the expressions on both sides must remain equal. Sometimes this is referred to as keeping the equation balanced.

a. What inverse operation was used in the Example?

b. How is the equation kept balanced when this inverse operation is used?

15 Solve each equation. Show your work as in the Example above.

a. $19 + x = 31$ **b.** $87 = y - 4$ **c.** $36w = 144$ **d.** $\frac{r}{6} = 13$

▶ **Two-Step Equations** **Some equations use more than one operation. For example, the rule of thumb for calculating the recommended amount of kitchen cupboard space for a family is given by the formula $c = 6p + 12$, where c is the number of square feet of cupboard space and p is the number of people in the family. The formula uses both multiplication and addition.**

16 Copy and complete the following to express the rule of thumb in words.

To find the number of square feet of kitchen cupboard space recommended for a family, ...

▶ **To find the recommended amount of kitchen cupboard space for a family of 3, you can evaluate the expression $6p + 12$ for $p = 3$. The order of operations tells you how to evaluate an expression.**

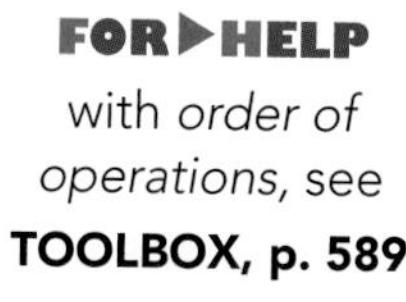
FOR▶HELP with *order of operations*, see **TOOLBOX, p. 589**

Evaluate the expression $6p + 12$ for $p = 3$.

p	**Start with the number.**	3
$6p$	**Multiply by 6.**	$6 \cdot 3 = 18$
$6p + 12$	**Add 12.**	$18 + 12 = 30$

17 Examine the Example above.

a. How much cupboard space is recommended for a family of 3?

b. Which operation was performed first, addition or multiplication? Why?

▶ **A real estate agent is writing an ad for a house she is selling and has calculated the kitchen cupboard space to be about 48 ft^2. The storage needs of how many people can be met by the given amount of space?**

18 **Try This as a Class**

a. Substitute 48 ft^2 for the cupboard space in the equation $c = 6p + 12$.

b. Which variable should the real estate agent solve for to find the number of people whose storage needs can be met?

▶ **The diagram below shows how to use math symbols and inverse operations to solve the equation $48 = 6p + 12$.**

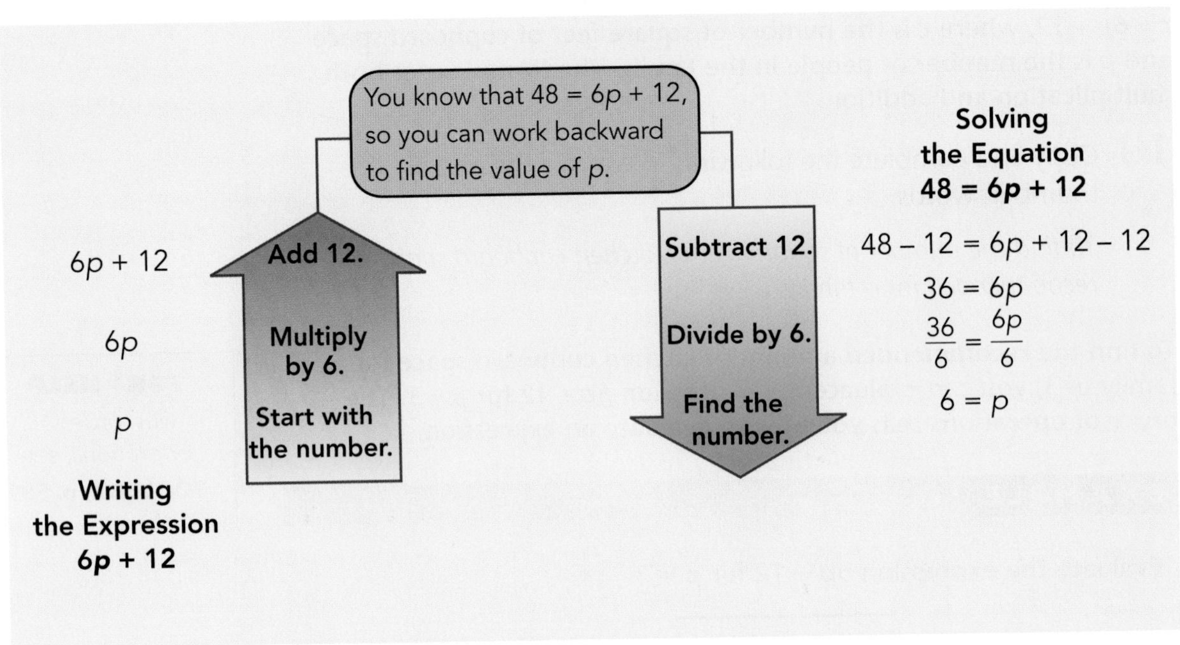

19 The diagram above shows the steps for solving the equation $48 = 6p + 12$.

a. What inverse operation is used to undo the multiplication $6p$?

b. Why do you *subtract 12* before you *divide by 6*?

c. How do you know in what order to use the inverse operations to solve an equation?

d. The storage needs of how many people can be met by the given amount of space?

e. Check the solution by substituting it into the original equation.

✓ QUESTION 20

...checks that you can use inverse operations to solve equations.

20 **✓ CHECKPOINT** Solve each equation. Show your work and check your solutions.

a. $8y + 16 = 24$ **b.** $2p - 7 = 15$ **c.** $4a = 10$

d. $\frac{n}{2} = 9$ **e.** $\frac{x}{2} + 3 = 11$ **f.** $\frac{r}{5} - 1 = 6$

HOMEWORK EXERCISES ▶ See Exs. 9–15 on pp. 45–46.

Exploration 3

Simplifying EXpressions

GOAL

LEARN HOW TO...
- simplify expressions

AS YOU...
- work with a rule of thumb about laundry

KEY TERMS
- terms
- like terms
- coefficient
- distributive property

▶ **The average person in the United States does an amazing 8493 loads of laundry in a lifetime! A rule of thumb states that the typical adult generates one load of laundry per week, while athletes, outdoor workers, and children generate two loads per week.**

"MAYBE WE SHOULDN'T HAVE LET THE LAUNDRY PILE UP FOR A YEAR."

21 Write an expression that represents the number of loads of laundry generated in x weeks.

a. by one child **b.** by one typical adult

c. by the child and the adult together

22 Evaluate your expression in Question 21(c) when $x = 4$.

▶ **Consider a family with one child and two adults where one of the adults is an outdoor worker. An expression for the number of loads of laundry generated by the family in x weeks is shown below.**

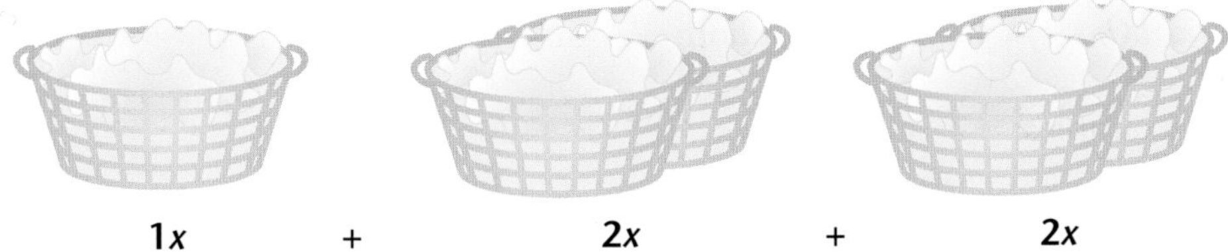

$1x \quad + \quad 2x \quad + \quad 2x$

▶ **The parts of an expression that are added are called terms. Each of the three terms in the expression $1x + 2x + 2x$ contains the variable x, which can be represented by the tile ▭. You can use algebra tiles to model an equivalent expression.**

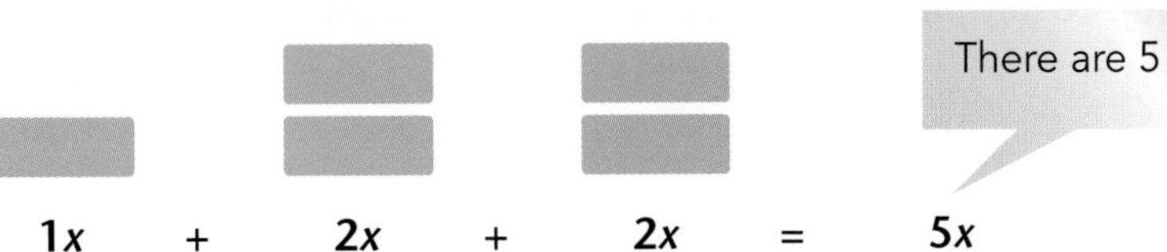

$1x + 2x + 2x = 5x$

23 **a.** How many loads of laundry will this family generate in $1\frac{1}{2}$ years, which is 78 weeks?

b. Did you use $1x + 2x + 2x$ or $5x$? Why?

▶ **The terms $1x$, $2x$, and $2x$ are *like terms.* Like terms have identical variable parts and can be combined by adding *coefficients.* The coefficient is the number part of the term.**

24 **Discussion** Use the table. Explain why the terms in the left column are *like* terms and the terms in the right column are *unlike* terms.

Like terms	Unlike terms
1, 13	4, $13x$
$2y$, $8y$	$2y$, $8y^2$
$3rs$, $4rs$	$3r$, $4rs$
$\frac{1}{4}m^2$, $7m^2$	$\frac{1}{4}m^2$, $7p^2$

25 **Try This as a Class**

a. Choose a value for x and substitute it in the expressions $2x + x$, $3x$, and $2x + 1$.

b. For which values of x does $2x + x = 3x$?

c. Are there values of x for which $2x + 1 = 3x$? If so, which ones?

d. Explain why $2x + x$ can be combined and written as $3x$, but $2x + 1$ cannot.

▶ **You can use the *distributive property of multiplication over addition* to write the expression $1x + 2x + 2x$ in another way.**

The distributive property of multiplication over addition says that for all numbers *a*, *b*, and *c*:

$$a(b + c) = ab + ac \qquad \text{and} \qquad ab + ac = a(b + c)$$

Examples:

$$7(5 + 2) = 7(5) + 7(2)$$
$$= 35 + 14$$

$$6 + 24 = 6(1) + 6(4)$$
$$= 6\ (1 + 4)$$

$$8(x + 3) = 8x + 8(3)$$
$$= 8x + 24$$

$$5x + 15 = 5x + 5(3)$$
$$= 5(x + 3)$$

You can use the distributive property of multiplication over addition to simplify the expression $1x + 2x + 2x$ to $5x$.

$$1x + 2x + 2x = (1 + 2 + 2)x$$
$$\downarrow$$
$$1x + 2x + 2x = 5x$$

26 **Try This as a Class** Use the distributive property of multiplication over addition to simplify the expression $2y + 11 + 4y - 2$.

27 **Discussion** Michael says there is also a distributive property of multiplication over subtraction because for all numbers a, b, and c,

$a(b - c) = ab - ac$ and $ab - ac = a(b - c)$.

Do you agree? Use examples to support your answer.

28 ✓ **CHECKPOINT** Combine like terms to simplify each expression.

a. $2w + 3w$ **b.** $2b^2 + b^2$ **c.** $3y + 7y - 6$

d. $4x - x + 1 + 3$ **e.** $5mn + 6mn$ **f.** $9q^2 + 7 - 2 - 3q$

✓ **QUESTION 28**

...checks that you can combine like terms.

▶ **Sometimes you can combine like terms to solve an equation.**

EXAMPLE

$$
\begin{aligned}
6x - x + 3 &= 18 \\
(6 - 1)x + 3 &= 18 \\
5x + 3 &= 18 \\
5x + 3 - 3 &= 18 - 3 \\
5x + 0 &= 15 \\
5x &= 15 \\
\frac{5x}{5} &= \frac{15}{5} \\
x &= 3
\end{aligned}
$$

Use the distributive property of multiplication over subtraction.

29 Show that 3 is a solution of the original equation $6x - x + 3 = 18$.

30 ✓ **CHECKPOINT** Solve each equation. Group and combine like terms if possible to simplify the equation before solving.

a. $3m + 5 + 10 = 45$ **b.** $12t - 4t + 2t = 30$

c. $21 = 5 + x + x$ **d.** $5p - 3p + 7 - 2 = 27$

✓ **QUESTION 30**

...checks that you can combine like terms to solve an equation.

HOMEWORK EXERCISES ▶ See Exs. 16–29 on pp. 46–47.

Section 3 Key Concepts

Key Terms

variable

constant

Writing Equations (pp. 33–35)

To write an equation for a word sentence, choose a variable to represent each of the quantities that are unknown or that may change. Any quantities that do not change are constants. Use symbols to repreent the relationships between the quantities.

Example

According to a rule that some caterers use, you should prepare 3 appetizers for each person at a party.

The number of appetizers (a) (is equal to) 3 (times) the number of people (p).

Equation: $a = 3 \cdot p = 3p$

solution of an equation

solve an equation

inverse operations

Solving Equations (pp. 35–38)

A value of a variable that makes an equation true is a solution of the equation. The process of finding solutions is called solving an equation. One way to solve an equation is to use inverse operations. Inverse operations are operations like addition and subtraction that undo each other.

Example

Solve:

$$\frac{y}{3} + 6 = 30$$

$$\frac{y}{3} + 6 - 6 = 30 - 6$$

$$\frac{y}{3} = 24$$

$$\frac{y}{3} \cdot 3 = 24 \cdot 3$$

$$y = 72$$

Check:

$$\frac{y}{3} + 6 = 30$$

$$\frac{72}{3} + 6 \stackrel{?}{=} 30$$

$$24 + 6 \stackrel{?}{=} 30$$

$$30 = 30$$

31 **Key Concepts Question** Explain how inverse operations were used to solve the equation in the second example.

Section 3 Key Concepts

Key Terms

Simplifying Expressions (pp. 39–41)

The parts of an expression that are added are terms. Terms with identical variable parts are like terms. To simplify some expressions and to solve some equations you can combine like terms by adding coefficients.

terms

like terms

coefficient

Example

Solve:

$$41 = 5x - 3x - 1$$
$$41 = 2x - 1$$
$$41 + 1 = 2x - 1 + 1$$
$$42 = 2x$$
$$\frac{42}{2} = \frac{2x}{2}$$
$$21 = x$$

Check:

$$41 = 5x - 3x - 1$$
$$41 \stackrel{?}{=} 5 \cdot 21 - 3 \cdot 21 - 1$$
$$41 \stackrel{?}{=} 105 - 63 - 1$$
$$41 \stackrel{?}{=} 42 - 1$$
$$41 = 41$$

Distributive Property (pp. 40–41)

distributive property

The distributive property of multiplication over addition says that for any numbers *a*, *b*, and *c*:

$a(b + c) = ab + ac$ and $ab + ac = a(b + c)$

The distributive property of multiplication over subtraction says that for any numbers *a*, *b*, and *c*:

$a(b - c) = ab - ac$ and $ab - ac = a(b - c)$

The distributive property allows you to combine like terms to simplify expressions and equations.

Examples

$$4(x + 8) = 4x + 4 \cdot 8$$
$$= 4x + 32$$

$$5x - 3x = (5 - 3)x$$
$$= 2x$$

32 Key Concepts Question

a. Simplify and then solve the equation $3x + 5 + 5x = 51$.

b. Check your solution. How do you know your solution is correct?

Section 3

Practice & Application Exercises

1. Leona makes flower arrangements so the flowers are about one and a half times the width of the container. Which equation represents this rule of thumb? Let a = the width of the arrangement and c = the width of the container.

   A. $1\frac{1}{2}c = a$ B. $1\frac{1}{2}a = c$ C. $c + 1\frac{1}{2} = a$

For Exercises 2–6, use variables to write each word sentence as an equation. Tell what each variable represents.

2. The total cost of tickets for a group of people at an amusement park is $29 per child plus $40 per adult.

3. The total distance of a bike trip divided by 50 gives the approximate number of days the trip will take.

4. To estimate a yearly salary from an hourly wage, double the hourly wage and multiply by 1000.

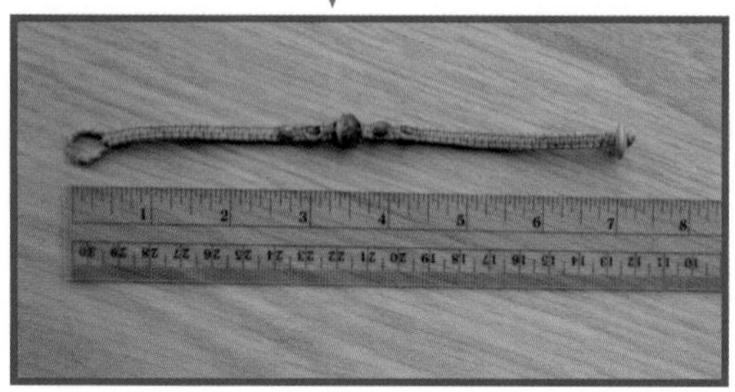

5. To estimate the beginning length of each cord needed to make a macramé bracelet, multiply the length you want the bracelet to be by 8.

6. The age of a lobster can be estimated by multiplying its weight in pounds by 7.

7. In the following rule of thumb and formula, C = temperature in degrees Celsius and F = temperature in degrees Fahrenheit.

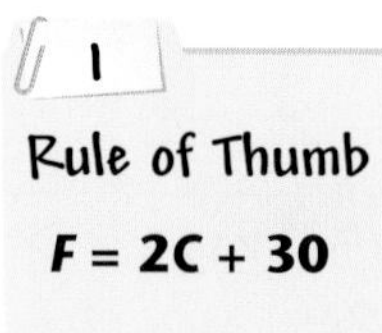

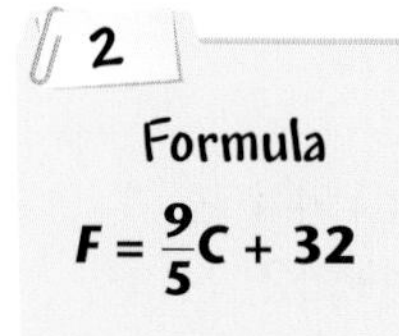

   a. Use the rule of thumb to convert 0°C, 15°C, and 100°C to Fahrenheit temperatures.

   b. Use the formula to convert 0°C, 15°C, and 100°C to Fahrenheit temperatures.

   c. For which Celsius temperature does the rule of thumb give the best estimate of the Fahrenheit temperature you found using the formula?

8. Your mass in kilograms multiplied by 0.08 is approximately equal to the volume of your blood in liters.

   a. Write an equation for this rule of thumb. Tell what each variable represents.

   b. According to this rule of thumb, how many liters of blood does a 50-kilogram person have?

9. Use inverse operations to solve each equation. Check your solution.

   a. $6 + x = 31$ b. $\frac{x}{12} = 105$ c. $6t = 21$

   d. $161 = 7y$ e. $39 = \frac{y}{4}$ f. $y - 18 = 27$

10. Check whether $x = 14$ is a solution for each equation below.

   a. $2x + 3 = 25$ b. $1 = \frac{x}{7} - 1$ c. $x - 14 = 0$

11. Which of the following is the preferred first step in solving the equation $16 = 6x - 7$?

   A. Add 7 to both sides of the equation.

   B. Subtract 7 from both sides of the equation.

   C. Divide each side of the equation by 6.

   D. Subtract 16 from each side of the equation.

12. Use inverse operations to solve each equation. Check your solution.

   a. $6 + 3x = 39$ b. $\frac{x}{12} + 8 = 105$ c. $6t - 8 = 154$

   d. $30 = 7y - 5$ e. $3y + 5 = 11$ f. $\frac{y}{4} + 1 = 7$

13. **Create Your Own** Write your own rule of thumb for something you estimate and then write it as an equation. Use your equation in two examples.

Oceanography Ships use the speed of sound in water to help find the water's depth.

14. a. The speed of sound in water is about five times the speed of sound in air. Write an equation for this rule of thumb.

   b. Assume that the speed of sound in ocean water is 1470 m/sec. At about what speed does sound travel in air?

This sonar image shows the ocean floor off the coast of California.

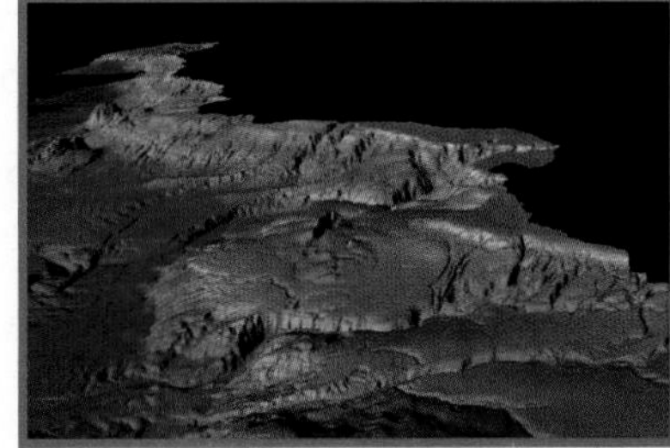

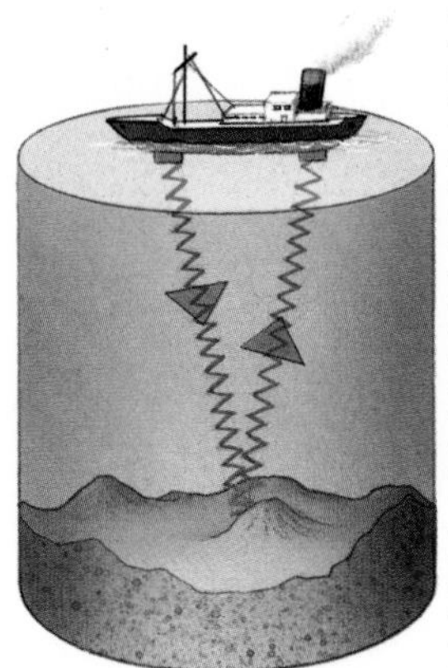

15. **Challenge** A sonar pulse from a ship is sent to the bottom the ocean. To find the distance the pulse has traveled, multiply the speed of sound in water by the amount of time it takes for the pulse to travel from the ship to the ocean floor and back to the ship. Assume that the speed of sound in water is 1470 m/sec.

    a. Suppose the sonar pulse returns in 2 sec. Explain why the ocean depth is 1470 m rather than 2940 m. (Hint: Draw a diagram of the path the sound travels.)

    b. Write a formula for finding ocean depth. Use your formula to find the ocean depth if the sonar pulse returns in 2.5 sec.

16. Which of the terms below are like terms?

    x^2 $\quad \frac{1}{2}x^2$ $\quad xy$ $\quad x^2y$ $\quad 2x^2$ $\quad xy^2$

If possible combine like terms to simplify each expression.

17. $17x + 4 - 3$ 18. $8rs - 6r$ 19. $16w + 3 + w$

20. $3t - 2t + 9t$ 21. $19n - 19n^2$ 22. $4xy + 4x - 4x$

23. $12y^2 + 6x + 3y^2 + x$ 24. $f^2 + 3f + 4f - 6$

25. **Geometry Connection** The perimeter of a rectangle can be represented by the equation $P = l + l + w + w$, where P = the perimeter, l = the length, and w = the width.

    a. Simplify the equation by combining like terms.

    b. If $l = 10$ in. and $w = 3$ in., what is the perimeter of the rectangle?

    c. Solve for w when $P = 50$ cm and $l = 18$ cm.

    d. Solve for l when $P = 15$ m and $w = 3$ m.

26. **Geometry Connection** Write an equation for finding the perimeter of each figure. Tell what each variable represents. Combine like terms when possible.

    a. equilateral triangle b. square

27. Find the length of one side of each figure in Exercise 26 when the perimeter is 36 yd.

28. Solve each equation. If possible, combine like terms to simplify each equation before solving.

    a. $3x + 8 - 5 = 27$ b. $72 = x + 2x + 3x$ c. $5m - 4 = 56$

Reflecting on the Section

29. The balance scales below are each balanced.

   a. What objects from Balance Scale A could be substituted for a cube on Balance Scale B?

   b. Use your answer to part (a) to find how many pencils it will take to balance one cylinder. Explain how you solved this problem. How is solving it like solving an equation?

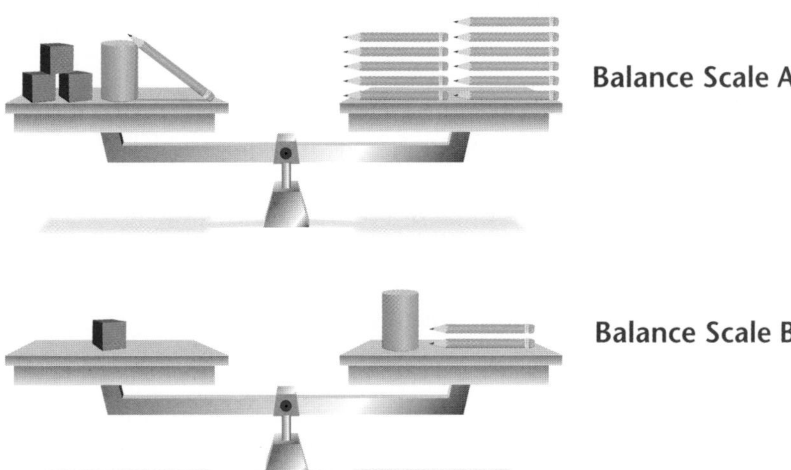

Visual THINKING

Exercise 29 checks to see if you can balance an equation.

Spiral Review

Choose a type of data display that you could use for each data set. Explain each choice of display. **(Module 1, pp. 9–10)**

30. the amounts of rainfall during the months of a certain year

31. the percentages of people who voted for various candidates in a student council election

Science In a thunderstorm, you see flashes of lightning before you hear the thunder from the lightning. This is because sound travels much more slowly than light. **(Module 1, p. 12)**

32. The speed of sound through air is about 1100 ft/sec.

   a. Suppose you want to explain to a friend how the speed of sound compares to the speed of a car. What units would you use to express the speed of sound for your friend? Explain.

   b. Express the speed of sound in the units you chose in part (a).

Section 3

Extra Skill Practice

Use variables to write each word sentence as an equation. Tell what each variable represents.

1. The camp cooks agree that the amount of hamburger they need to purchase for a trip is $\frac{1}{4}$ lb of hamburger for each camper and an extra 5 lb.

2. The total bus fare for a family is \$0.60 for each adult and \$0.10 for each child.

3. To estimate the monthly rent of an apartment in her city, Jenny multiplies the area in square feet of the apartment by \$0.90.

4. A mattress alone costs \$25 plus half the price of the box spring and mattress together.

Use inverse operations to solve each equation. Check your solution.

5. $3j + 2 = 95$
6. $5w = 30$
7. $\frac{m}{52} = 4$
8. $8 + 4z = 12$
9. $r - 131 = 17$
10. $27 = 14 + 2y$

If possible, combine like terms to simplify each expression.

11. $1y + 6y - 2y$
12. $5 + 11rz - 3z$
13. $t + 9t - 4$
14. $5p + 4p - 18pr$
15. $18r - 18rd + 18r$
16. $10v + 5k^3 - v + 20k^3$
17. $2h^3 + 4h$
18. $\frac{1}{2}xy + \frac{1}{4}x$
19. $7 + 5w - 4w + w^2$

Standardized Testing ▶ Multiple Choice

1. If $\frac{x}{3} - 23 = 4$, what does $2x$ equal?

   (A) 114 (B) 70 (C) 54 (D) 162

2. Combine like terms to simplify the expression $3x^2 + 10xy + x^2 - 7xy$. Which expression is correct?

   (A) $4x^2 + 3xy$ (B) $3x^2 + 3xy$ (C) $4x^4 + 3x^2y^2$ (D) $6x^6y^2$

Section 4 Scatter Plots

IN THIS SECTION

EXPLORATION 1
- Making a Scatter Plot

EXPLORATION 2
- Fitting a Line

Athletic Triumphs

Setting the Stage

The achievements of many athletes seem even more amazing when you think about the difficulties they have overcome.

At 5 ft 7 in., Anthony "Spud" Webb is much shorter than most National Basketball Association players. Yet he won the Slam-Dunk Competition at the 1986 NBA All-Star game. ▶

▲ In 1996, Lance Armstrong was given less than a 50% chance of surviving cancer. But he did survive, and in 2005 he won the grueling Tour de France bicycle race for the seventh year in a row.

▲ Marla Runyan has been legally blind since the age of 9, but it hasn't slowed her down! She finished eighth in the 1500 m run at the 2000 Olympics and fifth in the 2002 New York City marathon. In the 2004 Athens Olympics she competed in the 5000 m run.

Think About It

1 With a running start, Spud Webb could jump $3\frac{1}{2}$ ft off the floor.

  a. Estimate how high Spud's hand could have reached when he jumped.

  b. How did you make your estimate?

2 Shaquille O'Neal is 7 ft 1 in. tall. Do you think he could dunk a basketball without jumping? Explain your reasoning.

GOAL

LEARN HOW TO...
- organize data in a scatter plot

AS YOU...
- analyze data about height and jumping distance

KEY TERMS
- scale
- interval
- scatter plot

Exploration 1

Making a Scatter Plot

SET UP *Work in a group of six. You will need: • masking tape • tape measure or yardstick • ruler • graph paper*

▶ **Spud Webb's jumping ability was amazing, even for a professional athlete. How high would someone your age need to jump to be an amazing jumper? One way to find out is to gather data and use it to predict how high a 5 ft 7 in. eighth grade student might be expected to jump.**

3 **a.** Make a table like the one shown.

Jumping Data		
Student	Height (in.)	Jump height (in.)
Sarah	63	89
Milo	61	85

b. Measure the height of each person in your group. Record the heights in your table.

c. Follow the directions given below to measure each student's jump height to the nearest inch. Record the jump heights in your table.

First

Jump near a wall. Make two standing jumps, placing a piece of masking tape as high on the wall as possible.

Then

Record your jump height. Your jump height is the distance from the floor to your higher piece of masking tape.

4 **a.** Write an *ordered pair* like the one shown for each person in your group.

b. Write the ordered pairs on the board so each student can record the results for the entire class.

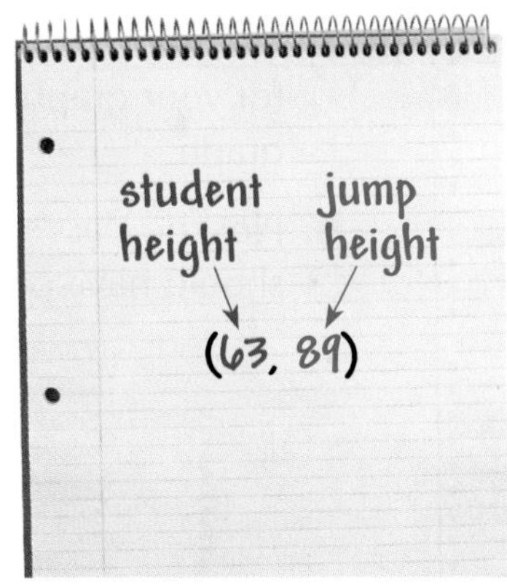

▶ **Sometimes it is easier to see how data are related by graphing the data. On a graph, the numbers written along an axis are its scale. The numbers on the scale can increase by ones, but when the data are spread over a large range it may be better to choose a scale that increases by twos, fives, tens, or some other number.**

5 **Try This as a Class** The questions below will help you plan how to graph your class's jumping data.

a. The horizontal axis of the graph will show student heights in inches. What are the greatest and least student heights?

b. Use the values from part (a) to decide what range of heights to show on the horizontal axis. Explain your thinking.

c. Use the range of heights to decide how many intervals you can fit along the horizontal axis. Explain your thinking.

d. Use your answers to parts (b) and (c) to choose a scale for the horizontal axis. Explain your decision.

e. The vertical axis will show jump height in inches. Decide what values will be shown and choose a scale for the vertical axis. Explain how you made your choices.

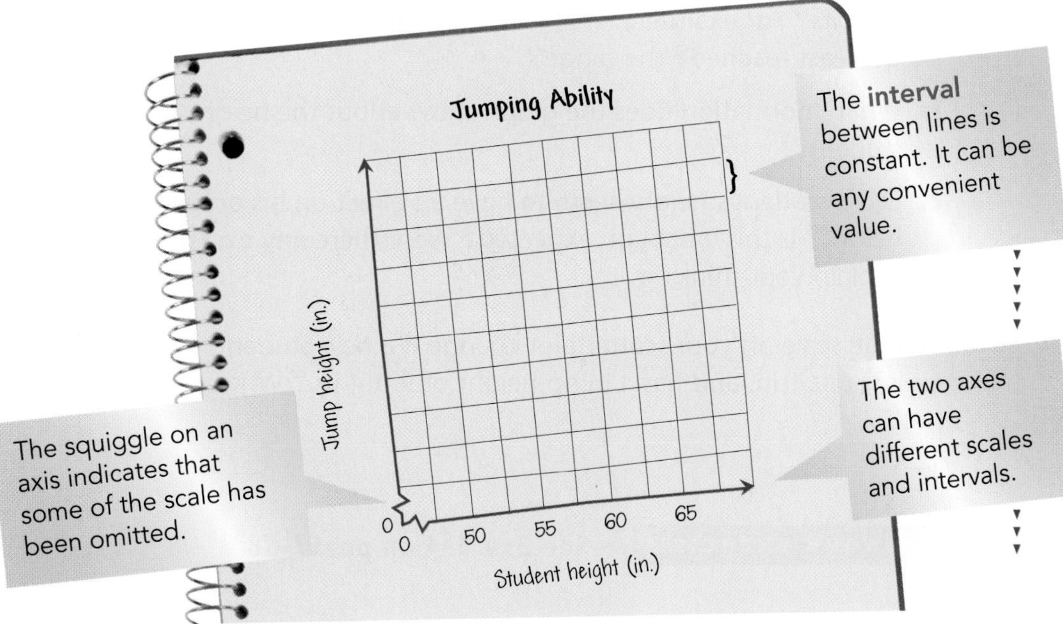

6 **a.** On graph paper draw and label the horizontal and vertical axes for your graph. Include the scale for each axis and a title for the graph.

b. Plot the class's jumping data on your coordinate grid. You should have one point for each member of the class.

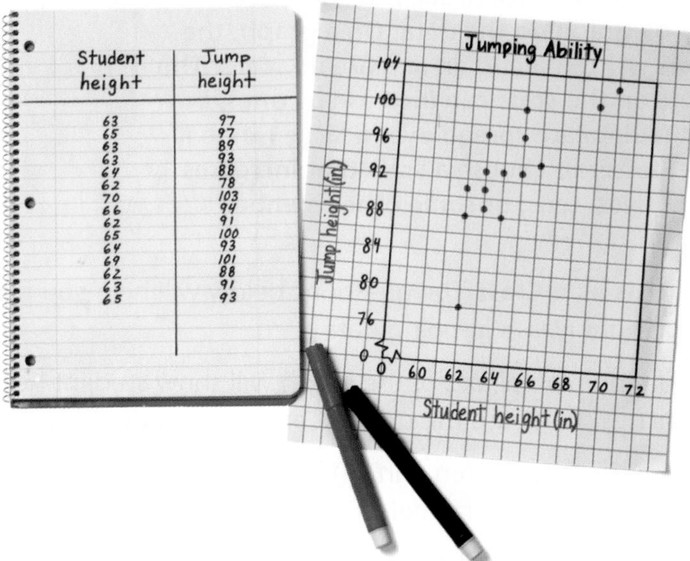

▶ **The graph you created is a *scatter plot*. A scatter plot is the graph of a set of data pairs. A scatter plot can help you to recognize patterns and make predictions.**

7 **Discussion** Use your scatter plot.

a. Looking at the scatter plot, what can you tell about the jump heights? For example, what is the greatest height reached? the least reached? the range?

b. What information does the graph show about the heights of the students?

c. Did a student's height seem to have an effect on his or her jump height? Is this what you expected? Were there any exceptions? Explain your thinking.

8 Will the scale on your scatter plot change if a new student in your class is 6 ft 1 in. and has a jump height of 9 ft 4 in.? Why or why not?

HOMEWORK EXERCISES ▶ See Exs. 1–4 on pp. 57–58.

Exploration 2

Fitting a LINE

GOAL

LEARN HOW TO...
- use a fitted line to make predictions

AS YOU...
- analyze data about the Tour de France and about students' jump heights

KEY TERMS
- positive correlation
- negative correlation
- fitted line

SET UP *You will need • Labsheet 4A • ruler • your scatter plot of jumping data from Exploration 1*

▶ **The scatter plot below compares the performances of the top 20 finishers in one of the Tour de France races. Each point represents a racer's time for the mountain time trial and his total time for the Tour de France.**

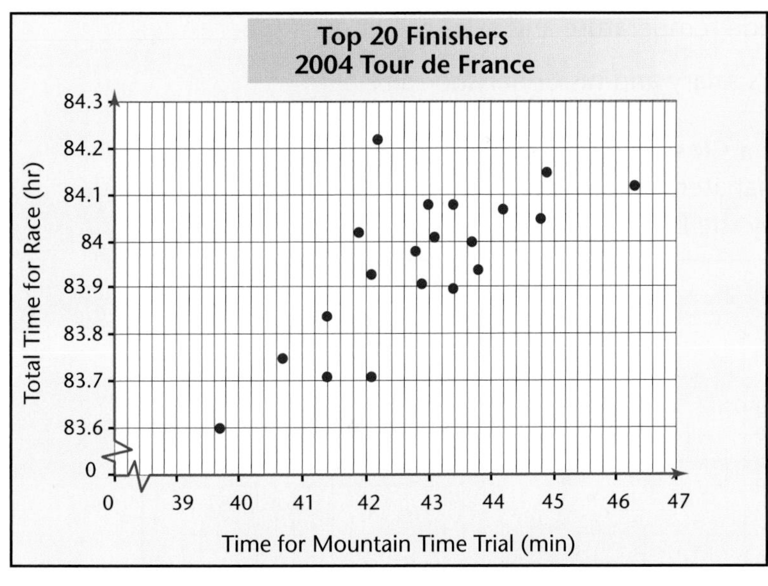

9 **a.** Lance Armstrong had the fastest total time for the race and the fastest time for the mountain time trial. Find the point on the scatter plot that shows his performance. What was his total time for the 2004 Tour de France?

b. Estimate Lance Armstrong's time for the mountain time trial.

c. For the top 20 finishers, the slowest time for the mountain time trial was 46.28 min and the slowest total time for the race was 84.22 hr. Did the same racer have both of these times? Explain.

10 **Discussion** What pattern do you notice in the points on the scatter plot?

▶ **Two variables that are related in some way are said to be correlated. There is a positive correlation if one variable tends to increase as the other increases. There is a negative correlation if one variable tends to decrease as the other increases.**

11 **Try This as a Class**

a. Is there a *positive correlation*, a *negative correlation*, or *no correlation* between the times for the mountain time trial and the total times for the race? Explain.

b. If there is a correlation, would you describe it as *strong* or *weak*? Why?

✓ QUESTION 12

...checks that you can determine if there is a correlation between two variables.

12 **✓ CHECKPOINT** Tell whether there is a *positive correlation*, a *negative correlation*, or *no correlation* between the two variables.

a. the height and weight of a stack of pennies

b. the outside temperature and sales of hot cocoa

c. an adult's salary and his or her shoe size

13 **Try This as a Class** The scatter plot below shows the number of Florida manatees killed by boats and the price of stocks as measured by the Dow Jones Industrial Average for 1983–2004.

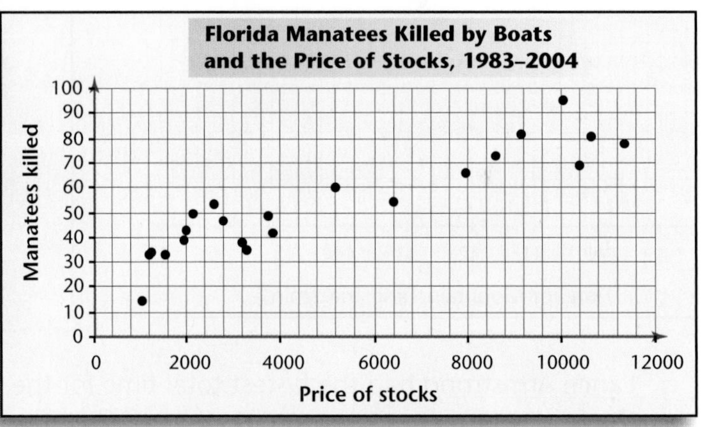

a. Is there a *positive correlation*, a *negative correlation*, or *no correlation* between the price of stocks and the number of manatees killed by boats?

b. Would it be correct to say that a rise in stock prices tends to cause an increase in the number of manatees killed by boats? Why or why not?

c. If a correlation exists between two variables, does that necessarily mean there is a cause-and-effect relationship between the variables? That is, does a change in one of the variables cause the other variable to change? Explain.

▶ **When the data points show a strong correlation, a fitted line can be drawn to show the pattern in the data and to help make predictions. An example of a fitted line is shown on the scatter plot of the Tour de France data.**

EXAMPLE

A fitted line is drawn so that most of the data points fall near it. About half of the points should be above the line and about half should be below it.

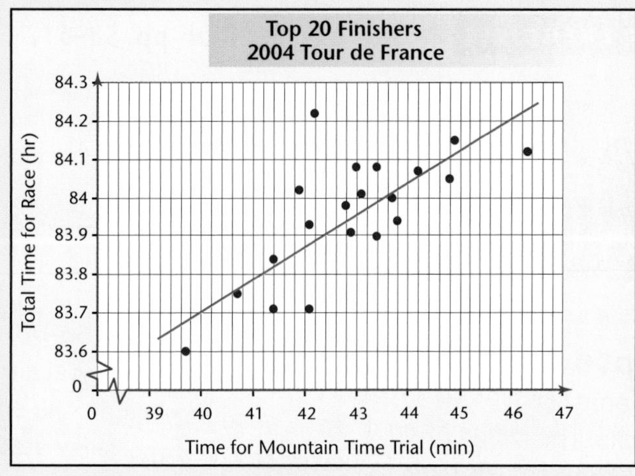

14 Discussion

a. How does the fitted line in the Example help you see that the racers who are faster on the mountain time trial are usually faster for the whole race?

b. Which points do not seem to follow this pattern?

c. Suppose a racer finishes the Mountain Time Trial in 41.2 min. Use the fitted line to predict his total time for the race.

▶ **The data points in a scatter plot do not always show a straight-line pattern. If you see a curved pattern or no pattern at all, it does not make sense to draw a fitted line.**

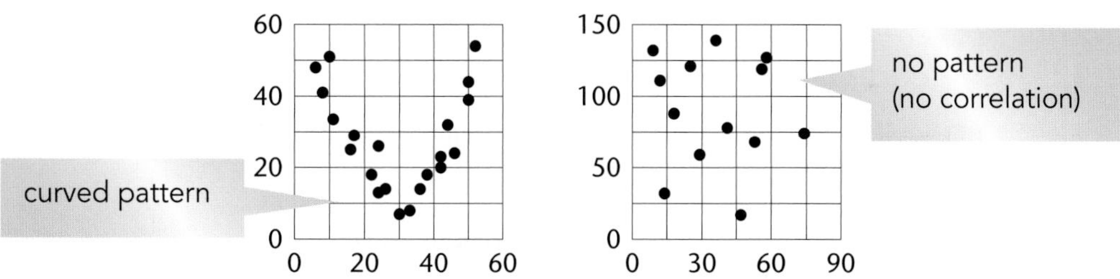

15 **Use Labsheet 4A.** You will examine scatter plots and make decisions about *Correlations and Fitted Lines.*

✓ QUESTION 16

...checks that you can draw a fitted line on a scatter plot and decide how well it represents the data.

16 **✓ CHECKPOINT** Draw a fitted line on your scatter plot from Exercise 6 in Exploration 1. Does the line represent your data well? Explain.

17 **a.** How can you use your fitted line from Question 16 to decide whether your class has any "amazing jumpers"?

b. Spud Webb is 5 ft 7 in. tall. What jump height would you expect for a student as tall as Spud Webb?

HOMEWORK EXERCISES See Exs. 5–18 on pp. 58–61.

Section 4 Key Concepts

Key Terms

scatter plot

scale

fitted line

Scatter Plots and Fitted Lines (pp. 51–53 and 55–56)

You can use a scatter plot to look for patterns in paired data and make predictions. The range of each data set determines the scale of each axis of the scatter plot. Sometimes the data show a strong correlation. When they do, you can draw a fitted line to show a pattern and help make predictions.

Example The scatter plot at the right compares how high a group of eighth grade students jumped to their heights. Because the correlation is strong, you can draw a fitted line.

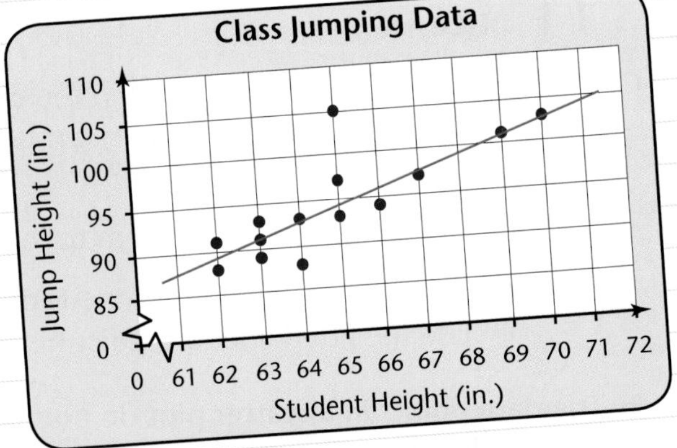

18 **Key Concepts Question** Use the scatter plot in the Example.

a. Describe the relationship between the students' heights and how high they jumped.

b. Predict the jump height for a 68 in. tall student.

c. Gerome's jump height was 105 in. About how tall is he? How does his jump height compare with those of other students?

Section 4 Key Concepts

Correlation (p. 54)

Two variables that are related in some way are said to be correlated. There is a positive correlation if one variable tends to increase as the other increases. There is a negative correlation if one variable tends to decrease as the other increases.

Positive correlation

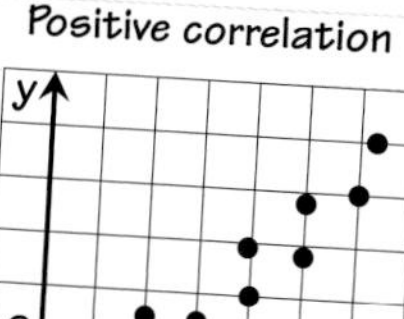

Negative correlation

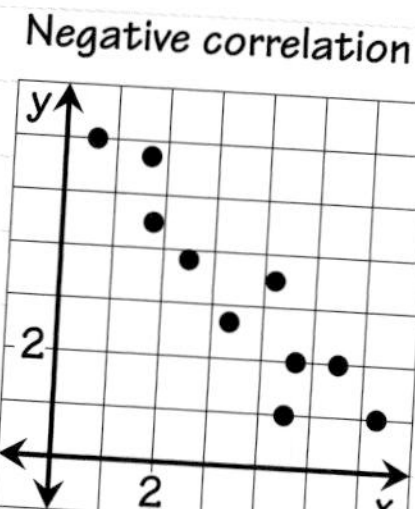

No correlation

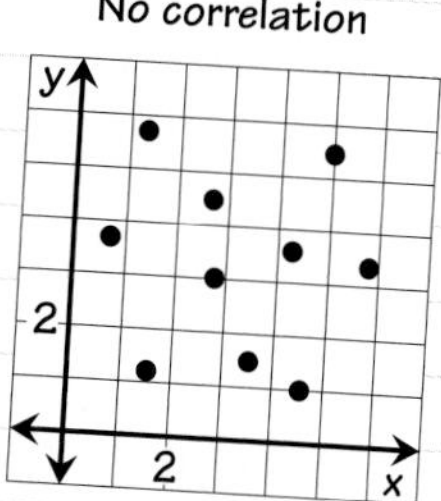

Key Terms

positive correlation

negative correlation

19 Key Concepts Question

a. Describe two real-world variables that have a negative correlation.

b. Does an increase in one of the variables in part (a) cause a decrease in the other variable? Explain your thinking.

Section 4 Practice & Application Exercises

YOU WILL NEED

For Exs. 1–3:
- Labsheet 4B

For Exs. 4 and 16:
- graph paper
- two colored pencils

For Ex. 17:
- small ball
- yardstick or meter stick
- graph paper

Use Labsheet 4B for Exercises 1–3. The scatter plot shows *World Record Marathon Times* for men and women of different ages.

1. **a.** What is the approximate age and record time of the oldest female marathon runner?

   b. What is the approximate age and record time of the youngest male marathon runner?

2. **a.** In what 10-year age range are the record times for men fastest?

   b. Does the fastest individual male time fall in this age range?

3. Writing Describe the pattern of the data points. Explain what it shows about the marathon runners and their times.

4. Some friends planned to travel at a rate of 12 km/hr on a 20 km bike trip. Several times during the trip they recorded the total distance traveled and the time elapsed. They also recorded the time it would have taken them at their planned rate of 12 km/hr. Their data are shown in the table below.

a. Make a scatter plot that compares distance and actual time. Put distance on the horizontal axis.

b. On the same graph, use a different color to plot ordered pairs (distance, planned time). Use these new points to make a line graph. (In a line graph, a segment is drawn to connect each point to the next point.)

Distance	Planned Time	Actual Time
0 km	0 min	0 min
2 km	10 min	6 min
4 km	20 min	22 min
6 km	30 min	32 min
10 km	50 min	45 min
14 km	70 min	58 min
15 km	75 min	60 min
17 km	85 min	77 min
20 km	100 min	90 min

c. How does the planned time compare with the actual time?

d. During what stage of the trip were people traveling the fastest? Explain how you found your answer.

Tell whether each graph shows a *positive correlation*, a *negative correlation*, or *no correlation* between the two variables.

5.

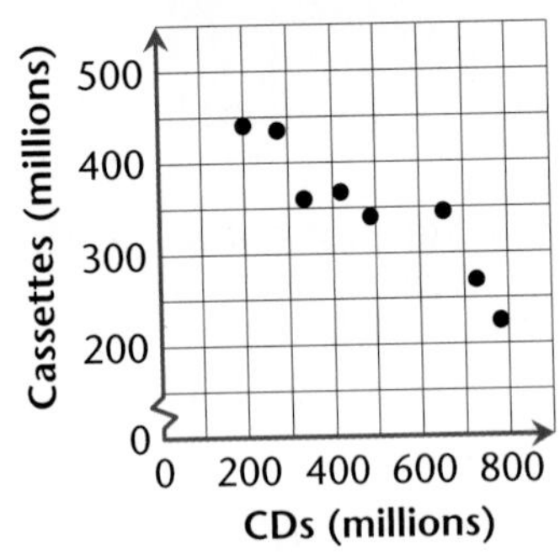

6.

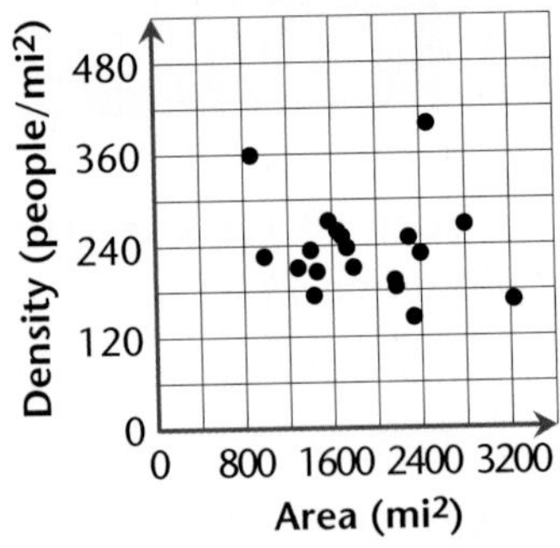

7. Tell whether each scatter plot appears to have a straight-line pattern, a curved pattern, or no pattern.

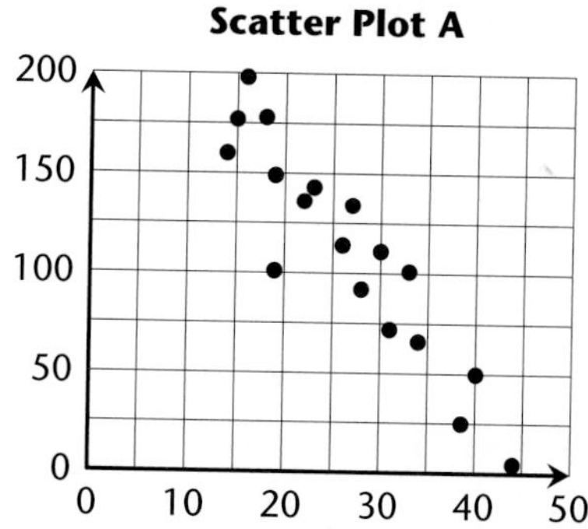

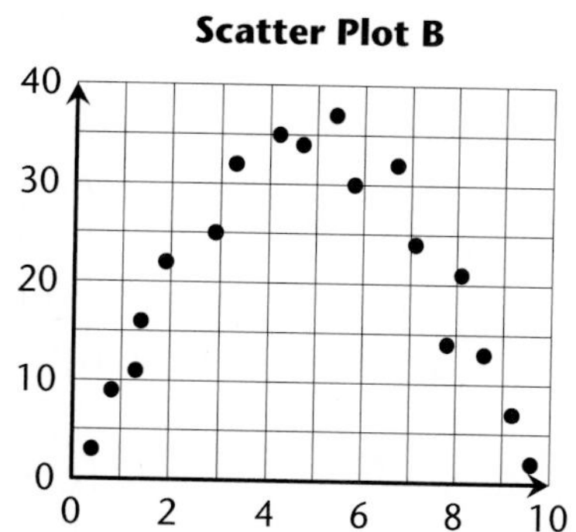

Biology **The table shows biological data for several animals.**

Animal	Body weight (kg)	Brain weight (g)	Heart rate (beats/min)	Life span (years)
Mouse	0.02	0.40	630	3.2
Hedgehog	0.79	3.5	250	6.0
Kangaroo	35	56	130	16
Pig	190	180	78	27
Cow	470	420	45	30
Elephant	2500	4600	30	69

Use the table to tell whether there is a *positive correlation*, a *negative correlation*, or *no correlation* between each pair of variables.

8. brain weight, body weight
9. heart rate, body weight
10. heart rate, brain weight
11. life span, body weight
12. life span, brain weight
13. life span, heart rate

14. One rule of thumb from someone living in New York City states that to predict the day's high temperature, add 18 degrees to the temperature at 6:00 A.M.

   a. Do you think this is a good rule of thumb? Explain how you can use the scatter plot at the right to convince someone you are right.

   b. Does it make sense to fit a line to the data in the scatter plot? Explain your reasoning.

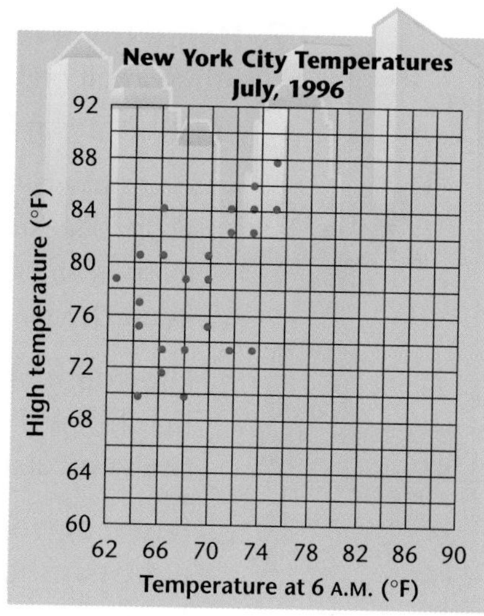

15. **Challenge** Suppose there is a positive correlation between x and y and a negative correlation between y and z. What kind of correlation is there between x and z? Explain.

16. a. **History** Make a scatter plot of the female employment data below. Put population age 16 and over on the horizontal axis and the number employed on the vertical axis. Add the male employment data to your scatter plot. Draw a fitted line for each set of data points.

Employment Status of United States Civilian Population in millions (1960–2005)

	Total Female Population		Total Male Population	
Year	Age 16 and over	Employed	Age 16 and over	Employed
1960	62	22	58	44
1965	67	25	62	46
1970	73	30	67	49
1975	80	34	73	51
1980	87	41	80	56
1985	94	47	84	60
1990	99	54	90	65
1995	103	58	95	67
2000	111	64	102	73
2005	117	66	110	76

b. Predict how many women will be employed when the total female population age 16 and over is 130 million.

c. About what will the number of males age 16 and older be if 90 million of them are employed?

17. **Home Involvement** Use a tennis ball, racquetball, or other small ball to compare drop height and bounce height. Have a friend or family member help you.

a. Drop the ball from five different heights. For each drop, measure the height the ball was dropped from and the height it reached on its first bounce. Record your data.

b. Use your data to make a scatter plot. Put drop height on the horizontal axis and bounce height on the vertical axis. Draw a fitted line if it makes sense.

c. Based on your scatter plot, do you think there is a relationship between drop height and bounce height? Explain.

Reflecting on the Section

18. Explain how scatter plots could be used in science class. Describe an actual problem or experiment where a scatter plot was used. You may want to interview a science teacher or student in your school to see how they use scatter plots.

RESEARCH

Exercise 18 checks that you know how to use a scatter plot.

Spiral Review

Find each answer. (Toolbox, p. 589)

19. 4^2 20. 2^4 21. $3 \cdot 2^3$ 22. $3.14 \cdot 2.5$

Find the area of each figure. (Toolbox, p. 595)

23. 24. 25.

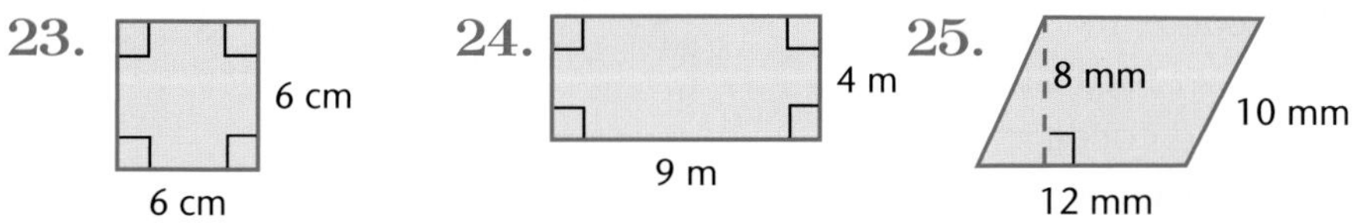

26. **Football** The heaviest football players are usually defensive linemen, linebackers, and offensive linemen. The box-and-whisker plots below compare the weights of these players on an NFL team. Use the box-and-whisker plots to tell whether each statement below is true or false. Explain your thinking. (Module 1, p. 23)

Weights (in lb) of players on an NFL team

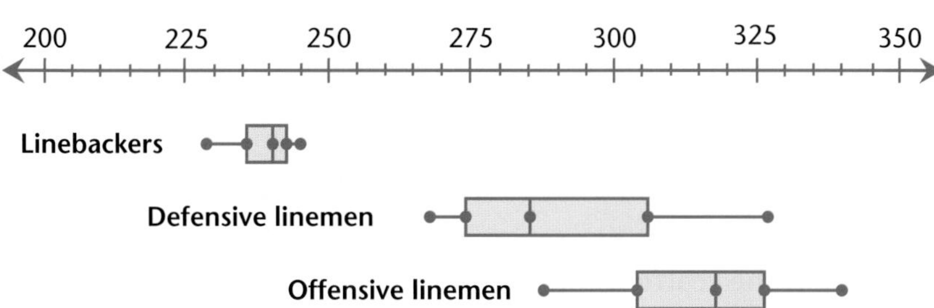

a. All of the linebackers weigh 245 lb or less.

b. About half of the defensive linemen weigh less than 285 lb.

c. At least one defensive lineman weighs less than all of the linebackers.

d. About 25% of the offensive linemen weigh more than the heaviest defensive linemen.

Section 4 Extra Skill Practice

You will need: • *graph paper* (Ex. 3)

Interpreting Data This scatter plot shows some records for the distance traveled by a human-powered vehicle in one hour.

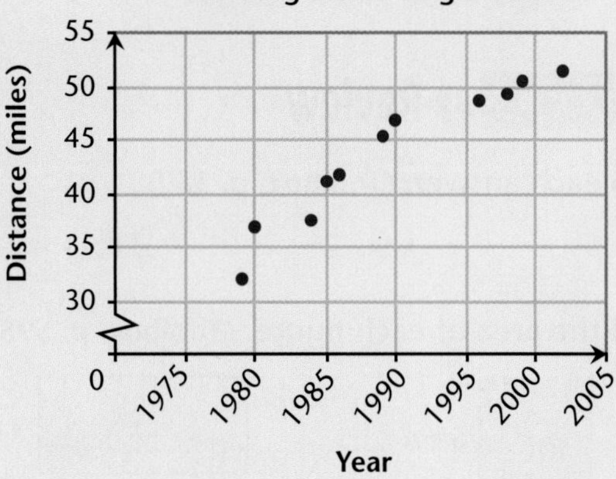

1. About how far is the longest distance record? In about what year was that record set?
2. Explain whether it makes sense to draw a fitted line for the scatter plot.
3. A snack shop owner is trying to decide how much hot cocoa to make each day. The owner records the high temperatures and cocoa sales each day for two weeks.

High temperature	77	72	75	70	71	68	69	65	64	60	55	58	54	51
Cups of cocoa sold	6	6	4	7	5	9	11	14	15	18	25	21	28	31

   a. Make a scatter plot of the data. Put high temperature on the horizontal axis. Choose a scale for each axis. Explain your choices.
   b. If it makes sense to draw a fitted line, draw one.
   c. Suppose one pot makes 10 cups of cocoa. How many pots should the owner make when the high temperature is 50°?

Standardized Testing ▶ Free Response

Sprint times for contestants in a race at a weekend picnic are shown in the scatter plot. The contestants' ages are also shown.

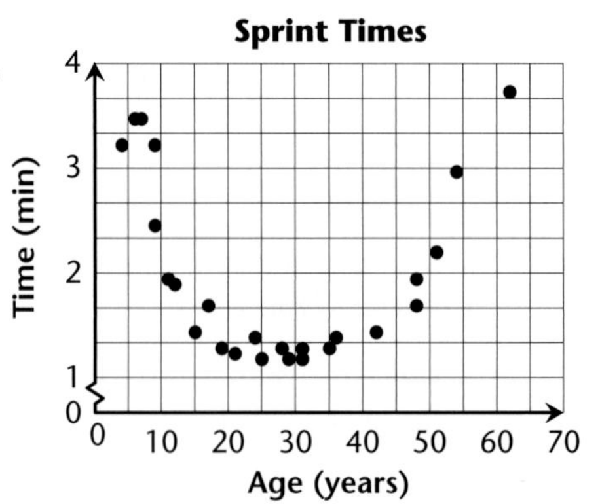

1. For what ages do the times appear to be decreasing? increasing?
2. Do the data appear to have a straight-line pattern or a curved pattern? Explain.

Section 5 Problem Solving and Mathematical Models

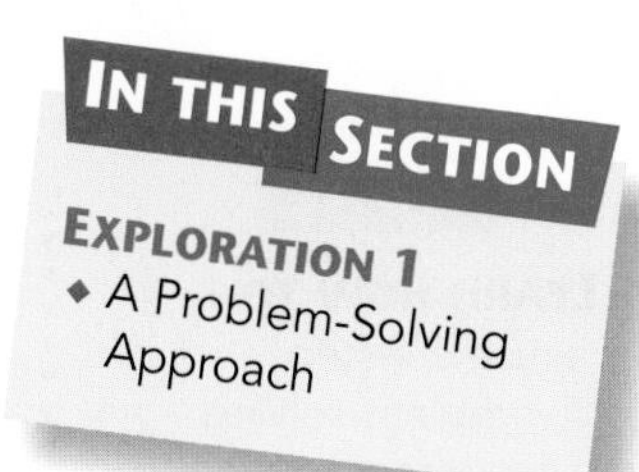

An AMAZING Lake

Setting the Stage

In this module, you have explored some amazing facts. Now you will learn about a lake with some surprising features.

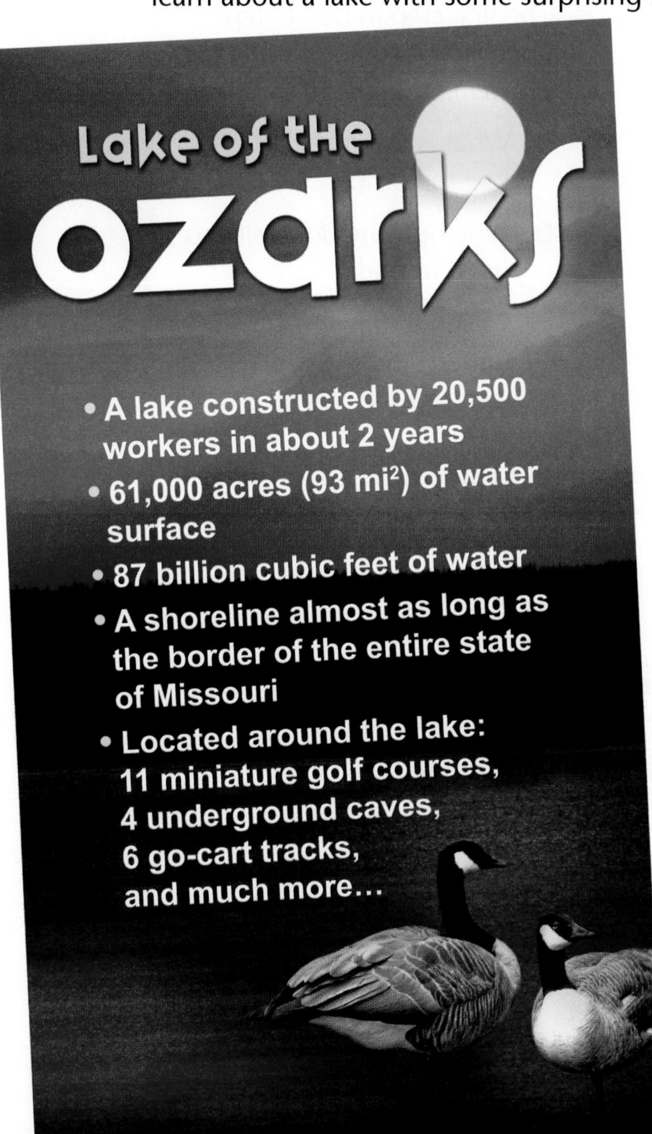

Think About It

1 **Discussion** Which claims on the travel brochure seem amazing? Why?

GOAL

LEARN HOW TO...
- use a 4-step problem-solving approach
- use tables, graphs, and equations to model relationships

AS YOU...
- learn about the Lake of the Ozarks

Exploration 1

A Problem-Solving Approach

SET UP *Work with a partner. You will need: • graph paper • a ruler • Labsheet 5A*

▶ **How can the Lake of the Ozarks have a perimeter almost as long as the border of Missouri even though the area of the lake is much less than the area of the state? To answer this question, you may want to use a 4-step problem solving approach.**

A 4-Step Problem-Solving Approach
- Understand the problem
- Make a plan
- Carry out the plan
- Look back

2 The first step in the 4-step approach is to *understand the problem.*

a. What is the question asking you to compare?

b. What information will you need to find?

c. To show that you understand the problem, restate it in your own words.

▶ **Once you understand the problem, the next step is to *make a plan* for solving it. The plan for solving a problem often involves using problem solving strategies.**

3 **Discussion**

a. How is finding the perimeter of a lake similar to finding the perimeter of a polygon?

b. How is finding the area similar to finding the area of a polygon?

c. How might exploring a simpler problem that involves polygons help solve the lake problem?

4 The third step is to *carry out the plan*. Complete parts (a)–(d) to apply the *solve a simpler problem* strategy.

a. Draw a 5-unit by 9-unit rectangle on graph paper.

b. Find the perimeter and the area of the rectangle.

c. Draw a polygon inside the rectangle that has a perimeter greater than the perimeter of the rectangle. Use only segments on the graph paper for the sides of the polygon.

d. Find the perimeter and the area of your polygon.

5 **Discussion** Explain how the Lake of the Ozarks could have a shoreline almost as long as the border of Missouri even though the area of the lake is much less than the area of state.

▶ **The final step is to *look back* to see if you can verify, extend, or generalize your solution.**

6 Explain how your plan helped you explain the brochure's claim about the lake's shoreline.

▶ **You discovered how the Lake of the Ozarks could have a shoreline almost as long as the border of the state of Missouri. You can extend your solution by determining the greatest possible perimeter the lake could have and still enclose 61,000 acres. Start by looking at a simpler problem.**

Use Labsheet 5A for Questions 7–9.

7 Follow the directions on the Labsheet to complete the *Rectangles with Area of 24 Square Units* table and graph.

8 **Try This as a Class** Use your graph on Labsheet 5A.

a. Does your graph show the perimeter of a rectangle with a width of 10 units? Explain.

b. Does your graph show the width of the rectangle with the least possible perimeter? Explain.

9 **a.** Draw a smooth curve to connect the points on the graph.

b. Use your graph to estimate the perimeter of a rectangle with a width of 10 units.

c. Use your graph to estimate the width and length of a rectangle with the least possible perimeter. Draw the rectangle.

10 **a.** How can you find the length of a rectangle with an area of 24 square units and a width of 16 units?

b. What is the length?

c. Write an equation that tells how to find the length of a rectangle with an area of 24 square units when you know the width. Use the variables *l* and *w* for the length and width.

d. Write an equation for the perimeter *P* of any rectangle when you know the length *l* and the width *w*.

e. Use the equations from parts (c) and (d) to find the perimeter of a rectangle with an area of 24 square units and a width of 16 units.

▶ **Mathematical Models Tables, graphs, and equations can be used as models to study mathematical relationships. You used them to explore relationships among the length, the width, and the perimeter of a rectangle.**

✓ QUESTION 11

...checks that you can use a mathematical model to study perimeter and area.

11 **✓ CHECKPOINT** Look back at the table, graph, and equations you made in Questions 7–10.

a. Suppose you want to quickly estimate the perimeter of a rectangle with an area of 24 square units and a width of 15 units. Which model would you use? Explain.

b. Suppose a rectangle with an area of 24 square units has a width of $\frac{1}{6}$ unit. Which model would you use to find the exact length? Why?

c. Is there a greatest possible perimeter for a rectangle with an area of 24 square units? Which model best shows this?

12 Do you think there is a greatest possible perimeter the Lake of the Ozarks could have and still enclose an area of 61,000 acres? Explain.

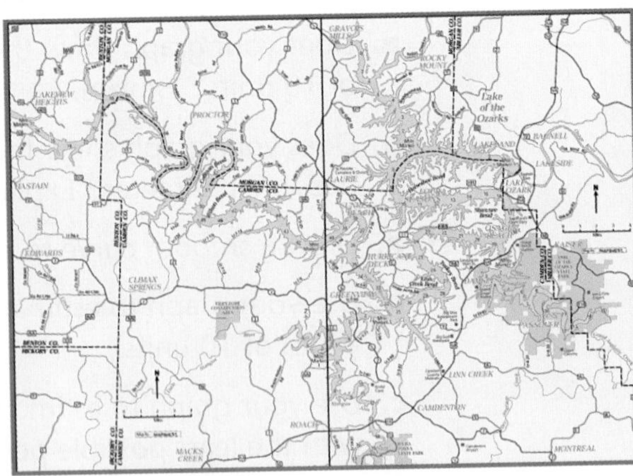

HOMEWORK EXERCISES See Exs. 1–6 on pp. 68–69.

4-Step Problem-Solving Approach (pp. 64–65)

Understand the Problem Identify the questions that need to be answered. Find the information you need to answer them. It may be helpful to restate the problem in your own words.

Make a Plan Choose a problem solving strategy such as solve a simpler problem, make a table, or use an equation. Decide what calculations, if any, are needed.

Carry out the Plan You may need to change your strategy or use a different approach, depending on how well your original plan works.

Look Back Is your solution reasonable? Could you solve the problem another way to verify your result? Can you generalize your solution or extend it to other situations or to solve other problems?

Mathematical Models (p. 66)

Tables, equations, and graphs can be used as mathematical models to study mathematical relationships.

Example Three ways to model a relationship between the perimeter P and the area A of a square with side length (s) are shown below.

Equations

$P = 4s$

$A = s^2$

Table

Perimeter (P)	Area (A)
4	1
8	4
12	9
16	16

Graph

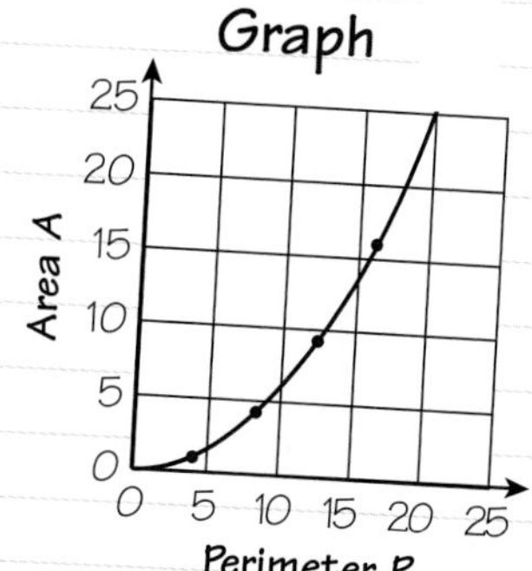

When data points fall in a curved pattern, a smooth curve can be drawn through the points as shown above.

13 Key Concepts Question

a. Explain how you could use one of the models above to find the area of a square with a perimeter 10 units long.

b. Explain how you could use a different model to estimate the perimeter of a square with area 20 square units.

Section 5

Practice & Application Exercises

YOU WILL NEED

For Ex. 4:
- Labsheet 5B

For Ex. 5:
- Labsheet 5C

Use the 4-step problem-solving approach for Exercises 1–3.

1. Jupiter revolves around the sun about once every 12 Earth years. Saturn revolves around the sun about once every 30 Earth years. In 1982, Jupiter and Saturn appeared very close to each other. About when will Jupiter and Saturn appear together again?

2. Four different types of tents are being used on a camping trip. They include 12-person, 6-person, 5-person, and 2-person tents. Find a possible combination of tents to sleep exactly 26 people in each situtation.

   a. Only one 12-person tent is used.

   b. The 12-person tent is not used.

   c. At least one 5-person tent is used.

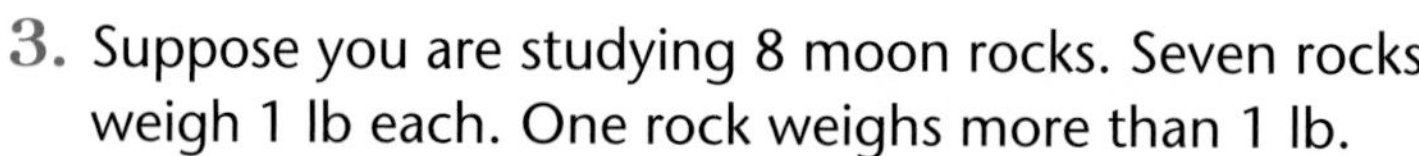

A balance scale is "balanced" when the weight of an object on one side equals the weight of an object on the other side.

3. Suppose you are studying 8 moon rocks. Seven rocks weigh 1 lb each. One rock weighs more than 1 lb.

   a. Describe how you can use a balance scale to find out which rock is the heaviest one.

   b. What is the least number of weighings you could use to find the heaviest rock?

4. **Use Labsheet 5B.**

   a. Complete the table and graph on Labsheet 5B.

   b. Estimate the width and length of the rectangle with the least perimeter. How do the width and the length compare?

   c. Find the exact length of a rectangle with an area of 30 square units and a width of $\frac{1}{6}$ unit. Which model (*table or graph*) did you use? Why?

   d. **Writing** Is there a greatest possible perimeter for a rectangle with an area of 30 square units? Explain.

5. **Use Labsheet 5C.** Suppose the perimeter of a rectangle is 28 units.

   a. Follow the directions on the labsheet to complete the table and graph of *Rectangles with Perimeter 28 Units.*

   b. Determine the width and the length of a rectangle with a perimeter of 28 units and the greatest area.

Reflecting on the Section

6. The polygons shown were made by placing square tiles side by side so each tile shares at least one full side with another tile. Each tile measures 1 unit by 1 unit.

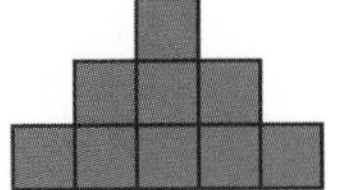
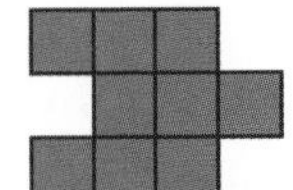

a. Find the perimeter of each polygon shown.

b. Use 9 squares to make a polygon with a 14-unit perimeter. Sketch your result.

c. What is the least possible perimeter for a polygon made with 9 squares?

d. What is the greatest possible perimeter for a polygon made with 9 squares?

Visual THINKING

Exercise 6 checks that you understand how the shape of a polygon can affect its perimeter.

Spiral Review

7. **Social Studies** Lake Baikal, located in southern Siberia, is the deepest lake in the world. At its deepest point its depth is 5371 ft. Lake Baikal is 395 mi long and varies in width from 16 mi to 50 mi. **(Module 1, p. 67)**

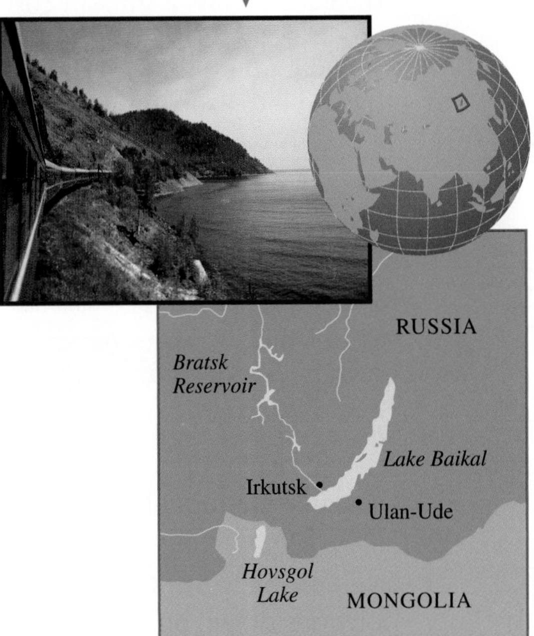

a. Find the area of a rectangle that is 395 mi long and 16 mi wide.

b. Find the area of a rectangle that is 395 mi long and 50 mi wide.

c. The area covered by Lake Baikal is 12,160 mi^2. How does this compare with the areas you found in parts (a) and (b)? Is this what you would expect? Explain your thinking.

8. a. Find the perimeter of a rectangle that is 395 mi long and 16 mi wide. **(Module 1, p. 67)**

b. Find the perimeter of a rectangle that is 395 mi long and 50 mi wide.

c. Lake Baikal has 1243 mi of shoreline. How does this compare with the perimeters you found in parts (a) and (b)?

Section 5 Extra Skill Practice

You will need: • *graph paper* (Exs. 2 and 4)

Use the 4-step problem-solving approach.

1. On a hike, a climber needs to measure 5 c of water to make soup. The climber has two pots, one that holds $3\frac{1}{2}$ pt and one that holds $1\frac{1}{2}$ pt. Explain how the climber can measure exactly 5 c of water.

Sheila was hired to organize a karate demonstration for a sports club's grand opening. She will use a space with an area of 48 square units.

2. On graph paper, draw 10 different rectangles that have an area of 48 square units.

3. Make a table for the lengths, widths, and perimeters of your 10 rectangles.

4. On a graph, plot the points for the width and perimeter of each rectangle. Put width on the horizontal axis and perimeter on the vertical axis. Draw a smooth curve to connect the points.

Write an equation or use the table or graph you made in Exercises 3 and 4 to complete Exercises 5 and 6.

5. Estimate the width and length of a rectangle with the least perimeter. Explain how you found your answer.

6. What is the exact width of a rectangle with a perimeter of 48 units and a length of 5 units? Explain how you found your answer.

Standardized Testing ▶ Performance Task

You will need: • *Labsheet 5D*

Pick's Formula is a formula for finding the area of a polygon drawn on dot paper. Complete the following exercises to discover Pick's Formula.

1. **Use Labsheet 5D.** Complete the table of values for the polygons drawn on the *Polygon Dot Paper.*

2. Try to guess a formula for the area *A* of any polygon in terms of the number of dots on its perimeter *P* and the number of dots in its interior *I*. You may want to get more data by drawing additional polygons.

FOR ASSESSMENT AND PORTFOLIOS

EXTENDED E2 EXPLORATION

A Special Number

The Situation

Study the number 1210. Do you notice anything special about it?

Look at the first digit in the number 1210. The 1 tells you how many 0s are in the entire number. The second digit, the 2, tells you how many 1s are in the number. This pattern continues for the other digits.

1 2 1 0

There is **1** *zero* in 1210.

There are **2** *ones* in 1210.

There is **1** *two* in 1210.

There are **0** *threes* in 1210.

The Problem

Create a 10-digit number that meets the following requirements.

- The first digit in the number tells how many 0s are in the entire number.
- The second digit tells how many 1s are in the entire number.
- The third digit tells how many 2s are in the entire number.
- The pattern continues through the tenth digit which tells how many 9s are in the entire number.

Something to Think About

- What is the sum of the digits in the number?
- What is the greatest digit that can occur in the number?

Present Your Results

Give your 10-digit number and explain what you did to find it. Is there more than one solution for the 10-digit number? How do you know?

Fact or Fiction?

Have you ever heard or read information that seemed too unlikely to be true? For example, "the average person eats 1095 lb of food a year!" or "The surface temperature of Venus is perfect for frying eggs."

For your module project you will look at similar claims and check to see if they are true or false. Then you will do research and gather data to write your own amazing claims. Finally, you will share your claims with your class by making a poster to display the evidence that shows your claims are true or false.

You will need:

- *Project Labsheet A*
- *poster board*
- *markers*

1 **Using a 4-Step Approach** Decide whether the following claim is reasonable. Use the 4-step problem-solving approach shown below to organize your work.

A stack of 200 billion pennies would reach from Earth to the moon.

Understand the Problem	Rewrite the claim in your own words. Decide what additional information you need to prove the claim.
Make a Plan	List some problem solving strategies you can try. Decide which strategy will be best.
Carry Out the Plan	As you carry out your plan, keep careful records of everything you do and the results of your work.
Look Back	Decide whether your solution is correct. If possible, check your solution by solving the problem another way.

Using Data Displays Many "amazing claims" are based on data. You will investigate to see whether the claim below is true.

Third basemen live longer than shortstops.

Use Project Labsheet A for Questions 2 and 3.

2 Find the mean, the median, and the mode(s) of each set of data in the stem-and-leaf plots showing Baseball Players' Life Spans.

3 Tell whether you think the claim on page 72 is true. Use the data and the displays to support your answer.

Collecting Data Sometimes it may be necessary to collect information to determine if a claim is true or false.

4 Work with a partner. Have your partner count the number of times you breathe in one minute. Then use the data collected to prove whether the following claim is true.

Human adults breathe about 23,000 times a day!

5 Choose a topic to research for your fact or fiction claim and gather data. You might want to explore the following subjects.

- Your Amazing Brain
- Extraordinary People in History

Finishing and Sharing You have written your own amazing claim and gathered data to show whether it is true or false. Now it is time to present your amazing claim to the world!

6 With a partner, create a poster showing your amazing claims. Think about interesting ways to illustrate your claims and the data you have gathered. Include enough information on the poster so that anyone reading it will be able to decide whether the claims are true or false.

7 Write the solutions for your amazing claims. Show how to determine whether your claims are true or false. You may include the solutions on your poster or keep them separate.

8 Tell where you found your information. For example, if you used a book, include the title, the author, and the page number. If you used information from a computer source, include the name of the program or website, and the name of the person or organization that created it.

"Cats: Nature's Masterwork"
by Stephen J. O'Brien
National Geographic, June, 1997

Information found:

MODULE 1
Review and Assessment

You will need: • *graph paper* (Ex. 10)

Periodical cicadas hatch at regular intervals. In Connecticut, they hatched in 1962, 1979, and 1996. (Sec. 1, Explor. 1, Sec. 5, Explor. 1)

1. The year 1996 was a leap year. Leap years generally occur every four years. When will the next hatching occur in a leap year?

2. Male cicadas make a buzzing noise by using muscles to vibrate a membrane. When making this noise, the muscles move 3 times each second. How many times do the muscles move in one hour?

Two package delivery companies each have 18 airplanes. The ages of the airplanes are shown in the table. Use the table for Exercise 3 and the box-and-whisker plots for Exercises 4 and 5. (Sec. 2, Explor. 1 and 2)

Company A	2, 3, 5, 6, 9, 15, 15, 12, 13, 17, 17, 17, 19, 18, 20, 20, 21, 26
Company B	1, 2, 3, 3, 5, 8, 7, 7, 6, 9, 12, 14, 16, 16, 25, 20, 19, 16

3. a. Use the data in the table to make a back-to-back stem-and-leaf plot of the ages of the airplanes of the two delivery companies.

   b. What does the shape of the plot tell you about the ages of the airplanes of the two companies?

   c. Find the mean, the median, and the mode(s) of each data set and record them in a table like the one on the right.

Company	A	B
mean	?	?
median	?	?
mode	?	?

4. The box-and-whisker plots below display the data from the table. For each box-and-whisker plot, find each value.

   a. the lower extreme
   b. the upper extreme
   c. the lower quartile
   d. the upper quartile

Airplane Ages (years)

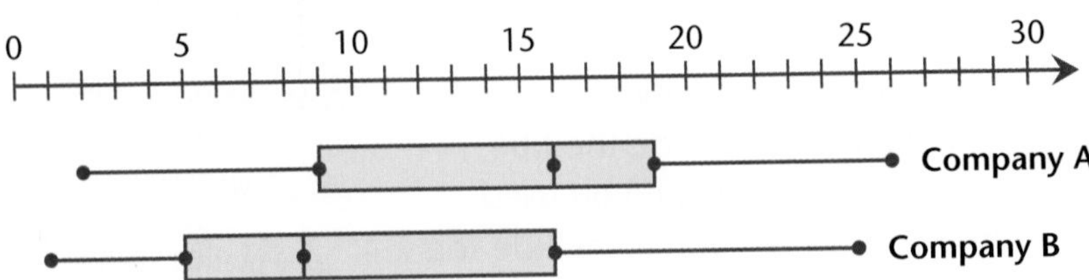

5. For which company is the statement below true? Explain how you can tell from the plots.

   At least 50% of the company's planes are less than 10 years old.

6. What type of data display could you use if you wanted to show the number of planes in each interval by age in years: 0–5, 6–10, 11–15, 16–20, 21–25, and 26–30? **(Sec. 2, Explor. 3)**

7. a. Admission to the 1893 World's Columbian Exposition in Chicago was $0.50 for people over age 12 and $0.25 for children aged 6–12. Children under 6 were free. Write an equation that represents the cost of tickets for any group of people attending the fair.

   b. How much would it have cost for a family of 3 adults, 1 baby, and 2 eight-year-olds to go to the Exposition? **(Sec. 3, Explor. 1)**

8. Use inverse operations to solve each equation. **(Sec. 3, Explor. 2)**

   a. $6y = 32$ b. $2 + 3x = 23$ c. $\frac{t}{4} + 3 = 9$ d. $3s - 16 = 11$

9. If possible, combine like terms to simplify each expression. **(Sec. 3, Explor. 3)**

   a. $rs + s + r$ b. $3y + 6y - y$ c. $2t - t + 4$ d. $3(m + 2)$

10. Cassandra drew 6 right triangles. The perimeter of each triangle was 32 cm. She measured the base and the height of each triangle to the nearest tenth of a centimeter. Then she found the area to the nearest tenth of a square centimeter. **(Sec. 4, Explor. 1 and 2)**

   a. Make a scatter plot of the data in the table.
      - Put base length on the horizontal axis and area on the vertical axis.
      - Use a straight line or a smooth curve to connect the points.

   b. Use your graph to estimate the length of the base of the triangle with the greatest area.

Base (cm)	Height (cm)	Area (cm^2)
1.5	15.2	11.4
2.9	14.4	20.9
5.9	12.4	36.6
7.9	10.8	42.7
9.3	9.4	43.7
11.9	6.6	38.7

Reflecting on the Module

11. **Writing** Describe a problem you solved outside of math class which involved using rates, equations, data displays, perimeter, or area. Explain how you solved the problem.

MODULE
2
AT THE
MALL

CONNECTING MATHEMATICS & The Theme

MODULE 2 SECTION OVERVIEW

1 Operations with Integers
As you discover how video games are created:
- Add and subtract integers
- Multiply and divide integers
- Find absolute values and opposites of integers

2 Operations with Fractions
As you explore a mall:
- Add and subtract positive and negative fractions
- Add and subtract positive and negative mixed numbers

3 Exploring Probability
As you find the chances of winning a contest:
- Find experimental probabilities
- Find theoretical probabilities
- Construct tree diagrams

4 Surveys, Proportions, and Percents
As you study the use of surveys:
- Summarize and interpret survey results
- Estimate percents using "nice" fractions or multiples of 10%
- Find percents using equations

5 Working with Percents
As you explore shopping in malls:
- Estimate percents
- Find percents of change

The Module Project — Designing a Game

There are many games that imitate life. But who makes up these games and how much of life do they imitate? In this module you will use mathematics to create your own board game about shopping in a mall. Then you will play your game, refine it, and share it with your class.

More on the Module Project
See pp. 150–151.

INTERNET
Resources and practice at
classzone.com

Section 1 Operations with Integers

IN THIS SECTION

EXPLORATION 1
- Adding Integers

EXPLORATION 2
- Subtracting Integers

EXPLORATION 3
- Multiplying and Dividing Integers

The VIDEO ARCADE

Setting the Stage

SET UP *Work in groups of two. You will need: • Labsheets 1A and 1B • 2 number cubes (red and blue) • colored disks*

Where can you go if you want to meet your friends, buy a stereo, experience virtual reality, enter a spaghetti-eating contest, or ride a roller coaster? A mall, of course!

Malls provide a wide variety of entertainment options for their visitors. Because of their popularity, many malls contain video arcades. Some arcade games require skill, others are based on chance, and some combine the two. The *Integer Invasion* games are simulations of video games similar to ones you might find in a video arcade.

Use Labsheets 1A and 1B. Play *Integer Invasion I* with a partner.

Think About It

1 What operation were you performing to find each coordinate in *Integer Invasion I*?

2 Use the results in your *Recording Sheet*. When will the sum of a positive integer and a negative integer be as described?

a. positive **b.** negative **c.** equal to 0

3 **a.** How can you find the sum of a positive integer and a negative integer without using a number line?

b. Does the order of the addends affect the sum? Explain.

▶ **Malls have become an important part of life for many people. In this module you will explore how mathematics is used at malls. You may find that math shows up when you least expect it.**

Exploration 1

Adding INTEGERS

SET UP *Work with a partner. You will need:* • *Labsheets 1A and 1B* • *2 number cubes (red and blue)* • *colored disks*

GOAL

LEARN HOW TO...
- add integers
- find the opposite of an integer
- find absolute values

AS YOU...
- simulate a video game

KEY TERMS
- integers
- quadrant
- opposite
- absolute value

▶ **In the game *Integer Invasion I* you plotted points on a coordinate grid in an attempt to hit celestial bodies. The coordinates of these points are *integers*. The integers are the numbers ... , –3, –2, –1, 0, 1, 2, 3, ...**

Use Labsheets 1A and 1B for Questions 4–8.

4 **Try This as a Class** Use the *Integer Invasion Game Board* on Labsheet 1B. In *Integer Invasion II*, each player will roll the number cubes and add the numbers rolled to determine the x-coordinate. Numbers on the blue cube are positive, and the ones on the red cube are negative.The y-coordinate will be determined by evaluating an expression.

a. Suppose Player A rolls a 4 and a –2 (a 2 on the red cube). Write an addition expression for the x-coordinate.

b. What is the x-coordinate?

c. To find the y-coordinate, substitute the value of x from part (a) into the expression $x + 5$ and perform the addition.

d. What are the coordinates of the point?

5 Play *Integer Invasion II* with a partner. Use the rules for *Integer Invasion I*, but evaluate the expression $x + (-3)$ to determine the y-coordinate. Record the coordinates in a *Recording Sheet* like the one below.

Blue	Red	x
6	2	4
?	?	?

$x + (-3)$	y
$4 + (-3)$	1
?	?

6 Use the results in your *Recording Sheet*.

a. Is the sum of two negative integers *positive* or *negative*?

b. How can you find the sum of two negative integers?

7 **Try This as a Class** Suppose in another game of *Integer Invasion II* the expression $x + 2$ is used to find the y-coordinate. For what values of x will the disk be placed as described?

a. above the horizontal axis

b. below the horizontal axis

c. on the horizontal axis

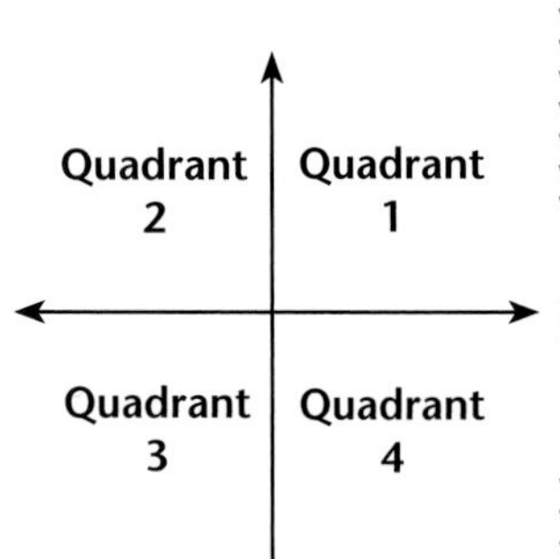

▶ **The axes on a coordinate plane divide the grid into four sections or quadrants. They are numbered counterclockwise as shown.**

8 **Use Labsheet 1B.** To find the y-coordinate, use the expression $x + (-2)$.

a. What must the value of x be to hit a planet in the first quadrant?

b. What must the value of x be to hit a planet in the third quadrant?

c. How does the value of x affect the quadrant in which the points are located?

✓ QUESTION 9

...checks that you can add integers.

9 **✓ CHECKPOINT** Find each sum.

a. $-8 + (-7)$ **b.** $12 + (-7)$ **c.** $2 + (-6)$ **d.** $-7 + 7$

10 The numbers –3 and 3 are **opposites**. So are 7 and –7. What is true about the sum of two opposites?

11 Find the opposite of each integer.

a. –17 **b.** 31 **c.** –215 **d.** 0

12 **Use Labsheet 1B.** A planet is located at (–5, 3) on the *Integer Invasion Game Board*. How far is the planet from each axis?

a. the vertical axis **b.** the horizontal axis

▶ **When you found the distance from the point (–5, 3) to the vertical axis, you found the *absolute value* of –5, or $|-5|$. The absolute value of a number is its distance from 0 on a number line.**

EXAMPLE

The distance from –5 to 0 is 5 units.

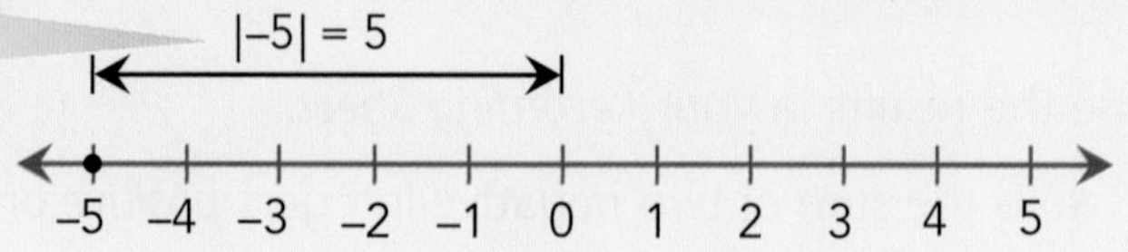

13 What other number has an absolute value of 5?

14 What two numbers have an absolute value of 15?

15 Find each absolute value.

a. $|-3|$ **b.** $|0|$ **c.** $|12|$ **d.** $|-17|$

Read $-x$ as "the opposite of x."

16 **Try This as a Class** Suppose in a new game, *Integer Invasion III*, you are given clues to determine the location of a disk on the game board. You have these two clues about the coordinates (x, y). What are the possible positions of the disk?

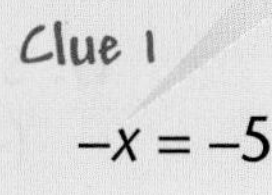

Clue 2

$|y| = 3$

17 ✓ **CHECKPOINT** Solve each equation.

a. $|x| = 2$ **b.** $-y = -3$ **c.** $|a| = 7$ **d.** $-b = 12$

✓ **QUESTION 17**

...checks that you can solve equations with opposites and absolute values.

HOMEWORK EXERCISES See Exs. 1–25 on p. 88.

Exploration 2

Subtracting INTEGERS

GOAL

LEARN HOW TO...
- subtract integers
- translate figures
- define a translation algebraically

AS YOU...
- explore translations on a coordinate grid

KEY TERMS
- translation
- image

SET UP *You will need: • Labsheet 1C • tracing paper*

▶ **When you played *Integer Invasion*, you attempted to hit a celestial body to score points. Game programmers may need to move these images to different locations on the grid to keep the game fresh. This type of move is a *translation*. A translation, or slide, moves each point of a figure the same distance in the same direction.**

18 **Use Labsheet 1C.** The labsheet shows a translation on a coordinate grid. Points A', B' and C' (read "*A* prime, *B* prime, and *C* prime") are the **images** of points *A*, *B*, and *C* after the translation. Follow the instructions for *Exploring Translations* to learn more about translations.

19 This table shows the coordinates of several points and their images after a translation.

Coordinates of the point	(3, 2)	(5, –7)	(0, –3)	(–5, 6)	(*x*, *y*)
Coordinates of the image	(2, 5)	(4, –4)	(–1, 0)	(–6, 9)	?

a. Describe the translation using the form ($x +$ __?__ , $y +$ __?__).

b. Suppose the same translation is used on the point (–45, –105). What are the coordinates of the image?

20 **Try This as a Class** Suppose you are programming a video game in which a jester is located at point (*x*, *y*).

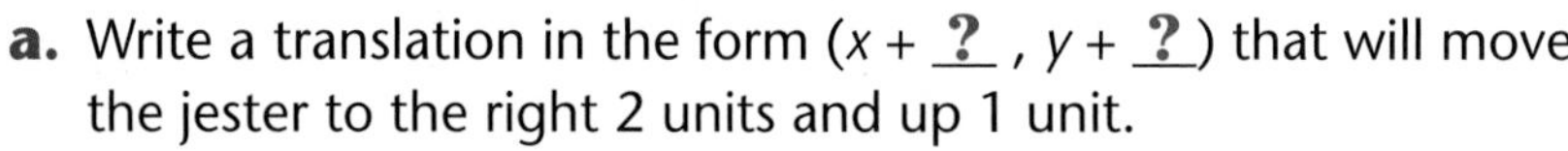

a. Write a translation in the form ($x +$ __?__ , $y +$ __?__) that will move the jester to the right 2 units and up 1 unit.

b. Use the form ($x -$ __?__ , $y -$ __?__) to write a translation that will move the jester to the left 3 units and down 5 units.

c. Rewrite the translation in part (b) in the form ($x +$ __?__ , $y +$ __?__).

d. Explain why any subtraction expression can be written as an addition expression.

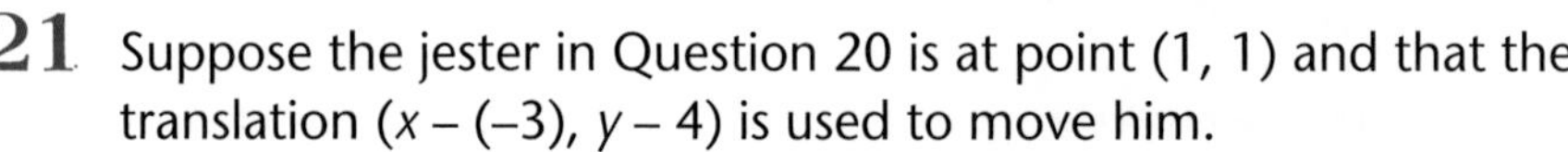

21 Suppose the jester in Question 20 is at point (1, 1) and that the translation ($x - (-3)$, $y - 4$) is used to move him.

a. Write 1 – (–3) as an addition expression.

b. What is the jester's new position after the translation ($x - (-3)$, $y - 4$)?

c. Describe this translation in words.

▶ **Subtracting Integers As you saw in Questions 20 and 21, you can write any subtraction problem as an addition problem.**

EXAMPLE

Find the difference: –8 – (–7).

The opposite of –7.

SAMPLE RESPONSE

$$\begin{aligned} -8 - (-7) &= -8 + [-(-7)] \\ &= -8 + 7 \\ &= -1 \end{aligned}$$

✓ QUESTION 22

...checks that you can subtract integers.

22 **✓ CHECKPOINT** Find each difference.

a. 23 – (–15) **b.** 12 – (–12) **c.** –80 – 22 **d.** –65 – (–43)

HOMEWORK EXERCISES See Exs. 26–35 on pp. 88–89.

Exploration 3

Multiplying and Dividing INTEGERS

GOAL

LEARN HOW TO...
- multiply and divide integers

AS YOU...
- explore linear equations

KEY TERM
- linear equation

SET UP *You will need: • Labsheet 1D • ruler*

▶ **Some video games display the path of an object such as a golf ball once it is hit or an asteroid moving through space. Programmers need to establish the paths for these visual effects. Multiplication and division may be used to create paths on a coordinate grid.**

23 **Use Labsheet 1D.**

a. Plot points *A, B, C* and *D* on the *Exploring Multiplication* coordinate plane.

b. Copy the table. Look for patterns to find the missing values.

x	–4	–3	–2	–1	0	1	2	3	4
y	–12	?	–6	?	0	?	6	9	?

c. What equation describes the relationship between x and y?

▶ **Multiplying Integers To find the y-coordinate of point A on Labsheet 1D you must multiply the x-coordinate, –4, by 3. You can use repeated addition to find the product.**

EXAMPLE

Use repeated addition to find 3 • (–4).

SAMPLE RESPONSE

Think: 3 groups of –4.

$$3 \cdot (-4) = (-4) + (-4) + (-4)$$
$$= -12$$

3 • (–4) can also be written as 3(–4).

24 **Try this as a Class** Use your table from Question 23(b).

a. Is the product of a positive integer and a negative integer *positive* or *negative*?

b. Describe how to find the product of a positive integer and a negative integer.

c. Use your method from part (b) to find the y-coordinate when the x-coordinate is –9.

25 **Use Labsheet 1D.**

a. Plot all the points from the table in Question 23(b) on the *Exploring Multiplication* coordinate plane.

b. If you connect all the points, what figure do you think will be formed?

c. Use a ruler to connect the points to see if your conjecture in part (b) was correct.

d. If you plot the point from Question 24(c), how do you think it will relate to the other points you plotted? Explain.

▶ **Linear Equations** **An equation whose graph is a straight line is a linear equation. Notice the word *line* in the word *linear*.**

26 **Try This as a Class**

a. Copy the table below. Look for patterns to find the missing values.

x	–4	–3	–2	–1	0	1	2	3	4
y	16	?	8	?	0	?	–8	–12	?

b. What equation describes the relationship between x and y?

c. Is the product of two negative integers *positive* or *negative*?

d. Describe how you can find the product of two negative integers.

27 **Use Labsheet 1D.**

a. Plot the points from your table in Question 26(a) on the *Exploring Multiplication* coordinate plane.

b. Connect the points using a ruler. How does this line compare with the one you drew in Question 25(c)?

c. **Discussion** How does the coefficient of x affect the graph of the line? Test your conjecture by graphing the equations $y = 5x$ and $y = -5x$.

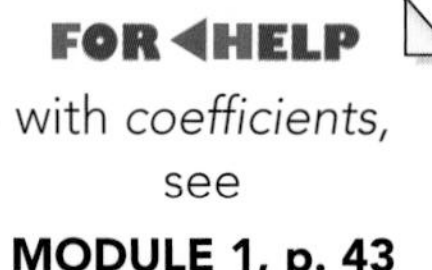
FOR ◀HELP with *coefficients*, see **MODULE 1, p. 43**

28 ✓ **CHECKPOINT** Find each product.

a. 3(–7) **b.** (–8)(–13) **c.** (–1)(–1) **d.** 7(–9)(8)

✓ **QUESTION 28**

...checks that you know how to multiply integers.

▶ **Dividing Integers In Exploration 2, you discovered that for every subtraction problem there is a related addition problem. This is also true for multiplication and division. For every division problem, there is a related multiplication problem.**

29 Write a multiplication equation related to 28 ÷ 7 = 4.

30 **a.** Write a multiplication equation related to –32 ÷ 8 = x.

b. What must the value of x be to make the multiplication equation you wrote for part (a) true?

c. What is the quotient –32 ÷ 8?

31 Write and solve a related multiplication equation to find each quotient.

a. 72 ÷ (–9) = x **b.** –16 ÷ 8 = x

c. –9 ÷ (–3) = x **d.** –24 ÷ (–6) = x

32 **Try This as a Class** You can find quotients without using multiplication.

a. Is the quotient –264 ÷ 12 *positive* or *negative*? Explain.

b. Explain how to divide two integers.

33 ✓ **CHECKPOINT** Find each quotient.

a. –18 ÷ (–3) **b.** $\frac{35}{-7}$ **c.** –150 ÷ 5 **d.** $\frac{-48}{-6}$

✓ **QUESTION 33**

...checks that you know how to divide integers.

34 **Discussion** Suppose you graph the equation $y = x \div (-2)$.

a. Do you think the graph will be a straight line? Explain.

b. Find the values of y for x = 4, 8, 12, and 16 and plot the points. Then connect the points.

c. How can you write the equation using a multiplication expression?

HOMEWORK EXERCISES ▶ See Exs. 36–55 on pp. 89–90.

Section 1 Key Concepts

Key Terms

integers

Adding and Subtracting Integers (pp. 79–81)

The integers are the numbers . . . , –3, –2, –1, 0, 1, 2, 3, ...
The sum of two integers may be positive, negative, or zero.

Examples $-3 + 5 = 2$ $\quad -4 + 1 = -3$
$12 + (-12) = 0$ $\quad -1 + (-9) = -10$

The difference of two integers may be positive, negative, or zero.

Examples $-4 - (-6) = 2$ $\quad 5 - 7 = -2$
$-3 - (-3) = 0$ $\quad -2 - 3 = -5$

absolute value

opposites

Absolute Value and Opposites (pp. 80–81)

The absolute value of a number tells you its distance from 0.

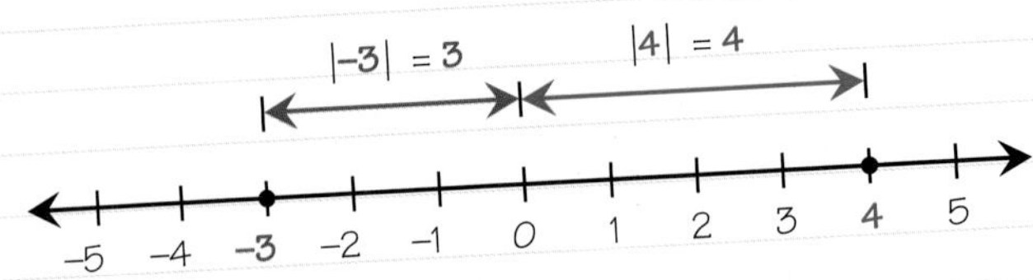

The integers 5 and –5 are opposites. To subtract an integer, add its opposite.

Examples $3 - 5 = 3 + (-5) = -2$
$7 - (-2) = 7 + (-(-2)) = 7 + 2 = 9$

Key Concepts Questions

35 The absolute value of –12 and the opposite of –12 are both 12. Is the absolute value of an integer always its opposite? Explain.

36 A negative integer and a positive integer are added. Describe the relationship between the integers being added if their sum is as described.

a. positive **b.** negative **c.** zero

Section 1 Key Concepts

Key Terms

translation

image

quadrants

linear equation

Translations (pp. 81–82)

A translation, or slide, moves each point of a figure the same distance in the same direction. A translation can be described by adding values to the coordinates of a point. The result of a translation is the image.

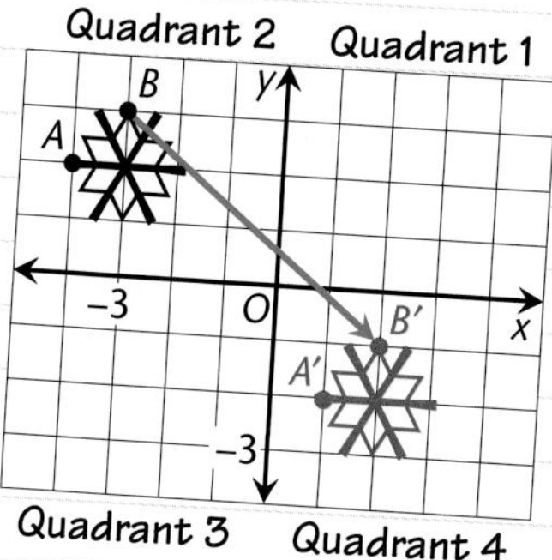

Original		Image
$A(-4, 2)$	→	$A'(1, -2)$
$B(-3, 3)$	→	$B'(2, -1)$

Translation: $(x + 5, y + (-4))$

Multiplying and Dividing Integers (pp. 83–85)

The product or quotient of two integers is:

- positive when both integers are positive or when both are negative.

Examples $-3(-8) = -3 \cdot (-8) = 24$ $\quad -24 \div (-8) = \frac{-24}{-8} = 3$

- negative when one integer is positive and the other is negative.

Examples $3(-8) = 3 \cdot (-8) = -24$ $\quad 24 \div (-3) = \frac{24}{-3} = -8$

Linear Equations (p. 82)

An equation whose graph is a straight line is a linear equation.

Examples $y = -3x$ and $y = x \div (-5)$ are linear equations.

37 **Key Concepts Question** When is the product of three integers as described?

a. positive

b. negative

c. zero

Section 1
Practice & Application Exercises

YOU WILL NEED

For Ex. 25:
- Labsheet 1B

For Ex. 35:
- graph paper

Find each sum.

1. $-23 + (-8)$
2. $91 + (-10)$
3. $-15 + 7$
4. $12 + (-12)$
5. $-88 + (-12)$
6. $4 + (-10) + 7$

Find the opposite of each integer.

7. -15
8. 101
9. 74
10. -62

Find each absolute value.

11. $|-47|$
12. $|53|$
13. $\left|8\frac{1}{2}\right|$
14. $|-0.43|$

15. Find two different integers with an absolute value of 7.

Solve each equation.

16. $|y| = 12$
17. $-w = 2$
18. $|z| = 0$
19. $-x = -5$

20. Joe earned $15 mowing lawns, then bought a radio for $11. The next day he earned $5 and spent $3 on arcade games. Write an addition expression for his income and expenses and find the sum.

Algebra Connection Find *y* when $x = -6$.

21. $y = x + 28$
22. $y = x + (-12)$
23. $y = x + 4$
24. $y = x + 6$

25. **Challenge** Suppose the value of *x* is –4. What equation could be used to determine the value of *y* so that a star is hit on the *Integer Invasion* game board? Explain how you found your equation.

Find each difference.

26. $5 - 9$
27. $18 - (-13)$
28. $2 - (-11)$
29. $-3 - (-3)$
30. $-10 - 4$
31. $-7 - (-19)$

32. **Weather** Suppose the temperature is –18°F at 6:00 A.M. and 23°F at 2:00 P.M. What is the difference in the temperatures?

33. The translation $(x + 2, y + (-3))$ is applied to figure *PQRST*.
    a. Give the coordinates of the image points *P′*, *Q′*, *R′*, *S′*, and *T′*.
    b. **Writing** Describe in words a translation that moves *PQRST* to the opposite side of the vertical axis.

34. After the translation $(x + 5, y + 2)$, the image of a point is (12, 16). What are the coordinates of the original point?

35. For each pair of coordinates, describe the translation in two ways, one using only addition and one using only subtraction. Then show each translation on a graph.

	Original	Image	Translations
a.	$L(2, 4)$	$L'(1, 5)$	$(x + \underline{?}, y + \underline{?})$ or $(x - \underline{?}, y - \underline{?})$
b.	$M(0, -7)$	$M'(2, -1)$	$(x + \underline{?}, y + \underline{?})$ or $(x - \underline{?}, y - \underline{?})$
c.	$N(-6, 3)$	$N'(-10, -3)$	$(x + \underline{?}, y + \underline{?})$ or $(x - \underline{?}, y - \underline{?})$

Find each product or quotient.

36. $8(-9)$ 37. $-16 \cdot 20$ 38. $-3(-8)(2)$ 39. $-2(-7)(-4)$

40. $-27 \div 9$ 41. $\frac{-56}{-8}$ 42. $\frac{72}{-3}$ 43. $-48 \div (-6)$

Algebra Connection Evaluate each expression when $a = -16$, $b = -4$, and $c = 48$.

44. ab 45. bc 46. $c \div a$ 47. $\frac{a}{b}$

Algebra Connection Find y when $x = -7$.

48. $y = 3x$ 49. $y = -12x$ 50. $y = 9x$ 51. $y = -6x$

52. **Football** On each of three consecutive plays, a football team loses 5 yd. Suppose lost yardage is represented by a negative integer.

a. Write a multiplication expression that describes the total change in yardage.

b. Find the total number of yards lost.

Use this information for Exercises 53 and 54: On a test, each correct answer scores 5 points, each incorrect answer scores –2 points, and each question left unanswered scores 0 points.

53. Suppose a student answers 15 questions on the test correctly, 4 incorrectly, and does not answer 1 question. Write an expression for the student's score and find the score.

54. **Challenge** Suppose you answer all 20 questions on the test. What is the greatest number of questions you can answer incorrectly and still get a positive score? Explain your reasoning.

Visual Thinking

Exercise 55 checks your understanding of opposites.

Reflecting on the Section

55. Suppose you multiply each coordinate of each point of a figure by –1. Describe the visual effect created by this operation.

Spiral Review

Find each quotient. Write each answer in lowest terms. **(Toolbox, p. 587)**

56. $\frac{3}{8} \div \frac{1}{4}$ 57. $\frac{7}{12} \div \frac{5}{6}$ 58. $\frac{33}{39} \div \frac{11}{13}$ 59. $\frac{10}{21} \div \frac{7}{9}$

Replace each ? with the number that will make the fractions equivalent. **(Toolbox, p. 585)**

60. $\frac{1}{5} = \frac{?}{30}$ 61. $\frac{1}{3} = \frac{?}{24}$ 62. $\frac{5}{8} = \frac{35}{?}$

63. $\frac{3}{10} = \frac{?}{110}$ 64. $\frac{3}{4} = \frac{21}{?}$ 65. $\frac{9}{16} = \frac{54}{?}$

Extension

Absolute Value Equations

The equation $|x + 1| = 3$ includes a variable inside the absolute value bars. You can use what you know about absolute value to find the values of x that make the equation true.

$$|x + 1| = 3$$

$$x + 1 = 3 \quad \text{or} \quad x + 1 = -3$$

66. Solve each equation above to find the values of x that make $|x + 1| = 3$ true.

Solve each equation.

67. $|y + 2| = 8$ 68. $|w - 5| = 10$ 69. $|-2z| = 4$

Section 1 Extra Skill Practice

Find each sum.

1. $-12 + 16$ 2. $27 + (-49)$ 3. $-130 + (-65)$ 4. $-78 + 25 + (-4)$

Find the opposite of each integer.

5. 512 6. -43 7. -1 8. 38

Find each absolute value.

9. $|29|$ 10. $|-83|$ 11. $\left|-3\frac{3}{4}\right|$ 12. $|-1.45|$

Find each difference.

13. $-32 - 45$ 14. $26 - (-13)$ 15. $-16 - (-22)$ 16. $55 - (-55)$

Find each product.

17. $-25(-10)$ 18. $4(-15)$ 19 $-7 \cdot 6$ 20. $-12(-5)$

Find each quotient.

21. $42 \div (-7)$ 22. $-88 \div 22$ 23. $\frac{-54}{-3}$ 24. $\frac{95}{-5}$

Simplify each expression.

25. $-14(-3)$ 26. $27 + (-33)$ 27. $-24 \div (-6)$

28. $52 - (-16)$ 29. $\frac{-76}{19}$ 30. $-41 + (-11)$

31. $64 \div (-4)$ 32. $9 \cdot (-7)$ 33. $-13 - 13$

Standardized Testing ▶ Open-ended

1. Give an example of two numbers that fit each description below. If no numbers fit the description, explain why.
   a. Both the sum and the product of 2 numbers are negative.
   b. The sum of 2 numbers is 0 and the product is positive.
   c. The sum of 2 numbers is positive and the quotient is negative.

2. A rectangle *ABCD* has two vertical sides that intersect the *x*-axis, and two horizontal sides that intersect the *y*-axis. Give a set of possible coordinates for *A*, *B*, *C*, and *D*. Then write the coordinates of *A′*, *B′*, *C′* and *D′* after the translation $(x - 4, y + 6)$.

Section 2 Operations with Fractions

IN THIS SECTION

EXPLORATION 1
- Working with Fractions

EXPLORATION 2
- Fraction Mindbender

EXPLORATION 3
- Working with Mixed Numbers

A WORLD CLASS WONDER

Setting the Stage

The West Edmonton Mall in Alberta, Canada, has over 800 stores, more than 110 eating establishments, and covers the equivalent of 48 city blocks. It is also the home of *Galaxyland*, the world's largest indoor amusement park. *Galaxyland* contains 25 rides and attractions, including the *Mindbender* roller coaster that reaches a top speed of 26.8 m/sec and a G-force of 5.2. It is easy to see why some people have called the West Edmonton Mall the eighth wonder of the world!

▲ The first descent on the *Mindbender* is 14 stories high.

Think About It

1 One story of a building is about 10 ft. Estimate the height of the *Mindbender*.

2 **a.** The 130-second ride covers 1280 m of track. To the nearest tenth, what is the average speed?

b. If the rollercoaster ran at top speed the entire length of the ride, about how many seconds would the ride last?

▶ **In this section, you will play *Fraction Mindbender*, a game of quick thinking and skill.**

Exploration 1

Working with FRACTIONS

GOAL

LEARN HOW TO...

- add and subtract positive fractions and mixed numbers
- add two or more negative fractions

AS YOU...

- prepare to play *Fraction Mindbender*

▶ **In the game *Fraction Mindbender*, you will try to create the greatest sum or difference by placing numbers in a fraction expression.**

3 **a.** Look at the *Fraction Mindbender* game board below. Find the sum and difference to determine which expression has the greater value.

Player A

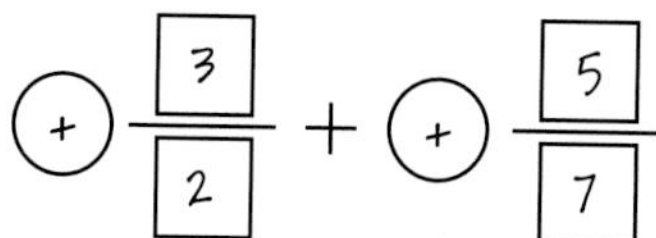

Player B

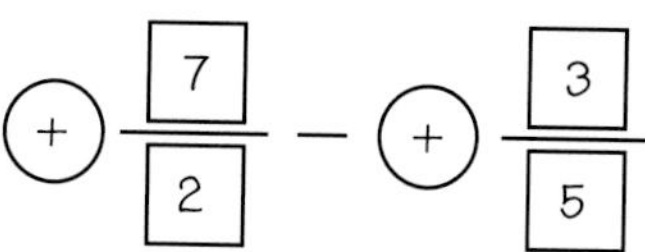

b. Rearrange the numbers 3, 2, 5, and 7 in the four boxes so Player A's sum is greater than the sum of the fractions shown. Give the new expression and the sum.

c. Rewrite the new expression from part (b) using mixed numbers.

FOR ▶ HELP with fractions, see **TOOLBOX, p. 586**

4 **Try This as a Class**

a. To find the difference $5\frac{3}{8} - 2\frac{7}{8}$ by subtracting the whole number and fractional parts separately, why would you need to regroup?

b. Regroup and find the difference.

c. Change the mixed numbers $5\frac{3}{8}$ and $2\frac{7}{8}$ to fractions.

d. Use the fractions you found in part (c) to find the difference in part (a).

e. Which method, regrouping or changing mixed numbers to fractions, do you prefer for finding the difference? Why?

▶ **Adding Negative Fractions** Sometimes during the game you may need to add two negative fractions. Look at the example below.

EXAMPLE

Find $-\frac{\boxed{2}}{\boxed{5}} + -\frac{\boxed{3}}{\boxed{4}}$

$$-\frac{2}{5} + \left(-\frac{3}{4}\right) = \frac{-8}{20} + \left(\frac{-15}{20}\right)$$

Rewrite each fraction with a common denominator.

$$= \frac{-8 + (-15)}{20}$$

Add the integers −8 + (−15) to find the new numerator, −23.

$$= \frac{-23}{20}$$
$$= -\frac{23}{20}$$
$$= -\left(\frac{20}{20} + \frac{3}{20}\right)$$
$$= -\left(1 + \frac{3}{20}\right)$$
$$= -1\frac{3}{20}$$

5 Discussion

a. How is adding two negative fractions similar to adding two positive fractions?

b. How is it different?

c. In the Example, when $-\frac{23}{20}$ was changed to a mixed number, what happened to the negative sign?

d. Explain how to add two negative fractions.

✓ QUESTION 6

...checks that you can add and subtract fractions and mixed numbers.

6 ✓ CHECKPOINT Find each sum or difference. Write all fractions in your answers in lowest terms.

a. $\frac{2}{9} + \frac{5}{6}$ **b.** $\frac{11}{12} - \frac{2}{3}$ **c.** $-\frac{3}{10} + \left(-\frac{5}{6}\right)$

d. $4\frac{2}{9} + 1\frac{1}{3}$ **e.** $-\frac{2}{3} + \left(-\frac{3}{4}\right)$ **f.** $5\frac{1}{2} - 3\frac{3}{8}$

HOMEWORK EXERCISES ▶ See Exs. 1–10 on p. 101.

Exploration 2

Fraction Mindbender

GOAL

LEARN HOW TO...
- add and subtract positive and negative fractions

AS YOU...
- play *Fraction Mindbender*

SET UP *Work with a partner. You will need:* • *Labsheet 2A* • *14 index cards*

▶ **Make a deck of cards and read the directions below to prepare to play *Fraction Mindbender*. You will try to create the greatest sum or difference using numbers and symbols in a fraction expression.**

Fraction *Mindbender*

Playing the Game

Labsheet 2A has 5 game boards for each player. A game is completed when each player fills in one game board.

Shuffle the deck of 14 cards, place it face down on the desk, and turn over the top card.

If a number is turned over, each player must write it in one of his or her four squares on the game board. If a symbol is turned over, each player must write it in one of his or her two circles.

Turn over cards from the top of the deck and record each number or symbol until you have filled your game board. Ignore any extra numbers or symbols you turn over.

Once all the squares and circles are filled, find each player's sum or difference. The player with the greater number wins.

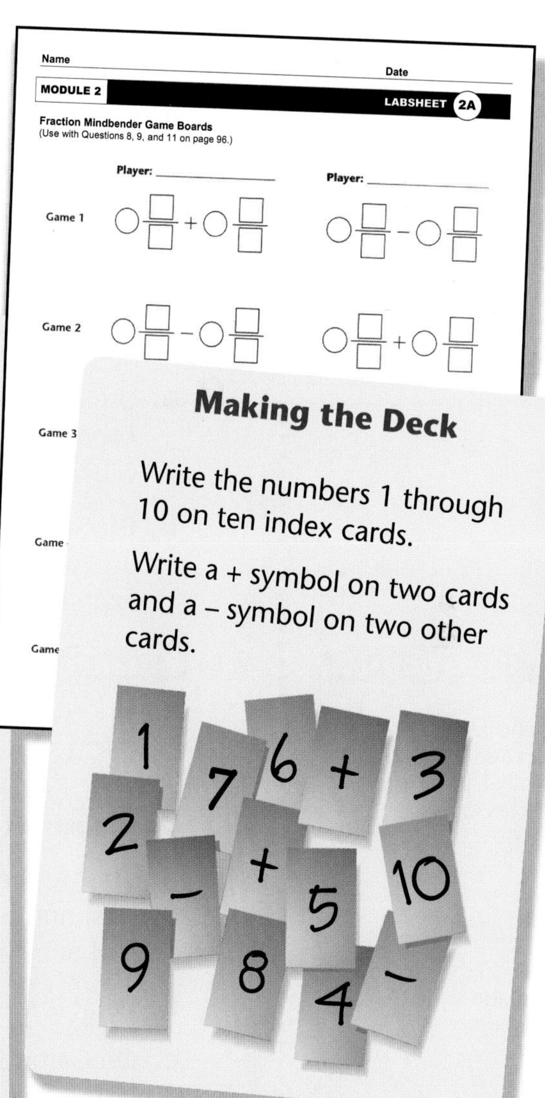

Making the Deck

Write the numbers 1 through 10 on ten index cards.

Write a + symbol on two cards and a – symbol on two other cards.

▶ Adding and Subtracting Positive and Negative Fractions

Positive and negative fractions can be added and subtracted the same way as integers. Before adding or subtracting, you may have to rewrite the fractions so the denominators are the same.

7 **Try This as a Class** Leeza and Rhea are playing *Fraction Mindbender*. Their game board shows that they have turned over the 8, 2, +, and 3 cards. The next card is a 6.

Player: Leeza **Player: Rhea**

$(+)\frac{8}{2} + \bigcirc\frac{\square}{3}$

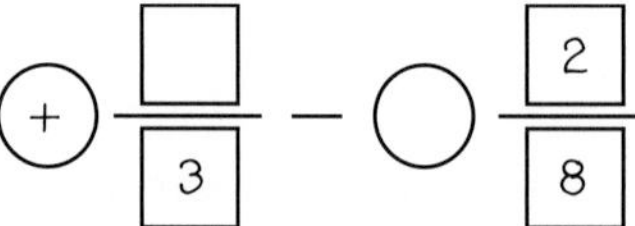

a. Can you tell who will win? Explain why or why not.

b. On the next draw, which symbol would be best for Rhea? Explain.

Use Labsheet 2A for Questions 8 and 9.

8 Play two games of *Fraction Mindbender* with your partner.

9 a. Use a new game board. Play another game of *Fraction Mindbender*, but this time the player with the lesser number wins.

b. **Discussion** Which part of the board do you think is best to use for this version of the game, the part with the subtraction expression or the part with the addition expression? Explain.

✓ QUESTION 10

...checks that you can add and subtract positive and negative fractions.

10 **✓ CHECKPOINT** Find each sum or difference.

a. $-\frac{1}{2}+\left(-\frac{3}{4}\right)$ b. $\frac{5}{6}-\left(-\frac{4}{3}\right)$ c. $-\frac{6}{10}+\frac{7}{8}$

11 **Use Labsheet 2A.** Use the remaining game boards.

a. Choose the symbols and numbers from the deck that give the least number. Fill in the boxes on Game 4 with the symbols and numbers you chose.

b. What is the least number?

c. On Game 5 choose the symbols and numbers that give the least positive number. Fill in the boxes with the symbols and numbers you chose.

d. What is the least positive number?

HOMEWORK EXERCISES ▶ See Exs. 11–21 on pp. 101–102.

Exploration 3

Working with MIXED NUMBERS

GOAL

LEARN HOW TO...
- add and subtract positive and negative mixed numbers

AS YOU...
- revisit the *Fraction Mindbender* game

SET UP *Work with a partner. You will need the game cards from Exploration 2.*

Mixed Number Mindbender allows for mixed numbers by including a box for a whole number in front of each fraction on the game board. To play this version, you will need to be able to add and subtract mixed numbers.

▶ **Adding Two Negative Mixed Numbers** **Compare adding two positive mixed numbers with adding two negative mixed numbers.**

EXAMPLE

Positive Mixed Numbers

$$5\frac{1}{8} + 2\frac{3}{4} = 5\frac{1}{8} + 2\frac{6}{8}$$
$$= 7\frac{7}{8}$$

Negative Mixed Numbers

$$-5\frac{1}{8} + \left(-2\frac{3}{4}\right) = -5\frac{1}{8} + \left(-2\frac{6}{8}\right)$$
$$= -\left(5\frac{1}{8} + 2\frac{6}{8}\right)$$
$$= -7\frac{7}{8}$$

Add the absolute values of the mixed numbers and place a negative sign on the sum.

Positive Mixed Numbers

$$3\frac{3}{5} + 1\frac{4}{5} = 4\frac{7}{5}$$
$$= 4 + 1\frac{2}{5}$$
$$= 5\frac{2}{5}$$

Negative Mixed Numbers

$$-3\frac{3}{5} + \left(-1\frac{4}{5}\right) = -\left(3\frac{3}{5} + 1\frac{4}{5}\right)$$
$$= -\left(4\frac{7}{5}\right)$$
$$= -\left(4 + 1\frac{2}{5}\right)$$
$$= -5\frac{2}{5}$$

12 Look at the examples on the previous page.

a. How are adding positive mixed numbers and adding negative mixed numbers alike?

b. How is adding two negative mixed numbers like adding two negative integers?

c. Describe the steps for adding two negative mixed numbers.

✓ **QUESTION 13**

...checks that you can add negative mixed numbers.

13 ✓ **CHECKPOINT** Add each pair of mixed numbers. Write all fractions in your answers in lowest terms.

a. $-3\frac{2}{9} + \left(-1\frac{5}{9}\right)$

b. $-8\frac{2}{5} + \left(-10\frac{8}{15}\right)$

c. $-5\frac{2}{3} + \left(-3\frac{6}{7}\right)$

▶ **Adding and Subtracting Mixed Numbers with Different Signs You can use your knowledge of operations with integers to write equivalent expressions with mixed numbers.**

14 For each expression, choose the expression on the right that is equivalent.

a. $4\frac{2}{9} - \left(-1\frac{1}{3}\right)$ $\quad 4\frac{2}{9} + 1\frac{1}{3}$ or $\frac{2}{9} - 1\frac{1}{3}$

b. $5\frac{1}{2} - 3\frac{3}{8}$ $\quad -5\frac{1}{2} + \left(-3\frac{3}{8}\right)$ or $5\frac{1}{2} + \left(-3\frac{3}{8}\right)$

▶ **Some of the fractions you added and subtracted during *Fraction Mindbender* may have been greater than 1 or less than –1.**

15 Discussion

a. How are fractions that are greater than 1 or less than –1 related to mixed numbers?

b. How can fractions that are greater than 1 or less than –1 be used to add or subtract mixed numbers?

16 **Try This as a Class** In a game of *Mixed Number Mindbender*, two players have filled in the game board as shown.

Player A

$(-)\ 4\frac{3}{5} + (+)\ 2\frac{1}{6}$

Player B

$(-)\ 1\frac{5}{6} - (+)\ 2\frac{3}{4}$

a. Change the mixed numbers to fractions to determine which player's game board has the greater value.

b. Describe how to add positive and negative mixed numbers using the method in part (a).

c. Describe how to subtract positive and negative mixed numbers using the method in part (a).

17 ✓ **CHECKPOINT** Add or subtract. Write all fractions in your answers in lowest terms.

a. $-3\frac{2}{5} + 1\frac{5}{9}$ **b.** $-4\frac{2}{5} - 5\frac{1}{10}$

c. $-\frac{2}{5} - \left(-3\frac{2}{3}\right)$ **d.** $6 + \left(-2\frac{7}{8}\right)$

✓ **QUESTION 17**

...checks that you can add and subtract positive and negative mixed numbers.

18 Charla and Maya are playing *Mixed Number Mindbender* and trying to obtain the *least* value. Their game board is shown below.

Charla

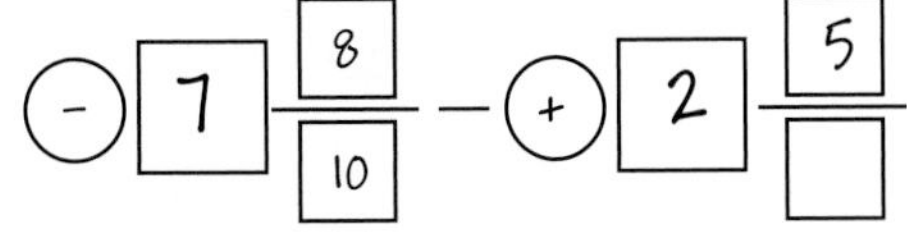

Maya

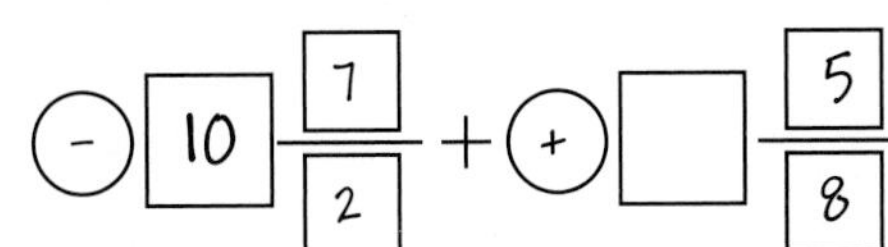

a. If the next card chosen is a 4, who will win?

b. Rewrite the expressions in part (a) as if both sign cards drawn had been negatives. How would this affect the value of each expression?

19 On your own paper, draw a *Mixed Number Mindbender* game board like the one in Question 18. Use the rules for playing the game from page 95 to play two games with a partner.

HOMEWORK EXERCISES ▶ See Exs. 22–38 on pp. 102–103.

Section 2 Key Concepts

Adding and Subtracting Fractions (pp. 93–96)

Positive and negative fractions can be added and subtracted the same way as integers. Make sure that the denominators of the fractions are the same before adding or subtracting.

Example

$$-\frac{5}{12}-\left(-\frac{1}{8}\right)=-\frac{5}{12}+\frac{1}{8}$$

Subtraction can be rewritten as adding the opposite.

$$=-\frac{10}{24}+\frac{3}{24}$$

Rewrite using the least common denominator.

$$=\frac{-10+3}{24}$$

$$=\frac{-7}{24}=-\frac{7}{24}$$

Example

$$-\frac{1}{5}+\left(-\frac{3}{10}\right)=\frac{-2}{10}+\left(\frac{-3}{10}\right)$$

$$=\frac{-2+(-3)}{10}$$

$$=\frac{-5}{10}$$

$-2 + (-3) = -5$

$$=\frac{-1}{2}=-\frac{1}{2}$$

Adding and Subtracting Mixed Numbers (p. 93 and pp. 97–99)

Positive and negative mixed numbers can be added and subtracted just like positive and negative fractions once they are rewritten as fractions.

Example $2\frac{5}{8}+\left(-1\frac{7}{8}\right)=\frac{21}{8}+\left(-\frac{15}{8}\right)=\frac{21+(-15)}{8}=\frac{6}{8}=\frac{3}{4}$

20 Key Concepts Question

a. Use the numbers 1, 4, 5, and 10, the symbols + and –, and the part of the game board shown at the right to create the greatest number you can.

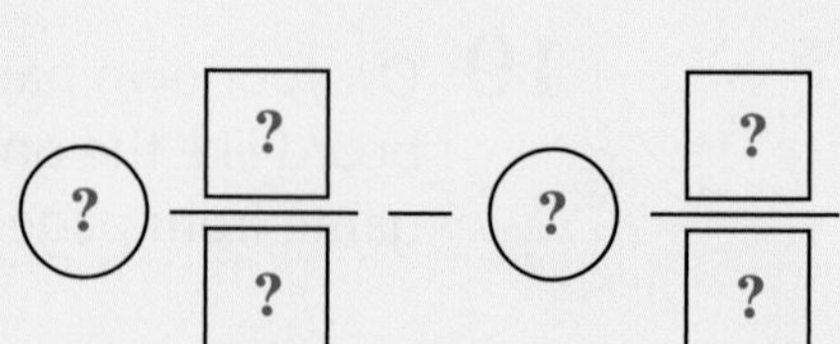

b. How would you answer part (a) if both of the symbols were –?

Section 2
Practice & Application Exercises

YOU WILL NEED

For Ex. 30:
- fraction calculator

Find each sum or difference. Write your answer in lowest terms.

1. $\frac{4}{9} + \frac{3}{8}$ 2. $\frac{1}{6} + \frac{2}{5}$ 3. $\frac{5}{14} - \frac{2}{7}$ 4. $\frac{5}{4} - \frac{7}{8}$

5. $-\frac{1}{12} + \left(-\frac{5}{12}\right)$ 6. $-\frac{5}{11} + \left(-\frac{3}{2}\right)$ 7. $-\frac{4}{9} + \left(-\frac{5}{9}\right)$ 8. $-\frac{1}{2} + \left(-\frac{2}{5}\right)$

9. **Sewing** A fabric store has the three pieces of scrap material shown below. An art teacher needs four pieces of material that are each $\frac{3}{8}$ yd long and 1 yd wide.

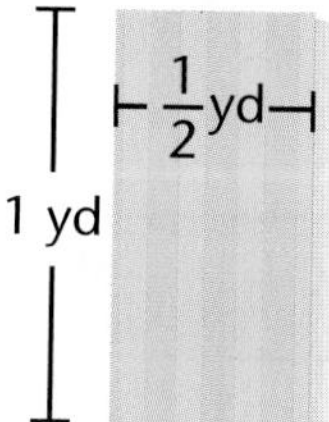

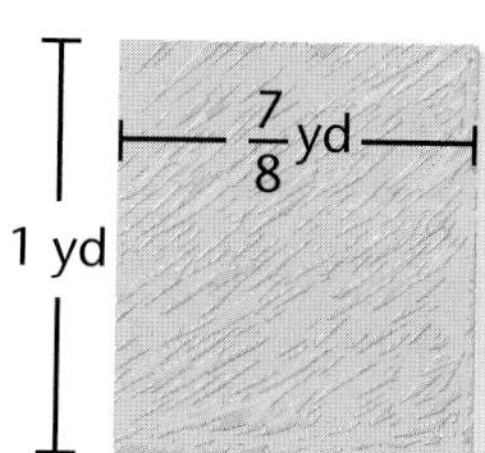

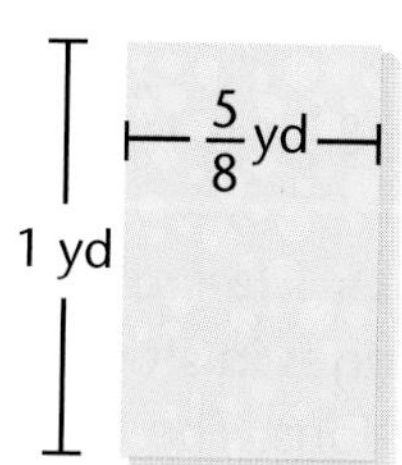

a. Is there enough fabric for the teacher?

b. How should the teacher cut the material? How much material will be left over from each original piece?

10. A carpenter is making a picture frame. The width of each piece of wood is $3\frac{5}{8}$ in. The top and the bottom pieces are $15\frac{3}{4}$ in. long and the two side pieces are $23\frac{3}{8}$ in. long. When the carpenter puts it together as shown, what will the outer dimensions of the picture frame be?

Find each sum or difference.

11. $-\frac{8}{12} + \left(-\frac{4}{12}\right)$ 12. $\frac{4}{11} - \frac{10}{11}$ 13. $-\frac{8}{15} + \frac{2}{5}$

14. $-\frac{7}{16} - \left(-\frac{3}{8}\right)$ 15. $\frac{3}{14} + \left(-\frac{6}{7}\right)$ 16. $\frac{3}{4} + \left(-\frac{5}{12}\right)$

17. $-\frac{3}{7} - \left(-\frac{1}{6}\right)$ 18. $-\frac{2}{3} - \frac{3}{5}$ 19. $-\frac{8}{15} - \frac{7}{20}$

20. **Writing** Suppose your friend missed today's class. Write a letter to the friend describing how to add and subtract positive and negative fractions. Include several examples.

21. **Patterns** The expressions below are part of a pattern.

$\frac{1}{2} - \frac{1}{4}$ $\quad$ $\frac{1}{2} - \frac{1}{4} + \frac{1}{8}$ $\quad$ $\frac{1}{2} - \frac{1}{4} + \frac{1}{8} - \frac{1}{16}$

a. Write the next two expressions in the pattern.

b. Evaluate each expression above and the two that you wrote for part (a).

c. Suppose you evaluated the thirtieth expression in the pattern. Do you think the result would be positive or negative? Explain.

Find each sum or difference.

22. $3\frac{2}{3} - 4\frac{1}{3}$

23. $-1\frac{4}{5} - 6\frac{1}{5}$

24. $-3\frac{1}{2} + \left(-1\frac{1}{4}\right)$

25. $8\frac{1}{4} + \left(-1\frac{7}{8}\right)$

26. $-4\frac{2}{3} - \left(-7\frac{1}{6}\right)$

27. $2\frac{5}{9} - \left(-3\frac{1}{3}\right)$

Stock Market Until August of 2000, changes in stock prices were reported as fractions. The table at the right shows how the price of a company's stock changed during one day.

Time	Stock change
9:30 A.M.	None
10:00 A.M.	$+\frac{1}{2}$
11:00 A.M.	$-\frac{1}{8}$
12:00 P.M.	$-\frac{9}{16}$
1:00 P.M.	$+\frac{1}{2}$
2:00 P.M.	$-\frac{3}{8}$
3:00 P.M.	$+\frac{1}{4}$
4:00 P.M.	$-\frac{1}{16}$

28. What was the change in the stock price from 9:30 A.M. to 11:00 A.M.?

29. How much did the stock change from 12:00 P.M. to 3:00 P.M.?

30. Fraction Calculator Suppose the price of the stock was \$36 at 9:00 A.M. Use a fraction calculator to find the price at 4 P.M. Is the total change from the beginning of the day to the end of the day positive or negative?

Mental Math Use mental math to find each sum or difference.

31. $-2\frac{3}{5} + \left(-4\frac{2}{5}\right)$

32. $4\frac{5}{6} + \left(-2\frac{5}{6}\right)$

33. $1\frac{3}{8} - \left(-1\frac{5}{8}\right)$

For Exercises 34–36, find the fraction described by each set of clues.

34. The fraction is between 0 and 1. If you add $\frac{2}{8}$ to it, the result is equivalent to $\frac{10}{16}$.

35. The fraction is between –1 and 0. If you subtract $\frac{2}{4}$ from it, the result is $-1\frac{1}{4}$.

36. **Challenge** The absolute value of a fraction is between 1 and 2. If you add $\frac{1}{8}$ to half the fraction the absolute value of the result is equivalent to $\frac{1}{2}$. What is the fraction?

37. **Challenge** Solve each equation for *n*.

a. $-3\frac{2}{3} + n = -1\frac{3}{8}$

b. $-5 = n - \left(-2\frac{1}{6}\right)$

Reflecting on the Section

Be prepared to discuss your response to Exercise 38 in class.

38. Two students each started to evaluate $-\frac{3}{10} - \left(-\frac{2}{15}\right)$ as shown.

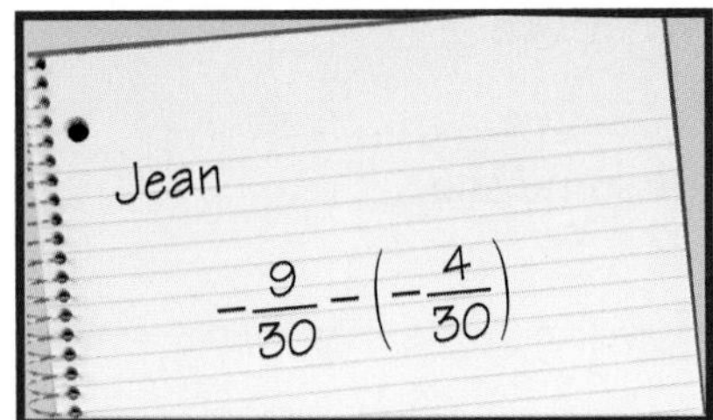

a. Describe what each student has done so far. Then write the next step for each student. Will their answers be the same?

b. Which method do you prefer? Explain your choice.

Discussion

Exercise 38 checks that you understand operations with fractions.

Spiral Review

Simplify each expression. **(Module 2, pp. 86–87)**

39. $28 + (-41)$ 40. $-12 \cdot (-8)$ 41. $72 \div (-8)$ 42. $-56 - 56$

43. The box-and-whisker plot models survey data from 16 countries. Find the lower extreme, the upper extreme, and the median of the data. **(Module 1, p. 23)**

Percent of People Who Would Like to Move to Another Country

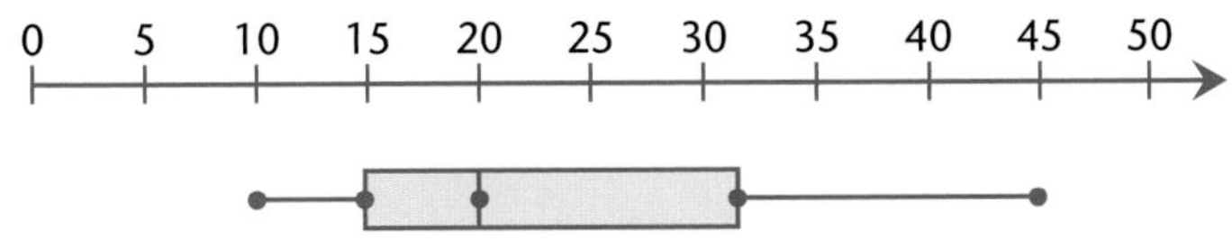

Section 2 Extra Skill Practice

Find each sum or difference.

1. $\frac{3}{5} - \frac{7}{2}$
2. $-\frac{1}{3} - \frac{2}{7}$
3. $\frac{4}{2} + \left(-\frac{7}{8}\right)$
4. $4\frac{1}{9} + \frac{7}{8}$
5. $\frac{2}{3} + \left(-1\frac{1}{3}\right)$
6. $-\frac{4}{9} - \left(-\frac{2}{7}\right)$
7. $-\frac{3}{10} + 2\frac{2}{5}$
8. $-\frac{3}{11} + \frac{2}{3} - \frac{9}{11}$
9. $-1\frac{7}{9} - 1\frac{2}{6}$
10. $6\frac{7}{9} - \left(-\frac{5}{8}\right)$
11. $\frac{5}{8} + 2\frac{1}{2}$
12. $-\frac{4}{9} - \left(-\frac{2}{3}\right) + 1\frac{1}{6}$

13. Johanna has decided to make her own party invitations. She has already bought the envelopes that are 7 in. long and 5 in. wide.
    a. She wants to have an extra $\frac{1}{6}$ in. of clearance around each edge of an invitation when it is placed in the envelope. What size should the invitations be?
    b. What size should the paper for each invitation be? Assume she folds the paper in half to make each invitation.

Standardized Testing ▶ Multiple Choice

1. Find $-7\frac{2}{3} + 5\frac{1}{5}$.

   (A) $-12\frac{13}{15}$ (B) $-2\frac{13}{15}$ (C) $-2\frac{3}{8}$ (D) $-2\frac{7}{15}$

2. The expression $-5\frac{7}{16} - 3\frac{5}{8}$ has the same value as what other expression?

   (A) $-3\frac{5}{8} - 5\frac{7}{16}$ (B) $5\frac{7}{16} + 3\frac{5}{8}$ (C) $5\frac{7}{16} + \left(-3\frac{5}{8}\right)$ (D) $-5\frac{7}{16} + 3\frac{5}{8}$

3. Which expression has a value that is less than $-\frac{2}{3}$?

   (A) $-\frac{3}{8} - \frac{2}{3}$ (B) $-\frac{3}{8} + \frac{2}{3}$ (C) $\frac{3}{8} + \left(-\frac{2}{3}\right)$ (D) $\frac{3}{8} - \frac{2}{3}$

Section 3 Exploring Probability

IN THIS SECTION

EXPLORATION 1
- Experimental Probability

EXPLORATION 2
- Theoretical Probability

EXPLORATION 3
- Tree Diagrams

The GRAND GIVEAWAY

Setting the Stage

When a new store opens at a mall, special promotions are often used to attract shoppers. The "Grand Giveaway" is such a promotion. Each customer is given the opportunity to spin a spinner to try to win a gift certificate for purchases in the store. Nancy and Becky are waiting to take their turns to spin the spinner. Nancy is second in line and Becky is third. The first person spins a 7 and wins a $100 gift certificate.

Spin and Win $$$$$	
Spinner number	Gift Certificate Value
1	$25
2	Sorry
3	$25
4	$10
5	$10
6	Sorry
7	$100
8	$10

Think About It

1 Which of Nancy's and Becky's statements do you agree with?

2 How can you decide which comments are correct?

GOAL

LEARN HOW TO...
- find experimental probabilities

AS YOU...
- simulate the *Grand Giveaway*

KEY TERMS
- experiment
- outcome
- equally likely
- event
- probability
- experimental probability

Exploration 1

EXPERIMENTAL PROBABILITY

SET UP *Work in a group of four. You will need: • Labsheets 3A and 3B • paper clip • pencil*

▶ **You can use a spinner to estimate Nancy's chances of winning a gift certificate in the "Grand Giveaway." Spinning the spinner is an example of an experiment. The result of an experiment is an outcome.**

3 "The spinner stops on 3" is one outcome of an experiment involving a spinner like the one shown on page 105.

a. List the other possible outcomes.

b. How many outcomes are there altogether?

c. Two outcomes are **equally likely** if they have the same chance of happening. What must be true about the spinner for the outcomes to be equally likely?

d. Is each of the eight numbers on the spinner equally likely to come up on each spin? How do you know?

▶ **Winning a gift certificate on a spin is an example of an *event*. An event is a set of outcomes of an experiment.**

4 Use the *Spin and Win $$$$$* table on page 105 to determine the outcomes that make up the following events.

a winning a gift certificate on a spin

b. winning a gift certificate with a value of at least $25 on a spin

Use Labsheets 3A and 3B for Questions 5–11.

5 Will moving to the back of the line improve Nancy's chances of winning a gift certificate? To find out, follow the directions for the *Grand Giveaway Experiment* on Labsheet 3A.

6 Use the data in the *Trials Table* to complete the first three rows in the *Group Results Table* on Labsheet 3B.

▶ **Experimental Probability To decide whether she should move to the back of the line, Nancy can determine whether the *probability* of spinning a winning number is the same or different for each person in line. A probability is a number from 0 through 1 that tells how likely it is that an event will occur.**

You can use the following ratio to find the *experimental probability* of an event.

$$\text{Experimental Probability} = \frac{\text{number of times an event occurs}}{\text{number of times the experiment is done}}$$

7 Use the data in the first three rows of the *Group Results Table* to find the experimental probabilities in the last three rows.

8 Compare the experimental probabilities for winning a gift certificate on the second, third, and fourth spins. Do you think you are more likely to win on any particular spin? Explain.

9 **Try This as a Class** Complete the following to see how increasing the number of trials can affect experimental probabilities.

a. Combine your group results with those of the other groups in the class and record the totals in the first four rows of the *Class Results Table*.

b. Find the experimental probability for each of the events in the last three rows and record them in the table.

10 **a.** Describe how the experimental probabilities of winning a gift certificate on the second, third, and fourth spins for your group compare with the probabilities for the whole class.

b. Which set of probabilities, the ones for your group or the ones for the class, do you think give a better indication of an event occurring? Why?

11 **Try This as a Class** Look back at the *Setting the Stage*. Use the probabilities in the *Class Results Table* to answer these questions.

a. Was Becky correct when she said moving to the back of the line would not make a difference? Why or why not?

b. Was Nancy correct when she said the first contestant was lucky to win a \$100 gift certificate on his spin? Explain.

✓ QUESTION 12

...checks that you can find experimental probabilities.

12 **✓ CHECKPOINT** A number cube has sides numbered 1 through 6. A pair of number cubes was rolled 20 times and the sum of the numbers was recorded in the *Trial Table*.

a. What are the possible outcomes of the experiment?

b. Based on this experiment, what sum or sums seem to be most likely to occur? What is the experimental probability that they occur?

c. What sum or sums seem to be least likely to occur? What is the experimental probability that they occur?

TRIAL TABLE

Trial	1	2	3	4	5	6	7	8	9	10
Sum	12	5	8	7	6	9	5	6	7	6

Trial	11	12	13	14	15	16	17	18	19	20
Sum	3	7	10	6	6	2	8	2	5	7

HOMEWORK EXERCISES ▶ See Exs. 1–16 on pp. 115–117.

GOAL

LEARN HOW TO...
- find theoretical probabilities
- recognize dependent and independent events

AS YOU...
- examine a promotional drawing

KEY TERMS
- theoretical probabilities
- dependent events
- independent events
- impossible event
- certain event

Exploration 2

THEORETICAL PROBABILITY

▶ **A second promotion, *Select a Number*, also takes place at the store each day. Four shoppers are selected at random and given a chance to win a gift certificate by drawing a numbered sphere from a box. The box contains five spheres that are numbered 1 through 5. The spheres are not put back into the box after they are drawn. Nancy is also second in line for *Select a Number*.**

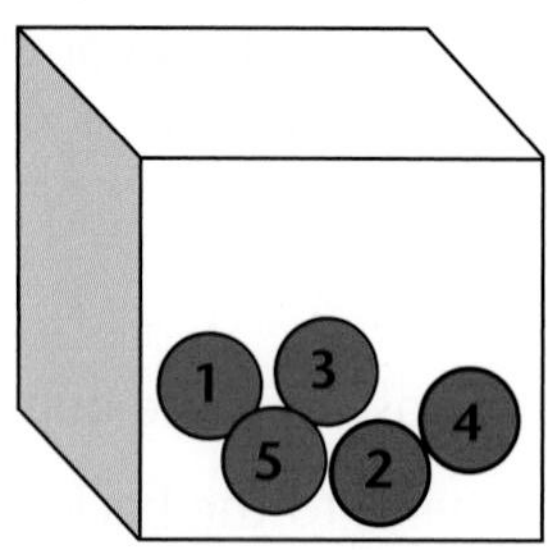

Select a Number and Win $$$$$	
Sphere number	Gift certificate value
1	$100
2	$25
3	$50
4	Sorry
5	Sorry

13 On the first draw, is each of the five spheres equally likely to be drawn? Why or why not?

▶ **Theoretical Probability** **Sometimes you can find the probability of an event without actually doing an experiment.**

If all of the outcomes of an experiment are equally likely, you can use this ratio to find the *theoretical probability* of an event.

$$\text{Theoretical Probability} = \frac{\text{number of outcomes that make up the event}}{\text{total number of possible outcomes}}$$

14 **a.** What is the theoretical probability that the first person in line wins a gift certificate?

b. **Discussion** Explain two ways to find the probability that the first person in line does *not* win a gift certificate.

c. What is the probability that the first person in line does *not* win a gift certificate?

▶ **When it is Nancy's turn to draw, one number has already been drawn from the box.**

15 Suppose the first person in line draws the sphere numbered 5.

a. What does the first person win?

b. How many spheres are left in the box? Is each of the spheres equally likely to be drawn?

c. What is the theoretical probability that Nancy will win a gift certificate if she draws next?

d. In this case, is Nancy's chance of winning a gift certificate better than, the same as, or worse than if she had been the first person to draw?

16 Suppose the first person in line had won a gift certificate.

a. If Nancy draws next, what is the theoretical probability that she will win a gift certificate?

b. Compare your answer in part (a) with your answer in Question 15(c). Does the outcome of the first draw affect the theoretical probability of winning a gift certificate on the second draw? Explain.

▶ **Dependent and Independent Events** In Questions 15 and 16, you discovered that the probability of winning a gift certificate on the second draw depends on the outcome of the first draw. If the probability that one event occurs is affected by whether or not another event occurs, the events are **dependent events**. If the probability of an event is not affected by whether or not another event occurs, the events are **independent events**.

17 Suppose you flip a nickel and get heads. Then you roll a number cube and get a five. Are these events *independent* or *dependent*?

...checks that you can find theoretical probabilities and identify dependent and independent events.

18 ✓ **CHECKPOINT** There are five numbered spheres in a box.

a. An odd-numbered sphere is drawn and not replaced before the second draw. What is the theoretical probability of getting an odd-numbered sphere on the second draw?

b. An odd-numbered sphere is drawn and replaced before the second draw. What is the probability of getting an odd-numbered sphere on the second draw?

c. In which experiment, the one in part (a) or the one in part (b), is the result of the second draw independent of the result of the first draw?

19 Consider the original situation of three winning numbers and two losing numbers in the *Select a Number* promotion.

a. Describe a sequence of draws in which the last person to draw cannot win a gift certificate. In this case winning on the last draw is an **impossible event**. What is the theoretical probability of this impossible event?

b. Describe a sequence of draws in which the last person to draw is sure to win a gift certificate. In this case, winning on the last draw is a **certain event**. What is the theoretical probability of this certain event?

20 Nancy thought it was "unlucky" for the first contestant in the *Select a Number* promotion to draw a losing number. Do you agree with Nancy? Explain.

HOMEWORK EXERCISES ▶ See Exs. 17–27 on pp. 117–118.

Exploration 3

TREE DIAGRAMS

GOAL

LEARN HOW TO...
- use a tree diagram to model and find theoretical probabilities

AS YOU...
- analyze a promotional drawing

KEY TERM
- tree diagram

SET UP *You will need Labsheet 3C.*

▶ **The Game Store at the mall attracts customers by encouraging people to come in and play a different game each day. Today's game is *WORD DRAW*. The rules of the game are simple.**

WORD DRAW

Each player is given a cup containing 4 letters.

Step 1 Without looking, each player removes one of the letters from his or her cup.

Step 2 The 3 remaining letters are then drawn out one at a time and placed in the order drawn to see if they make a three-letter word found in a dictionary.

Step 3 The 3 letters are returned to the cup and Step 2 is repeated 5 more times.

Players who make a word on at least two of their six tries win a prize.

▶ **Finding the experimental probability of an event can require many trials and take a long time, so it may be more efficient to find the theoretical probability. Using a *tree diagram* may help you find the theoretical probability of an event. A tree diagram can by used to show all the possible outcomes of an experiment.**

EXAMPLE

Roulan and Nancy played *WORD DRAW*. They each received a cup containing the letters A, T, E, and R. Without looking, Nancy removed the A and Roulan removed the R. They decided to make *tree diagrams* to find all the possible outcomes of drawing three letters one at a time.

Nancy's tree diagram with the A removed

1st Draw	2nd Draw	3rd Draw	Outcome
R	T	E	**RTE**
	E	T	**RET**
T	R	E	**TRE**
	E	R	**TER**
E	T	R	**ETR**
	R	T	**ERT**

Roulan's tree diagram with the R removed

1st Draw	2nd Draw	3rd Draw	Outcome
A	T	E	**ATE**
	E	T	**AET**
T	A	E	**TAE**
	E	A	**TEA**
E	T	A	**ETA**
	A	T	**EAT**

Use the tree diagrams in the Example for Questions 21 and 22.

21 **a.** What must Nancy do to get the outcome RTE?

b. How many outcomes are shown in each tree diagram?

c. Are the outcomes equally likely? Why or why not?

22 What is the theoretical probability of each event?

a. Nancy forms a word when she draws her letters one at a time.

b. Roulan forms a word when he draws his letters one at a time.

Use Labsheet 3C for Questions 23–26.

23 Roulan and Nancy are playing *WORD DRAW* for the Game Store's *Grand Prize Giveaway*. They win a $25 gift certificate if all four letters (A, E, T, and R), drawn one at a time, form the word TARE.

a. Complete the *Grand Prize Giveaway Tree Diagram* on Labsheet 3C.

b. How many possible outcomes are there?

c. What is the theoretical probability that A is drawn on the first draw?

d. Circle the part of the tree diagram that describes drawing A on the first draw.

24 Use the *Grand Prize Giveaway Tree Diagram*.

a. Suppose A is drawn on the first draw. What is the probability of drawing the T on the second draw?

b. If A and T are drawn on the first and second draws respectively, what is the probability of drawing the E on the third draw?

c. If A , T, and E are drawn on the first, second and third draws respectively, what is the probability of drawing the R on the fourth draw?

25 **a.** Three of the outcomes form words found in a dictionary. What are the three words?

b. What is the theoretical probability that a word will be formed?

c. What is the theoretical probability that either the word RATE or the word TEAR will be formed?

26 To win the gift certificate, a player must form the word TARE. What is the theoretical probability that a player will win?

27 **a.** Print the letters of the word RATIO on five identical slips of paper.

b. Turn each slip face down and thoroughly mix the slips.

c. Draw any three of the slips. Try to form a word with the three letters you picked.

d. Repeat the experiment 10 times.

e. What is the experimental probability that you can form a word when you draw any three letters from the pile?

f. **Try This as a Class** How could you find the theoretical probability that you can form a word when you draw any three letters from the pile?

g. Find the theoretical probability. How does it compare with the experimental probability in part (e)?

28 ✓ **CHECKPOINT** A number cube has sides numbered 1 through 6. Suppose you roll the number cube twice.

a. Make a tree diagram that shows all the possible outcomes.

b. Find the theoretical probability of rolling a 1 on the first roll and an odd number on the second roll.

...checks that you can make and use tree diagrams.

HOMEWORK EXERCISES See Exs. 28–33 on p. 119.

Section 3 Key Concepts

Key Terms

experiment

outcome

equally likely

event

probability

impossible event

certain event

experimental probability

theoretical probability

Outcomes and Events (p. 106)

An experiment is an activity whose results can be observed and recorded. The result of an experiment is an outcome. Outcomes are equally likely if they have the same chance of occurring. An event is a set of outcomes of an experiment.

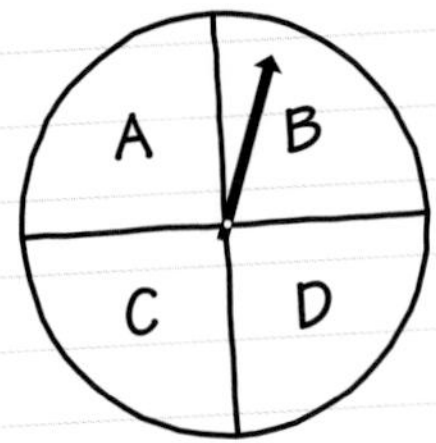

Example Suppose the experiment is to spin the spinner at the right once. The possible outcomes are A, B, C, and D. Spinning a B is an event. Spinning a consonant is also an event.

Experimental Probability (pp. 107–108)

A probability is a number from 0 through 1 that tells how likely something is to happen.

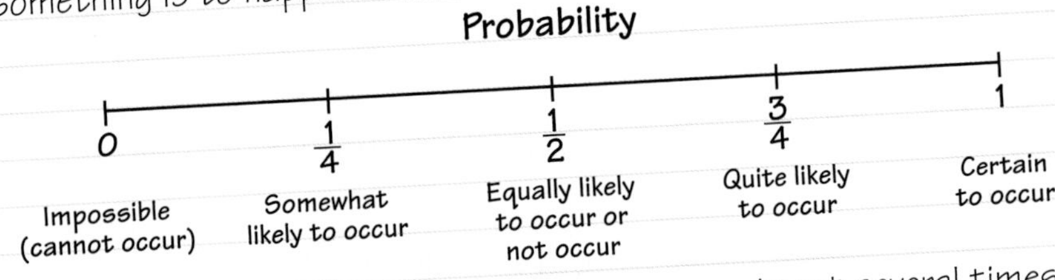

A probability that is found by repeating an experiment several times and recording the results is an experimental probability.

Example The table shows the results of spinning the spinner above 12 times.

The experimental probability of A is $\frac{2}{12}$ or $\frac{1}{6}$, of B is $\frac{3}{12}$ or $\frac{1}{4}$, of C is $\frac{3}{12}$ or $\frac{1}{4}$, and of D is $\frac{4}{12}$ or $\frac{1}{3}$.

Trial	Letter
1	C
2	D
3	D
4	A
5	C
6	B

Trial	Letter
7	D
8	A
9	B
10	C
11	D
12	B

Theoretical Probability (pp. 108–110)

A theoretical probability is found without doing an experiment.

Example Since the four outcomes (A, B, C, and D) on the spinner above are equally likely, the theoretical probability of spinning an A is $\frac{1}{4}$.

29 Key Concepts Question Based on the tables above, what is the experimental probability of spinning either an A or a C on the spinner above? What is the theoretical probability?

Section 3 Key Concepts

Key Terms

dependent events

independent events

tree diagram

Dependent and Independent Events (p. 110)

When the occurrence of one event affects the probability of the occurrence of another event, the events are dependent. Otherwise, they are independent.

Tree Diagrams (pp. 111–113)

A tree diagram can be used to show all the possible outcomes of an experiment.

Example The tree diagram at the right shows the possible outcomes of two flips of a coin.

The probability of flipping at least one head is $\frac{3}{4}$.

First flip	Second flip	Outcome
H	H	H H
	T	H T
T	H	T H
	T	T T

30 Key Concepts Question

a. Make a tree diagram that shows all the possible outcomes of spinning the spinner on page 114 twice.

b. How many possible outcomes are shown on your diagram?

c. What is the theoretical probability of spinning an A and then spinning a B?

Section 3 Practice & Application Exercises

YOU WILL NEED

For Ex. 9:
- a paper clip

A number cube with sides numbered 1–6 is rolled once.

1. What are the outcomes of the experiment?

2. Are the outcomes equally likely? Why or why not?

3. What outcomes make up the following events?

   a. rolling an odd number

   b. rolling an even number greater than 2

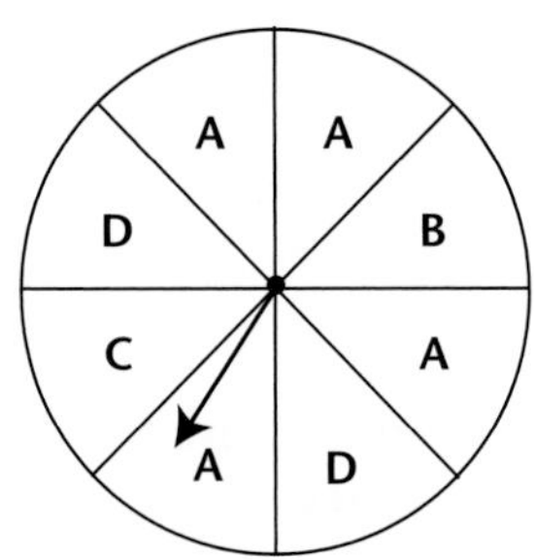

The spinner at the left is spun once.

4. What are the outcomes of the experiment?

5. Are the outcomes equally likely? Why or why not?

6. What outcomes make up the event "the spinner stops on a consonant"?

7. Is the spinner more likely to stop on a vowel or a consonant? Explain.

8. A penny is taped on the inside bottom of a bottle cap. The cap is then tossed in the air. The results for 12 tosses are shown in the Table. *Yes* means the cap landed with the penny up; *No* means the cap landed with the penny down.

Trial	1	2	3	4	5	6	7	8	9	10	11	12
Result	Yes	Yes	No	Yes	No	Yes	No	Yes	Yes	No	Yes	Yes

a. What is the experimental probability that the penny will land up?

b. Find the experimental probability that the penny lands down in two different ways.

9. An experiment consists of spinning the spinner at the right twice and finding the sum of the two numbers spun.

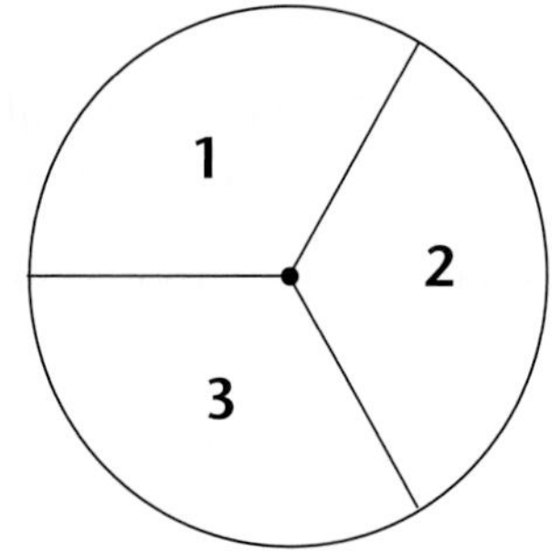

Make a copy of the spinner. Use a paper clip for a pointer. Perform the experiment 12 times and record the results in a table like the one below.

Trial	1	2	3	4	5	6	7	8	9	10	11	12
Sum	?	?	?	?	?	?	?	?	?	?	?	?

For Exercises 10–12, use the results in your table.

10. What is the experimental probability that the sum of the numbers spun is 3?

11. What sum(s) occurred most often?

12. What is the experimental probability of the sum(s) that occurred most often?

Games Use the information below for Exercises 13–16 and 28–30.

The game *Rock, Paper, Scissors* is played all over the world—not only as a form of recreation, but also as a way of settling disagreements.

The game uses the three different hand signs shown at the left. Two players pound the fist of one hand into the air three times. On the third beat each player displays one of the hand signs. Possible results are shown. If both players display the same symbol, the round is a tie.

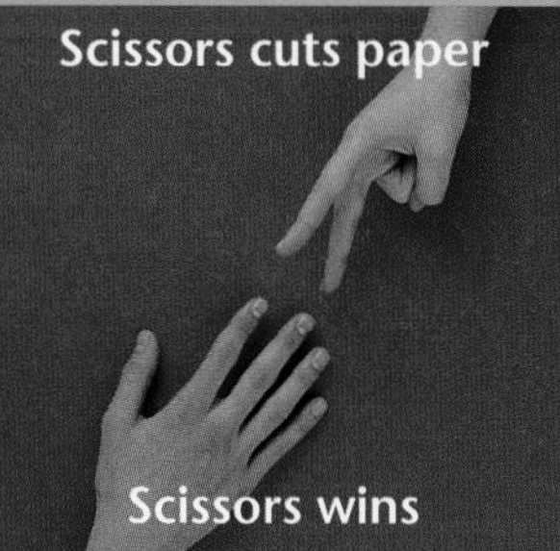

13. Play 20 rounds of *Rock, Paper, Scissors* with a partner. After each round, record each player's choice (using *R* for rock, *P* for paper, and *S* for scissors) and the result in a table like this one.

Round number	Player 1	Player 2	Result
1	R	P	Player 2 wins
2	S	S	Tie

14. Based on the results of your 20 rounds, what is the experimental probability of each result?

    a. Player 1 wins. b. Player 2 wins. c. There is a tie.

15. Did Player 1 or Player 2 win more often? How can you tell using the experimental probabilities in Exercise 14?

16. **Writing** Do you think playing *Rock, Paper, Scissors* is a fair way to settle a disagreement? Explain.

Interpreting Data Nate traced a circle, cut out a cardboard strip as shown, and used a thumbtack to make a spinner.

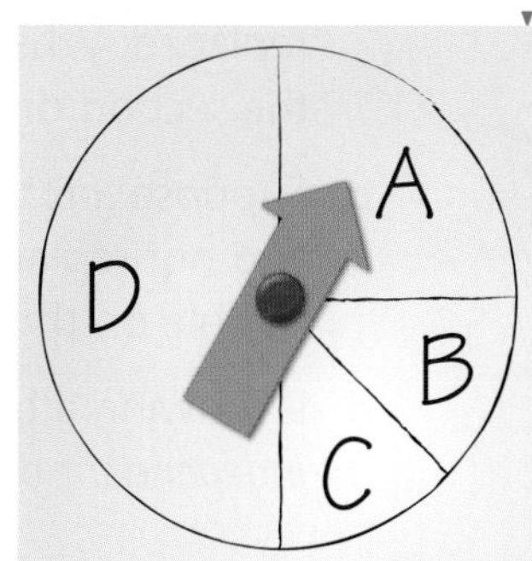

17. What appears to be the theoretical probability that the pointer will stop in each region?

    a. A b. B c. C d. D

Region	Frequency
A	9
B	5
C	5
D	21

18. Nate spun the pointer 40 times. The results are shown in the table. Use the data to calculate the experimental probability that the pointer will stop in each region.

    a. A b. B c. C d. D

For Exercises 19–21, a number cube with sides numbered 1 through 6 is rolled. Find each probability and plot it on a number line as on page 114. Label each point.

19. the theoretical probability of rolling a 7

20. the theoretical probability of rolling a number less than 5

21. the theoretical probability of rolling a number greater than 0

22. a. Which of the events in Exercises 19–21 are certain?

    b. Which of the events in Exercises 19–21 are impossible?

For Exercises 23–25, tell whether the events are equally likely.

23. "rolling an even number on a number cube with sides numbered 1 through 6" and "rolling an odd number using the same number cube"

24. "rolling a number less than 2 on a number cube with sides numbered 1 through 6" and "rolling a number greater than 3 using the same number cube"

25. "getting 2 heads and a tail on 3 flips of a coin" and "getting 2 tails and a head on 3 flips of the same coin"

26. **Open-ended** Describe an experiment that has three outcomes whose probabilities are $\frac{1}{2}$, $\frac{1}{3}$, and $\frac{1}{6}$.

27. In a bag of 20 marbles, 4 marbles are blue.

    a. One marble is drawn from the bag. What is the probability that it is a blue marble? That it is *not* a blue marble?

    b. Suppose a blue marble is drawn on the first draw and not replaced. What is the probability of drawing a blue marble on the second draw?

    c. Suppose another color (not blue) is drawn on the first draw and not replaced. What is the probability of drawing a blue marble on the second draw?

    d. Is drawing a blue marble on the second draw *dependent on* or *independent of* the first draw? Explain your answer.

28. a. Copy and complete the tree diagram shown at the right for the game *Rock, Paper, Scissors*.

b. How many outcomes are there?

c. What outcomes make up the event "Player 1 does not win"?

d. How is the event "Player 1 does not win" different from the event "Player 1 loses"?

Player 1	Player 2	Result
R	R	Tie
P		

29. **Writing** In a fair game, each player has an equal chance of winning. Is *Rock, Paper, Scissors* a fair game? Explain.

30. **Challenge** Suppose you notice that your partner never uses scissors.

a. Draw a tree diagram to show the possible outcomes if one player never uses scissors.

b. How would this affect your playing strategy?

31. a. Draw a tree diagram to show all the possible outcomes when a coin is flipped three times.

b. How many outcomes are there?

c. Do you think the outcomes are equally likely? Why or why not?

32. Use your tree diagram from Exercise 31 to find the theoretical probability of each event.

a. no heads b. exactly one head c. a head on the first flip

Reflecting on the Section

Write your response to Exercise 33 in your journal.

33. Describe two dependent events and two independent events.

Journal

Exercise 33 checks that you can apply ideas about probability.

Spiral Review

Find each sum or difference. (Module 2, p. 100)

34. $-\frac{1}{5}+\left(-\frac{7}{15}\right)$ 35. $\frac{5}{8}+\left(-4\frac{1}{2}\right)$ 36. $4\frac{1}{3}-\left(-\frac{9}{10}\right)$ 37. $-5\frac{11}{12}-\frac{3}{4}$

Combine like terms to simplify each expression. (Module 1, p. 43)

38. $12x-10x+1$ 39. $n^2-mn+mn$ 40. $2s+4st+6s$

Classsify each angle as *acute, right, obtuse,* or *straight*. (Toolbox, p. 592)

41. 85° 42. 140° 43. 180° 44. 95°

Section 3 Extra Skill Practice

The table shows the results of sixty flips of two coins. Use the table for Exercises 1 and 2.

Two Heads	One Head/ One Tail	Two Tails
14	28	18

1. What is the experimental probability of getting one head and one tail?

2. What is the experimental probability of getting two tails?

Suppose you roll the object shown. It has eight sides, numbered 1 through 8. All eight sides are equally likely. Find the theoretical probability of each of the events in Exercises 3–6.

3. rolling a 2

4. rolling a 7 or 8

5. rolling a number greater than 3

6. rolling a 2, 4, 6, or 8

7. In a sack of 25 apples, 8 are red, 10 are golden, and the rest are green.
   a. One apple is taken from the sack. What is the probability that it is golden? that it is green? that it is not green?
   b. If 2 red apples have been taken from the sack, what is the probability that the next apple taken will be red? will be green?
   c. Are the events below *dependent* or *independent*? Explain.
   Event 1: The first apple taken is golden.
   Event 2: The second apple taken is green.

8. José made a packing list for a weekend trip.
   a. Draw a tree diagram to show all the possible ways José could dress if he wears a pair of matching socks, a pair of pants, and a shirt.
   b. What is the theoretical probability that José wears the T-shirt with jeans and black socks?

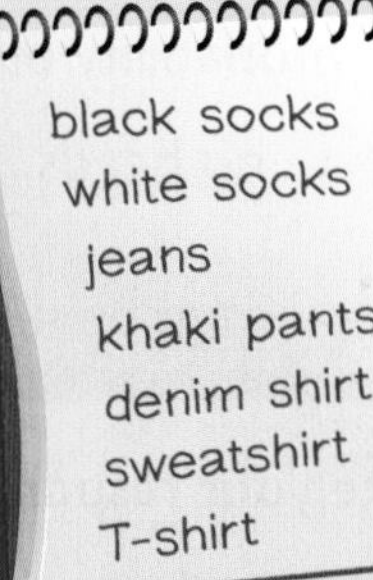

Standardized Testing ▶ Free Response

1. A spinner is divided into 6 segments, each labeled with a different positive integer. The theoretical probability of spinning a number less than 8 is 1. The theoretical probability of spinning a multiple of 3 is $\frac{1}{3}$, a multiple of 4 is $\frac{1}{6}$, and an odd number is $\frac{2}{3}$. Draw the spinner.

2. What is the theoretical probability of getting all heads or all tails when a coin is flipped 3 times? 4 times? 5 times? 50 times?

FOR ASSESSMENT AND PORTFOLIOS

EXTENDED E2 EXPLORATION

Is it a Boy or a Girl?

The Situation

The Ten O'Neil Girls

Between September of 1930 and July of 1952, Julia O'Neil of Boston, Massachusetts, gave birth to 12 children. The first child was a boy. The next 10 were girls, and the last was a boy.

The Problem

It is somewhat unusual for a woman to have 12 children. It is even more unusual for a woman to give birth to 10 girls in a row, as it would be for a woman to give birth to 10 boys in a row. What was the probability that the O'Neils would have 10 girls or 10 boys in a row?

Something to Think About

- What is the probability that all of the children born to a family have the same gender if the family consists of one child? two children? three children? four children? five children?
- Is there a pattern in these probabilities?

Present Your Results

Explain how you solved this problem. Include any representations that may be needed to make your explanation clear.

Section 4 Surveys, Proportions, and Percents

IN THIS SECTION

EXPLORATION 1
- Conducting a Survey

EXPLORATION 2
- Proportions and Percents

EXPLORATION 3
- Samples and Percent

Your OPINION COUNTS!

Setting the Stage

TEEN SURVEY

How often do you visit malls?

How do you get there?

What kinds of stores do you like?

According to a recent survey, average American teens spend more than $104 a week each, and about two-thirds of that money can be spent however they wish. Because of this buying power, store owners want to attract teens to malls. The store owners use surveys to answer questions like the ones at the left.

Think About It

1. One survey asked teens what mall features they found most appealing. About 35% chose movie theaters. What does 35% mean?

2. About how many dollars each per week can average American teens spend as they wish?

Exploration 1

Conducting a SURVEY

SET UP *Work in a group of four. You will need Labsheet 4A.*

GOAL

LEARN HOW TO...
- use percents, fractions, and decimals to summarize the results of a survey
- identify and correct biased survey questions

AS YOU...
- conduct a survey

KEY TERM
- biased question

▶ **To see how surveys can provide information, your group will conduct a survey.**

Use Labsheet 4A for Questions 3–5.

3 Answer the survey questions below. Record your group's results in the second column of each of the *Group Survey Results* tables.

Mall Survey

What kind of store do you think is most important at a mall? (Choose only one.)	How often do you go to a mall?
A. clothing	**A.** one or more times a week
B. shoes	**B.** once every 2 to 3 weeks
C. CD/DVD/video/music	**C.** once a month
D. sporting goods	**D.** less than once a month
E. department store	**E.** never
F. video arcade	

4 Suppose one out of four members of your group thinks a music store is most important at a mall. You can write this fact as a ratio in fraction form $\left(\frac{1}{4}\right)$, decimal form (0.25), or percent form (25%).

a. Use the *Group Survey Results* tables to record each of your group's ratios as a fraction, as a decimal, and as a percent.

b. Explain how you changed from the fraction form of the ratios to the decimal form.

c. How are the percent form and the decimal form of each ratio related?

d. Which form(s) of the ratio would you use to compare your group's results to those of another group? Why?

FOR ▶ HELP with *fractions, decimals, and percents*, see **TOOLBOX, p. 588**

5 Based on your group's results, do you think you can make an accurate prediction of the percent of the students in your class who rank clothing stores as the most important? Explain.

▶ **The way questions are asked can influence the results of a survey. For example, a group of students has been asked to plan an event to attract teenagers to a mall. A fashion show and a concert are possible events. The group will survey students to see which they prefer.**

6 Kelly and Sara suggest the survey questions shown.

a. Which question is more likely to get responses favoring the fashion show? Explain.

b. Which question is more likely to get responses favoring the concert? Explain.

c. Which activity do you think Kelly would prefer?

d. Which do you think Sara would prefer?

e. Will either Kelly's or Sara's question produce responses that accurately reflect students' opinions? Why or why not?

Kelly: Wouldn't a fashion show be a better way to attract teen shoppers than a concert?

Sara: Do you agree that a concert would be more fun than a fashion show?

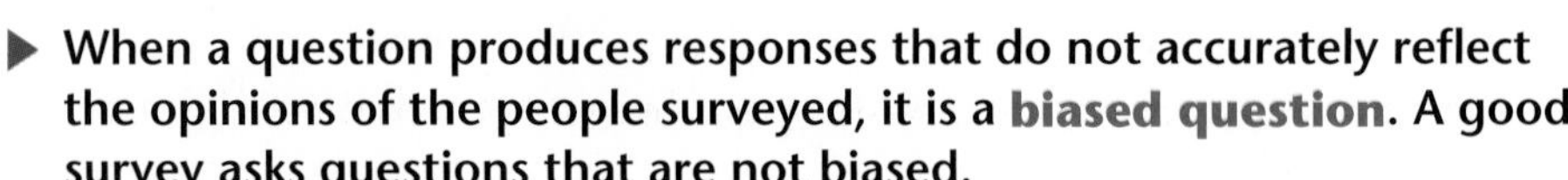

▶ **When a question produces responses that do not accurately reflect the opinions of the people surveyed, it is a biased question. A good survey asks questions that are not biased.**

7 Explain why each question below is biased. Then try rewriting each question so that it is not biased.

a. "Is recycling a waste of time?"

b. "Wouldn't building a new high school be a good idea?"

c. "Should all students be forced to take physical education?"

✓ QUESTION 8

...checks that you can write an unbiased survey question.

8 **✓ CHECKPOINT** Write an unbiased question that could be asked to find out whether a fashion show or a concert is a better way to attract students to the mall.

HOMEWORK EXERCISES ▶ **See Exs. 1–12 on p. 133.**

Exploration 2

Proportions and PERCENTS

GOAL

LEARN HOW TO...
- use proportional reasoning to estimate the percent of a number
- identify representative samples

AS YOU...
- make predictions based on a sample

KEY TERMS
- population
- sample
- representative sample
- proportion
- cross product

Some store owners at a mall think their sales will improve if more teenagers visit the mall. They know that about 40% of teenagers nationwide ride to malls with a parent or relative. They think a free shuttle service one Saturday each month might make it easier for the 4000 teenagers in the area to get to their mall. They survey 250 local teenagers (students in grades 8–11) to see whether they would use a shuttle.

▶ **A survey is used to gather information about a group called a population. It may not be practical to contact every member of the population, so a smaller group called a sample is surveyed. The survey results are used to make predictions about the entire population.**

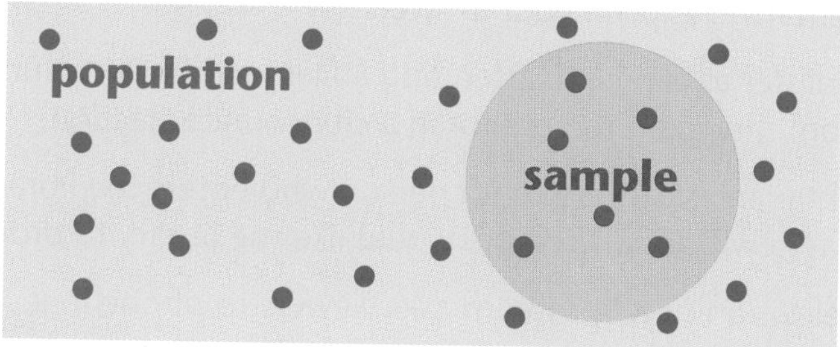

9 Discussion

a. What is the population that the store owners are trying to get information about?

b. What is the sample?

▶ **To make accurate predictions based on a sample, the sample must be representative of the whole population. A representative sample has the same characteristics as the population being studied.**

10 **Try This as a Class** Tell whether each group of students would be a representative sample for the survey about which event, a fashion show or a concert, would be better for attracting teenagers to a mall. Explain your thinking.

a. members of a girls' softball team

b. members of the All-City Band

c. every fifth student in line for lunch in the cafeteria

d. every student who takes a survey and completes it

✓ QUESTION 11

...checks that you can tell whether a sample is representative.

11 **✓ CHECKPOINT** Identify the intended population for each survey below. Also tell whether the sample from the population is representative. Explain your answers.

a. A pollster asks people attending a Democratic Party fundraiser whom they plan to vote for in a city council election.

b. A librarian asks every tenth person who enters the library what new books he or she would like the library to order.

c. A television news program asks viewers to phone in a vote for or against building a nuclear power plant.

12 **Discussion** Use the information about the mall given on page 125. Suppose 85 out of 250 teenagers surveyed by the store owners say they would use the shuttle.

a. Write the ratio of the number of teenagers who would ride the shuttle to the number of students in the sample as a percent.

b. Based on the results of the survey, do you think 2000 of the 4000 teenagers in the area will ride the shuttle? more than 2000 teenagers? fewer than 2000 teenagers? Explain.

▶ **Estimating with Percents** You can use the percent you found in Question 12 to estimate the total number of teenagers in the area who might ride the shuttle.

EXAMPLE

To estimate 34% of 4000, you can use the following methods.

Method 1 You can estimate 34% of 4000 by using the nearest "nice" fraction. 34% is close to $33\frac{1}{3}\%$, which equals the "nice" fraction $\frac{1}{3}$. So you can estimate $\frac{1}{3}$ of 4000.

Method 2 You can also estimate 34% of 4000 using multiples of 10%. A percent bar model shows how this method works.

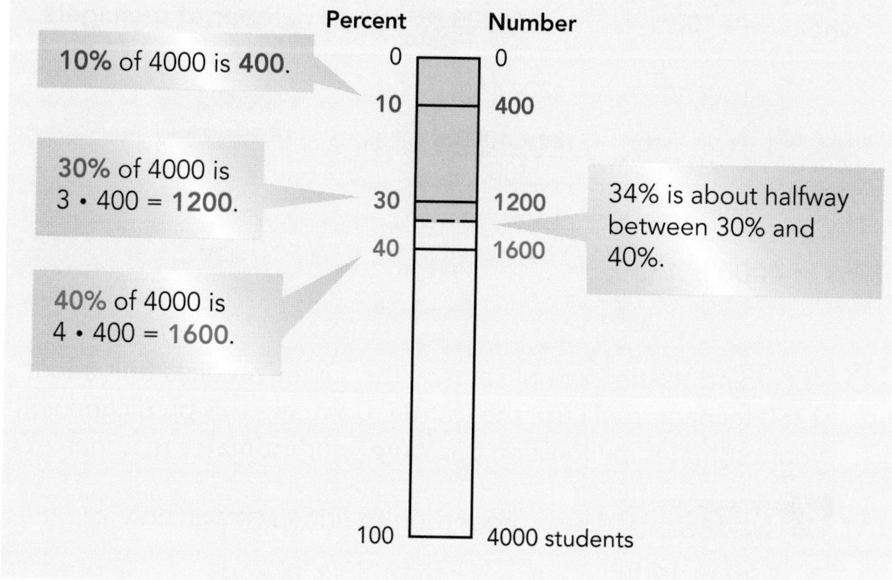

13 **a.** Refer to Method 1 in the Example. Estimate $\frac{1}{3}$ of 4000.

b. Refer to Method 2. Use the fact that 34% is about halfway between 30% and 40% to estimate 34% of 4000.

c. **Discussion** Which of your estimates from parts (a) and (b) would you use to predict how many teenagers in the area might use a shuttle to get to the mall? Explain.

14 ✓ **CHECKPOINT** Estimate to find each percent.

a. 26% of 600 **b.** 68% of 50

c. 74% of 3000 **d.** 21% of 150

...checks that you can estimate a percent of a number.

▶ **Using a Proportion** Another way to predict the number of teenagers who would ride the shuttle is to write and solve a proportion. A **proportion** is a statement that two ratios are equal.

EXAMPLE

Use a proportion to find 34% of 4000.

SAMPLE RESPONSE

Percent means "out of 100," so 34% means "34 out of 100" or $\frac{34}{100}$.

Let x = the number of teenagers who would ride the shuttle. The proportion can be written:

	Percent		Number	
part ⟶	34	=	x	⟵ number who would ride
whole ⟶	100		4000	⟵ total number of teenagers

$$\frac{34}{100} = \frac{x}{4000}$$

$$100 \cdot x = 34 \cdot 4000$$

$$x = \frac{34 \cdot 4000}{100}$$

$$x = 1360$$

In a proportion cross products are equal.

34% of 4000 is 1360.

15 According to the Example above, the survey predicts that about 1360 teenagers will use the shuttle. Compare this prediction with your estimates in Question 13. Were your estimates reasonable?

...checks that you can find the percent of a number.

16 ✔ **CHECKPOINT** Use a proportion to find each percent.

a. 37% of 1200 **b.** 93% of 250

17 **Try This as a Class** Suppose the survey convinced the store owners at the mall to run the shuttle. The first month 800 teenagers ride it.

a. The second month the number of riders is 125% of the number of riders in the first month. How many riders are there in the second month?

b. The third month the number of riders is 0.9% more than the number the second month. How many additional riders is this?

c. How many teenagers ride the shuttle the third month?

HOMEWORK EXERCISES ▶ See Exs. 13–27 on pp. 133–135.

Exploration 3

Samples and PERCENT

GOAL

LEARN HOW TO...
- write equations to solve percent problems
- find a representative sample

AS YOU...
- analyze the results of the Mall Survey

SET UP *You will need: • completed Labsheet 4A • Labsheet 4B*

18 For your survey on page 123, the population was the entire class. What was the sample?

▶ **Finding a Part You can use your group survey results to make predictions about the whole class.**

EXAMPLE

Suppose 75% of the members of a group go to the mall once a month. There are 31 students in the class. You can use this information to predict how many students in the class go to the mall once a month.

First	Describe what you want to find.	**75% of 31 is what number?**
Next	Write your sentence as an equation.	$0.75 \cdot 31 = x$
Then	Solve the equation.	$23.25 = x$

Use the fraction or **decimal equivalent** of 75%.

About 23 students in the class go to the mall once a month.

19 **Use Labsheet 4A.** Count the students in your class. Then use your *Group Survey Results* data to predict each number below.

a. the number of students in your class who visit the mall one or more times a week

b. the number of students in your class who rank clothing stores as the most important stores at the mall

c. the number of students in your class who rank video arcades as the most important

20 **Try This as a Class** Think about the groups who answered the survey for the *Group Survey Results* tables on Labsheet 4A. Do you think your group is representative of the whole class? Why or why not?

21 **Use Labsheets 4A and 4B.** Use the *Combined Group Survey Results* table to combine your group's survey data from Labsheet 4A with the data from two other groups. Try to choose two groups that will make the combined group as representative of the whole class as possible.

▶ **Finding a Percent** **You can use an equation to find the percent of students in your combined group who gave each response on the Mall Survey.**

EXAMPLE

Suppose 4 out of 12 students in a group go to the mall once a month. To find what percent of the group goes to the mall once a month, you can write an equation.

First	Describe what you want to find.	4 is what percent of 12?
Then	Write your sentence as an equation.	$4 = \frac{x}{100} \cdot 12$
		$4 = \frac{12}{100}x$

22 **Try This as a Class**

a. In the Example, why is x divided by 100?

b. Solve the equation in the Example.

Use completed Labsheet 4B for Questions 23–26.

✔ **QUESTION 23**

...checks that you can write and solve an equation to find a percent.

23 ✔ **CHECKPOINT** In Question 21, you combined your group's data with the data from two other groups. Use an equation to find the percent of the students in your combined groups who gave each of the responses described in Question 19.

24 Use the percents from Question 23 to predict the number of students in your class who gave each of the survey responses described in Question 19.

25 **Try This as a Class** Find the actual number of students in your class who gave each of the responses described in Question 19.

a. Compare your predictions in Questions 19 and 24 with the actual class results. Which predictions were more accurate?

b. Do you think your *original group* or your *combined group* was more representative of the class? Explain.

26 Suppose each group below answered the mall survey questions on page 123. Explain whether you think your combined class results from Question 25 can be used to predict their responses.

a. another class of students your age

b. a class of fifth grade students

c. the teachers at your school

▶ **Finding the Total** **You can use an equation to find the total when you know a part and the corresponding percent.**

EXAMPLE

In one class, 2 students said they never went to a mall. These students made up 8% of the class. To find the total number of students in the class, you can write and solve an equation.

First	Describe what you want to find.	2 is 8% of what number?
Then	Write your sentence as an equation.	$2 = 0.08 \cdot x$
		$2 = 0.08x$

27 Solve the equation in the Example. How many students were in the class?

28 ✓ **CHECKPOINT** Write and solve an equation to find each number.

a. 36 is 45% of what number?

b. 7% of what number is 28?

...checks that you can find a number when a percent of it is known.

HOMEWORK EXERCISES See Exs. 28–41 on pp. 135–136.

Section 4 Key Concepts

Key Terms

population

biased question

sample

representative sample

proportion

cross products

Surveys (pp. 123–124)

You can conduct a survey to get information about a population. A survey should not contain any biased questions.

Example The question "Do you agree that football is more fun to watch than golf?" is biased because it encourages a response favoring football. A better question is "Do you prefer to watch football or golf?"

Representative Samples (pp. 125–126)

When making a prediction based on surveys, usually only a sample of the population is used. Care must be taken to choose a representative sample that has the same characteristics as the whole population.

Example A survey asks parents of school-age children if they favor a new state tax to help fund education. The sample is not representative because it does not include state residents without school-age children.

Estimating Percents (p. 127)

You learned two ways to estimate the percent of a number. You can use a "nice" fraction or you can use multiples of 10%.

Finding Percents (pp. 128–131)

To find the exact percent of a number, you can write and solve a proportion or an equation.

Examples

Use a proportion to find 26% of 80.

part → / whole →
$$\frac{26}{100} = \frac{x}{80}$$
← part / ← whole

$$26 \cdot 80 = 100x$$

cross products

$$20.8 = x$$

Use an equation to find 26% of 80.

26% of 80 is what number?

$$0.26 \cdot 80 = x$$

$$20.8 = x$$

29 **Key Concepts Question** In a 2003 survey, 120 of the 400 teens surveyed got their spending money from a regular job, 43% got money from odd jobs, and 48% got an allowance.

a. What percent of the teens had a regular job?

b. How many of the teens got an allowance?

Section 4 Practice & Application Exercises

Write each percent as a fraction and as a decimal.

1. 40%
2. 74%
3. 115%

Write each decimal as a fraction and as a percent.

4. 0.67
5. 0.8
6. 0.005

Write each fraction as a decimal and as a percent.

7. $\frac{19}{100}$
8. $\frac{3}{8}$
9. $\frac{130}{200}$

Tell whether each question in Exercises 10–12 is biased. Rewrite each biased question so that it is no longer biased.

10. "Wouldn't Smith make a much better governor than Jones?"

11. "Which kind of movie do you like better—dramas or comedies?"

12. "Should teachers use video clips and movies to make their classes more interesting and effective?"

13. Suppose a middle school survey is given to find out if eighth graders should graduate a week before other students get out of school. The survey is given only to sixth graders.
    a. What is the population?
    b. What is the sample?
    c. Is this a representative sample? Why or why not?

Entertainment Some results from a survey of decision makers in the United States entertainment industry are shown below.

14. Explain whether you can conclude the following from this survey.

    A majority of people in the United States thinks that *viewers* and *ratings pressure* are most responsible for TV violence.

15. **Writing** How might the survey results differ if the question were asked to a representative sample of people in the United States?

Who would you say is most responsible for encouraging violence on television?

Response	Percent
Viewers	35%
Ratings pressure	33%
Network programmers	17%
Producers	5%
Writers	3%
Advertisers	2%
Program suppliers	1%
Directors	1%
Performers	2%
Outside media pressure	5%

Note: Due to rounding, percentages do not add up to 100%.

Estimate each percent. Tell which method you used.

16. 76% of 200 17. 67% of $99 18. 55% of 64

Marketing Use the information at the left for Exercises 19 and 20. Round decimal answers to the nearest unit.

In a survey of 1200 teens:

45.1% thought women's clothing was the most important type of store at the mall;

15% thought men's clothing was the most important;

30.9% of the teens said they go to the mall once a month with their parents.

19. a. Estimate how many of the teens thought women's clothing was the most important type of store. Then find the actual number.

b. Estimate how many of the teens thought men's clothing was the most important type of store. Then find the actual number.

20. a. Estimate how many of the 1200 teens said they go to the mall once a month with their parents.

b. **Alternative Method** Two methods for solving proportions are shown below. Use each method to find the number of teens surveyed who visit the mall once a month with their parents.

Undoing Method

Percent (part over whole) — Number (part over whole)

$$\frac{30.9}{100} = \frac{x}{1200}$$

$$1200 \cdot \frac{30.9}{100} = \frac{x}{1200} \cdot 1200$$

$$\underline{\ ?\ } = x$$

Multiply both sides by the least common denominator.

Equivalent Fraction Method

Percent (part over whole) — Number (part over whole)

$$\frac{30.9}{100} = \frac{x}{1200} \quad (\times\ ?)$$

What number times 100 is 1200?

$$\frac{30.9}{100} = \frac{x}{1200} \quad (\times 12)$$

$$\underline{\ ?\ } = x$$

c. Based on your estimate in part (a), do your answers in part (b) seem reasonable?

d. Which method in part (b) do you like best? Why?

Use a proportion to find each percent.

21. 16% of 210 22. 150% of 88 23. 42.2% of 500

24. 37.5% of 336 25. 105% of 20 26. 0.8% of 9000

27. In 1992, the Mall of America opened in Bloomington, Minnesota. Its area is about 4.2 million square feet. The table shows some of the largest malls in the United States. Use a percent to compare the area of each mall to the area of the Mall of America.

Mall	Area (square feet)
Woodfield Mall (Illinois)	2,700,000
The Galleria (Texas)	2,400,000
Tysons Corner Center (Virginia)	2,200,000

Use an equation to find each number or percent.

28. What is 40% of 80?

29. 0.5% of 90 is what number?

30. 30 is what percent of 125?

31. 2 is what percent of 200?

32. 65 is what percent of 50?

33. 17% of what number is 34?

34. 7.2 is 12% of what number?

35. 30 is 150% of what number?

36. **Writing** Compare the three examples in Exploration 3. How are they alike? How are they different?

37. The Park at MOA, an indoor theme park, is inside the Mall of America. It offers several different types of attractions. Use the information shown in the graph. Tell what percent of the attractions are each type.

a. rides

b. shops

c. food venues

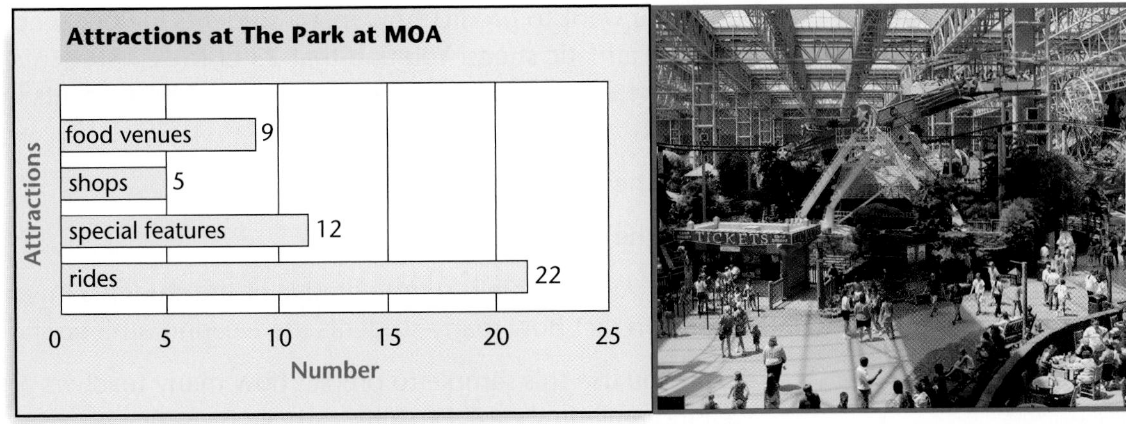

38. **Challenge** 20% of a number is 24 less than the number. What is the number?

39. You are planning to open a restaurant at a mall. To obtain information on the type of restaurant that would be most successful, you conduct a survey.

a. Give an example of a question you would ask on the survey.

b. What is the population?

c. Describe a representative sample.

40. The typical Monday night attendance at a movie theater in a mall is about 70 people. To increase attendance, the manager advertises that the first 45 customers on Monday nights will receive a movie poster. On the next Monday night, the first 45 customers were 60 percent of the total audience.

a. Use an equation to find the total audience size that night.

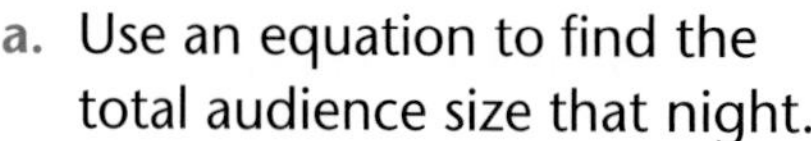

b. Do you think the poster giveaway helped increase attendance? Why or why not?

c. Suppose the posters cost the manager $2 each and the price of a ticket is $6. Was the promotion a good idea? Why?

Journal

Exercise 41 checks that you can use proportions and percents to analyze survey data.

Reflecting on the Section

Write your response to Exercise 41 in your journal.

41. Suppose you want to predict how many students in your school are wearing athletic shoes. You find that 23 of the 29 students in your class are wearing athletic shoes. There are 583 students in your school.

a. What is the population?

b. What is the sample?

c. Suppose your sample is representative of the students in your school. Predict how many students are wearing athletic shoes.

d. Could you use this sample to predict how many teachers are wearing athletic shoes? Explain.

Spiral Review

42. What is the least possible perimeter of a rectangle whose area is 36 m^2? (Module 1, p. 67)

Divide. Round each answer to the nearest tenth. (Toolbox, p. 582)

43. $50 \div 2.6$ 44. $680 \div 1.8$ 45. $9 \div 3.7$

Find each product. (Toolbox, p. 580)

46. $0.18 \cdot 10$ 47. $6.2 \cdot 0.01$ 48. $0.3 \cdot 100$ 49. $0.15 \cdot 1000$

Extension 

Sampling Methods

Several ways to take a sample from a population are described below.

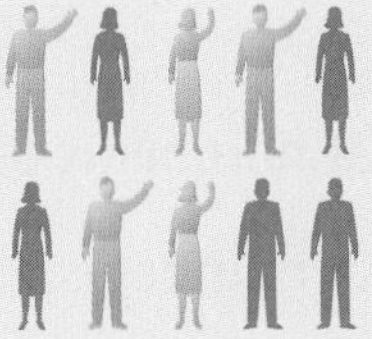

With *self-selected sampling,* you let people volunteer.

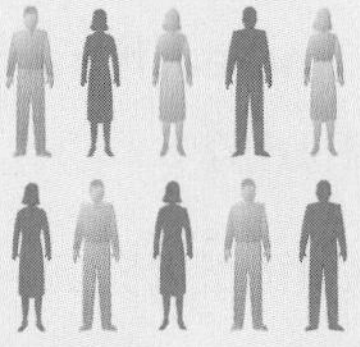

With *systematic sampling,* you use a pattern to select people, such as choosing every other person.

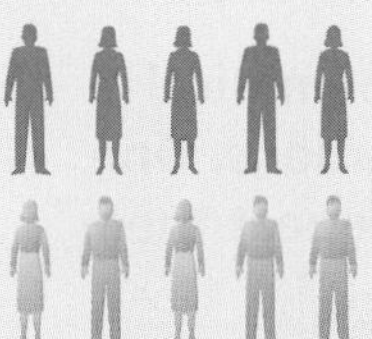

With *convenience sampling,* you choose easy-to-reach people, such as those in the first row.

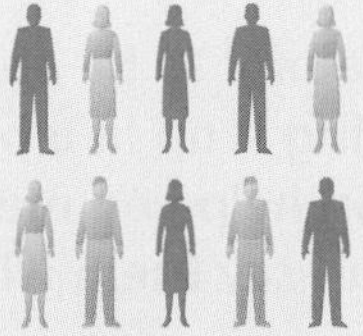

With *random sampling,* each person has an equally likely chance of being chosen.

50. What are some advantages and disadvantages of each sampling method described above?

51. Which sampling method is most likely to produce a sample that is representative of the population? Explain.

Section 4 Extra Skill Practice

Tell whether each question is biased. Rewrite each biased question so that it is no longer biased.

1. "Do you really think this town needs another grocery store?"
2. "Wouldn't the city be a more exciting place to live than the country?"
3. "Which football team do you like better—the Green Bay Packers or the Denver Broncos?"

Estimate to find each percent.

4. 78% of 900
5. 86% of 1500
6. 23% of 440
7. 48% of 37,000
8. 14% of 1500
9. 33% of $78
10. 11% of 82
11. 65% of 850

Use a proportion to find each percent.

12. 53% of 820
13. 12.5% of 48
14. 200% of 63
15. 86.9% of 10,000
16. 62% of 3480
17. 120% of 55
18. 28% of 470
19. 0.1% of 50,000

Use an equation to find each number or percent.

20. What is 80% of 165?
21. 15% of what number is 6?
22. 34 is what percent of 85?
23. 50% of what number is 931?
24. 190 is what percent of 304?
25. What is 32% of 6350?

Study Skills Recalling Useful Facts

Sometimes it is helpful to be able to quickly recall a mathematical fact without looking it up in a book or performing calculations. One technique that can help you memorize useful facts is to repeat them aloud until you can say them without hesitating.

1. Memorize the fraction equivalent of each common percent below by repeating it aloud.

   $50\% = \frac{1}{2}$ $25\% = \frac{1}{4}$ $20\% = \frac{1}{5}$

2. For each percent in Exercise 1, describe a situation in which it would be useful to recall the fraction equivalent quickly.
3. Name some other kinds of mathematical facts that you need to be able to recall quickly. Describe a situation in which quick recall of each fact can be helpful.

Section 5 Working with Percents

Exploration 1
- Estimating with Percents

Exploration 2
- Percent of Change

The PRICE i$ RIGHT, Isn't It?

Setting the Stage

For most people, shopping is the main attraction at the mall. Some people like to "shop 'til they drop," always looking for the best deals, while others buy on impulse. How about you? Do you compare prices to get the best deal?

One shopper tries to save money by comparing prices at two different stores.

Item	Higher Price	Lower Price
Top-selling CD	$18.99	$14.99
Brand-name jeans	$59.99	$54.99
Video game	$79.99	$49.48
Wristwatch	$29.99	$20.07
CD player	$179.99	$159.99

Think About It

1 Estimate the total amount of money the shopper can save by comparison shopping.

2 **a.** Find 10% of the higher price of each item shown above. Round your answers to the nearest cent.

b. For which items is the amount saved by comparison shopping greater than 10% of the higher price of the item?

c. For which items can the shopper save more than 20% of the higher price?

GOAL

LEARN HOW TO...
- estimate percents
- use mental math to find percents
- use percents to solve problems

AS YOU...
- play *Bargain Basement*

Exploration 1

Estimating with PERCENTS

SET UP *Work in a group of four. Your group will need: • one set of cards from Labsheet 5A • 4 index cards labeled A, B, C, and D*

▶ **Mental math and estimation are important skills for comparison shopping. In *Bargain Basement*, your team will compete to find or to estimate sale prices using mental math.**

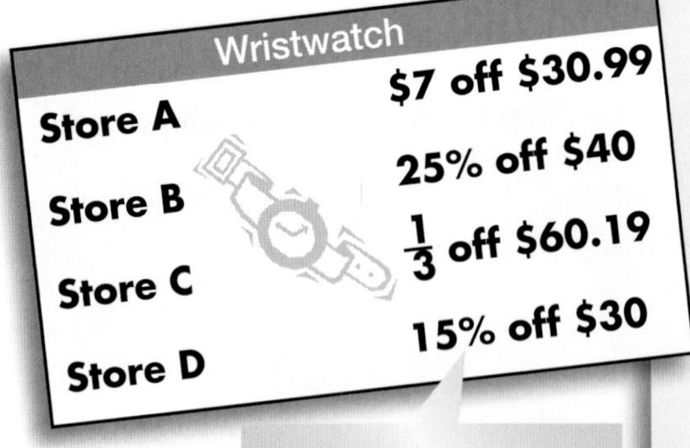

"15% off \$30" means \$30 – (15% of \$30).

Bargain Basement Game

Each team receives a set of cards. Each card lists four prices for the same item at four different stores.

Your teacher will call out an item. Locate that card. Work as a group to decide which price is the lowest.

The teams have one minute to decide which price is the lowest. When time is called, hold up the index card indicating your group's choice, either A, B, C, or D.

All teams with the correct choice earns 20 points.

Your teacher may call on your group to justify your choice or to choose the next item for which the class will determine the best buy.

3 Discussion

a. To find the amount of the discount at Store D, use mental math to find 15% of 30. Explain your thinking.

b. Find the sale price of the watch at Store D.

c. Find 85% of 30.

d. Explain why 85% of 30 represents the sale price of a \$30 item that is 15% off.

4 Discussion

a. Cheryl calculated the sale price for the watch at Store B by finding 75% of \$40. Explain why Cheryl's method works.

b. Use Cheryl's method to find the sale price of the watch at Store C.

c. Which of the four stores offers the best buy?

5 **Use Labsheet 5A.** Play a round of *Bargain Basement*. Be prepared to discuss the strategies your team used to determine the best buy.

HOMEWORK EXERCISES See Exs. 1–9 on pp. 144–145.

Exploration 2

PERCENT of CHANGE

GOAL

LEARN HOW TO...
- estimate percents of change

AS YOU...
- analyze sale prices

KEY TERMS
- percent of decrease
- percent of increase
- percent of change

SET UP *Work in a group of 3 or more.*

▶ **In Exploration 1, you saw how a percent discount is sometimes taken off the price of an item. A percent discount is an example of a *percent of decrease.* If you know the original value and the amount of the decrease, you can find the *percent of decrease.***

$$\text{Percent of decrease} = \frac{\text{amount of decrease}}{\text{original amount}} \cdot 100$$

EXAMPLE

A store advertises that all items are on sale for 40% off. A shopper sees this price tag on a denim jacket. Is the price of the jacket 40% off?

SAMPLE RESPONSE

First Find the amount of the decrease by subtracting the sale price from the original price.

Original price – sale price = amount of decrease

$60 – $38 = $22

Then Compare the amount of the decrease to the original amount.

$$x = \frac{22}{60} \cdot 100$$

$$x \approx 0.37 \cdot 100$$

$$x \approx 37$$

The denim jacket has been discounted by about 37%, not 40%.

6 Try This as a Class

a. Find the actual amount of decrease for a 40% discount on a \$60 jacket.

b. What should be the sale price of the jacket?

▶ **Percent of decrease can be used to describe a variety of situations.**

✓ QUESTION 7

...checks that you can find a percent of decrease.

7 ✓ CHECKPOINT According to one survey, an average shopper visited 2.9 outlets per week in 2000. By 2002 the number of outlets visited per week had declined to 1.9.

a. Estimate the percent of decrease in the number of outlets shoppers visited per week from 2000 to 2002.

b. Find the percent of decrease. Round to the nearest tenth of a percent. How does your answer compare with your estimate?

▶ **A *percent of increase* can be used to describe increases.**

$$\textbf{Percent of increase} = \frac{\text{amount of increase}}{\text{original amount}} \cdot 100$$

8 Discussion A store buys a book for \$12 and marks up the price to sell for \$20.

a. What was the amount of the markup?

b. Find the percent of increase after the markup.

9 a. In Question 8, the marked-up price of \$20 is what percent of the original price of \$12?

b. How did you get your answer?

10 Use estimation to determine which changes at the right represent the change described.

a. an increase of less than 50%

b. an increase of more than 100%

\$91 to \$118

40 mi/hr to 70 mi/hr

24 hr to 56 hr

\$0.49 to \$1

▶ **Percent of increase and percent of decrease are examples of percents of change.**

11 From 1990 to 2004, the number of people aged 25–29 in the United States changed from about 21.3 million to 19.6 million. Find the percent of change.

12 ✓ **CHECKPOINT** The average hourly wage in the United States in 1979 was \$6.33. In 1990, it was \$10.19. In 2005, it was \$16.11.

a. To the nearest percent, what was the percent of change from 1979 to 1990? from 1990 to 2005? from 1979 to 2005?

b. The 2005 hourly wage is what percent of the 1979 hourly wage? Round to the nearest percent.

✓ **QUESTION 12**

...checks that you can estimate and find a percent of change.

HOMEWORK EXERCISES ▶ See Exs. 10–17 on pp. 146–147.

Section 5 Key Concepts

Estimating Percents (pp. 140–141)

You can use mental math to estimate the percent of a number.

Example Estimate the sale price of an \$89 coat that is now on sale for 25% off.

25% off means you will pay 100% – 25% = 75% of the original cost.

$75\% = \frac{3}{4}$

$\frac{3}{4}$ of \$89 $\approx \frac{3}{4}$ of \$88

$\frac{3}{4}$ of \$88 = \$66

13 **Key Concepts Question** Suppose a store's sales decreased 19% from April to May and 19% from May to June.

a. Sales were \$9811 in April. Estimate the sales in May.

b. Use your answer to part (a) to estimate the sales in June.

c. Find the actual sales in May. Then use your answer to find the actual sales in June. Compare the answers with your estimates in parts (a) and (b).

Section 5

Key Concepts

Key Terms

percent of change

percent of decrease

percent of increase

Percent of Change (pp. 141–143)

Percent of decrease and percent of increase are examples of percents of change.

Example

A shirt that normally sells for $50 is on sale for $40. What is the percent of decrease in the price?

Original price	−	sale price	=	price decrease
$50	−	$40	=	$10

Since 10 is $\frac{1}{5}$ of 50 and $\frac{1}{5} = 20\%$ the $10 discount is 20% of $50. The percent of decrease is 20%.

Example

The original price of a toy was $18. It is marked up to sell for $20. What is the percent of increase in the price?

Increased price	−	original price	=	markup
$20	−	$18	=	$2

Since $2 is $\frac{1}{9}$ of $18, the percent of increase is about 11%.

14 **Key Concepts Question** Suppose a store's sales decreased 19% from April to May and 19% from May to June as in Question 13.

a. Uma thinks that since sales decreased 19% in May and 19% in June, they decreased the same number of dollars each month. Is she correct? Explain why or why not.

b. Did sales for the two months decrease by 38%? Explain.

Section 5

Practice & Application Exercises

1. Describe two different ways to estimate 69% of $59.98.

For Exercises 2–5, estimate the answer. Then find the exact answer.

2. 35% of 90 3. 22% of 240 4. 80% of 52 5. 9% of 1195

6. For each of the following discounts, determine what percent of the original price you will pay for the item.

a. 60% off b. 10% off c. 30% off

7. Nathan has been shopping online. Two companies are having sales on the same bicycle helmet. Which company is selling the item for less?

Hard Hats USA
15% off the original price of $45.

Bike Safely, Inc.
Regularly $50, now 20% off.

8. A store advertises that all items are 30–40% off. The original price is crossed out on each price tag, and the sale price is written below it. Use estimation or mental math to check that each markdown is within the advertised range. Tell which tags are marked incorrectly and explain how you know.

9. In a survey, 2051 teens in the United States were asked how they earned their spending money. Estimate the number of teens who made each of the responses below. Then find the actual number and compare it with your estimate.

About 47% said their parents gave them money when they needed it.

About 32% received a regular allowance.

About 45% did odd jobs.

About 26% worked part time.

About 11% worked full time.

10. 9.234 million spectators attended the National Hockey League's regular season games in 1995. In 2004, 22.065 million attended.

a. Estimate the percent of change in total spectators from 1995 to 2004.

b. Find the actual percent of change in total spectators from 1995 to 2004. How does it compare with your estimate?

Use the double bar graph for Exercises 11–13.

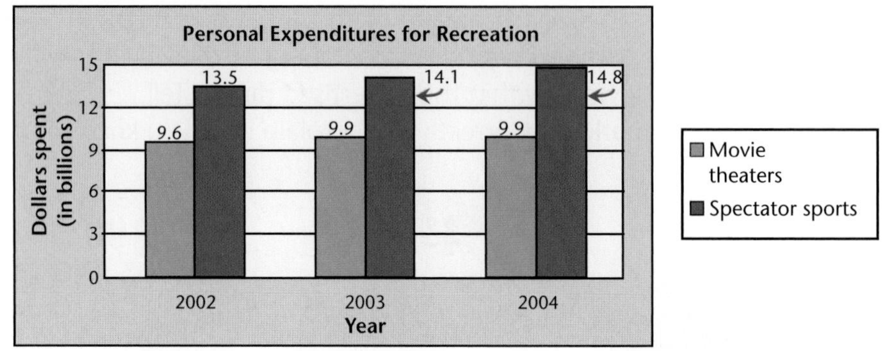

11. Describe the percent of change in the amount spent at movie theaters.

a. from 2002 to 2003 b. from 2003 to 2004

12. Describe the percent of change in the amount spent on sports.

a. from 2002 to 2003 b. from 2003 to 2004

13. Based on your answers in Exercises 11 and 12, how much money do you think was spent at movie theaters and sports in 2005?

14. a. The regular price of a necklace is $10 at two stores. At which store do you think the final sale price will be less? Why?

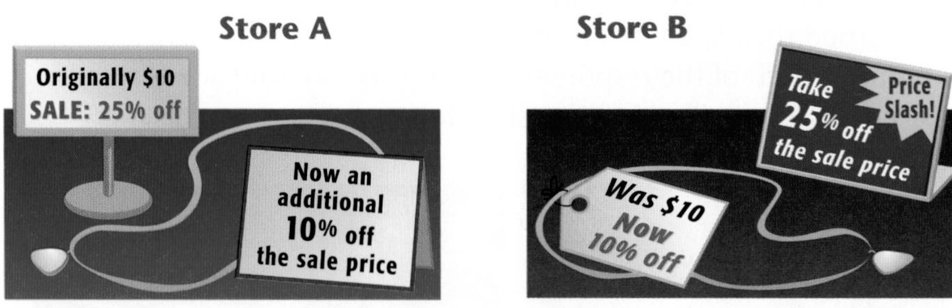

b. Find the final sale price of the necklace at each store. Was your prediction from part (a) correct? Explain.

c. Do you get the correct sale price if you add the two discounts together and then discount the price by that sum? Explain.

15. Find the percent of change. Be sure to tell whether it is a percent of increase or decrease. Round answers to the nearest percent.

a. \$9 to \$36

b. 55 mi/hr to 25 mi/hr

c. 12 min/day to 25 min/day

d. 2,654 people to 1,090 people

16. **Home Involvement**

a. Interview an adult born before 1970 to find the prices of three items in the past.

b. Compare each price with its equivalent today. In each case, what is the percent of change?

Item	Price then	Price now	Percent of change
movie	?	?	?
house	?	?	?
car	?	?	?

Reflecting on the Section

17. Find three sale ads in a newspaper or magazine that use percent discounts. Use estimation or mental math to determine the items on which you would save the greatest amount and the least amount. Do you always save the most with the greatest percent discount? Explain.

RESEARCH

Exercise 17 checks that you can apply percent of change.

Spiral Review

Use a proportion to find each percent. (Module 2, p. 132)

18. 28% of 5200

19. 2% of 485

20. 77% of 830

21. 100% of 61

22. 3.8% of 7900

23. 95% of 350

Find the greatest common factor and the least common multiple for each pair of numbers. (Toolbox, p. 584)

24. 10, 15

25. 12, 16

26. 21, 49

Replace each __?__ with >, <, or =. (Toolbox, p. 585)

27. $\frac{1}{4}$ __?__ $\frac{1}{3}$

28. $\frac{3}{8}$ __?__ $\frac{1}{2}$

29. $\frac{2}{3}$ __?__ $\frac{12}{18}$

30. $\frac{7}{8}$ __?__ $\frac{5}{6}$

Extension

Percent of Profit

Buyers are usually interested in the percent of decrease or increase in the cost of a product. Sellers are interested in how much the profit has changed. Profit is based on the selling price, *s*, of an item and the cost, *c*, of making an item. Two ways to calculate the percent of profit are shown at the right.

Percent of profit on cost = $\frac{s - c}{c}$

Percent of profit on selling price = $\frac{s - c}{s}$

31. Suppose a candy bar costs 35¢ to make, and sells for 50¢. What is the percent of profit on cost? What is the percent of profit on selling price?

32. Which percent of profit in Exercise 31 was greater? Do you think this will always be true? Explain your thinking.

Career Connection

Business Owner: Aricka Westbrooks

Aricka Westbrooks is the owner and manager of a company that sells fried turkeys.

33. Customers can purchase a fried turkey from Aricka Westbrooks's company at her store or by ordering online. Suppose that one year the company sold 450 Thanksgiving turkeys online. The next year, the number of Thanksgiving turkeys sold increased by 800. By what percent did the number of Thanksgiving turkeys sold online increase from the first year to the next?

34. Suppose that the number of turkeys the company sold online increased from 1347 last November to 1877 this November. The number of turkeys sold in the store increased from 2132 last November to 2500 this November. Which type of sales experienced greater growth? Explain.

For Exercises 1–6, estimate the answer. Then find the exact answer.

1. 55% of 340
2. 65% of 44
3. 7% of 48
4. 12% of 75
5. 38% of 160
6. 30% of 45

Use the bar graph for Exercises 7–9.

7. Find the percent of decrease in the price of unleaded gas from 2000 to 2002.
8. Find the percent of increase in the price of unleaded gas from 2002 to 2004.
9. Find the percent of increase in the price of unleaded gas from 2000 to 2004.

Average California Gasoline Prices

Year	Price (dollars)
2000	$1.66
2002	$1.51
2004	$1.97

10. A bicycle shop buys a new bike for $350 and sells it for $455.
    a. What is the amount of the markup?
    b. What is the percent of increase after the markup?

Use the table for Exercises 11–13.

11. Find the percent of decrease in the number of bald eagles from 1800 to 1974.
12. Find the percent of increase in the number of bald eagles from 1974 to 2000.
13. Find the percent of change in the number of bald eagles from 1800 to 2000.

Adult Bald Eagle Population in the Continental United States

Year	Number of adult eagles
1800	250,000
1974	1,582
2000	12,942

Standardized Testing ▶ Performance Task

For a Social Studies project, Diane and Rosa are ranking the 50 states based on the percent of increase in their populations from 2000 to 2005. Diane says New York's population increase was greater and should be ranked before North Carolina. Rosa disagrees. Who is right? Explain.

State	2000	2005
New York	18,998,889	19,254,630
North Carolina	8,078,429	8,683,242

Designing a Game

Many board games try to imitate what happens in real life. Working in a group, you will create a game that imitates shopping in a mall. You will play the completed game and refine it. Then your group will present the game to the class.

Getting Started You will start with a game board showing a map of a mall and an inventory list with prices. You will create rules, game pieces, game cards, and anything else needed to play the game. Your game will include math topics you learned about in this module, such as percents, proportions, and coordinate graphing.

SET UP

Work in a group.
You will need:

- *Project Labsheets A and B*
- *items for game pieces*
- *markers*
- *cardstock*
- *scissors*

Use Project Labsheets A and B.

1 Your game must use the *Game Board* and the *Inventory List*. Describe a possible goal for your game. In other words, how can someone win?

2 With your group, discuss possible rules for your game.

3 In your game, you will move from grid intersection to grid intersection on the *Game Board*. For each player, construct game pieces small enough to fit easily on the board.

4 Think about what might happen as a player visits the various stores on the game board. Construct cards like the ones below. You may also want to create game money to spend at the stores.

Game cards can include information on prices, sales, and discounts.

You may want to have different types of cards for entering stores, rolling the number cubes, or landing on certain spaces.

Writing Rules The rules of any game must be easy to understand and not leave room for arguments. Try to imagine playing your game and the situations you could encounter.

5 As a group, discuss the rules of your game. Describe how pieces can move. For example, will players roll number cubes? Spin a spinner? You can use your knowledge of coordinate graphing to move pieces on your game board.

6 Write down the official rules of the game. Make sure that the rules explain all aspects of the game.

7 **Playing the Game**

a. With your group, assemble the game and game pieces. Review the rules.

b. Play the game.

8 After you have played the game, discuss each question below in your group.

a. What math skills did you use while playing the game?

b. What worked well in your game?

c. What could you improve?

9 **Revising the Game** Make any changes necessary to improve your game. You may need to add or change rules.

10 As a group, prepare a presentation to give to the class. Each member of the group can present a part of the game. Include the following in your presentation.

the goal of the game	the rules
the mathematics used	the playing pieces
the cards	your own experience playing the game

MODULE 2 Review and Assessment

You will need: • *Review and Assessment Labsheet* (Ex. 14)

Evaluate each expression. (Sec. 1, Explors. 1, 2, and 3)

1. 123 + (–53)
2. 3 + (–18)
3. 5 – (–12)
4. –2 – 35
5. –6 • 15
6. (–24)(–8)
7. –72 ÷ 8
8. –108 ÷ (–9)
9. 6(–7)(–4) ÷ (–12)
10. –26 + 6 – (–20)
11. –36 + (–6) + (–8)
12. What numbers have an absolute value of 5? (Sec. 1, Explor. 1)
13. Explain what is meant by the *opposite* of a number. Give three examples. (Sec. 1, Explor. 1)
14. **Use the Review and Assessment Labsheet.** In the game *Cyber Spaceship*, a player guides a spaceship around moving obstacles. Follow the directions on the labsheet to draw the triangular obstacle after a translation. (Sec. 1, Explor. 2)

Find each sum or difference. (Sec. 2, Explors. 1, 2, and 3)

15. $-\frac{5}{6} + \frac{3}{8}$
16. $-\frac{4}{5} - \frac{2}{3}$
17. $-4\frac{3}{5} + 1\frac{2}{3}$
18. $3\frac{9}{10} - \left(-2\frac{3}{5}\right)$

For Exercises 19–21, suppose a 25¢ toy machine is usually full of colored bouncing balls, but most of the balls have been sold and only 1 blue, 1 yellow, and 2 red balls are left. You have two quarters to spend on balls. (Sec. 3, Explors. 1, 2, and 3)

19. Draw a tree diagram showing all the possible outcomes.
20. What is the theoretical probability of getting two red balls when you buy two balls?
21. Suppose you design an experiment to model the color of the first ball you buy from the machine. In each trial, you pull a ball from a bag, record the color, and then replace it. The results are shown in the table. What is the experimental probability of getting a red ball?

50 Trials		
Blue	Yellow	Red
14	10	26

22. Is the following question biased? If so, rewrite the question so that it is no longer biased. (Sec. 4, Explor. 1)

"Do you agree that students should have access to the Internet in order to improve their education?"

23. A middle school is conducting a survey to decide whether its spring dance should be open to students in grades 5–8 or just to students in grades 7 and 8. Tell whether each group of students would be a *representative sample* for the survey. Explain your thinking. (Sec. 4, Explor. 1)

a. all students whose last names begin with the letter "A"

b. the students in Mr. Marshall's eighth grade English class

24. In a survey of teens, 51% of the girls and 83% of the boys said athletic shoes were their favorite type of shoe. (Sec. 4, Explor. 2)

a. Suppose 1030 girls were surveyed. About how many of the girls said athletic shoes were their favorite type of shoe?

b. Suppose 639 boys answered that athletic shoes were their favorite type of shoe. How many boys were surveyed?

25. Of 500 New England youths surveyed, 90% said they visit a supermarket on a weekly basis. (Sec. 4, Explor. 3)

a. What was the sample? Do you think the sample was representative of all the young people in the United States? Explain.

b. Use mental math to find how many of the 500 youths surveyed visit a supermarket on a weekly basis.

Estimation For Exercises 26 and 27, estimate each answer. Explain how you found your estimate. (Sec. 5, Explor. 1)

26. An appliance store buys a television for $322 and marks up the price to $475 for resale. Estimate the percent of the markup.

27. A $66.50 item is discounted 30%. Estimate the sale price.

28. The table shows the average weekly allowances for kids by age, based on one survey. Determine the percent increase in allowance for each of the following. Round your answers to the nearest whole percent. (Sec. 5, Explor. 2)

a. age 13 to 14 b. age 13 to 15 c. age 12 to 16

Age	Average Allowance
12	$9.58
13	$9.52
14	$13.47
15	$15.57
16	$17.84

Reflecting on the Module

29. **Writing** Describe the mathematics you learned in this module. Discuss how you can use what you learned to be a better shopper.

MODULE 3

The Mystery of Blacktail Canyon

CONNECTING
MATHEMATICS & The Theme

Module 3 SECTION OVERVIEW

1 Square Roots and Measurement
As you learn about Anasazi ruins:
- Find and estimate square roots
- Describe patterns related to length, area, and volume

2 Equations and Graphs
As you investigate a car accident:
- Evaluate expressions with square roots and fraction bars
- Graph equations

3 Slope and Equations
As you search for a missing driver:
- Find the slope of a line
- Use an equation to make a prediction

4 Similar Figures and Constructions
As you estimate a cliff's height:
- Tell whether triangles are similar and make indirect measurements
- Find a perpendicular bisector of a chord

5 Scientific Notation and Decimal Equations
As you learn about carbon dating:
- Write very large numbers in scientific notation
- Solve equations involving decimals

6 Logical Thinking
As you solve the mystery:
- Use Venn diagrams to interpret statements with *and, or,* and *not*.

INTERNET
Resources and practice at
classzone.com

The Module Project: Solving a Mystery

Do you like a good mystery story? You will read *The Mystery of Blacktail Canyon* and learn to use mathematics to solve mysteries. Then you will gather clues to identify a thief and write the conclusion to the mystery.

More on the Module Project
See pp. 222–225.

Section 1 Square Roots and Measurement

In This Section

Exploration 1
- Finding Square Roots

Exploration 2
- Length, Area, and Volume

Ancient Sites of Mystery

Setting the Stage

In *The Mystery of Blacktail Canyon*, a crime is committed. In this module you will read the story and solve the mystery. With the help of story characters who use their mathematical knowledge to solve mysteries, you will collect evidence that will help you identify the criminal who has damaged an ancient site in Blacktail Canyon. Along the way, you will learn about the people who developed a culture in the North American desert.

The story takes place in the Four Corners region of the United States. Four Corners includes parts of Utah, Arizona, Colorado, and New Mexico.

Jim Cooper, one of the main characters, is an eighth grade student in Escavada, New Mexico. He is fascinated with mysteries, both ancient and modern. His new friend Nageela Ashilaka lives in Kenya, but travels everywhere with her father, Dr. B. B. Ashilaka, an expert on prehistoric dwellings. In spite of being confined to a wheelchair due to a disabling fall, Dr. Ashilaka continues his research with the help of his daughter.

◀ For centuries the Four Corners was inhabited by the *Anasazi* or *Ancestral Puebloans*. They often lived in villages, like Cliff Palace in Mesa Verde National Park in Colorado.

MAP OF BALCONY HOUSE

A Cliff Dwelling in Mesa Verde National Park, Colorado

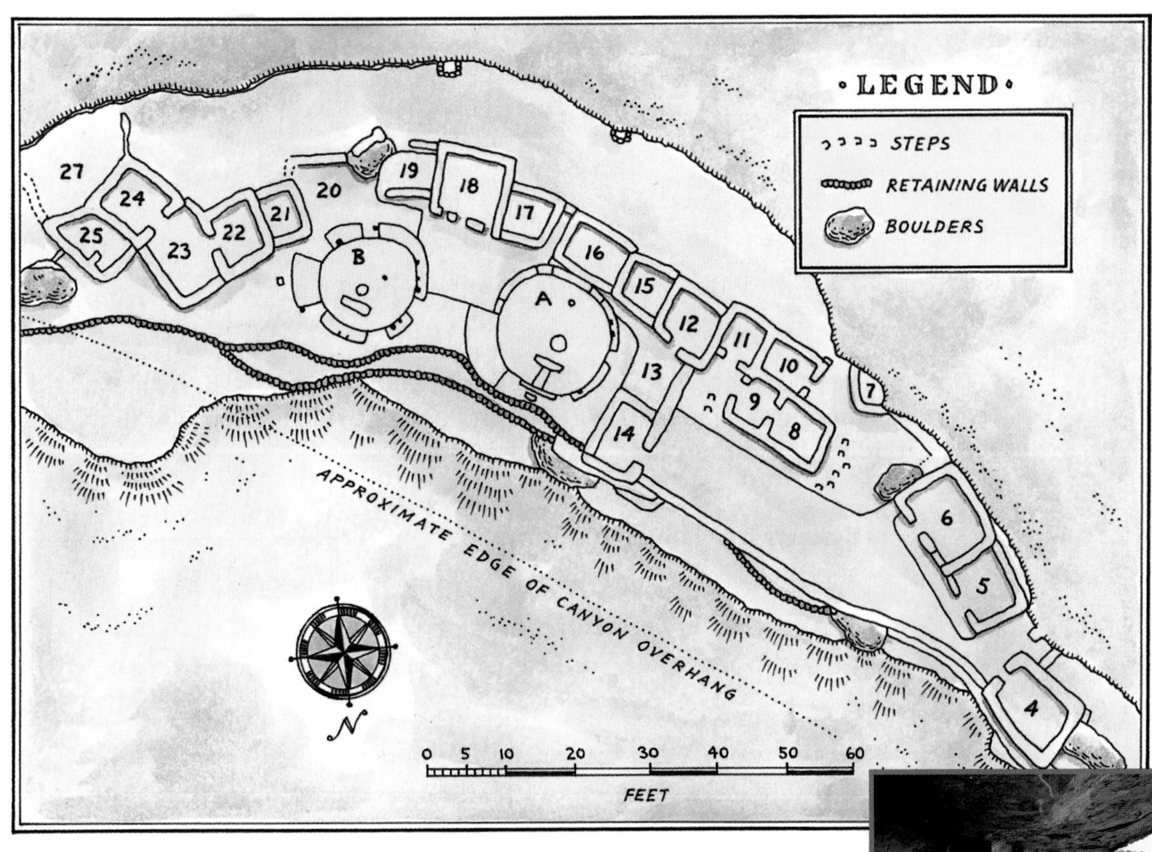

Think About It

Use the Map of Balcony House for Questions 1 and 2.

1 **a.** Copy the map scale onto the edge of a piece of paper.

b. Place your copy of the map scale on the map and use it to estimate the distance from the entrance of Room 4 to the northern-most corner of Room 25.

c. About how long would it take you to walk from Room 4 to Room 25?

2 **a.** What is the approximate shape of Room 24?

b. Estimate the area of Room 24. How does the area compare with the area of your classroom?

▲ Anasazi people began building Balcony House in the early 1200s. They lived there for less than 100 years.

GOAL

LEARN HOW TO...
- find and estimate square roots

AS YOU...
- find dimensions of a room at an archaeological site

KEY TERMS
- square root
- principal square root
- perfect square

Exploration 1

Finding $\sqrt{\text{Square Roots}}$

SET UP *Work with a partner. You will need a calculator.*

▶ **In *The Mystery of Blacktail Canyon*, archaeologist Dr. B. B. Ashilaka and his daughter, Nageela, are studying ancient ruins. Their work involves finding the dimensions of archaeological sites.**

3 Discussion The sketch shows a room at a site.

a. What is the approximate shape of the room?

b. Estimate the length of one side of the room. How did you make your estimate?

c. Let s = the length of one side of the room. Write an equation relating the area A of the room to s.

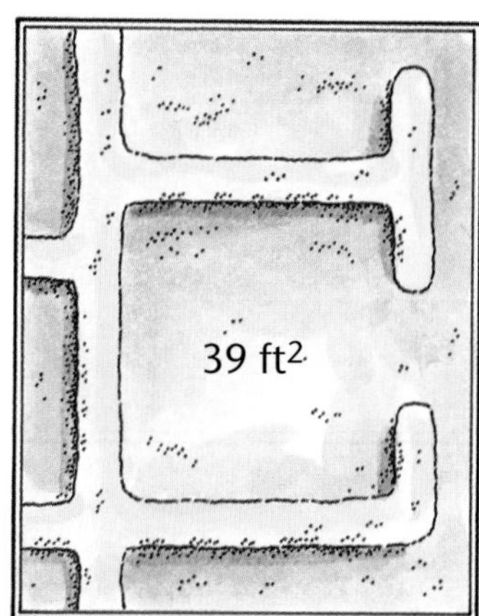

$A = s \cdot s$

$A = s^2$

s

s

▶ **The area of a square can be found by multiplying the length of one of the sides by itself, or by squaring the length of a side. The equation $A = s^2$ can also be used to find s, the length of a side of a square with area A.**

EXAMPLE

If a side of a square is 4 cm long, then $A = 4^2$, or 16. The area is 16 cm^2.

If the area of a square is 25 cm^2, then $s^2 = 25$, so $s = 5$. The length of a side is 5 cm.

4 In the Example on the previous page, the number 5 is a solution of the equation $s^2 = 25$ and is a *square root* of 25. What is another square root of 25?

▶ **If $A = s^2$, then s is a square root of A. Since $4^2 = 16$ and $(-4)^2 = 16$, both 4 and −4 are square roots of 16. The positive solution of $s^2 = 16$ is the principal square root of 16 and is indicated by $\sqrt{16}$.**

$\sqrt{16} = 4$ **The principal square root of 16 is 4.**

The same symbol with a negative sign, $-\sqrt{16}$, indicates the negative square root.

$-\sqrt{16} = -4$ **The negative square root of 16 is −4.**

5 Use mental math to find each value.

a. $\sqrt{81}$ **b.** $\sqrt{49}$ **c.** $\sqrt{1}$

d. $-\sqrt{9}$ **e.** $-\sqrt{64}$ **f.** $-\sqrt{144}$

▶ **The numbers 1, 4, 9, 16, and 25 are *perfect squares*. A perfect square is a number whose principal square root is a whole number.**

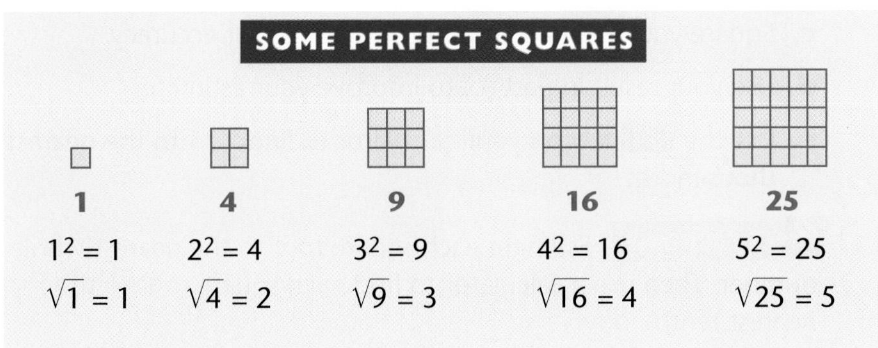

SOME PERFECT SQUARES

1	4	9	16	25
$1^2 = 1$	$2^2 = 4$	$3^2 = 9$	$4^2 = 16$	$5^2 = 25$
$\sqrt{1} = 1$	$\sqrt{4} = 2$	$\sqrt{9} = 3$	$\sqrt{16} = 4$	$\sqrt{25} = 5$

6 List the next five perfect squares after 25. Then list some numbers that are not perfect squares.

▶ **Estimating Square Roots** **In Question 3 you estimated $\sqrt{39}$. There are many situations in which you may need to estimate square roots.**

7 Calculator Use the $\sqrt{\ }$ key to approximate $\sqrt{39}$. Compare this approximation with your estimate from Question 3.

8 Try this as a Class

a. Follow these steps to make a table.

Step 1 List the first 25 **consecutive whole numbers** in the first column.

Step 2 Find and record the **principal square root** of each perfect square.

Step 3 Use a calculator to approximate the **principal square roots** of the other numbers.

n	$\sqrt{n}$
1	1
2	1.41
3	1.73
4	2
5	?
6	?
7	?
8	?

b. Look at the whole numbers between 4 and 9. Compare their square roots with $\sqrt{4}$ and $\sqrt{9}$.

c. Make some predictions about the square roots of the whole numbers between 25 and 36. Check your predictions.

9 **a.** Since 45 is not a perfect square, its principal square root is not a whole number. Is $\sqrt{45}$ closer to 6 or to 7? Explain how you know using the fact that $(6.5)^2 = 42.25$.

b. Estimate $\sqrt{45}$ to the nearest tenth. Do not use your calculator.

c. Square your estimate in part (b) to check for accuracy.

d. Use your result in part (c) to improve your estimate.

e. Use the [√] key on your calculator to find $\sqrt{45}$ to the nearest thousandth.

✔ QUESTION 10

...checks that you can estimate square roots.

10 **✔ CHECKPOINT** Estimate each square root to the nearest whole number. Then use a calculator to find each square root to the nearest tenth.

a. $\sqrt{55}$ **b.** $\sqrt{37}$ **c.** $\sqrt{62}$ **d.** $\sqrt{103}$

HOMEWORK EXERCISES ▶ See Exs. 1–23 on pp. 164–165.

Exploration 2

Length, AREA, and Volume

SET UP *Work with a partner. You will need 30 centimeter cubes.*

GOAL

LEARN HOW TO...
- describe patterns related to length, area, and volume

AS YOU...
- compare dimensions of rooms at an archaeological site

The Story So Far . . .

▶ **Dr. Ashilaka and his group of amateur archaeologists take a field trip to Blacktail Canyon. While there, a sudden cloudburst forces everyone into the ruins of one of the dwellings. Jim asks about the size of a smaller room behind the room they are in, and Dr. Ashilaka asks him to estimate the size of the larger and smaller rooms.**

"I know that my height and my arm span are about 5 feet. The big room is about twice my reach across the floor in both directions, and about twice my height. So, I guess it's about 10 by 10 by 10 feet. I can barely stand up in the center of the small room, and can just touch two walls. It must be about 5 by 5 by 5 feet." Jim looked puzzled. "I guess the big room is twice the size of the small one. But the funny thing is, it seems so much larger."

Dr. Ashilaka laughed and called Jim over. Nageela groaned and shook her head. She knew what was coming. She had heard the length, area, and volume lecture many times before.

11 **a.** Describe the shape of each room in the story.

b. Why does Jim say the big room is twice the size of the smaller room? Do you agree? Explain.

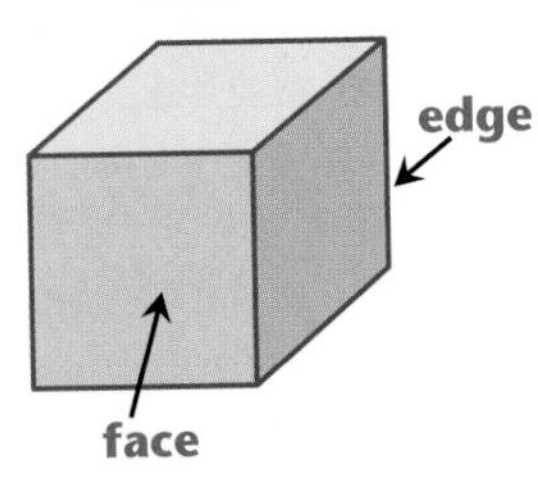

▶ **Jim made a very rough estimate of the sizes of the rooms. You can use cubes to learn more about how the sizes of the rooms compare.**

12 Build cubes with edges whose lengths are twice and three times those of a centimeter cube. Copy and complete the table.

Cube Measurements			
Length of an edge	1 cm	2 cm	3 cm
Perimeter of a face	4 cm	?	?
Area of a face	1 cm^2	?	?
Volume of the cube	1 cm^3	?	?

13 Let s = the length of an edge of a cube. Write expressions for the perimeter of a face, the area of a face, and the volume of the cube.

▶ **When you compare objects of different sizes, you need to know whether you are comparing lengths, areas, or volumes.**

14 **Try This as a Class** Study your answers in Question 12. Look for patterns for how the length, the area, and the volume of the cubes are related.

a. What is the *perimeter of a face* of a cube multiplied by when the length of an edge is multiplied by 2? by 3?

b. What is the *perimeter of a face* of a cube multiplied by if the length of an edge is multiplied by 4? by 5? by 10? by n?

c. Repeat parts (a) and (b) for the *area of a face*. What patterns do you notice?

d. Repeat parts (a) and (b) for the *volume of the cube*. What patterns do you notice?

15 Without building a cube, predict the area of a single face and the volume of a cube whose dimensions are fourteen times those of a centimeter cube.

...checks that you understand length, area, and volume relationships.

16 ✓ **CHECKPOINT** Jim Cooper made good estimates of the length, width, and height of each room, but he jumped to the wrong conclusion when comparing the volumes of the rooms. Explain Jim's mistake in the story on page 161. Use mathematics to support your answer.

HOMEWORK EXERCISES ▶ **See Exs. 24–29 on pp. 165–166.**

Section 1 Key Concepts

Key Terms

Squares and Square Roots (pp. 158–159)

Suppose $s^2 = n$. Then s is a square root of n. Every positive number has both a positive and a negative square root. The principal square root, indicated by $\sqrt{\ }$, is the positive square root.

square root

principal square root

perfect square

Example $5^2 = 25$ and $(-5)^2 = 25$, so both 5 and –5 are square roots of 25. The principal square root of 25 is written $\sqrt{25}$, or 5. 25 is a perfect square since $\sqrt{25}$ is a whole number.

Estimating Square Roots (pp. 159–160)

You can use various methods to estimate a square root.

Example

Method 1 Use a calculator: $\sqrt{5} \approx 2.24$.

Method 2 Estimate between two integers by looking for the closest perfect squares less than and greater than a number:
$\sqrt{4} < \sqrt{5} < \sqrt{9}$, so $2 < \sqrt{5} < 3$.
Note that $(2.5)^2 = 6.25$ and $5 < 6.25$. So, $\sqrt{5} < 2.5$ and $\sqrt{5}$ is closer to 2 than to 3.

Changing Dimensions (pp. 161–162)

When you compare sizes of objects, you need to know whether you are comparing lengths, areas, or volumes.

Example Suppose the length, width, and height of a prism are multiplied by 2 to create a larger prism. The areas of the faces of the larger prism are 2^2 or 4 times those of the smaller prism. The volume of the larger prism is 2^3 or 8 times the volume of the smaller prism.

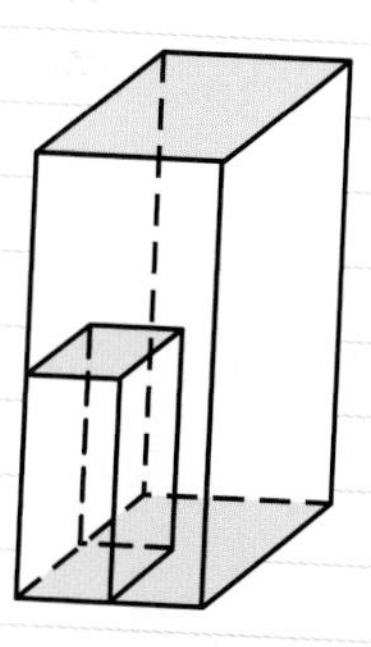

17 Key Concepts Question

a. Find the side length of a square whose area is 289 cm^2.

b. Suppose each side of the square in part (a) is multiplied by 5. What is the effect on the area of the square?

Section 1

Practice & Application Exercises

Mental Math **Use mental math to find each value.**

1. $\sqrt{100}$
2. $-\sqrt{144}$
3. $\sqrt{3600}$
4. $\sqrt{0.49}$
5. $\sqrt{\frac{16}{100}}$
6. $-\sqrt{9{,}000{,}000}$

7. The dimensions of a typical sheet of notebook paper are $8\frac{1}{2}$ in. by 11 in.
   a. What is the area of the paper?
   b. Suppose a square piece of paper has the same area. Estimate the dimensions of the square piece of paper to the nearest $\frac{1}{2}$ in.

8. **Estimation** Use the sketch of a floor plan.
   a. Estimate the width of the bathroom.
   b. Estimate the perimeter of the living room.
   c. Estimate the area of the kitchen.

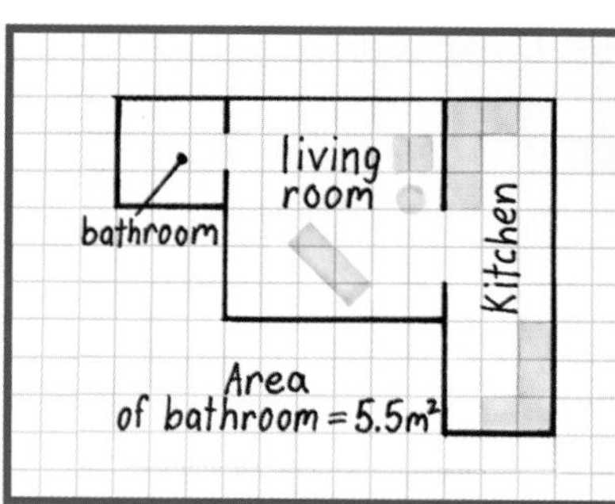

Estimation **Estimate each square root to the nearest tenth.**

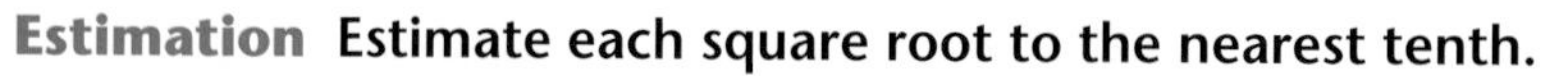

9. $\sqrt{39}$
10. $\sqrt{55}$
11. $\sqrt{12}$
12. $\sqrt{125}$

Copernicus, the crater nearest to the center in the photo, is an impact crater believed to be less than 1 billion years old.

13. **Challenge** The lunar crater Copernicus covers a circular area of about 6793 km^2. Estimate the diameter of the crater.

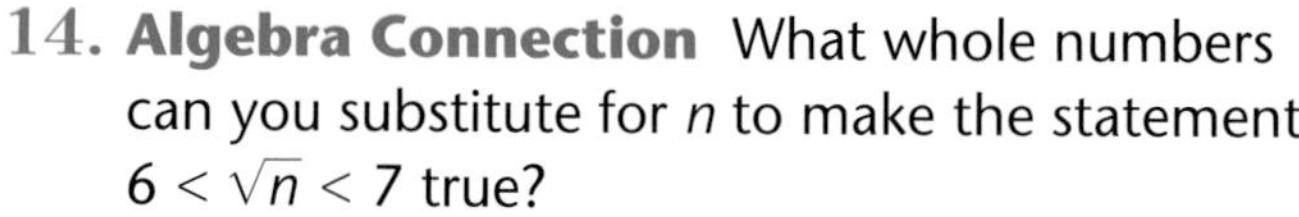

14. **Algebra Connection** What whole numbers can you substitute for *n* to make the statement $6 < \sqrt{n} < 7$ true?

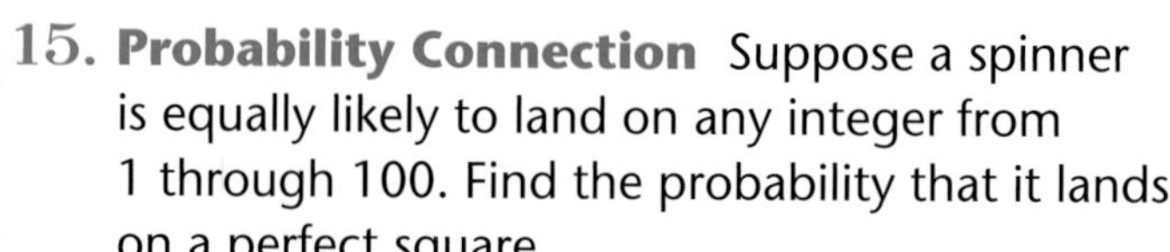

15. **Probability Connection** Suppose a spinner is equally likely to land on any integer from 1 through 100. Find the probability that it lands on a perfect square.

16. Rae says that every positive number is greater than or equal to its square root. Find examples to support her statement. Can you find a counterexample?

Choosing a Method **Find each value. Tell whether your answer is exact or an estimate.**

17. $-\sqrt{810,000}$
18. $\sqrt{810}$
19. $-\sqrt{33}$
20. $\sqrt{0.25}$
21. $\sqrt{1000}$
22. $\sqrt{0.0064}$

23. **Estimation** The area of a square plot of land is about 9500 yd^2. Estimate the length of a side and the perimeter of the plot of land.

24. **Writing** A homeowner figures that the cost of carpet for the walk-in closet will be one-third the cost of carpet for the bedroom. The carpet chosen is sold by the square foot. Do you agree with the homeowner? Explain.

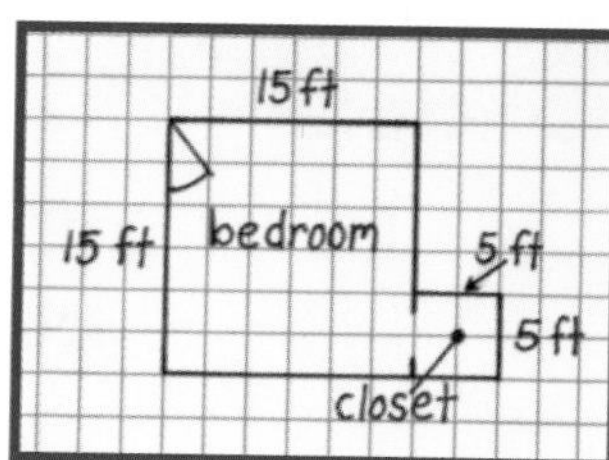

Air Conditioning **For Exercises 25–27, use the ad below.**

25. **Algebra Connection** Write an equation that you can use to estimate how much cooling capacity is needed for a room with a given floor area.

26. A room in Bob Lang's house is 10 ft x 15 ft. Another room is 20 ft x 30 ft. Bob estimates that he needs an air conditioner with twice as much cooling capacity for the larger room as for the smaller room.

 a. Sketch each room. Label the dimensions. Then find the cooling capacity needed for each room.

 b. Do you think Bob is correct? Explain.

27. One room in Maria Franco's house is 18 ft x 12 ft. Another room is 18 ft x 24 ft. Maria estimates that she needs an air conditioner with twice as much cooling capacity for the larger room as for the smaller room.

 a. Sketch each room. Label the dimensions.

 b. Do you think Maria is correct? Explain.

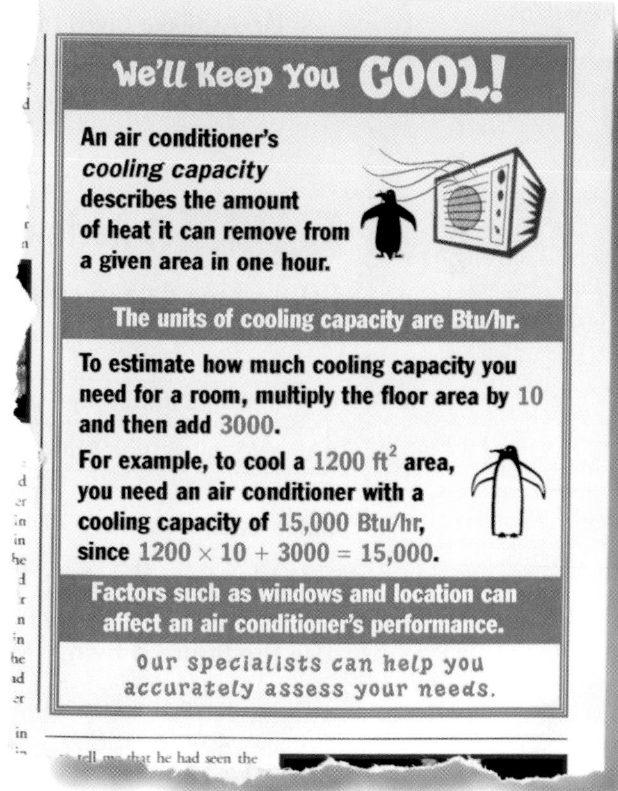

28. **Challenge** A company makes and sells small and large boxes. The same materials are used to make each size.

THIS END UP
10 in.
13 in.
12 in.

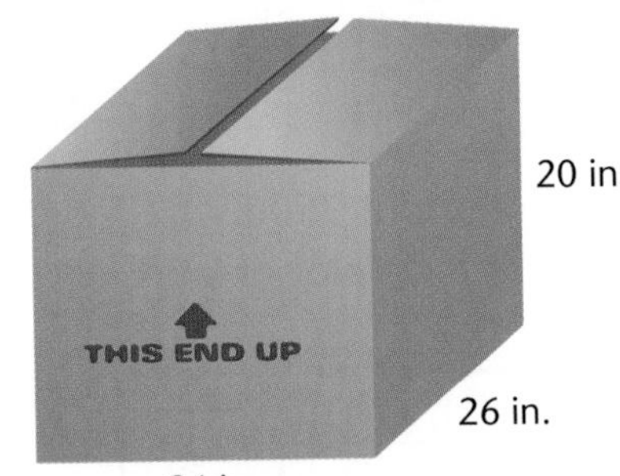

a. Compare the amount of cardboard needed to make each box. About how many times as much cardboard is needed for the large box?

b. The volume of the large box is about how many times the volume of the small box?

c. **Writing** The company plans to charge \$1.50 for a small box. How much do you think the company should charge for a large box?

Oral Report

Exercise 29 checks that you can compare length, area, and volume relationships.

Reflecting on the Section

Be prepared to report on the following topic in class.

29. In *The Mystery of Blacktail Canyon*, Dr. Ashilaka asks Jim to estimate the size of two rooms in a dwelling. When Jim is done, Dr. Ashilaka gives him a lecture about the relationships among length, area, and volume. Pretend you are Dr. Ashilaka and write what you would say to Jim. Then present your lecture to the class.

Spiral Review

30. Use the data to create a box-and-whisker plot. Identify any outliers. **(Module 1, p. 23)**

Amounts Raised by Students at a Charity Dance Marathon (dollars)
55, 60, 65, 70, 80, 80, 80, 90, 100, 110, 115, 150, 170, 175, 175, 450

Solve each equation. **(Module 2, p. 86)**

31. $|x| = 4$ 32. $|n| = 11$ 33. $-y = 19$ 34. $-r = -6$

Use the figure shown. **(Module 2, p. 87)**

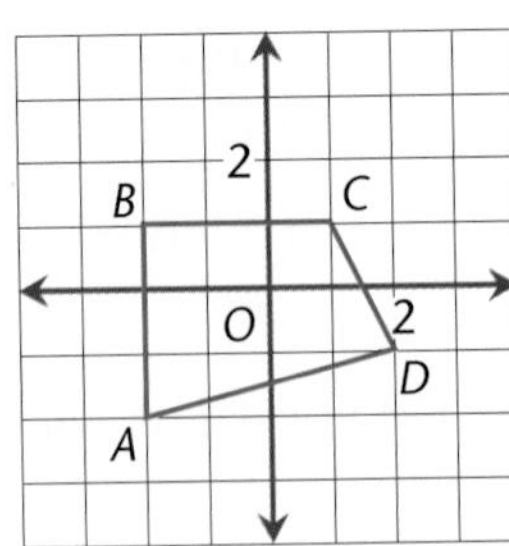

35. a. Give the coordinates of points *A*, *B*, *C*, and *D*.

b. Give the coordinates of the image points *A′*, *B′*, *C′*, and *D′* after a translation of $(x + 2, y)$.

Section 1 Extra Skill Practice

Mental Math Use mental math to find each value.

1. $\sqrt{490,000}$
2. $-\sqrt{16}$
3. $\sqrt{\frac{1}{100}}$
4. $\sqrt{0.01}$
5. $\sqrt{0.0036}$
6. $-\sqrt{2500}$
7. $\sqrt{0.0004}$
8. $\sqrt{\frac{4}{25}}$

Estimation Estimate each square root to the nearest tenth.

9. $\sqrt{50}$
10. $\sqrt{22}$
11. $\sqrt{136}$
12. $\sqrt{67}$
13. $\sqrt{43}$
14. $\sqrt{94}$
15. $\sqrt{32}$
16. $\sqrt{85}$

Choosing a Method Find each square root. Tell whether your answer is exact or an estimate.

17. $\sqrt{28.4}$
18. $-\sqrt{63}$
19. $\sqrt{6.25}$
20. $-\sqrt{9000}$
21. $\sqrt{4.81}$
22. $\sqrt{\frac{1}{36}}$
23. $\sqrt{0.64}$
24. $\sqrt{0.064}$
25. The volume of a cube is 64 cm^3. What will be its volume if its edge length is halved?

Study Skills ▸ Preparing for Assessment

Planning ahead is important when you prepare for a test. Try to study every day instead of waiting until the night before a test. Also, be sure to practice what you have learned. Some people find it helpful to make review cards for important ideas, rules, and formulas.

Suppose you have 3 days to prepare for a test on this section.

1. Make a list of the important ideas in the section.
2. Develop a plan for dividing up the section so that you can study part of it each day.
3. Write and solve some practice problems for the topics you plan to study each day.
4. Make review cards of important ideas, rules, and formulas in the section.

Section 2 Equations and Graphs

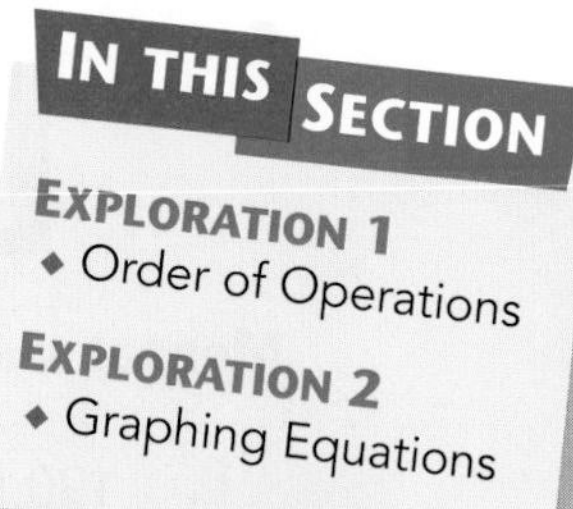

On the Road

Setting the Stage

SET UP *You will need Labsheet 2A.*

The Story So Far...

On the drive back from Blacktail Canyon, Jim and Nageela find Highway Patrol Officer Ferrel Yellow Robe investigating a single-car accident. The officer explains how he knows that the missing driver of the car was going too fast on the wet curve.

"When I investigate an accident, I check the road conditions, the length of the skid, and the condition of the tire tread. There's a chart that we use to figure the speed the car was going when the driver hit the brakes, or we can plug the numbers into a formula. Just routine."

To estimate the car's speed, Ferrel needs to know the distance the car skidded and a number called the *coefficient of friction*. This number is a measure of the friction between the car's tires and the road surface.

Think About It

1 *Friction* is the force that resists the motion of objects in contact with each other. Try pushing a notebook quickly, then slowly, across two different surfaces, such as carpet and wood. Describe the amount of friction present in each instance.

2 Suppose you ride a bike across dirt, ice, dry asphalt, and wet asphalt. Which surface do you think is the least safe? the safest?

▶ **Use Labsheet 2A for Questions 3–6. In the story on page 168, Officer Yellow Robe mentions a chart. This chart is called a *Nomogram*.**

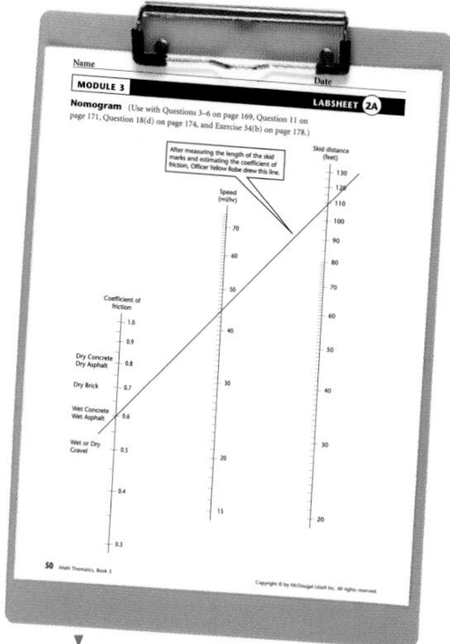

3 Officer Yellow Robe measures the skid distance and estimates the coefficient of friction at the crash site. He then uses the data to draw a line as shown on the labsheet.

a. Describe the road conditions. What is the coefficient of friction?

b. How long were the skid marks?

c. Estimate the car's speed when the driver hit the brakes.

4 An officer measures 45 ft skid marks on wet asphalt at a crash site. Use the *Nomogram* to estimate the car's speed.

5 A driver is traveling at 35 mi/hr on dry asphalt. Estimate how far the car will skid if the driver hits the brakes.

6 Can two cars traveling at the same speed leave different skid mark lengths? Explain.

Exploration 1

Order of Operations

GOAL

LEARN HOW TO...
- evaluate expressions with square roots and fraction bars

AS YOU...
- estimate speeds of cars involved in accidents

SET UP *You will need: • Labsheet 2A • calculator*

Nomograms are only one way to estimate speed from skid marks. Most of the time, accident investigators use two formulas to find the speed.

The formula shown at the right is used first to find a coefficient of friction for the road where the accident happened. An officer drives a patrol car at a certain speed and then hits the brakes to find a skid distance.

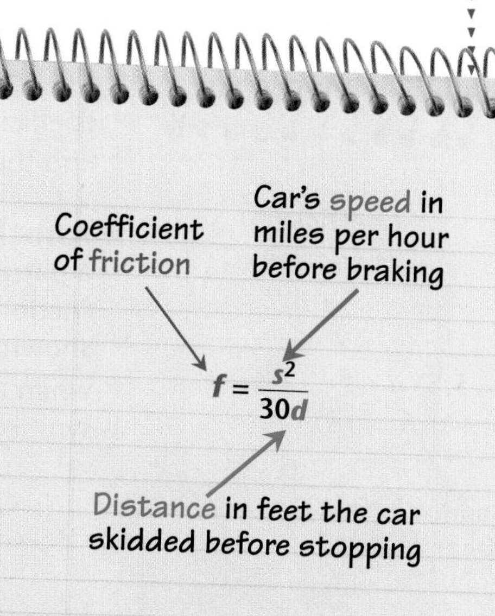

FOR ▶ HELP with *the order of operations*, see **TOOLBOX, p. 589**

EXAMPLE

Officer Patricia Hayes conducts a skid test at an accident site. She uses the formula $f = \frac{s^2}{30d}$ to find the coefficient of friction.

REPORTING OFFICER	LOCATION OF ACCIDENT
Hayes, Patricia	Mile 6, Adobe Road

DATE OF ACCIDENT			TIME OF ACCIDENT		AM	PM
Mo	Day	Yr	Hour	Min.		
05	19	07	3	41	☐	☒

Result of Skid Test

Speed before brakes were applied: 32 mi/hr

Skid distance: 50 ft

$f = \frac{s^2}{30d}$

$f = \frac{32^2}{30 \cdot 50}$

$f = \frac{1024}{1500} \approx 0.68$

The fraction bar is a grouping symbol. You may need to simplify the numerator and denominator before dividing.

The coefficient of friction is about 0.68.

▶ **For Questions 7 and 8, use the Example above.**

7 **Try This as a Class** Explain each step of Officer Hayes's work. How did she use the order of operations?

✓ QUESTION 8

...checks that you understand how to evaluate an expression with a fraction bar.

8 **✓ CHECKPOINT** To make sure her results are accurate, Officer Hayes conducts two skid tests. She finds the coefficient of friction for each test, and then finds an average.

a. In her second skid test, Officer Hayes's speed is 34 mi/hr and her skid distance is 60 ft. Find the coefficient of friction.

b. Use your answer to part (a) and the coefficient of friction from the Example to find the mean coefficient of friction.

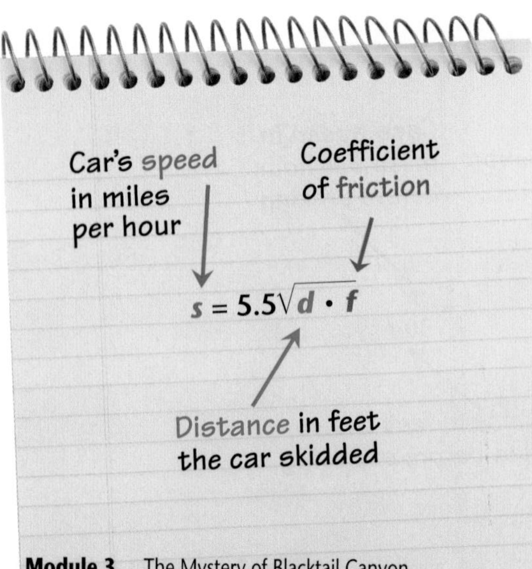

▶ **Another Grouping Symbol When a patrol officer knows the coefficient of friction, he or she can use the formula shown at the left to estimate a car's speed when the brakes were applied. The $\sqrt{\ }$ symbol in the formula is a grouping symbol.**

EXAMPLE

A car skids 49 ft in an accident. The investigating officer finds that the coefficient of friction is 0.75. Estimate the car's speed.

SAMPLE RESPONSE

Evaluate the formula $s = 5.5\sqrt{d \cdot f}$ for $d = 49$ and $f = 0.75$.

$s = 5.5\sqrt{49(0.75)}$

Perform the operations under the $\sqrt{\ }$ symbol first.

$s = 5.5\sqrt{36.75}$

Then find the square root of 36.75.

$s \approx 5.5(6.06)$

$s \approx 33$ mi/hr

The car's speed was approximately 33 mi/hr.

9 ✓ **CHECKPOINT** Find each value.

a. $1.65\sqrt{32 \cdot 2}$ b. $\dfrac{5-13}{2^3}$ c. $\dfrac{3-21}{-2(3)}$

d. $\sqrt{\dfrac{19+8}{3}}$ e. $12\sqrt{\dfrac{12}{56-8}}$ f. $8 + 2\sqrt{9 \cdot 4}$

QUESTION 9

...checks that you can find the value of an expression with grouping symbols.

10 Calculator You can use a calculator to simplify expressions with grouping symbols. For example, one way to simplify $5.5\sqrt{49(0.75)}$ is to enter a key sequence that uses parentheses to group operations under the $\sqrt{\ }$ symbol:

 49  0.75    5.5 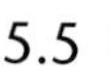

Does this key sequence work on your calculator? If not, describe another key sequence you could use.

11 **Use Labsheet 2A.** Suppose a car leaves 60 ft skid marks on dry gravel in a 30 mi/hr speed zone. Use the *Nomogram* and then the formula $s = 5.5\sqrt{d \cdot f}$ to estimate the car's speed. How do your answers compare? Was the driver speeding?

HOMEWORK EXERCISES See Exs. 1–20 on pp. 176–177.

GOAL

LEARN HOW TO...
- graph equations

AS YOU...
- investigate highway safety issues

KEY TERMS
- solution of the equation
- linear
- nonlinear

Exploration 2

SET UP *You will need: • Labsheet 2A • graph paper • graphing calculator (optional)*

▶ **To prevent highway collisions, it is important to leave enough "following distance" between your car and the car ahead of you. The table models a relationship between speed and recommended following distance that drivers have used for years. Some new guidelines call for even greater following distances.**

Use the table for Questions 12–14. You will use an equation and a graph to model the relationship between a car's speed and the recommended following distance.

Recommended Following Distances	
Speed of a car (mi/hr)	Following distance (ft)
10	15
20	30
30	45
40	60
50	75

12 **a.** Use the table to complete this equation:

Following distance = ? • speed

b. Follow these steps to graph the equation from part (a).

First Make a coordinate grid. You want to show how following distance depends on speed, so put following distance on the vertical axis. In general, when one quantity depends on another, put the dependent quantity on the vertical axis.

Next Write the data in the table as ordered pairs: (Speed, Following distance).

Then Plot the ordered pairs. Draw a smooth curve through the points or connect the points in order with segments.

c. A driver is traveling at 45 mi/hr. Use your graph and the equation to recommend a following distance to the driver.

d. Which model in part (c) did you find easier to use?

e. Which model gave the more accurate answer?

FOR ◀ HELP with *choosing a scale*, see **MODULE 1, p. 51**

13 Let s = the speed of a car in miles per hour. Let d = the recommended following distance in feet. Model the relationship in Question 12(a) with an equation using the variables s and d.

14 **Discussion** Some drivers estimate the distance between their car and the one ahead using a car length as a benchmark. At 50 mi/hr, how many car lengths would you recommend as a minimum following distance between two cars? Explain your thinking.

1 car length ≈ 15 ft

Your Car

Car in Front

▶ **The equation you wrote in Question 13 has two variables. An ordered pair of numbers that makes an equation with two variables true is a solution of the equation. The graph of an equation includes all possible solutions of the equation.**

EXAMPLE

Follow these steps to graph the equation $y = 2x + 1$.

First Make a table of values. Include several values so you can see the pattern in the points you plot. Include both positive and negative values of x.

x	y	(x, y)
–2	–3	(–2, –3)
–1	–1	(–1, –1)
0	1	(0, 1)
1	3	(1, 3)
2	5	(2, 5)

Then Plot the ordered pairs on a coordinate grid. Draw a curve or a line to show the pattern. Use arrowheads to show that the graph extends.

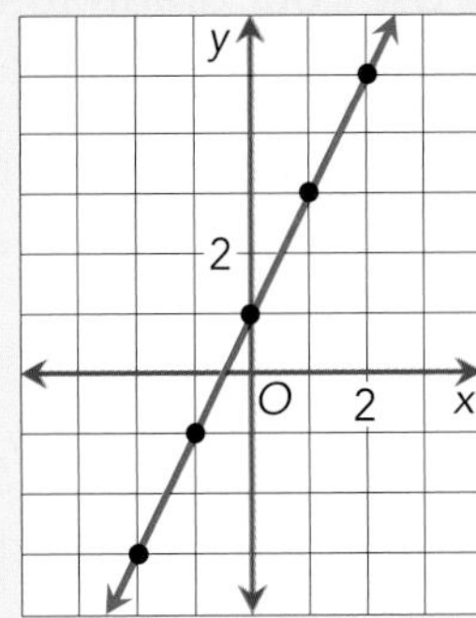

15 **Try This as a Class** Tell whether each ordered pair is a solution of the equation in the Example. Explain your thinking.

a. (–5, –9) **b.** (–4, 9) **c.** (3, 1) **d.** (9, 19)

✓ QUESTION 16

...checks that you can graph an equation.

16 ✓ CHECKPOINT Graph each equation.

a. $y = x$ **b.** $y = x - 4$ **c.** $y = -2x$

▶ **Linear and Nonlinear Graphs** **When the graph of an equation is a straight line, the graph and the equation are linear. Now you will look at a relationship whose graph is nonlinear.**

17 Copy and complete the table. Use the formula $s = 5.5\sqrt{d \cdot f}$ from page 170. (The coefficient of friction for dry concrete is 0.81.) Round all values to the nearest unit.

Skid Distance on a Dry, Concrete Road

Skid distance d (ft)	Speed s (mi/hr)	(d, s)
1	5	(1, 5)
7	13	(7, 13)
33	28	(33, 28)
57	37	(57, 37)
95	?	?
129	?	?
154	?	?

18 **a.** Plot all the points in the table on a coordinate grid. Then draw a smooth curve through them to graph the equation $s = 5.5\sqrt{d \cdot f}$.

b. Use your graph to estimate the speed of a car that leaves 19 ft skid marks on a road with a coefficient of friction of 0.81.

c. Use your graph to estimate how far a car traveling at 55 mi/hr on a dry, concrete road will skid when the driver slams on the brakes.

d. **Use Labsheet 2A.** Use the *Nomogram* to estimate how far a car traveling at 55 mi/hr on a dry, concrete road will skid. How does this estimate compare with your estimate from part (c)**?**

19 Graphing Calculator Graph each equation. Tell whether the graph is *linear* or *nonlinear*.

a. $y = x + 20$ **b.** $y = \sqrt{x}$ **c.** $y = 1 + \sqrt{x}$

HOMEWORK EXERCISES ▶ **See Exs. 21–34 on pp. 177–178.**

Section 2 Key Concepts

Key Terms

Order of Operations (pp. 169–171)

The order of operations is a set of rules for evaluating an expression so that the expression has only one value.

First Perform all calculations inside grouping symbols. Grouping symbols include parentheses, fraction bars, and square root symbols.

Next Evaluate any powers.

Next Perform multiplications and divisions in order from left to right.

Then Perform additions and subtractions in order from left to right.

Example $2\sqrt{6+3} = 2\sqrt{9} = 2(3) = 6$

Do the addition inside the square root symbol first.

solution of the equation

Graphing Equations (pp. 172–174)

The graph of an equation includes all possible solutions of the equation. Some graphs are linear. Some are nonlinear.

linear

nonlinear

Examples

Linear graph

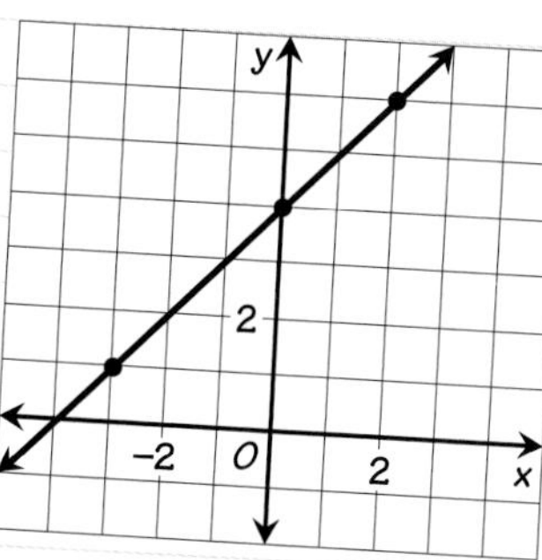

Nonlinear graph

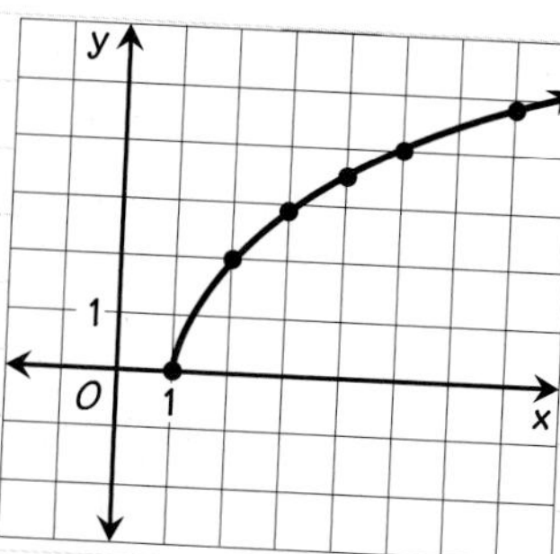

20 **Key Concepts Question** Use the equations graphed in the Examples above. For which equation is (10, 6) a solution? How do you know?

Section 2

Practice & Application Exercises

YOU WILL NEED

For Exs. 22-27 and 33:
- graph paper

For Exs. 30-32:
- graph paper or graphing calculator (optional)

For Ex. 34(b):
- Labsheet 2A

Evaluate each expression. Round decimals to the nearest hundredth.

1. $\frac{3 \cdot 10}{5 - 3}$
2. $\frac{2(8 - 3)}{5}$
3. $\frac{(-3)^2}{8 + 1 - 2(3)}$
4. $9\sqrt{2 \cdot 3}$
5. $-\sqrt{8 \cdot 2} + 7$
6. $\frac{\sqrt{16 - 4}}{6}$

Exercises 7–10 show the incorrect answers a student gave on a quiz. Describe the mistakes the student made.

7. $12 + 6 \div 3 = 6$
8. $3 \cdot 8 - 4 \cdot 5 = 100$
9. $\frac{3 + 5}{5} = 4$
10. $\sqrt{4 + 9} = 5$

Biology **Scientists use the expression below to measure how circular a lake is. The closer the value of the expression is to 1, the more circular the lake. Use the expression for Exercises 11–13.**

L = the length of the shoreline

$$\frac{L}{2\sqrt{\pi A}}$$

A = the surface area of the lake

Crater Lake lies in the "bowl" of an extinct volcano in Oregon.

11. The length of Crater Lake's shoreline is about 26 mi, and its surface area is about 21 mi^2. Evaluate the expression above for Crater Lake.

12. a. Suppose a lake is perfectly circular and has a 2 mi diameter. Evaluate the expression for this lake.

    b. Evaluate the expression for two other perfectly circular lakes. (You choose the diameters.) What pattern do you see?

13. a. Evaluate the expression for the Lake of the Ozarks. The length of its shoreline is about 1350 mi, and its surface area is about 93 mi^2.

    b. You learned about the Lake of the Ozarks on page 63. Would you have expected a value close to 1 for this lake? Explain.

Evaluate each expression when $b = 5$ and $c = -2$. Round decimal answers to the nearest hundredth.

14. $3\sqrt{b + c}$
15. $\frac{8b + 6}{c}$
16. $\frac{c^3}{bc}$
17. $\frac{b^2 + 8c}{9bc}$
18. $\frac{30b}{5 \cdot 3} - c$
19. $\frac{\sqrt{b^2 \cdot 36}}{c^2}$

20. **Challenge** Write a numerical expression that equals 5. Your expression should include a fraction bar, a $\sqrt{\ }$ symbol, and at least three different numerical operations.

21. **History** The article below first appeared in a November 1896 issue of *Scientific American.*

"An immense crowd assembled near the Hotel Metropole, London, November 14, to witness the departure of the motor carriages for their race to Brighton, 47 miles. The occasion of the race was the going into effect of the new law which opens up the highways to the use of the motor carriages. . . . under the old law self-propelled vehicles were not allowed to go faster than six miles an hour and had to be preceded by a horseman waving a red flag. . . . the race was won by the American Duryea motor wagon. The distance was covered in four hours."

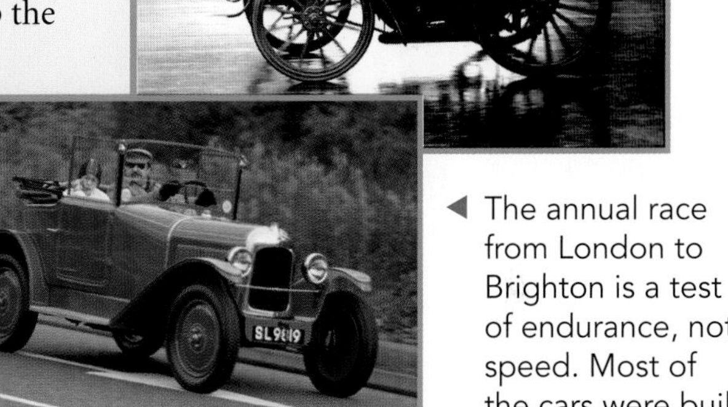

◀ The annual race from London to Brighton is a test of endurance, not speed. Most of the cars were built before 1918.

a. Find the average speed of the winning car. Write an equation for the distance d it could travel in h hours at this speed.

b. According to the article, what was the speed limit before the new law went into effect? Write an equation for the distance d a vehicle could travel in h hours at this speed.

c. Graph the equations from parts (a) and (b) on the same pair of axes. Use the graph to estimate how long it would take to finish the race if you traveled at the old speed limit.

Graph each equation.

22. $y = 2x - 3$

23. $y = -3x$

24. $y = -3x + 2$

25. $y = 4$

26. $y = 90 + x$

27. $y = 100 - x$

28. For which equations in Exercises 22–27 is (5, 95) a solution?

29. For which equation in Exercises 22–27 is (2.5, 4) a solution?

Graphing Calculator **Graph each equation. Tell whether the graph is *linear* or *nonlinear*.**

30. $y = x + \sqrt{5}$

31. $y = 2\sqrt{x}$

32. $y = 0.5x^2$

Radius r (cm)	Volume V (cm^3)
1	?
2	?
3	?
5	?
10	?
20	?

33. Geometry Connection A table, an equation, and a graph can all model the relationship between the radius r of a sphere and the volume V.

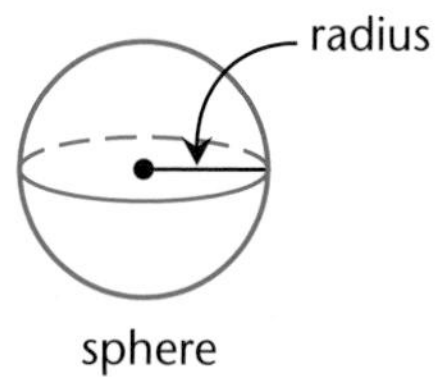

a. Copy and complete the table. Use the formula for the volume of a sphere, $V = \frac{4}{3}\pi r^3$. Round your answers to the nearest whole number.

b. Graph the data in the table. Is the graph *linear* or *nonlinear*?

c. The radius of a tennis ball is about 6.5 cm. Use the graph and the equation to estimate its volume.

Journal

Exercise 34 checks that you can use and interpret formulas and graphs.

Reflecting on the Section

Write your response to Exercise 34 in your journal.

34. In this section, you used both a formula and a nomogram to estimate the speed of a car based on skid mark length. Another formula you can use is $s = 2\sqrt{5d}$. This formula does not include friction as a variable.

Length of skid (ft)	Approximate speed of car (mi/hr)
1	$2\sqrt{5(1)} \approx 4.5$
5	?
15	?
35	?
55	?
75	?
100	?
150	?

a. Copy and complete the table using the formula $s = 2\sqrt{5d}$ to estimate the speed s for each skid length d.

b. **Use Labsheet 2A.** For what road conditions does the formula $s = 2\sqrt{5d}$ give a good estimate of a car's speed?

c. If you want to quickly estimate a car's speed based on skid length, which of the methods would you use? Why?

Spiral Review

Estimate each value. **(Module 3, p. 163)**

35. $\sqrt{8}$ **36.** $\sqrt{11}$ **37.** $\sqrt{15}$ **38.** $\sqrt{0.144}$

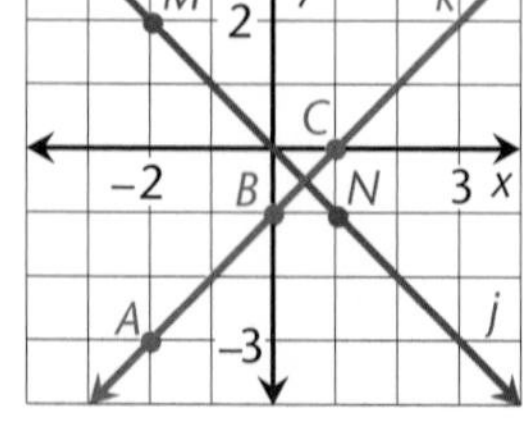

39. Use the coordinate plane shown. List the ordered pairs for the points labeled on line j and line k. **(Module 1, p. 51)**

For each rate, write a unit rate **(Module 1, p. 19)**

40. \$1.69 for 12 oz **41.** 5.2 mi in 18 hr **42.** \$280 for 3.75 hr

Section 2 Extra Skill Practice

You will need: • *graph paper* (Exs. 10–15 and 18–20)

Evaluate each expression. Round decimal answers to the nearest hundredth.

1. $\dfrac{8 \cdot 3}{5 + 9 - 2(4)}$
2. $8 + 6\sqrt{7 \cdot 4}$
3. $\dfrac{\sqrt{13 + 5}}{9}$
4. $(5 + 3)\sqrt{4(12)}$
5. $\dfrac{37 + 2(-5)}{3^3}$
6. $\sqrt{\dfrac{7}{11 - 3}}$

Evaluate each expression for $f = -3$ and $g = 4$. Round decimal answers to the nearest hundredth.

7. $\dfrac{2 - 6f}{g}$
8. $\dfrac{\sqrt{f^2 - 2g}}{g - f}$
9. $\dfrac{8 + g}{-2f}$

Graph each equation.

10. $y = 4x$
11. $y = 2x + 6$
12. $y = -2x + 12$
13. $y = 3x - 8$
14. $y = x - 9$
15. $y = 0.5x + 2$
16. For which equations in Exercises 10–15 is (7, –2) a solution?
17. For which equations in Exercises 10–15 is (4, 4) a solution?

Graph each equation. Tell whether the graph is *linear* or *nonlinear*.

18. $y = \sqrt{4x}$
19. $y = x^3 - 1$
20. $y = 1.5x + 2.5$

Standardized Testing ▶ Multiple Choice

1. Evaluate $\dfrac{\sqrt{7 + 2 \cdot 3^2}}{3 + 6 \div 3}$.

   A 1　　B 3　　C 9　　D 2.6

2. Which point lies on the graph of $y = 3x - 2$?

   A (0, 2)　　B (5, 17)　　C (6, 16)　　D (4, 2)

3. Which ordered pair is *not* a solution of $y = 3 - 8x$?

   A (0, 3)　　B (3, 21)　　C (–1, 11)　　D (–3, 27)

Section 3 Slope and Equations

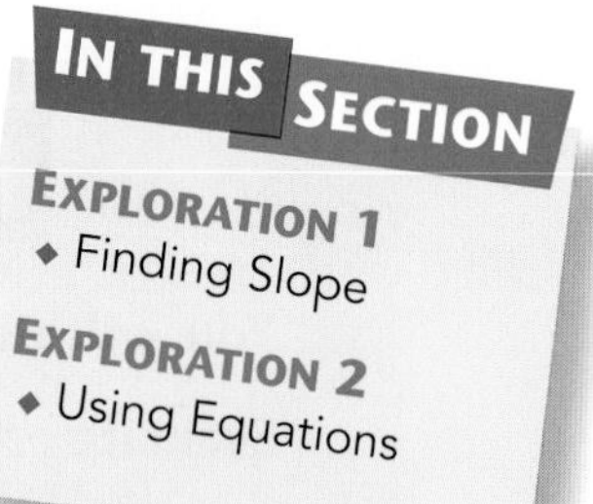

BIG foot

Setting the Stage

The Story So Far...

Jim, Nageela, and Officers Ferrel Yellow Robe and Charlotte Lopez search for the missing driver of an abandoned car. When Jim finds some footprints, the officers think they can make some deductions about the person who left them.

"Do you think these are the driver's footprints?" Nageela asked.

"They must be," said Ferrel. "Otherwise, the rain would have washed them away. Now we can tell how tall the driver is."

"How will you do that?" asked Jim. "All I can tell is which way the tracks are going."

"It's all right here in the sand," said Charlotte. "All you have to do is look. By the looks of the stride, this person could cover quite a bit of ground if he or she was in a hurry. If he got to the top of the canyon, he'd be back to the main road easily by now."

Think About It

1 How do you think a person's height can be determined by examining his or her footprints?

2 What can you tell about the person who made the footprints in the photo on this page? Explain your thinking.

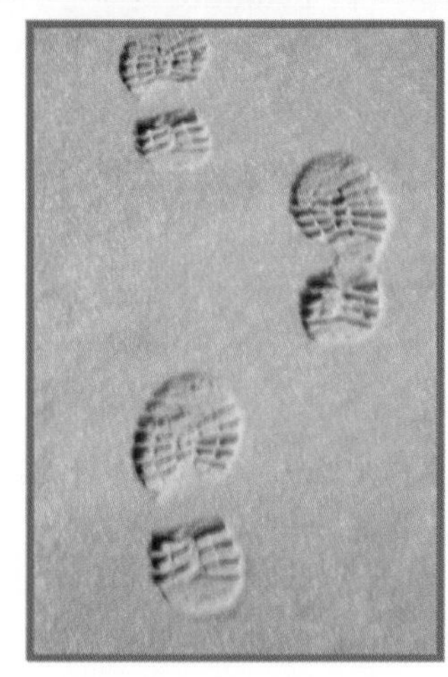

Exploration 1

Finding Slope

Set Up *Work with a partner.*

GOAL

Learn how to...
- find the slope of a line
- use equations and graphs to model situations

As you...
- compare walking rates

Key Terms
- slope
- rise
- run

▶ **In this exploration, you will use graphs to explore rates. The mathematics you will learn will help you find the height of the missing driver in Exploration 2.**

3 Look back at the story on page 180. What does Charlotte mean by the word *stride*? How does your stride affect the distance you can cover in a given amount of time?

4 **Discussion** The red and blue lines on the coordinate plane below show distances two different people can walk over time. You and your partner should each choose one of the lines.

a. Work on your own. Choose four different travel times. For each time, find the distance traveled and calculate the walking rate. Record your results in a table like the one shown.

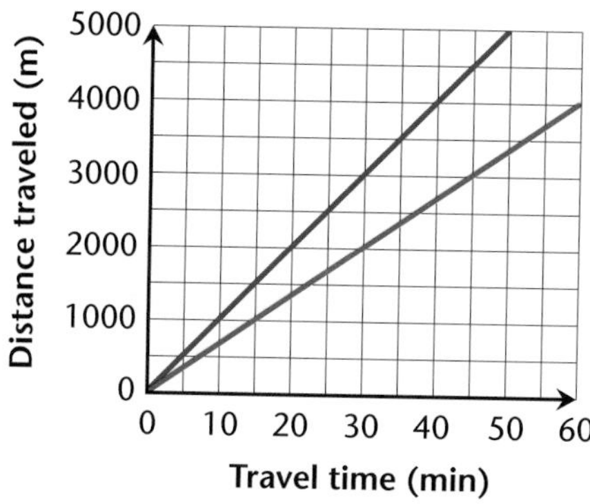

Time (min)	Distance (m)	Rate (m/min)
?	?	?
?	?	?
?	?	?
?	?	?

b. Compare your tables. Which person is walking at a faster rate?

c. How do the graphs show who is walking at a faster rate?

d. Suppose the missing driver in *The Mystery of Blacktail Canyon* has a faster walking rate than the rates you found. How would the graph of the driver's distance walked over time compare with the graphs shown?

▶ **Finding Slope** **The slope of a line is a ratio that measures the line's steepness.**

EXAMPLE

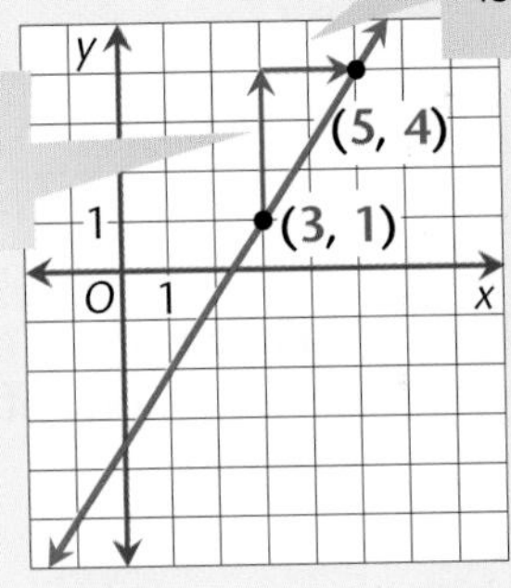

$$\text{Slope} = \frac{\text{rise}}{\text{run}}$$

$$\text{Slope} = \frac{3}{2}$$

The slope is $\frac{3}{2}$ or 1.5.

5 Try This as a Class

a. Use a different pair of points to find the slope of the line in the Example.

b. Does it matter which points you choose? Explain.

c. Why is the order in which you subtract one set of coordinates from the other set of coordinates important?

✓ **QUESTION 6**

...checks that you can find the slope of a line.

6 ✓ **CHECKPOINT** Find the slope of each line.

a.

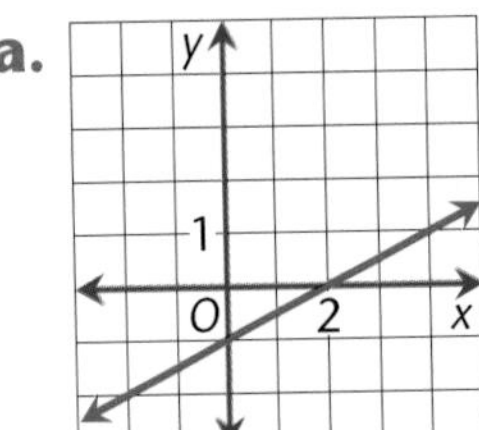

b.

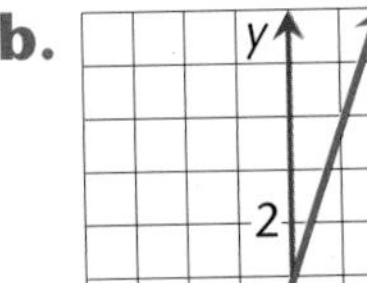

7 Look back at the graph in Question 4. Find the slope of each line. How does the slope compare with the person's walking rate?

▶ **Writing an Equation** **You can use an equation to model the distance a person walking at a steady rate can cover in a given amount of time.**

$$\text{Distance} = \text{rate} \cdot \text{time}$$
$$d = rt$$

8 Use the rates you found in Question 4. Write an equation that can be used to estimate the distance d each person can walk in t minutes. How is the slope you found in Question 7 related to your equation?

▶ **The slope of a line often gives you information about a situation. Sometimes you can use that information to write an equation.**

EXAMPLE

Use the graph to find the daily rate Crownpoint Car Rental charges. Then write an equation for the total cost of renting a car for a given number of days.

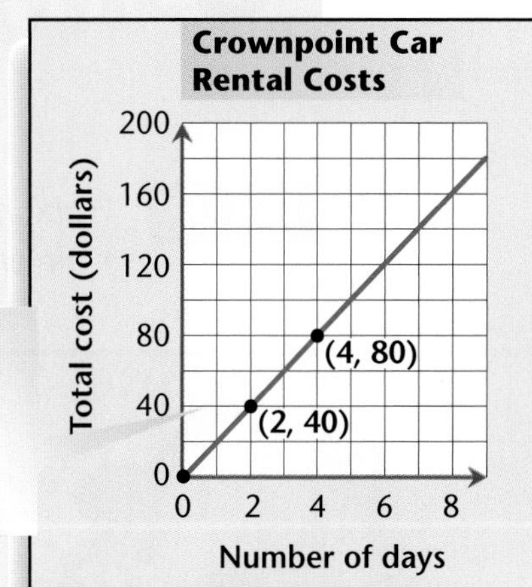

SAMPLE RESPONSE

First Find the daily rate. To find the daily rate, find the slope of the line. The slope is 20, so the rate is \$20 per day.

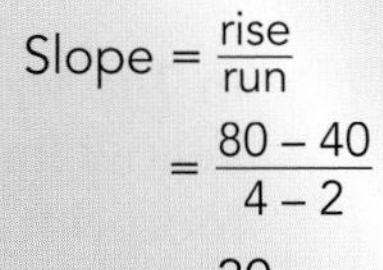

$$\text{Slope} = \frac{\text{rise}}{\text{run}} = \frac{80 - 40}{4 - 2} = 20$$

Next Write an equation. Let C = total cost and d = the number of days.

$$\text{Total cost} = \text{daily rate} \cdot \text{number of days}$$

$$C = 20d$$

Then Check your work. Choose at least two points from the graph. Check that their coordinates are solutions of the equation $C = 20d$.

Choose (3, 60). $60 = 20(3)$ ✔

Choose (4, 80). $80 = 20(4)$ ✔

9 **Try This as a Class** How does the graph in the Example show what the units of the daily rate are?

10 **Try This as a Class** Suppose Crownpoint Car Rental's rate becomes \$25 per day.

a. How will the graph of rental costs be different?

b. How will the equation be different?

11 ✔ **CHECKPOINT** Write an equation for the graph shown at the right. Give an example of a problem you can use your equation to solve.

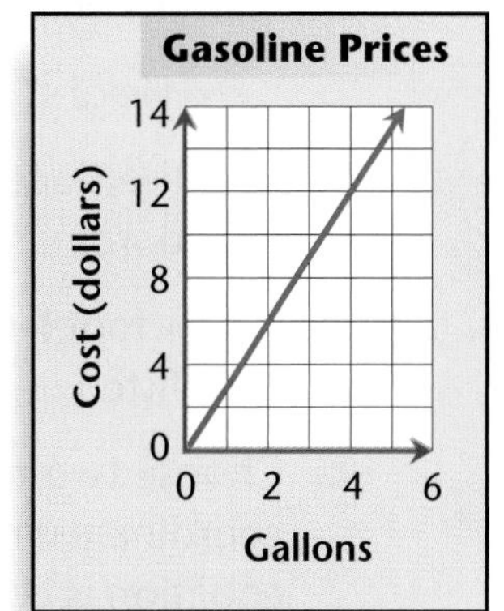

✔ **QUESTION 11**

...checks that you can apply the idea of slope to model a situation with an equation.

HOMEWORK EXERCISES ▶ See Exs. 1–7 on pp. 187–188

GOAL

LEARN HOW TO...
- use an equation to make a prediction

AS YOU...
- estimate heights from foot lengths

Exploration 2

Using Equ+ati=ons

SET UP *Work in a group of four. You will need: • Labsheet 3A • meter stick • masking tape • marker • graph paper*

▶ **In *The Mystery of Blacktail Canyon*, Officer Yellow Robe says that he can use the footprints Jim found to estimate the height of the missing driver. In this Exploration, you will use an equation to estimate heights from foot lengths.**

Use Labsheet 3A for Questions 12–14.

12 Follow the directions on the labsheet for collecting and recording data in the *Foot Length and Height Table.* You will use the data to make a scatter plot and a fitted line.

13 The footprint of the missing driver in *The Mystery of Blacktail Canyon* is 29 cm long. Use your fitted line to predict the person's height.

14 Suppose you guess that an equation for your fitted line follows the pattern below.

Height = slope • foot length

a. Find the slope of your fitted line. (You may need to estimate the coordinates of the points you use to find the slope.)

b. Let f = foot length and let h = height. Write an equation for your fitted line, based on the pattern described above.

c. Choose two points on your fitted line to see whether their coordinates make the equation true. Do you think your equation is correct? Explain.

▶ **In Question 14(c), you probably found that the equation in part (b) did not work for your fitted line. In Question 15, you will explore how to adjust the pattern to write an equation for your fitted line.**

15 **a.** Copy and complete the table below. As shown, use two different methods to predict height.

Method 1: Use your fitted line to make a prediction.

Method 2: Use your equation from Question 14 to make a prediction.

Then Find the difference between the two predictions.

Foot length (cm)	Height (cm) (Fitted line prediction)	Height (cm) (Equation prediction)	Difference
24 cm	?	?	?
26 cm	?	?	?
28 cm	?	?	?
30 cm	?	?	?

b. How do your predictions compare?

c. **Discussion** How would you revise the equation you wrote in Question 14? Explain your thinking.

16 Use your revised equation from Question 15 to predict the height of the missing driver. Compare your prediction with the one you made in Question 13.

17 ✓ **CHECKPOINT** Use the scatter plot.

a. Which equation can you use to predict a person's height h if you know his or her lower arm length a: $h = 4.5a$ or $h = 4.5a - 35$? Explain your choice.

b. Use the equation you chose to predict the height of someone whose lower arm length is 45 cm.

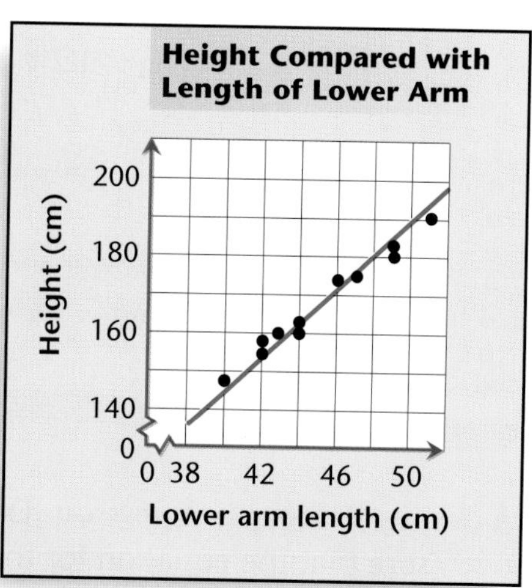

✓ **QUESTION 17**

...checks that you can use an equation of a fitted line to make predictions.

HOMEWORK EXERCISES ▶ **See Exs. 8–14 on pp. 188–189.**

Section 3 Key Concepts

Key Terms

slope

rise

run

Slope (pp. 181–183)

The slope of a line is the ratio of its rise to its run. Sometimes the slope of a line gives you information about an everyday situation.

Example Water is added to a tub at a steady rate. The graph shows the amount of water in the tub over time. The slope of the line is a rate.

$$\text{Slope} = \frac{\text{rise}}{\text{run}} = \frac{6-2}{3-1} = \frac{4}{2} = 2$$

Water is added to the tub at a rate of 2 gal/min.

Equations for Predictions (pp. 184–185)

You can use an equation of a fitted line to make predictions.

Example An equation of the fitted line shown is

$$w = 5.5h - 213,$$

where w = weight in pounds, and h = height in inches. You can predict that a 78 in. tall player will weigh about 216 lb.

$$w = 5.5(78) - 213$$

$$w \approx 216$$

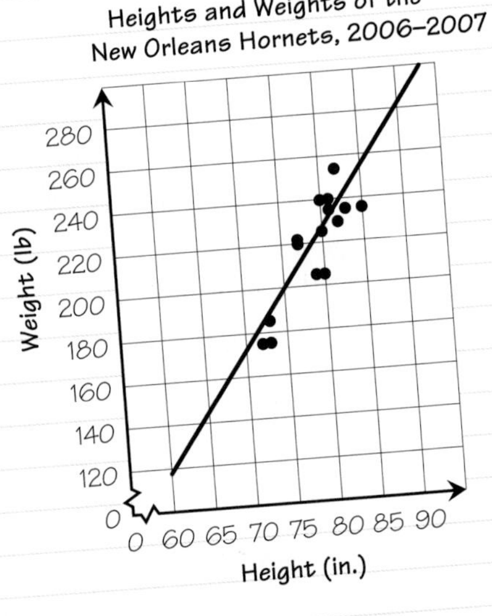

18 Key Concepts Question Explain how you can check to make sure that the equation for the fitted line in the second Example is the correct equation.

Section 3

Practice & Application Exercises

YOU WILL NEED

For Exs. 6(d), 12:
- graph paper

Find the slope of each line.

1. 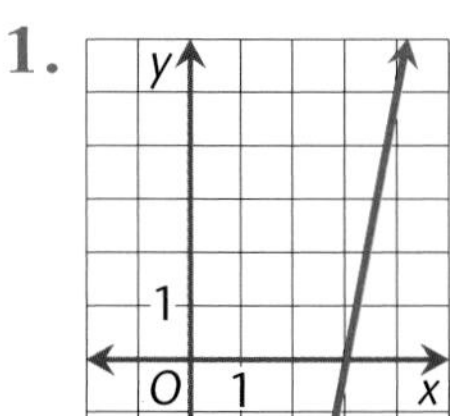

2. 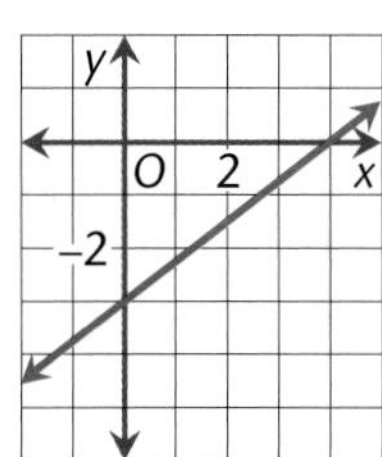

3. 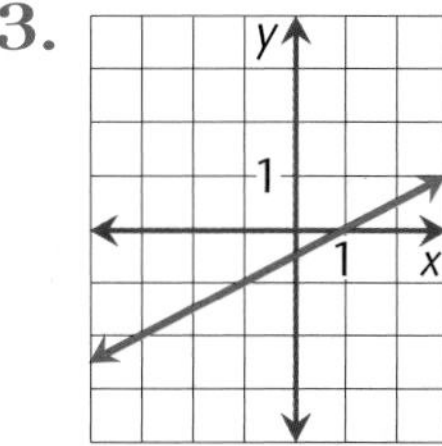

4. Darryl says that the slope of the line in Exercise 3 is 2. Explain what he did wrong.

5. **Race Walking** The first official world record in the 20 km race walk was set in 1918 by Niels Petersen of Denmark. In 1994, Bernardo Segura of Mexico set a new world record. The graph shows the average walking rates of these two athletes.

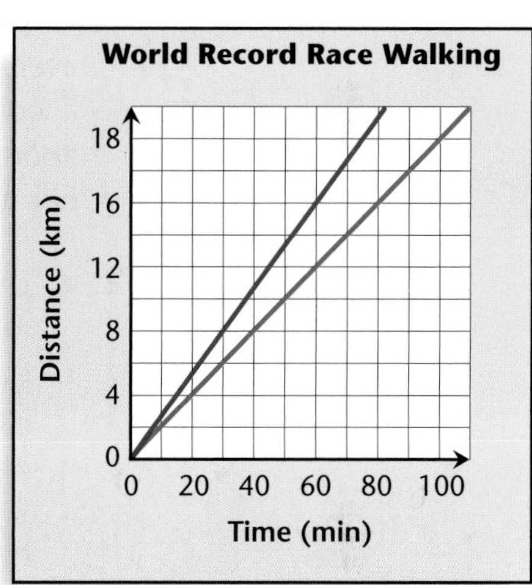

   a. Which line shows Segura's walking rate? Explain.

   b. Find each athlete's average rate.

   c. Write equations you can use to find the average distance each athlete walks in a given amount of time.

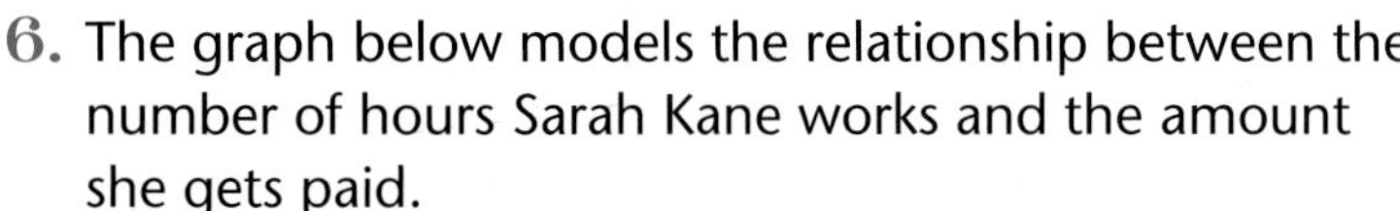

6. The graph below models the relationship between the number of hours Sarah Kane works and the amount she gets paid.

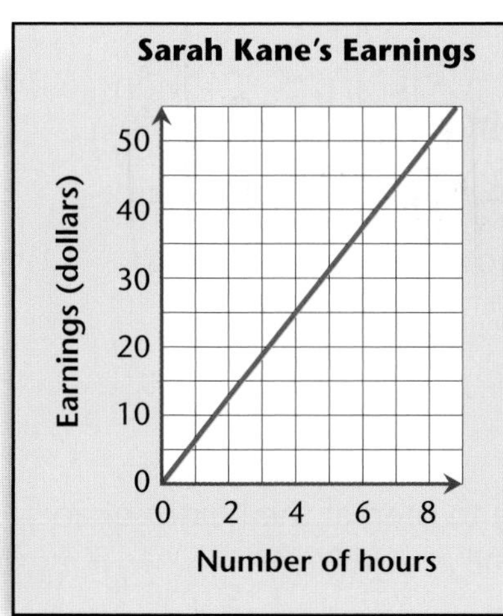

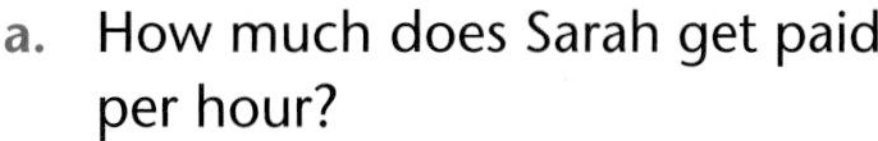

   a. How much does Sarah get paid per hour?

   b. Write an equation for the amount she makes based on the number of hours she works.

   c. Suppose Sarah gets an 8% raise in her hourly wage. Write a new equation to model the amount she makes.

   d. Graph the new equation. Find the slope of the graph.

7. **Challenge** Find the slope of a line that passes through the points (–2, 4) and (3, 4).

Match each equation with one of the lines. Explain your thinking.

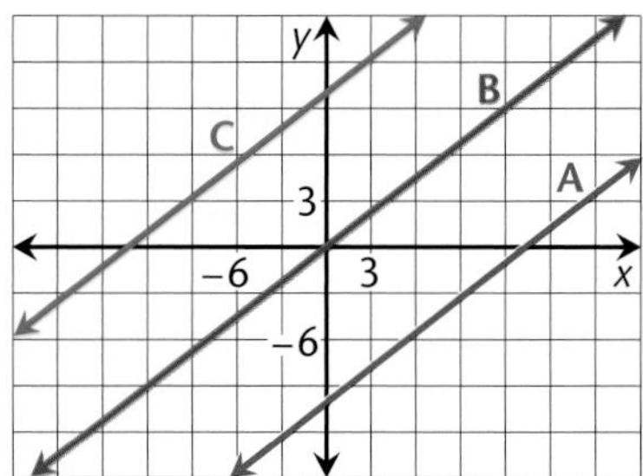

8. $y = 0.75x$

9. $y = 0.75x - 10$

10. $y = 0.75x + 10$

Human Development **In Module 1, you used a rule of thumb that said your adult height will be twice your height at age 2. In Exercises 11–13, you will re-examine that claim. Use the data in the table for the exercises.**

11. **Interpreting Data** On average, the height of a woman at age 18 is about how many times her height at age 2?

Heights of 10 Females (in centimeters)	
Height at age 2 (t)	Height at age 18 (h)
82.0	156.5
83.0	158.4
85.6	163.3
85.9	162.4
86.4	163.8
86.4	165.2
88.6	169.2
88.9	166.8
90.2	168.1
91.4	173.7

12. a. Use the data to make a scatter plot. Use the horizontal axis for t, the height at age 2, and the vertical axis for h, the height at age 18.

    b. Draw a fitted line. Then find its slope.

    c. Suppose you guess that an equation for your fitted line follows this pattern:

    height at age 18 = slope • height at age 2.

    Write an equation for your fitted line based on this pattern.

    d. As you did in Exploration 2, use two different methods to predict values for h.

    e. How would you revise the equation you wrote in part (c)? Explain your thinking.

13. Use your equation from Exercise 12(e) to predict the height of an 18-year-old woman who was 84 cm tall at age 2.

Reflecting on the Section

Be prepared to discuss your response to Exercise 14 in class.

14. In Exploration 2 you predicted height from foot length using data collected from a sample of people. Do you think the sample will enable you to reasonably predict the height of anyone in the world from the person's foot length? Explain.

Discussion

Exercise 14 checks that you understand how reasonable it is to make a prediction from a scatter plot.

Spiral Review

Evaluate each expression. (Module 3, p. 185)

15. $\frac{8(-4)}{-7+4}$ 16. $3\sqrt{8-(-8)}$ 17. $\frac{\sqrt{12 \cdot 3}}{8}$ 18. $\frac{(-12)^2}{11+1}$

19. Tell what inverse operation you would use to solve $\frac{x}{8} = 17$. Then solve the equation. (Module 1, p. 42)

Use a proportion to find each percent. (Module 2, p. 132)

20. 15% of 90 21. 22.5% of 118 22. 0.4% of 17

Use the 4-step problem solving approach for Exercises 23 and 24. (Module 1, p. 67)

23. To prepare for an upcoming sale, a grocery clerk plans to stack boxes for a display. The boxes will form a pyramid. The bottom row of boxes will hold 10 boxes. Each row will hold one box fewer than the row below. How many boxes will be in the pyramid?

24. You are helping to plan your school's sports banquet. There are two types of tables available. The rectangular tables seat 8 people and the round tables seat 6 people. Find a possible combination of tables to seat exactly 120 people given that you want to use some rectangular tables and some round tables.

Name the units in each rate. Then write a unit rate. (Module 1, p. 9)

25. \$30 for 6 pairs of socks

26. \$3.24 for 12 oranges

Section 3 Extra Skill Practice

Find the slope of each line.

1. 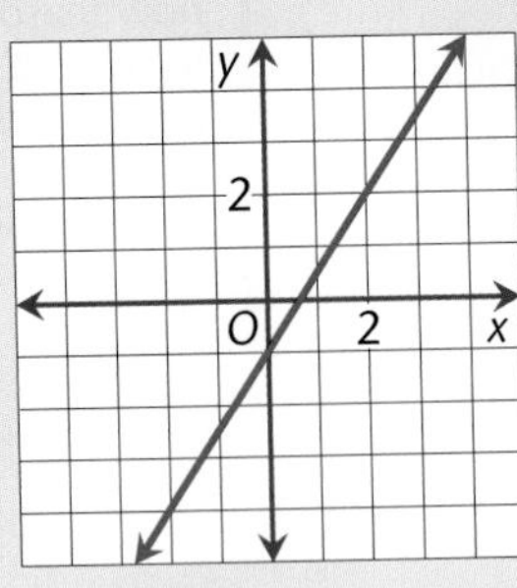

2. 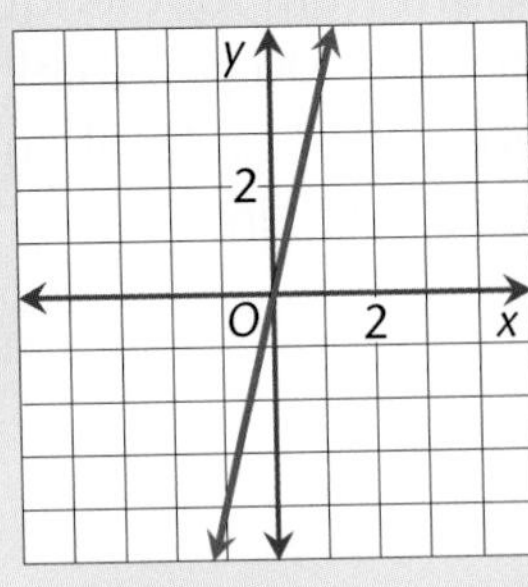

3. 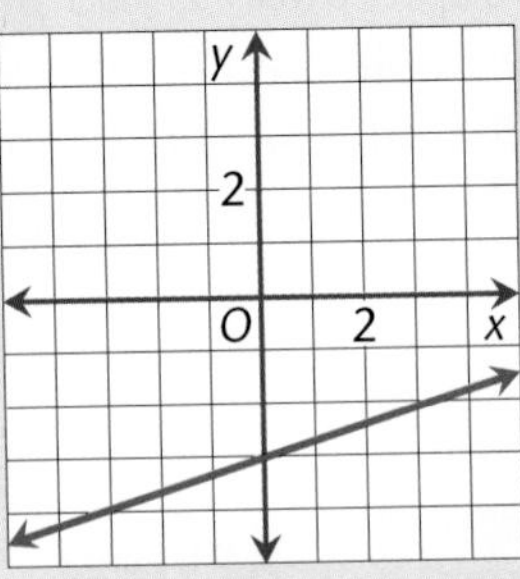

The scatter plot shows the number of pounds of ice used each day at a school lunch center based on the outdoor temperature. Use the scatter plot for Exercises 4–6.

Ice Used in School Lunch Center

Ice used (lb): 0, 80, 100, 120, 140, 160

Temperature (°F): 0, 30, 50, 70, 90

4. Predict the amount of ice used if the temperature is 70°F.

5. Find the slope of the fitted line.

6. Let t = the temperature in degrees Fahrenheit. Let p = the number of pounds of ice used. Which equation can you use to predict the number of pounds of ice used if you know the outdoor temperature?

A. $p = \frac{5}{3}t$ B. $p = \frac{3}{5}t + 10$ C. $p = \frac{3}{5}t - 10$ D. $p = \frac{5}{3}t + 10$

Standardized Testing ▶ Open-ended

Make up a story that explains the graph below. Write a title and appropriate labels and scales on the graph. Be sure to explain how the situation shown by the red line is different from the situation shown by the green line.

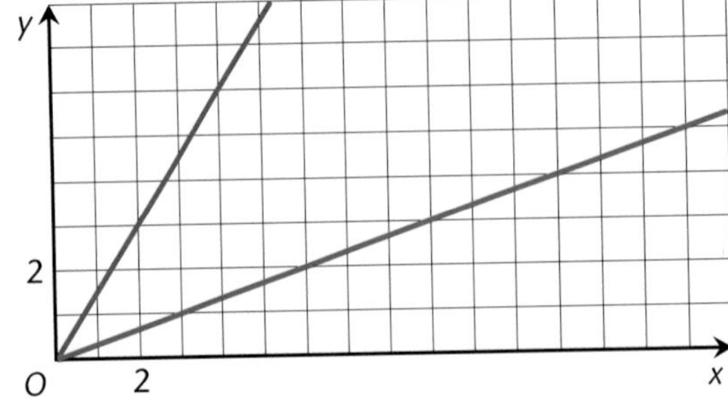

EXTENDED E2 EXPLORATION

FOR ASSESSMENT AND PORTFOLIOS

Mystery State

The Situation

Try the following puzzle. Is mystery or mathematics at work?

- Pick an integer between 1 and 10.
- Multiply your number by 6.
- Add 12.
- Divide by 3.
- Subtract 4.
- Divide by your original number.
- Add 4.
- Match the number with the corresponding letter of the alphabet (1 = A, 2 = B, *and so on*).
- Think of a state in the United States that begins with that letter.
- Look at the third letter of the name of the state. Think of a fruit that begins with that letter and grows in that state.
- Turn your book upside-down and look at the bottom of the page to complete the mystery.

The Problem

Explain why the mystery puzzle works. Then create a puzzle of your own and explain why it works.

Something to Think About

- How might examining a mystery puzzle with fewer steps help you?
- Does this puzzle work for any positive integer? Would it work for negative integers? decimals? fractions?

Present Your Results

Write your puzzle on a sheet of paper. Include the solution on the back. Explain why the puzzle above works, and why your mystery puzzle works.

You thought of oranges in Florida.

Similar Figures and Constructions

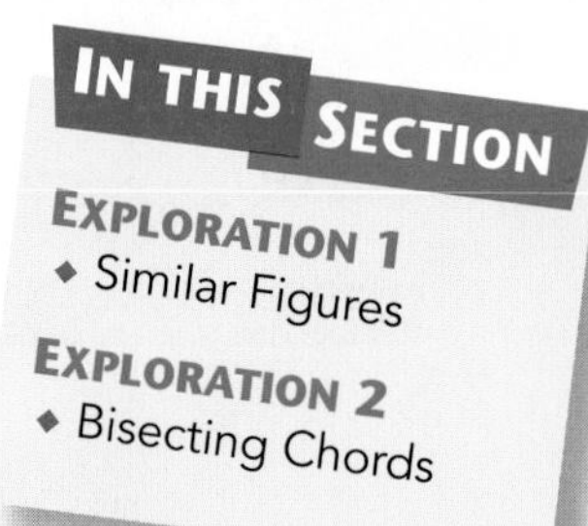

CLIFF DWELLERS

Setting the Stage

The Story So Far...

▶ **The missing driver's tracks lead to a previously undiscovered cliff dwelling. Nageela wonders if her 40 m rope will reach the site. Charlotte Lopez has a method for estimating the cliff height.**

She used her pocket knife to pry the ink cartridge out of the plastic body of the pen.

. . . Charlotte marked a spot on the ground, then paced off the distance to the foot of the cliff. Next, she had Jim stand between her marked spot and the cliff. Finally, she lay down with her head on the ground and sighted the top of Jim's head through the hollow pen.

"Take two steps back, Jim," she said.
"Good! Now, how tall are you?"

Drawing not to scale

Think About It

1 The diagram models the situation in the story selection. Which segment represents Jim? Which represents the cliff?

2 What kind of triangles do you see in the diagram?

Exploration 1

Similar Figures

Similar Figures

SET UP *You will need:* • *Labsheet 4A* • *centimeter ruler* • *protractor*

GOAL

LEARN HOW TO...
- tell whether triangles are similar
- make indirect measurements

AS YOU...
- estimate the height of a cliff

KEY TERMS
- similar
- corresponding angles
- corresponding sides

▶ **As you will see in this exploration, Charlotte Lopez uses *similar* figures to estimate the cliff height. Two figures are similar if they have the same shape, but not necessarily the same size. The figures below are similar.**

$\angle P$ and $\angle T$ are *corresponding angles.* **Corresponding angles** have the same measure.

$m\angle P = m\angle T$

Read $m\angle T$ as "the measure of angle T."

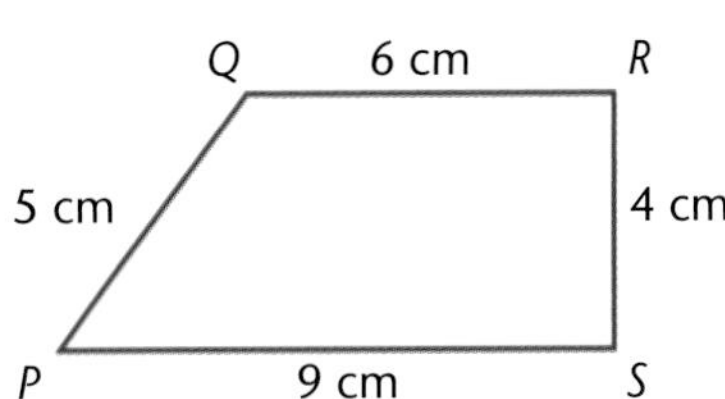

$\overline{PQ}$ and $\overline{TU}$ are *corresponding sides*. The lengths of **corresponding sides** are in proportion.

$$\frac{PQ}{TU} = \frac{QR}{UV}$$

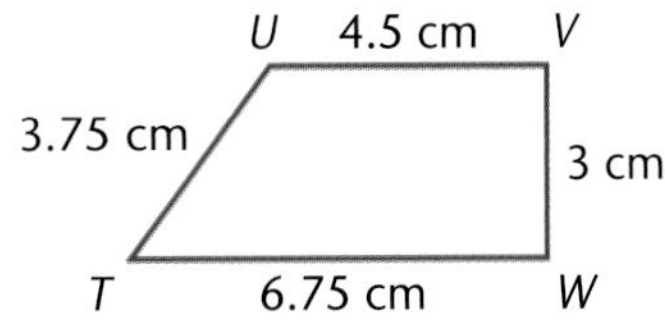

Read $\overline{TU}$ as "segment TU." Read TU as "the length of segment TU."

3 a. Try This as a Class Name all pairs of corresponding angles and corresponding sides in the figures above.

b. Find the ratios $\frac{PQ}{TU}$, $\frac{QR}{UV}$, $\frac{RS}{VW}$, and $\frac{PS}{TW}$. What do you notice?

4 ✓ CHECKPOINT The figures below are similar. Copy and complete each statement.

a. $m\angle C = m$ __?__

b. $\frac{BC}{FG} = \frac{?}{GH}$

c. $\frac{?}{AD} = \frac{EF}{?}$

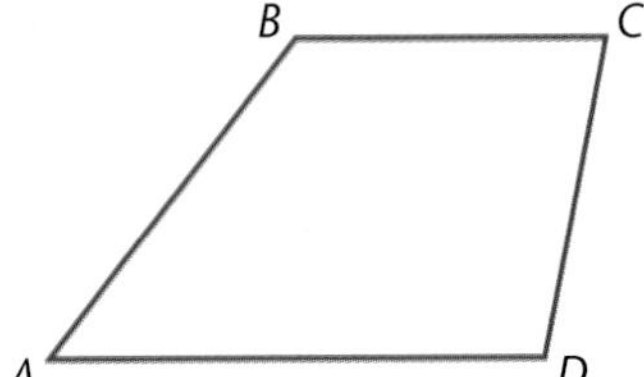

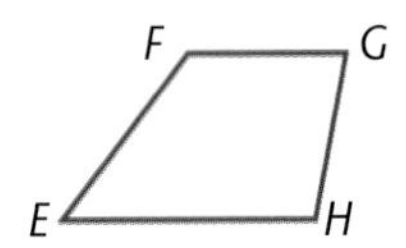

✓ QUESTION 4

...checks your understanding of the definition of similar figures.

▶ **Naming Similar Figures The symbol ~ means "is similar to." When you name similar figures, be sure to put their corresponding angles in the same order.**

5 **Try this as a Class** The triangles at the right are similar. Which of the statements below are written correctly? Explain your thinking.

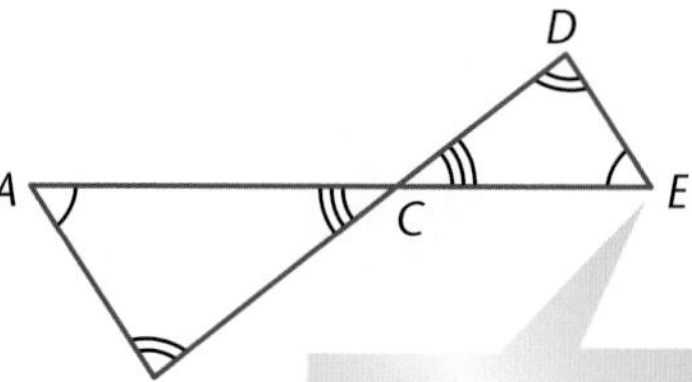

A. $\triangle ABC \sim \triangle CDE$

B. $\triangle ABC \sim \triangle EDC$

C. $\triangle BAC \sim \triangle DEC$

D. $\triangle ACB \sim \triangle ECD$

Symbols are used to show which angles have the same measure.

A vertex is a point where sides of a figure come together.

6 **Use Labsheet 4A.** You will use a protractor and a ruler to determine whether the *Two Triangles* are similar.

▶ **A Test for Similar Triangles Two triangles are similar if two angles of one triangle have the same measures as two angles of the other triangle.**

7 **Try This as a Class** The triangles from page 192 are shown below. The large triangle on the left can be divided into two smaller triangles as shown on the right.

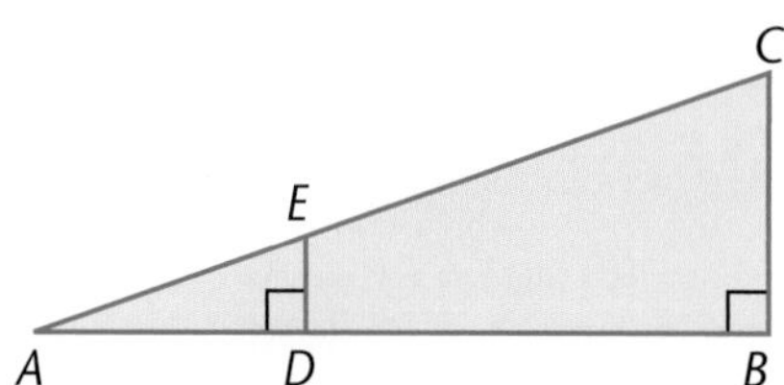

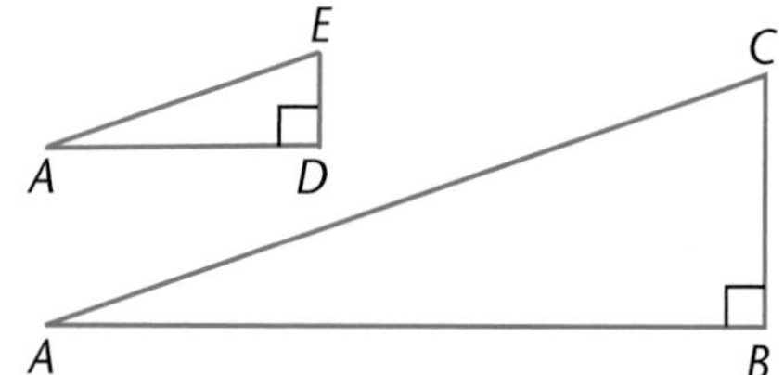

a. $\angle ABC$ and $\angle ADE$ are right angles. What does this tell you about their measures?

b. How do you know $\angle BAC$ and $\angle DAE$ have the same measure?

c. The sum of the measures of the angles of a triangle is 180°. Without using a protractor, what do you know about the measures of $\angle ACB$ and $\angle AED$? Explain.

d. Is $\triangle ABC \sim \triangle ADE$? How do you know?

8 **Discussion** Do you think the test for similar triangles would work for other figures? Explain.

▶ **Indirect Measurement In *The Mystery of Blacktail Canyon,* Charlotte cannot directly measure the height of the cliff. She can use similar figures to make an indirect measurement.**

EXAMPLE

To estimate the cliff height, Charlotte uses what she knows about similar triangles to write and solve a proportion.

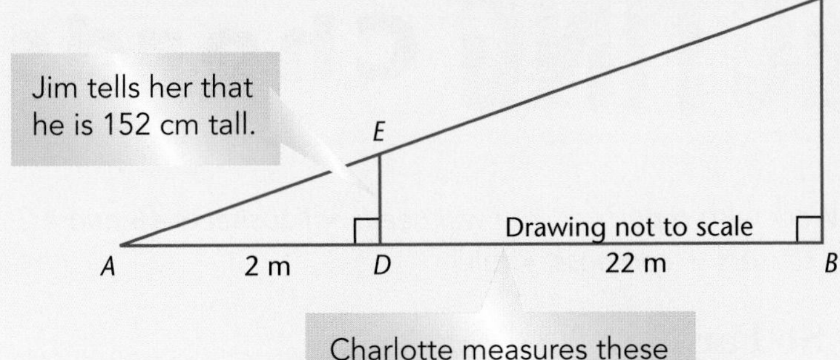

Jim tells her that he is 152 cm tall.

Charlotte measures these distances on the ground.

$$\frac{AB}{AD} = \frac{BC}{DE}$$

Substitute known values. Let $h = BC$, the unknown cliff height.

$$\frac{24}{2} = \frac{h}{1.52}$$

Convert Jim's height from 152 cm to 1.52 m.

$$24(1.52) = 2h$$

Use cross products.

$$18.24 = h$$

The cliff dwellings are about 18 m above the canyon floor.

▶ **Try This as a Class For Questions 9–11, use the Example.**

9 Suppose you do not convert Jim's height to meters. What answer do you get?

10 Can Charlotte use the proportion $\frac{DE}{BC} = \frac{DA}{BA}$ to find the cliff height? Explain.

11 In *The Mystery of Blacktail Canyon,* Nageela's climbing rope is 40 m long. She needs "as much going down as going up." Is her rope long enough to reach the cliff dwellings?

12 ✓ **CHECKPOINT** $\triangle RST \sim \triangle UVW$. Tell which missing side length you can find. Then find it.

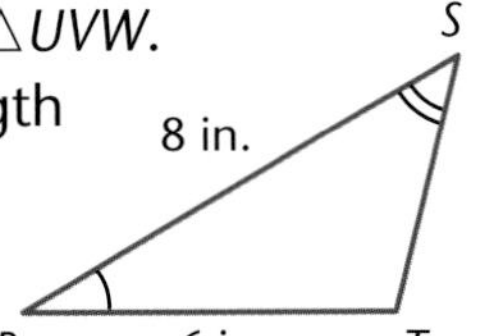

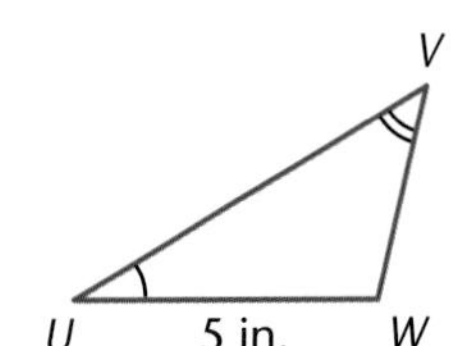

✓ **QUESTION 12**

...checks that you can use a proportion to find an unknown side length.

HOMEWORK EXERCISES See Exs. 1–14 on pp. 199–200.

GOAL

LEARN HOW TO...
- find a perpendicular bisector of a chord

AS YOU...
- estimate dimensions of artifacts

KEY TERMS
- chord
- perpendicular bisector

Exploration 2

BISECTING Chords

SET UP *Work with a partner. You will need:* • *Labsheets 4B and 4C* • *scissors* • *compass* • *ruler*

The Story So Far...

▶ **After using the rope to climb up the cliff, Nageela discovers broken pottery pieces in a dwelling. Jim is surprised that Nageela can estimate the original size of the pottery.**

"You mean you can tell the diameter of a platter just by tracing a little broken part? How do you do it?"

".... It's easy, really." Nageela knelt and drew a circle with her finger. "But first you have to know a few things about circles."

13 **Use Labsheet 4B.**

a. Cut out *Circle 1*. Fold the circle in half and draw a segment on the crease. Then rotate the circle and repeat with a new crease.

b. What is another name for the segments you drew? Where do they intersect? Would other segments constructed in the same way intersect at the same point?

c. Cut out *Circle 2* and fold it so points *K* and *L* meet. Draw a segment on the crease. Refold so points *M* and *N* meet. Draw a segment on the crease. Where do the segments intersect?

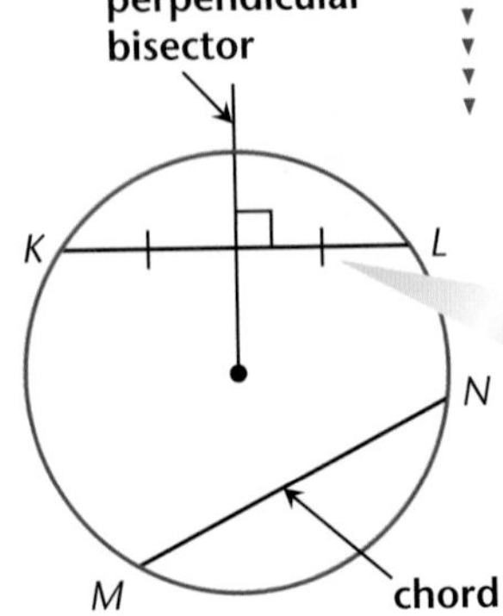

Symbols are used to show that the two halves of $\overline{KL}$ are equal in length.

14 **Try This as a Class** $\overline{KL}$ and $\overline{MN}$ are *chords*. A **chord** is a segment that joins two points on a circle. The segment you drew through each chord is a **perpendicular bisector**. Why is this a good name for these segments?

Circles

Student Resource

A circle is the set of all points in a plane that are a given distance from a point called the center of the circle.

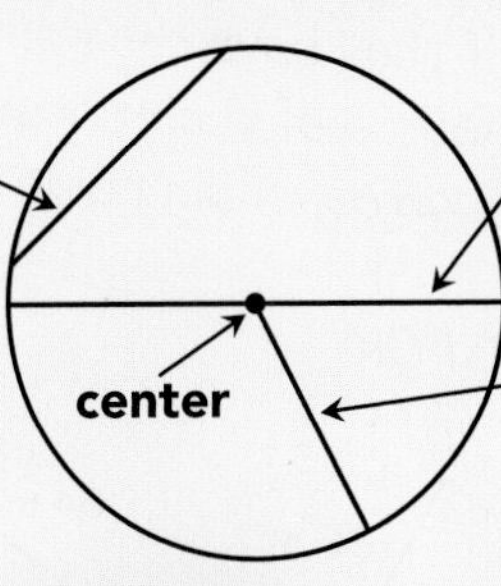

A **chord** is a segment that has both endpoints on the circle.

A **diameter** is a chord that passes through the center of the circle.

A **radius** is a segment that connects a point on the circle to the center.

Constructing a Circle

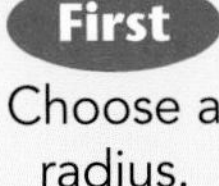

First Choose a radius.

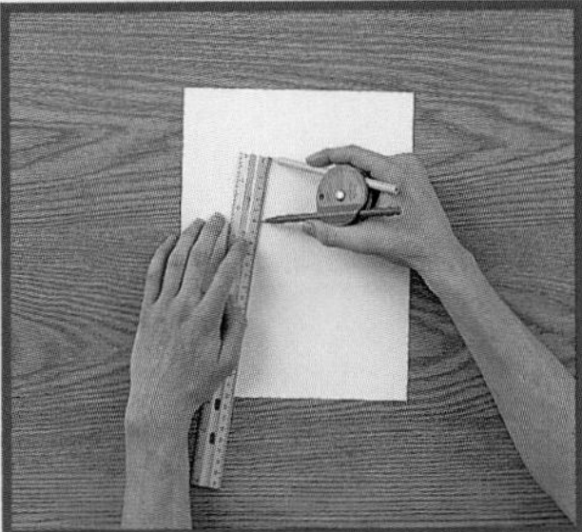

Then Draw the circle.

15 Discussion Use your compass to make a circle. Draw two chords. Then fold the circle to find the perpendicular bisector of each chord. What do you observe about the perpendicular bisectors of two chords drawn in the same circle?

▶ **Nageela found a pottery fragment that was originally part of a platter. Her first steps in estimating the platter's size are shown.**

First Nageela traced the pottery fragment's outline in the sand.

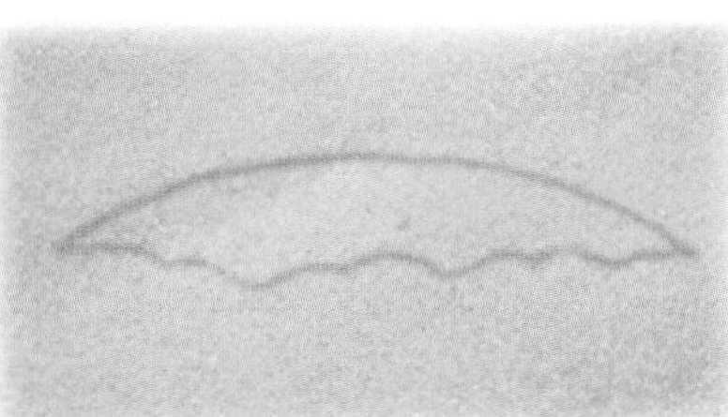

Then She drew two chords.

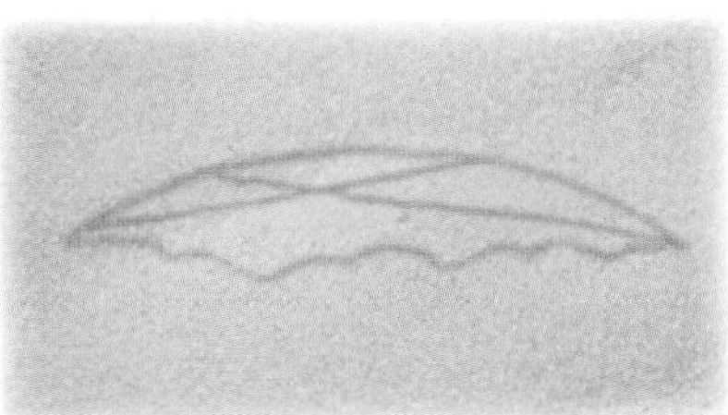

16 Discussion What do you think Nageela's next steps are?

17 ✓ CHECKPOINT Use Labsheet 4C. You will use perpendicular bisectors to estimate the original diameter of a *Circular Platter.*

...checks your understanding of perpendicular bisectors and chords.

See Exs. 15–19 on p. 201.

Section 4 Key Concepts

Key Terms

Similar Figures (pp. 193–195)

Two figures are similar if they have the same shape, but not necessarily the same size. The measures of their corresponding angles are equal, and the ratios of their corresponding side lengths are in proportion.

similar

corresponding angles

corresponding sides

Example 

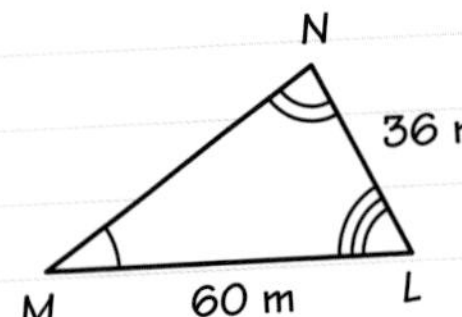

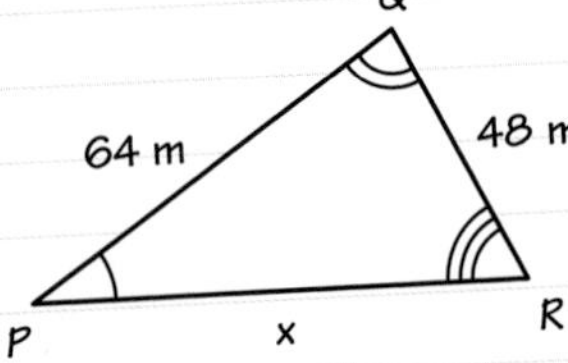

Similar Triangles and Indirect Measurement (pp. 194–195)

Two triangles are similar if two angles of one triangle have the same measure as two angles of the other. You can use similar triangles to make indirect measurements and find missing side lengths.

Example Find the length of $\overline{PR}$ in the diagram above.

Let x = PR. Solve for x.

$$\frac{ML}{PR} = \frac{NL}{QR}$$

$$\frac{60}{x} = \frac{36}{48}$$

$$x = 80$$

The length of $\overline{PR}$ is 80 m.

Circles and Chords (pp. 196–197)

chord

perpendicular bisector

The perpendicular bisectors of any two chords on a circle intersect at the center of the circle.

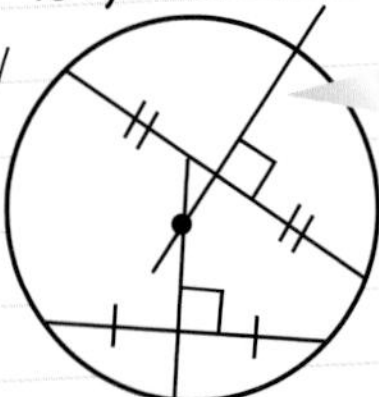

The perpendicular bisector forms a right angle with the chord. It divides the chord in half.

Key Concepts Questions

18 Use the triangles above. Find the length of $\overline{MN}$.

19 Draw a line segment on a piece of paper. Describe a method for dividing the segment into four parts with equal lengths.

Section 4
Practice & Application Exercises

YOU WILL NEED

For Ex. 11:
- ruler

For Exs. 20–21:
- graph paper

For Exs. 18, 33:
- compass

For Ex. 34:
- protractor

For Exercises 1–3, use similar figures *ABCD* and *MNQP*.

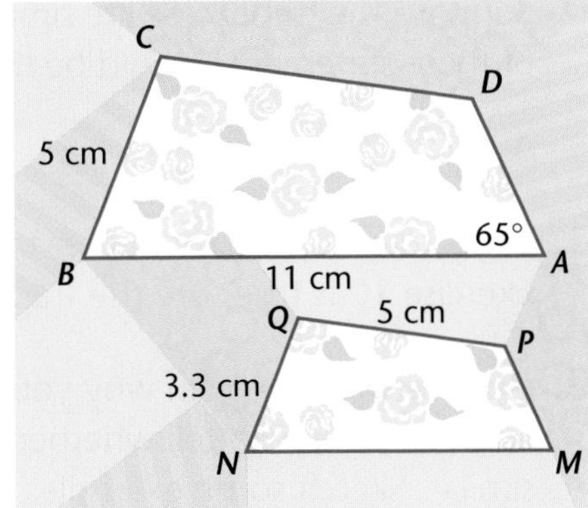

1. Find the ratio of the corresponding side lengths.

2. Copy and complete each statement.

   a. $m\angle A = m$ __?__

   b. $\frac{BA}{NM} = \frac{BC}{?}$

   c. $\frac{QP}{CD} = \frac{?}{AD}$

3. Find each measure.

   a. $m\angle M$ b. NM c. CD

For each pair of figures, write a mathematical statement saying the figures are similar.

4. 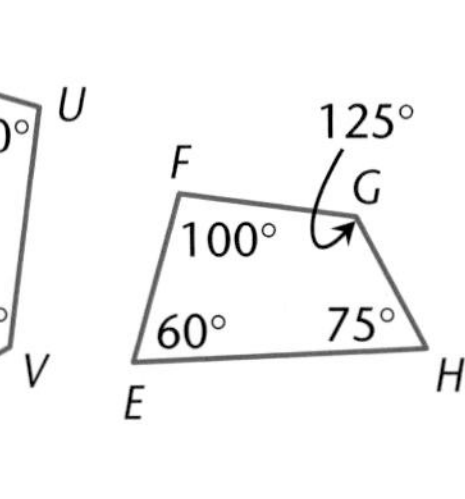

5. 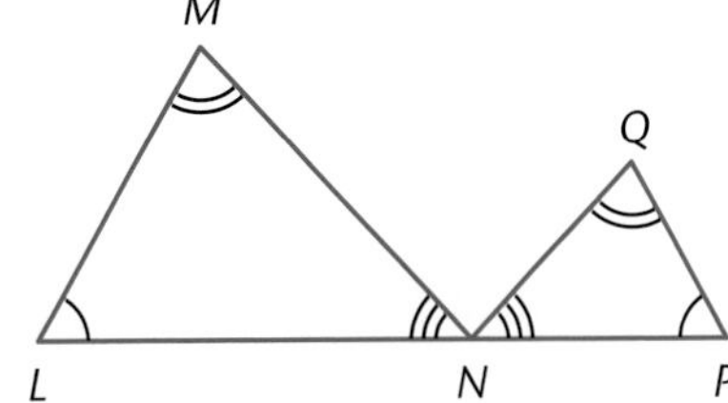

6. 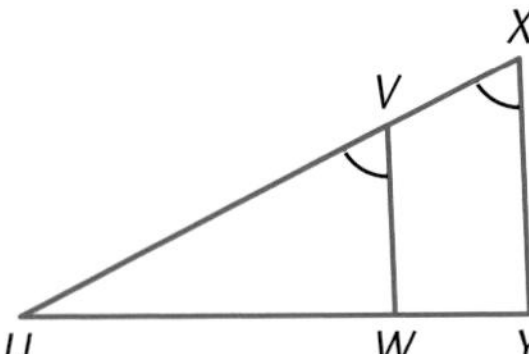

7. 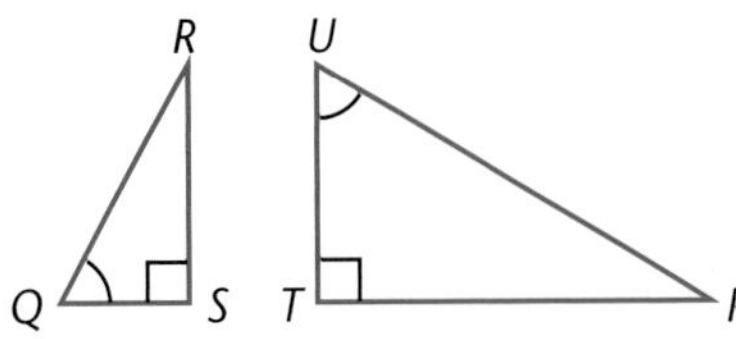

8. **Challenge** Suppose you push the triangles in Exercise 7 together, as shown. Name all the triangles you see. Without measuring, tell how you know that all the triangles are similar.

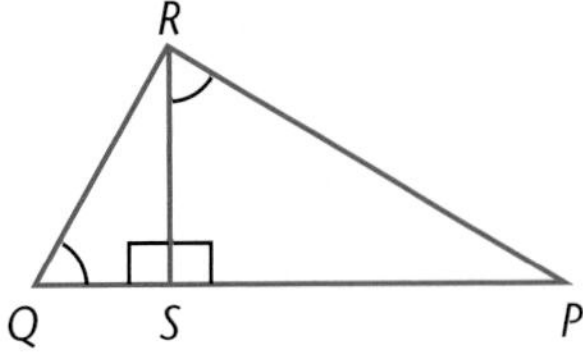

For Exercises 9–11, use the trapezoids *MNQR* and *NLPQ*.

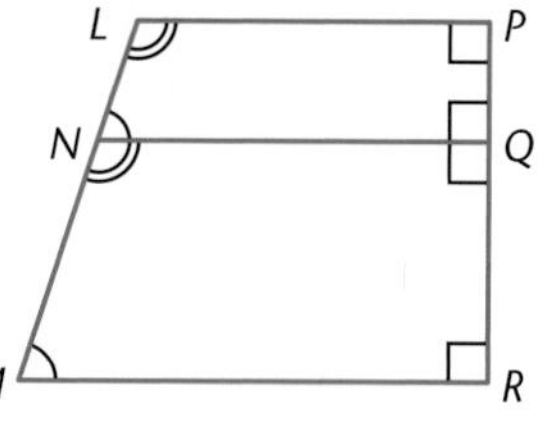

9. Byron assumes that the trapezoids are similar. Why do you think he might make that assumption?

10. Suppose the trapezoids are similar. Which of these statements would be true?

    A. $\frac{PQ}{QR} = \frac{MN}{NL}$ B. $\frac{PQ}{QR} = \frac{LP}{NQ}$

11. Use a ruler to check whether the statement you chose in Exercise 10 is true. Are the trapezoids similar? Why?

12. **Open-ended** Explain why you need to check more than the angle measures to tell whether the figures described below are similar. Sketch some examples to support your answers.

    a. 2 rectangles b. 2 trapezoids c. 2 parallelograms

13. **Challenge** Kasey can see the top of a 788 ft tall skyscraper over the top of a 15 ft flag pole at her school. She estimates that she is about 300 ft away from the flagpole. About how many miles is she from the skyscraper? (*Note*: 1 mi = 5280 ft)

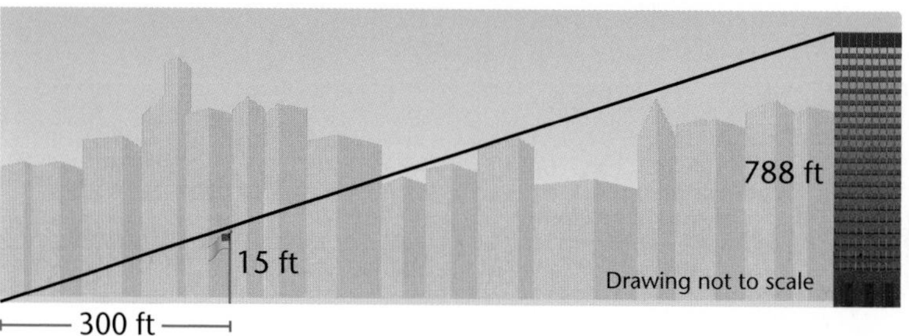

14. As shown by the diagram, you can think of rays of light from the sun as hitting the ground at the same angle.

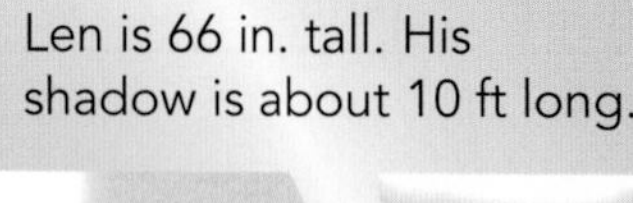

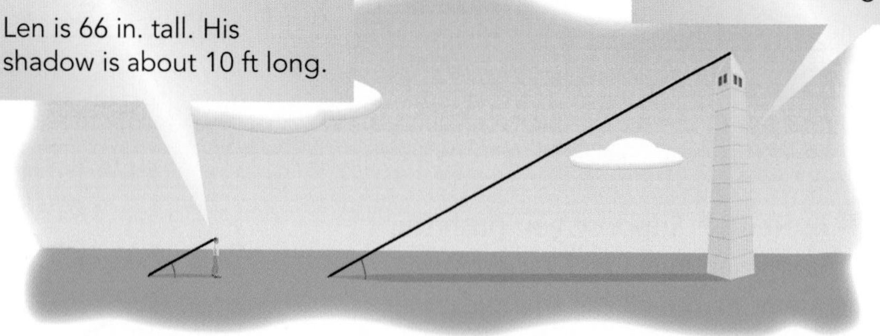

a. Explain how you know the triangles in the diagram are similar.

b. Estimate the height of the monument. Explain your method.

15. **Visual Thinking** Draw a large square on graph paper and cut it out. Use paperfolding to show that each of the four small triangles formed by the two diagonals is similar to each of the two larger triangles formed by just one diagonal.

16. a. Draw a rectangle and a diagonal. Then draw a smaller rectangle inside the first rectangle, as shown.

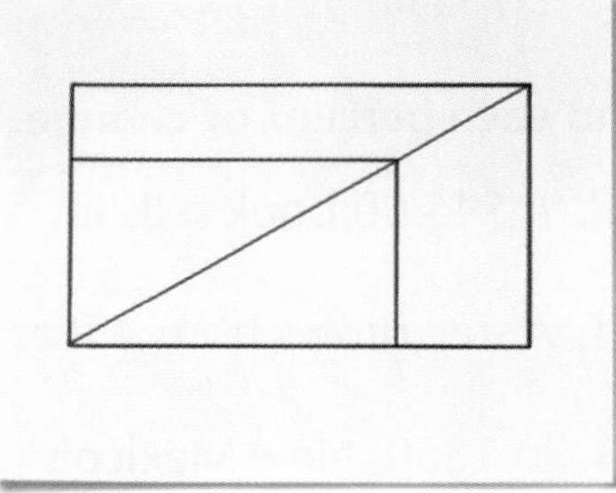

b. Do the rectangles appear to be similar? What do you need to check to make sure?

c. Repeat part (a) several times. Use different sizes of rectangles each time. Do all the rectangle pairs appear to be similar?

17. Use the method in Exercise 16 to make two parallelograms that are not rectangles. Does this method appear to produce similar parallelograms? Use examples to support your answer.

18. a. Draw a circle. Then draw two chords. The chords can be any length, but they should intersect. Connect the endpoints to form two triangles, as shown.

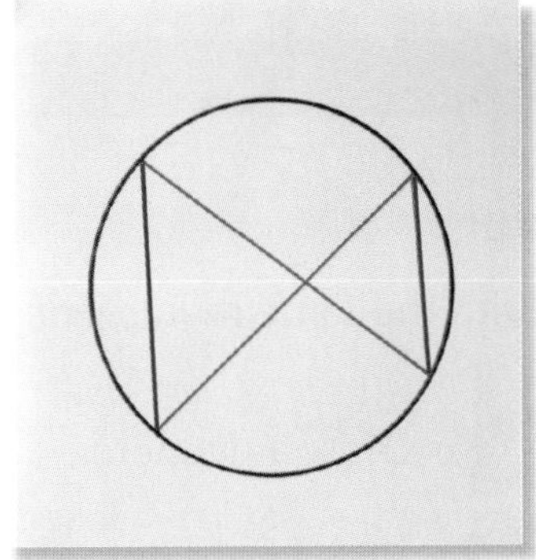

b. Repeat part (a) at least three times, using different chords.

c. What do you notice about the triangles in each circle?

Reflecting on the Section

19. The design below uses similar figures and segments that are perpendicular bisectors. Create your own design. Explain which figures in your design are similar, and give the ratio of the corresponding sides. Which segments are perpendicular bisectors?

Visual THINKING

Exercise 19 checks your understanding of similar figures and perpendicular bisectors of line segments.

Spiral Review

Plot each pair of points on a coordinate plane and draw a line through them. Find the slope of the line. (Module 3, p. 186)

20. (1, 1) and (–3, 3)

21. (0, –5) and (2, 3)

Find each percent of change. (Module 2, p. 144)

22. A \$45.00 book sells for \$30.00.

23. A tree grows from 4 ft to 5 ft 6 in.

24. In 1850, New Mexico's population was about 93,516. In 1860, it was about 61,547.

Find each product. (Toolbox, p. 589)

25. $3.6 \cdot 10^2$ 26. $0.4 \cdot 10^1$ 27. $249 \cdot 10^3$ 28. $0.007 \cdot 10^2$

29. $75.3 \cdot 10^4$ 30. $9.87 \cdot 10^5$ 31. $0.16 \cdot 10^2$ 32. $10.18 \cdot 10^6$

Extension 

Making a Conjecture

33. Draw five circles with the same radius. For each circle, follow these steps:

First Draw a diameter.

Then Choose a point on the circle and draw a triangle. The diameter should form one side of the triangle. Be sure to choose a different point for each circle.

Each vertex of the triangle should be on the circle.

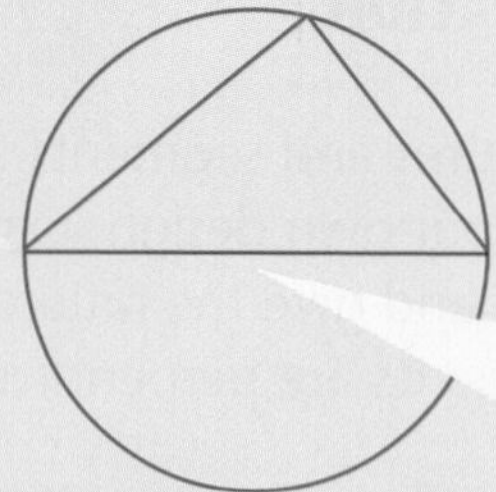

One side of the triangle should be the diameter of the circle.

34. Compare the angle measures of the triangles. Then make a conjecture about triangles drawn this way. Did the observations of other students support your conjecture?

Section 4 Extra Skill Practice

For Exercises 1–3, use the triangles shown. The triangles are similar.

1. Find the ratio of the corresponding side lengths.
2. Copy and complete each statement.

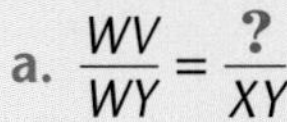

   a. $\frac{WV}{WY} = \frac{?}{XY}$

   b. $\frac{UV}{?} = \frac{?}{YW}$

   c. $\triangle UVW \sim$ __?__

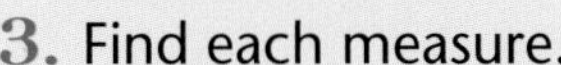

3. Find each measure.

   a. $m\angle X$ b. XW c. VW

You are standing on shore at point *A*. A raft is anchored in a bay at point *B*. Your friends Cathy, Damien and Ellen are standing at points *C*, *D*, and *E*.

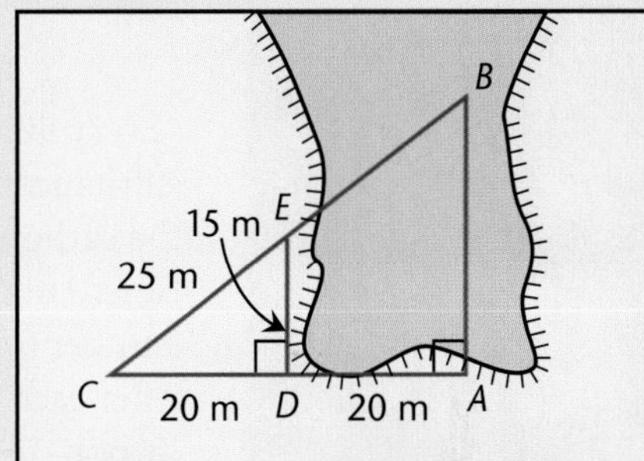

4. Which triangles are similar? How do you know?
5. Explain how your friends can help you find the distance from you to the raft by using similar triangles. Is there any information on the drawing that you will *not* need?
6. Find the distance from point *A* to point *B*.

Standardized Testing ▶ Free Response

1. $\overline{AB}$ is the perpendicular bisector of $\overline{CD}$.

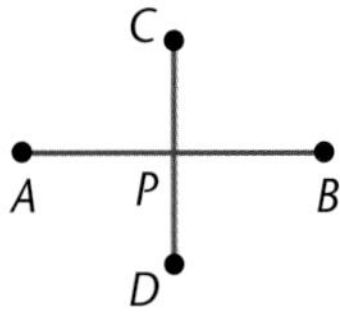

   a. Name two segments in the diagram that have the same measure.

   b. Name two angles in the diagram that have the same measure.

2. Suppose the measures of the corresponding sides of two similar rectangles are in the ratio 2 : 1. Give possible dimensions of the rectangles. Include a sketch of the rectangles with their dimensions labeled.

Section 5 Scientific Notation and Decimal Equations

EXPLORATION 1
- Using Scientific Notation

EXPLORATION 2
- Equations with Decimals

Setting the Stage

SET UP *You will need Labsheet 5A.*

The Story So Far...

▶ **Nageela visits Dr. Beatrice Leschensky, a scientist who is analyzing the bones found at the site. Dr. Leschensky explains how she uses *carbon dating* to estimate the age of the bones.**

"Every living creature contains a certain amount of a radioactive substance known as *carbon-14*. After a plant or an animal dies, the carbon-14 decays, so that there is less and less carbon-14 over time. After about 5730 years, only half the carbon-14 remains. After another 5730 years or so, only one fourth the carbon-14 remains. After each additional 5730 years, only half the previous amount of carbon-14 remains. By measuring the amount of carbon-14 in these bones, I was able to estimate their age. That's all there is to it."

Think About It

1 Scientists say that carbon-14 has a half-life of 5730 years. Why is *half-life* a good term to use?

2 What fraction of carbon-14 is left in an 11,460-year-old bone? in a 17,190-year-old bone? How do you know?

3 **Use Labsheet 5A.** Use a table and a graph to model the *Half-Life of Carbon-14*.

▶ **In this section, you will use mathematics to find out more about the bones found in the cliff dwelling in *The Mystery of Blacktail Canyon*.**

Exploration 1

Using Scientific Notation

SET UP *You will need:* • *Labsheet 5A* • *calculator*

GOAL

LEARN HOW TO...
- write very large numbers in scientific notation

AS YOU...
- estimate ages of bones

KEY TERMS
- scientific notation
- decimal notation

▶ **Here is a summary of Dr. Leschensky's report on the bones found in the cliff dwelling. Use the report for Questions 4–6.**

Carbon-14 Dating of Bone Samples

Bone sample	Gender	Bone type	Diameter (cm)	Length (cm)	Estimated age (years)
1	male	femur	3.3	38.9	$1.7 \cdot 10^2$
2	female	femur	3.1	35.6	$1.18 \cdot 10^3$

$10^3 = 10 \cdot 10 \cdot 10$

FOR ▶ HELP
with *powers*, see
TOOLBOX, p. 589

4 **a.** About how many years old was each bone sample?

b. To what year does each bone date back? (Assume *The Mystery of Blacktail Canyon* takes place in 2007.)

▶ **Writing Very Large Numbers** **The ages in Dr. Leschensky's report are written in *scientific notation.* Scientists use this notation as shorthand for writing some numbers.**

Decimal notation		**Scientific notation**
5,900,000,000	=	$5.9 \cdot 10^9$

A number greater than or equal to 1 and less than 10

A power of 10

5 **Try This as a Class** Tell whether each number is in scientific notation. Explain your answers.

a. $11.8 \cdot 10^7$ **b.** $6.9 \cdot 10^5$ **c.** $0.7 \cdot 10^{18}$ **d.** $1.2 \cdot 5^3$

6 Write each product as a number in decimal notation.

a. $9.3 \cdot 10^4$ **b.** $4.5 \cdot 10^5$ **c.** $3.8 \cdot 10^6$ **d.** $2.3 \cdot 10^1$

EXAMPLE

The age of the oldest fossils found on Earth is about 3,500,000,000. Write this age in scientific notation.

SAMPLE RESPONSE

First Move the decimal point to get a number greater than or equal to 1 and less than 10.

3,500,000,000

Then Count how many places the decimal point moves to decide on the power of 10.

$3.5 \cdot 10^9$

Decimal point moved 9 places to the left.

The fossils are about $3.5 \cdot 10^9$ years old.

7 **Try This as a Class** Jackie got a different answer for the Example above. Explain her mistake.

$3{,}500{,}000{,}000 = 35 \cdot 10{,}000{,}000 = 35 \cdot 10^8$

8 **Discussion** Describe how you can reverse the process in the Example to write $3.5 \cdot 10^9$ in decimal notation.

9 Calculator Many calculators use scientific notation to display very large numbers.

a. Use the key sequence below.

5.5 [×] 10 [=] [×] 10 [=] [×] 10 [=] [×] 10 [=] ...

Continue multiplying each product by 10 until your calculator switches to scientific notation. How is the number of times you pressed the [=] key related to the power of 10 on the display?

b. Your calculator may have a special key for entering numbers in scientific notation. For example, to enter $3.2 \cdot 10^{14}$, you might use one of these key sequences:

3.2 [EXP] 14　　　　3.2 [EE] 14

Find out the key sequence that your calculator uses. Then practice by entering $5.88 \cdot 10^{12}$. How does the number appear on the display?

...checks that you can write very large numbers in scientific notation.

10 **CHECKPOINT** Write each number in scientific notation.

a. 2390　　**b.** 4,500,000　　**c.** 365,000,000,000

11 **Use Labsheet 5A.** Look back at Dr. Leschensky's report on page 205. Bone sample 2 contains about $\frac{7}{8}$ of the original amount of carbon-14. Use your graph from Question 3 to estimate its age. How does this estimate compare with Dr. Leschensky's?

HOMEWORK EXERCISES See Exs. 1–10 on pp. 210–211.

Exploration 2

Equations with D.e.c.i.m.a.l.s

GOAL

LEARN HOW TO...
- solve equations involving decimals

AS YOU...
- estimate heights

The Story So Far...

Dr. Leschensky believes that the bones found in the cliff dwelling came from two skeletons, one male and one female. She explains how she can use the bones to learn more about these skeletons.

"We have a number of equations that help us predict the heights of people based on different bones of the body. . . . Since we have the measurements of two femurs, we will use these equations." She erased the chalkboard and wrote two formulas on it.

Male height from femur length	Female height from femur length
$h = 61.41 + 2.38f$	$h = 49.74 + 2.59f$

"You see, h represents height and f is femur length in centimeters.... When we use the formulas, we get close to the real height, but the answer may not be exact."

12 Look back at Dr. Leschensky's data from page 205 to estimate the height of each skeleton to the nearest centimeter. Explain why it may not be reasonable to make a closer estimate.

13 Dr. Leschensky is 172 cm tall. Write an equation you could use to estimate her femur length.

EXAMPLE

Jim's height is 152 cm. Nageela uses the formula $h = 61.41 + 2.38f$ to estimate his femur length to the nearest centimeter.

Substitute 152 for *h*. Then solve using inverse operations.

$$152 = 61.41 + 2.38f$$

$$152 - 61.41 = 61.41 + 2.38f - 61.41$$

$$90.59 = 61.41 - 61.41 + 2.38f$$

$$90.59 = 2.38f$$

$$\frac{90.59}{2.38} = \frac{2.38f}{2.38}$$

$$38.06 \approx f$$

Jim's femur is about 38 cm long.

14 **Try This as a Class** Describe the steps in the Example above. Tell which inverse operations were used.

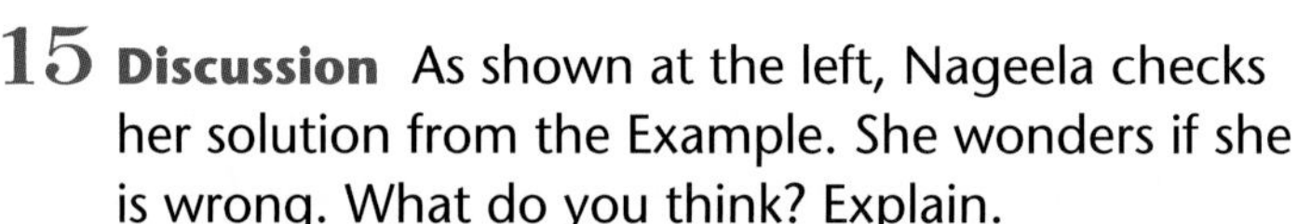

15 **Discussion** As shown at the left, Nageela checks her solution from the Example. She wonders if she is wrong. What do you think? Explain.

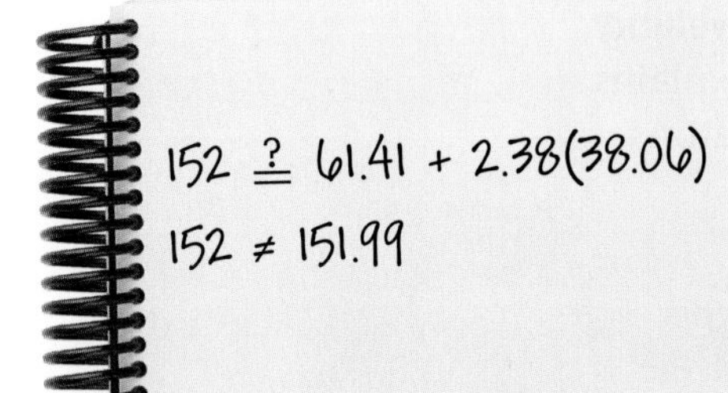

16 **Discussion** You can first multiply both sides of the equation shown in the Example by a power of ten to avoid working with decimals.

$$100(152) = 100(61.41 + 2.38f)$$

a. Copy this first step. Then finish solving the equation.

b. Show how you would use this method to solve $9.7 = 3 + 2.7x$. What power of ten did you use? Why?

✓ QUESTION 17

...checks that you can solve an equation involving decimals.

17 **✓ CHECKPOINT** Solve each equation. Round decimal solutions to the nearest hundredth and check your solutions.

a. $28.6 = 3.7x + 5.3$ **b.** $4.1 + 0.5n = 4.1$ **c.** $\frac{x}{9.8} + 1 = 10$

d. $0.57r - 3 = 8.2$ **e.** $\frac{m}{5.5} - 120 = 2.5$ **f.** $\frac{t}{4.5} - 13 = -12$

18 Estimate Dr. Leschensky's femur to the nearest centimeter by solving the equation you wrote in Question 13.

HOMEWORK EXERCISES See Exs. 11–26 on pp. 211–212.

Section 5 Key Concepts

Key Terms

decimal notation

scientific notation

Scientific Notation (pp. 205–207)

Scientific notation is a useful way to write large numbers. You can change between decimal notation and scientific notation.

Example

decimal notation → scientific notation

$320{,}000 = 3.2 \cdot 100{,}000 = 3.2 \cdot 10^5$

A number greater than or equal to 1 and less than 10

A power of ten

Example

scientific notation → decimal notation

$9.4 \cdot 10^3 = 9.4 \cdot 1000 = 9400$

Solving Equations with Decimals (pp. 207–208)

You can use inverse operations to solve equations with decimals.

Example

Solve $\frac{x}{3.3} + 1.6 = 4.8$.

$\frac{x}{3.3} + 1.6 - \mathbf{1.6} = 4.8 - \mathbf{1.6}$ Subtract **1.6** to both sides to undo the addition.

$\frac{x}{3.3} = 3.2$

$\mathbf{3.3}\left(\frac{x}{3.3}\right) = \mathbf{3.3}(3.2)$ Multiply both sides by **3.3** to undo the division.

$x = 10.56$

Key Concepts Questions

19 **a.** Which number is greater, $5.9 \cdot 10^8$ or $6.8 \cdot 10^7$?

b. Do you need to rewrite the numbers in decimal notation to be able to tell which is greater? Explain.

20 Show how to check the solution in the last Example.

Section 5
Practice & Application Exercises

YOU WILL NEED

For Ex. 7:
- calculator

For Exercises 1–4, write each number in decimal notation.

1. Approximate age of Earth: at least $4.5 \cdot 10^9$ years

2. The distance from Earth to the sun: about $9.3 \cdot 10^7$ mi

3. Speed of light: about $1.86 \cdot 10^5$ mi/sec

4. Distance light travels in a year: about $5.88 \cdot 10^{12}$ mi

5. Which numbers below are written in scientific notation? Explain.

   A. $7.987 \cdot 10^2$ B. $3.57 \cdot 10^{99}$ C. $82.1 \cdot 10^3$ D. $5.13 \cdot 2^{10}$

Astronomy **A *light-year* is the distance that light travels in a vacuum in one year. One light-year ≈ $5.88 \cdot 10^{12}$ miles. Use this fact and the bar graph below for Exercises 6–8.**

Approximate Distances to Galaxies Near Earth

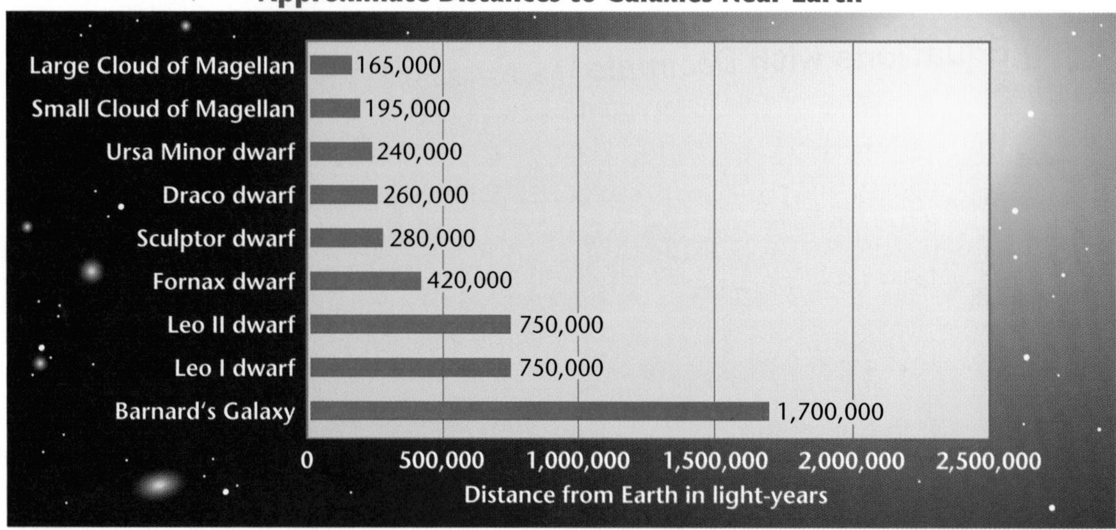

6. Which galaxy is a little more than 10 times as far from Earth as the Large Cloud of Magellan?

7. Calculator Find the distance to each galaxy in miles. Write your answers in scientific notation. Round the decimal part of each number to the nearest tenth.

8. **Challenge** Suppose a fictional space ship travels from Earth to the Large Cloud of Magellan in 3 weeks. Estimate its speed in miles per hour.

9. **Oceanography** On average, the ocean is about $3.795 \cdot 10^3$ m deep. Its deepest point is $11.033 \cdot 10^3$ m.

a. Which of these measurements is in scientific notation?

b. Give each measurement in kilometers. Use decimal notation.

FOR▶HELP with *the metric system*, see **TOOLBOX, p. 581**

10. **Population Growth** In 1650, the world population was about 470 million. In 2006, it was about 6.528 billion.

a. Write each population in scientific notation and in decimal notation.

b. **Estimation** Compare the 1650 and 1990 populations. About how many times greater is the 1990 world population?

Solve each equation. Round decimal answers to the nearest hundredth and check your solutions.

11. $12.5 = 2.5x$

12. $0.7x - 2 = 19$

13. $\frac{m}{0.3} = 8$

14. $12 = 0.5p + 2.5$

15. $12.4 = \frac{w}{2.4} + 2.4$

16. $\frac{n}{0.33} - 9 = 12.99$

17. $8.3 + 0.7n = 8.3$

18. $0.15p + 12.95 = 13.15$

19. $4.1x + 5.8 = 10$

20. $0.36 + 1.05x = 9.92$

Shoe Sizes The formulas below relate United States shoe size *s* to foot length *f* in inches. Use the formulas for Exercises 21–24.

Men's shoes	**Women's shoes**
$s = 3f - 22$	$s = 3f - 20.7$

21. Barry wears men's shoe size 10. Estimate his foot length to the nearest inch.

22. Tia wears women's shoe size 8. Estimate her foot length to the nearest inch.

23. Edie usually wears a women's size 10 shoe. She wants to try on a pair of men's running shoes. Running shoes come in whole and half sizes. What size should she try on?

24. According to these formulas and your foot length measurement in inches, what size shoe should you wear?

25. **Open-ended** If you buy shoes from another country, you may need to know your European shoe size. The formulas below relate European size e to United States size u. Write a word problem that can be solved by using one or both of the formulas.

Men's shoes	Women's shoes
$e = 1.29u + 30.8$	$e = 1.24u + 28.7$

RESEARCH

Exercise 26 checks that you know how scientific notation is applied.

Reflecting on the Section

26. Find three large numbers in a newspaper or encyclopedia. Write them in scientific notation and add labels that explain what the numbers mean.

Spiral Review

27. $\triangle ABC \sim \triangle ADE$. Find the length of $\overline{DE}$. (Module 3, p. 198)

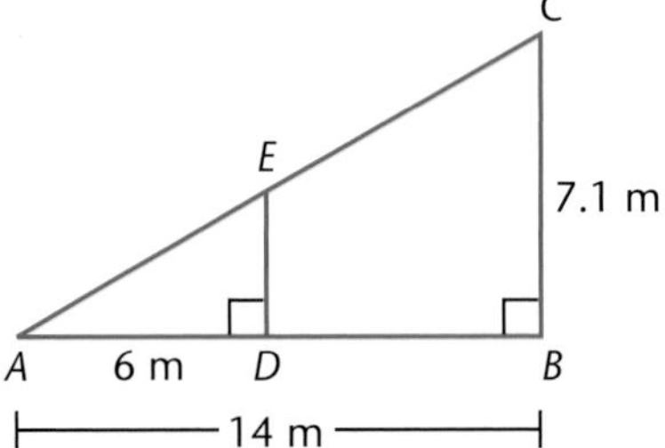

Find each sum or difference. (Module 2, p. 86)

28. –8 + 7
29. 6 – (–11)
30. 92 + (–2)
31. –15 – (–21)
32. –50 + 50
33. 0 – (–12)
34. –18 – (–5)
35. 3 – 5 + 8

Use the box-and-whisker plots. (Module 1, p. 23)

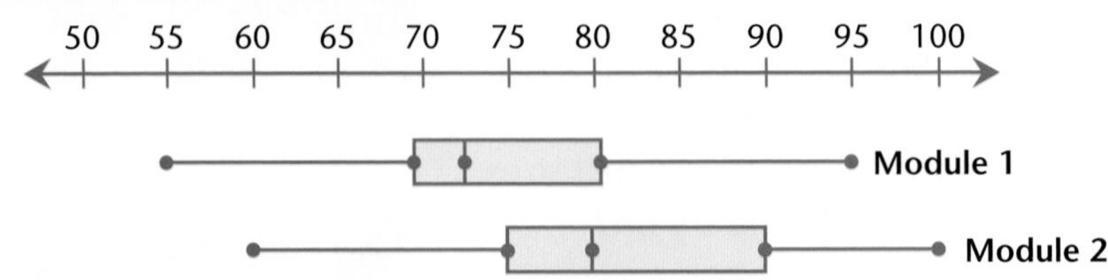

36. Estimate the median score on the Module 2 test.

37. Estimate the high score on the Module 1 test.

Section 5 Extra Skill Practice

Write each number in scientific notation.

1. 5,180,000
2. 870
3. 28,900,000
4. 3,120
5. 362,900,000,000
6. 15,000

Write each number in decimal notation.

7. $3.5 \cdot 10^8$
8. $5.23 \cdot 10^3$
9. $8.1 \cdot 10^5$
10. $6.91 \cdot 10^1$
11. $4.8 \cdot 10^{14}$
12. $2.25 \cdot 10^2$
13. $4.76 \cdot 10^4$
14. $1.853 \cdot 10^7$
15. $6 \cdot 10^{10}$

Solve each equation. Round decimal answers to the nearest hundredth and check your solutions.

16. $18.1 = 2.2k + 6.4$
17. $\frac{t}{8.1} + 13.5 = 29.9$
18. $0.39w + 4.5 = 8.4$
19. $24.6 + \frac{q}{0.2} = 30.1$
20. $5.08z + 6.17 = 16.47$
21. $32.91 = \frac{m}{3.34} + 12.83$
22. $15.6 = 1.6v + 7.36$
23. $38.62 = \frac{r}{6.49} + 27.53$
24. $1.2g + 110.9 = 121.7$
25. $0.02x + 0.13 = 6.16$
26. $\frac{c}{0.17} + 6.9 = 11.3$
27. $3.62n + 0.23 = 9.43$
28. $76.8y + 5.31 = 12.99$
29. $6.387 + 2.8p = 15.349$

Standardized Testing ▶ Multiple Choice

1. The area of the Pacific Ocean is about 166,000,000 km^2. How is this measure expressed in scientific notation?

   (A) 1.66 million km^2
   (B) $16.6 \cdot 10^7$ km^2
   (C) 1.668 km^2
   (D) $1.66 \cdot 10^8$ km^2

2. What is the value of y in the equation $16.8 = \frac{y}{1.2} + 4.8$?

   (A) 144 (B) 14.4 (C) 1.44 (D) 0.144

Section 6 Logical Thinking

IN THIS SECTION

EXPLORATION 1
- Using *And, Or, Not*

Whodunit?

Setting the Stage

The Story So Far...

The police know that the thief has blood type A. They also know that he or she did not go on Dr. Ashilaka's field trip. Jim and Nageela use a computer database at the police station to see which of the 22 suspects match up with these clues. But Jim thinks they have made a mistake.

"My first step was to search for suspects with blood type A. The computer found 11 people who match up. But then I ran a new search to find suspects who did not go on the field trip. Now look! Twelve people! That makes a total of 23 suspects, but there are only 22 suspects in the database! And I haven't even searched for suspects with the right height or hair color yet."

"Oh no," moaned Nageela. "You're right! We've done something wrong!"

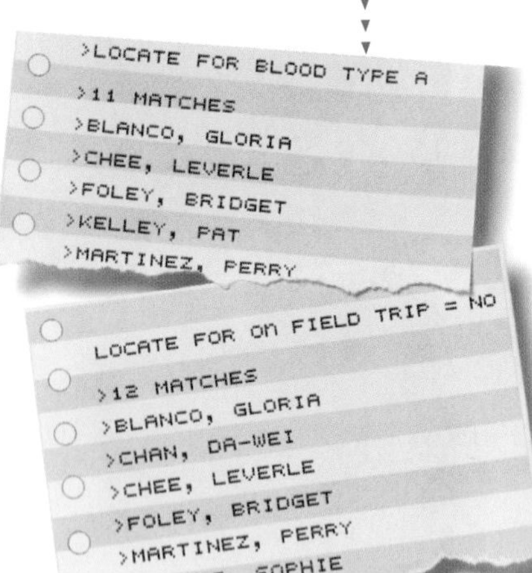

Think About It

1 What did Jim tell the computer to search for?

2 Do you think Jim and Nageela did something wrong? Use the printout from Jim's computer search to help explain your thinking.

Exploration 1

Using AND, OR, NOT

SET UP *Work as a class. You will need:* • *Labsheet 6A* • *tape*

GOAL

LEARN HOW TO...
- interpret statements with *and, or,* and *not*
- organize information in a Venn diagram

AS YOU...
- analyze clues in a mystery

KEY TERMS
- Venn diagram
- and
- or
- not

▶ **You will use a diagram to search for suspects who have blood type A and were absent from the field trip to Blacktail Canyon.**

3 **Use Labsheet 6A.** The *Suspect List* gives information about each of the 22 suspects in *The Mystery of Blacktail Canyon.* Your class should follow these steps:

- Your teacher will assign a suspect name to each student in the class. Write your suspect's name on a small slip of paper.
- Your teacher will draw a large diagram on the board. Tape your suspect's name in the correct part of the diagram.

4 Look back at the story on page 214. How could your class diagram help Nageela and Jim understand their mistake?

▶ **The diagram your class made is a *Venn diagram.* Venn diagrams are used to model relationships between groups. They can help you interpret statements that use the words *and, or,* and *not.***

EXAMPLE

This Venn diagram organizes information about eight pieces of pottery Nageela found on one shelf of a cliff dwelling. She used the letters A–H to label the pieces.

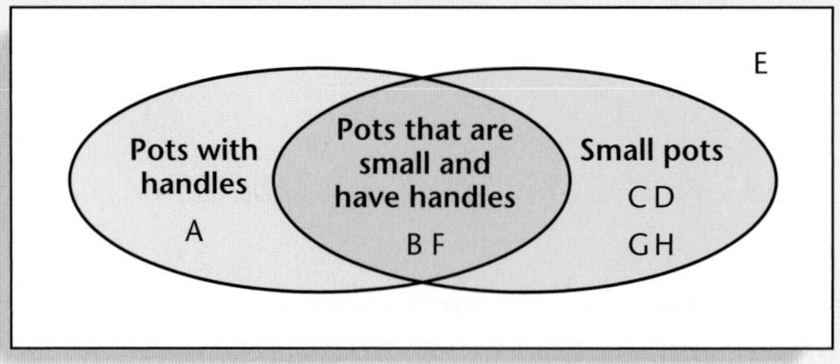

▶ **The diagrams below show groupings that use the words *and, or,* and *not.* Notice that the word *or* has special meaning in mathematics. It means *one or the other or both.***

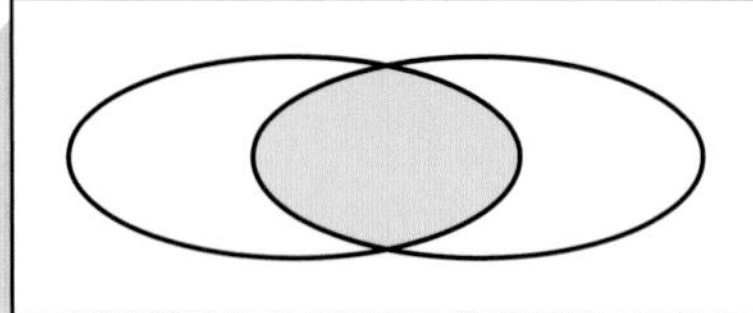
2 pots are small **and** have handles.

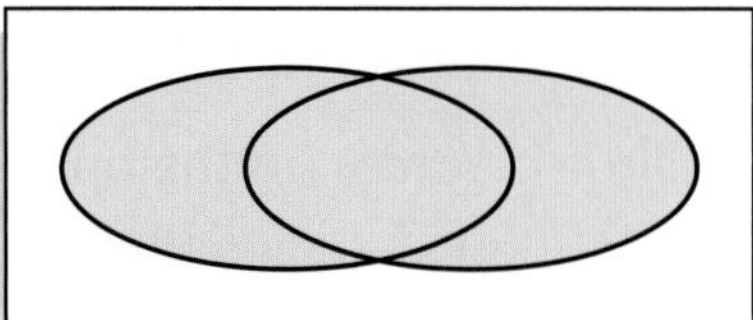
7 pots are small **or** have handles (or both).

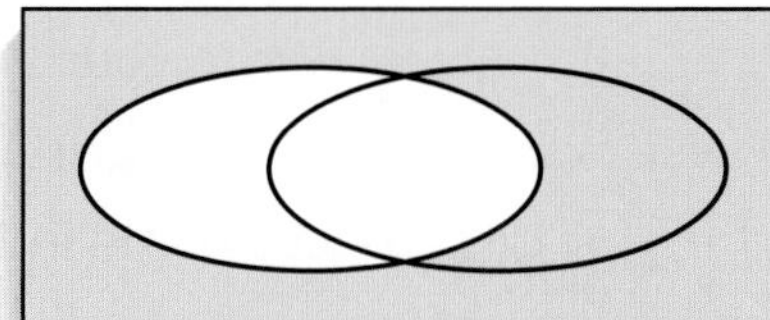
5 pots do **not** have handles.

5 **Try This as a Class** Use the Venn diagram from the Example.

a. How many pots are small? How many are *not* small?

b. How many pots have handles? How many do *not* have handles?

c. How many pots are *not* small *and* do *not* have handles?

d. To count the number of small pots or pots with handles, Angela says you should add the number of small pots and the number with handles to get 9. Do you agree? Explain.

6 **Try This as a Class** Use the Venn diagram of suspects your class created.

a. How many suspects do *not* have blood type A?

b. How many have blood type A *or* were absent from the field trip?

c. How many do *not* have blood type A *and* were not absent from the field trip?

d. In what group will Jim and Nageela find the thief?

7 ✓ **CHECKPOINT** Six friends were talking about whether they had been to Canada and Mexico. Paolo, Maria, Dan, and Jim have been to Mexico. Paolo, Maria, and Stacey have been to Canada. Rob has never visited either country. Use this information to make a Venn diagram. Shade the diagram to show which friends have been to Canada or Mexico.

✓ **QUESTION 7**

...checks that you can use a Venn diagram to interpret statements with *and*, *or*, and *not*.

HOMEWORK EXERCISES See Exs. 1–14 on pp. 218–220.

Section 6 Key Concepts

Key Terms

Venn Diagram (pp. 215–217)

A Venn diagram models relationships among groups. It can help you interpret statements that use the words and, or, and not.

Venn diagram

and

or

not

Example Joshua kept track of how many days in August were sunny and how many days were over 90°. He made the Venn diagram below.

Number of sunny days:
$21 + 5 = 26$

Number of days that were sunny or over 90°: $21 + 5 + 3 = 29$

Number of days that were not sunny and not over 90°: 2

8 **Key Concepts Question** Use the Venn diagram above.

a. How many days in August were not over 90°?

b. About what percent of the days in August were not over 90°? Give your answer to the nearest percent. Show how you got your answer.

Section 6 Practice & Application Exercises

YOU WILL NEED

For Exs. 22–24:
- compass
- metric ruler

Language Arts **In everyday English, the word *or* can be *exclusive* or *inclusive,* as shown below.**

Exclusive *Or*
Nao drives or takes a bus to work. Nao either drives or takes a bus, not both. She cannot do both at the same time.

Inclusive *Or*
Nao eats lunch or reads at noon. Nao can eat lunch, read, or do both activities at once.

For Exercises 1 and 2, tell whether the *or* used is *inclusive* or *exclusive.* (*Note*: All other exercises in this book use the inclusive *or.*)

1. Brad has saved enough money to buy either a touring bike *or* a mountain bike. He can afford only one bike.

2. On cold days, Maria wears a sweater *or* a jacket or both.

Track **For Exercises 3–6, use the Venn diagram below.**

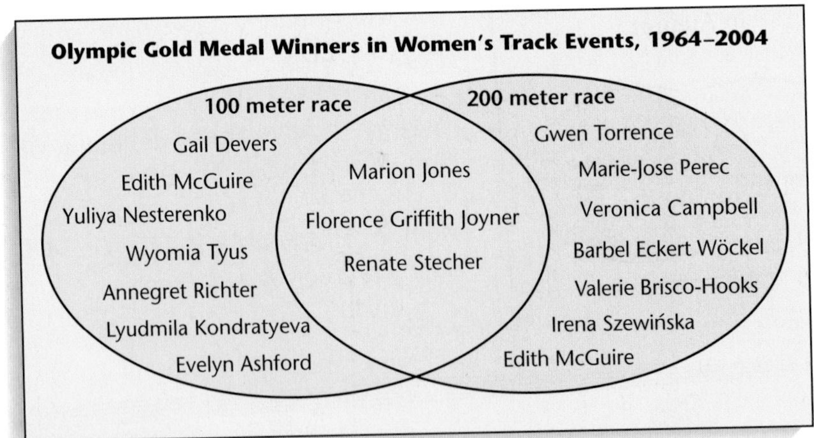

3. Which runners have won the 100 m race and the 200 m race?

4. How many runners have won the 100 m race?

5. How many runners have won the 100 m race or the 200 m race?

6. In the 1996 Olympics, Svetlana Masterkova won the gold medal in the 800 m race, but she has not won the gold medal in an Olympic 100 m or 200 m race. Describe where to put her name in the diagram on page 216.

For Exercises 7–10, use the Venn diagram at the right.

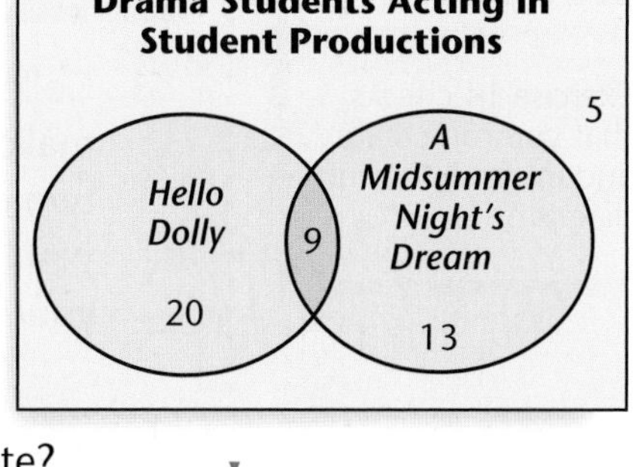

7. How many students acted in *Hello Dolly* or in *A Midsummer Night's Dream?*

8. a. How many drama students acted in both plays?

   b. How many drama students did not act in both plays?

9. The drama teacher estimates that about 60% of the students acted in *Hello Dolly.* How close is this estimate?

10. **Challenge** Suppose some students act in *The Marriage Proposal,* a short play with only three characters. Two of these students also act in both *Hello Dolly* and *A Midsummer Night's Dream.* The third student does not appear in either of these plays. Revise the Venn diagram to include this information.

Geography For Exercises 11 and 12, use the map below.

11. Make a Venn diagram that includes all 50 states. Use these categories:

    - States that border another country or a Great Lake
    - States that border an ocean

12. Use your Venn diagram to answer each question.

    a. How many states border another country or a Great Lake?

    b. How many states border an ocean?

    c. How many states border an ocean or a country or a Great Lake?

    d. How many states do not border an ocean?

    e. What percent of the states border an ocean and border a country or a Great Lake?

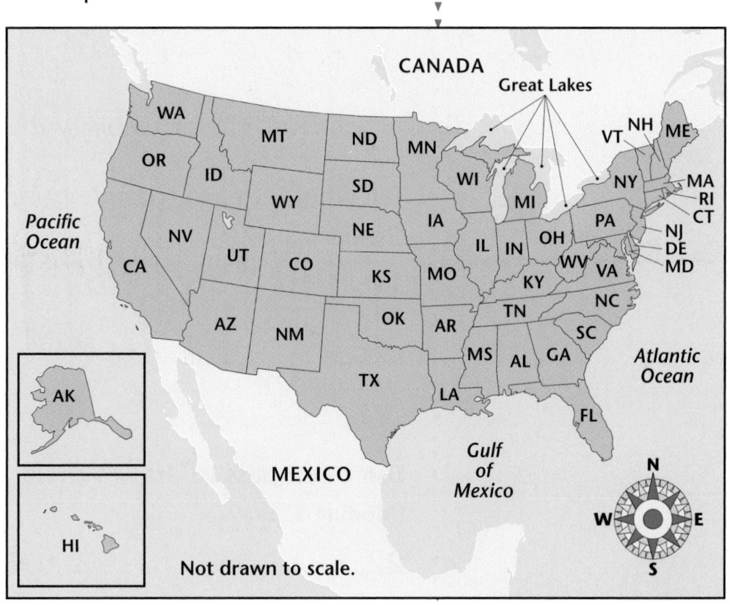

13. Open-ended Write a word problem that can be solved using a Venn diagram. Then solve the problem. Explain your solution using the words *and, or,* and *not.*

RESEARCH

Exercise 14 checks that you can create and interpret a Venn diagram.

Reflecting on the Section

14. Collect data from friends and family members and use the data to make a Venn diagram. For example, you may want to ask people two questions, such as, "Do you like to watch soccer?" and "Do you like to watch figure skating?" Share your Venn diagram with your class. Explain how you collected your data.

Spiral Review

Solve each equation. Round decimal answers to the nearest hundredth. **(Module 3, p. 209)**

15. $30.9 = 0.3x + 6$ 16. $\frac{p}{0.12} = 5$ 17. $24 = 13.2 + 0.7n$

18. The eighth grade class is asked to choose two students to help plan an event for the school's field day. Mary, John, Sue, and José all volunteer. The class decides to choose names out of a hat to decide who will help. **(Module 2, p. 118)**

a. Copy and complete the tree diagram showing the possible pairs of students who can be chosen.

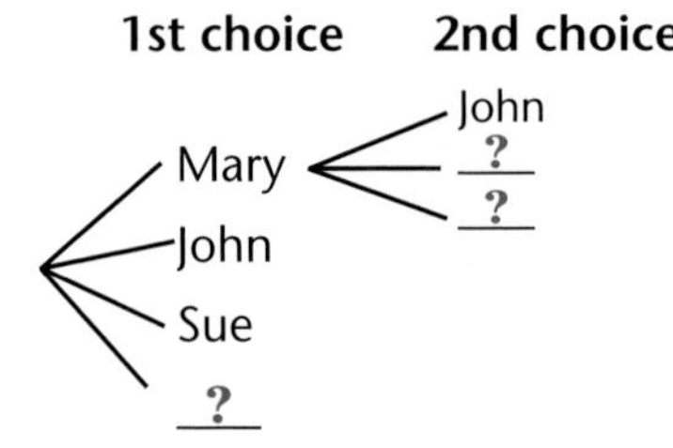

b. Find the probablility that José and Sue will help plan the trip.

Tell whether each triangle is *isosceles, equilateral,* or *scalene.* **(Toolbox, p. 593)**

19. 3 cm, 3 cm, 3 cm

20. 6.1 mm, 5.7 mm, 10.2 m

21. 2.5 in., 2.5 in., 1.9 in.

Use a compass to draw a circle with the given radius or diameter. **(Module 3, p. 197)**

22. $r = 1.5$ cm 23. $d = 5$ cm 24. $r = 6$ cm

Section 6 Extra Skill Practice

For Exercises 1–5, use the Venn diagram below. It shows the animals that a class chose for their research reports.

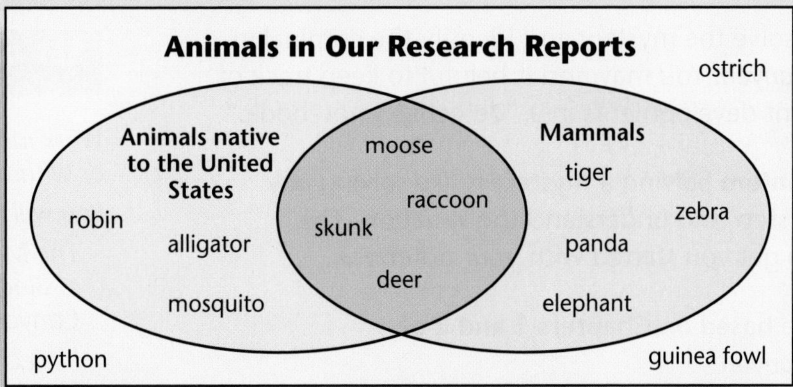

1. Which animals native to the United States are mammals?
2. Which animals are not mammals and not native to the United States?
3. How many animals are native to the United States?
4. The mosquito belongs to which category or categories?
5. A llama is a mammal that is native to South America. Describe where you would put a llama in the Venn diagram.
6. Make a Venn diagram of the days of the week. In one category put all the days you are at school. In another category put all the days that contain the letter *n*.

Standardized Testing ▶ Performance Task

Many letters of the alphabet show line symmetry. Some have a vertical line of symmetry, some have a horizontal line of symmetry, and some have both. Make a Venn diagram that organizes all 26 capital letters by the types of line symmetry they show.

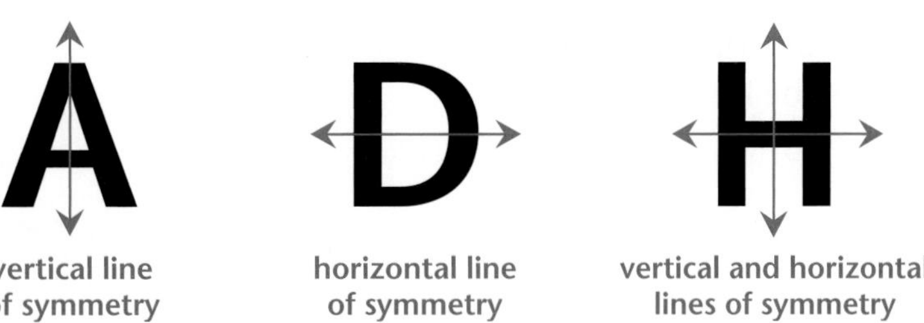

vertical line of symmetry — horizontal line of symmetry — vertical and horizontal lines of symmetry

Solving a Mystery

For this project, you will solve the mystery and identify the criminal in *The Mystery of Blacktail Canyon.* You may find it helpful to keep track of ideas, clues, and important developments in a "detective's notebook."

SET UP

Work individually or with a partner.

You will need:

- *The Mystery of Blacktail Canyon*
- *Project Labsheet A (Question 15)*

Understanding the Problem Solving a mystery is like solving any other problem. Your first step is to understand the situation. The questions below will help get you started with your notebook.

Project Questions 1–4 are based on Chapters 1 and 2 of *The Mystery of Blacktail Canyon.*

1 Why have Dr. Ashilaka and Nageela come to the Four Corners region? What do they hope to find?

2 What crime is Dr. Ashilaka afraid someone might commit?

3 Whom does Jim Cooper see at Dr. Ashilaka's lecture? What observations, if any, does Jim make about each person?

4 Why does Officer Yellow Robe think there is something strange about the rental car that had skidded to a stop at the edge of the washout?

Making Predictions In Chapter 3 of *The Mystery of Blacktail Canyon,* Officer Charlotte Lopez examines the footprints and the length of the stride of the person they are tracking. You used Charlotte's measurement of foot length to predict the missing driver's height in Section 3 on pages 184–185. You can also use her clue about the missing driver's stride length to get more information.

CLUE Measurements taken by Officer Lopez:

- **foot length: 29 cm**
- **stride length: 155 cm**

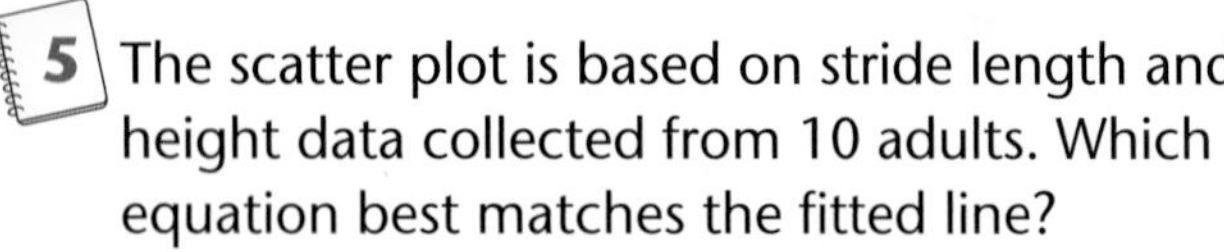

5 The scatter plot is based on stride length and height data collected from 10 adults. Which equation best matches the fitted line?

A. $y = 0.6x - 84$

B. $y = 0.6x$

C. $y = 0.6x + 84$

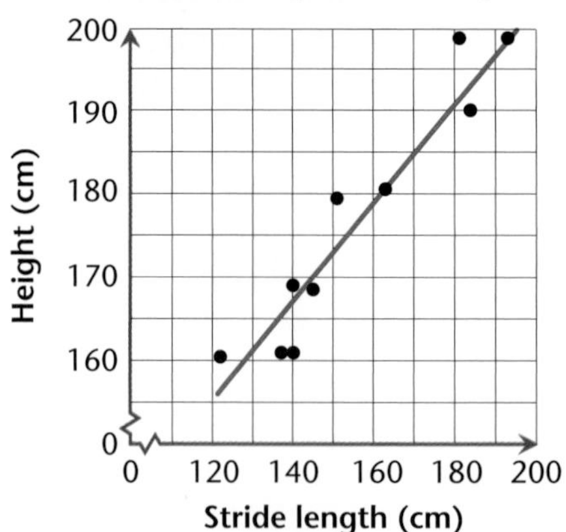

6 a. Use the equation you chose in Question 5 to predict the height of the driver from the stride length measurement.

b. Use this prediction and the one from Exploration 2 of Section 3 to give a reasonable range of heights for the driver.

Gathering and Reviewing Evidence To answer the questions below, you need to read Chapter 7 of *The Mystery of Blacktail Canyon.* You will use some of the skills you have learned to estimate the heights of two suspects, Ms. Weatherwax and Mr. Martinez.

7 How can knowing the heights of Ms. Weatherwax and Mr. Martinez help Jim and Nageela find the thief?

In Chapter 7 Jim measures Ms. Weatherwax's stride length. Her stride is about 22 hand-widths long. After leaving the school, Jim and Nageela find that Jim's hand is 7 cm wide.

8 How many centimeters long is Ms. Weatherwax's stride?

9 Look back at Questions 5 and 6. Use the information to estimate Ms. Weatherwax's height. Describe your method.

In the story, Jim measures Mr. Martinez's shadow length. At the same time, he also measures Nageela's height and shadow length. Use the diagrams below for Questions 10 and 11.

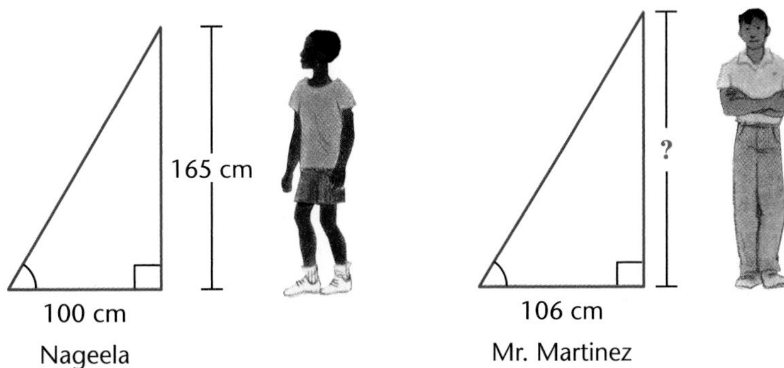

10 Are the triangles in the diagram similar? How do you know?

11 Find Mr. Martinez's height. Describe your method.

12 Summarize the clues you have gathered. Make sure you list everything you know or suspect about the thief. Below are some questions to consider.

- What do you know about the person's appearance?
- Do you know the person's height and foot size?
- How does knowing that the thief was injured help you?
- Did the suspect attend Dr. Ashilaka's lecture? the field trip? How do you know?
- Is the thief a stranger or someone who knows the area? Explain your reasoning.

Using a Venn diagram In Section 6, you narrowed down the list of suspects in *The Mystery of Blacktail Canyon.* You can narrow down the list further by identifying suspects whose height is the same as the height of the person who left the footprints in Blacktail Canyon.

Questions 13–15 are based on Chapter 8 of *The Mystery of Blacktail Canyon.*

13 Look back at your notes from Questions 5 and 6. About how tall do you think the person who left the footprints is?

14 Sketch the diagram shown. Shade your sketch to show where you would put suspects who fit the description of the thief.

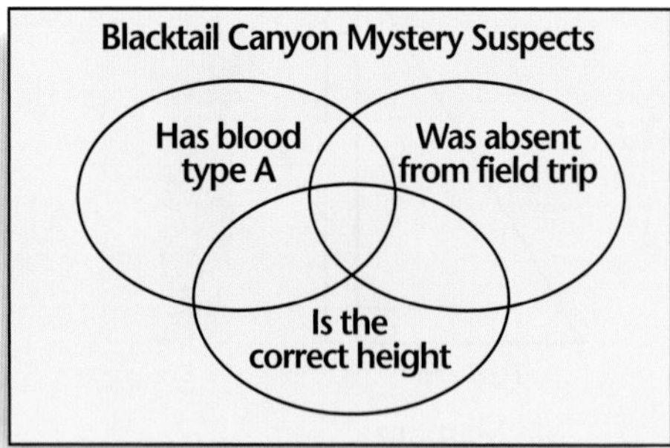

15 **Use Project Labsheet A.** Make a list of the people on the *Suspect List* who fit the description of the thief.

Drawing Conclusions Throughout this project, you have used mathematics to help identify a thief. You have discovered some characteristics of the guilty person, and you have narrowed a list of 22 possible suspects to three. Now you will receive more information from your teacher that will help you narrow the list even further.

SET UP

Work in a group of four.

You will need:

- *Project Labsheet B*
- *Your "detective's notebook" or journal*
- *Clues and transcripts chosen by your teacher*

16 Some information gathered during an investigation is useful. Some is not. Review the clue cards. Discuss the clues with your group. Write down the names of people you believe may have committed the crime. Explain why you feel these people and no others are guilty.

17 **Use Project Labsheet B** Complete the labsheet and review the interview transcripts from the police investigation. Who do you now believe committed the crime? Is your final suspect one of the people you chose in Question 16? Explain why you feel this person and no one else is guilty.

18 Have your teacher check your answers to Questions 16 and 17. If you made an error, review your evidence and revise your solution. Record your new conclusion, explaining your errors as well as your new answer.

Like you, Nageela and Jim think they know the identity of the thief. Ferrel, Jack, and Charlotte agree with their conclusion. At the end of Chapter 10, the five sleuths leave the station to catch the suspect.

19 What happens after the police, Nageela, and Jim leave the station? Write an ending to *The Mystery of Blacktail Canyon* in your journal.

MODULE 3 Review and Assessment

You will need • *graph paper* (Exs. 9–12) • *compass, ruler, and Review and Assessment Labsheet* (Ex. 18)

Find each value. Describe your method. Tell whether your answer is exact or an estimate. (Sec. 1, Explor. 1)

1. $\sqrt{0.09}$
2. $\sqrt{16,000}$
3. $-\sqrt{96}$
4. $\sqrt{\frac{4}{81}}$

5. Keith claims that the large can will hold twice as much as the small can. Is he correct? Explain. (Sec. 1, Explor. 2)

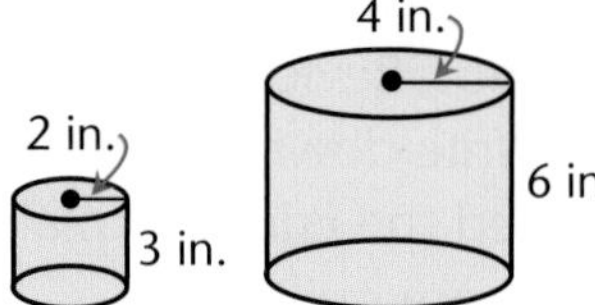

Find each value. (Sec. 2, Explor. 1)

6. $\frac{3(4) + 21}{\sqrt{102 + 19}}$
7. $\sqrt{\frac{8(3) + 2(-4)}{36}}$
8. $\frac{5^2}{4(-3) + 87}$

Graph each equation. Tell whether the graph is *linear* or *nonlinear*. (Sec. 2, Explor. 2)

9. $y = 4x - 3$
10. $y = -2x + 1$
11. $y = x^2 + 1$
12. $y = 3x - 6$

Find the slope of each line. (Sec. 3, Explor. 1)

13.
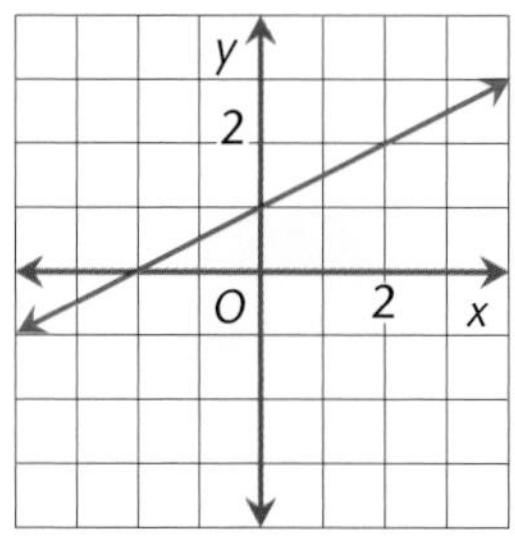

14.
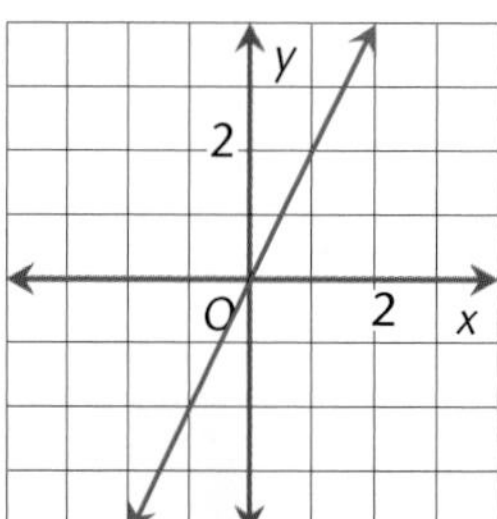

15.
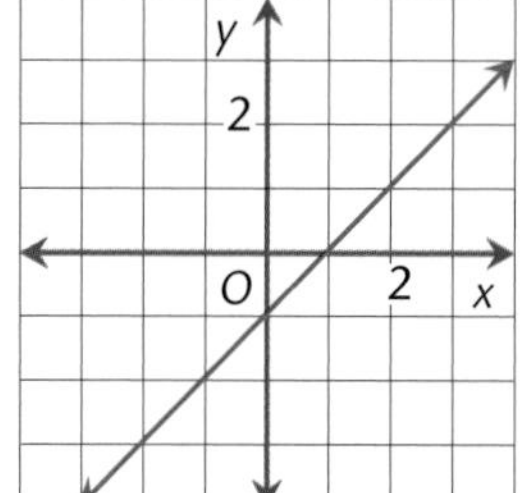

16. The scatter plot compares the populations of a number of counties in Texas in 2000 with the populations in 1990. The 1990 population is on the horizontal axis and the 2000 population is on the vertical axis. (Sec. 3, Explor. 2)

   a. Which equation best fits the fitted line on the scatter plot?
      I. $y = 1.2x - 660$
      II. $y = 1.2x$
      III. $y = x + 800$

   b. Use the equation you chose in part (a) to predict the 2000 population for a county that had a population of 6200 in 1990.

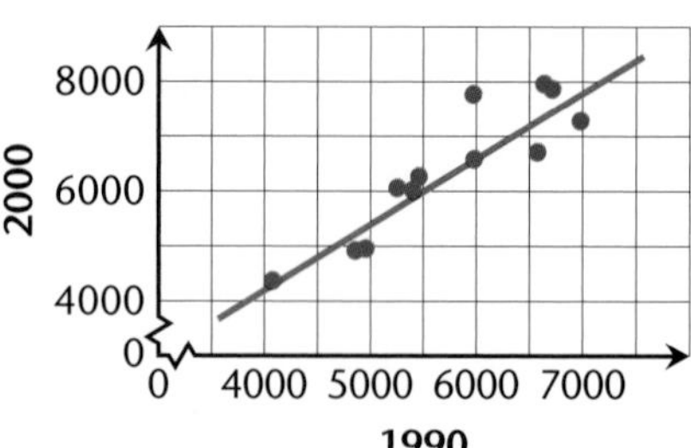

17. Estimate the height of the building if the person shown is about 6 ft tall. (Sec. 4, Explor. 1)

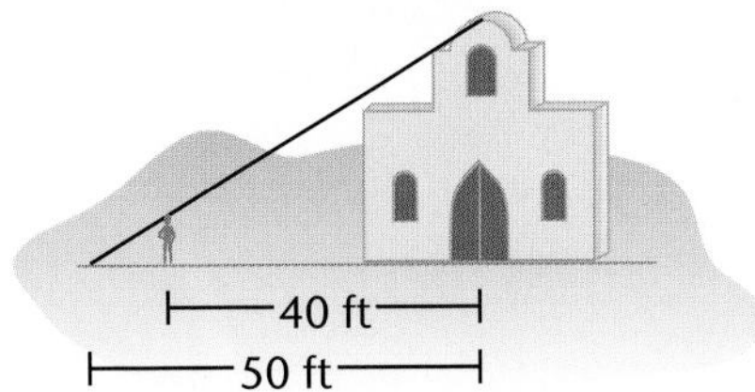

18. **Use the Review and Assessment Labsheet.** Follow the directions to find the diameter of the tree trunk. Mark a radius and a chord. (Sec. 4, Explor. 2)

Write each number in scientific notation. (Sec. 5, Explor. 1)

19. About 52,500,000 pet dogs lived in the United States in 1991.
20. The area of Mexico is about 762 thousand square miles.

For Exercises 21 and 22, write each product in decimal notation. (Sec. 5, Explor. 1)

21. The entrance to Mesa Verde Park is $6.95 \cdot 10^3$ ft above sea level.
22. The mesa dwellings were abandoned about $7 \cdot 10^2$ years ago.
23. **Writing** Jill Wu is an anthropologist. She finds the incomplete skeleton of a 180 cm tall male at a site. She thinks another bone (a tibia) found nearby is part of the same skeleton. Explain how she can use the formula $h = 78.62 + 2.52t$, where h = the height of the skeleton and t = the length of the tibia in centimeters, to see whether she is correct. (Sec. 5, Explor. 2)

For Exercises 24–27, use the table. (Sec. 6, Explor. 1)

Means of Transportation
airplane
bicycle
bus
car
helicopter
skateboard
skis
speedboat
train
truck

24. Make a Venn diagram that includes the means of transportation listed. Use the categories *Has Engine* and *Travels Only On Ground.*
25. Which means of transportation have an engine?
26. Which means of transportation have an engine and travel only on the ground?
27. Add two more means of transportation to the Venn diagram.

Reflecting on the Module

28. **Writing** Explain how mathematics is important to the work of a police officer. What kinds of mathematics are used in investigations?

MODULE 4

INVENTIONS

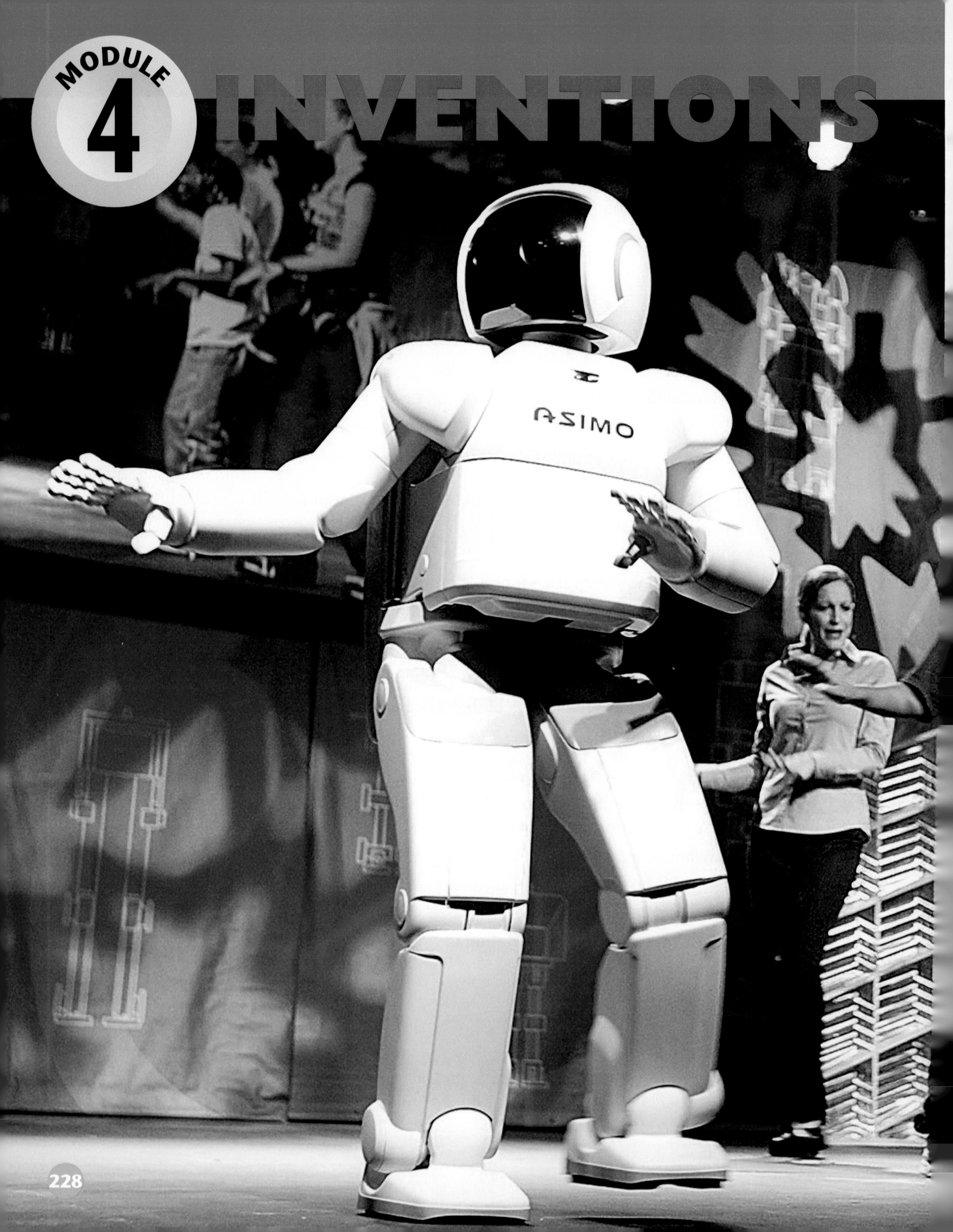

ASIMO

CONNECTING
MATHEMATICS & The Theme

SECTION OVERVIEW

1 Circumference, Area, and Volume

As you study the invention of pancakes:

- Find the circumference and area of a circle
- Find volumes of prisms, cylinders, and spheres

2 Working with Cylinders

As you read about tin cans:

- Find the surface area of a cylinder
- Find and interpret the ratio of surface area to volume

3 Slopes and Equations of Lines

As you explore TV sales:

- Identify positive, negative, zero, and undefined slopes
- Write equations of lines in slope-intercept form

4 Rational Numbers

As you learn to write fractions using the Egyptian number system:

- Recognize characteristics of rational numbers
- Solve equations containing rational numbers

5 Counting Techniques

As you learn about Braille:

- Find numbers of permutations
- Find numbers of combinations

6 Working with Probability

As you examine keys for locks:

- Find probabilities of events

The Module Project

Building a Ramp

The ancient Egyptians may have used ramps and cylinders to move the stone blocks that form the Pyramids of Giza. You will use mathematics to design and build your own model ramp and cylinders that you can use to move small objects.

More on the Module Project

See pp. 304–305.

INTERNET
Resources and practice at
classzone.com

Circumference, Area, and Volume

IN THIS SECTION

EXPLORATION 1
- Finding Circumference and Area

EXPLORATION 2
- Finding Volume

Perfect Pancakes

Setting the Stage

Ask people to describe a typical American breakfast and many will mention pancakes, but pancakes are popular all over the world. There are French *crêpes,* Russian *blini,* and German *Pfannkuchen,* to name just a few. Pancakes may be thick or thin, fried or baked, sweet, salty, or even spicy. But the typical American pancake is sweet and fluffy and served with syrup.

Today one pancake restaurant chain alone serves a total of nearly 2 million pancakes each day in the United States and Canada. The popularity of pancakes has led to inventions such as the pancake ring for making multiple pancakes at once, specialty pans that allow you to flip a pancake without removing it from the pan, and even griddles that allow you to cook special designs or lettering into your pancakes.

▲ This pancake ring makes four perfectly round $3\frac{1}{2}$ in. diameter pancakes.

Think About It

1 **a.** Estimate the minimum size skillet needed to use the pancake ring shown at the left.

b. Suppose an average pancake is $6\frac{1}{2}$ in. in diameter. How many pancakes laid side-by-side would fit across your classroom?

2 A catering service claims it has sold 30,000,000 pancakes that, if laid end-to-end, would stretch from Los Angeles to Springfield, Illinois, a distance of 1857 mi. About what diameter pancakes does the catering service sell?

▶ **In this module, you will learn about the history of certain inventions and see how these inventions relate to mathematics.**

Exploration 1

Finding Circumference and AREA

GOAL

LEARN HOW TO...
- find the circumference and area of a circle

AS YOU...
- interpret scatter plots

KEY TERMS
- circumference
- area

▶ **The circumference of a circle is the distance around it. The exact relationship between the circumference and the diameter of a circle is given by the formula $\frac{C}{d} = \pi$, or $C = \pi d$.**

3 a. Calculator Press the π key on a calculator. What number appears?

b. π is actually a letter from the Greek alphabet. Does this mean that it is a variable? Explain.

c. Which is a closer approximation for π, 3.14 or $\frac{22}{7}$? Explain.

4 Try This as a Class Some students measured the diameter and the circumference of several circular objects. Then they made a scatter plot and drew a fitted line.

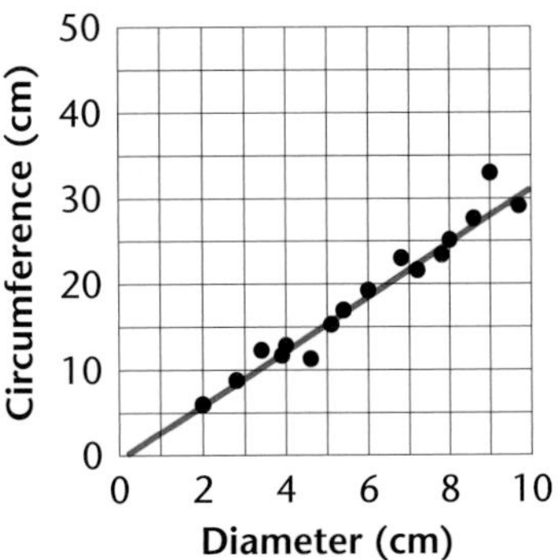

a. Does the scatter plot show a positive or negative correlation between the diameter and the circumference of a circle? Explain.

b. How do the data support the formula for the circumference of a circle?

c. Why is only Quadrant I used for the graph?

EXAMPLE

To find the circumference of a circle with a diameter of 20 cm, evaluate the expression πd when $d = 20$.

$$C = \pi d$$
$$= \pi(20)$$
$$\approx (3.14)(20)$$
$$\approx 62.8$$

To approximate the circumference, use 3.14 for π.

To find the exact circumference, substitute 20 for d. Use parentheses to show multiplication.

The circumference is about 62.8 cm.

5 **Discussion** You can also give the circumference in the Example in terms of π. Explain why the circumference is exactly 20π cm.

✓ QUESTION 6

...checks that you can find the circumference of a circle.

6 **✓ CHECKPOINT**

a. Find the exact circumference of a circle with $r = 6$ cm.

b. Approximate the circumference of a circle with $d = 15$ cm. Use 3.14 for π.

7 What length strip of metal is needed to make one of the four circular parts of the pancake ring shown on page 230?

▶ **The area of a circle is the number of square units of surface the figure covers. You can use the equation $A = \pi r^2$ to find the area of a circle when you know its radius.**

8 a. Name a circular object used in daily life. Describe the circumference of the object.

b. Describe the area of the object.

9 **Discussion** Which of the following best represents the relationship between a circle's area and its radius? How do you know?

Area Measurements of Circular Objects

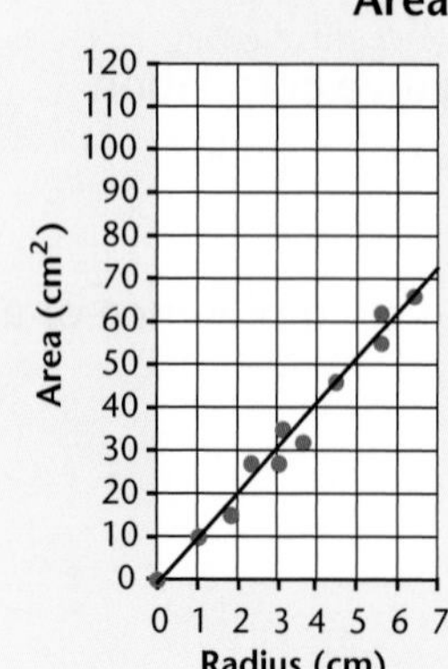

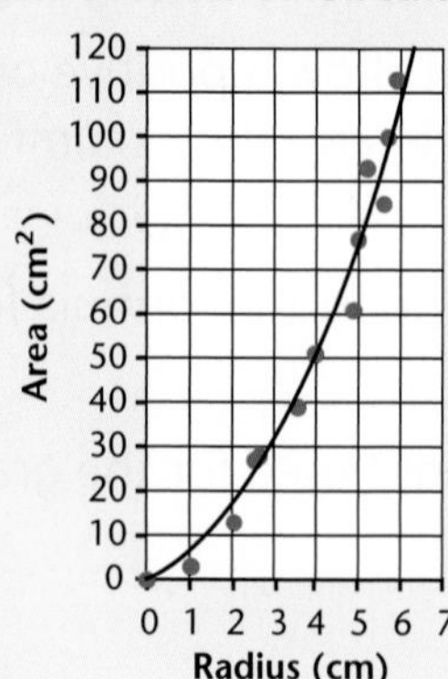

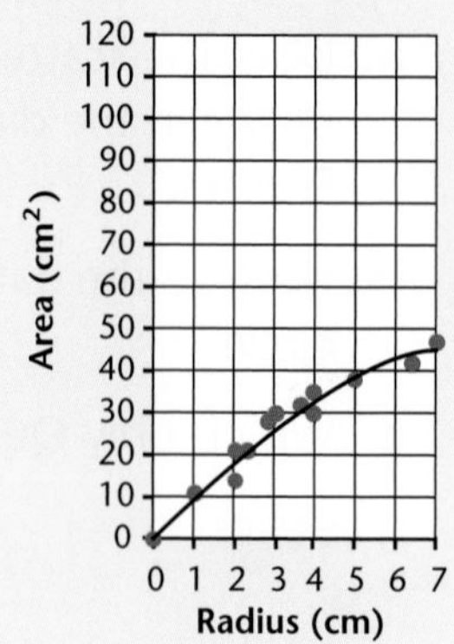

▶ **When you know a circle's radius, you can find both the exact area and an approximate area of the circle.**

FOR ▶ HELP with *exponents,* see **TOOLBOX, p. 589**

EXAMPLE

Find the area of a circle with a radius of 2.4 cm. Use 3.14 for π to find an approximate area.

2.4 cm

SAMPLE RESPONSE

Exact Area

$A = \pi r^2$

$= \pi(2.4)^2$

$= \pi(5.76)$

$= 5.76\pi$

The exact area is 5.76π cm^2.

Approximate Area

$A = \pi r^2$

$= \pi(2.4)^2$

$\approx (3.14)(5.76)$

≈ 18.0864

This is an approximation because 3.14 is an approximation for π.

An approximate area is 18.0864 cm^2.

▶ **Unless otherwise instructed, when you are asked to approximate the value of an expression involving π, use 3.14 for π and round to the nearest hundredth, if necessary.**

10 ✓ **CHECKPOINT** Find the exact area and an approximate area of each circle.

a. circle with $r = 6$ cm

b. circle with $d = 15.2$ cm

...checks that you can find the area of a circle.

11 You have been assigned to reinvent the pancake shape so that it will no longer be circular. The marketing department wants the new design to produce a pancake that has about the same area as a standard 5.5 in. diameter circular ring.

a. Sketch your design and label its dimensions.

b. Show how the area is equal to that of a 5.5 in. diameter circular ring.

c. How will the length of the metal strip needed for your design differ from the length needed for a 5.5 in. diameter ring?

HOMEWORK EXERCISES ▶ **See Exs. 1–9 on pp. 239–241.**

GOAL

LEARN HOW TO...
- find the volumes of prisms, cylinders, and spheres

AS YOU...
- investigate eating records

KEY TERMS
- prism
- polyhedron
- base
- cylinder
- sphere

Exploration 2

Finding VOLUME

SET UP *Work in a group of four. You will need • Labsheet 1A • metric ruler • 2 5-oz cans of modeling clay • plastic knife*

▶ **DO NOT TRY THESE AT HOME! Have you ever watched old movies where actors try to set a record swallowing goldfish? or eating pies? Setting eating records is dangerous to your health, but studying eating records can help you understand volume.**

- **Paul Hughes ate 39 jelly sandwiches in 60 min.**
- **Peter Dowdeswell ate 62 pancakes with butter and syrup in 6 min 58.5 sec.**

12 On average, what fraction of a sandwich did Paul Hughes consume per minute? Do you think this is an amazing feat?

▶ **Another way to decide whether Hughes's feat was amazing is to estimate the volume of what he ate. A stack of 39 jelly sandwiches would be shaped like a right *prism*. A prism is a polyhedron in which two of the faces, the bases, are congruent and parallel. The other faces are parallelograms. In a right prism, the other faces are rectangles.**

A **polyhedron** is a 3-dimensional object made up of flat surfaces, or **faces**, that are polygons.

Volume of a Prism
Volume = Area of the base × height
$V = Bh$

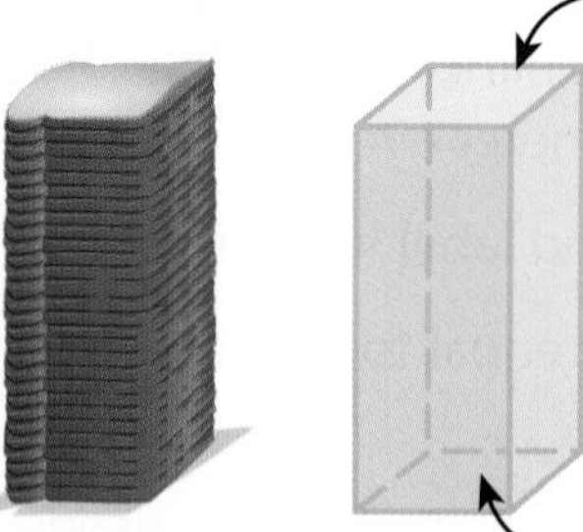

13 The shape of the bases of a prism determine the type of prism.

a. Why does it make sense to call the prism shown above a *rectangular* prism?

b. If the bases of a rectangular prism have length l and width w, what is another way to write the formula $V = Bh$ using l and w?

14 Each sandwich Paul Hughes ate measured 5 in. by 3 in. and was $\frac{1}{2}$ in. thick. Assume each sandwich is a rectangular prism.

a. Estimate the height of a stack of 39 sandwiches.

b. Find the actual height.

c. Find the area of the base of the stack of sandwiches.

d. Find the volume of the sandwiches Paul Hughes ate.

▶ **How does Peter Dowdeswell's record compare with Paul Hughes's record? To see, imagine a stack of 62 pancakes. The stack would be shaped like a *circular cylinder*. A cylinder is a 3-dimensional figure that has a curved surface and two flat, parallel, congruent bases. A circular cylinder has two circular bases.**

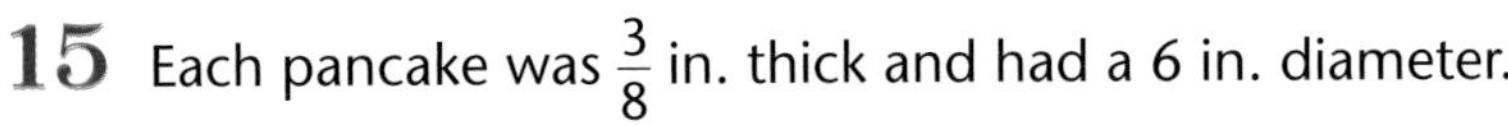

15 Each pancake was $\frac{3}{8}$ in. thick and had a 6 in. diameter.

a. Show with your hands the approximate height of the stack of 62 pancakes. Compare your estimate with others in your class.

b. Find the actual height of the stack of 62 pancakes.

▶ **You can use the formula for the volume of a prism to find the volume of a cylinder: Volume = area of base • height or $V = Bh$. In this book, all the cylinders are circular cylinders, so you can use the formula for the area of a circle to find B.**

EXAMPLE

Approximate the volume of a cylinder with a height of 10 in. and a diameter of 8 in.

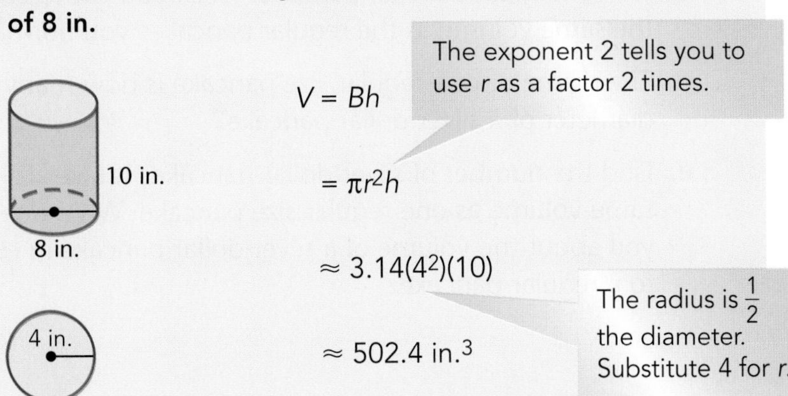

$V = Bh$

$= \pi r^2 h$

$\approx 3.14(4^2)(10)$

$\approx 502.4 \text{ in.}^3$

The exponent 2 tells you to use r as a factor 2 times.

The radius is $\frac{1}{2}$ the diameter. Substitute 4 for r.

The volume of the cylinder is about 502.4 in.^{3}

16 **a.** **Discussion** In the Example, why is the volume of the cylinder *about* 502.4 in.^{3} and not *exactly* 502.4 in.^{3}?

b. The volume of the cylinder in the Example is *exactly* 160π in.^{3} Explain why this is true.

17 **a.** Use the information in Question 15 to find the volume of the stack of pancakes eaten by Peter Dowdeswell.

b. Who ate a greater volume of food, Dowdeswell or Hughes?

✓ QUESTION 18

...checks that you can find the volumes of rectangular prisms and cylinders.

18 **✓ CHECKPOINT** Find the volume of each figure.

a. rectangular prism: $l = 5$ ft, $w = 8$ ft, $h = 9$ ft

b. cylinder: $r = 5$ cm, $h = 3$ cm

▶ **Silver dollar pancakes are so named because they are similar in size to silver dollars.**

19 **Try This as a Class**

a. Suppose you normally eat four regular 6 in. diameter pancakes before you feel full. If each pancake is about $\frac{1}{4}$ in. thick, find the volume of pancakes you normally eat.

b. Suppose you decide to try the new silver dollar size pancakes. Each one is 2 in. in diameter and about $\frac{1}{4}$ in. thick. Find the volume of one pancake.

c. How many silver dollar pancakes must you eat to consume the same volume as the regular pancakes you normally eat?

d. The diameter of a regular size pancake is how many times the diameter of a silver dollar pancake?

e. Find the number of silver dollar pancakes it takes to equal the same volume as one regular size pancake. What does this tell you about the volume of a silver dollar pancake in comparison to a regular pancake?

▶ **In American folklore, the fictional lumberjack Paul Bunyan was a man of enormous size, strength, and appetite. One legend involves his circular pancake griddle. It had a diameter of 236 ft, or 2832 in.!**

20 Suppose Paul Bunyan made a giant pancake that covered the entire circular pancake griddle and had a thickness of $\frac{3}{8}$ in.

a. Find the volume of the pancake in cubic inches.

b. How would the volume of the pancake compare with the volume of the 62 pancakes Peter Dowdeswell ate? (See Question 17(a).

▶ **A sphere is a 3-dimensional figure made up of a set of points that are an equal distance from a given point, called the center.**

21 An *Aebleskiver* is a traditional Scandinavian spherical shaped pancake. The seven molds of the pan are each the shape of a hemisphere (half-sphere), usually with a radius of 2 in. The pancake is flipped to create a sphere.

a. Suppose you wanted to make an *Aebleskiver* pan with molds one-half the diameter of the regular size holes. How might this affect the amount of pancake batter needed for each hole?

b. **Use Labsheet 1A.** Complete the activity and table.

c. Does a sphere with one-half the volume of a larger sphere have a diameter equal to one-half the diameter of the larger sphere? Explain.

▶ **The formula for the volume V of a sphere is $V = \frac{4}{3}\pi r^3$ where r = radius.**

22 **a.** Find the exact volume of a sphere with a radius of 1 in.

b. Find the exact volume of a sphere with a radius of $\frac{1}{2}$ in.

c. Compare the volumes. If one sphere's radius is one-half that of a second sphere, how do the diameters compare?

d. **Discussion** If you were to increase the radius of a sphere to 5 times its original size, how would this affect the volume of the sphere? Why?

HOMEWORK EXERCISES ▶ **See Exs. 10–26 on pp. 241–243.**

Section 1 Key Concepts

Key Terms

circumference

Circumference (pp. 231–232)

π is the ratio of the circumference of a circle to its diameter.

π is approximately equal to 3.14.

$$\frac{C}{d} = \pi$$

$$C = \pi d$$

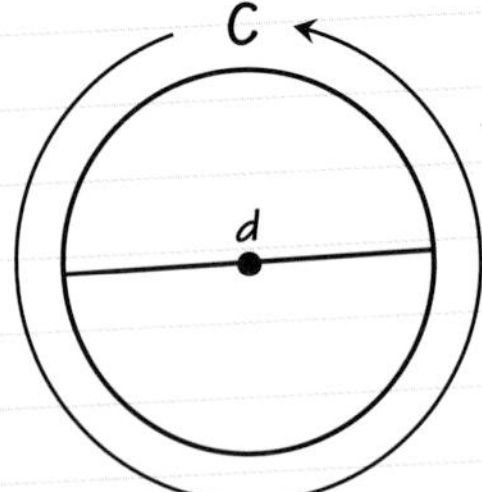

The circumference C of a circle is the distance around the circle.

area

Area (pp. 232–233)

The area A of a circle with radius r is equal to πr^2.

$A = 16\pi$ in.^{2} is the exact area of a circle with radius 4 in.

$A \approx 50.24$ in.^{2} is an approximation, since 3.14 is substituted for π.

polyhedron
face
prism
base

cylinder

Prisms and Cylinders (pp. 234–236)

A polyhedron is a 3-dimensional figure made up of flat surfaces, or faces, that are polygons. A prism is a polyhedron in which two faces, the bases, are congruent and parallel. The other faces are parallelograms.

A cylinder has a curved surface and two flat, parallel, congruent bases. In this book, all the cylinders have circular bases.

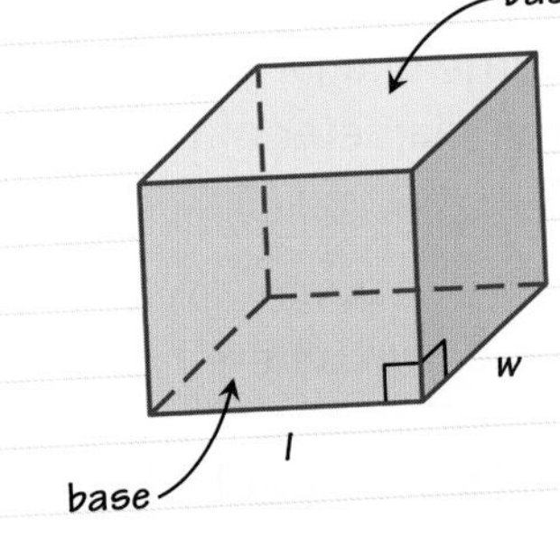

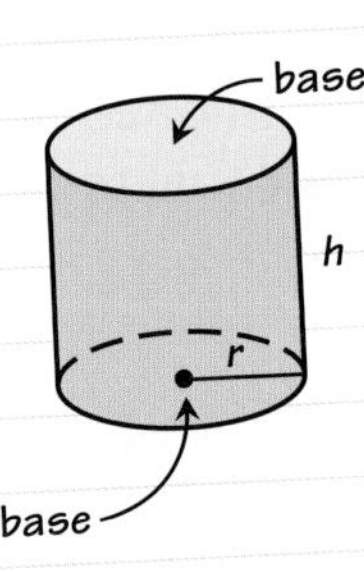

Use the formula $V = Bh$ to find the volume of a rectangular prism and a cylinder.

Key Concepts Questions

23 The formula for the circumference of a circle is sometimes written as $C = 2\pi r$, where r = the radius of the circle. Explain how this formula is related to the formula $C = \pi d$. Then find the circumference of a circle with radius 5 cm.

24 The height of a circular cylinder is 5 in. The diameter of a base is 4 in. Find its volume.

Section 1 Key Concepts

Key Term

Spheres (p. 237)

A sphere is a 3-dimensional figure made up of a set of points that are an equal distance from a given point, called the center.

sphere

The formula $V = \frac{4}{3}\pi r^3$ can be used to find the volume V of a sphere when the radius r is known.

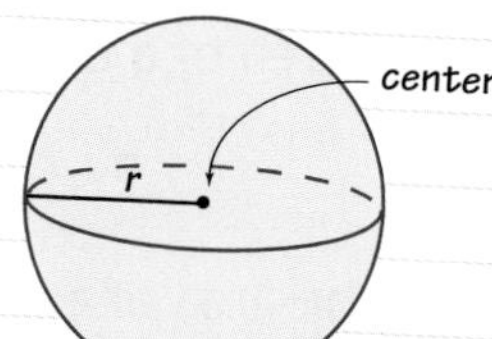

25 **Key Concepts Question** Find the volume of a sphere with a radius of 4 cm.

Section 1 Practice & Application Exercises

1. Find the exact circumference of a circle with the given radius or diameter.

   a. $r = 12$ m b. $d = 10$ ft c. $d = 1.1$ cm

2. Approximate the circumference of each circle in Exercise 1.

3. The smallest bicycle ever ridden had wheels with a diameter of 0.76 in. The largest bicycle ever ridden had wheels with a diameter of 10 ft.

   a. Find the circumference of a wheel on each bicycle.

   b. How far would each bicycle travel in one complete turn of its wheels?

   c. The world's smallest bicycle was ridden a distance of 13 ft 5 in. About how many turns did the wheels make?

   d. Suppose the wheels on the world's largest bicycle made as many turns as your answer to part (c). How far would it travel?

4. **Challenge** Suppose two identical circles just touch each other. Then a rectangle is drawn as shown. The distance d is the diameter of each circle.

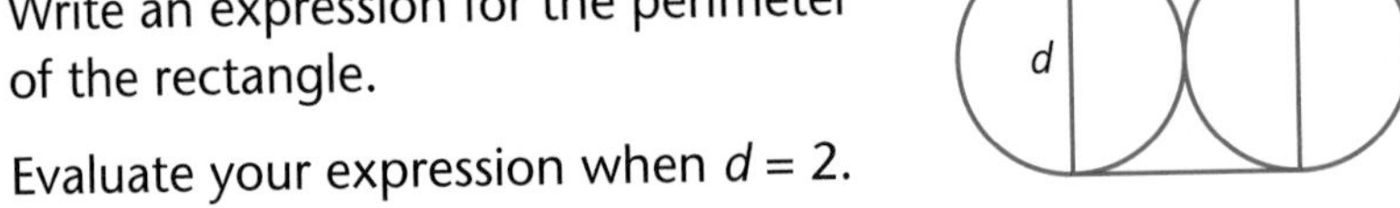

a. Write an expression for the perimeter of the rectangle.

b. Evaluate your expression when $d = 2$.

5. Find the exact area of a circle with the given radius or diameter.

a. $r = 8$ ft

b. $r = 30$ cm

c. $d = 1.4$ m

6. Approximate the area of each circle in Exercise 5.

7. **Costume Design** The Goodspeed Opera House in East Haddam, Connecticut, was a difficult place to perform the play *Bloomer Girl.* The hoop skirts in the women's 1860s costumes were too large for the narrow halls, stairways, and doors. Hoop skirts have a hoop around the hem of the skirt. This hoop can be made of steel.

a. The wardrobe master of the play said, "The real super hoops were about 11 ft in diameter, but if we had one in the show, it would cover about half the stage." Approximate the area the super hoop would cover.

b. According to the wardrobe master's comment, about what size (in square feet) is the opera house stage?

c. Find the length of steel needed to make a super hoop.

d. The women acting in *Bloomer Girl* ended up wearing hoop skirts that were 6 ft in diameter. Determine the length of steel needed to make each hoop.

e. About what fraction of the stage did a 6 ft diameter hoop cover?

8. Each vertex of square $ABCD$ is at the center of a circle with radius 5 cm. The circles just touch each other. Find the area of the shaded region.

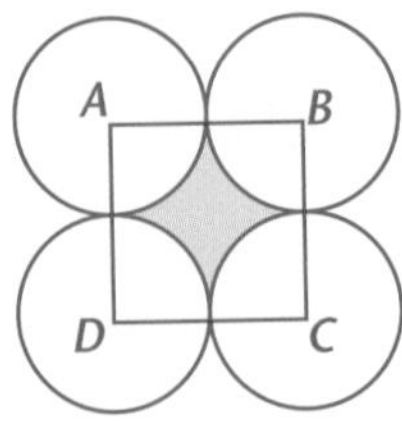

9. **Open-ended** One of the most unusual aircraft ever designed for the U.S. Navy was the Vought–Sikorsky V-173, also known as the "Flying Pancake." It was 26 ft 8 in. long and had a wingspan of 23 ft 4 in.

a. The Flying Pancake is round and flat. How do you know from just its measurements that its shape is not a circle?

b. Approximate the distance around the edge of the aircraft. Explain your method.

c. Approximate the area of the top of the Flying Pancake. Explain your method.

Find the volume of each figure.

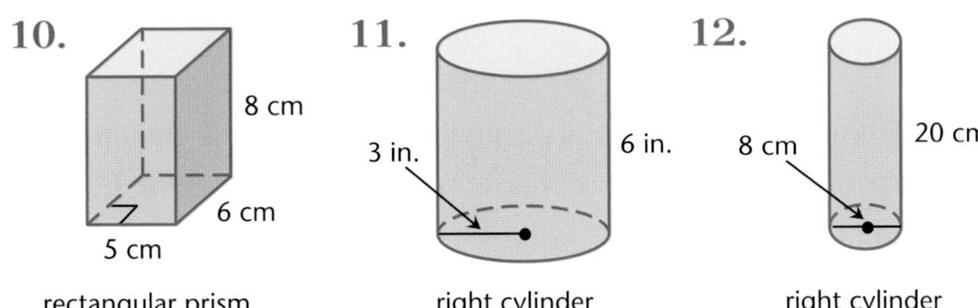

Find the volume of a cylinder with the given dimensions.

13. $r = 2$ cm, $h = 10$ cm

14. $r = 6.3$ cm, $h = 6.3$ cm

15. $r = 13$ cm, $h = 10$ cm

Find the volume of a rectangular prism with the given dimensions.

16. $l = 26$ cm, $w = 26$ cm, $h = 10$ cm

17. $l = 13$ cm, $w = 14$ cm, $h = 7$ cm

18. $l = 4$ cm, $w = 5$ cm, $h = 12$ cm

19. **Challenge**

a. The cylinder in Exercise 14 can fit into two of the rectangular prisms in Exercises 16–18. Which two prisms can it fit into?

b. The prism in Exercise 17 can fit into one of the cylinders in Exercises 13–15. Which cylinder can it fit into?

20. **Music** Sarah Hopkins, an Australian composer and performer, has experimented with the musical sounds of cylindrical instruments called "whirlies." Whirlies are played by whirling them through the air at different speeds. Differences in length and diameter affect the pitch and sound of each instrument.

Whirlies are flexible ▶ cylindrical hoses of various lengths and diameters.

	High Voiced Whirly	Deep Voiced Whirly
Diameter (mm)	25	32
Length (m)	1	1.75
Length (mm)	?	?
Volume (mm^3)	?	?

a. Copy and complete the table.

b. Sarah Hopkins also made a whirly that is exactly twice as long as a Deep Whirly. Its diameter is the same as the Deep Whirly's. How does doubling the length of a Deep Whirly affect its volume?

Beauclerc Elementary School in Jacksonville, Florida, made the largest popcorn box on record. The box was a rectangular prism 39 ft $11\frac{1}{2}$ in. long, 20 ft $8\frac{1}{2}$ in. wide, and 8 ft high.

21. a. Estimate the volume of the popcorn box. Calculate the actual volume of the popcorn box to the nearest cubic foot.

b. Suppose a regular-sized popcorn box is shaped like a rectangular prism $3\frac{1}{2}$ in. wide, $7\frac{1}{2}$ in. long, and $10\frac{1}{2}$ in. high. What is the volume of the box?

c. About how many regular-sized boxes of popped popcorn would be needed to fill the large popcorn box? Explain.

22. Find the exact volume of a sphere with the given dimension.

a. $r = 40$ in. b. $r = 5.1$ m c. $d = 2$ ft

23. Approximate the volume of each sphere in Exercise 22.

24. **Open-ended** Explore how doubling a circle's radius affects each of the following.

a. the circumference of the circle

b. the area of the circle

25. **Challenge** Two students have been exploring the effects of changing the base radius and height of a cylinder on its volume. Below are their conclusions. Decide whether each conclusion is *true* or *false* and explain why.

Tripling the height will triple the volume.

Tripling the radius will triple the volume.

Tripling both the height and the radius will triple the volume.

Reflecting on the Section

Write your response to Exercise 26 in your journal.

26. Rosa takes a carton of milk out of the refrigerator and empties it into the glass shown. Amazingly, the milk fills the glass so it is perfectly even with the rim. Was the milk carton full when Rosa began filling her glass? Explain your reasoning.

Journal

Exercise 26 checks that you can find and compare the volumes of two different containers.

Spiral Review

27. The table shows sales of CDs at a record store. Make a scatter plot using the data. Put hours of operation on the horizontal axis. If it makes sense to draw a fitted line, do so. (Module 1, p. 56)

Hours of Operation	54	48	60	65	40	60	48	56
CDs Sold	710	530	850	940	520	740	630	750

Find each quotient. (Toolbox, p. 582)

28. $0.141 \div 12$ 29. $6.2 \div 3.1$ 30. $12.4 \div 12$ 31. $150.62 \div 18$

Find each answer. (Toolbox, p. 589)

32. $4(2 + 3^2)$ 33. $5 \cdot 6 - 3$ 34. $11(6) \div 2$ 35. $16 - 8 + \frac{42}{6}$

Section 1 Extra Skill Practice

Find the exact circumference of each circle.

1. 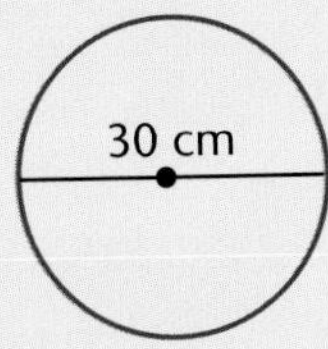

2. 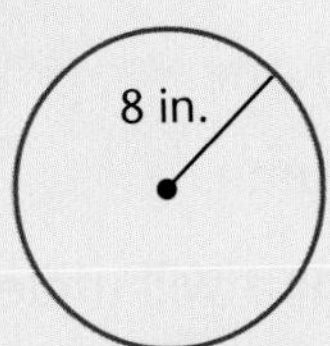

3. 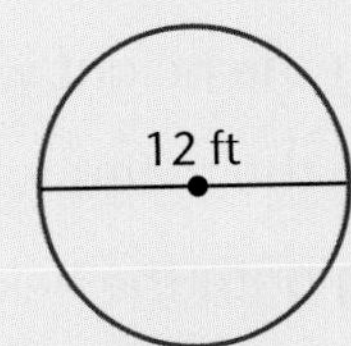

Find the exact area of each circle.

4. 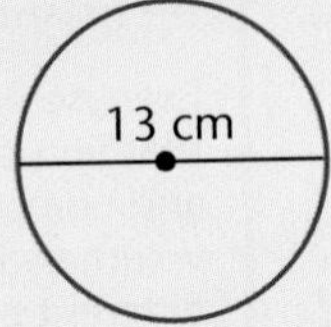

5. 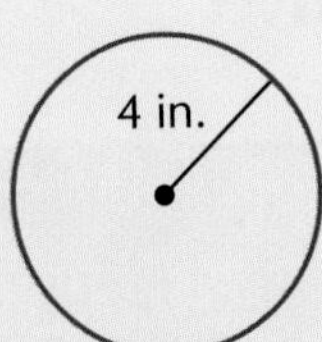

6. 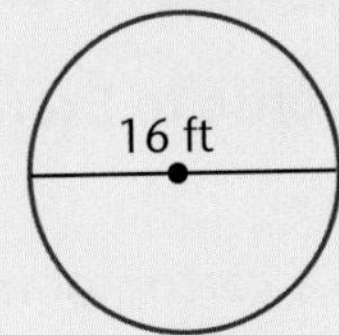

Approximate the volume of each prism, cylinder, or sphere.

7. 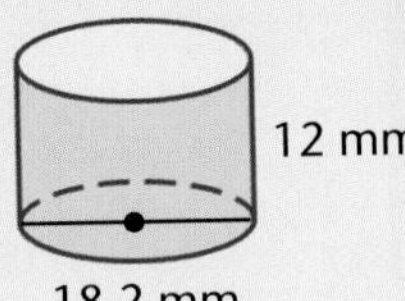

8. 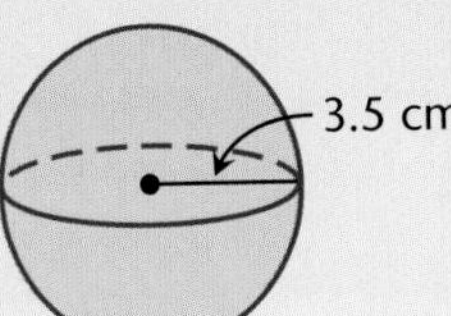

9. 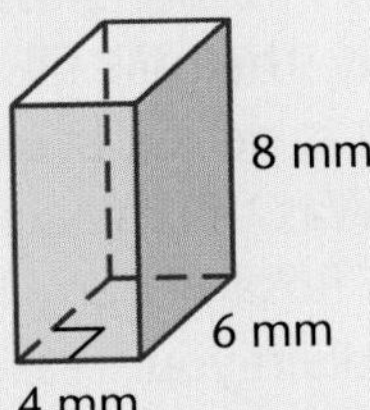

10. rectangular prisms:
    a. $l = 4$ ft, $w = 2\frac{1}{2}$ ft, $h = 5\frac{1}{2}$ ft
    b. $l = 6.3$ m, $w = 2.5$ m, $h = 5.9$ m

11. cylinders:
    a. $d = 10\frac{1}{2}$ in., $h = 17$ in.
    b. $d = 0.5$ mm, $h = 1.2$ mm

12. spheres:
    a. r = 10 in.
    b. $d = 6.4$ m

Standardized Testing ▶ Open-Ended

1. How are the formulas for finding the volume of a prism and a cylinder alike? How are they different?

2. Write a word problem that involves finding the volume of a prism or a cylinder found in your home.

Section 2 Working with Cylinders

EXPLORATION 1
- Surface Areas of Cylinders

EXPLORATION 2
- Surface Area and Volume

Setting the Stage

The French general Napoleon Bonaparte once said, "An army marches on its stomach." He was not exaggerating. Hunger and poor nutrition caused more casualties in Napoleon's armies than actual combat. In 1795, the French government offered a prize of 12,000 francs to anyone who could invent a way to preserve food for the military.

Nicolas Appert, a candy maker from Paris, won the prize in 1809. Appert found that food could be preserved for months by sealing it in glass jars and heating the jars in boiling water. Glass jars break easily, however, and soldiers needed stronger containers.

Peter Durand, an English inventor, solved this problem. Durand patented the use of metal cans for storing food. These cans were made of tin plate (iron coated with tin to prevent rusting) and came to be known as "tin cans." Tin cans were first used in 1813 to supply food to the British military.

Think About It

1. What two-dimensional shapes could you cut from a sheet of tin plate to make a tin can?

2. What factors might a manufacturer consider before designing a can?

GOAL

LEARN HOW TO...
- find the surface area of a cylinder

AS YOU...
- make a paper can

KEY TERM
- surface area

Exploration 1

Surface Areas of Cylinders

SET UP *You will need:* • *compass* • *metric ruler* • *scissors* • *tape* • $8\frac{1}{2}$ *in. by 11 in. sheet of paper*

▶ **A tin can is made by cutting two circles and a rectangle from a sheet of tin plate. The rectangle is rolled into a tube. The circles are added to the ends of the tube to form a cylinder.**

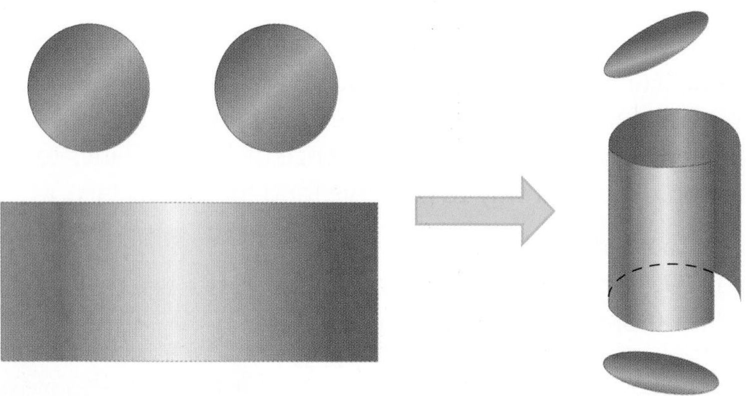

3 Think about the dimensions of cans you see in the supermarket. You can create your own can from a single sheet of paper.

a. Choose a realistic radius and height for your paper can. Give the radius and the height in centimeters.

b. Use a compass to draw two circles having the radius you chose in part (a). Label the radius of each circle *r* as shown.

c. Discussion In order for the tube and the circles to form a can, how should the length, *l*, of the rectangle pictured on the paper be related to the radius, *r*, of each circle?

d. Using the radius from part (a), calculate the length l of the rectangle to the nearest tenth of a centimeter.

e. How should the width, w, of the rectangle pictured on the paper be related to the height you chose in part (a)?

f. Draw a rectangle with the length and the width you found in parts (d) and (e). When drawing the rectangle, measure l and w to the nearest tenth of a centimeter.

g. Cut out the circles and the rectangle you drew. Tape the edges of the rectangle together with no overlap to form a tube. Tape the circles to the ends of the tubes to complete your can.

▶ **A cylinder's *surface area* is the sum of the areas of the circles and the rectangle that form the cylinder. In general, the surface area of a 3-dimensional figure is the combined area of the figure's outer surfaces.**

4 **Try This as a Class** Use the paper can you made in Question 3.

a. How is the area of each circle related to the can's radius?

b. How can you use the length and width of the rectangle to find its area?

c. How can you use the can's radius and height to find the area of the rectangle?

d. Use your answers from parts (a) and (c) to write a formula for the surface area, *S.A.*, of a cylinder in terms of its radius, r, and height, h.

e. Find the surface area of your paper can.

5 **✓ CHECKPOINT** Approximate the surface area of each can.

a.

b.

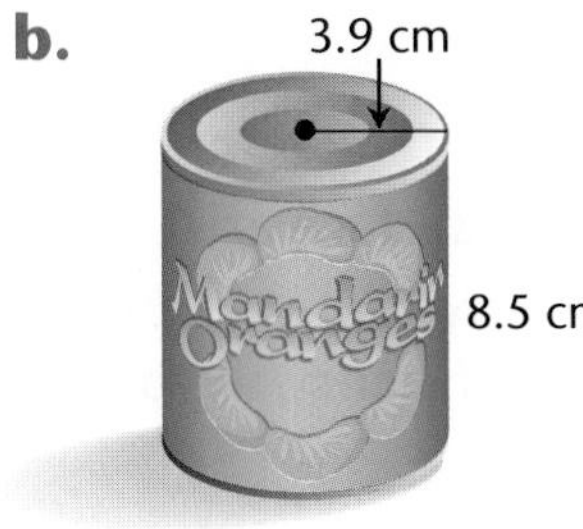

...checks that you can find a cylinder's surface area given its radius and height.

6 Which of the cans in Question 5 uses more metal? Explain.

HOMEWORK EXERCISES ▶ See Exs. 1–9 on p. 252.

GOAL

LEARN HOW TO...
- find and interpret the ratio of a cylinder's surface area to its volume

AS YOU...
- compare the efficiency of different cans

Exploration 2

Surface Area and Volume

SET UP *Work in a group. You will need: • Labsheet 2A • metric ruler • five cans with different sizes and shapes • calculator*

▶ **An *efficient* can is one that uses a small amount of metal compared to the amount of food or drink it holds.**

7 **Discussion** What are some advantages of efficient cans?

▶ **A small juice can uses about 300 cm^2 of metal and holds about 400 cm^3 of juice. A large juice can uses about 400 cm^2 of metal and holds about 600 cm^3 of juice.**

8 **Mental Math**

a. How much metal is used per cubic centimeter of juice for the small can?

b. How much metal is used per cubic centimeter for the large can?

c. How did you get your answers?

d. Which can is more efficient? Explain.

▶ **Using Ratios In Question 8 parts (a) and (b), you calculated the ratio of a can's surface area, *S.A.*, to its volume, *V*. The ratio $\frac{S.A.}{V}$ is one measure of the efficiency of the can. Your group will use this ratio to compare the efficiency of your cans.**

9 If the ratio $\frac{S.A.}{V}$ is greater for can A than for can B, what can you say about the efficiency of the cans? Explain.

10 **a.** Make a table like the one shown. Include rows for cans A–E.

Can	Diameter	Height	Radius	*S.A.*	*V*	$\frac{S.A.}{V}$
A	?	?	?	?	?	?
B	?	?	?	?	?	

FOR ◀HELP with *the volume of a cylinder, see* **MODULE 4, p. 235**

b. Measure the diameter and height of each of your cans to the nearest tenth of a centimeter. Record the measures in your table.

c. Complete the rest of the table.

d. Rank your cans from most efficient to least efficient.

11 ✓ **CHECKPOINT** Rank the cans shown from most efficient to least efficient. Explain your thinking.

✓ QUESTION 11

...checks that you can find and interpret the ratio of a cylinder's surface area to its volume.

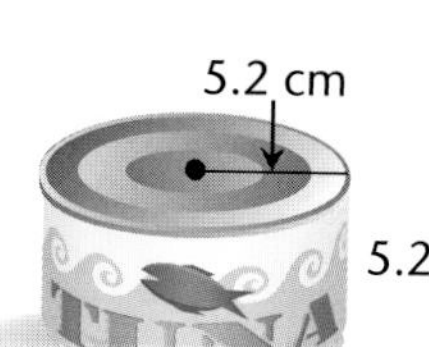

▶ **Of all cans having a given volume, which one uses the least metal? Canning companies often want to solve this problem, since using less metal reduces costs. You will explore this problem below.**

Use Labsheet 2A for Questions 12 and 13.

12 Labsheet 2A shows four cylinders.

a. Find each cylinder's surface area and volume.

b. What do you notice about the volumes?

13 **a.** What are the height and the radius of the cylinder with the least surface area?

b. What is the ratio of the cylinder's height to its radius?

14 **Try This as a Class** Of all cylinders having a given volume, the cylinder whose height is equal to its diameter (twice its radius) has the least surface area.

a. A snack food company plans to sell peanuts in cans with a volume of 800 cm^3. An engineer at the company found the dimensions of the can that has this volume and uses the least amount of metal. The engineer's solution starts like this:

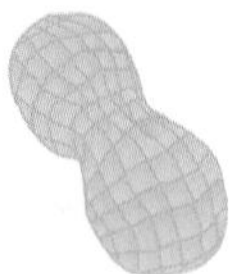

$$V = 800$$

$$\pi r^2 h = 800$$

$$\pi r^2(2r) = 800$$

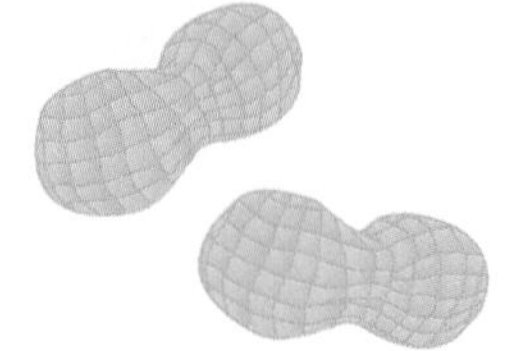

Explain each step of the solution so far.

b. Show that $\pi r^2(2r) = 800$ can be written as $r^3 \approx 127$.

c. Explain why the solution of $r^3 \approx 127$ must satisfy $5 < r < 6$.

d. Calculator Use a calculator and a guess-and-check strategy to find r to the nearest hundredth. What is the radius of the peanut can that uses the least amount of metal?

e. Find the height of the peanut can that uses the least amount of metal. How did you get your answer?

15 A company is producing cylindrical metal containers that are open at the top and that will hold 274 $in.^3$ of flour. The containers will have plastic lids. To find the dimensions of the container that uses the least metal, you can find the value of r for which $\pi r^3 = 274$, or $r^3 \approx 87$.

a. Of all open cylinders (cylinders with no tops) having a given volume, the cylinder whose height is equal to its radius has the least surface area. Explain how you can use this information and the formula for the volume of a cylinder to obtain $r^3 \approx 87$.

b. Use a calculator and a guess-and-check strategy to find r to the nearest hundredth.

c. What are the dimensions of the open cylindrical container that holds 274 $in.^3$ of flour and uses the least amount of metal?

16 **Discussion** Why might a food or drink manufacturer use a can that does not have the least surface area for its volume?

HOMEWORK EXERCISES See Exs. 10–19 on pp. 253–254.

Section 2 Key Concepts

Key Term

surface area

Surface Area of a Cylinder (pp. 246–247)

The surface area, S.A., of a cylinder with radius r and height h is given by the formula $S.A. = 2\pi r^2 + 2\pi rh$.

Example You can use the radius and height of the cylinder shown to find its surface area.

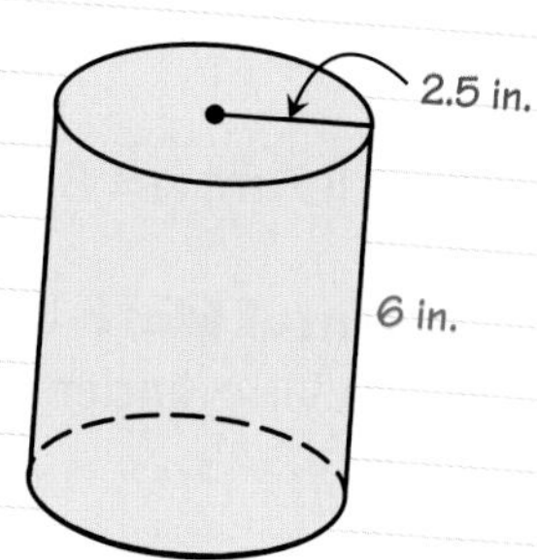

$$S.A. = 2\pi r^2 + 2\pi rh$$
$$\approx 2(3.14)(2.5)^2 + 2(3.14)(2.5)(6)$$
$$\approx 133.45$$

The cylinder's surface area is about 133.45 in.^{2}

Comparing Surface Area to Volume (pp. 248–250)

For a container (such as a can) with surface area S.A. and volume V, the ratio $\frac{S.A.}{V}$ is a measure of the container's efficiency. The smaller this ratio, the more efficient the container.

Example

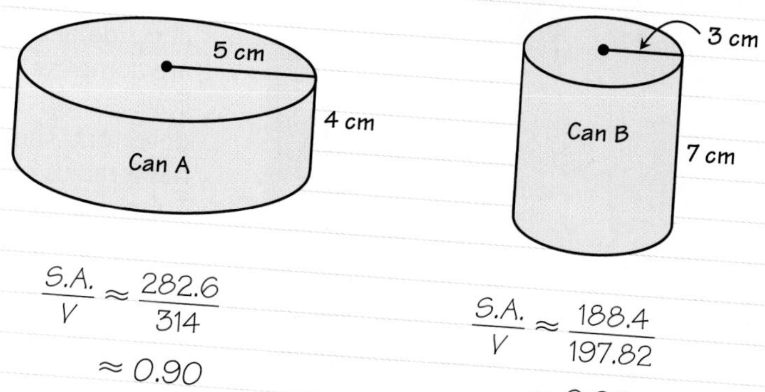

$$\frac{S.A.}{V} \approx \frac{282.6}{314} \approx 0.90$$

$$\frac{S.A.}{V} \approx \frac{188.4}{197.82} \approx 0.95$$

The ratio $\frac{S.A.}{V}$ is less for Can A than for Can B, so Can A is more efficient than Can B.

17 Key Concepts Question A coffee can has a radius of 8 cm and a height of 16 cm. A tomato sauce can has a radius of 3 cm and a height of 8 cm. Which can is more efficient? Explain.

Section 2

Practice & Application Exercises

For Exercises 1–6, find the surface area of a cylinder with the given radius *r* and height *h*.

1. $r = 2$ cm, $h = 7$ cm
2. $r = 1$ m, $h = 3$ m
3. $r = 6$ in., $h = 6$ in.
4. $r = 8$ ft, $h = 4$ ft
5. $r = 1.7$ m, $h = 8$ m
6. $r = 2.4$ in., $h = 9.6$ in.

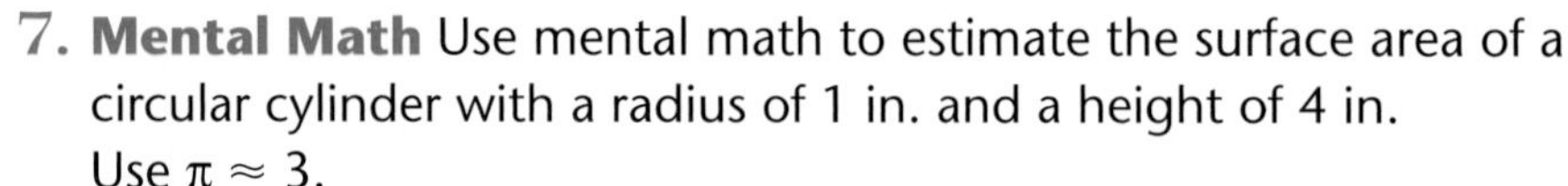

7. **Mental Math** Use mental math to estimate the surface area of a circular cylinder with a radius of 1 in. and a height of 4 in. Use $\pi \approx 3$.

Science Sometimes stars explode, releasing tiny particles called neutrinos that may eventually reach Earth. The sun is also a source of neutrinos. To detect neutrinos, scientists built the "Super Kamiokande," a huge cylindrical tank of water located in a mine near Toyama, Japan.

◀ The top, bottom, and side of the tank are completely covered with light detectors. The tank has a radius of about 20 m and a height of about 40 m.

8. Estimate the surface area of the tank.

9. The light detectors are mounted on rectangular frames like the one shown. Each frame is about 210 cm by 280 cm and holds 12 detectors.

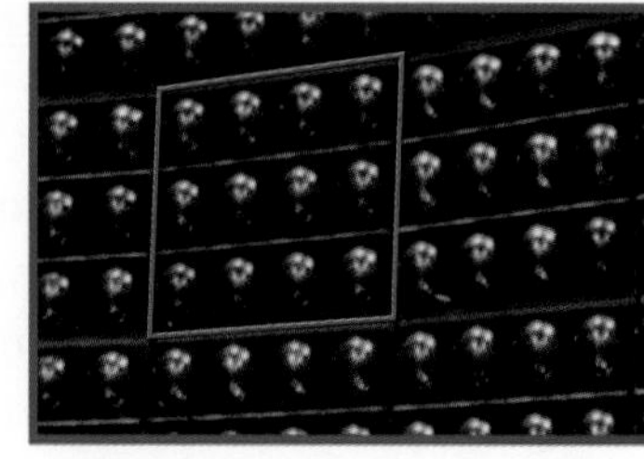

   a. About how many frames were needed to cover the inside of the tank?

   b. About how many light detectors were needed?

Find the ratio of surface area to volume for each can.

10. 11. 12.

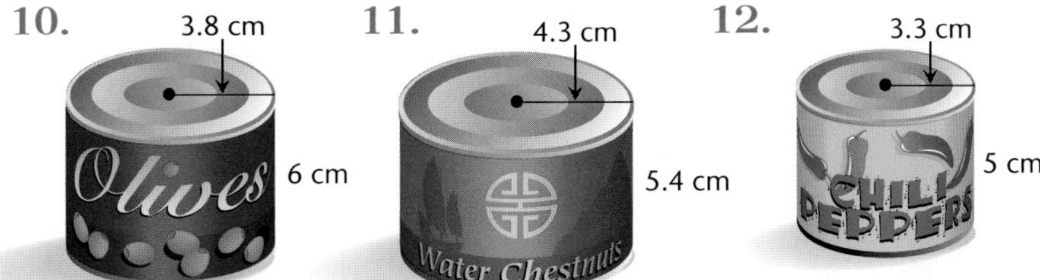

13. Use your answers for Exercises 10–12 to rank the cans shown above from most efficient to least efficient.

14. **Architecture** A *Quonset hut* is a building shaped like a half cylinder and made of corrugated steel. Examples of a Quonset hut and of a greenhouse also shaped like a half cylinder are shown.

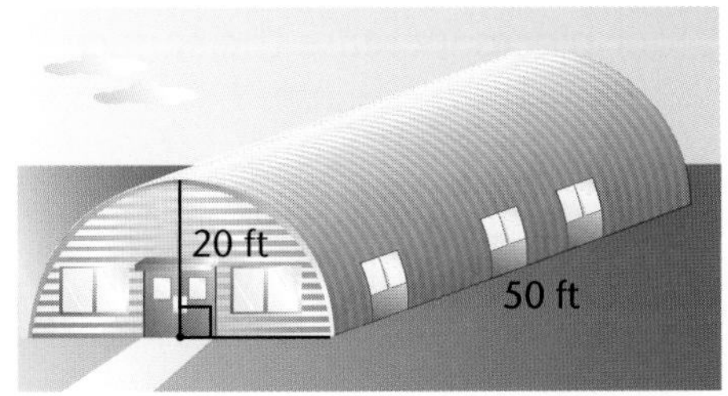

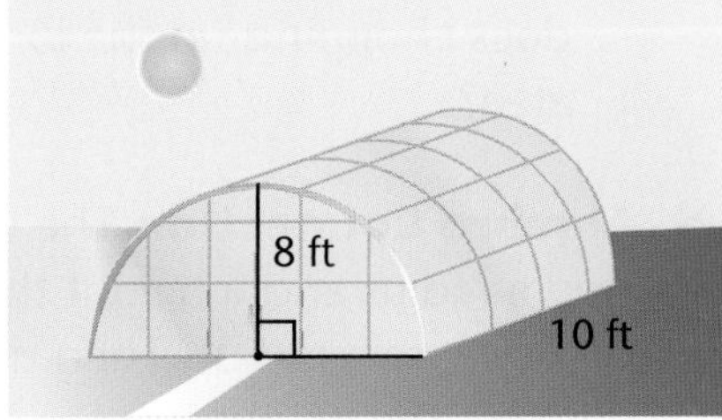

   a. Find the ratio of surface area to volume for each building. Include the floors of the buildings when calculating surface area.

   b. Which building encloses space more efficiently? Explain.

   c. **Writing** Would the more efficient of the two buildings be the better building in all situations? Why or why not?

Look back at your answers to Questions 12–14 on pages 249–250 in Exploration 2. Use what you learned to complete Exercises 15 and 16.

15. **Research** Go to a supermarket and look at some of the canned foods sold. Find a can that uses (approximately) the least amount of metal possible for its volume. Also find a can that uses a large amount of metal for its volume. Explain how you chose your cans.

16. **Agriculture** A farmer decides to roll hay into large cylindrical bales, each with a volume of 100 ft^3. (A bale this size will feed 2 horses for about a month.) To keep the bales dry, the farmer plans to seal them in plastic wrap. What should the dimensions of each bale be if the farmer wants to use the least amount of plastic wrap possible?

17. **Challenge** A log of firewood burns faster if you chop it into pieces before throwing it in a fireplace. This is because chopping a log increases the total area of wood exposed to the flames. For example, suppose you chop a log into four equal-sized pieces as shown.

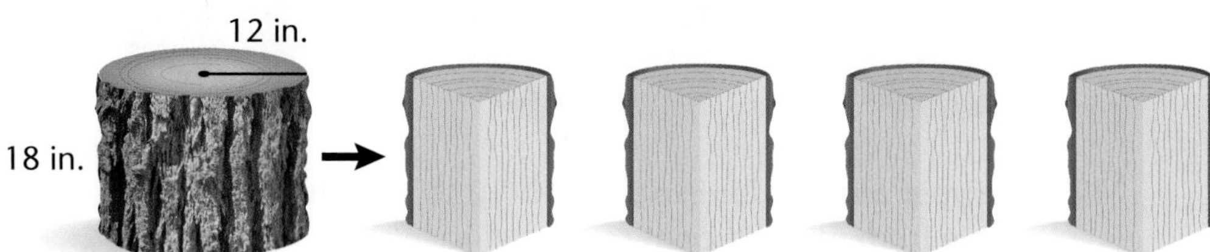

a. Find the surface area of the log before it was chopped up.

b. Find the combined surface area of the four chopped-up pieces.

c. Compare your answers from parts (a) and (b). By what percent does chopping up the log in four pieces increase the surface area?

18. **Algebra Connection** The surface area of a cylinder is 850 cm^2. Find a radius and a height that this cylinder could have. (Hint: First choose a radius. Then use the formula S.A. = $2\pi r^2 + 2\pi rh$ to solve for the height.)

Visual THINKING

Exercise 19 checks your understanding of the surface area of a cylinder.

Reflecting on the Section

19. Describe how you can find a cylinder's surface area either by using a formula or by thinking about the shapes that form the cylinder.

Spiral Review

Estimation Estimate each percent. (Module 2, p. 132)

20. 11% of 200 21. 19% of 3500 22. 79% of 660

Plot each pair of points on a coordinate plane and draw a line through them. Find the slope of the line. (Module 3, p. 186)

23. (0, 0) and (1, 4) 24. (4, 5) and (2, 1)

25. (–6, –3) and (–2, 7) 26. (4, –2) and (–3, 3)

27. The equation for finding the area of a triangle is $A = \frac{1}{2}bh$, where A is the area of a triangle, b is the length of the base of the triangle, and h is the height of the triangle. Find the area of each triangle below. (Toolbox, p. 595)

a.

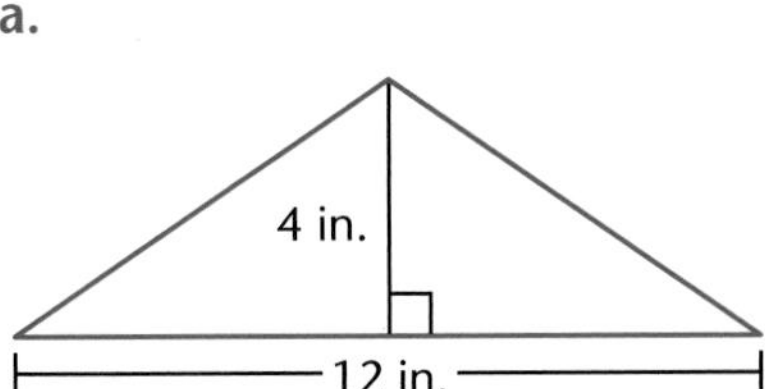

b.

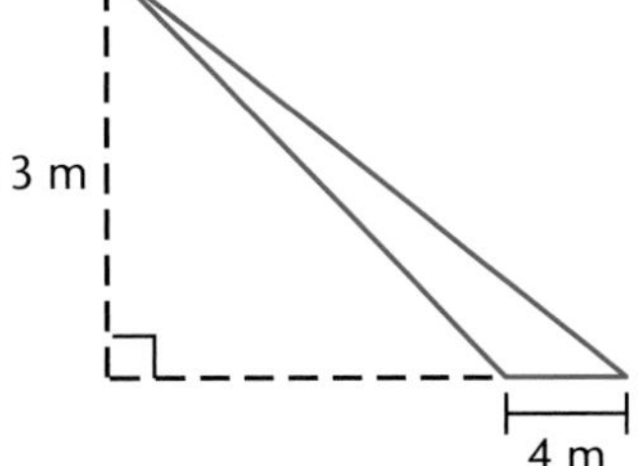

Extension 

Maximum Efficiency

28. Cylindrical containers have the maximum efficiency when the height is twice the radius ($h = 2r$). For these special cylinders, the efficiency ratio simplifies to $\frac{S.A.}{V} = \frac{3}{r}$.

a. Use the formula to complete the table below.

The Efficiency of Cylindrical Containers Whose Height is Twice the Radius			
Container Name	Height h	Radius r	Efficiency $\frac{3}{r}$
A	2	1	3
B	6	3	?
C	?	6	?
D	?	9	?
E	24	?	?

$\frac{3}{r} = \frac{3}{1} = 3$

b. From the results of your table, what do you think is happening to the ratio of surface area to volume when the radius increases?

c. Which container has the lowest efficiency ratio?

29. Find a radius and height in centimeters of a cylinder with maximum efficiency of 5.

30. Find a radius and height in centimeters of a cylinder with maximum efficiency of 0.1.

Section 2

Extra Skill Practice

Find the surface area of the cylinder with the given radius r and height h.

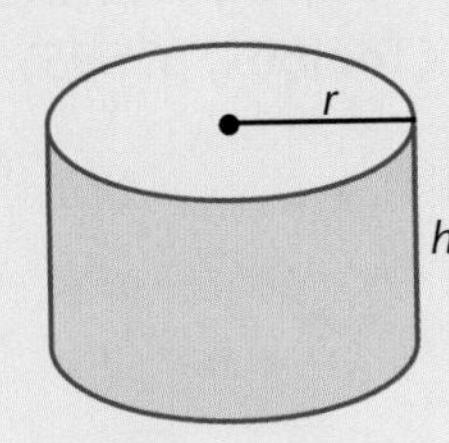

1. $r = 5$ in., $h = 3$ in.
2. $r = 3$ in., $h = 5$ in.
3. $r = 11$ cm, $h = 40$ cm
4. $r = 9.5$ cm, $h = 9.5$ cm
5. $r = 1.8$ m, $h = 6.2$ m
6. $r = 33$ ft, $h = 100$ ft

Find the ratio of surface area to volume for each cylinder.

7.
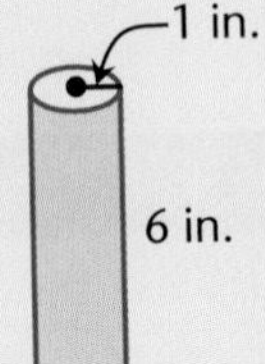

8.
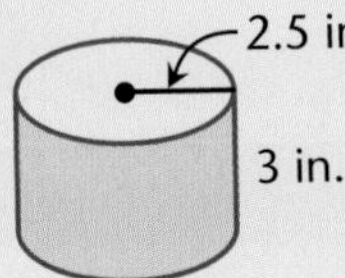

9.
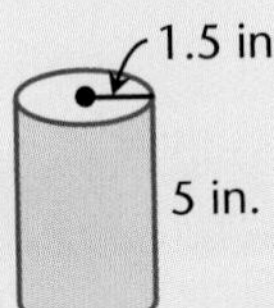

10.
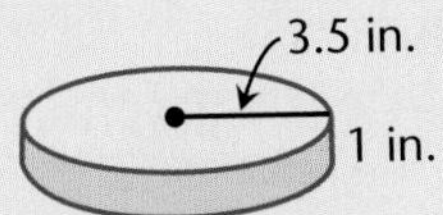

11.
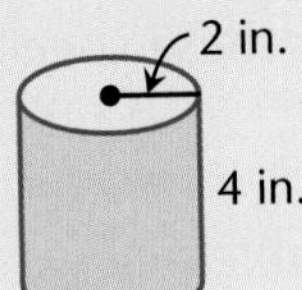

12.
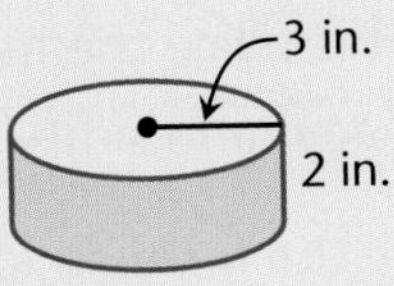

13. Suppose you have six plastic storage containers with the same dimensions as the cylinders in Exercises 7–12. Which container was made most efficiently? Explain.

Study Skills ▶ Comparing and Contrasting

When you compare and contrast objects or ideas, you consider how they are alike and how they are different. Comparing and contrasting can help you see how things are related and extend your understanding of what you have learned.

1. Compare and contrast the formulas for the surface area and volume of a cylinder.
2. Graph $y = 3x + 2$ and $y = -3x + 2$. Compare and contrast the lines that you graphed.
3. Give an example of when comparing and contrasting helped you make a decision.

EXTENDED E2 EXPLORATION

FOR ASSESSMENT AND PORTFOLIOS

Getting the Most Out of a Can

SET UP *You will need:* • *compass* • *ruler* • *scissors* • *tape* • $8\frac{1}{2}$ *in. by 11 in. sheet of paper*

The Situation

Most cans you find in a supermarket are designed to have a specific volume. However, a package manufacturer sometimes needs to design a can or other cylindrical container that uses a fixed amount of material and has the greatest volume possible.

The Problem

Make a "paper can" with the greatest volume possible by cutting and taping together two circles and a rectangle from an $8\frac{1}{2}$ in. by 11 in. sheet of paper. (The circles and the rectangle should all be from a single piece of paper and should not be a combination of several smaller pieces.)

Something to Think About

- How must the length of one side of the rectangle for your can be related to each circle's radius?
- Which dimension–the *radius* or the *height*– has a greater effect on the can's volume?
- Is it possible for you to make your can without wasting any paper?

Present Your Results

Give the radius and the height of the can you made, and explain how you chose those dimensions. Explain why you think it is not possible to make a can that has a greater volume. Show any diagrams, tables, or equations you used to solve the problem.

Section 3 Slopes and Equations of Lines

IN THIS SECTION

EXPLORATION 1
- Exploring Slope

EXPLORATION 2
- Slope-Intercept Form

Setting the Stage

If you try to buy a black-and-white TV today, you may have trouble finding one. Demand for black-and-white TVs has almost disappeared. In 1995, more than 98% of all TVs sold were color TVs.

Although the first color telecast was in 1953, it was not until 1970 that color TVs began outselling black-and-white TVs.

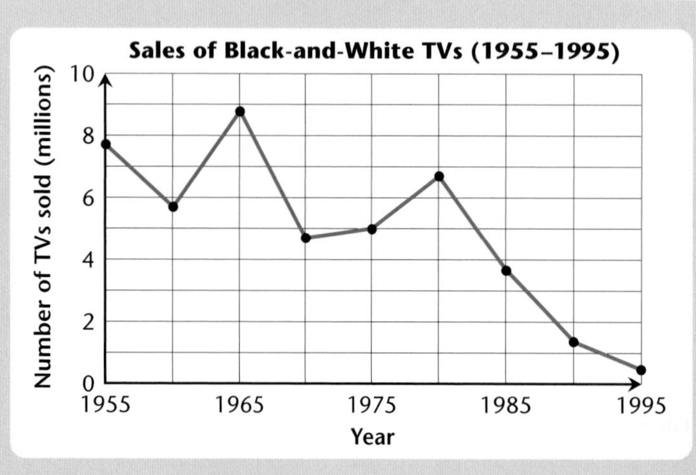

Think About It

1 About how many black-and-white TVs were sold in 1980?

2 In what year did sales of black-and-white TVs begin making a steady decline?

3 **Discussion** During which periods did sales of black-and-white TVs increase? decrease? How can you tell?

Exploration 1

Exploring Slope

GOAL

LEARN HOW TO...
- find and interpret positive and negative slopes
- identify slopes of horizontal and vertical lines

AS YOU...
- investigate TV sales

SET UP *You will need:* • *Labsheet 3A* • *graph paper*

▶ **In Module 3, you learned that the *slope* of a line is a ratio that measures the steepness of the line.**

$$\text{slope} = \frac{\text{rise}}{\text{run}} = \frac{\text{vertical change}}{\text{horizontal change}}$$

FOR ◀HELP with *slope*, see **MODULE 3, p. 186**

In this exploration, you will see how slope can give you other information about a line.

Use Labsheet 3A for Questions 4–9.

4 **Try This as a Class** Labsheet 3A shows the *Graph of Black-and-White TV Sales* that you saw in the *Setting the Stage*. Ordered pairs for certain points are included on the graph.

a. The first row of the table below the graph has been completed for you. Explain how the rise, run, and slope were found.

b. Why is the slope negative?

5 Complete the table on the labsheet. For each five-year period:

- Find the slope of the graph for each period.
- Tell whether the graph slants *up* or *down* from left to right.
- Tell whether TV sales were *increasing* or *decreasing*.

6 Look at the periods in the table where the graph's slope is positive.

a. For these periods, does the graph slant *up* or *down* from left to right?

b. Were sales of black-and-white TVs *increasing* or *decreasing*?

7 Repeat Question 6 for the periods where the graph's slope is negative.

8 **a.** Based on your observations from Questions 6 and 7, what can you say about the slope of a line that slants *up* from left to right?

b. What can you say about the slope of a line that slants *down* from left to right?

FOR ◀HELP
with *rates*, see
MODULE 1, p. 9

9 **Discussion** Look at the graph and the table on the labsheet.

a. By looking at the slopes in the table, how can you tell when sales were increasing most rapidly? decreasing most rapidly?

b. The graph's slope for the period 1955–1960 represents a decrease of TV sales at a rate of 0.4 million per year or 26% over a 5-year period. Describe the rate and the percent of decrease for the period 1985–1990.

✓ QUESTION 10

...checks that you understand the relationship between a line's appearance and its slope.

10 **✓ CHECKPOINT** Use the lines shown.

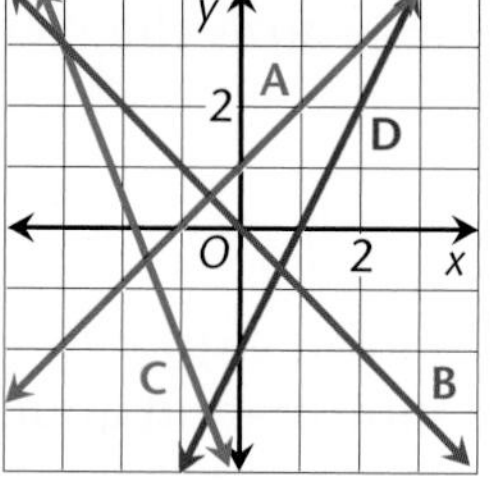

a. Which lines have slopes that are positive?

b. Which lines have slopes that are negative?

▶ **Horizontal and Vertical Lines You have seen that some lines have positive slopes and some have negative slopes. In Questions 11 and 12, you will explore the slopes of horizontal and vertical lines.**

11 **a.** Draw several horizontal lines on a coordinate plane.

b. Find the slope of each line.

c. What do you notice about the slopes?

12 **a.** Draw several vertical lines on a coordinate plane. Then try to find the slope of each line. What do you notice?

b. The slope of a vertical line is said to be *undefined*. Why do you think this is so?

✓ QUESTION 13

...checks that you can identify slopes of horizontal and vertical lines.

13 **✓ CHECKPOINT** Identify the slope of each line or tell if the slope is undefined.

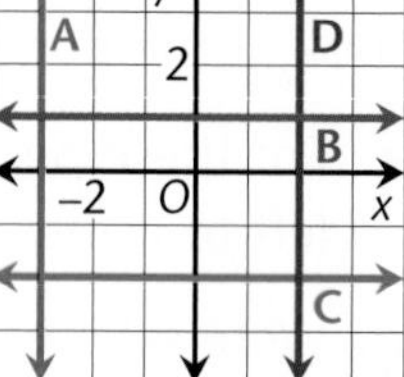

a. line A **b.** line B

c. line C **d.** line D

HOMEWORK EXERCISES ▶ **See Exs. 1–11 on pp. 265–266.**

Exploration 2

Slope-Intercept Form

SET UP *Work with a partner. You will need graph paper.*

GOAL

LEARN HOW TO...
- identify the *y*-intercept of a line
- write an equation of a line in slope-intercept form

AS YOU...
- model sales of DVD players and VCRs

KEY TERMS
- *y*-intercept
- slope-intercept form

▶ **The sale of VCRs was nearing its peak in 1997 when DVD players hit the market. Soon after the introduction of the DVD player, VCR sales began to decrease. In this exploration, you and your partner will look for relationships between lines and their equations as they relate to the sale of VCRs and DVD players.**

14 An electronics store sold 800 DVD players and 600 VCRs this year. Based on market trends, the store manager expects DVD sales to increase by about 160 DVD players per year and VCR sales to decrease by about 120 VCRs per year over the next five years.

a. You and your partner should each choose one of the tables below. Copy and complete your table.

Expected DVD Player Sales	
x = years from now	y = DVD players sold
0	800
1	800 + 160(1) = 960
2	800 + 160(2) = 1120
3	?
4	?
5	?

Expected VCR Sales	
x = years from now	y = VCRs sold
0	600
1	600 – 120(1) = 480
2	600 – 120(2) = 360
3	?
4	?
5	?

b. Make a scatter plot of the ordered pairs (x, y) in your table. What do you notice about the points in the scatter plot?

c. Draw a line through the points in your scatter plot. Find the slope of the line.

d. Look for a pattern in your table. Use the pattern to write an equation relating y and x.

15 **Discussion** Compare the equations that you and your partner wrote in Question 14(d) with the lines you drew in part (c).

a. How is the slope of each line related to the equation of the line?

b. Is there any other way in which the lines and the equations are related? Explain.

▶ **The *y*-intercept of a line is the *y*-coordinate of the point where the line crosses the *y*-axis.**

16 **a.** Look back at the lines you drew in Question 14. Give the *y*-intercept of each line.

b. How is the *y*-intercept of each line related to the line's equation?

c. What information do the *y*-intercepts give you about the sales of VCRs and DVD players?

✓ QUESTION 17

...checks that you can identify the y-intercept of a line.

17 **✓ CHECKPOINT** Give the *y*-intercept of each line.

a.

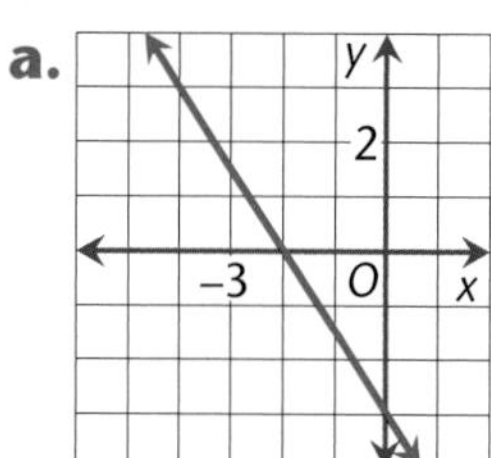

b.

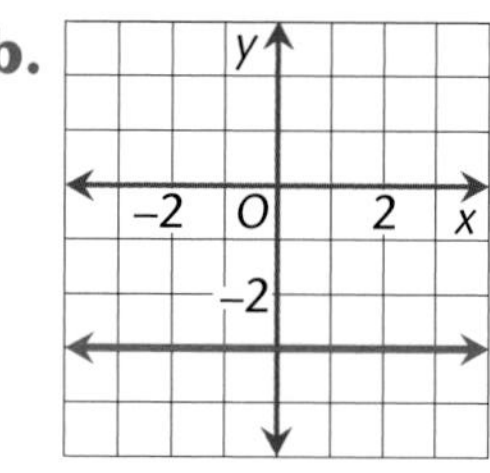

c.

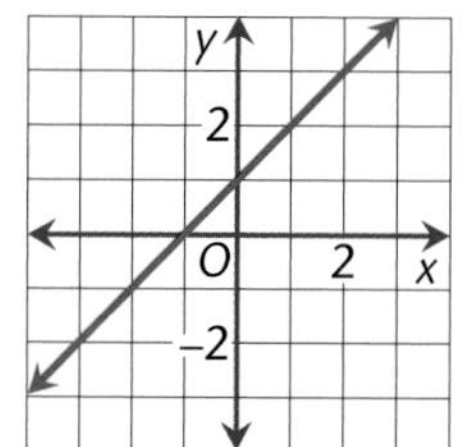

▶ **Suppose a line has slope *m* and *y*-intercept *b*. An equation of this line is $y = mx + b$. When an equation is in this form it is in slope-intercept form.**

EXAMPLE

To write an equation in slope-intercept form for the line shown, first find the line's slope and *y*-intercept.

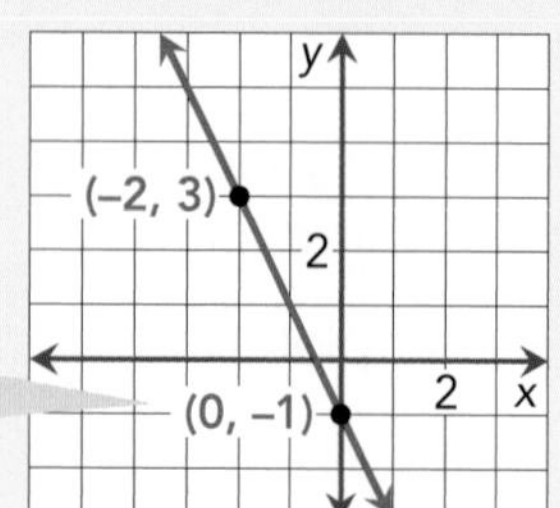

The *y*-intercept is –1.

$$\text{slope} = \frac{-1-3}{0-(-2)} = \frac{-4}{2} = -2$$

Then substitute the values for the slope *m* and the *y*-intercept *b* into $y = mx + b$.

$$y = -2x + (-1)$$

$$y = -2x - 1$$

18 **a.** Identify the slope and the y-intercept of the line with equation $y = -\frac{2}{3}x + 7$.

b. Suppose the slope of a line is 5 and its y-intercept is $\frac{1}{2}$. Write an equation of the line.

c. Is the equation $5x + y = 20$ in slope-intercept form? Explain.

19 **Try This as a Class** Use the coordinate plane shown.

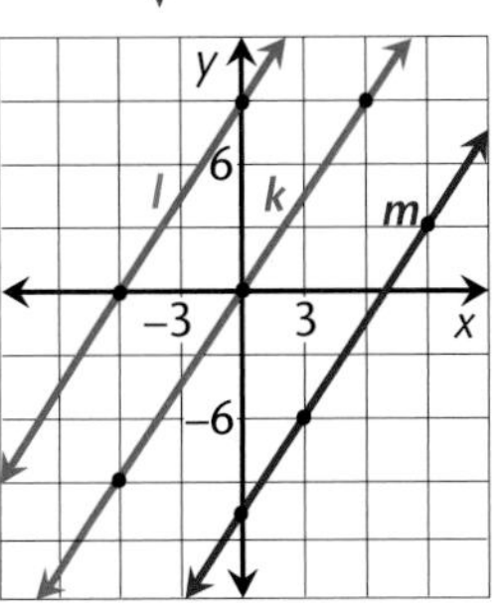

a. Find the slope of line k. Write an equation in slope-intercept form for the line.

b. Find the slope of line m. Write an equation in slope-intercept form for line m.

c. What do you notice about the two lines?

d. What do you notice about the two equations?

e. Suppose line l has the same slope as lines k and m. What does that tell you about line l?

f. Write an equation for line l in slope-intercept form.

g. Write an equation in slope-intercept form for a line that is parallel to lines m, k, and l.

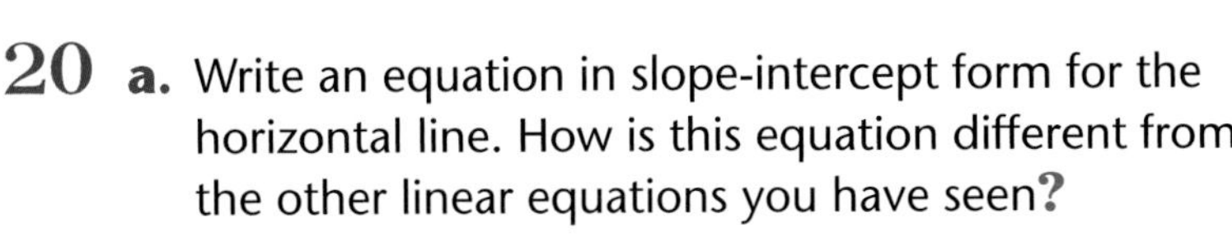

20 **a.** Write an equation in slope-intercept form for the horizontal line. How is this equation different from the other linear equations you have seen?

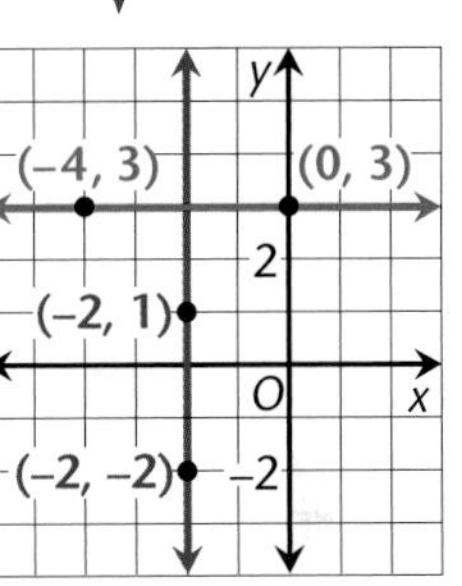

b. Can you write an equation in slope-intercept form for the vertical line? Explain.

c. What is true about the x-coordinate of each point on the vertical line? Use your answer to write an equation of the line.

d. How can you find an equation of a horizontal or vertical line just by looking at the coordinates of one point on the line?

21 ✓ **CHECKPOINT** For each line, write an equation in slope-intercept form.

a.

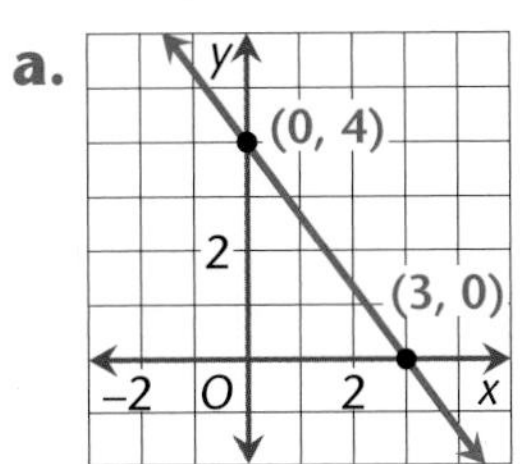

b.

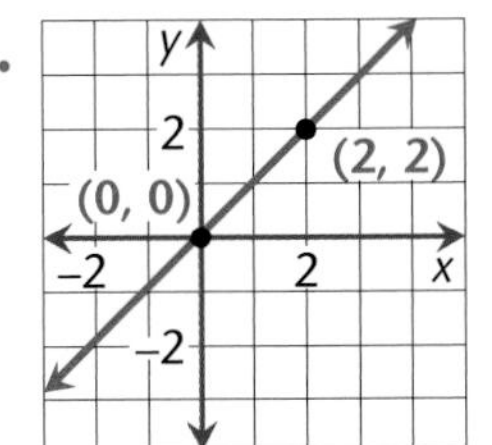

c.

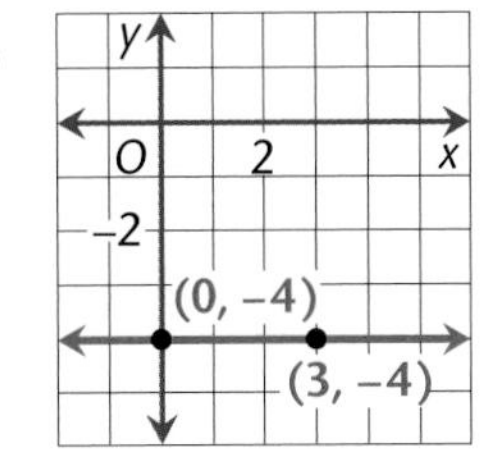

✓ **QUESTION 21**

...checks that you can write an equation of a line in slope-intercept form.

HOMEWORK EXERCISES ▶ See Exs. 12–29 on pp. 266–268.

Section 3 Key Concepts

Key Term

Slope (pp. 259–260)

The slope of a line can be positive, negative, zero, or undefined.

Positive slope

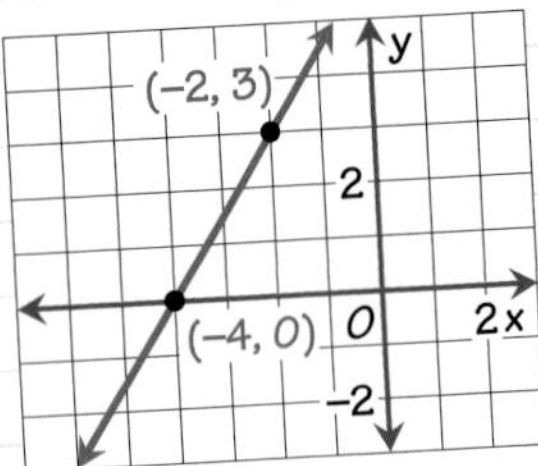

$$\frac{\text{vertical change}}{\text{horizontal change}} = \frac{3-0}{-2-(-4)} = \frac{3}{2}$$

Negative slope

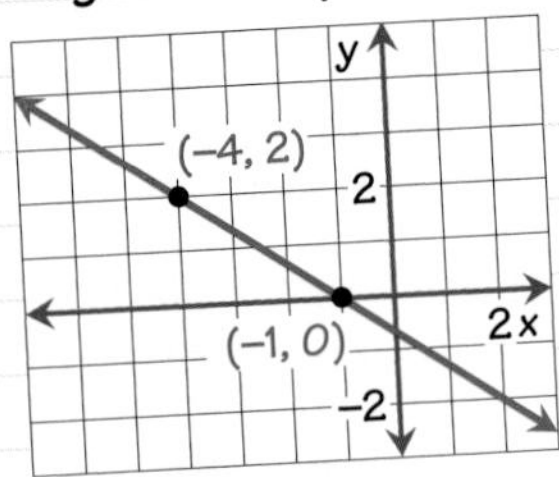

$$\frac{\text{vertical change}}{\text{horizontal change}} = \frac{0-2}{-1-(-4)} = -\frac{2}{3}$$

Zero slope

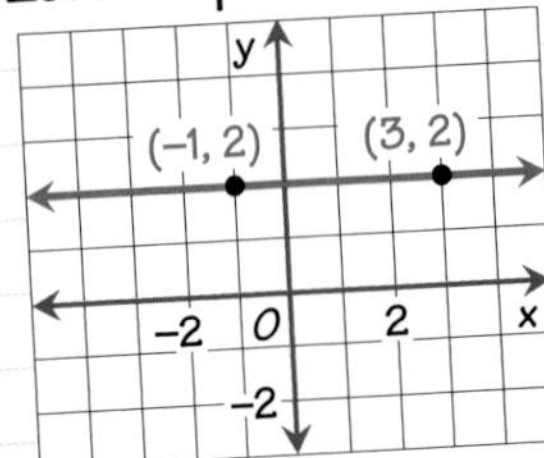

$$\frac{\text{vertical change}}{\text{horizontal change}} = \frac{2-2}{3-(-1)} = \frac{0}{4} = 0$$

Undefined slope

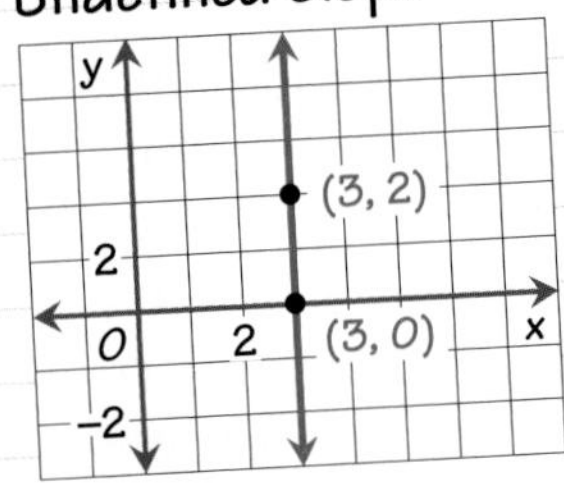

$$\frac{\text{vertical change}}{\text{horizontal change}} = \frac{2-0}{3-3} = \frac{2}{0} \leftarrow \text{undefined}$$

***y*-intercept**

y-intercept (p. 262)

The y-intercept of a line is the y-coordinate of the point where the line crosses the y-axis.

22 **Key Concepts Question** For each part, draw a line that satisfies the given condition(s).

a. The line has a negative slope and a *y*-intercept of 5.

b. The line has a slope that is undefined.

Section 3 Key Concepts

Key Term

Slope-Intercept Form (pp. 261–263)

If a line has slope m and y-intercept b, then an equation of the line is $y = mx + b$. This equation is in slope-intercept form.

slope-intercept form

Example Since the slope of the line shown is $\frac{1}{2}$ and the y-intercept is -3, an equation of the line is $y = \frac{1}{2}x + (-3)$, or $y = \frac{1}{2}x - 3$.

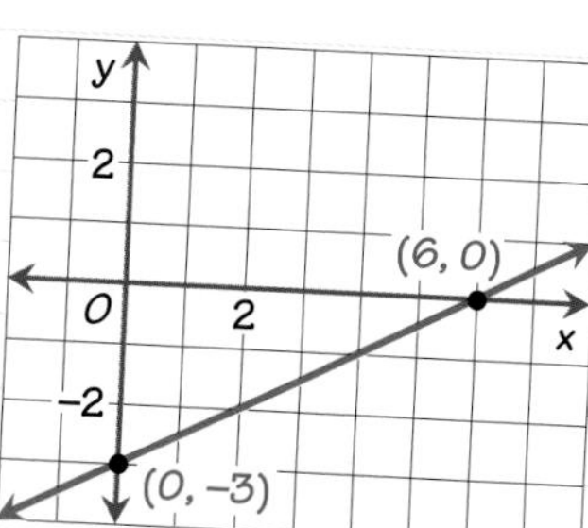

23 **Key Concepts Question** A line passes through the points (0, 5) and (2, 0). Is this enough information for you to write an equation of the line? If so, write an equation of the line in slope-intercept form. If not, explain why not.

Section 3 Practice & Application Exercises

YOU WILL NEED

For Ex. 22:
- graphing calculator or graph paper

For Exs. 23-28:
- graph paper

Find the slope of each line.

1.

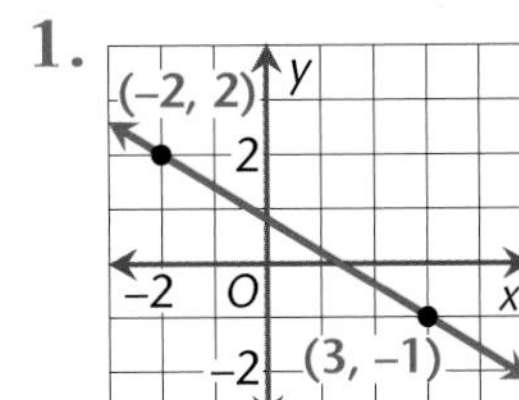

2.

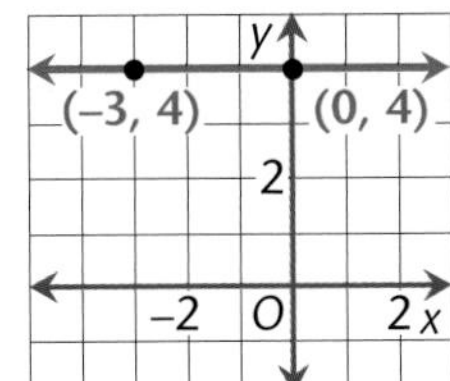

3.

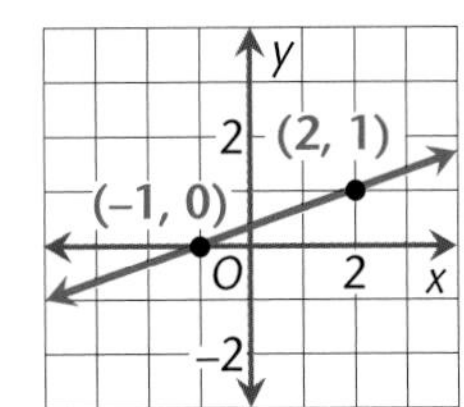

Find the slope of the line through the given points. You may find it helpful to plot the points and draw a line through them first.

4. (2, 7) and (4, 1)

5. (3, 8) and (6, 8)

6. (–9, –4) and (5, 0)

7. (–4, 4) and (3, –5)

8. Use the lines shown.

a. Which line has a positive slope?

b. Which line has a negative slope?

c. Which line has a slope of zero?

d. Which line has a slope that is undefined?

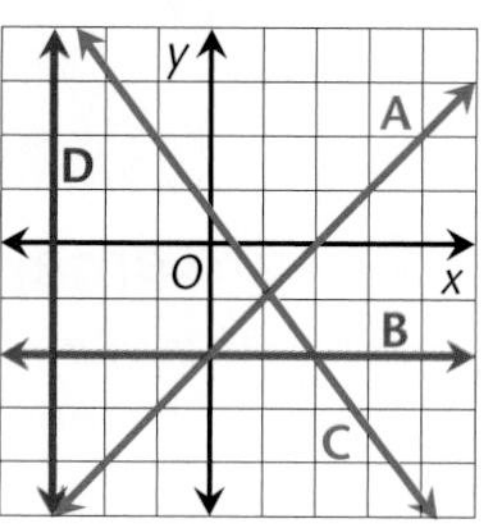

Endangered Species The Kemp's ridley sea turtle was listed as endangered by the United States government in 1970. While the species is now recovering, it is still endangered. Most Kemp's ridley turtles nest on a single beach in Mexico. The graph shows how the number of nests on the beach changed from 1970 to 1995.

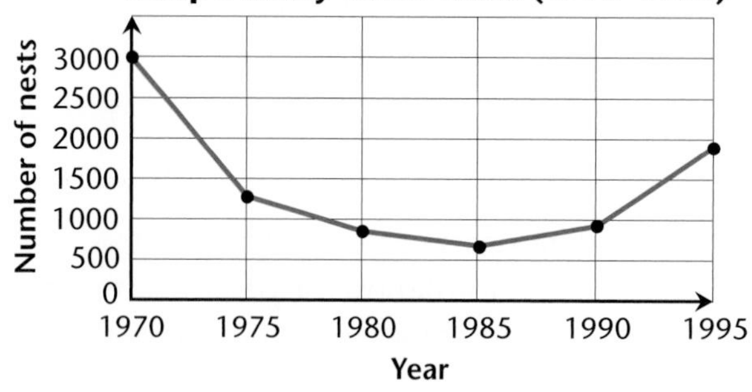

9. **Estimation** For each five-year period shown on the graph's horizontal axis, estimate the average annual rate of change in the number of turtle nests. Start with 1970–1975. Organize your results in a table.

10. During which five-year period from Exercise 9 did the number of turtle nests increase most rapidly? decrease most rapidly?

11. **Writing** Mexico and the United States decided to work together to protect the beach where the Kemp's ridley turtles nest. About when do you think they made this decision? Explain.

For each line, find the slope and the *y*-intercept.

12.

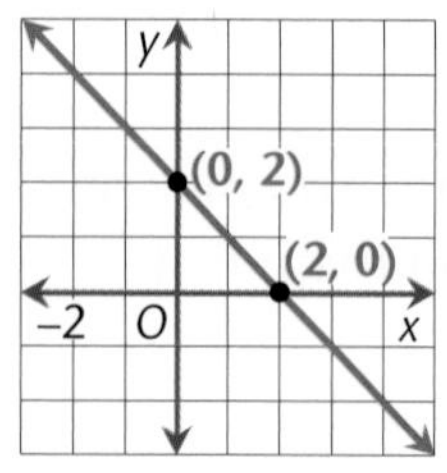

13.

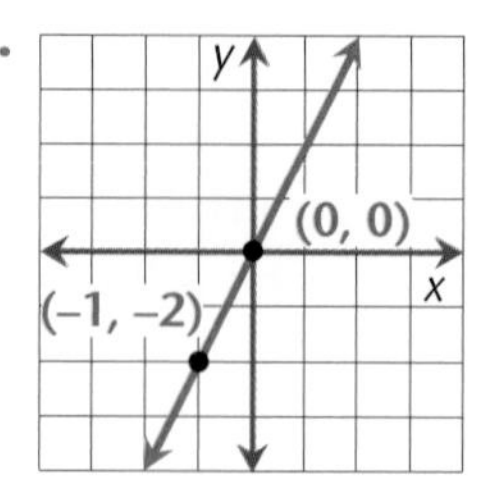

14.

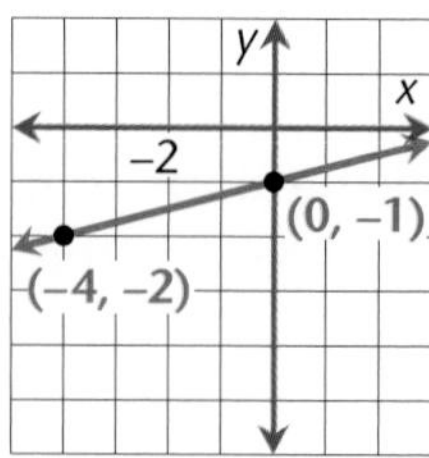

Environment Air pollution causes acid rain, which can damage the environment. From 1975 to 1978, scientists measured the acidity of rain and snow in a Colorado forest. The graph shows a fitted line that the scientists found for their data. Use the graph for Exercises 15–17.

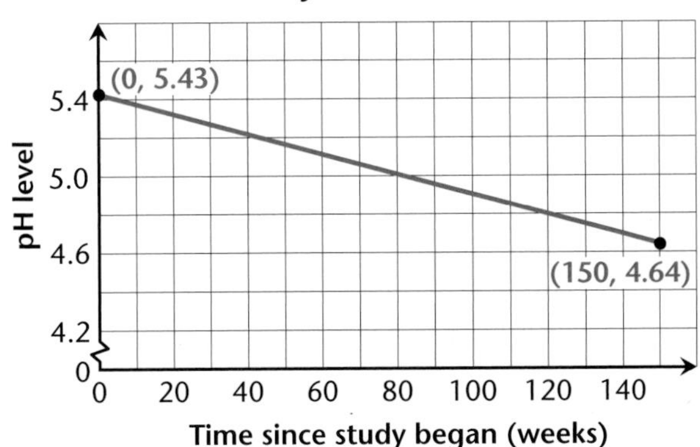

The acidity of rain or snow is given by a pH level. A decreasing pH level means that acidity is increasing.

15. **Interpreting Data** Did the environmental situation in the forest get better or worse during the years 1975–1978? Explain.

16. a. Identify the line's slope and y-intercept.
    b. What information does the slope give about the situation?
    c. What information does the y-intercept give about the situation?

17. The scientists' study ended after 150 weeks. Estimate the acidity of rain and snow in the forest 20 weeks after the study ended. Explain your thinking.

Write an equation in slope-intercept form for the line through the given points. You may find it helpful to plot the points and draw a line through them first.

18. (0, 7) and (1, 2)
19. (0, 4) and (2, 8)
20. (–5, 5) and (3, –1)
21. (–3, –5) and (4, –5)

22. Graphing Calculator Use a graphing calculator or graph paper to complete parts (a) and (b).
    a. Give the slope of the lines $y = x + 2$, $y = x + 3$, and $y = x + 4$. Then graph all three lines on the same coordinate plane. What do you notice about the lines? Write a statement about lines with the same slope.
    b. Graph $y = 2x + 1$, $y = 3x + 1$, and $y = 4x + 1$ on the same coordinate plane. How are the lines alike? How are they different?

23. Maria uses what she knows about slope-intercept form to graph the equation $y = \frac{3}{4}x + 2$.

The y-intercept is 2. Plot the point (0, 2).

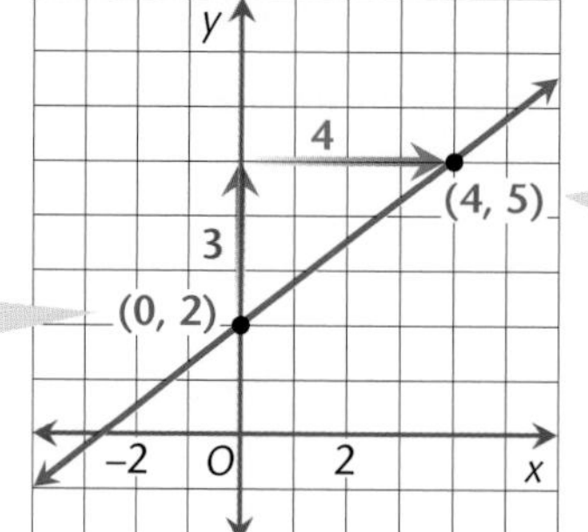

The slope is $\frac{3}{4}$. Count 3 units up and 4 units right. Plot a second point, then draw the line.

Use Maria's method to graph each equation.

a. $y = \frac{5}{2}x + 1$ b. $y = 4x - 5$ c. $y = \frac{1}{3}x - 1$

24. **Challenge** Graph each pair of lines on a coordinate plane.

a. $y = -2x$, $y = \frac{1}{2}x$ b. $y = 3x$, $y = -\frac{1}{3}x$ c. $y = \frac{2}{3}x$, $-\frac{3}{2}x$

d. Describe the relationship between the lines in each pair. Write equations for two other lines that have this relationship.

Graph each equation. Give the slope of each line.

25. $y = 8$ 26. $y = -4$ 27. $x = 3$ 28. $x = -1$

Reflecting on the Section

Discussion

Exercise 29 checks that you understand slopes and equations of lines.

Be prepared to discuss your response to Exercise 29 in class.

29. Given a graph of a line, what can you tell about its slope, even before you do any calculations? How can you find an equation of the line?

Spiral Review

30. Find the surface area of a cylinder that has a radius of 4 in. and a height of 10 in. **(Module 4, p. 251)**

Use an equation to find each percent or number. **(Module 2, p. 132)**

31. 33 is what percent of 60? 32. What is 15% of 30?

Write each number in scientific notation. **(Module 3, p. 209)**

33. 700 34. 2593 35. 101,000

Section 3

Extra Skill Practice

Find the slope of the line through the given points. You may find it helpful to plot the points and draw a line through them first.

1. (0, 1) and (1, 4)
2. (4, –3) and (2, 5)
3. (–1, –1) and (8, –4)
4. (3, –5) and (7, 5)
5. (5, –3) and (1, –3)
6. (6, –2) and (6, 6)

Use the lines shown for Exercises 7–10.

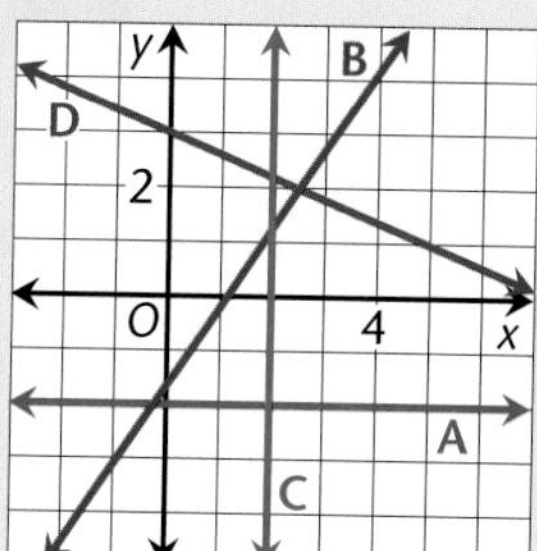

7. Which line has a positive slope?
8. Which line has a negative slope?
9. Which line has a slope of zero?
10. Which line has a slope that is undefined?

For each line, write an equation in slope-intercept form.

11.

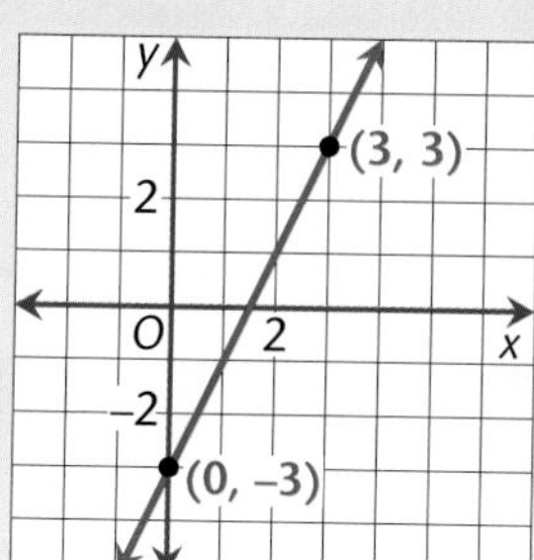

12.

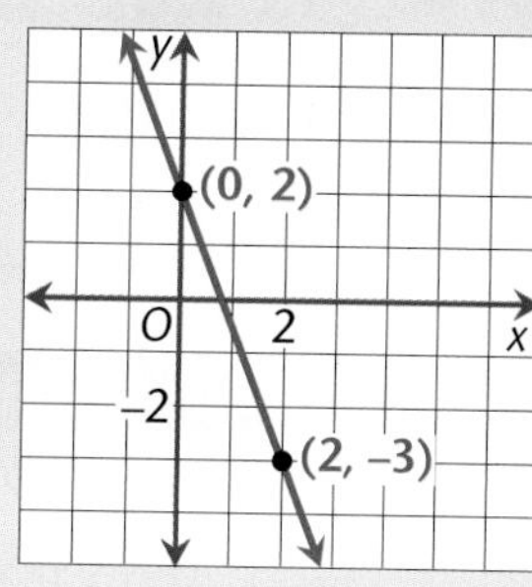

13.

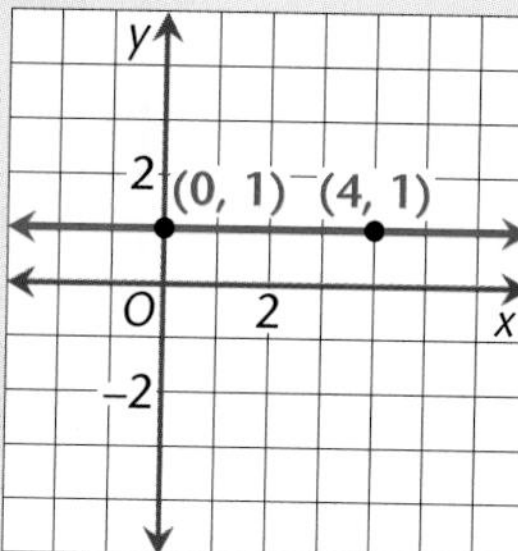

Write an equation in slope-intercept form for the line through the given points. You may find it helpful to plot the points and draw a line through them first.

14. (3, 7) and (5, 7)
15. (0, 5) and (5, 0)
16. (3, 4) and (–2, –2)

Standardized Testing ▶ Open-ended

Write an equation in slope-intercept form for a line that satisfies the given condition(s).

1. The line has a negative slope and a *y*-intercept of 4.
2. The line has a slope of 3 and a negative *y*-intercept.
3. The line has a slope of zero and a positive *y*-intercept.
4. The line is steeper than the line with equation $y = -2x + 7$.

Section 4 Rational Numbers

IN THIS SECTION

EXPLORATION 1
- Rational Numbers

EXPLORATION 2
- Equations with Rational Numbers

Writing Numbers

Setting the Stage

Throughout the ages, many systems have been invented for recording numbers. As early as 3400 B.C., the Egyptians had developed a system for using hieroglyphs to write numbers. They used tally marks for the first nine numerals and wrote symbols for the first few powers of ten.

<table>
<tr><th colspan="10">Egyptian Symbols for One Through Nine</th></tr>
<tr><td>Symbol</td><td>|</td><td>||</td><td>|||</td><td>||||</td><td>|||
	</td><td>		
		</td><td>			
		</td><td>			
			</td><td>				
			</td></tr>
<tr><td>Value</td><td>1</td><td>2</td><td>3</td><td>4</td><td>5</td><td>6</td><td>7</td><td>8</td><td>9</td></tr>
</table>

<table>
<tr><th colspan="3">Egyptian Symbols for Powers of Ten</th></tr>
<tr><th>Symbol</th><th>Description</th><th>Value</th></tr>
<tr><td>|</td><td>a vertical staff</td><td>1</td></tr>
<tr><td>∩</td><td>a heel bone or a yoke</td><td>10</td></tr>
<tr><td>𓍢</td><td>a scroll or a coil of rope</td><td>100</td></tr>
<tr><td>𓆼</td><td>a lotus flower</td><td>1000</td></tr>
<tr><td>𓂭</td><td>a pointing finger</td><td>10,000</td></tr>
<tr><td>𓆐</td><td>a fish or a tadpole</td><td>100,000</td></tr>
<tr><td>𓁨</td><td>an astonished man</td><td>1,000,000</td></tr>
</table>

▲ How do we know how the Egyptians wrote numbers? Much of our knowledge of Egyptian mathematics comes from the Rhind Papyrus. The papyrus contains information from sources dating back to about 1850 B.C.

Sometimes the Egyptians wrote the numerals from left to right or down the page, but most of the time they wrote them from right to left as in ||||∩𓍢𓍢𓍢𓆼𓆼𓆼𓆼𓆐. From the tables, you can see that

<table>
<tr><td>𓆐</td><td>represents</td><td>100,000</td></tr>
<tr><td>𓆼𓆼𓆼𓆼</td><td>represents</td><td>4,000</td></tr>
<tr><td>𓍢𓍢𓍢</td><td>represents</td><td>300</td></tr>
<tr><td>∩</td><td>represents</td><td>10</td></tr>
<tr><td>and ||||</td><td>represents</td><td>4</td></tr>
<tr><td></td><td>which all adds up to</td><td>104,314.</td></tr>
</table>

So the Egyptian numeral ||||𓍢𓍢𓍢𓆼𓆼𓆼𓆼𓆐 represents 104,314.

Think About It

1 What number does the Egyptian numeral represent?

2 Write 2396 as an Egyptian numeral.

Exploration 1

Rational Numbers

GOAL

LEARN HOW TO...
- recognize the characteristics of rational numbers
- use notation for repeating decimals

AS YOU...
- explore ratios and Egyptian fractions

KEY TERMS
- rational number
- terminating decimal
- repeating decimal

SET UP *Work with a partner. You will need a calculator.*

▶ **To record measurements such as the length of a side of a field or the amount of grain in a sack, the Egyptians had to invent a way to write fractions.**

For some common fractions they used special symbols such as for $\frac{1}{2}$, for $\frac{2}{3}$, and for $\frac{1}{4}$.

The symbol , which meant "part of," was used with a numeral to write fractions that have a numerator of 1. Here are a few examples with their modern equivalents:

↔ $\frac{1}{3}$ ↔ $\frac{1}{10}$ ↔ $\frac{1}{125}$ ↔ $2\frac{1}{2}$

All other fractions were written as sums of fractions with numerators of 1 and distinct denominators.

read from right to left, $\frac{1}{2} + \frac{1}{4}$ ↔ $\frac{3}{4}$

$\frac{1}{3} + \frac{1}{15}$ ↔ $\frac{2}{5}$

FOR◀HELP with *adding fractions*, see **MODULE 2, p. 100**

3 What is the modern equivalent of each fraction?

a. 

b. 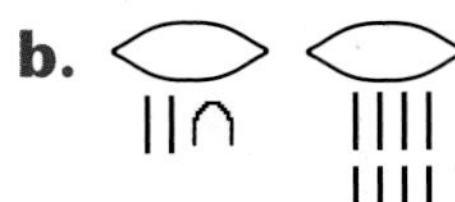

c. 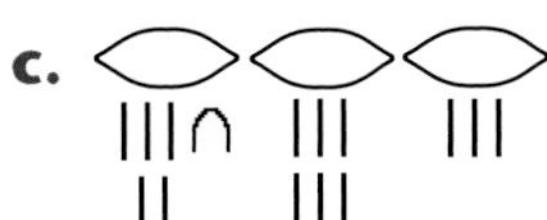

4 Use Egyptian symbols to represent each fraction.

a. $\frac{1}{25}$ **b.** $\frac{1}{100}$ **c.** $\frac{7}{8}$

▶ **The Egyptians' numeration system made it possible for them to write all the positive *rational numbers*. A rational number is a number that can be written in the form $\frac{a}{b}$ where a and b are integers and $b \neq 0$. In our system, we have many different ways of writing rational numbers.**

EXAMPLE

0.3 is a rational number because it can be written as $\frac{3}{10}$.

3.8 is a rational number because it can be written as $\frac{38}{10}$.

9 is a rational number because it can be written as $\frac{9}{1}$.

$-2\frac{1}{3}$ is a rational number because it can be written as $\frac{-7}{3}$.

5 Use your calculator to write each rational number as a decimal. Give the decimal displayed on the calculator. Do not round.

a. $\frac{1}{2}$ **b.** $\frac{1}{3}$ **c.** $\frac{4}{25}$ **d.** $\frac{3}{8}$ **e.** $\frac{5}{11}$

FOR▶HELP with *equivalent fractions*, see **TOOLBOX, p. 585**

6 For each fraction, try to write an equivalent fraction that has a power of 10 as its denominator.

a. $\frac{1}{2}$ **b.** $\frac{1}{3}$ **c.** $\frac{4}{25}$ **d.** $\frac{3}{8}$ **e.** $\frac{5}{11}$

7 **Discussion** In Question 6, were you able to write $\frac{1}{3}$ and $\frac{5}{11}$ as fractions with denominators that are powers of 10? Why or why not?

▶ **The rational numbers $\frac{1}{2}$, $\frac{2}{5}$, and $\frac{3}{8}$ can be written as *terminating decimals*. A terminating decimal contains a finite number of digits. Some rational numbers, such as $\frac{1}{3}$ and $\frac{5}{11}$, can be written as *repeating decimals*. A repeating decimal contains a digit or group of digits that repeats forever.**

8 **Try This as a Class** Any rational number can be written as a terminating or a repeating decimal. Explain how you can tell whether a particular fraction will be a *terminating* or a *repeating* decimal.

9 **a.** Without using your calculator, divide 7 by 11 and find the answer to five decimal places.

b. Explain how you know the decimal will continue to repeat beyond the place where you stopped dividing.

▶ **You can use a bar to show which digits in a decimal repeat.**

EXAMPLE

$$\frac{16}{33} = 0.484848... = 0.\overline{48}\text{, so}$$

$\frac{16}{33}$ is exactly equal to $0.\overline{48}$ and $-\frac{16}{33}$ is exactly equal to $-0.\overline{48}$.

10 Write your answer to Question 9(a) using a bar to show which digits repeat.

11 In the decimal $0.6\overline{3}$, only the digit 3 repeats, $0.6\overline{3} = 0.633333...$. Write each decimal below using six decimal places, as shown in the Example. Then write the decimals in order from least to greatest.

a. $0.8\overline{2}$ $\quad 0.\overline{828}$ $\quad 0.\overline{82}$ $\quad 0.822$

b. $-0.8\overline{28}$ $\quad -0.\overline{8}$ $\quad -0.8$ $\quad -0.82\overline{8}$

12 ✔ **CHECKPOINT** Write each rational number as a terminating or a repeating decimal. Then write the numbers in order from least to greatest.

a. $\frac{5}{37}$ $\quad$ **b.** $-3\frac{1}{4}$ $\quad$ **c.** 6 $\quad$ **d.** $-\frac{14}{16}$

✔ **QUESTION 12**

...checks that you can write a rational number as a terminating or a repeating decimal.

HOMEWORK EXERCISES ▶ See Exs. 1–7 on p. 278.

GOAL

LEARN HOW TO...
- solve equations containing rational numbers

AS YOU...
- investigate a problem from the Moscow Papyrus

Exploration 2

Equations With Rational Numbers

▶ **The Egyptians also invented ways to approximate surface areas and volumes. For example, one of the problems in the Moscow Papyrus explains how to find the surface area of a "basket". The third line of the basket problem shows that the diameter of the basket is $4\frac{1}{2}$ units long. Can you find this numeral in the hieroglyphics below?**

Scholars disagree ▶ about the shape of the basket referred to in the Moscow Papyrus (written in about 1850 B.C.). We will assume the basket was a hemisphere.

13 **Try This as a Class** The formula for the surface area of a sphere is $S.A. = 4\pi r^2$, where r is the radius of the sphere.

a. The surface area of the basket is similar to the surface area of the curved surface of a hemisphere. Write a formula for finding the area of the curved surface of a hemisphere.

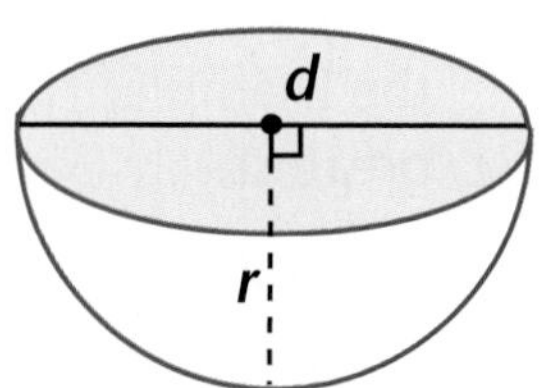

▲ a hemisphere with radius r and diameter d

b. The basket has a diameter of $4\frac{1}{2}$ units. What is the radius? Write your answer as a fraction.

c. Use the radius you found in part (b) to write an equation representing the exact surface area of the basket. Simplify the equation.

▶ **To approximate the surface area of the basket you would need to substitute a value such as 3.14 or $\frac{22}{7}$ for π in the equation you wrote. The Egyptians did not use these values for π. What value did they use and how does it compare to the approximations we often use today? Answer Questions 14 and 15 to find out.**

14 The next to last line of the basket problem is given below. It reads, "You get 32. Behold this is its surface!"

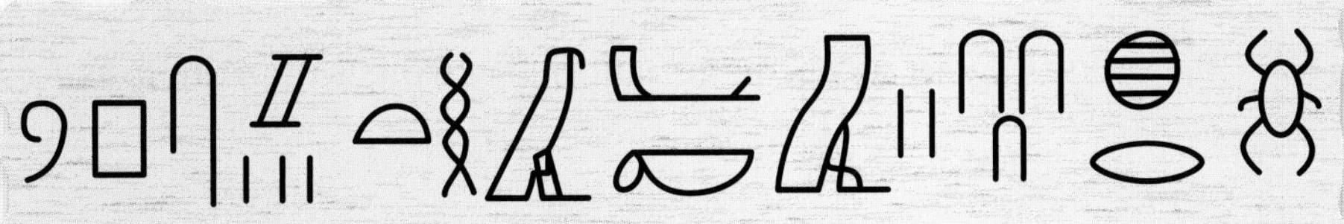

a. Use your equation from Question 13(c). Replace *S.A.* with 32 and choose a variable to represent the Egyptians' value for π. Replace π with the variable you chose.

b. To solve for the variable, you can undo the multiplication by dividing by the fraction. What fraction will you need to divide by to solve your equation?

▶ **The Egyptians invented ways to calculate with positive rational numbers, but methods for calculating with negative rationals were not invented until centuries later. The sign rules for multiplying and dividing negative rational numbers are the same as those for integers.**

EXAMPLE

Solve $8 = -\frac{4}{5}n$.

SAMPLE RESPONSE

$$8 = -\frac{4}{5}n$$

$$8 \div \left(-\frac{4}{5}\right) = -\frac{4}{5}n \div \left(-\frac{4}{5}\right)$$

Undo multiplication by dividing both sides of the equation by $-\frac{4}{5}$.

$$8 \cdot \left(-\frac{5}{4}\right) = -\frac{4}{5}n \cdot \left(-\frac{5}{4}\right)$$

To divide by $-\frac{4}{5}$, multiply by its reciprocal, $-\frac{5}{4}$.

$$-\frac{40}{4} = n$$

$$-10 = n$$

15 **a.** Use the Example as a guide to help solve your equation from Question 14(a) to find what fraction the Egyptians used for π.

b. What fraction did the Egyptians use for π? To what decimal is this close?

16 **Discussion** Describe the steps you would use to solve each equation.

a. $\frac{1}{8} = -\frac{9}{2}x$ **b.** $-4\frac{1}{2}x = 180$ **c.** $-\frac{2}{3}x + 5 = 11$

▶ Sometimes equations are written so that the variable is part of a fraction. In Questions 17–19 you will develop methods for solving equations like $\frac{3x}{5} = 10$.

17 One way to solve the equation $\frac{3x}{5} = 10$ is to rewrite it as $\frac{3}{5}x = 10$.

a. Solve $\frac{3}{5}x = 10$.

b. Check that your answer is a solution of the equation $\frac{3x}{5} = 10$.

18 Another way to solve $\frac{3x}{5} = 10$ is to first multiply both sides of the equation by 5.

a. Discussion Why is it helpful to use this as a first step?

b. Finish solving the equation.

19 Solve each equation.

a. $\frac{5y}{6} = 18$ **b.** $21 = \frac{-3n}{10}$ **c.** $\frac{-p}{8} + 10 = 20$

20 Consider the equation $-\frac{3}{4}x + \frac{1}{6} = \frac{11}{12}$.

a. What is the least common denominator of the fractions?

b. Multiply both sides of the equation by the LCD of the fractions and solve the resulting equation.

c. Check that your solution in part (b) is a solution of the original equation.

d. Discussion Could you solve the original equation by multiplying both sides by 48? What is the advantage of using the LCD instead?

21 Discussion

a. What would be your first step in solving $2n + 0.5 = -0.7$?

b. What would be your second step?

c. Solve $2n + 0.5 = -0.7$. What is the value of n?

✓ QUESTION 22

...checks that you can solve equations containing rational numbers.

22 ✓ CHECKPOINT Solve each equation and check your solution.

a. $-\frac{2}{3}y - \frac{1}{2} = 4$ **b.** $2.9 - 0.2x = 1.2$ **c.** $-1.1 = -0.5a - 1.2$

HOMEWORK EXERCISES ▶ **See Exs. 8–30 on pp. 278–280.**

Section 4 Key Concepts

Key Terms

rational number

terminating decimal

repeating decimal

Rational Numbers (pp. 271–273)

A rational number can be written in the form $\frac{a}{b}$, where a and b are integers and $b \neq 0$. When written as a decimal, a rational number either terminates or repeats.

rational numbers $\frac{13}{50} = 0.26$ (terminating decimal) $\quad \frac{8}{11} = 0.727272... = 0.\overline{72}$ (repeating decimal)

Equations with Rational Numbers (pp. 274–276)

You can solve equations that contain rational numbers. Recall that the sign rules for multiplying and dividing negative rational numbers are the same as those for multiplying and dividing integers.

Example

$$-\frac{3}{4}x + 5 = 10$$

$$-\frac{3}{4}x + 5 - 5 = 10 - 5$$ Subtract 5 from both sides.

$$-\frac{3}{4}x = 5$$

$$-\frac{3}{4}x \div \left(-\frac{3}{4}\right) = 5 \div \left(-\frac{3}{4}\right)$$ Divide both sides by $-\frac{3}{4}$.

$$-\frac{3}{4}x \bullet \left(-\frac{4}{3}\right) = 5 \bullet \left(-\frac{4}{3}\right)$$ To divide by $-\frac{3}{4}$ multiply by its reciprocal, $-\frac{4}{3}$.

$$x = -\frac{20}{3} = -6\frac{2}{3}$$

Key Concepts Questions

23 Check that $-6\frac{2}{3}$ is a solution of the equation $-\frac{3}{4}x + 5 = 10$.

24 Solve the equation $20 = -1.5y - 7$. Explain the steps you use.

Section 4
Practice & Application Exercises

1. What is the modern equivalent of each fraction?

a. 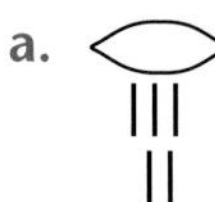
b. 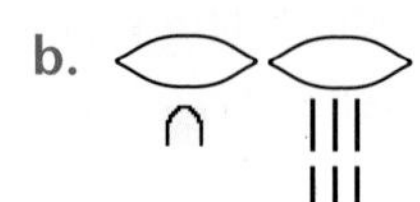
c. 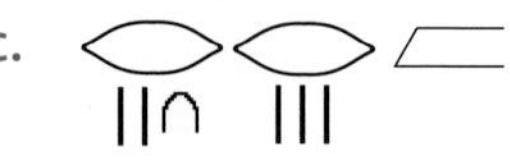

2. Use Egyptian symbols to represent each fraction.

a. $\frac{1}{125}$ b. $\frac{1}{1000}$ c. $\frac{4}{5}$

3. Write each rational number as a quotient of two integers.

a. -4 b. $\sqrt{16}$ c. 0.25 d. $2\frac{3}{7}$

4. Write each rational number as a terminating or repeating decimal.

a. $2\frac{3}{5}$ b. $\frac{9}{11}$ c. $\frac{8}{27}$ d. $\frac{7}{20}$

5. **Writing** Explain why 0.666667 is not exactly equal to $\frac{2}{3}$.

6. Write the repeating decimals below in order from least to greatest. Explain your thinking.

$0.1\overline{25}$ $0.12\overline{5}$ $0.\overline{12}$ $0.\overline{125}$

7. Write the numbers $\frac{16}{3}$, $-14.\overline{14}$, -1 , $5\frac{4}{9}$, 14.1, 5.33, and $-\sqrt{4}$ in order from least to greatest.

Solve each equation.

8. $\frac{3}{5}n = 15$
9. $10 = -1.25x$
10. $1\frac{2}{3}r = 120$
11. $\frac{5}{6}b + 15 = 14$
12. $9 = \frac{3}{4}h + 12$
13. $-2.25s - 7 = 20$
14. $\frac{2x}{3} = -7$
15. $15 = \frac{-5x}{3}$
16. $\frac{x}{5} - 2 = -3$
17. $3x + 6 = 4.5$
18. $-\frac{3}{4}x = \frac{11}{12}$
19. $-0.5x - 1.25 = 6.75$
20. $-\frac{4}{5}x + \frac{3}{5} = \frac{13}{25}$
21. $\frac{2}{3}x + 6 = \frac{4}{9}$
22. $6.25x + 3 = -4.5$

23. **Geometry Connection** The area of the triangle is 209 ft^2. Find the length of the base of the triangle.

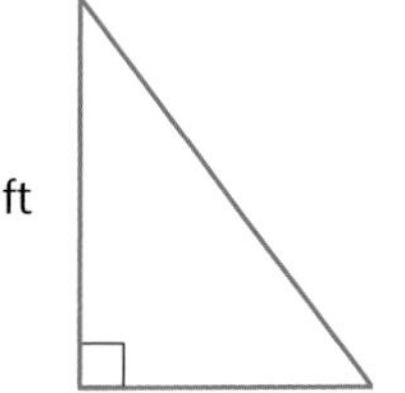

24. **Music** The City Youth Orchestra has four sections. The circle graph shows what fraction of the orchestra play in three of the sections.

    a. Let n be the fraction of the orchestra members that play brass instruments. Write an equation that shows that the sum of the fractional parts of the orchestra is 1.

    b. What fraction of the orchestra members play brass instruments? How did you find your answer?

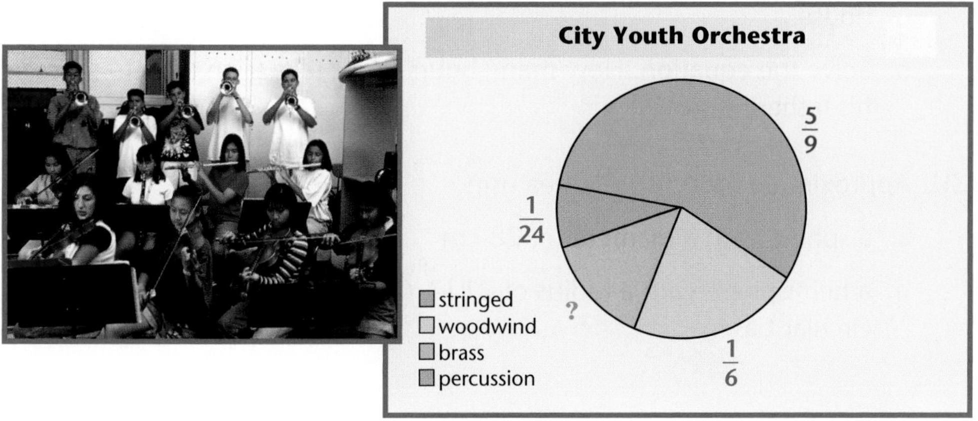

25. **Challenge** Soft drinks come in four sizes at a local convenience store: small, medium, large, and jumbo. The small is $\frac{1}{9}$ the size of the jumbo. The jumbo is 2 times the size of the large, and the medium is $\frac{1}{3}$ the size of the large. If the medium is 12 ounces, find the size of the jumbo, the large, and the small.

26. Jill was planning a hiking trip through Europe. To get a feel for metric distances, she converted miles to kilometers. To do this, she multiplied the number of miles by 1.6.

    a. Write an equation Jill could have used to estimate distances in kilometers given distances in miles.

    b. About how many kilometers is 55 mi?

    c. About how many miles is 120 km?

    d. How would she convert kilometers to miles?

27. The equation $C = \frac{5}{9}F - 17\frac{7}{9}$ can be used to convert degrees Fahrenheit (F) to degrees Celsius (C).

a. What is the Celsius temperature for 212°F?

b. What is the Fahrenheit temperature for –20°C?

c. Show that the formula $F = \frac{9}{5}C + 32$ is equivalent to $C = \frac{5}{9}F - 17\frac{7}{9}$.

28. a. Elian drives 345 mi from his home to a campground. He travels at an average rate of 57.5 mi/hr. He plans to stop on the way at his father's house, which is 161 miles from the campground. Explain why you can use the equation $345 - 57.5t = 161$ to find the time in hours it will take Elian to get to his father's house.

b. Solve the equation. How many hours will it take Elian to get to his father's house?

29. Approximate each surface area using $\frac{22}{7}$ for π.

a. a sphere with a diameter of 28 cm

b. a hemisphere with a radius of 21 in. (Include the area of the circular base.)

Discussion

Exercise 30 checks that you understand terminating and repeating decimals.

Reflecting on the Section

Be prepared to discuss your response to Exercise 30 in class.

30. a. Without dividing, determine whether each fraction is equivalent to a repeating decimal or to a terminating decimal. Explain your decision in each case.

$\frac{7}{40}$ $\qquad$ $\frac{5}{14}$ $\qquad$ $\frac{6}{15}$

b. Check your answers by dividing.

Spiral Review

Evaluate each expression. Round decimal answers to the nearest hundredth. (Module 3, p. 175)

31. $\frac{12 + 13}{7}$ $\qquad$ 32. $\frac{9}{2}\sqrt{6 + 5}$ $\qquad$ 33. $\frac{8}{12 - 3}$

Tell whether each ordered pair is a solution of the equation $y = -x + 2$. (Module 3, p. 175)

34. (0, 2) 35. (–1, –1) 36. (–2, 0) 37. (2, 4)

Solve each equation. Round decimal solutions to the nearest hundredth. (Module 3, p. 220)

38. $19 = 2.5x - 3.1$

39. $\frac{n}{4.4} + 39 = 52.6$

40. $3.7 + 0.06z = 11$

41. $\frac{r}{2} + 21 = 31.1$

Extension

Repeating Decimals

The decimal 0.25 can be written as the fraction $\frac{25}{100}$, or $\frac{1}{4}$. A repeating decimal such as $0.\overline{36}$ can also be written as a fraction.

Step 1 Write an equation. $x = 0.\overline{36}$

Step 2 Multiply both sides by 100 since $0.\overline{36}$ has two digits that repeat. $100x = 100(0.\overline{36})$

Step 3 Subtract $x = 0.\overline{36}$ from the resulting equation.

$$\begin{array}{r} 100x = 36.\overline{36} \\ -\quad x = -0.\overline{36} \\ \hline 99x = 36 \end{array}$$

Step 4 Solve for x and write the fraction in lowest terms. $x = \frac{36}{99} = \frac{4}{11}$

Step 5 Check that $\frac{4}{11} = 0.\overline{36}$. $4 \div 11 = 0.36363636\ldots$

Write each repeating decimal as a fraction in lowest terms. Check your solutions.

42. $0.\overline{48}$ 43. $0.\overline{2}$ 44. $0.\overline{123}$ 45. $0.5\overline{8}$

Section 4
Extra Skill Practice

Write each rational number as a quotient of two integers.

1. 1.37
2. $-\sqrt{25}$
3. 0.125
4. $5\frac{3}{8}$

Write each rational number as a terminating or repeating decimal.

5. $1\frac{3}{4}$
6. $\frac{7}{13}$
7. $\frac{8}{15}$
8. $\frac{9}{25}$
9. Order the numbers 0.35, $-\frac{3}{10}$, $-0.\overline{3}$, $\frac{2}{5}$, and $\frac{1}{3}$ from least to greatest.

Replace each __?__ with >, <, or =.

10. $-2.5\overline{8}$ __?__ -2.6
11. $-8.\overline{42}$ __?__ $-8.\overline{4}$
12. $-\frac{2}{3}$ __?__ $-\frac{5}{8}$
13. $-9\frac{5}{6}$ __?__ $-9.8\overline{3}$

Solve each equation.

14. $3.2x - 2.7 = -8.4$
15. $-2.5x + 3 = 5.75$
16. $2.6 = 2.7 + 2.5x$
17. $\frac{2}{3}x + 1 = \frac{1}{6}$
18. $\frac{3}{5} - \frac{2}{5}x = \frac{21}{25}$
19. $6\frac{1}{4} = -\frac{5}{12}x$
20. $\frac{1}{8}x = -3$
21. $3 = 5 + \frac{2}{3}y$
22. $4 = \frac{7}{3}m$
23. $0.5 = 0.75x + 1.25$
24. $-\frac{2}{5}m - \frac{1}{10} = \frac{3}{10}$
25. $3.2 + 0.4x = 1.2$
26. $\frac{3}{2}t + 30 = 15$
27. $2 = 4 - \frac{1}{4}s$
28. $6 - \frac{4}{9}x = \frac{1}{9}$

Standardized Testing ▶ Open-ended

Write a real-world problem that can be modeled by each equation.

1. $\frac{3}{5}y = 30$
2. $\frac{1}{2}n + 12 = 40$

Section 5 Counting Techniques

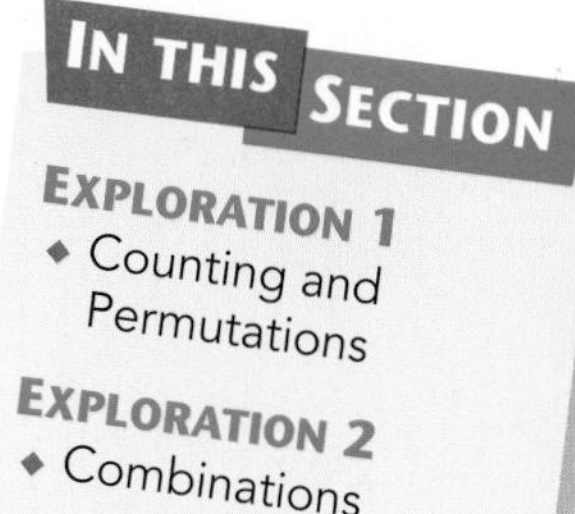

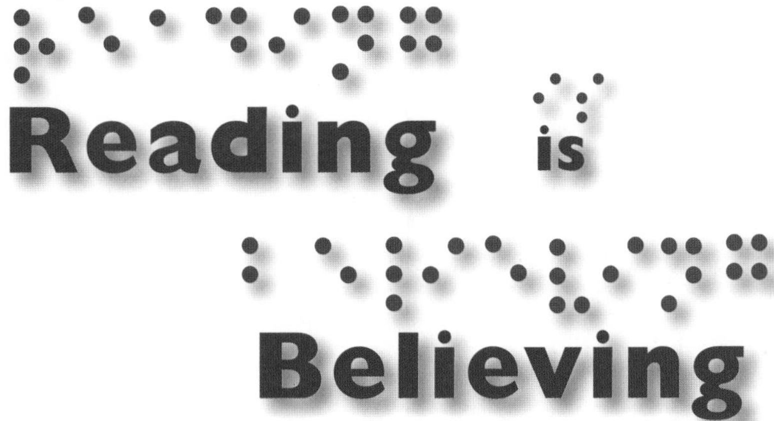

Setting the Stage

SET UP *You will need Labsheet 5A.*

Louis Braille (1809–1852) was blinded in an accident when he was only three years old. As a young boy, he anxiously awaited the day when he could go to school and learn to read. In her book *Seeing Fingers: The Story of Louis Braille,* Etta DeGering describes Louis's first year in school.

Seeing Fingers by Etta DeGering

Since Monsieur Becheret, the teacher, lectured one day and questioned the next, Louis did not find it too difficult to compete with his sighted classmates. After a few weeks he stood at the top of most of his classes.

In arithmetic he could often work a problem in his head as quickly as the other pupils on paper. But when it came to the reading and writing periods there was nothing for him to do. There were no books for blind boys to read and no way for them to write. This he learned the first day of school. When the primers were passed out, he held out his hand and was given one. He touched [his cousin] Jean to see how the reading was done. He held his book in the same way, but the pages told him no magic words.

"Are there no books for blind boys to read?" he asked the teacher.

When Monsieur Becheret said "None that I know of," Louis put his head down on his desk and wept.

Louis did not give up, however. Between the ages of 12 and 15, he created a code that he hoped would allow blind students to read. His code used groups of raised dots to represent letters of the alphabet. Today the code Louis created is called Braille in his honor. The Braille alphabet is shown below.

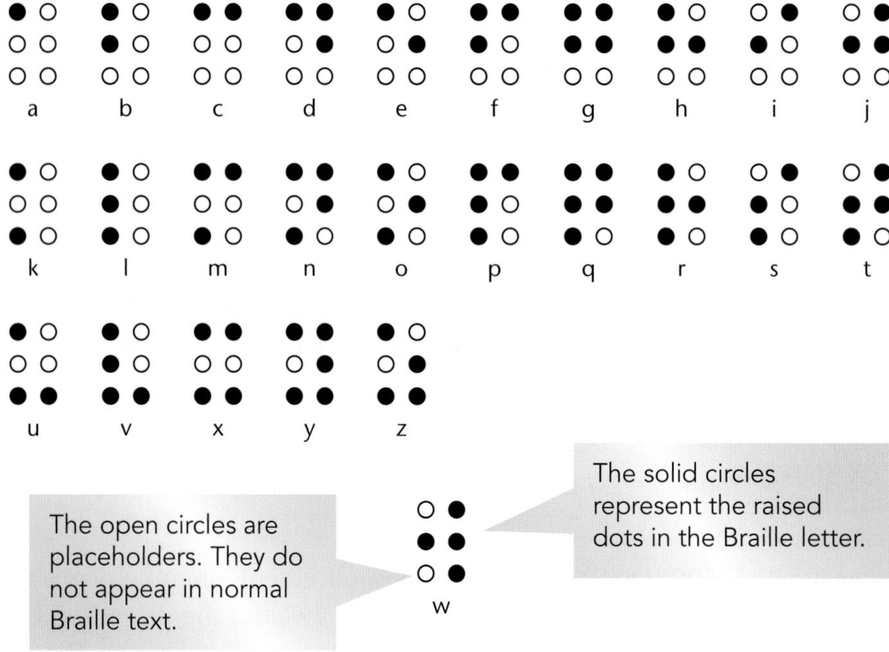

Notice that Braille letters are at most 2 dots wide and at most 3 dots high. The 6 possible dot positions form a Braille *cell*. The cell at the right shows how the dot positions are numbered.

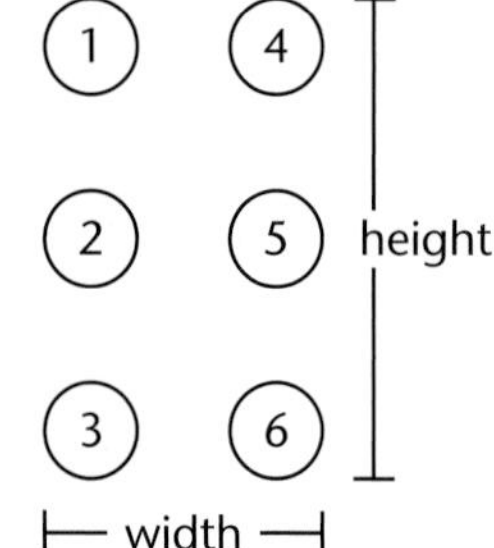

Think About It

1 **Use Labsheet 5A.** One day at school, Louis showed the Braille alphabet to some of his classmates. As his classmates discussed what the new alphabet would allow them to do, his friend Gabriel interrupted them excitedly. "Already I know the alphabet. I have written a sentence." Follow the directions on the labsheet to read *Gabriel's Sentence.*

▶ **In this section, you will discover why Louis Braille's decision to use 6 dot positions in a Braille cell was a very important one. You will also explore how he constructed the Braille alphabet.**

Exploration 1

Counting and Permutations

SET UP *You will need colored markers or pencils.*

GOAL

LEARN HOW TO...
- use the counting principle to count numbers of choices
- find the number of permutations of a group of objects

AS YOU...
- work with Braille symbols

KEY TERMS
- counting principle
- permutation

▶ **In this exploration, you will answer this question: What would have happened if Louis Braille had chosen fewer than 6 dot positions for his Braille cell?**

2 How many different symbols could Louis Braille have made if he had used only 1 dot position for the Braille cell?

▶ **You can use a tree diagram to find the number of different symbols you can make with a Braille cell that has 2 dot positions.**

Start	Choices for position 1	Choices for position 2	Symbol
	① Dot in position 1	①② Dot in position 2	● ●
		①② No dot in position 2	● ○
	① No dot in position 1	①② Dot in position 2	○ ●
		①② No dot in position 2	○ ○

3 Use the tree diagram on the previous page for a 2-position Braille cell.

a. How many choices are there for position 1 of the cell?

b. For each choice for position 1, how many choices are there for position 2?

c. How many different symbols can you make with a 2-position Braille cell?

4 **a.** Draw a tree diagram that lists the number of different symbols you can make with a 3-position Braille cell like the one shown. Use color to indicate the choices in your tree diagram, as was done in the diagram on the previous page.

b. How many choices are there for position 1? for position 2? for position 3?

c. How many different symbols can you make with a 3-position Braille cell?

d. How are your answers to parts (b) and (c) related?

e. Is this relationship also true for parts (a) and (b) of Question 3?

▶ **The relationship you described in Question 4(d) is called the counting principle. This principle says that the total number of ways a sequence of decisions can be made is the product of the number of choices for each decision.**

EXAMPLE

To find the number of different symbols you can make with a Braille cell that has only 4 dot positions, use the counting principle.

$$\text{number of symbols} = \text{choices for position 1} \times \text{choices for position 2} \times \text{choices for position 3} \times \text{choices for position 4}$$

$$= 2 \times 2 \times 2 \times 2$$

$$= 16$$

There are 2 choices for each position: have a raised dot, or do not have a raised dot.

You can make 16 different symbols with a Braille cell that has 4 dot positions.

5 **✓ CHECKPOINT** How many different symbols can you make with each type of Braille cell? Explain.

a. a 5-position Braille cell

b. a 6-position Braille cell

✓ QUESTION 5

...checks that you can use the counting principle to count numbers of choices.

6 **Discussion** Could Louis Braille have used a Braille cell with fewer than 6 positions for his code? Explain.

▶ **Today new technologies make it easier for blind people to go to school or hold a job. Braille keyboards and Braille printers enable the blind to communicate in written form. Electronic Braille displays are used to convert text on a computer screen into Braille text.**

▲ This student is using a small computerized device with a Braille keyboard. He is able to write in Braille and hear back what he has written by means of synthetic speech.

7 Max Jones uses a Braille keyboard and a Braille display at his job. He needs to choose a password for his company's e-mail system. He decides to use an arrangement of the letters in his first name. You can find the number of passwords from which Max can choose by using the counting principle.

a. How many choices are there for the first letter in an arrangement of the letters in *Max*?

b. After the first letter of the arrangement is chosen, how many choices are there for the second letter?

c. After the first and second letters of the arrangement are chosen, how many choices are there for the third letter?

d. **Discussion** Use the counting principle to find the number of different arrangements of the letters in *Max*. How many of these arrangements can Max use as a password? Explain your reasoning.

▶ **An arrangement of a group of items in a definite order is a permutation of the items. For example, AMX and MAX are permutations of the letters M, A, and X.**

8 **✓ CHECKPOINT** Find the number of permutations of the letters in each word.

a. HAT b. DEAL c. SIGNAL

✓ QUESTION 8

...checks that you can find the number of permutations of a group of items.

HOMEWORK EXERCISES ▶ See Exs. 1–12 on p. 293–295.

GOAL

LEARN HOW TO...
- find numbers of combinations

AS YOU...
- investigate the first ten letters of the Braille alphabet

KEY TERM
- combination

Exploration 2

Combinations

SET UP *You will need Labsheet 5B.*

▶ **In *Seeing Fingers: The Story of Louis Braille,* Etta DeGering describes how Louis created the first ten letters of the Braille alphabet.**

> The first ten letters had been the most difficult. [Louis] made them from different arrangements of the top four dots of the [Braille cell]. **A** was dot 1, **B** dots 1 and 2, **C** dots 1 and 4....

▶ **The first ten Braille letters (a-j) occupy the first row of the Braille alphabet on page 284. As the passage above states, each letter is formed using only dots in the top 4 positions of a Braille cell.**

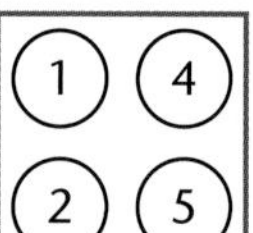

9 Draw all possible Braille symbols (including symbols that are not letters of the Braille alphabet) that have exactly 1 dot in the top 4 positions and no dots in the bottom 2 positions. How many symbols did you get?

Use Labsheet 5B for Questions 10 and 11.

10 You can use the unfinished *Tree Diagram* on the labsheet to find the Braille symbols with exactly 2 dots in the top 4 positions and no dots in the bottom 2 positions.

a. Finish drawing the tree diagram. How many paths through the tree diagram are there?

b. Does each path through the tree diagram represent a *different* Braille symbol? Explain.

c. How many Braille symbols are there with exactly 2 dots in the top 4 positions and no dots in the bottom 2 positions? Draw each symbol.

▶ **In Question 10, you formed Braille symbols by choosing 2 of the top 4 positions in a Braille cell. The order in which you chose the positions did not matter. An arrangement or selection of a group of items in which the order is not important is a combination of the items.**

11 **a.** Write a multiplication expression for the number of permutations you found in Question 10(a).

b. What fraction of the total number of permutations does the number of symbols you found in Question 10(c) represent?

12 **Try This as a Class** Use the counting principle.

a. Write a multiplication expression for the number of permutations of 3 dots selected from the 4 dot positions.

b. Try drawing all possible Braille symbols that have exactly 3 dots in the top 4 positions and no dots in the bottom 2 positions. How many symbols did you make?

c. What fraction of the total number of permutations does the actual number of symbols you found in part (b) represent?

13 **a.** Find the number of permutations of 4 dots selected from the dots in the top 4 positions of a Braille cell. Explain what you did.

b. How many Braille symbols have exactly 4 dots in the top 4 positions and no dots in the bottom 2 positions? Check by drawing the symbol(s).

c. What fraction of the total number of permutations does the number of symbols you drew represent?

14 **Try This as a Class** Use your results from Questions 9–13.

a. Copy and complete the table.

Number of dots in top 4 positions	Number of permutations	Number of Braille symbols	Fraction of permutations represented by the Braille symbol
1	?	?	?
2	?	?	?
3	?	?	?
4	?	?	?

b. The value of 5!, read "five factorial," is the product $5 \cdot 4 \cdot 3 \cdot 2 \cdot 1 = 120$. How does the factorial of the number of dots in the top 4 positions relate to its fraction of permutations?

15 **a.** How many Braille symbols can be formed that use exactly 2 dots when the dots occupy any of the 6 positions in a Braille cell?

b. **Discussion** Use what you discovered in Question 14(b) to describe a method you might use to find the number of combinations using exactly 2 dots when the dots occupy any of the 6 positions of a Braille cell. Compare your answer to your answer in part (a).

16 **a.** Look at the top 4 positions of the two Braille symbols shown below. How can you determine the 3-dot symbol from the 1-dot symbol?

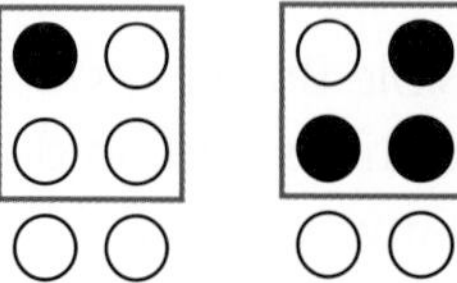

b. Explain why the number of symbols with 3 dots in the top 4 positions must equal the number of symbols with 1 dot in the top 4 positions. Use this fact and your results from Question 9 to check your answer to Question 12(b).

c. **Discussion** How would you use the results from part (b) to determine the number of symbols that can be made from placing exactly 3 dots in the top 4 positions and 1 dot in the bottom 2 positions? How many did you find?

✓ QUESTION 17

...checks that you can find numbers of combinations.

17 **✓ CHECKPOINT**

a. Suppose 2 of the letters in the word SWIFT are selected randomly. How many combinations of letters are possible?

b. In how many ways can a 3-person committee be selected from the 5 people in the Math Club?

HOMEWORK EXERCISES ▶ **See Exs. 13–19 on pp. 294–295.**

Section 5 Key Concepts

Key Term

Using a Tree Diagram to Count Choices (pp. 285–286)

You can use a tree diagram to count choices in a given situation.

Example Brian has a pair of **blue pants** and a pair of **gray pants**. He also has a **white shirt**, a **blue-striped shirt**, a **gray-striped shirt**, and a **plaid shirt**. The tree diagram shows that there are 8 different outfits Brian can wear.

The Counting Principle (p. 286)

counting principle

The total number of ways that a sequence of decisions can be made is the product of the number of choices for each decision.

Example In the Example above, Brian can choose his pants in 2 ways and his shirts in 4 ways. So Brian can choose $2 \cdot 4 = 8$ outfits.

Example Suppose a license plate can have any three letters followed by any three digits from 0 to 9 and that the letters and digits can repeat. Since there are 26 possible letters and 10 possible digits, the number of possible license plates is:

$$26 \cdot 26 \cdot 26 \cdot 10 \cdot 10 \cdot 10 = 17{,}576{,}000$$

26	26	26	10	10	10
choices for 1st letter	choices for 2nd letter	choices for 3rd letter	choices for 1st digit	choices for 2nd digit	choices for 3rd digit

18 Key Concepts Question In the license plate Example above, suppose a letter or digit can be used only once. How many plates are possible?

Section 5 Key Concepts

Key Terms

permutation

combination

Permutations (p. 287)

A permutation of a group of items is an arrangement of the items in a definite order.

Example A pizzeria offers 3 specialty pizzas: the Meat Combo (M), the Vegetarian (V), and the Supreme (S). Each way of arranging the pizzas on the menu is a permutation. You can find the number of permutations using the counting principle:

$$3 \cdot 2 \cdot 1 = 6$$

3 — choices for 1st pizza; 2 — choices for 2nd pizza; 1 — choices for 3rd pizza

Combinations (pp. 288–290)

A combination is a selection of items from a group where order is not important.

Example The Shaw family wants to buy 2 of the 3 specialty pizzas listed in the Example above. Since the order in which the pizzas are chosen is not important, each possible selection is a combination. You can use a tree diagram to find the number of combinations.

1st Pizza	2nd Pizza	Selection
M	V	M, V
	S	M, S
V	M	V, M
	S	V, S
S	M	S, M
	V	S, V

The selections with the same color are the same combination. There are 3 possible solutions.

19 **Key Concepts Question** Does counting the ways to choose 3 of 8 possible toppings for a pizza involve permutations or combinations? Explain.

Section 5
Practice & Application Exercises

YOU WILL NEED

For Ex. 26:
- Labsheet 5C

1. A certain model of car is available in 6 exterior colors: white, red, navy blue, forest green, tan, and maroon. The car is also available in 2 interior colors: black and gray.
   a. Draw a tree diagram showing the different color choices available for the exterior and interior of the car.
   b. In how many ways can you choose an exterior color and an interior color for the car?

2. **Consumer Electronics** Rosa Hernandez wants to buy a new TV and a new DVD player. A consumer magazine she reads rates 3 TVs and 5 DVD players as "best buys." If Rosa limits her choices to the "best buys," in how many ways can she choose a TV and a DVD player?

3. At a certain restaurant, dinners include one entrée, one vegetable, and one dessert from the menu shown.
   a. Draw a tree diagram showing the different dinners that a customer at the restaurant can order.
   b. How many different dinners can a customer order?

4. **Forensics** One method police can use to produce composite drawings of crime suspects is a kit containing clear plastic sheets that show facial features and can be combined to create likeness. One kit contains 195 hairlines, 99 eyes and eyebrows, 89 noses, 105 mouths, and 74 lower faces. How many different faces can be created?

Find the number of permutations of the letters in each word.

5. HI
6. TEA
7. MULE
8. BAKERY
9. SPINACH
10. CENTRIFUGAL

11. **Sports** In the Olympics, 8 swimmers participate in the final race of the women's 100-meter freestyle event. In how many different orders can the swimmers finish the race?

12. The keypad for the Allen's garage door opener has the 10 digits, 0–9. They must choose a code using 4 digits, none of which can be used more than once, to open the door. How many possible codes could they choose?

13. Mrs. McLeish requires her students to answer 2 of the 4 essay questions on a history test. How many combinations of 2 questions can Mrs. McLeish's students answer?

14. **Personal Finance** Ian finds 6 books in a bookstore that he would like to read, but he only has enough money to buy 4 of them. How many combinations of 4 books can Ian buy? (*Hint*: Choosing 4 books to buy is the same as choosing 2 books *not* to buy.)

15. Kaya has roses, lilies, tulips, daisies, and poppies growing in her flower garden. She wants to make a bouquet for a friend. How many combinations of types of flowers can Kaya have in the bouquet if she uses each of the following?

a. exactly 1 type of flower

b. exactly 2 types of flowers

c. exactly 3 types of flowers

d. at least 3 types of flowers

Geometry Connection A *complete graph* is a collection of points, called *vertices*, and segments, called *edges*, such that every pair of vertices is joined by an edge. One complete graph is shown below.

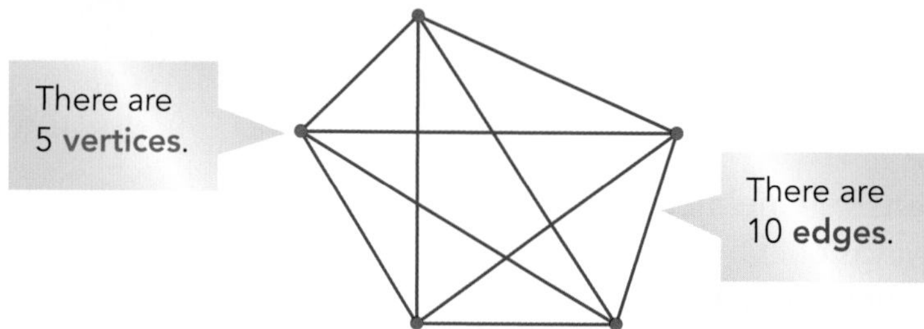

16. Copy the table. For each number of vertices in the table, draw a complete graph with that many vertices. In the table, record the number of edges each complete graph has.

Number of vertices	Number of edges
2	?
3	?
4	?
5	?
6	?

17. **Writing** Look at the table. Explain how you can use the number of vertices as well as the concepts you explored for combinations to determine the number of edges.

18. **Challenge** Write a formula for the number of edges, e, in a complete graph with v vertices.

Reflecting on the Section

Be prepared to report on the following topic in class.

19. Describe how a combination differs from a permutation. Use at least two real-world examples to help illustrate the difference.

Oral Report

Exercise 19 checks that you know the difference between a combination and a permutation.

Spiral Review

Find the slope of a line that passes through each pair of points. **(Module 3, p. 186)**

20. (3, 2) and (7, 5) 21. (5, 1) and (7, 4) 22. (3, 4) and (4, 6)

Find the theoretical probability of each outcome when you roll a six-sided number cube. **(Module 2, p. 114)**

23. rolling an even number 24. rolling a number less than 5

Extension

Pascal's Triangle

The triangle of numbers shown below is part of *Pascal's triangle*. You can use Pascal's triangle to solve problems involving combinations. To find the number of combinations of r objects taken from a group of n objects, locate the $(r + 1)$st entry in row n.

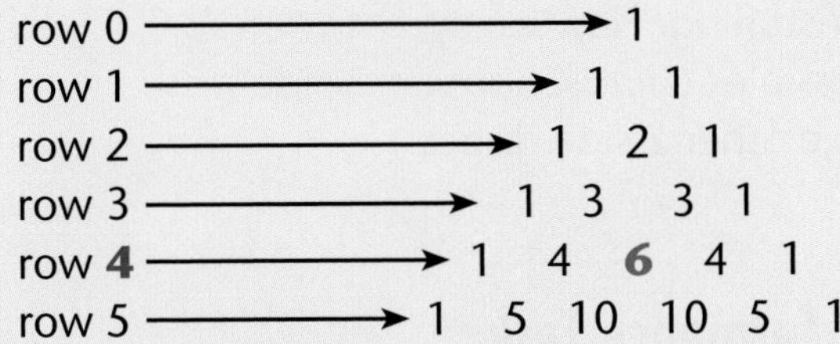

The number of combinations of 2 objects taken from a group of **4** objects is the 3rd entry in row **4**. There are **6** combinations.

25. **Writing** Look at the numbers in Pascal's triangle that are not equal to 1. Explain how each of these numbers is related to the two numbers directly above it.

26. **Use Labsheet 5C.** The labsheet shows the part of *Pascal's Triangle* given above. Use the pattern you found in Exercise 25 to complete rows 6–8 of Pascal's triangle.

27. Suppose you have 8 short-sleeved shirts and want to pack 4 of these shirts to take on a vacation to Florida. Use Pascal's triangle to find the number of ways you can choose the 4 shirts.

Section 5 Extra Skill Practice

1. At a video rental store, there are 6 comedies, 8 dramas, and 3 science fiction films that Maureen wants to see. In how many ways can she choose one of each type of movie to rent?
2. How many permutations are there of the letters in the word FLOWERS?
3. A president and a vice president are to be selected from a 6-member student council committee. In how many ways can the selection be made?
4. Two of the 5 players on a basketball team are to be selected as co-captains. In how many ways can the selection be made?
5. In how many ways can 4 people line up for a photograph?
6. In a group of 4 people, each person shakes hands with everyone else once. How many handshakes are there?
7. In how many ways can you complete a 10-question true-false test if every question must be answered?
8. In how many ways can you complete a 10-question multiple-choice test if there are 4 choices for each question and every question must be answered?
9. In how many ways can 8 books be arranged on a shelf?
10. A chicken dinner comes with any 3 of these side dishes: mashed potatoes, baked beans, corn, rice, or stuffing. How many combinations of 3 side dishes are possible? (*Hint*: Choosing 3 side dishes is the same as *not* choosing the other 2 side dishes.)

Standardized Testing ▶ Performance Task

Tonya makes 3 sketches of different classmates for her art class.

1. In how many ways can Tonya select 2 of the 3 sketches to include in her final portfolio? Is this a *permutation* problem or a *combination* problem? Explain.
2. After her art class is over, Tonya decides to hang all 3 of the sketches she made in a row on her bedroom wall. In how many ways can she arrange the sketches? Is this a *permutation* problem or a *combination* problem? Explain.

Section 6 Working with Probability

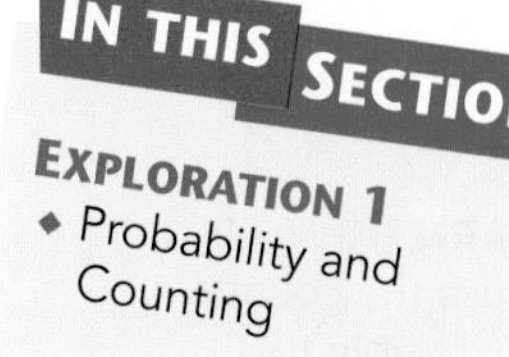

Lock It Up!

Setting the Stage

Have you ever misplaced your keys? You would not be as likely to lose special keys made in ancient Rome. Occasionally large bronze keys were made as long as your arm and weighed over 10 lb! It was a great relief in 1862 when Linus Yale, Jr. invented the modern combination lock. The only "key" needed to open a combination lock is a special sequence of numbers or letters.

Think About It

1 Suppose that the key for a combination lock is a 3-digit sequence using the numbers 1, 2, 3, 4, or 5, and that each number is used only once. Use the counting principle to find the number of possible 3-digit keys.

2 Create your own 3-digit key. Use any of the numbers 1, 2, 3, 4, or 5, but do not use any number more than once. Keep your key a secret for now.

3 For each group described below, do you think the probability that everyone chose a different key is closer to 0, 0.25, 0.50, 0.75, or 1?

a. a group of 4 students **b.** your entire class

GOAL

LEARN HOW TO...
- use the counting principle to determine the probability of an event

AS YOU...
- solve the duplicate key problem

Exploration 1

Probability and Counting

▶ **How likely is it that everyone in your class chose a different 3-digit key in Question 2? You can find out by looking at a simpler situation and thinking about probability.**

4 Suppose a 3-digit key can be made with only the numbers 1, 2, and 3, and each number cannot be used more than once in a key.

a. How many different keys are possible?

b. Use the numbers 1, 2, and 3 to list all the possible keys.

c. Suppose two people each choose one of the keys from part (b). The model at the left can be used to show all the ways they can choose two keys. Copy and complete the model. Mark each box with a **D** if the people choose different keys or with an **S** if they chose the same key.

2nd person's choice \ 1st person's choice	1-2-3	1-3-2	2-1-3	?	?	?
1-2-3	S	?	?	?	?	?
1-3-2	D	?	?	?	?	?
2-1-3	?	?	?	?	?	?
?	?	?	?	?	?	?
?	?	?	?	?	?	?
?	?	?	?	?	?	?

◀ The S shows that the 1st and 2nd persons both choose 1-2-3. The D shows that the 1st person chooses 1-2-3 but the 2nd person chooses 1-3-2.

5 Use your completed model from Question 4.

a. How many ways are there for two people to choose the keys? How does the model show this?

b. What is the probability that both people choose the same key?

c. What is the probability that both people choose different keys?

▶ **You can also use the counting principle to find the probability that the two people in Question 4 choose different keys.**

EXAMPLE

Two people each choose one of the six 3-digit keys. The probability that they choose *different* keys is given by this ratio:

$$\text{Probability that two people choose different keys} = \frac{\text{Ways to choose different keys}}{\text{Total ways to choose keys}}$$

Use the counting principle.

$$\text{Probability that two people choose different keys} = \frac{6 \cdot 5}{6 \cdot 6} = \frac{5}{6}, \text{ or about } 0.83$$

If each person can choose *any* key, the first person has **6** choices and the second person also has **6** choices.

If each person chooses a *different* key, the first person has **6** choices and the second person has **5** choices.

6 **Discussion** In the Example, why does the second person have 5 choices rather than 6?

7 **Try This as a Class** Suppose three people each choose one of the keys you listed in Question 4(b).

a. Find the total number of ways for three people to choose the keys.

b. How many ways can the three people all choose different keys?

c. What is the probability that everyone chooses a different key?

8 ✔ **CHECKPOINT**

a. Suppose four people each choose one of the keys you listed in Question 4(b). What is the probability that everyone will choose a different key?

b. What is the probability that everyone will choose a different key if there are 5 people choosing keys?

✔ **QUESTION 8**

...checks that you can use the counting principle to find probabilities.

9 **Try This as a Class** In Question 2, each person in your class chose a 3-digit key that uses the numbers 1, 2, 3, 4, or 5.

a. Find the probability that everyone in a group of four would choose a different 3-digit key.

b. Based on your answer to part (a), what percent of the time would you expect at least two members of a group to have the same key?

c. Form a group of four students. Check to see if any two people chose the same key.

d. How does the probability in part (a) compare to your answer to Question 3 on page 297?

e. Would you expect the probability that everyone in your class chose a different 3-digit key to be greater than or less than that for a group of four students? Explain.

f. Check to see if any two people in your class chose the same key.

HOMEWORK EXERCISES See Exs. 1–11 on pp. 301–302.

Section 6 Key Concepts

Probability and Counting (pp. 298–300)

You can use the counting principle to find some probabilities.

Example Suppose three 6-sided number cubes are rolled. The probability that the cubes show different numbers is given by this ratio:

$$\text{Probability the cubes show different numbers} = \frac{\text{Ways to roll different numbers}}{\text{Total ways to roll cubes}}$$

If different numbers must be rolled, there are 6 possibilities for the 1st cube, 5 possibilities for the 2nd cube, and 4 possibilities for the 3rd cube. If any numbers can be rolled, there are 6 possibilities for each cube.

$$\text{Probability} = \frac{6 \cdot 5 \cdot 4}{6 \cdot 6 \cdot 6}$$

$$= \frac{5}{9}, \text{ or about } 0.56$$

10 Key Concepts Question Suppose you roll three 4-sided number pyramids. The sides of each pyramid are numbered 1, 2, 3, and 4.

a. What is the probability that all the pyramids show different numbers on the bottom?

b. Is this probability *greater than, less than,* or *equal to* the probability for three 6-sided number cubes? Explain.

Section 6
Practice & Application Exercises

For Exercises 1–3, suppose three coins are tossed and the number of heads is recorded.

1. List all the possible outcomes when three coins are tossed.

2. What is the probability of getting 3 heads? 2 heads? 1 head? 0 heads?

3. What is the probability of getting at least one head?

4. **Government** Your Social Security number is a 9-digit number. Suppose the last four digits are chosen randomly from the numbers 0–9.

   a. How many sequences are possible for the last four digits?

   b. What is the probability of getting a 5 or 0 in the last digit?

   c. What is the probability of getting two 5s in the last two digits?

5. Suppose a license plate has 4 letters followed by a 1-digit number and then 3 more letters. The letters and number are chosen randomly.

   a. How many license plates are possible if the letters cannot repeat?

   b. Compare the probability that a license plate spells MATH4YOU with the probability that the first four letters spell MATH.

   c. Repeat parts (a) and (b) if the letters can be repeated.

6. **History** In a game popular in France during the seventeenth century, a player tried to roll a six-sided number cube four times without getting a 6. What is the probability that a player wins this game?

7. A student finds a combination lock in the hallway that uses a 3-number key based on the numbers from 0 to 24.

   a. How many possible keys are there for this type of lock?

   b. What is the probability the student will open the lock on the first try?

8. **Electronics** A certain model of automatic garage door opener can be assigned one of 512 possible codes. If the openers for two garage doors have the same code, then the transmitter for one door will also open the other door.

   a. Find the probability that two neighbors who each buy this brand of garage door opener get openers with different codes.

   b. **Writing** If you are one of the neighbors in part (a), do you want the probability you found to be high or low? Explain.

9. **Open-ended** Describe a real-world problem whose solution involves using the counting principle to find a probability.

10. **Challenge** Suppose a group of n people is randomly selected. For each value of n, find the probability that everyone in the group has a different birthday. (Assume no one is born on February 29 of a leap year, so that there are 365 equally likely birthdays possible.)

    a. $n = 5$ b. $n = 10$ c. $n = 20$

THINKING

Exercise 11 checks that you can find probabilities using a visual model.

Reflecting on the Section

The 1st person chooses yellow and the 2nd person chooses blue.

11. a. Suppose two people each choose 1 of 3 colors: red (R), yellow (Y), or blue (B). Explain how the model shows all the ways the people can choose their colors.

    b. What is the probability that the two people choose different colors? the same color?

Spiral Review

12. Michael Kiefer needs to choose 2 of his 4 suits to take on a business trip. How many combinations of 2 suits can Michael choose? **(Module 4, p. 292)**

13. **Choosing a Data Display** Some test scores for a science class are listed below. **(Module 1, p. 23)**

    78, 61, 94, 68, 52, 81, 70, 64, 53, 86, 99, 72, 87,
    59, 81, 75, 93, 81, 66, 75, 48, 96, 85, 77, 98, 41

    a. Display the scores using a stem-and-leaf plot.

    b. Display the scores using a box-and-whisker plot.

    c. Find the median and the mode of the test scores.

    d. Which display did you use to find each average in part (c)? Why?

Section 6 Extra Skill Practice

One model of a briefcase has a lock with three dials. Each dial can show a digit from 0 to 9. The lock opens when the dials are turned to a certain three-digit key, such as 2-0-7. Suppose Jamal, Lisa, and Kim each randomly choose a key for this model of briefcase. Find the probability of each outcome.

1. The last two digits in Jamal's key are both 8.
2. Each digit in Lisa's key is less than 7.
3. None of the digits in Kim's key are 0 or 5.
4. Each digit in Kim's key is either 0 or 5.
5. Jamal and Lisa have different keys.
6. Jamal, Lisa, and Kim have different keys.

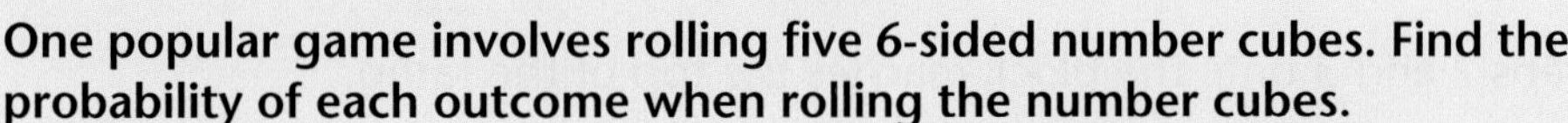

One popular game involves rolling five 6-sided number cubes. Find the probability of each outcome when rolling the number cubes.

7. all ones
8. all even numbers
9. all different numbers
10. all numbers greater than 2
11. no fours
12. all perfect squares

Standardized Testing ▶ Free Response

1. Suppose you flip a coin 4 times. What is the probability that you get all heads?
2. A certain two-person game is played with pegs that have 6 possible colors: black, blue, green, red, white, and yellow. Player 1 forms a sequence of 4 pegs that is not shown to Player 2, such as green-black-yellow-green. (The same color may be used more than once.) Player 2 tries to guess Player 1's sequence.
   a. What is the probability that Player 2 correctly guesses Player 1's sequence on the first try?
   b. What is the probability that Player 2 guesses the wrong color for every position in Player 1's sequence on the first try?

Building a Ramp

The ancient Egyptians built the Pyramids of Giza using thousands of stone blocks. The Egyptians may have used ramps and logs to roll the blocks into place. The diagrams show how you can model this process using a miniature ramp, several cylinders, and a small block.

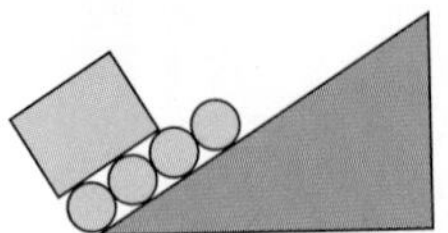

Step 1 Use one more cylinder than is needed to support the block.

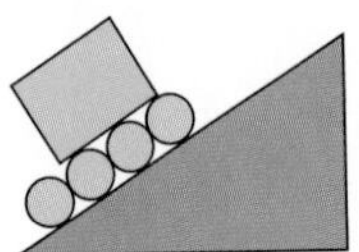

Step 2 Roll the block up the ramp to the edge of the highest cylinder. The cylinders will roll some as the block rolls.

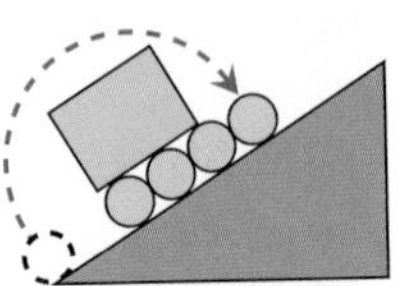

Step 3 Move the lowest cylinder to the front of the block.

Step 4 Repeat Steps 2 and 3 until the block reaches the top of the ramp.

SET UP

You will need:

- *Project Labsheet A*
- *ruler*
- *material for ramp*
- *material for cylinders*
- *small object (to be moved)*

For your module project, you will design and build a model ramp with cylinders that you can use to move small objects.

Working with Cylinders One step in building your model is choosing the diameter of the cylinders. The diameter may affect how much the cylinders cost and how easy they are to use.

Use Project Labsheet A for Questions 1–4.

1 The labsheet shows four diagrams of a *Ramp and Cylinders*. Use the diagrams to complete the table at the bottom of the labsheet.

2 As the diameter of the cylinders decreases, what happens to:

a. the number of cylinders you need to move the block?

b. the volume of material needed for all the cylinders?

3 How does the diameter of the cylinders affect the number of times you must move a cylinder from the lowest position to the highest position on the ramp?

4 What are some advantages of using cylinders with a small diameter? What are some disadvantages? Be sure to discuss how the diameter affects the cost and ease of use of the cylinders.

Choosing a Ramp's Slope Like the slope of a line, a ramp's slope is the ratio of its rise to its run. Suppose you want to design a ramp that is 6 ft wide and reaches 8 ft above the ground. The diagrams show four ramps with different slopes that you could design.

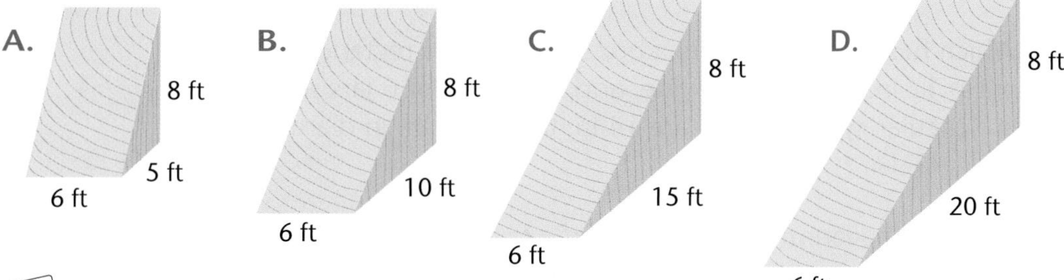

5 a. Find the slope of each ramp shown above.

b. How does a ramp's slope affect how much effort it takes to move an object a fixed distance (say, 4 ft) up the ramp?

c. For ramps of the same height, how does the slope of the ramp seem to affect the ramp's length?

6 Suppose the ramps shown are made of solid concrete, so that the cost of making a ramp depends on the ramp's volume. How does a ramp's slope affect its volume in the diagrams shown?

Building Your Ramp and Cylinders Before designing and building your own model ramp and cylinders, think about these factors:

- the size of the object you want to move up your ramp
- the number of cylinders you want to use, as well as each cylinder's diameter d and length l
- the height h and width w you want your ramp to have
- the desired steepness of your ramp as measured by the ramp's slope $\frac{h}{b}$, where b is the length of the ramp's base
- the advantages of certain ramp slopes and cylinder sizes

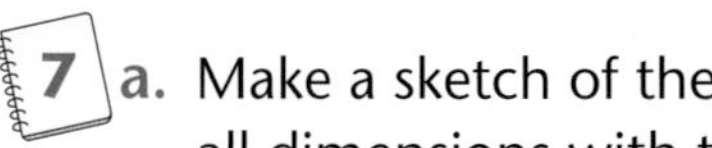

7 a. Make a sketch of the ramp and cylinders you plan to build. Label all dimensions with their measures.

b. Choose the materials you will use. The cylinders can be wooden dowels, markers, paper towel rolls, or other household items. Your ramp might be made from cardboard or wood.

c. Construct your ramp and cylinders. Then test how well your model works by trying to move a small object up the ramp using the procedure described on page 304.

MODULE 4 Review and Assessment

1. The Ferris wheel at the 1893 World's Columbian Exposition in Chicago had a diameter of 250 ft. Its 36 passenger cabs could hold a total of 2160 people. Suppose the cabs were evenly spaced. About how far apart would they have been? **(Sec. 1 Explor. 1)**

2. Which has greater volume: a box shaped like a rectangular prism 12 in. long, 11 in. wide, and 9 in. high or 6 jars shaped like circular cylinders that are 14 in. tall and 4 in. in diameter? **(Sec. 1 Explor. 2)**

3. Suppose the length of each edge of a cube is tripled. **(Sec. 1, Explor. 2)**
   a. How does the surface area of the new cube compare to the surface area of the original cube?
   b. How do the volumes of the two cubes compare?

Find the surface area of the cylinder with the given radius *r* and height *h*. Use $\pi = 3.14$. **(Sec. 2, Explor. 1)**

4. $r = 3$ cm, $h = 4$ cm 5. $r = 2$ in., $h = 6$ in. 6. $r = 1.5$ ft, $h = 12$ ft

Find the ratio of surface area to volume for each cylinder. Use $\pi = 3.14$. **(Sec. 2, Explor. 2)**

7.
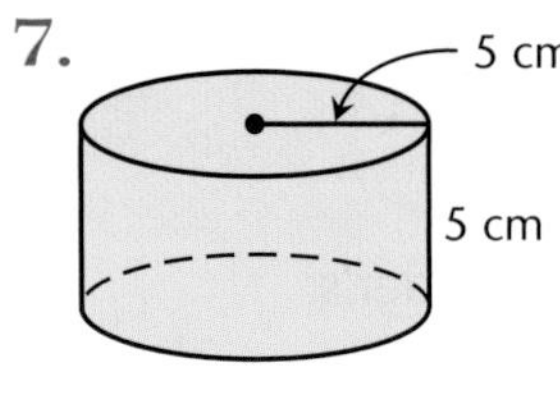

8.
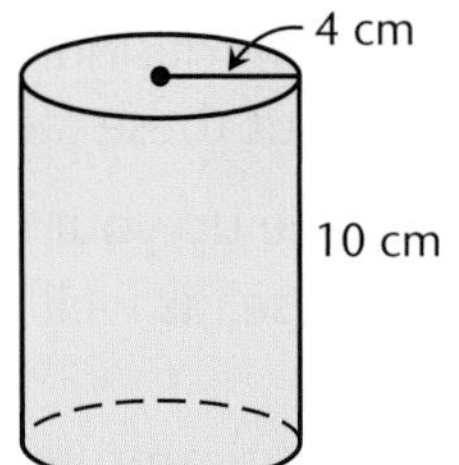

9.
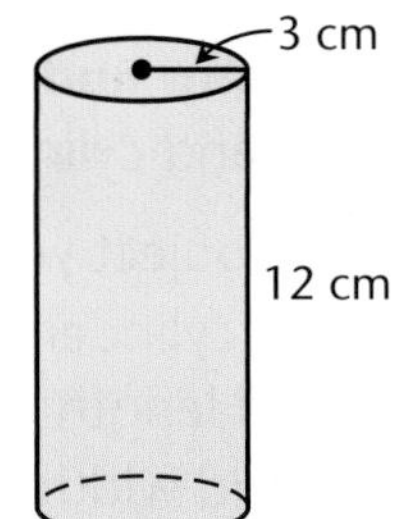

10. Suppose three cans have the same dimensions as the cylinders above. Which can is most efficient? Explain. **(Sec. 2, Explor. 2)**

For each line, find the slope and the *y*-intercept. Then write an equation of the line in slope-intercept form. **(Sec. 3, Explors. 1 and 2)**

11.
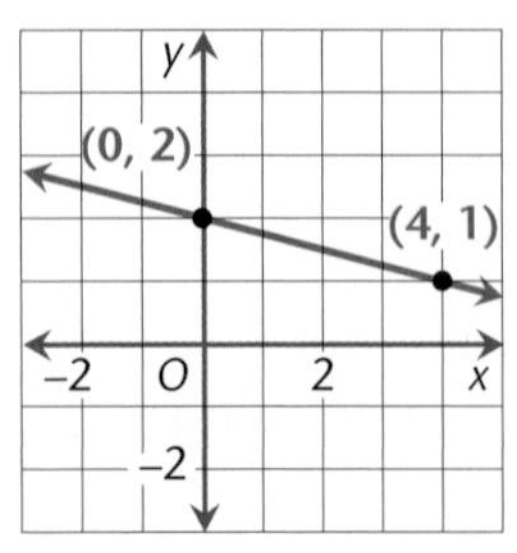

12.
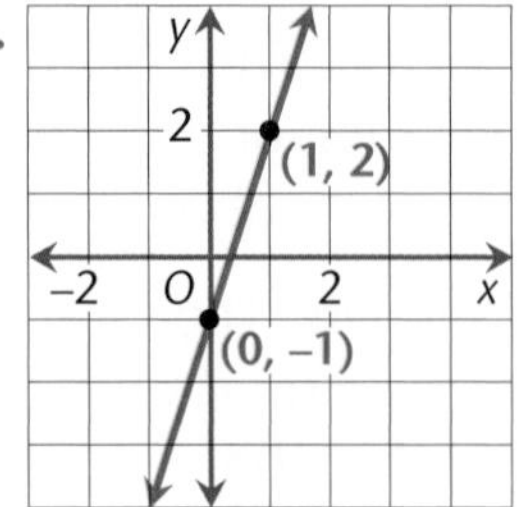

13.
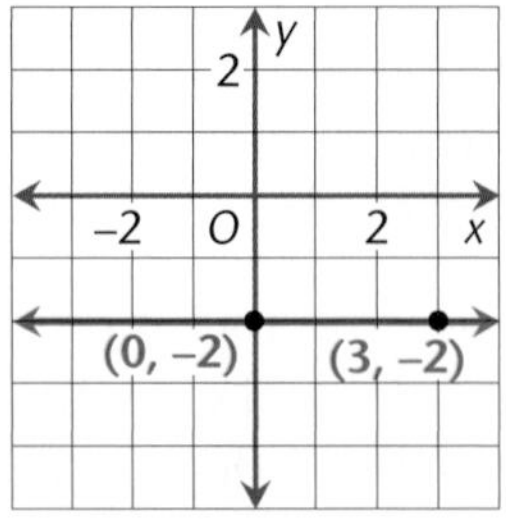

14. Explain why the slope of a vertical line is undefined. **(Sec. 3, Explor. 1)**

15. Write equations in slope-intercept form for 2 lines that are parallel. Explain why they are parallel. **(Sec. 3, Explor. 2)**

16. Write each rational number as a terminating or a repeating decimal. **(Sec. 4, Explor. 1)**

a. $\frac{5}{11}$ b. $-3\frac{1}{4}$ c. $\frac{14}{16}$

17. Write the numbers in order from least to greatest. **(Sec. 4, Explor. 1)**

$0.\overline{72}, \frac{5}{7}, 0.7\overline{2}, 0.72, \frac{3}{4}, -0.7, -\frac{8}{11}, -0.72, -\frac{3}{4}$

Solve each equation. **(Sec. 4, Explor. 2)**

18. $5 = -2.5x$ 19. $12 + \frac{2}{3}t = 4$ 20. $\frac{2}{3}b + 11 = 5$

21. At a local pizza parlor, 5 employees work on Saturday nights: Armand, Cathy, Ishana, Jim, and Susan. Employees must wear uniforms consisting of tan or black pants and red, green, or black shirts. **(Sec. 5, Explors. 1 and 2)**

a. How many different uniforms are possible?

b. On one Saturday night, all 5 employees decide to line up and sing "Happy Birthday" to a customer. In how many different ways can they line up?

c. Usually, 2 employees are needed to take telephone orders on Saturday nights. List all possible combinations of 2 employees who can be assigned to answer telephones.

22. A bank customer who uses an automatic teller machine (ATM) chooses a 4-digit password. **(Sec. 6, Explor. 1)**

a. How many different passwords are possible?

b. What is the probability that the first and last digits in a customer's password are both greater than 6?

Reflecting on the Module

23. **Writing** Make a list of what you think are the ten most important mathematical concepts in this module. Write and solve a problem that illustrates each concept.

MODULE 5

ARCHITECTS AND ENGINEERS

CONNECTING MATHEMATICS & The Theme

MODULE 5

SECTION OVERVIEW

1 Geometry and Perspective

As you model cube buildings:

- Explore volumes and surface areas
- Draw 3-dimensional figures and flat views

2 Geometry and Constructions

As you study 3-dimensional figures:

- Construct triangles
- Sketch nets for pyramids and prisms
- Construct angle bisectors
- Compare triangles for congruence

3 Working with Triangles

As you explore the pyramids:

- Classify triangles
- Find unknown side lengths of a right triangle

4 Surface Area and Volume

As you look at dwellings:

- Find surface areas of prisms and pyramids
- Find volumes of prisms, pyramids, and cones

5 Angles Formed by Intersecting Lines

As you study the Chunnel:

- Find the measures of angles formed by intersecting lines

6 Scale Drawings and Similar Figures

As you draw your classroom:

- Make scale drawings
- Find perimeters and areas of similar figures

The Module Project

Creating a Model Town

Have you ever thought about how you would design a house, an office, or a school? In this module, you will learn about nets and scale models and use these tools to design and construct a model building for your class's model town.

More on the Module Project
See pp. 386–387.

INTERNET
Resources and practice at
classzone.com

Geometry and Perspective

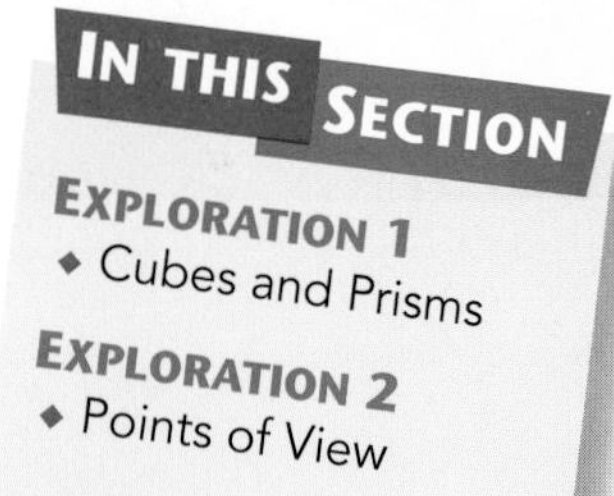

Where do you Stand?

Setting the Stage

This picture shows the Sears Tower in Chicago. At the time of its completion in 1974, it was the world's tallest building, with 110 stories and a height of 1454 ft.

When architects design buildings, they must be able to visualize the geometric figures within them and draw many different views.

The Sears Tower is actually a group of nine towers of various heights, so the tower's appearance changes when it is viewed from different sides.

Think About It

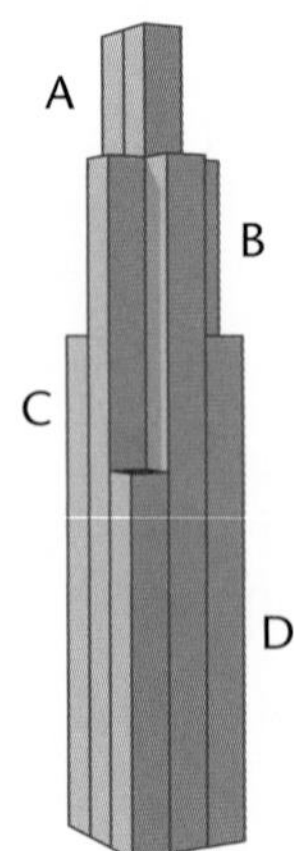

1 The cross sections below are drawn as if the viewer were looking down on the Sears Tower from above. Match the cross sections to the lettered areas in the diagram.

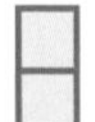 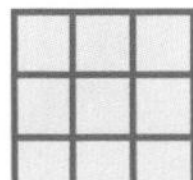 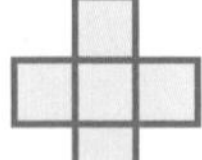 

2 Would the cross sections look the same if the viewer could look up at the building from below? Explain.

3 In the photo you can see two sides of the Sears Tower. Will it look the same when viewed from the corner formed by the two sides you cannot see? Explain.

▶ **In this module you will see how architects and engineers use mathematics to design and construct buildings and other structures.**

Exploration 1

GOAL

LEARN HOW TO...
- draw rectangular prisms and figures made with cubes
- find volumes and surface areas of figures made with cubes

AS YOU...
- use isometric dot paper

SET UP *You will need:* • *Labsheets 1A–1C* • *ruler* • *centimeter cubes*

▶ **When presenting project ideas, architects and engineers often show their clients drawings of the structures they are to build. These drawings give the viewer a sense of how the finished structures will look in three dimensions.**

Here are steps you can use to sketch a rectangular prism.

Step 1
Draw a rectangle.

Step 2
Draw a congruent rectangle behind and to the right of the original.

Step 3
Connect the corresponding corners. Use dashed segments for hidden edges.

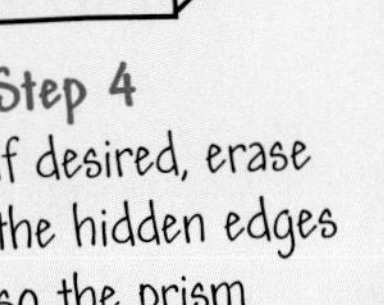

Step 4
If desired, erase the hidden edges so the prism appears solid.

4 **a.** Follow the steps above to sketch your own rectangular prism.

b. Repeat part (a), but place the second rectangle behind and to the left instead of behind and to the right. How is this view of the prism different from the view you drew in part (a)?

c. Sketch a prism that is wider than your original prism. Then sketch another prism that is shorter than your original prism.

▶ **You can also use special paper called *isometric dot paper* to help draw three-dimensional figures. The prefix *iso-* means "equal" and *metric* means "measure," so *isometric* means "equal measure."**

isometric dot paper

5 **Discussion** Look at the isometric dot paper. Why do you think it was given the name *isometric dot paper*?

▶ **Drawing Figures Made with Cubes** **Here are steps you can use to draw on isometric dot paper.**

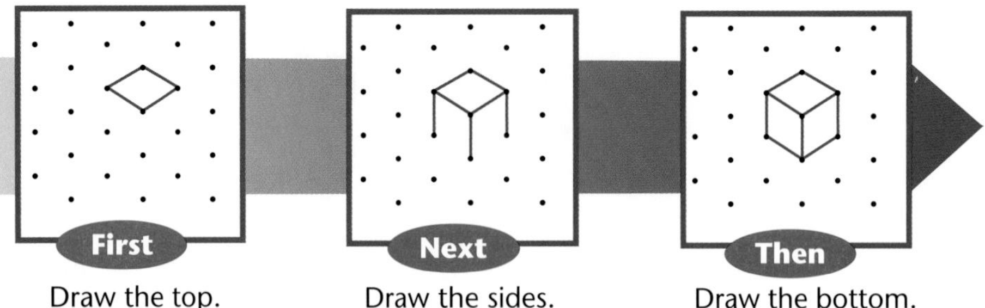

6 **Use Labsheet 1A.** Draw a cube on the *Isometric Dot Paper.*

7 **Use Labsheet 1B.** Follow the directions on the labsheet to make *Isometric Drawings.*

▶ **After architects meet with a client, there are often adjustments to be made to the drawings. An example is shown below.**

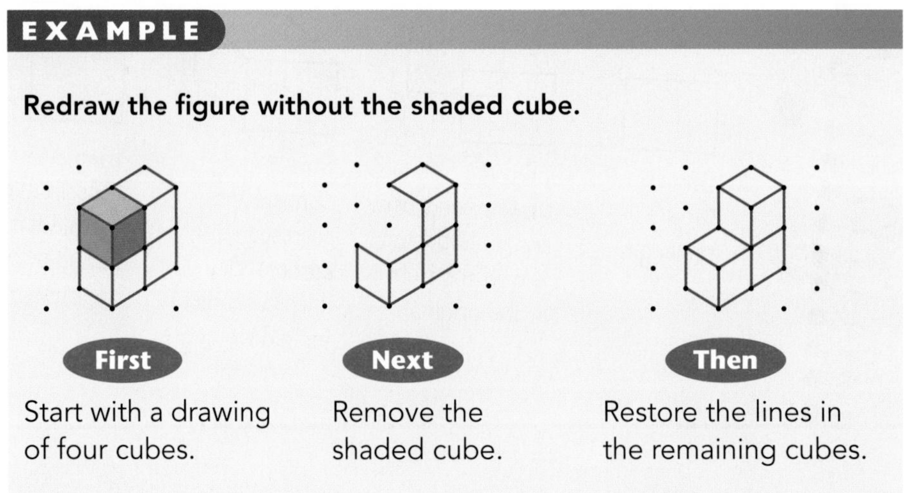

8 **Try This As a Class** Use centimeter cubes to build the two figures shown in the Example.

a. Compare the volumes of the figures.

b. Compare the surface areas of the figures.

Use Labsheet 1C for Questions 9 and 10.

9 Follow the directions on the labsheet to redraw each of the *Cube Figures.* You will find the volume and the surface area, including the base, before and after the change.

10 **a.** How did removing one block affect the volume of each of the *Cube Figures*?

b. How did it affect the surface area of the figures?

c. **Discussion** Were the volume and surface area affected in the same way for both figures? Explain.

11 ✓ **CHECKPOINT** **Use Labsheet 1A.** Draw a rectangular prism that is not a cube. Find its surface area and volume.

✓ QUESTION 11

...checks that you can draw a rectangular prism and find its surface area and volume.

HOMEWORK EXERCISES See Exs. 1–7 on pp. 317–318.

Exploration 2

Points of View

GOAL

LEARN HOW TO...
- draw 3-dimensional figures and flat views

AS YOU...
- model simple buildings with cubes

SET UP *You will need:* • *Labsheets 1A and 1D* • *centimeter cubes* • *ruler*

▲ front view

▲ back view

▲ side view

◀ Construction of the White House began in 1792. President and Mrs. John Adams became its first residents in 1800.

▶ **In Exploration 1 you used isometric dot paper to draw figures made with cubes. This type of drawing can be used to help show how a real building will appear. But, as you will see, one viewpoint does not always show you the whole building.**

12 The picture at the right shows the front and left sides of a building. Use centimeter cubes to build a model of the building. How many cubes did you use?

left front

13 Two other views of the building in Question 12 are shown below.

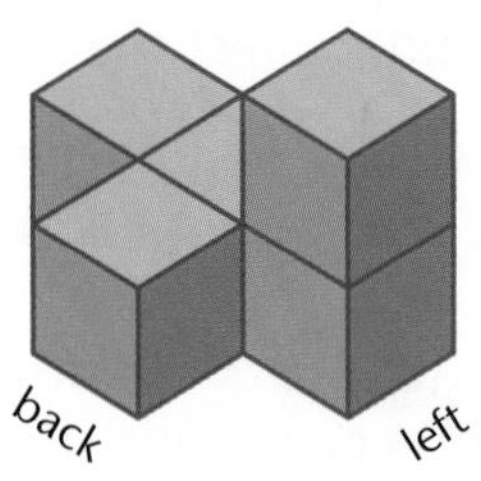

a. Add cubes to the model you built in Question 12 so the buildings will have the views shown above. How many cubes did you add?

b. What can be seen in these two views that was not visible in the first view?

c. **Use Labsheet 1A.** Sketch the building from the right-back view.

14 Why is it important to show different views of a building?

✓ QUESTION 15

...checks that you can draw three-dimensional figures from different points of view.

15 **✓ CHECKPOINT**

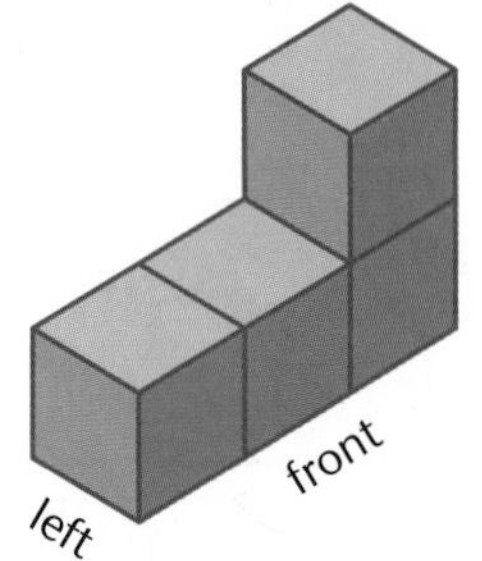

a. Suppose each cube in this building shares at least one face with another cube. Can there be more than four cubes in the building? Explain.

b. **Use Labsheet 1D.** Labsheet 1D has isometric dots and labeled viewpoints for *Three Views of a Building*. Use them to make isometric drawings of the building.

▶ **Flat Views The views of the buildings you have seen so far give them a three-dimensional appearance. Suppose you were to view the buildings straight on from any side. What you would see would appear flat and could be called a *flat view*.**

16 Use centimeter cubes to build the four-cube building shown in Question 15. Position it so that the flat view from the front of the building is as shown at the right.

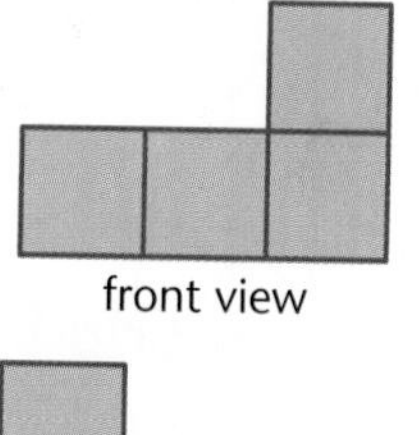

17 Flat views of two other sides of the building in Question 15 are shown. Sketch the right-side view of the building.

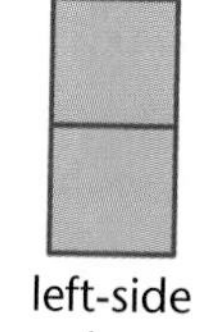

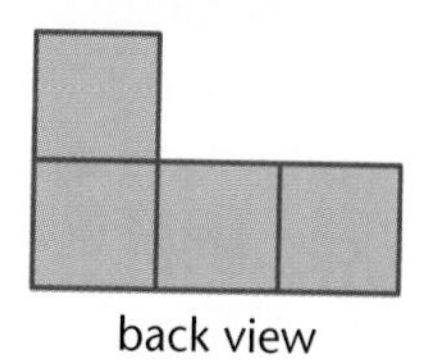

18 **a.** How are the front and back views of the building in Question 15 related?

b. How are the left- and right-side views related?

▶ **A flat view of the top of the building in Question 15 is shown at the right. This top view shows what the building looks like from directly above and also identifies each of the sides.**

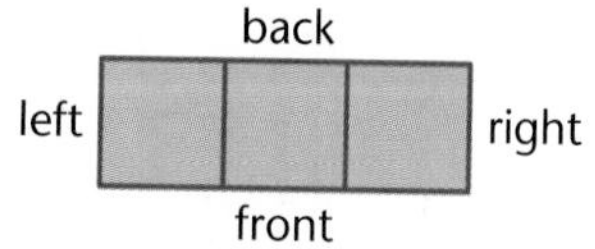

19 **a.** The building in Question 15 is not the only cube building that could have the flat view of the top shown above. Explain why.

b. Use flat views to draw the four side views of another building that has the same top view as shown above.

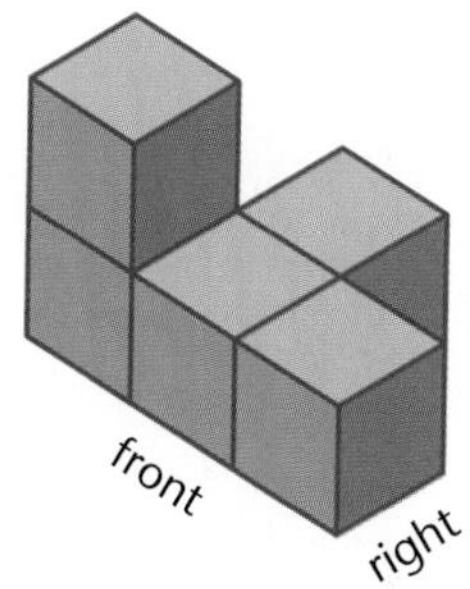

20 ✓ **CHECKPOINT** The building at the left contains only five cubes. Draw flat views of the building from each of the following viewpoints: front, back, left, right, and top.

✓ QUESTION 20

...checks that you can draw flat views from different viewpoints.

21 What is the maximum number of cubes that could be used to build a cube building with the following front and side views?

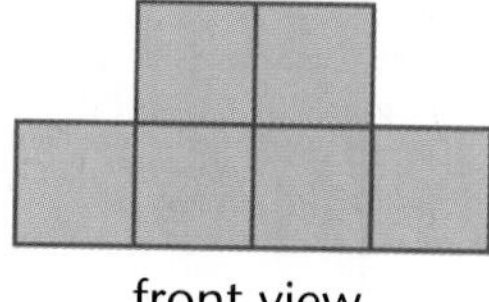

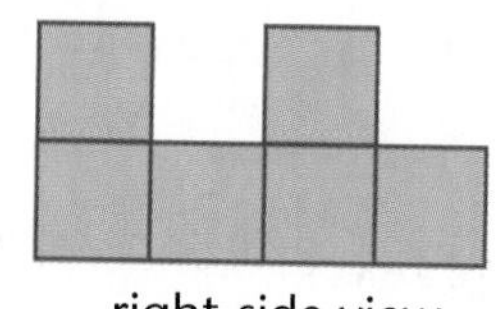

22 What is the minimum number of cubes that could be used to build the cube building in Question 21?

HOMEWORK EXERCISES ▶ See Exs. 8–15 on pp. 318–319.

Section 1 Key Concepts

Isometric Drawings (pp. 311–313)

Isometric dot paper can be helpful in drawing three-dimensional figures.

Example Four different views of the same figure are shown on isometric dot paper.

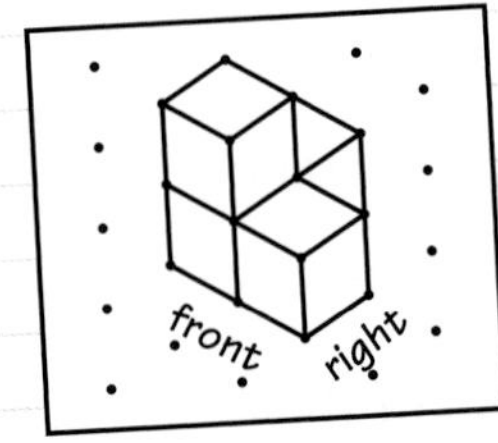

The volume is 4 cubic units. The surface area is 18 square units, including the base.

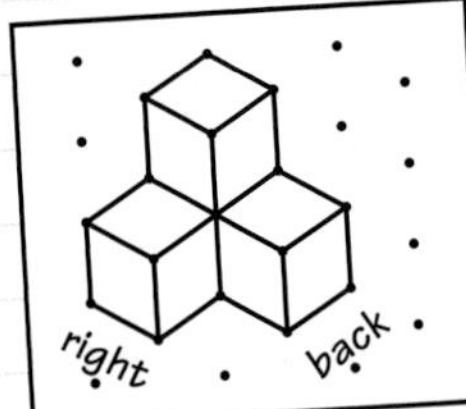

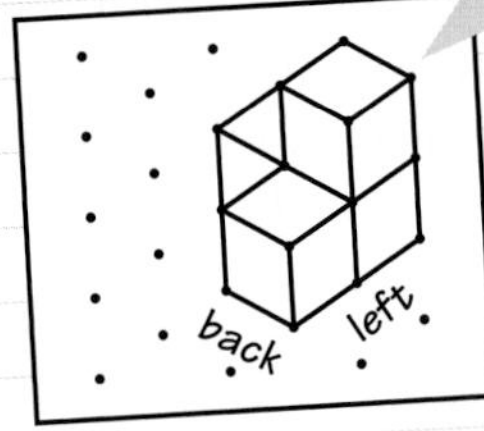

Flat Views (pp. 314–315)

Flat views of a building can be used to show what the building will look like when viewed directly from the front, back, left side, or right side, or from the top (directly above).

Example These are flat views of the building modeled above.

Side Views

front view | back view | left-side view | right-side view

Top View

back
left
right
front

Key Concepts Question

23 **Use Labsheet 1A.** Imagine removing the top cube from the figure above. On the *Isometric Dot Paper,* draw four different views of the new figure. Then draw five different flat views.

Section 1
Practice & Application Exercises

YOU WILL NEED

For Exs. 2, 3, 5–7, and 12–14:
- Labsheet 1A (2 copies)

For Ex. 11:
- ruler

For Ex. 15:
- Labsheet 1D

1. Sketch a cube using the steps on page 311 for drawing a rectangular prism.

Use the *Isometric Dot Paper* on Labsheet 1A for Exercises 2 and 3.

2. a. Draw a rectangular prism.

   b. Draw a rectangular prism that has the same height and width but is twice as long as the prism in part (a).

   c. Draw a rectangular prism that has the same height and length but is three times as wide as the prism in part (a).

   d. **Writing** Record the number of cubes, the surface area, and the volume of each rectangular prism you drew in parts (a)–(c). What relationships do you notice among these measurements?

3. How many different rectangular prisms can you draw that are made up of 12 cubes?

4. Prisms are named for their bases. Steps similar to those for drawing a rectangular prism can be used to sketch other prisms.

   a. Sketch a triangle.

   b. Sketch a congruent triangle that is placed behind and to the right of the triangle in part (a).

   c. Connect corresponding vertices to form a triangular prism.

   d. Sketch a prism as in parts (a)–(c) with a trapezoid (instead of a triangle) for a base.

Use Labsheet 1A. On the *Isometric Dot Paper,* draw the figure that results from removing the shaded cube(s). Then give the volume and the surface area of the figure before and after removing the cube(s). Assume that there are no gaps on the bottom layer. Also assume that the only hidden cubes are directly beneath the cubes on the top layer.

5.

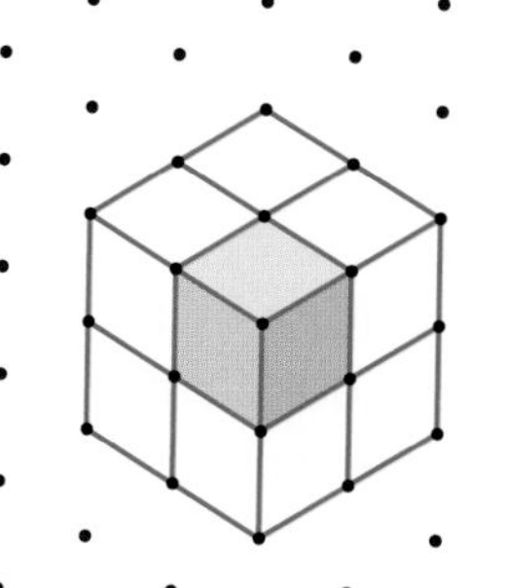

6.

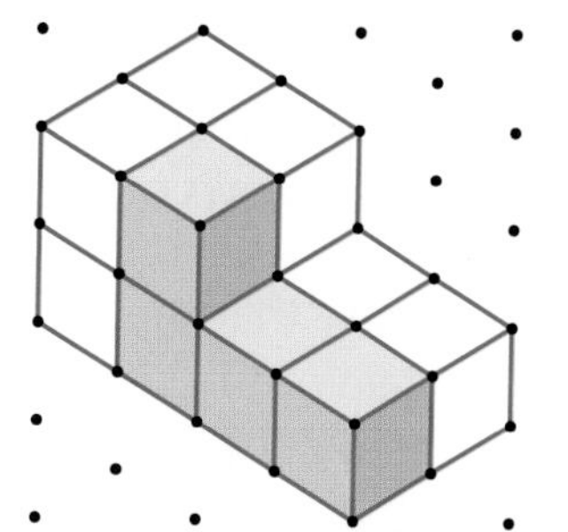

7. **Use Labsheet 1A.** A client has hired you to build an addition on the office building shown at the right.

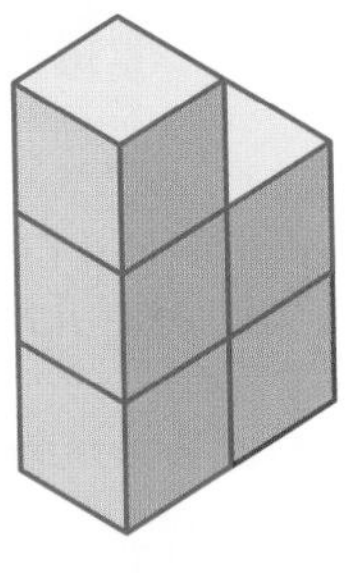

a. The pink face represents the place where the client might like to have the addition attached. On the *Isometric Dot Paper*, redraw the building with the addition in place. (Add only one cube.)

b. **Open-ended** Select another location where you might ask the client to consider adding the additional office space. Redraw the building with the addition in place.

For Exercises 8–10, tell whether each view shows the *front view*, the *left-side view*, or the *top view* of the canister at the right. (Ignore the design on the canister.)

8.

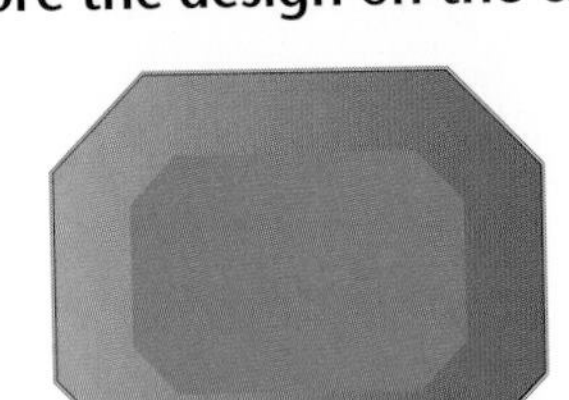

9.

10.

11. Assume the building at the right contains five cubes. Draw flat views of the building from each of the following viewpoints: front, back, left, right, and top.

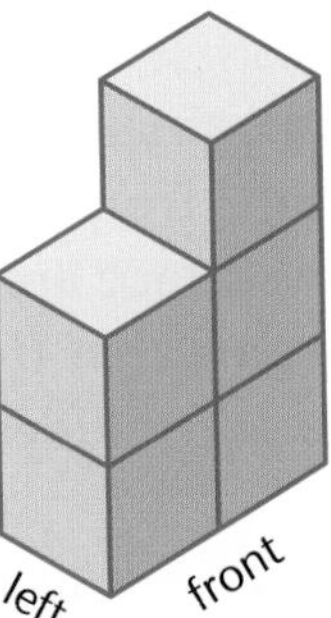

Use the *Isometric Dot Paper* on Labsheet 1A for Exercises 12–14.

12. Draw and label front-right, right-back, and back-left views of the building in Exercise 11.

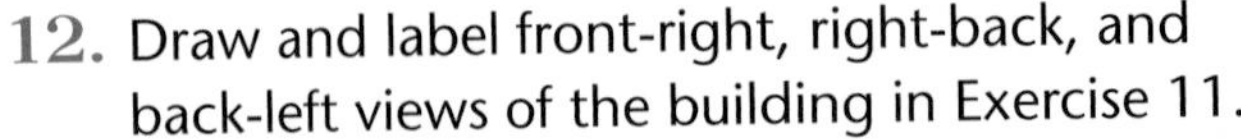

13. Suppose that the view shown in Exercise 11 is for a building containing six cubes. Think about where the hidden cube must be located if it shares at least one face with another cube. Then carry out the steps in Exercises 11 and 12 for the six-cube building.

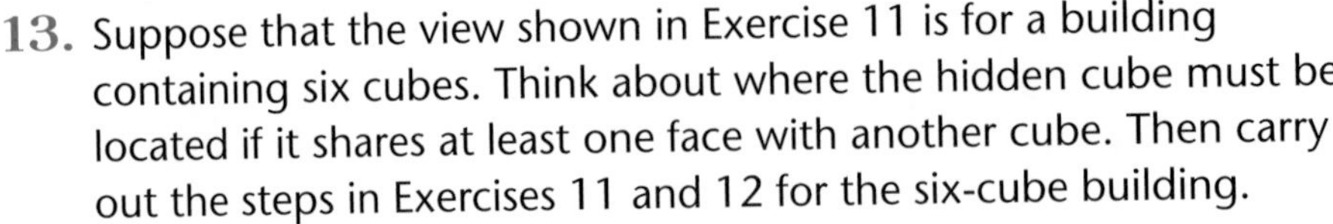

14. **Challenge** Five flat views of a figure made with cubes are shown. On *Isometric Dot Paper*, draw a view of the figure from the front-right corner.

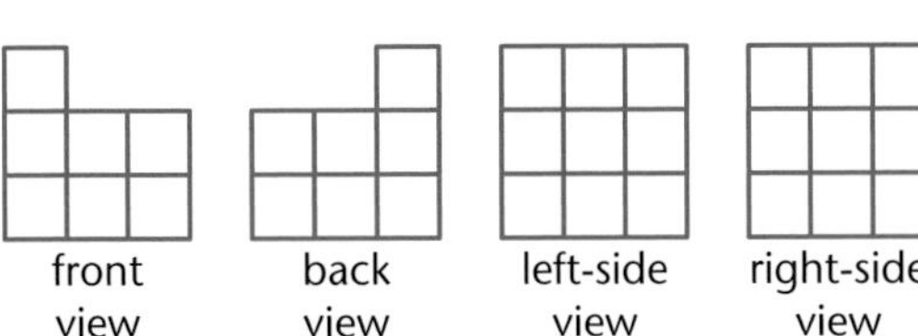

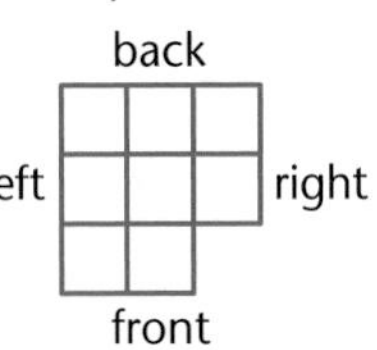

Reflecting on the Section

Exercise 15 checks that you can visualize figures made with cubes.

15. **Use Labsheet 1D.** A blue 3-dimensional figure and a green three-dimensional figure were put together to form the building shown below at the right. The two colors help you see how the figures fit together. Use shading to show how the blue and green figures below fit together to form each of the *Three Buildings* shown on the labsheet.

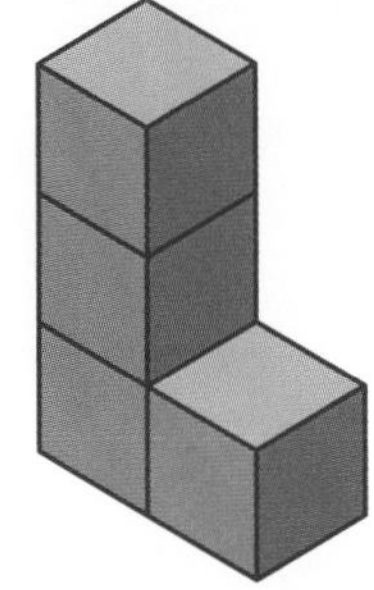

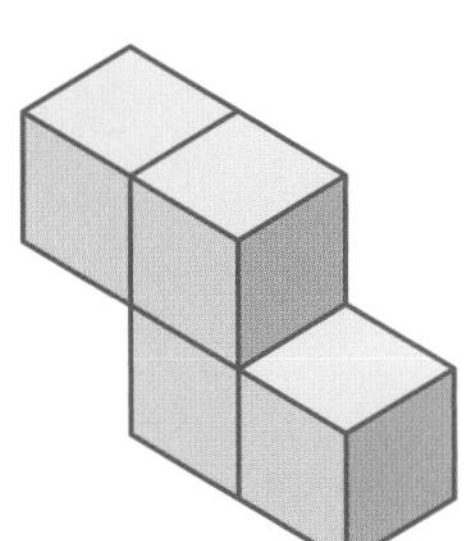

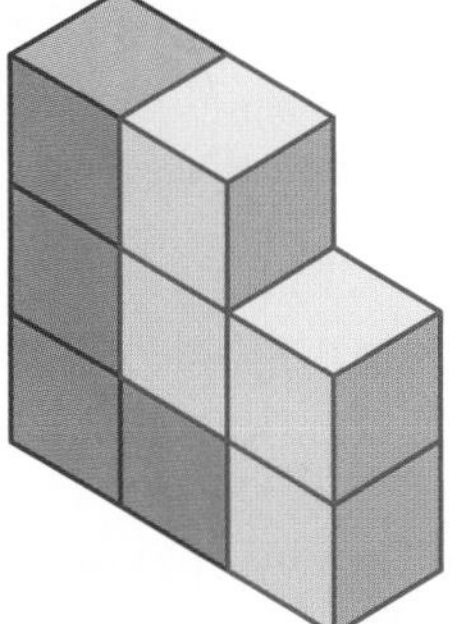

Spiral Review

16. Evetta, Luisa, and Yoko are auditioning for a part in a play. The order of their auditions will be determined by a random drawing. What is the probability of each event? **(Module 4, p. 300)**

    a. Evetta auditions first.
    b. Yoko does not audition last.

Use mental math to find each value. **(Module 3, p. 163)**

17. $\sqrt{36}$ 18. $\sqrt{9}$ 19. $\sqrt{144}$

Estimate each square root to the nearest tenth. **(Module 3, p. 163)**

20. $\sqrt{56}$ 21. $\sqrt{10}$ 22. $\sqrt{31}$

Find each sum or difference and write it in lowest terms. **(Module 2, p. 100)**

23. $\frac{3}{8} + \frac{1}{6}$ 24. $\frac{2}{5} + \left(-\frac{3}{4}\right)$ 25. $-\frac{13}{15} - \frac{41}{45}$

Section 1 Extra Skill Practice

You will need: • *Labsheet 1A* (Exs. 3–5, 8, and 9) • *ruler* (Exs. 3–5 and 7–9)

Follow the steps on page 311 for drawing a rectangular prism.

1. Sketch a rectangular prism whose height is twice its width.
2. Sketch a rectangular prism whose height is one-third its width.

Use the *Isometric Dot Paper* on Labsheet 1A. Draw all the different rectangular prisms that can be made from each number of cubes.

3. three cubes
4. four cubes
5. eight cubes
6. **Writing** Record the number of cubes, the surface area, and the volume of each rectangular prism you drew in Exercises 3–5. What relationships do you notice among these measurements?
7. Assume the building at the right contains five cubes. Draw flat views of the building from each of the following viewpoints: front, back, left, right, and top.

Use the *Isometric Dot Paper* on Labsheet 1A for Exercises 8 and 9.

8. Draw and label left-front, right-back, and back-left views of the building at the right.
9. Suppose that the view shown in Exercise 7 is for a building containing six cubes. Think about where the hidden cube must be located if it shares at least one face with another cube. Then carry out the steps in Exercises 7 and 8 for the six-cube building.

Study Skills — Identifying Weaknesses

When you complete a module or a section of a textbook, it can be helpful to identify anything that you do not fully understand. By writing out a list of questions to discuss with your teacher or other students, you can fill in any gaps in your understanding before moving on.

Describe a topic in this section about which you have questions. Write down your questions and try to obtain answers. Write the answers in your own words to be sure you understand them fully.

Section 2 Geometry and Constructions

IN THIS SECTION

EXPLORATION 1
- Constructing Triangles

EXPLORATION 2
- Constructing Nets

EXPLORATION 3
- Angles and Triangles

Building BLOCKS

KEY TERM
- congruent

Setting the Stage

Paul Spooner is a mechanical engineer of sorts. He designs and constructs moving sculptures made from paper and other simple materials. With scissors, glue, paper folding, and craftsmanship, Spooner's 2-dimensional patterns can be turned into playful 3-dimensional animals that you animate with the turn of a handle.

Over 45 separate pieces were put together to create the anteater sculpture. ▶

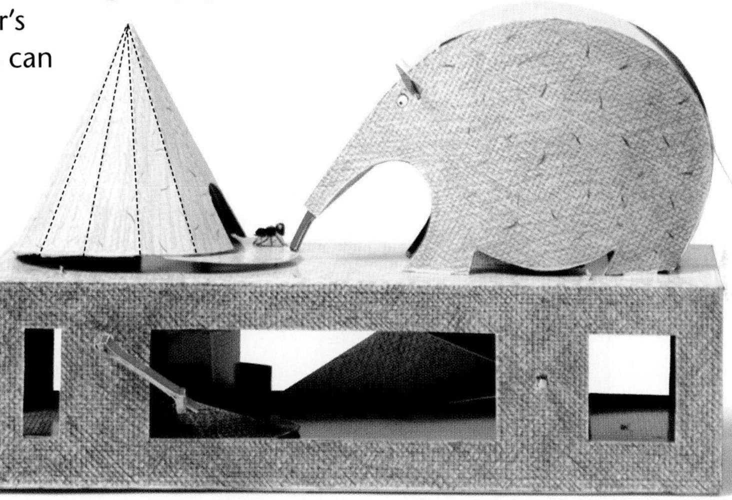

Think About It

1 What is the mathematical term for the general shape of the 3-dimensional figure the anteater is standing on in the photograph?

2 **a.** Describe the general shape of the anthill in the photograph.

b. What 2-dimensional shape is formed between two adjacent dashed lines on the anthill?

3 Two figures are **congruent** if they are the same shape and size. Do any of the figures in Spooner's sculpture appear to be congruent? Explain.

GOAL

LEARN HOW TO...
- name congruent figures
- apply the triangle inequality

AS YOU...
- construct triangles

KEY TERMS
- side-side-side rule
- triangle inequality

Exploration 1

Constructing TRIANGLES

SET UP *Work in a group of three. You will need: • compass • ruler • plain white paper • protractor*

▶ **In this exploration, you will learn about congruent triangles. You will also learn how to construct a triangle using a compass and a ruler.**

Student Resource

Constructing a Triangle

You can construct a triangle if you know its side lengths. The figures below show the steps for constructing a triangle that has side lengths of 4 in., $3\frac{1}{2}$ in., and 3 in.

Step 1 Draw a line segment 4 in. long. Label the endpoints *A* and *B*.

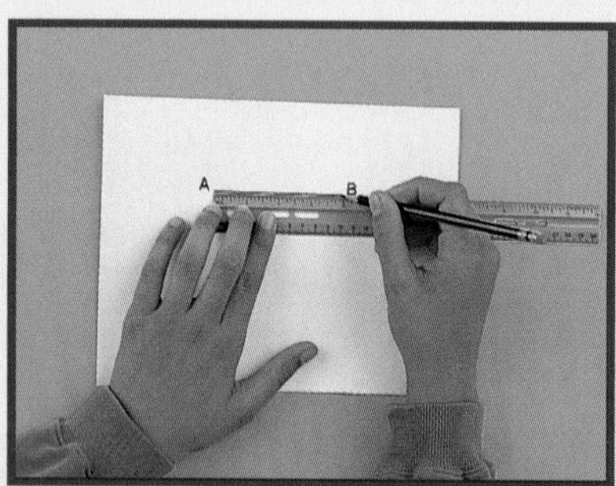

Step 2 Adjust the compass to a radius of $3\frac{1}{2}$ in. Put the compass point on *A* and draw an arc.

An **arc** is part of a circle.

Step 3 Adjust the compass to a radius of 3 in. Put the compass point on *B*. Draw another arc that intersects the first arc.

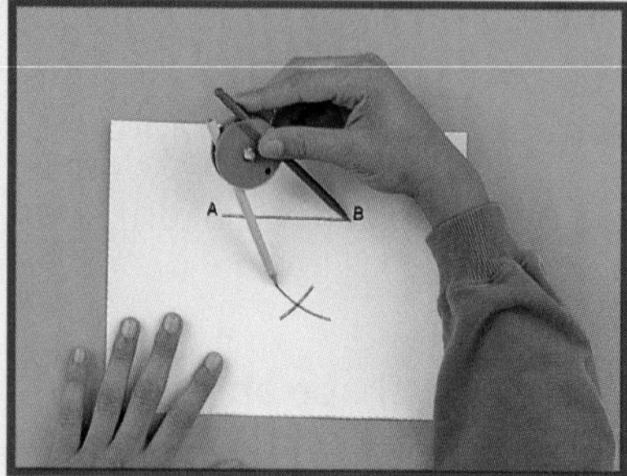

Step 4 Label the point where the arcs intersect *C*. Draw segments from *A* to *C* and from *B* to *C*.

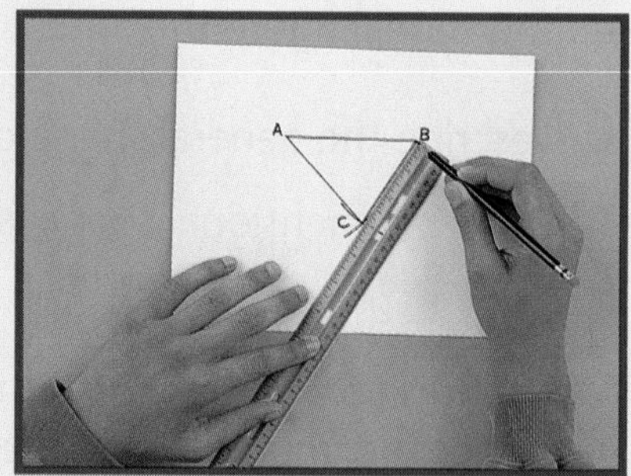

4 **a.** Each member of your group will construct a triangle with side lengths of 5 in., 4 in., and 3 in., starting with a different side length. (Use the *Student Resource* on the previous page.)

Person 1: Draw the 5 in. line segment first.

Person 2: Draw the 4 in. line segment first.

Person 3: Draw the 3 in. line segment first.

b. How do the three triangles compare?

$\angle A$ corresponds to $\angle D$.
$\overline{BC}$ corresponds to $\overline{EF}$.

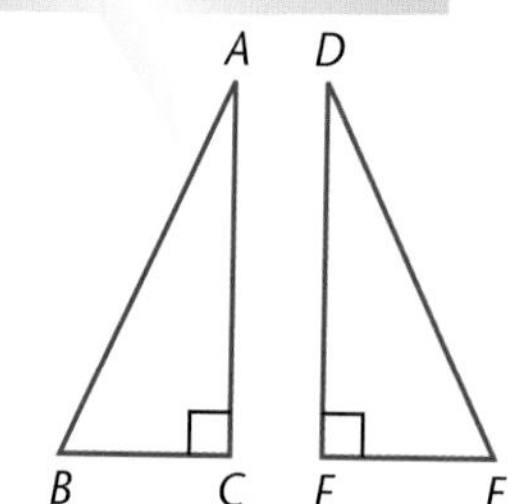

▶ **If two figures are congruent, it is possible to fit one figure onto the other so that all the corresponding parts match. In the diagram at the left, $\triangle ABC$ is congruent to $\triangle DEF$. This is written $\triangle ABC \cong \triangle DEF$. Corresponding angles of congruent triangles have the same measure, and corresponding sides are the same length.**

5 Are your triangles from Question 4 congruent? Explain.

6 **Discussion** Suppose you are given the statement $\triangle ABC \cong \triangle DEF$.

a. How can you tell which angles are corresponding angles?

b. How can you tell which sides are corresponding sides?

▶ **One way to determine if triangles are congruent is to measure the lengths of their sides. If the sides of one triangle have the same lengths as the sides of another triangle, the triangles are congruent. This is called the side-side-side rule.**

7 **a.** Label the vertices of each of the triangles your group made in Question 4. (Use different letters for each triangle.)

b. Write statements like the one in Question 6 telling that the triangles are congruent. Be sure to list the corresponding vertices in the same order.

8 ✓ **CHECKPOINT** Construct and label two congruent triangles. Explain how you know the triangles are congruent.

✓ **QUESTION 8**

...checks that you can identify congruent triangles.

9 Try to construct triangles with the given side lengths.

a. 2 in., 3 in., 2 in.

b. 1 in., 2 in., 3 in.

c. 1 in., 1 in., 1 in.

d. $1\frac{1}{2}$ in., $1\frac{1}{2}$ in., 4 in.

10 **Try This as a Class** Look at your work in Question 9.

a. How can you predict whether three side lengths can be used to construct a triangle? Explain.

b. Test your answer to part (a) by making up 3 side lengths that can be used to construct a triangle and 3 that cannot. Then try to construct each triangle.

▶ **The relationship among the side lengths of a triangle that you described in Question 10 is the triangle inequality.**

✓ **QUESTION 11**

...checks that you understand the relationship among the side lengths of any triangle.

11 ✓ **CHECKPOINT** Tell whether it is possible to construct a triangle with the given side lengths.

a. 2 cm, 4 cm, 6 cm

b. 3 cm, 9 cm, 8 cm

c. $\frac{1}{2}$ in., $\frac{1}{4}$ in., $\frac{3}{8}$ in.

d. 1.5 m, 4.9 m, 3.4 m

HOMEWORK EXERCISES ▶ See Exs. 1–11 on p. 332.

GOAL

LEARN HOW TO...
- identify and count parts of 3-dimensional figures
- create nets for pyramids and prisms

AS YOU...
- build a house with a modified mansard roof

KEY TERMS
- net
- pyramid
- tetrahedron
- base
- face
- edge
- vertex (plural: vertices)

Exploration 2

Constructing

SET UP *You will need:* • *Labsheets 2A and 2B* • *compass* • *ruler* • *scissors* • *tape*

▶ **You can use a compass and the straight edge of a ruler to create two-dimensional patterns for some of the 3-dimensional figures that Paul Spooner uses in his moving sculptures. A two-dimensional pattern that can be folded into a 3-dimensional figure is a net.**

12 The anthill in the *Setting the Stage* is a *pyramid*. Follow the steps below to construct a net to make a simple pyramid.

First

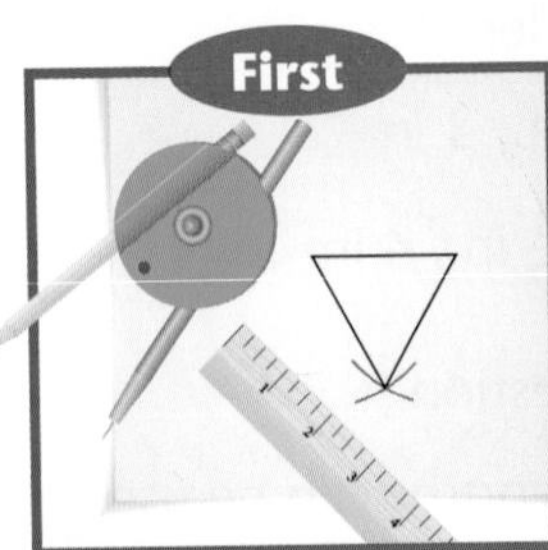

Use a compass and a straightedge to construct any equilateral triangle.

Next

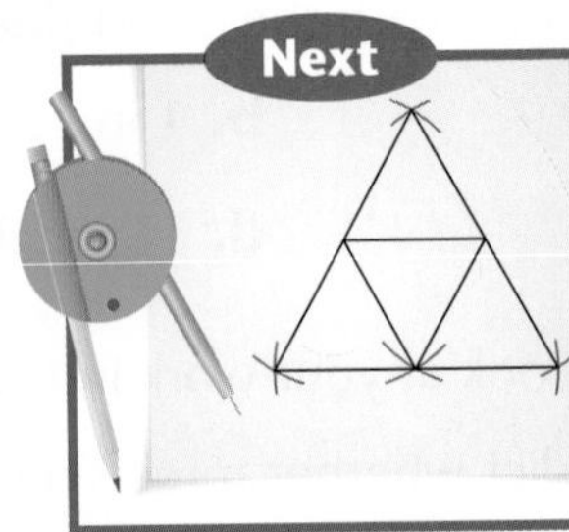

Construct another equilateral triangle on each side of the original triangle.

Then

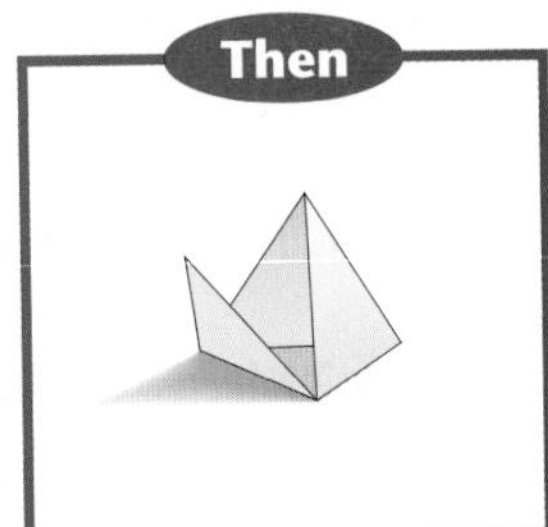

Cut out the net and fold it along the sides of the original triangle.

▶ **A pyramid is a polyhedron with one base that is a polygon. The other faces are triangles and meet at a common vertex. A pyramid with four triangular faces, including the base, is a tetrahedron.**

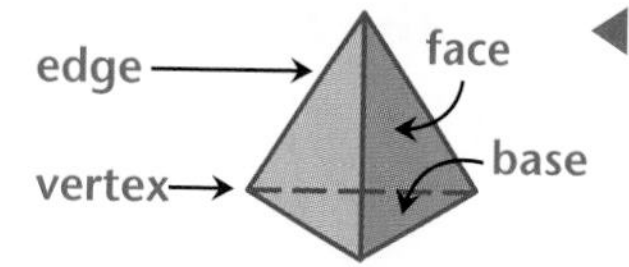

◀ A pyramid is named for the shape of its base. This tetrahedron may also be called a triangular pyramid.

13 Refer to the tetrahedron you made in Question 12.

a. How many edges does the tetrahedron have?

b. How many vertices?

c. How many faces, including the base?

d. How are the faces related? How can you tell?

14 ✓ **CHECKPOINT**

a. How many edges does a cube have?

b. How many vertices?

c. How many faces, including the base?

d. How are the faces related? How can you tell?

...checks that you can identify and count parts of a 3-dimensional figure.

▶ **Nets for Buildings** **Architects sometimes make nets to build cardboard models of the buildings they design. A model of a building allows an architect to see what the real building will look like and make changes before it is actually built.**

15 The roof of the house in the sketch below is a modified mansard roof. This type of roof creates extra space for living quarters in an attic.

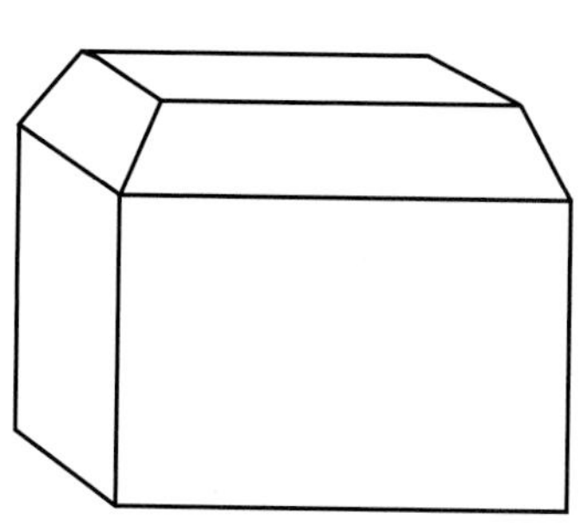

◀ The four-sided roof of this house is a mansard roof. Each side of the roof has two slopes, with the lower slope steeper than the upper slope.

a. What polygons are used to create the modified mansard roof? Sketch one face of the roof.

b. What polygons are used to create the vertical walls of the building? Sketch one wall.

Use the *Net for a House* on Labsheet 2A for Questions 16–18.

16 Follow the directions on the labsheet to make a model of a house with a modified mansard roof.

17 **a.** How many edges does the model have?

b. How many vertices does the model have?

c. How many faces, including the top and the bottom, does the model have?

18 **Discussion** How could you modify the *Net for a House* on Labsheet 2A to create a net for a rectangular prism?

✓ QUESTION 19

...checks that you can sketch a net for a prism.

19 **✓ CHECKPOINT** Sketch a net for a rectangular prism. Then find the number of edges, the number of vertices, and the number of faces, including the bases.

20 **Use Labsheet 2B.** In the mid 1700s, a Swiss mathematician named Leonhard Euler observed a relationship among the numbers of faces, edges, and vertices of a polyhedron.

a. Complete the *Three-Dimensional Figures* chart on the labsheet.

b. Look for a relationship among the number of faces, edges, and vertices. If you only know the number of faces and vertices, how can you determine the number of edges?

c. Write an equation that shows the relationship among the number of faces, vertices, and edges.

21 If a polyhedron has 7 faces and 10 vertices, how many edges will it have?

22 The 3-dimensional figure shown is an *icosahedron*. An icosahedron has 20 faces (all triangles) that are joined by 30 edges. How many vertices does an icosahedron have?

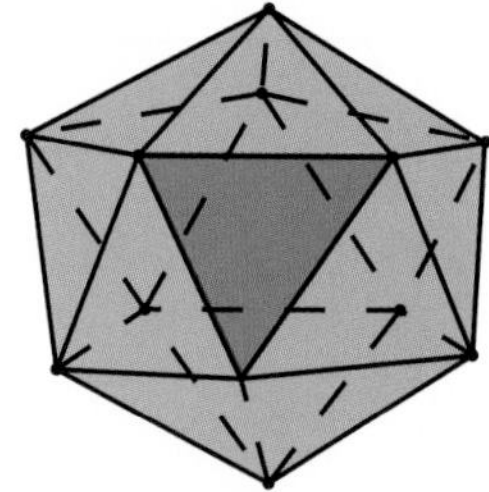

HOMEWORK EXERCISES ▶ See Exs.12–19 on pp. 332–334.

Exploration 3

Angles and Triangles

Goal

Learn how to...
- bisect an angle using a compass
- compare triangles using two sides and the included angle

As you...
- construct a net for a pyramid

Key Terms
- angle bisector
- included angle

Set up *Work with a partner. You will need:* • *plain paper* • *compass* • *ruler* • *scissors* • *protractor* • *tape*

▶ **At the right is a net for the anthill in Paul Spooner's paper anteater shown in the *Setting the Stage*. You need a protractor to draw this net, but some nets like it can be constructed by bisecting angles.**

The steps below show how to bisect an angle using a compass and a straightedge, such as the straight edge of a ruler.

Bisecting an Angle

Student Resource

First

Place the compass point on the vertex of the angle. Draw an arc that intersects both sides of the angle.

Next

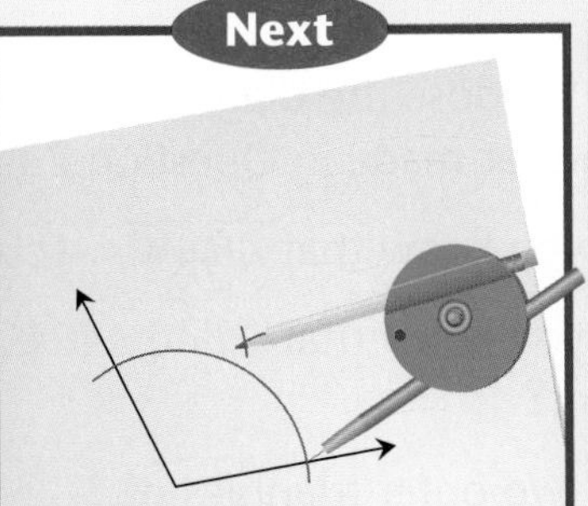

Place the compass point at one of the points where the original arc intersects the sides of the angle. Draw an arc inside the angle. Use the same compass setting to draw an arc from the other intersection point as shown.

Then

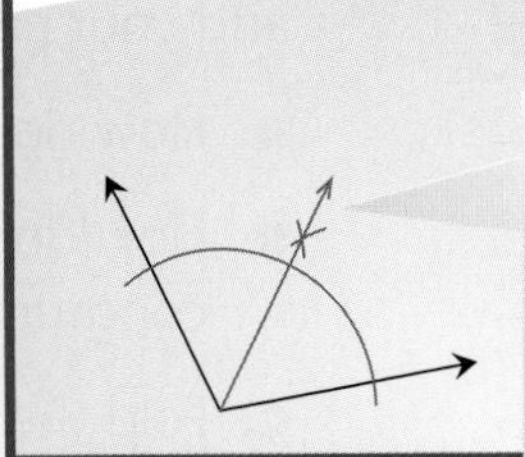

This ray is the **angle bisector**. It divides the original angle into two congruent angles.

Use a straightedge to draw a ray from the vertex of the angle through the point where the two arcs intersect.

23 Use a compass and a ruler. Follow the instructions below. The diagrams will help you and your partner draw nets for the triangular faces of two simple pyramids.

First

Draw an obtuse angle. Then follow the steps on page 327 to bisect the angle, using a large radius for the intial arc.

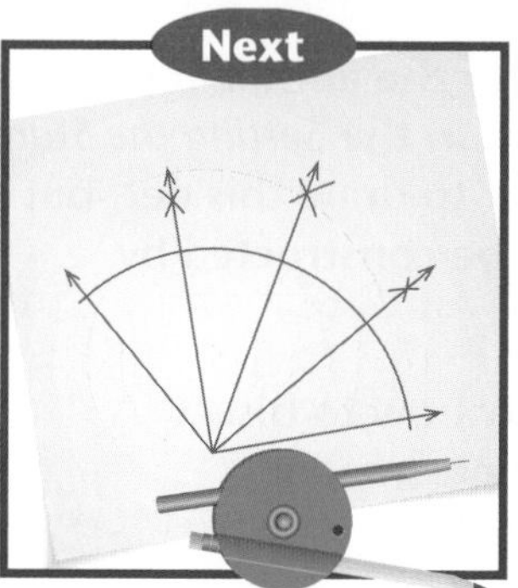

Next

Bisect each of the two new angles that you just formed. You do not have to draw the first arc again, just use the one already drawn.

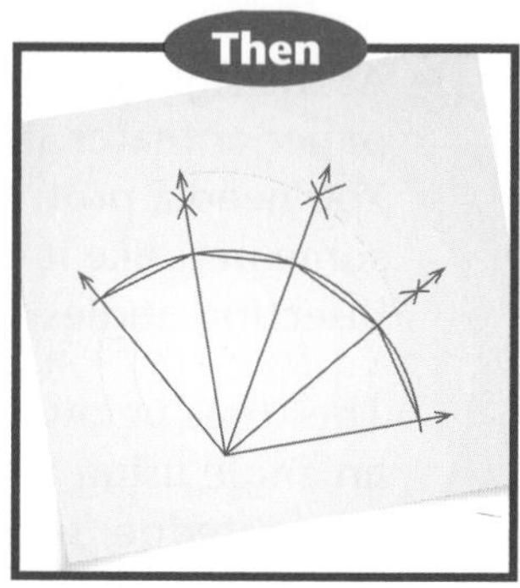

Then

Use a straightedge to connect the points where the arc intersects each ray. Cut out the net formed by the four triangles.

24 **Discussion** Suppose the diagram below represents the nets you and your partner made in Question 23.

a. How do you know that $\overline{AB}$, $\overline{AC}$, $\overline{AD}$, $\overline{AE}$, and $\overline{AF}$ are congruent?

b. How do you know that $\angle BAC$, $\angle CAD$, $\angle DAE$, and $\angle EAF$ are congruent?

c. Fold the two outer triangles of your net on top of the two inner triangles. Then fold again, so that all four triangles overlap. How are $\triangle BAC$, $\triangle CAD$, $\triangle DAE$, and $\triangle EAF$ related?

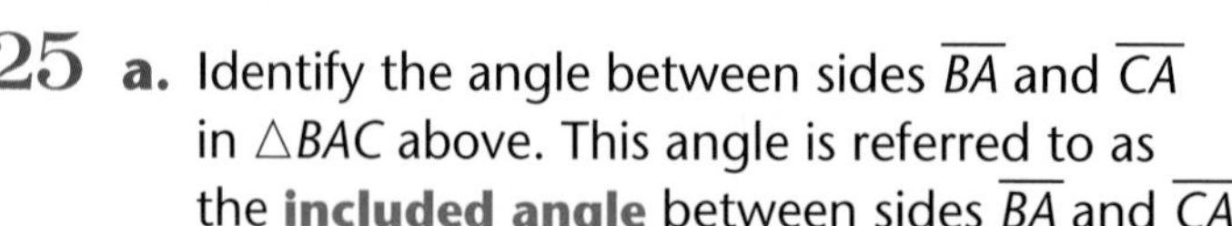

25 **a.** Identify the angle between sides $\overline{BA}$ and $\overline{CA}$ in $\triangle BAC$ above. This angle is referred to as the **included angle** between sides $\overline{BA}$ and $\overline{CA}$.

b. Identify the included angle between sides $\overline{AC}$ and $\overline{CB}$.

26 Use a ruler and a protractor to complete parts (a)–(e). You and your partner should each make a triangle.

a. Draw a triangle and label the vertices *A*, *B*, and *C*.

b. Draw a segment that is congruent to $\overline{AB}$. Label the endpoints of the new segment *P* and *Q*.

c. Draw an angle with the same measure as $\angle ABC$ that has *Q* as its vertex and $\overrightarrow{QP}$ as a side.

d. On the side of $\angle Q$ that does not contain point *P*, draw a segment with the same length as $\overline{BC}$ that has one endpoint at *Q*. Label the other endpoint *R*.

e. Connect points *P* and *R* to form another triangle.

f. Discussion How are $\triangle ABC$ and $\triangle PQR$ related? Explain.

27 **Try This as a Class** Suppose two sides and the included angle of one triangle are congruent to two sides and the included angle of another triangle. Based on the results of Questions 25 and 26, what do you think is the relationship between the two triangles?

28 ✓ **CHECKPOINT**

a. How are $\triangle ABC$ and $\triangle DEF$ related? Explain your reasoning.

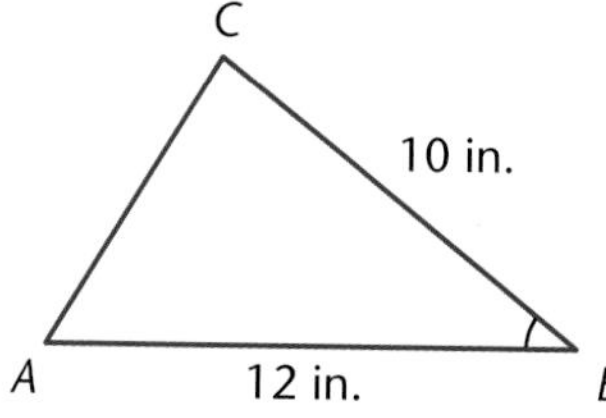

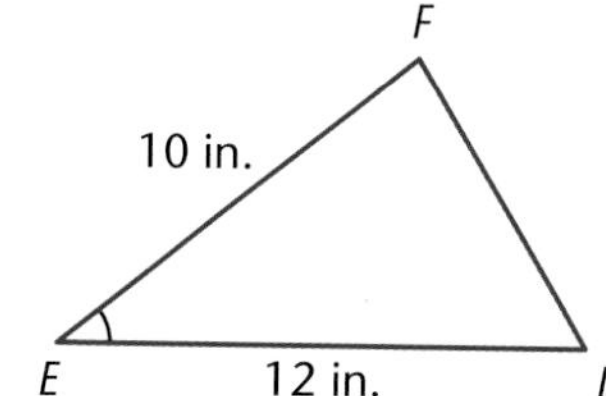

b. The diagram does *not* indicate that $\triangle ABC \cong \triangle EDF$. Why?

29 **a.** The net you made in Question 23 is made up of four congruent triangles. Tape two edges of the net together to form the sides of a pyramid.

b. What shape needs to be added to the net to form the base of the pyramid?

c. Make a sketch to show how you could change the net to include a base.

d. Discussion Compare the net you sketched in part (c) with the net that your partner sketched.

✓ **QUESTION 28**

...checks that you can compare triangles based on two sides and the included angle.

HOMEWORK EXERCISES See Exs. 19–28 on pp. 334–335.

Section 2

Key Concepts

Key Terms

Congruent Figures (pp. 321–322)

congruent

Figures are congruent if they have the same size and shape.

Congruent Triangles (pp. 323-324 and pp. 328–329)

side-side-side rule (SSS)

If the three sides of one triangle are congruent to the sides of another triangle, then the triangles are congruent. This is known as the side-side-side rule (SSS).

Example $\triangle RST \cong \triangle WXY$

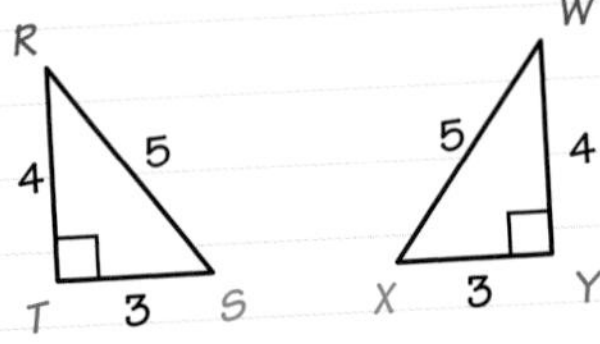

If two figures are congruent, then their corresponding parts are congruent. In the example above,

$\overline{ST}$ and $\overline{XY}$ are corresponding sides. $\overline{ST} \cong \overline{XY}$

$\triangle RST \cong \triangle WXY$

$\angle T$ and $\angle Y$ are corresponding angles. $\angle T \cong \angle Y$

included angle

If two sides and the included angle of one triangle are congruent to two sides and the included angle of another triangle, then the triangles are congruent. This is known as the side-angle-side rule (SAS).

Example $\triangle LMN \cong \triangle XYZ$

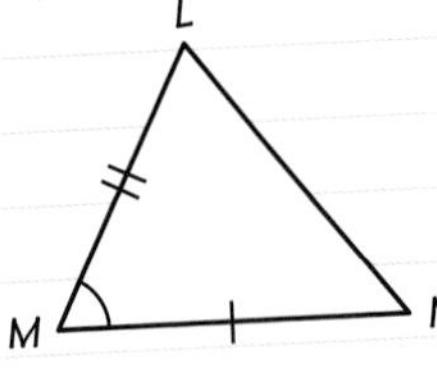

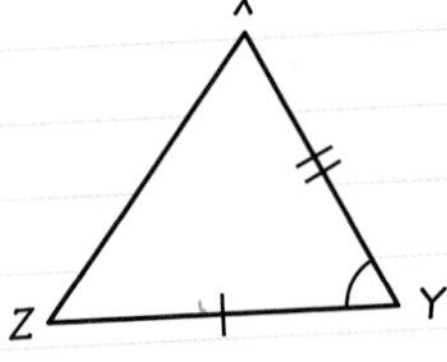

30 **Key Concepts Question** $\triangle CMD \cong \triangle TSQ$. List the corresponding sides and the corresponding angles of the triangles.

Section 2

Key Concepts

Triangle Inequality (pp. 323–324)

The triangle inequality states that the sum of the lengths of any two sides of a triangle is greater than the length of the third side.

Nets for Pyramids and Prisms (pp. 324–326)

A pyramid is a polyhedron with one base that is a polygon. The other faces are triangles and meet at a common vertex. Pyramids and other 3-dimensional figures can be built from 2-dimensional nets.

Examples This pyramid is a tetrahedron because it has four faces. All the faces, including the base, are triangles. Pairs of faces meet in segments called edges. A tetrahedron has 4 faces, 6 edges, and 4 vertices.

pyramid

edge
face
base
vertex

pyramid net

A rectangular prism has 6 faces, 12 edges, and 8 vertices.

prism

prism net

Bisecting Angles (pp. 327–328)

You can use a compass and a straightedge to bisect an angle.

Key Terms

triangle inequality

angle bisector

pyramid

net

tetrahedron

base

face

edge

vertex

Key Concepts Questions

31 Give three side lengths that could be used to construct a triangle and three side lengths that could not.

32 **a.** Sketch a net for a square pyramid. Draw the base in the center as in the pyramid net above.

b. How many edges does the square pyramid have? How many vertices? How many faces, including the base?

Section 2 Practice & Application Exercises

YOU WILL NEED

For Exs. 5–10:
- compass
- ruler

For Ex. 15:
- package for a real product
- ruler

For Exs. 16, 18, and 19:
- compass
- straightedge

Visual Thinking Without measuring or making any drawings, decide whether each set of line segments could form the sides of a triangle. Explain your thinking.

1. k, m, n

2. r, s, t

3. x, w, y

4. **Algebra Connection** A triangle has side lengths 3, 8, and x. Use inequalities to describe all the possible values of x.

Tell whether it is possible to construct a triangle with the given side lengths. If it is possible, construct the triangle.

5. 3 in., 2 in., 2 in.

6. 4 in., 1 in., 2 in.

7. 3 in., 3 in., 3 in.

8. 5 in., 2 in., 3 in.

9. 3 in., 2 in., $2\frac{1}{2}$ in.

10. $1\frac{3}{4}$ in., $1\frac{5}{8}$ in., $3\frac{3}{4}$ in.

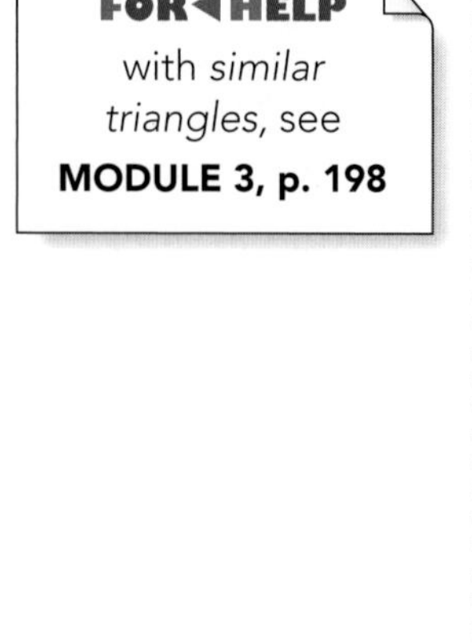

FOR HELP with *similar triangles*, see **MODULE 3, p. 198**

11. Compare the triangles below. Which appear to be similar? Which appear to be congruent? Explain how you can check. Then write mathematical statements like the ones in the Examples on page 330 telling which triangles are congruent.

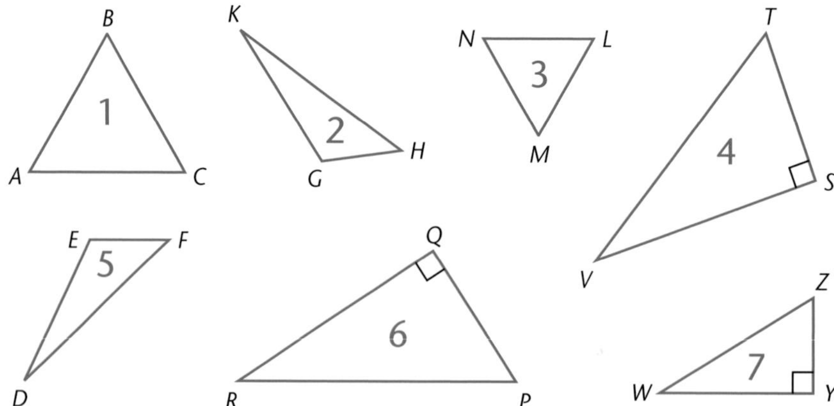

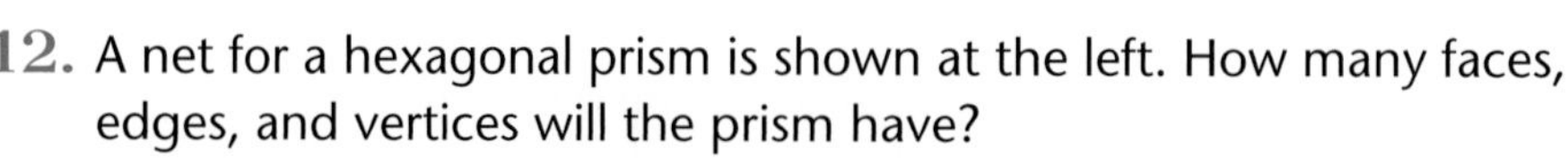

12. A net for a hexagonal prism is shown at the left. How many faces, edges, and vertices will the prism have?

13. **Open-ended** Sketch a net for a pentagonal prism. How many faces, edges, and vertices will the prism have?

14. **Open-ended** Sketch a net for a hexagonal pyramid. How many faces, edges, and vertices will the pyramid have?

15. **Home Involvement**

    a. Find a real product whose package is a prism.

    b. Estimate the area of each face and the total surface area of the package.

    c. Carefully unfold the package and sketch its net.

16. The base of a building does not have to be a rectangle. For example, a hexagon can form the base of a tower, a carousel, a ticket office, or a circus tent.

    a. Follow the steps below to construct a regular hexagon.

FOR ▶ HELP with *regular polygons*, see **TOOLBOX, p. 594**

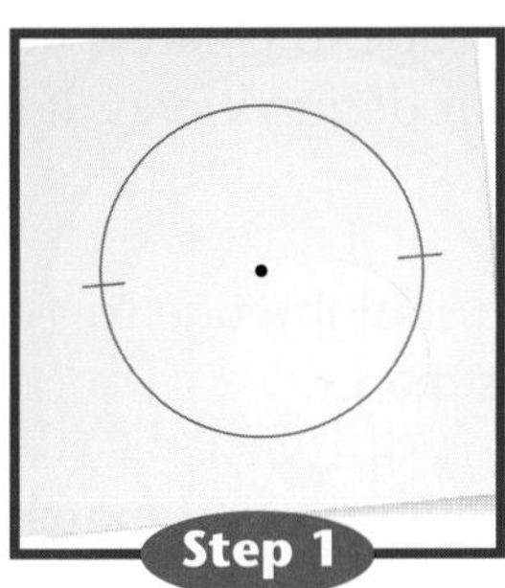

Step 1

Draw a circle with a compass. Leave the compass set to the circle's radius. Use a straightedge to mark the endpoints of a diameter.

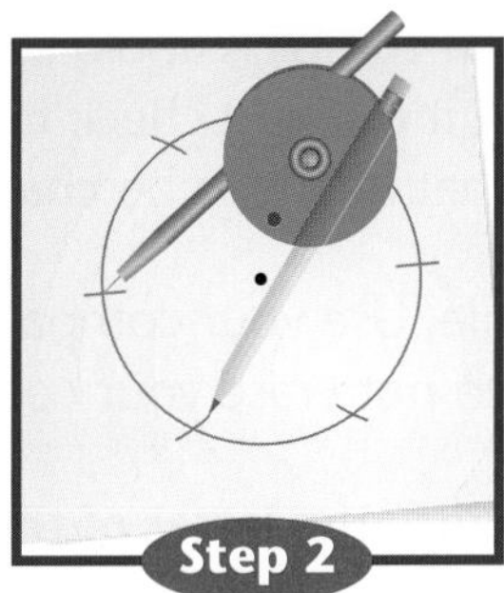

Step 2

Set the compass point on one endpoint of the diameter and mark two arcs that intersect the circle. Do the same for the other endpoint.

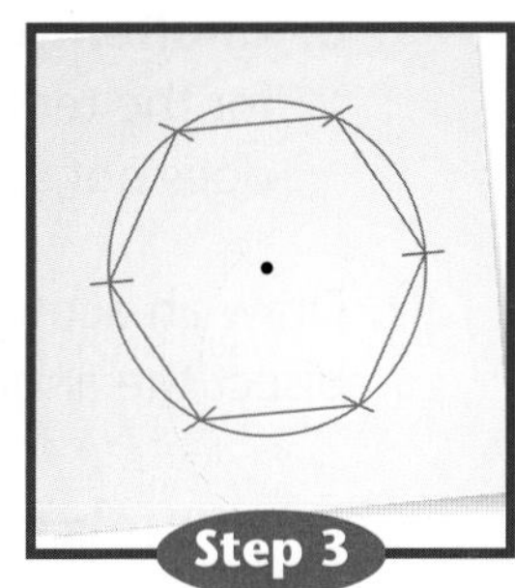

Step 3

Connect the six points to form a regular hexagon.

    b. In Step 3, what other polygon can you form by connecting the six points and drawing a diameter?

    c. What other polygon can you form by connecting every other point you drew on the circle in Step 2?

17. If a polyhedron has 9 faces and 9 vertices, how many edges will it have?

18. A *dodecahedron* is a 3-dimensional figure with 12 faces and 30 edges. How many vertices does a dodecahedron have?

19. a. The base of the tent pictured below is a regular hexagon. What shapes are the other faces of the tent?

b. Make a rough sketch of a net for the tent, including the base.

c. How many faces, edges, and vertices does the tent have?

d. **Challenge** Use a compass and a straightedge to create a net for the tent. Cut it out and check that your design works. If it does not, tell what needs to be changed.

20. Draw an acute angle. Use your compass and straightedge to bisect the angle. Do not erase your compass marks.

For Exercises 21–24, choose the letter of the polyhedron that matches each net.

A. triangular pyramid B. triangular prism C. octagonal pyramid D. octagonal prism

21.

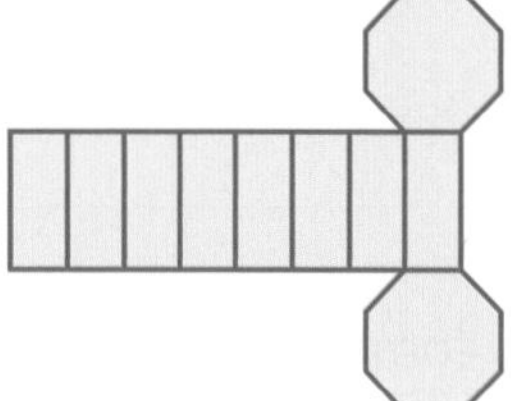

22.

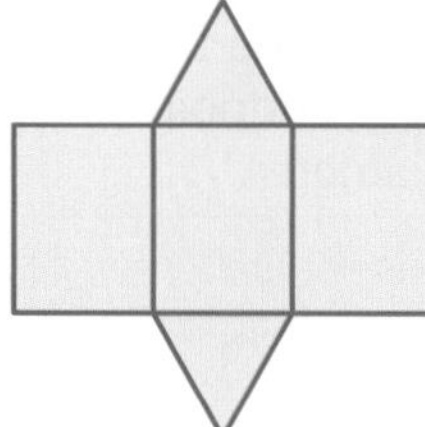

23.

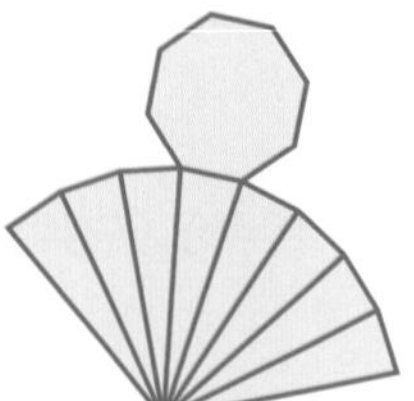

24.

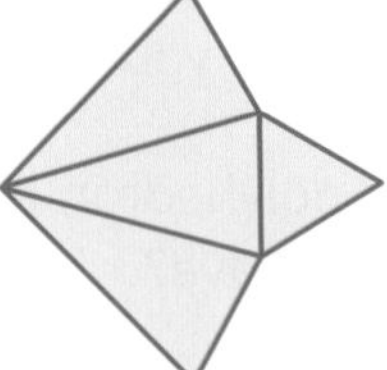

25. **Writing** Which net for a pyramid in Exercises 21–24 can be constructed using angle bisectors as on page 328? Which net for a pyramid cannot be constructed that way? Explain.

Tell whether the triangles in each pair are congruent. Explain.

26. $\triangle ABC$, $\triangle DEF$

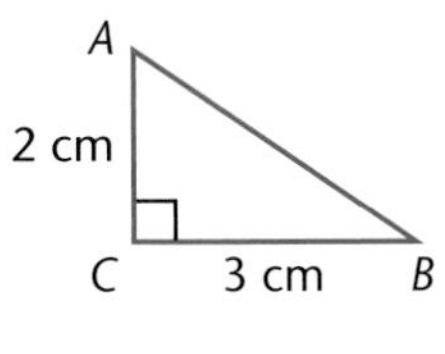

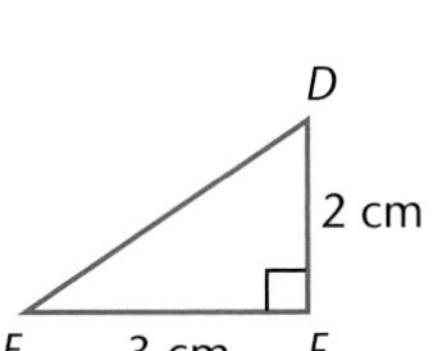

27. $\triangle PQS$, $\triangle RSQ$

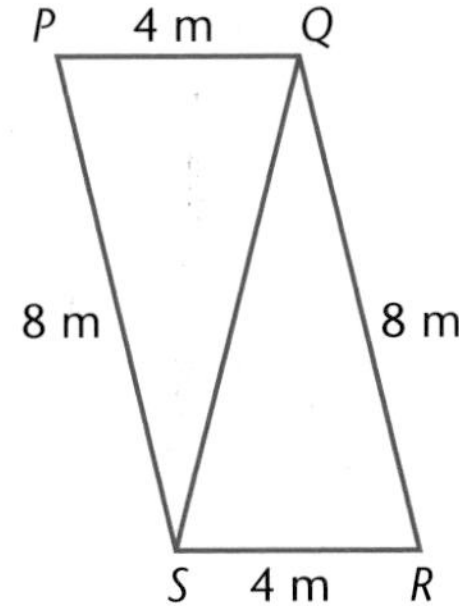

28. $\triangle ABC$, $\triangle WXY$

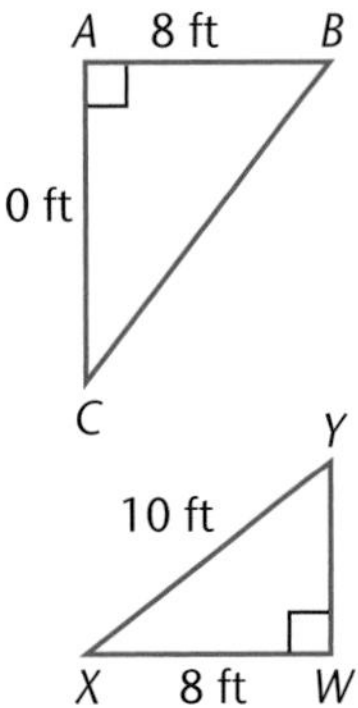

Reflecting on the Section

Be prepared to report on the following topic in class.

29. Describe how you can draw a right angle by constructing an angle bisector. Then describe how to use this construction to draw a net for a cube using a compass and a straightedge.

Oral Report

Exercise 29 checks that you can use constructions to draw nets.

Spiral Review

30. Assume the building at the right contains seven cubes. Think about where the hidden cubes must be located if they each share at least one face with another cube. Draw flat views of the building from each of the following viewpoints: front, back, left, right, and top. **(Module 5, p. 316)**

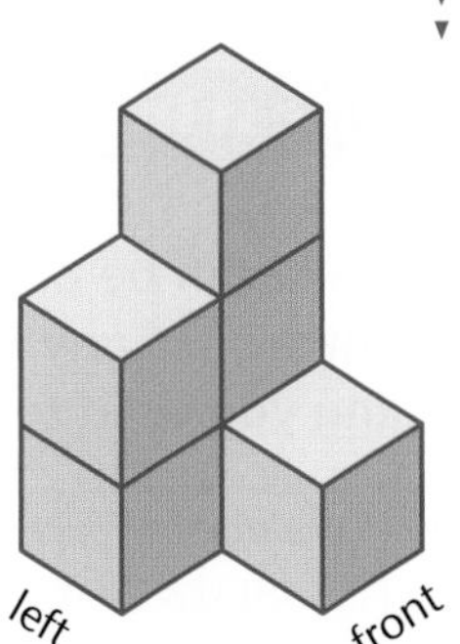

Solve each equation. **(Module 4, p. 277)**

31. $-2.4x = 72$

32. $-0.9y + 1.8 = 0.9$

33. $32 = -2.5z - 18$

34. $-2.7 = 5.4m$

35. $1.5n - 3.5 = -0.5$

36. $4 + 9.6k = 0.8$

37. $\frac{3}{5}a = 27$

38. $\frac{2}{3}b - 5 = 5$

39. $\frac{4}{3}c + 9 = 49$

Section 2 Extra Skill Practice

You will need: • *compass, straightedge* (Exs. 5–6) • *scissors, tape* (Ex. 5)

Tell whether it is possible to construct a triangle with the given side lengths.

1. 5 cm, 4 cm, 10 cm
2. $2\frac{5}{16}$ in., 4 in., $1\frac{5}{8}$ in.
3. 8 m, 24 m, 24 m
4. Sketch a net for each polyhedron. Then tell how many faces, edges, and vertices it will have.
   a. octagonal prism
   b. pentagonal pyramid
5. a. Make a rough sketch of a net for a hexagonal pyramid. Then use a compass and straightedge to create the net.
   b. Build the pyramid. If your net does not work, explain how to fix it.
6. Draw an obtuse angle. Use your compass and straightedge to bisect the angle. Do not erase your compass marks.

Tell whether the triangles in each pair are congruent. Explain.

7. $\triangle PQR$, $\triangle NML$

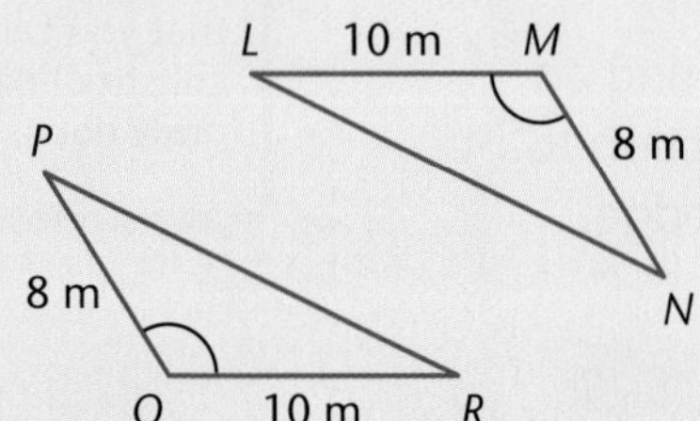

8. $\triangle ABD$, $\triangle CBD$

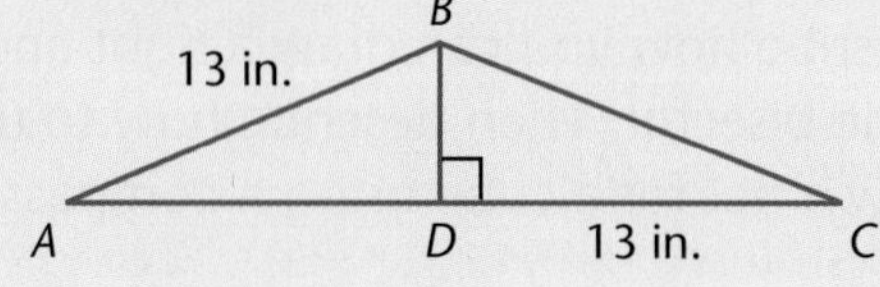

Standardized Testing ▶ Performance Task

Two identical pyramids can be put together with the bases attached to form a new polyhedron. Copy and complete the table below. Explain the reasoning you used to complete the table.

Number of sides on the base of each pyramid	Number of faces on the new polyhedron	Number of edges on the new polyhedron	Number of vertices on the new polyhedron
3	?	?	?
4	?	?	?
5	?	?	?
100	?	?	?

Section 3 Working with Triangles

In This Section

Exploration 1
- Triangle Side Length Relationships

Exploration 2
- The Pythagorean Theorem

Right ON!

Setting the Stage

Set Up *Work in a group of three or four. You will need: • scissors • centimeter grid paper • tape or glue • construction paper*

The pyramids at Giza in Egypt were built as tombs for Egyptian kings, their families, and their servants. King Khufu's pyramid, shown in the center at the right, is the largest pyramid ever built. Many skilled craftspeople and laborers worked together to build the pyramids at Giza. There were stonecutters and polishers, crews who transported the giant stones, and laborers called *rope stretchers.*

The rope stretchers tied equally spaced knots in a piece of rope. They knew they could form a right triangle with side lengths of 3, 4, and 5 units by arranging the rope as shown. The rope triangle was then used at a construction site to measure distances and to form 90° angles at the corners of a pyramid.

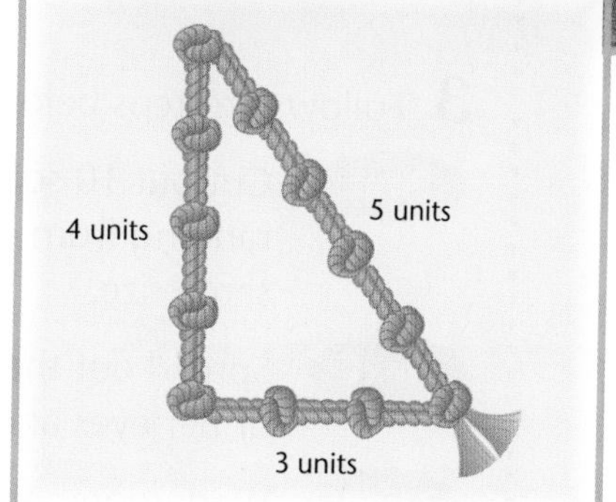

Think About It

1 **a.** Cut three squares from centimeter grid paper. One square should have sides 3 units long, one should have sides 4 units long, and one should have sides 5 units long.

b. Label each square with its area and the length of one side.

2 **a.** Use your three squares to form a triangle. Tape the arrangement into place on construction paper. Label the two shorter sides *a* and *b* and the longest side *c*.

b. Is the triangle a right triangle? Explain how you can check.

c. What is the relationship between the areas of the two smaller squares and the area of the largest square?

d. Do you think this relationship is the same for all triangles? How can you find out?

▶ **Your discovery about the 3-4-5 triangle is part of a larger pattern. In this section, you will learn more about the relationship among side lengths of triangles.**

GOAL

LEARN HOW TO...
- identify different types of triangles by looking at their side lengths

AS YOU...
- work with paper squares

Exploration 1

TRIANGLE Side Length Relationships

SET UP *Work in a group of three or four. You will need: • Labsheet 3A • centimeter grid paper • scissors • construction paper • tape or glue • protractor*

3 Follow the steps below with your group.

First Cut out 10 squares from the grid paper with side lengths ranging from 6 cm to 15 cm. No two squares should be the same size.

Next Spread out the squares. Have one group member close his or her eyes and choose a square. Set this square aside.

Then Work together to try to form 3 triangles with the remaining 9 squares. (The triangles do not have to be right triangles.)

4 **a.** Are there some sets of squares that will not form a triangle? If so, explain why.

b. Tape or glue each triangle to construction paper.

Use Labsheet 3A for Questions 5 and 6.

5 Follow the directions on the labsheet to complete the *Triangle Table* for the triangles made by your group.

6 **Try This as a Class** Share your group's data from the *Triangle Table* with the other groups in your class.

a. Use the extra spaces in the *Triangle Table* to record the data from other groups for any triangles that your group did not make.

b. How many different triangles did your class find altogether? Do you think that these are all the possible arrangements? How could you find out?

c. Look at the last two columns in the *Triangle Table*. What do you notice about the relationship between the sum of the areas of the smaller squares and the area of the largest square for an acute triangle? a right triangle? an obtuse triangle?

FOR ▶ HELP with *classifying triangles*, see **TOOLBOX, p. 593**

▶ **A triangle may appear to be a right triangle even if it is not. If you know the side lengths of a triangle, you can tell what type of triangle it is.**

EXAMPLE

Tell whether a triangle with side lengths of 12 in., 16 in. and 21 in. is a right triangle.

SAMPLE RESPONSE

$(12)^2 + (16)^2 \stackrel{?}{=} (21)^2$

$144 + 256 \neq 441$

This triangle is not a right triangle.

For a right triangle, if you square the lengths of the two shorter sides and add the results, the sum must equal the length of the longest side squared.

7 Is the triangle in the Example *obtuse* or *acute*? Explain.

8 ✓ **CHECKPOINT** Tell whether a triangle with the given side lengths is *acute*, *right*, or *obtuse*.

a. 11 cm, 13 cm, 20 cm

b. 16 mm, 18 mm, 10 mm

c. 17 in., 15 in., 8 in.

d. 6.5 cm, 4.2 cm, 7.9 cm

✓ **QUESTION 8**

...checks that you can use the lengths of the sides of a triangle to determine what type of triangle it is.

9 Give the side lengths of a triangle (other than a 3-4-5 triangle) that the Egyptian rope stretchers could have used to form a right angle. Sketch a picture of a rope triangle with these new side lengths.

HOMEWORK EXERCISES ▶ **See Exs. 1–7 on p. 344.**

GOAL

LEARN HOW TO...
- use the Pythagorean theorem to find an unknown side length of a right triangle

AS YOU...
- explore the dimensions of the I.M. Pei Pyramid

KEY TERMS
- Pythagorean theorem
- hypotenuse
- leg

Exploration 2

The PYTHAGOREAN Theorem

Architect I.M. Pei designed a pyramid as part of the Louvre Museum in Paris, France. The pyramid, shown below, utilizes many right triangles in its structure. In his design, the architect relied on the work of Pythagoras, a Greek mathematician who made an important discovery about right triangles.

The **Pythagorean theorem** says that in a right triangle the square of the length of the *hypotenuse* is equal to the sum of the squares of the lengths of the *legs*. The **hypotenuse** is the side opposite the right angle. The **legs** are the sides adjacent to the right angle.

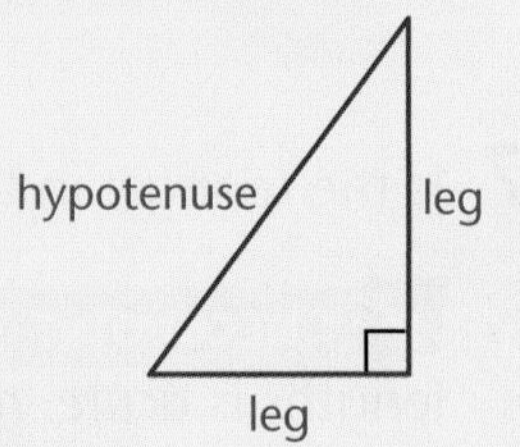

10 **Try This as a Class** Use the diagram above.

a. Let a and b represent the lengths of the legs of the right triangle. Let c represent the length of the hypotenuse. Restate the Pythagorean theorem as an equation relating a, b, and c.

b. Suppose you know the length of each leg in a right triangle. How can you use the equation you wrote in part (a) to find the length of the hypotenuse?

11 ✓ **CHECKPOINT** A skateboard ramp has a height of 3 ft on one side and extends 13 ft along the ground. What is the approximate distance a skateboarder will travel from the top to the bottom of the ramp?

✓ **QUESTION 11**

...checks that you can use the Pythagorean theorem to find the length of the hypotenuse of a right triangle.

▶ **You can use the Pythagorean theorem to find the length of one side of a right triangle if you know the lengths of the other two sides.**

EXAMPLE

Use the Pythagorean theorem to find the unknown side length of the triangle below.

SAMPLE RESPONSE

The hypotenuse is given, so you need to find the length of one leg.

Let a = the unknown side length.

$$a^2 + b^2 = c^2$$
$$a^2 + 9^2 = 17^2$$
$$a^2 + 81 = 289$$
$$a^2 + 81 - 81 = 289 - 81$$
$$a^2 = 208$$
$$a \approx 14.42$$

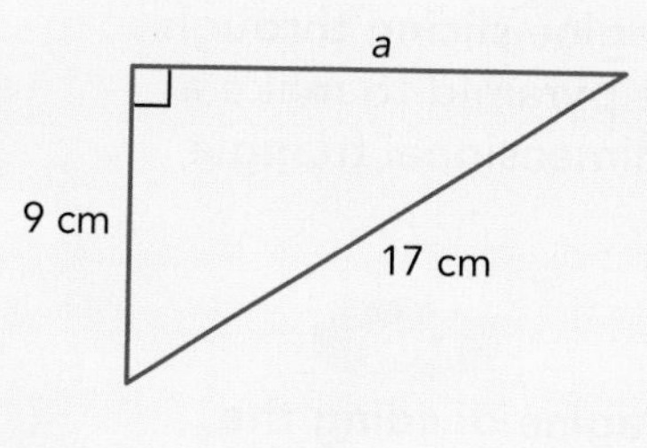

The length of the unknown side is about 14.42 cm.

FOR◀HELP with *square roots*, see **MODULE 3, p. 163**

Use the Example to answer Questions 12–14.

12 How can you tell from looking at the triangle that the unknown side length is a leg of the triangle, and not the hypotenuse?

13 In the equations in the Example, why was 81 subtracted from both sides before solving for a?

14 Why is the length of the third side not an exact measurement?

15 ✓ **CHECKPOINT** For each triangle, find the unknown side length. Round to the nearest hundredth.

a. 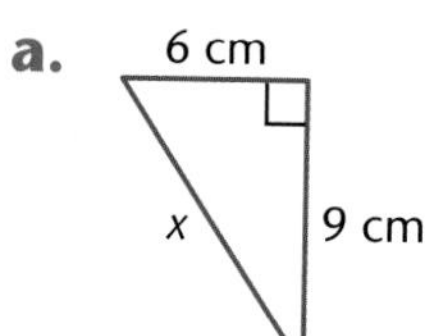

b. 141 m, x, 100 m

c. x, 12 mm, 7 mm

✓ **QUESTION 15**

...checks that you can use the Pythagorean theorem to find an unknown side length.

16 Suppose the length of the hypotenuse of a right triangle is $\sqrt{90}$, and the lengths of the legs are equal. Find the length of the legs. Round your answer to the nearest hundredth.

▶ **The Louvre pyramid is a square pyramid. The height of the pyramid is 71 ft and each side of the base is 116 ft long. The *slant height* of the pyramid is the height of each of the faces. You can use the Pythagorean theorem to find the slant height.**

EXAMPLE

To find the slant height of the Louvre pyramid:

First
Imagine slicing through the pyramid to make a 2-dimensional triangle.

Then
Imagine dividing the 2-dimensional triangle into two congruent right triangles.

Now
Use the Pythagorean theorem to find the slant height.

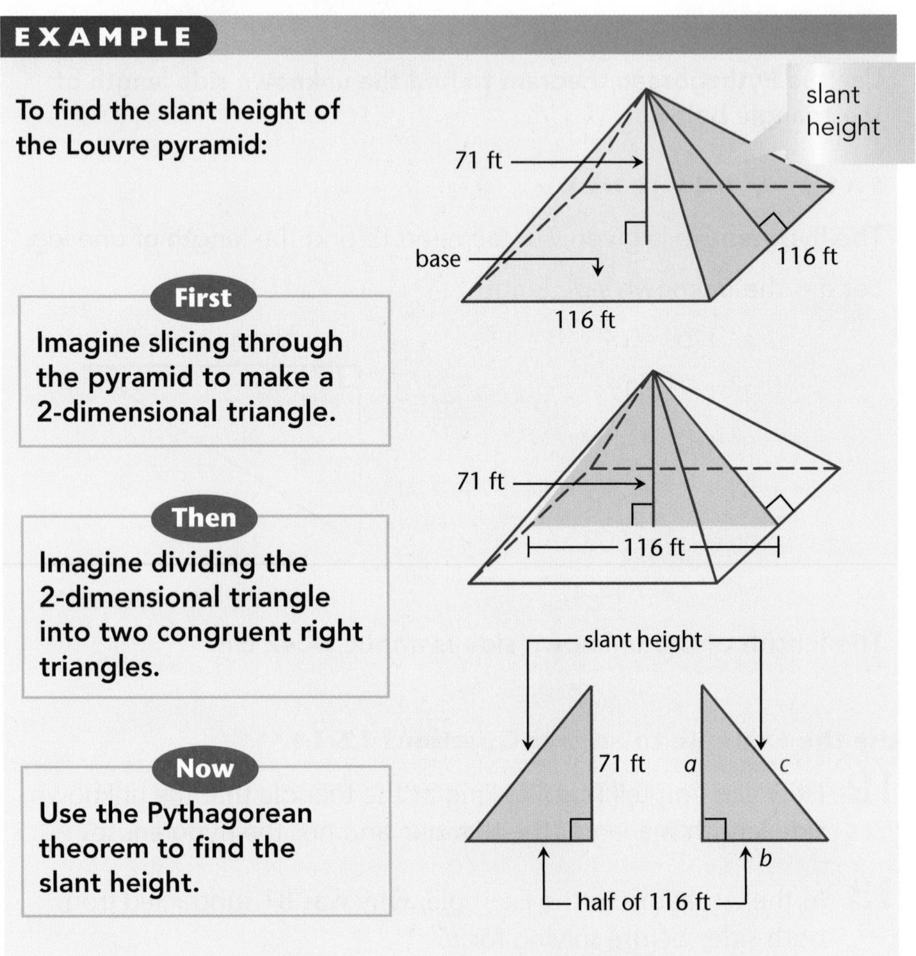

17 **Try This as a Class** Use the Example above.

a. Use the Pythagorean theorem to find the length of the hypotenuse of one of the congruent right triangles.

b. Find the slant height of the Louvre pyramid to the nearest foot.

c. Now that you know the slant height of the pyramid, explain how you can find the area of one triangular face of the pyramid.

HOMEWORK EXERCISES ▶ **See Exs. 8–21 on pp. 344–346.**

Section 3 Key Concepts

Key Terms

Side Lengths of Triangles (pp. 338–339)

If you know the side lengths of a triangle, you can identify it as acute, right, or obtuse. Let c equal the length of the longest side of the triangle and a and b equal the lengths of the two shorter sides.

If $a^2 + b^2 > c^2$, then the triangle is acute.

If $a^2 + b^2 = c^2$, then the triangle is right.

If $a^2 + b^2 < c^2$, then the triangle is obtuse.

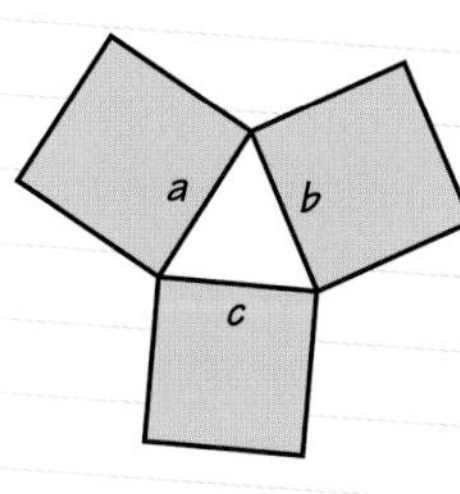

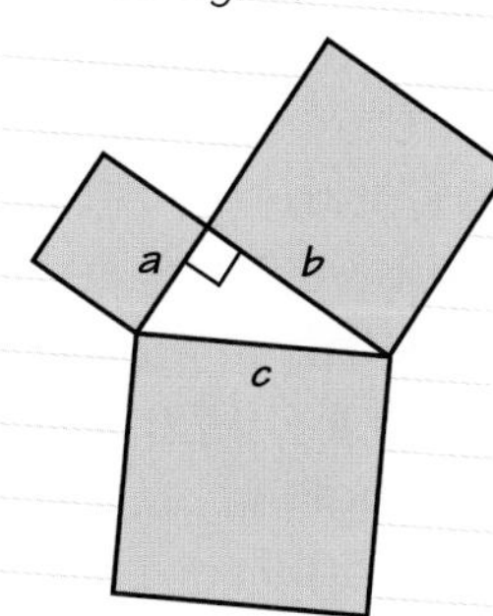

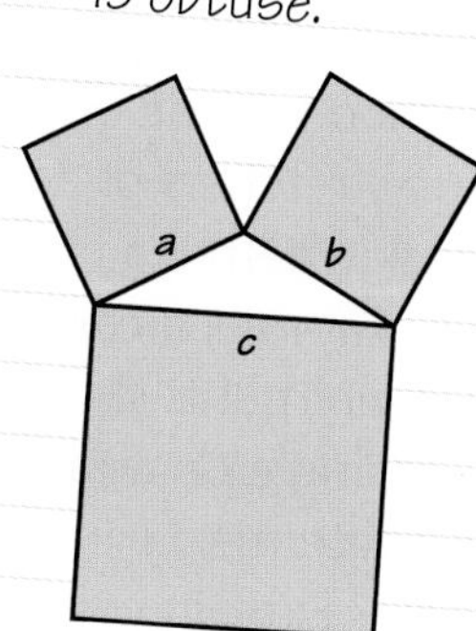

The Pythagorean Theorem (pp. 340–342)

In a right triangle, the sum of the squares of the lengths of the **legs** is equal to the square of the length of the **hypotenuse**, the longest side of the triangle. This relationship is known as the Pythagorean theorem.

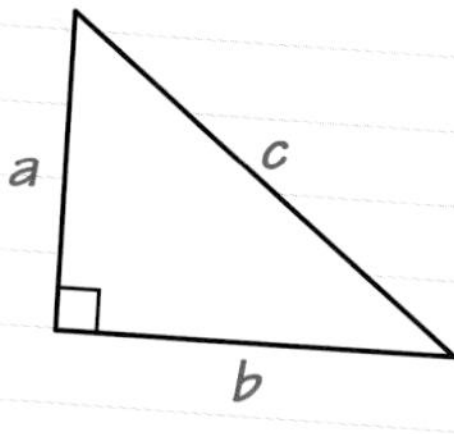

$$a^2 + b^2 = c^2$$

Pythagorean theorem

leg

hypotenuse

Key Concepts Question

18 Yuka drew a right triangle and labeled the side lengths as shown. Assume the legs are labeled correctly. Explain why the hypotenuse must be labeled incorrectly. Then use the lengths of the legs to find the correct length of the hypotenuse.

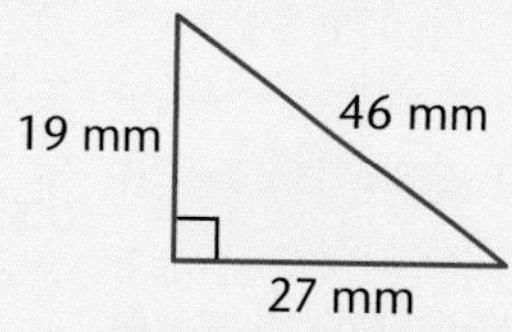

19 Is a triangle with side lengths of 5.4 cm, 9.2 cm, and 7.8 cm *acute*, *right*, or *obtuse*?

Section 3 Practice & Application Exercises

YOU WILL NEED

For Ex. 14:
- graph paper

For Ex. 28:
- Labsheet 3B

Tell whether a triangle with the given side lengths is *acute, right,* or *obtuse.*

1. 5 cm, 12 cm, 13 cm
2. 5 mm, 9 mm, 7 mm
3. 8 in., 10 in., 9 in.
4. 11.5 m, 6.2 m, 7 m
5. 16 cm, 20 cm, 17 cm
6. 15 mm, 12 mm, 9 mm
7. **Carpentry** Carpenters can use a method like the one used by the rope stretchers of ancient Egypt to check whether a corner is "square." For example, a carpenter took the measurements shown to check a right angle on a table. Is the angle opposite the 21 in. diagonal a right angle? Explain your thinking.

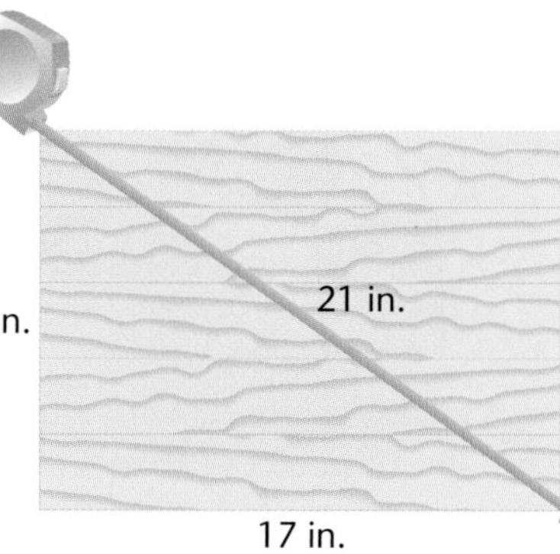

For each right triangle, find the unknown side length. Give each answer to the nearest hundredth if necessary.

8. 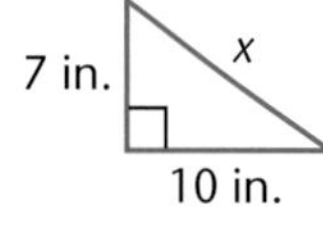

9. 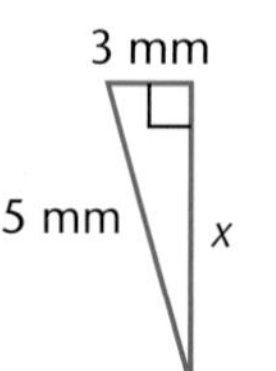

10. 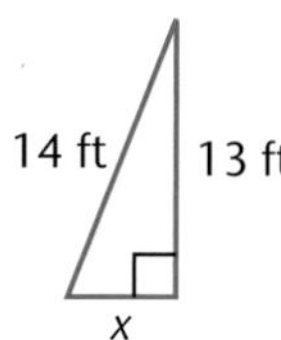

11. 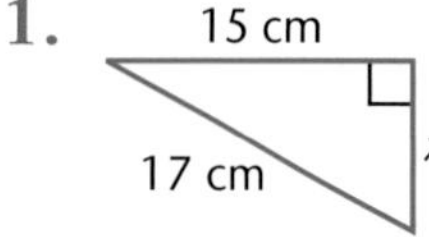

12. 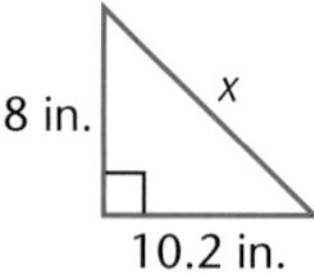

13. 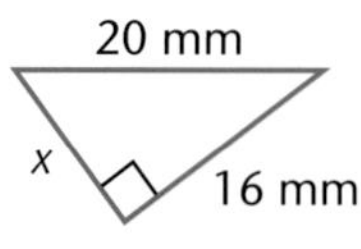

Hey Sharon!
Here are the directions to the party!
Hope you can make it!
First drive 70 mi north on Highway 9.
Then drive 80 mi west on Route 16.
Then drive 40 mi north on Highway 7.
Then drive 30 mi east on Route 14.

14. **Visual Thinking** Sharon Ramirez receives directions for a party. Use graph paper to sketch Sharon's route. Draw a single segment connecting Sharon's house and her friend's house. Find the distance represented by the segment.

15. Can a circular trampoline with a diameter of 16 ft fit through a doorway that is 10 ft high and 8 ft wide? (Assume that the legs of the trampoline can be removed.) Explain your answer.

16. The size of a television set is indicated by the length (to the nearest inch) of a diagonal of the screen.

a. Which of the following would be considered a 30 in. TV?

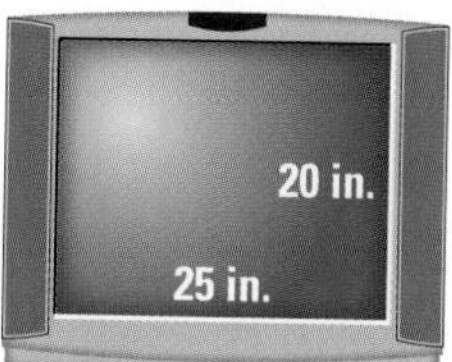

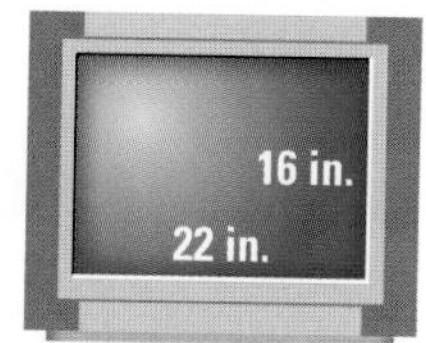

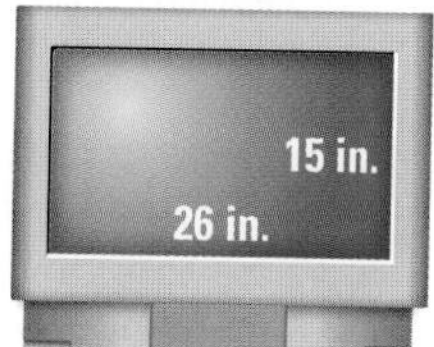

b. A store advertises a 25 in. TV with an aspect ratio of 4:3. That means that the ratio of the width of the screen to its length is 4:3. Find the length and width of the screen. Explain your method.

17. **Architecture** Many building codes specify that the ratio of the rise of a stair to its tread cannot exceed the ratio 3:4.

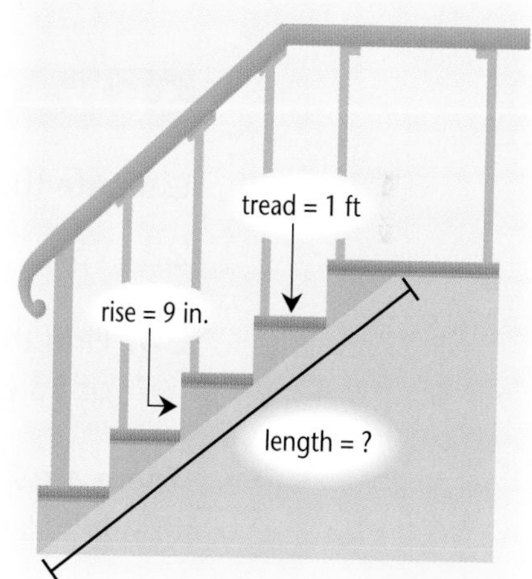

a. Find the ratio of the rise to the tread on the staircase shown. Does the staircase shown follow the building code described above?

b. What is the length of the line along the staircase shown?

c. **Research** Measure the rise and the tread of a stair in your home or school. Find the ratio of the rise to the tread. Does the staircase follow the building code described above?

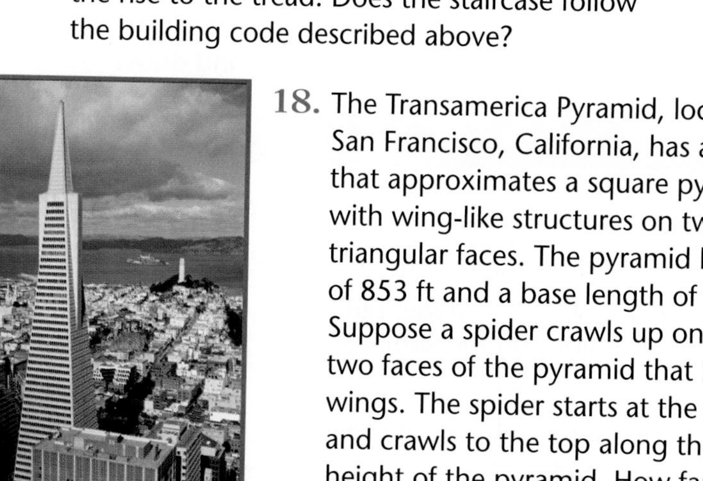

18. The Transamerica Pyramid, located in San Francisco, California, has a shape that approximates a square pyramid with wing-like structures on two of the triangular faces. The pyramid has a height of 853 ft and a base length of 175 ft. Suppose a spider crawls up one of the two faces of the pyramid that have no wings. The spider starts at the bottom and crawls to the top along the slant height of the pyramid. How far does the spider crawl?

19. **Challenge** Find the next 3 terms in the sequence 3, 4, 5, 6, 8, 10, 9, 12, 15, … . Explain how you got your answer.

20. A maintenance worker needs to repair a light fixture mounted on a building. She leans a 20 ft ladder against the building with the foot of the ladder 5 ft from the building. How far up the building does the ladder reach? Round your answer to the nearest hundredth.

Reflecting on the Section

Oral Report

Exercise 21 checks that you can explain how to use the Pythagorean theorem.

21. Imagine you just discovered the relationship among the side lengths of a right triangle. Unfortunately, no one believes your discovery is very important. Write a persuasive speech explaining how useful your discovery is. Make visual aids to use with your speech.

Spiral Review

Estimate the square root to the nearest tenth. (Module 3, p. 163)

22. $\sqrt{57}$ 23. $\sqrt{148}$ 24. $\sqrt{12}$

25. Find the surface area of a can with a diameter of 7 cm and height of 13 cm. (Module 4, p. 251)

There are 7 red apples and 5 green apples in a paper bag.
(Module 2, p. 114)

26. What is the probability of drawing a red apple at random?

27. Suppose a green apple is drawn first and not replaced. What is the probability of getting a green apple on a second draw?

Extension

A Pythagorean Puzzle

28. **Use Labsheet 3B.** Hundreds of proofs have been written for the Pythagorean theorem. Many are in the form of diagrams that illustrate the theorem. Follow the directions on the labsheet to complete a *Pythagorean Puzzle.*

a. What do you notice about the relationship between the two smaller squares and the large one you built?

b. How might this puzzle be used to justify the Pythagorean theorem?

c. Through research, see if you can find other ways to "prove" the Pythagorean theorem.

Section 3

Extra Skill Practice

For Exercises 1–4, tell whether a triangle with the given side lengths is *acute*, *right*, or *obtuse*.

1. 6 in., 12 in., 14 in.
2. 7.5 m, 18 m, 19.5 m
3. 8 mm, 10 mm, 12.8 mm
4. 21 ft, 25 ft, 33 ft

For each triangle, find the unknown side length. Round each answer to the nearest hundredth if necessary.

5.

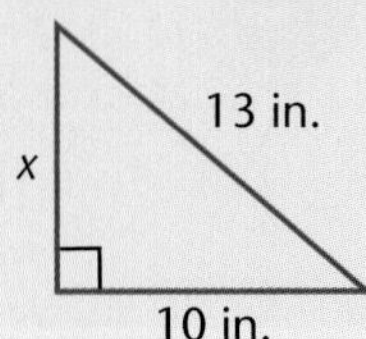

6. 9 ft, 8 ft, x

7.

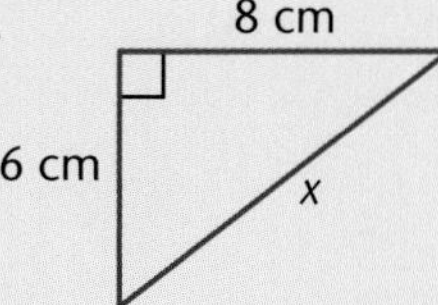

Tell whether the given side lengths could be the side lengths of a right triangle. Explain why or why not.

8. 4.5 cm, 6 cm, 7.5 cm
9. 3 in., 3 in., 5 in.
10. 2.5 m, 6 m, 6.5 m
11. 6 m, 6 m, 10 m
12. a. Find the exact length of the hypotenuse of each right triangle in the spiral at the right.
    b. What pattern do you notice?

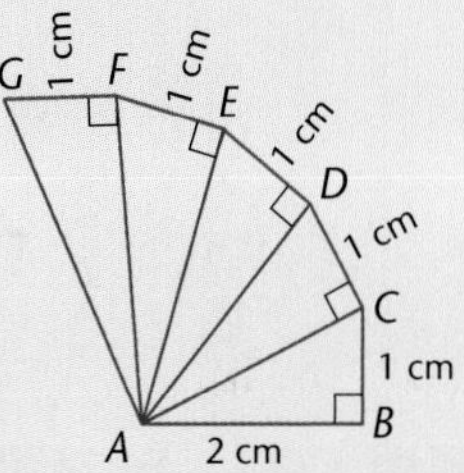

Standardized Testing ▶ Performance Task

1. The lengths of the two shortest sides of a triangle are given. What is a possible length of the third side if the triangle is acute? right? obtuse?
   a. 6 cm, 4.5 cm
   b. 2 in., $5\frac{1}{2}$ in.
2. Find the combined area of all four triangular faces of the pyramid. Assume the triangular faces are congruent.

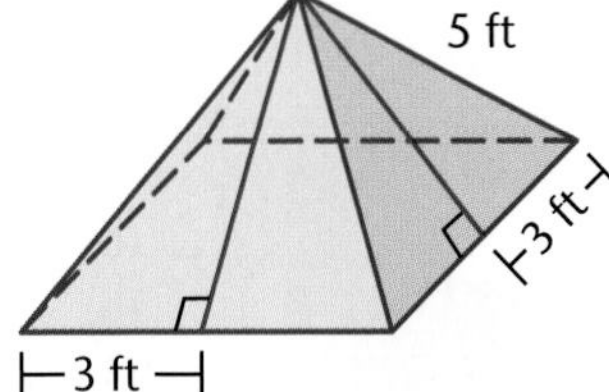

Section 4 Surface Area and Volume

In This Section

Exploration 1
- Surface Areas of Prisms and Pyramids

Exploration 2
- Volumes of Prisms, Pyramids, and Cones

Where You Live

Setting the Stage

People around the world build homes to keep them safe and comfortable in their environments. The design of the buildings and the materials used for construction depend on local conditions. In the passage below from *Black Star, Bright Dawn* by Scott O'Dell, Bright Dawn describes how she and her friends Katy and Oteg made an igloo.

Black Star, Bright Dawn

by Scott O'Dell

I had helped to make an igloo at school, so I showed her how to cut the blocks. I handed them to Oteg and he put them side by side in a circle. When he had one row, he trimmed off the top edges so that each of the blocks slanted in.

We worked until there was a circle three rows high. It was not yet an igloo, but it helped to shield us from the bitter wind. . .

At dawn we began again on the igloo. One by one Oteg added rows of blocks until they met above the top. He got down on his knees, cut a round hole in the wall, and crawled out. The cracks between the blocks were filled with soft snow. The opening at the top of the dome was closed with a piece of clear ice.

Think About It

1 Igloos have a dome shape that encloses a large volume for a given surface area.

a. What does *volume* mean? **b.** What does *surface area* mean?

c. What do volume and surface area tell you about a structure?

2 Why would it be desirable to have a large volume compared to the surface area?

Exploration 1

SURFACE AREAS of PRISMS and PYRAMIDS

GOAL

LEARN HOW TO...
- find surface areas of prisms and pyramids

AS YOU...
- explore the shape of an adobe house

KEY TERM
- regular pyramid
- slant height

SET UP *You will need: • Labsheet 4A • metric ruler • scissors*

Long ago, people did not always have a choice of building materials. In the Southwest, *adobe houses* were built from baked mud bricks because mud was usually available. Rooms of an adobe house were built roughly in the shape of a rectangular prism.

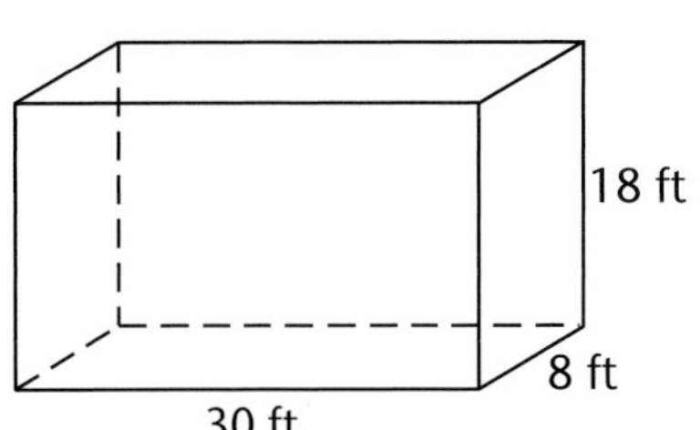

3 **a.** Sketch a net for the rectangular prism shown above. Use the dimensions shown to label the length of each edge of the net.

b. The surface area of the prism is the total area of all six faces, including the bases. Find the area of each face of the prism. Then find the surface area of the prism.

▶ **You can find the surface area (*S.A.*) of any prism by adding the areas of all the faces.**

EXAMPLE

To find the surface area of the trapezoidal prism shown, you need to use the formula $A = \frac{1}{2}(b_1 + b_2)h$ for the area A of a trapezoid with height h and base lengths b_1 and b_2.

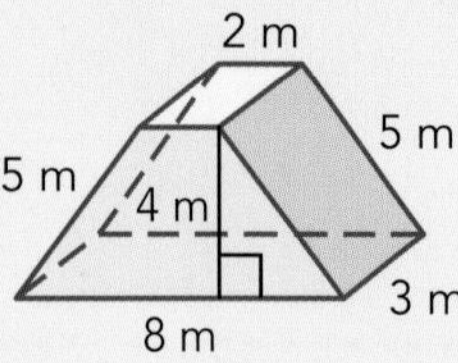

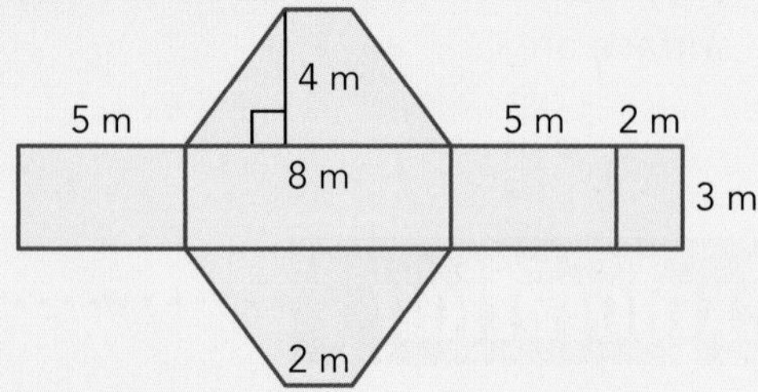

$$\begin{aligned} S.A. &= \text{areas of trapezoids} + \text{areas of rectangles} \\ &= 2\left[\frac{1}{2}(8 + 2)4\right] + (5 \cdot 3) + (8 \cdot 3) + (5 \cdot 3) + (2 \cdot 3) \\ &= 40 + 15 + 24 + 15 + 6 \\ &= 100 \end{aligned}$$

The surface area of the trapezoidal prism is 100 m^2.

4 Discussion

a. In the example, why is the figure called a trapezoidal prism?

b. How is sketching the net of a figure helpful in finding its surface area?

5 Sketch a net for each prism. Label the length of each edge.

a.

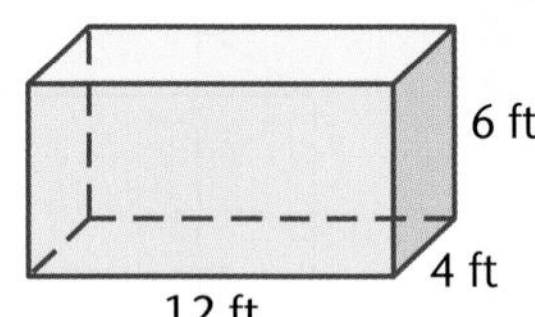

b.

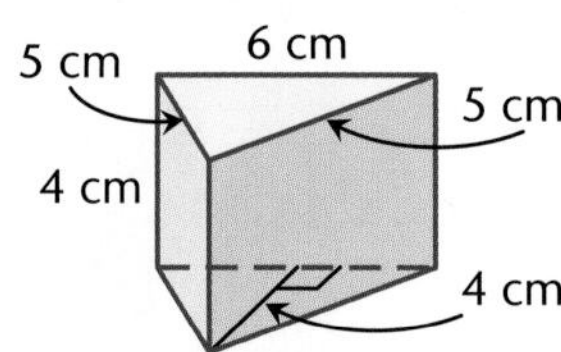

✓ QUESTION 6

...checks that you can find the surface area of a prism.

6 **✓ CHECKPOINT** Find the surface area of each prism in Question 5.

▶ **Surface Area of a Pyramid You can use a method similar to the one in the Example to find the surface area of a pyramid.**

7 **Use Labsheet 4A.** Follow the directions to make a square pyramid.

▶ **The pyramid in Question 7 is a regular pyramid, because the base is a regular polygon and its other faces are congruent isosceles triangles. The slant height of a regular pyramid is the height of a triangular face.**

8 Try This as a Class

a. How is the slant height of the pyramid different from the height of the pyramid?

b. Explain how to use the slant height of the pyramid, the length of an edge of the base, and the Pythagorean theorem to find the height of the pyramid. Then find the height.

c. Measure the height of your pyramid. How does the height you calculated in part (b) compare with your measurement?

d. Did you need the height of the pyramid to find its surface area? Explain.

▶ **The surface area of a regular pyramid can be found using the height of one of the triangular faces.**

EXAMPLE

Find the surface area of the square pyramid.

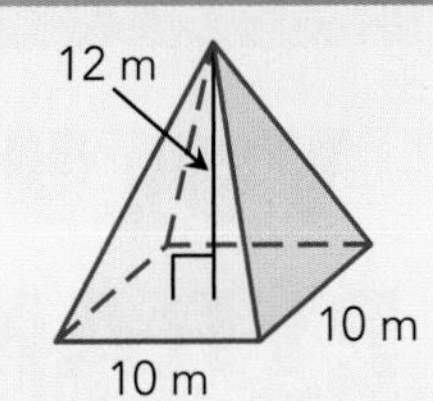

SAMPLE RESPONSE

Use the Pythagorean theorem to find the slant height, c.

$$5^2 + 12^2 = c^2$$

$$169 = c^2$$

$$13 = c$$

$$\text{S.A.} = \left(\begin{array}{c}\text{area of}\\ \text{base}\end{array}\right) + 4 \times \left(\begin{array}{c}\text{area of one}\\ \text{triangular face}\end{array}\right)$$

$$= 10 \cdot 10 + 4\left(\frac{1}{2} \cdot 10 \cdot 13\right)$$

$$= 100 + 260$$

$$= 360$$

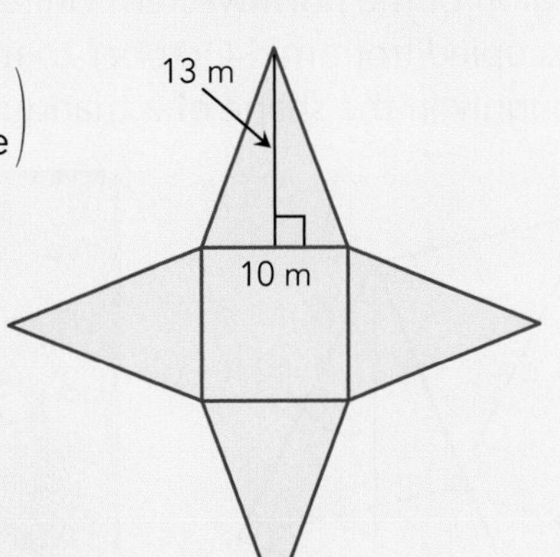

The surface area of the square pyramid is 360 m^2.

9 Discussion

a. Why is it necessary to find the slant height of the pyramid in the Example on page 351 in order to calculate the surface area of the pyramid?

b. In the Example, a right triangle is used to find the slant height of the pyramid. The length of one leg of this triangle is the height of the pyramid. Explain why the length of the other leg is 5 m.

✓ QUESTION 10

...checks that you can find the surface area of a pyramid.

10 ✓ CHECKPOINT Find the surface area of each square pyramid.

a.

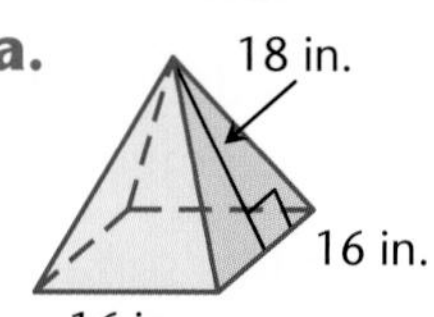

b.

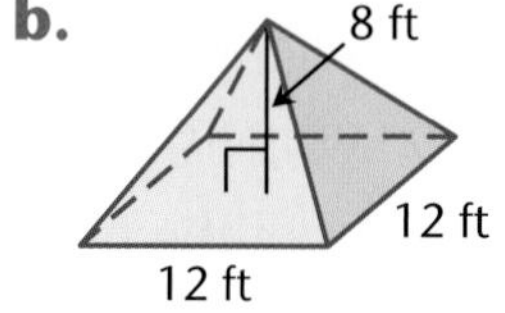

c.

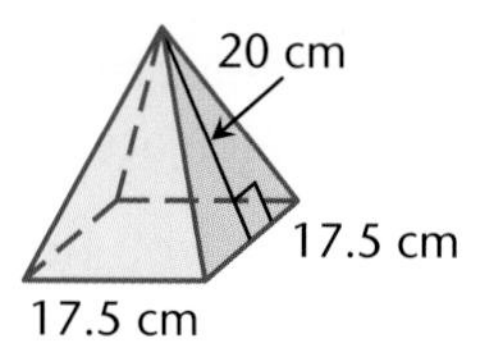

HOMEWORK EXERCISES See Exs. 1–8 on p. 357.

GOAL

LEARN HOW TO...
- find volumes of prisms, pyramids, and cones

AS YOU...
- look at models of block pyramids and prisms

KEY TERM
- circular cone

Exploration 2

VOLUMES of PRISMS, PYRAMIDS, and CONES

SET UP *You will need Labsheet 4B.*

Winter *mat houses* were once used by people living in the Plateau region of the northwestern United States. These homes were usually occupied from mid-October to mid-March. A mat house was built roughly in the shape of a triangular prism.

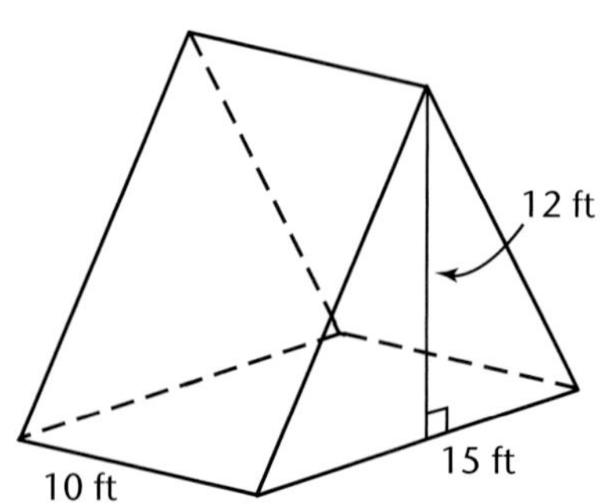

11 In Module 4 you learned how to use the formula

Volume = area of base × height, or $V = Bh$

to find the volume of a cylinder or a rectangular prism. This formula can also be used to find volumes of prisms with other bases.

a. Discussion How can you use this formula to find the volume of the triangular prism on page 352?

b. Calculate the volume of the triangular prism.

▶ **Volume of a Pyramid The Great Pyramid of Giza is made from blocks of stone. The sides are jagged, but they look smooth when viewed from afar, as if the block pyramid had straight edges and flat faces. Now you will look at block pyramids and block prisms to discover the relationship between the volume of a pyramid and the volume of a prism with the same base and height.**

Use Labsheet 4B for Questions 12–14.

12 Follow the directions on the labsheet to complete the *Table of Volumes.*

13 Look at the Volume Ratio column of the table. What patterns do you notice in the values?

14 **Discussion** If the last column of the table were continued, the ratio for the 50th entry would be 0.343 and the ratio for the 100th entry would be 0.338. What "nice" fraction do the ratios appear to be approaching?

15 **Try This as a Class** Use your answer to Question 14.

a. The volume of a prism is about how many times the volume of a pyramid that has the same base and height?

b. Using V for the volume, B for the area of the base, and h for the height, write a formula for the volume of a pyramid.

c. Use your formula from part (b) to find the volume of a pyramid that has the same base and height as the triangular prism on page 352.

16 ✓ **CHECKPOINT** Find the volume of each 3-dimensional figure.

a. triangular prism

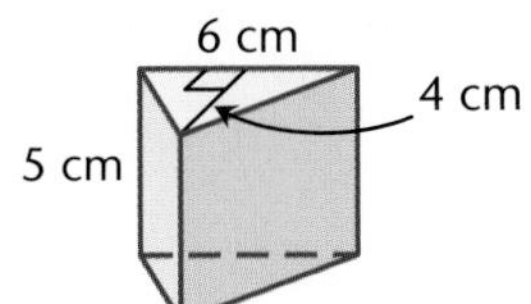

b. square pryamid

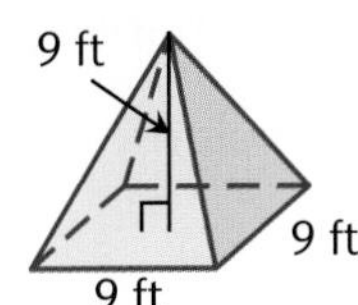

✓ **QUESTION 16**

...checks that you can find volumes of prisms and pyramids.

▶ **Volume of a Cone** **The relationship between the volume of a cone and the volume of a cylinder with the same base and height is the same as the relationship between the volume of a pyramid and the volume of a prism with the same base and height.**

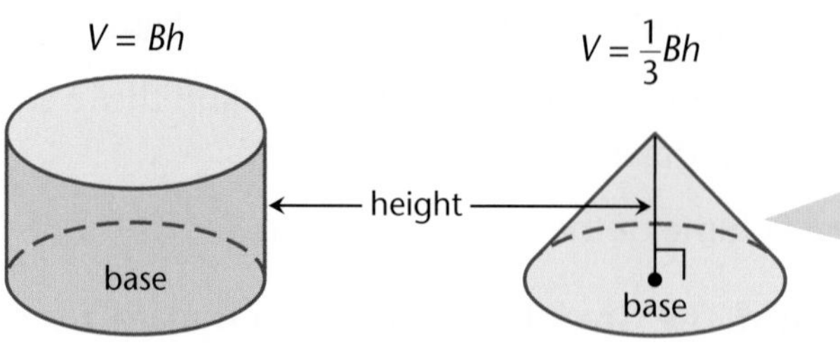

A **circular cone** is a 3-dimensional figure with a circular base and a vertex that are not in the same plane.

▶ **All the cones in this book have circular bases. You can refer to them as cones rather than as *circular cones*.**

17 **Try This as a Class**

a. How would you find the area of the base of a cone?

b. Write a formula for the volume of a cone in terms of the radius of the base *r* and the height *h*.

c. The radius of the base of a cone is 5 ft, and the height of the cone is 10 ft. Use the formula you wrote in part (b) to find the volume of the cone.

✓ QUESTION 18

...checks that you can find the volume of a cone.

18 **✓ CHECKPOINT** The shape of tepees used by Native American peoples on the Great Plains resembles a cone. A typical tepee might have stood 18 ft high and had a diameter of 15 ft at its base. Estimate the volume of such a tepee.

▶ **Most buildings are made up of a variety of 3-dimensional figures. The shape below is an alternate representation of a mat house. It is a triangular prism with half of a cone at either end.**

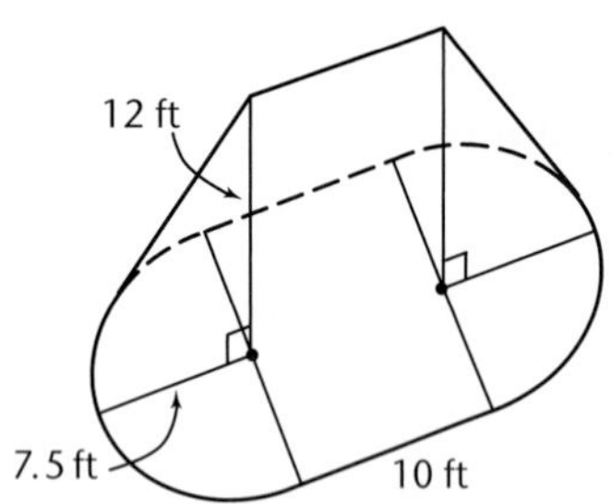

19 **a.** **Discussion** Describe how you would find the volume of a mat house shaped like the figure above.

b. Find the volume.

HOMEWORK EXERCISES See Exs. 9–21 on pp. 358–359.

Section 4 Key Concepts

Surface Areas of Prisms and Pyramids (pp. 349–352)

The surface area of a pyramid or a prism is the sum of the areas of the faces of the figure, including the base or bases. You can use a net to help you find the surface area.

Example

right square prism

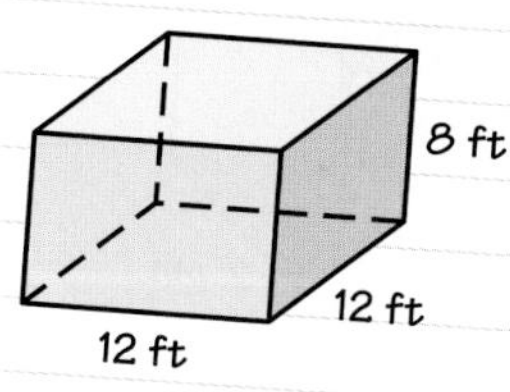

net for the prism

12 ft
B
8 ft
8 ft
8 ft
12 ft
A
C
E
F
12 ft
D

S.A. = area A + area B + area C + area D + area E + area F
$= (8 \cdot 12) + (8 \cdot 12) + (12 \cdot 12) + (8 \cdot 12) + (8 \cdot 12) + (12 \cdot 12)$
$= 96 + 96 + 144 + 96 + 96 + 144$
$= 672$

The surface area of the prism is 672 ft^2.

The base of a regular pyramid is a regular polygon, and its other faces are congruent isosceles triangles. You use the slant height of a pyramid rather than the height of the pyramid to find its surface area.

regular pyramid

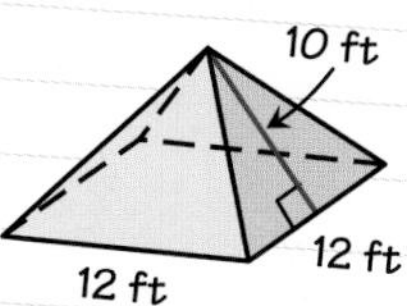

Key Terms

regular pyramid

slant height

20 Key Concepts Question

a. Find the surface area of the pyramid above.

b. If you stack the pyramid directly on top of the prism above, what will be the surface area of the new figure? Explain.

Section 4 Key Concepts

Key Term

Volumes of Prisms (p. 353)

You can use the formula Volume = area of base × height, or $V = Bh$, to find the volume of any prism. Many buildings consist of two or more 3-dimensional figures. To find the volume, you add the volumes of the parts.

Example

Volume of rectangular prism

$$V = Bh = (12 \cdot 25)18 = 5400$$

Volume of triangular prism

$$V = Bh = \left(\frac{1}{2} \cdot 12 \cdot 8\right)25 = 1200$$

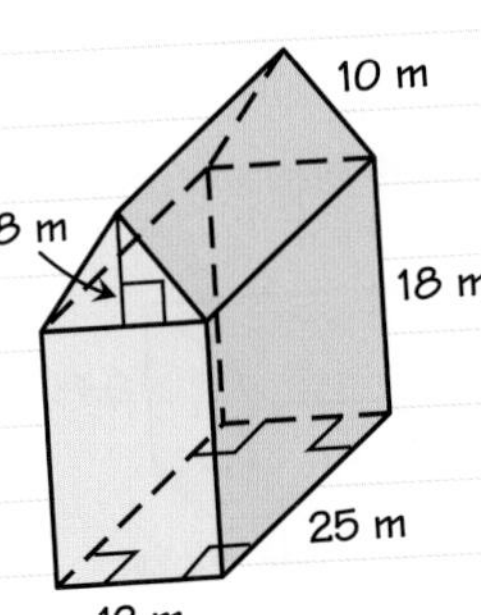

The total volume is 6600 m^3.

circular cone

Volumes of Pyramids and Cones (pp. 353–354)

The volume of a pyramid is one-third the volume of a prism with the same base and height. The volume of a cone is one-third the volume of a cylinder with the same base and height.

The formula Volume = $\frac{1}{3}$ × area of base × height, or $V = \frac{1}{3}Bh$, can be used to find the volume of a pyramid or a cone.

Example

$$V = \frac{1}{3}Bh$$

$$= \frac{1}{3} \cdot \pi r^2 \cdot h$$

$$\approx \frac{1}{3} \cdot (3.14) \cdot 3^2 \cdot 5$$

$$\approx 47.1$$

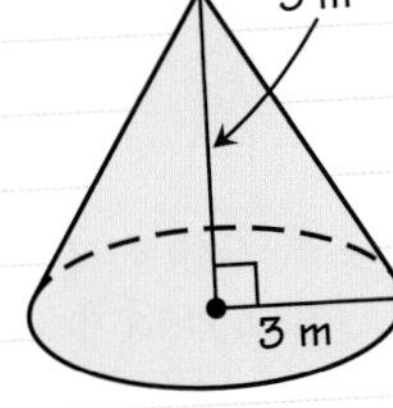

The volume of the cone is about 47.1 m^3.

21 Key Concepts Question

a. Find the volume of the prism and the volume of the pyramid on page 355.

b. If you stack the pyramid directly on top of the prism, what will be the volume of the new figure?

Section 4
Practice & Application Exercises

YOU WILL NEED

For Exs. 27–28:
- Labsheets 4C and 4D
- scissors
- paper clip

Find the surface area of each rectangular or triangular prism. Round answers to the nearest hundredth if necessary.

1. 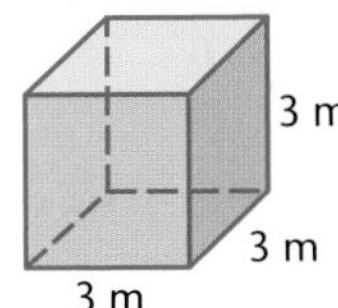

2. 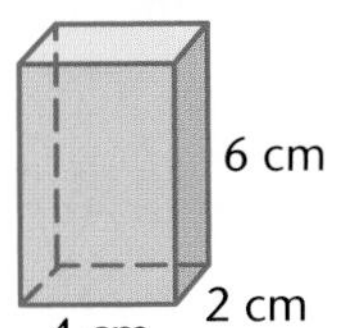

3. 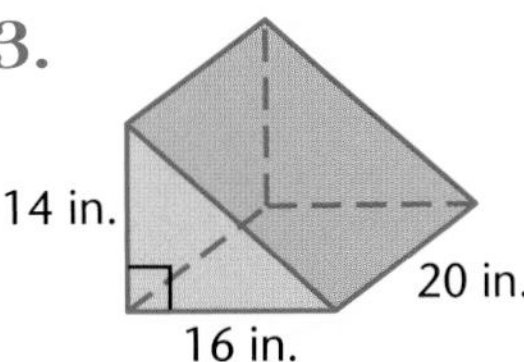

Find the surface area of each square pyramid. Round answers to the nearest hundredth if necessary.

4. 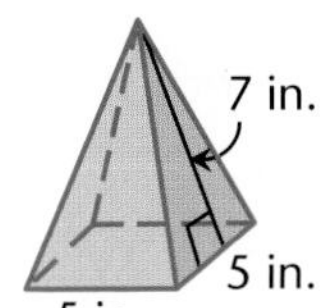

5. 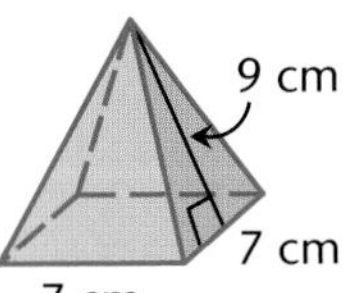

6. 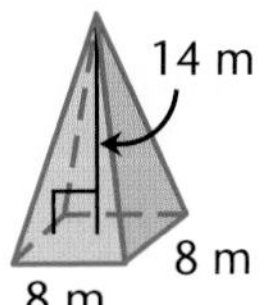

7. **Challenge** Many products are packaged in boxes that are the shape of a rectangular prism. In some cases more unusual shapes are used. A net for a box designed to hold a desk lamp is shown.
   a. Find the surface area of the box.
   b. Sketch a view of the box that looks three-dimensional.
   c. Find the volume of the box.

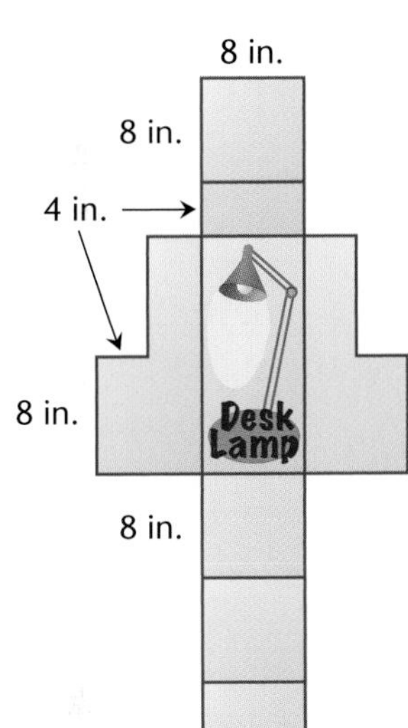

8. The figure below represents a Navajo *hogan* like the one shown in the photograph. The base is a square and the edges that form the peak of the roof are each 8 ft long.
   a What two 3-dimensional figures combine to form the figure shown?
   b. Sketch a net of the figure. Label the edges with their lengths.
   c. Find the surface area of the figure to the nearest hundredth.

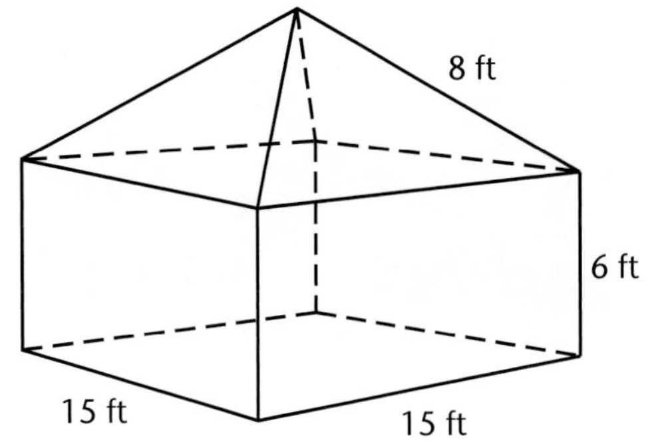

Find the volume of each pyramid or cone with the given height and base. Round answers to the nearest hundredth if necessary.

9. height = 3 in.

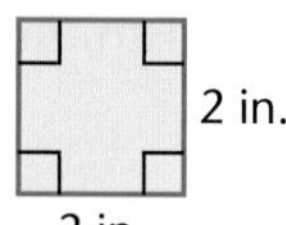

10. height = 4 cm

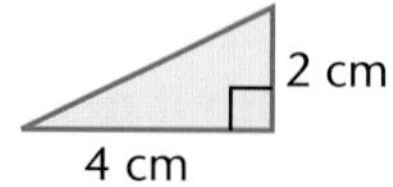

11. height = 2 m

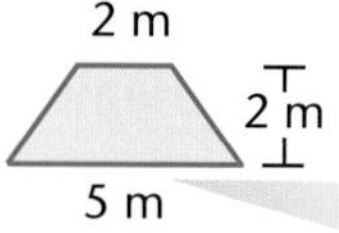

The base is a trapezoid.

12. height = 23.5 ft

13. height = 20 mm

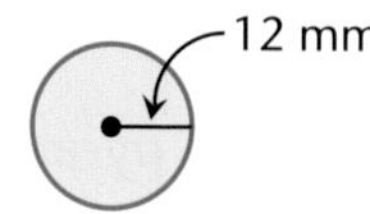

14. height = 14 yd

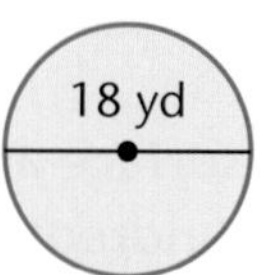

15. The diagram represents a *yurt*, which is a dwelling used by nomadic tribes. The walls of a yurt fold up, making it easy to put up and take down. It is also very weather resistant.

   a. What two 3-dimensional figures combine to form the yurt?

   b. Find the volume of the yurt in the diagram.

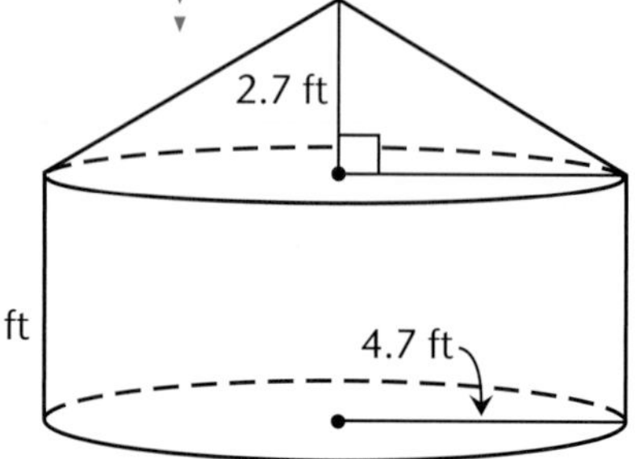

16. The Christa McAuliffe Planetarium in Concord, New Hampshire, incorporates a square pyramid in its design. Each side of the pyramid's base is 724 in. long. The height of the pyramid is 360 in.

   a. Find the volume of the pyramid.

   b. Find the total area of the triangular faces of the pyramid. Round your answer to the nearest hundredth.

Find the surface area and the volume of each composite figure.

17. 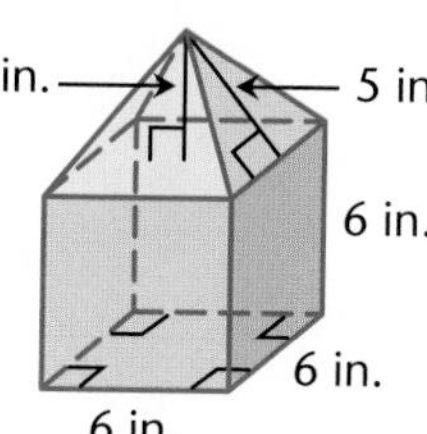

18. 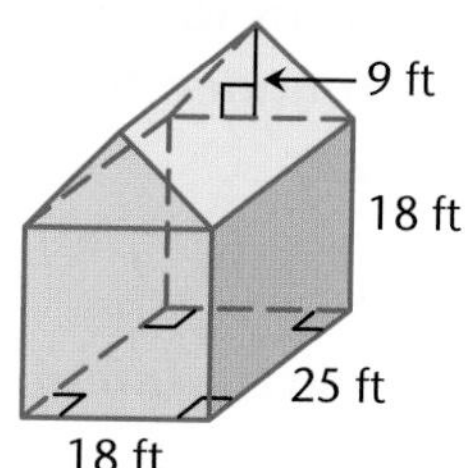

19. **Challenge** Find the surface area and the volume of the figure at the right. (*Hint*: The heights of the triangles are different.)

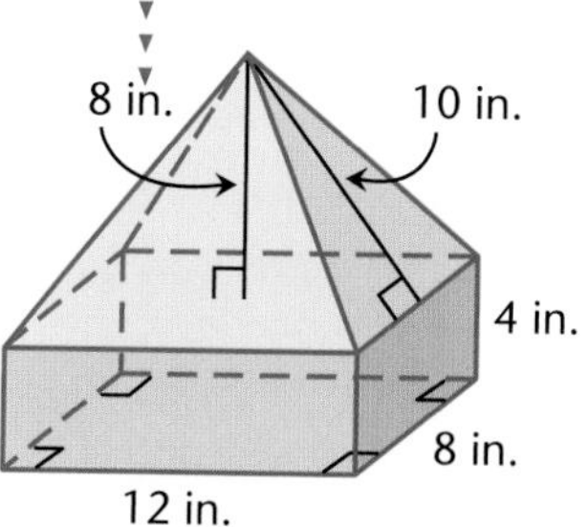

20. **Open-ended** Sketch a 3-dimensional figure made up of two or more 3-dimensional figures. Then sketch a net of the figure. Find its surface area and volume.

Reflecting on the Section

Write your response to Exercise 21 in your journal.

21. Draw a sketch of a house that you have seen. Describe how you can estimate its surface area and volume. Explain why the surface area and volume might be useful information about the house.

Journal

Exercise 21 checks that you understand surface area and volume.

Spiral Review

Tell whether the triangles in each pair are congruent. Explain your reasoning. **(Module 5, p. 330)**

22. $\triangle FED$, $\triangle RQP$

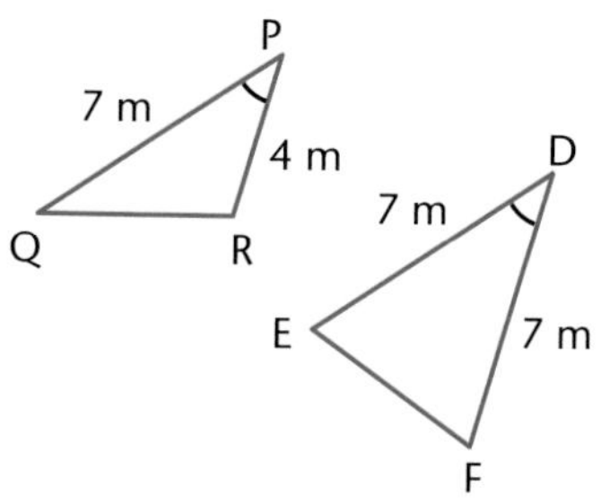

23. $\triangle WZX$, $\triangle YZX$

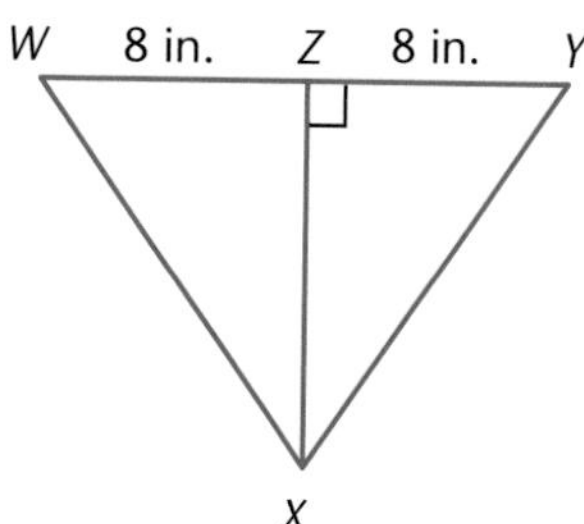

Write an equation in slope-intercept form of a line that has the given slope and *y*-intercept. **(Module 4, p. 265)**

24. slope = 3, *y*-intercept = 2

25. slope = –4, *y*-intercept = 5

The box-and-whisker plot below models 51 T-shirt prices from 18 different Internet sites. All prices are rounded to the nearest dollar. (Module 1, p. 23)

T-Shirt Prices on the Internet

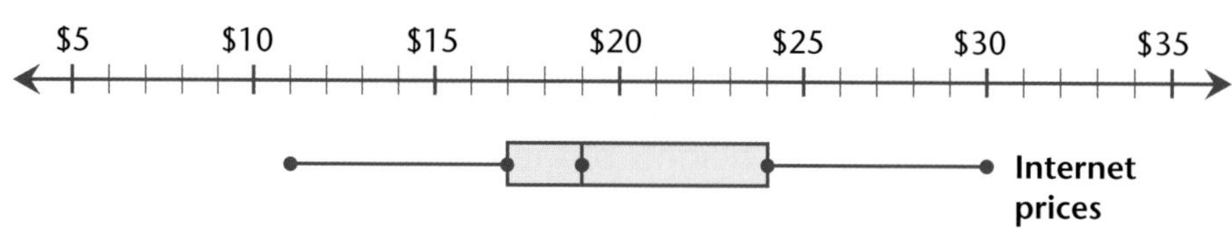

26. a. About what percent of the T-shirt prices are greater than or equal to $17?

    b. About what percent of the T-shirt prices are between the lower quartile and the upper quartile?

    c. About what percent of the prices are less than or equal to $19?

Extension 

Surface Areas of Cones

Use Labsheets 4C and 4D for Exercises 27 and 28.

27. Follow the *Pattern for a Cone* directions on Labsheet 4C to form a cone. Then find the *Dimensions of a Cone* as you complete Labsheet 4D.

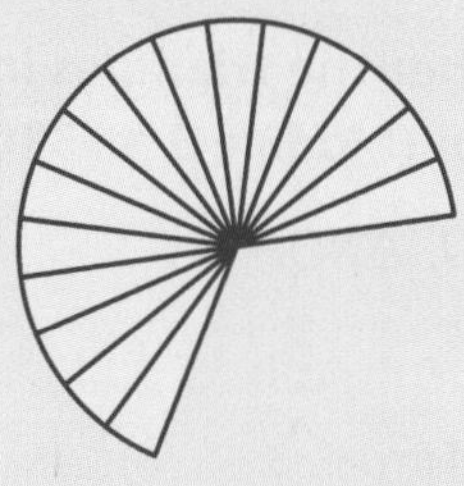

28. Suppose the partial circle from Labsheet 4C is divided into sections and they are rearranged to form a figure like a parallelogram.

    a. What is a good approximation of the height of the "parallelogram"? Why?

    b. What is a good approximation of the length of a base of the "parallelogram"? How can you tell?

    c. Use your answers from parts (a) and (b) to find an expression for the area of the "parallelogram." This expression represents the surface area of the cone, not including the circular base of the cone.

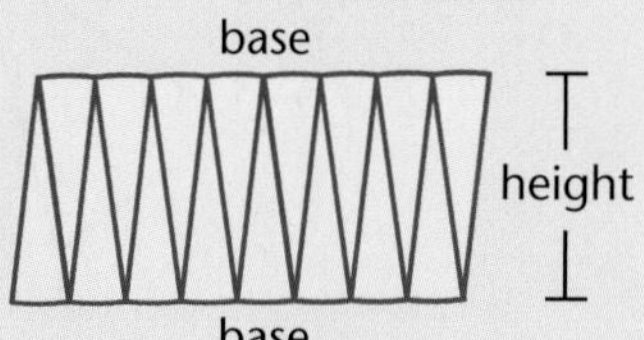

Extra Skill Practice

Find the surface area of each prism or pyramid. Round to the nearest hundredth if necessary.

1\.

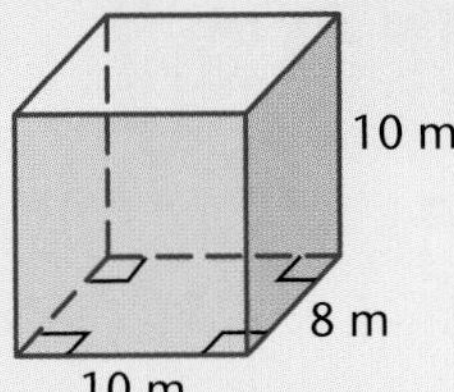

2\.

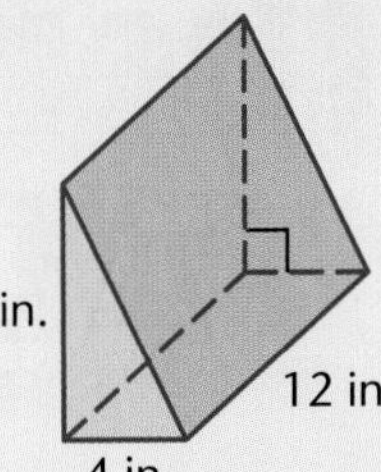

3\.

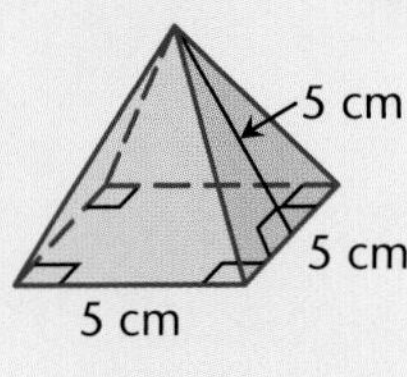

For Exercises 4 and 5, round answers to the nearest hundredth if necessary.

4. The height of a cone is 2 m and the radius of the base is 4 m. Find the volume.
5. The height of a square pyramid is 9 ft and the length of each side of the base is 0.5 ft. Find the volume.
6. The volume of a cone is $64y^3$. Find the volume of a cylinder with the same base area and height as the cone.

Find the surface area and the volume of each figure. Round answers to the nearest hundredth if necessary.

7\.

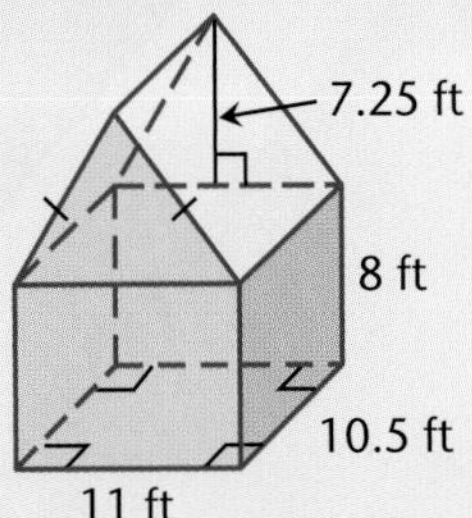

8\.

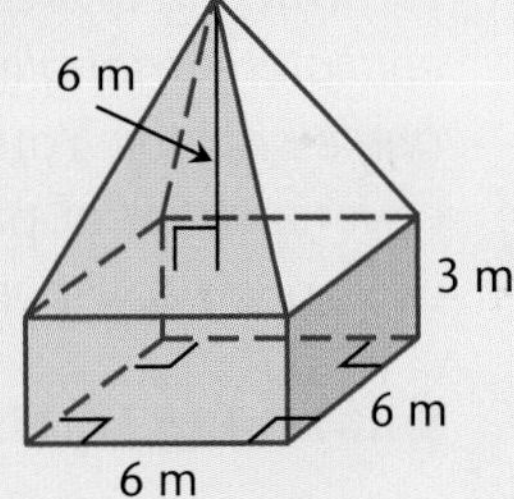

Standardized Testing ▶ Open-ended

1. Sketch a square pyramid and a square prism that have the same volume. Label the heights and the dimensions of the bases.
2. For each situation, sketch two rectangular prisms that fit the description. Label the length of each edge.
   a. The volume of one prism is three times the volume of the other.
   b. The volume of one prism is eight times the volume of the other.
   c. The surface area of one prism is twice the surface area of the other.

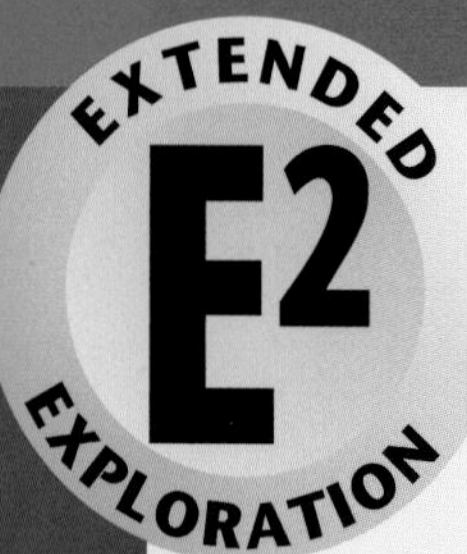

FOR ASSESSMENT AND PORTFOLIOS

Mathematical ART

SET UP *You will need: • compass • ruler • $8\frac{1}{2}$ in. by 11 in. plain paper • colored pencils or markers*

The Situation

Some very beautiful artwork is based on geometric designs. The design shown was created using a compass and the straight edge of a ruler.

The Problem

Create your own design using two or three of the following constructions: *constructing a circle, a triangle or equilateral triangle, a hexagon, or an angle bisector*. Your design should almost cover a sheet of paper, and you should use only a compass and a straightedge.

Something to Think About

- Do you want your design to be symmetrical?
- How can you make variations on the constructions you have already learned to make your designs more interesting?
- How else can you add to your design?

Present Your Results

Create a poster displaying your design. Add color if you wish. On a separate sheet of paper, describe how you used constructions to make your design. Also note anything special you used in your design that was not one of the constructions mentioned above.

Section 5 Angles Formed by Intersecting Lines

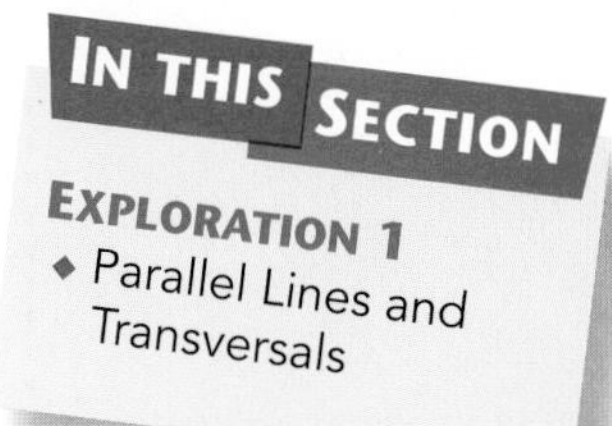

Meet Me in the MIDDLE

Setting the Stage

SET UP *Work with a partner. You will need:* • *Labsheets 5A and 5B* • *protractor* • *metric ruler*

In 1750, as part of a competition to improve trade links between France and England, an engineer proposed that a tunnel be built under the English Channel. Over 230 years later, engineering companies were bidding for the job.

The tunnel was to be built by two teams of workers: one digging from England and one digging from France. The idea was for each team to build one half of the *Chunnel*, as the English Channel Tunnel has become known. The two halves would meet in the middle.

According to Derek Wilson in his book *Breakthrough, Tunnelling the Channel,* one company submitted a very low bid to construct the Chunnel. The company was asked if it had carefully planned for the meeting of the two halves. The reply was, "Oh well, if we miss you'll get two tunnels for the price of one."

Think About It

Use Labsheets 5A and 5B for Questions 1 and 2.

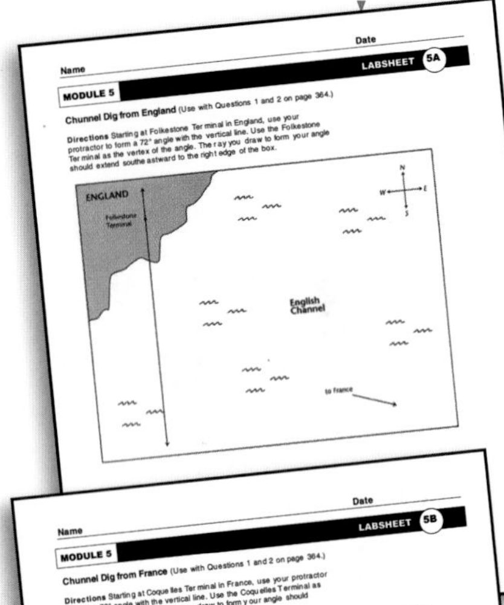

Name Date

LABSHEET 5A

MODULE 5

Chunnel Dig from England (Use with Questions 1 and 2 on page 364.)

Directions Starting at Folkestone Terminal in England, use your protractor to form a 72° angle with the vertical line. Use the Folkestone Terminal as the vertex of the angle. The ray you draw to form your angle should extend southeastward to the right edge of the box.

Name Date

LABSHEET 5B

MODULE 5

Chunnel Dig from France (Use with Questions 1 and 2 on page 364.)

Directions Starting at Coquelles Terminal in France, use your protractor to form a 72° angle with the vertical line. Use the Coquelles Terminal as the vertex of the angle. The ray you draw to form your angle should extend northwestward to the left edge of the box.

1 **a.** Work with a partner. One of you should complete the *Chunnel Dig from England* while the other completes the *Chunnel Dig from France*. Follow the directions on each labsheet to dig a portion of a mock Chunnel.

b. Fold Labsheet 5A along the right edge of the box and line up the right edge of the box with the left edge of the box on Labsheet 5B.

c. Do your two halves of the tunnel line up? If not, measure to the nearest millimeter the gap between the two ends.

2 The distance from Folkestone to Coquelles along a straight line is about 29 mi.

a. Estimate the actual distance represented by the value you found in Question 1(c).

b. In the drawings on your labsheets, 1 cm represents 1 mi. How many miles does 1 mm on the drawing represent?

c. Use the result from part (b) and your measurement from Question 1(c). Find the size, in miles, of the gap between the ends of your two tunnels. How big is the gap in feet?

FOR ▶ HELP
with *measurements and conversions,* see
TABLE OF MEASURES, p. 601
TOOLBOX, p. 581

Exploration 1

Parallel Lines AND Transversals

SET UP *Work in a group. You will need:* • *ruler* • *protractor*

GOAL

LEARN HOW TO...
- identify and find the measures of pairs of angles formed by intersecting lines

AS YOU...
- learn about the construction of the Chunnel

KEY TERMS
- supplementary, complementary angles
- supplement, complement
- transversal
- alternate interior, alternate exterior, vertical, corresponding angles

▶ **In the Chunnel Dig activity you completed, you did not have precision equipment to line up the two tunnels. The following questions will help you see why the tunnels would meet if precise measurements could be made.**

3 The angle that the tunnel makes with the north-south line drawn at the Folkestone Terminal can be described as 72° *east of south.*

a. How many degrees east of north is the tunnel? Answer this question by measuring the angle on Labsheet 5A.

b. Explain how you can obtain the measure of the angle in part (a) *without* using a protractor by recognizing that the north-south line creates a straight angle.

c. Using the phrases *west of north* and *west of south*, give two ways to describe the angle that the tunnel makes with the north-south line drawn at the Coquelles Terminal in France.

▶ **In Question 3, you found pairs of supplementary angles. Two angles whose measures have a sum of 180° are supplementary angles. Each angle is a supplement of the other angle.**

4. Two of the angles below are supplementary. Name these angles.

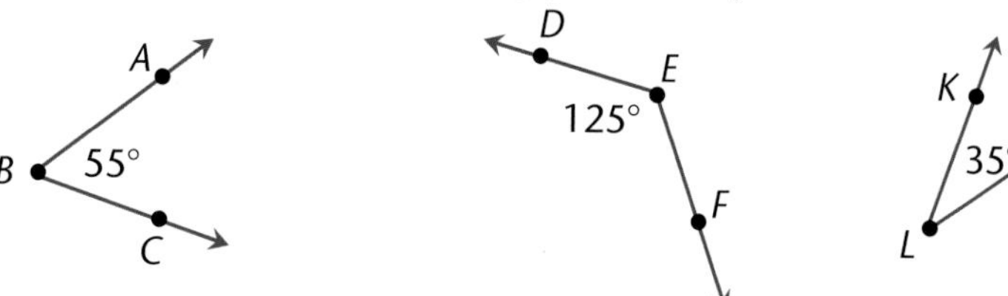

5 ✓ **CHECKPOINT** Suppose $\angle P$ and $\angle R$ are supplementary. If $m\angle P = 82°$, what is $m\angle R$?

✓ **QUESTION 5**

...checks that you can find the supplement of an angle.

6 In the Chunnel Dig activity, suppose that east-west lines were also drawn at the terminals in England and France.

a. Measure the angle that the tunnel makes with an east-west line drawn at Folkestone Terminal in England. Describe the angle using the phrase *south of east.*

b. How is the angle in part (a) related to the angle 72° east of south?

c. *Without* using a protractor, determine the measure of the angle that the tunnel makes with an east-west line drawn at Coquelles Terminal in France. Then describe the angle using the phrase *north of west.*

▶ **In Question 6, you found pairs of *complementary angles.* Two angles whose measures have a sum of 90° are complementary angles. Each angle is a complement of the other angle.**

✓ QUESTION 7

...checks that you can find the complement of an angle.

7 ✓ CHECKPOINT Find the complement of each angle.

a. 22° **b.** 50° **c.** 18° **d.** 84°

8. A **transversal** is a line that intersects two or more lines in a plane at separate points. In the diagram, line *t* is a transversal of lines *m* and *n*.

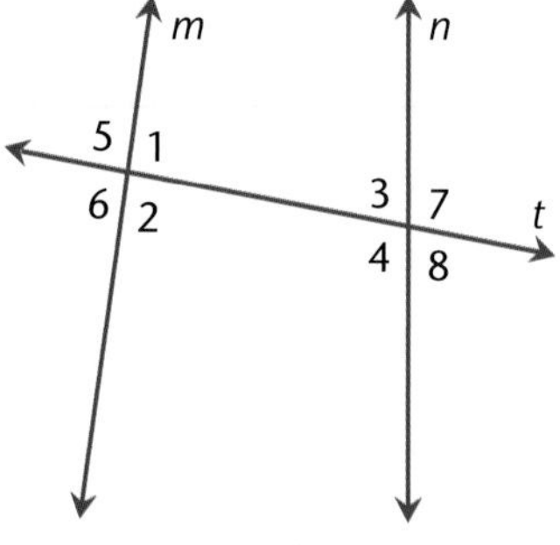

a. Angles 1 and 4 are **alternate interior angles**. Angles 6 and 7 are *not* alternate interior angles. Identify another pair of alternate interior angles.

b. Angles 6 and 7 are **alternate exterior angles**. How does this name describe the location of the angles?

c. Identify another pair of alternate exterior angles.

9 Discussion Use a ruler and a protractor.

a. Draw a pair of parallel lines cut by a transversal. Measure the angles formed.

b. What do you notice about pairs of alternate interior angles?

c. What do you notice about pairs of alternate exterior angles?

d. Compare your results with those of other group members.

e. Repeat parts (a)–(d) with nonparallel lines. What do you notice?

10 **Try This as a Class** Suppose two lines are cut by a transversal.

a. What can you conclude about the measures of the alternate interior angles?

b. What seems to be true about the measures of the alternate exterior angles?

11 **Discussion** Lines *p* and *q* in the diagram are parallel.

a. Describe what vertical angles are.

b. Give three examples of vertical angles.

c. Describe what corresponding angles are.

d. Give three examples of corresponding angles.

$\angle 4$ and $\angle 6$ are **vertical angles.**

$\angle 5$ and $\angle 7$ are **corresponding angles.**

Arrowheads indicate parallel lines.

12 **Try This as a Class** Use the diagram in Question 11.

a. What relationship do you think exists between vertical angles formed by intersecting lines?

b. What relationship do you think exists between corresponding angles formed when parallel lines are cut by a transversal?

▶ **Angle Measures You can use the relationships between pairs of angles, including supplementary angles, to find measures of angles formed when parallel lines are cut by a transversal.**

13 **Discussion** Use the diagram in Question 11. Suppose $m\angle 6$ is 56°. Explain how to find each angle measure.

a. $m\angle 5$ **b.** $m\angle 2$ **c.** $m\angle 8$

14 ✓ **CHECKPOINT** Use the diagram at the right.

a. Name all the pairs of alternate interior angles, alternate exterior angles, vertical angles, and corresponding angles.

b. Suppose lines *p* and *n* are parallel and $m\angle 1$ is 60°. Find $m\angle 8$, $m\angle 5$, and $m\angle 4$.

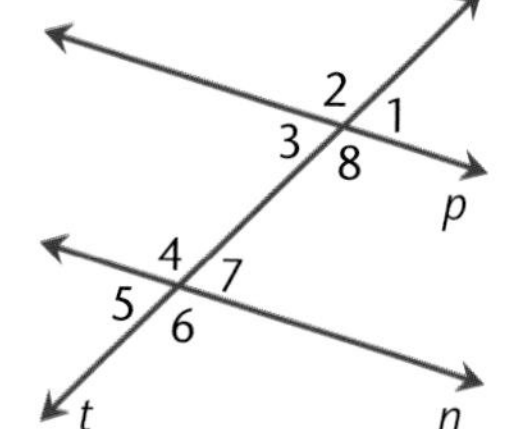

✓ **QUESTION 14**

...checks that you can identify and find the measures of pairs of angles formed by intersecting lines.

HOMEWORK EXERCISES ▶ **See Exs. 1–37 on pp. 369–371.**

Section 5 Key Concepts

Key Terms

Supplementary and Complementary Angles (pp. 365–366)

supplementary angles

complementary angles

Two angles whose measures have a sum of 180° are supplementary angles. Two angles whose measures have a sum of 90° are complementary angles.

Examples

supplement

$\angle LKN$ is a supplement of $\angle NKP$.

complement

$\angle MKN$ is a complement of $\angle NKP$.

Intersecting Lines and Transversals (pp. 366–367)

vertical angles

When two lines intersect they form four angles. Angles that have the same vertex and whose sides are opposite rays are vertical angles, and they are always congruent.

$\angle 1 \cong \angle 3$, so $m\angle 1 = m\angle 3$. $\angle 2 \cong \angle 4$, so $m\angle 2 = m\angle 4$.

transversal

A transversal is a line that intersects two or more lines in a plane at separate points. When two lines are cut by a transversal, various angles are formed.

alternate interior angles

- **Alternate interior angles** are between the two lines and are on opposite sides of the transversal.

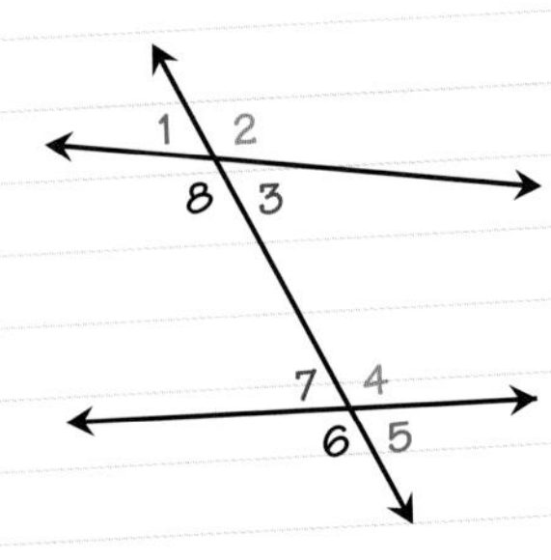

alternate exterior angles

- **Alternate exterior angles** are outside of the two lines and are on opposite sides of the transversal.

corresponding angles

- **Corresponding angles** are in the same position with respect to two lines and a transversal.

15 Key Concepts Question

a. Which two angles in $\triangle ABC$ are complements?

b. What is the measure of $\angle B$?

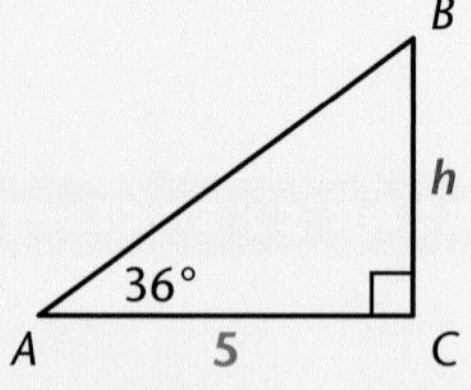

Section 5 Key Concepts

Parallel Lines and Transversals (pp. 366–367)

When parallel lines are cut by a transversal, there are special relationships among the angles formed.

- Alternate interior angles are congruent.
  $m\angle 3 = m\angle 7$ $\quad m\angle 4 = m\angle 8$
- Alternate exterior angles are congruent.
  $m\angle 1 = m\angle 5$ $\quad m\angle 2 = m\angle 6$
- Corresponding angles are congruent.
  $m\angle 2 = m\angle 4$ $\quad m\angle 3 = m\angle 5$
  $m\angle 1 = m\angle 7$ $\quad m\angle 6 = m\angle 8$

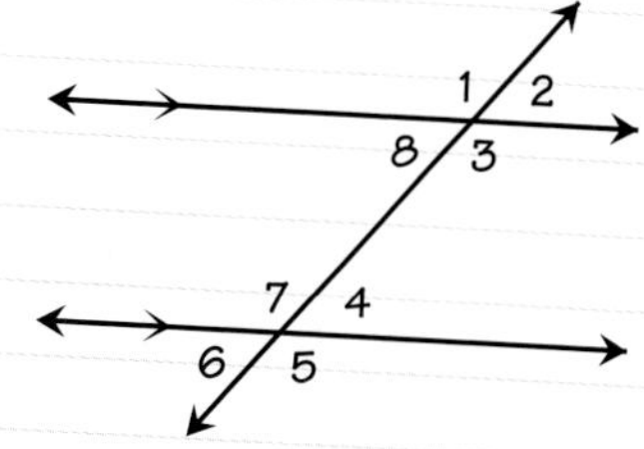

16 **Key Concepts Question** Use the parallel lines diagram above. Suppose the measure of $\angle 8$ is 50°. What is the measure of $\angle 2$? of $\angle 6$? of $\angle 4$? Explain.

Section 5 Practice & Application Exercises

Mental Math **Use mental math to find the supplement of each angle.**

1. 60°
2. 132°
3. 90°
4. 18°
5. 45°
6. 24°
7. 120°
8. 98°

Mental Math **Use mental math to find the complement of each angle.**

9. 63°
10. 19°
11. 48°
12. 81°
13. 12°
14. 22°
15. 36°
16. 74°

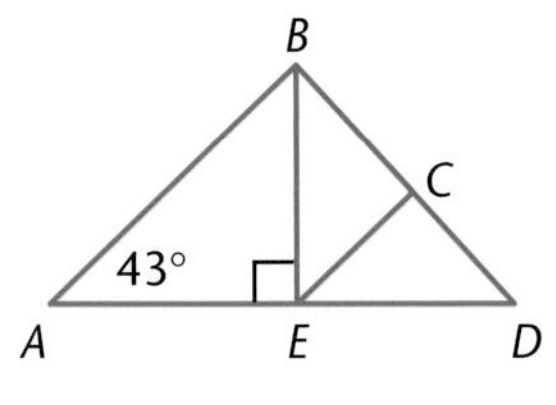

Use the diagram at the left for Exercises 17–19.

17. Name an angle that is a supplement of $\angle AEC$.

18. Name an angle that is a complement of $\angle BEC$.

19. Name an angle that is a supplement of $\angle BCE$.

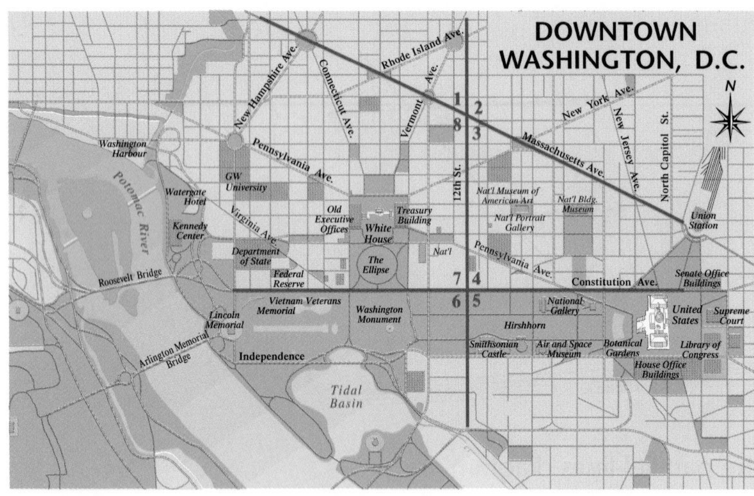

The map shows part of the street layout of Washington, D.C. In the diagram, 12th St. is a transversal of Massachusetts Ave. and Constitution Ave. Replace each ? with the correct angle.

20. $\angle 2$ and ? are vertical angles.

21. $\angle 6$ and ? are corresponding angles.

22. $\angle 3$ and ? are alternate interior angles.

23. $\angle 5$ and ? are alternate exterior angles.

In the diagram, line p is parallel to line q and line r is parallel to line s. Find each angle measure.

24. $m\angle 7$

25. $m\angle 5$

26. $m\angle 4$

27. $m\angle 6$

28. $m\angle 1$

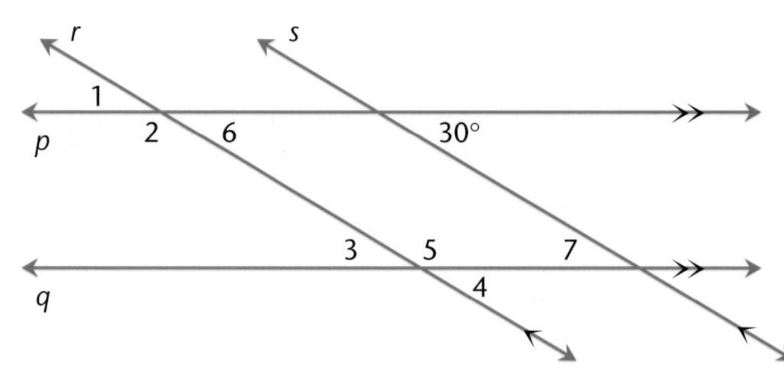

For Exercises 29–31, use the diagram below. Lines m and n are parallel.

29. Find the measures of angles 1–6.

30. What is the sum of the measures of angles 1 and 2?

31. What is the sum of the measures of angles 5 and 6?

32. **Writing** Lines p and q are parallel. Use the relationships between supplementary angles and between corresponding angles to explain why $m\angle 4 = m\angle 8$.

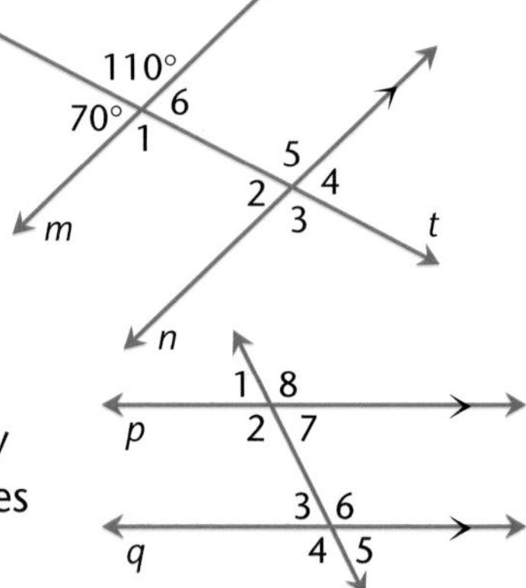

33. **Algebra Connection** Line *m* and line *n* are parallel. What is the value of *x*? What is the value of *y*? Explain your reasoning.

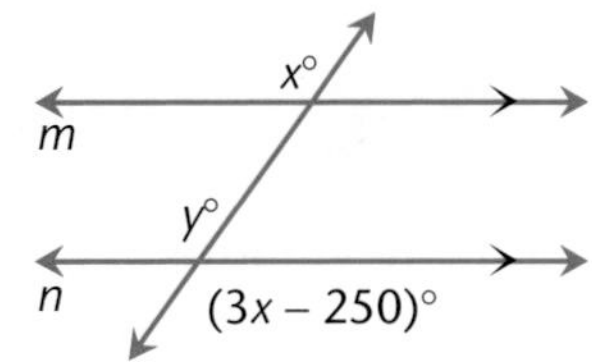

Algebra Connection For Exercises 34 and 35, write and solve an equation to find the value of each variable.

34.

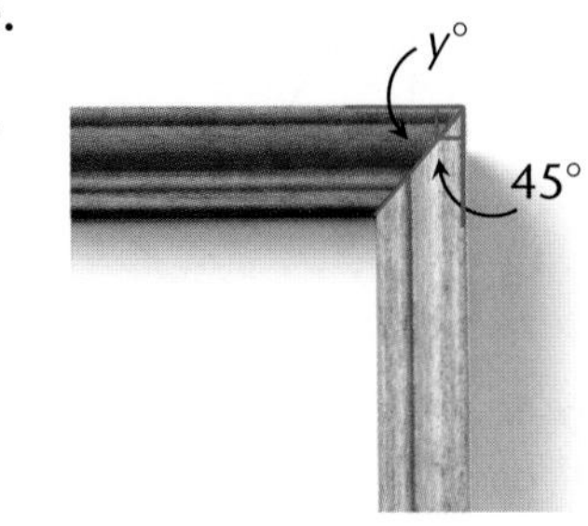

35.

36. **Challenge** In the 3rd century B.C., Eratosthenes used the fact that sunbeams are parallel to estimate Earth's circumference. At noon on the summer solstice, Eratosthenes measured the shadow cast by a pole in Alexandria. He knew that at noon the sun would be directly over Syene and would cast no shadow there.

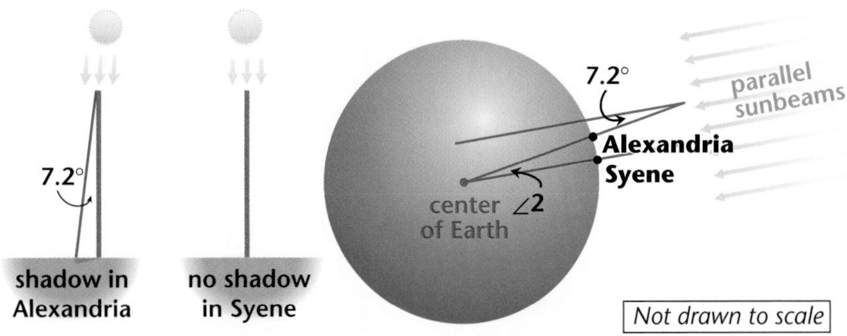

a. What is the measure of $\angle 2$ in the diagram? Explain.

b. Eratosthenes believed the distance between Alexandria and Syene was 5000 *stades*, or about 575 mi. Use this distance to estimate Earth's circumference in miles. Explain your method.

Reflecting on the Section

Be prepared to discuss your response to Exercise 37 in class.

37. A highway is to be built to join Town A and Town B. If road *r* is parallel to road *s*, are the measures of the angles correctly labeled? Explain why or why not.

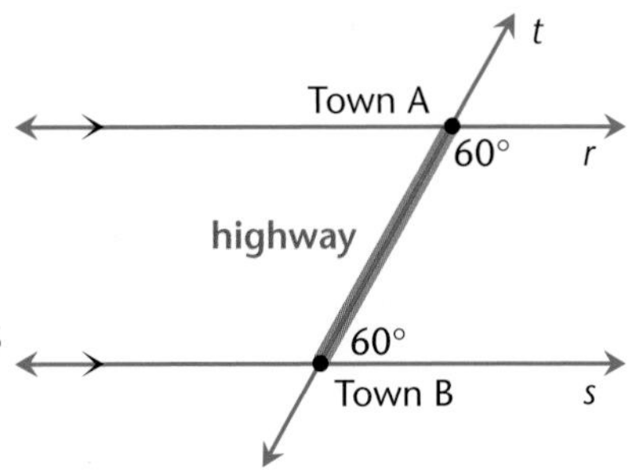

Discussion

Exercise 37 checks that you understand the relationships between pairs of angles formed by a transversal.

Spiral Review

Find the volume of each circular cone or regular pyramid. Round answers to the nearest hundredth if necessary. (Module 5, p. 356)

38. 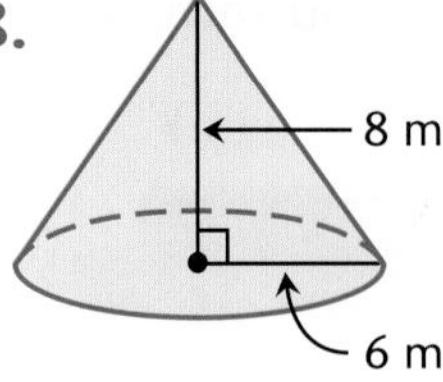

39. 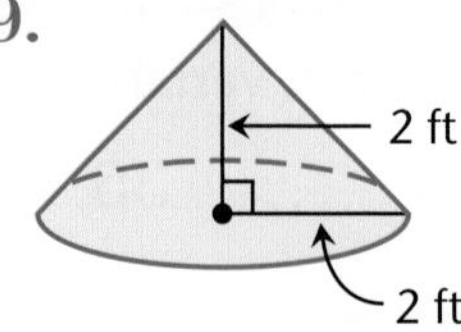

40. 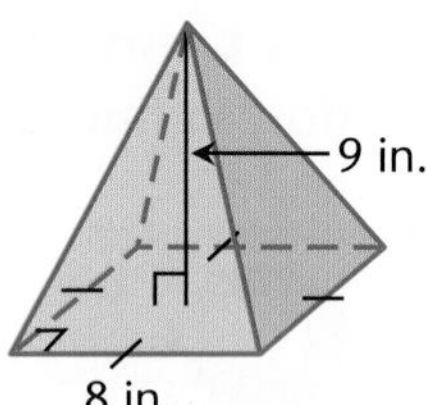

Copy and complete each equation. (Table of Measures, p. 601; Toolbox, p. 581)

41. 28 in. = __?__ ft
42. 1.5 mi = __?__ ft
43. 3 yd = __?__ in.
44. 36 mm = __?__ cm
45. 248 cm = __?__ m
46. 2.6 km = __?__ m

Career Connection

Surveyor: Wendy Lathrop

You have learned that if two parallel lines are cut by a transversal, then alternate interior angles are congruent. It is also true that if two lines are cut by a transversal and alternate interior angles are congruent, then the two lines are parallel. Surveyor Wendy Lathrop has used this second fact while surveying boundary lines.

47. The diagram shows how Wendy Lathrop would construct angles to survey around several objects.
    a. What is the relationship between line *AB* and line *CD*? Explain your reasoning.
    b. In order to project line *AB* beyond the tree through point *E*, what must the measure of ∠*DEF* be?

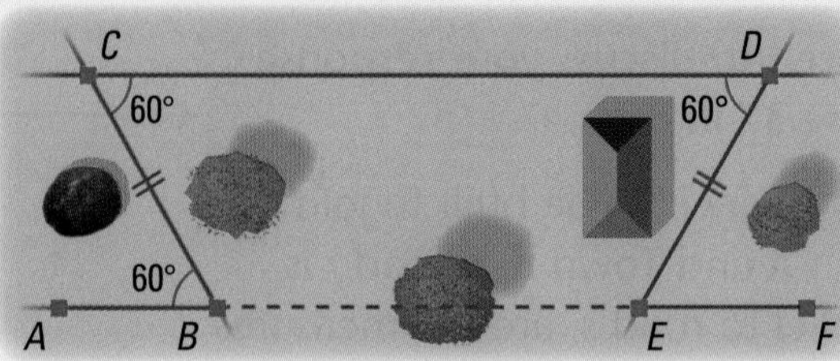

Section 5 Extra Skill Practice

Find the supplement of each angle.

1. 102°
2. 81°
3. 152°
4. 13°

Find the complement of each angle.

5. 8°
6. 27°
7. 58°
8. 89°

For Exercises 9–13, use the diagram.

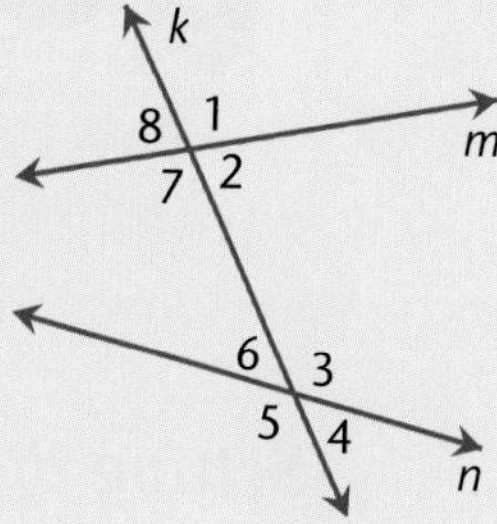

9. Is line *k* a transversal? Explain.
10. Identify each pair of vertical angles.
11. Identify each pair of corresponding angles.
12. Identify each pair of alternate interior angles.
13. Identify each pair of alternate exterior angles.

In the diagram, line *k* is parallel to line *p*. Find each measure.

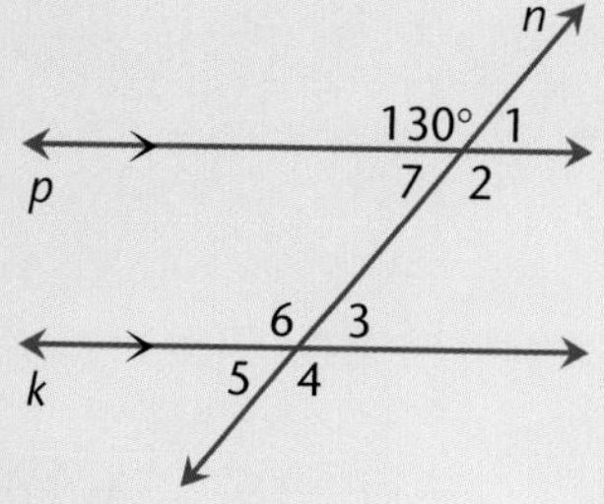

14. $m\angle 1$
15. $m\angle 7$
16. $m\angle 6$
17. $m\angle 5$
18. $m\angle 3$

Standardized Testing ▶ Multiple Choice

1. Line *n* is parallel to line *k*. Lines *p* and *q* are transversals that intersect at a point on line *n*. Which of the following statements is not true?

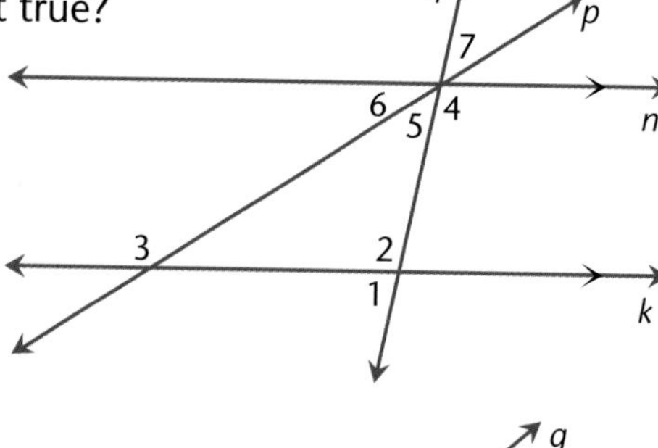

   A. $m\angle 2 = m\angle 4$
   B. $m\angle 1 = 180° - m\angle 2$
   C. $m\angle 6 = m\angle 7$
   D. $m\angle 1 = m\angle 5 + m\angle 6$

2. Line *n* is parallel to line *k* and line *q* is a transversal. If $m\angle 1 = 40°$ and $m\angle 2 = 75°$, what is $m\angle 3$?

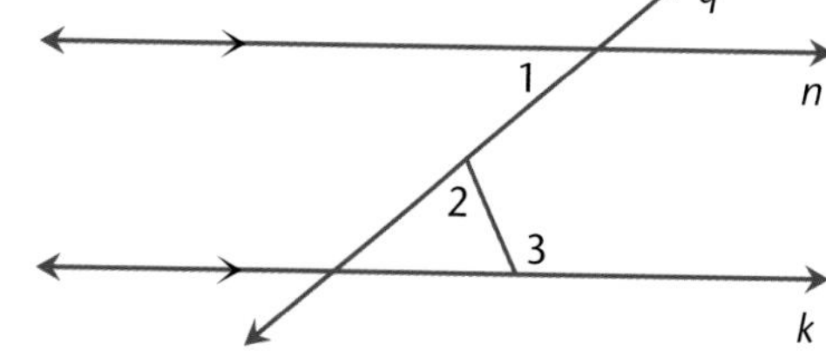

   A. 65°
   B. 115°
   C. 140°
   D. 75°

Scale Drawing and Similar Figures

IN THIS SECTION

EXPLORATION 1
- Scale Drawings

EXPLORATION 2
- Perimeters and Areas of Similar Figures

BUILDING MODELS

Setting the Stage

An architect designing a building will draw a floor plan to show the rooms of the building in proportion to one another. You may have used such a floor plan to help locate an exhibit in a museum, a store in a mall, or even a classroom in your school. The floor plan below is for the first floor of the Cesar Chavez Elementary School in Chicago, Illinois.

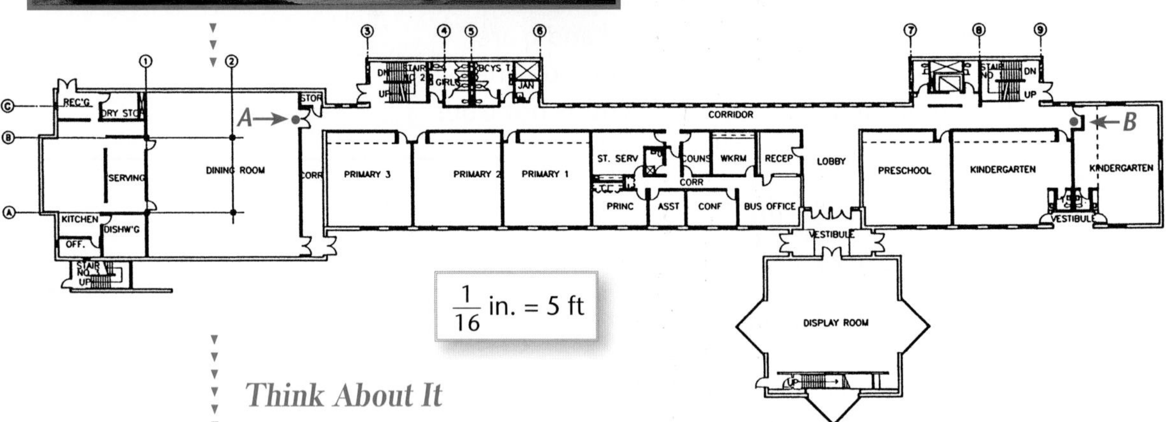

Think About It

1 How does the plan designate a doorway?

2 How many feet are represented by 1 in. on the drawing?

3 Estimate the length of the long corridor from the dining room to the kindergarten at the other end of the building, that is from *A* to *B*.

Exploration 1

SCALE DRAWINGS

GOAL

LEARN HOW TO...
- make a scale drawing

AS YOU...
- measure and draw your classroom

KEY TERM
- scale

SET UP *Work in a group. You will need: • Labsheet 6A • ruler • tape measure • plain or graph paper*

▶ **The floor plan on page 374 is an example of a *scale drawing* with a *scale* of 1 in. to 80 ft. The scale is the ratio of a length in the drawing to the corresponding length in the actual school.**

To make a scale drawing, you need to choose a scale and convert the actual measurements to those for the drawing. You will practice these skills by making scale drawings of your desktop and your classroom.

EXAMPLE

Students in Rosa's class were asked to measure the length and width of their rectangular desktops and make scale drawings that would fit on a 4 in. by 6 in. card.

Step 1 Rosa measured the length and width of her desktop and labeled a sketch of the desktop with the actual measurements. Rosa's school desktop measured 24 in. by 18 in.

Step 2 She used the scale of $\frac{1}{2}$ in. to 3 in. for her scale drawing.

Step 3 Rosa set up proportions to find the length x in inches and width y in inches for the scale drawing of her desktop.

$$\begin{matrix}\text{length in drawing} \rightarrow \\ \text{actual length} \rightarrow\end{matrix} \frac{x}{24} = \frac{\left(\frac{1}{2}\right)}{3} \text{ and } \frac{y}{18} = \frac{\left(\frac{1}{2}\right)}{3} \begin{matrix}\leftarrow \text{length in drawing} \\ \leftarrow \text{actual length}\end{matrix}$$

4 **Discussion** Use the information in the Example.

a. What do the measures $\frac{1}{2}$ in. and 3 in. in the scale represent?

b. Why do you think Rosa chose a scale of $\frac{1}{2}$ in. to 3 in. for her scale?

▶ **Rosa could have used equivalent fractions or cross products to solve the proportions for the length and width of the desktop in her scale drawing.**

EXAMPLE

Rosa's desktop is 24 in. long and 18 in. wide. The scale she selected for the scale drawing of her desktop was $\frac{1}{2}$ in. to 3 in. Solve the proportion to find the length of the desktop in her scale drawing.

length in drawing → $\frac{x}{24} = \frac{\left(\frac{1}{2}\right)}{3}$ ← actual length

Use Equivalent Fractions or **Use Cross Products**

Use Equivalent Fractions:

$$\frac{x}{24} = \frac{\left(\frac{1}{2}\right)}{3} \quad (\times 8)$$

$$x = \frac{1}{2} \cdot 8$$

$$x = 4 \text{ in.}$$

Use Cross Products:

$$\frac{x}{24} = \frac{\left(\frac{1}{2}\right)}{3}$$

$$3x = \frac{1}{2} \cdot 24$$

$$3x = 12$$

$$x = 4 \text{ in.}$$

In the scale drawing, the length of her desktop was 4 in.

5 **a.** In the equivalent fractions example above, why is $\frac{1}{2}$ multiplied by 8?

b. Use one of the methods in the Example to find the width of the desktop in Rosa's scale drawing.

c. Did her drawing fit on the card?

▶ **Before making a scale drawing of her classroom, Rosa made a sketch of the floor plan. She included the door, her desk, and a table on the sketch since she wanted to show them on her scale drawing.**

Next she measured the length and width of the classroom and the locations of the door, her desk, and the table and recorded the measurements. Her partially completed measurements table is shown on Labsheet 6A.

Then she chose an appropriate scale and used it to find the measurements for the scale drawing and recorded them in the measurements table. Finally, using the measurements in her table, she drew the scale drawing shown on Labsheet 6A.

6 **Use Labsheet 6A.**

a. Complete Rosa's table of measurements for her scale drawing.

b. Based on Rosa's scale drawing, about how far is the actual distance from the center of the doorway to the center of the front edge of the table?

▶ **Before you make a scale drawing that includes any of the features of your classroom, make a sketch and label it with the actual measurements.**

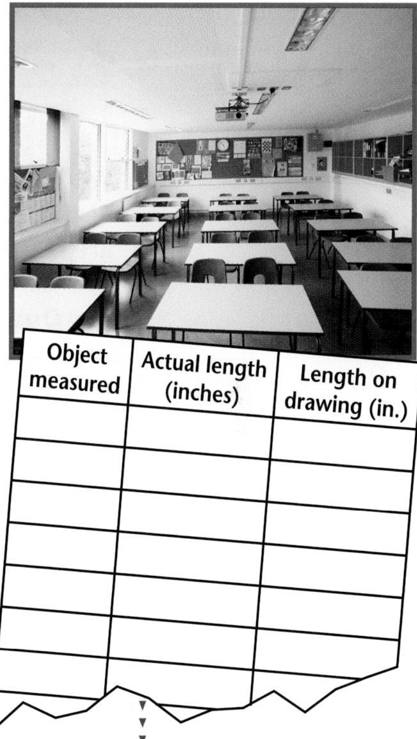

Object measured	Actual length (inches)	Length on drawing (in.)

7 **Try This as a Class** You will be making a scale drawing of your classroom on an $8\frac{1}{2}$ in. by 11 in. piece of paper. Think about the size of your classroom and what it contains.

a. Copy the table. To the nearest inch, measure the length of each wall of your classroom, the dimensions and location of your desk, any doors, and one other feature. Record the actual measurements in the table.

b. Select an appropriate scale and use it to find the measurements for the scale drawing. Record your answers in the table.

c. Make a scale drawing of your classroom using the measurements you found in part (b).

8 **Discussion** Compare your scale drawing with those of your classmates.

a. Do all the drawings use the same scale?

b. Do they all look the same? Why or why not?

9 Pick a feature in your classroom such as a tabletop, a door, or a window.

a. What would be the dimensions of the feature in a scale drawing with a scale of 2 in. to 1 ft?

b. Is this a good scale to use? Why or why not?

10 ✓ **CHECKPOINT** Make a scale drawing of one wall of your classroom. Include at least one feature and the scale.

...checks that you can make a scale drawing.

HOMEWORK EXERCISES ▶ **See Exs. 1–8 on p 382.**

GOAL

LEARN ABOUT..

- relationships between perimeters and areas of two similar figures

AS YOU...

- find the perimeter and the area of your classroom floor

Exploration 2

PERIMETERS and AREAS of SIMILAR FIGURES

SET UP *Work with a partner. You will need: • scale drawings and classroom measurements from Exploration 1 • ruler*

▶ **You can use the scale on a drawing to find the perimeter and the area of the actual figure if you know how the perimeters of similar objects are related and how the areas are related.**

For Questions 11–13, use the table below.

	Measurement on scale drawing (in inches or square inches)	Actual measurement (in inches or square inches)	Ratio of measurement on scale drawing to actual measurement
length of front wall	?	?	?
length of back wall	?	?	?
length of right wall	?	?	?
length of left wall	?	?	?
perimeter of classroom floor	?	?	?
area of classroom floor	?	?	?

11 Copy the table. Use the measurements of your classroom and your scale drawing from Question 7 on page 377 to complete the first four rows of the table.

12 **a.** Find the perimeter of your scale drawing and the perimeter of your actual classroom floor.

b. Find the ratio of the perimeters. What do you notice?

13 **a.** Find the area of your scale drawing and the area of your actual classroom floor.

b. Find the ratio of the areas. What do you notice?

14 **Try This as a Class** Use your answers to Questions 12 and 13.

a. How is the perimeter of a scale drawing related to the actual perimeter?

b. How is the drawing's area related to the actual area?

▶ **You can use what you have learned about the relationship between perimeters and areas of similar figures to find unknown measurements.**

EXAMPLE

$\triangle ABC$ is similar to $\triangle DEF$. Use the information in the diagram to find the perimeter of $\triangle DEF$.

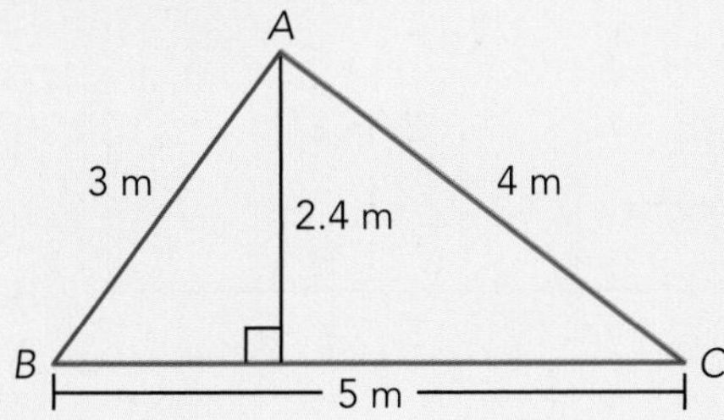

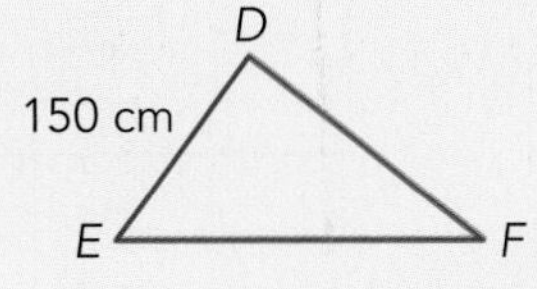

SAMPLE RESPONSE

First Find the scale. It is the ratio of *DE* to *AB*.

Recall that *AB* is read as "the length of segment *AB*."

$$\text{scale} = \frac{DE}{AB} = \frac{150 \text{ cm}}{3 \text{ m}} = \frac{50 \text{ cm}}{1 \text{ m}}$$

Next Use the fact that the ratio of the perimeters is the same as the scale to write a proportion.

$$\frac{\text{Perimeter of } \triangle DEF}{\text{Perimeter of } \triangle ABC} = \frac{50 \text{ cm}}{1 \text{ m}}$$

Then Solve the proportion. Let P = the perimeter of $\triangle DEF$.

$$\frac{P}{3 \text{ m} + 4 \text{ m} + 5 \text{ m}} = \frac{50 \text{ cm}}{1 \text{ m}}$$

$$\frac{P}{12 \text{ m}} = \frac{50 \text{ cm}}{1 \text{ m}}$$

$$12 \text{ m} \cdot \frac{P}{12 \text{ m}} = 12 \text{ m} \cdot \frac{50 \text{ cm}}{1 \text{ m}}$$

$$P = 600 \text{ cm}$$

The perimeter of $\triangle DEF$ is 600 cm or 6 m.

15 **Try This as a Class** Use the triangles in the Example.

a. What is the ratio of the area of $\triangle DEF$ to the area of $\triangle ABC$? How do you know?

b. Find the area of $\triangle ABC$. Use it and your answer to part (a) to find the area of $\triangle DEF$.

16 The scale drawing below is for the offices of a small business.

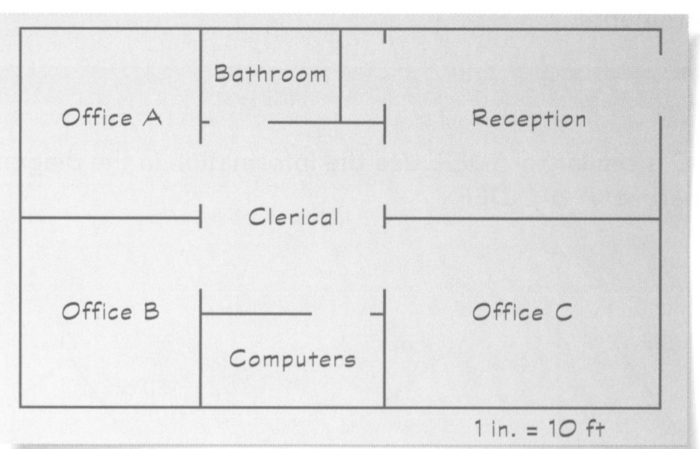

a. Measure to find the perimeter and the area of Office C in the scale drawing.

b. Use your answer to part (a) and the scale to find the perimeter and the area of the actual Office C.

c. The area of the actual computer room is 50 ft^2. Without measuring, find the area of that room in the scale drawing.

✓ QUESTION 17

...checks that you can use a scale to find perimeters and areas.

17 ✓ CHECKPOINT Each pair of figures is similar. Find each missing perimeter or area.

a. Perimeter of $\triangle ACD$ = 72 in.
Perimeter of $\triangle ABE$ = __?__

Area of $\triangle ACD$ = 216 in.^{2}
Area of $\triangle ABE$ = __?__

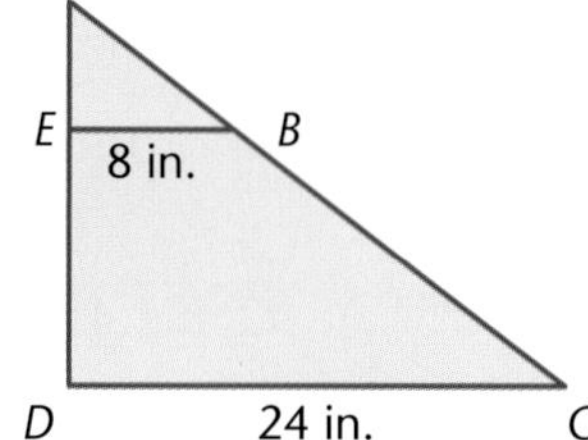

b. Perimeter of $WXYZ$ = 30 yd
Perimeter of $PQRS$ = __?__

Area of $WXYZ$ = 50 yd^2
Area of $PQRS$ = __?__

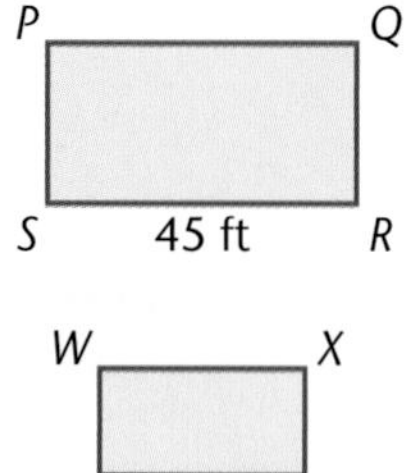

HOMEWORK EXERCISES ▶ See Exs. 9–22 on pp. 383–384.

Section 6

Key Concepts

Key Term

Scale Drawings (pp. 375–377)

The scale of a drawing is the ratio of a length on the drawing to the length of the corresponding part of the actual object. To find out how long to make a segment in a scale drawing, you can use a proportion.

scale

Example A building is 30 ft high. Find the height h of the building in a scale drawing if the scale is 1 in. to 10 ft.

height in drawing → $\frac{h}{30 \text{ ft}} = \frac{1 \text{ in.}}{10 \text{ ft}}$ ← actual height

$$10h = 30$$
$$h = 3$$

The height of the building in the scale drawing is 3 in.

Perimeters and Areas of Similar Figures (pp. 378-380)

If the ratio of corresponding sides of similar figures is $\frac{a}{b}$, then the ratio of their perimeters is $\frac{a}{b}$, and the ratio of their areas is $\frac{a^2}{b^2}$.

Example Parallelogram $ABCD$ is similar to parallelogram $PQRS$.

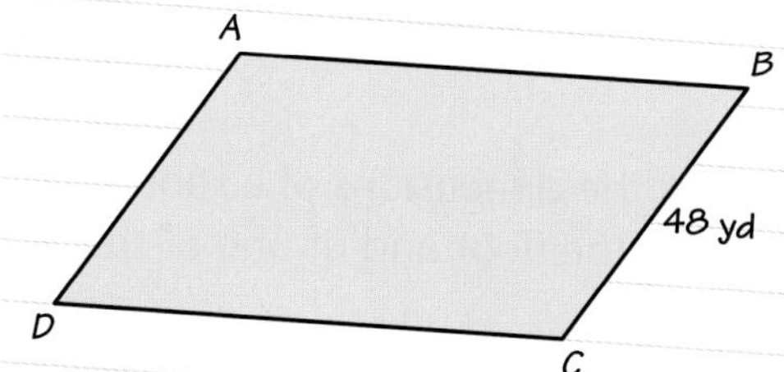

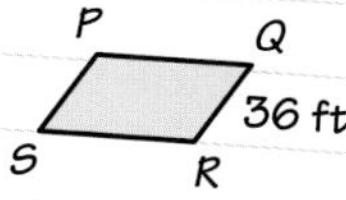

The scale is 36 ft to 48 yd, or 3 ft to 4 yd.

$$\frac{\text{Perimeter of } PQRS}{\text{Perimeter of } ABCD} = \frac{3 \text{ ft}}{4 \text{ yd}}$$

$$\frac{\text{Area of } PQRS}{\text{Area of } ABCD} = \left(\frac{3 \text{ ft}}{4 \text{ yd}}\right)^2 = \frac{9 \text{ ft}^2}{16 \text{ yd}^2}$$

18 Key Concepts Question Use the parallelograms in the Example.

a. The perimeter of $ABCD$ is 256 yd. Find the perimeter of $PQRS$.

b. The area of $PQRS$ is 1800 ft^2. Find the area of $ABCD$.

YOU WILL NEED

For Exs. 1–5, 7, and 8:
- ruler
- plain or graph paper

For Exs. 17–19 and 22:
- ruler

Section 6

Practice & Application Exercises

1. The scale drawing below uses the scale $\frac{1}{16}$ in. to 5 ft. Make a scale drawing of the gymnasium using the scale $\frac{1}{8}$ in. to 5 ft.

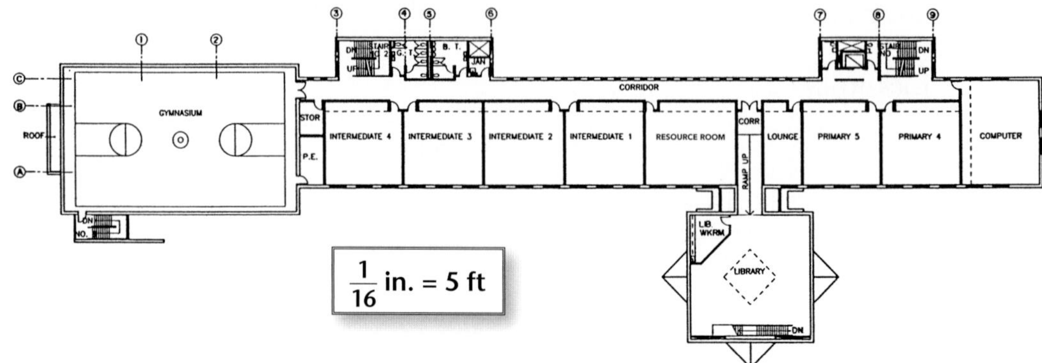

In Exercises 2–4, the dimensions of several objects are given. Make a scale drawing of the top view, the front view, and the right-side view of each object. Include the scale.

2. A dictionary is 12 in. long, 9 in. wide, and 3 in. thick.

3. A credit card is 85 mm long, 55 mm wide, and 1 mm thick.

4. The base of a rectangular prism is 24 ft long and 18 ft wide. The height is 36 ft.

5. **Estimation** Estimate and then find the dimensions of a room in your home. Make a scale drawing of the floor and of one of the four walls. Include the scale(s).

6. **Writing** Describe the process you went through to choose the scale for one of the scale drawings you made in Exercises 2–5.

7. **Open-ended** Choose an object that is more complex than a single rectangular prism and make detailed scale drawings of the top view, the front view, and the right-side view.

8. **Create Your Own** Make a scale drawing of the floor and all four walls of your ideal bedroom. Include the doors, windows, closets, and furniture in your drawing, and identify the scale.

The perimeter of a room is 16 yd and the area of the room is 16 yd^2. What would be the perimeter and the area of the room in a scale drawing with each of the following scales?

9. 1 in. to 36 in.

10. 1 ft to 4 yd

11. 3 in. to 4 yd

12. **Writing** Describe the process you went through to find the answer in Exercise 11.

The two figures in each diagram are similar. Use the given information to replace each __?__ with the correct measurement. Round answers to the nearest hundredth if necessary.

13. Area of $\triangle ABC = 5.25$ cm^2
Area of $\triangle XYZ \approx$ __?__

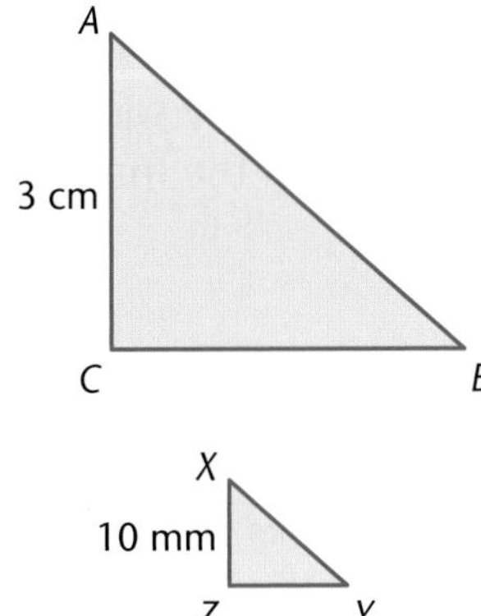

14. Perimeter of *STUV* = 58 ft
Perimeter of *DEFG* = __?__

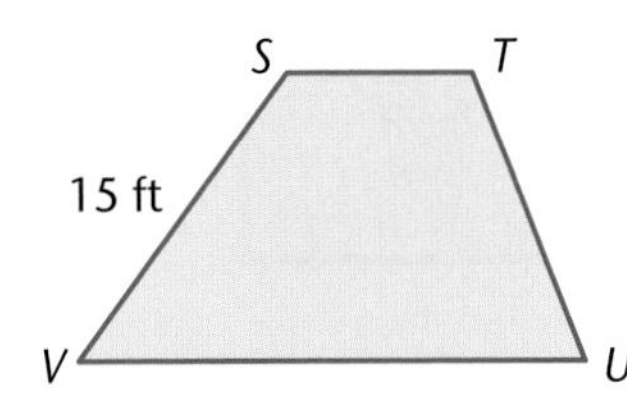

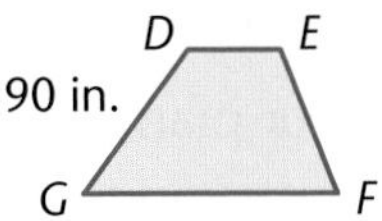

15. Area of *PQRSTU* $\approx$ 9353.1 ft^2
Area of *ABCDEF* $\approx$ __?__

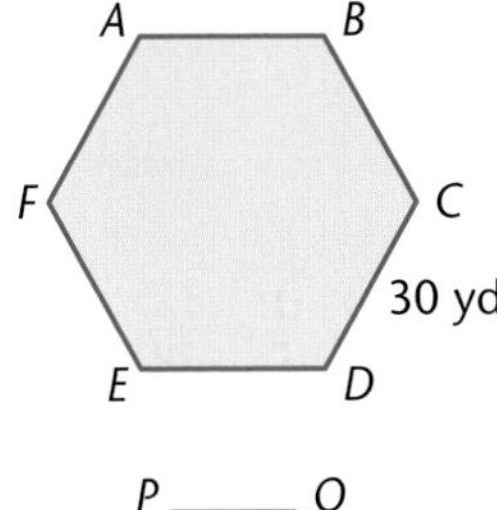

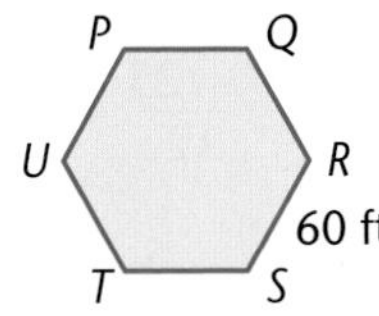

16. Perimeter of *WXYZ* = 16.5 m
Perimeter of *KLMN* = __?__

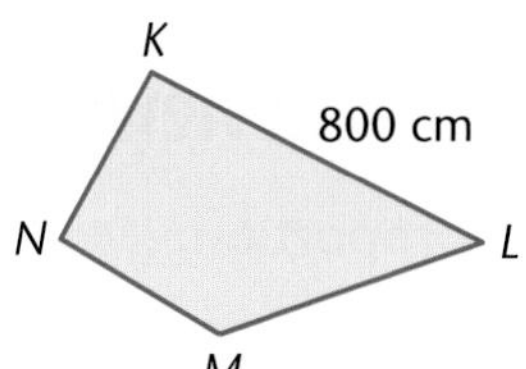

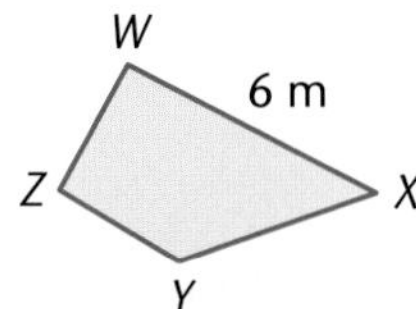

17. **Challenge** Use a ruler and the trapezoids in Exercise 14.

a. Find all the unknown side lengths of the trapezoids.

b. Find the height of each trapezoid.

The scale on the map of Minneapolis is 3 in. to 10 mi.

18. **Estimation** Estimate the perimeter of the city on the map. Then use your answer to estimate the actual perimeter of the city.

19. **Estimation** Estimate the actual length of the section of the Mississippi River that runs through the city.

20. The actual city covers about 58.7 mi^2. How many square inches is this on the map?

21. There are about 3.6 mi^2 of inland water in the actual city. How many square inches of water is this on the map?

RESEARCH

Exercise 22 checks that you can interpret the scale on a scale drawing.

Reflecting on the Section

22. Find a floor plan. Some possible sources are books about architecture and magazines about homes. Use the scale on the floor plan to estimate the perimeter and the area of the actual floor.

Spiral Review

Solve each proportion. (Module 2, p. 132)

23. $\frac{x}{24} = \frac{0.5}{3}$
24. $\frac{x}{7} = \frac{5}{14}$
25. $\frac{n}{7} = \frac{32}{28}$
26. $\frac{n}{26} = \frac{\left(\frac{1}{4}\right)}{13}$
27. $\frac{24}{9} = \frac{52}{y}$
28. $\frac{0.125}{12} = \frac{m}{132}$

Graph each equation. (Module 3, p. 175)

29. $y = x + 3$
30. $y = -2$
31. $y = 5 - 2x$

1. A 6 ft tall man is drawn 4 in. tall in a scale drawing. What is the scale?

2. The dimensions of a room in a scale drawing are 8 cm by 5 cm. The scale is 2 cm to 1 m. Find the dimensions of the actual room.

The dimensions of some objects are given. Make a scale drawing of the top view, the front view, and the right-side view of each object. Include the scale.

3. A rectangular prism is 27 ft long, 12 ft wide, and 36 ft high.

4. The base of a rectangular prism is 5 m long and 5 m wide. The height of the prism is 11 m.

The two polygons in each diagram are similar. Find the unknown perimeter or areas.

5. Perimeter = 30 in.

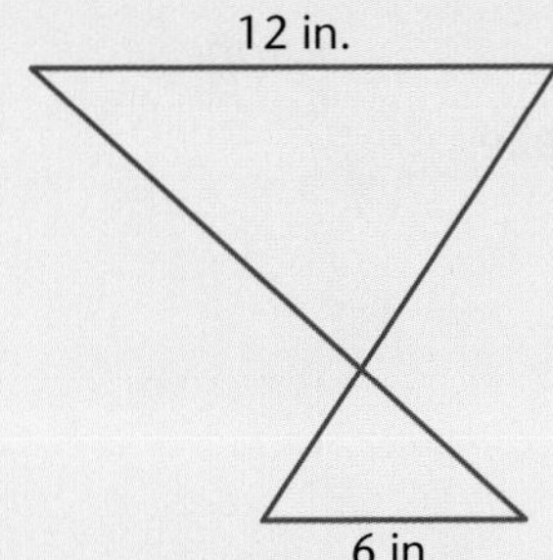

Perimeter = ___?___

6. Area = 500 mm²

20 mm

5 cm

Area = ___?___

7. Area = 405 ft²

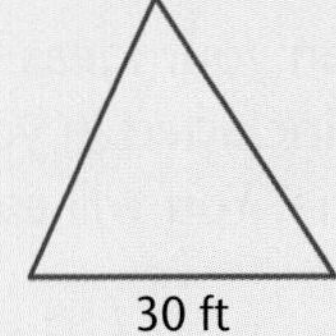

120 in.

Area = ___?___

Standardized Testing ▶ Multiple Choice

1. A door is 8 ft high. How high is the door in a scale drawing that uses the scale 1 in. to 2 ft?

   A 0.25 in. B 2 in. C 4 in. D 16 in.

2. *ABCD* and *EFGH* are similar parallelograms. If the perimeter of *ABCD* is 80 ft, the length of $\overline{AD}$ is 10 ft, and the length of the corresponding side $\overline{EH}$ is 5 ft, what is the perimeter of *EFGH*?

   A 40 ft B 20 ft C 15 ft D 30 ft

Creating a Model Town

When architects and urban planners design housing developments and business districts, they draw plans and build models to show people how the buildings will look. For your module project, you and your classmates will draw plans for a model town and then build it.

SET UP

Work individually and as a class.

You will need:

- *graph paper (optional)*
- *ruler*
- *large sheets of sturdy paper*
- *colored pencils or markers*
- *scissors*
- *tape*

Sketching Nets One way to create a model for a building is to make a net that can be folded into the shape of the building.

1 Work as a class.

a. Brainstorm ideas for your town. Will you make houses, offices, stores, or some combination of buildings? How many styles of buildings will there be? You may want to look at books or magazines to help generate ideas.

b. Based on your ideas from part (a), decide which buildings will be included in your town and who will design and make each one. You will each make one building.

2 a. Sketch a view of your building that gives it a three-dimensional look.

b. Sketch a net for your building.

c. Label your sketches with the dimensions that the actual building would have. (*Hint*: Begin with dimensions of buildings you are familiar with.)

3 What polygons are used to create the floor, the walls, and the roof of your building?

Surface Area and Volume The surface area of a building determines how much siding, roofing, and flooring material is needed. The volume of a building determines what size heating and cooling systems should be installed.

Use your sketches from Question 2.

4 Find the surface area of your building.

5 Find the volume of your building.

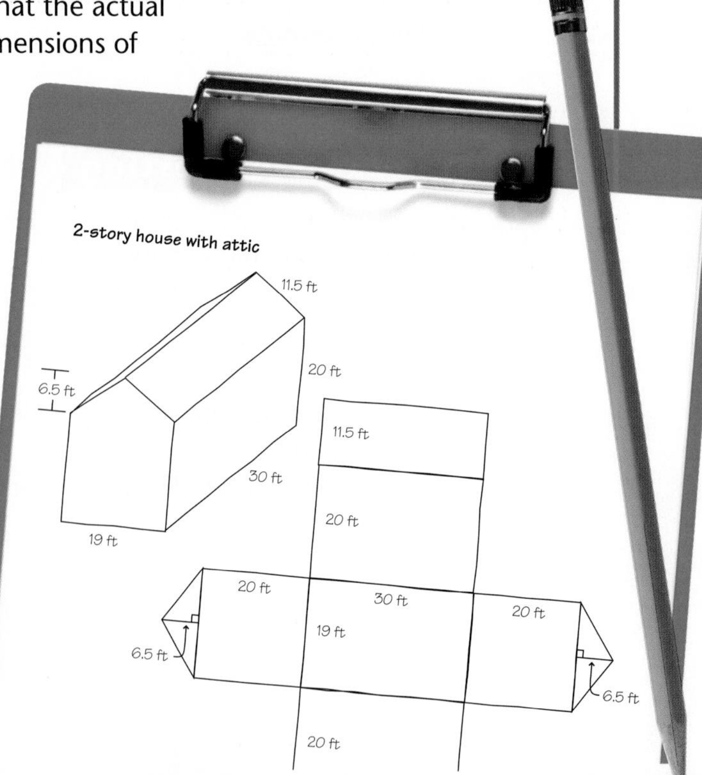

Scale Drawings You can use scale drawings to show details of the various parts of your building.

6 Use your sketch from Question 2. What actual dimensions will you use for the exterior doors and the windows of your building? Explain why you chose these dimensions.

7 **Discussion** Describe to another student the scale you would like to use for your building and discuss how each scale presented would affect the size of the final model.

You have made sketches and discussed scales to use for your models. To complete the project, you will build a three-dimensional model of your building and help to put together your class's model town.

8 Work as a class. Compare the scales you discussed in Question 7. Together choose a scale that you will all use to create the buildings for your model town.

9 Use the net you sketched in Question 2. On sturdy paper, make a net for your building using the scale from Question 8.

10 Add to your net features such as doors and windows using the scale from Question 8.

11 Use colored pencils or markers to add other details to your net.

12 Cut out your net and fold along the edges to form your building. Then tape the edges together.

13 Work as a class to arrange your buildings to form a model town. Use the same scale for the streets that you did for each building.

MODULE 5 Review and Assessment

You will need: • *ruler* (Exs. 2, 21, and 23)

For Exercises 1 and 2, assume that the figure at the right is made of centimeter cubes. Also assume that there are no hidden cubes. (Sec. 1, Explors. 1 and 2)

front
right

1. a. Find the surface area and the volume of the figure.

   b. Find the surface area and the volume of the figure without the green cubes.

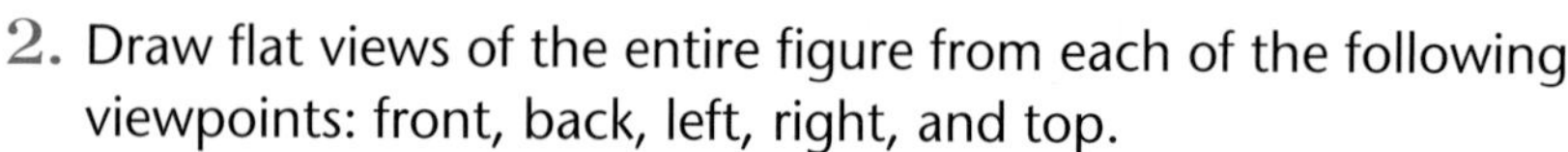

2. Draw flat views of the entire figure from each of the following viewpoints: front, back, left, right, and top.

3. a. Sketch a net for an octagonal pyramid. (Sec. 2, Explor. 2)

   b. How many faces, edges, and vertices will the pyramid have? (Sec. 2, Explor. 2)

For Exercises 4 and 5, explain whether the triangles in each pair are congruent. If the triangles are congruent, write the relationship between them using symbols. (Sec. 2, Explor. 3)

4.

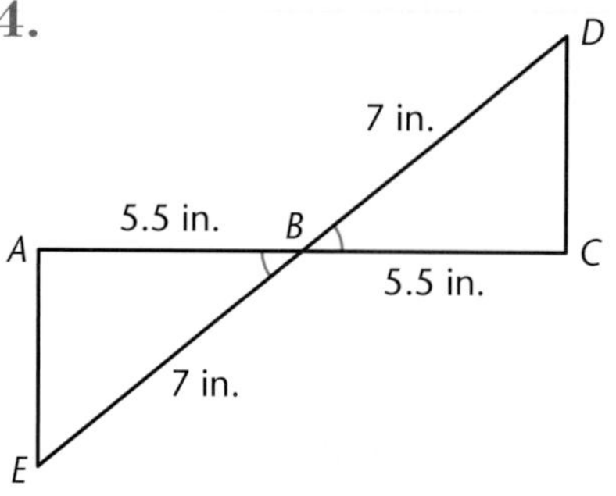

5.

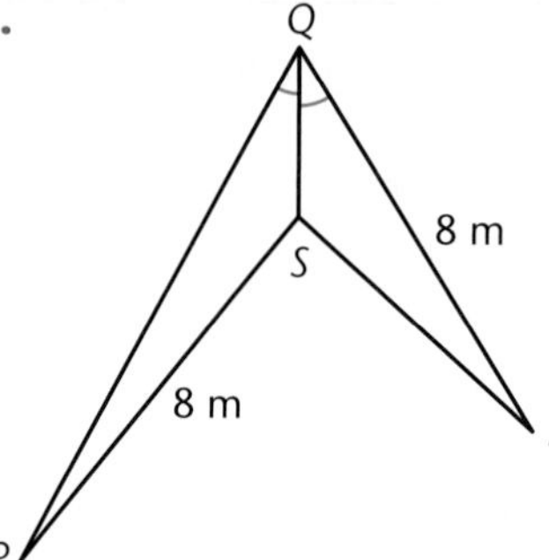

6. Beth wants to plant a rectangular garden in her backyard. If she uses the measurements shown will her garden be rectangular? Explain. (Sec. 3, Explor. 1)

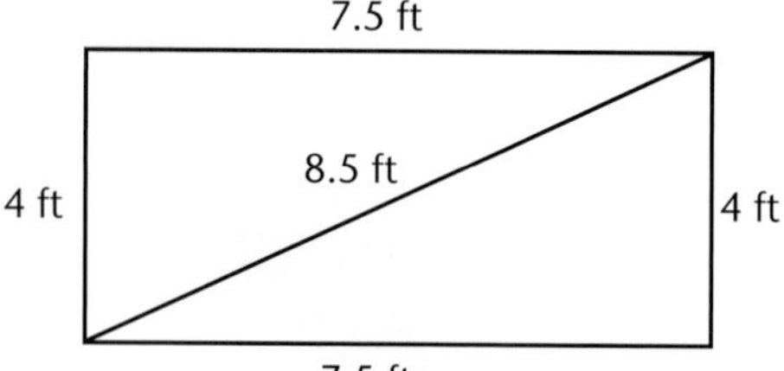

For each triangle, find the unknown side length. (Sec. 3, Explor. 2)

7.

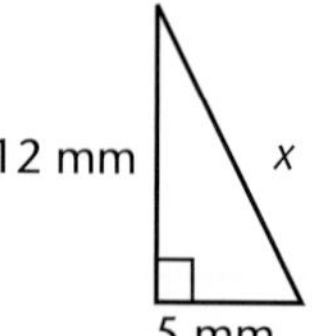

8.

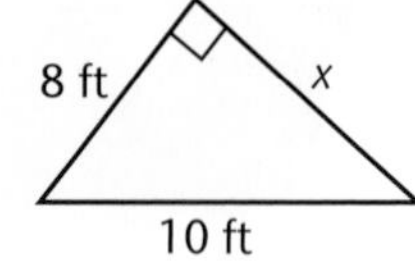

9.

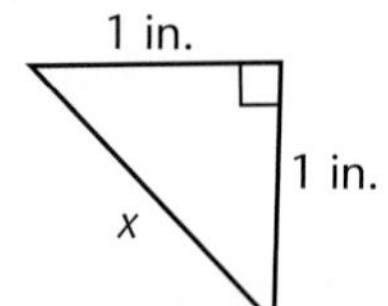

Find the surface area and the volume of each figure. (Sec. 4, Explors. 1 and 2)

10.

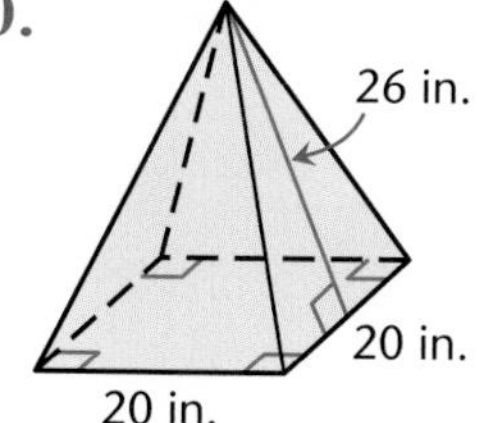

11.

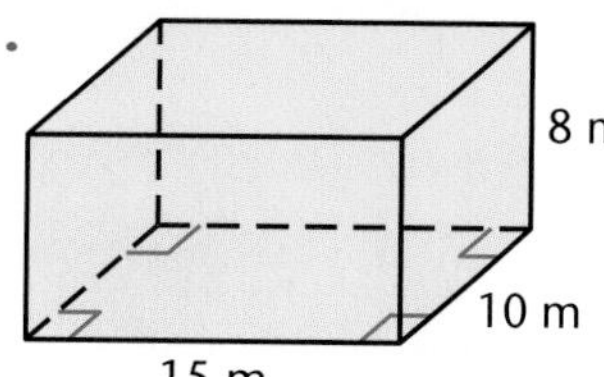

12.

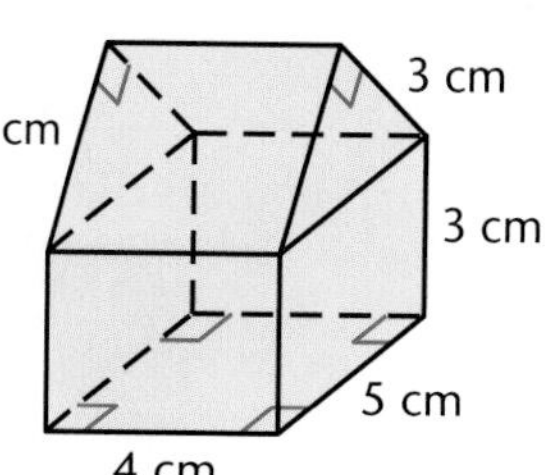

13. The volume of a cylinder is 51 cm^3. What is the volume of a cone with the same base and height as the cylinder? (Sec. 4, Explor. 2)

For Exercises 14–17, use the diagram. Line *k* is parallel to line *n* and the measure of ∠3 is 105°. (Sec. 5, Explor. 1)

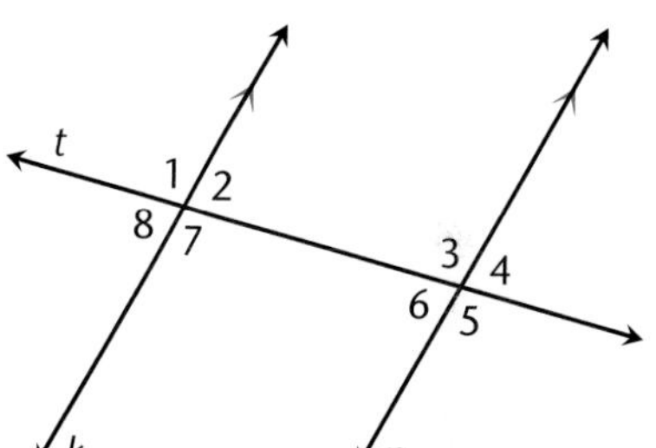

14. Identify and find the measure of the alternate interior angle to ∠3.

15. Identify and find the measure of the corresponding angle to ∠6.

16. Identify and find the measure of the alternate exterior angle to ∠8.

17. Find the measure of ∠5. Explain your method.

Use the diagram for Exercises 18–20. (Sec. 5, Explor. 2)

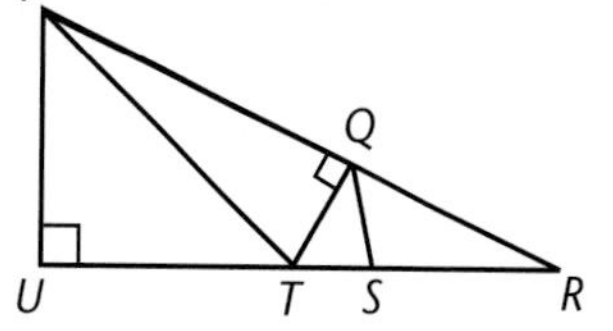

18. Which angle is a supplement of ∠*UTQ*?

19. Which angle is a complement of ∠*SQR*?

20. Suppose $m\angle UPT = 40°$. Find $m\angle PTR$.

21. Use the scale $\frac{1}{2}$ in. to 1 ft. Make a scale drawing of a rectangular window that is 3 ft wide and 1.5 ft high. (Sec. 6, Explor. 1)

22. The scale on a map is 1 cm to 2 km. The perimeter of a lake on the map is 14 cm and its area on the map is 12 cm^2. Find the actual perimeter and area of the lake. (Sec. 6, Explor. 2)

Reflecting on the Module

23. Sketch two rectangular prisms with different dimensions. Then make scale drawings of the figures from different views. Find the surface area and the volume of each figure.

MODULE 6

Visualizing Change

CONNECTING
MATHEMATICS & The Theme

SECTION OVERVIEW

1 Graphs and Functions

As you study rainfall data:

- Use tables and graphs to model changes in data
- Use equations, tables, and graphs to represent functions

2 Linear Equations and Problem Solving

As you study different savings plans:

- Use linear equations, tables, and graphs to solve problems
- Simplify and solve equations
- Use the distributive property

3 Modeling Exponential Change

As you learn about compound interest:

- Use tables and equations to solve problems involving exponential growth

4 Algorithms and Transformations

As you model a gymnast's change in position:

- Use algorithms to transform geometric shapes
- Reflect geometric shapes

5 Exploring Quadratic Functions

As you model the paths of aircraft and the shapes of bridge cables:

- Explore the shape and symmetry of parabolas
- Recognize and simplify quadratic equations

The Module Project

Modeling Change in a Story

Leaves change color, caterpillars change into butterflies, and day changes into night. In this project, you will write a story that involves changes and use mathematics to model them.

More on the Module Project

See pp. 452–453.

INTERNET
Resources and practice at
classzone.com

Section 1 Graphs and Functions

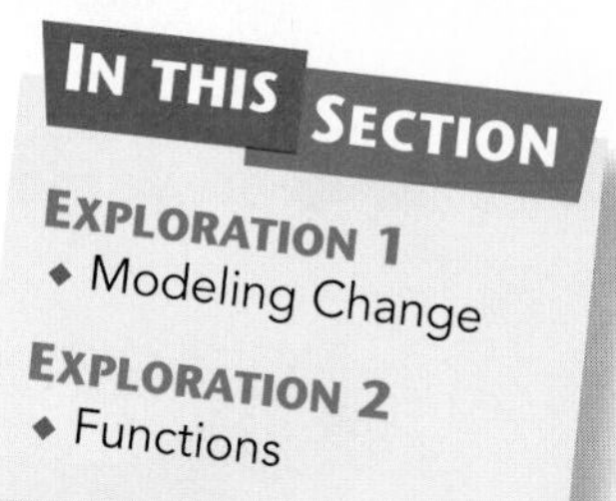

Time for a Change

Setting the Stage

Suppose you are asked to describe a rainfall. You might paint a picture, write a story, or compose a piece of music. Barbara M. Hales decided to write the poem shown below.

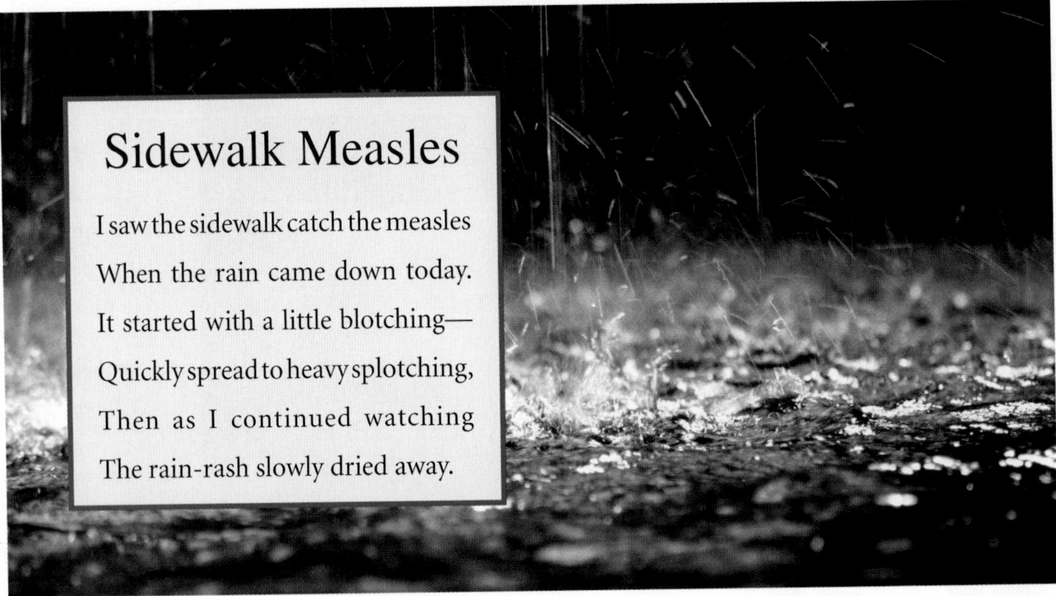

Sidewalk Measles

I saw the sidewalk catch the measles
When the rain came down today.
It started with a little blotching—
Quickly spread to heavy splotching,
Then as I continued watching
The rain-rash slowly dried away.

Think About It

1 Which graph below do you think best describes how the rainfall changes over time in the poem?

A.

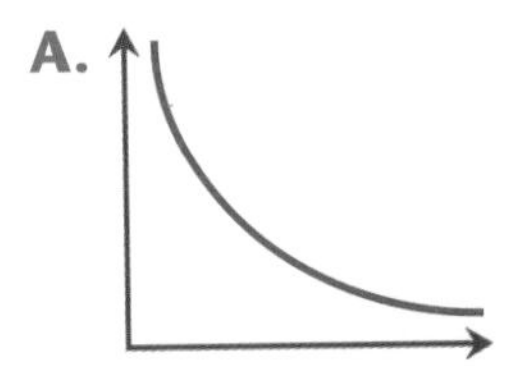

B.

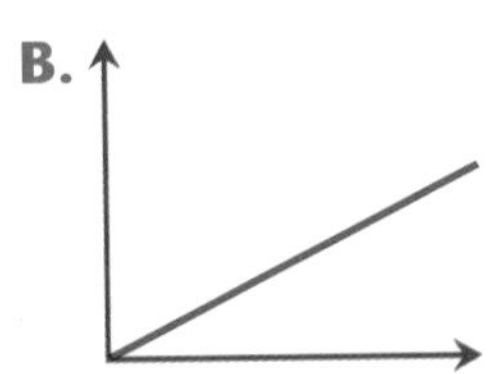

C.

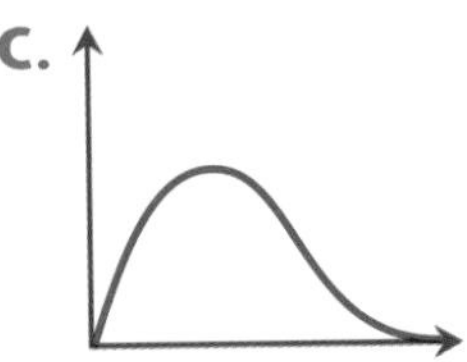

2 a. How did the rainfall change in the poem?

b. How was this change shown in the graph you chose in Question 1?

3 What labels would you use for the horizontal and vertical axes of the graph you chose in Question 1?

▶ **The world around you is constantly changing. A graph is one way to model change. Throughout this module you will choose and develop mathematical models that can help you visualize change.**

Exploration 1

Modeling Change

GOAL

LEARN HOW TO...
- use tables and graphs to model changes in data

AS YOU...
- explore how the shape of a container affects changes in water level

SET UP *Work in a group of three. You will need: • water • clear plastic cup • metric ruler • clear container • graph paper*

▶ **Rainfall can cause dramatic changes in the water level of lakes and rivers. For example, from 1963 to 1987, the water level in Utah's Great Salt Lake varied by as much as 20 ft. The surface area of the lake went from 950 mi^2 to 3,300 mi^2. These changes were due in part to the shape of the lake bed.**

In this exploration, you will model rainfall on a lake by pouring water into a container. Each group in your class should choose a container with a different shape. As you add water to the container, your group will measure the change in water level.

4 **Discussion** Suppose you were to pour water into your group's container. How can you use a graph to show the change in water level inside the container?

5 **a.** Before you start your experiment, look at your group's container. How do you think the water level will change as water is poured into the container?

b. Use your prediction to sketch a graph of the water level as the container is filled.

6 Follow the steps below to perform the experiment.

Step 1 Mark your cup so that the same amount of water will be poured into the container each time. This amount will be called a "unit."

Step 2 Fill the cup with water up to the mark you made in Step 1. Pour the water into the container.

Step 3 Measure the water level to the nearest millimeter.

Step 4 Record the measurement in a table like the one shown.

Step 5 Repeat Steps 2–4 until the container is almost full. As you finish filling the container, you may need to estimate what fraction of a unit you use to completely fill it. Do not let the container overflow.

7 **a.** Use your table to make a graph that shows how the water level depends on the number of units of water in the container. Connect the data points with a smooth curve.

b. Compare your graph from part (a) with the one you drew in Question 5. How accurate was your prediction?

FOR◀HELP with *choosing a scale*, see **MODULE 1, p. 51**

▶ **To get an idea of how something is changing, look at how one variable changes as the other variable increases by a fixed amount.**

8 **Try This as a Class** Compare your results with other groups' results.

a. For which containers did the water level increase by the same amount each time water was added?

b. For which containers did the water level change by a different amount each time water was added?

c. Which graphs are linear?

d. Which graphs are nonlinear?

e. Suppose you repeated the experiment using the container shown at the right. Describe what you think your graph would look like. Explain your thinking.

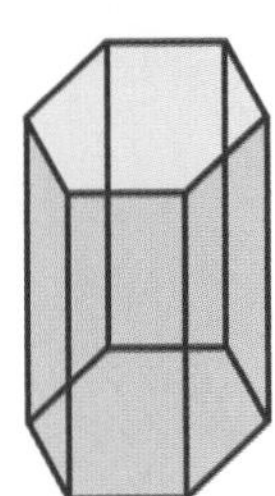

FOR◀HELP with *linear and nonlinear graphs*, see **MODULE 3, p. 175**

9 **Try This as a Class** Consider all groups' results.

a. For which groups did the water level in the container rise the fastest?

b. How can you use your graphs to answer part (a)?

c. How does the shape of the container affect how fast the water level rises?

10 Two cylindrical containers are shown below. Equal amounts of water are poured into both containers.

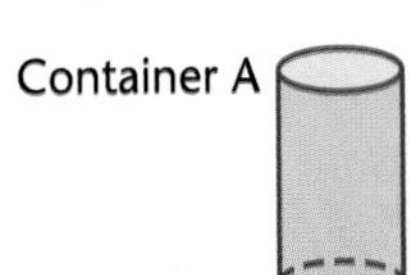

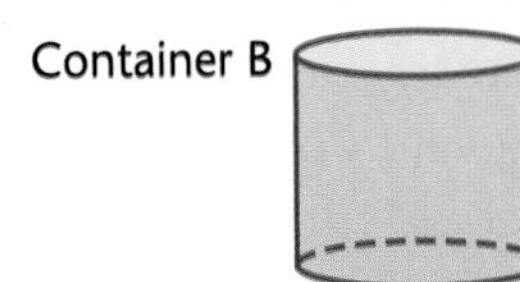

a. For which container does the water level rise faster?

b. A graph of the water level for Container A is shown. How would a graph of the water level for Container B compare with this graph?

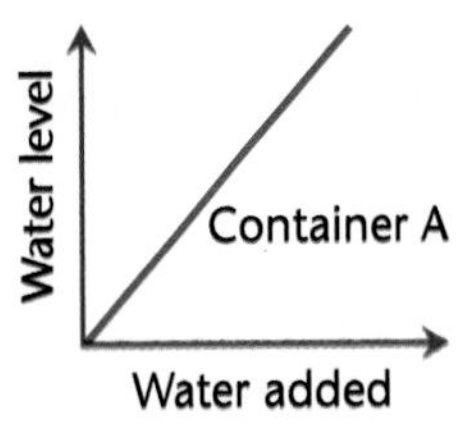

✓ QUESTION 11

...checks that you can use tables and graphs to interpret data.

11 **✓ CHECKPOINT**

a. Match each table with one of the graphs below.

Table A: Height of a ball thrown in the air as time passes

Time (seconds)	0	0.5	1	1.5	2	2.5
Height (feet)	0	27	40	45	42	31

Table B: Bacteria growth in a heated swimming pool

Time (days)	0	0.5	1	1.5	2	2.5
Bacteria count	1500	2121	3000	4242	6000	8485

Table C: Speed conversion chart

mi/hr	0	10	20	30	40	50	60	70
km/hr	0	16	32	48	64	81	97	113

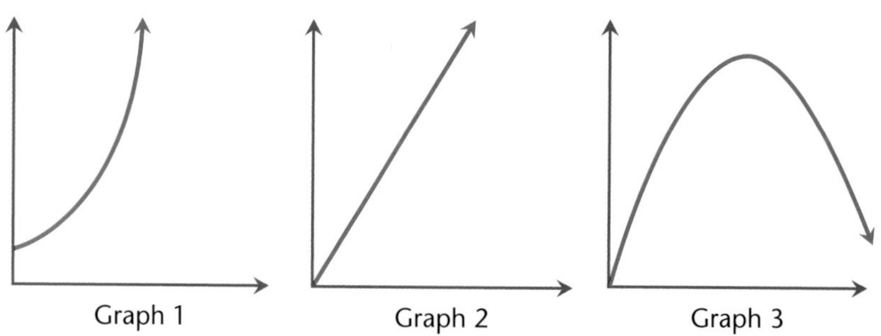

Graph 1 Graph 2 Graph 3

b. Explain why you chose that graph and tell what the labels on the horizontal and vertical axes should be.

12 On page 393, you read about the Great Salt Lake. Suppose a lake bed is approximately cone-shaped, as shown at the right. A long, steady rain causes the water level to rise. Sketch a graph that could model the water level over time.

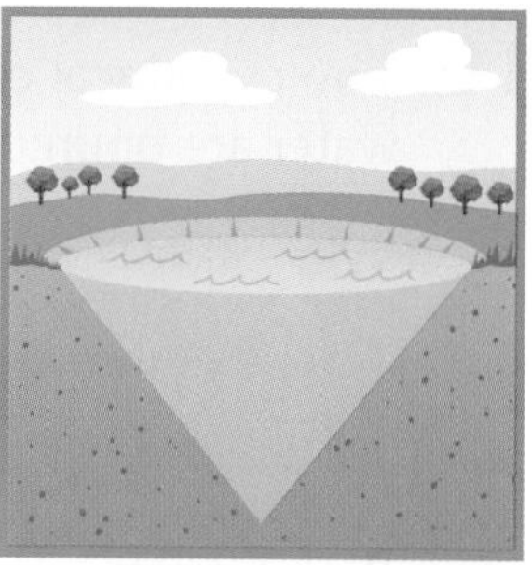

HOMEWORK EXERCISES ▶ See Exs. 1–9 on pp. 401–402.

Exploration 2

LEARN HOW TO...
- use tables, graphs, and equations to represent functions

AS YOU...
- compare different rainfall data

KEY TERM
- function

FUNCTIONS

SET UP *Work with a partner.*

▶ **In Exploration 1, you used a graph to show the relationship between the amount of water poured into a container and the water level inside the container.**

13 Use the phrases *amount of water added* and *water level* to complete the following sentence. Explain your thinking.

In the experiment performed in Exploration 1, the __?__ depended on the __?__.

▶ **Your graph in Question 7 represented a *function*. A function is a relationship between input and output. For each input value, there is *exactly* one output value. Output is a function of input.**

14 **a.** Explain why the data you collected in your experiment represent a function. What is the input? the output?

b. Use the phrase *is a function of* to rewrite the completed statement from Question 13.

15 For five days, Mei recorded the data shown at the right. She concluded that the amount of rainfall for any given day is a function of the high temperature for that day.

a. How do you think Mei came to this conclusion?

b. Suppose Mei recorded these data for a year. Do you think she would still say that daily rainfall is a function of daily high temperature? Why or why not?

c. In general, do you think that daily rainfall is a function of daily high temperature? Explain.

Daily high temperature (°F)	Amount of rainfall (in.)
81	0.4
75	0
79	0.5
80	1.2
74	0.5

▶ **A function may be represented using a rule that relates one variable to another. A function rule is typically an equation that gives the output in terms of the input.**

16 A driver is maintaining the same rate of travel during a long-distance trip on a highway. The table shows the total distances the driver travels for various amounts of driving time.

Time (hours)	1	3	6	8
Distance (miles)	55	165	330	440

a. Describe the relationship between the distance traveled and the number of hours traveled using the phrase *is a function of.*

b. Let x = the number of hours driven and let y = the distance traveled in miles. Explain why the equation $y = 55x$ is a rule for the function in part (a).

17 **Discussion** Tell whether y is a function of x. Explain your thinking.

a. x = the amount of time that the sky is cloudy
y = the amount of rain that falls

b. x = the rate at which you read
y = the time you take to read a book

c. x = the number of pounds of grapes purchased
y = the cost of the grapes

d. x = a person's height
y = the foot length of someone with that height

18 Suppose it starts raining steadily at noon. The rain falls for the rest of the afternoon at a rate of 0.2 inch per hour.

a. Let y = the amount of rain that has fallen since noon. Let x = the number of hours since noon. Explain why the value of y is a function of the value of x.

b. Write an equation that represents this function.

▶ **You can use a table of values or a graph to tell whether an equation represents a function.**

EXAMPLE

Given an equation relating x and y, you can tell whether y is a function of x by comparing input and output values in a table or a graph.

a. $y = x^2$ For every value of **x**, there is exactly one value of **y**. The equation represents a function.

Input (x)	Output (y)
−2	4
−1	1
0	0
1	1
2	4

b. $x = y^2$ For some values of **x**, there are two different values of **y**. The equation does not represent a function.

Input (x)	Output (y)
0	0
1	−1 and 1
4	−2 and 2

19 **Try This as a Class** Refer to the Example.

a. How are the two graphs alike? How are they different?

b. Use the table for each equation to find the value(s) of y when $x = 1$. Then use the graph of each equation.

c. How can you use a table of values to tell whether an equation represents a function? How can you use a graph?

20 ✓ **CHECKPOINT** For each equation or graph, tell whether y is a function of x. Explain your thinking.

a. $y = 7x$

b. $2 + x = y^2$

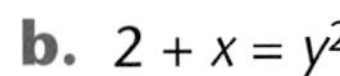

c.

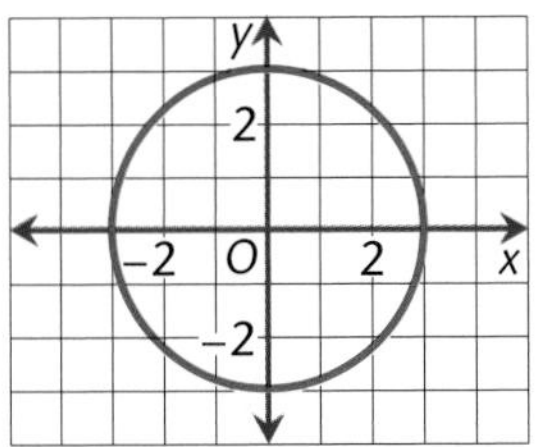

d.

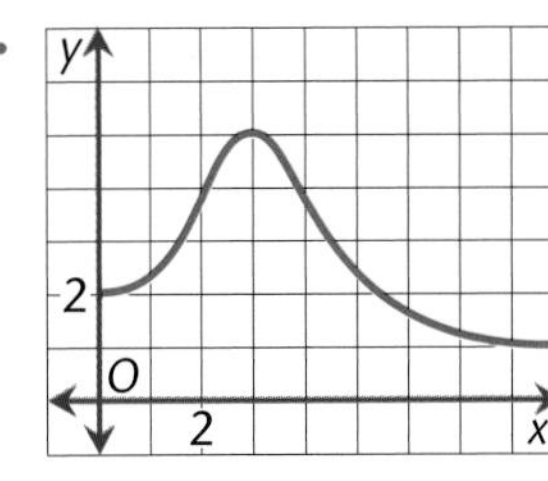

✓ **QUESTION 20**

...checks that you can identify a function.

HOMEWORK EXERCISES See Exs. 10–26 on pp. 403–404.

Section 1 Key Concepts

Modeling Change (pp. 393–396)

You can use tables and graphs to model and analyze changes in data.

Example Suppose you measured the amount of gasoline in two different automobile tanks.

Car A The table shows that the number of gallons of gasoline in the tank increases by the same amount each minute as gasoline is pumped into the tank. The data points lie on a straight line.

Time (min)	Gallons in the tank
0	1
1	5
2	9
3	13

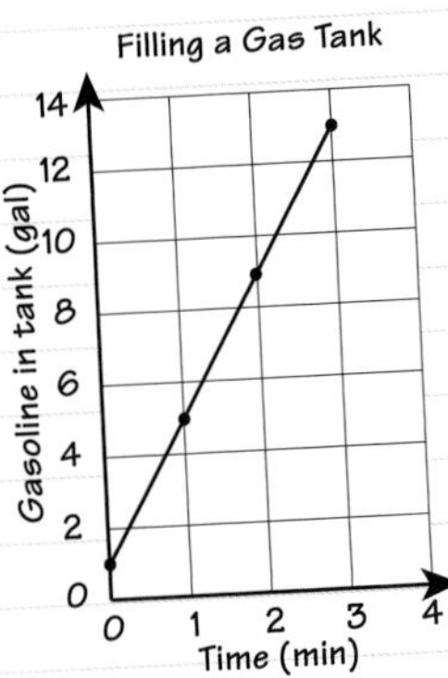

Car B The table shows that the number of gallons of gasoline in the tank decreases by a different amount every 20 minutes while the car is being driven. The graph is always decreasing, but not in a straight line.

Time (min)	Gallons in the tank
0	14
20	13
40	11
60	10.5
80	10.5
100	9

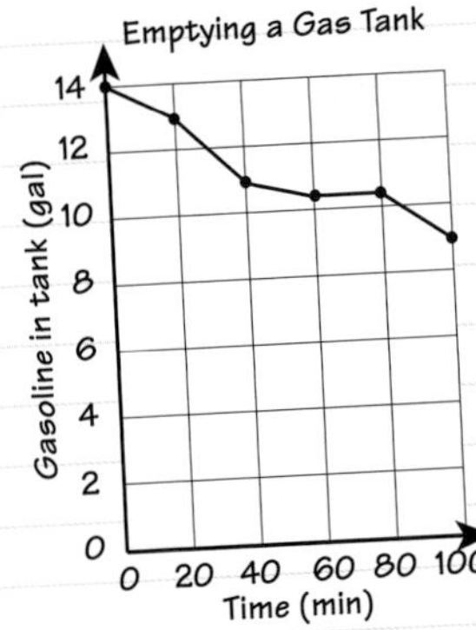

21 Key Concepts Question

a. How much gasoline is in Car A's tank after $2\frac{1}{2}$ min? Explain how you used either the table or the graph to find the answer.

b. Describe a situation that the graph for Car B might represent.

Section 1 Key Concepts

Key Term

function

Functions (pp. 397–399)

A function is a relationship that pairs each input with exactly one output. You can use equations, tables, and graphs to represent functions.

Example A number y is 1 more than 3 times a number x.

Equation

$y = 3x + 1$

Table

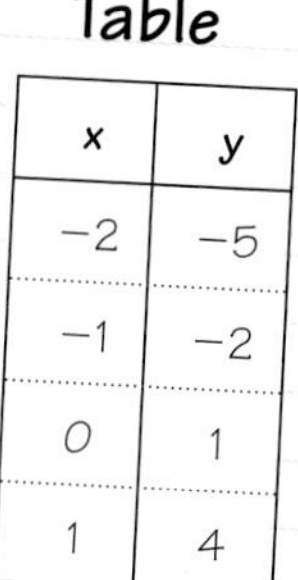

x	y
−2	−5
−1	−2
0	1
1	4

Graph

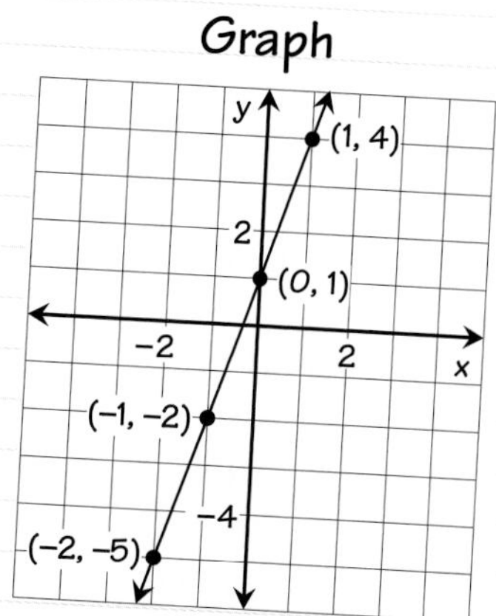

22 Key Concepts Question Do the graphs and tables on page 400 represent functions? If so, list the input values and the corresponding output values. If not, explain why.

Section 1 Practice & Application Exercises

YOU WILL NEED

For Ex. 5:
- Labsheet 1A

For Exs. 6, 7, 25, and 29–32:
- graph paper

Suppose water is steadily poured into each of the containers below. Which graph models the water level in each container over time?

1. 

2. 

3. 

4. 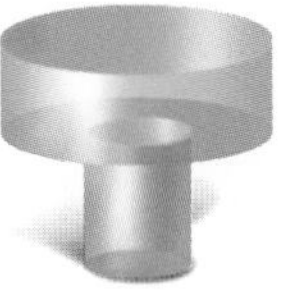

A. 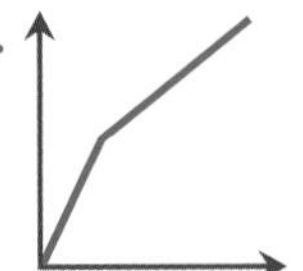

B. 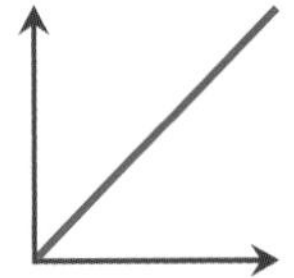

C. 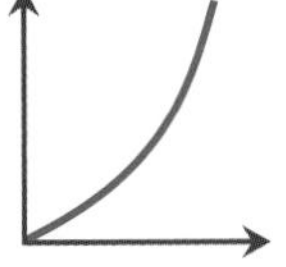

D. 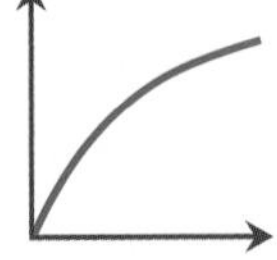

5. **Use Labsheet 1A.** You will match a verbal description or a table with each of the *Graphs Without Labels*.

6. **Open-ended** Sketch a graph that could model the following bike ride. You ride a bicycle for some time at a constant speed. Then you slow down for a stop sign, stop and look both ways, then speed up again.

7. **Create Your Own** Write a story or a poem that describes a change over time. Use a graph to illustrate your story or poem.

The oldest surviving ▶ water clock is from Egypt, 14th century B.C.

History In ancient times, people used containers filled with water to tell time. The water dripped out a hole in the base of the water clock at a nearly constant rate. People could tell the time by comparing the water level with hour marks on the container. Use this information for Exercises 8 and 9.

8. Which graph would you expect to model the change in water level inside the water clock shown above? Why?

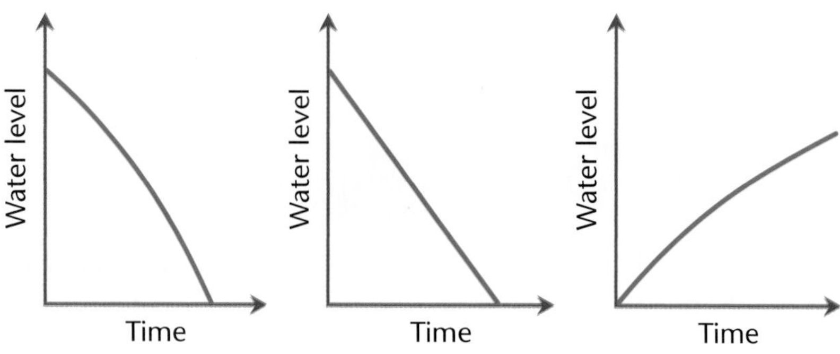

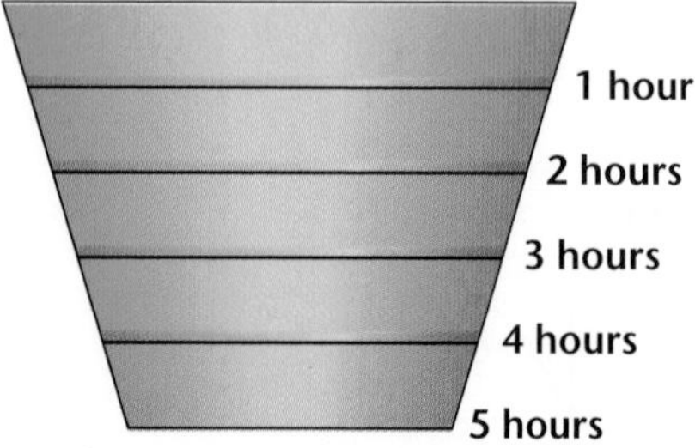

9. **Challenge** An artist drew a sketch of the inside of a water clock to show that after one hour, the level is at the first hour mark, after two hours, the level is at the second hour mark, and so on. The artist makes the distances between the marks the same. Are the marks spaced correctly? Explain.

10. Suppose you have \$230 saved. You get a job that pays \$25 a week. You decide to add all of your earnings to your savings.

a. Describe a function based on this situation.

b. Identify the input and output.

c. Write an equation to represent the function.

NUMBER	DATE	DESCRIPTION OF TRANSACTION	PAYMENT/ DEBIT	DEPOSIT/ CREDIT	BALANCE
					\$ 230.00
	5/3	Deposit	\$	\$ 25.00	\$ 25.00
					255.00
	5/10	Deposit		25.00	25.00
					280.00
	5/17	Deposit		25.00	25.00
					305.00

Writing For each pair of variables, tell whether y is a function of x. Explain your thinking.

11. x = the number of \$12 concert tickets sold
y = the amount of money made from selling the tickets

12. x = the age of any given office building
y = the height of that office building

13. x = the time of year
y = the time at which the sun rises where you live

For each equation or graph, tell whether y is a function of x.

14. $7x = y$ 15. $x = 7$ 16. $x^2 - 1 = y$ 17. $2x = y^2$

18.

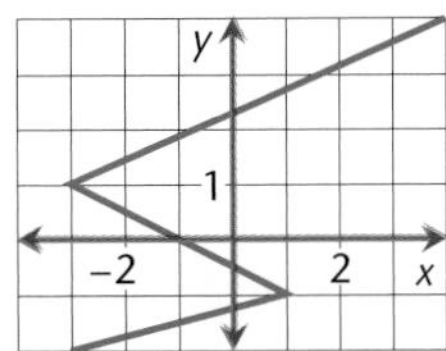

19.

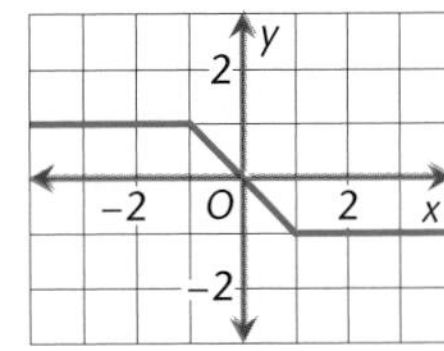

20. **Geometry Connection**

a. Is the area of a square a function of its side length? Explain.

b. Is the side length of a square a function of its area? Explain.

For Exercises 21–23, a rule for a function is given. Write an equation to represent the function.

21. Divide a number by 5. 22. Multiply a number by −1.

23. Multiply a number by itself, then divide the result by 2.

24. **Home Involvement** Make up a rule for a function like those in Exercises 21–23. Keep your rule secret. Have someone give you a number to use as the input. Tell the person the output for that number. The person should make a table of the input and output pairs. Have the person try to guess the rule.

25. **Earth Science** In 1993, heavy rains in the Midwest caused the Mississippi River to flood its banks. By April 4, the water had risen 2.1 in. above the banks of the river. It continued to rise at an average rate of 0.4 in. per day for the next six days.

a. Let y = the height of the river above the bank x days after April 4. Write an equation for y in terms of x.

b. Describe reasonable values for each of the variables in your equation. Explain your thinking.

c. Graph your equation.

d. Tell whether y is a function of x.

Discussion

Exercise 26 checks that you can identify and represent a function.

Reflecting on the Section

26. In this section, you have seen how graphs and tables can be used to illustrate change.

a. Describe a quantity that changes over time. Explain how you could use a table and graph to represent the change.

b. Is the change you described in part (a) a function? Explain.

Spiral Review

27. The perimeter of a rectangular garden is 136 m. Its area is 960 m^2. Find the perimeter and the area of a scale drawing of the garden with a scale of 1 cm to 2 m. **(Module 5, p. 381)**

28. Find the value of x. Round to the nearest hundredth. **(Module 5, p. 343)**

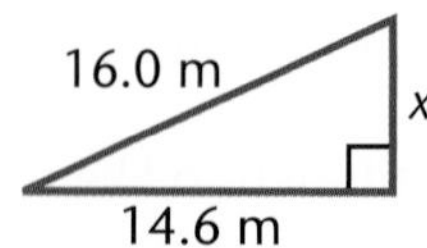

Graph each equation. Give the slope of each line.
(Module 4, pp. 264–265)

29. $y = x + 1$ 30. $y = -x$ 31. $y = -3$ 32. $y = -x - \frac{1}{2}$

Section 1 Extra Skill Practice

Match each container with a graph that shows the water level as a function of the amount of water in the container.

1. 

2. 

3. 

4. 

A. 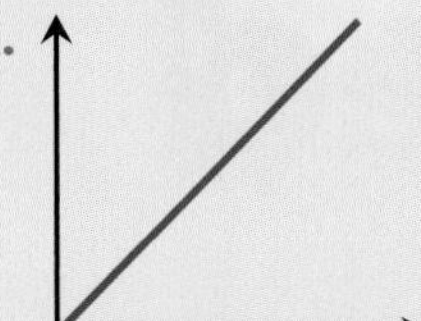

B. 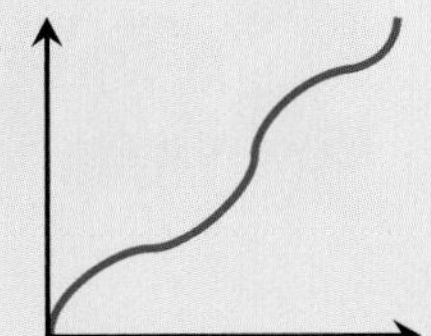

C. 

D. 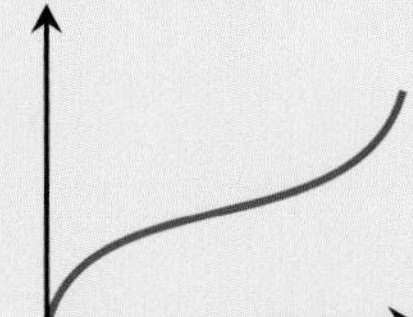

For each equation or graph, tell whether y is a function of x.

5. $2x = 2y$

6. $y = x - 7$

7. $2y = x^2$

8. $2x = y^2$

9. 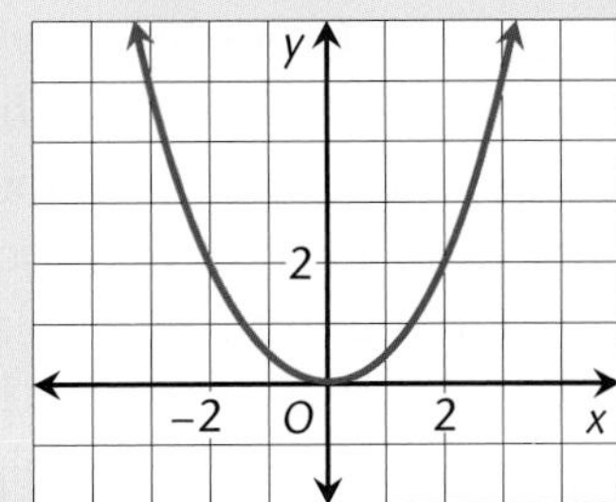

10. 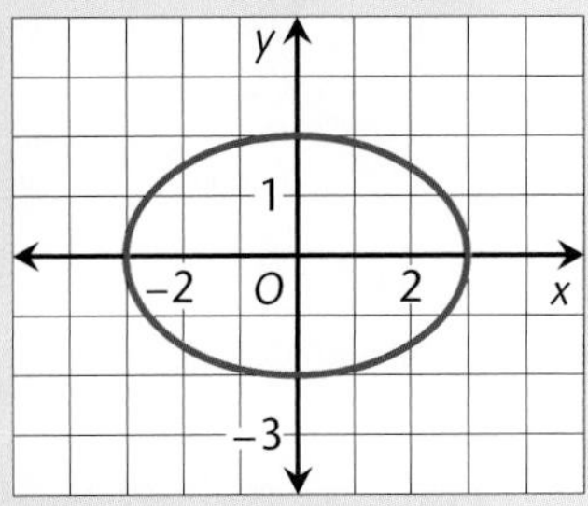

Study Skills ▶ Managing Your Time

Whether you are working independently or in a group to complete a short-term activity or a long-term project, time management should be part of your preparation.

1. In Exploration 1, you worked in a group to conduct an experiment to explore how the shape of a container affects water level. Did your group finish the experiment in the available time? What strategies can you use in planning your time so that you will always finish group activities?

2. Before you begin working on the module project on pages 452–453, make a plan for how you will complete all of the steps so that you finish the entire project on time.

Section 2 Linear Equations and Problem Solving

IN THIS SECTION

EXPLORATION 1
- Linear Change

EXPLORATION 2
- Multi-Step Equations

a Penny Saved

Setting the Stage

A penny may not seem like very much, but you would be surprised at how quickly pennies add up.

Students at the Lovell J. Honiss School in Dumont, New Jersey, set a goal of filling two five-gallon jugs with pennies. Although they quickly met their goal, they continued to save pennies. In the end, they filled four jugs and raised over $1000 to help the homeless.

In Hartland, Michigan, students in the Hartland Consolidated Schools collected pennies for the Meals on Wheels program. They collected over $10,000, enough to fund the program for a year.

Think About It

1 **a.** About how may pennies does a five-gallon jug hold? How do you know?

b. Suppose the Hartland students collected the pennies over 50 school days. On average, about how many pennies were collected each day?

2 Would the pennies collected at the Hartland Consolidated Schools cover your classroom floor? the gymnasium floor? Explain.

▶ **In this section, you will use equations, tables, and graphs to model problems involving the growth of savings over time.**

Exploration 1

Linear Change

GOAL

LEARN HOW TO...
- use equations, tables, and graphs to solve problems

AS YOU...
- investigate different savings plans

KEY TERM
- linear equation

SET UP *Work with a partner. You will need: • graph paper • graphing calculator (optional)*

▶ **How quickly can you save $1000? It all depends on how much you start with, and how much you add to your savings over time.**

3 **Discussion** Read the savings plans described below. Without doing any calculations, tell which person you think will reach the $1000 goal first. Explain your thinking.

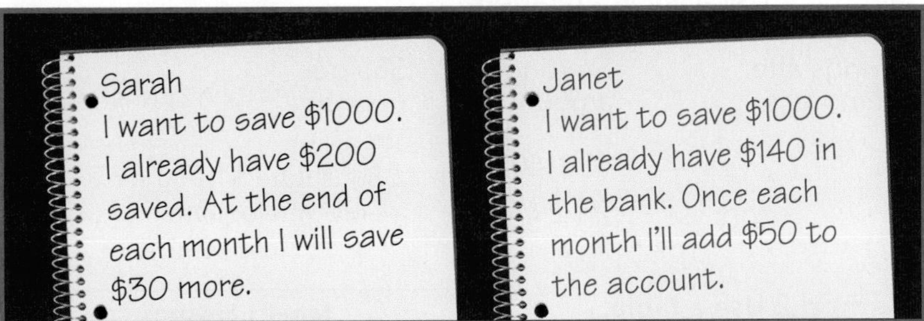

4 **a.** Copy and extend the table to show how much Sarah will save throughout the first year of her plan.

b. Use your table to find the number of months it will take Sarah to save $1000. Describe your method.

Sarah's Savings	
Number of months (x)	Amount saved (y)
0	200
1	230
...	...

5 **a.** Plot the ordered pairs (x, y) for the data in your table on a coordinate grid. What do you notice about the points?

b. Draw a line through the points on your graph. Extend the line and use it to find the number of months it will take Sarah to save $1000.

c. **Discussion** Find the point on the line whose x-coordinate is $6\frac{1}{2}$. Does the value of the y-coordinate of this point represent Sarah's savings after $6\frac{1}{2}$ months? Explain.

▶ **The growth of Sarah's savings over time is an example of linear change. You can use a *linear equation* to represent linear change. A linear equation is an equation whose graph is a line. A linear equation whose graph is not a vertical line represents a function.**

FOR◀HELP with *slope-intercept form*, see **MODULE 4, p. 265**

6 **a.** Find the slope m and the y-intercept b of the line you drew in Question 5(b). Use these values to write an equation for the line in slope-intercept form.

b. Substitute values for x in the equation from part (a). Solve for y. Do the values you get match the values in your table?

▶ **You can use equations, tables, and graphs to model problems involving linear change.**

EXAMPLE

Janet has \$140. She adds \$50 to her savings at the end of each month. When will she have \$1000?

Method 1 **Use a linear equation.**

Savings after x months = Starting amount + \$50 per month • x months

$$y = 140 + 50x$$

$$1000 = 140 + 50x$$

Substitute **\$1,000** for y. Solve the equation for x.

Method 2 **Use a table.**

Keep adding \$50 to Janet's savings for each month until she reaches the \$1000 goal.

Janet's Savings

Number of months	Amount saved
0	140
1	190
2	240
...	...

Method 3 **Use a graph.**

Graph $y = 140 + 50x$ and $y = 1000$ on the same pair of axes.

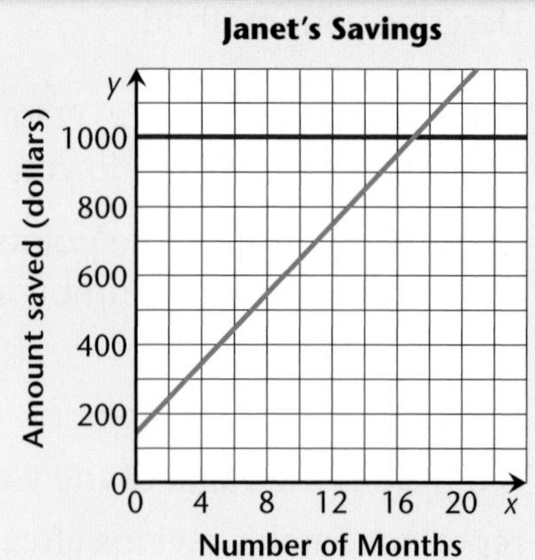

7 **Try This as a Class** Refer to the Example on page 408. You will use each model to find how long it will take Janet to save $1000.

a. Solve the equation in the Example. How can you use the solution to find out when Janet will have saved $1000?

b. Show how to use the table to find out how long it will take Janet to save $1000.

c. Show how to use the graph to find out how long it will take Janet to save $1000.

d. Which method do you prefer? Why?

8 Plot the data for Janet's savings from the Example on page 408 on the same pair of axes as the graph you made in Question 5. What does the intersection of the two lines tell you?

9 ✓ **CHECKPOINT** The Hartland Consolidated students collected $10,000 in pennies. Suppose your class was given a gift of $650 and saved $175 each week. With your partner, use an equation, a table, or a graph to find out how many weeks it would take to save $10,000. Explain why you chose the model you did.

✓ **QUESTION 9**

...checks that you can model and solve a problem about linear change.

10 **Discussion** Find a group in your class that chose a different model than you did for Question 9.

a. Show the other group how you got your answer.

b. Compare the advantages and disadvantages of using an equation, a table, and a graph to model the growth of a savings plan.

HOMEWORK EXERCISES ▶ See Exs. 1–8 on pp. 414–415.

GOAL

LEARN HOW TO...
- solve equations that involve simplifying
- use the distributive property

AS YOU...
- model savings plans

KEY TERM
- distributive property

Exploration 2

Multi-Step Equations

▶ **On page 407, you read about two people who are each trying to save \$1000. Sarah has \$200 and saves another \$30 each month. Janet is starting with \$140 and saves an additional \$50 each month.**

11 **Discussion** In Question 8 on page 409, you used a graph to find when the two girls will have saved equal amounts of money. How could you use tables to solve this problem?

▶ **You can also use an equation to find out when the girls will have the same amount.**

EXAMPLE

For each plan, model the amount saved after x months.

Sarah's savings = 200 + 30x **Janet's savings = 140 + 50x**

Then write a new equation.

When will **Sarah's savings** equal **Janet's savings?**

Sarah's savings = Janet's savings

200 + 30x = 140 + 50x

To find out when the amounts saved are equal, solve the equation for x.

12 **Try This as a Class** The final equation in the Example has a variable on both sides of the equal sign.

a. What would be your first step in solving an equation like this one? Explain your thinking.

b. When will Sarah and Janet have the same amount?

✓ QUESTION 13

...checks that you can solve equations with variables on both sides.

13 **✓ CHECKPOINT** Solve each equation.

a. $18 + 3x = x + 24$ **b.** $9 + 2x = 12 + 5x$ **c.** $4x - 7 = 2 - 3x$

d. $5 - x = 25 + x$ **e.** $-12 + 7x = 3x + 8$ **f.** $-5x - 8 = -7x + 1$

▶ **One way to save money is in a savings bank *certificate of deposit* (CD). You deposit an amount of money and agree not to take any money out for a certain amount of time. In return, the bank pays a higher than usual interest rate.**

14 Suppose you deposit $1000 into a one-year CD. The expression $1000(1 + x)$ models the amount of money you will have after one year. What do you think x represents?

▶ **In Module 1 you learned the distributive property. Recall that all four of the following statements are true for all numbers a, b, and c.**

$a(b + c) = ab + ac$	$ab + ac = a(b + c)$
$a(b - c) = ab - ac$	$ab - ac = a(b - c)$

15 **a.** Use the distributive property to rewrite the expression $1000(1 + x)$.

b. Show that the expression in Question 14 and the expression you wrote in part (a) have the same value when $x = 0.04$.

c. How much money will you have after one year at 4% interest?

▶ **You can use the distributive property to rewrite an expression involving parentheses.**

EXAMPLE

Rewrite $5(3 - 2x)$ without parentheses.

$$5(3 - 2x) = 5(3) - 5(2x)$$
$$= 15 - 10x$$

Use the distributive property.

16 **a.** In Module 1, you used the distributive property to combine like terms, such as $2x + 3x = (2 + 3)x = 5x$. Which version of the distributive property did you use?

b. Which version of the distributive property is used in the Example above to rewrite an expression involving parentheses?

17 ✓ **CHECKPOINT** Use the distributive property to rewrite each expression without parentheses.

a. $5(2x - 3)$

b. $-2(5 + x)$

c. $3(6m + 7)$

d. $7(8m - 1)$

✓ **QUESTION 17**

...checks that you can use the distributive property.

▶ **Sometimes you may want to use the distributive property to solve an equation.**

EXAMPLE

Hector earns the same amount babysitting every week. Each week he saves all but \$10 of his earnings. If he has \$160 after 8 weeks, how much does he earn each week?

SAMPLE RESPONSE

Let x = the amount Hector earns each week. Then $x - 10$ = the amount he saves each week.

$$160 = 8(x - 10)$$
$$160 = 8x - 80$$
$$240 = 8x$$
$$30 = x$$

Use the distributive property.

Hector earns \$30 each week babysitting.

18 Two students tried to solve the equation $-4(2 - x) = 6$.

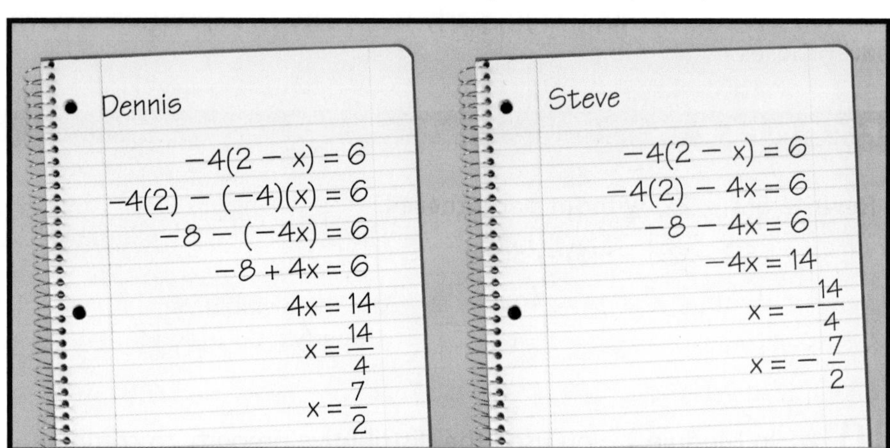

a. Which student solved the equation correctly? What mistake did the other student make?

b. What would be your first step in solving $-2(3 - x) = 8$?

19 **Discussion** How would you solve $-3(x - 1) = 2(5 - x)$?

20 ✓ **CHECKPOINT** Solve each equation.

a. $4(x - 1) = 12$ **b.** $-2(3 - x) = 3x + 1$ **c.** $3(2x - 1) = x + 13$

✓ **QUESTION 20**

...checks that you can use the distributive property to solve an equation.

HOMEWORK EXERCISES ▶ **See Exs. 9–30 on pp. 415–417.**

Section 2

Key Concepts

Key Term

linear equation

Modeling Linear Change (pp. 407–409)

When a quantity changes by the same amount at regular intervals, the quantity shows linear change. You can use a linear equation to model linear change. You can also use a table or a graph.

Example Lynda borrowed **\$175** from her parents. She pays them back **\$10** a week. Her sister Maria borrowed **\$200** and pays back \$15 a week. Who will finish paying off her loan first?

Write an equation for each person. Let $y =$ the amount the person owes after x weeks.

Lynda
$y = 175 - 10x$

Maria
$y = 200 - 15x$

Number of weeks	Amount Lynda owes	Amount Maria owes
0	175	200
1	165	185
2	155	170
4	135	140
5	125	125
6	115	110
...	...	...
13	45	5
14	35	0

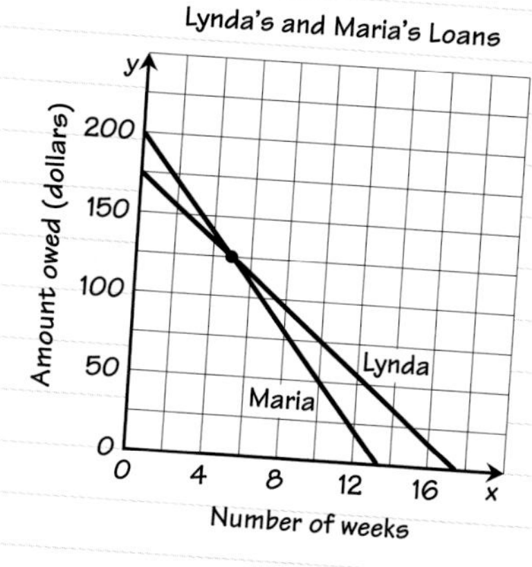

Maria only has to pay \$5 in the 14th week.

After five weeks, they owe the same amount of money. After that, Maria is paying more per week than Lynda, so she will pay off her loan first.

21 Key Concepts Question In the Example above, how does the graph show when the sisters owe the same amount of money?

Section 2

Key Concepts

Key Term

distributive property

Solving Equations (pp. 410–412)

To solve some equations, you may need to use the distributive property and combine like terms.

Example

$$-3(1 + 4x) + 2x = 5x$$

Use the distributive property.

$$-3(1) + (-3)(4x) + 2x = 5x$$

$$-3 + (-12x) + 2x = 5x$$

Combine like terms.

$$-3 - 10x = 5x$$

Add 10x to both sides.

$$-3 - 10x + 10x = 5x + 10x$$

$$-3 = 15x$$

$$-\frac{3}{15} = \frac{15x}{15}$$

$$-\frac{1}{5} = x$$

22 **Key Concepts Question** Look back at the Example on page 413. Explain how to write and solve an equation to find out when the sisters owe the same amount of money.

Section 2

Practice & Application Exercises

YOU WILL NEED

For Exs. 2–7, 17, 29, and 30:
- graph paper or graphing calculator (optional)

1. The equation $y = 75x + 90$ models Bruce's savings after x weeks. Describe his savings plan in words.

Graph each pair of equations on the same pair of axes. Find the point where the graphs intersect and label its coordinates.

2. $y = 25x$ and $y = 20x + 10$
3. $y = 10 - 2x$ and $y = 4 - x$
4. $y = 18 - 3x$ and $y = 6$
5. $y = 50 - 4x$ and $y = 20 + x$

6. A school plans to rent a boat for a dolphin-watching trip. Rental company A charges a boat rental fee of \$375 plus \$125 per hour. Rental Company B charges a boat rental fee of \$175 plus \$150 per hour.

   a. Use a table or graph. For how many hours will the total cost of renting a boat from Company A be \$1500?

   b. Use your answer to part (a). What would the cost of renting a boat from Company B for that number of hours be?

   c. Use your table or graph. For what number of hours will the boat rental cost be the same for both companies?

   d. Explain why you could solve the equation $375 + 175x = 175 + 125x$ to answer part (c).

   e. Solve the equation in part (d). Compare the result to your answer in part (c).

7. Suppose you have \$5000 in savings. You start spending your savings at a rate of \$150 per month. Your friend has \$200 and adds \$150 to his savings every month. Use a table or a graph to answer the questions below.

   a. When do you run out of money?

   b. How much has your friend saved by that time?

   c. When will you and your friend have the same amount of money?

   d. How much money will you each have then?

8. Look back at Exercise 7. Show how to write and solve equations to answer parts (a) and (b).

Use the distributive property to rewrite each expression without parentheses.

9. $-5(m + 12)$ 10. $3(1 + 8p)$ 11. $8(-5 - x)$

12. $10(0.5 - 0.5w)$ 13. $6(3x - 1)$ 14. $(1 - 2t)2$

15. **Alternative Method** Anne used a different method to solve the equation $160 = 8(x - 10)$ in the Example on page 412. She first divided both sides of the equation by 8.

a. Why do you think she did this?

b. What do you think she did next?

c. Do you prefer her method or the method used in the Example? Explain.

16. It costs \$3 to park at Bay Beach if you buy a special sticker for your car. A sticker costs \$50 and can be used all summer. It costs \$8 to park without a sticker.

a. Write two equations that model your cost of parking at the beach n times, one if you have a sticker and one if you do not have a sticker.

b. **Writing** Under what circumstances would you save money by buying a sticker? Explain your th inking.

17. a. Use an equation to find a common solution of $y = 5x$ and $y = 2x + 3$. Are there other common solutions? Explain.

b. Graph the equations from part (a) on the same pair of axes. How can you use the graph to find a common solution of the two equations?

c. Graph $y = 3x + 4$ and $y = 3x - 2$ on the same pair of axes. Do these equations have any common solutions? Explain.

Solve each equation.

18. $25x + 200 = 50x + 50$

19. $4t = -10t - 28$

20. $3 = 2(m - 3)$

21. $-3 - 6h = 3(2h + 3)$

22. $15m + 30 - 2m = 2m$

23. $8(2x - 1) = 5(2x + 3)$

24. $2(5 - x) = -2x - 5 + x$

25. $5 - 3(1 - m) = 2(m - 5)$

Geometry Connection For each diagram, use the given area to find the value of x.

FOR ▶ HELP with using formulas from geometry, see **TOOLBOX, p. 595**

26. Area = 25 m^2

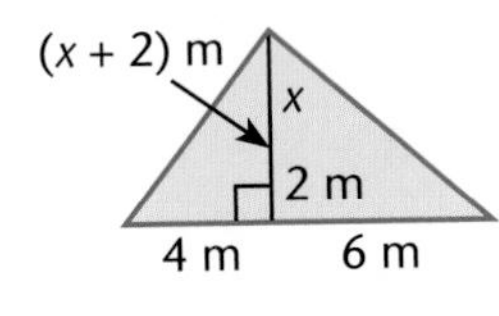

triangle

27. Area = 24 ft^2

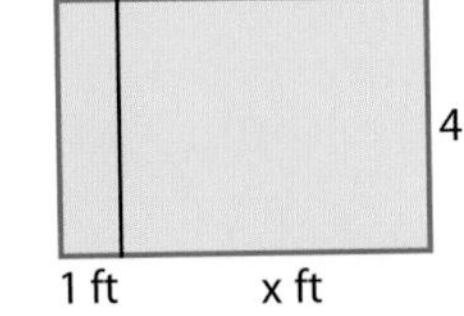

rectangle

28. Area = 35 cm^2

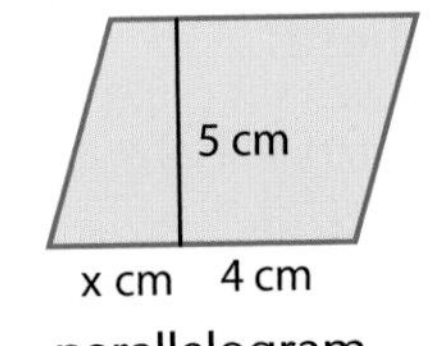

parallelogram

29. You can use graphs to solve equations like $3x + 8 = 2(x + 5)$.

a. Graph $y = 3x + 8$ and $y = 2(x + 5)$ on the same pair of axes. Find the x-coordinate of the point where the graphs intersect.

b. Check to see that the x-coordinate you found in part (a) is the solution of $3x + 8 = 2(x + 5)$.

c. Use graphs to solve $-5 = -3(-1 - x) + 7$. Check your solutions.

Reflecting on the Section

Write your response to Exercise 30 in your journal.

30. Suppose you have $100 in savings. How much money would you like to have saved in 10 years? Make a plan that involves linear change for achieving this savings goal. Describe your plan in words. Use an equation, a table, and a graph to model your plan.

Journal

Exercise 30 checks that you can model change.

Spiral Review

31. Suppose you raise a flag up a pole. Which of the graphs below best models this situation? Explain your choice(s). (Module 6, p. 400)

a.

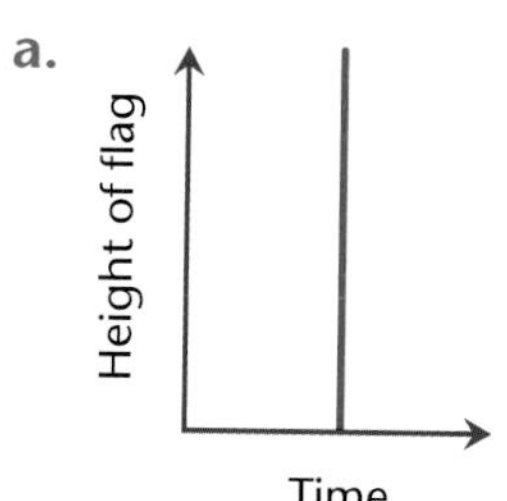

b.

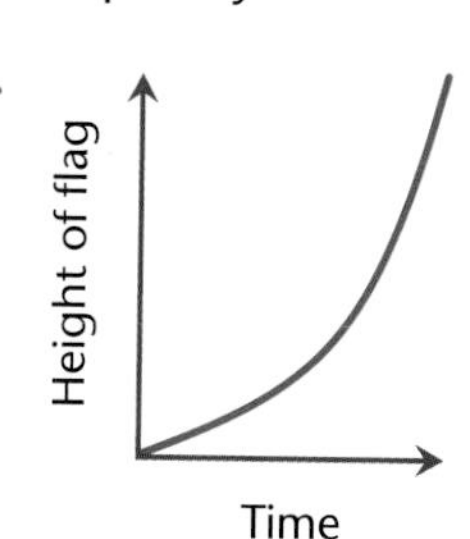

c.

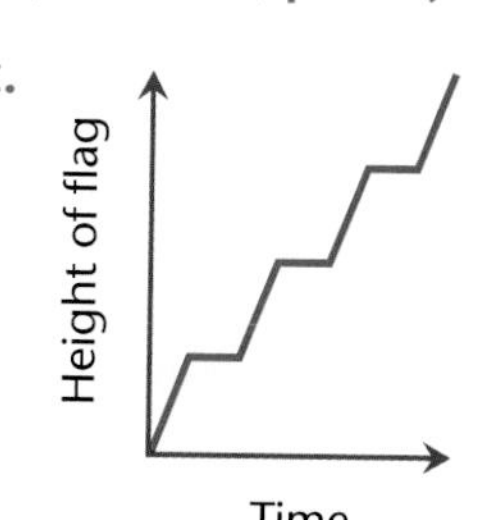

Write each rational number as a terminating or repeating decimal. (Module 4, p. 277)

32. $\frac{3}{7}$ 33. $\frac{6}{11}$ 34. $-2\frac{1}{5}$ 35. $\frac{5}{8}$

Rewrite each product as a power. (Toolbox, p. 589)

36. (5.2)(5.2)(5.2)(5.2)

37. $3 \cdot 3 \cdot 3 \cdot 3 \cdot 3 \cdot 3 \cdot 3 \cdot 3$

38. $16 \cdot 16 \cdot 16 \cdot 16 \cdot 16$

39. $\frac{3}{5} \cdot \frac{3}{5} \cdot \frac{3}{5} \cdot \frac{3}{5} \cdot \frac{3}{5} \cdot \frac{3}{5}$

Section 2 Extra Skill Practice

You will need: • *graph paper or graphing calculator (optional)* **(Exs. 1–4)**

Graph each pair of equations on the same pair of axes. Find the point where the graphs intersect and label its coordinates.

1. $y = 10x$ and $y = 5x + 20$
2. $y = 15 - 3x$ and $y = 5 - x$
3. $y = 12 - 4x$ and $y = 3$
4. $y = 25 - 2x$ and $y = 10 + x$

Solve each equation.

5. $3x - 4 = x + 10$
6. $6 + 2x = 5x + 9$
7. $12 + x = -3 + 4x$
8. $7x + 4 = 2x - 11$
9. $-3x - 2 = -9 - 4x$
10. $-7x + 5 = 8x - 1$
11. $3x = 18 - 3x$
12. $14x + 6 = -2x - 2$
13. $-5x - 9 = 3x + 17$

Use the distributive property to rewrite each expression without parentheses.

14. $5(x - 3)$
15. $-3(2 + 3x)$
16. $4(-1 - 6x)$
17. $(2x + 1)6$
18. $3(x - 3)$
19. $(7 - 4x)2$
20. $x(x + 1)$
21. $x(x + 4)$
22. $(4x - 1)3$

Solve each equation.

23. $2(x - 1) = 3x + 4$
24. $-w + 2(5w - 6) - 4w = -3(-w - 10)$
25. $3y + 5 + 2y = 5(2y + 1)$
26. $2 - 4(h - 4) = 10(2h - 3)$
27. $4k - 15(k - 2) = 17k + 9$
28. $8 + 5m(m - 3) = 12 - m(3 - 5m)$
29. $6 - 2t = 3(2t + 4)$
30. $3b(4 - 2b) - 6b = -b(6b + 7) + 104$

Standardized Testing ▶ Open-ended

1. Describe a real-life situation that can be modeled by the equation $y = 5x + 30$.
2. Write an expression that involves parentheses. Then use the distributive property to rewrite the expression without parentheses.
3. Write an equation that can be solved by using the distributive property. Then solve your equation.

FOR ASSESSMENT AND PORTFOLIOS

EXTENDED E² EXPLORATION

Choosing the Right Plan

SET UP *You will need graph paper.*

The Situation

The Smith family is planning to subscribe to a cellular phone service. They have three payment plans from which to choose.

The Problem

The Smiths are not sure which plan they should choose. Evaluate each plan described at the right. Use mathematical models such as equations, tables, and graphs to make recommendations for choosing a plan.

Something to Think About

- What factors should the Smiths consider when choosing a payment plan?
- How can you model the three plans using equations, tables, and graphs?

Present Your Results

Write a letter to the Smith family explaining the advantages and disadvantages of each service plan. Give useful advice to the Smiths about choosing a plan. Include the mathematical models you used to come up with your recommendations.

Modeling Exponential Change

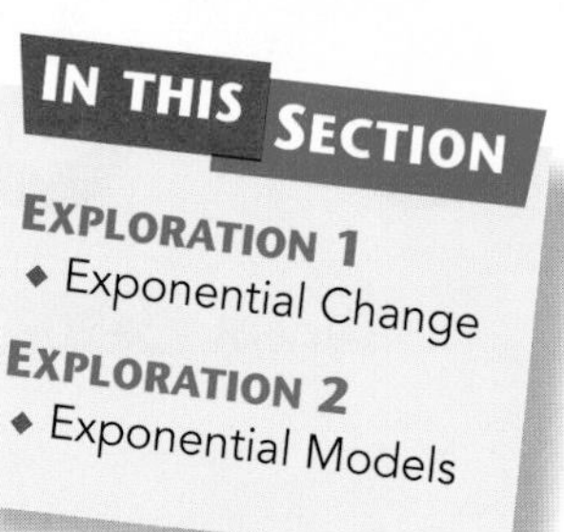

How Sweet It Is

Setting the Stage

In Roald Dahl's *Charlie and the Chocolate Factory*, Charlie Bucket's family is so poor that he only gets a chocolate bar once a year.

Only once a year, on his birthday, did Charlie Bucket ever get to taste a bit of chocolate. The whole family saved up their money for that special occasion, and when the great day arrived, Charlie was always presented with one small chocolate bar to eat all by himself.

...he would take a *tiny* nibble...

The next day, he would take another tiny nibble, and so on, and so on. And in this way, Charlie would make his ten-cent bar of birthday chocolate last him for more than a month.

Roald Dahl, *Charlie and the Chocolate Factory*

Think About It

Suppose on the first day, Charlie eats half the chocolate bar. The next day, he eats half the remaining chocolate bar, and continues to eat half the remaining chocolate each day after that.

1 Will Charlie eat the same amount of chocolate each day? Explain.

2 How long do you think the chocolate bar will last?

Exploration 1

Exponential CHANGE

GOAL

LEARN HOW TO...
- model exponential change

AS YOU...
- use paper folding to model eating a chocolate bar

SET UP *You will need: • a rectangular sheet of paper • graph paper • graphing calculator (optional)*

▶ **In Question 2, you estimated how long Charlie Bucket's chocolate bar would last if he ate half of the remaining chocolate each day. In this exploration, you will use paper folding to model this situation.**

3 **a.** Fold a sheet of paper in half. With no folds there is one layer. After one fold there are two layers.

0 folds
1 layer
area = 1

1 fold
2 layers
area of a layer = **?**

b. If the area of the unfolded paper is one square unit, what is the area of each layer after you fold the paper once**?**

c. Record the number of folds, the number of layers, and the area of each layer in a table like the one shown.

d. Fold your paper as many times as possible. Extend and fill in your table each time you fold the paper.

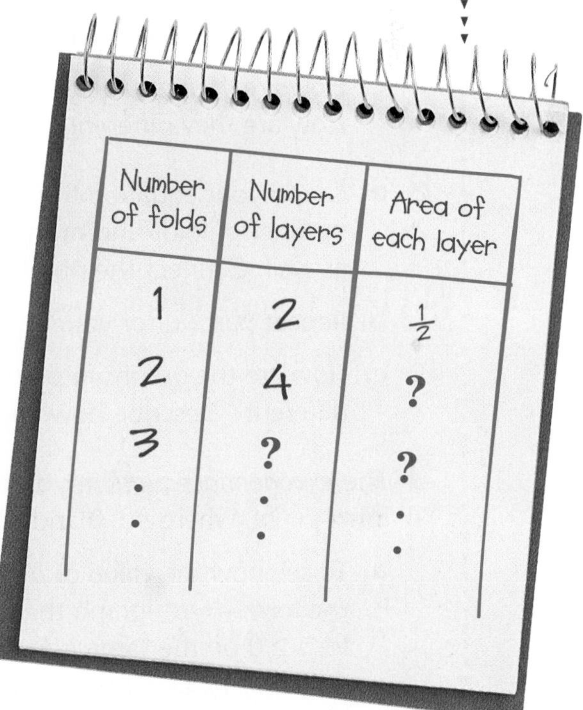

Number of folds	Number of layers	Area of each layer
1	2	$\frac{1}{2}$
2	4	?
3	?	?
⋮	⋮	⋮

Number of folds	Number of layers	Area of each layer	Number of layers as a power	Area of each layer as a power
1	2	$\frac{1}{2}$	2^1	$\left(\frac{1}{2}\right)^1$
2	4	?	?	?
3	?	?	?	?
⋮	⋮	⋮	⋮	⋮

For Questions 4–7, use your completed table from Question 3.

4 Suppose you could continue folding the paper.

a. What would happen to the number of layers as the number of folds increased?

b. What would happen to the area of each layer?

5 Add two columns to your table, as shown. Write the number of layers as a power of 2 and the area of each layer as a power of $\frac{1}{2}$.

6 Suppose you could fold the paper ten times. Predict how many layers there would be. Then predict the area of each layer. Explain your reasoning.

▶ **As you folded the paper, the number of layers and the area of each layer changed *exponentially*. You can use equations and graphs to model exponential change.**

7 **Try This as a Class** Let x = the number of folds.

a. Let y = the number of layers. Write an equation for y in terms of x. Explain why when $x = 0$, $y = 1$.

b. Let y = the area of each layer. Write an equation for y in terms of x. Explain why when $x = 0$, $y = 1$.

c. How are your equations in parts (a) and (b) alike? How are they different?

8 **a.** Graph your equation from Question 7(a). Plot points for the number of folds and number of layers in your table. Plot (0, 1) as well. Connect the points with a smooth curve.

b. Repeat part (a) for your equation from Question 7(b).

c. How are the graphs in parts (a) and (b) alike? How are they different? Describe how each graph changes as x increases.

9 The *exponential equations* you have seen so far have all had the form $y = b^x$, where $b > 0$ and $x \geq 0$.

a. To see how the value of b affects the graph of an equation in the form $y = b^x$, graph the equations $y = 3^x$, $y = 4^x$, and $y = 7^x$ for $x \geq 0$ on the same pair of axes. For each graph, include the point (0, 1). Describe the differences and the similarities in the curves.

b. How would you describe the graph of an equation in the form $y = b^x$, where $b > 1$ and $x \geq 0$?

c. How is your graph of the equation $y = \left(\frac{1}{2}\right)^x$ from Question 8(b) different from the graphs in part (a)?

d. Why do you think the graphs are different?

10 ✓ **CHECKPOINT** Look back at the excerpt from *Charlie and the Chocolate Factory* on page 420. What fraction of the original candy bar would Charlie have left after 1 month (30 days) if he eats half of what is left each day?

✓ **QUESTION 10**

...checks that you understand exponential change.

HOMEWORK EXERCISES ▶ **See Exs. 1–5 on pp. 427–428.**

Exploration 2

Exponential MODELS

GOAL

LEARN HOW TO...
- write an equation to model compound interest
- use tables and equations to solve problems

AS YOU...
- model price changes and the growth of a savings account

KEY TERM
- exponential equation

SET UP *Work with a partner. You will need a calculator.*

▶ **Much has changed since 1964, when *Charlie and the Chocolate Factory* was first published. The price of a candy bar is more than five times what it was then.**

11 In 1960, a candy bar cost about 10¢. Suppose this price is raised 5 times to reach 50¢. Work with your partner to find a way to change 10 to 50 in 5 steps using each method.

Step	Price
0	10¢
1	?
2	?
3	?
4	?
5	50¢

a. *Add* the same number at each step. Tell what number you added. Copy and complete the table for each step.

b. *Multiply* by the same number at each step. Use guess and check to find the number. Tell what number you multiplied by. Copy and complete the table for each step.

▶ **Savings can grow as quickly as prices if you deposit money in a savings account that earns interest. The amount of money increases exponentially, even if you do not make any more deposits.**

12 **a.** Suppose you deposit $1000 into an account that pays 8% annual interest. Find 8% of $1000 to determine the amount of interest you will earn in one year.

b. What is the new total in your account at the end of one year?

▶ **How much money will you have in a savings account after 10, 20, or 30 years? To find out, look for a pattern.**

EXAMPLE

Suppose you deposit $2000 into an account that earns 5% annual interest. After one year, you will have 100% of your deposit plus an additional 5% interest.

Initial deposit + Interest after one year

(1.00)(2000) + (0.05)(2000)

You can use the distributive property to rewrite this expression:

(1.00)(2000) + (0.05)(2000) = (1.00 + 0.05)(2000)

= (1.05)(2000)

= 2100

After one year, there will be $2100 in the account.

13 Refer to the situation described in the Example.

a. Suppose you leave your money in the account for two years. How much money will you have at the end of the second year? Explain how you got your answer.

b. Copy the table and complete it by continuing the pattern in the *Expression* column.

Year	Amount in account at beginning of year	Expression	Amount in account at end of year
1	$2000	1.05 • 2000	$2100
2	$2100	1.05 • 1.05 • 2000	?
3	?	?	?
4	?	?	?
5	?	?	?

c. **Discussion** Describe the pattern in the *Expression* column.

14 **a.** At the end of two years, the amount of money in the account described in the Example is given by the expression 1.05 • 1.05 • 2000. Rewrite this expression using exponents.

b. Calculator Use exponents to write an expression for the amount of money in your account at the end of 20 years. Use the y^x key to evaluate the expression.

▶ **The growth of money in a savings account that earns annual interest is an example of an exponential function. You can represent an exponential function with an exponential equation in this form:**

$$y = a \cdot b^x$$

amount after x years (y); starting amount (a); growth factor (b)

15 **Try This as a Class** The equation $2923.08 = 1500 \cdot (1.1)^7$ gives the amount in an account after a certain number of years.

a. How much money was originally deposited into the account?

b. How many years was the money in the account?

c. How much money is in the account after this number of years?

d. What is the growth factor? What is the interest rate?

16 ✓ **CHECKPOINT** Suppose you deposit $4000 in an account that earns 6% annual interest. Write an equation that models the amount y in the account after x years. How much will be in the account after each period of time?

a. 1 year **b.** 12 years **c.** 20 years

✓ **QUESTION 16**

...checks that you can write and use an exponential equation to solve problems.

17 **Discussion** Look back at Question 11 on page 423.

a. Suppose the price of a candy bar starts at $0.10 and increases by $0.01 each year. Write an equation for the price after x years.

b. Suppose the price starts at $0.10 and increases by 10% each year. Write an equation for the price after x years.

Price of candy bar	$.01 yearly increase	10% yearly increase
After 10 years	?	?
After 20 years	?	?
After 30 years	?	?
After 40 years	?	?

c. Use your equations to copy and complete the table. Compare the predicted prices over time.

HOMEWORK EXERCISES See Exs. 6–17 on pp. 428–429.

Section 3 Key Concepts

Key Term

exponential equation

Exponential Change (pp. 421–423)

Some exponential equations have the form $y = b^x$, where $b > 0$ and $x \geq 0$. You can use an equation in this form to model some types of exponential change.

Example Suppose a piece of paper has an area of 1 square unit. You fold the paper into thirds. Then you fold the paper into thirds again. You keep repeating this process.

Number of regions after x steps = 3^x

Area of each region after x steps = $\left(\frac{1}{3}\right)^x$

Step 0
Regions: 1
Area of each region: 1

Step 1
Regions: 3
Area of each region: $\frac{1}{3}$

Step 2
Regions: 9
Area of each region: $\frac{1}{9}$

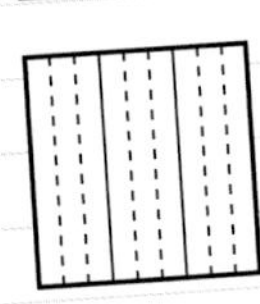

Exponential Models (pp. 423–425)

When you deposit money into a savings account that earns annual interest, the amount of money in the account grows exponentially over time. You can model a relationship like this one with an exponential equation in the form $y = \mathbf{a} \cdot \mathbf{b}^x$.

starting amount

amount after **x** years $\quad y = a \cdot b^x \quad$ growth factor

Example Suppose you deposit **$1800** into a savings account that earns 3% annual interest. To find out how much money you will have after **5** years, you can write an equation.

$$y = 1800 \cdot (1.03)^x$$

When $x = 5$, $y = 1800 \cdot (1.03)^5 \approx 2086.69$.

You will have about $2087 after 5 years.

18 Key Concepts Question In the Example above about the savings account, how is the number 1.03 related to the interest rate? Explain why you use 1.03 as a factor five times.

Section 3

Practice & Application Exercises

YOU WILL NEED

For Ex. 16:
- graph paper or a graphing calculator

1. In the Example about folding paper into thirds on page 426, two equations are given. Match each equation with one of the graphs below. Explain your thinking.

A.
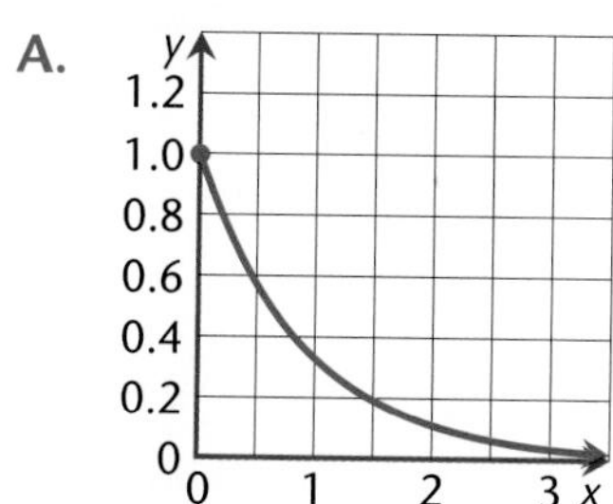

B.
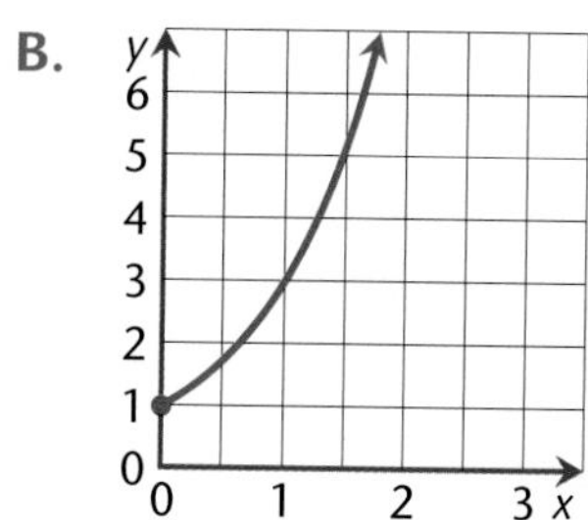

2. **Geometry Connection** In the diagram, the area of each regular hexagon is $\frac{3}{4}$ the area of the next larger hexagon. If the area of the outer hexagon is 1 square unit, what is the area of the smallest hexagon?

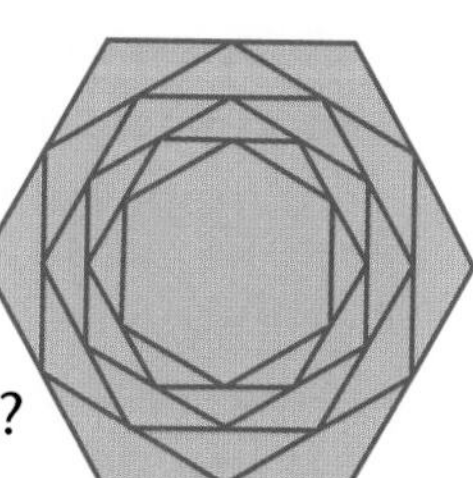

3. Suppose someone in your class starts a rumor. This student tells the rumor to two other students. Each of these students repeats the rumor to two other students. This pattern continues.

   a. Suppose it takes one minute to find two students and tell them the rumor. Copy and extend the table for the first ten minutes after the rumor starts.

Number of minutes	Number of new people hearing the rumor	Total number of people who have heard the rumor
0	1	1
1	2	3

   b. Write and solve an equation to find the **number of new people who *hear* the rumor** one hour after it was started.

   c. How is this problem like the paper folding activity in Exploration 1?

   d. **Visual Thinking** Show how you can use a tree diagram to model this situation.

4. **Challenge** Use the information in Exercise 3. Write an equation that models the **total number of people who *have heard* the rumor** after x minutes.

5. **Writing** Jane graphed three equations on the same graphing calculator screen, but cannot tell which graph goes with each equation. Explain how she can tell just by looking at the graphs.

1st equation: $y = \left(\frac{1}{3}\right)^x$
2nd equation: $y = 4^x$
3rd equation: $y = \left(\frac{3}{2}\right)^x$

6. a. Suppose you deposit \$500 into an account that earns 9% annual interest. Write an equation that shows the amount of money in the account after x years.

   b. How much money will be in the account after 10 years?

   c. About how many years will it take for the amount of money in the account to reach \$2000? How did you get your answer?

7. Write an equation in the form $y = a \cdot b^x$ to model each situation. Tell what the variables x and y represent.

   a. The student population of a school with 1200 students is predicted to grow at a rate of 4% each year.

   b. Marcia is training for a marathon. She runs 5 km this weekend. For the next several weeks, she will increase her distance by 10% each weekend.

8. **Open-ended** Describe a situation like the ones in Exercise 7. Write a word problem about the situation that you could use an exponential equation to solve. Give the solution of your problem.

9. **Algebra Connection** Are the equations you wrote in Exercise 7 functions? Explain.

Evaluate each expression for the given value of the variable.

10. $4 \cdot 3^x$; $x = 3$
11. $4 \cdot \left(\frac{1}{2}\right)^x$; $x = 4$
12. $100 \cdot 0.4^x$; $x = 2$
13. $\frac{1}{2} \cdot 2^x$; $x = 5$
14. $\frac{2}{3} \cdot 6^x$; $x = 3$
15. $5 \cdot \left(\frac{1}{3}\right)^x$; $x = 4$

16. **Population Growth** Exponential equations in the form $y = a \cdot b^x$ are often used to model population growth. For example, suppose the population of a town is 10,000 and is predicted to grow at a rate of 3% each year.

a. Write an equation to model the population y after x years.

b. Graph your equation. Your graph should show the town's population for the next 30 years.

c. In about how many years will the population double?

d. Suppose the population of the town grows at a rate of 6% each year. Predict how many years it will take the population to double. Check your prediction by writing and graphing an equation.

Reflecting on the Section

Be prepared to discuss your response to Exercise 17 in class.

17. **Discussion** Suppose you win a $25,000 college scholarship on a TV quiz show. You are given two options for collecting your scholarship money. What are the advantages and disadvantages of each option? Which option would you choose? Why?

Discussion

Exercise 17 checks that you can use an exponential equation to model a problem situation.

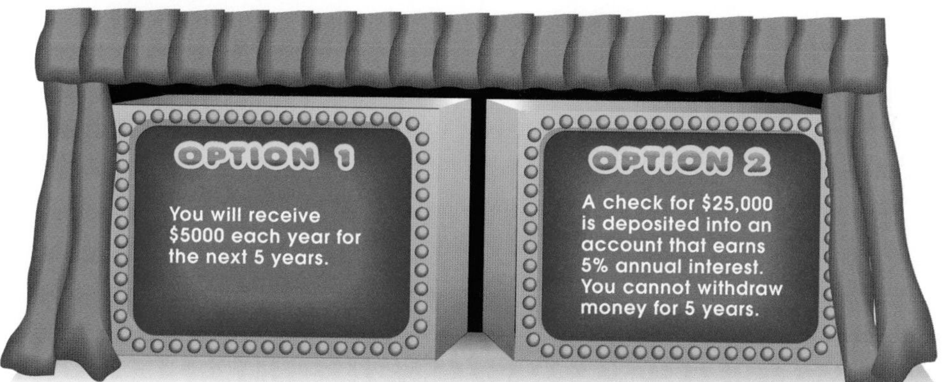

Spiral Review

Solve each equation. (Module 6, p. 414)

18. $13x + 15 = 185 - 4x$

19. $-6 - 2p = -(3 - 4p)$

20. After the translation $\left(x - 2, y + \frac{1}{2}\right)$, the image of a point is (5, 0). What are the coordinates of the original point? (Module 2, p. 87)

Career Connection

Wildlife Veterinarian: William Karesh

As a wildlife veterinarian, William Karesh studies disease and nutrition. He may help a monkey with malaria or an elephant with an infected toe. Many infections are caused by bacteria that reproduce exponentially.

21. Suppose 2 bacteria infect an animal. In 20 min, each of these bacteria splits into 2 bacteria, so that there are 4 bacteria. In another 20 min, these 4 bacteria each split into 2 bacteria. This pattern continues over time.

a. How many bacteria will there be after 2 hr? after 6 hr? How did you get your answers?

b. How does exponential growth help explain what can happen if an infection is not treated quickly?

Extension 

Exponential Decay

Most of the situations you modeled in this section involved *exponential growth*. You can also use an equation in the form $y = a \cdot b^x$ to model *exponential decay*. For example, suppose you pay \$18,000 for a new car. You plan to sell the car in a few years, but know that the car will be worth less and less as time goes on. The value of the car is depreciating (losing value) at a rate of 12% a year.

22. About how much will your car be worth after 1 year? after 2 years? after 3 years? How did you get your answers?

23. Let y = the value of your car after x years. An equation for y in terms of x is $y = 18{,}000(0.88)^x$. The number 0.88 is the *decay factor*. How is the decay factor related to the rate of depreciation?

24. In Exploration 1, you found the area of each layer as you folded a sheet of paper. Was this an example of exponential growth or exponential decay? Explain.

Section 3 Extra Skill Practice

Write an equation in the form $y = a \cdot b^x$ to model each situation. Tell what the variables x and y represent.

1. A baseball card worth $150 is projected to increase in value by 8% a year.
2. A TV station's local news program has 60,000 viewers. The managers of the station plan to increase viewership by 5% a month.
3. A bakery produces 2000 loaves of bread on an average day. In order to meet demand for an upcoming holiday, the bakers want to increase production by 10% a day.

Evaluate each expression for the given value of the variable.

4. $18 \cdot 4^x$; $x = 6$
5. $\frac{3}{5} \cdot 5^x$; $x = 7$
6. $0.35 \cdot 9^x$; $x = 4$
7. $\frac{4}{3} \cdot 3^x$; $x = 8$
8. $8 \cdot \left(\frac{1}{4}\right)^x$; $x = 6$
9. $\frac{3}{2} \cdot \left(\frac{2}{3}\right)^x$; $x = 4$

Write an equation to find out how much money you will have in each situation.

10. You deposit $2000 into an account for 1 year at 3% annual interest.
11. You deposit $200 into an account for 10 years at 3% annual interest.
12. You deposit $600 into an account for 4 years at 7% annual interest.
13. You deposit $1500 into an account for 8 years at 4% annual interest.

Standardized Testing ▶ Performance Task

1. A store is having a sale on sweaters. On the first day the price of a sweater is reduced by 20%. The price will be reduced another 20% each day until the sweater is sold. Gustav thinks that on the fifth day of the sale the sweater will be free. Is he right? Explain.
2. Carlos plans to deposit $1000 into one of two banks. For four years, he will leave any interest earned in the account, but make no other deposits or withdrawals. At the end of each year Bank A pays interest at a rate of 6% of the total amount in the account, while Bank B pays interest at a rate of 7% of the original amount deposited. Which bank should Carlos choose? Explain.

Algorithms and Transformations

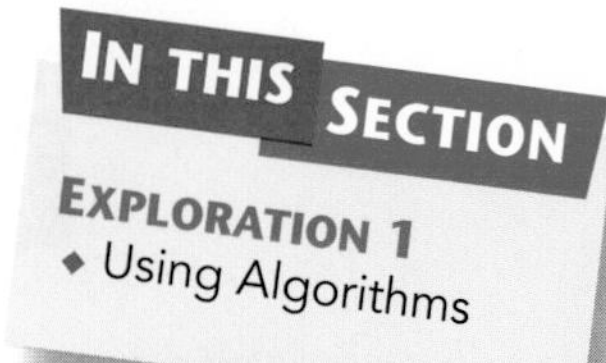

Setting the Stage

Computer graphics can be used to model motion. For example, Olympic gymnasts in training are videotaped performing a floor routine or vault. A computer analyzes the tape and recreates the motion. Sometimes these tapes are broken down into stick figure sequences like the one below. Sports scientists study these sequences to help improve equipment and reduce injury among athletes.

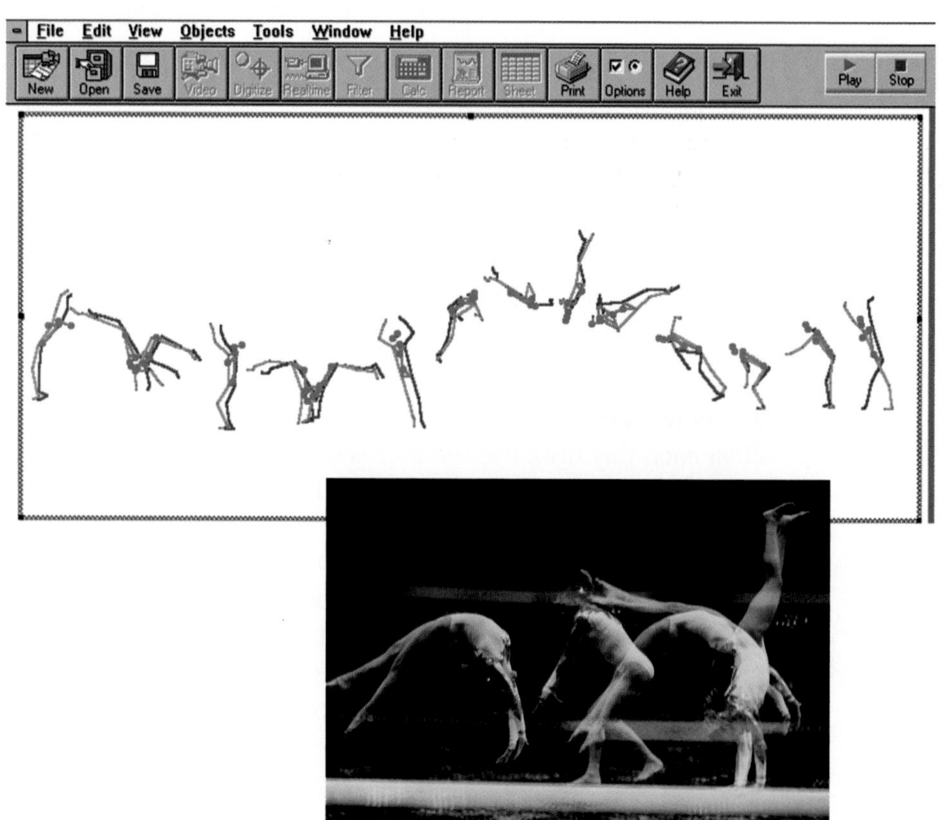

Think About It

Suppose the computer simulation on page 432 is shown in the first quadrant of a coordinate plane. You want to give instructions that will move the figure through the routine.

1 What information do you need to include in your instructions?

2 How can you use coordinates to describe changes in the gymnast's position?

▶ **Movement of a figure on a computer screen can be created by assigning coordinates to points on the figure and giving instructions for moving each point. In this section you will explore how to represent movements using a series of instructions.**

Exploration 1

Using Algorithms

SET UP *You will need:* • *Labsheet 4A* • *graph paper*

GOAL

LEARN HOW TO...
- use algorithms to transform geometric shapes
- reflect geometric shapes

AS YOU...
- model a gymnast's change in position

KEY TERMS
- transformation
- algorithm
- reflection

▶ **In Module 2 you learned how to translate objects. You can use translations and other *transformations* to represent simple motions. A transformation is a change in an object's shape, size, or position.**

3 The figures below show positions before and after a move.

original figure

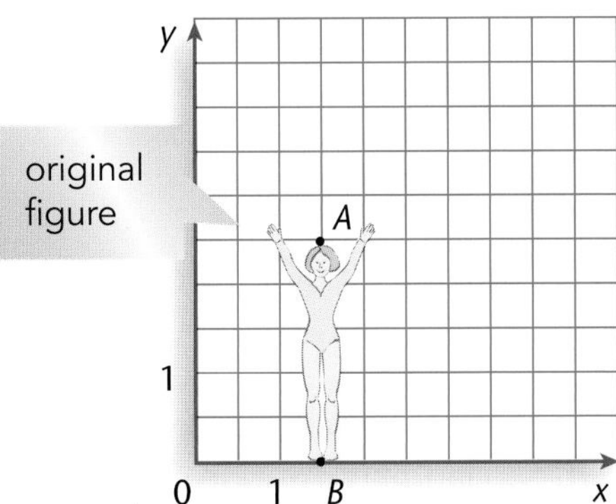

image

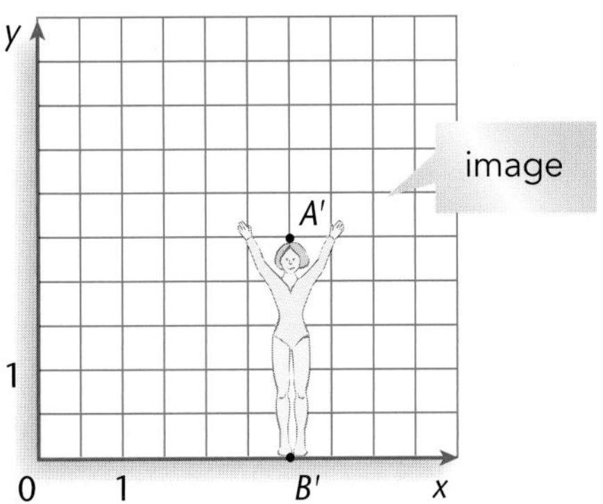

a. Are the image and the original figure congruent? Explain.

b. How can you transform the original figure to get the image?

FOR ◀ HELP with *translations,* see **MODULE 2, p. 87**

▶ **Animation that models movement may combine a series of steps. You can use an *algorithm* to describe these steps. An algorithm is a step-by-step set of instructions you can follow to accomplish a goal.**

The Example below shows an algorithm for creating a very simple representation of the key positions of a gymnast's jump.

EXAMPLE

Suppose a gymnast is videotaped jumping on a balance beam. At the peak of the jump, the gymnast is 2 units to the right and 1 unit higher than her starting position. After landing, she is 2 units to the right and 1 unit lower than when she was in the peak position.

Use an algorithm to create a simple representation of the gymnast's key positions in a coordinate plane.

SAMPLE RESPONSE

Step 1

Plot points to show the gymnast's starting position.

$A = (x, y)$

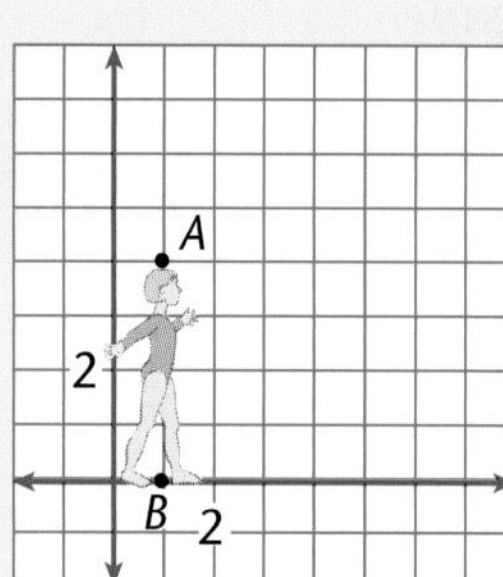

Step 2

Translate each point 2 units to the right and 1 unit up.

$A' = (x', y') = (x + 2, y + 1)$

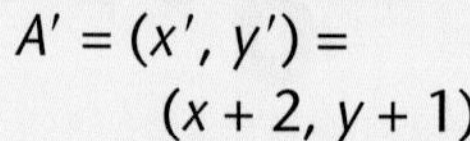

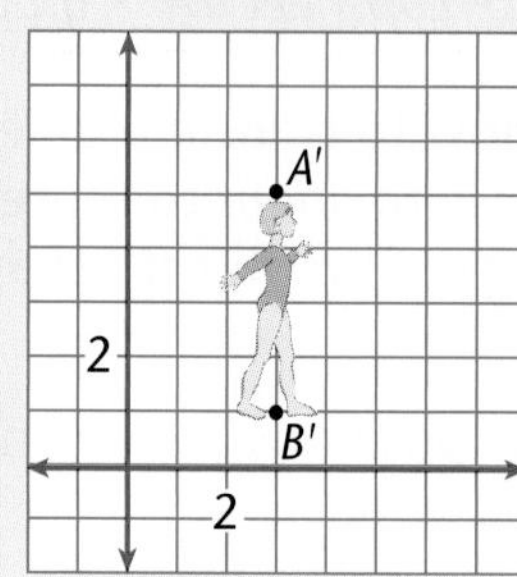

Step 3

Translate each point 2 units to the right and 1 unit down.

$A'' = (x'', y'') = (x' + 2, y' - 1)$

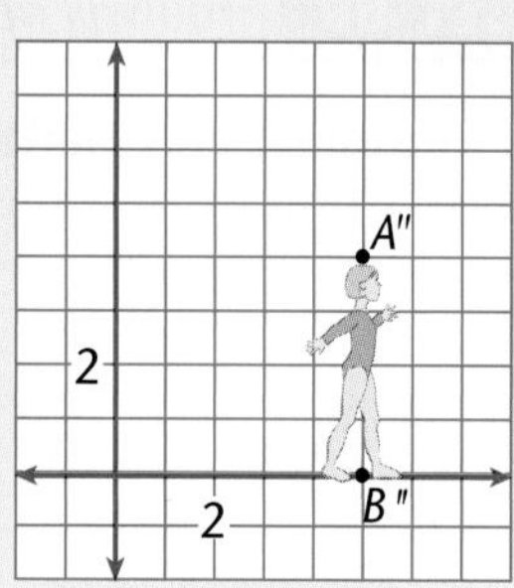

4 Give the coordinates of points A, A', and A'' in the Example.

✓ QUESTION 5

...checks that you can use an algorithm to describe a series of transformations.

5 **✓ CHECKPOINT** Write an algorithm for moving a point from (0, 0) to (2, −3) and then to (2, 3).

6 **a.** Write an algorithm that moves the gymnast in the Example directly from the starting position to the landing position.

b. How is your algorithm different from the one in the Example? How is it similar?

▶ **Animation that models movement may be made up of different types of transformations. The Example below shows a reflection.**

EXAMPLE

The triangle is *reflected* across the *y*-axis. We say that $\triangle A'B'C'$ is the reflection of $\triangle ABC$. Note that the triangles are congruent and the *y*-axis is the perpendicular bisector of every segment joining corresponding points on $\triangle ABC$ and $\triangle A'B'C'$.

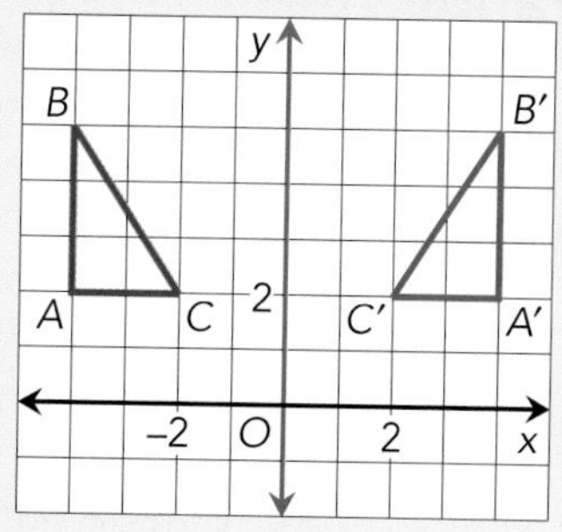

7 **Discussion** Look at the Example above. Compare the coordinates of points *A* and *A'*. Then compare the coordinates of points *B* and *B'* and the coordinates of points *C* and *C'*. Describe any patterns you see.

8 **Try This as a Class** The vertices of $\triangle JKL$ are $J(1, -4)$, $K(5, -2)$, and $L(3, 0)$.

a. Write an algorithm for reflecting $\triangle JKL$ across the *y*-axis of a coordinate plane. Then perform the steps of your algorithm.

b. Compare $\triangle JKL$ and its reflection. Are the two figures congruent? How could you check?

9 **Use Labsheet 4A.** Sometimes there is more than one way to write an algorithm, depending on the order in which you perform the steps.

a. Draw a figure on the blank grid to complete a *Sequence of Transformations.* Describe the steps that transform the original figure to its image.

b. Compare your sequences with those of other students. Did everyone perform the same steps in the same order?

10 ✓ **CHECKPOINT** In a coordinate plane, draw a triangle with vertices at points $M(-2, -4)$, $N(-2, -2)$, and $O(0, 0)$. Then write an algorithm for reflecting $\triangle MNO$ across the *x*-axis and then across the *y*-axis.

...checks that you can write an algorithm for a reflection.

HOMEWORK EXERCISES See Exs. 1–20 on pp. 437–440.

Section 4 Key Concepts

Key Terms

transformation

Transformation (p. 433)

A transformation is a change made to an object's shape, size, or position. Two types of transformations are translations and reflections.

algorithm

Algorithms (p. 434)

An algorithm is a set of steps that you can follow to accomplish a goal.

Example Write an algorithm for the transformation shown.

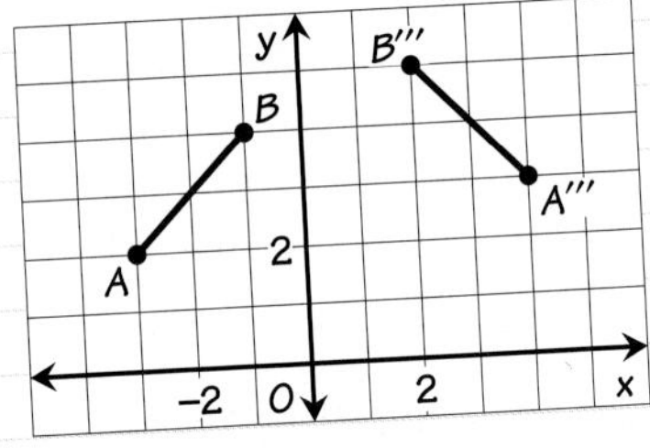

Step 1 Reflect each point across the y-axis.
$(x', y') = (-x, y)$

Step 2 Translate each point up 1 unit.
$(x'', y'') = (x', y' + 1)$

Step 3 Translate each point right 1 unit.
$(x''', y''') = (x'' + 1, y'')$

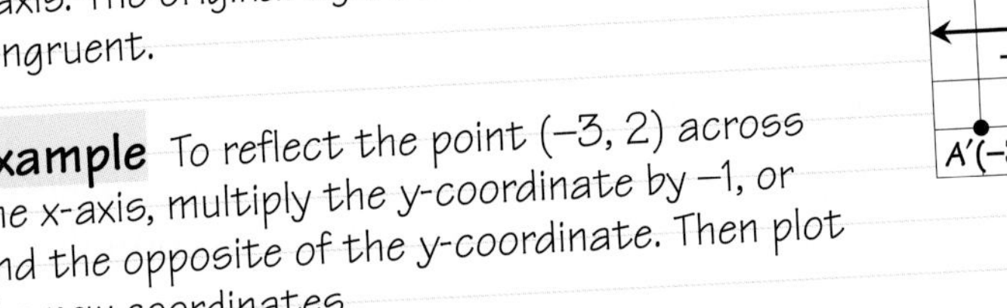

The algorithm $(x''', y''') = (-x + 1, y + 1)$ moves $\overline{AB}$ in the Example to its image $\overline{A'''B'''}$ in one step.

reflection

Reflection (p. 435)

A reflection is a transformation where a figure is flipped across a line such as the x-axis or the y-axis. The original figure and its reflection are congruent.

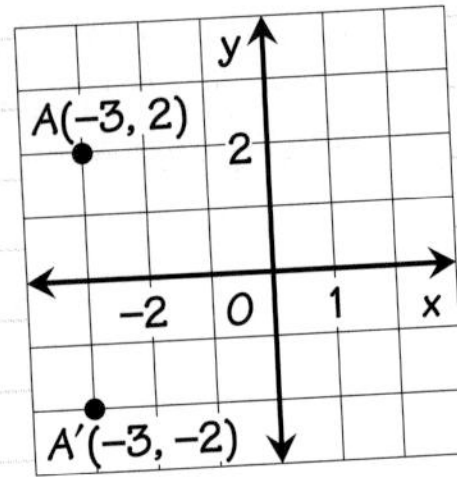

Example To reflect the point (–3, 2) across the x-axis, multiply the y-coordinate by –1, or find the opposite of the y-coordinate. Then plot the new coordinates.

11 **Key Concepts Question** Write a two-step algorithm for the transformation shown.

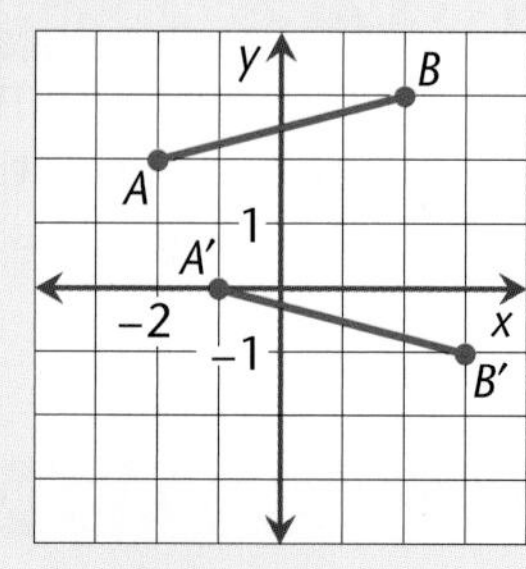

Section 4 Practice & Application Exercises

You will need

For Ex. 1–7, 9, 14–17, and 19:
- graph paper

For Exercises 1 and 2, sketch a stick figure in a coordinate plane. Label a point for each foot and a point for the head. Use algorithms to create simple models of the key positions of the head and each foot for the movement described. (If necessary, write a separate algorithm for each point.) Show the steps of your algorithms in a coordinate plane.

1. jumping up and down in place

2. standing in place and then doing a split

For each figure in Exercises 3–6:

a. **Copy the figure on graph paper.**

b. **Reflect the figure across the given axis or axes. Draw the reflection(s) in the same coordinate plane.**

3. the y-axis

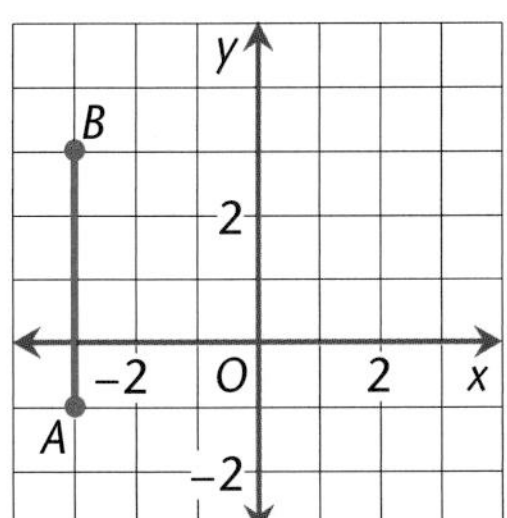

4. the x-axis

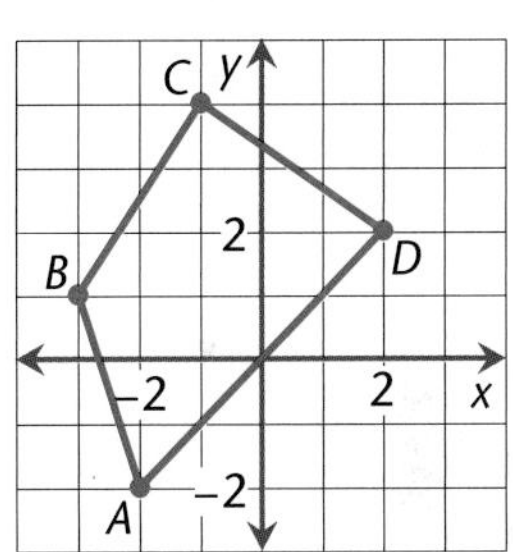

5. the x-axis, then the y-axis

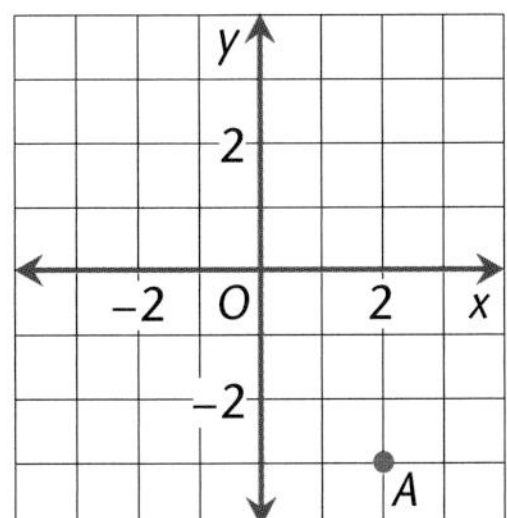

6. the y-axis, then the x-axis

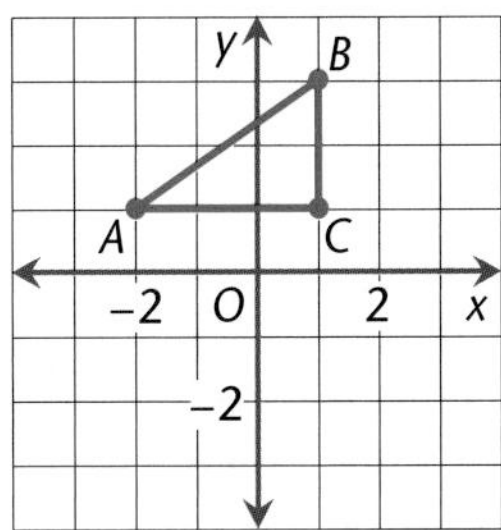

7. Copy the original figure from Exercise 6. Reflect the triangle across the x-axis and then across the y-axis. How does the final image compare to the final image in Exercise 6?

Art **The first and last steps in creating a design are shown.**

8. Write an algorithm that can be used to create the design.

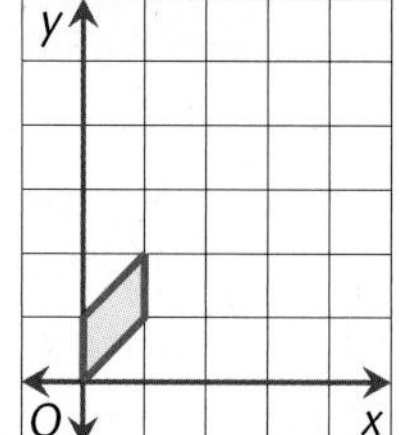

9. **Create Your Own** Sketch a repeating design and write an algorithm that can be used to create it.

Write an algorithm that can be used to create each transformation.

10.

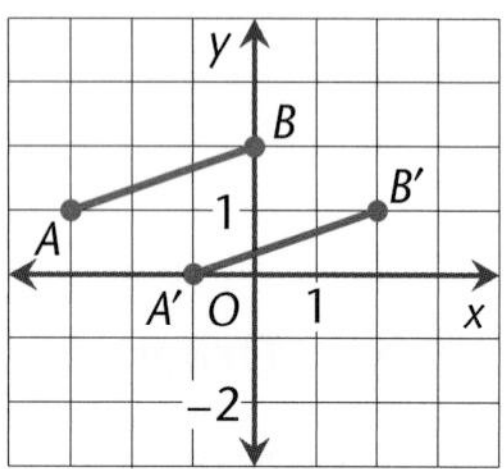

11.

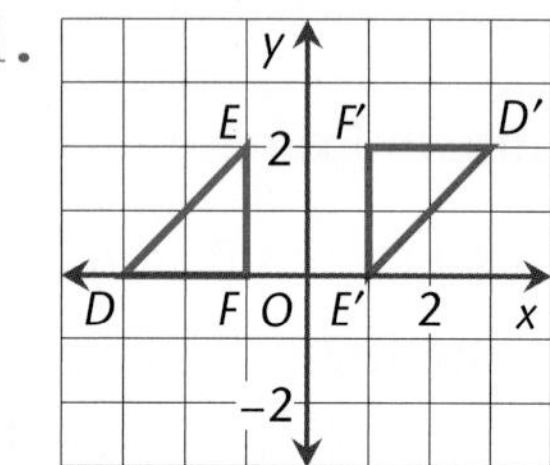

12. **Alternative Method** In the diagram at the right, $\triangle AB'C'$ was created by rotating $\triangle ABC$ 180° clockwise about the origin. Describe how to transform $\triangle ABC$ to $\triangle AB'C'$ using reflections.

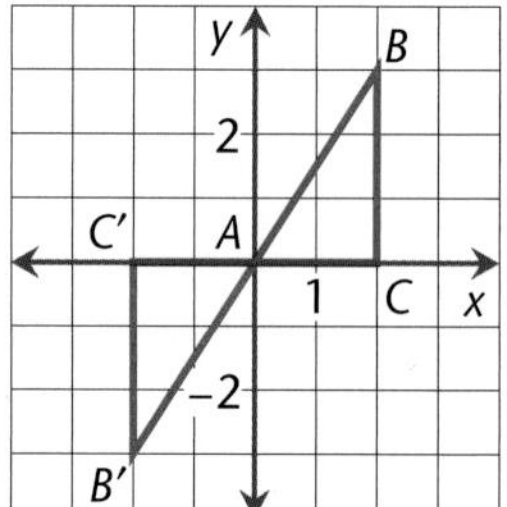

13. In the diagram at the right, $\triangle DE'F'$ was created by rotating $\triangle DEF$ 90° clockwise about the origin. Do you think it is possible to transform $\triangle DEF$ to $\triangle DE'F'$ using only reflections across the *x*- and *y*-axes? Explain.

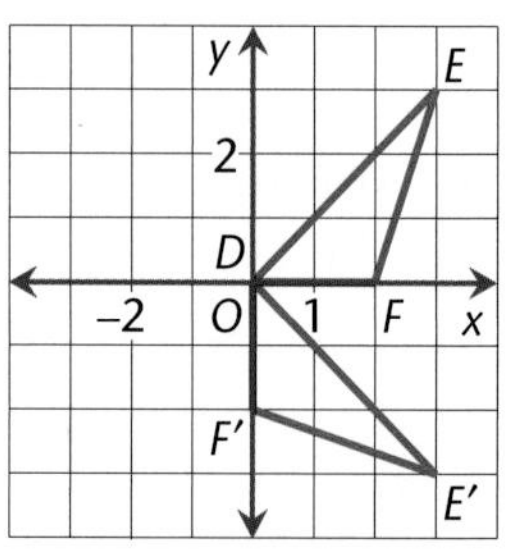

14. The diagram at the right shows a triangle and its reflection across the line $y = x$. Compare the coordinates of each point on the original figure with the coordinates of the corresponding point on the reflection. Write an algorithm for reflecting a figure across the line $y = x$. Draw a figure in a coordinate plane and use it to test your algorithm.

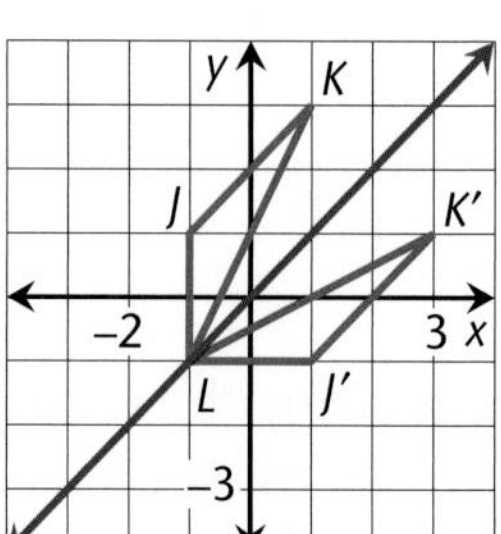

15. You can use an algorithm to model a change that involves stretching. The transformation shown is represented by the algorithm below.

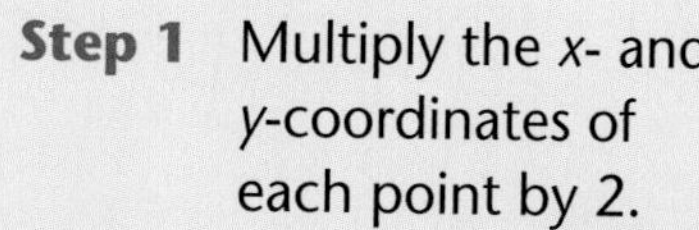

Step 1 Multiply the x- and y-coordinates of each point by 2.

Step 2 Translate each point up 1 unit.

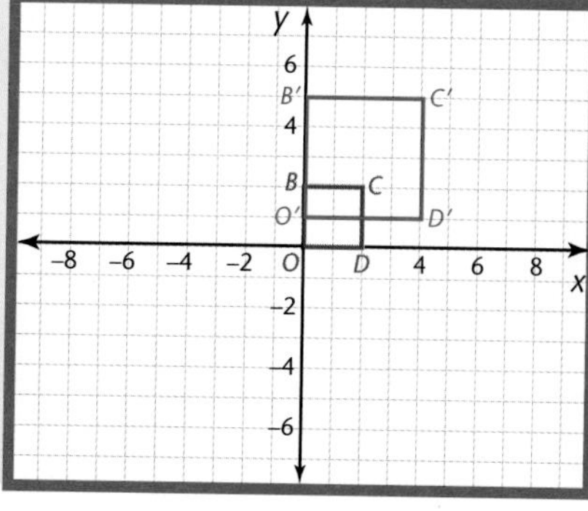

a. Draw square $OBCD$ with coordinates $O(0, 0)$, $B(0, 2)$, $C(2, 2)$ and $D(2, 0)$. Translate the square up 1 unit. Then multiply each coordinate by 2. Draw the final image.

b. Compare your results from part (a) with the transformation shown. Does the order in which you perform the steps matter?

16. Copy the figure below. Then use the algorithm to transform the figure.

Step 1 Multiply the x- and y-coordinates of each point by 3.

Step 2 Reflect each point over the x-axis.

Step 3 Translate each point up 12 units.

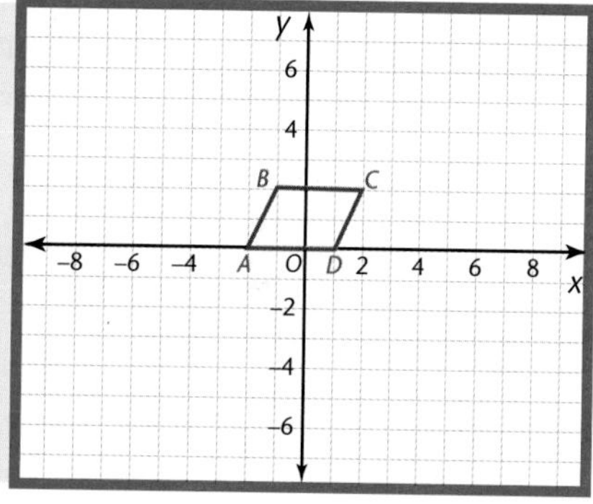

17. You already know how to stretch a figure using multiplication. You can also use multiplication to shrink a figure. Draw the figure below. Then use the algorithm to transform the figure.

Step 1 Multiply the x- and y-coordinates of each point by $\frac{1}{2}$.

Step 2 Translate each point to the left 1 unit.

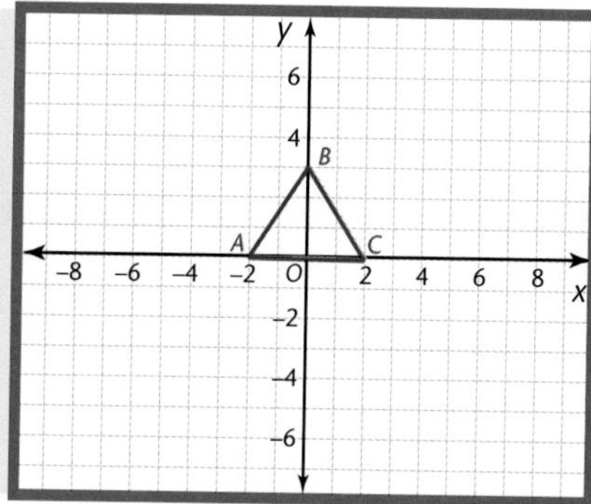

18. **Challenge** What value must you multiply each coordinate of the points on the original figure by to create the final image?

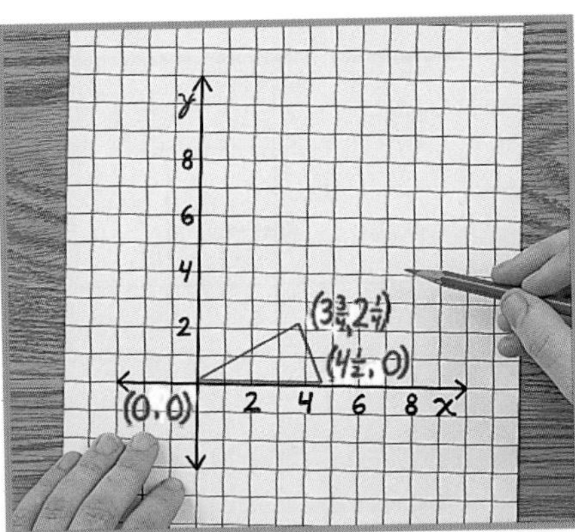

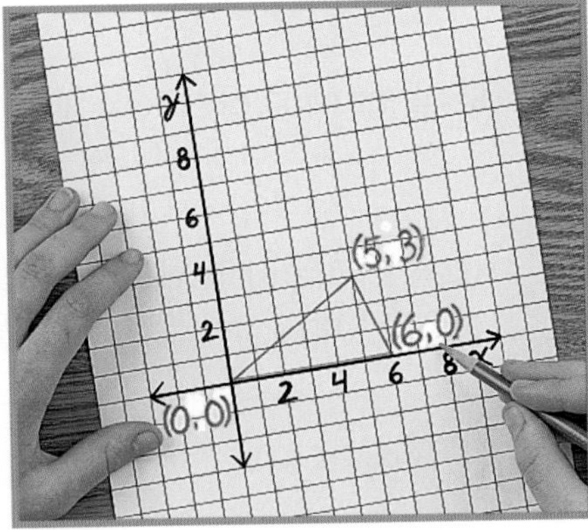

19. **Create Your Own** Work in a group of three. Agree on a figure to transform, and an algorithm with 3 or 4 steps. Each person should follow the steps in a different order. Compare your results.

Reflecting on the Section

Journal

Exercise 20 checks that you understand algorithms.

Write your response to Exercise 20 in your journal.

20. Write two different algorithms for the transformation shown.

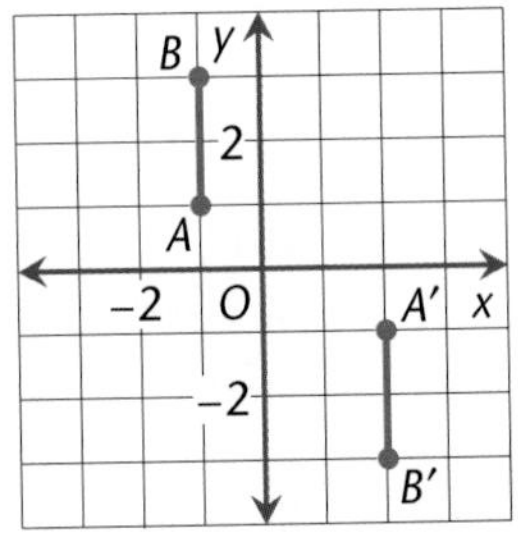

Spiral Review

Evaluate each expression when $x = 3$. (Module 6, p. 426)

21. 3^x

22. $2 \cdot \left(\frac{1}{4}\right)^x$

23. $(4x)^3$

24. In the diagram, line s is parallel to line t. Find each angle measure. (Module 5, pp. 368–369)

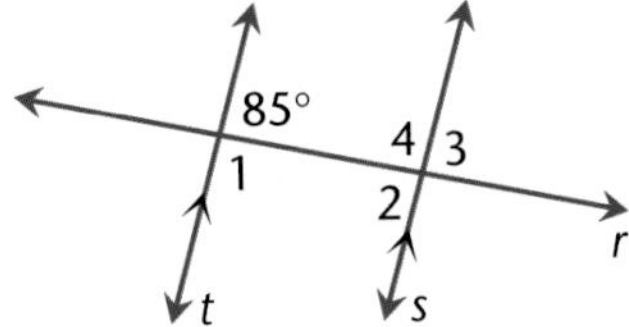

Mental Math Use mental math to find each value. (Module 3, p. 163)

25. $-\sqrt{144}$

26. $\sqrt{0.0001}$

27. $\sqrt{\frac{1}{81}}$

28. $-\sqrt{\frac{49}{225}}$

Extra Skill Practice

You will need: • *graph paper* (Exs. 7–9)

Write an algorithm for moving the point as specified.

1. from (0, 0) to (3, –3)
2. from (1, 4) to (3, 5)
3. from (–2, 5) to (0, 7) and then to (2, 5)

Explain how to perform the following reflection(s).

4. Reflect point (–1, 4) across the *y*-axis.
5. Reflect point (0, 3) across the *x*-axis.
6. Describe at least three different ways to transform point *A*(2, 5) to point *A*′(2, –5).

Sketch the original figure and the final image of the reflection(s).

7. Reflect across the *x*-axis.

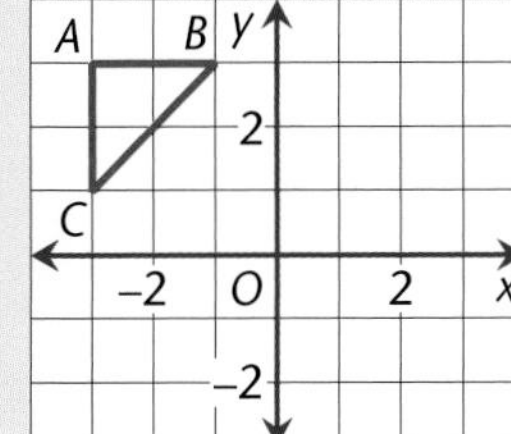

8. Reflect across the *y*-axis and then across the *x*-axis.

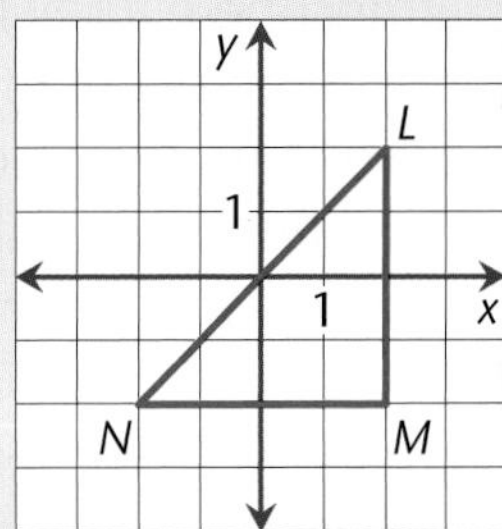

9. Write an algorithm that involves a reflection and a translation.

Standardized Testing ▶ Multiple Choice

1. △*ABC* is translated 8 units to the right and 5 units down. What are the coordinates of point *A* if the coordinates of point *A*′ are (6, 7)?

   A (8, –5) B (11, –1) C (–2, 12) D (14, 2)

2. Which transformation cannot be represented by an algorithm that involves multiplication?

   A reflection over the *x*-axis
   B reflection over the *y*-axis
   C a translation
   D stretching a figure

Section 5 Exploring Quadratic Functions

IN THIS SECTION

EXPLORATION 1
- Parabolas

EXPLORATION 2
- Quadratic Functions

It's All in the Curve

Setting the Stage

How does it feel to orbit Earth? Before NASA astronauts even leave the atmosphere, they have a chance to find out. Specially modified airplanes help astronauts get used to the near-weightless conditions they will experience in space. The airplanes zoom upward and back down, following part of a curve called a *parabola*. As the airplanes reach the top of the parabola, the astronauts feel weightless for a short period of time. For the KC-135 NASA used from 1995 to 2004, the feeling of weightlessness lasted 15-25 seconds.

Think About It

1 During a training flight aboard the KC-135, the astronauts usually flew along the curve of 40 parabolas. About how much time did they spend feeling weightless on a training flight?

2 The section of the curve where the astronauts felt weightless is part of a parabola. Describe it. Does it show symmetry? Explain.

▶ **In this section, you will learn about objects and situations that can be modeled by parabolas.**

Exploration 1

Parabolas

SET UP *Work in a group of four. You will need graph paper or a graphing calculator (optional).*

GOAL

LEARN HOW TO...
- predict the shape of a parabola

AS YOU...
- use equations and graphs to model events and objects

KEY TERMS
- parabola
- line of symmetry
- vertex of a parabola

▶ **A parabola is a type of curve. In the photos below, the main cable of the Golden Gate Bridge and the path of the water can be modeled with parabolas. You can represent a parabola with an equation.**

EXAMPLE

The graph of the equation $y = 0.0239x^2$ models the curve formed by a main cable on the Golden Gate Bridge.

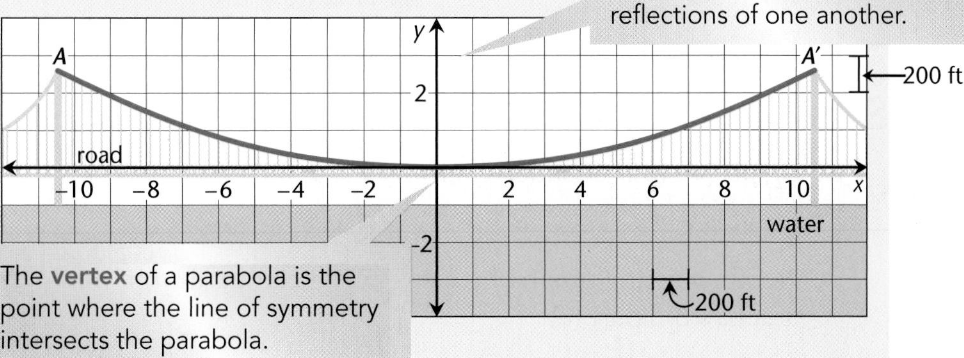

The *y*-axis is the **line of symmetry** for this parabola because it divides the curve into two parts that are reflections of one another.

The **vertex** of a parabola is the point where the line of symmetry intersects the parabola.

3 Give the coordinates of the vertex of the parabola in the Example.

4 Discussion

a. Describe the relationship between the x-coordinates of points A and A' in the Example on page 443.

b. Describe the relationship between the y-coordinates.

c. Are there other points with coordinates that have the same relationships?

▶ **All equations in the form $y = ax^2$, where $a \neq 0$, have graphs that are parabolas. The value of a determines the shape of the parabola.**

5 Use graph paper or a graphing calculator.

a. Graph the equations $y = x^2$ and $y = -x^2$ on the same pair of axes.

b. How are the graphs alike?

c. How are they different?

6 Each person in your group should use graph paper or a graphing calculator to graph one of the following sets of equations on the same pair of axes. How do you think the value of a affects the shape of the graph of an equation in the form $y = ax^2$?

a. $y = x^2$	$y = 2x^2$	$y = 3x^2$	$y = 4x^2$
b. $y = x^2$	$y = -2x^2$	$y = -3x^2$	$y = -4x^2$
c. $y = x^2$	$y = 0.25x^2$	$y = 0.07x^2$	$y = \frac{1}{3}x^2$
d. $y = x^2$	$y = -0.25x^2$	$y = -0.07x^2$	$y = -\frac{1}{3}x^2$

7 Try This as a Class How does the graph of an equation in the form $y = ax^2$ compare with the graph of $y = x^2$ in each case?

a. when $a > 1$

b. when $0 < a < 1$

c. when $a < -1$

d. when $-1 < a < 0$

8 The graph of an equation in the form $y = ax^2 + c$ is also a parabola.

a. Graph the four equations below on the same pair of axes.

$y = x^2 + 1$ $\quad y = x^2 + 2$ $\quad y = x^2 + 3$ $\quad y = x^2 + 4$

b. Predict how the graph of $y = x^2 + 5$ will compare with the graphs from part (a).

c. Predict how the graphs of $y = 0.5x^2 - 1$ and $y = 0.5x^2 - 2$ will compare with the graph of $y = 0.5x^2$. Then check your predictions by graphing all three equations on the same pair of axes.

9 ✓ **CHECKPOINT**

a. Predict how the graph of $y = -0.25x^2$ will compare with the graph of $y = x^2$.

b. Predict how the graph of $y = 2x^2 - 3$ will compare with the graph of $y = 2x^2$.

c. Check your predictions by graphing all four equations on the same pair of axes.

✓ **QUESTION 9**

...checks that you can make predictions about parabolas.

HOMEWORK EXERCISES See Exs. 1–8 on pp. 448–449.

Exploration 2

Quadratic Functions

GOAL

LEARN HOW TO...

- recognize quadratic equations
- simplify quadratic expressions

AS YOU...

- explore the physics of sports

KEY TERM

- quadratic function

SET UP *You will need graph paper or a graphing calculator.*

▶ **One common place to "see" parabolas is at a sporting event such as a basketball game. When a ball is thrown, its path can be represented by a parabola.**

EXAMPLE

The equation $y = -0.05x^2 + 0.7x + 5$ describes the path of a basketball after it is tossed.

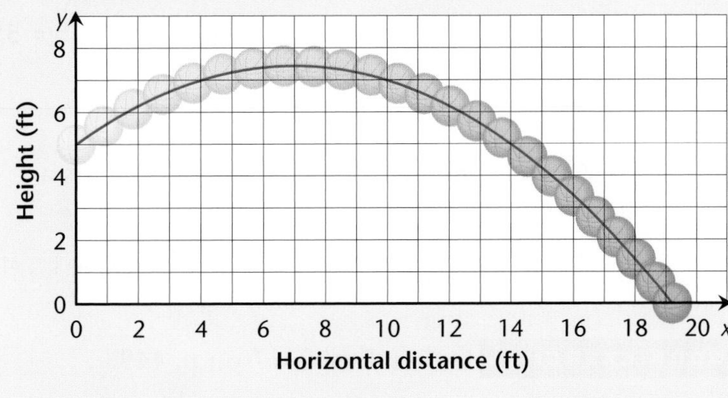

Refer to the Example on page 445 for Questions 10 and 11.

10 **a.** What do the variables x and y represent in the equation?

b. Does the equation model every basketball throw? Explain.

c. What was the maximum height the ball reached?

d. When it hit the floor, how far was the ball from the person who tossed it?

11 Why do you think part of the parabola is missing?

▶ **The equation and graph in the Example represent a *quadratic function*. A quadratic function can be represented by an equation in this form:**

$$y = ax^2 + bx + c, \text{ where } a \neq 0$$

12 **Try This as a Class** Identify the values of a, b, and c in the equation $y = -0.05x^2 + 0.7x + 5$.

13 In Exploration 1, you explored graphs of equations in the form $y = ax^2$. What were the values of b and c in these equations?

14 **Discussion** Explain why the equation $y = 0x^2 + 5x + 3$ does *not* represent a quadratic function. What kind of function is it?

▶ **Sometimes it is difficult to tell if an equation represents a quadratic function. It may be helpful to rewrite the equation.**

EXAMPLE

To see whether $y = 3(2x + 4) - x + 2x^2$ models a quadratic function, rewrite the equation in the form $y = ax^2 + bx + c$.

$$\begin{aligned} y &= 3(2x + 4) - x + 2x^2 \\ &= 3(2x) + 3(4) - x + 2x^2 \\ &= 6x + 12 - x + 2x^2 \\ &= 2x^2 + 6x - x + 12 \\ &= 2x^2 + 5x + 12 \end{aligned}$$

Use the distributive property.

Regroup and combine like terms.

The equation represents a quadratic function where $a = 2$, $b = 5$, and $c = 12$.

✓ QUESTION 15

...checks that you can identify a quadratic function.

15 **✓ CHECKPOINT** Tell whether each equation represents a quadratic function.

a. $y = 5x^2 - 3x$

b. $y = -2(2x^2 + 3x) + 1 + 4x^2$

HOMEWORK EXERCISES ▶ **See Exs. 9–17 on p. 449.**

Section 5

Key Concepts

Key Terms

parabola

vertex

line of symmetry

quadratic function

Parabolas (pp. 443-445)

A parabola is a U-shaped curve. The vertex of a parabola is the point at which the line of symmetry intersects the curve. The graphs of equations in the form $y = ax^2$ where $a \neq 0$ are parabolas.

Example The graph of $y = -2x^2$ is narrower than the graph of $y = -0.5x^2$ because $|-2| > |-0.5|$. Both graphs are "upside-down" compared to the graph of $y = x^2$ because the coefficient of x^2 is negative.

x	$y = -0.5x^2$	$y = -2x^2$
−2	−2	−8
−1	−0.5	−2
0	0	0
1	−0.5	−2
2	−2	−8

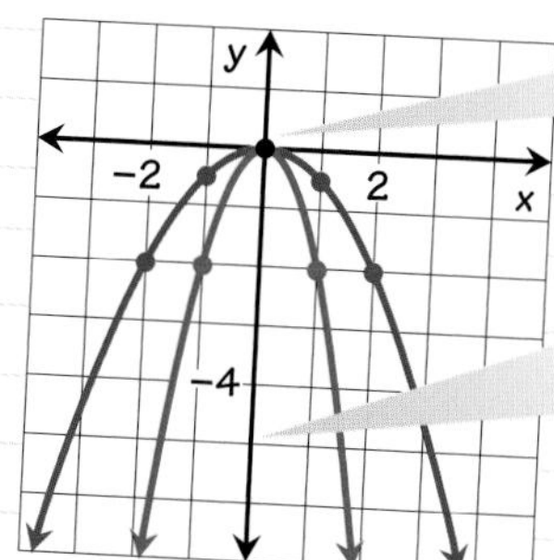

The vertex of each parabola is (0, 0).

The line of symmetry of each parabola is the *y*-axis.

To graph the parabola $y = ax^2 + c$, translate the graph of $y = ax^2$ up c units if $c > 0$ or down $|c|$ units if $c < 0$.

Quadratic Functions (pp. 445–446)

A quadratic function is represented by an equation in the form $y = ax^2 + bx + c$, where $a \neq 0$. Its graph is a parabola.

Example To see whether $y = 4x^2 - 2x - x^2 + 2x - 5$ represents a quadratic function, rewrite it in the form $y = ax^2 + bx + c$.

$$\begin{aligned} y &= 4x^2 - 2x - x^2 + 2x - 5 \\ &= 4x^2 - x^2 - 2x + 2x - 5 \\ &= 3x^2 + 0x - 5 \quad \text{Combine like terms.} \\ &= 3x^2 - 5 \end{aligned}$$

The equation represents a quadratic function where $a = 3$, $b = 0$, and $c = -5$.

16 **Key Concepts Question** Tell whether each equation models a quadratic function. If so, sketch the graph of the function. Identify the vertex and the line of symmetry of the parabola.

a. $y = -x^2 + 4(x^2 - 3) - 3x^2$ **b.** $y = -2(x^2 + 1) + x^2$

Section 5 Practice & Application Exercises

YOU WILL NEED

For Exs. 5, 7, and 18
- graph paper

For Exs. 9, 17, and 26:
- graph paper or graphing calculator (optional)

Match each equation with one of the parabolas at the right.

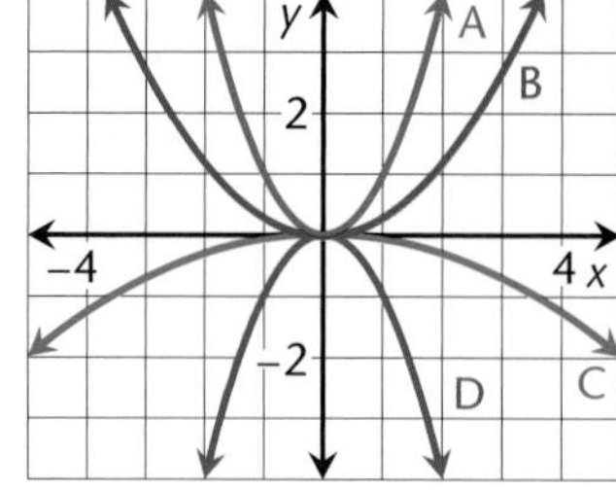

1. $y = 0.3x^2$
2. $y = x^2$
3. $y = -x^2$
4. $y = -0.08x^2$

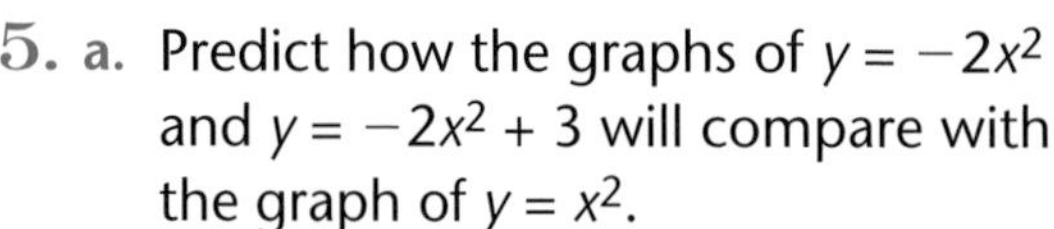

5. a. Predict how the graphs of $y = -2x^2$ and $y = -2x^2 + 3$ will compare with the graph of $y = x^2$.
   b. Check your prediction by graphing all three equations on the same pair of axes.

6. a. For each parabola give the coordinates of the vertex and the equation of the line of symmetry.

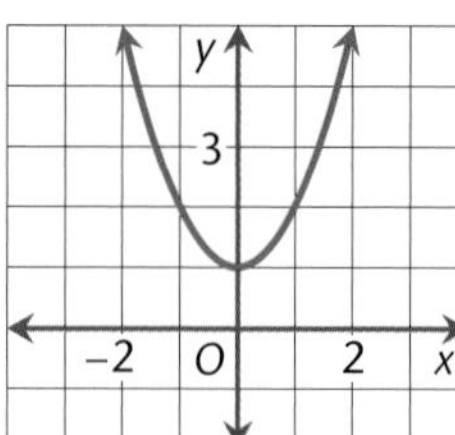

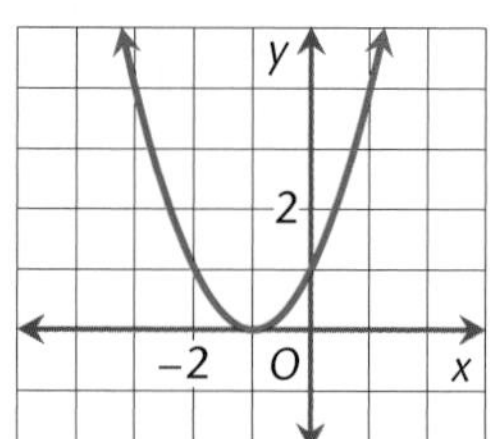

   b. Write an equation for the parabola on the left.

7. **Physics** The observation deck of the Tower of the Americas in San Antonio, Texas, is 622 ft above the ground. You can use the formula $h = 622 - 16t^2$ to find the height h (in feet) of an object t seconds after it is dropped from the observation deck.
   a. Find the values of h for $t = 0, 1, 2, \ldots, 7$.
   b. Use your answer to part (a) to plot eight ordered pairs (t, h). Connect the points with a smooth curve.
   c. About how long does it take an object dropped from the observation deck to hit the ground? How do you know?
   d. Reflect the curve you drew in part (b) across the y-axis. Does this part of the parabola make sense in this real-life situation? Explain.
   e. Give the coordinates of the vertex of the parabola you drew in parts (b) and (d).

FOR HELP with *reflections*, see **MODULE 6, p. 436**

8. a. Use the graph in the Example on page 443 to estimate the height of point A above the road. Then use the equation $y = 0.0239x^2$ to make the same height estimate. (*Hint:* Use the scale on the x-axis to approximate the x-coordinate of A.)

   b. About how high is point A above the water?

   c. Estimate the length of the main cable that stretches from point A' to point A.

9. A ball is thrown upward with an initial speed of 32 ft/sec. The equation $h = -16t^2 + 32t + 4$ gives the height h (in feet) of the ball t seconds after it is thrown.

   a. Explain why this equation is a quadratic function. Identify the values of a, b, and c in the equation.

   b. Graph the equation. Show where the graph crosses the h-axis and about where the graph crosses the t-axis. Also draw the line of symmetry.

   c. How high does the ball go?

   d. After how many seconds does it begin to fall?

   e. To the nearest tenth of a second, how long does it stay in the air?

Rewrite each equation in the form $y = ax^2 + bx + c$. Tell whether the equation represents a quadratic function.

10. $y = 7x + 8 - 3x + 5$

11. $y = 3(x - 4)$

12. $y = 2(x^2 - 7) - 2x^2$

13. $y = 6x^2 - 2x - 3x^2$

14. $y - 3 = x^2 + 7x - 5$

15. $y + x^2 = x^2 - 2x + 5$

16. **Challenge** An ordered pair of numbers that make an equation true is a solution of the equation. Find a common solution for the equations $y = x^2 - 2$ and $y = -x^2 + 2$.

Reflecting on the Section

Write your response to Exercise 17 in your journal.

17. You have explored linear, exponential, and quadratic functions. How can you tell from looking at an equation what type of function it represents? How can you tell from looking at a graph? Include examples in your explanation.

Journal

Exercise 17 checks that you can identify quadratic functions and graphs.

Spiral Review

18. The points $A(3, 5)$, $B(7, 4)$, and $C(6, 1)$ are vertices of a triangle. Draw $\triangle ABC$ and its image after a reflection across the x-axis. (Module 6, p. 436)

Find the complement of each angle. (Module 5, p. 369)

19. 16° 20. 78° 21. 31° 22. 88°

A survey is given to find out whether taxes should be used to build a playground. The survey is given to parents in the town. (Module 2, p. 132)

23. What is the population? What is the sample?

24. Is this a representative sample? Why or why not?

Extension 

Finding the Vertex

In this section you learned that all quadratic functions can be written in the form $y = ax^2 + bx + c$. All quadratic functions can also be written in the form $y - k = a(x - h)^2$, which is sometimes more useful.

25. Study the equations and graphs below. What do the values of h and k tell you about the vertex of each parabola?

$y - 1 = (x - 2)^2$ $k = 1$ $h = 2$

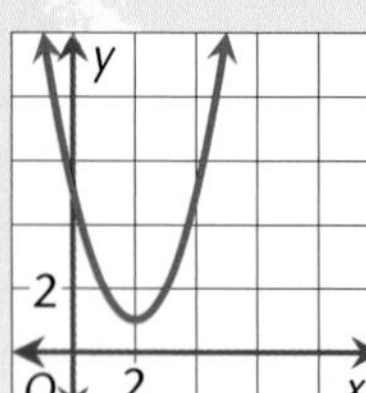

$y - 3 = (x + 3)^2$ $k = 3$ $h = -3$

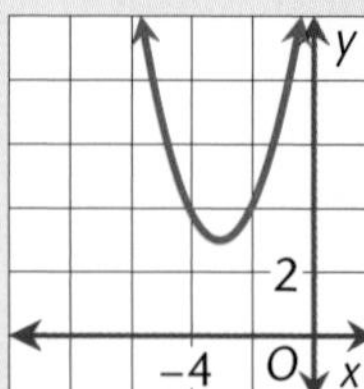

$y + 2 = (x + 4)^2$ $k = -2$ $h = -4$

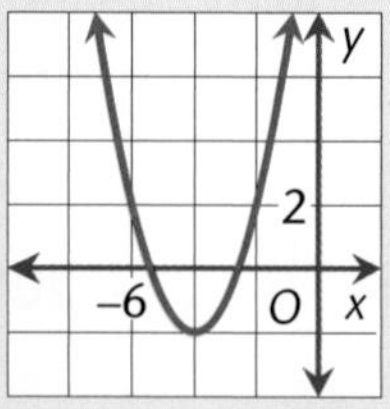

26. Make a prediction about the vertex of the graph of each equation. Then check your prediction by graphing the equation using graph paper or a graphing calculator. (*Hint:* Before graphing, rewrite the equation so that y is alone on one side of the equals sign.)

a. $y + 7 = (x - 2)^2$ b. $y - 2 = (x - 1)^2$ c. $y = (x + 3)^2$

Section 5 Extra Skill Practice

You will need: • *graph paper* (Exs. 1–6)

Predict how the graph of each equation will compare with the graph of $y = x^2$. Then check your prediction by graphing both equations on the same pair of axes.

1. $y = 5x^2$
2. $y = 0.1x^2$
3. $y = x^2 + 1$
4. $y = -x^2$
5. $y = -3x^2 - 2$
6. $y = -\frac{2}{3}x^2$

For each parabola give the coordinates of the vertex and the equation of the line of symmetry.

7. 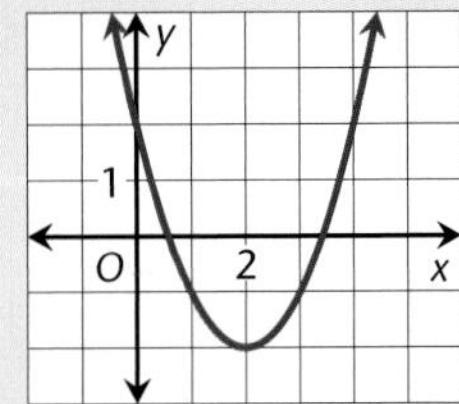

8. 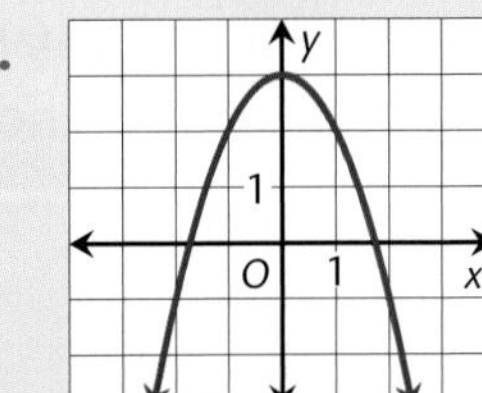

Rewrite each equation in the form $y = ax^2 + bx + c$. Tell whether the equation represents a quadratic function.

9. $y = 2x^2 + 7x - x^2$
10. $y = 3(x - 6) + 2(x + 1)$
11. $x^2 - 5x = 2(x^2 - 5) + y$
12. $y = 3(x + 4)$
13. $y - 2x^2 = 2(3 - x^2)$
14. $2 - 3(x + 7) = 1 - 2(x^2 + 3x) - y$
15. $y + 7 = x^2(2x - 5)$
16. $y + 8x^3 - 4 = -2(-2x^2 + x) - 4(x^3 + 9)$

Standardized Testing ▶ Free Response

1. Describe how the graphs of the following equations are the same and how they are different.

   $y = x^2$ $\quad\quad$ $y = \frac{1}{2}x^2$ $\quad\quad$ $y = 2x^2$ $\quad\quad$ $y = x^2 + 4$

2. Tell whether each equation represents a quadratic function.

   a. $y = -5x^2 + 3x + 2 + 5(x^2 + 4)$

   b. $y = 2(3x + 1) - 7x^2 + 4$

   c. $y = 3x - 6x + 3x^2 + 4x + 5$

   d. $y = 4x^2 + x - 4x^2 - 2$

Modeling Change in a Story

SET UP

You will need:

- *graph paper*
- *Project Labsheet A*

In this project you will experiment with using different mathematical models to describe changes. Then you will write a story using these mathematical models as illustrations.

Graphing Change Over Time Many stories involve change. You may be able to model the change with a graph. An example is the story of "Jack and the Beanstalk." In the story, a poor boy named Jack sells his family's cow for some magic beans. The beans sprout into a giant beanstalk that Jack climbs. He finds a wealthy giant at the top of the beanstalk, steals the giant's riches, and then chops down the beanstalk to protect himself from the giant. The graph shown models one change in the story.

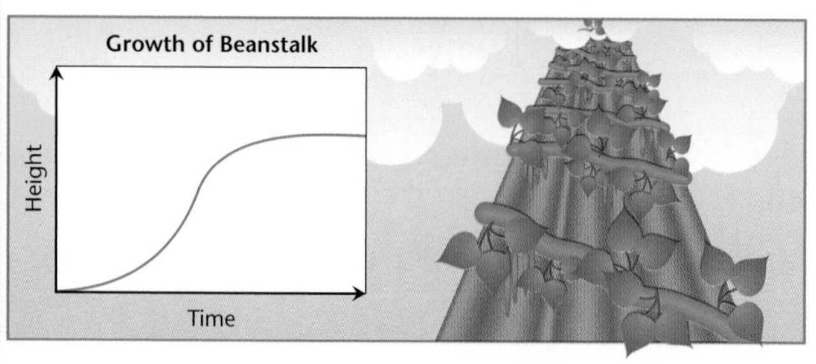

1 Describe in words the change modeled by the graph.

2 Draw a graph that could represent Jack's height above the ground, from the beginning to the end of the story. Give the graph a title and label the axes.

Linear Models Many stories involve travel. You can use equations, tables, and graphs to model changes in distance over time.

3 Suppose Brad leaves his house at 3:00 P.M. and heads west on his bike. His speed is 8 mi/hr. His friend John is 10 mi west of Brad's house. He starts walking toward Brad's house at 3:00 P.M. His speed is 4 mi/hr.

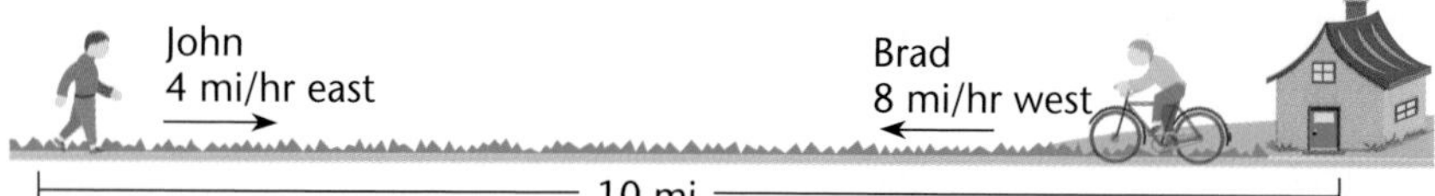

Time after 3:00 P.M. (hours)	Brad's distance from Brad's house (miles)	John's distance from Brad's house (miles)
0	0	10
0.25	2	9
0.50	?	?
0.75	?	?
1.00	?	?

John's speed is 4 mi/hr, so in 0.25 hr, he travels 1 mi and is $10 - 1 = 9$ mi from Brad's house.

a. Copy and complete the table to model Brad's and John's distances from Brad's house. Then estimate when Brad and John will meet.

b. Let x = the number of hours after 3:00 P.M. and y = the distance from Brad's house. Use the table to write two equations, one that models Brad's distance from his house over time, and one that models John's distance from Brad's house over time.

c. Graph your equations from part (b) on the same pair of axes. How does your graph show when John and Brad will meet?

d. Show how you can write and solve an equation to find out when John and Brad will meet.

4 Describe a situation that involves a change in distance over time like the one in Question 3. Explain how you could model the change.

Algorithms for Change You know how to translate, stretch, and reflect figures in a coordinate plane. Each of these transformations can create a different visual effect that you can use to illustrate a story.

5 **Use Project Labsheet A.**

a. Imagine that the frames on the Project Labsheet are frames of film. Describe the visual effect of each transformation.

b. Follow the directions for the *Blank Film Frames* to create a visual effect using a series of transformations.

Illustrating a Story Any of the models you have experimented with can be used to represent change in a story. It all depends on the story.

6 Work with a partner to discuss possible story ideas. Each of you should write down at least three possible ideas. Each idea should involve a change that can be represented by at least one of the following.

- an equation, a table, or a graph
- transformations on a coordinate plane

7 a. On your own, choose the story idea that appeals to you. Write a draft of the story. Include the mathematical models you plan to use as illustrations.

b. Exchange drafts and models with a partner. Share helpful comments and suggestions for improvement.

8 Write the final draft of your story. Include your mathematical models.

MODULE 6 Review and Assessment

You will need: • *graph paper* (Exs. 10, 23–26)
• *graph paper or graphing calculator (optional)* (Ex. 27)

Match each situation with a graph. Explain your thinking. (Sec. 1, Explor. 1)

1. the number of sunlight hours per day throughout the year
2. your height from birth to age 18
3. the length of the grass in your yard during the summer

A. 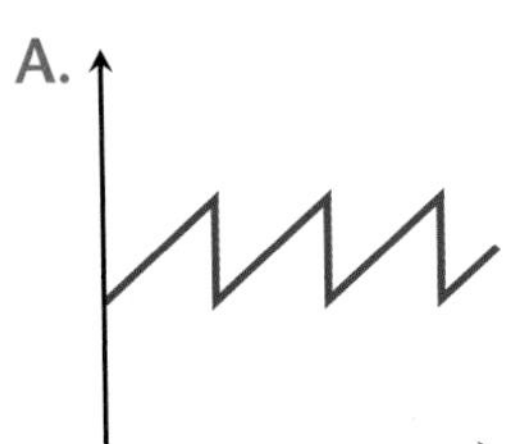

B.

C. 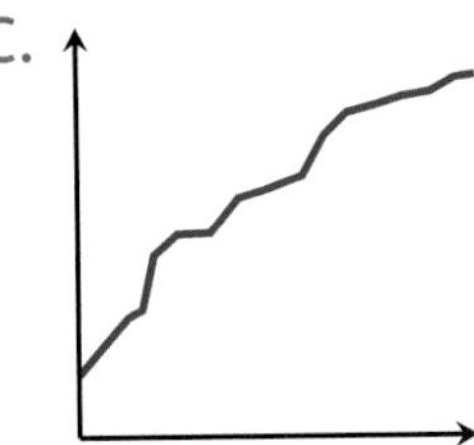

For each equation, tell whether y is a function of x. (Sec. 1, Explor. 2)

4. $y = 6x$
5. $x = 6y^2$
6. $2x = 2y$
7. $y = x^2 - 4$
8. $y = |x|$
9. $x = |y|$

10. Olivia Murk paid \$20,000 for her car. Her car is losing value at the rate of \$500 per year. Write an equation to model this situation. Then use your equation, a table, or a graph to determine what her car will be worth in 10 years. (Sec. 2, Explor. 1)

Solve each equation. (Sec. 2, Explor. 2)

11. $3x - 10 = 7 + 2x$
12. $5(x - 2) = 10$
13. $-4x - 7 = -2(x + 3)$
14. $20 - (x - 5) = 3(3x + 5)$
15. $7x - 2(x + 5) = 5(5x + 9)$
16. $5 - 6x = -2(2x - 1) - 20$

17. Joe starts walking at the rate of 3 ft/sec. His total distance traveled can be modeled by the equation $y = 3x$, where y = distance in feet and x = time in seconds. Ten seconds later, Lidia starts jogging at the rate of 5 ft/sec. Her total distance traveled can be modeled by the equation $y = 5(x - 10)$. When will Lidia's distance traveled equal Joe's? (Sec. 2, Explor. 2)

Evaluate each expression for the given value of the variable. (Sec. 3, Explors. 1 and 2)

18. 10^x; $x = 4$ 19. $\left(\frac{3}{4}\right)^x$; $x = 2$ 20. $3 \cdot 2^x$; $x = 5$ 21. $5 \cdot \left(\frac{1}{5}\right)^x$; $x = 3$

22. Irene Ehler deposits $100 in a savings account that earns 5% annual interest. Write an equation that models the amount of money y in the account after x years. Use your equation to determine how much money will be in the account after 25 years. (Sec. 3, Explor. 2)

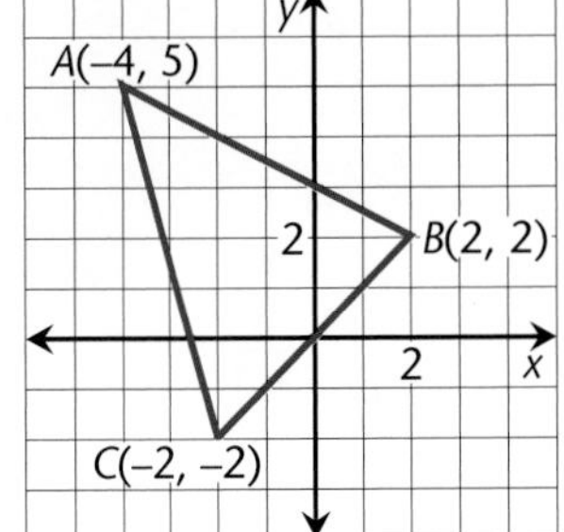

23. Use the triangle at the right. Write an algorithm for reflecting $\triangle ABC$ across the y-axis and then translating it up 3 units. Then draw the image. (Sec. 4, Explor. 1)

Make a sketch showing how you think the graphs of the given equations will compare with the graph of $y = x^2$. (Sec. 5, Explor. 1)

24. $y = 2x^2$; $y = -2x^2$ 25. $y = 0.5x^2$; $y = 10x^2$ 26. $y = x^2 + 2$; $y = x^2 - 5$

27. A ball is thrown upward with an initial speed of 15 m/sec. The equation $h = -4.9t^2 + 15t + 1$ models the height h (in meters) of the ball t seconds after it is thrown. (Sec. 5, Explor. 2)

   a. Graph the equation and sketch the line of symmetry for the parabola.

   b. About how long does it take the ball to hit the ground?

   c. Give the approximate coordinates of the vertex of the parabola.

Rewrite each equation in the form $y = ax^2 + bx + c$. Tell whether the equation represents a quadratic function. (Sec. 5, Explor. 2)

28. $y = 5 - x^2$

29. $y + 7 = 2(x^2 - 3) + x$

30. $x^2 - 2x - y = x^2 + 7x + 4$

31. $x^2 + 4(x^2 - 2x) = -2(x - 3) + y + 3$

Reflecting on the Module

32. **Writing** In this module you studied linear, exponential, and quadratic functions. Give an example of each type of equation. Describe a real-life situation that could be modeled by each type of equation.

DULE 7

The Algebra Connection

Math and Careers

Mathematics appears in many places. In this module project you will conduct an interview with an individual who uses mathematics in his or her job. After gathering information about the person, the job, and the type of math used, you will present your findings to the class.

More on the Module Project
See pp. 512–513.

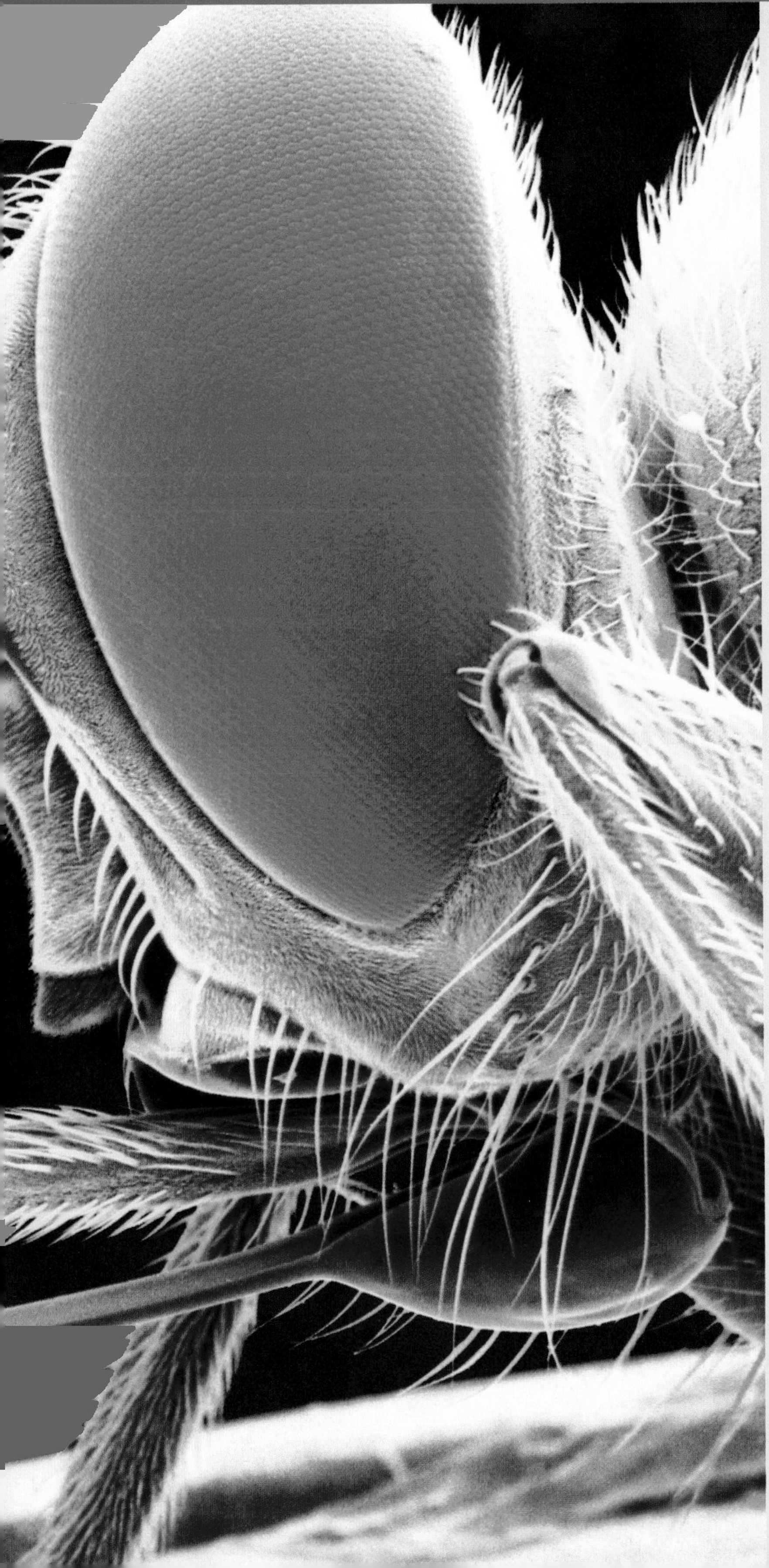

MATHEMATICS The & Theme

SECTION OVERVIEW

1 Working with Exponents

As you read about the use of telescopes and microscopes:

- Multiply and divide powers
- Simplify powers with zero and negative exponents

2 Simplifying Radicals

As you study a mathematician's work:

- Identify irrational numbers
- Use the product and quotient properties of square roots to simplify square roots
- Simplify radical expressions

3 Graphing and Solving Inequalities

As you learn how engineers use data to design car seats, seat heights, and theater seating:

- Write and graph inequalities
- Solve simple inequalities
- Solve multi-step inequalities

4 Polynomials and Factoring

As you examine Leonardo da Vinci's work:

- Use algebra tiles to model binomials and their products
- Multiply binomials
- Use algebra tiles to factor quadratics

INTERNET
Resources and practice at
classzone.com

Working with Exponents

In This Section

Exploration 1
- Properties of Exponents

Exploration 2
- Zero and Negative Exponents

Big and Small

Setting the Stage

There is a lot in the universe that your eyes cannot see without help—objects as big as planets and stars and as small as blood cells and bacteria. The invention of the telescope and the microscope made these objects visible.

In 1924, Edwin Hubble was using a telescope to investigate the Andromeda Nebula, believed to be a gaseous cloud inside our own Milky Way Galaxy. Hubble calculated the distance to one of the stars in the nebula to be over 1,000,000 light-years, which placed it outside the Milky Way. (A light-year is the distance light travels in one year.) Scientists realized that the universe was much larger than they had presumed.

The Hubble Space Telescope, named for Edwin Hubble, orbits Earth 353 miles above its surface and has produced some of the clearest astronomical images ever recorded.

Think About It

1 Why do you think the Hubble Space Telescope provides clearer images of astronomical objects than telescopes located on Earth?

2 The Andromeda Nebula (now called the M31 Galaxy) is about 2,000,000 light-years away. The Hubble Space Telescope has identified a galaxy 10 times that distance from Earth. About how far from Earth is that galaxy?

▶ **In this module, you will see how algebra is connected to the world around us and used in many walks of life.**

Exploration 1

Properties of Exponents

GOAL

LEARN HOW TO...
- multiply and divide powers

AS YOU...
- work with astronomical distances

KEY TERMS
- product of powers property
- quotient of powers property

SET UP *You will need a calculator.*

▶ **In 1995, the Hubble Space Telescope sent an image of the giant star Betelgeuse (pronounced *beetle juice*) to Earth. This was the first detailed image of a star other than the sun. However, the image actually showed what the star looked like hundreds of years ago! The diagram explains why.**

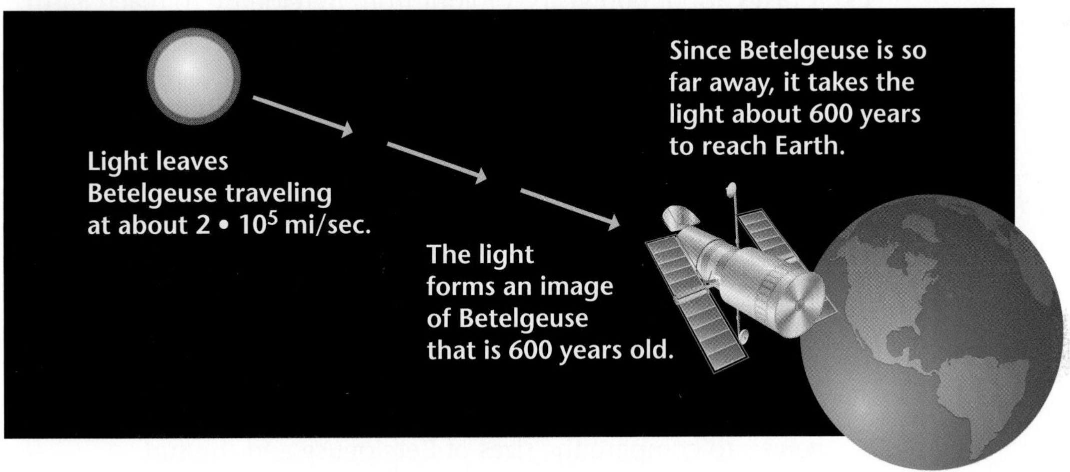

▶ **How many miles is it from Betelgeuse to Earth? You can use the information in the diagram to find out.**

3 You first need to convert the speed of light given in the diagram from miles per second to miles per year.

a. Show that there are about $3 \cdot 10^7$ seconds in one year.

b. Explain why the product of $2 \cdot 10^5$ and $3 \cdot 10^7$ approximates the speed of light in miles per year.

c. Explain why the product in part (b) can be written as $6 \cdot (10^5 \cdot 10^7)$.

FOR ▶ HELP with *powers*, see **TOOLBOX, p. 589**

4 **a.** How many factors of 10 are in the product $10^5 \cdot 10^7$?

b. Use your answer from part (a) to write $6 \cdot (10^5 \cdot 10^7)$, the speed of light in miles per year, as $6 \cdot 10^k$ for some integer k.

c. How is the exponent in 10^k related to the exponents in $10^5 \cdot 10^7$?

5 Write each product as a single power. Use a calculator to check each answer.

a. $10^2 \cdot 10^3$ **b.** $3^6 \cdot 3^6$ **c.** $2^{10} \cdot 2^7$

6 Complete this rule for multiplying powers with the same base: $b^m \cdot b^n = b^?$. This is the **product of powers property**.

...checks that you can use the product of powers property to multiply powers.

7 ✓ **CHECKPOINT** Write each product as a single power.

a. $10^3 \cdot 10^4$ **b.** $5^9 \cdot 5^2$ **c.** $a \cdot a^7$ **d.** $b^5 \cdot b^8 \cdot b^2$

8 It takes about 600 years for light from Betelgeuse to reach Earth.

a. Write 600 in scientific notation.

b. Use your answer from part (a), the speed of light in miles per year from Question 4, and the product of powers property to show that Betelgeuse is about $36 \cdot 10^{14}$ mi from Earth.

FOR ◀HELP with *scientific notation*, see **MODULE 3, p. 209**

9 **a.** Explain why $36 \cdot 10^{14}$ is not in scientific notation.

b. Use the product of powers rule to write $36 \cdot 10^{14}$ in scientific notation. (*Hint*: $36 = 3.6 \cdot 10^1$.)

10 Betelgeuse is huge, even for a star. You can use a *quotient of powers* to compare the sizes of Betelgeuse and the sun.

a. The diameter of Betelgeuse is roughly 10^9 mi. The diameter of the sun is roughly 10^6 mi. Write a fraction that represents the ratio of Betelgeuse's diameter to the sun's diameter.

b. Rewrite the fraction showing all of the factors of 10 in the numerator and in the denominator. Then write the fraction as a single power of 10. (*Hint:* Look for factors that divide out.)

c. How is the exponent of this single power of 10 related to the exponents of the powers in the numerator and denominator of the fraction you wrote in part (a)?

d. The diameter of Betelgeuse is about how many times as great as the diameter of the sun?

11 Write each quotient as a single power. Use a calculator to check each answer.

a. $\frac{10^6}{10^2}$ b. $\frac{10^8}{10^3}$ c. $\frac{6^7}{6^4}$ d. $\frac{2^{13}}{2^5}$

12 Complete this rule for dividing powers with the same base: $\frac{b^m}{b^n} = b^?$. This is the **quotient of powers property**.

13 ✓ **CHECKPOINT** Write as a single power.

a. $\frac{10^{50}}{10^{30}}$ b. $\frac{5^{19}}{5^{14}}$ c. $\frac{a^7}{a^2}$ d. $\frac{c^{11}}{c \cdot c^7}$

✓ **QUESTION 13**

...checks that you can use the quotient of powers property to divide powers.

HOMEWORK EXERCISES ▶ **See Exs. 1–28 on pp. 465–466.**

Exploration 2

Zero and Negative Exponents

GOAL

LEARN HOW TO...

- simplify powers with zero and negative exponents
- represent small numbers in scientific notation and in decimal notation

AS YOU...

- investigate dimensions of real-world objects

SET UP *You will need:* • *calculator* • *Labsheet 1A*

▶ **Look at the images shown. As you go from one image to the next in the series, the width of the field of view decreases by a factor of 10.**

▶ **In Exploration 1 you explored exponents greater than or equal to 1. An exponent may also be an integer less than 1.**

14 Written as a fraction, the ratio of the width of view of the first photo on page 461 to itself is $\frac{1000}{1000}$.

a. Write the numerator and the denominator of the fraction as a power of 10.

b. Use the *quotient of powers property* to write the quotient in part (a) as a single power.

c. Write the fraction $\frac{1000}{1000}$ in lowest terms.

15 Use a calculator to evaluate each power.

a. 2^0 **b.** 9^0 **c.** 75^0 **d.** $(3.14)^0$

16 Based on your results from Questions 14 and 15, what is the value of b^0 for any positive number b?

17 **Use Labsheet 1A** Follow the directions and answer the questions on the *Powers of 10* labsheet.

18 Let n be a positive integer. Complete this equation: $\frac{1}{10^n} = 10^?$.

19 **Try This as a Class** Use the expression $3^2 \div 3^4$.

a. Write the division expression as a fraction. Then write the numerator and denominator as whole numbers without exponents. Write the fraction in lowest terms.

b. Use the quotient of powers property to write the quotient as a single power.

c. Let b be any positive number and n be any positive integer. Complete this equation: $b^{-n} = \frac{1}{?}$

✓ QUESTION 20

...checks that you can simplify powers with zero and negative exponents.

20 **✓ CHECKPOINT** Write each power as a whole number or a fraction without exponents.

a. 6^0 **b.** 8^{-1} **c.** 3^{-4} **d.** 5^{-3}

▶ **You can use negative exponents to write small numbers in scientific notation. For example, a red blood cell's diameter is $7.5 \cdot 10^{-3}$ mm.**

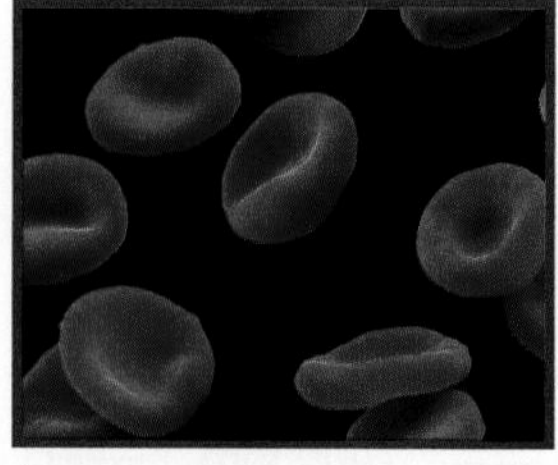

▲ This photograph shows a group of red blood cells.

21 **a.** Explain why $7.5 \cdot 10^{-3}$ is in scientific notation.

b. Evaluate $7.5 \cdot 10^{-3}$. Give the answer as a decimal.

22 Use a calculator to write each number as a decimal.

a. $9 \cdot 10^{-3}$ **b.** $5.2 \cdot 10^{-1}$ **c.** $4.26 \cdot 10^{-2}$

23 Look for a pattern in your answers to Questions 21 and 22. Explain how you can change a small number from scientific notation to decimal notation *without* using a calculator.

24 ✓ **CHECKPOINT** Write each number as a decimal without using a calculator.

a. $2 \cdot 10^{-4}$ **b.** $8.4 \cdot 10^{-5}$ **c.** $6.31 \cdot 10^{-8}$

> ✓ **QUESTION 24**
>
> ...checks that you can change small numbers from scientific notation to decimal notation.

▶ **In Questions 21–24, you changed small numbers from scientific notation to decimal notation. You can also reverse this procedure.**

EXAMPLE

In 1996, scientists used an electron microscope to study a meterorite from Mars. The photograph shows tiny tube-shaped forms found inside the meterorite. A typical form is about 0.00000007 m long. Write this length in scientific notation.

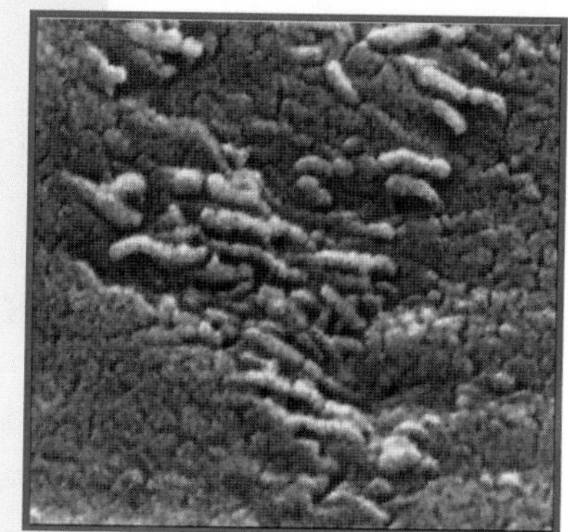

Decide how many places the decimal point in 0.00000007 must be moved to get a number that is at least 1 but less than 10.

$$0.00000007 = \mathbf{7} \cdot 0.00000001$$

(8 places)

$$= \mathbf{7} \cdot \frac{1}{100{,}000{,}000}$$

Note that $1 \le \mathbf{7} < 10$.

$$= \mathbf{7} \cdot \frac{1}{10^{\mathbf{8}}}$$

$$= \mathbf{7} \cdot 10^{\mathbf{-8}}$$

25 Describe a shortcut for writing 0.00000007 in scientific notation.

26 ✓ **CHECKPOINT** Write each number in scientific notation.

a. 0.4 **b.** 0.0089 **c.** 0.00000123

> ...checks that you can change small numbers from decimal notation to scientific notation.

HOMEWORK EXERCISES ▶ **See Exs. 29–52 on pp. 466–467.**

Section 1 Key Concepts

Key Terms

product of powers property

quotient of powers property

Product of Powers Property (pp. 459–460)

To multiply powers with the same base, add the exponents.

Examples $2^5 \cdot 2^3 = 2^{5+3} = 2^8$ $\quad c^4 \cdot c^7 = c^{4+7} = c^{11}$

Quotient of Powers Property (pp. 460–461)

To divide powers with the same nonzero base, subtract the exponents.

Examples $\frac{3^{13}}{3^4} = 3^{13-4} = 3^9$ $\quad \frac{y^8}{y^6} = y^{8-6} = y^2$

Zero and Negative Exponents (pp. 461–462)

If b is any positive number and n is any positive integer, then $b^0 = 1$ and $b^{-n} = \frac{1}{b^n}$.

Examples $5^0 = 1$ $\quad 5^{-2} = \frac{1}{5^2} = \frac{1}{25}$

Scientific Notation with Small Numbers (pp. 462–463)

You can change small numbers in scientific notation to decimal notation. You can also change small numbers in decimal notation to scientific notation.

Examples

$3.8 \cdot 10^{-5} = 3.8 \cdot \frac{1}{10^5}$

$= 3.8 \cdot 0.00001$

$= 0.000038$ (5 places)

$0.000729 = 7.29 \cdot 0.0001$ (4 places)

$= 7.29 \cdot \frac{1}{10^4}$

$= 7.29 \cdot 10^{-4}$

Key Concepts Questions

27 Write b^7 as a product of two powers. Is there only one product that you can write? Explain.

28 Negative exponents are used to write small numbers in scientific notation. What precisely is a "small number" in this situation?

Section 1 Practice & Application Exercises

YOU WILL NEED

For Ex. 51:
- scientific calculator

Write each product as a single power.

1. $10^4 \cdot 10^2$
2. $10^5 \cdot 10^8$
3. $2^3 \cdot 2^6$
4. $5^5 \cdot 5^5$
5. $3^9 \cdot 3$
6. $7^2 \cdot 7^6 \cdot 7^3$
7. $a \cdot a^3$
8. $c^2 \cdot c^{10}$
9. $b^4 \cdot b^4$
10. $d^8 \cdot d^{12}$
11. $w^{60} \cdot w^{20}$
12. $t^5 \cdot t \cdot t^7$

Oceanography In his book *The Perfect Storm,* Sebastian Junger describes how the amount of energy in ocean waves depends on the wind speed.

Unfortunately for mariners, the total amount of wave energy in a storm doesn't [depend on the first power of] wind speed, but [on the] fourth power. The seas generated by a forty-knot wind aren't twice as violent as those from a twenty-knot wind, they're seventeen times as violent. A ship's crew watching the anemometer [an instrument that measures wind speed] climb even ten knots could well be [in great danger].

◀ As the anemometer spins in the wind, revolutions per minute are converted to miles per hour to calculate the wind speed.

13. The equation $h = 0.019s^2$ gives the height h (in feet) of waves caused by wind blowing at a speed of s knots. (One knot is slightly faster than 1 mi/hr.) The equation $E = 8h^2$ gives the energy E (in foot-pounds) in each square foot of a wave with height h.

    a. Write an equation that relates E and s. (*Hint:* First write $E = 8h^2$ as $E = 8 \cdot h \cdot h$. Then use the fact that $h = 0.019s^2$ to write another equation for E.)

    b. Junger says that wave energy depends on the fourth power of wind speed. Is this true? Explain.

    c. What is the wave energy per square foot when the wind speed is 20 knots? when the wind speed is 40 knots?

    d. Is the wave energy for a 40-knot wind about 17 times the wave energy for a 20-knot wind, as Junger states?

14. **Open-ended** Junger says that even a 10-knot increase in wind speed can be very dangerous. For what intervals does a 10-knot increase in wind speed cause a great increase in wave energies?

Write each quotient as a single power.

15. $\frac{10^6}{10^4}$
16. $\frac{10^9}{10^3}$
17. $\frac{2^5}{2}$
18. $\frac{3^{10}}{3^7}$
19. $\frac{7^{15}}{7^6}$
20. $\frac{5^3 \cdot 5^8}{5^2}$
21. $\frac{a^5}{a^2}$
22. $\frac{b^6}{b^5}$
23. $\frac{c^{12}}{c^6}$
24. $\frac{d^7}{d}$
25. $\frac{u^{95}}{u^{52}}$
26. $\frac{v^{18}}{v^4 \cdot v^3}$

27. **Challenge** Write $\frac{a^5b^9}{ab^4}$ as the product of a power of a and a power of b.

Biology The average weight w (in pounds) of an Atlantic cod aged t years can be modeled by the equation $w = 1.16(1.44)^t$.

28. **a.** Find the ratio of the weight of a 5-year-old cod to the weight of a 2-year-old cod. Express this ratio as a power of 1.44.

    b. A 5-year-old cod weighs how many times as much as a 2-year-old cod?

29. A newly-hatched Atlantic cod is about 5 mm long. Does the given equation produce a reasonable weight for $t = 0$? Explain.

Write each power as a whole number or fraction without exponents.

30. 8^0
31. 3^{-2}
32. 2^{-3}
33. 5^{-1}

Write each expression without using zero or negative exponents.

34. a^0
35. b^{-6}
36. c^{-10}
37. $4w^{-2}$

38. **Personal Finance** Many people invest in stocks as a way to save for retirement. Based on the history of stock prices, the amount A you need to invest in order to have D dollars after n years can be estimated using this equation:

$$A = D(1.105)^{-n}$$

a. How much money would you need to invest in stocks now to have \$1,000,000 after 10 years? after 20 years? after 40 years?

b. Writing Explain why your answers from part (a) show the importance of starting to save for retirement at an early age.

Write each number as a decimal.

39. $9 \cdot 10^{-1}$
40. $3 \cdot 10^{-2}$
41. $1.8 \cdot 10^{-4}$
42. $4.4 \cdot 10^{-7}$
43. $2.65 \cdot 10^{-6}$
44. $7.523 \cdot 10^{-8}$

Write each number in scientific notation.

45. 0.3
46. 0.0087
47. 0.00025
48. 0.00001199
49. 0.000000006
50. 0.000000408

51. **Probability Connection** If you flip a coin n times, the theoretical probability of getting n heads is 2^{-n}.

   a. Find the probability of getting 25 heads in 25 flips. Write your answer in scientific notation.

   b. Compare your answer from part (a) with the probability of winning a common type of state lottery (about $7.15 \cdot 10^{-8}$).

Reflecting on the Section

Write your response to Exercise 52 in your journal.

52. Write a quiz that covers the mathematical topics presented in this section. Include at least two questions for each topic. Then make an answer key for your quiz.

Journal

Exercise 52 checks that you understand and can apply the mathematical ideas in this section.

Spiral Review

53. Give the slope and the y-intercept of the line with equation $y = -2x + 9$. (Module 4, p. 265)

54. **Estimation** Between which two consecutive integers does $\sqrt{60}$ lie? (Module 3, p. 163)

Solve each equation. (Module 1, p. 42)

55. $\frac{x}{3} = 4$
56. $\frac{w}{13} + 2 = 7$
57. $6 = \frac{t}{85}$

Solve each equation. (Module 4, p. 277)

58. $-0.75s - 1.35 = 4.65$
59. $14 = \frac{2}{3}n + 2$

Career Connection

Scientist: France Córdova

Dr. France Córdova was Chief Scientist at the National Aeronautics and Space Administration (NASA) from 1993–1996. She studied small, dense, rapidly spinning stars called *pulsars,* which result when a giant star undergoes a supernova explosion.

60. A pulsar's *mass density*—its mass per unit volume—is about 10^{11} kg/cm^3. (A handful of material from a pulsar would weigh more than all the people on Earth combined!) The volume of a typical pulsar is about 10^{19} cm^3. Find the mass of a pulsar with this volume.

61. Pulsars rotate very rapidly. The *period* of a pulsar is the time required for one rotation. The fastest-rotating pulsar known has a period of about 0.00156 sec. Write this period in scientific notation.

Extension 

Extending the Properties of Exponents

In this section, you applied the product and quotient of powers properties to expressions containing only positive exponents. Also, the quotient of powers property was applied only to quotients where the exponent in the numerator was greater than the exponent in the denominator. However, both properties work for any exponents.

Examples:

$3^{-2} \cdot 3^7 = 3^{-2+7} = 3^5$ $\qquad$ $\frac{5^8}{5^{11}} = 5^{8-11} = 5^{-3}$ or $\frac{1}{5^3}$

62. Show that $3^{-2} \cdot 3^7 = 3^5$ and $\frac{5^8}{5^{11}} = 5^{-3}$ without using the product of powers and quotient of powers properties. (*Hint*: Write 3^{-2} and 5^{-3} using positive exponents.)

Write each product as a single power.

63. $2^{-1} \cdot 2^3$ $\qquad$ 64. $10^9 \cdot 10^{-4}$ $\qquad$ 65. $a^6 \cdot a^{-10}$ $\qquad$ 66. $x^{-3} \cdot x^{-5}$

Write each quotient as a single power.

67. $\frac{3^5}{3^7}$ $\qquad$ 68. $\frac{7^2}{7^{-12}}$ $\qquad$ 69. $\frac{b^{-8}}{b^{-3}}$ $\qquad$ 70. $\frac{y^{-2}}{y^{10}}$

Section 1 Extra Skill Practice

Write each product as a single power.

1. $6^4 \cdot 6^3$
2. $9^{10} \cdot 9^{17}$
3. $11^{11} \cdot 11^{23}$
4. $2^2 \cdot 2^{21} \cdot 2$
5. $b^3 \cdot b^9$
6. $h^5 \cdot h^{19}$
7. $k^{33} \cdot k^{48}$
8. $n^7 \cdot n^8 \cdot n^9$

Write each quotient as a single power.

9. $\frac{10^{12}}{10^2}$
10. $\frac{9^6}{9}$
11. $\frac{8^{21}}{8^{19}}$
12. $\frac{6^{15}}{6^4 \cdot 6^7}$
13. $\frac{p^8}{p^5}$
14. $\frac{z^{57}}{z^{39}}$
15. $\frac{m^{82}}{m^{78}}$
16. $\frac{t^{26}}{t^7 \cdot t^{11}}$

Write each power as a number without exponents.

17. 24^0
18. 6^{-3}
19. 11^{-2}
20. 4^{-4}
21. 13^{-1}

Write each expression without using zero or negative exponents.

22. h^{-3}
23. p^{-8}
24. k^0
25. $3b^{-7}$
26. $12g^{-32}$

Write each number as a decimal.

27. $8 \cdot 10^{-3}$
28. $3.6 \cdot 10^{-4}$
29. $6.14 \cdot 10^{-7}$
30. $1.271 \cdot 10^{-8}$

Write each number in scientific notation.

31. 0.06
32. 0.000412
33. 0.000001013
34. 0.000000761

Standardized Testing ▶ Multiple Choice

1. Simplify $3^4 \cdot 3^5$.

   A 3^9 B 3^{20} C 9^9 D 9^{20}

2. Simplify $\frac{2^{15}}{2^3}$.

   A 5 B 2^5 C 2^{12} D 2^{18}

3. Simplify 8^{-2}.

   A $\frac{1}{4}$ B $\frac{1}{8}$ C $\frac{1}{16}$ D $\frac{1}{64}$

4. Which number is *not* in scientific notation?

   A $4.3 \cdot 10^{-5}$ B $1 \cdot 10^4$ C $7.01 \cdot 10^{-8}$ D $12 \cdot 10^{-3}$

Section 2 Simplifying Radicals

IN THIS SECTION

EXPLORATION 1
- Simplifying Square Roots

EXPLORATION 2
- Radical Expressions

Brahmagupta's Discovery

KEY TERMS
- radical sign
- radicand

$A = bh$

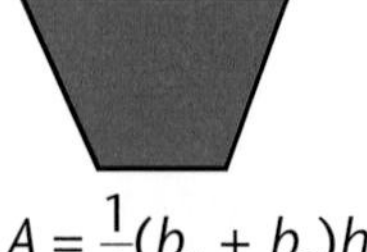

$A = \frac{1}{2}(b_1 + b_2)h$

Setting the Stage

The formulas shown at the left can be used to find the areas of parallelograms and trapezoids. But how do you find the area of a quadrilateral that is neither a parallelogram nor a trapezoid? Around 628 A.D., a Hindu mathematician named Brahmagupta discovered a formula for finding the area of a quadrilateral that is *inscribed* in a circle. His formula uses the principal square root of an expression involving the side lengths and perimeter of the quadrilateral.

$$A = \sqrt{(s-a)(s-b)(s-c)(s-d)}$$

The symbol $\sqrt{\ }$ is called a **radical sign**.

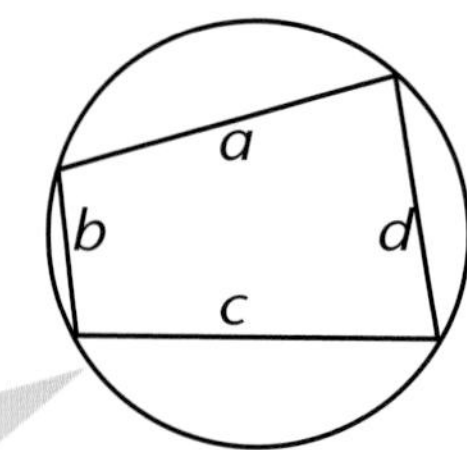

In this formula, a, b, c, and d represent the lengths of the sides of the quadrilateral, and s represents half of the perimeter of the quadrilateral.

$$s = \frac{a+b+c+d}{2}$$

When all its vertices lie on a circle, a quadrilateral is *inscribed* in the circle.

Think About It

1 Find the area of the quadrilateral above if $a = 12$ mm, $b = 6$ mm, $c = 9$ mm, and $d = 7$ mm. Round to the nearest hundredth.

2 Was the **radicand**, the value under the radical sign, a perfect square? Explain how you know.

3 The value you obtained in Question 1 is the approximate area. How can you write the exact area of the quadrilateral?

Exploration 1

Simplifying $\sqrt{\text{Square Roots}}$

GOAL

LEARN HOW TO...
- identify irrational numbers
- simplify square roots

AS YOU...
- find the exact area of an inscribed quadrilateral

KEY TERMS
- irrational
- simplest form (of a square root)
- product property of square roots
- quotient property of square roots

SET UP *Work with a partner.*

▶ **A square root like $\sqrt{4900}$, which equals 70, is a rational number because 70 is a perfect square. But a square root like $\sqrt{4400}$, which equals 66.332495. . . (whose digits neither terminate nor repeat), is an *irrational* number. An irrational number cannot be written as the quotient of two integers. When written as a decimal, an irrational number does not terminate or repeat.**

4 **Discussion** Which of the following numbers are irrational? Explain how you know.

a. $\sqrt{144}$ **b.** $\sqrt{10}$ **c.** $1.\overline{87}$ **d.** π

▶ **Many square roots can be *simplified*.**

FOR HELP with *square roots*, see **MODULE 3, p. 163**

A square root is in **simplest form** if the following are true.
- There are no perfect square factors other than 1 in the radicand.
- There are no fractions in the radicand.
- There are no square roots in the denominator of a fraction.

Examples: $\sqrt{6}$ and $\frac{\sqrt{7}}{2}$

Nonexamples: $\sqrt{8}$, $\sqrt{\frac{25}{81}}$, and $\frac{5}{\sqrt{4}}$

5 **a.** Simplify $\sqrt{4}$. Simplify $\sqrt{25}$. Multiply the simplified answers.

b. Multiply $4 \cdot 25$. Find the principal square root of the result.

c. How does $\sqrt{4} \cdot \sqrt{25}$ compare with $\sqrt{4 \cdot 25}$?

d. Choose any two perfect squares and use them in place of 4 and 25 in parts (a)–(c). What do you notice?

▶ **The product property of square roots states that for all positive numbers a and b,**

$$\sqrt{a \cdot b} = \sqrt{a} \cdot \sqrt{b}.$$

6 Try This as a Class

a. Use the product property of square roots to simplify each of the following.

$\sqrt{64 \cdot 9}$ $\sqrt{81 \cdot 4 \cdot 36}$ $\sqrt{9 \cdot 49}$

b. How can you write 900 as the product of two perfect squares, each greater than 1? Use the result and the product property of squares to simplify $\sqrt{900}$.

c. Write the radicand of each of the following as a product of perfect squares and then simplify.

$\sqrt{2500}$ $\sqrt{576}$ $\sqrt{324}$

▶ **Simplifying Irrational Numbers The product property of square roots can be used to simplify square roots.**

EXAMPLE

Simplify $\sqrt{45}$.

Think of perfect squares greater than 1. The first such number is 4, but 4 is not a factor of 45. The next is 9, and 9 is a factor of 45, so rewrite 45 as 9 • 5. Then use the product property of square roots.

SAMPLE RESPONSE

$$\begin{aligned}\sqrt{45} &= \sqrt{9 \cdot 5}\\ &= \sqrt{9} \cdot \sqrt{5}\\ &= 3 \cdot \sqrt{5}\end{aligned}$$

The radicand 5 can not be factored into perfect squares, so $\sqrt{5}$ is in simplest form.

In simplest form, $\sqrt{45} = 3\sqrt{5}$.

✓ **QUESTION 7**

...checks that you can simplify square roots.

7 ✓ **CHECKPOINT** Simplify each square root.

a. $\sqrt{75}$ **b.** $\sqrt{8}$ **c.** $\sqrt{216}$

8 Try This As a Class Replace the variables a and b using several different pairs of perfect squares. Simplify each expression. Which statements appear to be true?

a. $\sqrt{a} + \sqrt{b} = \sqrt{a + b}$ **b.** $\sqrt{a} - \sqrt{b} = \sqrt{a - b}$ **c.** $\sqrt{\frac{a}{b}} = \frac{\sqrt{a}}{\sqrt{b}}$

9 **a.** Why is $\sqrt{\frac{25}{49}}$ not in simplest form?

b. Show that $\sqrt{\frac{25}{49}} = \frac{\sqrt{25}}{\sqrt{49}}$.

▶ **The quotient property of square roots states that for all positive numbers *a* and *b*,**

$$\sqrt{\frac{a}{b}} = \frac{\sqrt{a}}{\sqrt{b}}.$$

10 ✓ **CHECKPOINT** Simplify each expression.

a. $\sqrt{\frac{81}{4}}$ **b.** $\sqrt{\frac{15}{16}}$ **c.** $\sqrt{\frac{7}{36}}$

✓ **QUESTION 10**

...checks that you can simplify a square root with a fractional radicand.

11 Why is $\frac{3}{\sqrt{2}}$ not in simplest form?

▶ **To eliminate a square root in the denominator of a fraction, you can multiply the numerator and denominator of the fraction by a square root that will make the radicand in the denominator a perfect square.**

12 Copy and replace each **?** with the correct number.

$$\frac{3}{\sqrt{2}} = \frac{3}{\sqrt{2}} \cdot \frac{?}{\sqrt{2}} = \frac{?}{\sqrt{2 \cdot ?}} = \frac{?}{\sqrt{?}} = \frac{?}{?}$$

13 What could you multiply the numerator and denominator of each fraction by to obtain an equivalent fraction that does not have a radical sign in its denominator?

a. $\frac{3}{\sqrt{5}}$ **b.** $\frac{19}{\sqrt{10}}$ **c.** $\frac{2}{\sqrt{31}}$ **d.** $\frac{10}{\sqrt{15}}$

14 ✓ **CHECKPOINT** Simplify each expression in Question 13.

✓ **QUESTION 14**

...checks that you can simplify a fraction with a square root in the denominator.

15 A quadrilateral with sides *a*, *b*, *c*, and *d* is inscribed in a circle. Use Brahmagupta's formula to find the exact area. Be sure your answer is in simplest form.

a. $a = 12$ mm
$b = 6$ mm
$c = 9$ mm
$d = 7$ mm

b. $a = 5$ in.
$b = 1\frac{1}{2}$ in.
$c = 5$ in.
$d = 2\frac{1}{2}$ in.

HOMEWORK EXERCISES ▶ **See Exs. 1–8 on p. 478.**

GOAL

LEARN HOW TO...
- simplify radical expressions

AS YOU...
- explore square roots, cube roots, and fourth roots

KEY TERMS
- radical expression
- cube root

Exploration 2

$\sqrt{\text{Radical Expressions}}$

SET UP *Work with a partner.*

▶ **You can use other properties along with the product and quotient properties of square roots to simplify square roots. In some cases you can use the product of powers property that you learned in Section 1.**

16 Use the fact that $5^3 = 5^2 \cdot 5$ to show that $\sqrt{5^3}$ is equal to $5\sqrt{5}$.

17 In Question 16, you used the fact that $\sqrt{5^2} = 5$. Suppose you want to simplify $\sqrt{a^2}$.

a. Simplify $\sqrt{a^2}$ when $a = 9$, when $a = 7$, and when $a = 21$.

b. Simplify $\sqrt{a^2}$ when $a = -9$, when $a = -7$, and when $a = -21$.

c. What do you notice about $\sqrt{a^2}$ when a is positive?

d. What do you notice about $\sqrt{a^2}$ when a is negative?

e. Explain why $\sqrt{a^2} = |a|$ for all values for a.

▶ **The product property of square roots can be used to simplify *radical expressions*. A radical expression is an expression that contains a radical with one or more variables in the radicand.**

EXAMPLE

Simplify $\sqrt{16a^3}$. Assume a represents a positive number.

SAMPLE RESPONSE

$\sqrt{16a^3} = \sqrt{16 \cdot a^2 \cdot a}$	Rewrite $\sqrt{16a^3}$ as $\sqrt{16 \cdot a^2 \cdot a}$.
$= \sqrt{16} \cdot \sqrt{a^2} \cdot \sqrt{a}$	Use the product property.
$= 4 \cdot \lvert a \rvert \cdot \sqrt{a}$	Simplify perfect squares.
$= 4 \cdot a \cdot \sqrt{a}$	Rewrite $\lvert a \rvert$ as a.

In simplest form, $\sqrt{16a^3} = 4a\sqrt{a}$.

18 Discussion

a. In the example, why could you write $|a|$ as a?

b. Why was a^3 written as $a^2 \cdot a$?

c. In simplifying $\sqrt{a^5}$, how would you rewrite a^5?

d. Simplify $\sqrt{a^5}$. Assume a is a positive number.

19 ✓ CHECKPOINT Simplify each radical expression. Use the product property of square roots when necessary. Assume all variables represent positive numbers.

a. $\sqrt{9x^8}$ **b.** $\sqrt{36x^9}$ **c.** $\sqrt{x^3y^{16}}$ **d.** $\sqrt{y^{50}}$

✓ QUESTION 19

...checks that you can simplify radical expressions.

20 a. Which of the radicands in Question 19 are perfect squares?

b. Explain how you can tell if a radicand containing variables is a perfect square.

▶ **Sometimes formulas contain a *cube root.* If $A = s^3$, then s is a cube root of A. Cube roots can be written with the symbol $\sqrt[3]{}$. For example, $\sqrt[3]{64}$ represents the cube root of 64.**

In words	Using a radical symbol				Simplified
the cube root of 64	$\sqrt[3]{64}$	=	$\sqrt[3]{4 \cdot 4 \cdot 4}$	=	4

21 Why is $\sqrt[3]{64}$ equal to 4?

22 If $\sqrt[3]{n} = 5$, what is the value of n?

23 Every positive number a has two square roots, $\sqrt{a}$ and $-\sqrt{a}$. For example, 8 and -8 are both square roots of 64.

a. Are 5 and –5 both cube roots of $\sqrt[3]{125}$? Why or why not?

b. What is $-\sqrt[3]{125}$?

c. What is $\sqrt[3]{-125}$?

24 a. What does $\sqrt[3]{-8}$ equal?

b. If $\sqrt[3]{n} = -3$, what is the value of n?

▶ **The product and quotient properties of square roots generalize to other radicals. For example, for all positive numbers *a* and *b*,**

$$\sqrt[3]{ab} = \sqrt[3]{a} \cdot \sqrt[3]{b} \text{ and } \sqrt[3]{\frac{a}{b}} = \frac{\sqrt[3]{a}}{\sqrt[3]{b}}.$$

25 $2\sqrt[3]{2}$ is in simplest form, but $\sqrt[3]{16}$ is not. Explain why.

26 Use the product or quotient property shown above to simplify each expression.

a. $\sqrt[3]{216}$ **b.** Simplify $\sqrt[3]{48}$ **c.** $\sqrt[3]{\frac{8}{27}}$

27 **Try This as a Class**

a. n^6 is a perfect cube because $n^2 \cdot n^2 \cdot n^2$ or $(n^2)^3 = n^6$. Simplify $\sqrt[3]{n^6}$.

b. What is the next power of *n* that is a perfect cube?

c. Simplify $\sqrt[3]{n^8}$.

d. Simplify $\sqrt[3]{4n^{12}m^9}$.

28 Students in a class were asked to write *the cube root of five raised to the fourth power* in radical form. One student wrote $\sqrt[3]{5^4}$; the other wrote $\left(\sqrt[3]{5}\right)^4$.

a. Simplify each expression.

b. How are the expressions alike? How are they different?

29 **Discussion** The $\sqrt[3]{}$ symbol represents the third root (or cube root) of the radicand. What do you think $\sqrt[4]{64}$ represents?

30 Which of the following is the simplest form of $\sqrt[4]{64}$?

$2\sqrt[4]{4}$ $4\sqrt[4]{2}$ 4 16

✓ QUESTION 31

...checks that you can simplify cube roots and fourth roots.

31 **✓ CHECKPOINT**

a. Simplify each expression.

$\sqrt[3]{16}$ $\sqrt[3]{-24}$ $\sqrt[4]{16}$ $\sqrt[4]{32}$

b. Are any of the expressions in part (a) irrational? Explain how you can tell.

HOMEWORK EXERCISES ▶ **See Exs. 9–13 on p. 479.**

Section 2 Key Concepts

Key Terms

Irrational Numbers (p. 471)

A number that cannot be written as the quotient of two integers is irrational. As a decimal, an irrational number will not terminate or repeat. For example, $\sqrt{4}$ is rational because $\sqrt{4} = 2$. $\sqrt{8}$ is irrational because the radicand 8 is not a perfect square.

irrational
radical sign
radicand

Simplifying Square Roots (pp. 471–475)

A square root is in simplest form if the following are true.

- There are no perfect square factors other than 1 in the radicand.
- There are no fractions in the radicand.
- There are no square roots in the denominator of a fraction.

simplest form (of a square root)

The product and quotient properties of square roots can be used to simplify radical expressions. A radical expression is an expression that contains a radical with one or more variables in the radicand.

$$\sqrt{a \cdot b} = \sqrt{a} \cdot \sqrt{b} \qquad \sqrt{\frac{a}{b}} = \frac{\sqrt{a}}{\sqrt{b}}$$

product property of square roots

quotient property of square roots

radical expression

Examples

Simplify $\sqrt{8}$. $\sqrt{8} = \sqrt{4} \cdot \sqrt{2} = 2\sqrt{2}$

Simplify $\sqrt{\frac{3}{4}}$. $\sqrt{\frac{3}{4}} = \frac{\sqrt{3}}{\sqrt{4}} = \frac{\sqrt{3}}{2}$

Cube Roots (p. 475)

If $A = s^3$, then s is a cube root of A. The cube root of a number can be represented using the symbol $\sqrt[3]{}$.

cube root

Examples $4^3 = 64$, so $\sqrt[3]{64} = 4$

$$\sqrt[3]{9m^5n^{15}} = \sqrt[3]{9m^3m^2n^{15}}$$

$$= mn^5\sqrt[3]{9m^2}$$

m^5 can be rewritten as $m^3 \cdot m^2$. m^3 and n^{15} are perfect cubes.

32 Key Concepts Question Show how to use the product and quotient properties of radicals to simplify each expression.

a. $\sqrt{\frac{13}{100}}$

b. $\sqrt[3]{54n^7m^9}$

Section 2

Practice & Application Exercises

1. Tell whether each number is *rational* or *irrational.*

a. $\sqrt{17}$ **b.** $\frac{16}{3}$ **c.** $-14.\overline{14}$ **d.** $\sqrt{49}$

2. The number π is irrational. However, the rational numbers $\frac{22}{7}$ and 3.14 are often used to approximate π. Why do you think rational numbers are sometimes used in place of irrational numbers?

3. a. Suppose the digits of the decimal 0.12112111211112... continue to follow the same pattern forever. Write the next six digits.

b. Why is $0.\overline{12}$ rational and 0.12112111211112... irrational, even though they both continue forever?

4. Jodie uses her calculator to find a decimal value for $\frac{8}{23}$. Her calculator displays 0.3478261, so she decides $\frac{8}{23}$ is an irrational number. Do you agree with her? Why or why not?

5. Around 75 A.D., Heron of Alexandra discovered the formula $A = \sqrt{s(s - a)(s - b)(s - c)}$ for finding the area of a triangle when only the lengths a, b, and c of the sides are known. In the formula, s represents one-half the perimeter of the triangle.

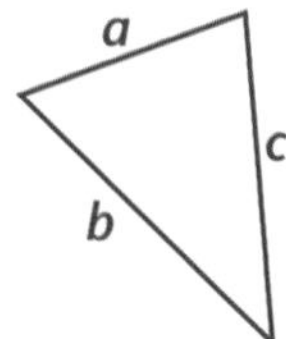

a. Find the exact area of a triangle with side lengths 8 cm, 6 cm and 4 cm. Write your answer in simplest form.

b. Find the exact area of an equilateral triangle with side length 10 in. Write your answer in simplest form.

c. Use a calculator to find the approximate area of each triangle in parts (a) and (b). Round to the nearest tenth.

6. Simplify.

a. $\sqrt{60}$ **b.** $\sqrt{12}$ **c.** $\sqrt{484}$ **d.** $\sqrt{\frac{5}{49}}$

7. Which of the following are in simplest form? Explain.

a. $\frac{\sqrt{3}}{50}$ **b.** $\frac{50}{\sqrt{3}}$ **c.** $\sqrt{\frac{50}{3}}$ **d.** $\frac{\sqrt{50}}{3}$

8. Simplify the expressions in Exercise 7 that are not already written in simplest form.

For Exercises 9–11 assume all variables represent positive numbers.

9. Simplify each radical expression. Use the product and quotient properties of square roots when possible.

   a. $\sqrt{121x^6}$ b. $\sqrt{y^{29}}$ c. $\sqrt{\frac{6}{m^{10}}}$ d. $\frac{\sqrt{b^5}}{\sqrt{b^3}}$

10. Simplify each expression.

   a. $\sqrt[3]{40}$ b. $\sqrt[3]{10n^{18}}$ c. $\sqrt[4]{625}$ d. $\sqrt[4]{a^4b^6}$

11. **Challenge** A radical expression is simplified to $9ab^3\sqrt[4]{ab^3}$. What was the original expression?

$$\sqrt[4]{?} = 9ab^3\sqrt[4]{ab^3}$$

12. Consider the expression $\sqrt[n]{64}$ where n is a positive integer. For which values of n is the expression rational? Name a value of n that makes the expression irrational. Explain your choices.

Reflecting on the Section

Write your answer to Exercise 13 in your journal.

13. Two students are discussing whether the number represented by the expression $\sqrt[3]{n^2}$ is rational or irrational. The first student says it is always irrational, while the second says you cannot tell since it depends on the value of n. With whom do you agree? Justify your choice.

Journal

Exercise 13 checks that you can simplify radical expressions and identify irrational numbers.

Spiral Review

Rewrite each equation in the form $y = ax^2 + bx + c$. Tell whether the equation represents a quadratic function. **(Module 6, p. 447)**

14. $y = 3x^2 - 5x - x^2$ 15. $y = x(2x - 4)$ 16. $x(x + 2) = 16y + x^2$

Find each sum or difference. **(Module 2, p. 100)**

17. $-32\frac{1}{5} - \frac{3}{5}$ 18. $-3\frac{1}{2} + \left(-3\frac{1}{8}\right)$ 19. $-6\frac{2}{3} - \left(-3\frac{1}{4}\right)$

20. In the diagram $\triangle ABC \sim \triangle XYZ$. Find the length of $\overline{AB}$. **(Module 3, p. 198)**

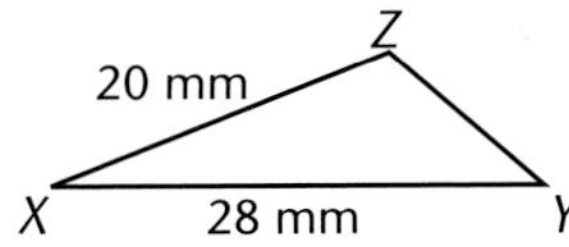

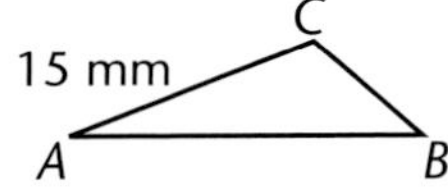

Section 2 Extra Skill Practice

Tell whether each number is *rational* or *irrational*.

1. $3.\overline{6}$
2. $\frac{36}{11}$
3. $\sqrt{3}$
4. 1.87
5. $\sqrt{16}$
6. -19
7. $\sqrt{27}$
8. $\sqrt{35}$
9. 3.454454445...
10. Which expression(s) could be used to simplify $\sqrt{24}$? Explain.

    $\sqrt{6} \cdot \sqrt{4}$ $\sqrt{4} \cdot 6$ $\sqrt{4} + \sqrt{4} + \sqrt{16}$

Simplify each expression. Assume all variables represent positive numbers.

11. $\sqrt{140}$
12. $\sqrt{44}$
13. $\sqrt{250}$
14. $\sqrt{28}$
15. $\sqrt{98}$
16. $\sqrt{320}$
17. $\sqrt{\frac{10}{81}}$
18. $\sqrt{\frac{14}{9}}$
19. $\sqrt{\frac{32}{81}}$
20. $\frac{11}{\sqrt{3}}$
21. $\frac{2}{\sqrt{5}}$
22. $\frac{\sqrt{9}}{25}$
23. $\frac{40}{\sqrt{2}}$
24. $\sqrt{49n^{10}}$
25. $\sqrt{x^3y^8}$
26. $\sqrt[3]{343}$
27. $\sqrt[3]{125}$
28. $\sqrt[4]{48}$
29. $\sqrt[4]{1296}$
30. $\sqrt[3]{54n^5}$
31. $\sqrt[3]{r^3s^5t^9}$

Standardized Testing ▶ Multiple Choice

1. Which of the following numbers is an irrational number?

   Ⓐ 40 Ⓑ $\sqrt{108}$ Ⓒ $\frac{29}{28}$ Ⓓ $3.\overline{51}$

2. Which expression is written in simplest form?

   Ⓐ $\sqrt{\frac{3}{5}}$ Ⓑ $3\sqrt{8}$ Ⓒ $\frac{\sqrt{4}}{9}$ Ⓓ $\frac{\sqrt{11}}{11}$

FOR ASSESSMENT AND PORTFOLIOS

EXTENDED E2 EXPLORATION

Sum Fun!

7	5	8
6	4	7
9	7	10

The Situation

	5	3	6
2	7	5	8
1	6	4	7
4	9	7	10

~~7~~	~~5~~	(8)
(6)	~~4~~	~~7~~
~~9~~	(7)	~~10~~

Six numbers are chosen randomly and placed along the edge of a grid as shown. Corresponding numbers are then added to complete each box in the 3 × 3 grid.

A number is circled and all other numbers that share the same row and same column are crossed out. The process is repeated with the available numbers until only one number remains in each row and in each column. The sum of the circled numbers is 21.

Copy the grid and choose a different starting number to circle. Find the sum of the circled numbers. Repeat this several times.

The Problem

Find out what the sum of the circled numbers on any sum-generated grid will be before any numbers are circled.

Something to Think About

- What happens if different random numbers are chosen to generate the grid?
- If the grid is completed using variables for the six random numbers, what is the sum of the circled expressions? What if the variables are rearranged along the outside of the grid? How is the sum affected?
- Does the trick work with other size grids? Must the grids have an equal number of columns and rows or could a grid be 3 × 4?

Present Your Results

Explain why this puzzle works and how you could predict the sum for any size grid. Include an explanation of how you used algebra to solve this problem.

Section 3 Graphing and Solving Inequalities

IN THIS SECTION

EXPLORATION 1
- Graphing Inequalities

EXPLORATION 2
- Solving Simple Inequalities

EXPLORATION 3
- Multi-Step Inequalities

Setting the Stage

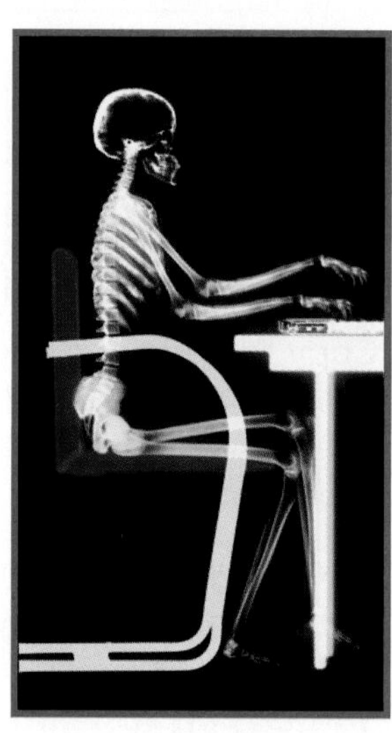

How high should the seat of a chair be so it is comfortable for most people? How can children ride safely and comfortably in a car? To get answers to questions like these, the person to call is a *human factors engineer*. These engineers make use of data about people—heights, weights, leg lengths, and so on. They use the information to help design buildings, furniture, tools, appliances, and cars that are comfortable for as many people as possible.

To decide how high to make the seat of a chair, for example, a human factors engineer would study the data below on *popliteal height*.

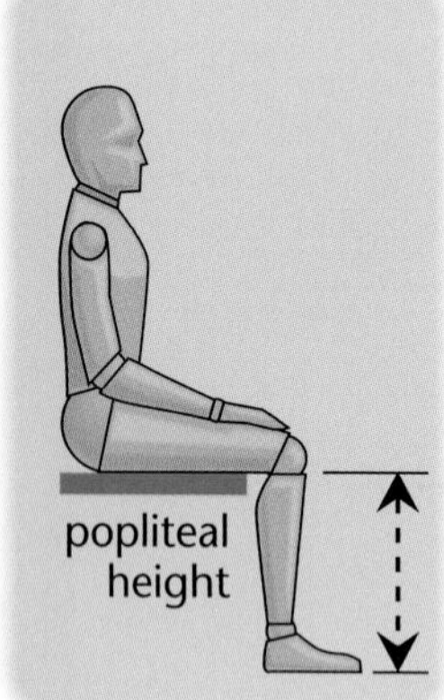

▲ *Popliteal height* is the distance from the floor to the underside of the knees when a person is seated.

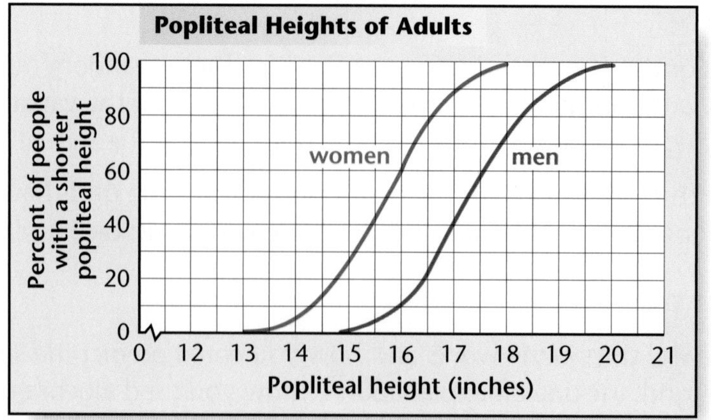

Think About It

1 About what percent of adult women have a popliteal height less than 17 in.? about what percent of adult men?

2 The popliteal height of 5% of women is less than how many inches?

3 Can you tell from the graph if any men have a popliteal height less than the number of inches you found in Question 2? Explain.

Exploration 1

Graphing INEQUALITIES

GOAL

LEARN HOW TO...
- write and graph inequalities

AS YOU...
- study car seat safety for children

KEY TERM
- inequality

▶ **Seats in cars are designed mainly for the safety and comfort of adults, therefore the National Highway Traffic Safety Administration (NHTSA) offers guiding principles for children riding in vehicles. Some of the principles can be represented using inequalities. An inequality is a mathematical sentence that compares two quantities using the symbols <, >, ≤, or ≥.**

EXAMPLE

Infants up to age one weighing less than 20 lb should always be secured in a rear-facing safety seat in the back seat of a vehicle. Write and graph an inequality to describe the weight restriction.

SAMPLE RESPONSE

$w < 20$ where w is weight in pounds.

The open circle shows that 20 is not on the graph.

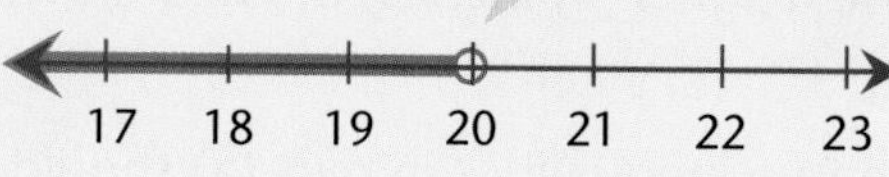

4 **Discussion**

a. In the inequality $w < 20$, what does the symbol $<$ mean?

b. How do you know that the graph does not include 20? How do you know that it includes values less than 17?

5 According to NHTSA, an infant weighing 20 lb or more before age one should ride in a rear-facing safety seat rated for heavier infants.

a. Write an inequality that describes the weight restriction in this situation. Use the symbol ≥ (read as *is greater than or equal to*).

b. The graph of the inequality from part (a) is shown below. Why is the circle filled in?

▶ **Sometimes two inequalities are combined to form one inequality.**

EXAMPLE

Children older than one year weighing from 20 lb to 40 lb may ride in a forward-facing safety seat in the back seat of a vehicle. Write and graph an inequality that describes this weight restriction.

SAMPLE RESPONSE

$w \geq 20$ represents a weight greater than or equal to 20 lb.
$w \leq 40$ represents a weight less than or equal to 40 lb. Together they can be written as $20 \leq w \leq 40$, where w is the weight in pounds.

You can read $20 \leq w \leq 40$ as "w is greater than or equal to 20 and less than or equal to 40."

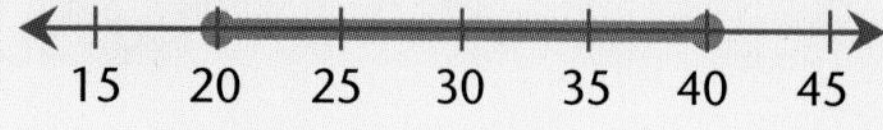

$20 \leq w \leq 40$ can also be read as "20 is less than or equal to w and w is less than or equal to 40."

6 **Try This as a Class** NHTSA recommends that children weighing over 40 lb use booster seats until they reach a height of 4 ft 9 in.

a. Write and graph an inequality for the weights (in pounds) of children who should use booster seats. Write and graph an inequality for the heights (in inches) of children who should use booster seats.

b. Explain why the two inequalities in part (a) should not be combined into one inequality.

7 The graph shows the percent of child safety seats that studies show are used incorrectly. Write an inequality represented by the graph.

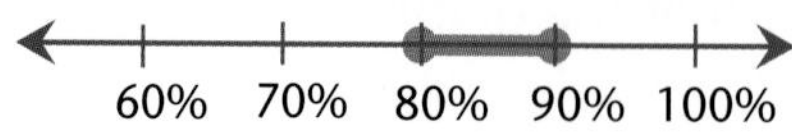

8 ✓ **CHECKPOINT** Write and graph each inequality.

a. n is less than or equal to 65.

b. x is greater than –250.

c. r is less than 16 but greater than 5.

✓ **QUESTION 8**

...checks that you can write and graph an inequality.

HOMEWORK EXERCISES See Exs. 1–6 on p. 490.

Exploration 2

Solving Simple Inequalities

GOAL

LEARN HOW TO...
- solve inequalites that involve one operation

AS YOU...
- study the seat heights of chairs

KEY TERMS
- solution of an inequality
- solve an inequality

▶ **Some human factors engineers recommend that for comfort, the height of a chair seat should be less than or equal to the popliteal height of the person sitting in it plus 1.5 in. Adding 1.5 in. adjusts for the thickness of the soles and heels of the person's shoes.**

9 a. Use h for the seat height and p for the popliteal height. Write an inequality for the recommended height of a chair seat.

b. Substitute 15 for p in the inequality in part (a). A value of a variable that makes an inequality true is a **solution of the inequality**. Are 16.5 in. and 19 in. solutions of your new inequality? Why or why not?

c. A student claims that a 2 in. chair would be comfortable for a person with a 15 in. popliteal height because 2 is a solution of the inequality $h \leq 15 + 1.5$. Is 2 a solution? Is it realistic?

10 **Try This as a Class** Suppose the seat height of a chair is 17 in.

a. Substitute 17 in. for the seat height in the inequality from Question 9(a). Write the new inequality.

b. People with what popliteal heights would be comfortable in such a chair? Explain how you found your answer.

c. Use the graph on page 482. About what percent of adult women would not be comfortable in the chair? About what percent of adult men would not be comfortable?

▶ **In Question 10(c), you solved the inequality $17 \le p + 1.5$ by finding all of the solutions of the inequality. In Questions 11–13, you will investigate some of the operations used to solve inequalities.**

11 Choose two different numbers (the numbers can both have the same sign, or they can have opposite signs). Write an inequality that compares the numbers.

12 Perform each operation below to both sides of the original inequality you wrote in Question 11. Then write the correct inequality symbol between the two new numbers.

a. Add 5. **b.** Subtract 5. **c.** Multiply by 5.

d. Divide by 5. **e.** Add –2. **f.** Subtract –2.

g. Multiply by –2. **h.** Divide by –2. **i.** Add $-\frac{1}{4}$.

j. Subtract $-\frac{1}{4}$. **k.** Multiply by $-\frac{1}{4}$. **l.** Divide by $-\frac{1}{4}$.

13 **Try This as a Class** Look back at your results from Question 12. Tell how you think the operations described affect the inequality.

a. Adding or subtracting the same number on both sides

b. Multiplying or dividing both sides by the same nonzero number

▶ **The properties found in Question 13 can be used to solve inequalities.**

EXAMPLE

Adding or subtracting the same number on both sides of an inequality does not affect the inequality.

$$x - 7 \le -2$$

$$x - 7 + 7 \le -2 + 7$$

$$x \le 5$$

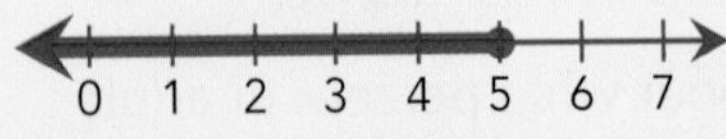

Multiplying or dividing both sides of an inequality by a *negative* number **reverses the inequality**.

$$-6x > 18$$

$$\frac{-6x}{-6} < \frac{18}{-6}$$

$$x < -3$$

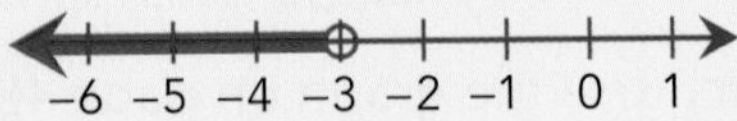

14 **Discussion** How would you check the solutions of the inequalities in the Example? How is this different than checking the solution of an equation?

15 ✓ **CHECKPOINT** Solve. Check and then graph each solution.

a. $36 < x + 13$ **b.** $\frac{x}{3} \geq -2$ **c.** $-7x > -63$

✓ **QUESTION 15**

...checks that you can solve inequalities that involve one operation.

16 One manufacturer decided that the seat height of a non-adjustable chair should be at least 16 in. Using the inequality from Question 9(a), an inequality for the popliteal heights of the people who would be comfortable in a chair with a seat height of 16 in. is $16 \leq p + 1.5$.

a. Solve $16 \leq p + 1.5$. People with what popliteal heights would be comfortable in the chair?

b. Use the graph on page 482. About what percent of adult women would not be comfortable in the chair? About what percent of adult men would not be comfortable?

c. Why do you think the company decided on this seat height instead of a greater one?

HOMEWORK EXERCISES ▶ See Exs. 7–21 on p. 491.

Exploration 3

MULTI-STEP INEQUALITIES

GOAL

LEARN HOW TO...
- solve inequalities that have more than one operation

AS YOU...
- plan the arrangement of the seats in a theater

▶ **In this exploration, you will use human factors engineering to design comfortable seating for a theater.**

17 To provide comfortable seating, the width of a theater seat should be from 20 to 26 in. and the depth of each row should be from 34 to 42 in.

a. What is the least area in square feet needed for a person to have a comfortable seat? What is the greatest area needed? (*Hint:* 1 ft^2 = 144 $in.^2$)

b. What seat width and row depth would you recommend for each seat in a theater? Why?

c. Based on your recommendation, how many square feet would be needed for each seat in a theater?

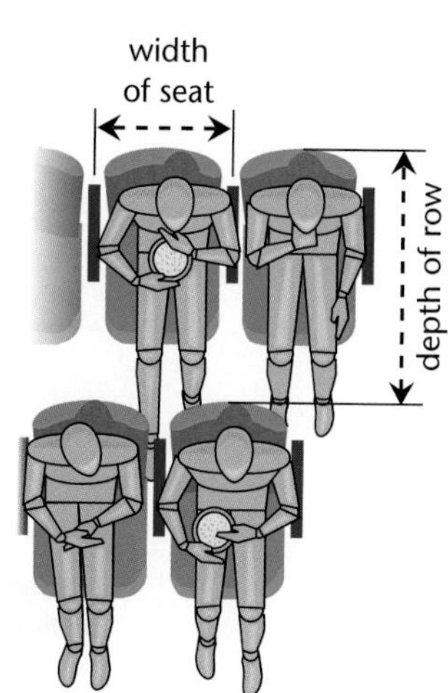

18 A new theater will be 48 ft long and 36 ft wide. Two aisles are needed, one down the center of the theater and one between the front row and the screen. The aisles will be 4 ft wide.

a. Make a sketch of the theater showing the locations and dimensions of the aisles.

b. What is the total area of the theater? of the aisles?

19 **Try This as a Class** The total area of the theater, *t*, must be greater than or equal to the area per seat times the number of seats, *s*, plus the area of the aisles, *a*. Use the area per seat that you recommended in Question 17(c).

a. Write an inequality relating *t*, *s*, and *a*.

b. Use your answers to Question 18(b) to write an inequality for the number of seats the theater can hold.

c. The inequality in part (b) uses both addition and multiplication. What are their inverse operations?

d. In what order would you use the inverse operations to solve the inequality in part (b)? Why?

e. About how many seats can the theater hold?

✓ QUESTION 20

...checks that you can solve inequalities that involve two operations.

20 **✓ CHECKPOINT** Solve each inequality.

a. $14 < 5x - 9$ **b.** $-\frac{x}{2} - 3 \geq -2$ **c.** $-3x + 17 > -4$

21 **a.** Use the aisle width and the theater width from Question 18 and the seat width you chose in Question 17(b) to write an inequality involving *s*, the number of seats.

b. Suppose that, in each row, there will be the same number of seats on either side of the aisle. How many seats can you have in each row?

c. Use the row depth you chose in Question 17(b). How many rows can you have?

d. How many seats will fit in the theater? How does this compare with your answer to Question 19(e)?

22 **Discussion** Human factors engineers recommend that the rows of seats be staggered as in the diagram on page 487. How would this affect the number of seats you can have in the theater?

HOMEWORK EXERCISES ▶ See Exs. 22–38 on pp. 492–493.

Section 3 Key Concepts

Key Terms

Inequalities (pp. 483–485)

The symbols <, >, ≤, and ≥ are used to write inequalities. Inequalities can be graphed on a number line.

inequality

Example A number is greater than or equal to −2 and less than 3.

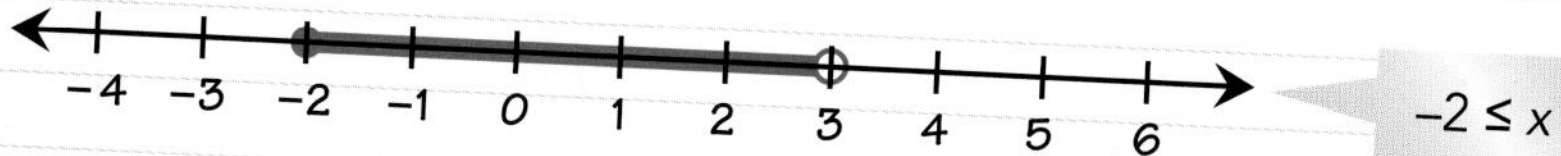

$-2 \le x < 3$

Solving Inequalities (pp. 485–488)

A value of a variable that makes an inequality true is a solution of the inequality. All the solutions together are called the solution of the inequality. When you find them, you are solving the inequality.

solution of an inequality

solve an inequality

Example

$$-3x + 2.5 < 11.8$$

$$-3x + 2.5 - 2.5 < 11.8 - 2.5$$

Subtracting the same number does not affect the inequality.

$$-3x < 9.3$$

$$\frac{-3x}{-3} > \frac{9.3}{-3}$$

Dividing by a *negative* number reverses the inequality.

$$x > -3.1$$

You can use inverse operations to solve inequalities. However, you must be sure to reverse the inequality symbol whenever you multiply or divide both sides by a negative number.

Key Concepts Questions

23 Explain why in the first Example above there is a closed circle on −2 and an open circle on 3.

24 **a.** Solve $-2a - 3 = 5$ and graph the solution.

b. Solve $-2a - 3 \ge 5$ and graph the solution.

c. How is the solution of $-2a - 3 \ge 5$ similar to the solution of $-2a - 3 = 5$? How is it different?

Section 3

Practice & Application Exercises

Write an inequality to describe each situation. Then graph each inequality on a number line.

1. The price of the ticket for a concert was more than $25.

2. The temperature today ranged from –10°F to 3°F.

3. The elevation of the house was less than 50 ft above sea level.

4. At a theater, people 55 years old and older pay a reduced admission price.

5. **Geometry Connection** The graph of the inequality $a \geq 7$ is a *ray*, because it is a part of a line and has one endpoint. The graph of the inequality $2 \leq b \leq 6$ is a *segment*, because it is a part of a line and has two endpoints.

   a. Graph each of the inequalities above on a number line and label the endpoints.

   b. A segment has endpoints at –3 and 1. Write an inequality that has this segment as its graph.

   c. A ray has an endpoint at 10 and includes points to the left on a number line. Write an inequality that has this ray as its graph.

6. **Writing** A student graphed the inequality $-2 < x \leq 4$ as shown below. Explain what is wrong with the graph.

–4 –2 0 2 4 6

7. Is 6 a solution of the inequality $-8 + x < 2$? Explain.

Solve each inequality. Check and graph each solution.

8. $a + 17 < 37$

9. $8 + w \geq 10$

10. $-13 > b - 7$

11. $x - (-3) \leq 8$

12. $96 \leq 12n$

13. $-0.5z > -6.5$

14. $\frac{y}{2} < 2.5$

15. $-7 \geq \frac{q}{-1.5}$

16. $-\frac{2}{3}x < 6$

For Exercises 17–20, write and solve an inequality for each situation.

17. Seven more than a number is less than seven.

18. The opposite of a number is greater than or equal to five.

19. A family needs to drive 95 miles in less than 1 hour and 45 minutes. What average speed must they drive?

20. **Building Codes** The Uniform Building Code requires that there be at least 20 ft^2 of space for each person in a classroom. Suppose a classroom is 28 ft long and 18 ft wide. How many people can be in the classroom?

21. **Theater Design** Rows in a theater are often elevated so each person can look over the head of the person in front of him or her. Theater floors must either be sloped or have steps. Whether the floor can be sloped depends on the depth of the row d and the amount of rise r. A floor can only be sloped if $r \leq \frac{d}{8}$.

    a. A rise of 5 in. will give the maximum visibility for the greatest number of people. How deep can the rows be if the floor is sloped and has a rise of 5 in.?

    b. Many theaters have 32-inch-deep rows. What is the maximum rise for a sloped floor?

    c. A certain theater chain claims to give everyone an unobstructed view of the screen. Suppose the rise is 10.8 in. What is the minimum row depth for a sloped floor?

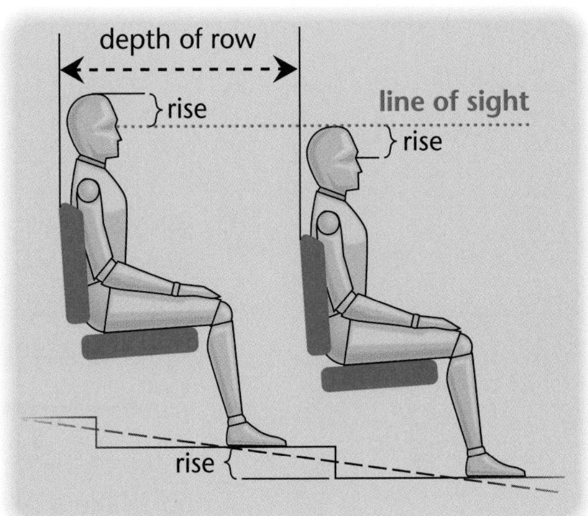

    d. Why do you think the theaters in part (c) have stepped floors?

    e. What are some advantages of a stepped floor?

    f. What are some advantages of a sloped floor?

For Exercises 22–26, write and solve an inequality for each situation.

22. Two times a number minus 13 is less than 47.

23. Twenty-four minus half of a number is greater than or equal to 132.

24. The difference when 1.57 is subtracted from 3 times a number is less than or equal to 10.62.

25. Suppose you can rent a snowmobile for an initial fee of \$25, plus \$12.50 per hour. For how many hours can you rent a snowmobile and still spend less than \$90?

26. A landowner has 200 acres of land and wants to keep at least 20 acres. The rest will be divided and sold in 12-acre lots. How many of these lots can the land owner offer for sale?

Solve each inequality. Check and graph each solution.

27. $-5b + 77 \geq 92$

28. $-8z + 9 \geq 93$

29. $-32 + (-41x) \leq -155$

30. $1.2a - 0.97 < 2.63$

31. $\frac{3}{4}y + \frac{11}{16} > \frac{19}{16}$

32. $\frac{8}{9} - \frac{1}{3}m < \frac{23}{27}$

33. $5.95 - 2.95x > -11.75$

34. $49y + 249 \leq -976$

35. **Create Your Own** For each graph, create three inequalities that when solved would produce the solution shown in the graph.

a. 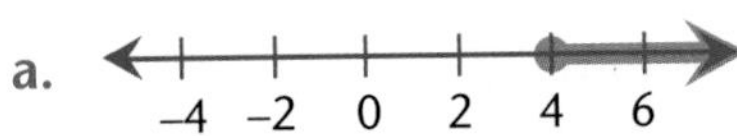

b. 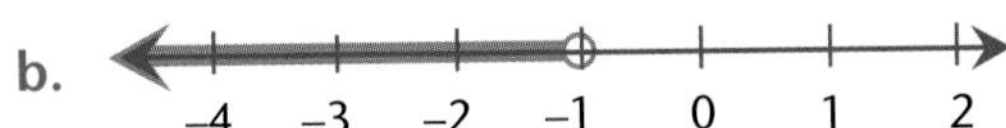

36. Riley's Factory produces energy bars for a sports company. The weight of each bar must be within a certain number of ounces or it is rejected. The graph below shows the range for the weights that are acceptable.

5.7 5.8 5.9 6.0 6.1 6.2 6.3

a. Make a graph that represents the weights that are rejected.

b. Complete the sentence: If a bar weighs __?__ or __?__ it is rejected.

37. **Challenge** G-forces make a roller coaster thrilling, but extreme G-forces can make a rider pass out. A roller coaster designer can use the following inequality to keep the G-forces less than 3.5 G, a safe level according to one designer.

$$3.5\text{ G} > \frac{[\text{speed of the car (in ft/sec)}]^2}{32.2 \times \text{radius of the curve (in feet)}}$$

a. If the speed of the car is 35 mi/hr, what is the minimum radius of the curve? Round to the nearest tenth. (*Hint:* 1 mi = 5280 ft)

b. If the radius of the curve is 10 ft, what is the maximum speed in miles per hour? Round to the nearest tenth.

c. Do you think it is reasonable to design a roller coaster to go around a curve at 100 mi/hr? Explain.

The amount of G-force you feel depends on the car's speed and the curve of the track, which can be thought of as part of the circle.

Reflecting on the Section

Write your response to Exercise 38 in your journal.

38. You can solve the inequality $\frac{x}{-2} < 5$ by multiplying both sides by –2.

$$\frac{x}{-2} < 5$$

$$-2 \cdot \frac{x}{-2} > -2 \cdot 5$$

$$x > -10$$

Explain why multiplying by x to solve the inequality $\frac{2}{x} < 5$ might lead to an error.

Journal

Exercise 38 checks that you understand how to solve inequalities.

Spiral Review

Use the diagram to find each angle measure. **(Module 6, p. 438)**

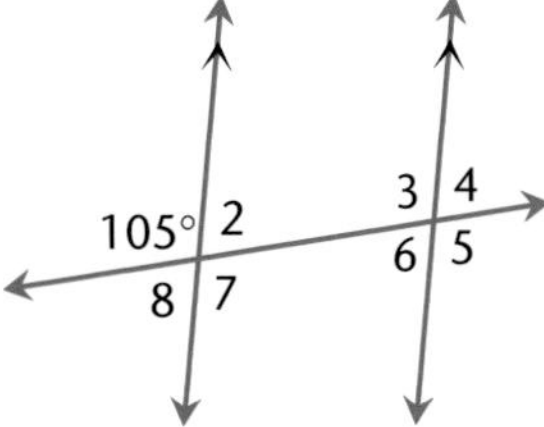

39. $m\angle 3$

40. $m\angle 5$

41. $m\angle 7$

Solve each proportion. **(Module 2, p. 132)**

42. $\frac{x}{100} = \frac{3}{5}$

43. $\frac{9}{h} = \frac{2}{3}$

44. $\frac{1}{2} = \frac{x}{4.5}$

Section 3
Extra Skill Practice

Write an inequality to describe each situation. Then graph each inequality on a number line.

1. The woman was at least 20 years old, but not yet 25.
2. The number of fish in the tank is always less than 10.
3. The price is \$10 or more.
4. The number is greater than or equal to 2 and less than 7.

Solve each inequality. Check and graph each solution.

5. $x + 4 \le 2$
6. $-2 + x < 3$
7. $16a > 2$
8. $60 > -4c$
9. $a - 2 \ge 4$
10. $x - \frac{4}{3} \ge 3$
11. $-0.2u < 8$
12. $15 \ge \frac{m}{3}$
13. $\frac{n}{-3} < 9$
14. $-\frac{3}{4}q < 12$
15. $\frac{x}{5} < -\frac{3}{5}$
16. $\frac{3}{2} \le -6a$

Write and solve an inequality for each situation.

17. Five more than a number is greater than two.
18. Three minus twice a number is less than eight.
19. You will spend at least \$10 if you buy a melon for \$2.88 and 4 lb of grapes. What do grapes cost per pound?

Solve each inequality. Check and graph each solution.

20. $3x - 5 \le 6$
21. $-4w - 18 \ge 2$
22. $2 > 6 + 7c$
23. $-36x + 15 < 24$
24. $14 \le -112a - 42$
25. $4.5x + 0.8 > 3.5$
26. $4.5 - 0.25x \ge 3.25$
27. $7.8 - 2.3n < 3.2$
28. $\frac{a}{-2} + 7 < 8$
29. $\frac{x}{3} - 1 < \frac{3}{4}$
30. $\frac{7}{5} + \frac{y}{10} \le -\frac{2}{5}$
31. $12 - \frac{1}{2}m \ge 3\frac{1}{4}$

Standardized Testing ▶ Free Response

1. The edges of the base of a square pyramid are each 14 in. long. For what values of the height h will the volume of the pyramid be less than 5880 in.^{3}?
2. A camera shop charges \$12 to develop a roll of film plus \$0.45 for each extra print. How many extra prints can Stephanie get if she has \$20 to spend for photographs?

Section 4 Polynomials and Factoring

IN THIS SECTION

EXPLORATION 1
- Multiplying Binomials

EXPLORATION 2
- Factoring Quadratics

The Art of Quadratics

Setting the Stage

Leonardo da Vinci, born on April 15, 1452, was a man of many talents. He was a famous artist, musician, mathematician, scientist, philosopher, writer, architect, sculptor, and inventor.

Da Vinci, like many other painters past and present, often used geometric shapes, ratios, and patterns in his paintings. *The Mona Lisa*, painted by Leonardo more than 450 years ago, is one of the world's most famous paintings.

◀ Leonardo da Vinci's painting entitled *The Mona Lisa*

▲ This chalk drawing is believed to be a self-portrait of Leonardo da Vinci in his later years of life.

Think About It

▶ **The width of the painting is 53 cm and the height is 77 cm. Suppose a frame of width x centimeters is placed around the painting as shown.**

1 Write an expression for the width of the painting when the frame is included.

2 Write an expression for the height of the painting when the frame is included.

3 **a.** What is the area of the painting without the frame?

b. How might you express the area of the painting including the frame?

GOAL

LEARN HOW TO...
- multiply binomials

AS YOU...
- work with algebra tiles and find areas of various rectangles

KEY TERMS
- polynomial
- monomial
- term
- binomial
- trinomial

Exploration 1

Multiplying Binomials

SET UP *Work with a partner. You will need:* • *Labsheet 4A* • *algebra tiles*

▶ **In the *Setting the Stage*, you wrote *polynomial* expressions for the height and the width of the framed *Mona Lisa* painting. A polynomial is a *monomial* or a sum of monomials. The table shows some different types of polynomials.**

	Examples
A **monomial** is a number or a variable or a product of a number and one or more variables. (Each monomial is a **term**.)	2 $3x^2$ $-st$
A **binomial** is a polynomial with exactly two terms.	$4x + 3$ $3t^2 + 2s$
A **trinomial** is a polynomial with exactly three terms.	$3x^2 + 2x + 1$ $25n + 4 - 17t$

4 **a.** Which type of polynomial did you use to represent the width of the painting, including the frame, in the *Setting the Stage*?

b. Does the expression you wrote for the area of the framed painting have the form of a polynomial? Explain.

▶ **Algebra tiles can be used to model polynomials. When using algebra tiles, a negative or positive term can be identified by the color of the tile or by a negative or positive sign on the tile.**

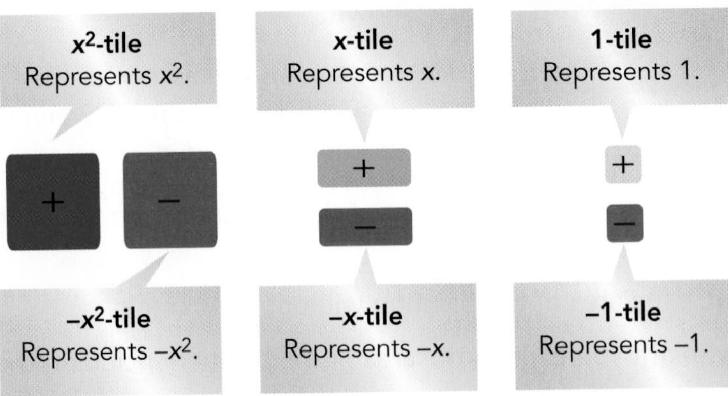

EXAMPLE

Write the polynomial represented by the group of algebra tiles.

Two x^2-tiles → $2x^2$

Two $-x$-tiles → $-2x$

One x-tile → x

One 1-tile → 1

The polynomial is:

$$2x^2 + (-2x) + x + 1 = 2x^2 + (-x) + 1$$
$$= 2x^2 - x + 1$$

5 **Discussion** Name the polynomial represented by each group of algebra tiles. Tell whether each polynomial is a *monomial, binomial,* or *trinomial.*

a. 

b. 

c. 

d. 

e. 

f. 

6 **a.** Use algebra tiles to model the polynomial $x^2 + 2x + 3$.

b. Is there only one way to model $x^2 + 2x + 3$? Explain.

▶ **The expression $(2x + 77)(2x + 53)$ represents the area of the framed *Mona Lisa* painting. Can $(2x + 77)(2x + 53)$ be expressed as a polynomial? If so, will it be a monomial, binomial, or trinomial? To answer these questions, let's first look at a simpler example.**

7 Complete each of the steps below to model the product $(x + 2)(2x + 1)$.

Step 1 Model each binomial with algebra tiles. Arrange the first binomial vertically and the second binomial horizontally as shown.

Step 2 The binomials define a rectangular region with width $(2x + 1)$ and height $(x + 2)$. Fill in the region with the appropriate tiles to form the *product rectangle.*

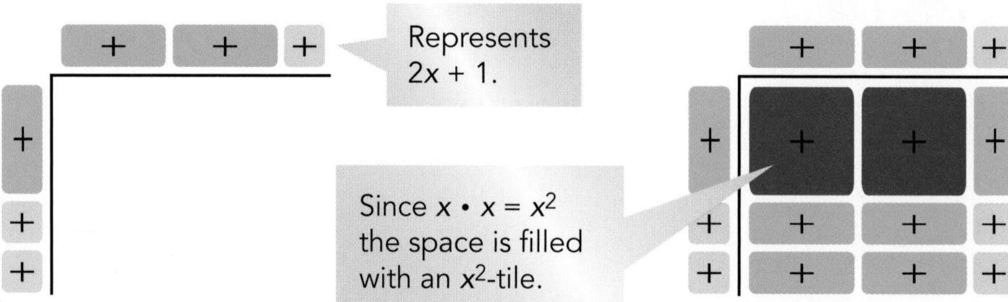

Represents $x + 2$.

Step 3 Read the expression represented by the product rectangle, combining like terms if necessary. This model represents the expression $2x^2 + 5x + 2$. This is the product of the two binomials.

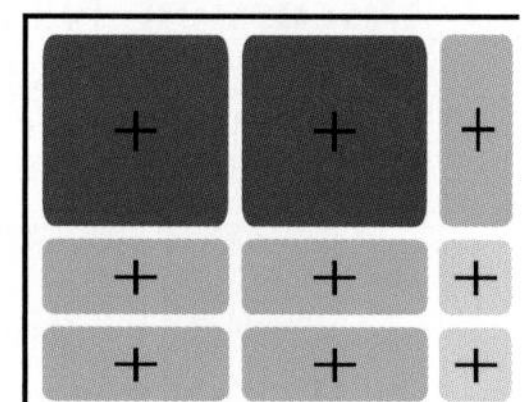

▶ **The expression in Step 3 is written in *descending order of exponents.* The exponents of the variable decrease from left to right.**

$$2x^2 + 5x + 2$$

x^2, then x^1, then x^0. (Think of 2 as $2x^0$ because $x^0 = 1$).

You should write polynomials in descending order of exponents.

8 **a.** Now rearrange the horizontal and the vertical binomials from Question 7 so the second binomial is vertical and the first binomial is horizontal and follow Steps 1–3 again.

b. Compare your answer to the one in Question 7. What does this tell you about multiplication of binomials?

✓ QUESTION 9

...checks that you can use algebra tiles to multiply two binomials.

9 **✓ CHECKPOINT** Use algebra tiles to find the product of the binomials.

a. $(x + 2)(x + 1)$ **b.** $(x + 3)(x + 4)$ **c.** $(x + 3)(2x + 5)$

▶ **You can use algebra tiles to multiply binomials where the terms are joined by subtraction. First rewrite all expressions involving subtraction as equivalent expressions involving addition. Then model the binomials with algebra tiles, using the red tiles to represent negative terms.**

10 How would you write $(x + 2)(2x - 1)$ without subtraction signs?

11 **Use Labsheet 4A.** Follow the directions for *Multiplying Binomials* to find the product $(x + 2)(2x - 1)$.

12 **Try This As a Class**

a. Use algebra tiles to model $(x - 2)(x - 3)$.

b. In which situations does a negative tile appear in the product?

c. In which situations does a positive tile appear in the product?

13 **CHECKPOINT** Use algebra tiles to find the product of the binomials. Combine like terms.

a. $(x - 2)(x - 1)$ **b.** $(2x - 1)(x + 3)$

...checks that you can use algebra tiles to multiply binomials containing subtraction signs.

▶ **The example below shows how you can multiply binomials using algebra tiles and a table.**

EXAMPLE

Multiply $(x - 2)(2x + 3)$.

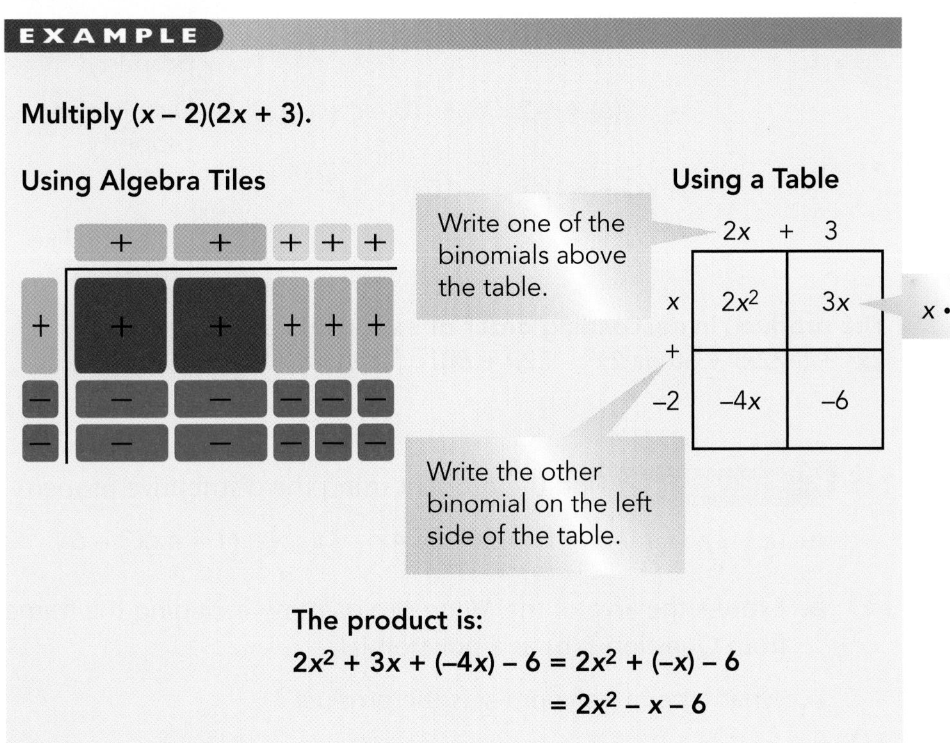

The product is:

$$2x^2 + 3x + (-4x) - 6 = 2x^2 + (-x) - 6$$
$$= 2x^2 - x - 6$$

14 **Discussion**

a. Explain how the table was used to find the product. Compare this model to the algebra tile model.

b. Did you have to rewrite the product in descending order of exponents? Explain.

15 Find the product of each pair of binomials using a table. Show your work.

a. $(3x + 2)(2x + 1)$ **b.** $(x + 4)(-x + 4)$ **c.** $(x + 3)(x - 3)$

16 Use algebra tiles to check your answers in Question 15.

17 **a.** Would it be easier to use algebra tiles or a table to find the product $(2x - 15)(3x + 20)$? Why?

b. Find the product $(2x - 15)(3x + 20)$. Show your work.

▶ **You can also find a product of binomials by using the distributive property twice.**

FOR ◀ HELP with *the distributive property, see* **MODULE 6, p. 411**

EXAMPLE

Find the product (10 – 2x)(6 – x).

Rewrite all subtractions as additions.

$(10 - 2x)(6 - x) = (10 + (-2x))(6 + (-x))$

$= (10 + (-2x))6 + (10 + (-2x))(-x)$ Distributive property

$= 10(6) + (-2x)(6) + 10(-x) + (-2x)(-x)$ Distributive property

$= 60 + (-12x) + (-10x) + 2x^2$

$= 60 + (-22x) + 2x^2$ Combine like terms.

The product, in descending order of exponents, is $2x^2 + (-22x) + 60$ or $2x^2 - 22x + 60$.

✓ **QUESTION 18**

...checks that you can use the distributive property to find the product of two binomials.

18 ✓ **CHECKPOINT** Find the product using the distributive property.

a. $(x + 3)(3x + 2)$ **b.** $(4x - 3)(4x + 3)$ **c.** $(1 - 4x)(3 - 6x)$

19 **a.** Express the area of the *Mona Lisa* painting including the frame from Question 3(b) as a polynomial.

b. What type of polynomial is the product?

20 When is the product of two binomials a binomial? a trinomial? Explain.

HOMEWORK EXERCISES ▶ **See Exs. 1–25 on pp. 508–509.**

Exploration 2

Factoring Quadratics

GOAL

LEARN HOW TO...
- factor quadratics

AS YOU...
- work with algebra tiles

KEY TERM
- factor

SET UP *Work with a partner. You will need algebra tiles.*

Leonardo's artwork includes sketches of various inventions such as a catapult, designed to throw projectiles great distances. The path that a projectile follows can be modeled by a quadratic equation.

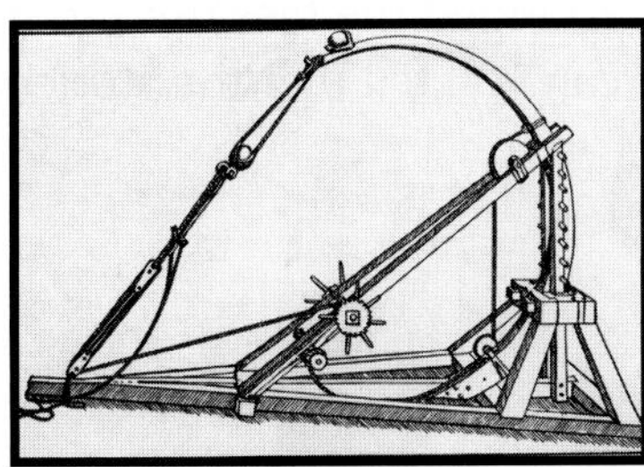

The expression $ax^2 + bx + c$ in the quadratic equation $y = ax^2 + bx + c$ is called a *quadratic polynomial* because the greatest exponent of the variable is 2. In a future course, you will learn that you may be able to solve a quadratic equation by factoring a quadratic polynomial.

▶ **In this exploration you will learn to *factor* quadratic polynomials.**

21 The product $x^2 + 4x + 3$ can be represented by the product rectangle of algebra tiles below.

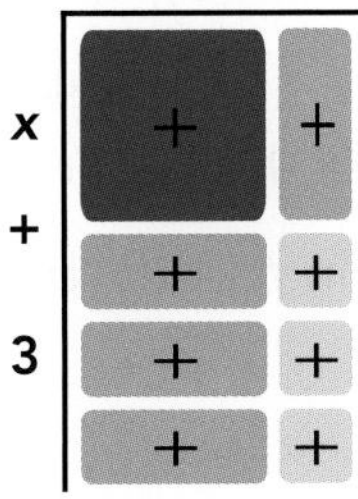

a. The height of the product rectangle is $x + 3$. Explain why.

b. Write the expression for the width of the product rectangle.

▶ **To factor a quadratic polynomial, or simply *quadratic*, you must find the factors whose product is the quadratic. For example, you know that**

$$(x + 5)(x - 2) = x^2 + 3x - 10.$$

Then $x + 5$ and $x - 2$ are factors of $x^2 + 3x - 10$.

22 **a.** Look at your work from Question 21. What are the factors of $x^2 + 4x + 3$?

b. Multiply the binomials in part (a) to check that they are the factors of $x^2 + 4x + 3$.

23 **Try This As a Class**

a. Use algebra tiles to model $x^2 + 4x + 4$.

b. One student arranged the tiles used to model $x^2 + 4x + 4$ as shown. How can you tell that the student did *not* find the factors of $x^2 + 4x + 4$?

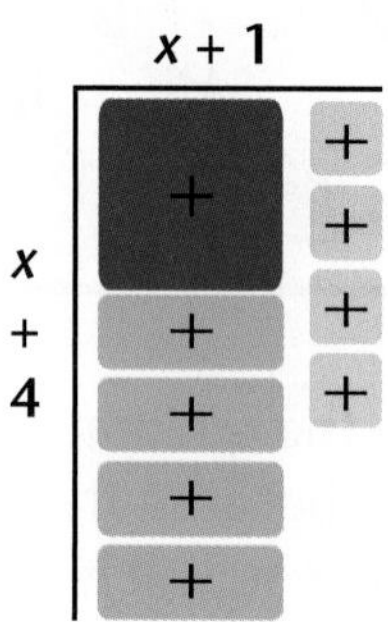

c. Experiment with arranging the algebra tiles until you complete a product rectangle. What are the height and width of your rectangle?

d. What are the factors of $x^2 + 4x + 4$?

24 **a.** Use algebra tiles to model $x^2 + 5x + 4$.

b. Arrange the tiles into a rectangle to find the factors of $x^2 + 5x + 4$. What are the factors?

c. Check your answer in part (b) by multiplying the factors.

25 Consider your work from Questions 23 and 24.

a. The last term of each quadratic in Questions 23 and 24 is 4. Name all the factor pairs of 4.

b. How do the factor pairs of 4 appear in the expressions for the length and width of each product rectangle?

c. **Discussion** If you were to factor $x^2 + 6x + 8$, what factor pairs do you think might appear in the expressions for the length and width of the product rectangle? Explain.

d. Use the factor pairs you found in part (c) and algebra tiles to help you factor $x^2 + 6x + 8$.

26 **✓ CHECKPOINT** Use algebra tiles to factor each trinomial. Multiply the factors to check your answer.

a. $x^2 + 5x + 6$ **b.** $x^2 + 7x + 6$

✓ QUESTION 26

...checks that you can factor a quadratic using algebra tiles.

27 **Try This as a Class** Look back at the quadratics you have factored so far. Suppose a quadratic is written in the form $x^2 + bx + c$ where b and c are positive.

a. Explain how you can use c to help find the factors of the quadratic.

b. Explain how the factors of c are related to b.

28 Factor $x^2 + 10x + 9$ into two binomials by using 9's factor pairs. Check your answer by multiplying the binomials or by using algebra tiles.

▶ **Algebra tiles can also be used to factor quadratics of the form $x^2 + bx + c$ when either b or c is negative.**

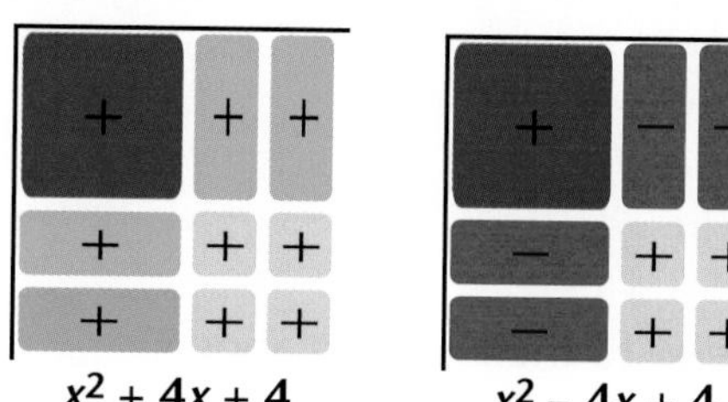

$x^2 + 4x + 4$ $x^2 - 4x + 4$

29 **a.** Use algebra tiles to represent $x^2 - 6x + 9$.

b. Arrange the tiles in a rectangle. What are the factors of $x^2 - 6x + 9$?

▶ **In some cases, tiles must be added to form a product rectangle for a quadratic.**

EXAMPLE

Use algebra tiles to factor $x^2 + x - 6$.

SAMPLE RESPONSE

First: Model the quadratic with algebra tiles.

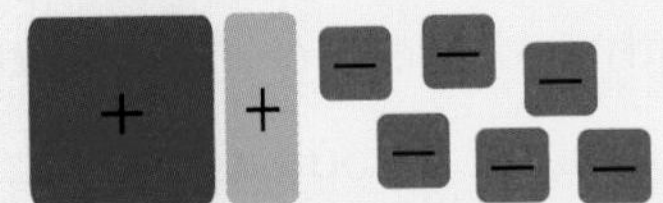

Next: Arrange the tiles to form a rectangle. It helps to start with the x^2-tile in the upper left corner and the 1-tiles in the lower right. Remember that the edges of tiles that are lined up together must have the same edge length.

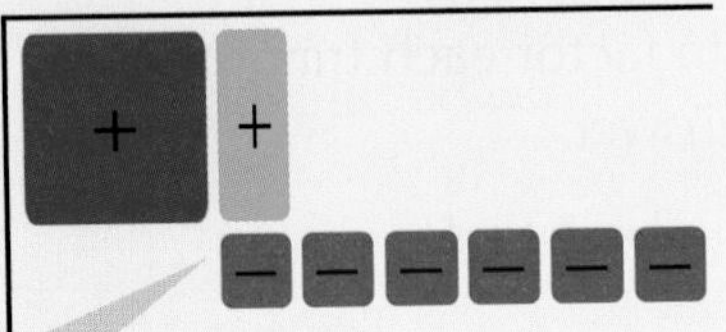

$1 \cdot 6 = 6$, so try arranging the six -1-tiles in a 1 by 6 rectangle.

2 and 3 are also factors of 6, so try arranging the six -1-tiles in a 2 by 3 rectangle.

Then: Add the same number of tiles to the height and width so they fill in the spaces and form a rectangle.

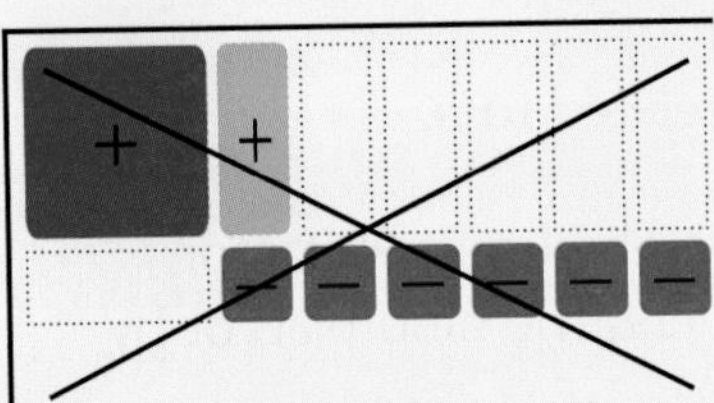

Not possible, because you cannot add the same number of x-tiles to the width as you do to the height when the 1-tiles are arranged in 1 row of 6.

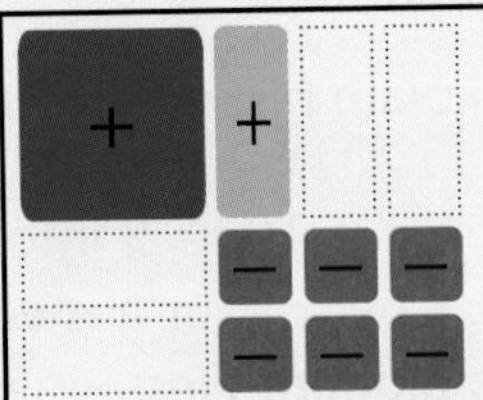

Two x-tiles and two $-x$-tiles can be added to form a rectangle, so factors of 2 and 3 will work.

30 **Discussion** Refer to the Example above.

a. Why do you have to add an equal number of x-tiles and $-x$-tiles? What would happen if you did not add an equal number of each?

b. Where would you place the two $-x$-tiles? Why?

c. How can you check that you have arranged the tiles correctly?

d. What are the factors of $x^2 + x - 6$?

31 Rafaela claims her model represents $x^2 + x - 6$. She has completed the rectangle by adding three x-tiles and three $-x$-tiles as shown below.

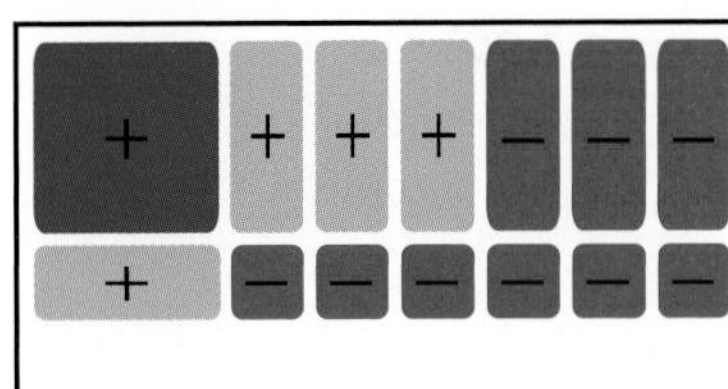

a. What two factors does her model represent?

b. Check Rafaela's solution by multiplying the two factors.

c. What would you tell Rafaela to help her correctly use algebra tiles to factor polynomials?

32 Refer to the Example on the preceding page.

a. Could you have factored $x^2 + x - 6$ by arranging the 1-tiles in 6 rows of 1? Why or why not?

b. Could you have factored $x^2 + x - 6$ by arranging the 1-tiles in 3 rows of 2? Why or why not?

33 **Try This as a Class** Use algebra tiles to factor $x^2 - 9x + 8$.

34 ✓ **CHECKPOINT** Use algebra tiles to factor each quadratic. Multiply the factors to check your answer.

a. $x^2 + 5x + 6$ **b.** $x^2 + 4x - 5$ **c.** $x^2 - 2x - 3$

✓ **QUESTION 34**

...checks that you can factor quadratics using algebra tiles.

35 Tyrell says that $x^2 - 4x + 5$ cannot be factored. Use what you have learned along with algebra tiles to prove whether or not he is right.

36 From your work with algebra tiles, you have seen that when the quadratic $x^2 + bx + c$ is factored into the product of two binomials $x + m$ and $x + n$, m and n are factors of c and $m + n = b$. What can you say about the signs of m and n in each of the following cases? Give examples to support your answers.

a. $b > 0$ and $c > 0$

b. $b < 0$ and $c > 0$

c. $c < 0$ ($b > 0$ *or* $b < 0$)

HOMEWORK EXERCISES See Exs. 26–47 on pp. 509–510.

Section 4 Key Concepts

Key Terms

monomial
term

polynomial
binomial
trinomial

Multiplying Binomials (pp. 496–500)

A monomial is a number or a variable or a product of a number and one or more variables. Each monomial is called a term.

A polynomial is a monomial or a sum of monomials. A binomial is a polynomial with exactly two terms. A trinomial is a polynomial with exactly three terms.

The product of two binomials can be found by using algebra tiles, a table, or the distributive property.

Example Multiply $(x + 2)(x - 3)$.

Represent each binomial with tiles, one as the height and one as the width. Then complete the product rectangle.

Using Algebra Tiles

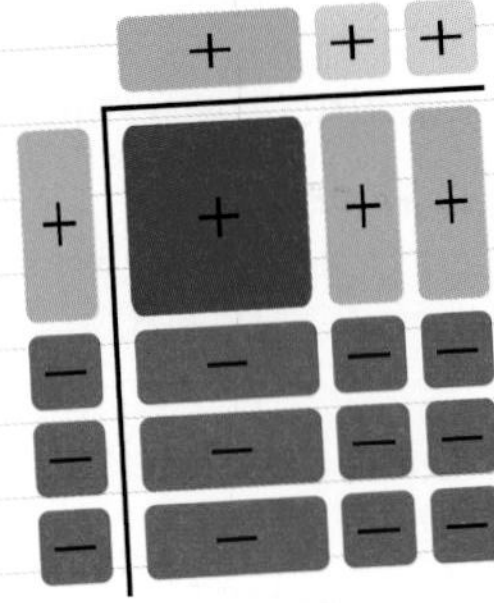

Write one of the binomials on the left side of the table.

Using a Table

Write the other binomial above the table.

	x +	2
x	x^2	$2x$
+ −3	$-3x$	-6

$x^2 + (-3x) + 2x - 6 = x^2 - x - 6$

Using the Distributive Property

$$\begin{aligned}(x + 2)(x - 3) &= (x + 2)(x + (-3)) \\ &= (x + 2)x + (x + 2)(-3) \\ &= x^2 + 2x + (-3x) + (-6) \\ &= x^2 + (-x) + (-6) \\ &= x^2 - x - 6\end{aligned}$$

The product $(x + 2)(x - 3)$ is equal to $x^2 - x - 6$.

x^2, $-x$, and -6 are each monomials, and $x^2 - x - 6$ is a trinomial.

37 Key Concepts Question

a. Multiply $(x - 5)(x - 4)$.

b. Is the product in part (a) a monomial, binomial, or trinomial?

Section 4

Key Concepts

Key Term

factor

Factoring Quadratics (pp. 501–505)

To factor a quadratic, you need to find the factors whose product is the quadratic. In the example on page 506, $x - 3$ and $x + 2$ are the factors of the quadratic $x^2 - x - 6$. The factors of a quadratic can be found by using algebra tiles.

Example Factor $x^2 - 9$.

Model $x^2 - 9$ with tiles. Arrange the x^2-tiles and the 1-tiles in opposite corners of the rectangle, so that you will be able to make a product rectangle.

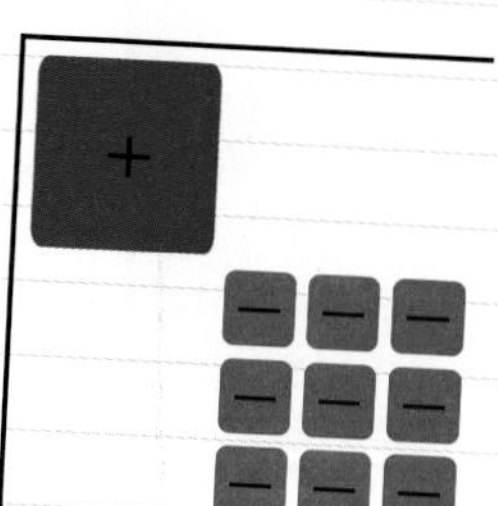

Add three x-tiles and three –x-tiles to complete the product rectangle.

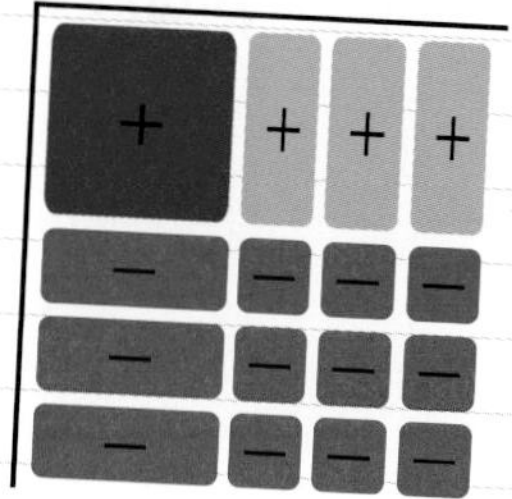

Adding an equal number of x-tiles and –x-tiles does not affect the product.

Then read the height and width of the product rectangle. So, $x^2 - 9 = (x - 3)(x + 3)$.

38 Key Concepts Question

a. In the Example above the nine 1-tiles were arranged in 3 rows of 3. What other possible arrangement might have been tried if this arrangement had not worked?

b. Use the distributive property to show that the product $(x - 3)(x + 3)$ is equal to $x^2 - 9$.

c. Factor $x^2 - 16$.

Section 4

Practice & Application Exercises

YOU WILL NEED

- algebra tiles

Use algebra tiles to find the product of the binomials.

1. $(x + 1)(x + 2)$
2. $(x + 4)(x + 4)$
3. $(x + 2)(2x + 1)$

Name the polynomial represented by each group of tiles and tell whether it is a monomial, binomial, or trinomial.

4. 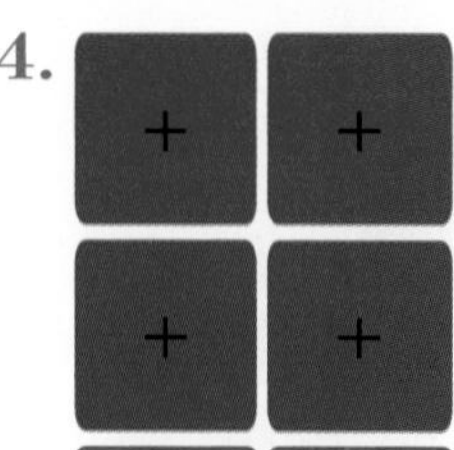

5.

6. 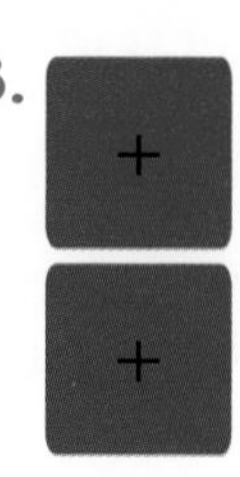

Use algebra tiles to find the product of the binomials. Combine like terms.

7. $(x - 2)(x + 3)$
8. $(x + 2)(x - 1)$
9. $(x - 2)(x + 1)$
10. $(x + 4)(x - 4)$
11. $(x - 1)(x + 1)$
12. $(x + 3)(x - 4)$

Use a table to find the product of the binomials. Show your work.

13. $(x + 3)(x + 2)$
14. $(2x - 3)(x - 3)$
15. $(-x - 3)(x + 3)$
16. $(5x - 4)(-x + 6)$
17. $(2 - x)(4 - 2x)$
18. $(-x - 5)(-x - 12)$

Use the distributive property to find the product of the binomials.

19. $(x + 5)(x + 8)$
20. $(x + 9)(x + 9)$
21. $(x + 12)(2x + 3)$
22. $(9 + 5x)(4 - x)$
23. $(3 - 7x)(4 - 3x)$
24. $(-x + 1)(6x - 23)$

25. A poster of Leonardo da Vinci's sketch of a woman is about one and a half times as high as it is wide. The sketch is to be placed in a 4 in. wide frame.

a. How many inches will the frame add to the poster's height? to its width?

b. Write the binomial that represents the height of the poster with the frame.

c. Write the binomial that represents the width of the poster with the frame.

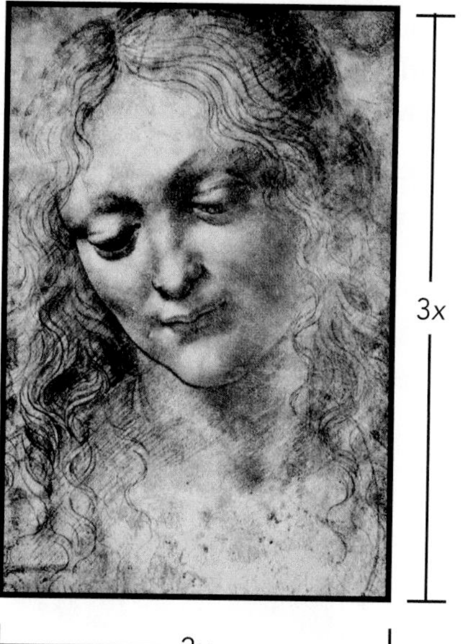

Not actual size

d. What polynomial expression represents the total area of the poster and the frame?

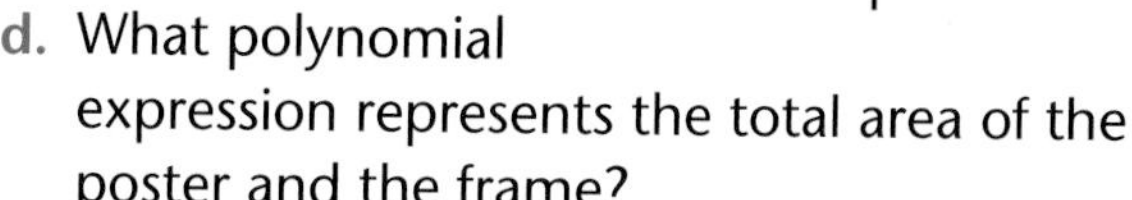

Find the binomials whose product is represented by each product rectangle. Multiply the two binomials to check your answer.

26.

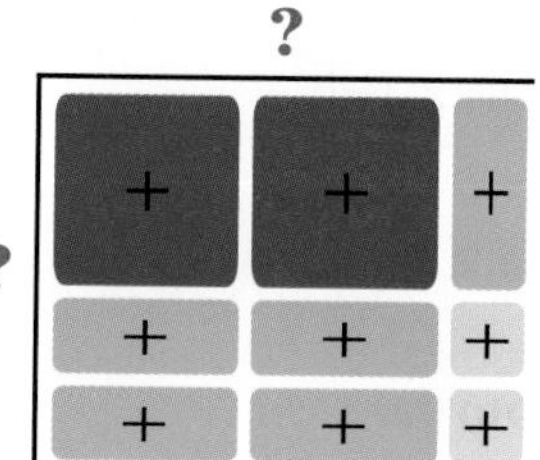

27.

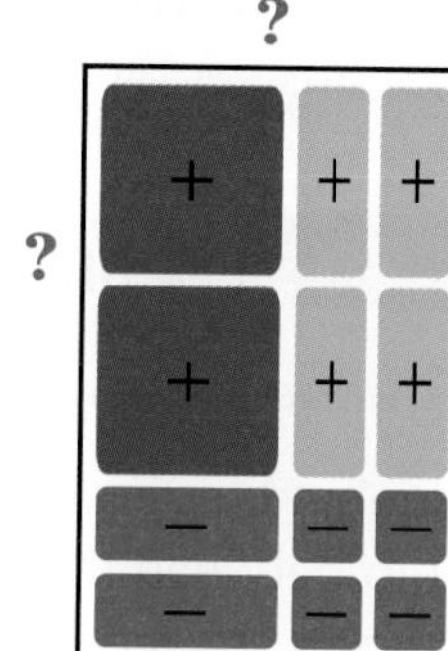

28.

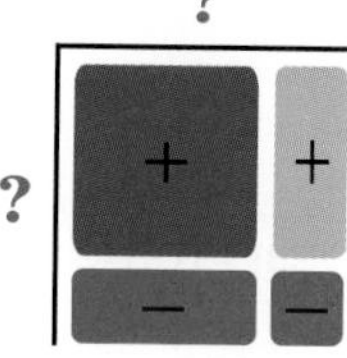

29.

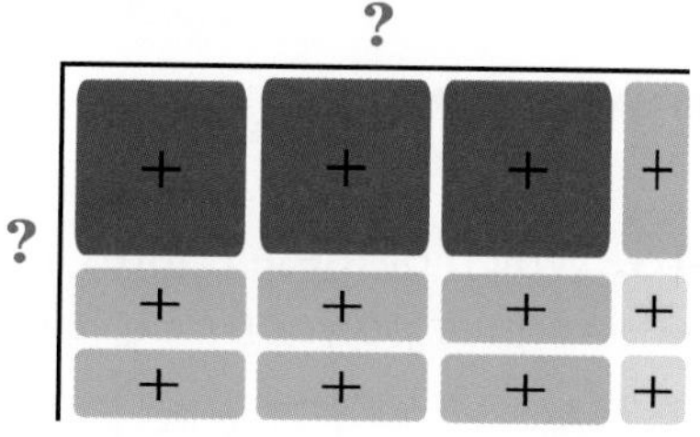

Use algebra tiles to factor each quadratic. Multiply the factors to check your answer.

30. $x^2 + 2x + 1$

31. $x^2 + 5x + 6$

32. $x^2 + 6x + 5$

33. $x^2 + 4x + 3$

34. $x^2 + 3x + 2$

35. $x^2 + 8x + 7$

If possible, use algebra tiles to complete the product rectangle, and find the factors of the quadratic. Multiply the factors to check your answer. If the trinomial cannot be factored explain why.

36. $2x^2 - x - 3$

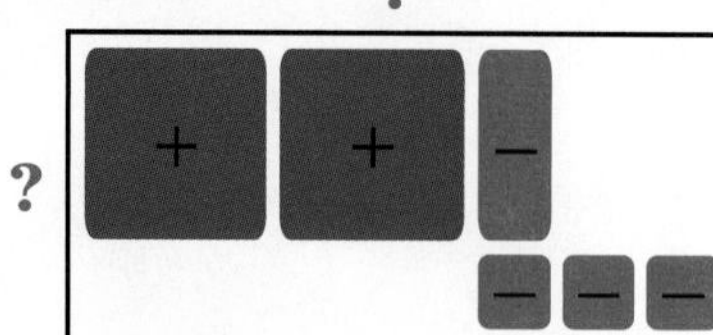

37. $x^2 + x - 5$

38. $x^2 - 4x - 5$

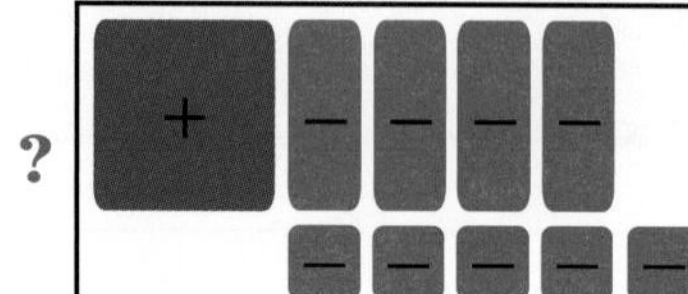

39. $x^2 - 5x - 6$

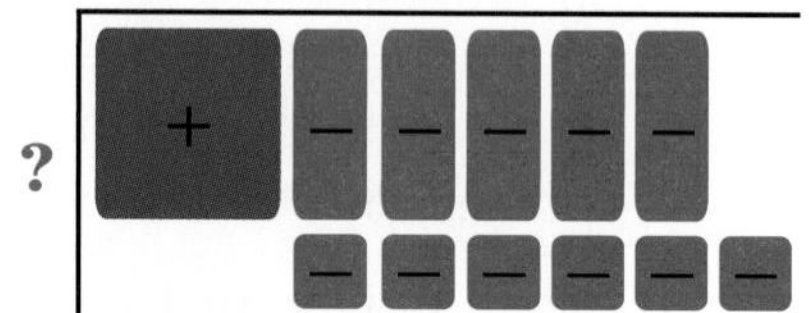

Use algebra tiles to factor each quadratic. Multiply the factors to check your answers.

40. $x^2 + 3x - 4$

41. $x^2 - 2x + 1$

42. $x^2 - x - 6$

43. $x^2 - 8x + 7$

44. $x^2 - 5x + 4$

45. $x^2 - 4$

46. Use factor pairs of 10 to factor $x^2 + 7x + 10$ into two binomials. Check your answer by multiplying the binomials.

Journal

Exercise 47 checks that you understand how to use algebra tiles to represent a polynomial and its factors.

Reflecting on the Section

Write your response to Exercise 47 in your journal.

47. Sketch algebra tiles arranged in a product rectangle. Explain the relationship between the polynomial that the product rectangle represents and the length and width of the product rectangle.

Spiral Review

48. Which of these figures are polygons? Which appears to be a regular polygon? Explain your thinking. **(Toolbox, p. 594)**

A. B. C. D.

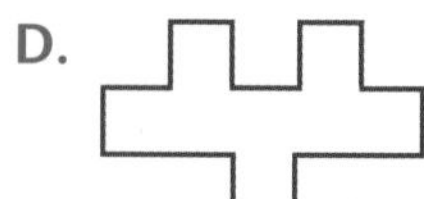

Solve each inequality. Check and graph each solution. **(Module 7, p. 489)**

49. $n - 3 \geq 5$

50. $55 > -11y$

51. $\frac{x}{2} - 6 \leq -7$

Section 4 Extra Skill Practice

You will need: • algebra tiles (Exs. 2–4 and 11–16)

1. Write the polynomial represented by the group of algebra tiles. Tell whether each polynomial is a monomial, binomial, or trinomial.

a. 

b.

c. 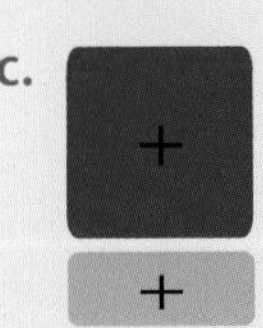

d. 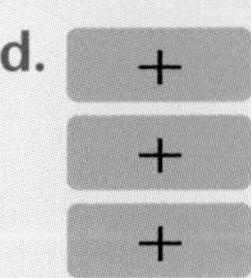

Use algebra tiles to find the product of the binomials.

2. $(x + 3)(x + 1)$
3. $(2x - 3)(x + 1)$
4. $(x - 3)(x - 2)$

Use a table to find the product of the binomials. Show your work.

5. $(-2x + 5)(x - 7)$
6. $(x + 7)(x - 7)$
7. $(3x + 5)(2x + 5)$

Use the distributive property to find the product of the binomials.

8. $(4x - 1)(3x + 2)$
9. $(1 - 6x)(3 + 9x)$
10. $(3x + 2)(5x - 2)$

Use algebra tiles to factor the quadratic. Multiply the factors to check your answer.

11. $x^2 + 4x + 3$
12. $x^2 - x - 6$
13. $x^2 - 4$
14. $x^2 + 6x + 5$
15. $x^2 - 3x + 2$
16. $x^2 - 2x - 3$

Standardized Testing ▶ Open-ended

1. Find two trinomials that have $x + 3$ as a factor.
2. Give a binomial that can be factored into two binomials.

Math and Careers

People who use mathematics in their occupations may be found in the most unusual places. Did you know that, to ensure load safety, elevator operators at the Empire State Building in New York City estimate the weight of visitors and their equipment as they enter the elevator?

In this project you will interview an individual who uses mathematics in his or her occupation and then present your findings to the class.

Getting Started

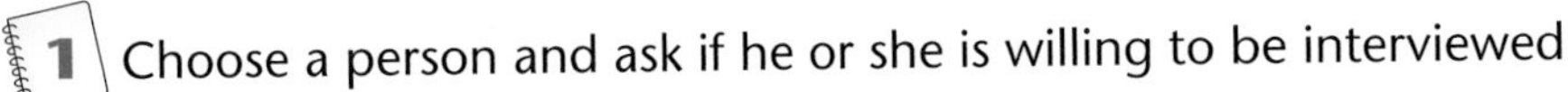

1 Choose a person and ask if he or she is willing to be interviewed.

2 Write 5 to 10 questions you would like answered.

- Questions should ask for specific information.
- Ask questions that will give background information such as the training and education required to perform the job.
- Ask questions about exactly how the person uses math in this occupation. In particular, ask whether he or she uses algebra.

3 Set up an appointment to visit with the individual, or conduct an email or phone interview.

Conducting the Interview

4 During the interview take careful notes. Be sure to record specific mathematics applications used by the individual.

5 If possible, obtain pictures of the individual performing his or her job.

Organizing Your Presentation

6 Look at the information you gathered. Which pieces of information are relevant to the presentation? Which pieces best show how mathematics is used in this occupation?

7 Choose one or more visual aids that will create a clear portrait of the work life of your interview subject. You may choose to create a poster, a bulletin board, or a computer slide show presentation, or use any other means to present your information to the class.

8 Think about how you will present your information. Discuss your ideas with a classmate. Based on the feedback from your classmate, make necessary changes to your presentation.

9 Prepare the final draft of your presentation.

Making Your Presentation

10 Share with the class what you learned about the individual you interviewed.

- Speak clearly and loudly enough for everyone to hear you.
- Use voice inflection to make your presentation interesting.
- Show pictures, charts, or other visual aids to draw attention to specific points you want to make.
- Be prepared to answer questions about the person you interviewed and his or her occupation.

MODULE 7 Review and Assessment

You will need: • *algebra tiles* (Exs. 37–41)

Write each product or quotient as a single power. (Sec. 1, Explor. 1)

1. $10^8 \cdot 10^3$
2. $a^4 \cdot a^5$
3. $\frac{2^{10}}{2^3}$
4. $\frac{b^{23}}{b^{19}}$

Write each power as a whole number or fraction without exponents. (Sec. 1, Explor. 2)

5. 4^0
6. 11^{-2}
7. 3^{-3}
8. 2^{-6}

Write each number in decimal notation. (Sec. 1, Explor. 2)

9. $5 \cdot 10^{-2}$
10. $8.03 \cdot 10^{-4}$
11. $1.266 \cdot 10^{-7}$

12. Rock fragments ejected through the air or water from a volcano are called *tephra*. Geologists classify tephra by size according to a measurement called the *intermediate axis*. The classes of tephra according to the intermediate axis a are given in the table. Rewrite each inequality in the table so that the numbers in the inequality are expressed in scientific notation. (Sec. 1, Explor. 2)

Types of Tephra

Name	intermediate axis a (meters)
ash	$a < 0.002$
lapilli	$0.002 \le a \le 0.064$
bombs	$a \ge 0.064$

Tell whether each number is *rational* or *irrational*. (Sec. 2, Explor. 1)

13. $\sqrt{75}$
14. $\sqrt{36}$
15. $\sqrt{\frac{25}{9}}$
16. $-0.\overline{12}$

17. Show how to use the product property of square roots to simplify $\sqrt{108}$. (Sec. 2, Explor. 1)

Simplify each expression. Assume all variables represent positive numbers. (Sec. 2, Explor. 2)

18. $\sqrt{96}$
19. $\sqrt{\frac{13}{64}}$
20. $\sqrt{500}$
21. $\sqrt{\frac{17}{100}}$
22. $\sqrt{\frac{8}{49}}$
23. $\frac{5}{\sqrt{6}}$
24. $\sqrt[3]{64}$
25. $\sqrt{x^4y^5}$

Graph each inequality on a number line. (Sec. 3, Explor. 1)

26. $w > -10$ 27. $1 < z \le 4$ 28. $-2 < y \le 0$ 29. $-3 \le v$

Solve each inequality. Check and graph each solution. (Sec. 3, Explors. 2 and 3)

30. $2a \le 10$ 31. $-0.4n + 0.2 \le 1.6$ 32. $\frac{n}{3} < -3$

33. A rectangular community garden is 100 m long by 70 m wide. The community will set aside 50 m^2 of the garden to plant trees. The rest of the garden space will be split into sections. The area of each section will be at least 20 m^2. Write and solve an inequality to find the number of sections the garden will contain. (Sec. 3, Explor. 3)

Use the distributive property to find the product of the binomials. (Sec. 4, Explor. 1)

34. $(x + 4)(2x + 3)$ 35. $(5 - x)(3 - 6x)$ 36. $(10x - 2)(10x + 2)$

Find the binomials whose product is represented by each product rectangle. Multiply the two binomials to check your answer. (Sec. 4, Explor. 2)

37.

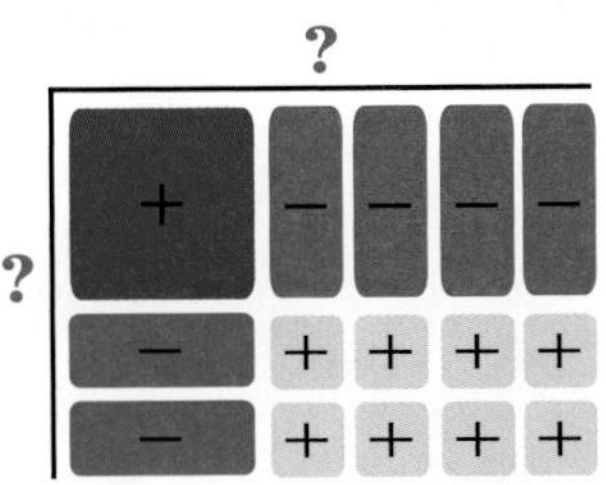

38.

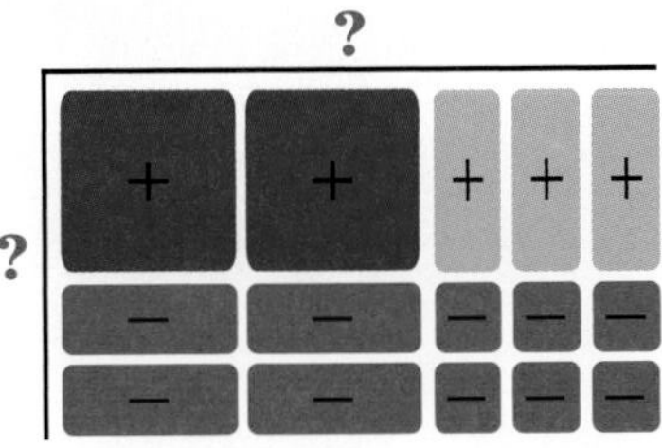

Use algebra tiles to factor each quadratic. Multiply the factors to check your answer. (Sec. 4, Explor. 2)

39. $x^2 + 5x + 4$ 40. $x^2 - 5x + 4$ 41. $x^2 - 3x - 4$

Reflecting on the Module

42. According to the U.S. Department of Labor, math skills are one of the top ten skills employers would like their employees to have. Explain how some of the algebra skills learned in this module might be used at work. Describe a specific situation and give an example.

MODULE 8

MATH-Thematical MIX

CONNECTING

MATHEMATICS

The & Theme

SECTION OVERVIEW

1 Patterns and Sequences

As you revisit Amazing Feats and Facts:

- Identify and analyze arithmetic and geometric sequences
- Write an equation for a sequence

2 Polygons and Rotational Symmetry

As you revisit Architects and Engineers:

- Find the sum of the measures of interior angles of a polygon
- Describe rotational symmetry

3 Properties of Quadrilaterals

As you revisit The Mystery of Blacktail Canyon:

- Classify quadrilaterals

4 Geometry and Probability

As you revisit At the Mall:

- Find probabilities using areas

5 Tangent, Sine, and Cosine

As you revisit Inventions:

- Use the tangent, sine, and cosine ratios to find unknown side lengths in right triangles

The Module Project

Looking for Patterns

Mathematics is filled with patterns and sequences. In this project you will use a visual pattern made up of borders on a grid to explore sequences and geometric probability. You will then create your own design that can be used to model a sequence.

More on the Module Project
See pp. 574–575.

INTERNET
Resources and practice at
classzone.com

Patterns and Sequences

IN THIS SECTION

EXPLORATION 1
- Arithmetic and Geometric Sequences

EXPLORATION 2
- Exploring Sequences

Amazing Feats and Facts

Setting the Stage

In the story *Two of Everything* by Lily Toy Hong, Mr. Haktak, while out digging in his garden one spring day, finds a large pot buried there. As he carries the heavy pot home, his purse containing his last 5 gold coins falls to the ground. He picks up the purse, tosses it into the pot and takes the pot home to Mrs. Haktak.

As Mrs. Haktak leaned over to peer into the pot, her hairpin—the only one she owned—fell in. She felt around in the pot, and suddenly her eyes grew round with surprise. "Look!" she shouted. "I've pulled out TWO hairpins, exactly alike, and TWO purses, too!" Sure enough, the purses were identical, and so were the hairpins. Inside each purse were five gold coins!

Think About It

1 How many coins will Mrs. Haktak pull out of the pot if she puts in a purse containing 20 coins? 80 coins?

2 Considering the way the pot works, is it possible for Mrs. Haktak to pull 51 coins from the pot? Explain.

Exploration 1

+ Arithmetic + and × Geometric × Sequences

GOAL

LEARN HOW TO...
- identify arithmetic and geometric sequences
- write an equation for any term in a sequence

AS YOU...
- explore the patterns in *Two of Everything*

KEY TERMS
- sequence
- term
- arithmetic sequence
- geometric sequence

3 Suppose Mr. Haktak puts 1 purse containing 5 coins into the pot. When he reaches in, he pulls out 2 identical purses. The next time he puts in 2 identical purses and pulls out 4. But then he begins to fear that he will lose all of his money. So, the third time he puts only 3 purses into the pot. The fourth time he puts in 4 purses and so on.

a. How many purses will he take out of the pot after putting them into the pot the third time?

b. How many purses will he take out after the sixth time he puts purses into the pot? How do you know?

▶ **Describing Sequences The number of purses pulled out of the pot each time is a *sequence*. A sequence is an ordered list of numbers or objects called terms.**

You can use a table to organize the terms of a sequence.

EXAMPLE

To find each term after the first term of the sequence below, add 4 to the previous term.

Term number	1	2	3	4	5	6
Term	3	7	11	15	19	23

+4 +4 +4 +4 +4

$$7 + 4 = 11$$

4 Make a table for the sequence you found in Question 3. The term numbers are the numbers of purses put in the pot, and the terms are the numbers of purses pulled out after each time purses are put in.

a. How is each term in your sequence related to the previous one?

b. Use the pattern in part (a) to predict how many purses Mr. Haktak will pull out of the pot after putting 10 purses in.

FOR HELP with *constants and variables*, see **MODULE 1, p. 42**

▶ **The sequences in the Example on page 519 and in Question 4 are *arithmetic sequences*. An arithmetic sequence is one in which each term after the first is found by adding a constant to the previous term. The constant may be positive or negative.**

You can write an equation that uses the term number to find a term in an arithmetic sequence.

5 Look at the arithmetic sequence below.

Term number	1	2	3	4	5	6
Term	2	7	12	17	22	27

a. What constant do you add to each term to obtain the next term?

b. How many times did you add the constant from part (a) to the first term to get the second term? the third term? the fourth?

c. What is the relationship between the number of times the constant was added and the *term number* for each term?

d. Write an equation that uses the term number n to find the nth term t of the sequence.

6 **a.** Use the equation you wrote in Question 5(d) to find the 12th term in the sequence.

b. Check your answer from part (a) by extending the sequence. If your answer from part (a) is not correct, write an equation that will give you the correct result.

c. **Try This as a Class** The equation you wrote is specific to this arithmetic sequence. How could you write it so it would apply to *any* arithmetic sequence?

✓ QUESTION 7

... checks that you can write and use an equation for an arithmetic sequence.

7 **✓ CHECKPOINT** Write an equation that uses the term number n to find the nth term t of each arithmetic sequence. Then find the 13th term.

a. 5, 12, 19, 26, ...

b. 300, 289, 278, 267, ...

▶ **In the story, Mrs. Haktak wanted her fortune to grow more quickly. Every time she took purses out of the pot she put all the coins into one purse and put it back into the pot.**

8 **a.** There were 5 coins in the first purse Mrs. Haktak put in the pot. How many coins did she have when she pulled purses out the first time? the second time?

b. The process describes a sequence. The term numbers are the numbers of times she puts a single purse into the pot. The terms are the numbers of coins she has after pulling purses out each time. Make a table to show the first 6 terms in the sequence.

c. How is each term related to the preceding term?

▶ **The sequence in Question 8 is a *geometric sequence.* A geometric sequence is one in which each term after the first is found by multiplying the previous term by a non-zero constant.**

You can write an equation that uses the term number to find a term in a geometric sequence.

9 Look at the geometric sequence in the table at the right.

Term Number	Term
1	2
2	4
3	8
4	16
5	32
6	64

a. What constant do you multiply each term by to obtain the next term?

b. By what power of the constant in part (a) can you multiply the first term to get the second term? the third? the fourth?

c. What is the relationship between the power of the constant and the term number?

d. Write an equation that uses the term number n to find the nth term t of the geometric sequence.

10 **Try This as a Class** Suppose the first term in a sequence is 2 and each successive term is found by multiplying the previous term by 3. Write an equation that can be used to find any term in the sequence.

11 Rewrite your equation from Question 10 so that it could be used to find any term in *any* geometric sequence.

12 ✓ **CHECKPOINT** Identify each sequence as *arithmetic* or *geometric*. Then write an equation for the sequence.

a. 2, 9, 16, 23, ... **b.** $3x, 3x^2, 3x^3, 3x^4, \ldots$

... checks that you can identify and write equations for arithmetic and geometric sequences.

HOMEWORK EXERCISES ▶ See Exs. 1–12 on p. 526.

GOAL

LEARN HOW TO...
- analyze sequences

AS YOU...
- explore the Fibonacci sequence

KEY TERM
- Fibonacci sequence

Exploration 2

Exploring Sequences

▶ **In Exploration 1 you explored arithmetic and geometric sequences. Some sequences are neither arithmetic nor geometric yet follow a definite pattern.**

His neighbors called him *Bigollone,* which means "the blockhead." His real name was Leonardo Fibonacci, and he was not a blockhead at all. He was a mathematician who loved to "play around" with numbers. In 1202 he published a book in which he introduced a fascinating mathematical problem.

Suppose two newborn rabbits, male and female, are put into a cage. How many rabbits will there be at the end of one year if this pair of rabbits produces another pair every month, and every new pair of rabbits produces another new pair every month? All rabbits must be two months old before they can produce more rabbits.

Here is what happens in the first three months after the first pair of newborn rabbits are put in the cage:

Start Start with **1st pair** of newborn rabbits.

Month 1 **1st pair** are growing.

Month 2 **1st pair** are adults. They produce **2nd pair** of rabbits.

Month 3 **1st pair** produce **3rd pair** of rabbits.
2nd pair are growing.

13 Solve Fibonacci's rabbit problem. Start by creating a model or diagram that shows the total number of rabbit pairs over the first six months of the year. Find a way to show newborn, growing, and adult rabbits.

14 Use your model in Question 13 to help complete a table like the one shown.

Month	Number of rabbit pairs			Total number of rabbit pairs
	Newborn	Growing	Adult	
Start	1	0	0	1
1	0	1	?	?
2	?	?	?	?

15 The number pattern in the last column of the table you made in Question 14 is known as the **Fibonacci sequence**. The numbers in the sequence are sometimes called *Fibonacci numbers*.

Fibonacci sequence						
1	1	2	3	5	?	?
↓ 1st term	↓ 2nd term	↓ 3rd term				

a. How are any two consecutive terms in the Fibonacci sequence used to find the next term in the sequence?

b. Use the pattern you found in part (a) to complete the table above.

c. What is the answer to the rabbit problem? Explain how you got your answer.

16 **Discussion** The sum of the first, second, and third terms in the Fibonacci sequence is one less than the fifth term of the sequence. The sum of the second, third, and fourth terms is 2 less than the sixth term. Find a similar relationship for sums of other terms in the sequence.

▶ **The Fibonacci sequence follows a pattern without using a constant as in arithmetic and geometric sequences. Other sequences may also follow patterns that do not use constants.**

17 Triangles are constructed as shown below. To create each successive triangle in the sequence, small congruent triangles are added to the previous triangle as shown.

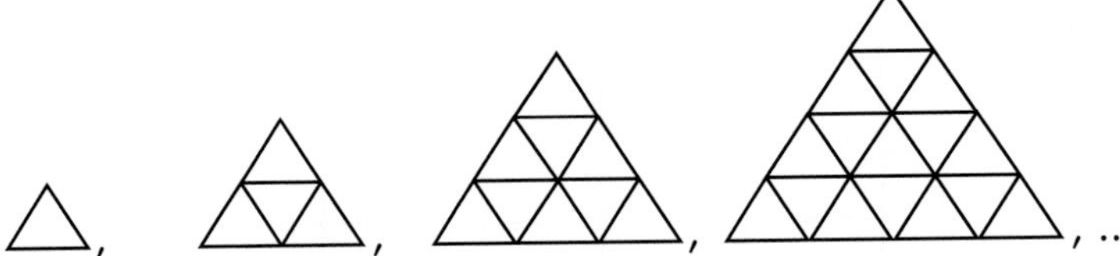

a. Write a rule to show how the number of small triangles in each term relates to the term number of this sequence.

b. What do you call the numbers in this sequence?

18 **Try This as a Class** The arrays below represents the first four terms in the sequence of *triangular numbers*.

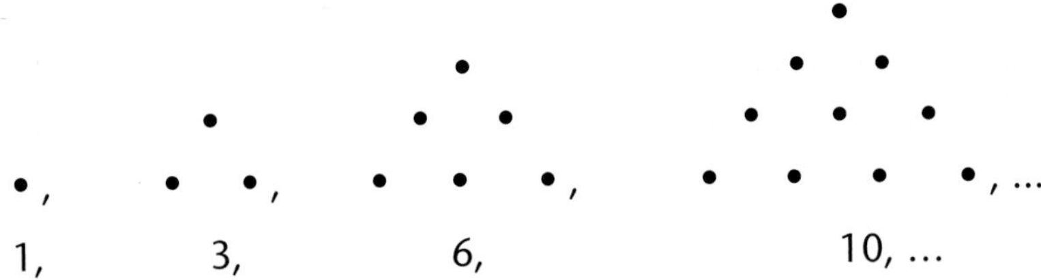

a. Describe any patterns you notice in how the terms of the sequence are related to each other or in how the number of dots in each term is related to the term number.

b. Use the pattern you noticed in part (a) to find the next three terms in the sequence.

✓ QUESTION 19

...checks that you can find patterns in sequences.

19 **✓ CHECKPOINT** Look for a pattern in each sequence. Then find the next three terms.

a. 2, 6, 12, 20, 30, ...

b. 400, 396, 388, 372, 340, ...

c. 4, 7, 13, 25, 49, ...

d. –3, 6, –12, 24, –48, ...

20 In Exploration 1 you saw how Mr. Haktak tried to conserve some of his money by setting some of the bags of money aside rather than putting them all into the pot.

a. How many total bags did he have set aside before using the pot the second time? the third time? the fourth time? the fifth time? the sixth time?

b. How is the sequence created by the terms you recorded in part (a) related to the other sequences in this section?

HOMEWORK EXERCISES ▶ **See Exs. 13–20 on pp. 527–528.**

Section 1 Key Concepts

Arithmetic Sequences (pp. 519–520)

A sequence is an ordered list of numbers or objects called terms. An arithmetic sequence is one in which each term after the first is found by adding a constant to the previous term.

Example The sequence 1, 3, 5, 7, ... describes the number of triangles in each figure.

1, 3, 5, 7, ...

Geometric Sequences (p. 520)

In a geometric sequence, each term after the first is found by multiplying the previous term by a nonzero constant.

Example The sequence 1, 5, 25, 125, ... describes the number of shaded squares in each figure.

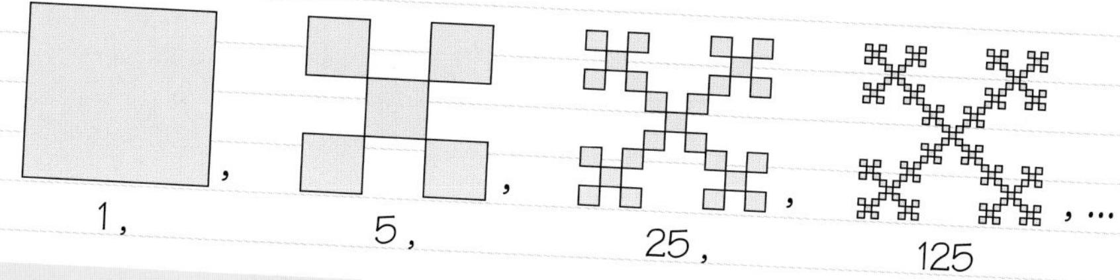

1, 5, 25, 125, ...

Other Sequences (pp. 522–524)

In the Fibonacci sequence each term after the second is the sum of the two previous terms.

1, 1, 2, 3, 5, 8, 13, ...

In the following sequence, the differences of pairs of consecutive terms increase by 1.

1, 3, 6, 10, 15, 21, ...

Key Terms

sequence

term

arithmetic sequence

geometric sequence

Fibonacci sequence

Key Concepts Questions

21 Is the sequence 3, 8, 13, 18, 23, ... *arithmetic* or *geometric*? Explain.

22 Write an equation that uses the term number n to find the nth term t of the sequence 1, 5, 25, 125....

Section 1 Practice & Application Exercises

YOU WILL NEED

For Exs. 21–22:
- grid paper
- ruler

For Exs. 23–24:
- protractor

For Ex. 27
- Labsheet 1A

Identify each sequence as *arithmetic*, *geometric*, or *neither*.

1. $\frac{1}{2}, \frac{1}{4}, \frac{1}{8}, \frac{1}{16}, \ldots$

2. 4, 6, 9, 13, ...

3. 94, 47, 23.5, 11.75, ...

4. –24, –13, –2, 9, ...

5. 0.7, 1.1, 1.5, 1.9, ...

6. 4, 9, 16, 25, ...

Find the next three terms in each sequence.

7. 5, 6, 8, 11, ...

8. 128, 32, 8, 2, ...

9. $10x, 20x^2, 40x^3, 80x^4, \ldots$

10. $\frac{1}{3}, \frac{3}{3}, \frac{5}{3}, \frac{7}{3}, \ldots$

11. Write an equation that uses the term number n to find the nth term t of each sequence.

Sequence I

Term number	1	2	3	4	5	...	n
Term	3	5	7	9	11	...	t

Sequence II

Term number	1	2	3	4	5	...	n
Term	2	6	18	54	162	...	t

12. **Challenge** At age 10, Carl Gauss, a future mathematician, was given a challenging problem by his teacher. The teacher expected the students in his class to struggle with the problem, but Carl solved the problem in a matter of seconds by finding a pattern.

The Problem: *Add the first one hundred positive integers.*

a. Make a table showing a sequence whose nth term t is the sum of the first n positive whole numbers.

b. Look for a pattern that relates a term to the product of its term number and the next term number.

c. Use the pattern in part (b) to write an equation for the sequence.

d. Solve Gauss's problem.

13. **Music** Use the piano keyboard shown.

a. How many *whole* black keys are there in an octave?

b. How many white keys are there in an octave?

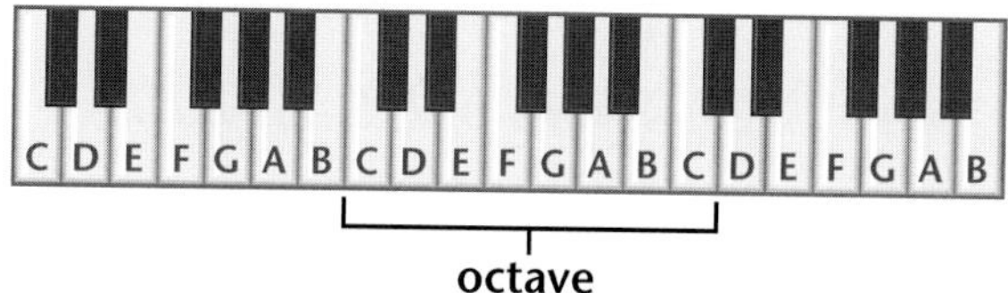

c. What is the total number of keys in an octave?

d. How are your answers to parts (a)–(c) related to the Fibonacci sequence?

14. **Biology** A male bee is called a *drone* and has only a mother because it develops from an unfertilized egg. A female bee has a mother and a father because it develops from a fertilized egg.

a. The figure below shows the "family tree" of a drone. You read the tree from the bottom up. Copy the family tree and extend it to six generations back.

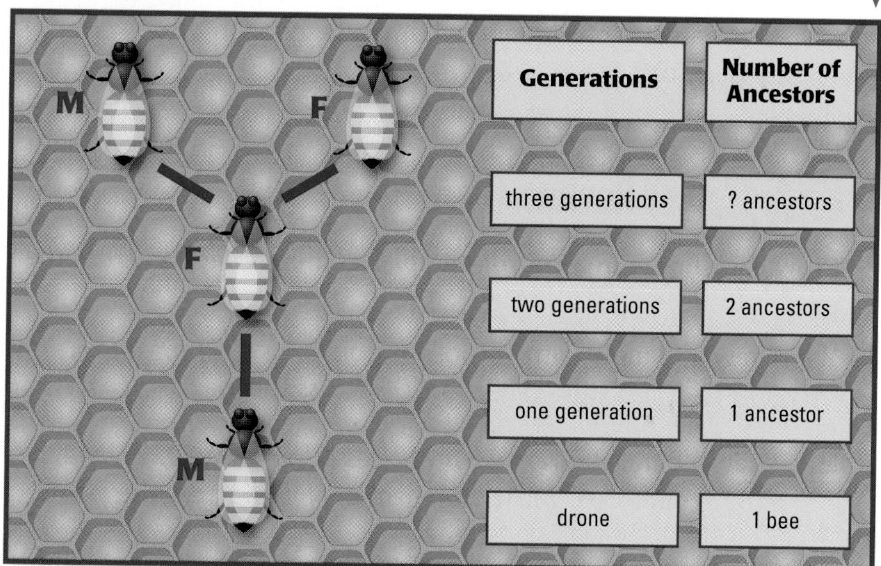

b. Use your family tree to find the total number of bees in each generation. What pattern do you see?

c. Without extending the diagram, find the total number of ancestors the drone would have eight generations back. Explain how you got your answer.

15. **Writing** Kanesha wrote a sequence using the rule *multiply the previous term by 2 and subtract 3.*

a. What is the fifth term of the sequence if the first term is 6?

b. Will each new term always be an odd number? Explain your thinking.

Describe the pattern in each sequence. Then use the pattern to write the next three terms of the sequence.

16. 4, 4.5, 5.5, 7, 9, ...

17. 1, 4, 13, 40, 121, ...

18. 8, 7, 5, 2, −2, ...

19. 1, 3, 9, 27, 81, ...

Reflecting on the Section

Visual THINKING

Exercise 20 checks that you understand sequences.

20. In the figure at the right, the tiling begins with a blue tile. The yellow tiles show the next set of tiles in the sequence. The red tiles are the third set of tiles in the sequence.

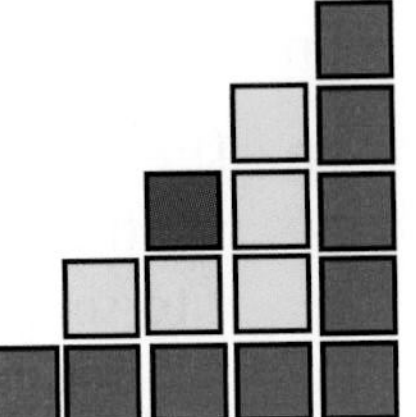

a. If this pattern continues, how many tiles will be needed for the tenth set of added tiles in the sequence?

b. Describe the pattern you found in words and with an equation.

c. What kind of sequence did you describe in part (b)?

Spiral Review

Draw each figure in a coordinate plane, then reflect it across the given axis. (Module 6, p. 436)

21. Draw a triangle with vertices at points $C(-4, 2)$, $D(-4, 5)$, and $E(-2, 2)$. Then reflect $\triangle CDE$ across the x-axis.

22. Draw a parallelogram with vertices at points $M(2, 2)$, $N(4, 5)$, $P(8, 5)$, and $Q(6, 2)$. Then reflect $\square MNPQ$ across the y-axis.

Use a protractor to measure each angle in the figure. Then answer Exercises 23–26. (Module 5, p. 369)

23. What is the measure of an angle that is a complement of $\angle CAD$?

24. What is the measure of an angle that is a supplement of $\angle CEB$?

25. Name an angle that is a complement of $\angle AEB$.

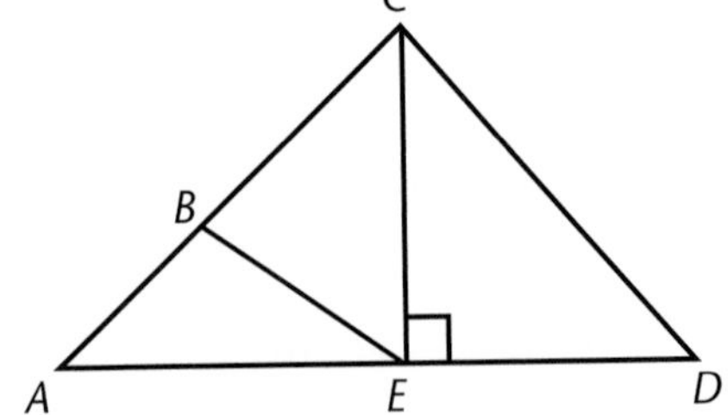

26. Name an angle that is a supplement of $\angle CBE$.

Extension

The Koch Snowflake

Many objects in nature such as trees and snowflakes can be modeled by geometric shapes called *fractals*. The Koch snowflake is a fractal.

Use Labsheet 1A for Exercise 27.

27. a. Complete the third and fourth rows of the table.

    b. Describe the patterns in the sequences formed by the entries in the second and third columns. Then describe how each entry in the third column relates to entries in the other columns.

    c. Complete the last row in the table by writing an expression for the *n*th term of each sequence.

Career Connection

Digital Artist: Junpei Sekino

When Junpei Sekino was 10 years old he won first prize for the junior division in a national printmaking contest in Japan. He now combines art and mathematics to create fractal art.

Junpei Sekino uses fractals to show the beautiful patterns in mathematics, as in his digital art, *Fractal Sphere,* below.

28. Computers are often used to generate fractals and other patterns. Follow the steps below to get an idea of how computers are used to create patterns.

    First Draw a coordinate grid. Label the *x*-axis and the *y*-axis from 0 to 10.

    Next Evaluate the expression *xy* for all pairs (*x*, *y*) on the grid section you drew with *x* and *y* whole numbers. For example, for (2, 3), the value is $2 \cdot 3 = 6$.

    Then Plot and color the point for each coordinate on your grid using the following rules.

    - If *xy* is a multiple of 10, color the point green.
    - If *xy* is an odd number, color the point blue.
    - If *xy* is neither of these, color the point red.

29. What patterns do you see on your grid? What do you think would be the result if the numbers on the grid went to 100?

Section 1 Extra Skill Practice

Write a rule for finding a term of each sequence. Then find the next three terms.

1. $x, 1 + x, 2 + x, 3 + x, \ldots$
2. 64, 16, 4, 1, ...
3. 4, –20, 100, –500, ...
4. 24, 26, 30, 36, ...
5. $\frac{1}{2}, \frac{2}{6}, \frac{4}{18}, \frac{8}{54}, \ldots$
6. 14, 9, 4, –1, ...
7. Tell whether each of the sequences in Exercises 1–6 is *arithmetic*, *geometric*, or *neither*.
8. Describe the similarities and differences between arithmetic and geometric sequences.
9. Each of the following figures is made up of squares congruent to the first one in the sequence.

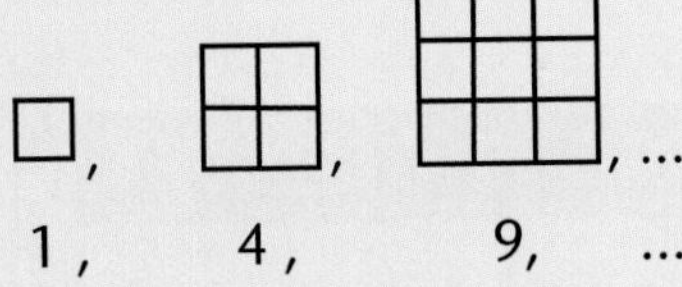

1, 4, 9, ...

   a. What is the 10th term in the sequence?

   b. What is the nth term in the sequence?

10. To what sequence is the sequence 3, 4, 7, 11, 18, ... related? Explain.

Study Skills Test-Taking Strategies

There are many different types of test questions, including multiple choice, free response, open-ended, and performance task. The Standardized Testing feature in this book has provided practice with these types of questions.

1. When you answer a multiple choice question, it is important to read all the choices before you decide which one is correct. Look back at Question 1 in the Standardized Testing feature on page 213. Explain why each choice is either correct or incorrect.
2. When you complete a performance task, it is important to show all your work. Look back at the performance task in the Standardized Testing feature on page 221. Describe the steps that you should show in your solution.

EXTENDED E2 EXPLORATION

FOR ASSESSMENT AND PORTFOLIOS

Changing SHAPE

The Situation

Some fractals can be constructed in surprising ways. Here are the first six steps for constructing a fractal called the *Sierpinski triangle* using circles.

The Problem

Find a method for determining the number of circles in each step. Then find the number of circles that would be needed for Steps 7–9.

Something to Think About

- How were the figures in each step created?

Present Your Results

Explain how you solved the problem and why your method worked. Use tables and drawings to support your explanation.

Section 2 Polygons and Rotational Symmetry

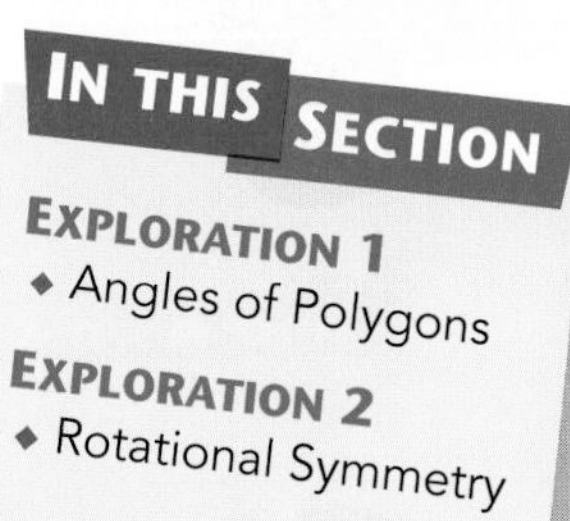

IN THIS SECTION

EXPLORATION 1
- Angles of Polygons

EXPLORATION 2
- Rotational Symmetry

ARCHITECTS and ENGINEERS

Setting the Stage

When designing houses or commercial properties, many architects take into account the natural environment around them. Landscape architects may design walkways and use plants to enhance a building's architecture or help draw the viewer's eye away from undesirable features. Architects may use nature's influence in the design or decoration of a building. Some examples are shown below.

Ceramic wall tile

Spiral staircase

Outdoor patio

Think About It

1 How is nature's influence evident in the tile design?

2 What item in nature might the architect of the spiral staircase have been thinking about when designing it? Explain.

3 How does the patio design complement the geometry of the doors of the entryway?

Exploration 1

Angles of POLYGONS

LEARN HOW TO...
- find the sum of the measures of the interior angles of a polygon

AS YOU...
- look for patterns in polygons

SET UP *Work with a partner. You will need: • Labsheets 2A and 2B • ruler • scissors • plain white paper*

▶ **Many different patio designs can be made using pre-formed stones called *pavers*. The rectangle is considered one of the most basic shapes for pavers, although combinations of rectangular pavers can be used to create more complicated designs.**

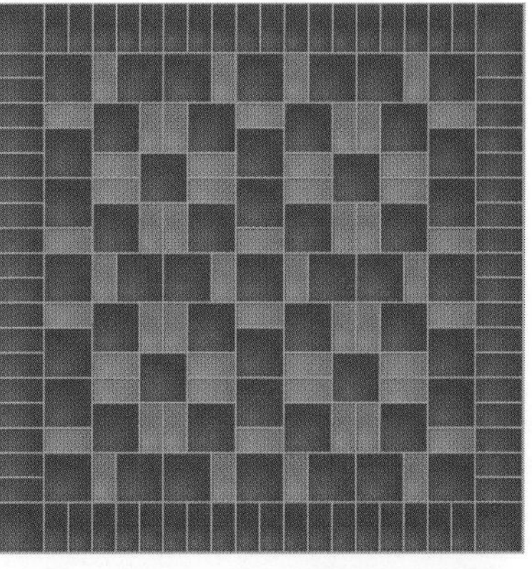

4 **Discussion** The pavers in both patio designs at the right fit together with no overlaps or gaps.

a. Why do rectangles fit together so well?

b. The patio designs shown use a combination of different size squares and rectangles that are not squares. Would it be possible to use only one size rectangle to build a design that fits together with no gaps or overlaps? If so, describe a design. If not, explain why not.

c. Suppose you were to design a patio with pavers shaped like the polygons below. Do you think copies of either polygon would fit together without overlaps or gaps? Explain.

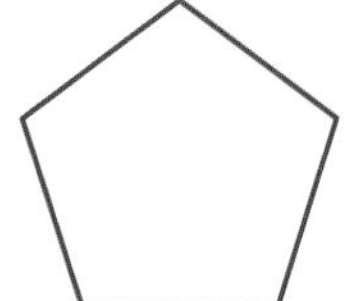
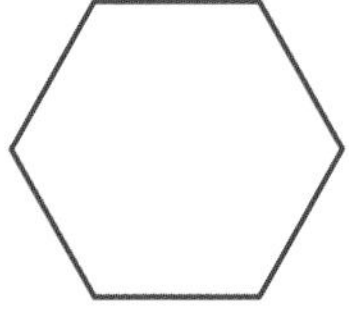

5 **Use Labsheet 2A.** Work with a partner to create two designs using *Pentagons and Hexagons*.

6 **a.** Which polygon from Labsheet 2A can be copied to fit together without gaps or overlaps?

b. Why do you think copies of one polygon fit together without gaps or overlaps and copies of the other polygon do not?

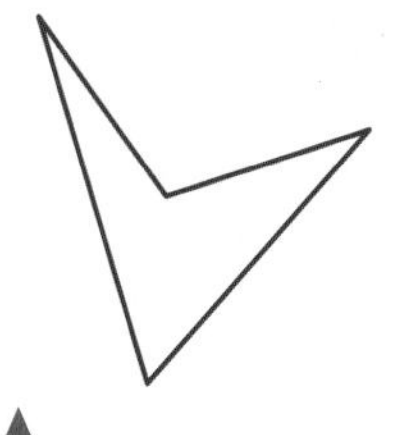

▲ concave polygon

▶ **The pentagons and hexagons you used to create your designs are examples of *convex* polygons. A polygon is convex if all its diagonals lie inside the polygon. A polygon that is not convex is *concave*. To decide whether copies of a convex polygon will fit together without gaps or overlaps, it helps to think about the *interior angles* of the polygon.**

Use Labsheet 2B for Questions 7 and 8.

7 Follow the directions on the labsheet for finding *Patterns in Polygons*. You will explore the relationship between the number of sides of a convex polygon and the measure of its interior angles.

8 **Discussion**

a. How is the number of triangles in each polygon related to the number of sides of the polygon?

b. How can you find the sum of the measures of the interior angles of any convex polygon?

✓ **QUESTION 9**

...checks that you can find the sum of the measures of the interior angles of a polygon.

9 ✓ **CHECKPOINT** Find the sum of the measures of the interior angles of each convex polygon.

a. heptagon (7-sided polygon) **b.** nonagon (9-sided polygon) **c.** decagon (10-sided polygon)

10 The interior angles of a *regular polygon* are congruent.

FOR ▶ HELP with *regular polygons*, see **TOOLBOX, p. 594**

a. What is the measure of one interior angle of a regular hexagon?

b. What is the measure of one interior angle of a regular pentagon?

11 Which of the following expressions could be used to find the measure of one interior angle of a regular polygon with n sides?

$\frac{(n-2)180}{n}$ $\quad$ $n(n-2)180$ $\quad$ $\frac{(n-2)}{180n}$

12 Use what you know about the interior angles of convex polygons to explain what you observed about pentagons and hexagons in Question 6. (*Hint*: Find the sum of the angle measures where the polygons have a common vertex.)

HOMEWORK EXERCISES ▶ **See Exs. 1–13 on pp. 538–539.**

Exploration 2

Rotational Symmetry

SET UP *You will need:* • *Labsheet 2C* • *protractor*

GOAL

LEARN HOW TO...
- describe rotational symmetry

AS YOU...
- discover patterns in nature and architecture

KEY TERMS
- rotational symmetry
- minimum rotational symmetry

Have you ever been drawn to the beauty of a flower or amazed by a starfish on the beach? Some people would claim that the object's symmetry is what caught your eye. So it's no wonder that many architects incorporate symmetry into their designs in hopes of catching the public's eye.

▶ **Fort Jefferson is on Garden Key off the Gulf Coast of Florida. Its design is based on *rotational symmetry*. A figure has rotational symmetry if it fits exactly on itself after being rotated less than 360° around a center point.**

Use Labsheet 2C with Questions 13–15.

13 Use the Fort Jefferson design and your protractor to find *Rotational Symmetries*.

▶ **The minimum rotational symmetry of a figure is the least angle measure, greater than 0° but less than 360°, that you could rotate a copy of an object for it to match with the original.**

14 What is the minimum rotational symmetry for the Fort Jefferson design?

15 Try This as a Class

a. How could you find the minimum rotational symmetry of the Fort Jefferson design without using a protractor?

b. How can you use the minimum rotational symmetry of a figure to find all its rotational symmetries?

16 Without using a protractor, find the minimum rotational symmetry of each flower on these iron gates.

a.

b.

17 Objects in nature may seem symmetrical, though they do not have perfect symmetry. Tell which figures appear to have rotational symmetry. For those that do, name all the rotational symmetries they appear to have.

a.

b.

c.

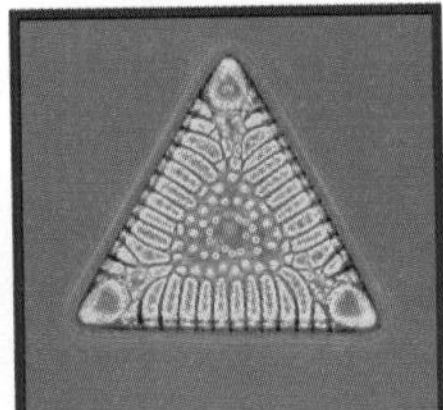

✓ QUESTION 18

...checks that you can use rotational symmetry to create shapes.

18 **✓ CHECKPOINT** Sketch a shape that has rotational symmetries of 90°, 180°, and 270°.

19 At first glance the design below appears to have multiple rotational symmetries. Explain why it does not. Identify its only rotational symmetry.

◀ Folk-art designs like this one are a common outdoor sight in some areas of Pennsylvania.

HOMEWORK EXERCISES ▶ See Exs. 14–18 on pp. 539–540.

Section 2 Key Concepts

Key Terms

Interior Angles of Polygons (pp. 533–534)

The sum of the measures of the interior angles of a convex polygon depends on the number of sides. The equation $S = 180°(n - 2)$ gives the sum S of the measures of the interior angles of a polygon with n sides.

Example

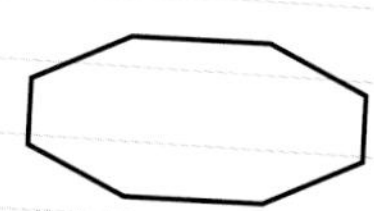

This is an 8-sided polygon, so $S = 180°(8 - 2) = 1080°$.

In a regular 8-sided polygon each angle would measure 135° since $1080 \div 8 = 135$.

Rotational Symmetry (pp. 535–536)

rotational symmetry

minimum rotational symmetry

An object has rotational symmetry if it fits exactly on itself after a rotation of less than 360° around a center point.

Example This figure has rotational symmetries of 90°, 180° and 270°. Its minimum rotational symmetry is 90°.

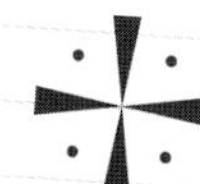

This figure does not have rotational symmetry.

Key Concepts Questions

20 What is the sum of the measures of the interior angles of a 12-sided convex polygon?

21 What is the minimum rotational symmetry of each figure?

a.

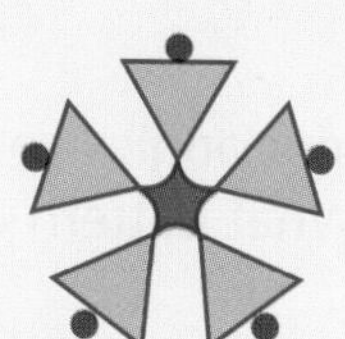

b.

Section 2

Practice & Application Exercises

YOU WILL NEED

For Ex. 11:
- protractor

For Ex. 13:
- cardboard or thick paper
- scissors
- ruler

Find the sum of the measures of the interior angles of each polygon.

1. 

2. 

3. 

4. 

Find the unknown angle measure in each polygon.

5. 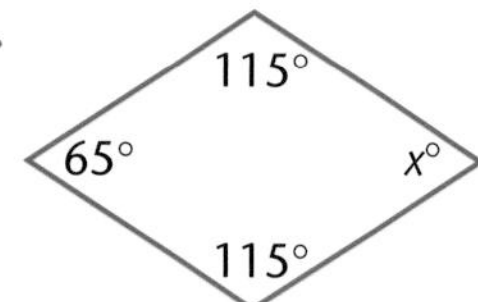

6. 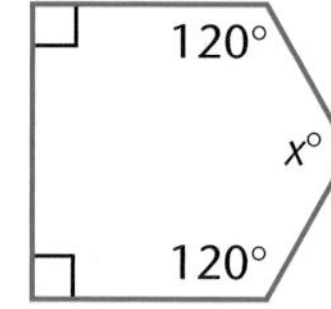

7. 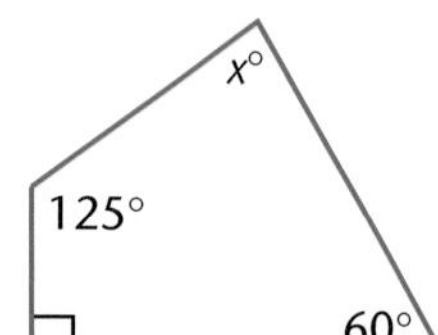

8. 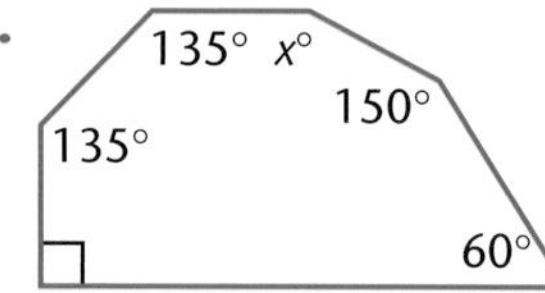

Find the measure of one interior angle of each regular polygon. Round your answers to the nearest hundredth.

9. 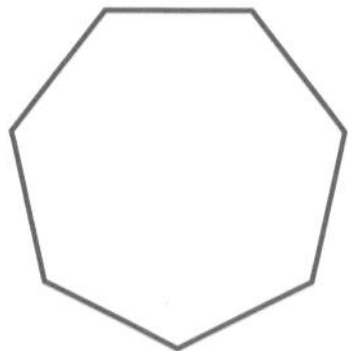

10. 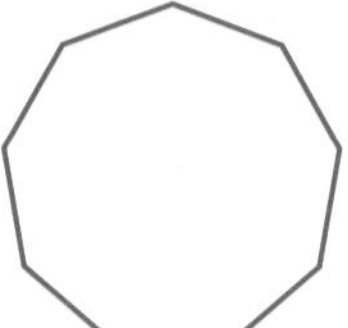

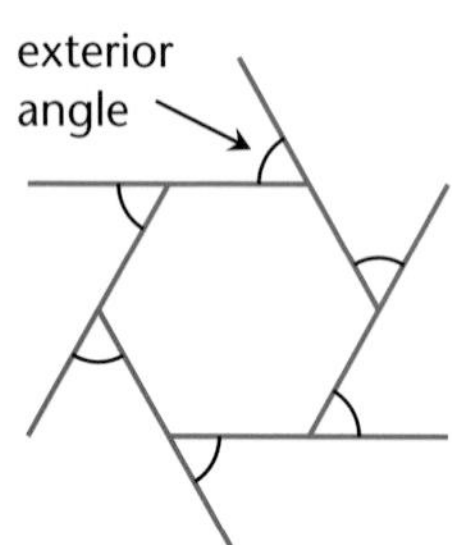

11. **Challenge** Look for a pattern in the sum of the measures of the *exterior angles* of a polygon.

    a. Draw several polygons with different numbers of sides. Draw one exterior angle at each vertex.

    b. Find the sum of the measures of the exterior angles you sketched. Record your results in a table. What pattern do you notice?

12. Patio designs such as the one shown at the right can be created from a paver stone in which a square is attached to a regular octagon. Use the measures of interior angles to explain why this paver shape can create a patio design with no gaps or overlaps.

13. A *tessellation* is a repeating pattern of shapes that cover a plane with no gaps or overlaps.

a. Draw and cut out a triangle or a quadrilateral. Trace around it several times to create a tessellation.

b. On Labsheet 2A, you discovered that a regular hexagon could create a tessellation. Can a tessellation be made using any other regular polygons? Explain your thinking.

c. This tessellation uses regular hexagons and equilateral triangles. List two other combinations of regular polygons that could be used to create a tessellation. Make a sketch of these new combinations of polygons.

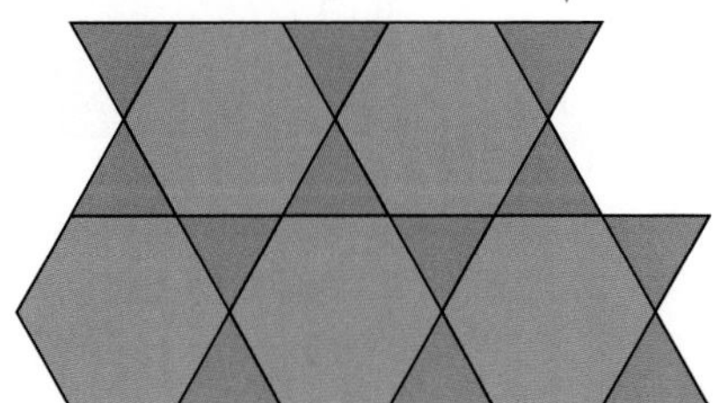

14. A figure has a minimum rotational symmetry of 30°. What other rotational symmetries does the figure have?

15. **Japanese Family Crests** In Japan, family crests are used to distinguish one family from another. Crests are typically carried on by a family's eldest son. Sometimes the patterns are modified by the younger males to show their heritage and differentiation. An example of a modified crest is shown below.

Original igeta | **Igeta with a ring** | **Igeta with angular ring** | **Compounded igeta** | **Stacked igeta**

Igeta means "well crib" and refers to a framework that supports a well.

a. What is the minimum rotational symmetry of the original igeta?

b. Do the modified igetas have the same rotational symmetry as the original igeta? Explain.

16. **Create Your Own** Create 3 different designs that involve rotational symmetry. Use a different minimum rotational symmetry for each design. List all the rotational symmetries for each design.

17. Use the objects shown.

A B C

D E F

a. Tell which objects appear to have rotational symmetry. For each of these, find the minimum rotational symmetry and explain how you found your answer.

b. A figure has *line symmetry* if one half of the figure is the mirror image of the other half. Tell which objects appear to have line symmetry.

c. Make a Venn diagram that organizes the objects into these categories: objects that have line symmetry, objects that have rotational symmetry, objects that have both types of symmetry, and objects that have neither type of symmetry.

Reflecting on the Section

Journal

Exercise 18 checks that you understand the formula for finding the sum of the measures of the interior angles of a polygon.

Write your response to Exercise 18 in your journal.

18. Use the equation $S = 180°(n - 2)$ to explain why it is impossible to have an n-sided polygon for which the sum of the measures of the interior angles is 600°.

Spiral Review

Multiply. Write each product in descending order of exponents. **(Module 7, p. 506)**

19. $(x + 5)(x - 10)$ 20. $(2x - 4)(x - 7)$ 21. $(6x + 1)(6x - 1)$

22. Evaluate $5 \cdot 10^x$ for $x = 4$. **(Module 3, p. 209)**

Find the sum of the measures of the interior angles of each convex polygon.

1. a 100-sided polygon
2. an 11-sided polygon
3. an 18-sided polygon

Find the unknown angle measure in each polygon.

4.

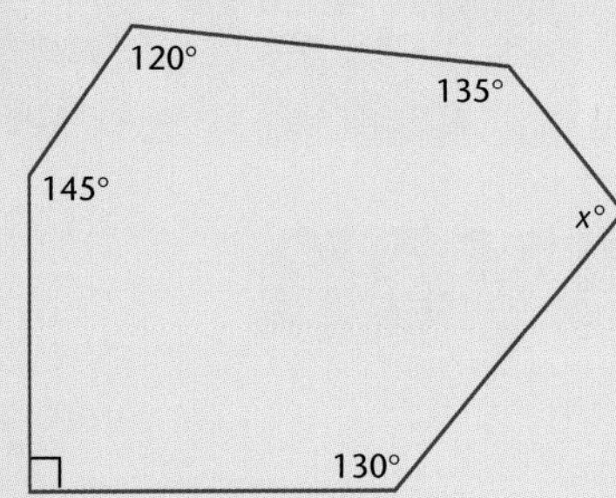

5.

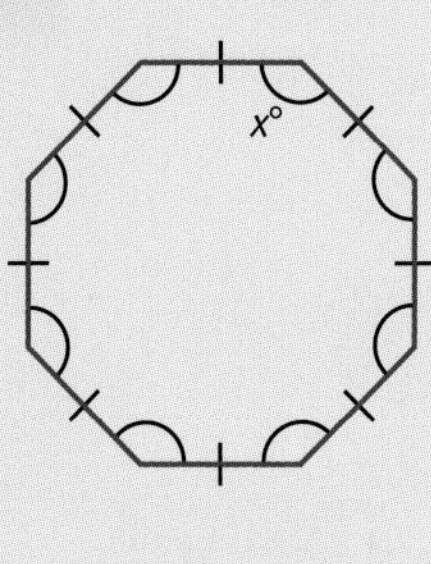

Tell whether each figure appears to have rotational symmetry. If the figure has rotational symmetry, give the minimum rotational symmetry and tell what other rotational symmetries it has.

6.

7.

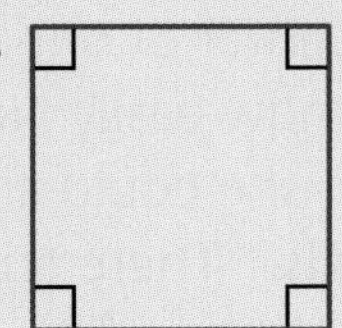

8.

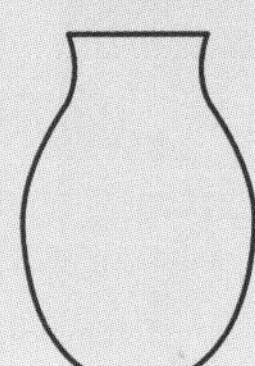

9.

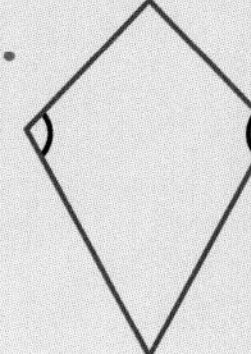

10.

11.

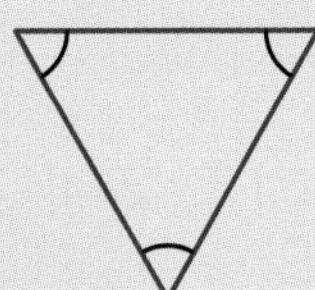

12.

13.

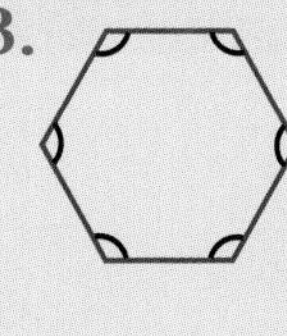

Standardized Testing ▶ Free Response

1. Each measure below is the sum of the measures of the interior angles of a convex polygon. How many sides does each polygon have?

   a. 360°   b. 1800°   c. 5940°

2. A convex polygon has a minimum rotational symmetry of 45°. How many sides does the polygon have?

Section 3 Properties of Quadrilaterals

IN THIS SECTION

EXPLORATION 1
- Sides, Diagonals, and Angles
- Using Coordinates

The Mystery of Blacktail Canyon

Setting the Stage

As the mystery at Blacktail Canyon unfolded, Nageela found broken pieces of pottery. By drawing chords and their perpendicular bisectors, she was able to locate the center of one of the circular pieces. Jim, suprised at how easily Nageela used mathematics, wondered if she could also unravel the mystery of quadrilaterals. "There are so many of them. How can I tell them apart?" Jim asked. Nageela told him that quadrilaterals have properties that distinguish them from each other. "Let me show you," she said. Nageela drew a rectangle, then added diagonal lines.

Think About It

1 Are the diagonals of the rectangle the same length?

2 Are the diagonals of the rectangle perpendicular? Explain.

3 Do the diagonals bisect each other? Explain.

4 How do you think the diagonals of other rectangles compare to those of the one above?

Exploration 1

Sides, Diagonals, and Angles

SET UP *You will need:* • *ruler* • *Labsheets 3A and 3B* • *protractor* • *scissors*

GOAL

LEARN HOW TO...
- classify quadrilaterals

AS YOU...
- investigate the properties of the sides, diagonals, and angles of quadrilaterals

KEY TERMS
- parallelogram
- rectangle
- rhombus
- trapezoid
- square
- kite
- opposite angles
- consecutive angles

Use Labsheet 3A for Questions 5–7.

5 Follow the instructions on the labsheet for identifying *Characteristics of Quadrilaterals*. You'll use a protractor and ruler to make measurements. Then you'll mark right angles, sides with equal lengths, and parallel sides.

▶ ***Quadrilaterals* can be classified according to their properties. Because different quadrilaterals can have the same properties, the quadrilaterals on Labsheet 3A may have more than one name.**

6 **a.** A **parallelogram** is a quadrilateral that has two pairs of parallel sides. Identify all the parallelograms on the labsheet.

b. A **rectangle** is a quadrilateral that has four right angles. Identify all the rectangles on the labsheet.

c. A **rhombus** is a quadrilateral that has four congruent sides. Identify all the rhombuses on the labsheet.

d. A **trapezoid** is a quadrilateral that has exactly one pair of parallel sides. Identify all the trapezoids on the labsheet.

e. Use your results from parts (a)–(c) to give a definition for a **square**. Then identify all the squares on the labsheet.

7 **Try This as a Class** Complete the Venn diagram on Labsheet 3A. Decide on a category label for each oval. Then write the letter for each quadrilateral in the appropriate space on the Venn diagram.

8 ✓ **CHECKPOINT** List as many names as possible for each quadrilateral. Which name is most precise?

a.

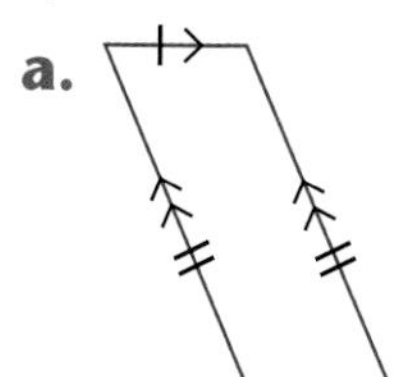

b.

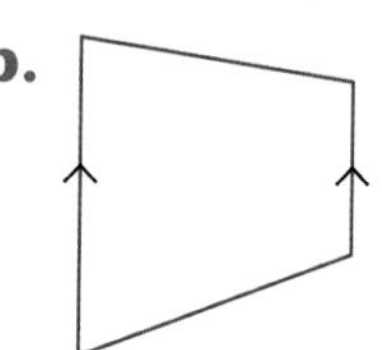

c.

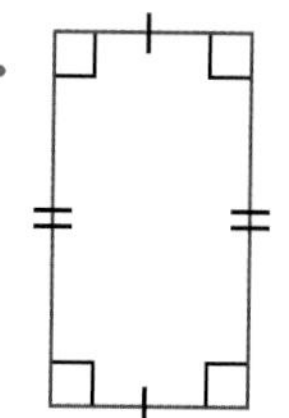

✓ **QUESTION 8**

...checks that you can classify quadrilaterals.

▶ **In the *Setting the Stage* you explored the diagonals of a rectangle. Now you will compare the diagonals of other quadrilaterals and use that information to identify their properties.**

A kite is a quadrilateral with two pairs of consecutive congruent sides, but opposite sides are not congruent.

9 **a.** On a piece of paper, draw a square, a parallelogram, a rhombus, a trapezoid, and a kite like the ones shown below.

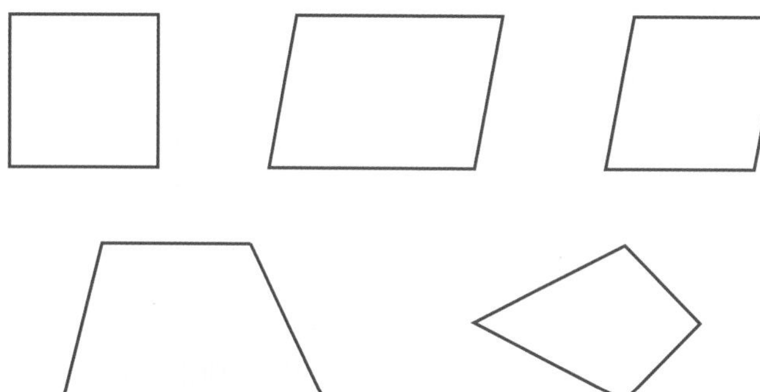

b. Draw the diagonals in each figure.

c. In which figure(s) are the diagonals congruent?

d. In which figure(s) do the diagonals bisect each other?

e. In which figure(s) are the diagonals perpendicular?

f. Do any of the figures have diagonals that are perpendicular bisectors of each other? If so, which one(s)?

FOR ◀ HELP *with perpendicular bisectors, see* **MODULE 3, p. 198**

Use Labsheet 3B for Questions 10–12.

10 **a.** Draw the diagonals of each quadrilateral in the *Properties of Quadrilaterals* table.

b. Use a ruler and a protractor to make measurements. In the *Diagonal Properties* column, record whether the diagonals are bisectors, are perpendicular, are neither, or are both.

c. What generalization can you make about quadrilaterals whose diagonals are perpendicular bisectors?

11 **a.** Are there any quadrilaterals whose diagonals are congruent? If so, which ones?

b. What must be true about a parallelogram if its diagonals are congruent?

▶ **You have seen how quadrilaterals can be classified by their diagonals. Quadrilaterals can also be classified by the properties of their angles.**

12 Use the following questions to complete the *Angle Properties* column in the *Properties of Quadrilaterals* table.

a. How many of the quadrilaterals in the table have four congruent angles? Which quadrilaterals are they?

b. Which quadrilaterals have two pairs of congruent angles? Name the angle pairs that are congruent.

c. Which quadrilateral has only one pair of congruent angles?

d. Is it possible to draw a quadrilateral, other than the one in part (c), that has only one pair of congruent angles? Explain.

- **In a quadrilateral, angles whose vertices are the endpoints of the same diagonal are opposite angles.**
- **In a quadrilateral, angles whose vertices are the endpoints of the same side are consecutive angles.**

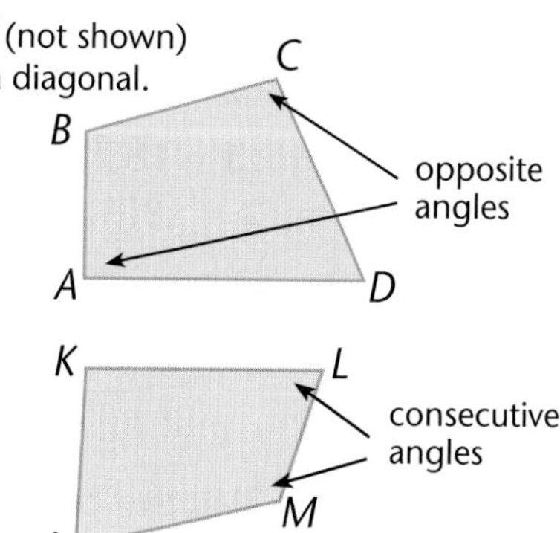

13 **Try This as a Class** Follow the steps below.

- Draw a quadrilateral with at least one pair of parallel sides and cut it out.
- Trace the quadrilateral onto a sheet of plain paper.
- Label the vertices of the original figure *A, B, C,* and *D* so that $\overline{BC}$ is parallel to $\overline{AD}$. Then label the corresponding vertices of the traced figure A', B', C', and D'.

a. Are $\angle C$ and $\angle D$ *opposite angles* or *consecutive angles*?

b. Rotate the figure you cut out and position it so that $\angle C$ and $\angle D'$ have the same vertex and $\overline{CD}$ and $\overline{D'C'}$ overlap.

c. What is the measure of the angle formed by $\angle C$ and $\angle D'$?

d. What other angles form an angle with the same measure as in part (c)?

e. Will the measures of consecutive angles that are between parallel sides of a quadrilateral always have the same sum as those in parts (c) and (d)? Explain.

FOR ◀ HELP
with *transversals*, see
MODULE 5, p. 368

14 **Use Labsheet 3B.** Find the sums of the measures of pairs of consecutive angles for the quadrilaterals in the table. Then tell which quadrilaterals in the table have the same diagonal and angle properties as a parallelogram.

▶ **Transversals You can use transversals to show why the angle properties of quadrilaterals hold true.**

EXAMPLE

Show that the consecutive angles between two parallel sides of a quadrilateral are supplementary.

Extend the sides of the quadrilateral to show the transversals.

$m\angle\mathbf{2} = m\angle\mathbf{4}$ since they are corresponding angles.

Since $m\angle\mathbf{2} + m\angle\mathbf{3} = 180°$, then $m\angle\mathbf{4} + m\angle\mathbf{3} = 180°$.

So ∠3 and ∠4 are supplementary.

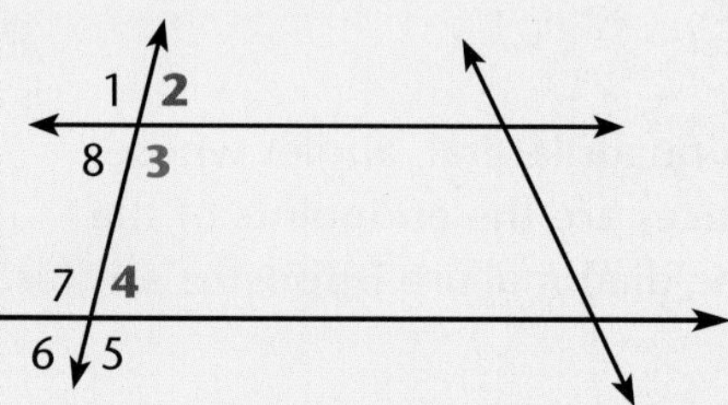

15 **Discussion** Will the consecutive angles between *nonparallel* sides of a quadrilateral be supplementary? Explain.

16 **Try This as a Class** Use transversals to show that opposite angles of a parallelogram are congruent.

✓ QUESTION 17

...checks that you can distinguish quadrilaterals by their properties.

17 **✓ CHECKPOINT** Use the table on Labsheet 3B to tell which quadrilateral is described. There may be more than one answer.

a. The diagonals bisect each other and are congruent. All angles are congruent.

b. The diagonals are perpendicular bisectors of each other. Opposite angles are congruent.

c. Consecutive angles are supplementary. The diagonals do not bisect each other and are not perpendicular.

d. The diagonals are perpendicular to each other. One pair of opposite angles is congruent.

e. The diagonals are perpendicular bisectors of each other. All angles are congruent.

HOMEWORK EXERCISES ▶ See Exs. 1–11 on pp. 550–551.

Exploration 2

Using Coordinates

SET UP *Work in a group of four. You will need:* • *graph paper*

GOAL

LEARN HOW TO...
- find the distance between points on a coordinate grid
- find the midpoint of a segment on a coordinate grid

AS YOU...
- use coordinate geometry to identify quadrilaterals and explore their properties.

▶ **When a quadrilateral is plotted on a coordinate grid, you can use coordinates and the properties of quadrilaterals to determine what type of quadrilateral it is.**

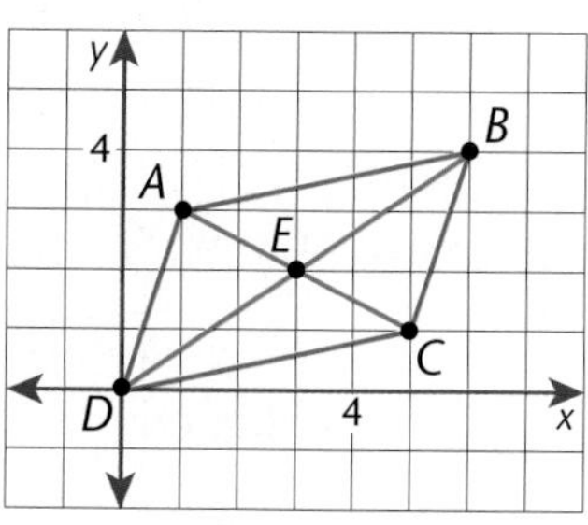

18 **Discussion** Quadrilateral *ABCD* on the grid at the left appears to be a parallelogram. How can you show that a quadrilateral is a parallelogram?

19 One way to show that *ABCD* is a parallelogram is to use slopes to show that its opposite sides are parallel.

a. Have each person in your group find the slope of one of the segments $\overline{AB}$, $\overline{BC}$, $\overline{CD}$, and $\overline{DA}$.

b. Are the opposite sides of the quadrilateral parallel? Explain.

FOR◀HELP with *slopes of parallel lines*, see **MODULE 4, p. 263**

▶ **If both pairs of opposite sides of a quadrilateral are congruent, then the quadrilateral is a parallelogram.**

20 **a.** **Try This as a Class** Use the Pythagorean theorem to find the length of $\overline{CD}$.

b. Have each person in your group find the length of one of the segments $\overline{AB}$, $\overline{BC}$, and $\overline{DA}$.

c. Is the quadrilateral a parallelogram? Explain.

FOR◀HELP with the *Pythagorean theorem*, see **MODULE 5, p. 343**

21 **a.** *E* is the midpoint of both diagonals of parallelogram *ABCD*. What are the coordinates of *E*?

b. How is the *x*-coordinate of *E* related to the *x*-coordinates of points *D* and *B*? of points *A* and *C*?

c. Answer part (b) for the *y*-coordinates of the points.

22 **Try This as a Class** Based on the results in Question 21, how can you use the coordinates of the endpoints of a segment to find the coordinates of the midpoint of the segment?

✓ QUESTION 23

...checks that you can find the length and the midpoint of a segment on a coordinate grid.

23 **✓ CHECKPOINT** The endpoints of $\overline{XY}$ are $X(-2, -1)$ and $Y(6, 5)$. (*Hint:* It may help to plot the points on a coordinate grid.)

a. Find the length of $\overline{XY}$.

b. Find the coordinates of the midpoint of $\overline{XY}$.

▶ **Coordinate geometry can also be used to verify the properties of quadrilaterals and to verify conjectures about figures.**

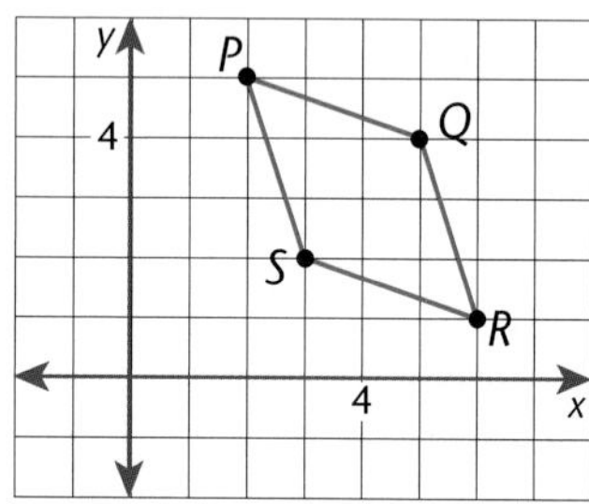

24 **a.** Have each member of your group find the length of one side of quadrilateral *PQRS*.

b. Explain why quadrilateral *PQRS* is both a rhombus and a parallelogram.

25 Based on your discoveries in Exploration 1, the diagonals of quadrilateral *PQRS* should be perpendicular and bisect each other.

a. Verify that the diagonals $\overline{PR}$ and $\overline{QS}$ bisect each other.

b. Find the slope of each diagonal.

c. Are the diagonals perpendicular? Why or why not?

FOR▶HELP

with *slopes of perpendicular lines*, see

MODULE 4, p. 268

26 **a.** Plot the points $W(2, 6)$, $X(6, 8)$, $Y(8, 2)$, and $O(0, 0)$ on a coordinate grid.

b. Draw segments $\overline{WX}$, $\overline{XY}$, $\overline{YO}$, and $\overline{OW}$. Is quadrilateral *WXYO* a special quadrilateral? Explain.

c. Have each member of your group find the coordinates of the midpoint of one side of quadrilateral *WXYO*. Plot the midpoints on your graph.

d. Draw segments to form a new quadrilateral *EFGH* where *E*, *F*, *G*, and *H* are the midpoints of $\overline{WX}$, $\overline{XY}$, $\overline{YO}$, and $\overline{OW}$ respectively.

e. What type of quadrilateral is *EFGH*? Justify your answer.

HOMEWORK EXERCISES ▶ See Exs. 12–16 on pp. 551–552.

Section 3

Key Concepts

Properties of Quadrilaterals (pp. 543–546)

The chart shows some special types of quadrilaterals. Each quadrilateral belongs to the family of quadrilaterals linked to it above and has its same properties. So, for example, a square is also a rectangle, a parallelogram, and a quadrilateral. The chart and the Example identify some of the properties of quadrilaterals.

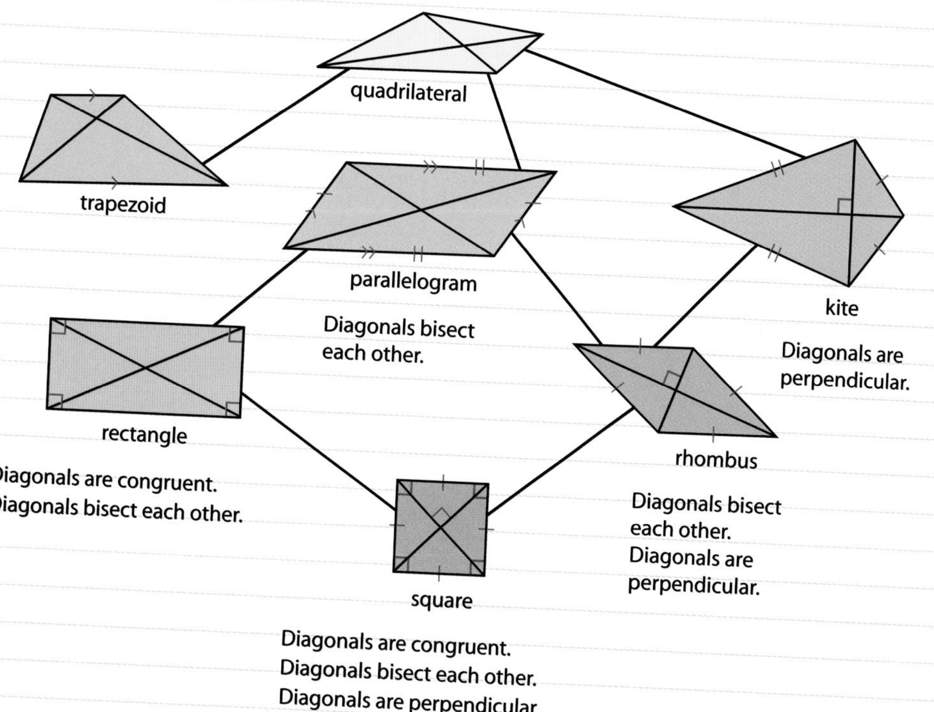

Example

Opposite angles of a parallelogram are congruent, and consecutive angles of a parallelogram are supplementary.
If both pairs of opposite sides of a quadrilateral are congruent, then the quadrilateral is a parallelogram.

Key Terms

parallelogram

rectangle

rhombus

trapezoid

square

kite

opposite angles

consecutive angles

27 **Key Concepts Question**

a. What angle and diagonal properties do a rhombus and a parallelogram that is not a rhombus have in common?

b. What properties make them different?

Section 3 Key Concepts

Distance Between Points (pp. 547–548)

The Pythagorean theorem can be used to find the distance between two points on a coordinate grid.

Example Find the distance between points $A(2, 5)$ and $B(6, 2)$.

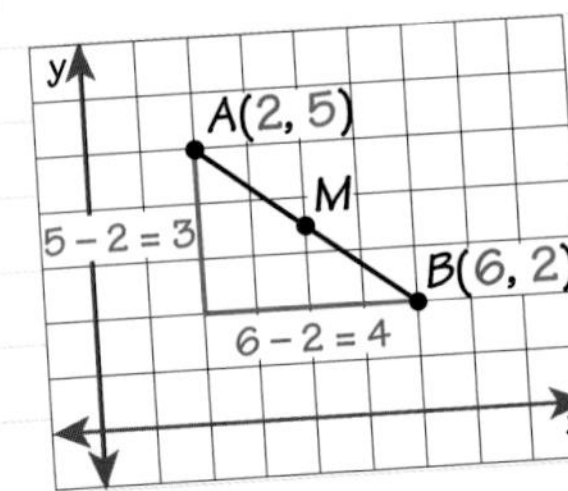

$$AB^2 = 3^2 + 4^2$$
$$\sqrt{AB^2} = \sqrt{3^2 + 4^2}$$
$$AB = \sqrt{9 + 16}$$
$$= \sqrt{25}$$
$$= 5$$

Midpoints of Segments (pp. 547–548)

The x-coordinate of the midpoint of a segment is the mean of the x-coordinates of the endpoints of the segment, and the y-coordinate is the mean of the y-coordinates of the endpoints.

Example The coordinates of the midpoint M of $\overline{AB}$ above are $\left(\frac{2+6}{2}, \frac{5+2}{2}\right) = \left(\frac{8}{2}, \frac{7}{2}\right) = \left(4, 3\frac{1}{2}\right)$.

28 **Key Concepts Question** Find the length and the coordinates of the midpoint of the segment with endpoints $Y(9, 8)$ and $Z(-3, 3)$.

Section 3 Practice & Application Exercises

YOU WILL NEED

For Exs. 12 and 14:
- graph paper

Tell whether each statement in Exercises 1–5 is *True* or *False*. Explain your answer.

1. The sum of the measures of the consecutive angles between two parallel sides of a quadrilateral is 180°.

2. A quadrilateral whose diagonals bisect each other is a parallelogram.

3. A rhombus has congruent opposite angles.

4. A square is the *only* quadrilateral whose diagonals are congruent.

5. If a quadrilateral has only one pair of congruent angles it *must* be a trapezoid.

Open-ended Draw and label a quadrilateral that fits each description.

6. A quadrilateral with congruent opposite angles, neither of which have measure 90°.

7. A quadrilateral whose diagonals are perpendicular and bisect each other.

8. A quadrilateral with at least one pair of congruent sides and one diagonal that is a perpendicular bisector of the other diagonal.

9. A quadrilateral whose diagonals do not bisect each other and that has at least one pair of angles that are supplementary.

10. **Challenge** Use what you know about the properties of congruent triangles to show that the diagonals of rectangle *ABCD* at the right are congruent.

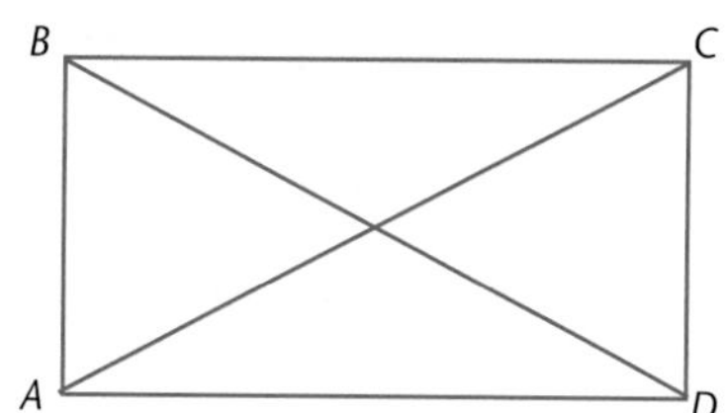

11. Draw a Venn diagram like the one below. Use the following quadrilaterals: rectangle, square, rhombus, parallelogram, kite, and trapezoid. Write the name of the quadrilateral in the most appropriate region.

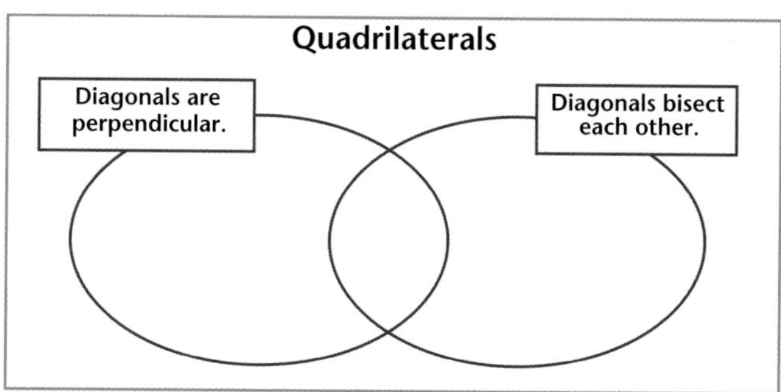

12. Find the length of the segment with the given endpoints. Then find the coordinates of the midpoint of the segment. (*Hint:* It may help to plot the points on a coordinate grid.)

a. (0, 3) and (0, –5) b. (8, 1) and (2, 9) c. (3, 5) and (–2, –7)

13. **Challenge** The coordinates of one endpoint of a segment are (6, 4) and the coordinates of the midpoint of the segment are $(1\frac{1}{2}, 5)$. What are the coordinates of the other endpoint?

14. a. Plot the points $A(0, 0)$, $B(-2, 3)$, $C(4, 7)$, and $D(6, 4)$ on a coordinate grid.

    b. Show that $ABCD$ is a rectangle by first showing that $ABCD$ is a parallelogram, and then that each angle is a right angle.

15. Verify each statement for square $WXYZ$.

    a. The diagonals are congruent.

    b. The diagonals bisect each other.

    c. The diagonals are perpendicular.

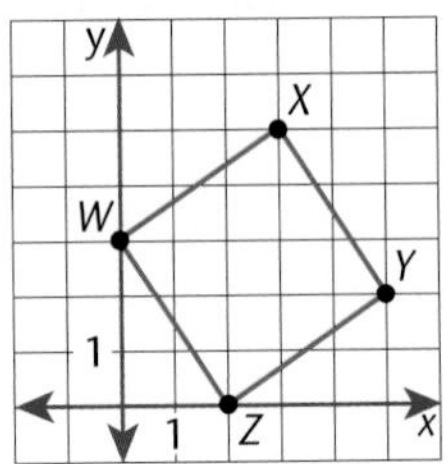

Journal

Exercise 16 checks that you can justify properties of quadrilaterals.

Reflecting on the Section

Write your response to Exercise 16 in your journal.

16. Give an example of how a transversal can be used to justify a property of a quadrilateral. Use a diagram to show your thinking.

Spiral Review

Tell whether each equation represents a quadratic function. If so, rewrite the equation in the form $y = ax^2 + bx + c$. **(Module 7, p. 447)**

17. $y = 4(x - 3) + 7$

18. $y - 8x = 15x^2 + 3(2 - 5x)$

For each right triangle find the unknown side length. **(Module 5, p. 343)**

19. 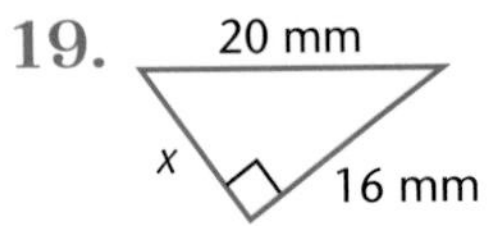

20. 15 cm, 17 cm, x

21. 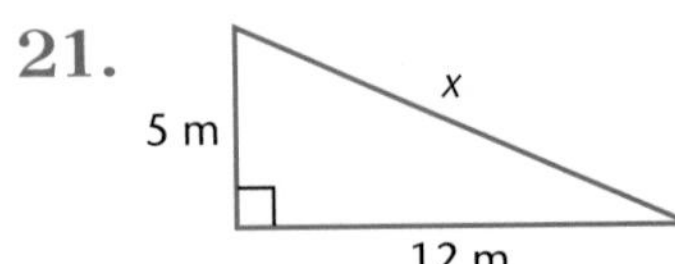

22. 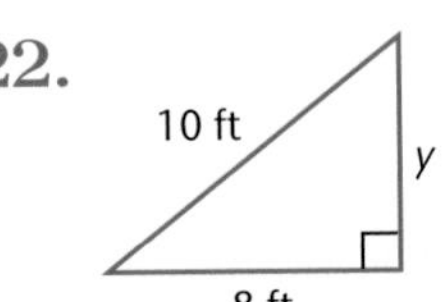

Write each expression without using zero or negative exponents. **(Module 7, p. 464)**

23. x^{-1}

24. c^{-5}

25. n^0

26. $3y^{-4}$

Section 3 Extra Skill Practice

List the angle properties for each of the quadrilaterals.

1. 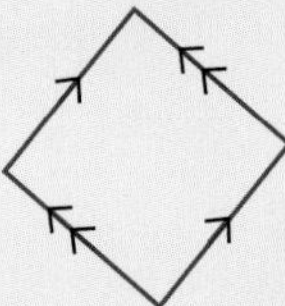

2. 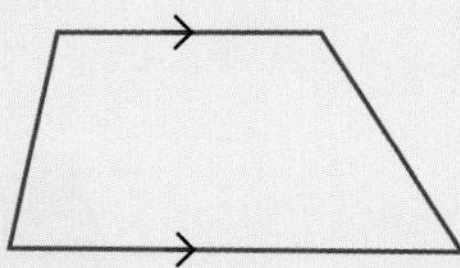

List the diagonal properties for each of the quadrilaterals.

3. 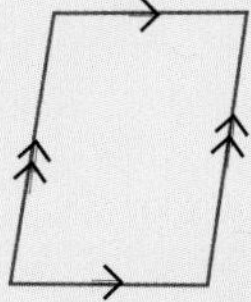

4. 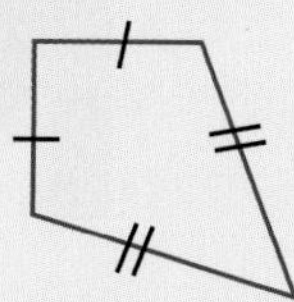

Tell whether each statement is *True* or *False*. Explain your answer.

5. A rhombus has *all* the properties of a parallelogram.
6. Opposite angles of a trapezoid *may* be congruent.
7. A kite has *some* of the diagonal properties of a rectangle.
8. A parallelogram has *at least* one pair of supplementary angles.
9. The opposite angles of *some* parallelograms are not congruent.
10. A square is the only quadrilateral whose diagonals are perpendicular bisectors of each other.
11. Find the length of the segment with the given endpoints. Then find the coordinates of the midpoint of the segment.
    a. (–2, 5) and (4, 13) b. (3, –4) and (8, 8) c. (0, 7) and (8, –8)

Standardized Testing ▶ Open-ended

1. Name a type of quadrilateral that always has the given properties.
   a. Both pairs of opposite angles are congruent.
   b. Diagonals do not bisect each other.
   c. Diagonals are congruent and bisect each other.
   d. Consecutive angles between parallel sides are supplementary.
2. List the angle and diagonal properties of the quadrilateral at the right.

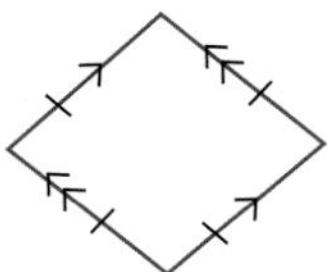

Geometry and Probability

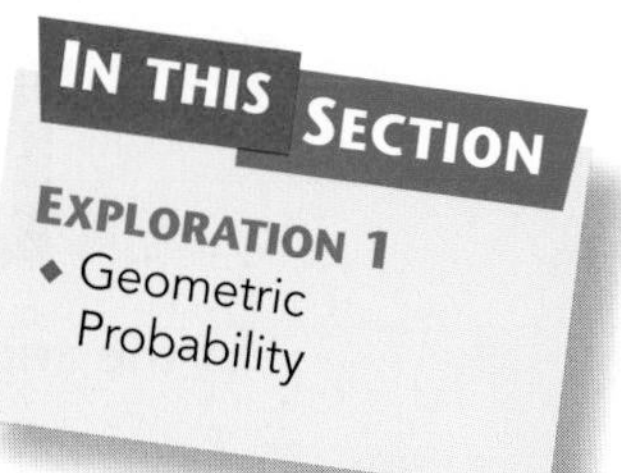

AT THE MALL

Setting the Stage

Visit a mall in Providence, Rhode Island, the Ozarks of Missouri, or Edmonton, Alberta, and you could enjoy a movie in one of the many IMAX theaters across North America. Dome-shaped screens up to 8 stories high and 83 ft wide, along with 12,000 watts of digital sound give the viewer the sensation of being in scenes such as a *NASCAR* speedway race or an underwater expedition to the *Titanic* shipwreck.

The IMAX movie *Titanica* was filmed during a high-risk international expedition 12,500 ft beneath the surface of the Atlantic Ocean. The film crew was not the first to find the wreckage. Over the years, a number of different expeditions tried to find the *Titanic's* final resting place. One of the most challenging problems faced by searchers was locating the exact spot where the *Titanic* sank in 1912. The *Titanic* reported her position when she struck the iceberg. Another ship, the *Carpathia*, reported the location of the lifeboats it picked up some time later. Still, no one knew exactly where the *Titanic* lay.

The bow of the *Titanic* ▶ after nearly 80 years under water.

Think About It

1 A team of searchers from the United States and France predicted that the *Titanic's* final resting place was likely to be in the region outlined with dashed lines on the map below. Estimate the area in square kilometers of this predicted shipwreck region.

2 In 1985, the French ship *Le Suroit* searched in the pink shaded region. Due to strong currents and other factors, *Le Suroit* could not search the entire predicted shipwreck region. Estimate how many square kilometers of the predicted shipwreck region *Le Suroit* covered in its search.

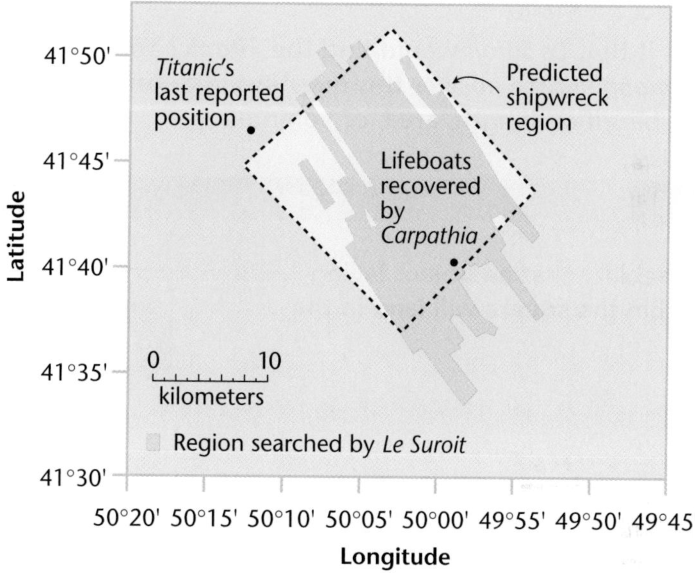

▶ **Knowledge about historical events, ocean currents, and other conditions helped the people who eventually found the *Titanic* predict where the ship might be found. In this section, you will use mathematics to explore the probability of finding the *Titanic*.**

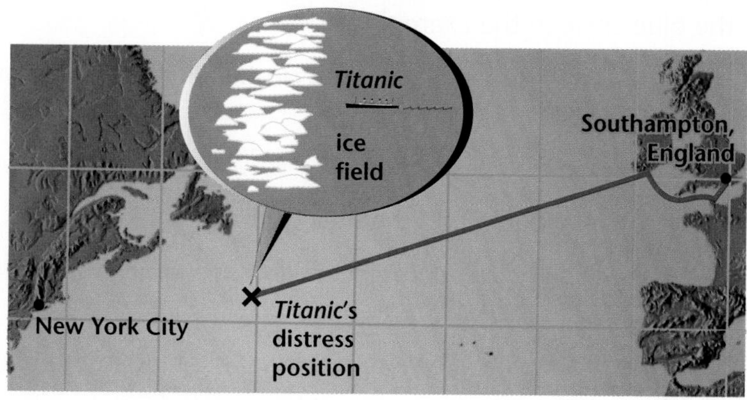

GOAL

LEARN HOW TO...
- find probabilities using areas

AS YOU...
- examine the area where a shipwreck occurred

KEY TERMS
- geometric probability
- complementary events

Exploration 1

Geometric Probability

SET UP *You will need:* • *Labsheet 4A* • *metric ruler*

▶ **How likely was it that *Le Suroit* would find the *Titanic*? You can use *geometric probability* to answer this question. A geometric probability is based on length, area, or volume.**

EXAMPLE

Find the probability that an object falling randomly within the square will land in the blue circle.

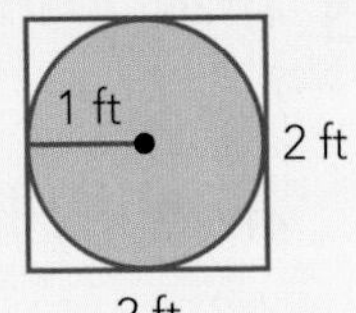

SAMPLE RESPONSE

$$P(\text{landing in the shaded circle}) = \frac{\text{area of circle}}{\text{area of square}} \approx \frac{3.14 \text{ ft}^2}{4 \text{ ft}^2} = 0.785$$

The probability of landing in the shaded circle is about 78.5%.

You write the probability of event A as $P(A)$.

3 **Try This as a Class** Suppose a circle of radius 0.5 ft is removed from the blue circle in the Example above.

a. How do you think this will affect the probability of landing in the blue region?

b. Make a sketch of the new figure.

c. Explain how you could find the area of the new blue region.

d. Find the probability that an object falling randomly on the new figure will land in the blue region.

e. What is the probability that an object will *not* land in the blue region?

4 ✓ **CHECKPOINT** Find the probability that an object falling randomly on each figure will land in the blue region.

a.

4 ft

2 ft

1 ft

b.

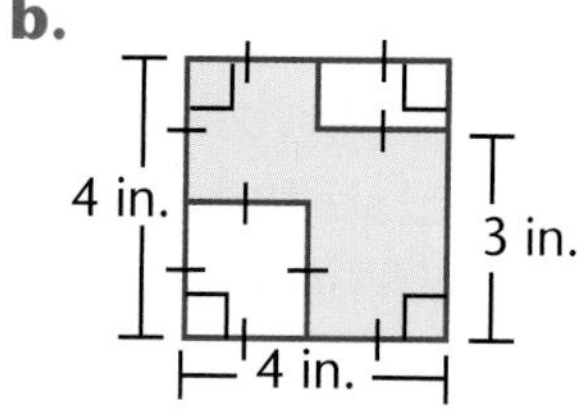

✓ **QUESTION 4**

...checks that you can find geometric probabilities.

▶ **The events in parts (d) and (e) of Question 3 are *complementary events.* Two events are complementary events if one or the other must occur but they cannot both occur. In Question 3 the object cannot land both in the blue region and not in the blue region at the same time.**

5 **a.** Find the probability that an object falling randomly on each figure in Question 4 will *not* land in the blue region.

b. What do you notice about the sum of the probabilities of two complementary events?

6 Use your answers to Questions 1 and 2 on page 556. Assume the *Titanic* lay in the predicted shipwreck region.

a. Estimate the probability that the *Titanic* lay in the region *Le Suroit* searched.

b. Based on your answer to part (a), what is the probability that the *Titanic* did *not* lay in the region *Le Suroit* searched?

▲ *Le Suroit* used sonar to look for the *Titanic.*

7 **Use Labsheet 4A.** Suppose you are on a ship that is *Searching for the Titanic.* Follow the directions on the labsheet to estimate the probability that the *Titanic* lies in your search region.

HOMEWORK EXERCISES ▶ See Exs. 1–10 on pp. 558–559.

Section 4 Key Concepts

Key Terms

geometric probability

Geometric Probability (pp. 556–557)

Probabilities that are based on length, area, or volume are called geometric probabilities.

Example Suppose an object randomly falls onto the figure shown. What is the probability that the object will land in the orange region?

Total area of the figure = **4** in.^{2}

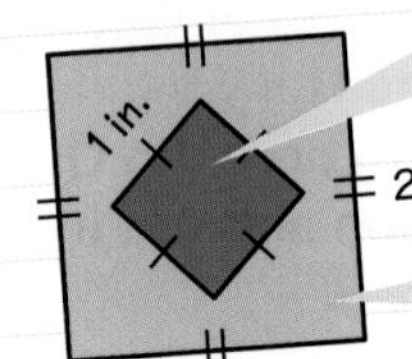

Area of blue region = **1** in.^{2}

Area of orange region = **3** in.^{2}

The probability that the object will land in the orange region is $\frac{3}{4}$.

complementary events

Complementary Events (p. 557)

The sum of the probabilities of complementary events is 1.

P(the event occurs) = 1 − P(the event does not occur).

8 Key Concepts Question Use the Example above.

a. How was the probability of landing in the orange region found?

b. What is the probability of landing in the blue region?

Section 4 Practice & Application Exercises

YOU WILL NEED

For Exs 14-16
- graph paper

1. Suppose the probability that event A will occur is 0.6. Find the probability that event A will *not* occur.

2. **Visual Thinking** A 12 in. by 14 in. rectangular cake is divided into 2 in. squares. If a piece is chosen at random, what is the probability that the piece is from the outside edge of the cake?

Find the probability that an object falling randomly on each figure will land in the shaded area. Round your answers to the nearest hundredth.

3. 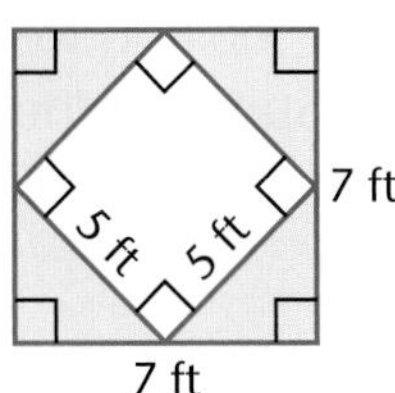

4. 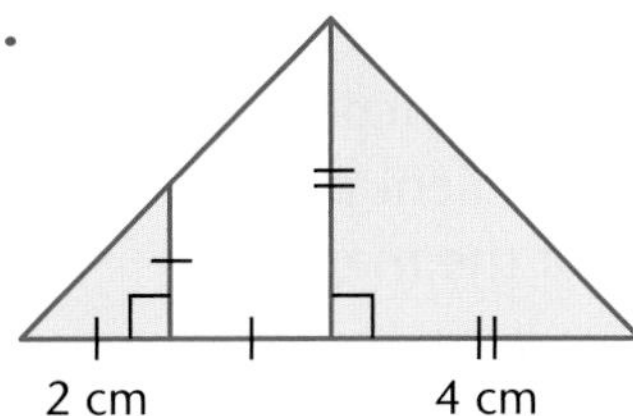

5. 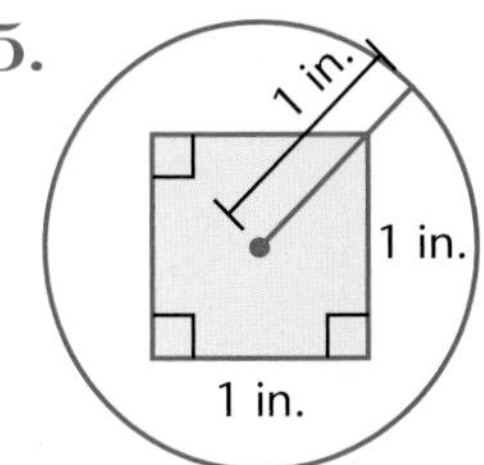

6. 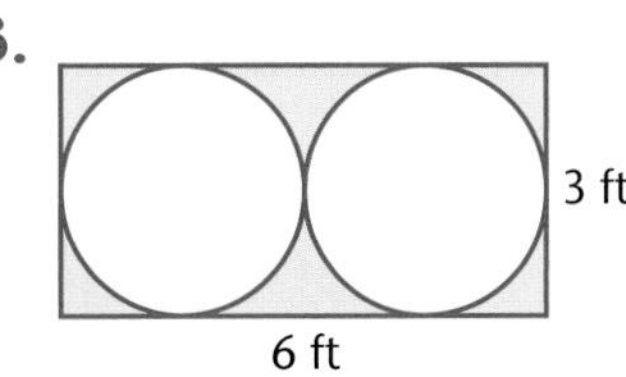

7. Denise lost her ring while playing volleyball. Assume that the ring is equally likely to be anywhere in the entire region shown.

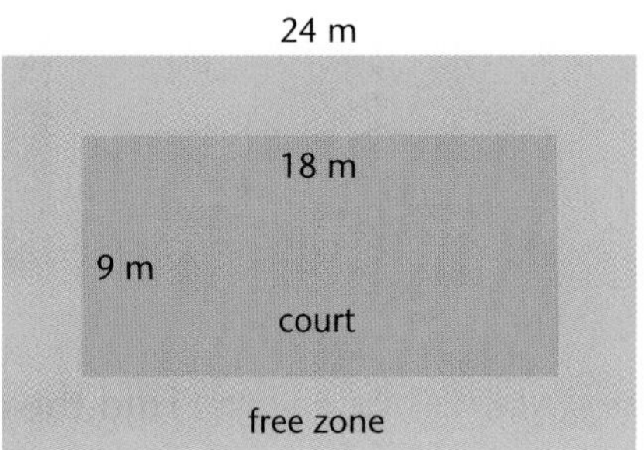

   a. Find the probability that Denise's ring is on the court.

   b. Find the probability that it is in the free zone.

8. **Social Studies** In the 1950s, there was a significant increase in the rat population in northern Borneo. In an attempt to control the rat population, cats were parachuted into the remote regions.

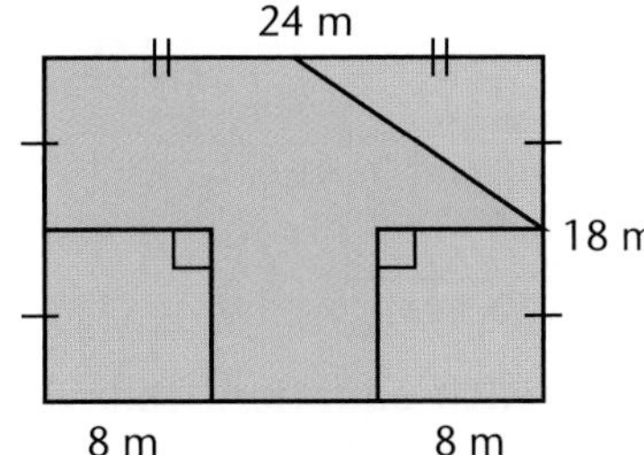

   a. Suppose the cats landed randomly on the rectangular field shown. Find the probability that a cat landed in the tan region.

   b. Find the probability that a cat landed in the green region.

9. *Barm brack* is a spongy cake served in Ireland. Traditionally, a ring is baked inside the cake. If the cake is divided into 10 equal-sized slices, find each probability.

   a. *P*(your slice contains the ring)

   b. *P*(your slice does not contain the ring)

Journal

Exercise 10 checks that you can use geometric probability.

Reflecting on the Section

Write your answer to Exercise 10 in your journal.

10. Murphy's Law for Maps states: "If a place you're looking for can lie on the inconvenient parts of a map, it will." Suppose the inconvenient parts of a map are within 2 cm on either side of a fold of the map.

a. Explain why it might be inconvenient if a place that you are looking for lies on the fold of a map.

b. Find the total area of the map below.

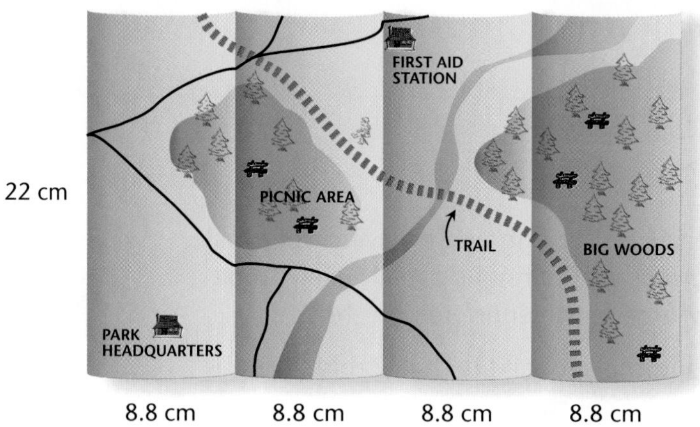

c. Find the probability that a place chosen randomly lies on an inconvenient part of the map.

Spiral Review

Tell whether each triangle is *acute, right,* or *obtuse.* (Module 5, p. 343)

11. 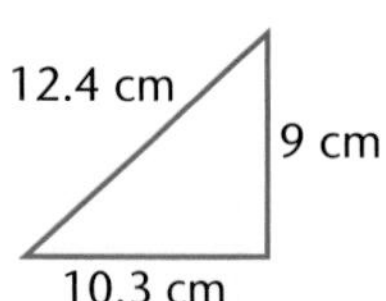

12. 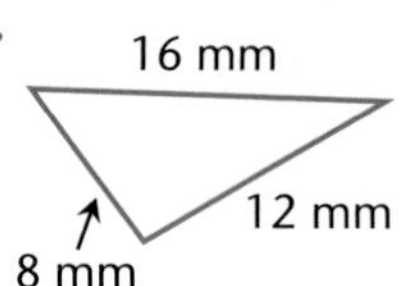

13. 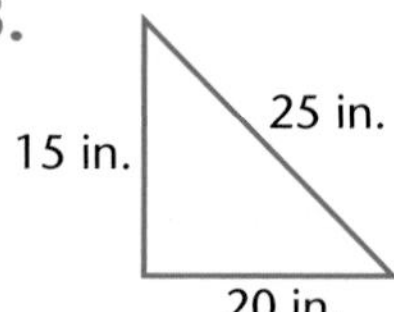

Graph each equation. Tell whether the graph is *linear* or *nonlinear.* (Module 3, p. 175)

14. $y = 3x$

15. $y = -\sqrt{x}$

16. $y = -\frac{1}{2}x - 1$

Find the volume of each cylinder. Round your answers to the nearest hundredth. (Module 4, p. 238)

17. $r = 10$ mm
$h = 6$ mm

18. $d = 4.6$ in.
$h = 11.2$ in.

19. $d = 9.2$ cm
$h = 14$ cm

Section 4 Extra Skill Practice

Suppose that during a storm, a hiker gets lost in the square region shown. Assume it is equally likely that he is anywhere in the region.

1. What is the probability that the hiker is in the white region?
2. What is the probability that the hiker is in the tan region?
3. What is the probability that the hiker is in the red region?
4. What is the probability that the hiker is not in the white region?

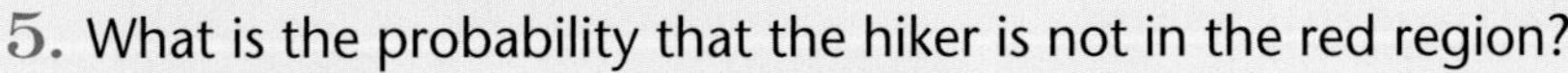

5. What is the probability that the hiker is not in the red region?

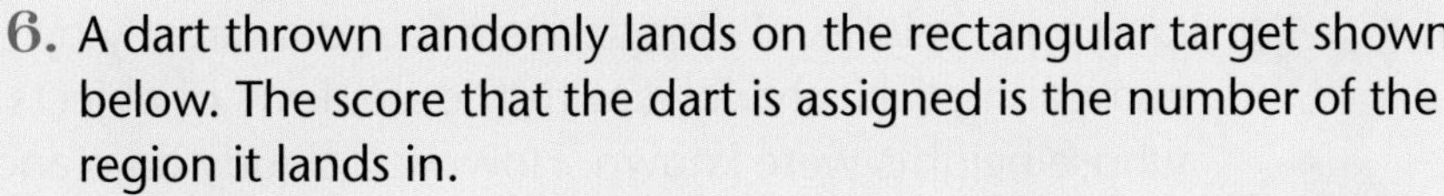

6. A dart thrown randomly lands on the rectangular target shown below. The score that the dart is assigned is the number of the region it lands in.
   a. What is the probability that the dart's score is less than 3?
   b. What is the probability that the dart's score is an even number?

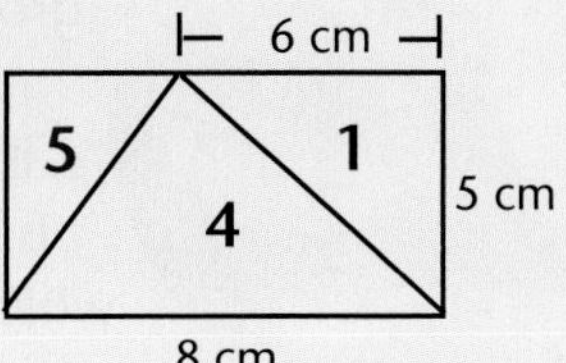

7. Sketch a target that has a shaded region with a 60% chance of being hit when a dart thrown randomly lands on the target.

Standardized Testing ▶ Multiple Choice

1. Which of the following could be the probabilities of complementary events?

   (A) 80% and 80% (B) 1 and 0.1 (C) $\frac{3}{8}$ and $-\frac{3}{8}$ (D) 0.45 and 0.55

2. What is the probability that an object falling randomly onto the figure shown will land in the green region?

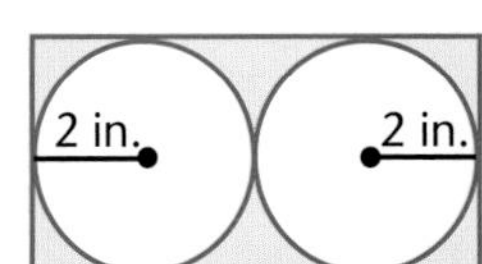

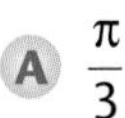

   (A) $\frac{\pi}{3}$ (B) $\frac{1}{3}$ (C) $1 - \frac{\pi}{4}$ (D) $\frac{\pi}{4}$

Tangent, Sine, and Cosine

IN THIS SECTION

EXPLORATION 1
- The Tangent Ratio

EXPLORATION 2
- The Sine and Cosine Ratios

INVENTIONS

Setting the Stage

Long ago, heights of objects were found indirectly by comparing their shadows with the shadows of objects whose heights were known. However, cloudy days and a growing interest in astrology and astronomy created a need for new measuring instruments. One of the first instruments designed for measuring the angle between a star and the horizon was the *astrolabe*, which many scholars believe was invented by the Greek mathematician Hypatia, one of the first notable female mathematicians.

A simple astrolabe can be constructed from a protractor, straw, and weighted string. By sighting the top of an object, the astrolabe can be used to find angle measures of a right triangle formed by the object, the person using the astrolabe, and the line of sight to the top of the object.

▲ Astrolabes are used primarily for measuring the positions of stars, but they can also be used to find the heights of objects.

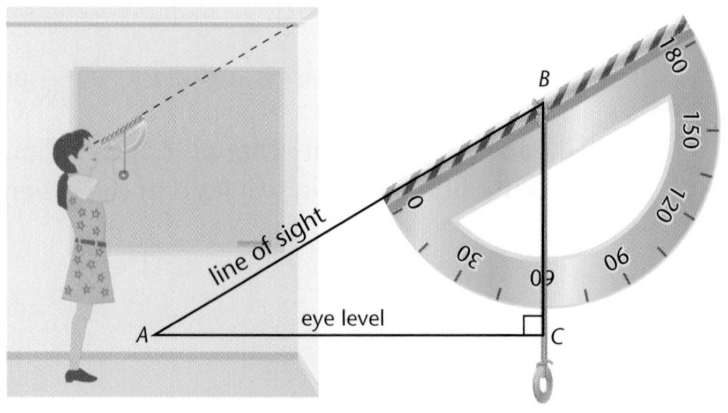

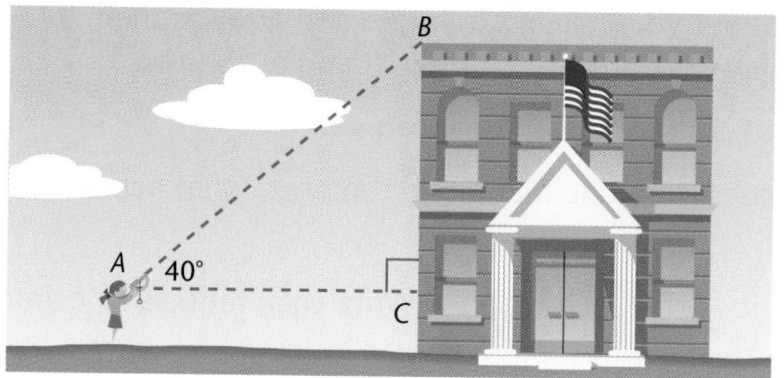

◀ Adriana uses an astrolabe to sight the top of her school. She finds that the measure of ∠*B* in the diagram is 50°.

Think About It

1 Adriana's astrolabe gives her the measure of ∠*B*. From that measure she calculates that the measure of ∠*A*, the angle of elevation, is 40°. How does she know that $m\angle A = 40°$?

2 What happens to the measure of the angle of elevation if Adriana steps closer to the building, but keeps her eye sighted on the top of the building?

Exploration 1

The Tangent Ratio

GOAL

LEARN HOW TO...
- use the tangent ratio to find unknown side lengths in right triangles

AS YOU...
- investigate heights of objects

KEY TERM
- tangent

SET UP *Work in a group. You will need: • protractor • metric ruler • scissors • calculator*

▶ **How can an astrolabe be used to find the heights of objects? In this exploration, you will study a ratio that will help you answer this question.**

3 Each person in your group should complete these steps:

Step 1 Draw a right triangle, △*ABC*, such that ∠*C* is the right angle and $m\angle A = 40°$. The triangles your group draws should be different sizes.

Step 2 Measure the lengths of sides $\overline{BC}$ and $\overline{AC}$ to the nearest tenth of a centimeter. Label $\overline{BC}$ and $\overline{AC}$ with their lengths.

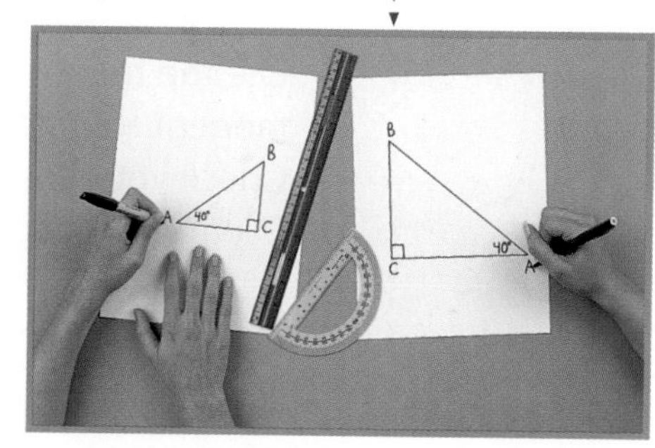

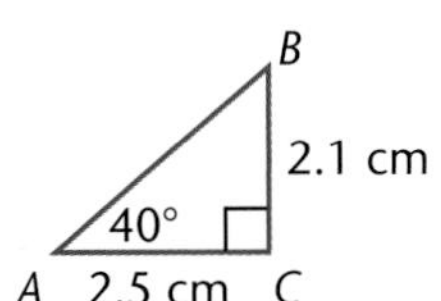

4 **Discussion** Cut out your group's triangles and arrange them in order from smallest to largest. A sample triangle is shown.

a. Are all the triangles similiar? How can you tell?

b. As BC increases from one triangle to the next, what happens to AC ?

c. Find the ratio $\frac{BC}{AC}$ for each triangle. Write each ratio as a decimal rounded to the nearest hundredth. What do you notice?

d. What seems to be true for any right triangle with a 40° angle?

5 Calculator Enter this key sequence on a calculator: TAN 4 0 . How does the number in the display compare with the ratios your group calculated in Question 4?

▶ **In a right triangle, the tangent of an acute angle is the ratio of the length of the leg opposite the angle to the length of the leg adjacent to the angle. The tangent of an angle *A* is written "tan *A*."**

$$\tan A = \frac{\text{opposite}}{\text{adjacent}}$$

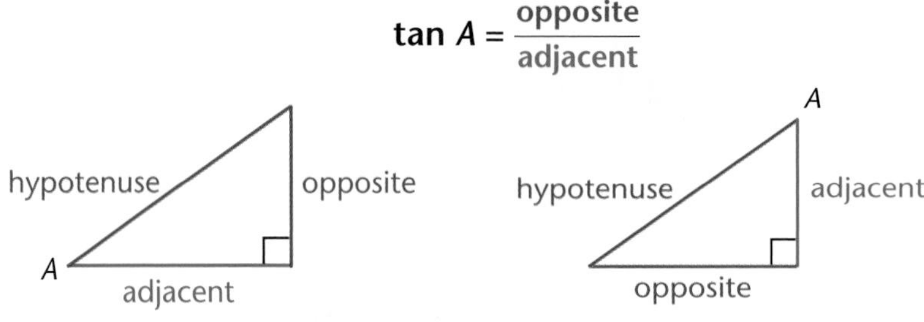

6 **Try This as a Class**

a. In $\triangle ABC$, which leg is opposite $\angle B$?

b. Which leg is adjacent to $\angle B$?

c. Write the tangent ratio for $\angle B$.

d. Write the tangent ratio for $\angle A$.

e. Why can't you write a tangent ratio for $\angle C$?

A
b
c
C
a
B

7 Use the triangle shown to find each tangent rounded to the nearest hundredth. Check your answers with a calculator. (*Note*: Side lengths are approximate.)

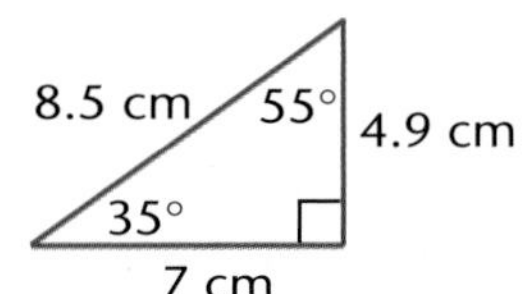

a. tan 35° **b.** tan 55°

8 **a.** Copy the table. Then use a calculator to complete it.

Angle measure	10°	20°	30°	40°	50°	60°	70°	80°	89°
Tangent	?	?	?	?	?	?	?	?	?

b. What happens to the tangent as the angle measure increases?

c. **Discussion** Try finding tan 90° on your calculator. What happens? Why do you think this happens?

▶ **You can use what you know about the tangent ratio to measure the heights of objects indirectly.**

9 Look back at the *Setting the Stage*. Suppose that, in addition to the angle of elevation, Adriana knows her distance from the school and the height of her eyes above ground.

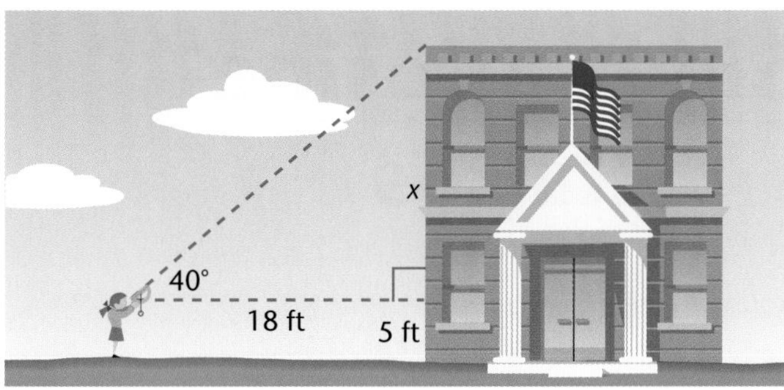

a. Write an equation relating tan 40° and x.

b. Find tan 40°. Use your answer to solve your equation for x.

c. What is the height of the school?

10 **Try This as a Class** Use the triangle.

a. Write an equation relating tan 39° and x.

b. How is your equation different from the equation you wrote in Question 9?

c. How can you solve this new type of equation?

d. Find the value of x.

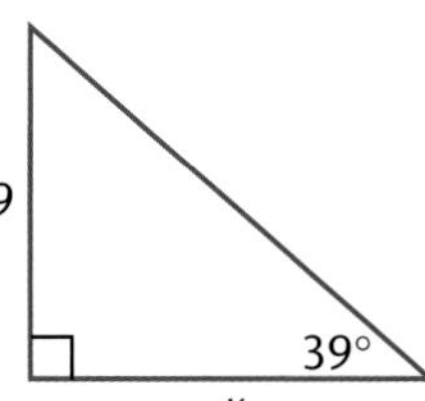

✓ QUESTION 11

...checks that you can use the tangent ratio to find unknown side lengths in right triangles.

11 **✓ CHECKPOINT** Find the value of each variable.

a.

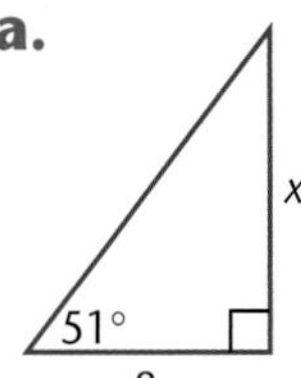

b.

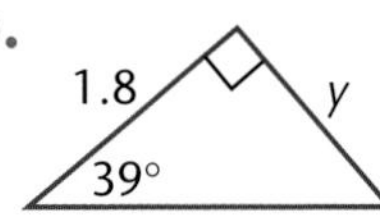

c.

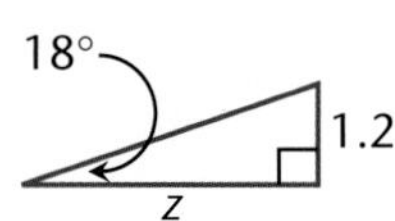

HOMEWORK EXERCISES ▶ **See Exs. 1–10 on pp. 569–570.**

GOAL

LEARN HOW TO...
- use the sine and cosine ratios to find unknown side lengths in right triangles

AS YOU...
- investigate right triangles

KEY TERMS
- sine
- cosine

Exploration 2

The Sine and Cosine Ratios

SET UP *You will need a calculator.*

▶ **Like the tangent ratio, the sine and the cosine of an acute angle of a right triangle are ratios of side lengths. These ratios are defined below.**

You write the sine of ∠A as "sin A."

$$\sin A = \frac{\textbf{opposite}}{\textbf{hypotenuse}}$$

You write the cosine of ∠A as "cos A."

$$\cos A = \frac{\textbf{adjacent}}{\textbf{hypotenuse}}$$

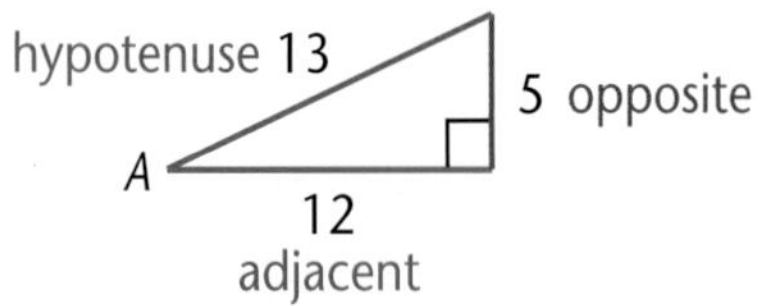

12 Use the triangle above to find each ratio.

a. sin A **b.** cos A

13 **a.** Calculator In the right triangle above, $m\angle A \approx 22.6°$. On a calculator, enter SIN 2 2 . 6 to find sin A. Then enter COS 2 2 . 6 to find cos A.

b. Do your answers in part (a) agree (approximately) with your answers to Question 12?

14 **Try This as a Class** Use $\triangle ABC$ at the right.

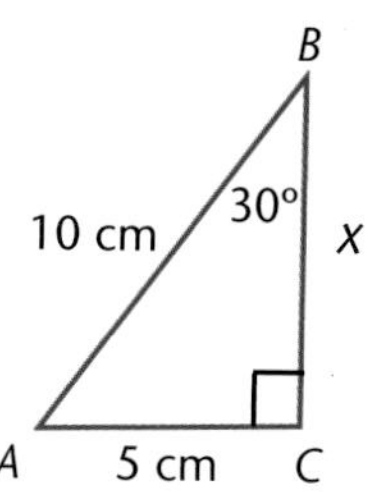

a. Write an equation relating cos B and x.

b. Find cos 30°. Use your answer to solve your equation for x. Round your answer to the nearest hundredth of a centimeter.

c. Show how you could find x using the sine ratio.

d. Could you use the tangent ratio to find the value of x? Explain.

e. Use the Pythagorean theorem to find the value of x. Round your answer to the nearest hundredth of a centimeter. How does the result compare with the value you found in part (b)?

15 Assume you know the measure of $\angle M$ and the side lengths shown on each right triangle. Determine whether you could use the sine, the cosine, or the tangent of $\angle M$ to find the value of x.

a.

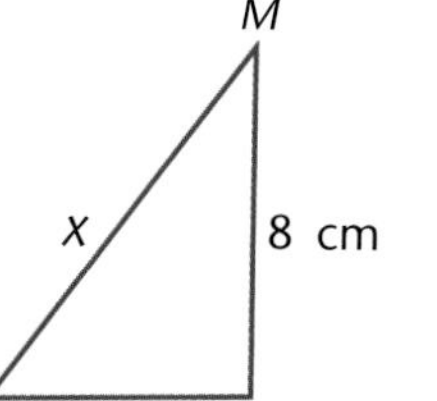

b.

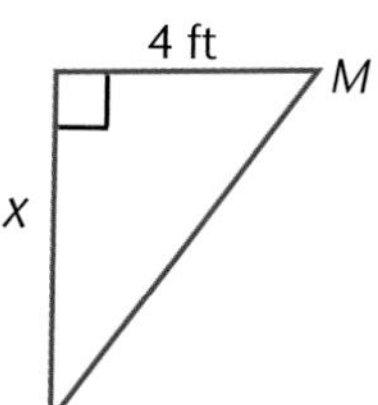

c.

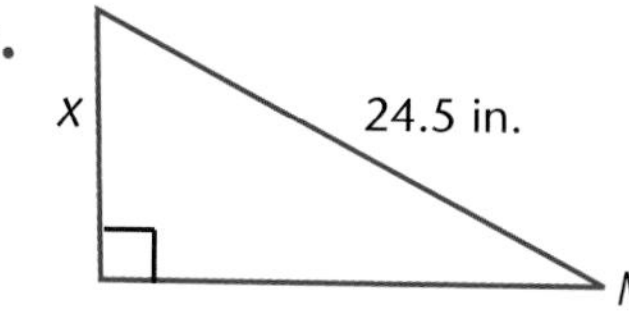

d.

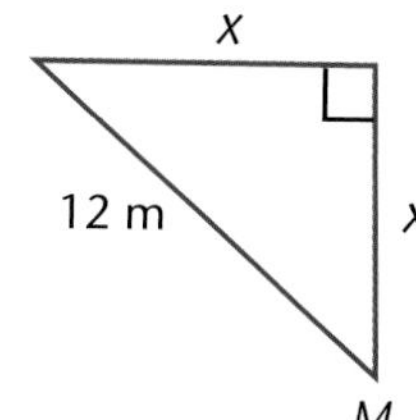

16 ✓ **CHECKPOINT** While flying her kite at the park, Maureen let out all 25 m of her kite string. The measure of the angle of elevation of the kite was 65°. She made this sketch when she returned home.

How far above the ground was the kite flying?

✓ **QUESTION 16**

...checks that you can use the sine or cosine ratio to find unknown side lengths in a right triangle.

HOMEWORK EXERCISES See Exs. 11–22 on pp. 570–572.

Section 5 Key Concepts

Key Terms

The Tangent Ratio (pp. 563–566)

tangent

In a right triangle, the tangent of an acute angle is the ratio of the length of the leg opposite the angle to the length of the leg adjacent to the angle. You can use the tangent ratio to find unknown side lengths in a right triangle.

Example You can use the tangent ratio to find the value of h in $\triangle ABC$.

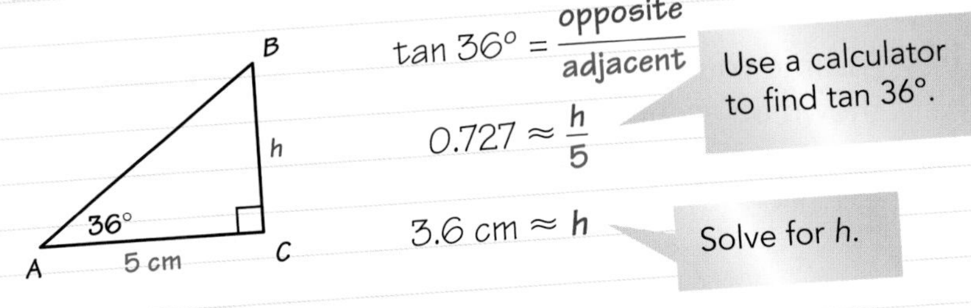

$$\tan 36^\circ = \frac{\text{opposite}}{\text{adjacent}}$$

$$0.727 \approx \frac{h}{5}$$

$$3.6 \text{ cm} \approx h$$

The Sine and Cosine Ratios (pp. 566–567)

sine

cosine

In a right triangle, the sine of an acute angle is the ratio of the length of the leg opposite the angle to the length of the hypotenuse. The cosine is the ratio of the length of the leg adjacent to the angle to the length of the hypotenuse. Like the tangent ratio, the sine and cosine ratios can be used to find unknown side lengths in a right triangle.

Example Find the length of the hypotenuse $\overline{AB}$ in $\triangle ABC$ above.

$$\cos 36^\circ = \frac{\text{adjacent}}{\text{hypotenuse}}$$

Use a calculator to find cos 36°.

$$0.809 \approx \frac{5}{AB}$$

$$0.809 \cdot AB \approx 5$$

Solve for AB.

$$AB \approx \frac{5}{0.809}$$

$$AB \approx 6.2 \text{ cm}$$

17 Key Concepts Question Use $\triangle ABC$ in the Example above. Show how you can use the sine ratio to find AB.

Section 5
Practice & Application Exercises

For Exercises 1–3, use the triangle to find the given tangent. Check each answer with a calculator. (*Note:* Side lengths are approximate.)

1. tan 45°

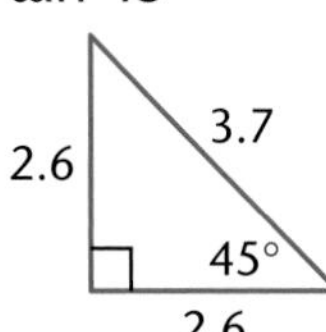

2. tan 65°

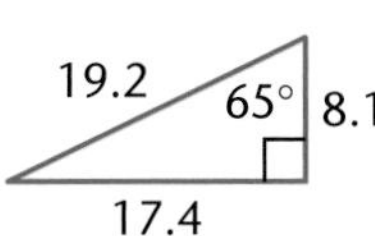

3. tan 28°

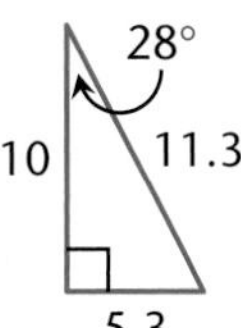

4. **Architecture** Mark uses an astrolabe to sight the top of the Sears Tower in Chicago.

Not drawn to scale

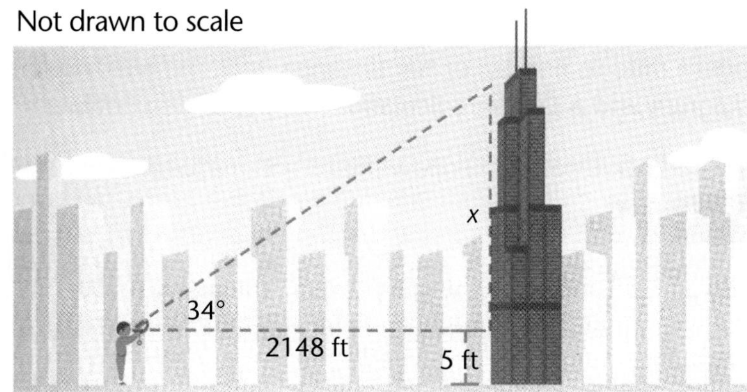

   a. About how tall is the Sears Tower?

   b. Suppose Mark changes his position so that the angle of elevation is now 32°. About how far from the Sears Tower is he standing?

Find the value of each variable. Round your answers to the nearest hundredth.

5.

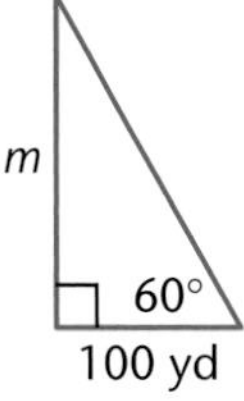

6.

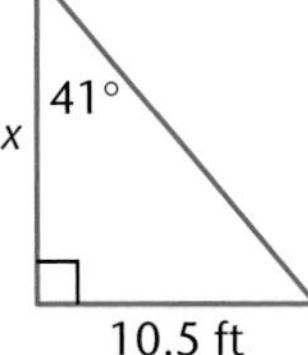

7.

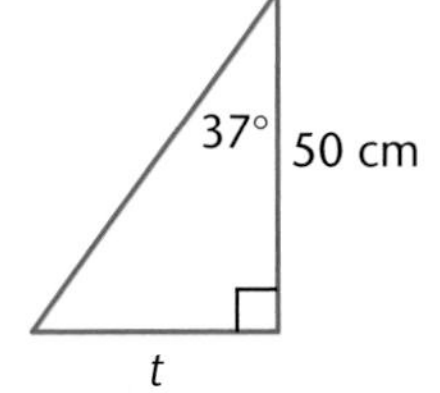

8. **Research** Look up the height of a famous building in an encyclopedia or other source. Describe how a person could use this height and the tangent ratio to find his or her distance from the building. Include a diagram and sample calculation.

YOU WILL NEED

For Exs 1–22:
- calculator

For Ex. 8:
- encyclopedia

For Ex. 10:
- Labsheet 5A
- protractor
- drinking straw
- string (8 in.)
- weight (such as a washer)
- tape

9. **Challenge** The angle of depression from an airplane to the outskirts of a city measures 5.8°. The airplane is flying 6 mi above the ground at a speed of 200 mi/hr. How much time will elapse before the airplane begins passing over the city?

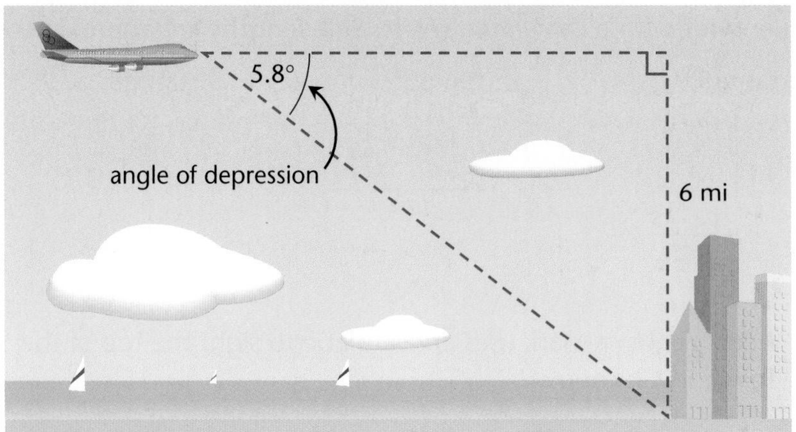

Not drawn to scale

10. **Create Your Own**

  a. **Use Labsheet 5A.** Follow the directions for *Making an Astrolabe.*

  b. Use your astrolabe to sight the top of objects such as buildings, trees, or lamp posts. Record in a sketch the angle of elevation and your horizontal distance from the object. Then use the tangent ratio to calculate the object's approximate height.

For Exercises 11–13, use each right triangle to find the given sine or cosine. Check each answer with a calculator. (*Note:* Side lengths are approximate.)

11. sin 50°

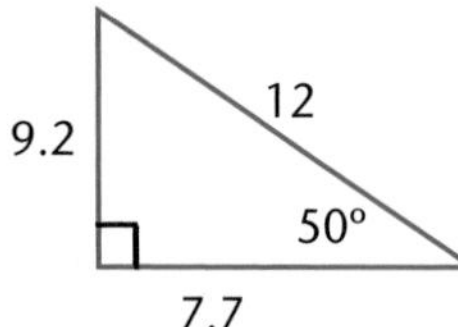

12. sin 40°

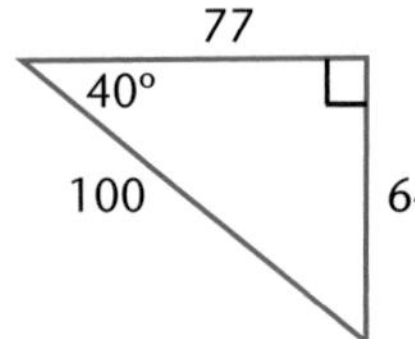

13. cos 75°

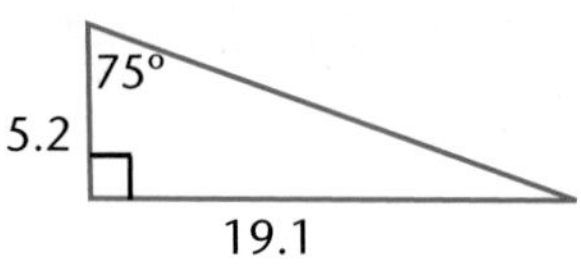

14. **Writing** Benny used his calculator to find sin 45° and cos 45°. The calculator screen displayed the same answer for each. Benny is convinced he pressed a wrong key. Use a diagram to show him why sin 45° = cos 45°.

15. In Exploration 1 you used the tangent ratio to find the height of the building Adriana had sighted in her astrolabe. Explain why you cannot use the sine or cosine ratio to find the height of the building.

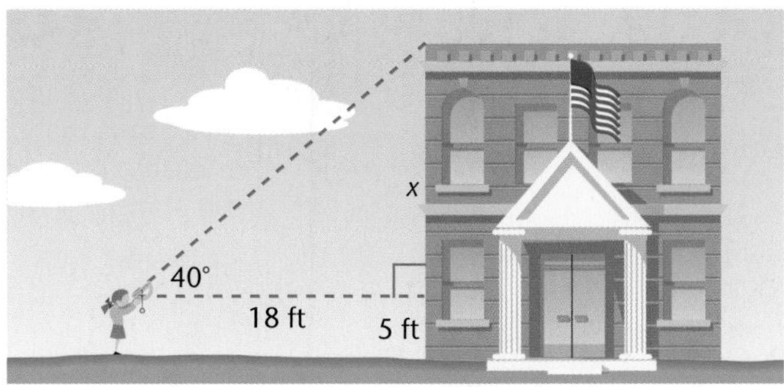

Find the value of each variable. Round your answers to the nearest hundredth.

16. 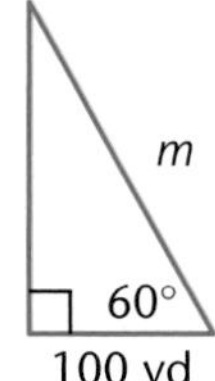

17. 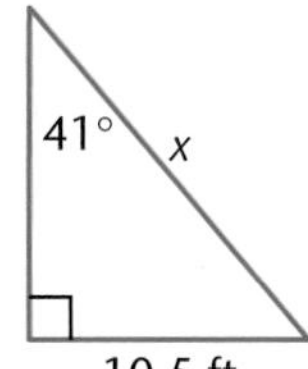

18. 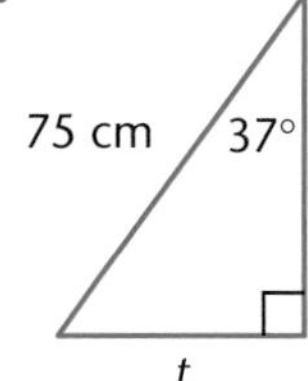

19. **Challenge** The cosine of $\angle B$ in a right triangle is 0.25.

a. What is the approximate measure of $\angle B$? Make a sketch of the triangle and describe how you found the angle measure.

b. Is this the only triangle for which $\cos B = 0.25$? Explain how you know.

20. A painter places an extension ladder 7 ft from the base of a building so that it is at an angle of 65° with the ground.

a. Make a sketch of the right triangle formed by the ladder, ground, and building. Include the angle measure and distance from the building.

b. How far does the painter have the ladder extended? Round to the nearest tenth of a foot.

21. **Ramps and Angles** An engineer designing a ramp often has to be concerned about the angle that the ramp makes with the ground. For example, the *American National Standards Institute* (ANSI) limits the possible angles for a wheelchair ramp like the one shown.

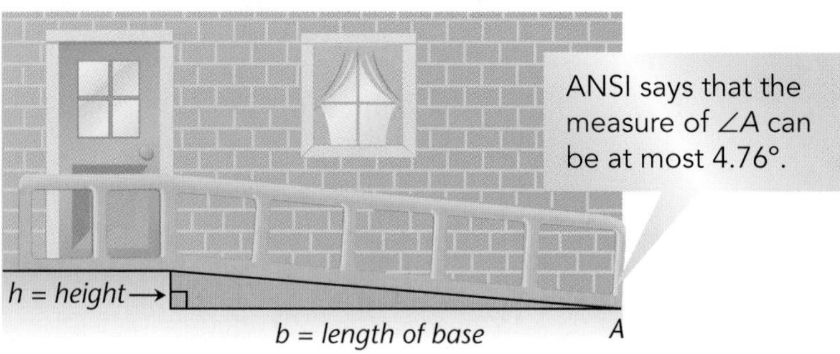

a. Write an equation involving tangent that relates $\angle A$, h, and b.

b. Michelle is designing a wheelchair ramp that is supposed to reach a door 2 ft above the ground and have an angle of 4.76°. What should the length of the ramp's base be?

Journal

Exercise 22 checks that you understand and can apply the sine, cosine, and tangent ratios.

Reflecting on the Section

22. Use the definitions of sine, cosine, and tangent to show that $\tan A = \frac{\sin A}{\cos A}$ for any acute $\angle A$ in a right triangle.

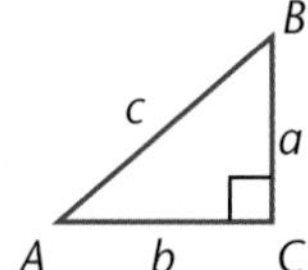

Spiral Review

23. Write each expression as a single power. **(Module 7, p. 464)**

a. $3^5 \cdot 3^8$ b. $\frac{a^{22}}{a^{15}}$

Describe the pattern in each sequence. Then use the pattern to find the next three terms of the sequence. (Module 8, p. 525)

24. 11, 22, 44, ...

25. $x + 2$, $2x + 3$, $3x + 4$, ...

26. Make a tree diagram that shows all the possible outcomes when you flip a coin 3 times. **(Module 2, p.115)**

Section 5

Extra Skill Practice

Use the triangle to find the given tangent. Check each answer with a calculator. (*Note:* Side lengths are approximate.)

1. tan 61°

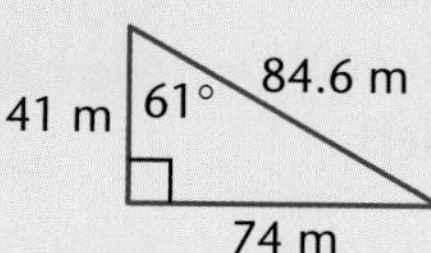

2. tan 22°

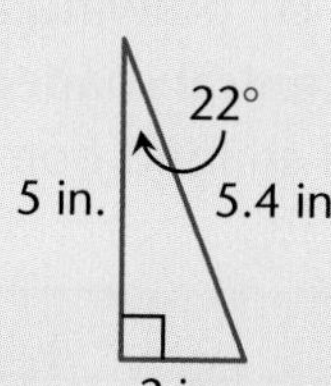

3. tan 67°

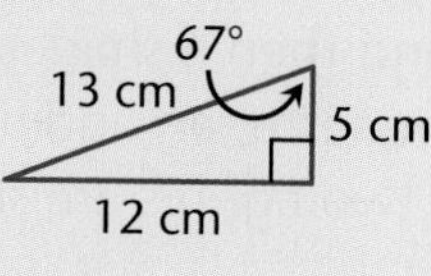

4. For each triangle in Exercises 1–3, find the sine of the given angle.

5. For each triangle in Exercises 1–3, find the cosine of the given angle.

Find the value of each variable. Round your answers to the nearest hundredth.

6.

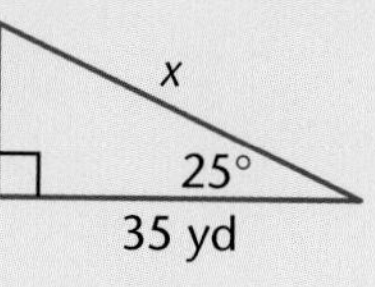

7.

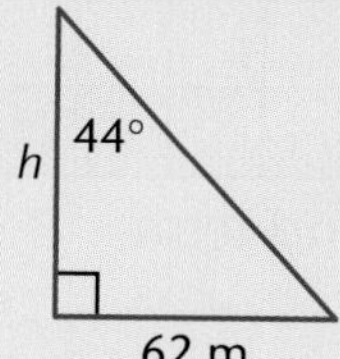

8.

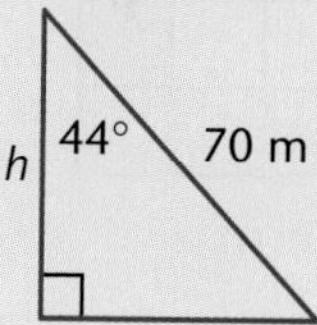

9. A ramp must reach a door 3 ft off the ground. If the ramp's angle of elevation is 4°, find the length ℓ of the ramp to the nearest tenth of a foot.

Standardized Testing ▶ Multiple Choice

1. Suppose $\angle A$ and $\angle B$ are two angles of a triangle. Which statement *cannot* be true?

   (A) $\angle A$ and $\angle B$ are complements.
   (B) $\angle A$ and $\angle B$ are supplements.
   (C) $m\angle A + m\angle B < 90°$
   (D) $m\angle A + m\angle B > 90°$

2. What is the approximate value of y?

   (A) 21.72
   (B) 10.53
   (C) 34.27
   (D) 39.19

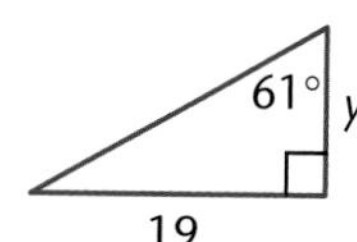

Looking for Patterns

Set Up

You will need:

- *graph paper*
- *calculator*

Sequences The sequence below was started by drawing an unshaded border and then a shaded border around a central shaded square. In each successive term, an additional unshaded and shaded border are added. The first two figures are shown.

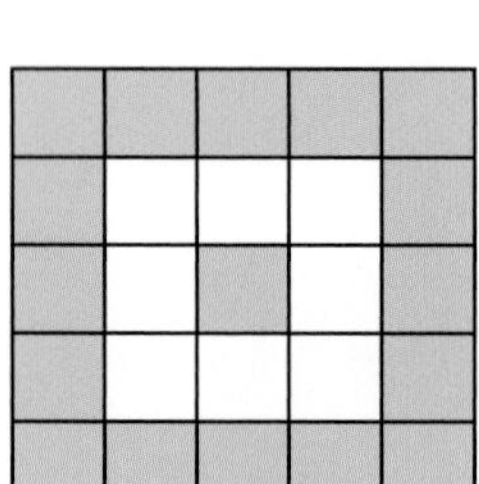

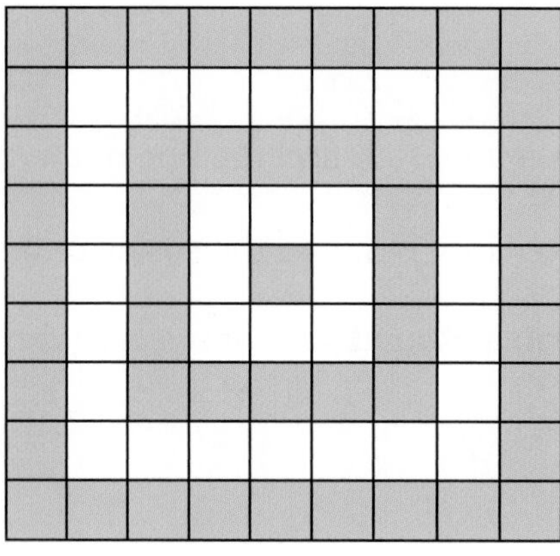

, , ...

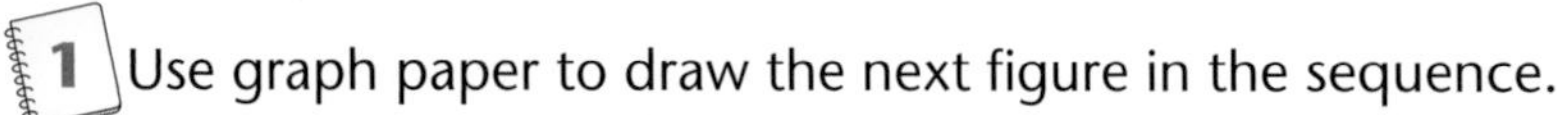

1 Use graph paper to draw the next figure in the sequence.

2 How many squares the size of the central square are shaded in each term?

a. the first term b. the second term c. the third term

3 Look at the pattern of shaded squares in each figure. Use it to find the number of shaded squares for the next two terms in the sequence.

4 Is the sequence of the number of shaded squares arithmetic, geometric, or neither? Explain.

Rotational Symmetry

5 Does the geometric figure representing the first term have rotational symmetry? If so, name all its symmetries.

6 Will any of the succeeding terms have rotational symmetry? How do you know?

Geometric Probability

7 A computer randomly selects a point within the design of each geometric figure. For each of the first five terms, find the probability that the point selected is in a shaded region.

8 What happens to the probability as more borders are added?

9 Will the probability ever reach 0? ever reach 1? Explain.

10 Predict the geometric probability that the computer selects a point in the shaded region of the 20th term in the sequence. Explain your reasoning.

Designing Your Own Pattern

11 a. Design a sequence using a pattern of quadrilaterals. Begin with a figure that has rotational symmetry.

b. Sketch the first three figures of your sequence.

c. Is it possible for the first term of a sequence to have rotational symmetry, but for succeeding terms not to have rotational symmetry? Make a sketch to support your answer.

12 Explain two different ways that someone could find the next term in your sequence.

13 Explore geometric probability using your sequence. Write a summary of your findings.

MODULE 8

Review and Assessment

Write a rule for finding a term of each sequence. Then find the next three terms. (Sec. 1, Explors. 1 and 2)

1. $\frac{1}{y}, \frac{1}{y^2}, \frac{1}{y^3}, \frac{1}{y^4}, ...$

2. 1, 10, 19, 28, ...

3. 1, 0.5, 0.25, 0.125, ...

4. 3, 8, 14, 21, 29, ...

Tell whether each of the following sequences is *arithmetic, geometric,* or *neither.* (Sec. 1, Explors. 1 and 2)

5. 2, –4, 8, –16, ...

6. 4, 11, 32, 95, ...

7. , , , ...

8. 1, 1, 2, 3, 5, ...

9. In this module you discovered the formula for finding the sum of the measures of the interior angles of a convex polygon. Suppose you cannot remember the formula. Describe a method for finding the sum of the interior angles of the polygon shown. (Sec. 2, Explor. 1)

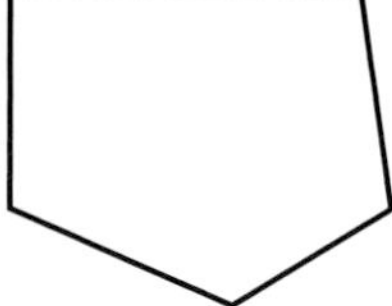

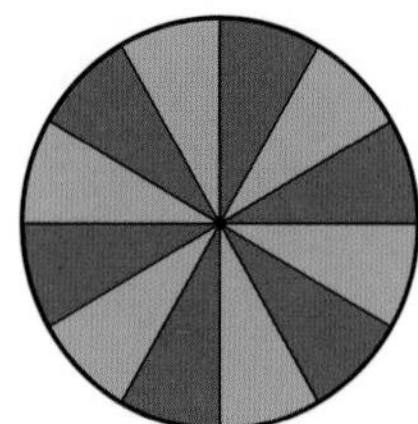

10. a. A carpenter designs and makes wooden tabletops. Find the minimum rotational symmetry of the design at the left.

    b. List all the other rotational symmetries in the design. (Sec. 2, Explor. 2)

11. A quadrilateral has congruent opposite angles and diagonals that bisect each other. Tell what types of quadrilateral it might be. Include sketches with your answer. (Sec. 3, Explor. 1)

For each of the following quadrilaterals, name the quadrilateral, then list at least three of its diagonal or angle properties. (Sec. 3, Explor. 1)

12. 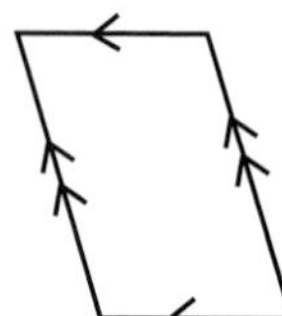

13. 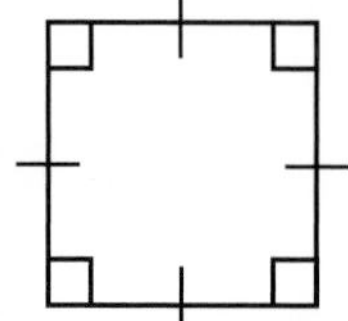

14. 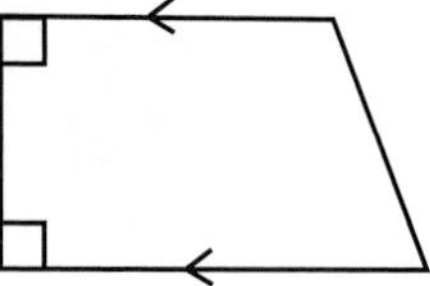

Find the length of the segment with the given endpoints. Then find the coordinates of the midpoint of the segment.
(Sec. 3, Explor. 2)

15. (0, 4) and (0, 10)   16. (1, 1) and (9, 7)   17. (1, 2) and (–3, 5)

18. Verify that each statement is true for rectangle *ABCD*.

a. The diagonals are congruent.

b. The diagonals bisect each other.

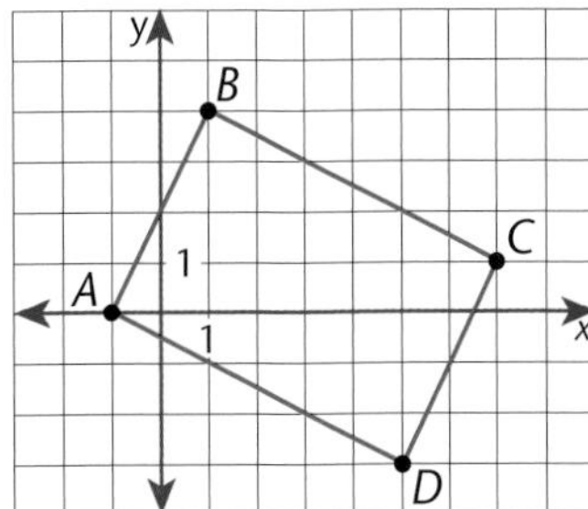

An object falls at random onto the figure shown. (Sec. 4, Explor. 1)

0.5 mi 0.5 mi
1 mi 1 mi
1 mi

19. What is the probability that the object lands in the yellow region?

20. Alter the figure so that the probability that the object lands in the yellow region is 0.75.

Find the value of each variable. Round your answers to the nearest hundredth. (Sec. 5, Explors. 1 and 2)

21.
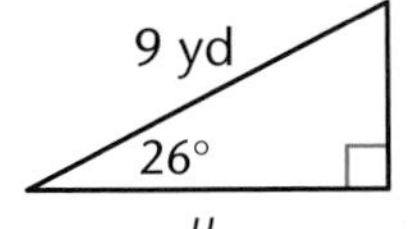

22.
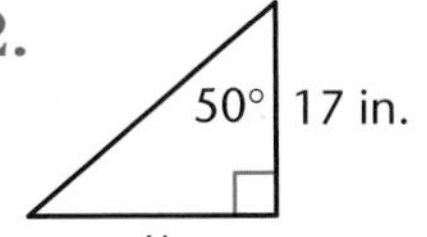

23.
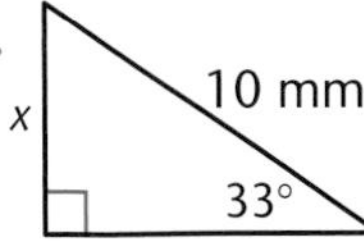

Reflecting on the Module

24. In this module, each section relates to the theme of a previous module. Some of the math concepts in this module relate to the math concepts of previous modules.

a. Choose two math concepts that relate to a math concept studied in an earlier module.

b. Explain how the concepts are related.

CONTENTS

STUDENT RESOURCES

STUDENT RESOURCES

TOOLBOX

NUMBERS and OPERATIONS

Decimal Place Value

To compare two numbers in decimal form, first write each number using the same number of decimal places.

EXAMPLE

Replace each ? with >, <, or =.

a. 0.63 ? 0.8 **b. 0.02 ? 0.002**

SOLUTION **a.** 0.63 ? **0.80**

Rewrite **0.8** as **0.80.**

0.63 < 0.80

b. 0.020 ? 0.002

Rewrite **0.02** as **0.020.**

0.020 > 0.002

EXAMPLE

Round each number to the nearest tenth.

a. 0.846 **b. 6.371**

SOLUTION Look at the digit in the hundredths place. Is it 5 or greater?

a. 0.846

Not 5 or greater. Do not change.
Drop the final digits.

0.8

b. 6.371

Greater than 5. Add 1 to the tenths place.
Drop the final digits.

6.4

Replace each ? with >, <, or =.

1. 0.4 ? 0.83
2. 0.65 ? 0.9
3. 0.750 ? 0.750
4. 0.163 ? 0.16
5. 0.12 ? 0.120
6. 0.8 ? 0.08
7. 0.5 ? 0.49
8. 0.3 ? 0.285
9. 0.1375 ? 0.18
10. 0.060 ? 0.06
11. 0.428 ? 0.73
12. 0.35 ? 0.25

Round each number to the nearest tenth.

13. 0.25
14. 0.81
15. 3.829
16. 1.657

Continued on next page

Round each number to the nearest hundredth.

17. 0.634 18. 7.852 19. 0.0499 20. 5.927

Round each number to the nearest thousandth.

21. 1.0375 22. 0.9932 23. 8.3096 24. 0.02405

Multiplying Whole Numbers and Decimals

To multiply by a number with more than one digit, you can break the number into parts.

EXAMPLE

Find each product.

a. 425 • 312 **b. 0.081 • 0.02**

SOLUTION **a.**

425		
× 312		
850	←	Multiply 425 by 2 ones.
4250	←	Multiply 425 by 1 ten.
127500	←	Multiply 425 by 3 hundreds.
132,600	←	Add the partial products.

b.

0.081	←	3 decimal places
× 0.02	←	2 decimal places
0.00162	←	5 decimal places in the product

Find each product.

1. 62 × 21
2. 48 × 25
3. 263 × 109
4. 3704 × 58
5. 1696 × 43
6. 75,080 × 243
7. 1.8 × 3
8. 5.7 × 2.2
9. 9.07 × 5
10. 4.61 × 1.7
11. 8.95 × 2.36
12. 92 × 4.73
13. 0.06 × 0.03
14. 5.004 × 1.01
15. 0.048 × 0.04
16. 640.8 × 0.012

Multiplying and Dividing by 10, 100, and 1000

**To multiply by a power of 10, move the decimal point to the right.
To divide by a power of 10, move the decimal point to the left.
Use zeros as placeholders if necessary.**

EXAMPLE

Find each product or quotient.

a. 143.628 • 100 **b. 0.057 ÷ 1000**

SOLUTION

a. 143.628 • **100** = 143.628

= 14,362.8

Move the decimal point **two** places to the right.

b. 0.057 ÷ 1**000** = 0000.057

= 0.000057

Move the decimal point **three** places to the left.
Add zeros as placeholders.

To convert from one metric measure to another, multiply or divide by a power of 10. Use the Table of Measures on page 601.

EXAMPLE

Complete the equation: 15 mm = ? cm

SOLUTION

10 mm = 1 cm

15 mm = (15 ÷ 10) cm

15 mm = 1.5 cm

Millimeters are a smaller unit than centimeters, so divide.

For Exercises 1–6, find each product or quotient.

1. 51.83 • 10
2. 9.8 • 100
3. 30.042 ÷ 10
4. 0.067 • 1000
5. 29.4 ÷ 100
6. 0.056 • 10
7. To convert from kilometers to meters, should you *multiply* or *divide* by 1000?

Complete each equation. Use the Table of Measures on page 601.

8. 68 cm = ___?___ m
9. 13 km = ___?___ m
10. 27 m = ___?___ cm
11. 3560 m = ___?___ km
12. 4.8 m = ___?___ mm
13. 4540 mg = ___?___ g

Dividing Whole Numbers and Decimals

When you divide, you may have to add zeros to the dividend. When dividing by a decimal, move both decimal points the same number of decimal places to the right, until the divisor is a whole number. Then follow the same rules as for dividing whole numbers.

EXAMPLE

Find the quotient $6\overline{)83}$. Round your answer to the nearest tenth.

SOLUTION

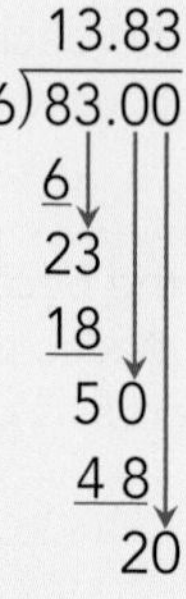

To round to the nearest tenth, carry out the division to the hundredths place. Then round.

To the nearest tenth, the quotient is 13.8.

EXAMPLE

Find the quotient: $0.05\overline{)4.8}$

SOLUTION

$0.05\overline{)4.80}$

Move the decimal point two places to the right. Write a zero.

Divide. ⟶ $5\overline{)480}$ = 96 (45, 30, 30, 0)

The quotient is 96.

Find each quotient. Round each answer to the nearest tenth.

1. $8\overline{)198}$
2. $15\overline{)265}$
3. $32\overline{)488}$

Find each quotient. Round each answer to the nearest hundredth.

4. $9\overline{)68}$
5. $16\overline{)851}$
6. $11\overline{)547}$

Find each quotient. If necessary, round each answer to the nearest tenth.

7. $1.8\overline{)25.2}$
8. $5.4\overline{)243}$
9. $6.4\overline{)54.4}$
10. $4.5\overline{)1180}$
11. $0.32\overline{)308}$
12. $0.027\overline{)26.136}$

Divisibility Rules

A number is divisible by another number if the remainder is zero when you divide the second number by the first. It is not possible to divide a number by zero. The table shows divisibility tests you can use to tell if a number is divisible by another number.

Divisible by	Test
2	The last digit is 0, 2, 4, 6, or 8.
3	The sum of the digits is divisible by 3.
4	The number formed by the last two digits is divisible by 4.
5	The last digit is 0 or 5.
6	The number is divisible by both 2 and 3.
8	The number formed by the last three digits is divisible by 8.
9	The sum of the digits is divisible by 9.
10	The last digit is 0.

EXAMPLE

Is 79,120 divisible by 8?

SOLUTION The number formed by the last three digits, 120, is divisible by 8.
Yes, 79,120 is divisible by 8.

EXAMPLE

Is 5742 divisible by 9?

SOLUTION The sum of the digits, $5 + 7 + 4 + 2 = 18$, which is divisible by 9.
Yes, 5742 is divisible by 9.

EXAMPLE

Is 818 divisible by 6?

SOLUTION 818 is divisible by 2, because the last digit is 8. 818 is not divisible by 3, because $8 + 1 + 8 = 17$, which is not divisible by 3.
No, 818 is not divisible by 6.

Test each number for divisibility.

1. Is 378 divisible by 4?
2. Is 657 divisible by 3?
3. Is 4695 divisible by 5?
4. Is 5934 divisible by 2?
5. Is 3511 divisible by 10?
6. Is 2178 divisible by 6?
7. Is 2043 divisible by 9?
8. Is 80,256 divisible by 8?

Finding Factors and Multiples

A common factor of two numbers is a number that is a factor of both numbers. For example, 4 is a common factor of 60 and 100, because $60 = 4 \cdot 15$ and $100 = 4 \cdot 25$.

The greatest common factor (GCF) of two numbers is the greatest number that is a common factor of the two numbers.

EXAMPLE

Find the GCF of 60 and 100.

SOLUTION Write the prime factorizations of 60 and 100.

$$60 = 2 \cdot 2 \cdot 3 \cdot 5$$
$$100 = 2 \cdot 2 \cdot 5 \cdot 5$$

Circle the numbers that are in *both* factorizations.

Multiply the numbers you circled.

The GCF of 60 and 100 is $2 \cdot 2 \cdot 5 = 20$.

A common multiple of two numbers is a number that is a multiple of both numbers. For example, 72 is a common multiple of 12 and 9, because $12 \cdot 6 = 72$ and $9 \cdot 8 = 72$.

The least common multiple (LCM) of two numbers is the least number that is a common multiple of the numbers.

EXAMPLE

Find the LCM of 9 and 12.

SOLUTION Find the GCF of 9 and 12.

$$9 = 3 \cdot 3$$
$$12 = 2 \cdot 2 \cdot 3$$

The GCF is 3.

Multiply the GCF by the numbers you did not circle.

The LCM of 9 and 12 is $3 \cdot 3 \cdot 2 \cdot 2 = 36$.

Find the GCF and the LCM of each pair of numbers.

1. 42, 60
2. 24, 36
3. 33, 110
4. 80, 120
5. 30, 90
6. 125, 420
7. 165, 315
8. 114, 138
9. 275, 495
10. 50, 98
11. 77, 81
12. 46, 69

Finding Equivalent Fractions and Ratios

Fractions that name the same part of a whole are equivalent fractions. A fraction is in lowest terms if the GCF of the numerator and the denominator is 1.

EXAMPLE

a. Complete $\frac{48}{60} = \frac{?}{240}$.

b. Write $\frac{48}{60}$ in lowest terms.

SOLUTION a. $\frac{48}{60} = \frac{48 \cdot \mathbf{4}}{60 \cdot \mathbf{4}} = \frac{192}{240}$

60 • **4** = 240, so multiply by **4**.

b. $\frac{48}{60} = \frac{48 \div \mathbf{12}}{60 \div \mathbf{12}} = \frac{4}{5}$

The GCF of 48 and 60 is **12**, so divide by **12**.

A ratio is a comparison of two numbers using division. The ratio of *a* and *b*, $b \neq 0$, can be written *a* to *b*, *a* : *b*, or $\frac{a}{b}$. To compare ratios, first write them as fractions. Then compare the fractions.

EXAMPLE

Replace the ? with >, <, or =. 3 : 16 ___?___ 5 : 24

SOLUTION Write 3 : 16 as $\frac{3}{16}$ and 5 : 24 as $\frac{5}{24}$.

Then write the fractions using a common denominator.

$\frac{3}{16} = \frac{3 \cdot 3}{16 \cdot 3} = \frac{9}{\mathbf{48}}$ and $\frac{5}{24} = \frac{5 \cdot 2}{24 \cdot 2} = \frac{10}{\mathbf{48}}$

The LCM of 16 and 24, **48**, is the least common denominator.

Since $\frac{9}{48} < \frac{10}{48}$, 3 : 16 < 5 : 24.

Replace each ? with the number that will make the fractions equivalent.

1. $\frac{2}{7} = \frac{?}{21}$
2. $\frac{14}{15} = \frac{?}{60}$
3. $\frac{12}{20} = \frac{?}{10}$
4. $\frac{15}{45} = \frac{?}{9}$

Write each fraction in lowest terms.

5. $\frac{9}{15}$
6. $\frac{4}{12}$
7. $\frac{18}{20}$
8. $\frac{6}{9}$

Replace each ? with >, <, or =.

9. $\frac{3}{10}$ ___?___ $\frac{9}{30}$
10. 5 : 12 ___?___ 7 : 8
11. 15 to 36 ___?___ 1 to 27

Adding and Subtracting Fractions

To add or subtract fractions, write the fractions using a common denominator. Then add or subtract the numerators of these fractions.

EXAMPLE

Find the sum: $\frac{3}{8} + \frac{2}{5}$

SOLUTION

$$\frac{3}{8} + \frac{2}{5} = \frac{15}{40} + \frac{16}{40}$$

The least common denominator is 40. Write each fraction with a denominator of 40.

$$= \frac{15+16}{40}$$

Add the numerators.

$$= \frac{31}{40}$$

EXAMPLE

Find the difference: $\frac{11}{12} - \frac{2}{3}$

SOLUTION

$$\frac{11}{12} - \frac{2}{3} = \frac{11}{12} - \frac{8}{12}$$

The least common denominator is 12. Write $\frac{2}{3}$ as $\frac{8}{12}$.

$$= \frac{11-8}{12}$$

Subtract the numerators.

$$= \frac{3}{12}$$

Write the answer in lowest terms.

$$= \frac{1}{4}$$

Find each sum or difference. Write each answer in lowest terms.

1. $\frac{1}{3} + \frac{1}{4}$
2. $\frac{3}{8} + \frac{3}{4}$
3. $\frac{15}{16} - \frac{5}{8}$
4. $\frac{2}{7} + \frac{2}{3}$
5. $\frac{5}{8} - \frac{5}{9}$
6. $\frac{10}{11} - \frac{3}{4}$
7. $\frac{13}{20} - \frac{3}{10}$
8. $\frac{4}{15} + \frac{2}{5}$
9. $\frac{1}{6} + \frac{7}{12}$
10. $\frac{13}{18} - \frac{2}{9}$
11. $\frac{4}{7} - \frac{5}{11}$
12. $\frac{2}{7} + \frac{1}{6} + \frac{2}{21}$
13. $\frac{23}{24} - \frac{5}{12} - \frac{1}{8}$
14. $\frac{3}{2} + \frac{9}{5}$
15. $\frac{1}{2} - \frac{1}{6} + \frac{5}{12}$

Multiplying and Dividing Fractions

To multiply two fractions, multiply the numerators and the denominators.

EXAMPLE

Find the product: $\frac{9}{10} \cdot \frac{2}{3}$

SOLUTION $\frac{9}{10} \cdot \frac{2}{3} = \frac{9 \cdot 2}{10 \cdot 3}$ — Multiply the **numerators** and the **denominators**.

$= \frac{18}{30}$

$= \frac{3}{5}$ — Write the answer in lowest terms.

To divide by a fraction, multiply by its reciprocal. Change mixed numbers to fractions before multiplying or dividing.

EXAMPLE

Find the quotient: $1\frac{5}{6} \div 2\frac{1}{3}$

SOLUTION $1\frac{5}{6} \div 2\frac{1}{3} = \frac{11}{6} \div \frac{7}{3}$ — Write each mixed number as a fraction.

$= \frac{11}{6} \cdot \frac{3}{7}$ — Multiply by the **reciprocal** of the second number.

$= \frac{33}{42}$

$= \frac{11}{14}$ — Write the answer in lowest terms.

Find each product. Write each answer in lowest terms.

1. $\frac{4}{5} \cdot \frac{1}{3}$
2. $\frac{1}{14} \cdot \frac{2}{7}$
3. $\frac{1}{3} \cdot \frac{9}{10}$
4. $\frac{7}{12} \cdot \frac{8}{21}$
5. $\frac{3}{8} \cdot 16$
6. $\frac{8}{15} \cdot 1\frac{1}{2}$
7. $1\frac{4}{5} \cdot 1\frac{2}{3}$
8. $18 \cdot \frac{5}{6}$

Find each quotient. Write each answer in lowest terms.

9. $\frac{1}{4} \div \frac{1}{2}$
10. $\frac{3}{10} \div \frac{2}{5}$
11. $\frac{1}{3} \div \frac{1}{8}$
12. $\frac{3}{10} \div \frac{6}{25}$
13. $6 \div \frac{4}{5}$
14. $\frac{3}{10} \div 3$
15. $1\frac{1}{2} \div \frac{1}{4}$
16. $2\frac{2}{9} \div 1\frac{1}{4}$

Writing Fractions, Decimals, and Percents

You can write a fraction as a decimal or as a percent. Percent means "per hundred," so to write a fraction as a percent, start by finding an equivalent fraction with 100 as the denominator.

EXAMPLE

Write $\frac{2}{5}$ as a decimal and as a percent.

SOLUTION

$$\frac{2}{5} = \frac{2 \cdot \mathbf{20}}{5 \cdot \mathbf{20}}$$

Find an equivalent fraction with 100 as the denominator.

$$= \frac{40}{100}$$

$$= 0.40$$

$$= 40\%$$

$$\mathbf{\frac{2}{5} = 0.40 = 40\%}$$

EXAMPLE

Write 72% as a decimal and as a fraction in lowest terms.

SOLUTION

$$72\% = 0.72$$

$$= \frac{72}{100}$$

$$= \frac{18}{25}$$

Write the fraction in lowest terms.

The chart shows some common percent, decimal, and fraction equivalents.

$1\% = 0.01 = \frac{1}{100}$	$33\frac{1}{3}\% = 0.\overline{3} = \frac{1}{3}$	$66\frac{2}{3}\% = 0.\overline{6} = \frac{2}{3}$
$10\% = 0.1 = \frac{1}{10}$	$40\% = 0.4 = \frac{2}{5}$	$75\% = 0.75 = \frac{3}{4}$
$20\% = 0.2 = \frac{1}{5}$	$50\% = 0.5 = \frac{1}{2}$	$80\% = 0.8 = \frac{4}{5}$
$25\% = 0.25 = \frac{1}{4}$	$60\% = 0.6 = \frac{3}{5}$	$100\% = 1$

Write each fraction as a decimal and as a percent.

1. $\frac{19}{20}$
2. $\frac{4}{25}$
3. $\frac{1}{1000}$
4. $\frac{31}{50}$

Write each percent as a decimal and as a fraction in lowest terms.

5. 80%
6. 87.5%
7. 64%
8. 120%

Write each decimal as a percent and as a fraction in lowest terms.

9. 0.48
10. 0.85
11. 0.125
12. 3.5

Using Order of Operations

When you evaluate an expression that contains more than one operation, perform the operations in the order shown below.

1. First do all work inside parentheses.
2. Then evaluate any powers.
3. Then do all multiplications and divisions in order from left to right.
4. Then do all additions and subtractions in order from left to right.

A power is the product when a number or an expression is used as a factor a given number of times. For example, $3 \cdot 3 \cdot 3 \cdot 3 \cdot 3$ is the fifth power of 3 and can be written as 3^5. In 3^5, 3 is the base and 5 is the exponent.

Sometimes multiplication is written with parentheses. For example, $3(4) = 3 \cdot 4$.

EXAMPLE

Find each answer.

a. $2(11) + 20 \div (7 - 5)$

b. $5 \cdot 2^3 - 6$

SOLUTION

a. $2(11) + 20 \div (7 - 5) = 2(11) + 20 \div 2$ — Do work inside parentheses first.

$= 22 + 10$ — Do multiplication and division.

$= 32$ — Add.

b. $5 \cdot \mathbf{2^3} - 6 = 5 \cdot \mathbf{8} - 6$ — Evaluate the power first: $\mathbf{2^3 = 2 \cdot 2 \cdot 2 = 8}$

$= 40 - 6$ — Multiply.

$= 34$ — Subtract.

Find each answer.

1. $4^2 - 1$
2. $6(8 - 5)$
3. $7 \cdot 2^3$
4. $5 \cdot 6 - 17$
5. $3 \cdot 10 \div 6$
6. $(9 \div 3)^2$
7. $9 \div 3^2$
8. $15 + 42 \div 7 - 17$
9. $15 + 2(11 - 4)$
10. $4^2 + 5(2^3 - 3)$
11. $2 \cdot 3^2 - 4(7 - 3)$
12. $3(6 + 2) \div 4(9 - 7)$

Comparing Integers

Integers are the numbers ... –3, –2, –1, 0, 1, 2, 3, ... To compare two integers, use a number line. The greater number is to the right of the lesser number on a horizontal number line.

EXAMPLE

Graph each pair of integers on a number line. Then replace each ? with > or <.

a. –3 _?_ 2 **b. 2 _?_ –3**

SOLUTION

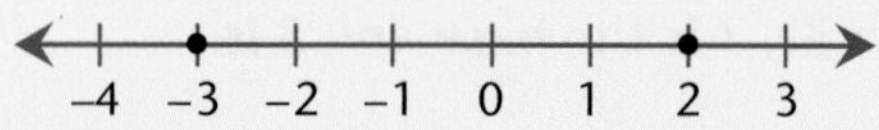

The greater number is always to the right of the lesser number.

Since 2 is to the right of –3, 2 is the greater number and –3 is the lesser number.

a. –3 < 2 **b.** 2 > –3

EXAMPLE

Use a number line to write the integers 3, 5, and –2 in order from least to greatest.

SOLUTION Graph each number on a number line.

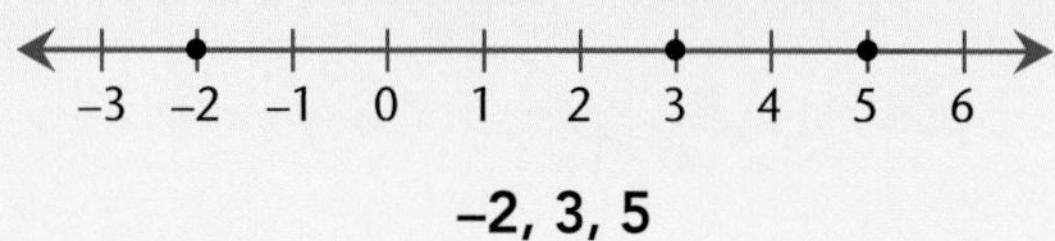

–2, 3, 5

Replace each ? with > or <.

1. 4 _?_ –6
2. –3 _?_ –1
3. –5 _?_ 0
4. –2 _?_ 4
5. 0 _?_ –7
6. –1 _?_ –4
7. 5 _?_ 1
8. –8 _?_ 8
9. –4 _?_ 2

Use a number line to write each group of integers in order from least to greatest.

10. –5, 1, –4
11. 0, –3, 2
12. –2, –4, –1
13. 3, 4, –5
14. –3, 0, –6
15. 2, –2, 6
16. 1, –1, 0, –2
17. 0, –4, –7, –2
18. 5, –3, 2, –6

Locating Points in a Coordinate Plane

You can use an ordered pair to describe the location of a point in a coordinate plane. The first number in an ordered pair is the horizontal coordinate and the second number is the vertical coordinate.

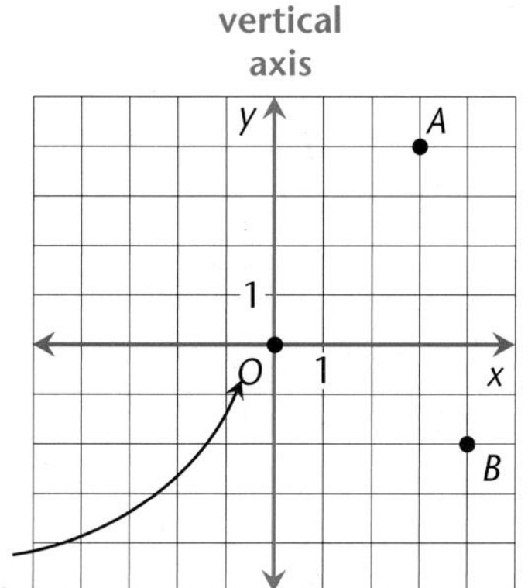

The coordinates of point *A* are (3, 4).

The coordinates of point *B* are (4, –2).

The origin is at (0, 0).

EXAMPLE

Graph each point.

a. **(–5, –1)**

b. **(0, 3)**

SOLUTION

a. From the origin, move **5 units left** and **1 unit down**.

b. From the origin, move 3 units up.

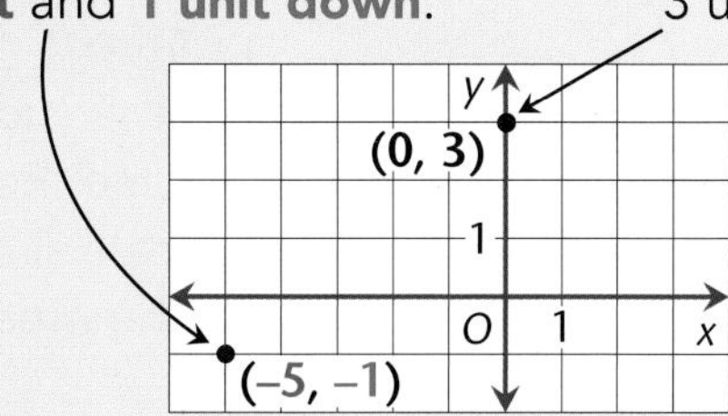

Use the diagram at the right. Give the coordinates of each point.

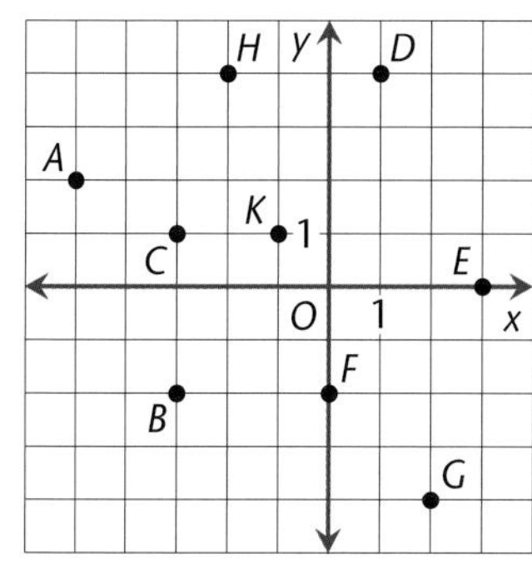

1. *A*
2. *B*
3. *C*
4. *D*
5. *E*
6. *F*
7. *G*
8. *H*
9. *K*

Graph each point in a coordinate plane.

10. (2, 3)
11. (4, –3)
12. (0, –5)
13. (–1, –2)
14. (–5, 2)
15. (–4, 0)
16. (1, –5)
17. (–1, 1)
18. (0, 0)

Measuring Angles

An angle is formed by two rays, called *sides* of the angle, with the same endpoint, called the *vertex*. Angles are measured in degrees. You use a protractor to measure an angle.

An angle whose measure is between 0° and 90° is an acute angle.	**An angle whose measure is 90° is a right angle.**
An angle whose measure is between 90° and 180° is an obtuse angle.	**An angle whose measure is 180° is a straight angle.**

EXAMPLE

Use a protractor to measure ∠*S*.

SOLUTION

Step 1 Place the center mark of the protractor on the vertex.

Step 2 Place the 0° mark on one side of the angle.

Step 3 Read the number where the other side of the angle crosses the scale. Read the number on the bottom scale since you used its 0° mark.
The measure of ∠*S* is 65°.

Use a protractor to measure each angle. Then tell whether the angle is *acute, right, obtuse,* or *straight*.

1. 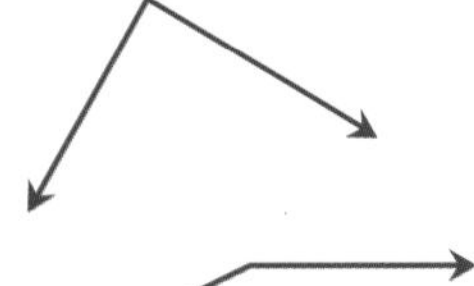

2. 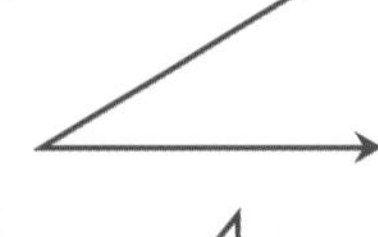

3. 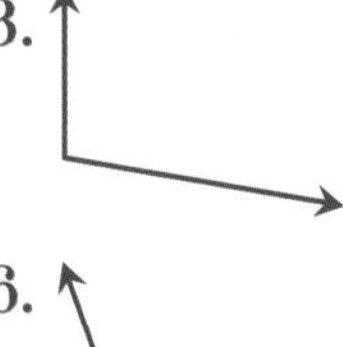

4. 

5. 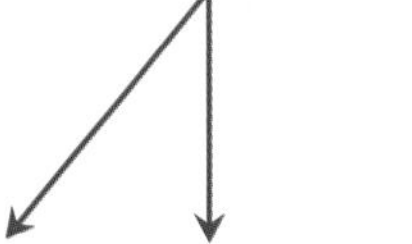

6. 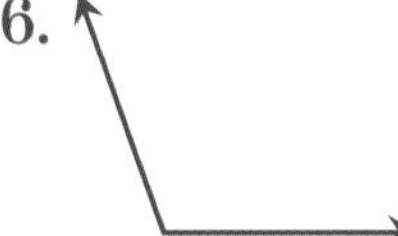

Classifying Triangles

To classify a triangle, you can use the measures of its angles or the relationship between the lengths of its sides. The sum of the measures of the angles of a triangle is 180°.

An acute triangle has three acute angles. 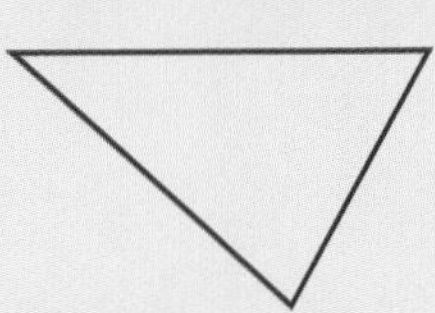	**A right triangle has one right angle.** 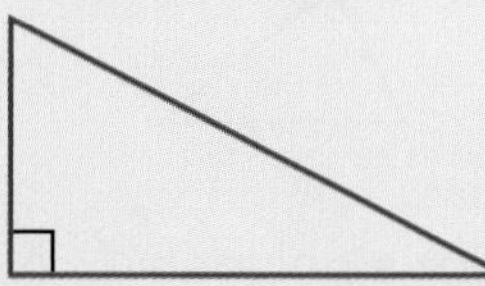	**An obtuse triangle has one obtuse angle.** 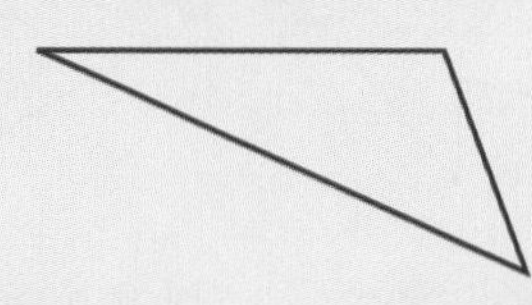
A scalene triangle has no sides of equal length. 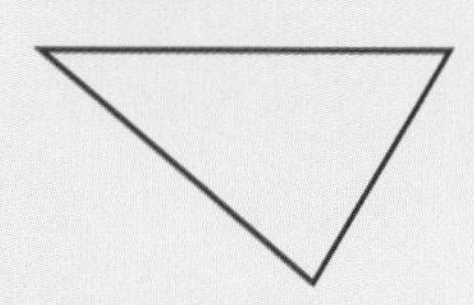	**An isosceles triangle has at least two sides of equal length.** 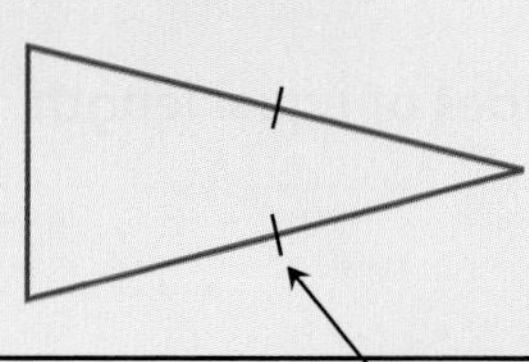	**An equilateral triangle has three sides of equal length.** 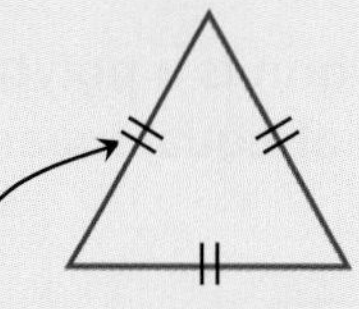

Sides marked alike are equal in length.

Tell whether each triangle is *acute, right,* or *obtuse.*

1. 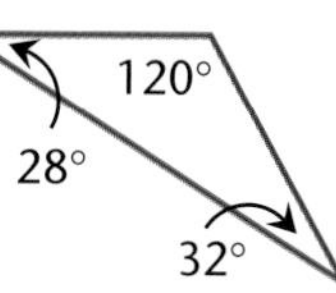

2. 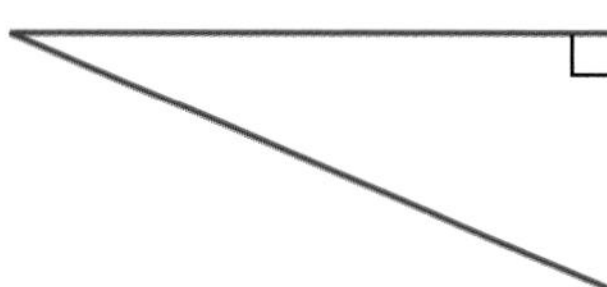

3. 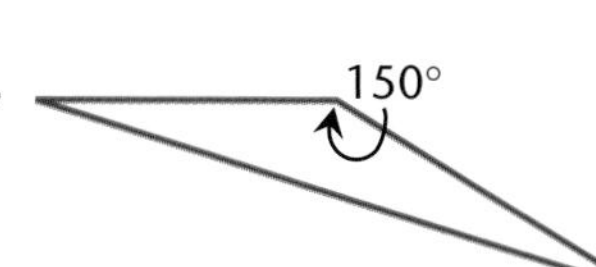

4. 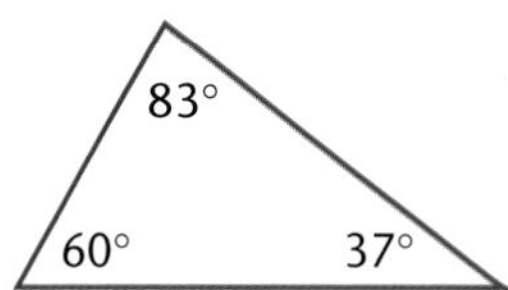

Tell whether each triangle is *scalene, isosceles,* or *equilateral.*

5. 25 cm 14 cm 25 cm

6. 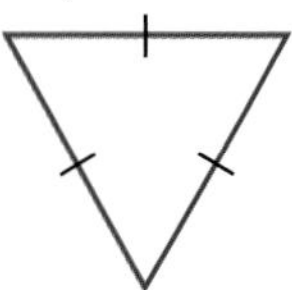

7. 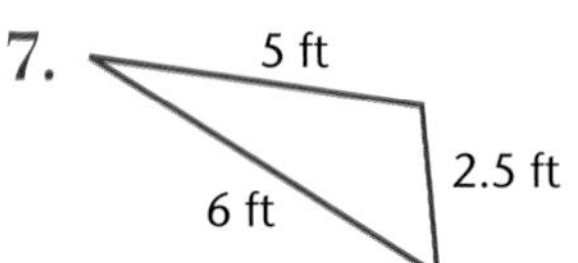

8. 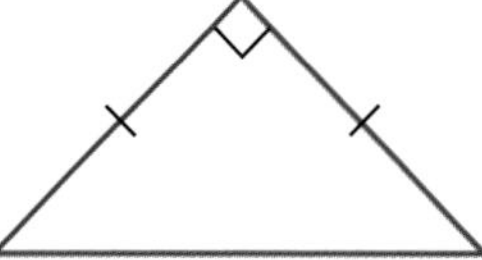

Identifying Polygons

A polygon is a closed plane figure formed by three or more segments that do not cross each other.

A polygon

Not a polygon (not closed)

Not a polygon (crosses itself)

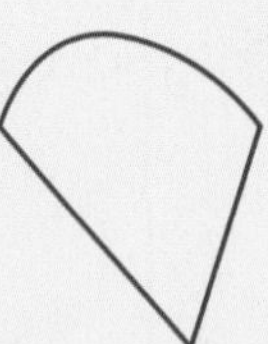

Not a polygon (not formed by segments)

A regular polygon is a polygon with all sides of equal length and all angles of equal measure.

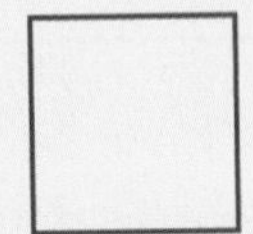

Regular polygon

Not a regular polygon (Angles are of equal measure but sides are not of equal length.)

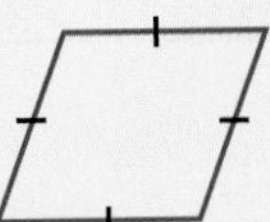

Not a regular polygon (Sides are of equal length, but angles are not of equal measure.)

Which of these figures are polygons? Which appear to be regular polygons? Explain your thinking.

1. 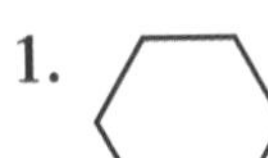
2. 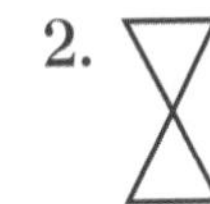
3. 
4. 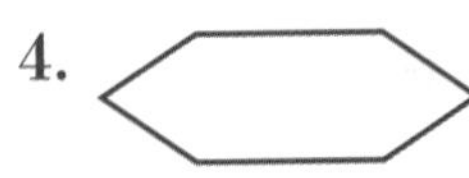
5. 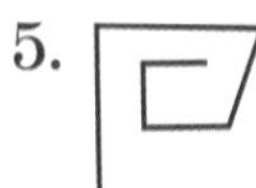
6. 
7. 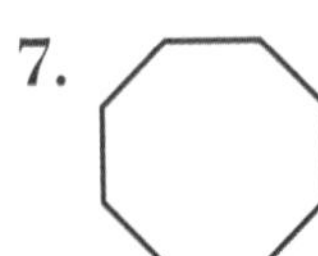
8. 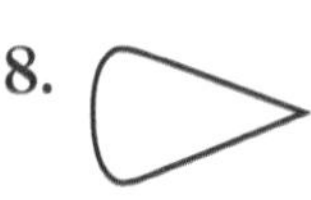

Using Formulas from Geometry

To find the perimeter, area, or volume of a figure, use the Table of Formulas on page 602.

EXAMPLE

Find the perimeter and the area of the rectangle.

SOLUTION

$P = 2l + 2w$ ← Use the formula for the perimeter of a rectangle.
$= 2 \cdot \mathbf{11} + 2 \cdot \mathbf{5}$ ← Substitute **11** for *l* and **5** for *w*.
$= 32$ ← Evaluate.

$A = lw$ ← Use the formula for the area of a rectangle.
$= \mathbf{11} \cdot \mathbf{5}$ ← Substitute **11** for *l* and **5** for *w*.
$= 55$ ← Evaluate.

The perimeter is 32 cm. The area is 55 cm^2.

EXAMPLE

Find the volume of the right rectangular prism.

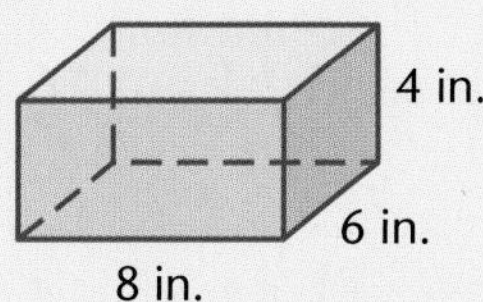

SOLUTION

$V = Bh$ ← Use the formula for the volume of a rectangular prism.
$= \mathbf{48} \cdot \mathbf{4}$ ← *B* stands for the area of the base, which is **8** • **6** = **48**. Substitute **48** for *B* and **4** for *h*.
$= 192$ ← Evaluate.

The volume is 192 in.^{3}.

Find the perimeter and the area of each figure.

1. triangle

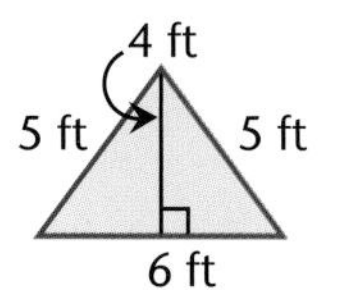

2. parallelogram

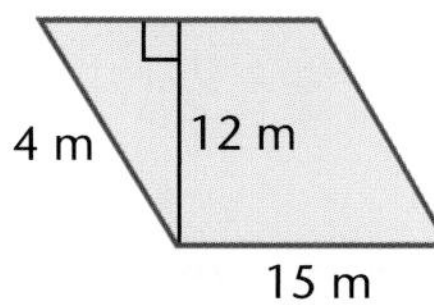

3. trapezoid

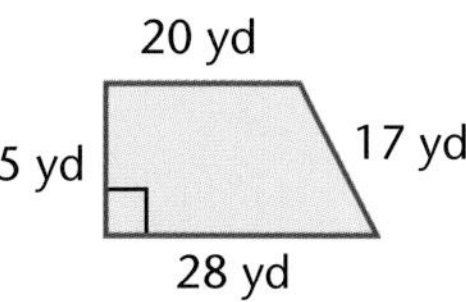

Find the volume of each right rectangular prism.

4. 8 cm, 6 cm, 10 cm

5.

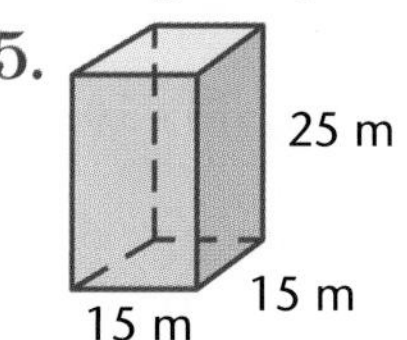

6.

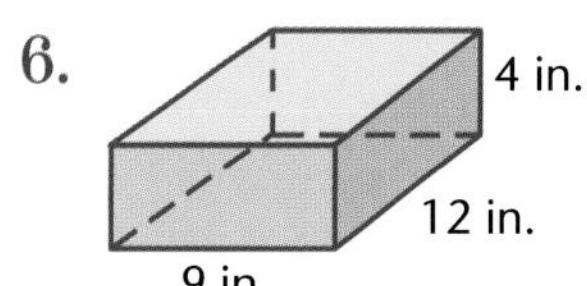

Finding the Mean, Median, Mode, and Range

You can use different numbers to describe a data set.

Mean: The sum of the data items, divided by the number of data items.

Median: The middle number or the average of the two middle numbers when the data items are listed in order.

Mode: The most frequently occurring item, or items, in a data set. There may be more than one mode or no mode.

Range: The difference between the largest and the smallest data items.

EXAMPLE

Find the mean, the median, the mode, and the range of the data set.

14, 18, 19, 16, 14, 20, 12, 18, 14

SOLUTION $\text{Mean} = \frac{14 + 18 + 19 + 16 + 14 + 20 + 12 + 18 + 14}{9} \approx 16.1$

There are **9** data items.

The mean is about 16.1.

Median: 12 14 14 14 **16** 18 18 19 20

List the numbers in order.

Find the **middle** number.

The median is 16.

Mode: 14 appears more often than any other number.

The mode is 14.

Range: The smallest number is 12. The largest number is 20.
Subtract to find the range: 20 – 12 = 8.

The range is 8.

Find the mean, the median, the mode, and the range of each data set.

1. 29, 38, 32, 37, 29
2. 18, 14, 15, 16, 20, 17
3. 3.6, 2.5, 4.2, 3.3, 5.4
4. 34, 34, 34, 34, 34, 34, 34
5. 4, 1, 1, 0, 2, 3, 5, 2
6. 145, 95, 90, 120, 105, 85, 95

Choosing a Data Display

Use a **bar graph** to compare numbers of data items that are grouped into categories.

Votes for School Color

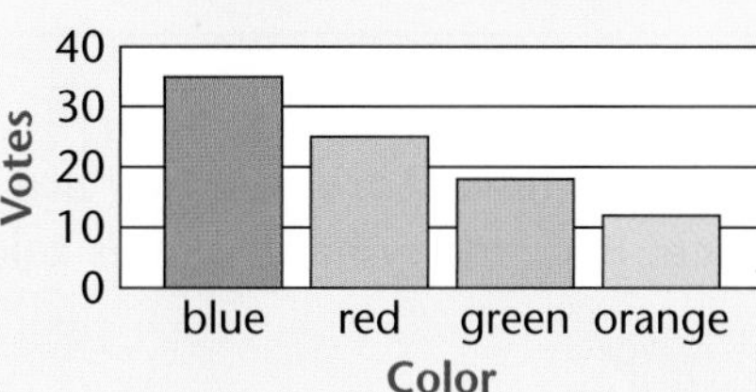

Use a **histogram** to compare numbers of data items that are grouped into numerical intervals.

Ages of Actors in a Play

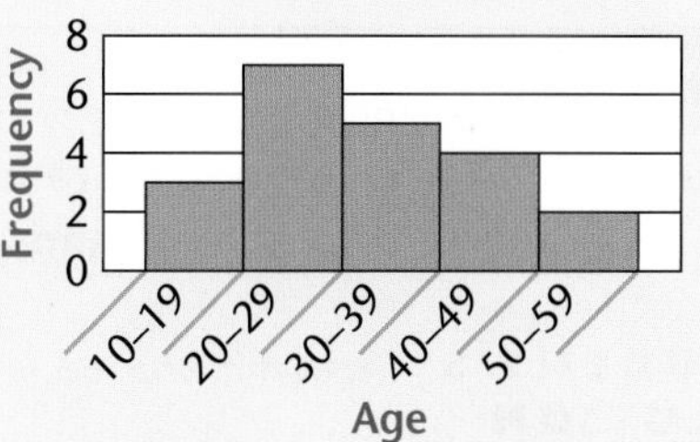

Use a **box-and-whisker plot** to show the median, the quartiles, and the extremes of a data set.

Ages of Actors in a Play

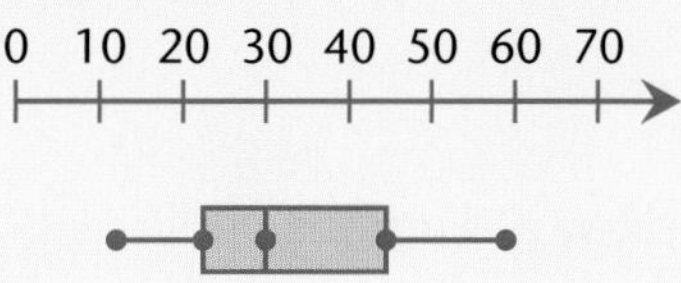

Use a **stem-and-leaf plot** to show each value in a data set and to group the values into intervals.

Ages of Actors in a Play

Stem	Leaves
1	2 5 8
2	1 3 4 4 7 9
3	0 2 5 8 9
4	3 6 6 7
5	5 9

4 | 3 means 43 years old.

Use a **scatter plot** to show a relationship between two sets of data.

Corn Production

Millions of acres harvested: 0, 60, 65, 70, 75

Millions of acres planted: 0, 70, 74, 78, 82

Use a **line graph** to show how data values change over time.

Corn Production

Millions of acres harvested: 0, 60, 65, 70, 75

Year: 1990, 1992, 1994, 1996

Use a **circle graph** to show the division of a whole into parts.

Votes for School Color

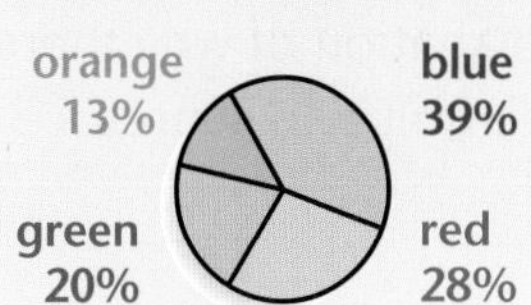

Using Self-Assessment Scales

One way to improve your problem solving skills is to use the Student Self-Assessment Scales on page 599. Use whichever scales apply to a problem you have solved to assess your work in mathematics.

EXAMPLE

PROBLEM **Five people are hired to work at a new store. As they are introduced they shake hands exactly once. How many handshakes take place?**

A STUDENT'S SOLUTION

Person A shakes 4 hands.

Person B shakes 3 more hands.

Person C shakes 2 more hands.

Person D shakes 1 more hand.

Person E has no more hands to shake.

There were ten total handshakes.

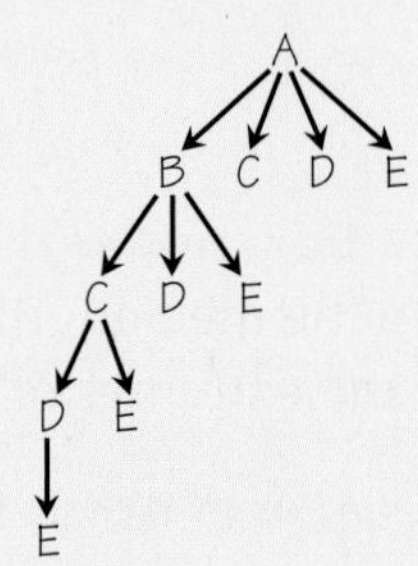

The problem was understood, the plan was to draw a diagram, a diagram was drawn, and the problem was solved. However, the solution was not verified. This solution scores a 4 on the Problem Solving Scale.

Mathematical vocabulary and symbols do not play a large role in this problem. The Mathematical Language Scale does not apply.

The representation chosen was helpful. The diagram shows why the answer is correct. This solution scores a 5 on the Representations Scale.

The problem was solved, but no patterns or generalizations were discussed. This solution scores a 1 on the Connections Scale.

The presentation of the problem shows there are 10 handshakes. A further explanation of why there are not more solutions would be helpful. This solution scores a 3 on the Presentation Scale.

Extended Exploration activities to which these scales can be applied are found on pages 71, 121, 191, 257, 362, 419, 481, and 531.

Student Self-Assessment Scales

Student Resource

If your score is in the shaded area, explain why on the back of this sheet and stop.

☆ *The star indicates that you excelled in some way.*

Problem Solving

1 — I did not understand the problem well enough to get started or I did not show any work.

2

3 — I understood the problem well enough to make a plan and to work toward a solution.

4

5 — I made a plan, I used it to solve the problem, and I verified my solution.

Mathematical Language

1 — I did not use any mathematical vocabulary or symbols, or I did not use them correctly, or my use was not appropriate.

2

3 — I used appropriate mathematical language, but the way it was used was not always correct or other terms and symbols were needed.

4

5 — I used mathematical language that was correct and appropriate to make my meaning clear.

Representations

1 — I did not use any representations such as equations, tables, graphs, or diagrams to help solve the problem or explain my solution.

2

3 — I made appropriate representations to help solve the problem or help me explain my solution, but they were not always correct or other representations were needed.

4

5 — I used appropriate and correct representations to solve the problem or explain my solution.

Connections

1 — I attempted or solved the problem and then stopped.

2

3 — I found patterns and used them to extend the solution to other cases, or I recognized that this problem relates to other problems, mathematical ideas, or applications.

4

5 — I extended the ideas in the solution to the general case, or I showed how this problem relates to other problems, mathematical ideas, or applications.

Presentation

1 — The presentation of my solution and reasoning is unclear to others.

2

3 — The presentation of my solution and reasoning is clear in most places, but others may have trouble understanding parts of it.

4

5 — The presentation of my solution and reasoning is clear and can be understood by others.

TABLE OF SYMBOLS

SYMBOL		Page
$=$	equals	**3**
$\div$	divided by	**4**
%	percent	**6**
$\times$	times	**6**
$\approx$	is approximately equal to	**9**
$\cdot$	times	**9**
$>$	is greater than	**30**
$<$	is less than	**30**
-6	negative 6	**30**
$+$	plus	**34**
$\frac{1}{4}$	1 divided by 4	**34**
$^\circ$	degrees	**35**
( )	parentheses—a grouping symbol	**40**
y^2	y used as a factor 2 times	**40**
$-$	minus	**43**
(x, y)	ordered pair of numbers	**51**
$-x$	the opposite of x	**80**
$\lvert x \rvert$	the absolute value of x	**80**
A'	A prime—point A goes to point A' after a transformation	**81**
$\sqrt{x}$	positive, or principal, square root of x	**159**
π	pi, a number approximately equal to 3.14	**176**
$\angle A$	angle A	**193**
$m\angle A$	the measure of angle A	**193**

SYMBOL		Page
$\overline{AB}$	segment AB	**193**
AB	length of segment AB	**193**
$\sim$	is similar to	**194**
	equal angle measures	**194**
$\triangle ABC$	triangle ABC	**194**
	right angle	**194**
	equal side lengths	**196**
2 : 1	ratio of 2 to 1	**203**
$\neq$	is not equal to	**208**
...	and so on	**273**
$0.\overline{63}$	repeating bar—the digits 6 and 3 repeat	**273**
5!	5 factorial	**289**
$\cong$	is congruent to	**321**
[ ]	brackets—a grouping symbol	**350**
	parallel sides	**367**
3^{-4}	$\frac{1}{3^4}$	**462**
$\sqrt[3]{x}$	cube root of x	**475**
$\sqrt[4]{x}$	fourth root of x	**476**
$\geq$	is greater than or equal to	**484**
$\leq$	is less than or equal to	**484**
$P(A)$	the probability of event A	**556**
$\tan A$	tangent of angle A	**564**
$\sin A$	sine of angle A	**566**
$\cos A$	cosine of angle A	**566**

TABLE OF MEASURES

Time

60 seconds (sec)	=	1 minute (min)
60 minutes	=	1 hour (hr)
24 hours	=	1 day
7 days	=	1 week
4 weeks (approx.)	=	1 month
365 days 52 weeks (approx.) 12 months	=	1 year
10 years	=	1 decade
100 years	=	1 century

METRIC

Length

10 millimeters (mm)	=	1 centimeter (cm)
100 cm 1000 mm	=	1 meter (m)
1000 m	=	1 kilometer (km)

Area

100 square millimeters (mm^2)	=	1 square centimeter (cm^2)
10,000 cm^2	=	1 square meter (m^2)
10,000 m^2	=	1 hectare (ha)

Volume

1000 cubic millimeters (mm^3)	=	1 cubic centimeter (cm^3)
1,000,000 cm^3	=	1 cubic meter (m^3)

Liquid Capacity

1000 milliliters (mL)	=	1 liter (L)
1000 L	=	1 kiloliter (kL)

Mass

1000 milligrams (mg)	=	1 gram (g)
1000 g	=	1 kilogram (kg)
1000 kg	=	1 metric ton (t)

Temperature — **Degrees Celsius (°C)**

0°C	=	freezing point of water
37°C	=	normal body temperature
100°C	=	boiling point of water

UNITED STATES CUSTOMARY

Length

12 inches (in.)	=	1 foot (ft)
36 in. 3 ft	=	1 yard (yd)
5280 ft 1760 yd	=	1 mile (mi)

Area

144 square inches ($in.^2$)	=	1 square foot (ft^2)
9 ft^2	=	1 square yard (yd^2)
43,560 ft^2 4840 yd^2	=	1 acre (A)

Volume

1728 cubic inches ($in.^3$)	=	1 cubic foot (ft^3)
27 ft^3	=	1 cubic yard (yd^3)

Liquid Capacity

8 fluid ounces (fl oz)	=	1 cup (c)
2 c	=	1 pint (pt)
2 pt	=	1 quart (qt)
4 qt	=	1 gallon (gal)

Weight

16 ounces (oz)	=	1 pound (lb)
2000 lb	=	1 ton (t)

Temperature — **Degrees Fahrenheit (°F)**

32°F	=	freezing point of water
98.6°F	=	normal body temperature
212°F	=	boiling point of water

TABLE OF FORMULAS

RECTANGLE

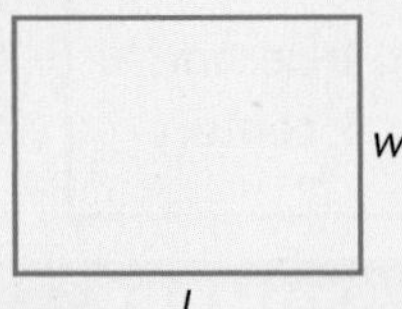

Area = lw

Perimeter = $2l + 2w$

PARALLELOGRAM

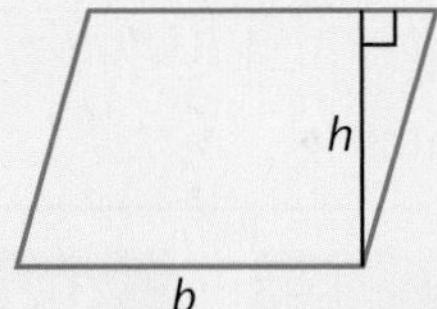

Area = bh

TRIANGLE

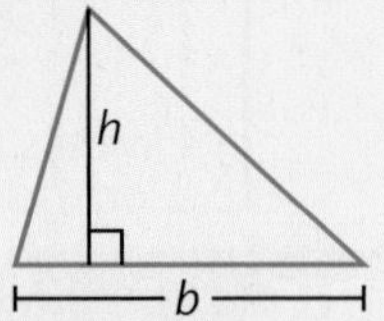

Area = $\frac{1}{2}bh$

CIRCLE

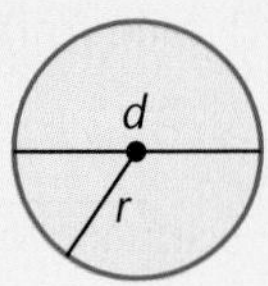

Circumference = πd, or $2\pi r$

Area = πr^2

TRAPEZOID

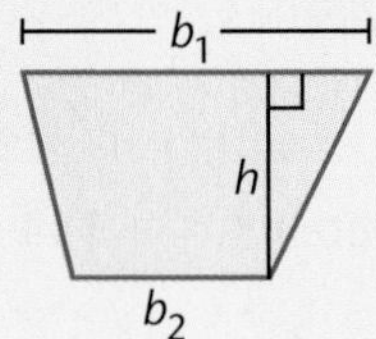

Area = $\frac{1}{2}(b_1 + b_2)h$

PRISM

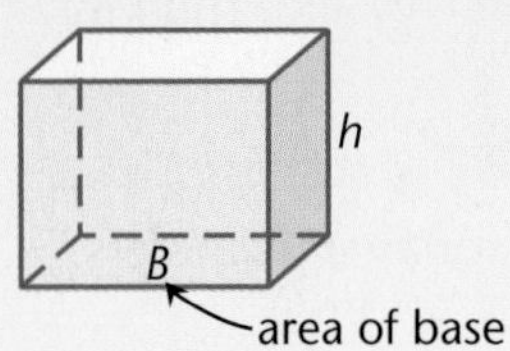

Surface Area =
sum of areas of faces

CYLINDER

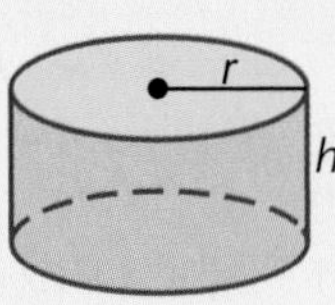

Volume = $\pi r^2 h$

Surface Area = $2\pi r^2 + 2\pi rh$

PYRAMID

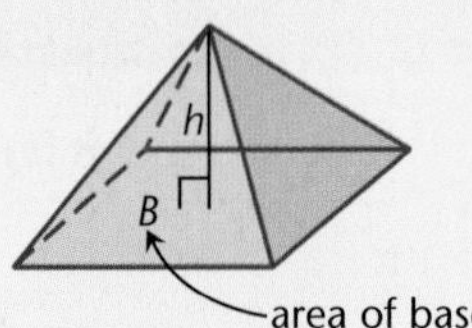

Volume = $\frac{1}{3}Bh$

Surface Area =
sum of areas of faces

CONE

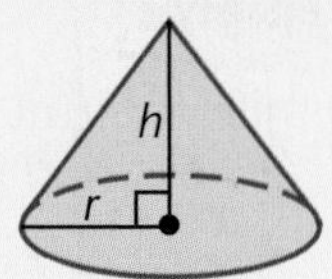

Volume = $\frac{1}{3}\pi r^2 h$

POWERS

$b^0 = 1$ $\qquad b^{-n} = \frac{1}{b^n}$

$b^m \cdot b^n = b^{m+n}$

$\frac{b^m}{b^n} = b^{m-n}$

DISTANCE

Distance = rate • time

$d = rt$

PYTHAGOREAN THEOREM

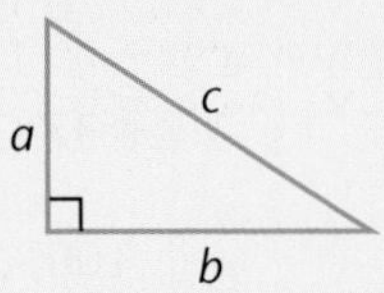

$a^2 + b^2 = c^2$

GLOSSARY

A

absolute value (p. 80) A number's distance from 0 on a number line.

acute angle (p. 592) An angle whose measure is greater than 0° but less than 90°.

acute triangle (p. 593) A triangle that has three acute angles.

algorithm (p. 434) A step-by-step set of instructions you can follow to accomplish a goal.

alternate exterior angles (p. 366) When two lines are cut by a transversal, these angles are outside of the two lines and are on opposite sides of the transversal.

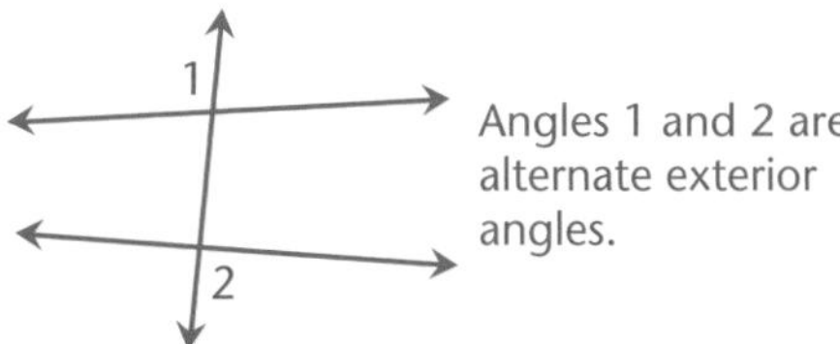

alternate interior angles (p. 366) When two lines are cut by a transversal, these angles are between the two lines and are on opposite sides of the transversal.

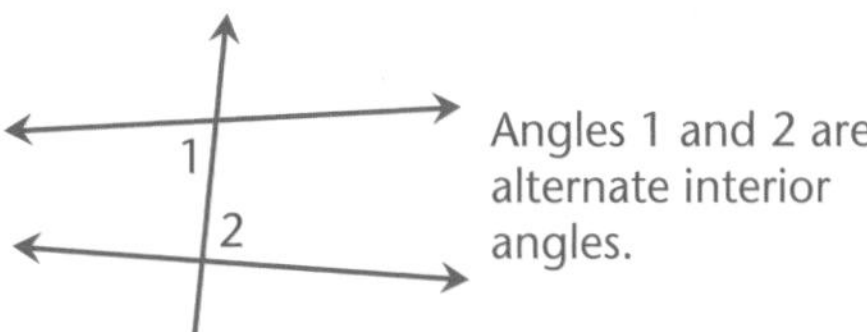

angle (p. 592) A figure formed by two rays, called sides, with the same endpoint, called the vertex.

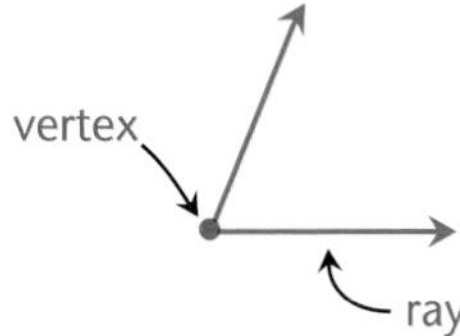

angle bisector (p. 327) A ray that divides an angle into two congruent angles is an angle bisector of the angle.

arc (p. 322) A part of a circle.

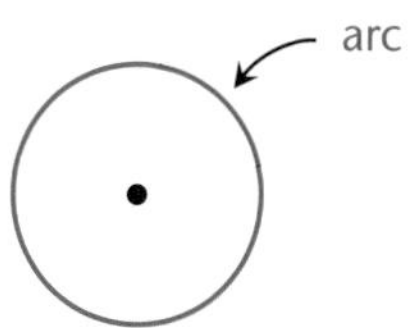

area (p. 232) The area of a plane figure is the number of square units of surface area the figure covers.

arithmetic sequence (p. 520) A sequence in which each term after the first is found by adding a constant to the previous term.

B

base (p. 589) *See* exponent.

base of a space figure (pp. 234, 325) *See* prism, cylinder, pyramid, *and* cone.

biased question (p. 124) A question that produces responses that do not accurately reflect the opinions of the people surveyed.

binomial (p. 496) A polynomial with exactly two terms.

box-and-whisker plot (p. 18) A plot that shows how data are distributed by dividing the data into 4 groups. The *box* contains about the middle 50% of the data values. The two *whiskers* each contain about 25% of the data values.

Average January Temperature in 50 U.S. Cities

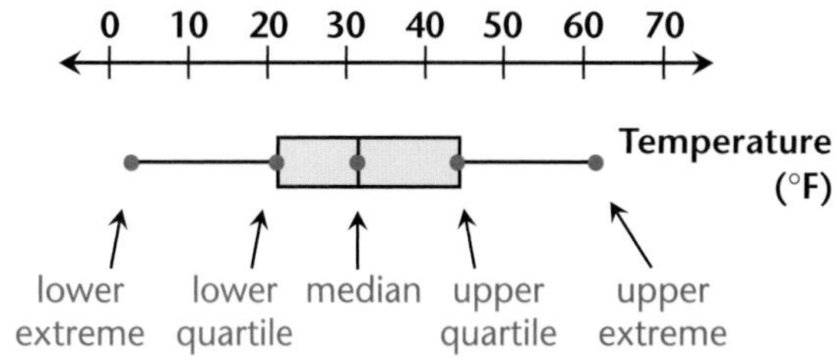

C

center (p. 197) *See* circle.

certain event (p. 110) An event that is sure to occur. It has a probability of 1.

chord (p. 196) A segment that has both endpoints on a given circle. *See also* circle.

circle (p. 197) The set of all points in a plane that are a given distance from a point called the center of the circle.

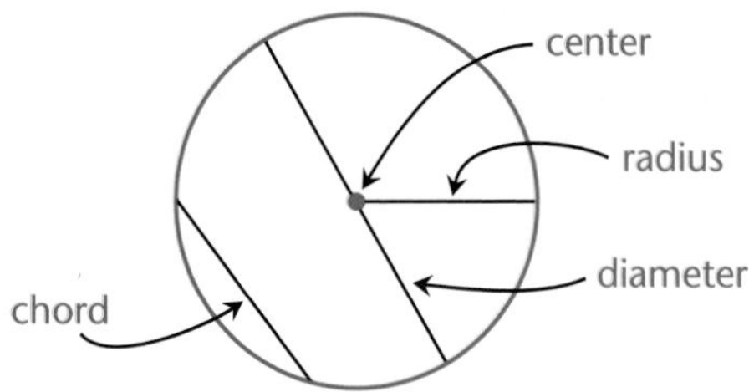

circle graph (p. 5) A graph that shows the division of a whole into parts, each represented by a sector.

circumference (p. 231) The distance around a circle.

coefficient (p. 40) The numerical factor of a term.

combination (p. 289) A selection of items in which order is not important.

complement (p. 366) One angle is the complement of a second angle if the two angles are complementary angles.

complementary angles (p. 366) Two angles whose measures have a sum of 90°.

complementary events (p. 557) Two events where one or the other must occur but they cannot both occur.

concave (p. 534) A polygon that is not convex is concave. *See also* polygon.

cone (p. 354) A space figure with one curved base and a vertex.

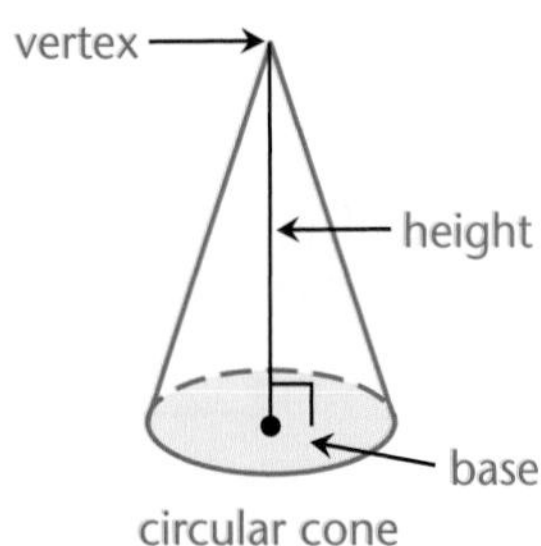

circular cone

congruent (p. 321) Having the same shape and size.

consecutive angles (p. 545) Angles in a quadrilateral whose vertices are the endpoints of the same side.

constant (p. 33) A quantity that does not change.

convex (p. 534) A polygon is convex when all of its diagonals lie in the interior of the polygon. *See also* polygon.

coordinate grid or plane (p. 591) A grid with a horizontal axis and a vertical axis that intersect at a point called the *origin* with coordinates (0, 0). Each point on the grid is identified by an ordered pair of coordinates that give the point's location left or right of the vertical axis and up or down from the horizontal axis.

corresponding angles (p. 362) When two lines are cut by a transversal, these angles are in the same position with respect to the two lines and the transversal.

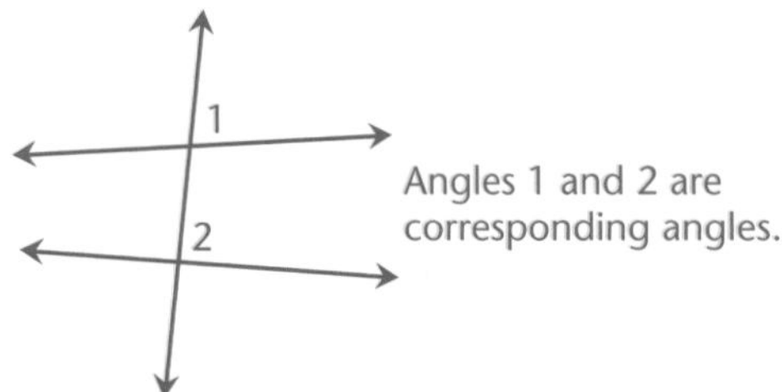

corresponding parts (p. 193) When two figures are similar, for each angle or side on one figure there is a similar angle or side on the other figure. The corresponding angles have the same measure. The corresponding sides are in proportion.

cosine (p. 566) In a right triangle, the cosine of an acute angle A is the ratio of the length of the leg adjacent to angle A to the length of the hypotenuse; $\cos A = \frac{\text{adjacent}}{\text{hypotenuse}}$. *See also* tangent.

counting principle (p. 286) The total number of ways a sequence of decisions can be made is the product of the number of choices for each decision.

cross products (p. 128) Equal products formed from a pair of equivalent ratios by multiplying the numerator of each fraction by the denominator of the other fraction.

cube (p. 169) A prism with six square faces.

cube root (p. 475) If $A = s^3$, then s is a cube root of A. Cube roots can be written with the symbol $\sqrt[3]{}$.

cylinder (p. 235) A space figure that has a curved surface and two parallel, congruent bases.

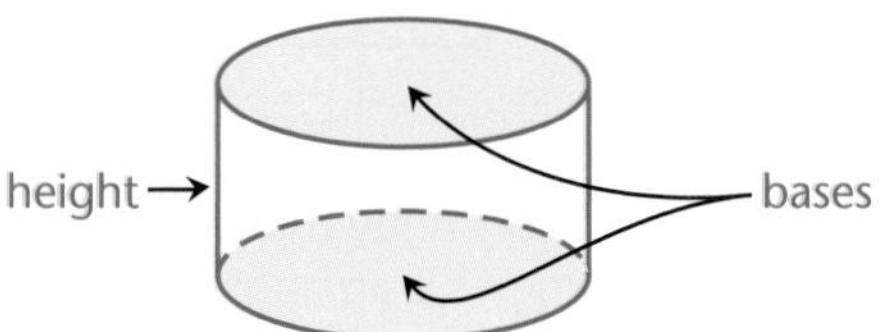

D

decimal notation (p. 205) A number is in decimal notation when it is written as a decimal, without using any powers. *See also* scientific notation.

dependent events (p. 110) Events for which the probability of one is affected by whether or not the other event occurs.

diameter (p. 197) A segment whose endpoints are on a given circle and that passes through the center of the circle. The length of a diameter is called *the* diameter. *See also* circle.

distributive property (pp. 40, 411) For all numbers a, b, and c: $a(b + c) = ab + ac$ and $ab + ac = a(b + c)$.

E

edge of a space figure (p. 325) A segment where two faces of a space figure meet. *See also* prism *and* pyramid.

equally likely (p. 106) Two outcomes that have the same chance of happening are equally likely.

equation (p. 33) A mathematical sentence stating that two quantities or expressions are equal.

equilateral triangle (p. 593) A triangle that has three sides of equal length.

equivalent rates (p. 4) Equivalent rates are equal rates that may be expressed using different units. For example $\frac{8 \text{ oz}}{25¢}$ and $\frac{2 \text{ lb}}{\$1}$ are equivalent rates.

evaluate (p. 37) To find the value of an expression for given values of the variables.

event (p. 106) A set of outcomes of an experiment.

experiment (p. 106) An activity whose results can be observed and recorded.

experimental probability (p. 107) A probability determined by repeating an experiment a number of times and observing the results. It is the ratio of the number of times an event occurs to the number of times the experiment is done.

exponent (p. 589) A raised number that tells the power of the base.

$$2^3 = 2 \cdot 2 \cdot 2 = 8$$

exponent; base; 8 is the 3rd power of 2.

exponential equation (p. 425) An equation of the form $y = a \cdot b^x$, where a is the starting amount, b is the growth factor, and y is the amount after x units of time.

F

face of a space figure (pp. 234, 325) A flat surface of a space figure. *See also* prism *and* pyramid.

factor a polynomial (p. 502) Find the factors whose product is the polynomial.

fair game (p. 119) A game in which every player has an equal chance of winning.

Fibonacci sequence (p. 523) The sequence 1, 1, 2, 3, 5, 8, 13, ... Each term after the second is the sum of the two previous terms.

fitted line (p. 55) A line drawn on a scatter plot to show a pattern in the data. *See also* scatter plot.

flat view (p. 314) A view of an object straight on from any side.

frequency (p. 5) The number of items in a category or numerical interval.

frequency table (p. 5) A table that shows the frequency of items in each category or numerical interval.

function (p. 397) A relationship that pairs each input value with exactly one output value.

G

geometric probability (p. 556) A probability based on length, area, or volume.

geometric sequence (p. 520) A sequence in which each term after the first is found by multiplying the previous term by a nonzero constant.

greatest common factor (GCF) (p. 584) The greatest number that is a factor of each of two or more numbers.

growth factor (p. 425) *See* exponential equation.

H

half-life (p. 204) The amount of time it takes for a radioactive substance to reduce to half of its original amount.

histogram (p. 7) A graph that shows the frequencies of numerical values that fall within intervals of equal width.

hypotenuse (p. 340) In a right triangle, the side opposite the right angle. *See also* right triangle.

I

image (p. 81) The figure that results from a transformation.

impossible event (p. 110) An event that cannot occur. It has a probability of 0.

included angle (p. 328) An angle of a polygon whose vertex is the shared point of two sides of the polygon.

independent events (p. 110) Events for which the probability of one is not affected by whether or not the other event occurs.

inequality (p. 483) A mathematical sentence that compares two quantities using the symbols $>$, $<$, $\geq$, or $\leq$.

integer (pp. 79, 590) Any number in the set of numbers ... –3, –2, –1, 0, 1, 2, 3, ...

interval (p. 51) The step between grid lines on a scale.

inverse operations (p. 36) Operations that undo each other, like addition and subtraction or multiplication and division.

irrational number (p. 471) A number that cannot be written as the quotient of two integers.

isosceles triangle (p. 593) A triangle that has at least two sides of equal length.

K

kite (p. 544) A quadrilateral with two pairs of consecutive congruent sides, but opposite sides are not congruent.

L

leaf (p. 16) *See* stem-and-leaf plot.

least common denominator (p. 585) The least common multiple of the denominators of two or more fractions.

least common multiple (LCM) (p. 584) The least number that is a multiple of each of two or more numbers.

legs (p. 340) In a right triangle, the sides adjacent to the right angle. *See also* right triangle.

like terms (p. 40) Terms of an expression that have identical variable parts.

line symmetry (p. 540) When one half of a figure is the mirror image of the other half, the figure has line symmetry.

line of symmetry (p. 443) A line that divides a figure into two parts that are reflections of each other. *See also* parabola.

linear (p. 174) When the graph of an equation is a straight line, the equation and its graph are linear.

linear equation (pp. 84, 408) An equation whose graph is a straight line.

lower extreme (p. 18) The least data value in a data set. *See also* box-and-whisker plot.

lower quartile (p. 18) The median of the data in the lower half of a data set. *See also* box-and-whisker plot.

lowest terms (p. 585) A fraction is in lowest terms when the greatest common factor of the numerator and the denominator is 1.

M

mean (p. 596) The sum of the data in a numerical data set divided by the number of data items.

median (p. 596) When the data in a data set are ordered in numerical order, the median is the middle number or the mean of the two middle numbers.

midpoint (p. 547) The point of a segment that divides it into two congruent segments.

minimum rotational symmetry (p. 535) The smallest number of degrees a figure can be rotated and fit exactly on itself. *See also* rotational symmetry.

mode (p. 596) The most frequently occurring item, or items, in a data set. A data set can have no mode.

monomial (p. 496) A number or a variable or a product of a number and one or more variables.

N

negative correlation (p. 54) The relationship between two variables when one variable tends to decrease as the other increases.

net (p. 324) A two-dimensional pattern that can be folded into a space figure.

prism

prism net

"nice" fraction (p. 127) A fraction that can easily be converted to a decimal or a percent or that makes computations easier.

nonlinear (p. 174) When the graph of an equation is not a straight line, the equation and its graph are nonlinear.

O

obtuse angle **(p. 592)** An angle whose measure is between 90° and 180°.

obtuse triangle **(p. 593)** A triangle that has one obtuse angle.

opposite **(p. 80)** A number and its opposite are the same distance from 0 on a number line but on opposite sides. The opposite of 3 is –3.

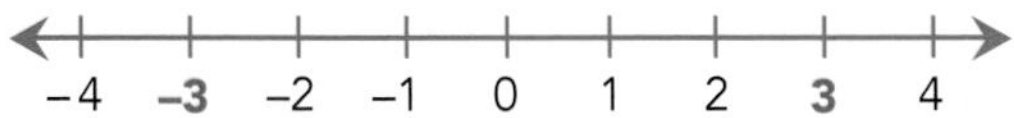

opposite angles **(p. 545)** Angles in a quadrilateral whose vertices are the endpoints of the same diagonal.

order of operations **(p. 589)** The correct order in which to perform mathematical operations in an expression: operations inside grouping symbols first, exponents next, then multiplication or division from left to right, and finally addition or subtraction from left to right.

outcome **(p. 106)** The result of an experiment.

P

parabola **(p. 443)** The graph of a quadratic function.

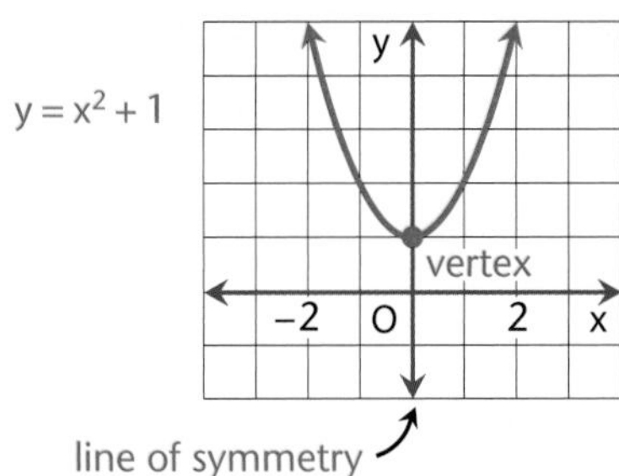

parallelogram **(p. 543)** A quadrilateral that has two pairs of parallel sides.

percent **(p. 588)** Percent means "per hundred" or "out of one hundred."

percent of change **(p. 142)** The percent by which an amount increases or decreases from its original amount.

percent of decrease **(p. 141)** The ratio of the amount of decrease to the original amount.

percent of increase **(p. 142)** The ratio of the amount of increase to the original amount.

perfect square **(p. 159)** A number whose principal square root is a whole number.

permutation **(p. 287)** An arrangement of a group of items in which order is important.

perpendicular bisector **(p. 196)** A segment, line, or ray that forms a right angle with a segment and divides the segment in half.

polygon **(p. 594)** A closed plane figure formed by three or more segments that do not cross each other.

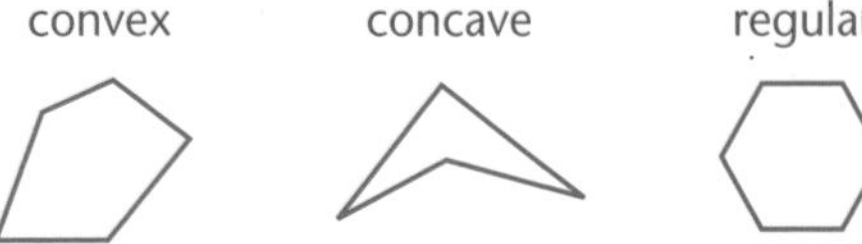

polyhedron **(p. 234)** A 3-dimensional object made up of flat surfaces, or faces, that are polygons.

polynomial **(p. 496)** A monomial or a sum of monomials.

population **(p. 125)** The entire group being studied.

positive correlation **(p. 54)** The relationship between two variables when one variable tends to increase as the other increases.

power **(p. 589)** *See* exponent.

principal square root **(p. 159)** The positive square root.

prism **(p. 234)** A polyhedron in which two of the faces, the bases, are congruent and parallel. The other faces are parallelograms. In a *right* prism, the other faces are rectangles.

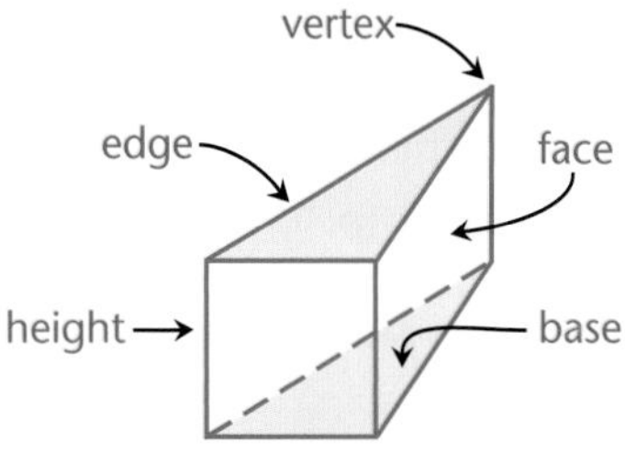

right triangular prism

probability **(p. 107)** A number from 0 to 1 that tells how likely it is that an event will happen.

product of powers property **(p. 460)** To multiply powers with the same base, add the exponents: $b^m \cdot b^n = b^{m+n}$.

product property of square roots **(p. 472)** For all positive numbers a and b, $\sqrt{a \cdot b} = \sqrt{a} \cdot \sqrt{b}$.

proportion **(p. 128)** A statement that two ratios are equal.

pyramid **(p. 325)** A space figure with one base that can be any polygon. The other faces are triangles that meet at a common vertex.

square pyramid

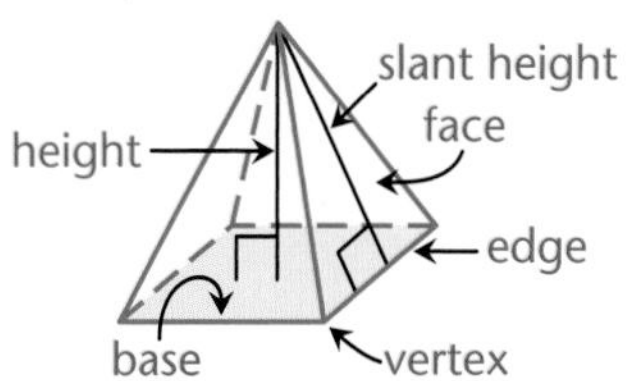

Pythagorean theorem (p. 340) In a right triangle, the square of the length of the hypotenuse is equal to the sum of the squares of the lengths of the legs.

Q

quadrant (p. 79) The four parts of a coordinate grid divided by the axes.

quadratic function (p. 446) A function that can be represented by an equation in the form $y = ax^2 + bx + c$, where $a \neq 0$.

quadrilateral (p. 543) A polygon with four sides.

quotient of powers property (p. 460) To divide powers with the same nonzero base, subtract the exponents: $\frac{b^m}{b^n} = b^{m-n}$.

quotient property of square roots (p. 473) For all positive numbers a and b, $\sqrt{\frac{a}{b}} = \frac{\sqrt{a}}{\sqrt{b}}$.

R

radical expression (p. 474) An expression that contains a radical with one or more variables in the radicand.

radical sign (p. 470) The symbol $\sqrt{\ }$.

radicand (p. 470) The value under a radical sign.

radius (plural: radii) (p. 197) A segment whose endpoints are the center and any point on a given circle. The length of a radius is called *the* radius. *See also* circle.

range (p. 596) The difference between the greatest data value and the least data value in a data set.

rate (p. 6) A ratio that compares two quantities measured in different units.

ratio (p. 585) The quotient you get when one number is divided by a second number not equal to zero.

rational number (p. 272) A number that can be written in the form $\frac{a}{b}$, where a and b are integers and $b \neq 0$.

reciprocals (p. 587) Two numbers whose product is 1.

rectangle (p. 543) A quadrilateral that has four right angles.

reflection (p. 435) A transformation where a figure is flipped across a line such as the x-axis or the y-axis.

regular polygon (p. 594) A polygon with all sides of equal length and all angles of equal measure. *See also* polygon.

regular pyramid (p. 351) A pyramid with a base that is a regular polygon and whose faces are congruent isosceles triangles.

repeating decimal (p. 272) A decimal that contains a digit or a group of digits that repeats forever.

representative sample (p. 125) A sample whose characteristics are similar to those of the entire population.

rhombus (p. 543) A quadrilateral that has four sides of equal length.

right angle (p. 592) An angle whose measure is 90°.

right triangle (p. 593) A triangle that has one right angle.

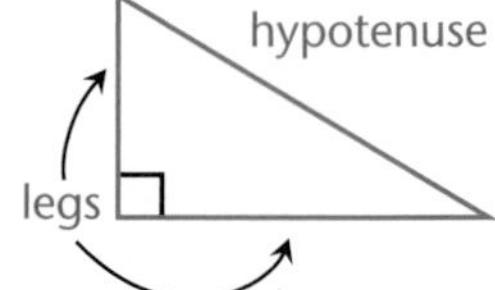

rise (p. 182) *See* slope.

rotation (p. 535) A turn of a figure about a fixed point, the center of rotation, a certain number of degrees either clockwise or counterclockwise.

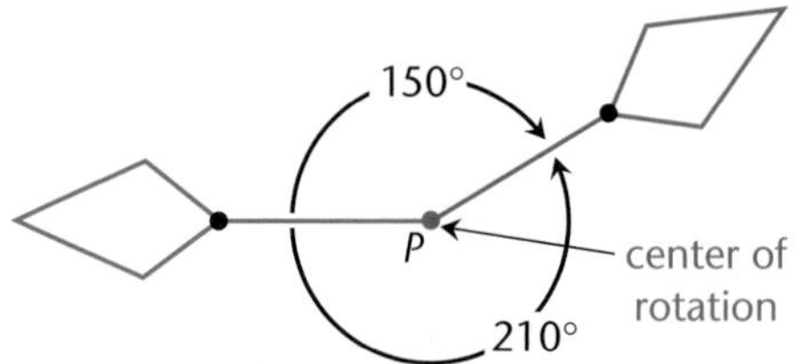

rotational symmetry (p. 535) When a figure fits exactly on itself after being rotated less than 360° around a center point, the figure has rotational symmetry.

The minimum rotational symmetry is 72°

run (p. 182) *See* slope.

S

sample (p. 125) A small group from the population.

scale of a drawing (p. 375) The ratio of a length on a drawing to a corresponding length on the actual object.

scale on a graph (p. 57) The numbers written along an axis of a graph.

scalene triangle (p. 593) A triangle that has no sides of equal length.

scatter plot (p. 52) A graph that compares two sets of data. It can be used to look for relationships between data sets.

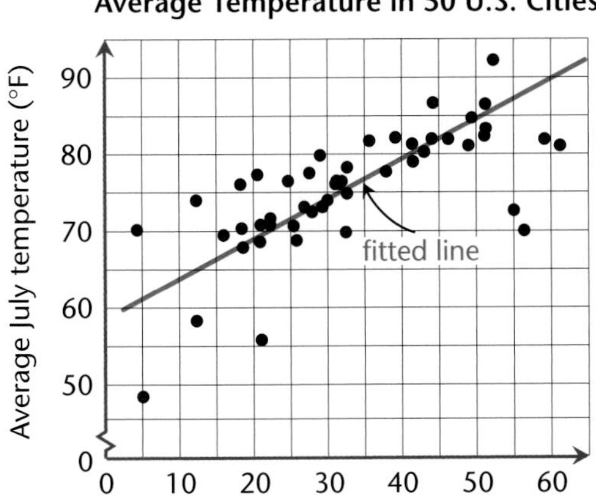

scientific notation (p. 205) A number is in scientific notation when it is written as the product of a number that is at least one but less than 10 and a power of ten.

decimal notation $\longrightarrow 5263.4 = 5.2634 \cdot 10^3 \longleftarrow$ scientific notation

sector (p. 5) A wedge-shaped region in a circle bounded by two radii and an arc. Can be used to refer to part of a circle graph.

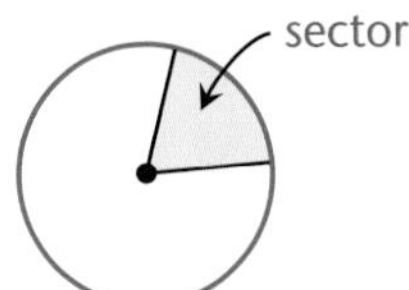

sequence (p. 519) An ordered list of numbers or objects.

side-side-side rule (p. 323) If the sides of one triangle have the same lengths as the sides of another triangle, the triangles are congruent.

similar (p. 193) Figures that have the same shape, but not necessarily the same size.

simplest form of a square root (p. 471) A square root is in simplest form if the following are true: There are no perfect square factors other than 1, there are no fractions in the radicand, and there are no square roots in the denominator of a fraction.

sine (p. 566) In a right triangle, the sine of an acute angle A is the ratio of the length of the leg opposite angle A to the length of the hypotenuse; $\sin A = \frac{\text{opposite}}{\text{hypotenuse}}$. *See also* tangent.

slant height (p. 351) The height of a triangular face of a pyramid. In a regular pyramid, the slant heights are all the same length. *See also* pyramid.

slope (p. 182) The ratio of the vertical change to the horizontal change along a line. Slope is a measure of a line's steepness.

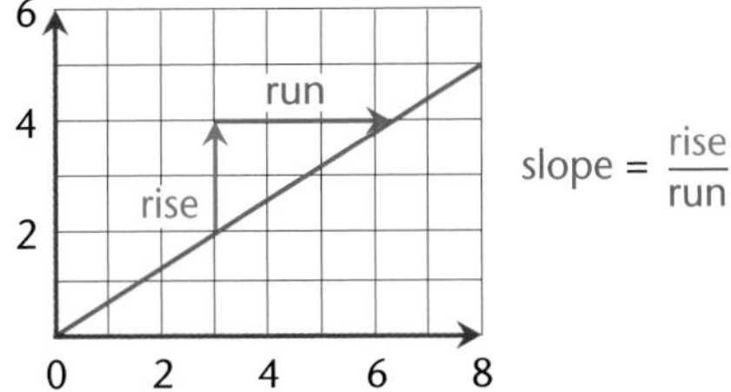

slope-intercept form (p. 262) An equation of a line in the form $y = mx + b$, where m is the slope and b is the y-intercept.

solution of an equation (pp. 35, 173) A value of a variable that makes an equation true. Also an ordered pair of numbers that make an equation with two variables true.

solution of an inequality (p. 485) A value of a variable that makes an inequality true is a solution of the inequality. All the solutions together are called the solution of the inequality.

solve an equation (p. 35) Find all the solutions of an equation.

solve an inequality (p. 486) Find all the solutions of an inequality.

sphere (p. 237) A 3-dimensional figure made up of a set of points that are an equal distance from a given point, called the center.

square (p. 543) A quadrilateral that has four right angles and four sides of equal length.

square root (p. 159) If $s^2 = n$, then s is a square root of n. For example, 5 and -5 are square roots of 25.

stem (p. 16) *See* stem-and-leaf plot.

stem-and-leaf plot (p. 16) A display of data where each number is represented by a *stem* (the left-most digits) and a *leaf* (the right-most digits).

straight angle (p. 592) An angle whose measure is 180°.

supplement (p. 365) One angle is the supplement of a second angle if the two angles are supplementary angles.

supplementary angles (p. 365) Two angles whose measures have a sum of 180°.

surface area (p. 247) The combined area of a figure's outer surfaces.

T

tangent (p. 564) In a right triangle, the tangent of an acute angle is the ratio of the length of the leg opposite the acute angle to the length of the leg adjacent to the angle.

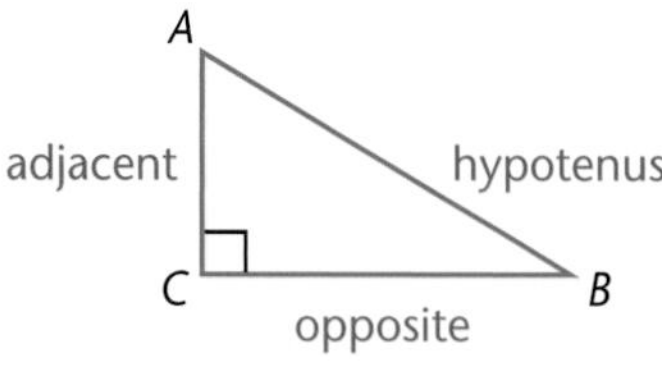

$$\tan A = \frac{\text{opposite}}{\text{adjacent}}$$

term of an expression (p. 39) The parts of an expression that are added together are called terms.

term number (p. 519) A number indicating the position of a term in a sequence.

term of a polynomial (p. 496) A monomial.

term of a sequence (p. 519) A number or object in a sequence.

terminating decimal (p. 272) A decimal that contains a finite number of digits.

tessellation (p. 539) A covering of a plane with polygons that has no gaps or overlaps.

tetrahedron (p. 325) A pyramid with four triangular faces, including the base.

theoretical probability (p. 109) The ratio of the number of outcomes that make up the event to the total number of possible outcomes if all the outcomes are equally likely. Theoretical probability can be determined without actually doing an experiment.

transformation (p. 433) A change in an object's shape, size, or position. *See also* reflection, rotation, and translation.

translation (p. 81) A transformation that moves each point of a figure the same distance in the same direction.

transversal (p. 366) A line that intersects two or more lines in a plane at separate points.

trapezoid (p. 543) A quadrilateral that has exactly one pair of parallel sides, called *bases.*

The perpendicular distance between bases of a trapezoid is the height.

base 2

height

base 1

tree diagram (p. 111) A diagram that can be used to show all the possible outcomes of an experiment.

triangle inequality (p. 324) The sum of the lengths of any two sides of a triangle is greater than the length of the third side.

trinomial (p. 496) A polynomial with exactly three terms.

U

unit rate (p. 7) A ratio that compares a quantity to one unit of another quantity.

unlike terms (p. 40) Terms that do not have identical variable parts.

upper extreme (p. 18) The greatest data value in a data set. *See also* box-and-whisker plot.

upper quartile (p. 18) The median of the data in the upper half of a data set. *See also* box-and-whisker plot.

V

variable (p. 33) A quantity, usually represented by a letter, that is unknown or that changes.

Venn diagram (p. 215) A diagram used to model relationships among groups.

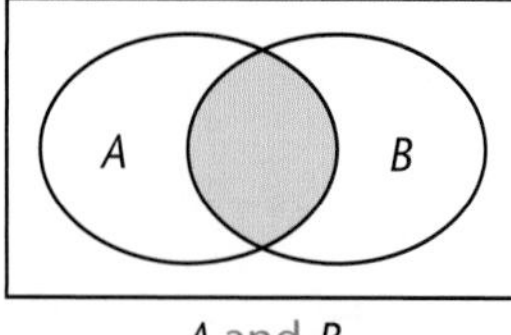

A and *B*

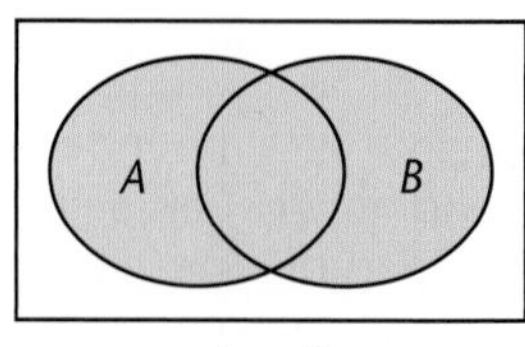

A or *B*

vertex of a parabola (p. 443) The point where a parabola intersects its line of symmetry. *See also* parabola.

vertex of a plane figure (p. 592) A point where sides of a figure, such as an angle or a polygon, come together. *See also* angle.

vertex of a space figure (plural: vertices) (p. 325) A point where three or more edges of a space figure meet. *See also* prism *and* pyramid.

vertical angles (p. 367) Angles that have the same vertex and whose sides are opposite rays.

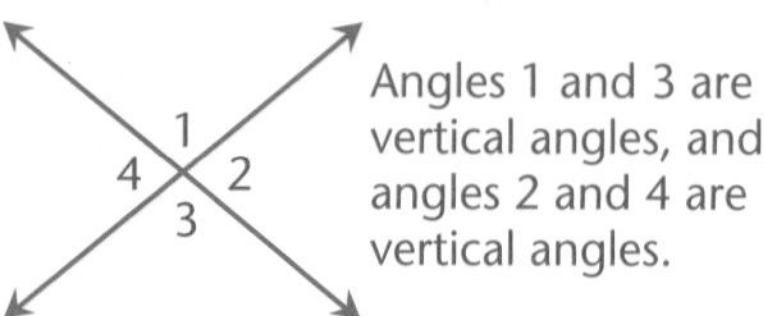

Y

***y*-intercept (p. 262)** The *y*-coordinate of the point where a line crosses the *y*-axis.

INDEX

D

M

N

O

P

S

T

CREDITS

ACKNOWLEDGMENTS
392 "Sidewalk Measles" by Barbara M. Hales, from *The Sky Is Full of Song,* selected by Lee Bennett Hopkins. Reprinted by permission of Barbara M. Hales. **518** *Two of Everything* by Lily Toy Hong. Text and illustrations copyright © 1993 by Lily Toy Hong. Excerpt and cover image reprinted by permission of Albert Whitman & Company. All rights reserved.

PHOTOGRAPHY
1 © Don Mason/Corbis; **2** *left* © George D. Lepp/Corbis; *bottom left* © Danny E Hooks/Shutterstock; *center* © Lightscapes Photography, Inc./Corbis; *bottom right* © James Woodson/Getty Images; *right* © Jupiterimages; **4** © Andy Rouse/Getty Images; **11** RMIP/Richard Haynes/McDougal Littell/Houghton Mifflin Co.; **15** © Gillain Allen/AP Images; **21** © Tim Boyle/Getty Images; **26** *top* © Michael Ochs Archives/Corbis; *bottom* © 2007 AP Images; **28** © Kmitu/Shutterstock; **29** © Paul Warner/AP Images; **30** Courtesy of Charles Cunningham; **32** RMIP/Richard Haynes/McDougal Littell/Houghton Mifflin Co.; **44** Bonnie Spence/McDougal Littell/Houghton Mifflin Co.; **45** © W. Haxby, LDEO/Photo Researchers, Inc.; **46** © Richard Ward/Getty Images; **49** *top* © PhotoDisc; *left* © NBAE/Getty Images; *center* © AFP/Getty Images; *right* © Anne Ryan/NewSport/Corbis; **50** RMIP/Richard Haynes/McDougal Littell/Houghton Mifflin Co.; **53** © Wolfgang Rattay/Reuters/Corbis; **54** *left* © Jeff Greenberg/Alamy; *center* © Brandon Cole Marine Photography/Alamy; **60** RMIP/Richard Haynes/McDougal Littell/Houghton Mifflin Co.; **61** © Scott Boehm/Getty Images; **63** *all* © PhotoDisc; **66** © GeoNova; **69** © Wolfgang Kaehler Photography; **72** © Paul Jasienski/Getty Images; **75** © Bettmann/Corbis; **76–77** © Richard Chung/Reuters/Corbis; **78** © Jeff Greenberg/The Image Works; **89** © Jonathan Daniel/Getty Images; **92** Courtesy of West Edmonton Mall; **105** *left, right* RMIP/Richard Haynes/McDougal Littell/Houghton Mifflin Co.; **117** *all* RMIP/Richard Haynes/McDougal Littell/Houghton Mifflin Co.; **122** © Veer Incorporated; **125** © Dana White/PhotoEdit; **126** *top left* © Ariel Skelley/Corbis; *top right* © Geri Engberg/The Image Works; *center left* © Peter Hvizdak/The Image Works; *center right* © Spencer Grant/PhotoEdit; **135** *both* © Mark Erickson/Getty Images; **139** © Bob Daemmrich/PhotoEdit; **145** *top left, top center, top right, center left* School Division, Houghton Mifflin Company; *center right* © PhotoObjects/Jupiterimages; *center* © Comstock/Jupiterimages; *bottom right* © Index Stock Imagery; **148** Courtesy of Aricka Westbrooks; **151** RMIP/Richard Haynes/McDougal Littell/Houghton Mifflin Co.; **154–155** © Craig Lovell/Corbis; **156** © Ira Block/Getty Images; **157** © Luc Novovitch/Alamy; **164** NASA; **168** © David R. Frazier Photgraphy/Alamy; **171** © William Albert Allard/National Geographic/Getty Images; **173** *left* © Gregorz Slemp/Shutterstock; *right* © Tomasz Pietryszek/Shutterstock; **174** © Mike Powell/Getty Images; **176** © Georg Gerster/Photo Researchers, Inc.; **177** *top* © Mary Evans Picture Library/The Image Works; *center* © Adam Woolfitt/Corbis; **180** © Darren Greenwood/Design Pics/Corbis; **184** RMIP/Richard Haynes/McDougal Littell/Houghton Mifflin Co.; **189** © Robin Nelson/PhotoEdit; **196** © Buddy Mays/Corbis; **197** *both* RMIP/Richard Haynes/McDougal Littell/Houghton Mifflin Co.; **204** © James King-Holmes/Photo Researchers, Inc.; **211** © Tony Freeman/PhotoEdit; **215** RMIP/Richard Haynes/McDougal Littell/Houghton Mifflin Co.; **225** RMIP/Richard Haynes/McDougal Littell/Houghton Mifflin Co.; **228–229** © John D. Russell/AP Images; **230** © Newedel/StockFood Munich; **231** RMIP/Richard Haynes/McDougal Littell/Houghton Mifflin Co.; **236** © Henrick Freek/StockFood Munich; **237** © Ted Streshinsky/Corbis; **240** © 20th Century Fox/The Kobal Collection; **241** © National Air and Space Museum, Smithsonian Institution (SI 97-16746); **242** © Carl Ericsson/www.harmonicwhirlies.com; **243** RMIP/Richard Haynes/McDougal Littell/Houghton Mifflin Co.; **245** © Jean-Loup Charmet/Bridgeman Art Library; **246** RMIP/Richard Haynes/McDougal Littell/Houghton Mifflin Co.; **249** RMIP/Richard Haynes/McDougal Littell/Houghton Mifflin Co.; **252** *both* Coutesy of Kamioka Observatory, ICRR (Institute for Cosmic Ray Research), The University of Tokyo; **253** © imagebroker/Alamy; **258** © Bettmann/Corbis; **261** *left* © PhotoDisc; *right* © Valery Potapova/Shutterstock; **266** © Tim Keatley/Alamy; **267** © Charles D. Winters/Photo Researchers, Inc.; **270** © Visual Arts Library (London)/Alamy; **279** *top* © Michael Newman/PhotoEdit; *bottom* © Mike Siluk/The Image Works; **283** © Albert Harlingue/Roger-Viollet/The Image Works; **287** © Owen Brewer/Zuma Press, Inc.; **297** *left* © RubberBall/SuperStock; *center* © James Lauritz/Getty Images; *right* © AAAC/Topham/The Image Works; **308–309** © Eckehard Schulz/AP Images; **310** © Stock Montage, Inc./Alamy; **311** © Artville **313** *left, center* © Alex Wong/Getty Images; *right* Library of Congress, Negative No. DC-37-164; **314** RMIP/Richard Haynes/McDougal Littell/Houghton Mifflin Co.; **318** School Division, Houghton Mifflin Company; **321** School Division/Houghton Mifflin Company (Construction from Spooner's Moving Animals by Paul Spooner); **322** *all* RMIP/Richard Haynes/McDougal

Littell/Houghton Mifflin Co.; **325** © Jochen Helle/age fotostock; **328** RMIP/Richard Haynes/McDougal Littell/ Houghton Mifflin Co.; **337** © Richard Nowitz/Getty Images; **338** RMIP/Richard Haynes/McDougal Littell/ Houghton Mifflin Co.; **340** © Paul Hardy/Corbis; **345** © Charles O. Cecil/Alamy; **348** *right* © Bryan & Cherry Alexander/Photo Researchers, Inc.; *left* © Chris Rainier/Corbis; **349** © Mary Steinbacher/Alamy; **352** © National Anthropological Archives, Smithsonian Institution (41,887); **354** © National Anthropological Archives, Smithsonian Institution (41,886-Z); **357** © Alison Wright/Corbis; **358** *right* © Eric Martin/Alamy; *bottom, bottom left* Courtesy of Christa McAuliffe Planetarium; **362** *all* School Division, Houghton Mifflin Company; **363** © qaphotos.com/Alamy; **364** RMIP/ Richard Haynes/McDougal Littell/Houghton Mifflin Co.; **372** Courtesy of Wendy Lathrop; **374** © Steve Hall/ Hedrich Blessing; **377** © Simon Jarratt/Corbis; **386** School Division, Houghton Mifflin Company; **387** RMIP/Richard Haynes/McDougal Littell/Houghton Mifflin Co.; **390–391** © Firefly Productions/Corbis; **392** © Andrew Chin/Shutterstock; **393** School Division, Houghton Mifflin Company; **394** *both* RMIP/Richard Haynes/McDougal Littell/Houghton Mifflin Co.; **396** © Jim Wark/Index Stock Imagery; **402** © SSPL/The Image Works; **404** © Dynamic Graphics Group/Creatas/ Alamy; **406** © Joel Sartore/Getty Images; **407** RMIP/ Richard Haynes/McDougal Littell/Houghton Mifflin Co.; **409** RMIP/Richard Haynes/McDougal Littell/Houghton Mifflin Co.; **410** RMIP/Richard Haynes/McDougal Littell/ Houghton Mifflin Co.; **415** © Craig Tuttle/Corbis; **417** © Michelle D. Bridwell/PhotoEdit; **428** *both* RMIP/ Richard Haynes/McDougal Littell/Houghton Mifflin Co.; **429** © Richard Laird/Getty Images; **430** *top* Courtesy of William Karesh; *bottom* © Tomislav Stajduhar/ Shutterstock; **432** © Duomo/Corbis; **437** RMIP/Richard Haynes/McDougal Littell/Houghton Mifflin Co.; **440** *both* RMIP/Richard Haynes/McDougal Littell/ Houghton Mifflin Co.; **442** NASA; **443** *left* © Thinkstock/Corbis; *right* © Justin Pumfrey/Getty Images; **448** © James Davis Photography/Alamy; **449** © Neil Rabinowitz/Corbis; **456–457** © BSIP/Photo Researchers, Inc.; **458** © Time & Life Pictures/Getty Images; **462** © Andrew Syred/Getty Images; **463** NASA; **465** © Philippe Giraud/Corbis; **466** © Hans Leijnse/Foto Natura/Minden Pictures; **468** Courtesy of France Córdova; **478** RMIP/Richard Haynes/McDougal Littell/ Houghton Mifflin Co.; **482** © Digital Vision/Getty Images; **490** *top left* © Daniel Dempster Photography/ Alamy; *top right* © Alan Kearney/Getty Images; *center left* © Caroline von Tumpling-Manning/Getty Images; *center right* © Gary Conner/PhotoEdit; **495** *right Self-Portrait* (ca. 1512), Leonardo da Vinci © Bettmann/Corbis; *bottom left Mona Lisa,* Leonardo da Vinci © Stuart Gregory/ Getty Images; **501** *Ballista That Threw Two Stones,* Leonardo da Vinci © Bettmann/Corbis; **509** *Head of a Woman,* Leonardo da Vinci. Charcoal on paper. © British Museum, London, UK/ Alinari/The Bridgeman Art Library; **512** © Bob Daemmrich/The Image Works; **513** RMIP/Richard Haynes/McDougal Littell/Houghton Mifflin Co.; **516–517** © Josh Westrich/zefa/Corbis; **522** © PhotoDisc; **529** *both* Courtesy of Junpei Sekino; **532** *left* © Gary James Calder/Shutterstock; *center* © Don Hammond/Design Pics/Corbis; *right* © Tim Street-Porter/ Beateworks/Corbis; **535** *left* © Barbara Strnadova/Photo Researchers, Inc.; *center* © Bob Krist/Corbis; *right* © Ronald Weir/Albaimages/Alamy; **536** *top left* © AA World Travel Library/Alamy; *top right* © Ingo Jezierski/Corbis; *center left* © Visuals Unlimited/Corbis; *center* © Roland Birke/OKAPIA/Photo Researchers, Inc.; *center right* © M.I. Walker/Photo Researchers, Inc.; *bottom* © SuperStock, Inc.; **538** *all* © PhotoDisc; **540** *top left* © Andrew G. Wood/Photo Researchers, Inc.; *top center* © John Burbidge/Photo Researchers, Inc.; *top right* © Rod Planck/Photo Researchers, Inc.; *left* © Richard Cummins/ SuperStock; *center* © M.I. Walker/Photo Researchers, Inc.; *right* © Visuals Unlimited/Corbis; **542** © George H. H. Huey/Corbis; **554** *bottom right* © Ralph White/Corbis; *center* © The Mariner's Museum/Corbis; **557** © Emory Kristof/National Geographic Image Collection; **562** *center* © Bridgeman Art Library; *bottom* © Werner Forman/ Art Resource, NY; **563** RMIP/Richard Haynes/McDougal Littell/Houghton Mifflin Co.; **571** © John Arsenault/ Getty Images; **575** RMIP/Richard Haynes/McDougal Littell/Houghton Mifflin Co.

ILLUSTRATION

34 Robin Storesund/McDougal Littell/Houghton Mifflin Co.; **39** Jeremy Spiegel/McDougal Littell/Houghton Mifflin Co.; **68, 112, 117** Robin Storesund/McDougal Littell/Houghton Mifflin Co.; **156, 157, 158** Chris Costello/McDougal Littell/Houghton Mifflin Co.; **161, 192, 221, 223** Betsy James/McDougal Littell/Houghton Mifflin Co.; **230, 274, 275, 345** Robin Storesund/ McDougal Littell/Houghton Mifflin Co.; **370** Magellan Geographix; **372** Robin Storesund/McDougal Littell/ Houghton Mifflin Co.; **374, 380** Courtesy of Ross Barney Architects; **419** Robin Storesund/McDougal Littell/Houghton Mifflin Co.; **432** Courtesy of Vicon Motion Systems, Inc., Centennial, CO; **461, 527, 533, 539, 560** Robin Storesund/McDougal Littell/Houghton Mifflin Co.

All other illustrations by McDougal Littell/Houghton Mifflin Co. or School Division/Houghton Mifflin Co.

SELECTED ANSWERS

MODULE 1

Section 1, Practice and Application (p. 10)

1. miles and hours; 60 mi/hr **3.** 480,000 **5.** not equivalent **9. a.** about 99 kicks/min **b.** At about 119 kicks/min, this rate is greater than Constance Constable's. **11.** Sample Response: The unit price given for cinnamon is $0.99 per ounce. What is the cost of 6 oz? Answer: $5.94 **13. a.** about 29,523,810 mi/month **b.** about 971,178 mi/day **c.** about 40,466 mi/hr **d.** Sample Response; miles per hour; It is more common to measure speed in miles per hour. **15.** 8

17. a. Source of China's 2004 GDP

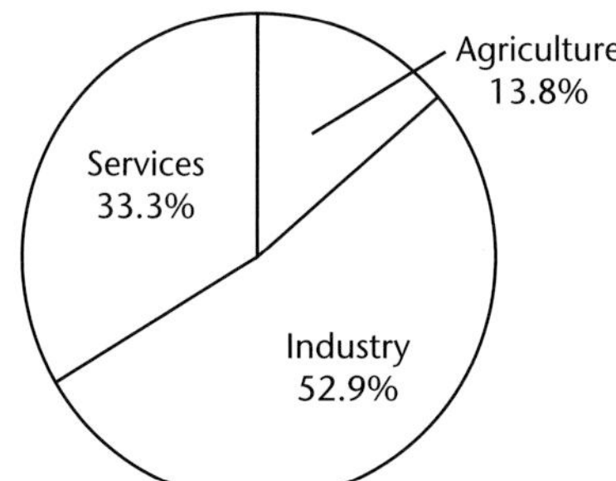

b. Source of India's 2004 GDP

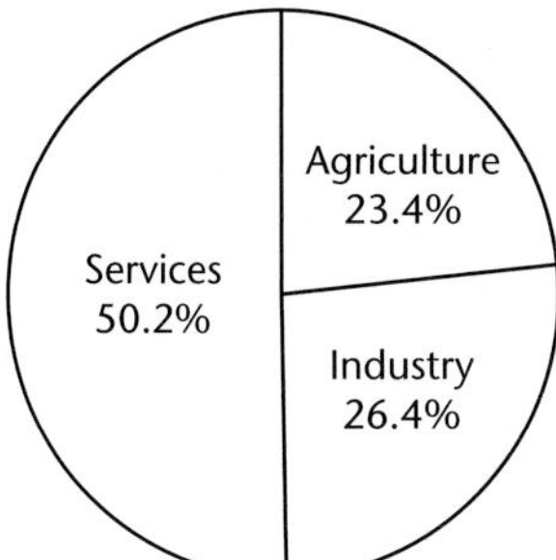

c. Source of Pakistan's 2004 GDP

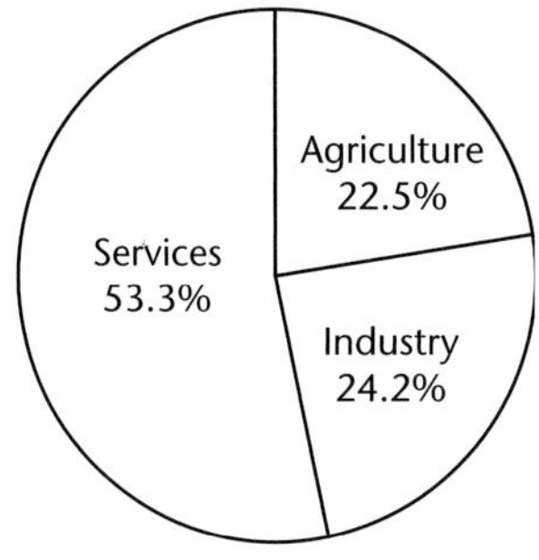

19. The sum of the percents is only 90%.

21. Correct Responses Out of 96 Trials

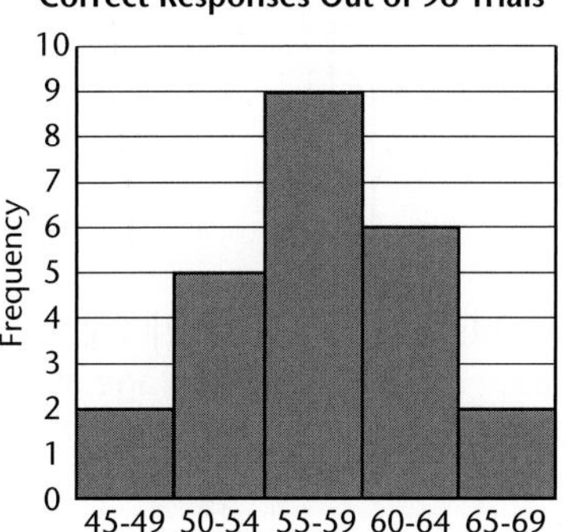

Spiral Review (p. 13)

25. mean: about 9.84, median: 9.8, modes: 9.8 and 10; range: 0.4 **26.** $\frac{2}{5}$ **27.** $\frac{4}{5}$ **28.** $\frac{1}{5}$ **29.** $\frac{7}{20}$

Extra Skill Practice (p. 14)

1. not equivalent **3.** 10%; The circle graph represents 100%; 100% – (60% + 30%) = 10% **5.** 1200 Cal

7.

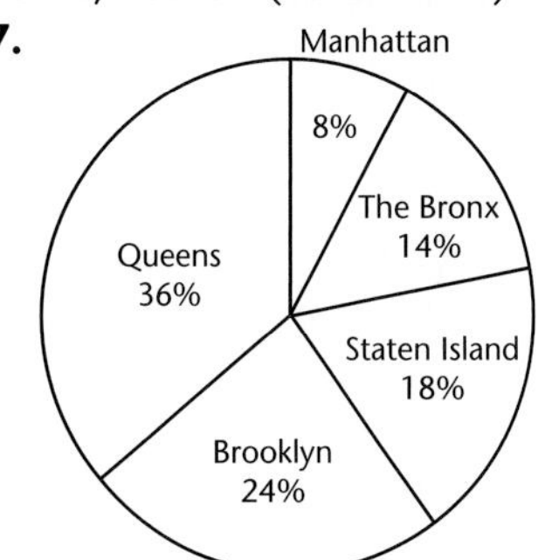

Standardized Testing (p. 14)

1. C **2.** B

SELECTED ANSWERS

Section 2, Practice and Application (p. 24)

1. a.

Age when Awarded Grammy for Best Female Vocal Performance

Country		Pop
4	1	
4	2	3 3 3 3 5
7 5 4 3 3 3 1	3	0 0 0 0 2 3
8	4	1
6	5	
	6	
4	7	

5 | 3 | represents an age of 35. | 2 | 3 represents an age of 23.

b. Sample Response: Ages of country winners are much more spread out than pop winners, although the greatest numbers of winners for both pop and country are in their 30s. **3. a.** Class A: 54, Class B: 45 **b.** Class A: 100, Class B: 100 **c.** Class A: 65, Class B: 70 **d.** Class A: 95, Class B: 85 **7. a.** lower extreme = 1, upper extreme = 40; the range of the data. You know Elvis had at least one hit make it to #1 and at least one make it only to #40 on the charts. **b.** 16 **c.** about 50% **9. a.** These are the data values that range from the line inside the box (the median) to the end of the upper whisker (the upper extreme). **b.** Answers will vary. Sample Response: Elvis because more than $\frac{1}{2}$ of his hits stayed at #1 for 4 or more weeks, whereas the Beatles had less than 25% of their #1 hits stay for 4 weeks or longer. The median is greater for Elvis, and for the Beatles, the median is equal to Elvis's lower quartile value showing that only about 50% of the Beatles' hits were at #1 for 2 weeks or more while about 75% of Elvis's hits were at #1 for 2 weeks or more.

11. a–b.

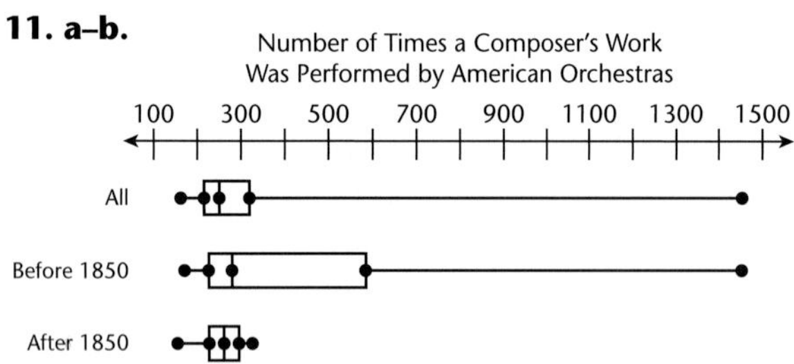

Spiral Review (p. 30)

19. 288 **20.** about 0.92 **21.** about 0.06 **22.** \$5.25 **23.** 3 and 5 only **24.** none **25.** 2 only **26.** 3 only **27.** > **28.** > **29.** >

Career Connection (p. 30)

31. Sample Response: 230, 350, 490 (any score below the median which is about 510)

Extra Skill Practice (p. 31)

1. a. Ages of Academy Award Winners

Actors		Actresses
6	2	1 5 5 6 8 9
9 8 7 7 6 5 2 1	3	1 3 3 3 3 4 5 5 8 9
7 6 5 5 3 3 2 0	4	1 2 5 9 9
7 4 2 2	5	
1 0	6	1
6	7	4
	8	0

| 2 | 5 represents an age of 52. | 4 | 2 represents an age of 42.

b. With the exception of a few actresses, the actresses were mainly in their 20s, 30s or 40s when receiving an Academy Award. For men, the awards were earned at slightly older ages, mainly 30s, 40s and 50s. Only one actor was in his 20s as compared to six actresses.

c. Actor: mean = 44.75, median 43, modes = 37, 43, 45, 52.

Actress: mean = 39.125, median = 34.5, mode = 33.

Sample Response: For actors, there are too many modes to be a good representation of the data. The mean is a good representation of the actors' ages. For the actresses, the mean is a bit high, probably due to the two ages of 74 and 80; therefore, the mode or the median is a better representation. There were four actresses at age 33 and four others were within 2 yrs of that age when they won, so I would choose the mode. **3.** Sample Response: Very unusual; Among the actors and actresses listed, she is the only person in her 80s to receive an Academy Award, and only 1 of 3 actresses over the age of 49. **5.** bar graph; A bar graph compares data items grouped into categories. **7.** circle graph; A circle graph shows the division of a whole into parts.

Standardized Testing (p. 31)

1. D **2.** A

Section 3, Practice and Application (p. 44)

1. A **3.** Let t = total distance of the trip, d = number of days; $\frac{t}{50} = d$ **5.** Let c = beginning length of cord, f = finished length of the bracelet; $c = 8f$ **7. a.** 30°F, 60°F, 230°F **b.** 32°F, 59°F, 212°F **c.** 15°C **9. a.** 25 **b.** 1260 **c.** 3.5 **d.** 23 **e.** 156 **f.** 45 **11.** A **13.** Answers will vary. **17.** $17x + 1$ **19.** $17w + 3$ **21.** not possible, unlike terms **23.** $15y^2 + 7x$ **25. a.** $P = 2l + 2w$ **b.** 26 in. **c.** 7 cm **d.** 4.5 m **27.** triangle: 12 yd, square: 9 yd

Spiral Review (p. 47)

30. Sample Response: a bar graph; The data fall into categories. **31.** Sample Response: a circle graph; The data are given in percentages. **32. a.** Sample Response: mi/hr; The speed of a car is usually given in mi/hr. **b.** 750 mi/hr

Extra Skill Practice (p. 48)

1. Let t = total amount of hamburger used in pounds and c = the number of campers; $t = 0.25c + 5$ **3.** Let r = rent and a = area of the apartment; $r = 0.9a$ **5.** 31 **7.** 208 **9.** 148 **11.** $5y$ **13.** $10t - 4$ **15.** $36r - 18rd$ **17.** no like terms **19.** $7 + w + w^2$

Standardized Testing (p. 48)

1. D **2.** A

Section 4, Practice and Application (p. 57)

1. a. 92 yr, 6.5 hr **b.** 6 yr, just under 5.5 hr **5.** negative correlation **7.** Plot A: straight-line pattern; Plot B: curved pattern **9.** negative correlation **11.** positive correlation **13.** negative correlation **17.** Answers will vary.

Spiral Review (p. 61)

19. 16 **20.** 16 **21.** 24 **22.** 7.85 **23.** 36 cm^2 **24.** 36 m^2 **25.** 96 mm^2 **26. a.** True; The upper extreme for linebackers is 245. **b.** True; The median for the defensive linemen is 285 lb. **c.** False; The upper extreme for the linebackers is about 245 lb and the lower extreme for the defensive linemen is about 270 lb. **d.** True; The upper whisker of the offensive linemen contains 25% of the data values and it begins at the same value as the upper extreme of the defensive linemen plot.

Extra Skill Practice (p. 62)

1. 52 miles; 2002 **3. a–b.** Sample Response: I chose a horizontal scale of 40 to 90 because the temperatures range from 51° to 77°. I chose a vertical scale of 0 to 35 because the cups of cocoa sold range from 4 to 31.

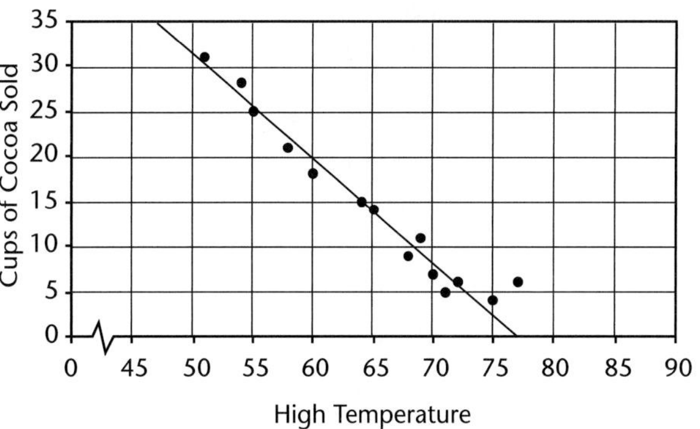

c. 3 pots

Standardized Testing (p. 62)

1. approximately 7 through 22; approximately 35 through 62 **2.** curved pattern; The data decreases, then levels off, then increases. This creates a curve.

Section 5, Practice and Application (p. 68)

1. 2042 **3. a.** Sample Response: Weigh 4 rocks on each side. Take the heavier side, divide it in half, and weigh 2 rocks on each side. Take the heavier side, divide it in half and weigh 1 rock on each side. **b.** 3 weighings

5. a.

Rectangles with Perimeter 28 Units															
Length	0	1	2	3	4	5	6	7	8	9	10	11	12	13	14
Width	14	13	12	11	10	9	8	7	6	5	4	3	2	1	0
Area	0	13	24	33	40	45	48	49	48	45	40	33	24	13	0

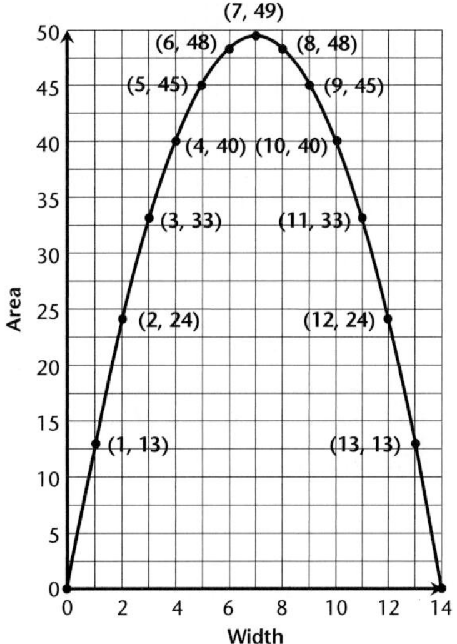

b. The length and width of the rectangle with the greatest area is 7 units and the area is 49 square units.

SELECTED ANSWERS

Spiral Review (p. 69)

7. a. area: 6320 sq mi **b.** area: 19,750 sq mi **c.** It is about in the middle. Sample Response: Yes; I would expect the average width to be about 33 mi which would make the area of this lake about 13,000 sq. mi. **8. a.** perimeter: 822 mi **b.** perimeter: 890 mi **c.** The actual perimeter is greater than either of the two that were calculated. The shoreline must have many inlets.

Extra Skill Practice (p. 70)

1. Sample Response: Measure two $3\frac{1}{2}$ pt pots of water then remove three $1\frac{1}{2}$ pt pots of water.

3.

Rectangles with Area of 48 Square Units										
Length	1	2	3	4	6	8	12	16	24	48
Width	48	24	16	12	8	6	4	3	2	1
Perimeter	98	52	38	32	28	28	32	38	52	98

5. about 7 units; Sample Response: I used the graph to find the least perimeter.

Standardized Testing (p. 70)

1.

Polygon	A	B	C	D	E	F	G	H	I
Area (A)	1	$1\frac{1}{2}$	2	$3\frac{1}{2}$	4	4	6	$6\frac{1}{2}$	8
Number of dots on perimeter (P)	4	5	6	7	8	6	10	9	8
Number of dots inside (I)	0	0	0	1	1	2	2	3	5

2. $A = \frac{P}{2} + I - 1$

Review & Assessment (pp. 74–75)

1. 2064 **2.** 10,800

3. a.

Ages of Airplanes by Company

Company A		Company B
9 6 5 3 2	0	1 2 3 3 5 6 7 7 8 9
9 8 7 7 7 5 5 3 2	1	2 4 6 6 6 9
6 1 0 0	2	0 5

2|1| represents an age of 12 years. |1|4 represents an age of 14 years.

3. b. Sample Response: Most of the planes owned by Company A are older than the planes owned by Company B. **c.** Company A: mean: about 14.2, median: 16, mode: 17; Company B: mean: 10.5, median: 8.5, mode: 16

4. a. Company A: lower extreme = 2
Company B: lower extreme = 1
b. Company A: upper extreme = 26
Company B: upper extreme = 25
c. Company A: lower quartile = 9
Company B: lower quartile = 5
d. Company A: upper quartile = 19
Company B: upper quartile = 16

5. Company B. The median for Company B is below 10, so more than 50% of the planes are under 10 years old.

6. histogram **7. a.** $t = 0.50a + 0.25c$ **b.** \$2.00 **8. a.** $5\frac{1}{3}$ **b.** 7 **c.** 24 **d.** 9 **9. a.** not possible **b.** $8y$ **c.** $t + 4$ **d.** $3m + 6$

10. a.

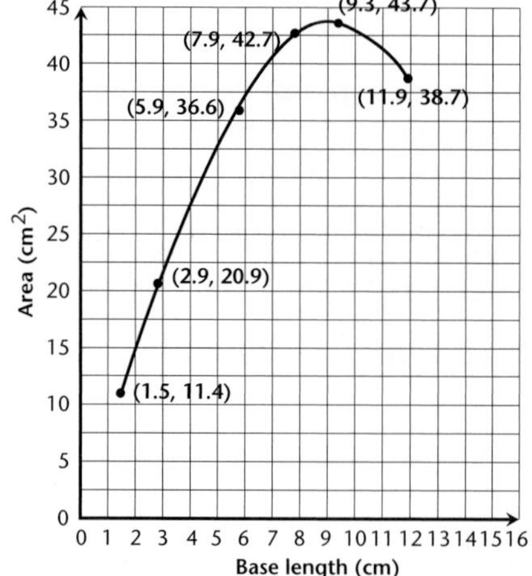

b. about 9 cm

MODULE 2

Section 1, Practice and Application (p. 88)

1. –31 **3.** –8 **5.** –100 **7.** 15 **9.** –74 **11.** 47 **13.** $8\frac{1}{2}$ **15.** 7, –7 **17.** –2 **19.** 5 **21.** 22 **23.** –2 **27.** 31 **29.** 0 **31.** 12 **33. a.** $P'(5, -2)$, $Q'(5, -1)$, $R'(4, 0)$, $S'(3, -1)$, $T'(3, -2)$ **35. a.** –1, 1; 1, –1 **b.** 2, 6; –2, –6 **c.** –4, –6; 4, 6 **37.** –320 **39.** –56 **41.** 7 **43.** 8 **45.** –192 **47.** 4 **49.** 84 **51.** 42 **53.** 15(5) + 4(–2) + 1(0); 67

Spiral Review (p. 90)

56. $1\frac{1}{2}$ **57.** $\frac{7}{10}$ **58.** 1 **59.** $\frac{30}{49}$ **60.** 6 **61.** 8 **62.** 56 **63.** 33 **64.** 28 **65.** 96

Extension (p. 90)

67. 6, –10 **69.** –2, 2

Extra Skill Practice (p. 91)

1. 4 **3.** –195 **5.** –512 **7.** 1 **9.** 29 **11.** $3\frac{3}{4}$ **13.** –77 **15.** 6 **17.** 250 **19.** –42 **21.** –6 **23.** 18 **25.** 42

27. 4 **29.** –4 **31.** –16 **33.** –26

Standardized Testing (p. 91)

1. a. Sample Response: –7, 5 **b.** None. Two numbers with sums of 0 are opposites. The product of opposites is always less than or equal to 0. **c.** Sample Response: 10 and –5 **2.** Sample Response: $A(-3, 2)$, $B(3, 2)$, $C(3, -2)$, $D(-3, -2)$; $A'(-7, 8)$, $B'(-1, 8)$, $C'(-1, 4)$, $D'(-7, 4)$

Section 2, Practice and Application (p. 101)

1. $\frac{59}{72}$ **3.** $\frac{1}{14}$ **5.** $-\frac{1}{2}$ **7.** –1 **9. a.** yes **b.** Use one piece from the $\frac{1}{2}$ yd remnant, two pieces from the $\frac{7}{8}$ yd remnant, and one piece from the $\frac{5}{8}$ yd remnant; $\frac{1}{8}$ yd; $\frac{1}{8}$ yd; $\frac{1}{4}$ yd **11.** –1 **13.** $-\frac{2}{15}$ **15.** $-\frac{9}{14}$ **17.** $-\frac{11}{42}$ **19.** $-\frac{53}{60}$ **21. a.** $\frac{1}{2}-\frac{1}{4}+\frac{1}{8}-\frac{1}{16}+\frac{1}{32}$; $\frac{1}{2}-\frac{1}{4}+\frac{1}{8}-\frac{1}{16}+\frac{1}{32}-\frac{1}{64}$ **b.** $\frac{1}{4}, \frac{3}{8}, \frac{5}{16}, \frac{11}{32}, \frac{21}{64}$ **c.** Sample response: positive; The fraction to be subtracted will be smaller than the value of the twenty-ninth expression. **23.** –8 **25.** $6\frac{3}{8}$ **27.** $5\frac{8}{9}$ **29.** $\frac{3}{8}$ **31.** –7 **33.** 3 **35.** $-\frac{3}{4}$

Spiral Review (p. 103)

39. –13 **40.** 96 **41.** –9 **42.** –112 **43.** lower extreme = 10; upper extreme = 45; median = 20

Extra Skill Practice (p. 104)

1. $-2\frac{9}{10}$ **3.** $1\frac{1}{8}$ **5.** $-\frac{2}{3}$ **7.** $2\frac{1}{10}$ **9.** $-3\frac{1}{9}$ **11.** $3\frac{1}{8}$ **13. a.** $4\frac{2}{3}$ in. by $6\frac{2}{3}$ in. **b.** Possible answers: $4\frac{2}{3}$ in. by $13\frac{1}{3}$ in. or $9\frac{1}{3}$ in. by $6\frac{2}{3}$ in.

Standardized Testing (p. 104)

1. D **2.** A **3.** A

Section 3, Practice and Application (p. 115)

1. 1, 2, 3, 4, 5, 6 **3. a.** 1, 3, 5 **b.** 4, 6 **5.** No; while landing on each sector is equally likely, the number of sectors for each outcome are not equal. **7.** 4 sectors are labeled with vowels and 4 are labeled with consonants, so the spinner is just as likely to stop on a vowel as a consonant. **9.** Results will vary. **11.** Answers will vary. (Theoretically, 4 occurs most often, then 5 and 3.) **13.** Results will vary. **15.** Answers will vary. You can tell which player won most often by comparing the probabilities. The player with the greater probability won most often.

17. a. $\frac{1}{4}$ **b.** $\frac{1}{8}$ **c.** $\frac{1}{8}$ **d.** $\frac{1}{2}$

19. 0; 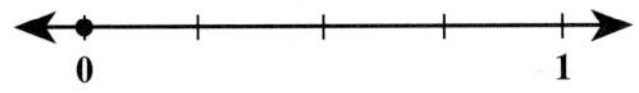

21. 1; 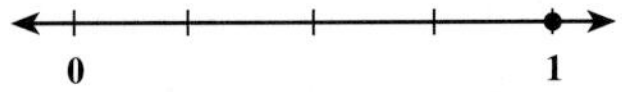

23. equally likely **25.** equally likely **27. a.** $\frac{1}{5}, \frac{4}{5}$ **b.** $\frac{3}{19}$ **c.** $\frac{4}{19}$ **d.** dependent on; The outcome of the first draw affects the probability of drawing a blue ball on the second draw.

31. a. Flip 1 Flip 2 Flip 3 Outcomes

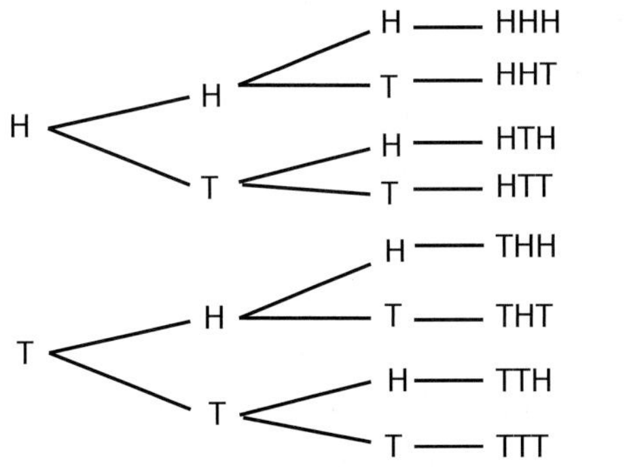

b. 8 outcomes **c.** Yes; The outcomes on each flip are equally likely.

Spiral Review (p. 119)

34. $-\frac{2}{3}$ **35.** $-3\frac{7}{8}$ **36.** $5\frac{7}{30}$ **37.** $-6\frac{2}{3}$ **38.** $2x + 1$ **39.** n^2 **40.** $8s + 4st$ **41.** acute **42.** obtuse **43.** straight **44.** obtuse

Extra Skill Practice (p. 120)

1. $\frac{7}{15}$ **3.** $\frac{1}{8}$ **5.** $\frac{5}{8}$ **7. a.** golden: $\frac{2}{5}$; green: $\frac{7}{25}$; not green: $\frac{18}{25}$ **b.** red: $\frac{6}{23}$, green: $\frac{7}{23}$ **c.** The events are independent if the first apple is replaced before the second apple is taken. If the first apple is not replaced, the events are dependent.

Standardized Testing (p. 120)

1.

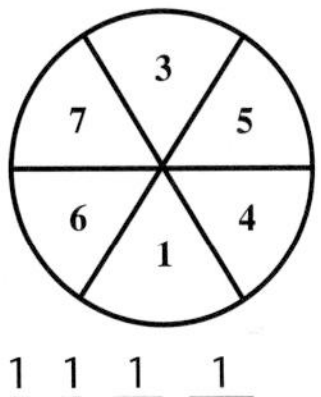

2. $\frac{1}{4}, \frac{1}{8}, \frac{1}{16}, \frac{1}{2^{49}}$

Section 4, Practice and Application (p. 133)

1. $\frac{2}{5}$; 0.4 **3.** $\frac{23}{20}$; 1.15 **5.** $\frac{4}{5}$; 80% **7.** 0.19; 19% **9.** 0.65; 65% **11.** not biased **13. a.** middle school students **b.** sixth grade students **c.** No; Sample Response: Sixth graders are not representative of the entire school. **17.** about \$66, nice fraction; about \$64, using multiples of 10% **19. a.** Estimates will vary: about 540; 541 **b.** Estimates will vary: about 180; 180 **21.** 33.6 **23.** 211 **25.** 21 **27.** Woodfield Mall: about 64%; The Galleria: about 57%; Tysons Corner Center: about 52% **29.** 0.45 **31.** 1% **33.** 200 **35.** 20 **37. a.** about 46% **b.** about 10% **c.** about 19%

39. a. Sample Response: Would you be more likely to eat at a new Italian or a new Chinese restaurant in the mall? **b.** people who visit the mall **c.** Sample Response: every 5th person entering the mall

Spiral Review (p. 137)

42. 24 m **43.** 19.2 **44.** 377.8 **45.** 2.4 **46.** 1.8 **47.** 0.062 **48.** 30 **49.** 150 **51.** Random sampling; Each person in the population has an equally likely chance of being chosen and represented.

Extra Skill Practice (p. 138)

1. Sample Response: biased; "How do you feel about a grocery store being built in this town?" **3.** not biased **5.** about 1275 **7.** about 18,500 **9.** about \$26 **11.** about 567 **13.** 6 **15.** 8690 **17.** 66 **19.** 50 **21.** 40 **23.** 1862 **25.** 2032

Study Skills (p. 138)

2. Answers will vary. Sample response: At a store with items on sale for 50%, 25%, or 20% off. **3.** Answers will vary.

Section 5, Practice and Application (p. 144)

1. Sample Response: Change 69% to the "nice" fraction $\frac{2}{3}$, then find $\frac{2}{3}$ of 60. Find 10% of \$60 and then multiply by 7. **3.** about 48; 52.8 **5.** about 120; 107.55 **7.** Hard Hats USA **9.** about 1000, 964; about 650, 656; about 900, 923; about 500, 533; about 200, 226. **11. a.** about a 3.1% increase **b.** 0% increase **13.** Sample Response: Movies about 9.9 billion, sports about 15.5 billion. **15. a.** 300% increase **b.** 55% decrease **c.** 108% increase **d.** 59% decrease

Spiral Review (p. 147)

18. 1456 **19.** 9.7 **20.** 639.1 **21.** 61 **22.** 300.2 **23.** 332.5 **24.** GCF 5; LCM 30 **25.** GCF 4, LCM 48 **26.** GCF 7, LCM 147 **27.** $<$ **28.** $<$ **29.** $=$ **30.** $>$

Extension (p. 148)

31. about 43%; 30%

Career Connection (p. 148)

33. about 178%

Extra Skill Practice (p. 149)

1. about 170; 187 **3.** about 3.5; 3.36 **5.** about 64; 60.8 **7.** about 9% **9.** about 19% **11.** about 99.4% **13.** about 95% decrease

Standardized Testing (p. 149)

Sample Response: Rosa is correct. New York only had a 1.3% increase in population while North Carolina had a 7.5% increase.

Review & Assessment (pp. 152)

1. 70 **2.** –15 **3.** 17 **4.** –37 **5.** –90 **6.** 192 **7.** –9 **8.** 12 **9.** –14 **10.** 0 **11.** –50 **12.** –5 and 5

13. Sample Response: The opposite of a number is the integer you add to that number to get a sum of 0; –2 and 2, –7 and 7, –0.34 and 0.34.

14.

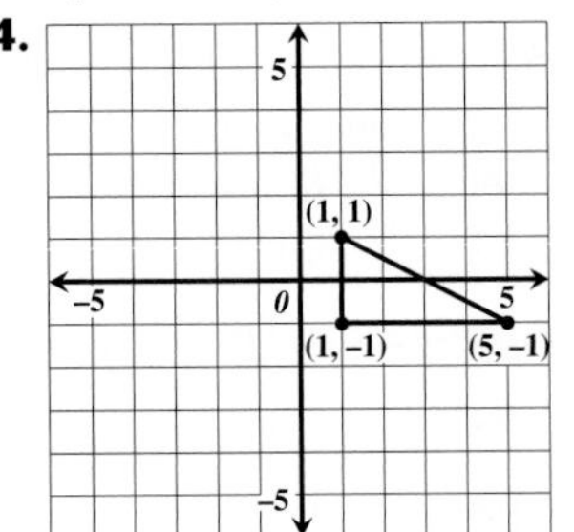

15. $-\frac{11}{24}$ **16.** $-1\frac{7}{15}$ **17.** $-2\frac{14}{15}$ **18.** $6\frac{1}{2}$

19.

First Ball	Second Ball	Outcome
B	Y	BY
	R_1	BR_1
	R_2	BR_2
Y	B	YB
	R_1	YR_1
	R_2	YR_2
R_1	Y	R_1Y
	B	R_1B
	R_2	R_1R_2
R_2	Y	R_2Y
	B	R_2B
	R_1	R_2R_1

20. $\frac{1}{6}$ **21.** $\frac{13}{25}$ **22.** Yes; Should students have access to the Internet? **23. a.** representative; This group should have the same characteristics as the rest of the population. **b.** not representative; Students in grades 5–7 are not represented. **24. a.** about 525 **b.** about 770 **25. a.** 500 New England youths; Sample Response: No; the sample is too small and only from one region of the country. **b.** 450 youths **26.** about 50%: the markup is \$153 and $\frac{153}{322} \approx \frac{1}{2} = 50\%$. **27.** about \$44.50; $30\% \approx \frac{1}{3}$ and $\frac{1}{3}$ of \$66 = \$22, so \$66.50 – \$22 = \$44.50. **28. a.** 41% **b.** 64% **c.** 86%

MODULE 3

Section 1, Practice and Application (p. 164)

1. 10 **3.** 60 **5.** $\frac{2}{5}$ **7. a.** $93\frac{1}{2}$ in.^{2} **b.** $9\frac{1}{2}$ in. × $9\frac{1}{2}$ in. **9.** about 6.2 **11.** about 3.5 **15.** $\frac{1}{10}$ **17.** –900; exact **19.** about –5.7; estimate **21.** about 31.6; estimate **23.** length of side ≈ 97.5 yd; perimeter of plot ≈ 390 yd **25.** $c = 10a + 3000$ where c represents the cooling capacity and a represents the floor area

27. a. 18 ft, 24 ft; cooling capacity: 7320 Btu/hr — 18 ft, 12 ft; cooling capacity: 5160 Btu/hr

b. No; Sample Response: 7320 is only about 1.5 • 5160 so she needs about 1.5 times the cooling capacity for the larger room.

Spiral Review (p. 166)

30.

Amounts Raised by Students at a Charity Dance Marathon (dollars)

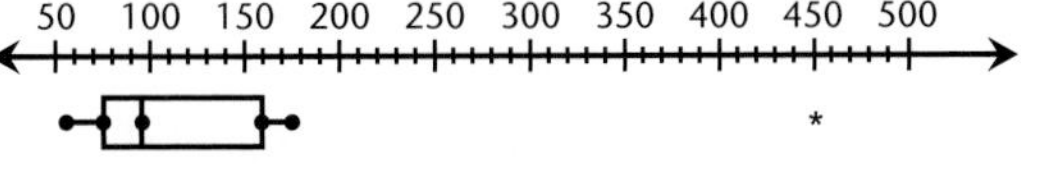

31. 4 or –4 **32.** 11 or –11 **33.** –19 **34.** 6
35. a. $A(-2, -2)$, $B(-2, 1)$, $C(1, 1)$, $D(2, -1)$
b. $A'(0, -2)$, $B'(0, 1)$, $C'(3, 1)$, $D'(4, -1)$

Extra Skill Practice (p. 167)

1. 700 **3.** $\frac{1}{10}$ **5.** 0.06 **7.** 0.02 **9.** about 7.1 **11.** about 11.7 **13.** about 6.6 **15.** about 5.7 **17.** about 5.3; estimate **19.** 2.5; exact **21.** about 2.2; estimate **23.** 0.8; exact **25.** 8 cm^3

Study Skills (p. 167)

1.–4. Answers will vary.

Section 2, Practice and Application (p. 176)

1. 15 **3.** 3 **5.** 3 **7.** The operations were done in order from left to right instead of doing the division and then the addition. **9.** The 5 in the numerator was divided by 5 but the 3 was not. The numerator should have been evaluated before dividing by 5. **11.** about 1.6
13. a. about 39.5 **b.** Sample Response: No. The Lake of the Ozarks isn't even close to a circle. It is very long and skinny, so the ratio shouldn't be very close to 1.
15. –23 **17.** –0.1 **19.** 7.5 **21. a.** 11.75 mi/hr; $d = 11.75h$ **b.** 6 mi/hr; $d = 6h$

c.

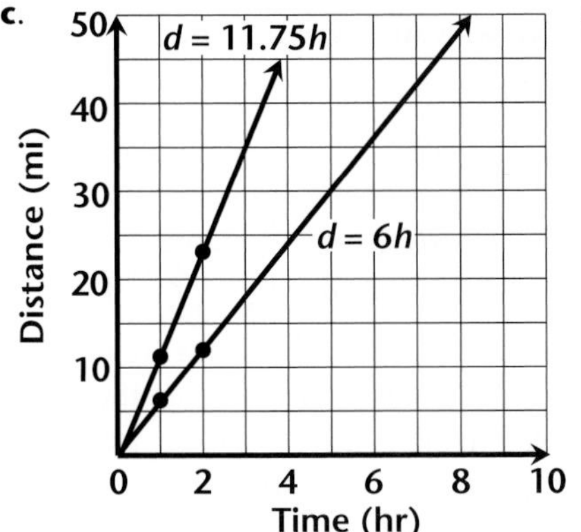

about 8 hr

23.

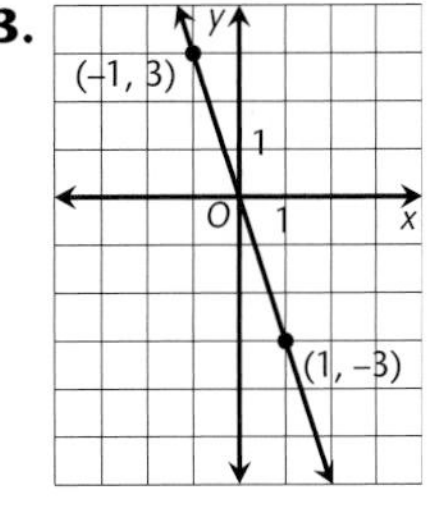

25.

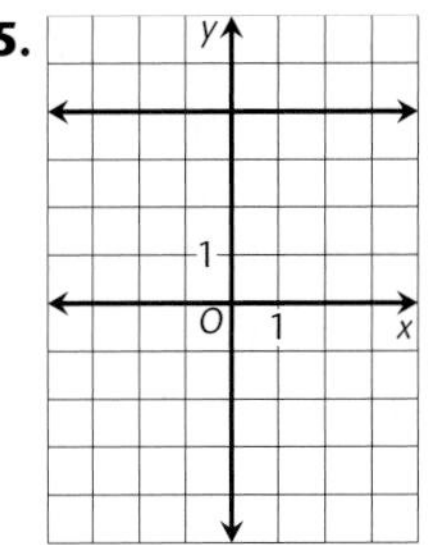

27.

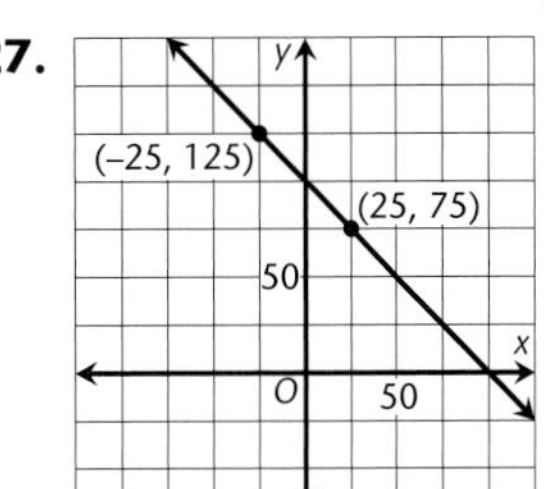

29. $y = 4$

31. nonlinear

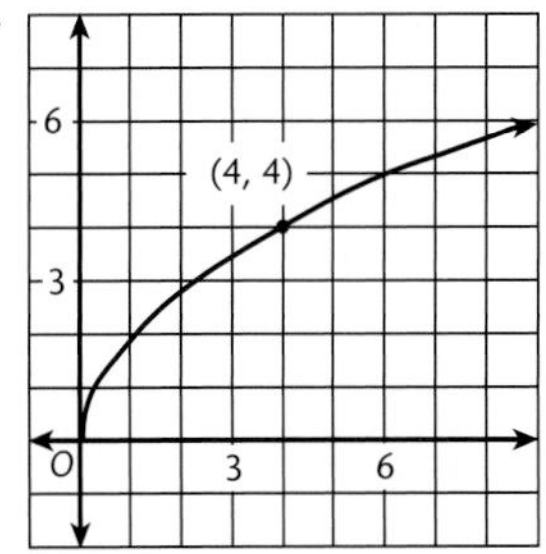

33. a.

Radius r (cm)	Volume V (cm^3)
1	4
2	34
3	113
5	524
10	4189
20	33,510

b.

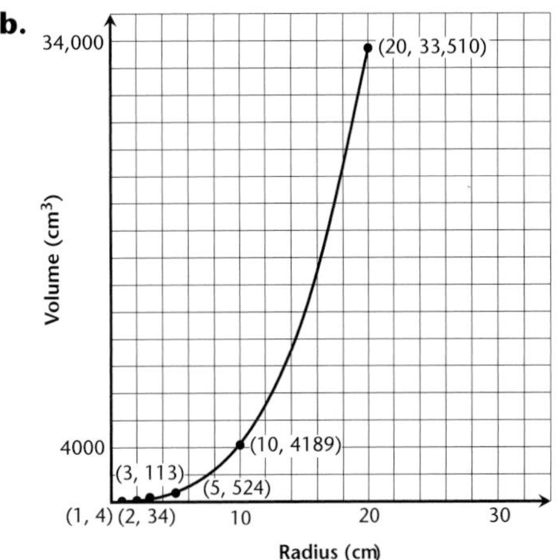

c. about 1150 cm^3

SELECTED ANSWERS

Spiral Review (p. 178)

35. about 2.8 **36.** about 3.3 **37.** about 3.9 **38.** about 0.4 **39.** $A(-2, -3)$, $B(0, -1)$, $C(1, 0)$, $M(-2, 2)$, $N(1, -1)$ **40.** $0.14/oz **41.** 0.29 mi/hr **42.** $74.67/hr

Extra Skill Practice (p. 179)

1. 4 **3.** 0.47 **5.** 1 **7.** 5 **9.** –6

11.

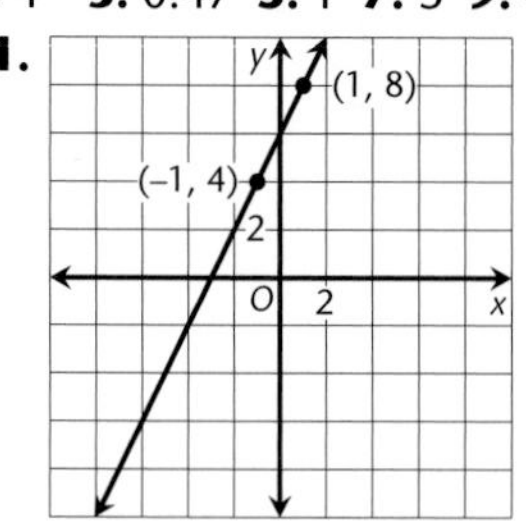

13.

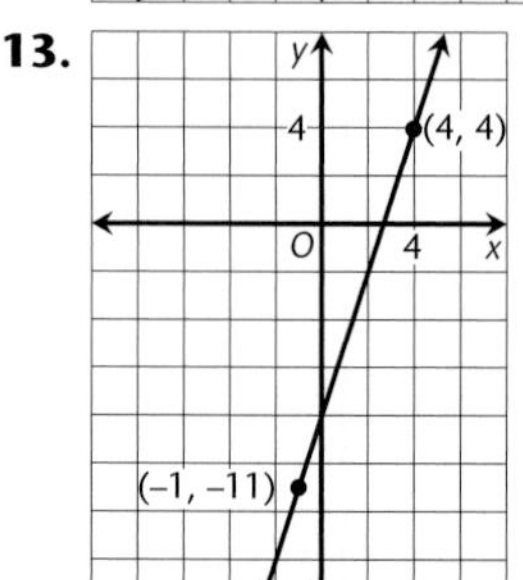

15.

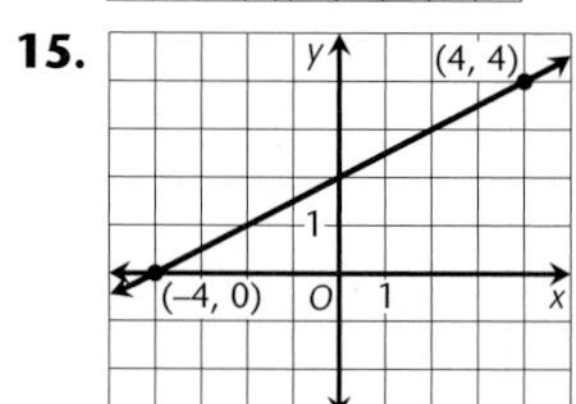

17. $y = -2x + 12$; $y = 3x - 8$; $y = 0.5x + 2$

19.

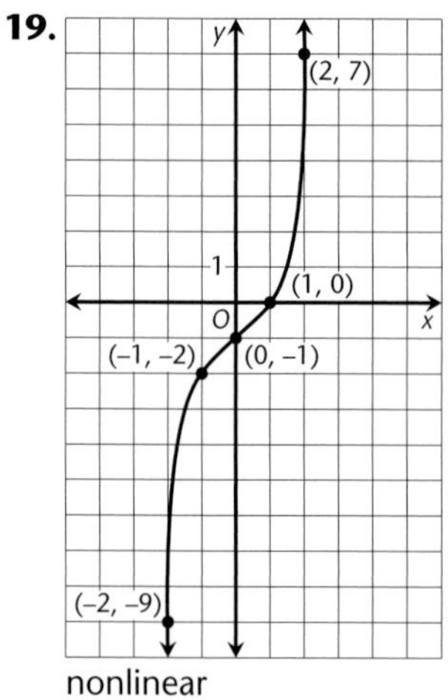

nonlinear

Standardized Testing (p. 179)

1. A **2.** C **3.** B

Section 3, Practice and Application (p. 187)

1. 5 **3.** $\frac{1}{2}$ or 0.5 **5. a.** the blue line; Sample Response: Since the blue line is steeper than the red line, it represents a faster walking rate. **b.** Segura's walking rate = 16 km/hr or about 0.27 km/min; Petersen's walking rate = 12 km/hr or 0.2 km/min **c.** Segura: $d = 0.27t$ where d = distance (km) and t = time (min) or $d = 16t$ where d = distance (km) and t = time (hr) Petersen: $d = 0.2t$ where d = distance (km) and t = time (min) or $d = 12t$ where d = distance (km) and t = time (hr) **9.** A; slope = 0.75, (0, –10) is on the line. **11.** about 1.9; Sample Response: I divided the height of each woman at age 18 by her height at age 2. All of the answers rounded to 1.9, so the average is about 1.9. **13.** 160.1 cm

Spiral Review (p. 189)

15. $10\frac{2}{3}$ **16.** 12 **17.** $\frac{3}{4}$ **18.** 12 **19.** multiply by 8; $x = 136$ **20.** 13.5 **21.** 26.55 **22.** 0.068 **23.** 55 boxes **24.** Possible answers: 3 round and 16 rectangular, 6 round and 12 rectangular, 9 round and 8 rectangular, 12 round and 4 rectangular **25.** dollars and pairs of socks; $5/pair **26.** dollars and oranges; $0.27/orange

Extra Skill Practice (p. 190)

1. $\frac{3}{2}$ or 1.5 **3.** $\frac{1}{3}$ **5.** slope $= \frac{160 - 110}{90 - 60} = \frac{5}{3}$

Standardized Testing (p. 190)

Answers will vary. Sample Response: Two people hiked up a trail to a mountain lake, a distance of 8 km. They both left the trailhead at the same time, the more experienced hiker averaging 1.5 km/hr and the other averaging $\frac{1}{3}$ km/hr. The faster hiker reached the lake in $5\frac{1}{3}$ hr. However, after hiking 12 hr, the novice hiker was only half way to the lake and decided to pitch camp and continue on in the morning.
vertical axis: distance from trailhead in kilometers
horizontal axis: time in hours
The red line represents the faster hiker, so it is steeper than the green line which represents the slower hiker.

Section 4, Practice and Application (p. 199)

1. $\frac{5}{3.3}$ **3. a.** 65° **b.** 7.26 cm **c.** about 7.58 cm **5.** $\triangle LMN \sim \triangle PQN$ **7.** $\triangle QRS \sim \triangle UPT$ **9.** Sample Response: Because the corresponding angles of trapezoids *MNQR* and *NLPQ* have the same measures. **11.** $\frac{PQ}{QR} = \frac{0.8}{1.4} \approx 0.57$ and $\frac{LP}{NQ} = \frac{2.5}{2.8} \approx 0.89$. Since the ratios are not equal, the trapezoids are not similar. **15.** Use the folded paper to show that the angles of each smaller triangle have the same measures as the angles of the larger triangles.

17. Yes; Sample Response: The corresponding angles of the parallelograms have the same measure, and the corresponding sides are in proportion, so the parallelograms are similar.

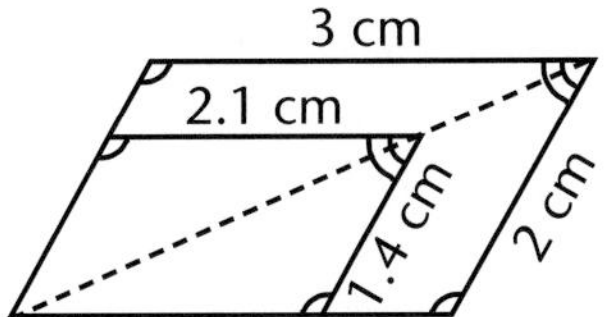

19. Answers will vary.

Spiral Review (p. 202)

20.

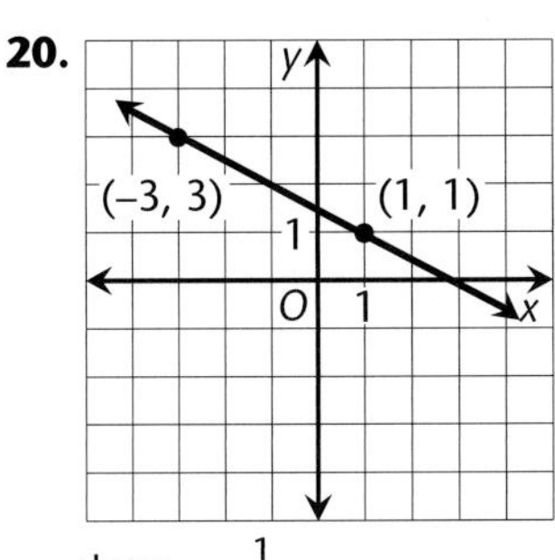

slope = $-\frac{1}{2}$

21.

slope = 4

22. $33\frac{1}{3}$% decrease **23.** 37.5% increase **24.** about 34% decrease **25.** 360 **26.** 4 **27.** 249,000 **28.** 0.7 **29.** 753,000 **30.** 987,000 **31.** 16 **32.** 10,180,000

Extension (p. 202)

33. Answers will vary.

Extra Skill Practice (p. 203)

1. $\frac{3}{8}$ or $\frac{8}{3}$ **3. a.** 90° **b.** 12 **c.** 40 **5.** Use the proportion $\frac{BA}{ED} = \frac{AC}{DC}$. Substitute the known distances and solve for x: $\frac{x}{15} = \frac{40}{20}$; CE is not needed.

Standardized Testing (p. 203)

1. a. $\overline{PC}$ and $\overline{PD}$ **b.** any two of $\angle CPA$, $\angle CPB$, $\angle DPA$, and $\angle DPB$ **2.** Sample Response:

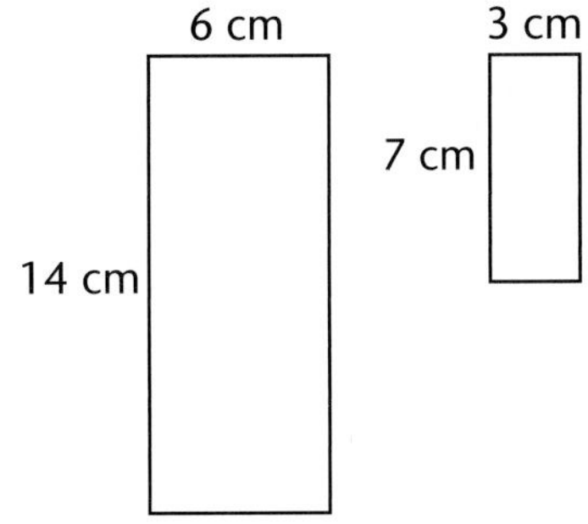

Section 5, Practice and Application (p. 210)

1. 4,500,000,000 yr **3.** 186,000 mi/sec **5.** A and B are in scientific notation. The numbers are written as a product of a number that is greater than or equal to 1 and less than 10 and a power of 10. C is not in scientific notation because 82.1 is greater than 10, and D is not in scientific notation because 2^{10} is not a power of 10.

7. Large Cloud of Magellan: $9.7 \cdot 10^{17}$ mi
Small Cloud of Magellan: $1.1 \cdot 10^{18}$ mi
Ursa Minor dwarf: $1.4 \cdot 10^{18}$ mi
Draco dwarf: $1.5 \cdot 10^{18}$ mi
Sculptor dwarf: $1.6 \cdot 10^{18}$ mi
Fornax dwarf: $2.5 \cdot 10^{18}$ mi
Leo II dwarf: $4.4 \cdot 10^{18}$ mi
Leo I dwarf: $4.4 \cdot 10^{18}$ mi
Barnard's Galaxy: $1.0 \cdot 10^{19}$ mi

9. a. $3.795 \cdot 10^{3}$ **b.** 3.795 km and 11.033 km
11. 5 **13.** 2.4 **15.** 24 **17.** 0 **19.** 1.02 **21.** 11 in.
23. size $8\frac{1}{2}$ or 9

Spiral Review (p. 212)

27. about 3.0 m **28.** –1 **29.** 17 **30.** 90 **31.** 6 **32.** 0 **33.** 12 **34.** –13 **35.** 6 **36.** about 80 **37.** about 95

Extra Skill Practice (p. 213)

1. $5.18 \cdot 10^{6}$ **3.** $2.89 \cdot 10^{7}$ **5.** $3.629 \cdot 10^{11}$
7. 350,000,000 **9.** 810,000
11. 480,000,000,000,000 **13.** 47,600
15. 60,000,000,000 **17.** 132.84 **19.** 1.1
21. 67.07 **23.** 71.97 **25.** 301.5 **27.** 1.33 **29.** 3.20

Standardized Testing (p. 213)

1. D **2.** B

Section 6, Practice and Application (p. 218)

1. exclusive or **3.** Marion Jones, Florence Griffith Joyner, and Renate Stecher **5.** 17 **7.** 42 students **9.** About 62% of the students acted in *Hello Dolly*, so she was only off by 2%.

11.

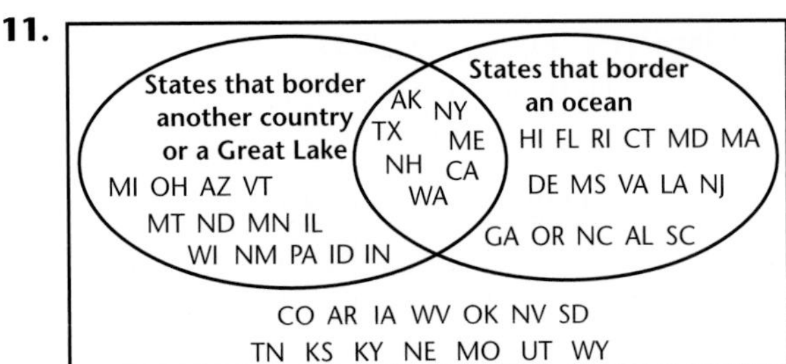

Spiral Review (p. 220)

15. 83 **16.** 0.6 **17.** 15.43

18. a.

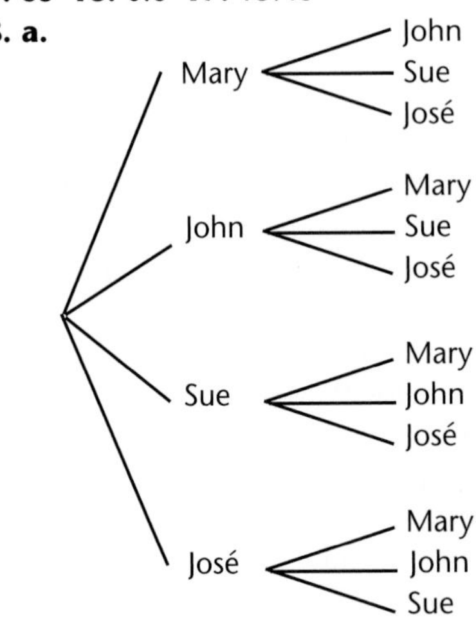

b. $\frac{1}{6}$ **19.** equilateral and isosceles **20.** scalene **21.** isosceles

Extra Skill Practice (p. 221)

1. moose, raccoon, skunk, deer **3.** 7 animals **5.** in the blue part of the oval labeled "Mammals"

Standardized Testing (p. 221)

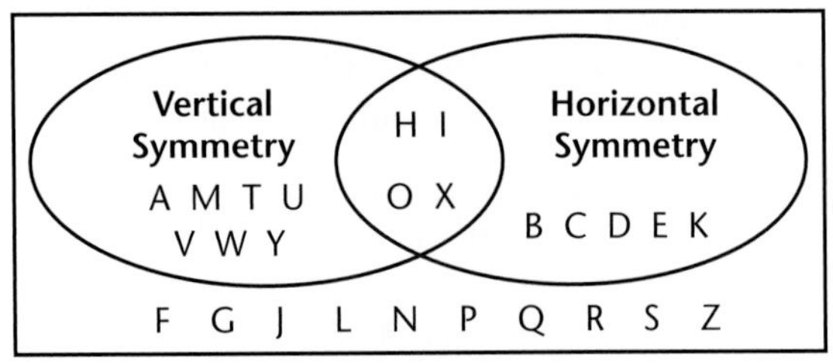

Review and Assessment (p. 226)

1. 0.3; mental math; exact **2.** about 126.5; calculator; estimate **3.** about –9.8; calculator; estimate **4.** $\frac{2}{9}$; mental math; exact **5.** No; Sample Response: He is comparing linear dimensions. Since the radius and height of the large can are twice those of the small can, the volume is 8 times greater. **6.** 3 **7.** $\frac{2}{3}$ **8.** $\frac{2}{9}$

9. linear

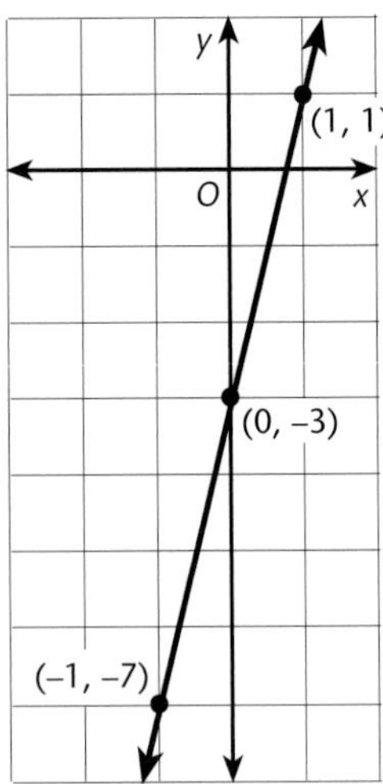

10. linear

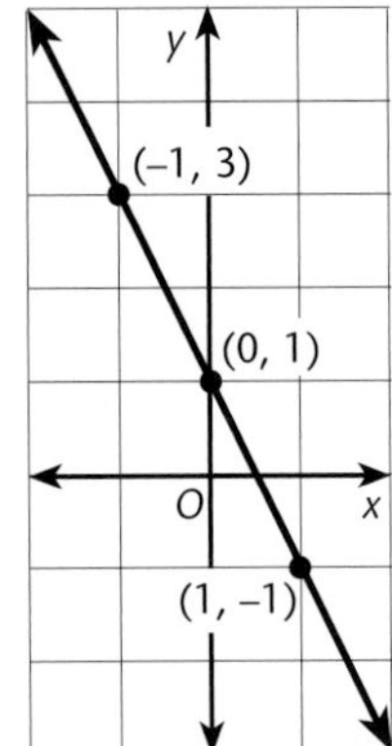

11. nonlinear

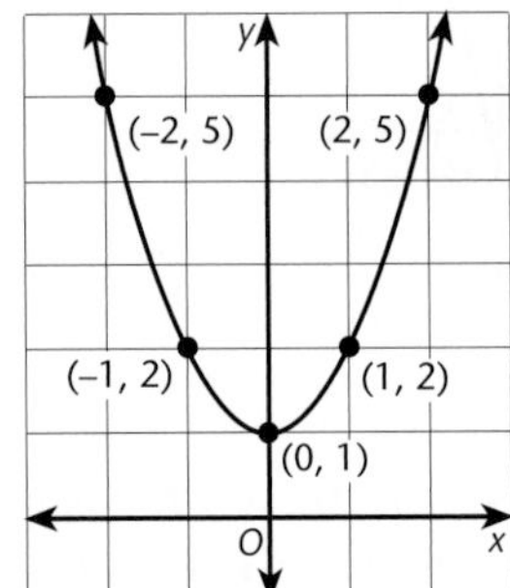

12. linear

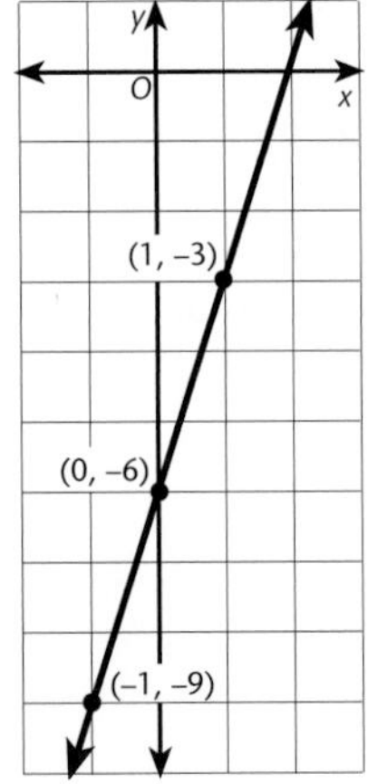

13. $\frac{1}{2}$ **14.** 2 **15.** 1 **16. a.** I **b.** 6780 **17.** about 30 ft **18.** about 22 cm or $8\frac{5}{8}$ in. **19.** $5.25 \bullet 10^7$ **20.** $7.62 \bullet 10^5$ **21.** 6950 ft **22.** 700 yr
24.

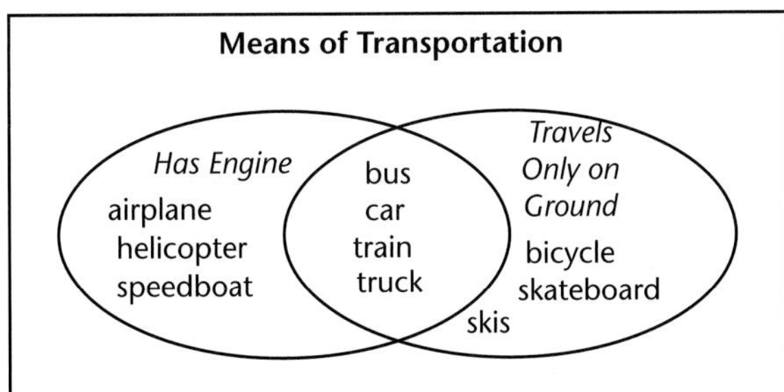

25. airplane, helicopter, speedboat, bus, car, train, truck **26.** bus, car, train, truck **27.** Sample Response: raft (neither), motorcycle (both)

MODULE 4

Section 1, Practice and Application (p. 239)

1. a. 24π m **b.** 10π ft **c.** 1.1π cm **3. a.** smallest bicycle: about 2.39 in.; largest bicycle: about 31.4 ft **b.** smallest bicycle: about 2.39 in.; largest bicycle: about 31.4 ft **c.** about 68 **d.** about 2135.2 ft **5. a.** 64π ft^2 **b.** 900π cm^2 **c.** 1.96π m^2 **7. a.** about 95 ft^2 **b.** about 190 ft^2 **c.** about 34.54 ft **d.** about 18.84 ft **e.** about $\frac{1}{6}$ **11.** 54π in.^{3} or about 169.56 in.^{3} **13.** 40π cm^3 or about 125.6 cm^3 **15.** 1690π cm^3 or about 5306.6 cm^3 **17.** 1274 cm^3 **19. a.** 16 and 17 **b.** 15 **21. a.** about 6400 ft^3, about 6620 ft^3 **b.** 275.625 in.^{3} **c.** about 41,503; Multiply the volume of the large popcorn box by $12^3 = 1728$ to convert it to in.^{3}. Then divide that volume by the volume of the regular size box to get an estimate. **23. a.** 267,946.67 in.^{3} **b.** 555.37 m^3 **c.** 4.19 ft^3

Spiral Review (p. 243)

27.

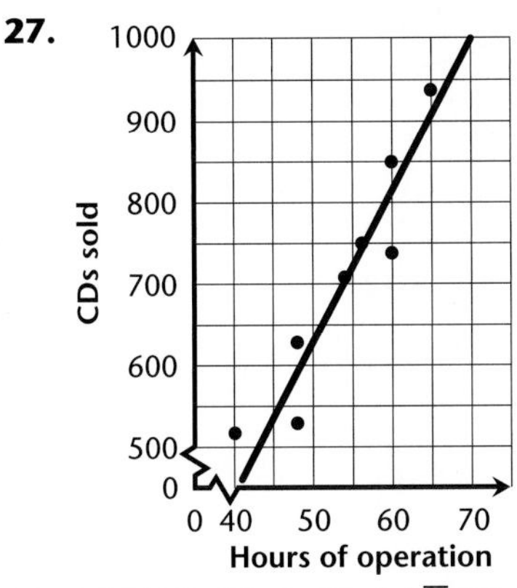

28. 0.01175 **29.** 2 **30.** $1.0\overline{3}$ **31.** $8.36\overline{7}$ **32.** 44 **33.** 27 **34.** 33 **35.** 15

Extra Skill Practice (p. 244)

1. 30π cm **3.** 12π ft **5.** 16π in.^{2} **7.** 3120.28 mm^3 **9.** 192 mm^3 **11. a.** 1471.29 in.^{3} **b.** 0.24 mm^3

Standardized Testing (p. 244)

1. Sample Response: Both use the formula $V = Bh$. The base of a prism is a polygon, so the area of its base, B, will always be exact. The base of a cylinder is a circle, so the formula for the area of its base is $B = \pi r^2$ and will only be exact when left in terms of π. **2.** Sample Response: A cereal box has a length of 10 in., a width of 3 in., and a height of 14 in. What is the volume of the cereal box? Answer: 420 in.^{3}

Section 2, Practice and Application (p. 252)

1. 113.04 cm^2 **3.** 452.16 in.^{2} **5.** 103.56 m^2 **7.** about 30 in.^{2} **9. a.** about 1282 frames **b.** about 15,384 light detectors **11.** about 0.84 **13.** water chestnuts, olives, chili peppers **15.** Answers will vary.

Spiral Review (p. 254)

20. about 20 **21.** about 700 **22.** about 560

23.

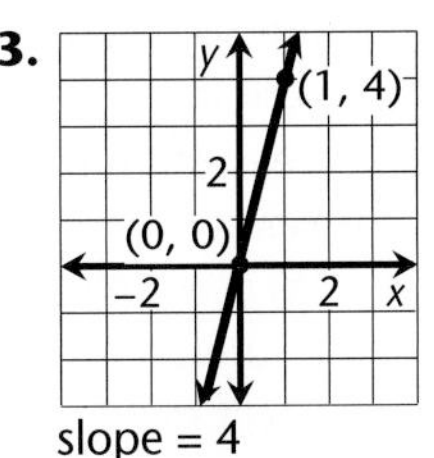

slope = 4

24.

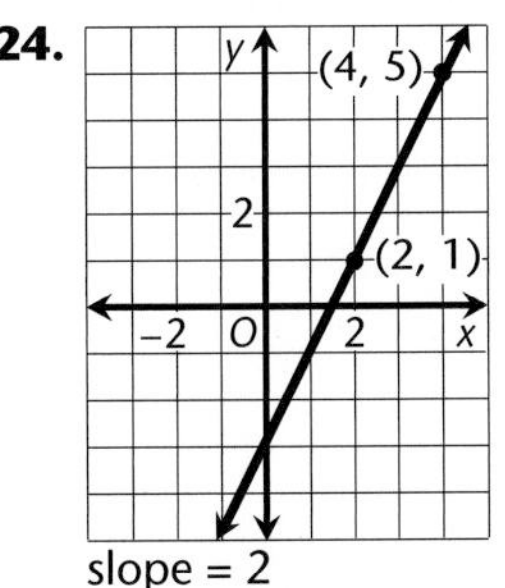

slope = 2

25.

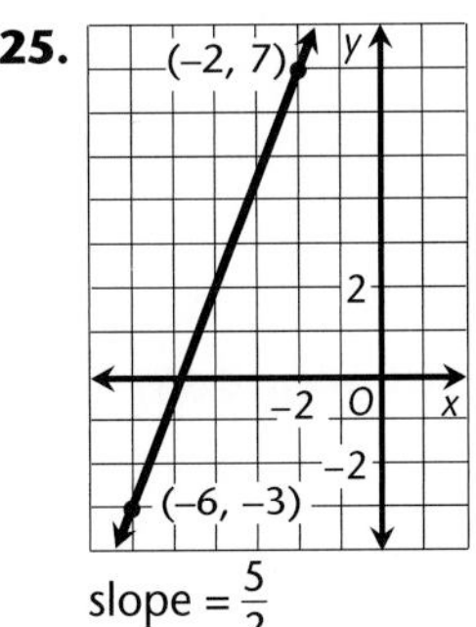

slope = $\frac{5}{2}$

SELECTED ANSWERS

26.

slope $= -\frac{5}{7}$

27. a. $A = 24 \text{ in.}^2$ **b.** $A = 26 \text{ m}^2$

Extension (p. 255)

29. Sample Response: radius: 0.6 cm; height: 1.2 cm

Extra Skill Practice (p. 256)

1. 251.2 in.^2 **3.** 3523.08 cm^2 **5.** 90.432 m^2 **7.** $2.\overline{3}$ **9.** $1.7\overline{3}$ **11.** 1.5 **13.** The cylinder with a radius of 2.5 in. and a height of 3 in.; The ratio of surface area to volume is lowest.

Study Skills (p. 256)

1. Sample Response: The two formulas are alike in that they both use π, r, and h. They are different in that the formula for surface area ($2\pi r^2 + 2\pi rh$) uses both multiplication and addition and has an answer in square units, while the formula for volume ($\pi r^2 h$) uses only multiplication and has an answer in cubic units.
2. Sample Response: The lines both intersect the y-axis at 2 and appear to be equally steep, although the first line slopes up to the right while the second slopes down to the right.

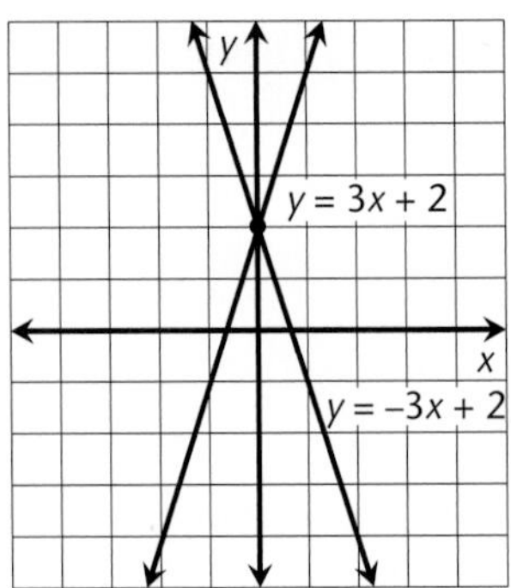

3. Answers will vary.

Section 3, Practice and Application (p. 265)

1. $-\frac{3}{5}$ **3.** $\frac{1}{3}$ **5.** 0 **7.** $-\frac{9}{7}$

9. Accept reasonable estimates.

Kemp's Ridley Turtle Nests (1970–1995)	
Time Period	Rate of Change (number of turtle nests/year)
1970–1975	–350
1975–1980	–75
1980–1985	–50
1985–1990	65
1990–1995	200

11. Sample Response: 1985; The number of nests began to increase in 1985. **13.** slope: 2; y-intercept: 0 **15.** It got worse; The line shows a decrease in pH which means that the acidity of the rain increased. **17.** about 4.58; Sample Response: I assumed the trend would continue, so I solved the equation $y = -0.005x + 5.43$ for $x = 170$. **19.** $y = 2x + 4$ **21.** $y = -5$

23. a.

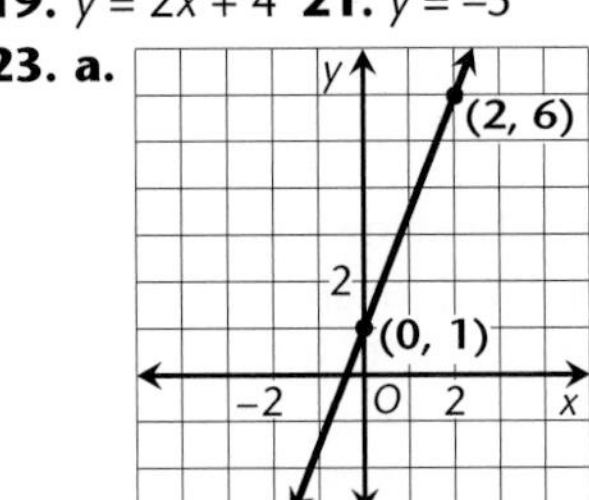

b.

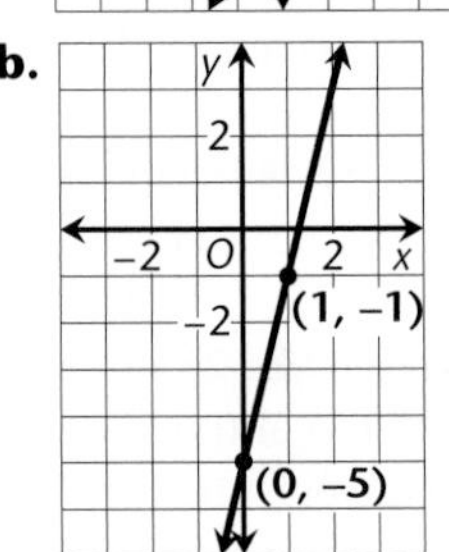

c.

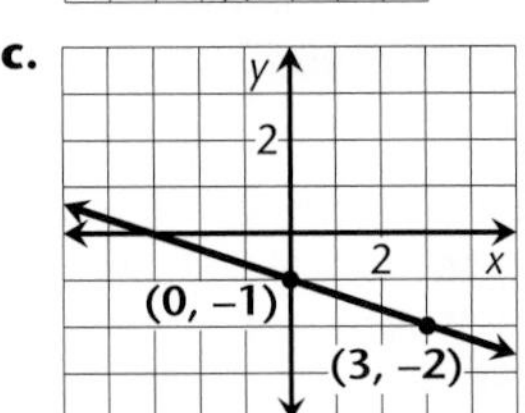

25.

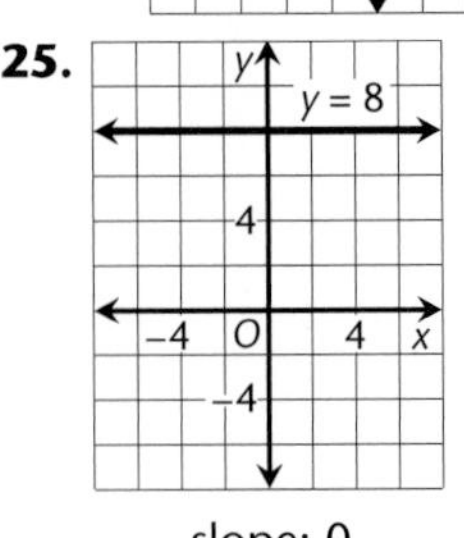

slope: 0

27. 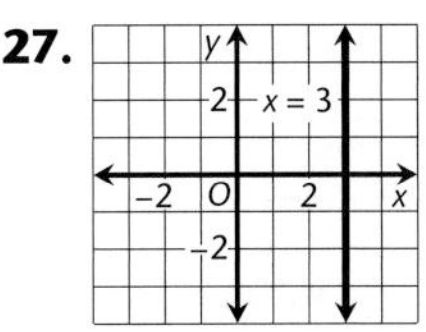

slope: undefined

Spiral Review (p. 268)

30. 351.68 in.^{2} **31.** 55% **32.** 4.5 **33.** $7 \cdot 10^2$ **34.** $2.593 \cdot 10^3$ **35.** $1.01 \cdot 10^5$

Extra Skill Practice (p. 269)

1. 3 **3.** $-\frac{1}{3}$ **5.** 0 **7.** line B **9.** line A **11.** $y = 2x - 3$ **13.** $y = 1$ **15.** $y = -x + 5$

Standardized Testing (p. 269)

1–4. Sample responses are given. **1.** $y = -5x + 4$ **2.** $y = 3x - 2$ **3.** $y = 2$ **4.** $y = -3x + 7$

Section 4, Practice and Application (p. 278)

1. a. $\frac{1}{5}$ **b.** $\frac{1}{6} + \frac{1}{10} = \frac{8}{30} = \frac{4}{15}$ **c.** $\frac{1}{2} + \frac{1}{3} + \frac{1}{12} = \frac{11}{12}$ **3. a.** $\frac{-4}{1}$ **b.** $\frac{4}{1}$ **c.** $\frac{1}{4}$ **d.** $\frac{17}{7}$ **7.** $-14.\overline{14}$, $-\sqrt{4}$, -1, 5.33, $\frac{16}{3}$, $5\frac{4}{9}$, 14.1 **9.** −8 **11.** $-\frac{6}{5}$ or $-1\frac{1}{5}$ **13.** −12 **15.** −9 **17.** −0.5 **19.** −2.5 **21.** $-\frac{25}{3}$ or $-8\frac{1}{3}$ **23.** 22 ft **27. a.** 100°C **b.** −4°F

c.

$$\begin{aligned} F &= \frac{9}{5}C + 32 \\ F - 32 &= \frac{9}{5}C \\ \frac{5}{9}(F - 32) &= C \\ \frac{5}{9}F - \frac{5}{9} \cdot 32 &= C \\ \frac{5}{9}F - \frac{160}{9} &= C \\ \frac{5}{9}F - 17\frac{7}{9} &= C \end{aligned}$$

29. a. about 2464 cm^2 **b.** about 4158 cm^2

Spiral Review (p. 280)

31. 3.57 **32.** 14.92 **33.** 0.89 **34.** yes **35.** no **36.** no **37.** no **38.** 8.84 **39.** 59.84 **40.** 121.67 **41.** 20.2

Extension (p. 281)

43. $\frac{2}{9}$ **45.** $\frac{53}{90}$ (multiply by 10)

Extra Skill Practice (p. 282)

1. $\frac{137}{100}$ **3.** $\frac{1}{8}$ **5.** 1.75 **7.** $0.5\overline{3}$ **9.** $-0.\overline{3}, -\frac{3}{10}, \frac{1}{3}, 0.35, \frac{2}{5}$ **11.** > **13.** = **15.** −1.1 **17.** $-\frac{5}{4}$ **19.** −15 **21.** −3 **23.** −1.5 **25.** −5 **27.** 8

Standardized Testing (p. 282)

1. Answers will vary. Sample responses are given. Kelly saves $\frac{3}{5}$ of all the money she earns. How much must she earn to save $30? **2.** Answers will vary. Sample responses are given. Moses purchased a $12 single CD and a half-priced boxed set. The total cost was $40. What was the regular price of the boxed set?

Section 5, Practice and Application (p. 293)

1. a.

Exterior Color	Interior Color	Combination
white	black	white, black
	gray	white, gray
red	black	red, black
	gray	red, gray
navy blue	black	navy blue, black
	gray	navy blue, gray
forest green	black	forest green, black
	gray	forest green, gray
tan	black	tan, black
	gray	tan, gray
maroon	black	maroon, black
	gray	maroon, gray

b. 12 ways

3. a.

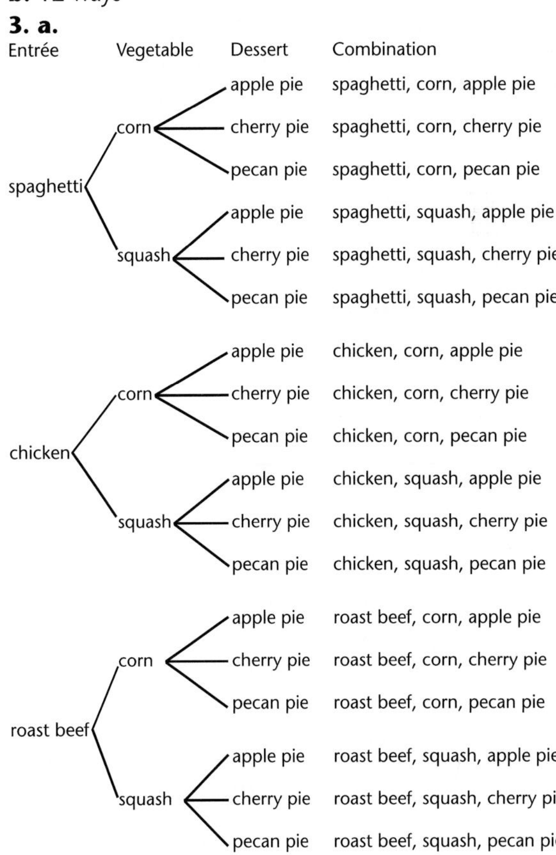

b. 18 dinners

5. 2 **7.** 24 **9.** 5040 **11.** 40,320 orders **13.** 6 combinations **15. a.** 5 **b.** 10 **c.** 10 **d.** 16

Spiral Review (p. 295)

20. $\frac{3}{4}$ **21.** $\frac{3}{2}$ **22.** 2 **23.** $\frac{1}{2}$ **24.** $\frac{2}{3}$

Extension (p. 295)

27. 70 ways

Extra Skill Practice (p. 296)

1. 144 ways **3.** 30 ways **5.** 24 ways **7.** 2^{10} or 1024 ways **9.** 40,320 ways

Standardized Testing (p. 296)

1. 3 ways; combinations problem; The order in which she selects her sketches is not important. **2.** 6 ways; permutations problem; The order in which she hangs her sketches is important.

Section 6, Practice and Application (p. 301)

1. HHH, HHT, HTH, HTT, THH, THT, TTH, TTT

3. $\frac{7}{8} = 0.875$ **5. a.** $3.315312 \cdot 10^{10}$

b. MATH4YOU: $\frac{1}{26 \cdot 25 \cdot 24 \cdot 23 \cdot 10 \cdot 22 \cdot 21 \cdot 20} = \frac{1}{3.315312 \cdot 10^{10}}$

MATH: $\frac{1 \cdot 1 \cdot 1 \cdot 1 \cdot 10 \cdot 22 \cdot 21 \cdot 20}{26 \cdot 25 \cdot 24 \cdot 23 \cdot 10 \cdot 22 \cdot 21 \cdot 20} = \frac{1}{358{,}800}$

A license plate on which the first four letters spell MATH is about 92,400 times more likely than the license plate MATH4YOU. **c.** 80,318,101,760 or $26^7 \cdot 10$ license plates; MATH4YOU: $\frac{1}{26^7 \cdot 10}$; MATH as first four letters: $\frac{1 \cdot 1 \cdot 1 \cdot 1 \cdot 10 \cdot 26^3}{26^7 \cdot 10} = \frac{1}{456{,}976}$. A license plate on which the first four letters spell MATH is 175,760 times more likely than the license plate MATH4YOU.

7. a. 15,625 keys **b.** $\frac{1}{15{,}625}$

Spiral Review (p. 302)

12. 6 combinations

13. a. Science Test Scores

Stem	Leaf
4	1 8
5	2 3 9
6	1 4 6 8
7	0 2 5 5 7 8
8	1 1 1 5 6 7
9	3 4 6 8 9

7 | 2 = 72

b. Science Test Scores

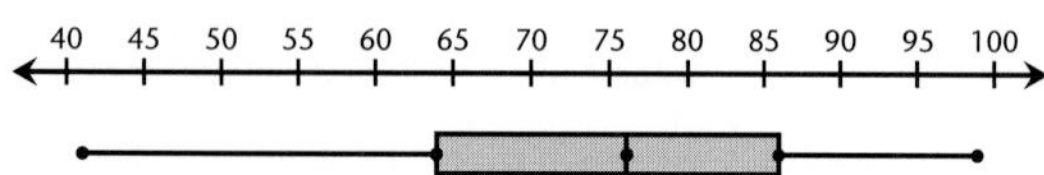

c. median: 76, mode: 81 **d.** Either the stem-and-leaf plot or the box-and-whisker plot could be used to find the median, but only the stem-and-leaf plot could be used to find the mode.

Extra Skill Practice (p. 303)

1. $\frac{1}{100} = 0.01$ **3.** $\frac{64}{125} = 0.512$ **5.** $\frac{999}{1000} = 0.999$ **7.** $\frac{1}{7776} \approx 0.00013$ **9.** $\frac{5}{54} \approx 0.093$ **11.** $\frac{3125}{7776} \approx 0.40$

Standardized Testing (p. 303)

1. $\frac{1}{16} = 0.0625$ **2. a.** $\frac{1}{1296} \approx 0.00077$ **b.** $\frac{625}{1296} \approx 0.48$

Review and Assessment (p. 306)

1. 21.81 ft **2.** the box **3. a.** 9 times greater **b.** 27 times greater **4.** 131.88 cm^2 **5.** 100.48 $in.^2$ **6.** 127.17 ft^2 **7.** 0.8 **8.** 0.7 **9.** $0.8\overline{3}$ **10.** The can in Ex. 8; It has the lowest ratio of surface area to volume.

11. slope: $-\frac{1}{4}$; y-intercept: 2; $y = -\frac{1}{4}x + 2$ **12.** slope: 3; y-intercept: –1; $y = 3x - 1$ **13.** slope: 0; y-intercept: –2; $y = -2$ **14.** Sample Response: The run of a vertical line is always 0. To calculate the slope division by zero is necessary. Since division by zero is undefined, the slope must also be undefined. **15.** Sample Response: $y = mx$ and $y = mx + b$. (Students may substitute any numbers for m and b in the equations as long as the slope (m) is the same in both equations.) They are parallel because the slope is the same in both equations. **16. a.** $0.\overline{45}$ **b.** –3.25 **c.** 0.875 **17.** $-\frac{3}{4}, -\frac{8}{11}$, –0.72, –0.7, $\frac{5}{7}$, 0.72, $0.7\overline{2}$, $0.\overline{72}$, $\frac{3}{4}$ **18.** –2 **19.** –12 **20.** –9 **21. a.** 6 uniforms **b.** 120 ways **c.** Armand and Cathy, Armand and Ishana, Armand and Jim, Armand and Susan, Cathy and Ishana, Cathy and Jim, Cathy and Susan, Ishana and Jim, Ishana and Susan, Jim and Susan. **22. a.** 10^4 or 10,000 passwords **b.** $\frac{9}{100} = 0.09$

MODULE 5

Section 1, Practice and Application (p. 317)

1. Sample Response:

3. 4 prisms: $1 \cdot 1 \cdot 12$; $1 \cdot 2 \cdot 6$; $1 \cdot 3 \cdot 4$; $2 \cdot 2 \cdot 3$

5.

Figure before removing cubes: S.A. = 24 $unit^2$, V = 8 $unit^3$; Figure after removing cubes: S.A. = 24 $unit^2$, V = 7 $unit^3$

7. a. 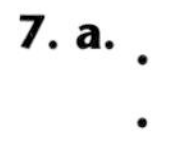

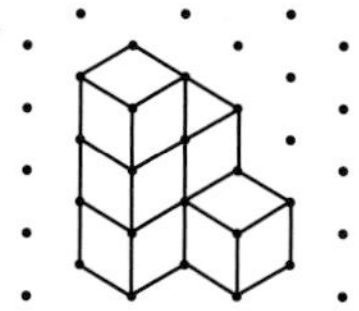

b. Sample Responses:

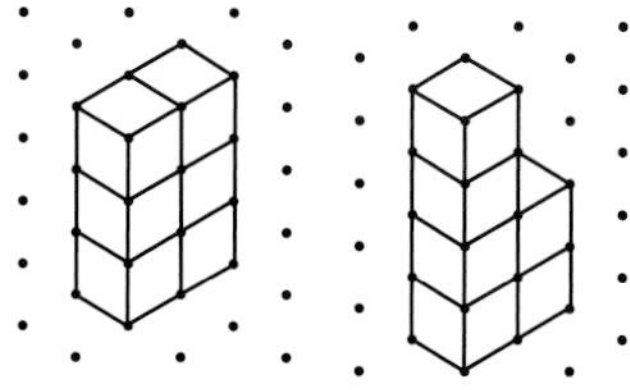

9. front view

11.

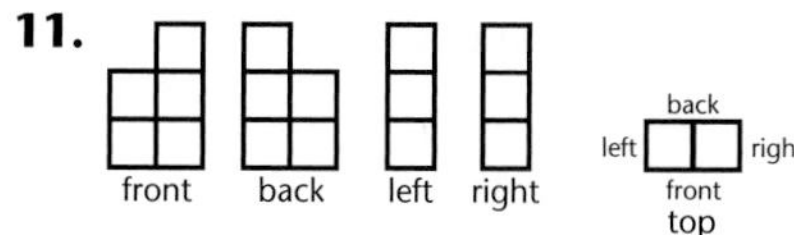

13.

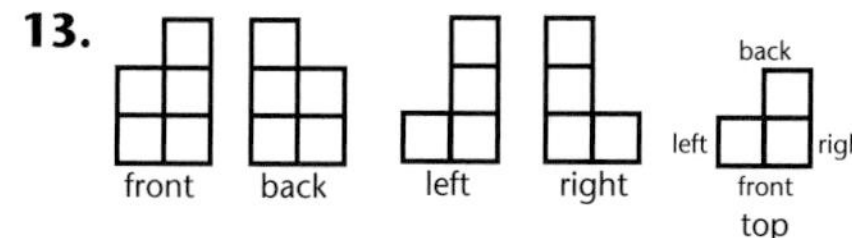

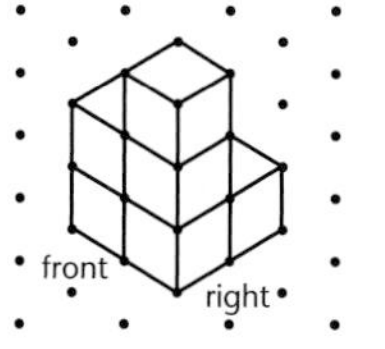

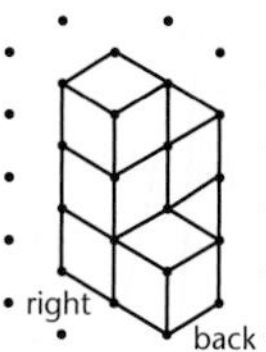

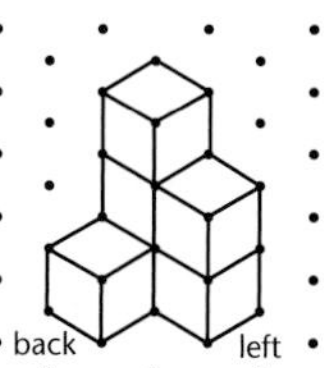

Spiral Reveiw (p. 319)

16. a. $\frac{1}{3}$ or about 0.33 **b.** $\frac{2}{3}$ or about 0.67 **17.** 6 **18.** 3 **19.** 12 **20.** 7.5 **21.** 3.2 **22.** 5.6 **23.** $\frac{13}{24}$ **24.** $-\frac{7}{20}$ **25.** $-1\frac{7}{9}$

Extra Skills Practice (p. 320)

1. Sample Response: 

3. 

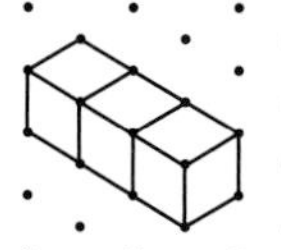

5.

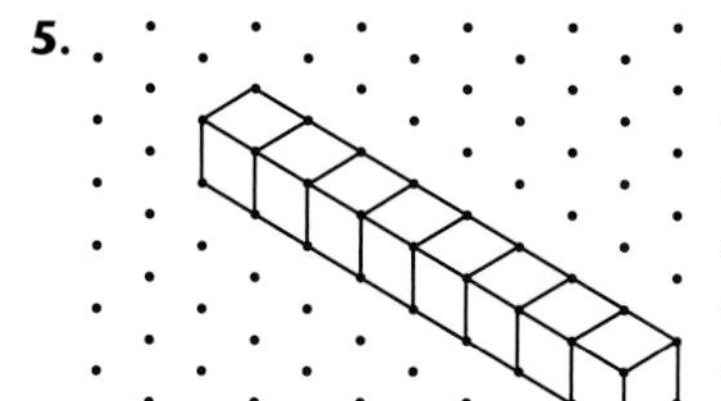

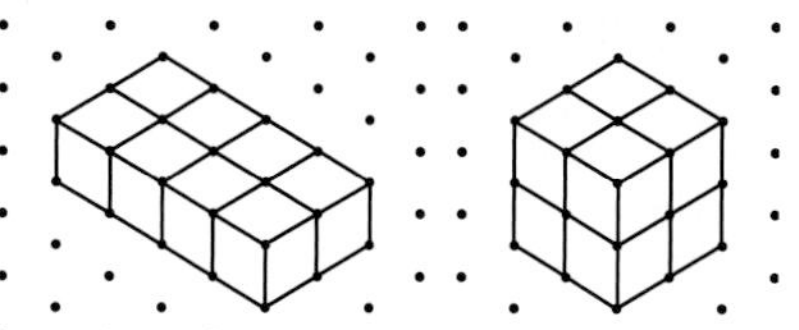

7.

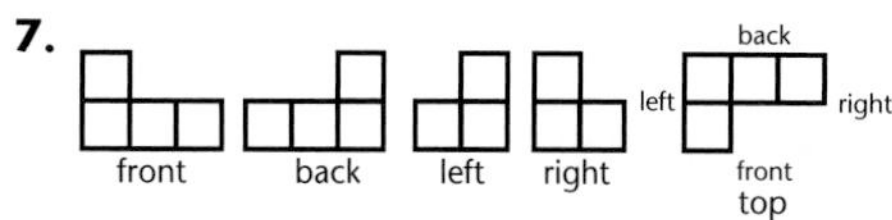

9.

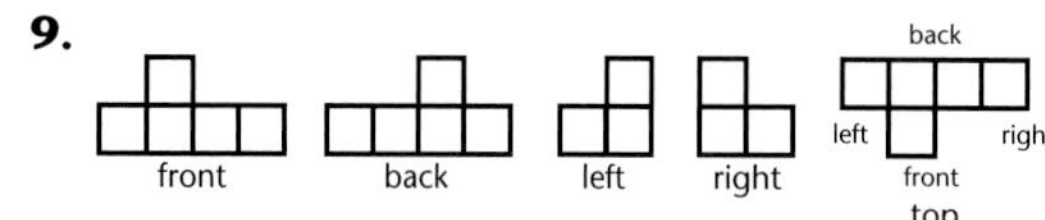

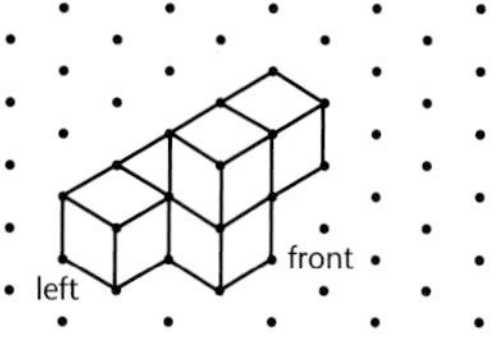

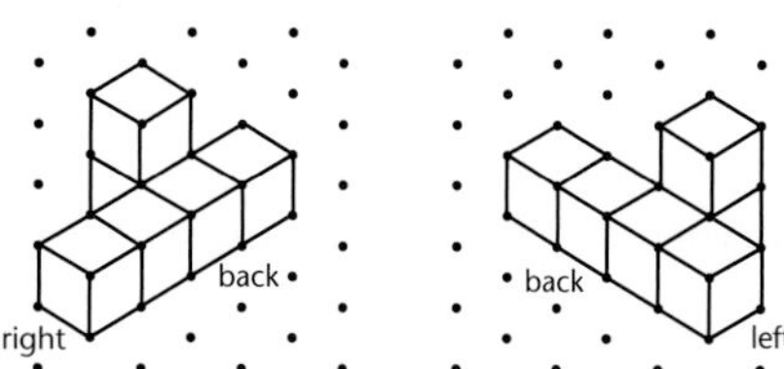

Section 2, Practice and Application (p. 332)

1. No; The sum of the lengths of segments *k* and *m* is less than the length of segment *n*, so the segments will not form a triangle. **3.** Yes; The sum of the lengths of segments *x* and *w* is greater than the length of segment *y*, so these three segments will form a triangle. **5.** Yes **7.** Yes **9.** Yes **11** similar: 1 and 3, 2 and 5, 4, 6, and 7; congruent: 2 and 5, 4 and 6; For similar triangles, check the type of triangle and the angle measures. For congruent triangles, use the side-side-side or side-angle-side rule. $\triangle GHK \cong \triangle EFD$, $\triangle STV \cong \triangle QPR$

15. a–c. Answers will vary. **17.** 16 edges

19. a. triangles and rectangles

b. Sample sketch:

c. 13 faces, 24 edges, 13 vertices **21.** D **23.** C

SELECTED ANSWERS

Spiral Review (p. 335)

30.

front back left right; back left right front top

31. –30 **32.** 1 **33.** –20 **34.** –0.5 **35.** 2 **36.** $-0.\overline{3}$ **37.** 45 **38.** 15 **39.** 30

Extra Skill Practice (p. 336)

1. No **3.** Yes

5. a. Sample Response:

7. Congruent; Two sides and the included angle of $\triangle PQR$ are congruent to two sides and the included angle of $\triangle NML$.

Standardized Testing (p. 336)

Number of sides on the base of each pyramid	Number of faces on the new polyhedron	Number of edges on the new polyhedron	Number of vertices on the new polyhedron
3	6	9	5
4	8	12	6
5	10	15	7
100	200	300	102

Section 3, Practice and Application (p. 344)

1. right **3.** acute **5.** acute **7.** Sample Response: Yes; the square root of the sum of the squares of the legs is about 20.81, which is close to 21. Allowing for measurement errors, the angle is probably a right angle.
9. 14.70 mm **11.** 8 cm **13.** 12 mm **15.** No; the diagonal of the door opening is only about 12.81 ft.
17. a. Yes; 9 in.:12 in. = 3:4 **b.** 75 in. **c.** Answers will vary.

Spiral Review (p. 346)

22. 7.5 **23.** 12.2 **24.** 3.5 **25.** 362.67 cm^2 **26.** $\frac{7}{12}$
27. $\frac{4}{11}$

Extra Skill Practice (p. 347)

1. obtuse **3.** acute **5.** 8.31 in. **7.** 10 cm **9.** No; $3^2 + 3^2 \neq 5^2$ **11.** No; $6^2 + 6^2 \neq 10^2$

Standardized Testing (p. 347)

1. Possible answers are given. **a.** acute: $6 < x < 7.5$ right: $x = 7.5$ obtuse: $7.5 < x < 10.5$
b. acute: $5.5 < x < \sqrt{34.25}$ right: $x = \sqrt{34.25}$ obtuse: $\sqrt{34.25} < x < 7.5$
2. 48 ft^2

Section 4, Practice and Application (p. 357)

1. 54 m^2 **3.** 1249.21 in.^{2} **5.** 175 cm^2 **9.** 4 in.^{3}
11. 4.67 m^3 **13.** 3014.4 mm^3 **15. a.** a cylinder and a cone **b.** 339.88 ft^3 **17.** *S.A.* = 240 in.^{2}, V = 264 in.^{3}

Spiral Review (p. 359)

22. not congruent; Corresponding sides $\overline{PR}$ and $\overline{DF}$ are not congruent. **23.** congruent; SAS **24** $y = 3x + 2$
25. $y = -4x + 5$

Extension (p. 360)

27. Labsheet 4D answers are given. **a.** $2\pi r$ **b.** the circumference of the partial circle **c.** the radius of the partial circle

Extra Skill Practice (p. 361)

1. 520 m^2 **3.** 75 cm^2 **5.** 0.75 ft^3 **7.** *S.A.* is about 730.35 ft^2, V = 1342.69 ft^3

Standardized Testing (p. 361)

1. Sample response:

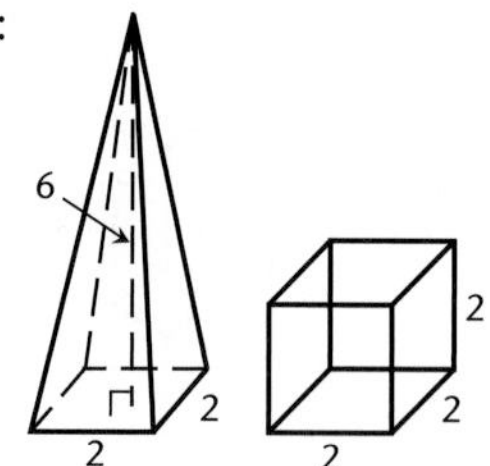

2. Sample responses are given.

a.

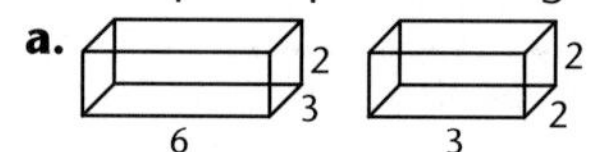

b.

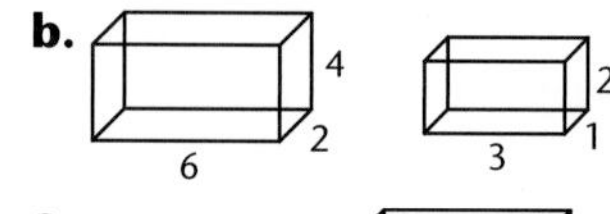

c.

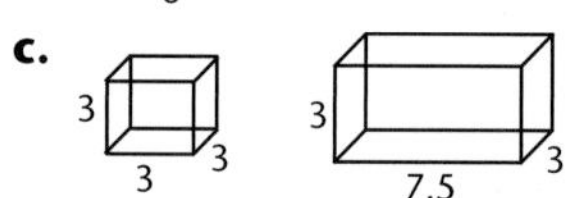

Section 5, Practice and Application (p. 369)

1. 120° **3.** 90° **5.** 135° **7.** 60° **9.** 27° **11.** 42° **13.** 78°
15. 54° **17.** $\angle CED$ **19.** $\angle DCE$ **21.** $\angle 8$ **23.** $\angle 1$
25. 150° **27.** 30° **29.** $m\angle 1 = 110°$; $m\angle 2 = 70°$; $m\angle 3 = 110°$; $m\angle 4 = 70°$; $m\angle 5 = 110°$; $m\angle 6 = 70°$
31. 180° **33.** $x = 125$; $y = 125$; $(3x - 250)$ and x are the measures of alternate exterior angles, and since lines m and n are parallel, the measures of alternate exterior angles are equal. Thus, $3x - 250 = x$. Solving $3x - 250 = x$ for x gives $x = 125$. y and x are the measures of corresponding angles, and since the measures of corresponding angles are equal, $y = x = 125$.
35. $y + 45 = 90$; $y = 45°$

Spiral Review (p. 372)

38. 301.44 m^3 **39.** 8.37 ft^3 **40.** 192 $in.^3$ **41.** 28 in. = $2\frac{1}{3}$ ft **42.** 1.5 mi = 7920 ft **43.** 3 yd = 108 in. **44.** 36 mm = 3.6 cm **45.** 248 cm = 2.48 m **46.** 2.6 km = 2600 m

Career Connection (p. 372)

47. a. Since the alternate interior angles formed by the transversal $\overline{CB}$ are congruent, the lines are parallel. **b.** 60°

Extra Skill Practice (p. 373)

1. 78° **3.** 28° **5.** 82° **7.** 32° **9.** Yes, it intersects lines *m* and *n* at different points. **11.** $\angle 1$ and $\angle 3$, $\angle 2$ and $\angle 4$, $\angle 5$ and $\angle 7$, $\angle 6$ and $\angle 8$ **13.** $\angle 1$ and $\angle 5$, $\angle 4$ and $\angle 8$ **15.** 50° **17.** 50°

Standardized Testing (p. 373)

1. C **2.** B

Section 6, Practice and Application (p. 382)

1. Based on measurements of $1\frac{5}{16}$ in. by $\frac{13}{16}$ in., the new scale drawing should be a $2\frac{5}{8}$ in. by $1\frac{5}{8}$ in. rectangle.

3. Scale may vary. Sample Response:

Scale: 5 mm = 1 mm

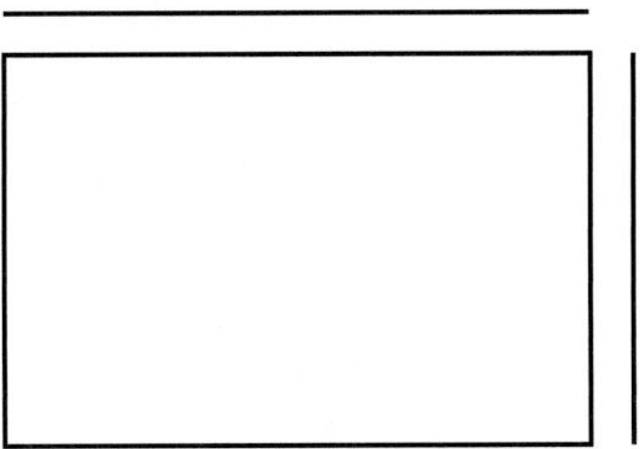

5. Answers will vary. **9.** 16 in.; 16 $in.^2$ **11.** 12 in.; 9 $in.^2$ **13.** 58.3 mm^2 **15.** 2338.28 yd^2 **19.** Sample Response: about 11.5 mi **21.** 0.324 $in.^2$

Spiral Review (p. 384)

23. 4 **24.** 2.5 **25.** 8 **26.** $\frac{1}{2}$ **27.** 19.5 **28.** 1.375

29.

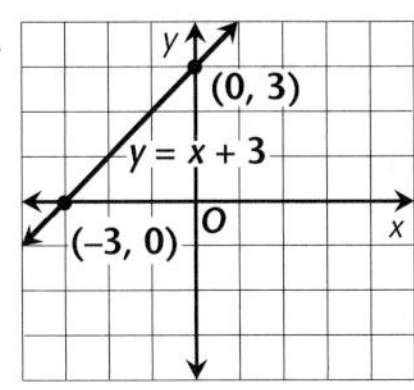

30.

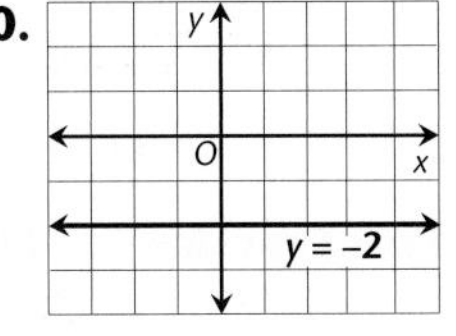

31.

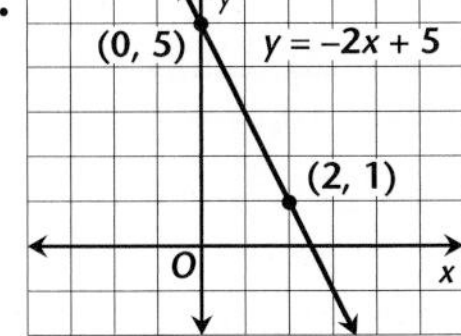

Extra Skill Practice (p. 385)

1. Answers will vary. They must be equivalent to $\frac{4 \text{ in.}}{6 \text{ ft}} = \frac{1 \text{ in.}}{1.5 \text{ ft}}$. **3.** Scale and views may vary. Sample Response: Scale: $\frac{1}{4}$ in. = 12 ft

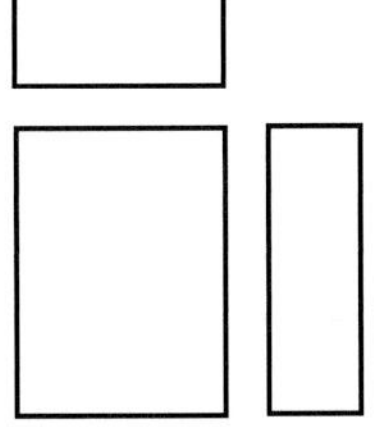

5. 15 in. **7.** 6480 $in.^2$

Standardized Testing (p. 385)

1. C **2.** A

Review and Assessment (p. 388)

1. a. surface area = 26 cm^2; volume = 6 cm^3 **b.** surface area = 18 cm^2; volume = 4 cm^3

2.

front back

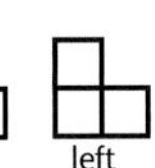

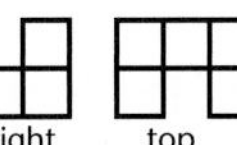

3. a.

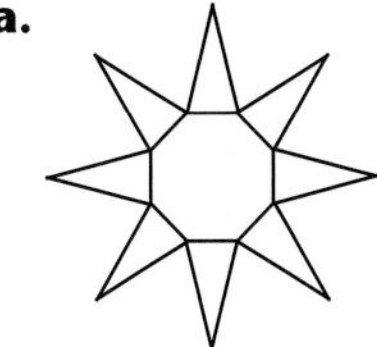

b. 9 faces, 16 edges, 9 vertices **4.** $\triangle ABE \cong \triangle CBD$ because two sides and the included angle of $\triangle ABE$ are congruent to two sides and the included angle of $\triangle CBD$ (SAS). **5.** Two sides of $\triangle PQS$ are congruent to two sides of $\triangle RQS$, but the included angles are not congruent, so the triangles are not congruent. **6.** Since $7.5^2 + 4^2 = 56.25 + 16 = 72.25 = 8.5^2$, the two triangles will be right triangles, and the quadrilateral will be a rectangle. **7.** 13 mm **8.** 6 ft **9.** $\sqrt{2}$ in. **10.** *S.A.* = 1440 $in.^2$; *V* = 3200 $in.^3$ **11.** *S.A.* = 700 m^2; *V* = 1200 m^3 **12.** *S.A.* = 114 cm^2; *V* = 84 cm^3 **13.** 17 cm^3 **14.** $\angle 7$; 105° **15.** $\angle 8$; 75° **16.** $\angle 4$; 75° **17.** 105°; Sample response: $\angle 3$ and $\angle 5$ are vertical angles, so $m\angle 3 = m\angle 5 = 105°$. **18.** $\angle RTQ$ **19.** $\angle SQT$ **20.** 130° **21.** Scale drawing should be $1\frac{1}{2}$ in. by $\frac{3}{4}$ in. **22.** perimeter = 28 km; area = 48 km^2

MODULE 6

Section 1, Practice and Application (p. 401)

1. B **3.** D **5.** The first graph matches the second table; the second graph matches the second description; The third graph matches the first table; The fourth graph matches the first description; The fifth graph matches the third description. **7.** Answers will vary.

11. Yes. The amount of money made depends on the number of tickets sold. **13.** Yes. In one location there is only one sunrise time for each day of the year. **15.** not a function **17.** not a function **19.** function **21.** $y = \frac{x}{5}$ **23.** $y = \frac{x^2}{2}$ **25. a.** $y = 0.4x + 2.1$ **b.** (0, 2.1), (1, 2.5), (2, 2.9), (3, 3.3), (4, 3.7), (5, 4.1), (6, 4.5); The values of x range from 0 to 6 since the river rose for 6 days. The values of y will be between 2 and 4.5 since the original height above the bank was 2.1 in. and it increased at a rate of 0.4 in. for 6 days. **c.**

Height of the River Above the Banks (in.)

Days After April 4

d. Yes, y is a function of x.

Spiral Review (p. 404)

27. Perimeter is 68 cm, area is 240 cm^2 **28.** 6.55 m

29. (−1, 0) (0, 1) slope = 1

30. (0, 0) (2, −2) slope = −1

31. slope = 0

32. $(-\frac{1}{2}, 0)$ $(0, -\frac{1}{2})$ slope = −1

Extra Skill Practice (p. 405)

1. B **3.** D **5.** function **7.** function **9.** function

Study Skills (p. 405)

1. Answers will vary. Set specific goals in the beginning and specify the time in which they need to be completed, appoint a group leader to make sure your project is on schedule. **2.** Answers will vary.

Section 2, Practice and Application (p. 414)

1. Bruce has \$90 in his savings account and he deposits \$75 each week without withdrawing any money. **3.** (6, −2) **5.** (6, 26) **7. a.** at 34 months **b.** \$5300 **c.** at 16 months **d.** \$2600 **9.** $-5m - 60$ **11.** $-40 - 8x$ **13.** $18x - 6$ **15. a.** to eliminate the multiplication required by the distributive property **b.** added 10 to both sides of the equation **c.** Preferences will vary. **17. a.** (1, 5); No; There is only one solution of the equation $5x = 2x + 3$.

b.

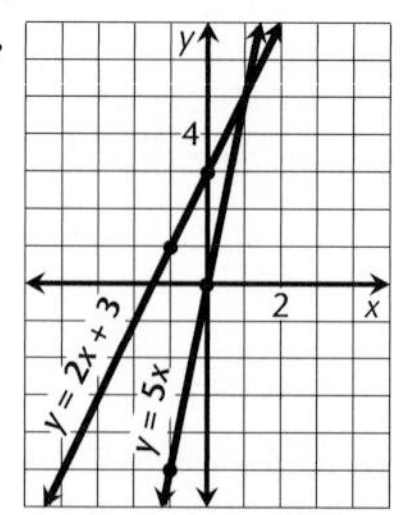

Find the point of intersection of the two graphs.

c.

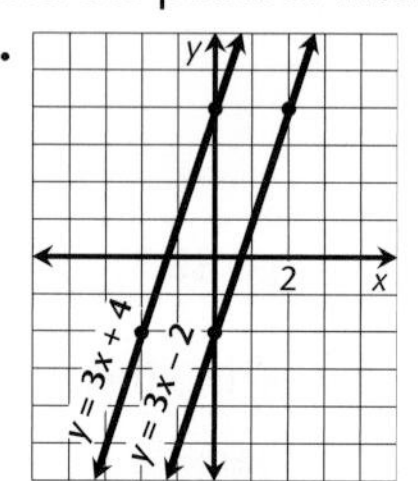

No; The graphs are parallel lines and do not intersect. **19.** −2 **21.** −1 **23.** $\frac{23}{6}$ **25.** −12 **27.** 5 ft

29. a.

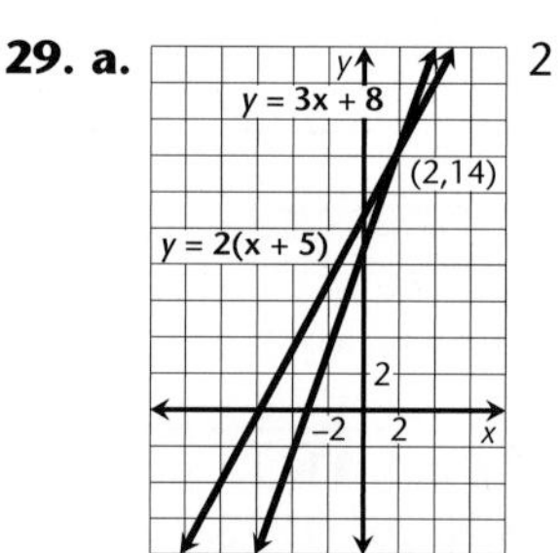

b. 3(2) + 8 = 6 + 8 = 14; 2(2 + 5) = 2(7) = 14 **c.** −5

Spiral Review (p. 417)

31. C; The graph shows the height of the flag increasing in stages with several pulls of a rope followed by brief rest periods. **32.** $0.\overline{428571}$ **33.** $0.\overline{54}$ **34.** $-2.\overline{2}$ **35.** 0.625 **36.** 5.2^4 **37.** 3^8 **38.** 16^5 **39.** $\left(\frac{3}{5}\right)^6$

Extra Skill Practice (p. 418)

1. **3.**

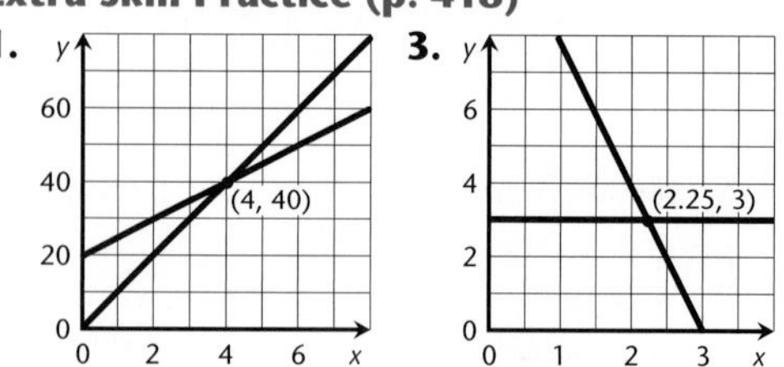

5. 7 **7.** 5 **9.** −7 **11.** 3 **13.** $-3\frac{1}{4}$ **15.** $-6 - 9x$ **17.** $12x + 6$ **19.** $14 - 8x$ **21.** $x^2 + 4x$ **23.** −6 **25.** 0 **27.** $\frac{3}{4}$ **29.** $-\frac{3}{4}$

Standardized Testing (p. 418)

1. Answers will vary. **2.** Answers will vary. Sample Response: $2(12x + 4)$; $24x + 8$ **3.** Answers will vary. Sample Response: $5(2x - 1) = 75$; $x = 8$

Section 3, Practice and Application (p. 427)

1. A: Area of each region after x steps $= \left(\frac{1}{3}\right)^x$; B: Number of regions after x steps $= 3^x$; As x increases, $\left(\frac{1}{3}\right)^x$ decreases and 3^x increases.

3. a.

Number of minutes	Number of new people hearing the rumor	Total number of people who have heard the rumor
0	1	1
1	2	3
2	4	7
3	8	15
4	16	31
5	32	63
6	64	127
7	128	255
8	256	511
9	512	1023
10	1024	2047

b. $y = 2^x$; When $x = 60$, $y = 2^{60}$. **c.** Sample Response: It shows exponential growth with powers of 2.

3. d.

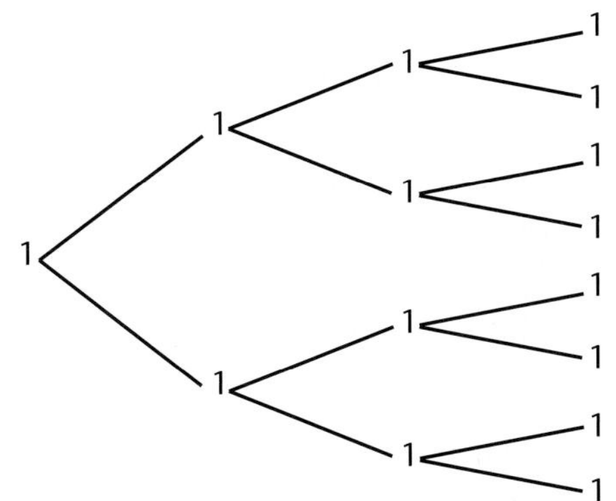

7. a. $y = 1200 \cdot (1.04)^x$ where y represents the enrollment and x represents the number of years.
b. $y = 5 \cdot (1.1)^x$ where y represents the distance Maria runs each week and x represents the number of weeks.
9. Yes; For every value of x there is only one value of y.
11. $\frac{1}{4}$ **13.** 16 **15.** $\frac{5}{81}$

Spiral Review (p. 429)

18. 10 **19.** $-\frac{1}{2}$ **20.** $\left(7, -\frac{1}{2}\right)$

Career Connection (p. 430)

21. a. 128 bacteria; 524,288 bacteria; Possible Answers: Write an equation, complete a table, or sketch a graph. Equation: $y = 2 \cdot 2^x$ where x represents the number of 20 min intervals that have passed. **b.** Sample Response: It shows how quickly the bacteria grow and so, how rapidly the infection worsens.

Extension (p. 430)

23. The decay factor is the rate of depreciation subtracted from 1.

Extra Skill Practice (p. 431)

1. $y = 150 \cdot (1.08)^x$ where y represents the value of the baseball card and x represents the number of years.
3. $y = 2000 \cdot (1.10)^x$ where y represents the value of the number of loaves of bread and x represents the number of days. **5.** 46,875 **7.** 8748 **9.** $\frac{8}{27} \approx 0.3$
11. $y = 200 \cdot (1.03)^{10}$, \$268.78
13. $y = 1500 \cdot (1.04)^8$, \$2052.85

Standardized Testing (p. 431)

1. No. Each day the new price, not the original price, is being reduced 20%, so on the fifth day the price will be about 67% off the original price. **2.** Bank B; The amount he will earn at Bank A is $y = 1000(1.06)^4 = \$1262.48$ and the amount he will earn at Bank B is $y = 1000 + 1000(0.07)(4) = \$1280$. He will make \$17.52 more than at Bank A.

Section 4, Practice and Application (p. 437)

1. Sample Response: $(x', y') = (x, y + 5)$; $(x'', y'') = (x', y' - 5)$

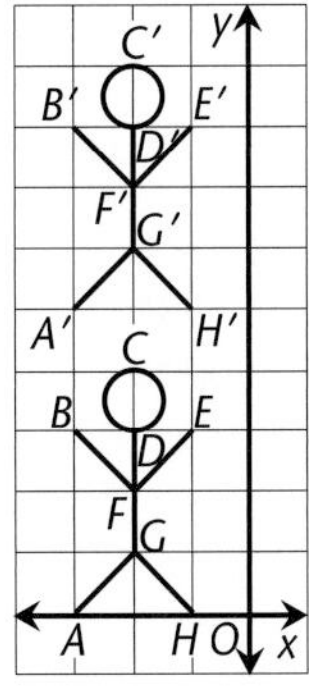

3.

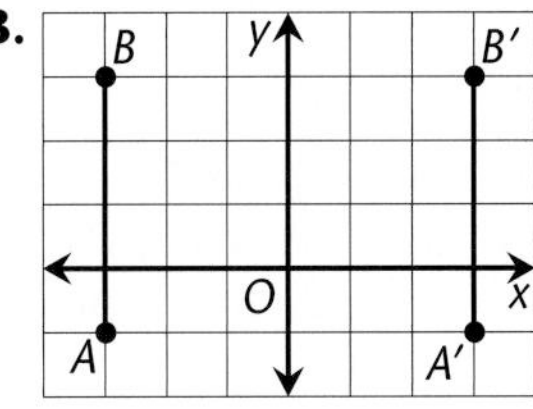

5.

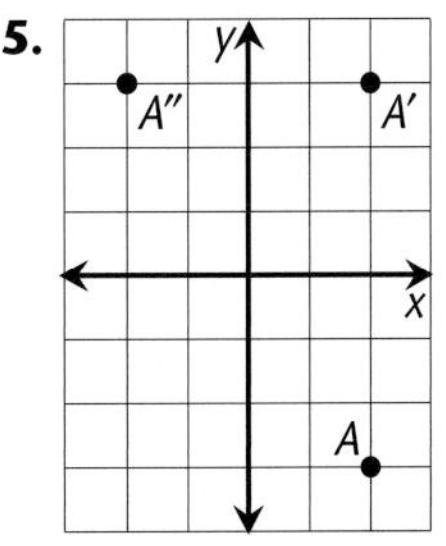

SELECTED ANSWERS

7. 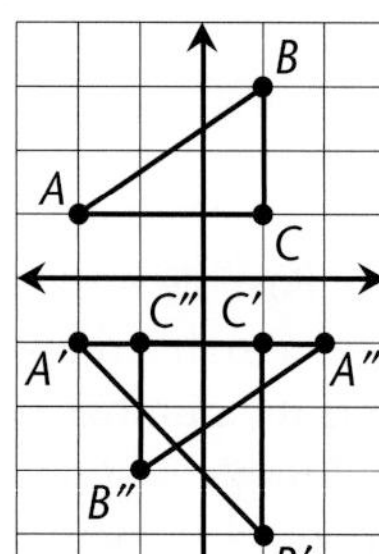

It is the same.

9. Answers will vary. **11.** $(x', y') = (x, -y)$; $(x'', y'') = (-x', y')$; $(x''', y''') = (x'', y'' + 2)$ **13.** No; Sample Response: $\triangle DE'F'$ is on the same side of the y-axis as $\triangle DEF$ and is not the image of $\triangle DEF$ reflected across the x-axis.

15. a. 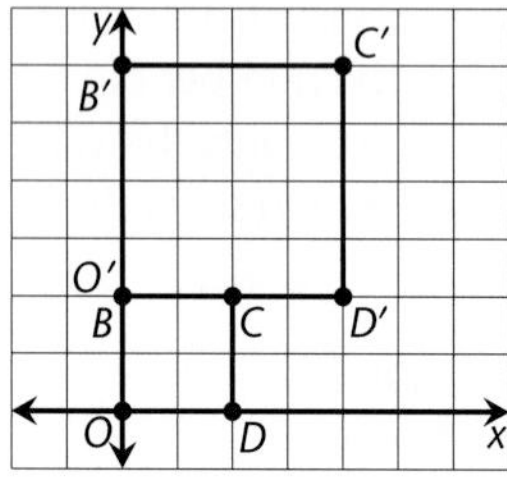

b. Yes

17. 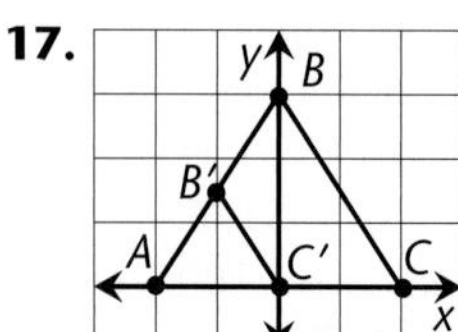

19. Answers will vary.

Spiral Review (p. 440)

21. 27 **22.** $\frac{1}{32} = 0.03125$ **23.** 1728 **24.** $m\angle 1 = m\angle 4 = 95°$; $m\angle 2 = m\angle 3 = 85°$ **25.** −12 **26.** 0.01 **27.** $\frac{1}{9}$ **28.** $-\frac{7}{15}$

Extra Skill Practice (p. 441)

1. $(x', y') = (x + 3, y - 3)$ **3.** $(x', y') = (x + 2, y + 2)$; $(x'', y'') = (-x' + 2, y' - 2)$ **5.** Sample Response: Plot the point with the same x-coordinate and the opposite y-coordinate.

7. 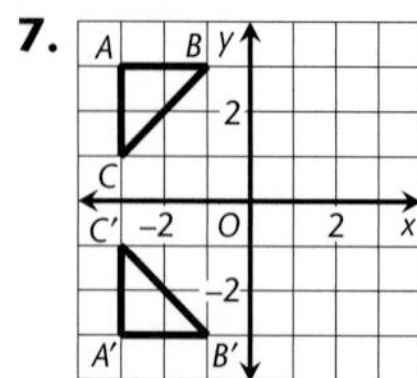

9. Answers will vary.

Standardized Testing (p. 441)

1. C **2.** C

Section 5, Practice and Application (p. 448)

1. B **3.** D **5. a.** Answers may vary. Sample Response: The graph of $y = -2x^2$ will have the same vertex and axis of symmetry as the graph of $y = x^2$, but the parabola will be narrower and open downward. The graph of $y = -2x^2 + 3$ is the same as the graph of $y = -2x^2$ except that it is shifted up 3 units so its vertex is at (0, 3) instead of (0, 0).

b. $y = x^2$; $y = -2x^2 + 3$; $y = -2x^2$

7. a. 622, 606, 558, 478, 366, 222, 46, −162

b. (0, 622), (1, 606), (2, 558), (3, 478), (4, 366), (5, 222), (6, 46), (7, −162)

c. about 6.25 sec; The graph crosses the x-axis at about $x = 6.25$.

d. 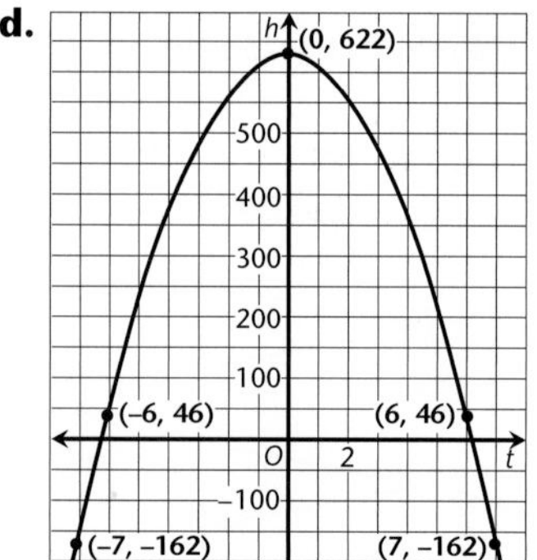

No; When the object is dropped, $t = 0$. Negative time values do not make sense in this situation.

e. (0, 622) **9. a.** It is in the form $y = ax^2 + bx + c$ and $a \neq 0$; $a = -16$, $b = 32$, $c = 4$

9. b. 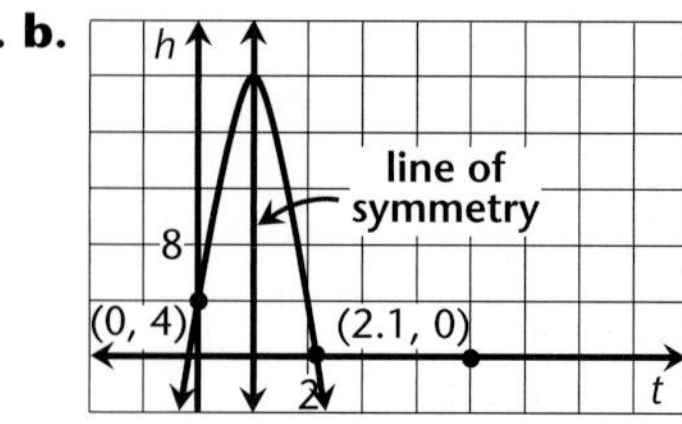

c. 20 ft **d.** 1 sec **e.** about 2.1 sec **11.** $y = 3x - 12$; not a quadratic function **13.** $y = 3x^2 - 2x$; quadratic function **15.** $y = -2x + 5$; not a quadratic function

Spiral Review (p. 450)

18.

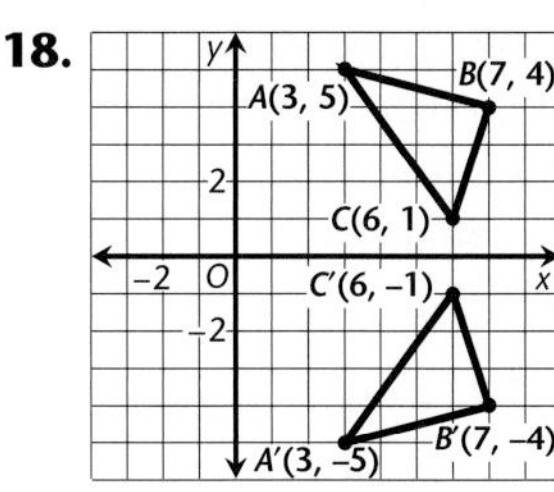

19. 74° **20.** 12° **21.** 59° **22.** 2° **23.** taxpayers; parents **24.** No; Taxpayers who are not parents are not represented.

Extension (p. 450)

25. The value of h is the x-coordinate and the value of k is the y-coordinate of the vertex of the parabola.

Extra Skill Practice (p. 451)

1. same vertex and axis of symmetry, narrower

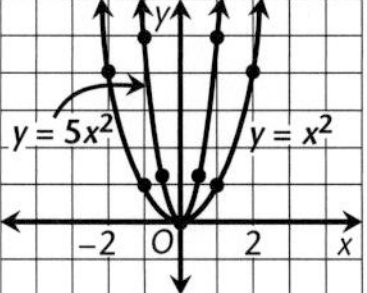

3. same shape and axis of symmetry, vertex (0, 1) instead of (0, 0)

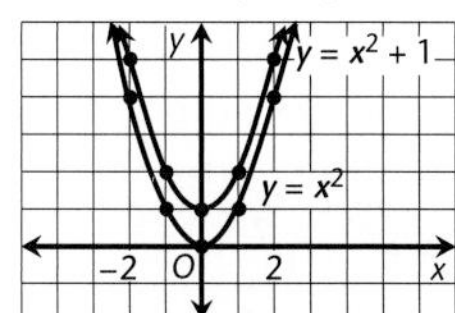

5. same axis of symmetry, narrower, vertex at (0, –2) instead of (0, 0), opens in opposite direction

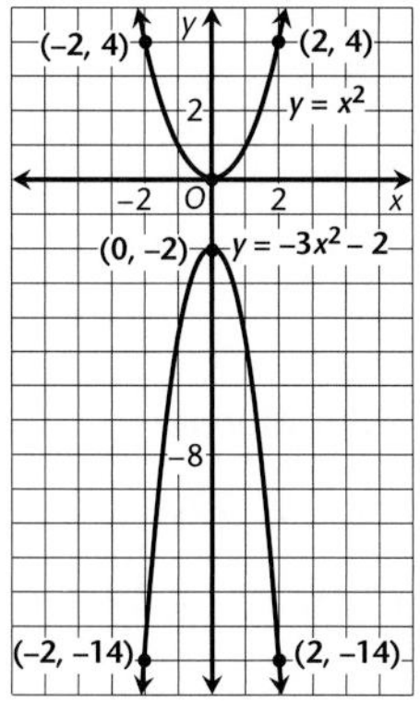

7. The vertex is at (2, –2) and the line of symmetry is a vertical line through the point (2, –2). **9.** $y = x^2 + 7x$; quadratic function **11.** $y = -x^2 - 5x + 10$; quadratic function **13.** $y = 6$; not a quadratic function **15.** $y = 2x^3 - 5x^2 - 7$; not a quadratic function

Standardized Testing (p. 451)

1. Sample Response: All the graphs are parabolas that open up and have the same line of symmetry (the y-axis); the graphs of $y = x^2$, $y = \frac{1}{2}x^2$, and $y = 2x^2$ all have vertex (0, 0) but the graph of $y = x^2 + 4$ has vertex (0, 4). **2. a.** not a quadratic function **b.** quadratic function **c.** quadratic function **d.** not a quadratic function

Review and Assessment (p. 454)

1. B; The hours increase gradually to a maximum and then decrease gradually to a minimum. **2.** C; Height increases at varying rates. **3.** A; The length of the grass in the summer increases then sharply decreases each time it is cut and then begins to grow again.
4. function **5.** not a function **6.** function **7.** function **8.** function **9.** not a function
10. $y = 20{,}000 - 500x$; $15,000

Years	Value ($)
0	20,000
1	19,500
2	19,000
3	18,500
4	18,000
5	17,500
6	17,000
7	16,500
8	16,000
9	15,500
10	15,000

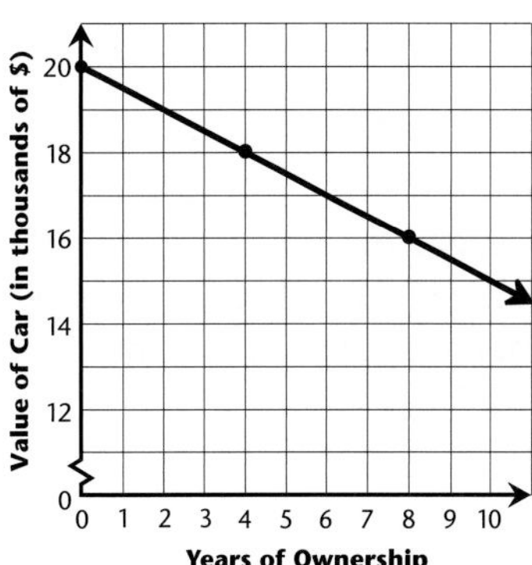

11. 17 **12.** 4 **13.** –0.5 **14.** 1 **15.** –2.75 **16.** 11.5
17. at 25 sec **18.** 10,000 **19.** $\frac{9}{16}$ **20.** 96 **21.** $\frac{1}{25}$
22. $y = 100 \cdot (1.05)^x$; $338.64

SELECTED ANSWERS

23. $(x', y') = (-x, y)$; $(x'', y'') = (x', y' + 3)$

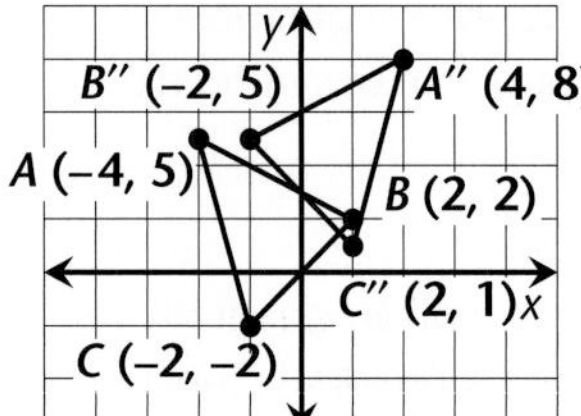

24.

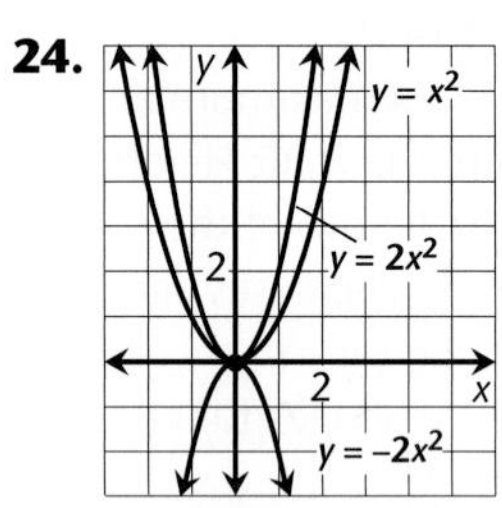

25.

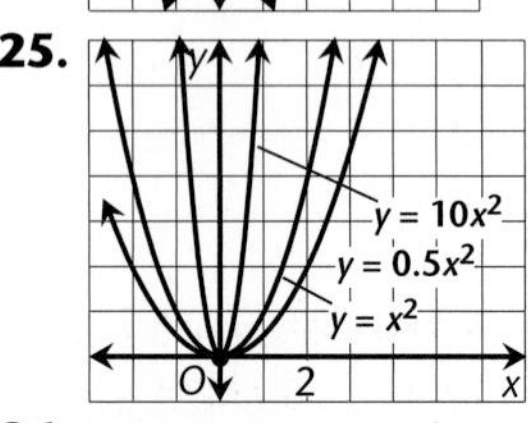

26.

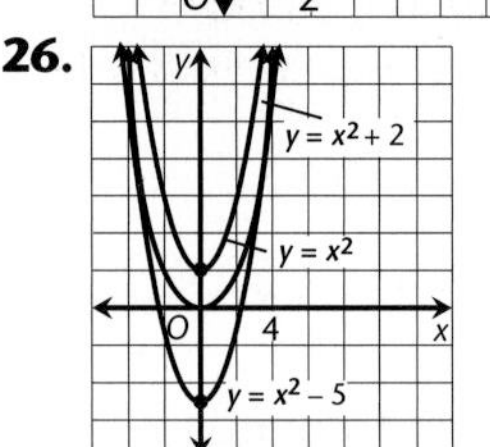

27. a.

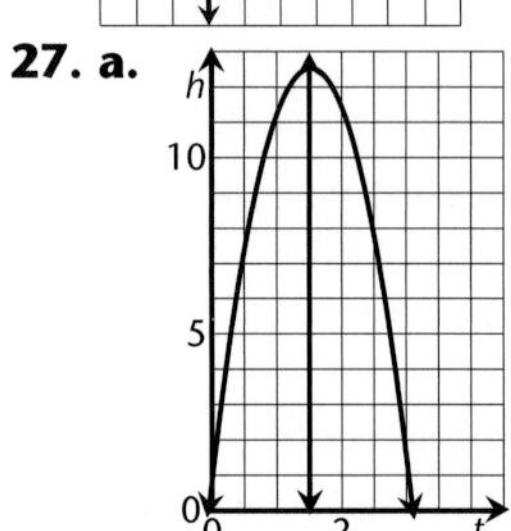

b. about 3.1 sec **c.** (1.5, 12.5) **28.** $y = -x^2 + 5$; quadratic function **29.** $y = 2x^2 + x - 13$; quadratic function **30.** $y = -9x - 4$; not a quadratic function **31.** $y = 5x^2 - 6x - 9$; quadratic function

MODULE 7

Section 1, Practice and Application (p. 465)

1. 10^6 **3.** 2^9 **5.** 3^{10} **7.** a^4 **9.** b^8 **11.** w^{80}
13. a. $E = 0.002888s^4$ **b.** Yes, in the equation s is raised to the 4th power. **c.** 462.08 foot-pounds; 7393.28 foot-pounds **d.** Yes, 7393.28 ÷ 17 = 434.899 which is close to 462.08. But it is actually 16 times the wave energy; 7393.28 ÷ 17 = 462.08. **15.** 10^2
17. 2^4 **19.** 7^9 **21.** a^3 **23.** c^6 **25.** u^{43}

29. No, if you substitute 0 for t in the formula, you get $w = 1.16(1.44)^0 = 1.16 \cdot 1$ or 1.16 lb, which is not a reasonable weight for a fish that is less than 5 mm long.
31. $\frac{1}{9}$ **33.** $\frac{1}{5}$ **35.** $\frac{1}{b^6}$ **37.** $\frac{4}{w^2}$ **39.** 0.9 **41.** 0.00018
43. 0.00000265 **45.** $3 \cdot 10^{-1}$ **47.** $2.5 \cdot 10^{-4}$
49. $6 \cdot 10^{-9}$ **51. a.** $2^{-25} \approx 2.98 \cdot 10^{-8}$ **b.** The probability of winning the state lottery is about 2.4 times greater than flipping 25 heads in 25 flips of a coin.

Spiral Review (p. 467)

53. slope = –2, y-intercept = 9 **54.** 7 and 8 **55.** 12
56. 65 **57.** 510 **58.** –8 **59.** 18

Career Connection (p. 468)

61. $1.56 \cdot 10^{-3}$ sec

Extension (p. 468)

63. 2^2 **65.** a^{-4} **67.** 3^{-2} **69.** b^{-5}

Extra Skill Practice (p. 469)

1. 6^7 **3.** 11^{34} **5.** b^{12} **7.** k^{81} **9.** 10^{10} **11.** 8^2 **13.** p^3
15. m^4 **17.** 1 **19.** $\frac{1}{121}$ **21.** $\frac{1}{13}$ **23.** $\frac{1}{p^8}$ **25.** $\frac{3}{b^7}$
27. 0.008 **29.** 0.000000614 **31.** $6 \cdot 10^{-2}$
33. $1.013 \cdot 10^{-6}$

Standardized Testing (p. 469)

1. A **2.** C **3.** D **4.** D

Section 2, Practice and Application (p. 478)

1. a. irrational **b.** rational **c.** rational **d.** rational
3. a. 111112 **b.** $0.\overline{12}$ repeats the same digits 121212... where as 0.121121112 changes because the number of ones after each 2 increases by one as the pattern continues. **5. a.** $A = \sqrt{9(1)(3)(5)} = 3\sqrt{15}$ cm^2
b. $A = \sqrt{15(5)(5)(5)} = 25\sqrt{3}$ in.^{2} **c.** about 11.6 cm^2; about 43.3 in.^{2} **7. a.** yes **b.** no **c.** no **d.** no
9. a. $11x^3$ **b.** $y^{14}\sqrt{y}$ **c.** $\frac{\sqrt{6}}{m^5}$ **d.** b

Spiral Review (p. 479)

14. $y = 2x^2 - 5x$; yes **15.** $y = 2x^2 - 4x$; yes
16. $y = \frac{1}{8}x$; no **17.** $-2\frac{4}{5}$ **18.** $-6\frac{5}{8}$ **19.** $-3\frac{5}{12}$ **20.** 21 mm

Extra Skill Practice (p. 480)

1. rational **3.** irrational **5.** rational **7.** irrational
9. irrational **11.** $2\sqrt{35}$ **13.** $5\sqrt{10}$ **15.** $7\sqrt{2}$ **17.** $\frac{\sqrt{10}}{9}$
19. $\frac{4\sqrt{2}}{9}$ **21.** $\frac{2\sqrt{5}}{5}$ **23.** $20\sqrt{2}$ **25.** $xy^4\sqrt{x}$ **27.** 5 **29.** 6
31. $rst^3\sqrt[3]{s^2}$

Standardized Testing (p. 480)

1. B **2.** D

Section 3, Practice and Application (p. 490)

1. $p > 25$

3. $e < 50$

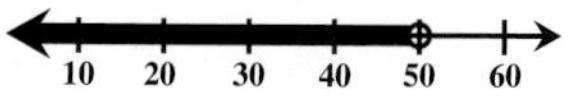

5. a.

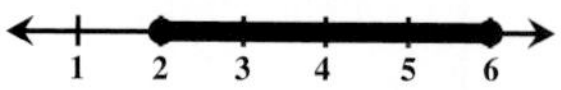

b. $-3 \le s \le 1$ **c.** $r \le 10$ **7.** Yes, when substituted for the variable, the left side equals –2 which is less than 2.

9. $w \ge 2$

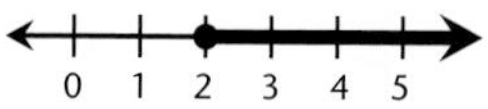

11. $x \le 5$

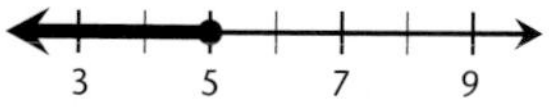

13. $z < 13$

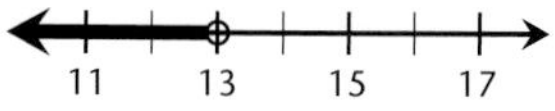

15. $q \ge 10.5$

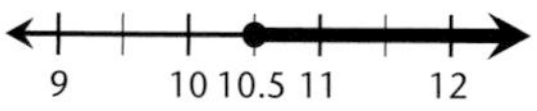

17. $7 + n < 7$; $n < 0$ **19.** $1.75s \ge 95$; $s \ge 54.3$; at least 54.3 mi/hr **21. a.** up to 40 in. **b.** 4 in. **c.** 86.4 in. **d.** The rows would have to be so far apart that they would lose too much seating if they used a sloped floor. **e.** Sample Response: More rows are possible with a stepped floor because of a higher rise and shorter row depth. **f.** Sample Response: A sloped floor may be safer, since people may be less likely to trip in low light. **23.** $24 - 0.5n \ge 132$; $n \le -216$ **25.** $12.50h + 25 < 90$; $h < 5.2$; less than 5.2 hr

27. $b \le -3$

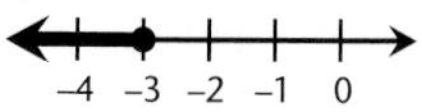

29. $x \ge 3$

31. $y > \frac{2}{3}$

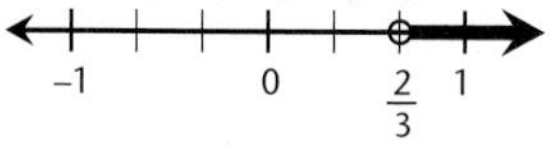

33. $x < 6$

35. a. Answers will vary. Sample Response: $x - 3 \ge 1$, $12x \ge 48$, $-2x \le -8$ **b.** Answers will vary. Sample Response: $x + 5 < 4$, $7x < -7$, $\frac{x}{2} < -\frac{1}{2}$

Spiral Review (p. 493)

39. 105° **40.** 105° **41.** 105° **42.** 60 **43.** 13.5 **44.** 2.25

Extra Skill Practice (p. 494)

1. $20 \le w < 25$

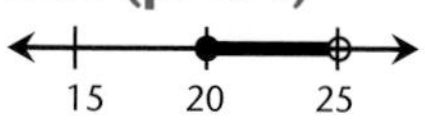

3. $p \ge 10$

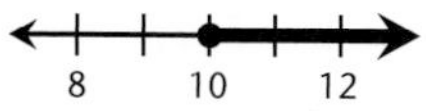

5. $x \le -2$

7. $a > \frac{1}{8}$

9. $a \ge 6$

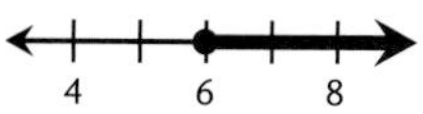

11. $u > -40$

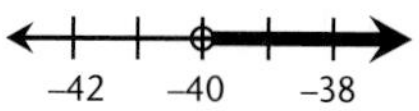

13. $n > -27$

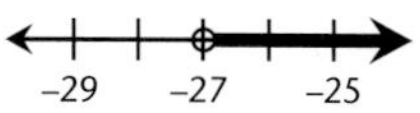

15. $x < -3$

17. $5 + n > 2$; $n > -3$ **19.** $2.88 + 4g \ge 10$; $g \ge 1.78$; at least \$1.78 **21.** $w \le -5$ **23.** $x > -0.25$ **25.** $x > 0.6$

27. $n > 2$ **29.** $x < \frac{21}{4}$ **31.** $m \le 17\frac{1}{2}$

Standardized Testing (p. 494)

1. less than 90 in. **2.** 17 or fewer prints

Section 4, Practice and Application (p. 508)

1. $x^2 + 3x + 2$ **3.** $2x^2 + 5x + 2$ **5.** $x^2 - 4x + 3$ trinomial **7.** $x^2 + x - 6$ **9.** $x^2 - x - 2$ **11.** $x^2 - 1$ **13.** $x^2 + 5x + 6$ **15.** $-x^2 - 6x - 9$ **17.** $2x^2 - 8x + 8$ **19.** $x^2 + 13x + 40$ **21.** $2x^2 + 27x + 36$ **23.** $21x^2 - 37x + 12$ **25. a.** 8 in.; 8 in. **b.** $(3x + 8)$ in. **c.** $(2x + 8)$ in. **d.** $6x^2 + 40x + 64$ in.^{2} **27.** $(x + 2)(2x - 2) = 2x^2 + 2x - 4$ **29.** $(3x + 1)(x + 2) = 3x^2 + 7x + 2$ **31.** $(x + 2)(x + 3)$ **33.** $(x + 3)(x + 1)$ **35.** $(x + 7)(x + 1)$ **37.** Not possible; The only factors of 5 are 1 and 5 and this does not produce the correct product rectangle. **39.** $(x - 6)(x + 1)$ **41.** $(x - 1)(x - 1)$ **43.** $(x - 7)(x - 1)$ **45.** $(x + 2)(x - 2)$

Spiral Review (p. 510)

48. B and D are polygons. B appears to be regular because all 4 sides appear to be the same length and all 4 angles appear to have the same measure (90°).

49. $n \ge 8$

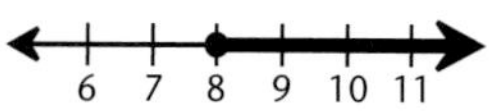

50. $y > -5$

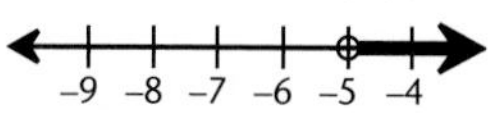

51. $x \le -2$

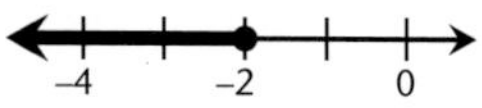

Extra Skill Practice (p. 511)

1. a. $x^2 - 2x + 1$; trinomial **b.** $2x^2 - 3x + 2$; trinomial **c.** $x^2 + x$; binomial **d.** $3x$; monomial **3.** $2x^2 - x - 3$ **5.** $-2x^2 + 19x - 35$ **7.** $6x^2 + 25x + 25$ **9.** $-54x^2 - 9x + 3$ **11.** $(x + 3)(x + 1)$ **13.** $(x + 2)(x - 2)$ **15.** $(x - 2)(x - 1)$

Standardized Testing (p. 511)

1. Answers will vary. Sample Response: $x^2 + 6x + 9$; $2x^2 + 5x - 3$ **2.** Answers will vary. Sample Response: $x^2 - 4 = (x - 2)(x + 2)$; $x^2 - 1 = (x + 1)(x - 1)$

Review and Assessment (p. 514)

1. 10^{11} **2.** a^9 **3.** 2^7 **4.** b^4 **5.** 1 **6.** $\frac{1}{121}$ **7.** $\frac{1}{27}$ **8.** $\frac{1}{64}$ **9.** 0.05 **10.** 0.000803 **11.** 0.0000001266 **12.** ash: $a < 2 \cdot 10^{-3}$; lapilli: $2 \cdot 10^{-3} \le a \le 6.4 \cdot 10^{-2}$; bombs: $a \ge 6.4 \cdot 10^{-2}$ **13.** irrational **14.** rational **15.** rational **16.** rational **17.** Sample Response: $\sqrt{108} = \sqrt{36 \cdot 3} = \sqrt{36} \cdot \sqrt{3} = 6\sqrt{3}$ **18.** $4\sqrt{6}$ **19.** $\frac{\sqrt{13}}{8}$ **20.** $10\sqrt{5}$ **21.** $\frac{\sqrt{17}}{10}$ **22.** $\frac{2\sqrt{2}}{7}$ **23.** $\frac{5\sqrt{6}}{6}$ **24.** 4 **25.** $x^2y^2\sqrt{y}$

26. 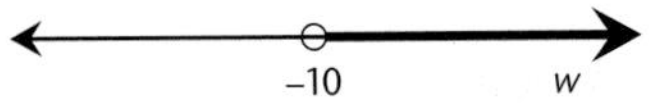

27. 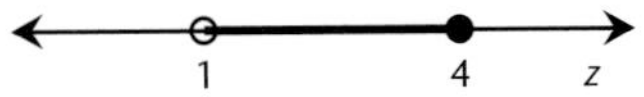

28. 

29. 

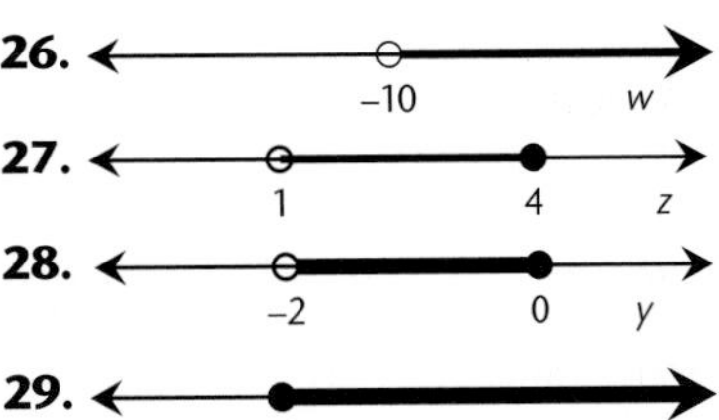

30. $a \le 5$ 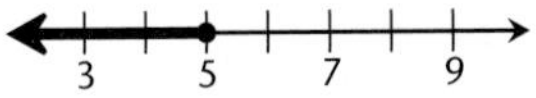

31. $n \ge -3.5$ 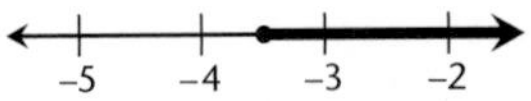

32. $n < -9$ 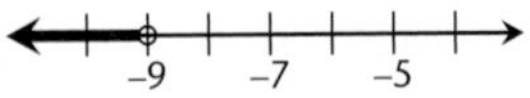

33. Sample Response: $6950 \ge 20s$; $s \le 347.5$; At most, the garden can contain 347 sections.
34. $2x^2 + 11x + 12$ **35.** $6x^2 - 33x + 15$ **36.** $100x^2 - 4$
37. $(x - 2)(x - 4)$ **38.** $(x - 2)(2x + 3)$ **39.** $(x + 1)(x + 4)$
40. $(x - 1)(x - 4)$ **41.** $(x + 1)(x - 4)$

MODULE 8

Section 1, Practice and Application (p. 526)

1. geometric (multiply by $\frac{1}{2}$) **3.** geometric (multiply by 0.5) **5.** arithmetic (add 0.4) **7.** 15, 20, 26 **9.** $160x^5$, $320x^6$, $640x^7$ **11.** Sequence 1: $t = 2n + 1$, or $n + (n + 1)$, or $2(n + 1) - 1$; Sequence 2: $t = 2 \cdot 3^{n-1}$
13. a. 5 whole black keys **b.** 8 white keys **c.** 13 keys **d.** They are terms 5–7 of the Fibonacci sequence.
15. a. 51 **b.** Yes; Sample Response: Multiplying by 2 will give you an even number and subtracting 3 will make that number odd. **17.** Add 3, then 3^2, then 3^3, 3^4... to each successive term; 364, 1093, 3280 **19.** The terms are consecutive powers of 3, starting with 3^0; $3^5 = 243$, $3^6 = 729$, $3^7 = 2187$

Spiral Review (p. 528)

21. 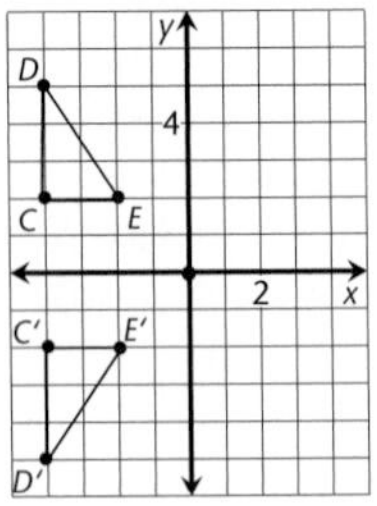

22. 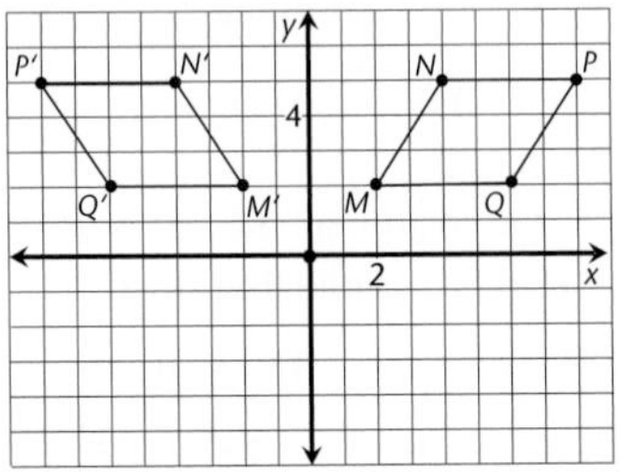

23. 48° (based on $m\angle CAD = 42°$) **24.** 123° (based on $m\angle CEB = 57°$) **25.** $\angle BEC$ **26.** $\angle ABE$

Extension (p. 529)

27. a.

Steps	Number of segments	Length of each segment	Total perimeter at this stage
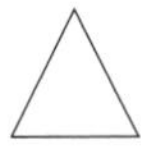	3	1 unit	3 units
	12	$\frac{1}{3}$ unit	$\frac{12}{3}$ = 4units
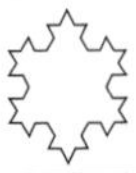	48	$\frac{1}{9}$ unit	$\frac{48}{9}$ units
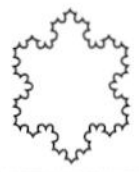	192	$\frac{1}{27}$ unit	$\frac{192}{27}$ units
:	:	:	:
n	$3 \cdot 4^{n-1}$	$\frac{1}{3^{n-1}}$	$\frac{3 \cdot 4^{n-1}}{3^{n-1}}$

b. The number of line segments in each stage is multiplied by 4 to obtain the number of line segments in the next stage. The length of each segment in one stage is multiplied by $\frac{1}{3}$ to get the length of each segment in the next stage. To get the total perimeter at each stage, you multiply the entry in the "Number of segments" column by the entry in the "Length of each segment" column.
c. See table in part (a).

Career Connection (p. 529)

29. The outside edge is green dots. Inside the green dot edge, the following patterns occur from left to right; blue, red, blue, red, blue, red, blue, red, blue—rows 1, 3, 7 and 9; red, red, red, red, green, red, red, red, red—rows 2, 4, 6, and 8; blue, green, blue, green, blue, green, blue, green, blue—row 5; The pattern would repeat itself every 10 rows.

Extra Skill Practice (p. 530)

1. Add 1 to the previous term; $4 + x$, $5 + x$, $6 + x$
3. Multiply the previous term by –5; 2500, –12,500, 62,500 **5.** Multiply the previous term by $\frac{2}{3}$; $\frac{16}{162}$, $\frac{32}{486}$, $\frac{64}{1458}$ **7.** 1: arithmetic; 2: geometric; 3: geometric; 4: neither; 5: geometric; 6: arithmetic **9. a.** 100 **b.** n^2

Study Skills (p. 530)
1. Sample Response: Choices A and C are not correct because they are not in scientific notation. Choice B is not correct because 16.6 is not between 1 and 10. Choice D is correct because it is in scientific notation.
2. Sample Response: Draw a rectangle. Inside the rectangle, draw two intersecting ovals. Put letters with no vertical or horizontal symmetry in the rectangle outside the ovals. Put letters with only horizontal symmetry in one oval and letters with only vertical symmetry in the other oval. Put letters with both horizontal and vertical symmetry in the intersection of the ovals.

Section 2, Practice and Application (p. 538)
1. 1080° **3.** 360° **5.** 65° **7.** 85° **9.** 128.57°
13. b. Yes; a square and an equilateral triangle; They have interior angles whose measure is a factor of 360°. **c.** Sample Response: octagons and squares, triangles and squares. **15. a.** 180° **b.** All but the stacked igeta which does not have rotational symmetry. **17. a.** A: 72°; Divide 360° by 5; B: 180°; Divide 360° by 2; E: 20°; Divide 360° by 18; F: 60°; Divide 360° by 6 **b.** A, B, D, E, and F
c.

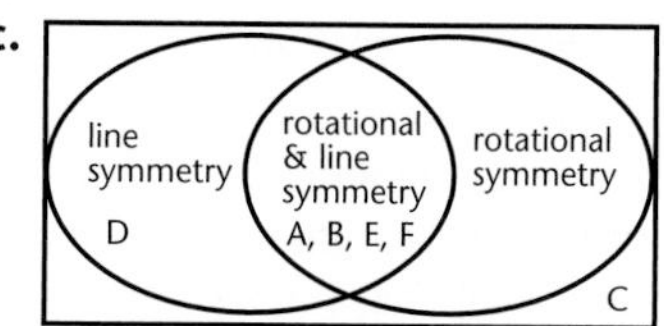

Spiral Review (p. 540)
19. $x^2 - 5x - 50$ **20.** $2x^2 - 18x + 28$ **21.** $36x^2 - 1$
22. 50,000

Extra Skill Practice (p. 541)
1. 17,640° **3.** 2880° **5.** 135° **7.** minimum: 90°; 180°, 270° **9.** no rotational symmetry **11.** minimum: 120°; 240° **13.** minimum: 60°; 120°, 180°, 240°, 300°

Standardized Testing (p. 541)
1. a. 4 sides **b.** 12 sides **c.** 35 sides **2.** 8 sides

Section 3, Practice and Application (p. 550)
1. True; This was shown in the Example on page 546.
3. True; A rhombus is a parallelogram and a parallelogram has opposite angles that are congruent.
5. False; A trapezoid may not have a pair of congruent angles. Also, a kite has only one pair of congruent angles.
7. Sample Response

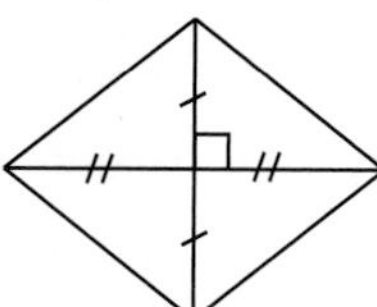

9. Sample Response

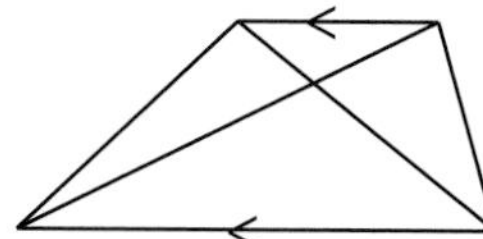

11.

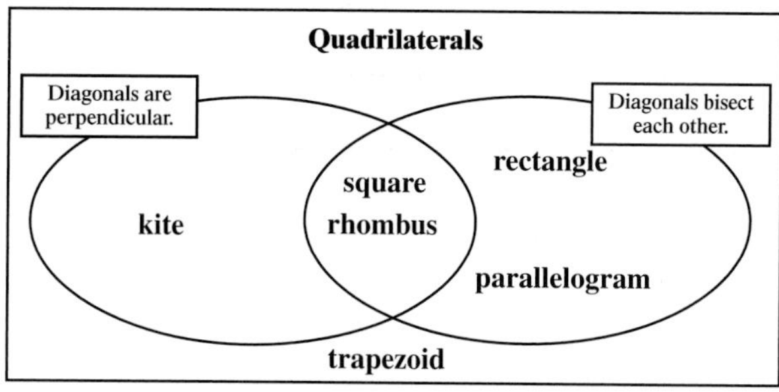

15. a. $XY = WY = \sqrt{26}$ **b.** Let $\overline{WY}$ and $\overline{XZ}$ intersect at point M. The coordinates of M are (2.5, 2.5). $WM = MY = \frac{\sqrt{26}}{2}$ and $WM = MY = \frac{\sqrt{26}}{2}$, so $\overline{WY}$ and $\overline{XZ}$ bisect each other. **c.** slope of $\overline{WY} = -\frac{1}{5}$; slope of $\overline{XZ} = 5$; The product of the slopes is –1, so the diagonals are perpendicular.

Spiral Review (p. 552)
17. No **18.** Yes; $y = 15x^2 - 7x + 6$ **19.** 12 mm
20. 8 cm **21.** 13 m **22.** 6 ft **23.** $\frac{1}{x}$ **24.** $\frac{1}{c^5}$ **25.** 1 **26.** $\frac{3}{y^4}$

Extra Skill Practice (p. 553)
1. Opposite angles are congruent; consecutive angles are supplementary. **3.** Diagonals bisect each other.
5. True; a rhombus is a parallelogram. **7.** False; the diagonals of a kite are perpendicular, but the diagonals of a rectangle are not perpendicular (unless the rectangle is a square). The diagonals of a rhombus are not congruent and do not bisect each other, while the diagonals of a rectangle are congruent and bisect each other.
9. False; the opposite angles of all parallelograms are congruent. **11. a.** 10; (1, 9) **b.** 13; (5.5, 2)
c. 17; $(4, -\frac{1}{2})$

Standardized Testing (p. 553)
1. a. rectangle, square, parallelogram, rhombus
b. trapezoid, kite **c.** rectangle, square, rhombus
d. trapezoid, parallelogram, rectangle, square, rhombus **2.** Opposite angles are congruent, and consecutive angles are supplementary; Diagonals are congruent and are perpendicular bisectors of each other.

Section 4, Practice and Application (p. 558)
1. 0.40 or 40% **3.** $\frac{24}{49} \approx 0.49$ or 49% **5.** $\frac{1}{\pi} \approx 0.32$ or 32% **7. a.** 0.45 or 45% **b.** 0.55 or 55% **9. a.** 0.10 or 10% **b.** 0.90 or 90%

Spiral Review (p. 560)
11. acute **12.** obtuse **13.** right

SELECTED ANSWERS

14. 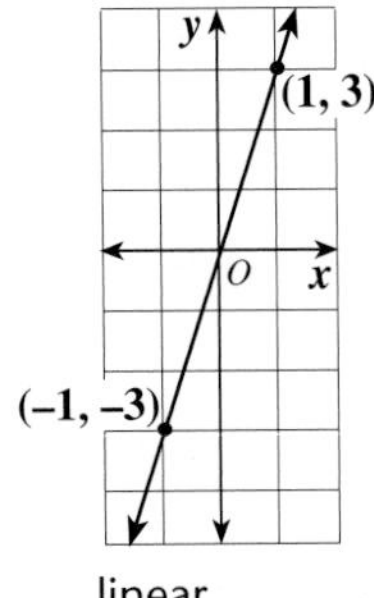

linear

15. 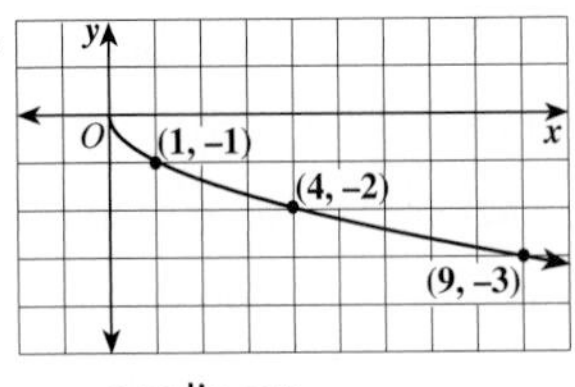

nonlinear

16. 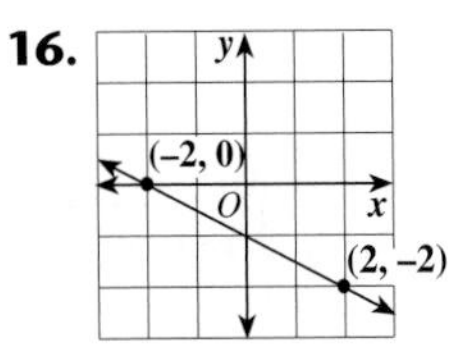

linear

17. about 1884 mm^3 **18.** about 186.04 $in.^3$ **19.** about 930.19 cm^3

Extra Skill Practice (p. 561)

1. 0.50 or 50% **3.** 0.25 or 25% **5.** 0.75 or 75% **7.** Answers will vary.

Standardized Testing (p. 561)

1. D **2.** C

Section 5, Practice and Application (p. 569)

1. 1 **3.** about 0.53 **5.** 173.21 yd **7.** 37.68 cm **11.** 0.77 **13.** 0.26 **15.** The length of the hypotenuse is unknown. **17.** 16.00 ft **21. a.** $\tan A = \frac{h}{b}$ **b.** about 24 ft

Spiral Review (p. 572)

23. a. 3^{13} **b.** a^7 **24.** Multiply the previous term by 2; 88, 176, 352 **25.** Add $x + 1$ to the previous term; $4x + 5$, $5x + 6$, $6x + 7$

26. 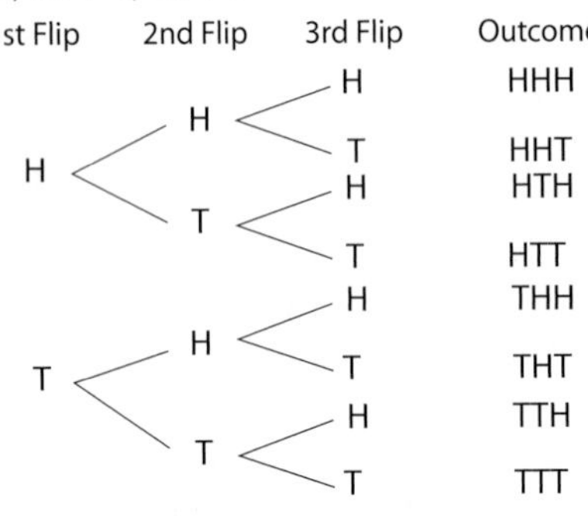

Extra Skill Practice (p. 573)

1. $\frac{74}{41} \approx 1.80$ **3.** $\frac{12}{5} = 2.75$ **5.** 0.48; 0.93; 0.38 **7.** 64.20 m **9.** 43.0 ft

Standardized Testing (p. 573)

1. B **2.** B

Review and Assessment (p. 576)

1. Multiply the previous term by $\frac{1}{y}$ (or divide by y); $\frac{1}{y^5}, \frac{1}{y^6}, \frac{1}{y^7}$ **2.** Add nine to the previous term; 37, 46, 55 **3.** Divide the previous term by 2 (or multiply by 0.5); 0.0625, 0.03125, 0.015625 **4.** Add 1 more than was added to the previous term; 38, 48, 59 **5.** geometric, multiply by –2 **6.** neither **7.** arithmetic, add 2 **8.** neither **9.** Possible answers: Use a protractor to measure all the angles and find their sum; Choose one vertex and draw segments to each of the other vertices to divide the polygon into 3 triangles. The sum of the measures of the angles in each triangle is 180°, so multiply 180° by 3. **10. a.** 60° **b.** 120°, 180°, 240°, 300° **11.** parallelogram, rectangle, square, rhombus. **12.** parallelogram; both pairs of opposite angles are congruent, consecutive angles are supplementary, diagonals bisect each other **13.** square; all angles are congruent, consecutive angles are supplementary, diagonals are congruent, diagonals bisect each other, diagonals are perpendicular **14.** trapezoid; consecutive angles between parallel lines are supplementary, diagonals do not bisect, diagonals are not perpendicular, diagonals are not congruent, opposite angles are not congruent, one pair of congruent angles **15.** 6 units; (0, 7) **16.** 10 units; (5, 4) **17.** 5 units; (–1, 3.5) **18. a.** $AB = \sqrt{2^2 + 4^2} = \sqrt{16 + 4} = \sqrt{20}$ and $BC = \sqrt{6^2 + 3^2} = \sqrt{36 + 9} = \sqrt{45}$, so $AC = \sqrt{20 + 45} = \sqrt{65}$. Because $ABCD$ is a rectangle and therefore a parallelogram, $CD = AB = \sqrt{20}$ and $AD = BC = \sqrt{65}$. Then $BD = \sqrt{20 + 45} = \sqrt{65}$.
b. The midpoint of $\overline{AC}$ is $\left(\frac{-1+7}{2}, \frac{0+1}{2}\right) = \left(3, \frac{1}{2}\right)$. The midpoint of $\overline{BD}$ is $\left(\frac{1+5}{2}, 4 + \left(\frac{-3}{2}\right)\right) = \left(3, \frac{1}{2}\right)$. So, the diagonals bisect each other. **19.** 0.50 or 50%
20. Sample Response: 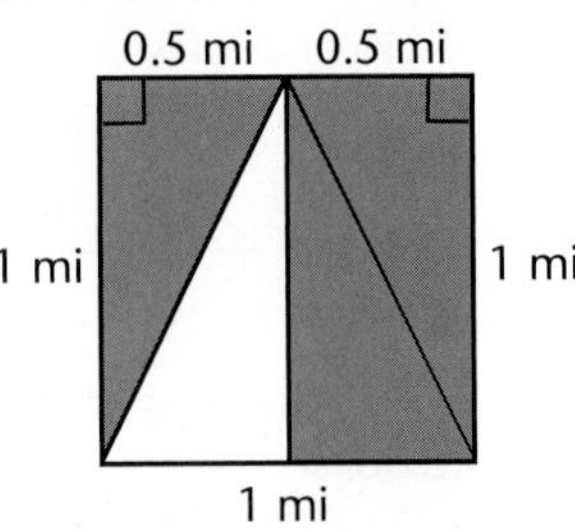

21. 8.09 yd **22.** 20.26 in. **23.** 5.45 mm

TOOLBOX ANSWERS

NUMBERS AND OPERATIONS

Decimal Place Value (p. 579)

1. < **2.** < **3.** = **4.** > **5.** = **6.** > **7.** > **8.** > **9.** < **10.** = **11.** < **12.** > **13.** 0.3 **14.** 0.8 **15.** 3.8 **16.** 1.7 **17.** 0.63 **18.** 7.85 **19.** 0.05 **20.** 5.93 **21.** 1.038 **22.** 0.993 **23.** 8.310 **24.** 0.024

Multiplying Whole Numbers and Decimals (p. 580)

1. 1302 **2.** 1200 **3.** 28,667 **4.** 214,832 **5.** 72,928 **6.** 18,244,440 **7.** 5.4 **8.** 12.54 **9.** 45.35 **10.** 7.837 **11.** 21.122 **12.** 435.16 **13.** 0.0018 **14.** 5.05404 **15.** 0.00192 **16.** 7.6896

Multiplying and Dividing by 10, 100, and 1000 (p. 581)

1. 518.3 **2.** 980 **3.** 3.0042 **4.** 67 **5.** 0.294 **6.** 0.56 **7.** Multiply **8.** 0.68 **9.** 13,000 **10.** 2700 **11.** 3.56 **12.** 4800 **13.** 4.54

Dividing Whole Numbers and Decimals (p. 582)

1. 24.8 **2.** 17.7 **3.** 15.3 **4.** 7.56 **5.** 53.19 **6.** 49.73 **7.** 14 **8.** 45 **9.** 8.5 **10.** 262.2 **11.** 962.5 **12.** 968

Divisibility Rules (p. 583)

1. No **2.** Yes **3.** Yes **4.** Yes **5.** No **6.** Yes **7.** Yes **8.** Yes

Finding Factors and Multiples (p. 584)

1. 6; 420 **2.** 12; 72 **3.** 11; 330 **4.** 40; 240 **5.** 30; 90 **6.** 5; 10,500 **7.** 15; 3465 **8.** 6; 2622 **9.** 55; 2475 **10.** 2; 2450 **11.** 1; 6237 **12.** 23; 138

Finding Equivalent Fractions and Ratios (p. 585)

1. 6 **2.** 56 **3.** 6 **4.** 3 **5.** $\frac{3}{5}$ **6.** $\frac{1}{3}$ **7.** $\frac{9}{10}$ **8.** $\frac{2}{3}$ **9.** = **10.** < **11.** >

Adding and Subtracting Fractions (p. 586)

1. $\frac{7}{12}$ **2.** $1\frac{1}{8}$ **3.** $\frac{5}{16}$ **4.** $\frac{20}{21}$ **5.** $\frac{5}{72}$ **6.** $\frac{7}{44}$ **7.** $\frac{7}{20}$ **8.** $\frac{2}{3}$ **9.** $\frac{3}{4}$ **10.** $\frac{1}{2}$ **11.** $\frac{9}{77}$ **12.** $\frac{23}{42}$ **13.** $\frac{5}{12}$ **14.** $3\frac{3}{10}$ **15.** $\frac{3}{4}$

Multiplying and Dividing Fractions (p. 587)

1. $\frac{4}{5}$ **2.** $\frac{1}{49}$ **3.** $\frac{3}{10}$ **4.** $\frac{2}{9}$ **5.** 6 **6.** $\frac{4}{5}$ **7.** 3 **8.** 15 **9.** $\frac{1}{2}$ **10.** $\frac{3}{4}$ **11.** $\frac{8}{3}$ or $2\frac{2}{3}$ **12.** $\frac{5}{4}$ or $1\frac{1}{4}$ **13.** $\frac{15}{2}$ or $7\frac{1}{2}$ **14.** $\frac{1}{10}$ **15.** 6 **16.** $\frac{16}{9}$ or $1\frac{7}{9}$

Writing Fractions, Decimals, and Percents (p. 588)

1. 0.95; 95% **2.** 0.16; 16% **3.** 0.001; 0.1% **4.** 0.62; 62% **5.** 0.8; $\frac{4}{5}$ **6.** 0.875; $\frac{7}{8}$ **7.** 0.64; $\frac{16}{25}$ **8.** 1.2; $\frac{6}{5}$ or $1\frac{1}{5}$ **9.** 48%; $\frac{12}{25}$ **10.** 85%; $\frac{17}{20}$ **11.** 12.5%; $\frac{1}{8}$ **12.** 350%; $\frac{7}{2}$ or $3\frac{1}{2}$

Using Order of Operations (p. 589)

1. 15 **2.** 18 **3.** 56 **4.** 13 **5.** 5 **6.** 9 **7.** 1 **8.** 4 **9.** 29 **10.** 41 **11.** 2 **12.** 3

Comparing Integers (p. 590)

1. > **2.** < **3.** < **4.** < **5.** > **6.** > **7.** > **8.** < **9.** < **10.** –5, –4, 1 **11.** –3, 0, 2 **12.** –4, –2, –1 **13.** –5, 3, 4 **14.** –6, –3, 0 **15.** –2, 2, 6 **16.** –2, –1, 0, 1 **17.** –7, –4, –2, 0 **18.** –6, –3, 2, 5

GEOMETRY AND MEASUREMENT

Locating Points in a Coordinate Plane (p. 591)

1. (–5, 2) **2.** (–3, –2) **3.** (–3, 1) **4.** (1, 4) **5.** (3, 0) **6.** (0, –2) **7.** (2, –4) **8.** (–2, 4) **9.** (–1, 1)

10–18.

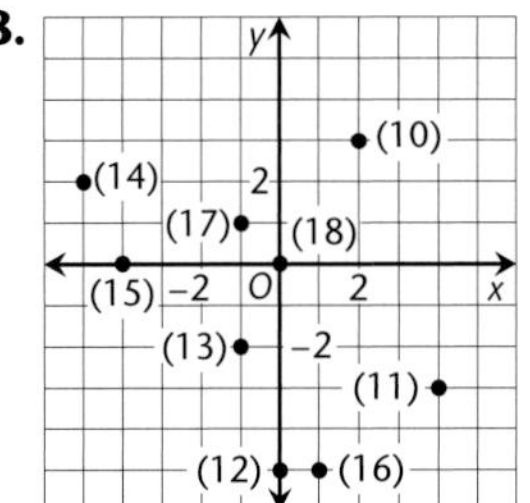

Measuring Angles (p. 592)

1. 90°; right **2.** 30°; acute **3.** 100°; obtuse **4.** 155°; obtuse **5.** 40°; acute **6.** 110°; obtuse

Classifying Triangles (p. 593)

1. obtuse **2.** right **3.** obtuse **4.** acute **5.** isosceles **6.** equilateral and isosceles **7.** scalene **8.** isosceles

Identifying Polygons (p. 594)

1. Regular polygon; closed, formed by 6 segments that do not cross each other; angles appear to be of equal measure, sides appear to be of equal length. **2.** Not a polygon; crosses itself. **3.** Not a polygon; not formed by segments **4.** Polygon; closed, formed by 6 segments that do not cross each other. **5.** Not a polygon; not closed

6. Polygon; closed, formed by 4 segments that do not cross each other. **7.** Regular polygon; closed, formed by 8 segments that do not cross each other; angles appear to be of equal measure, sides appear to be of equal length. **8.** Not a polygon; not formed by segments

Using Formulas from Geometry (p. 595)

1. $P = 16$ ft; $A = 12$ ft^2 **2.** $P = 58$ m; $A = 180$ m^2 **3.** $P = 80$ yd; $A = 360$ yd^2 **4.** 480 cm^3 **5.** 5625 m^3 **6.** 432 in.^{3}

DATA ANALYSIS

Finding the Mean, Median, Mode, and Range (p. 596)

1. mean: 33; median: 32; mode: 29; range: 9 **2.** mean: $16\frac{2}{3}$; median: 16.5; mode: none; range: 6 **3.** mean: 3.8; median: 3.6; mode: none; range: 2.9 **4.** mean: 34; median: 34; mode: 34; range: 0 **5.** mean: 2.25; median: 2; modes: 1 and 2; range: 5
6. mean: 105; median: 95; mode: 95; range: 60